Yearbook on International Communist Affairs 1986

Yearbook on International Communist Affairs 1986

Parties and Revolutionary Movements

EDITOR: Richard F. Staar

ASSISTANT EDITOR: Margit N. Grigory

AREA EDITORS

Thomas H. Henriksen	•	Africa
William Ratliff	•	The Americas
Ramon H. Myers	•	Asia and the Pacific
Richard F. Staar John B. Dunlop	•	Eastern Europe and the Soviet Union
James H. Noyes	•	The Middle East
Dennis L. Bark	•	Western Europe

HOOVER INSTITUTION PRESS

Stanford University, Stanford, California

The text of this work is set in Times Roman;
display headings are in Melior. Typeset by
Harrison Typesetting, Inc., Portland, Oregon.
Printed and bound by Braun-Brumfield, Inc.,
Ann Arbor, Michigan.

Hoover Press Publication 332

First printing, 1986
Manufactured in the United States of America
90 89 88 87 86 9 8 7 6 5 4 3 2 1

International Standard Book Number 0-8179-8321-X
International Standard Serial Number 0084-4101
Library of Congress Catalog Number 67-31024

Contents

ASIA AND THE PACIFIC

EASTERN EUROPE AND THE SOVIET UNION

THE MIDDLE EAST

WESTERN EUROPE

Preface

This edition of the *Yearbook*, the twentieth consecutive one, includes profiles by 76 contributors, covering 107 parties and revolutionary movements as well as ten international communist fronts and two regional organizations (the Council for Mutual Economic Assistance and the Warsaw Pact). In addition, 32 biographic sketches of prominent communist leaders follow individual profiles. The names and affiliations of contributors are given at the end of each essay.

The *Yearbook* offers data on the organization, policies, activities, and international contacts during all of calendar 1985 of communist parties and Marxist-Leninist movements throughout the world. Information has been derived primarily from published sources, including official newspapers and journals, as well as from radio transmissions monitored by the U.S. Foreign Broadcast Information Service. Dates cited in the text without indicating a year are for 1985.

Whether to include a party or group that espouses a quasi-Marxist-Leninist ideology, yet may not be recognized by Moscow as "communist," always remains a problem. It applies specifically to certain among the so-called national liberation movements and, more important, even to some ruling parties. In making our decisions, the following criteria have been considered: rhetoric, the organizational model, participation in international communist meetings and fronts, and adherence to the USSR's foreign policy line. It seems realistic to consider the regime of Nicaragua, for example, in the same category as that of Cuba. The ruling parties in the so-called "vanguard revolutionary democracies" appear to be clearly affiliated with the world communist movement. They also are discussed in the Introduction.

Our thanks go to the librarians and staff at the Hoover Institution for checking information and contributing to the bibliography. The latter was compiled by the *Yearbook* assistant editor, Mrs. Margit N. Grigory, who also remained in contact with contributors.

Richard F. Staar
Hoover Institution

* * *

The following abbreviations are used for frequently cited publications and news agencies:

CSM	*Christian Science Monitor*
FBIS	*Foreign Broadcast Information Service*
FEER	*Far Eastern Economic Review*
IB	*Information Bulletin* (of the *WMR*)
JPRS	*Joint Publications Research Service*
LAT	*Los Angeles Times*
NYT	*New York Times*
WMR	*World Marxist Review*

WP	*Washington Post*
WSJ	*Wall Street Journal*
YICA	*Yearbook on International Communist Affairs*
ACAN	Agencia Central Americano Noticias
ADN	Allgemeiner Deutscher Nachrichtendienst
AFP	Agence France-Presse
ANSA	Agenzia Nazionale Stampa Associata
AP	Associated Press
BTA	Bulgarska Telegrafna Agentsiya
ČETEKA	Československá Tisková Kancelář
DPA	Deutsche Presse Agentur
KPL	Khaosan Pathet Lao
MENA	Middle East News Agency
MTI	Magyar Távirati Iroda
NCNA	New China News Agency
PAP	Polska Agencja Prasowa
UPI	United Press International
VNA	Vietnam News Agency

Party Congresses

Country	*Congress*	*Date (1985)*
Egypt	2d	late 1984 or early 1985
Sweden (VPK)	27th	3–6 January
France	25th	6–10 February
Bolivia	5th	9–13 February
Netherlands	29th	1–3 March
Finland	Extraordinary	23 March
Hungary	13th	25–28 March
Colombia	Nat'l conference	30 March
Portugal	Nat'l conference	30 March
Canada	26th	5–8 April
Great Britain	Special	18–20 May
Bolivia	Extraordinary	2–5 August
Guyana	22d	3–4 August
People's Democratic Republic of Yemen	3d	11–16 October
Kampuchea	5th	13–16 October
Venezuela	7th	24–27 October
New Zealand (SUP)	7th	26–27 October
Iceland	Biennial	7–10 November
Benin	2d	18–24 November
Japan	17th	19–25 November
Angola	2d	2–9 December
Israel	20th	2–4 December
Uruguay	Nat'l conference	22 December
India (CPM)	12th	25–29 December

Register of Communist Parties

Status: * ruling # unrecognized
+ legal 0 proscribed

Country: *Party(ies)/Date Founded*	*Mid-1985 Population (est.) (World Factbook)*	*Communist Party Membership (claim or est.)*	*Party Leader (sec'y general)*	*Status*	*Last Congress*	*Last Election (percentage of vote; seats in legislature)*
AFRICA (12)						
Angola	7,953,000					
Popular Movement for the Liberation of Angola (MPLA), 1956 (MPLA-PT, 1977)		35,000 cl.	José Eduardo dos Santos	*	Second 2–9 Dec. 1985	(1980); all 203 MPLA approved
Benin	4,015,000					
People's Revolutionary Party of Benin (PRPB), 1975		no data	Mathieu Kerekou (chairman, CC)	*	Second 18–24 Nov. 1985	(1984); all 196 PRPB approved
Congo	1,798,000					
Congolese Labor Party (PCT), 1969		9,000 est.	Denis Sassou-Ngouesso (chairman)	*	Third 23–30 July 1984	95.0 (1984); all 153 PCT approved
Ethiopia	34,483,000 *(1985–86 Political Handbook)*					
Workers' Party of Ethiopia (WPE), 1984		50,000 est.	Mengistu Haile Mariam	*	First (Const.) 6–10 Sept. 1984	n/a
Lesotho	1,512,000					
Communist Party of Lesotho (CPL), 1962		no data	Jacob M. Kena	0 (tolerated)	Seventh Nov. 1984	n/a (1985)

Mozambique	13,776,000					
Front for the Liberation of Mozambique (FRELIMO), 1962		110,323 cl. (*African Communist* 4th quarter, 1983)	Samora Moisés Machel	*	Fourth 26–29 Apr. 1983	(1977); all 226 FRELIMO approved
Nigeria	91,178,000					
Socialist Working People's Party (SWPP), 1978 (Socialist Workers and Farmers Party, 1963)		no data	Dapo Fatogun (may no longer be)	0	First Nov. 1978	(1983)
Réunion	537,000					
Réunion Communist Party (PCR), 1959		7,000 cl.	Paul Vergès	+	Fifth 12–14 July 1980	31.10 (1985); 11 of 45 left coal., 7 for PCR (local assembly); none in Paris
Senegal	6,755,000					
Independence and Labor Party (PIT), 1981 (Parti Africain de l'Indépendence, 1957)		no data	Amath Dansoko	+	Second 28 Sept.–2 Oct. 1984	0.5 (1983); none
South Africa	32,465,000					
South African Communist Party (SACP), 1921		no data	Moses Mabhida	0	Sixth Dec. 1984 or early 1985, in London	n/a
Sudan	21,761,000					
Sudanese Communist Party (SCP), 1946		9,000 est.	Muhammad Ibrahim Nugud Mansur	+	Fourth (legal) 31 Oct. 1967	n/a
Zimbabwe	8,667,000					
Zimbabwe African National Union (ZANU-PF), 1963		no data	Robert Mugabe	*	Fifth 8–12 Aug. 1984	76.0 (1985); 64 of 100 (64 of 80 reserved for blacks)
TOTAL	224,900,000	220,323				

Country: Party(ies)/Date Founded	*Mid-1985 Population (est.) (World Factbook)*	*Communist Party Membership (claim or est.)*	*Party Leader (sec'y general)*	*Status*	*Last Congress*	*Last Election (percentage of vote; seats in legislature)*
THE AMERICAS (29)						
Argentina	30,708,000					
Communist Party of Argentina (PCA), 1918		70,000 est.	Athos Fava	+	Extraord. 5–6 Sept. 1983	2.0 (1985); none FREPU coalition
Bolivia	6,195,000					
Communist Party of Bolivia (PCB), 1950		500 est.	Simón Reyes Rivera	+	Fifth 9–13 Feb. 1985 Extraord. 2–5 Aug. 1985	2.21 (1985); 4 of 130 FPU coalition
Brazil	137,502,000					
Brazilian Communist Party (PCB), 1960 (Communist Party of Brazil, 1922)		15,000 est.	Giocondo Dias	+	Seventh (called National Meeting of Communists) Jan. 1984	(1985)
Canada	25,399,000					
Communist Party of Canada (CPC), 1921		2,500 est.	William Kashtan	+	Twenty-sixth 5–8 Apr. 1985	0.05 (1984); none
Chile	11,882,000					
Communist Party of Chile (CPC), 1922		20,000 West. est. 120,000 USSR est.	Luís Corvalán Lepe	0	Sixteenth June 1984 (clandestine in Chile and abroad)	n/a
Colombia	29,506,000					
Communist Party of Colombia (PCC), 1930		12,000 est.	Gilberto Vieira	+	Fourteenth 7–11 Nov. 1984	1.2 (1982); 3 of 199

Costa Rica	2,655,000					
Popular Vanguard Party (PVP), 1931		3,500 est. (prior to split)	Humberto Vargas Carbonell	+	Fifteenth 15–16 Sept. 1984	3.2 (1982); 4 of 57 United People's Coalition
Costa Rican People's Party (PPC), split from PVP, 1984		no data	Manuel Mora Valverde	+	Fourteenth 10–11 Mar. 1984	n/a
Cuba	10,105,000					
Cuban Communist Party (PCC), 1965		434,143 cl.	Fidel Castro Ruz	*	Second 17–20 Oct. 1981	(1981); all 499 PCC approved
Dominican Republic	6,588,000					
Dominican Communist Party (PCD), 1944		750 est.	Narciso Isa Conde	+	Third 15–17 Mar. 1984	7.1 (1982); none
Ecuador	8,884,000					
Communist Party of Ecuador (PCE), 1928		500 est.	René Mauge Mosquera	+	Tenth 27–29 Nov. 1981	3.6 (1984); 2 of 71 Broad Leftist Front, FADI 4.0 (1984) in pres. elec. for Mauge, FADI cand.
El Salvador	5,072,000					
Communist Party of El Salvador (PCES), 1930 (one of five in FMLN)		1,000 est.	Shafik Jorge Handal	0	Seventh Aug. 1979	n/a (1985)
Grenada	110,000					
Maurice Bishop Patriotic Movement (MBPM), 1984		no data	Kenrick Radix (chairman)	+	n/a	5.0 (1984); none
Guadeloupe	333,000					
Communist Party of Guadeloupe (PCG), 1958		3,000 est.	Guy Daninthe	+	Eighth 27–29 Apr 1984	(1985); 24 of 42 left coal. (local assembly); 1 of 3 in Paris
Guatemala	8,335,000					
Guatemalan Party of Labor (PGT), 1952		500 est.	Carlos González	0	Fourth Dec. 1969	n/a (1985)
Guyana	798,000					
People's Progressive Party (PPP), 1950		200 est.	Cheddi Jagan	+	Twenty-second 3–5 Aug. 1985	16.8 (1985); 8 of 53 elected members

Country: Party(ies)/Date Founded	*Mid-1985 Population (est.) (World Factbook)*	*Communist Party Membership (claim or est.)*	*Party Leader (sec'y general)*	*Status*	*Last Congress*	*Last Election (percentage of vote; seats in legislature)*
Haiti	5,762,000					
Unified Party of Haitian Communists (PUCH), 1968		350 est.	René Théodore	0	First 1979	n/a (1984)
Honduras	4,394,000					
Honduran Communist Party (PCH), 1954 (one of six in the MHR, 1982)		650 est.	Rigoberto Padilla Rush (claims to be) Mario Sosa Navarro (actual leader)	0	Third Mar. 1977	n/a (1981)
Jamaica	2,428,000					
Workers' Party of Jamaica (WPJ), 1978		50 est.	Trevor Munroe	+	Third 14–21 Dec. 1984	(1983)
Martinique	327,000					
Martinique Communist Party (PCM), 1957		1,000 est.	Armand Nicolas	+	Eighth 12–13 Nov. 1983	(1985); 7 of 46 (local assembly); none in Paris
Mexico	79,662,000					
Unified Socialist Party of Mexico (PSUM), 1981		40,800 cl.	Pablo Gómez Alvarez	+	Second 9–14 Aug. 1983	3.24 (1985); 12 of 400
Nicaragua	3,038,000					
Nicaraguan Socialist Party (PSN), 1937		no data	Gustavo Tablada	+	Tenth Oct. 1973	1.3 (1984); 2 of 96
Sandinista Front of National Liberation (FSLN), 1960		4,000 cl.	Daniel Ortega (coord. of Executive Commission)	*		63.0 (1984); 61 of 96
Panama	2,038,000					
People's Party of Panama (PPP), 1943		35,000 cl. (500–1,000 militants)	Rubén Darío Souza	+	Sixth 8–10 Feb. 1980	(1984); none

Paraguay	3,722,000					
Paraguayan Communist Party (PCP), 1928		4,000 est.	Antonio Maidana (arrested 1980) Julio Rojas (acting)	0	Third 10 Apr. 1971	n/a (1983)
Peru	19,532,000					
Peruvian Communist Party (PCP), 1930		5,000 est.	Jorge del Prado Chavez	+	Eighth Extraord. 27–31 Jan. 1982	26.0 (1984); 48 of 180 United Left coal. (6 PCP repr. of 48)
Puerto Rico	3,300,520					
Puerto Rican Communist Party (PCP), 1934		125 est.	Frank Irrizarry	+	unknown	0.3 (1984); none
Suriname	377,000					
Revolutionary People's Party (RVP), 1981 (quasi-independent within 25 FM)		100 est.	Edward Naarendorp	+	First 1981	n/a
United States of America	238,848,000					
Communist Party USA (CPUSA), 1919		17,500 cl.	Gus Hall	+	Twenty-third 10–13 Nov. 1983	0.01 (1984); none
Uruguay	2,936,000					
Communist Party of Uruguay (PCU), 1920		7,500 est.	Rodney Arismendi	+	Twentieth Dec. 1970	6.0 (1984); none Frente Amplio coal.
Venezuela	17,810,000					
Communist Party of Venezuela (PCV), 1931		4,000 est.	Alonso Ojeda Olachea	+	Seventh 24–27 Oct. 1985	2.0 (1983); 3 of 195
TOTAL	668,246,520	683,668				

ASIA AND THE PACIFIC (20)

Australia	15,700,000					
Communist Party of Australia (CPA), 1920		1,000 est.	Judy Mundey	+	Twenty-eighth 4 Nov. 1984	negl. (1984); none
Socialist Party of Australia (SPA), 1971		500 est.	Peter Dudley Symon	+	Fifth 28 Sept.–1 Oct. 1984	negl. (1984); none

Country: Party(ies)/Date Founded	*Mid-1985 Population (est.) (World Factbook)*	*Communist Party Membership (claim or est.)*	*Party Leader (sec'y general)*	*Status*	*Last Congress*	*Last Election (percentage of vote; seats in legislature)*
Bangladesh	101,408,000					
Communist Party of Bangladesh (CPB), 1948		3,000 est.	Muhammed Farhad	+	Third Feb. 1980	(1981)
Burma	36,919,000					
Burmese Communist Party (BCP), 1939		3,000 cl.	Thakin Ba Thein Tin (chairman)	0	Third 9 Sept.–2 Oct. 1985	n/a
China	1,041,346,000					
Chinese Communist Party (CCP), 1921		over 40,000,000 cl.	Hu Yaobang	*	Twelfth 1–11 Sept. 1982	(1981); all 3,202 CCP approved
India	762,507,000					
Communist Party of India (CPI), 1928		478,500 cl.	C. Rajeswara Rao	+	Twelfth 21–28 Mar. 1982	2.71 (1984); 6 of 544
Communist Party Marxist (CPM), 1964		271,500 cl.	E. M. S. Namboodiripad	+	Twelfth 25–30 Dec. 1985	5.96 (1984); 22 of 544
Indonesia	173,103,000					
Indonesian Communist Party (PKI), 1920 (split)		2,200 est. incl. exiles	Jusuf Adjitorop (pro-Beijing faction) Satiadjaya Sudiman (pro-Moscow faction)	0	Seventh Extraord. Apr. 1962	n/a
Japan	120,691,000					
Japan Communist Party (JCP), 1922		470,000 cl.	Tetsuzo Fuwa (Presidium chairman) Kenji Miyamoto (CC chairman)	+	Seventeenth 19–25 Nov. 1985	9.43 (1983); 26 of 511
Kampuchea	6,249,000					
Kampuchean People's Revolutionary Party (KPRP), 1951		7,500 est.	Heng Samrin	*	Fifth 13–16 Oct. 1985	99.0 (1981); all 117

Party of Democratic Kampuchea (PDK), or Kampuchean Communist Party (KCP), 1951		no data	Pol Pot	0	Third 14 Dec. 1975	n/a
Korea (North)	20,082,000					
Korean Workers' Party (KWP), 1949		3,000,000 cl.	Kim Il-song	*	Sixth 10–15 Oct. 1980	100 (1982); all 615 KWP approved
Laos	3,584,803 (1985 census)					
Lao People's Revolutionary Party (LPRP), 1955		42,000 cl.	Kaysone Phomvihane	*	Third 27–30 Apr. 1982	(Dec. 1975) Supreme People's Assembly (all 46 appointed by LPRP)
Malaysia	15,664,000					
Communist Party of Malaya (CPM), 1930		3,425 est.	Chin Peng	0	1965 (last known)	n/a (1984)
Communist Party of Malaysia (MCP), 1983		800 est.	Ah Leng	0	unknown	n/a (1984)
Mongolia	1,912,000					
Mongolian People's Revolutionary Party (MPRP), 1921		80,200 cl.	Jambyn Batmonh (Dzambiin Batmunkh)	*	Eighteenth 26–31 May 1981	99.0 (1981); all 370 MPRP approved
Nepal	16,996,000					
Nepal Communist Party (NCP), 1949 (factions)		5,000 est. (75% pro-Beijing and neutral)	Man Mohan Adhikary	0	Third 1961 (before split; right wing held its own third in 1963)	n/a
New Zealand	3,295,000					
Communist Party of New Zealand (CPNZ), 1921		50 est.	Richard C. Wolfe	+	26–28 Jan. 1979 (first since 1966)	(1984); none
Socialist Unity Party (SUP), 1966		175 est.	George H. Jackson	+	Seventh 26–27 Oct. 1985	0.5 (1984); none
Pakistan	99,199,000					
Communist Party of Pakistan (CPP), 1948		under 200 est.	Ali Nazish	0 (since 1954)	First (cland.) 1976	n/a

Country: Party(ies)/Date Founded	Mid-1985 Population (est.) (World Factbook)	Communist Party Membership (claim or est.)	Party Leader (sec'y general)	Status	Last Congress	Last Election (percentage of vote; seats in legislature)
Philippines	56,808,000					
Philippine Communist Party (PKP), 1930		200 est.	Felicismo Macapagal	+	Eighth 1980	n/a (1985)
Communist Party of the Philippines, Marxist-Leninist (CPP), 1968		15,000 cl.	Rafael Baylosis	0	Re-establishment 26 Dec. 1968	n/a (1984)
Singapore	2,562,000					
Communist Party of Malaya, branch (CPM), 1930		200 est.	Chin Peng	0	unknown	n/a (1984)
Sri Lanka	16,206,000					
Communist Party of Sri Lanka (CPSL), 1943		6,000 est.	Kattorge P. Silva	+	Twelfth 27–29 Jan. 1984	1.9 (1977); 1 of 168
Thailand	52,700,000					
Communist Party of Thailand (CPT), 1942		1,000 est.	Virat Angkhatha-vorn (active leader)	0	Fifth (cland.) Feb. 1984	n/a
Vietnam	60,492,000					
Vietnamese Communist Party (VCP), 1930		1,750,000 cl.	Le Duan	*	Fifth 27–31 March 1982	97.9 (1981); 496 of 614 all VCP endorsed
TOTAL	2,607,423,803	46,141,450				

EASTERN EUROPE AND USSR (9)

Country: Party(ies)/Date Founded	Mid-1985 Population (est.) (World Factbook)	Communist Party Membership (claim or est.)	Party Leader (sec'y general)	Status	Last Congress	Last Election (percentage of vote; seats in legislature)
Albania	2,968,000					
Albanian Party of Labor (APL), 1941		122,600 cl.	Ramiz Alia April 1985	*	Eighth 1–8 Nov. 1981	99.9 (1982); all 250 Democratic Front

Bulgaria	8,980,000					
Bulgarian Communist Party (BCP), 1903		912,000 cl.	Todor Zhivkov	*	Twelfth 31 Mar.–4 Apr. 1981	99.9 (1981); all 400 Fatherland Front
Czechoslovakia	15,503,000					
Communist Party of Czecho-slovakia (KSC), 1921		1,650,000 cl.	Gustáv Husák	*	Sixteenth 6–10 Apr. 1981	99.0 (1981); all 350 National Front
Germany: German Democratic Republic	16,701,000					
Socialist Unity Party (SED), 1946		2,293,289 cl. (*Neues Deutschland*, 1/9/86)	Erich Honecker	*	Tenth 11–16 Apr. 1981	99.9 (1981); all 500 National Front
Hungary	10,645,000					
Hungarian Socialist Worker's Party (HSWP), 1956		870,992 cl.	János Kádár	*	Thirteenth 25–28 Mar. 1985	98.9 (1985); all 352 Patriotic People's Front
Poland	37,236,000					
Polish United Workers' Party (PUWP), 1948		2,112,191 cl. (*Trybuna Ludu*, 1/8/86)	Wojciech Jaruzelski	*	Ninth Extraord. 14–20 July 1981	78.8 (1985); all 460 Fatherland Front
Romania	22,772,000					
Romanian Communist Party (RPC), 1921		3,500,000 cl.	Nicolae Ceaușescu	*	Thirteenth 19–22 Nov. 1984	97.8 (1985); all 369 Socialist Democracy and Unity Front
USSR	277,930,000					
Communist Party of the Soviet Union (CPSU), 1898		18,500,000 cl.	Mikhail S. Gorbachev (Mar. 1985)	*	Twenty-sixth 23 Feb.–4 Mar. 1981	99.9 (1984); all 1,500 CPSU approved (71.4% are CPSU members)
Yugoslavia	23,137,000					
League of Communists of Yugoslavia (LCY), 1920		2,188,943 cl.	Vidoje Zarkovič (president of Presidium)	*	Twelfth 26–29 June 1982	(1982); all 308 Socialist Alliance (all LCY approved)
TOTAL	415,872,000	32,150,015				

Country: Party(ies)/Date Founded	Mid-1985 Population (est.) (World Factbook)	Communist Party Membership (claim or est.)	Party Leader (sec'y general)	Status	Last Congress	Last Election (percentage of vote; seats in legislature)
MIDDLE EAST (15)						
Afghanistan	14,792,000					
People's Democratic Party of Afghanistan (PDPA), 1965		140,000 cl.	Babrak Karmal	*	Nat'l Conf. 14–15 Mar. 1982	(1978)
Algeria	22,025,000					
Socialist Vanguard Party (PAGS), 1920		450 est.	Sadiq Hadjeres (first secretary)	0	Sixth Feb. 1952	n/a (1982)
Bahrain	427,000					
Bahrain National Liberation Front (NLF/B), 1955		negligible	Yusuf al-Hassan al-Ajajai	0	unknown	n/a
Egypt	48,305,000					
Egyptian Communist Party (ECP), 1921		500 est.	Farid Mujahid	0	Second 1984 or early 1985	n/a
Iran	45,191,000					
Communist Party of Iran (Tudeh Party), 1941 (dissolved May 1983)		1,500 est.	Nureddin Kianuri (imprisoned)	0	1965	3.0 (1980); none
Iraq	15,507,000					
Iraqi Communist Party (ICP), 1934		no data	Aziz Muhammad	0	Third 4–6 May 1976	n/a (1984)
Israel	4,255,000 (incl. E. Jerusalem, Israeli Central Bureau of Statistics)					
Communist Party of Israel (CPI, "RAKAH"), 1948 (Palestine Communist Party, 1922)		1,500 est.	Meir Vilner	+	Twentieth 4–7 Dec. 1985	3.4 (1984); 4 of 120

Jordan	2,794,000					
Communist Party of Jordan (CPJ), 1951		no data	Fa'iq Warrad	0	Second Dec. 1983	n/a
Lebanon	2,619,000					
Lebanese Communist Party (LCP), 1924		5,000 est.	George Hawi	+	Fourth 1979	(1972)
Morocco	24,258,000					
Party of Progress and Socialism (PPS), 1974 (Moroccan Communist Party, 1943)		2,000 est.	'Ali Yata	+	Third 25–27 Mar. 1983	2.30 (1984); 2 of 306
Palestine Communist Party (PCP), 1982	4,500,000 Palestinians	200 est.	Bashir al-Barghuti (presumed)	0 (tolerated)	First presumably in 1984	n/a
Saudi Arabia	11,152,000					
Communist Party of Saudi Arabia (CPSA), 1975		negligible	Mahdi Habib	0	Second Aug. 1984	n/a
Syria	10,535,000					
Syrian Communist Party (SCP), 1944		5,000 est.	Khalid Bakhdash	+	Fifth May 1980	0.78 (1981); none
Tunisia	7,352,000					
Tunisian Communist Party (PCT), 1934		2,000 est.	Muhammad Harmel (first secretary)	+	Eighth Feb. 1981	0.78 (1981); none
Yemen (PDRY)	2,211,000					
Yemen Socialist Party (YSP), 1978		26,000 cl.	Ali Nasir Muhammad al-Hasani	*	Third 11–16 Oct. 1985	(1978); all 111 YSP approved
TOTAL	215,923,000	164,150				

WESTERN EUROPE (23)

Austria	7,540,000					
Communist Party of Austria (KPO), 1918		12,000 est.	Franz Muhri (chairman)	+	Twenty-fifth 13–15 Jan. 1984	0.66 (1983); none

Country: Party(ies)/Date Founded	*Mid-1985 Population (est.) (World Factbook)*	*Communist Party Membership (claim or est.)*	*Party Leader (sec'y general)*	*Status*	*Last Congress*	*Last Election (percentage of vote; seats in legislature)*
Belgium	9,856,000					
Belgian Communist Party (PCB-KPB), 1921		10,000 est.	Louis van Geyt (president)	+	Twenty-fourth Mar. and Dec. 1982 (two stages)	1.2 (1985); none
Cyprus	670,000					
Progressive Party of the Working People (AKEL), 1941 (Communist Party of Cyprus, 1922)		14,000 cl.	Ezekias Papaioannou	+	Fifteenth 13–15 May 1982	27.4 (1985); 15 of 56
Denmark	5,109,000					
Communist Party of Denmark (DKP), 1919		10,000 est.	Poul Emanuel (secretary) Jørgen Jensen (chairman)	+	Twenty-seventh 12–15 May 1983	0.7 (1984); none
Finland	4,894,000					
Finnish Communist Party (SKP), 1918		50,000 cl.	Esko Vainionpaa	+	Twentieth 25–27 May 1984 Extraord. 23 Mar. 1985	14.0 (1983); 27 of 200
France	55,094,000					
French Communist Party (PCF), 1920		610,000 cl.	Georges Marchais	+	Twenty-fifth 6–10 Feb. 1985	16.2 (1981); 44 of 491
Germany: Federal Republic of Germany	59,262,000 (excl. W. Berlin)					
German Communist Party (DKP), 1968		44,500 est.	Herbert Mies (chairman)	+	Seventh 6–8 Jan. 1984	0.2 (1983); none
Great Britain	56,437,000					
Communist Party of Great Britain (CPGB), 1920		16,000 est.	Gordon McLennan	+	Thirty-eighth 12–15 Nov. 1983 Special 18–20 May 1985	0.03 (1983); none

New Communist Party of Britain (NCPB), 19? (*New Kabul Times*, 12/24/85)		no data	Eric Trevett	+	Fifth 23–24 Nov. 1985	no data
Greece	9,966,000					
Communist Party of Greece (KKE), 1921		42,000 est.	Kharilaos Florakis	+	Eleventh 15–18 Dec. 1982	9.9 (1985); 13 of 300
Communist Party of Greece–Interior (KKE-I), 1968		12,000 est.	Yiannis Banias (Leonidas Kyrkos, chairman, de facto leader)	+	Third 17–23 May 1982	1.8 (1985); none
Iceland	241,000					
People's Alliance (AB), 1968		3,000 est.	Svavar Gestsson (chairman)	+	Biennial Congr. 7–10 Nov. 1985	17.3 (1983); 10 of 60
Ireland	3,590,000					
Communist Party of Ireland (CPI), 1933		500 est.	James Stewart	+	Eighteenth 14–16 May 1982	(1982); none
Italy	57,149,000					
Italian Communist Party (PCI), 1921		1,588,376 cl.	Alessandro Natta	+	Sixteenth 2–6 Mar. 1983	29.9 (1983); 198 of 630
Luxembourg	367,000					
Communist Party of Luxembourg (CPL), 1921		600 est.	René Urbany (chairman)	+	Twenty-fourth 4–5 Feb. 1984	4.9 (1984); 2 of 64
Malta	332,002 (Malta Office of Statistics)					
Communist Party of Malta (CPM), 1969		200 est.	Anthony Vassallo	+	Extraord. 18–25 May 1984	(1981); none
Netherlands	14,459,000					
Communist Party of the Netherlands (CPN), 1909		10,000 est.	Elli Izeboud	+	Twenty-ninth 1–4 Mar. 1985	1.8 (1982); 3 of 150
Norway	4,160,000					
Norwegian Communist Party (NKP), 1923		5,500 est.	Hans I. Kleven (chairman)	+	Eighteenth 30 Mar.–2 Apr. 1984	0.2 (1985); none
Workers' Communist Party (AKP), 1973		10,000 est.	Kjersti Ericsson	+	Third (or Fourth?) Dec. 1984	(1985); none

Country: Party(ies)/Date Founded	*Mid-1985 Population (est.) (World Factbook)*	*Communist Party Membership (claim or est.)*	*Party Leader (sec'y general)*	*Status*	*Last Congress*	*Last Election (percentage of vote; seats in legislature)*
Portugal	10,045,000					
Portuguese Communist Party (PCP), 1921		200,753 cl.	Álvaro Cunhal	+	Tenth 8–11 Dec. 1983	15.49 (1985); 38 of 250 United People's Alliance Coalition
San Marino	23,000					
Communist Party of San Marino (PCS), 1941		300 est.	Ermenegildo Gasperoni (chairman) Umberto Barulli (gen. secy.)	+	Tenth 1980	24.3 (1983); 15 of 60
Spain	38,629,000					
Spanish Communist Party (PCE), 1920		86,000 cl.	Gerardo Iglesias	+	Eleventh 14–18 Dec. 1983	3.8 (1982); 4 of 350
Communist Party (PC), 1984		35,000 cl.	Ignacio Gallego	+	First 13–15 Jan. 1984	n/a
Sweden	8,338,000					
Left Party Communists (VPK), 1921		17,500 cl.	Lars Werner (chairman)	+	Twenty-seventh 3–6 Jan. 1985	5.4 (1985); 19 of 349
Communist Workers' Party (APK), 1977		5,000 cl.	Rolf Hagel (chairman)	+	Twenty-seventh 1983	0.1 (1982); none
Switzerland	6,512,000					
Swiss Labor Party (PdAS), 1921		4,500 est.	Armand Magnin	+	Twelfth 21–22 May 1983	0.9 (1983); 1 of 200
Turkey	51,259,000					
Communist Party of Turkey (TCP), 1920		negligible	Haydar Kutlu	0	Fifth Oct. or Nov. 1983	n/a (1983)

West Berlin	1,870,000 (*1985–86 Political Handbook*)					
Socialist Unity Party of West Berlin (SEW), 1949		4,500 est.	Horst Schmitt	+	Seventh 25–27 May 1984	0.6 (1985); none
TOTAL	405,802,002	2,792,229				
GRAND TOTAL	4,538,167,325	82,151,835				

INTERNATIONAL FRONT ORGANIZATIONS

Organization (11)	*Year Founded*	*Headquarters*	*Claimed Membership*	*Affiliates*	*Countries*
Afro-Asian Peoples' Solidarity Organization	1957	Cairo	unknown	87	–
Asian Buddhist Conference for Peace	1970	unknown	unknown	15	12
Christian Peace Conference	1958	Prague	unknown	–	ca. 80
International Association of Democratic Lawyers	1946	Brussels	25,000	–	ca. 80
International Organization of Journalists	1946	Prague	180,000	–	120 plus
International Union of Students	1946	Prague	10,000,000	120	112
Women's International Democratic Federation	1945	East Berlin	200,000,000	135	117
World Federation of Democratic Youth	1945	Budapest	150,000,000	ca. 270	123
World Federation of Scientific Workers	1946	London	500,000	ca. 40	70 plus
World Federation of Trade Unions	1945	Prague	ca. 206,000,000	92	81
World Peace Council	1950	Helsinki	unknown	–	142 plus

Introduction
The Communist World, 1985

At the beginning of 1985 the first deputy chief of the International Department in the Central Committee of the Communist Party of the Soviet Union (CPSU), Vadim V. Zagladin, stated that "fraternal parties now exist in 95 countries" and constitute "more than 80 million fighters"—which is almost exactly what he had reported in 1984. He also claimed that "more than 1.5 billion people already have become involved with the building of socialism and the struggle to build communism."[1]

A much less precise Moscow radio broadcast at the end of 1985 alleged that the "communist movement functions in almost one hundred countries of the world" and that "it unites about 90 million people."[2] Such use of inflated figures is not unusual and, hence, official Soviet claims must be treated with caution. The hyperbole probably is intended to suggest a massive and monolithic worldwide movement, described in the draft of the new CPSU program as follows:

> This is the epoch of the transition from capitalism to socialism and communism, of the historic competition of the two world sociopolitical systems, the epoch of socialist and national liberation revolutions, of the collapse of colonialism, the epoch of the struggle of the chief motive forces of social development—world socialism, the workers' and communist movement, the peoples of the liberated states, and the mass democratic movements—against imperialism and its policy of aggression and oppression and for democracy and social progress.[3]

The so-called workers' and communist movement in actual fact has been unable to organize a world conference during the past seventeen years. Only three such meetings have been held (1957, 1960, 1969) since the last one under Comintern auspices in 1935, which called for a united front.

Early this past year, the daily newspaper of the League of Communists in Yugoslavia (LCY) asserted that "the proposal to convene a world conference of communist and workers' parties has been repeated here in Moscow three times in only two months . . . The journal *Kommunist*, the CPSU Central Committee organ, stressed in two consecutive issues the urgent need for a gathering of the communist world."[4]

The LCY, through its Presidium, rejected the call for a world conference. Subsequent reports indicated that the Italian, and probably other West European parties, would not attend. The Chinese long have been on record against any such gathering. Finally, the new CPSU leader, Mikhail S. Gorbachev, in an interview with an Italian party functionary, described the idea of a world conference as inappropriate.[5]

The Register of Communist Parties above lists the 95 entities in which communist parties theoretically operate. In certain instances, where they have been banned, it is difficult if not impossible to know whether any activity takes place inside the country. The CPSU apparently acknowledges two (and in the case of Spain, perhaps even three) parties in Australia, Finland, Costa Rica, Great Britain, India, New Zealand, Nicaragua, Spain, and Sweden. Communist movements also exist in territories not recognized as sovereign by international law: Guadeloupe, Martinique, Palestine, Puerto Rico, Réunion, and West Berlin.

The *Yearbook* also includes twelve of the approximately twenty "revolutionary democratic" parties,[6] most of which are in power and adhere to Marxism-Leninism. Those discussed exist in Afghanistan, Angola, Bahrain, Benin, Congo, Ethiopia, Grenada, Kampuchea, Mozambique, Nicaragua, South Yemen, and Zimbabwe. Only the ones in Bahrain and Grenada are not ruling. The Register also lists those significant movements *unrecognized* by the CPSU. They are frequently pro-Chinese.

Each party is listed under the appropriate geographic region. If the designation happens to be other than "Communist Party of . . .," the acronym is provided in the Register and the full name in the essays. All population estimates are derived from the latest edition of the *World Factbook*.[7] Party membership figures are either official claims or 31 December 1985 estimates by the profile contributor. Other information in the Register includes the name of each party's leader, dates of congresses, legal status, and results of the latest parliamentary elections (where relevant).

The CPSU claims an increase of 250,000, for a total membership of 18,750,000, an 8 percent growth since the twenty-sixth congress in 1981.[8] The twenty-seventh congress convened from 26 February through 6 March 1986 in Moscow. Most other ruling movements throughout the Soviet bloc will hold their congresses between March and June of 1986. The exceptions are Romania (1984) and Hungary (1985), which had congresses before the CPSU did.

It is the West European communist parties that have been losing electoral support, most notably those in Spain and France. This has also meant declining membership figures. The Communists in Spain are split into three groups and the French movement has lost influence over the General Confederation of Labor. A new party, the League of Communists in the Netherlands (VCN), claims about a thousand members.[9] Finland now has two parties, and a split also occurred in England; the new faction seems to have crystallized into the New Communist Party of Britain. Its secretary is Eric Trevett.[10]

The most publicized change in the leadership of a ruling movement occurred on 11 March 1985, when Mikhail Gorbachev succeeded the late Konstantin Chernenko. Outside the bloc (although in Eastern Europe), only Enver Hoxha died in power. His personally selected successor, Ramiz Alia, promptly assumed power. The party chairman in Greece is de facto leader rather than the secretary general, and the same applies to Japan. Changes in top leadership were registered in Bolivia, Finland, Honduras, Norway (AKP), Paraguay, Saudi Arabia, San Marino, and Venezuela, as reflected in the Register. The ruling party in South Yemen changed its leadership after a violent two-week revolt in which thousands were killed.[11]

A total of some 21 congresses took place during the year. In one case, that of Egypt, the clandestine meeting was held either in late 1984 or early 1985. Conferences were one-day affairs. The second congress of the MPLA-PT in Angola, held in early December, was attended by CPSU Politburo member Geidar Aliev. The importance attached to a ruling party can be seen from the rank of the chief Soviet delegate sent to its congress.

Three movements achieved legal status during the year, one in Africa and two in Latin America. As a result of a coup d'état in the Sudan, the communist party in that country received permission from the new rulers to function openly.[12] A new civilian government in Brazil lifted the ban on communist activities, which had been outlawed since 1922 (except for 1945–1947). The party announced that it will compete in the November 1986 parliamentary elections.[13] Finally, the movement in Uruguay, after twelve years of illegality, surfaced during March and held a national conference at the end of the year.[14]

Communist parties, recognized as such by Moscow, rule in the same fifteen countries as last year. Their total membership is approximately 75 million—of the world strength of about 80 million claimed by Zagladin. The pro-Soviet core of ten "socialist commonwealth" Council for Mutual Economic Assistance (CMEA) members is weaker in communist party strength than the other five states in this category. Otherwise, local movements have representatives in governments only on Réunion and Martinique, in San Marino, and in Syria.

Ruling parties in Zimbabwe, Hungary, Poland, and Romania held pro forma elections to parliament and "won" confirmation of their status. However, even official figures showed that 22 percent of the Polish electorate voted against the regime slate, with the percentage most probably much higher. Outside the bloc,[15] the Communists fared worse: they lost two seats in Belgium and their percentage of the vote declined by 5.4 percent on Cyprus, 1 percent in Greece, and 2.5 percent in Portugal. They dropped from 16.2 to 9.8 percent of the vote on 16 March 1986 in France. Other highlights from the different areas follow.

Sub-Saharan Africa. Even the South African Communist Party (SACP) remained uncertain about the "state of incipient civil war" and remained concerned that the workers would be diverted "from the true road of revolution." Moscow radio continued to provide its transmitters to the African National Congress for broadcasts in Zulu.[16] SAPC general secretary Moses Mabhida died in exile at Maputo, Mozambique.

The MPLA-PT congress in Angola, mentioned above, voted the ouster of pro-Soviet hard-liner Lucio Lara from the Politburo and ejected the foreign minister and the air force commander from the Central Committee. Despite the foregoing, the USSR continued supplying military equipment, which reached about $2 billion in value by year's end.[17] Soviet-bloc military troops and advisers have suffered casualties in combat against the guerrilla UNITA movement.

Mozambique celebrated a decade of independence and also faced an insurgency by RENAMO. Although relying on Soviet-bloc military hardware and instructors, the regime in Maputo reportedly accepted 12,000 troops from neighboring Zimbabwe.[18] President Samora Machel appeared to be conducting a "nonaligned" foreign policy by visiting first President Reagan and later General Secretary Gorbachev.

Small, landlocked Lesotho allowed its Communists to function openly, although not in the electoral process. They were listed as the sixty-sixth party on the editorial board of the *World Marxist Review*, in effect notable recognition by the CPSU. After a military coup toppled the government, the new military authorities expelled 107 members of the African National Congress from Lesotho to Zambia.[19]

Zimbabwe, the former Rhodesia, held parliamentary elections in July at which the ruling ZANU-PF picked up 7 more seats and now holds 64 of the 80 reserved for blacks. Prime Minister Robert Mugabe traveled to Moscow in early December for a state visit. In his speech there, he declared Marxism-Leninism to be the leadership's philosophy.[20] Mugabe also pledged increasing friendship and cooperation with the USSR.

The Workers' Party of Ethiopia is reportedly preparing a constitution that will institute a people's democratic republic. In the meantime, the government is dealing with rebel movements by resettling approximately 1.5 million people under the pretext of a severe drought and famine. As many as 300,000 (some 20 percent) will die in the process, according to Doctors Without Borders. About 100,000 have already lost their lives in the brutal resettlement process.[21]

Mathieu Kerekou, president of the People's Revolutionary Party of Benin (PRPB), finally succeeded in purging from the Politburo and the PRPB Michel Alladaye, the last survivor among the officers who staged the 1972 coup that brought Kerekou to power. At the party congress in November, Kerekou appeared to consolidate his position; most of the newly elected Politburo members seemed loyal to him. On the other hand, PRPB control over the country was challenged for the first time in ten years. Unrest surfaced among high school and university students, and worsening economic conditions spelled additional trouble.

The Americas. Fidel Castro hosted a conference of communist party representatives from Latin America and Caribbean countries during 12–14 June at Havana. It issued predictable denunciations of the United States.[22] Cuba itself has established government-to-government relations with sixteen Latin American countries. Only Colombia, Brazil (as of year's end), Chile, Paraguay, El Salvador, Costa Rica, and Honduras have no contacts with the Castro regime, which received a $600 million equivalent line of credit from Argentina. The Cuban foreign legion now totals 44,000 troops, mostly in Africa.

Peace talks between the FSLN guerrillas and the Salvadoran government made no progress during the year. The latter has the upper hand, despite a geographical widening of the conflict.[23] While the five insurgent groups have attempted to establish a single Marxist-Leninist party, the Democratic Revolutionary (political) Front denounced terrorism from exile and gave signs of returning to El Salvador to participate in the democratic process.

Truce between government and guerrillas in Colombia virtually ended conflict with FARC, although it did not involve ELN. The most spectacular terrorist action of the year occurred in November, after M-19 seized the palace of justice in Bogota. All 35 guerrillas and 64 of the hostages were killed when troops stormed the building.

The Communists in Chile also supported terrorism. This kept them out of the National Accord alliance, established in September by many opposition groups. The party operates out of Buenos Aires, and its newspaper, *El Siglo*, purportedly is published in the "deep underground."[24]

In other countries, the communist movements supported the democratic process in Costa Rica, Brazil, and Uruguay, where constitutional governments were restored during 1985. The party in Uruguay held a national conference after a twelve-year ban on its activities.[25] In Ecuador, the party held minor membership in a broadly based opposition front.

By contrast, the communist movement in Peru comprised the largest group in the United Left Political

Front (IU). The latter holds about one-fourth of the seats in each house of parliament. IU consists of four parties, two coalitions, and smaller groups, as well as individuals. Maoist guerrillas called Sendero Luminoso were capable of undertaking coordinated attacks almost anywhere in the country. Their fanaticism would appear to militate against cooperation with other movements.

The Sandinistas in Nicaragua continued harsh restrictions against the population, even closing down the official radio station of the Roman Catholic Church. They are openly aligned with Cuba and the Soviet bloc in their foreign policies, dependent upon these allies for weapons to combat the 16,000 to 20,000 armed men who are fighting to overthrow the communist regime.[26]

Asia and the Pacific. Communist leaders in Cambodia, China, North Korea, Laos, and Vietnam have pursued similar policies with minor deviations by those in Pyongyang. Kim Il-song continued to position his son as successor. Relations with Moscow became closer, and more than twenty USSR delegations visited North Korea. All its ports and airspace are now open to the Soviet military, which promised delivery of about 50 MiG-23 fighters to Pyongyang by the end of 1985.[27]

A major purge in the People's Republic of China (PRC) replaced 29 province party secretaries, 131 Central Committee members, and one-third of the Politburo. Older leaders were moved out to accommodate younger ones, supposedly favoring Deng Xiaoping's reform policies. A similar shake-up took place in the government. The rectification campaign for screening "third echelon" cadres in the party thus far has involved about 960,000 members. Of these some 60,000 have been expelled. The next stage will deal with the 13.5 million cadres in local organs, large enterprises, and higher education. The number of regional military commands has been consolidated from eleven to eight, and seven of the commanders were replaced.[28]

Economic reforms have alternated between relaxation and tighter controls. The latter involved foreign exchange restrictions during 1985 and a crackdown on corruption within the party. At the same time, Deng has reduced central planning, enlarged the flexible pricing system, and continued a small free-market sector.

Continuing their occupation of Kampuchea, some 150,000 Vietnamese troops are still at war with the opposition in that country. They also have engaged in heavy shelling and border skirmishes with PRC troops.[29] Serious economic problems affect Hanoi. However, the ruling party intends to pursue a massive resettlement campaign to eliminate villages and create 426 district agrocomplexes. A quarter of a million individuals would live in each complex, with about 25,000 individuals farming an average of 20,000 hectares of land.

Little has changed in countries where Communists have legal status or are tolerated. Even when Bangladesh lifted a ten-month ban on all political activities, the opposition groups, including the pro-Soviet communist party and other Marxist organizations, rejected the government's terms.[30]

The Communist Party of India—Marxist (CPM), the smaller of the two communist parties in India, held a congress at the end of the year at Calcutta, which re-elected its general secretary. The congress received coverage in three separate articles that emphasized its support for Soviet foreign policy initiatives.[31] The CPM won one seat of seven in supplementary elections to parliament from Assam province in mid-December.

As for neighboring Burma, the clandestine propaganda radio station of the Burmese Communist Party, operating out of Yunnan province in mainland China, went off the air on 16 April 1985. Apparently it was a casualty of the growing rapprochement between Rangoon and Beijing, the BCP's principal supporter over the last twenty years.

The Japanese Communist Party (JCP) has yet to reach its target half-million membership level, despite strenuous efforts. The leader, Kenji Miyamoto, accused the government of responsibility for the August 1985 plane crash in which 520 persons (including several JCP leaders) died. He also attacked it for expanding national defense. However, the JCP frequently pursues a line critical of both Moscow and Beijing.

Where local communist movements are banned, the parties vary in strength. The pro-Chinese New People's Army (NPA) in the Philippines did expand its terrorist activities in the countryside and simultaneously attempted to use "united front" tactics in metropolitan areas. Corazon Aquino even met with jailed communist leaders and stated she would accept them into her government if she won the 7 February 1986 elections.[32] This statement was later repudiated by Mrs. Aquino, although she did release all imprisoned Communists after becoming president.

The NPA has penetrated between 5 (government figures) and 20 percent (U.S. intelligence) of the 40,000 villages in the Philippines, so that party membership must have grown substantially. The National Democratic Front umbrella organization in the cities embraces workers, women, Moro revolutionaries, Christians, peasants, youth, and teachers.[33]

By the end of 1985, armed Thai insurgents had dwindled to a few hundred as a result of massive defections. (They totaled about 12,000 in 1978.) The communist party's united front efforts in the cities of Thailand have been virtually abandoned.

The Indonesian government executed Mohammed Munir, a member of the PKI Politburo. Three other leaders met the same fate in July. The few who survive now live in China, the Soviet Union, and Eastern Europe.

The Middle East. Communist and workers' parties of Arab countries issued a pronouncement about the situation in Lebanon. It attacked both the United States and Israel, calling upon the peoples of the Middle East to activate a mass movement that would lead to evacuation of all occupied territories. A longer statement appeared at mid-year. A third called for an end to the Iraq-Iran war, and the fourth urged support of Arab Palestinians against "aggressive, expansionist, and racist" Tel Aviv.[34]

A significant change in Soviet policy could be noted when clandestine broadcasts in Persian from Baku began personal attacks on Khomeini and even called for an armed uprising against his "despotic medieval regime." The once significant Tudeh party has been reduced to a few imprisoned leaders. Khomeini commuted their death sentences as a bargaining chip in a futile attempt to reduce Moscow's support for Baghdad. The opposite has occurred, even though remnants of the Iraqi Communists are fighting in guerrilla actions with the Kurds in the far north against the central government.

Despite the claim that party membership had increased by 25,000 since last year,[35] and despite the support of 118,000 Soviet troops in the field plus another 30,000 just across the border, the ruling party in Afghanistan is split into Parcham and Khalq factions. This precipitated a gun battle at the Arg palace between corresponding army groups in September. During the year 1985, Soviet advisers attempted to shift the balance of power toward the Parcham, to which party leader Babrak Karmal belongs.[36]

The other, more important, development occurred in South Yemen. The president called a meeting of his Politburo on 13 January 1986, did not appear, but had his gunmen kill many of his critics. The factional strife resulted in about 13,000 dead.[37] Although an estimated 4,000 Soviet civilians were evacuated during the struggle, with 1,000 military personnel remaining, the USSR-backed prime minister was in Moscow the whole time and returned to Aden as acting president.

Western Europe. The second conference of communist and workers' parties from the eastern Mediterranean, the Near and Middle East, and the Red Sea areas took place in January at Nicosia on Cyprus. A long, four-page declaration by fourteen movements, plus other unnamed and presumably clandestine ones, called for joint action in the region.[38] (The first such conference was held in 1981 at Athens.)

West European parties alone met during the summer for two days in Paris, where the eighteen delegations discussed the "economic crisis" in capitalist countries.[39] In general, however, the year 1985 witnessed disunity and decline within these movements.

The French Communists held a congress in February, where they decided to give up former attempts to forge a "unity of the left" with the socialists. Only 90 percent of the delegates voted for the leadership, with one dissenter dropped from the Politburo. The party moved toward the 16 March 1986 parliamentary elections with only about 11 percent public support. A former communist intellectual called the process "an irreversible regression."[40] Those elections saw a drop from 44 to 35 seats in the 577-member parliament.

The situation in Spain is even worse, because there are now three main parties. In late April 1985, the PCE Central Committee expelled its previous leader, Santiago Carrillo, and replaced his followers in regional bodies. A rival pro-Soviet group (PC) had been established in January 1984. Finally, a new

"Marxist Revolutionary" Spanish Communist Party was registered in October 1985 by the ousted Carrillo. The CPSU recognizes at least the first two, although Gorbachev has received only the PC leader Ignacio Gallego to date.[41]

The last member of the Big Three is the Italian Communist Party (PCI), which lost 50,000 members during the past year. More important, it no longer controls big cities like Rome, Venice, Milan, Turin, and Parma, as a result of May 1985 local elections.[42] Alessandro Natta, who succeeded Berlinguer as PCI leader in 1984, introduced the "leftist alternative" to woo the socialists. In mid-December this line received the support of the Central Committee, even though it probably has as little chance of success as the 1973–1979 "historic compromise."

A situation not unlike that in Spain developed within the communist movement of Finland (SKP). Parallel party organizations were formed by pro-Soviet hard-liners in eight of the seventeen districts prior to the May 1985 congress. The majority prevailed, however, and the rebels were replaced by loyalists in the fall. The losers sent a delegation to Moscow toward the end of the year.[43]

Regarding other communist parties, the one on Cyprus (AKEL) dropped from first to third place in the December 1985 elections.[44] Until then it had been the strongest in public support throughout Western Europe. The same happened to the larger party (KKE) in Greece, which fell below 10 percent of the vote and lost its parliamentary status as a "party," although not its thirteen seats. Finally, the movement in Great Britain also split in mid-year 1985, when the hard-line minority was expelled and yet won control over the communist newspaper *Morning Star*. The weakness of the party in Portugal can be seen from the fact that it ran as part of the electoral Alliance for the Unity of the People, subsequently supporting a dissident socialist and, in the runoff on 16 February 1986, former socialist prime minister Mario Soares, who became president.[45]

Eastern Europe and the USSR. The new Soviet general secretary saw every other bloc leader (with the exception of Nicolae Ceauşescu of Romania) on different occasions and met all of them together at the Warsaw Treaty Organization (WTO) extension ceremony and the CMEA meeting that launched an ambitious science and technology program. Actually four summits took place during 1985: in Moscow (March), Warsaw (April), Sofia (October), and Prague (November).[46]

Albanian Communists buried their first and, until 11 April 1985, only leader for the preceding four decades. Heir apparent Ramiz Alia has had no difficulty in establishing himself and continuing the policies of Enver Hoxha. New were the number of delegations from Western Europe, although no improvement occurred with Yugoslavia because of the Albanian minority in Kosovo.[47]

Another kind of ethnic issue involved Bulgaria, where the Turks were being forced to adopt Slavic names and stop speaking their native language in public. The standard of living in general began to deteriorate, and the New Economic Mechanism underwent criticism early in the year. One full member of the ruling Politburo and a candidate for membership were dismised, perhaps as scapegoats.[48]

The leadership in Czechoslovakia announced a hard-line approach regarding any "market-oriented concepts," after Gustáv Husák had conferred with Gorbachev in Moscow. An interview given by a Secretariat member to the West German weekly *Der Spiegel* about the "Prague Spring" was refuted in the Italian communist newspaper by Alexander Dubček, who broke a sixteen-year silence on those events.[49]

The East Germans sponsored a conference on criteria for effective communist party work, attended by representatives from eleven movements around the world, and held at the Karl Marx Higher Party School in East Berlin.[50] In general, the year was good for the German economy. Erich Honecker lost three members of his Politburo: he dismissed rival Konrad Naumann; Herbert Haeber retired for "health reasons"; and Honecker probably had no part in the death of Defense Minister Karl-Heinz Hoffmann. The purge of Naumann paved the way for Egon Krenz to become heir apparent.[51]

The party congress in Hungary again gave support to the 1968 New Economic Mechanism, even though it is having problems. The conclave was followed by national elections, where more than one candidate ran from each constituency. None of this, of course, means genuine pluralism. Within the bloc, there is talk of "socialist diversity," which the party leadership apparently would like to practice.[52]

The situation in Poland resembles that of Hungary after 1956 and Czechoslovakia after 1968. The communist regime has proclaimed "normalization" and the end of organized opposition. Yet in the capital city of Warsaw, only 127,000 inhabitants belong to the ruling party.[53] Authorities have intensified their drive against dissidents, whose strength could be estimated during national elections in October. Officially, some 22 (according to the underground Solidarity movement, 34) percent boycotted the event. By year's end, the number of political prisoners had exceeded three hundred, and the Roman Catholic Church was being attacked openly.[54]

Romania's cult of personality has no comparison in Eastern Europe, even though its economy is the weakest of the region. Although officially only 2.3 percent of the electorate voted against the regime's slate in the March elections, there were reports of peasant riots in December. Adverse publicity in the United States could lead to revocation of Romania's most-favored-nation status in trade relations.[55]

Five years after the death of Josip Broz Tito, a crisis faces Yugoslavia. The man and the system have been criticized for what has happened to the economy. With an inflation rate of more than 100 percent and a foreign currency debt surpassing the official $23 billion at the end of 1985, it is impossible to see how these problems can be overcome. The League of Communists (LCY) lost 75,000 members, mostly blue-collar workers, who resigned in just the month of November.[56] The problem of ethnic Albanians (77 percent of the population) in Kosovo province, mentioned above, will not disappear until autonomy is granted.

The Communist Party of the Soviet Union seems to be emerging from its 28-month leadership transition. After less than a year in power, Gorbachev approached the twenty-seventh party congress with his enemies and rivals gone from the Politburo or Secretariat. In their place are allies (appointed by Andropov) and his own clients, promoted before and at the congress.[57]

In many ways, the new leader reminds one of N. S. Khrushchev: the same *muzhik* background, a master politician, and a man "with iron teeth." His education in law, which he never practiced, makes him even more dangerous than does his avowed admiration for Stalin. Three police generals are on the Politburo—Aliev, Chebrikov, and Shevardnadze—but no army generals except for aging Defense Minister Sokolov, who holds only candidate (nonvoting) membership. These are not hopeful signs for the future.

Richard F. Staar
Hoover Institution

NOTES

1. V. V. Zagladin, "On the Contemporary Communist Movement," *Tribuna* (Prague), no. 5, 30 January 1985, p. 3.
2. Moscow radio, Tass in English; Foreign Broadcast Information Service, *Daily Report: Soviet Union* (Washington, D.C., hereafter *FBIS-SOV*), 16 December 1985, p. CC/3. These figures also are attributed to Zagladin.
3. Moscow, *Pravda*, 3 January 1986, p. 4.
4. Belgrade, *Borba*, 7 February 1985, p. 7
5. Belgrade radio, 7 February 1985 (translated in *FBIS-Eastern Europe*, 8 February 1985, p. I/5); Kevin Devlin, "PCI Against World Conference," *RAD Background Report* (Munich: Radio Free Europe–Radio Liberty [hereafter, RFE-RL], 14 March 1985); Milan, *L'Unità*, 22 May 1985, as cited in Budesinstitut für ostwissenschaftliche und internationale Studien, Report no. 28 (Cologne: June 1985), p. 4.
6. See Richard F. Staar, *USSR Foreign Policies After Detente* (Stanford: Hoover Institution Press, 1985), table 1.3, p. 14, for a list of the twenty countries with a "socialist" orientation and the names of their movements.
7. U.S. Central Intelligence Agency, *World Factbook, 1985* (Washington, D.C.: U.S. Government Printing Office, 1985), CR WF 85-001.
8. Malcolm Haslett, "Gorbachev's Long Term Plans," *BBC Current Affairs Talk*, no. 83 (15 October 1985).
9. James M. Markham, "Sharp Decline by Communists in Western Europe," *New York Times*, 3 February 1986, pp. 1 and 6; Rotterdam, *NRC Handelsblad*, 4 November 1985, p. 3.

10. *Kabul New Times*, 24 December 1985.
11. John Kifner, "The Battle for Southern Yemen," *New York Times*, 30 January 1986, pp. 1 and 4.
12. Interview with the general secretary, M. I. Nugud, in *L'Humanité* (Paris); reported by *Pravda*, 27 April 1985, p. 5.
13. Statement by the general secretary, Giocondo Dias, in *Pravda*, 11 December 1985, p. 5.
14. Tass report from Montevideo in *Pravda*, 24 December 1985, p. 4.
15. Kevin Devlin, "The Nonruling Communist Parties," in "Eastern Europe in 1985," *RAD Background Report*, no. 150 (Munich: RFE-RL, 27 December 1985), pp. 49–54.
16. R. S. Nyameko, "SACTU Celebrates Its 30th Birthday," *African Communist* (London), no. 100, 1985, p. 55; and Moscow radio in Zulu to Southern Africa, 9 December 1985; translated in *FBIS-SOV*, 16 December 1985. *Pravda*, on 11 March 1986, announced Mabida's death.
17. *New York Times*, 30 December 1985.
18. Radio Truth (clandestine from South Africa), 12 September 1985; translated in *FBIS-Africa*, 13 September 1985.
19. Alan Cowell's articles in the *New York Times*, 26 January and 2 February 1986.
20. "Speech by Comrade R. Mugabe," *Pravda*, 3 December 1985, p. 4.
21. Clifford D. May, "Moving Ethiopians Causes a Dispute," *New York Times*, 28 January 1986, pp. 1 and 4; "Today's Holocaust," editorial in the *Wall Street Journal*, 27 January 1986, p. 26.
22. Moscow radio, Tass in English, 15 June 1985; *FBIS-SOV*, 18 June 1985, p. K/1.
23. See articles by James LeMoyne in the *New York Times*, 10 and 12 January 1986.
24. Tass dispatch from Buenos Aires in *Pravda*, 8 January 1986, p. 4.
25. Tass from Montevideo, *Pravda*, 24 December 1985, p. 4.
26. AP dispatch from Managua, *New York Times*, 3 January 1986; see James LeMoyne, "Most Contras To Pull Out of Nicaragua," ibid., 30 January 1986, for figures.
27. Tokyo, *Sankei Shimbun*, 7 October and 26 December 1985; *Far Eastern Economic Review*, 26 September and 26 December 1985; *Pravda*, 25 December 1985, 22 January 1986.
28. *Far Eastern Economic Review*, 22 August 1985, p. 45; Beijing radio in Chinese, 18 September 1985; *FBIS-China*, 19 September 1985, p. K/18.
29. Joseph A. Reaves, *Sunday Star-Bulletin* (Honolulu), 8 September 1985; Barbara Crossette (from Hanoi), "Vietnam Reports Chinese Troops Have Stepped Up Border Attacks," *New York Times*, 5 January 1986; UPI dispatch from Peking, "China 'Wiped Out' Vietnamese Forces," *San Francisco Examiner and Chronicle*, 2 February 1986, p. A-8.
30. Special correspondent in Madras, *Pravda*, 6 January 1986, p. 5, and *Pravda*, 31 December 1985, p. 4; *Bangladesh Times*, 18 January 1985.
31. Tass dispatches from Calcutta in *Pravda*, 26, 27, and 30 December 1985.
32. *San Francisco Examiner*, 29 December 1985, pp. A-1 and A-15.
33. Guy Sacerdoti and Philip Bowring, "Marx, Mao and Marcos," *Far Eastern Economic Review*, 21 November 1955, p. 55.
34. Tass dispatch from Beirut in *Pravda*, 22 March 1985, p. 4, *Pravda*, 21 June 1985, p. 4, Tass from Damascus, *Pravda*, 7 August 1985, p. 5; and Moscow radio in English, 3 November 1985, in *FBIS-SOV*, 4 November 1985, for quotation.
35. Dispatch from Kabul by a special correspondent in *Pravda*, 16 January 1986, p. 5.
36. Craig Carp, "Afghanistan: Six Years of Soviet Occupation," *Special Report* no. 135 (Washington, D.C.: U.S. Department of State, December 1985), pp. 8–10.
37. John Kifner, "Southern Yemen Offers 'Good Neighbor Policy,'" *New York Times*, 1 February 1986 (dispatch from Aden).
38. "Consolidating Joint Action," *WMR Information Bulletin* (April 1985), pp. 6–9.
39. *Pravda*, 14 June 1985, p. 5; Brussels, *Le Drapeau rouge*, 15–16 June 1985, p. 6.
40. Devlin, "Nonruling Communist Parties," pp. 49–50; quotation from James Markham, "Sharp Decline by Communists," p. 1.
41. Devlin, "Nonruling Communist Parties."
42. See interview with PCI secretariat member Ugo Pecchioli in *L'Unità*, 1 November 1985, pp. 1 and

16, on membership losses; E. J. Dionne, Jr., "Italy's Communists Have Lost Their Grip," *New York Times*, 6 October 1985.

43. Devlin, "Nonruling Communist Parties," pp. 52–53; see also the "Statement by the Committee for SKP Organizations," *Pravda*, 18 December 1985, p. 5 (the SKP is the pro-Soviet minority).

44. Special correspondent in Athens, "Results of Elections," *Pravda*, 11 December 1985, p. 5.

45. Special correspondent in Lisbon, "Success of Democratic Forces," *Pravda*, 20 December 1985, p. 5; *San Francisco Examiner and Chronicle*, 26 January 1986; *New York Times*, 30 January 1986.

46. Vladimir Kusin, "Eastern Europe in 1985," in *RAD Background Report* no. 150 (Munich: RFE-RL, 27 December 1985), pp. 2–5; Vadim Zagladin, interview in *Rabotnichesko delo* (Sofia), 3 January 1986, pp. 1 and 6; translated in *FBIS-SOV*, 15 January 1986, p. CC/4.

47. See Elez Biberaj, "Albania After Hoxha: Dilemmas of Change," *Problems of Communism*, vol. 34, no. 6 (November–December, 1985), pp. 32–47.

48. Tass dispatch from Sofia, "Plenum of BCP Central Committee," *Pravda*, 26 January 1986, p. 4.

49. *L'Unità*, 21 November 1985, pp. 1 and 18; translated in *FBIS-Eastern Europe*, 25 November 1985, pp. D/7–8.

50. *World Marxist Review* (September 1985), pp. 62–78.

51. Paris radio, AFP in English, 26 November 1985; *FBIS-Eastern Europe*, 27 November 1985, p. E/1; William Drozdziak, "New Leader Emerging," *Washington Post*, 12 December 1985, pp. A-1 and A-27 (dispatch from East Berlin).

52. Paul Lewis, "Voter Choice in Hungary," *New York Times*, 23 January 1985; Budapest radio, MTI in English, 17 March 1985; in *FBIS-Eastern Europe*, 18 March 1985, p. F/2.

53. Special correspondent from Warsaw, "Fraternal Parties," *Pravda*, 5 January 1986, p. 4; *Zycie partii*, 4 December 1985, pp. 3–4.

54. Janusz Bugajski, "Poland's Anti-Clergy Campaign," *Washington Quarterly*, vol. 8, no. 4 (Fall 1985), pp. 157–68.

55. Roger Thurow, "Balkan Paradox," *Wall Street Journal*, 27 January 1986; Ion Mihai Pacepa, "A Defector's Story," *San Francisco Chronicle*, 29 January 1986, pp. C1–2.

56. Official figures give the inflation rate as 79.5 percent and the debt as $20 billion. See AP dispatch from Belgrade, *Wall Street Journal*, 4 February 1986; Henry Kamm, "In Post-Tito Yugoslavia," *New York Times*, 18 December 1985.

57. For a list of the new Politburo and Secretariat members, see *Pravda*, 7 March 1986.

AFRICA

Introduction

The year 1985 in Africa below the Sahara witnessed both successes and setbacks for Marxist ruling parties, revolutionary movements, and communist parties. One success for a communist party arose in Sudan, where after fourteen years of underground existence the party resurfaced after the military coup overthrowing the regime of Jaafar Numeiri. The Réunion Communist Party gained almost one-third of the vote in the March cantonal (county) elections. However, the ruling Congolese Party of Labor and the People's Revolutionary Party of Benin both felt serious challenges from student unrest. Even the South African Communist Party feared mixed blessings from the unsettled state of affairs in South Africa. The continued riots, sabotage, and disturbances in the country were viewed by the SACP as fostering "a state of recipient civil war," but the party worried that "economism, trade union politics and workerism" could "divert the workers from the true road of revolution" (*African Communist*, no. 100, p. 55). The ruling Marxist parties in Angola and Mozambique faced another year of internal rebellion and problem-ridden economies.

Among the major events of 1985 was the Second Congress of Angola's ruling Marxist-Leninist party, the Popular Movement for the Liberation of Angola–Labor Party (MPLA-PT) in December. Attended by over 700 delegates, the congress exhibited signs of tension within the highest party ranks. After declarations of unity by MPLA-PT leaders, a major purge took place with the ouster of pro-Soviet hardliner Lucio Lara from the Politburo and two of his key allies—former foreign minister Santos Onambwe and Air Force commander Henrique Carreira from the Central Committee. Congress sessions also drew attention to the spreading antigovernment insurgency in the countryside. The MPLA-PT government received up to $2 billion worth of Soviet military equipment in the last two years (*NYT*, 30 December). Troops and advisers also came from the Soviet bloc to counter guerrilla opposition from Jonas Savimbi's National Union for the Total Independence of Angola (UNITA). The Soviet Union and Cuba suffered casualties in a major effort to roll back UNITA advances. South African forces intervened to challenge the MPLA-PT and Soviet-backed counteroffensive.

Sudan saw the most favorable advances for a communist party in sub-Saharan Africa in 1985. Having been fourteen years underground as a proscribed movement, the Sudanese Communist Party (SCP) surfaced after the ouster of the military government of Jaafar Numeiri by General Abdel Rahman Siwar el-Dahab on 6 April. The Siwar el-Dahab regime legalized the SCP, and its secretary general, Muhammad Ibrahim Nugud Mansur, emerged with other officials from clandestinity while still others returned from exile. Nugud initially participated in meetings with the Transitional Military Council (TMC) to discuss the creation of the provisional government and plans for election. Later, he complained that the TMC was acting autocratically. The SCP held mass rallies in Khartoum and Omdurman, and Nugud castigated the United States for alleged interference in Sudanese internal affairs, called for socioeconomic transformations for the masses, and called for resolution of the insurgency in southern Sudan.

This insurgency had reignited during 1983 and had once again absorbed the central government. Led by a former army commander, Colonel John Garang, the Marxist-Leninist Sudanese People's Liberation Movement (SPLM) has sought to become the "sole people's organization" in Sudan. The SPLM refused to recognize the legitimacy of the TMC and claimed that the army simply "stole victory from the masses" and that the Siwar el-Dahab government represents "Numeiryism without Numeiri." The SCP holds that the rebellion in the southern region can only be solved through the formation of a broad front of political forces. The SCP closely parrots the radical Arab Communist line on Middle East politics.

The chairman of the People's Revolutionary Party of Benin (PRPB), Mathieu Kerekou, experienced an uneven year. On the one hand, he finally succeeded in purging Michel Alladaye from the PRPB Politburo and from the party itself; Alladaye was the last survivor of the group of officers who staged the 1972 coup bringing Kerekou to power. At the party congress in November, Kerekou appeared to consolidate his position. Most of the newly elected Politburo members seemed to be loyal to Kerekou. On the other hand, the PRPB's control over the country was challenged for the first time in ten years. Unrest surfaced among high school and university students, a group that causes problems for many Third World countries. The worsening economic conditions also spelled trouble for Kerekou and perhaps the PRPB.

The ruling Congolese Party of Labor (PCT) and the regime of President Denis Sassou-Ngouesso were also challenged by student unrest. Although traditionally supportive of the government, students held massive demonstrations to protest the decision to introduce a competitive examination for high school graduates seeking a university scholarship as part of an austerity policy. The unrest gave hardline ideologues an opportunity to challenge what they perceived as Sassou-Ngouesso's relatively pragmatic policies. In December, a month after announcing the new educational policy, the government made several changes to deal with the demonstrations and austerity efforts.

In February the PCT held a joint colloquium on ideology with the Communist Party of the Soviet Union (CPSU) that took place in Brazzaville. It was the fifth such meeting and its chief purpose was, as stated by Pierre Nze, Politburo member and PCT secretary for external affairs, "to exchange experience in order to achieve a better understanding of the socialist system." That same month the planning minister visited China and declared: "We have something to learn from China's planning experience." These events serve to underscore what many feel are the heterodox ideological views of the PCT.

The most tumultuous events of the year took place in South Africa, where rioting and sabotage carried over from 1984 as some elements of the African population protested the apartheid policies of the Pretoria government. Although thc South African Communist Party (SACP) took heart at the spreading violence, Joe Slovo, a non-African Communist, warned that if the people's victory is dominated by the aspirant black capitalist class or middle class, then South Africa could be taken down the capitalist rather than the communist road. The SACP Central Committee, therefore, aimed to have the African working class play its role in accomplishing the political and military tasks of the national democratic revolution. Internationally, the SACP maintained its unswerving loyalty to the Soviet Union. The MPLA-PT in Angola and the Front for the Liberation of Mozambique (FRELIMO), both staunch Marxist-Leninist parties, continued to practice more pragmatic policies toward the West for aid and private investment while maintaining firm ties with the Soviet Union by exchanging high-level visitors and signing various agreements.

Mozambique celebrated its tenth anniversary of independence from Portugal with large-scale demonstrations. However, the country continued to face a worsening economy and an expanding antigovernment insurgency by the Mozambique National Resistance (RENAMO). FRELIMO's counterinsurgency campaign required it to depend more on foreign forces and equipment than in past years. Although it relied on the Soviet bloc for military hardware and advisers, Mozambique saw the first significant deployment of foreign soldiers when Zimbabwe dispatched several thousand troops into Mozambique, primarily to protect the route to Beira. One source reported 12,000 Zimbabwan troups deployed in Mozambique in September (Radio Truth, 12 September; *FBIS*, 13 September). FRELIMO also turned to arming villagers and creating local militias to combat RENAMO's attacks. To increase domestic food production, Mozambique's Council of Ministers, or cabinet, announced economic liberalization measures. It also sought to reduce the role of state wholesale enterprises. These government intermediate structures have been held responsible for delays, waste, and corruption. Yet the government policies seek to promote "commercial ethics" in the farming sector. At the fourteenth session of the People's Assembly, the delegates heard that 1986 will be a difficult year in spite of the government's efforts to liberalize agricultural production. In September, Mozambican president Samora Machel visited the United States and met with President Reagan; he also journied to Moscow for discussions with General Secretary Mikhail Gorbachev.

To the south of Mozambique, in land-locked Lesotho, the Communist Party of Lesotho (CPL) also had a mixed year. Although the CPL operated openly during the year, it failed to achieve legal status and did not participate in the national elections. Its standing, however, increased in the Communist world when the CPL attained acceptance as the 66th Communist Party to be represented on the editorial council of the *World Marxist Review*. Lesotho itself also achieved greater Soviet recognition as evidenced by the dispatch of a resident ambassador from the Soviet Union in July. By October the ambassador's staff had reached 27 members, another sign of Soviet interest in southern Africa.

In nearby Zimbabwe, the Zimbabwe African National Union (ZANU) increased its parliamentary majority to 64 seats out of 100 in July in the first general election since independence. The election outcome once again demonstrated ZANU's reliance on the Shona ethnic group. The opposition party, Zimbabwe African People's Union (ZAPU), lost seats despite its secure hold among the Ndebele population. Zimbabwe, therefore, remained a deeply divided state. Other signs of ethnic cleavage surfaced in renewed assassinations and detention of ZAPU followers. Although President Robert Mugabe professes international nonalignment, his domestic policies continue toward his ultimate goal of a one-party Marxist state. For instance, ZANU recently established an ideological institute (the Chitepo College of Marxism and Leninism). The state continued its gradual expansion into the private sector, and the government moved farther in its efforts to control all the media.

Off the southeast coast of Africa on the island of Réunion, the Réunion Communist Party (PCR) improved electoral standing by gaining 31.1 percent of the vote in the March cantonal (county) election. In February the PCR held its first mass assembly to discuss the problems facing the country; the assembly centered on agricultural production, unemployment, and economic development. The PCR leadership renewed the party's goals for Réunion's autonomy from France.

Up the coast in Ethiopia, the Workers Party of Ethiopia (WPE) enunciated that its primary goal in 1985 was to formulate a new constitution that would lead to the creation of the People's Democratic Republic of Ethiopia. With respect to severe famine problems, the WPE continued its resettlement of a reported half-million families from north to south in spite of criticism from Western relief organizations. The latter held that forced population shifts took place in order to diminish support for the secessionist movements in the north and that the coercive movement of people resulted in many needless deaths. The Soviet Union supplied the trucks and planes for transport of the northern refugees. Ethiopia contended that the resettlement program was undertaken to provide destitute northern farmers with fertile land and access to water.

Across the continent in Senegal, the pro-Soviet Independence and Labor Party (PIT) showed few signs of domestic vitality. A more significant opposition force emerged with the formation of the Democratic Senegalese Alliance (ADS), which comprised four Marxist parties and the largest opposition party. The Ministry of the Interior proscribed ADS from political activity until it declared itself a political party and was recognized as such, emphasizing that alliances of political parties were illegal. The real threat to the government, however, stems from Islamic consciousness and mobilization, not the several splintered communist groups.

In Nigeria the Communist Party organization appeared dead or driven deeply underground as a result of the general repression of political debate by the government of Major General Muhammadu Buhari. With the ouster of the Buhari regime in late August by Army chief of staff Major General Ibrahim Babangida, a wave of political tolerance began. By years end, however, there were no measurable signs of political activity by the Socialist Working People's Party (SWPP), which had been the most prominent Marxist party.

A country of continuing interest, although it is not included in the following profiles, deserves attention in this introduction because of developments that began in 1984. Burkina Fasso (formerly Upper Volta) underwent a military coup that ushered into power the National Council of the Revolution (CNR) on 4 August 1984. Although the new government, led by Captain Thomas Sankara, has proved eclectic—making its ideology difficult to classify neatly—the regime's policies have nevertheless moved leftward. For example, it has declared all land to be the property of the state. Additionally, the government has initiated a mass literacy campaign, carried out massive vaccination drives, and extended health care to rural areas—all efforts that are similar to newly installed left-wing governments in Africa. The Sankara government also set up the Committee for the Defense of the Revolution (CDR), another common feature of Communist regimes to control their population. The CDR's monthly magazine, *Lolowulen* (Red star) carried an article by one of the government officials stating: "The revolution of August 4, 1984, is a democratic and popular revolution, that is, a struggle through which the democratic and revolutionary forces in Burkina strive to eliminate the domination of imperialism and to break the bourgeois, reactionary, conservative, and backward social forces that are opposed to the people's economic and social progress."

Yet activists in the capital city of Ouagadougou have been quoted as saying that "socialism is not on the agenda" (Ernest Harsch, "Burkina revolution brings gains," *Intercontinental Press*, 29 April, p. 238). The general director of *Carrefour Africain*, a weekly magazine, explained: "Marx, Engels, Lenin, we [agree] with the general framework. But little that they wrote applies directly to a country like Burkina. We're trying to apply it to conditions of extreme underdevelopment, in which classes are not very clearly defined and there is no bourgeoisie like those that exist in Europe. And our proletariat numbers only 20,000" (ibid.).

Another difficulty for the new government in establishing a coherent ideology stems from the many factions that make up the revolution. In fact, some of the organizations have split into two groups—one joining the CNR and the other remaining in opposition. Of the most significant among the major pre-coup organizations is the Patriotic League for Development (Lipad), which usually looks to Moscow for political inspiration. Lipad was the largest single organization on the left before it fractured into several groups. One minister in government held a leadership position in Lipad and other Lipad members head important projects. However, others have come into conflict with Sankara and the CDR. In an interview, Sankara even had to defend his government's policies from charges of fascism (*Liberation*, 5 June; *FBIS*, 25 June). He added in another interview that "I consider the Cuban revolution a symbol of courage and determination" (*Intercontinental Press*, 29 April, p. 233). Despite the CNR leadership and the Burkinabè intellectuals wrestling with the application of classical Marxist texts to such an economically undeveloped country, there seems little doubt about the leftward, centralizing thrust of the governmental policies.

Thomas H. Henriksen
Hoover Institution

Angola

Population. 7,953,000
Party. Popular Movement for the Liberation of Angola–Labor Party (Movimento Popular de Libertação de Angola–Partido do Trabalho; MPLA-PT)
Founded. 1956 (renamed, 1977)
Membership. 35,000 (*FBIS*, 5 December)
Secretary General. José Eduardo dos Santos
Politburo. 11 members
Central Committee. 90 members (increased from 60 members in 1985)
Status. Ruling party
Last Congress. Second, 9–11 December 1985

Last Election. 1980; all 203 candidates MPLA-PT approved
Auxiliary Organizations. MPLA Youth (JMPLA), Organization of Angolan Women (OMA), Angolan Teachers Association, National Union of Angolan Workers (UNTA)
Publications. No data

The ruling Marxist-Leninist political party of Angola, the MPLA-PT, was founded as the MPLA in 1956. The party was a secret movement to resist Portuguese rule in Angola and was led for the most part by urban-based *mesticos* and intellectuals with roots in the Portuguese Communist Party. (Its subsequent history is outlined in prior editions of the *YICA*.) In 1974–1975, the MPLA was catapulted into power in Luanda by virtue of covert support from influential members of the revolutionary military leadership in Lisbon as well as massive external support from Cuba and the Soviet Union in the military showdown with the two other major factions in Angolan politics, Holden Roberto's National Front for the Liberation of Angola (Frente Nacional de Libertação de Angola; FNLA) and Jonas Savimbi's National Union for the Total Independence of Angola (União Nacional para a Independência Total de Angola; UNITA).

The MPLA was renamed the MPLA-PT in December 1977 at the first major post-independence party congress. The party's chief ideologist, Lucio Lara, considered the move necessary to enhance the role of labor in the governing party (which was allocated at least 20 percent of party congress seats by statute) and to reinforce the development of Angola in a Marxist direction.

Organization and Leadership. The MPLA-PT and its Central Committee monopolize political power in the half of the country under the control of the central government. Day-to-day control is exercised by a much smaller group, the eleven-member Politburo, headed by the current president of Angola and chairman of the MPLA-PT, José Eduardo dos Santos. Dos Santos was educated in the Soviet Union and is married to a Russian. In the period since 1980, a vast political infrastructure has been created on paper, consisting of a People's Assembly, provincial assemblies, and a number of electoral colleges meant to represent the various constituencies appropriate to a Marxist-Leninist state. In the course of 1985, for instance, the People's Assembly met on 20–21 February and again on 24–26 July; the agendas included not only routine budgetary and administrative items, but also the ratification of laws to attribute wider powers to military tribunals and to send temporary workers to the German Democratic Republic (GDR) (*FBIS*, 9 July).

A major event in 1985 was the party's Second Congress held in December, an event that required much preparation. Following a national party conference on 14–19 January, on 8 February the Politburo created a national preparatory commission, which organized meetings throughout the year for the many subcommissions. Dos Santos asked for conditions that would allow "open, frank, and honest discussion of our problems" (*FBIS*, 29 April). On 26 September a meeting of the Central Committee was devoted to that upcoming meeting (ibid., 1 October).

The Second Congress involved over 700 delegates representing the 35,000 MPLA-PT members. Soviet Politburo member Geydar Aliyev led the Moscow delegation to the Angolan congress, as did Socialist Unity Party (SED) Politburo member Werner Krolikowski for the GDR delegation (*Pravda*, 4 December; *FBIS*, 5 December). Following the proclamations of unity by MPLA-PT leaders and the departure of Aliyev for Moscow, a major purge of party leadership occurred. Pro-Soviet hardliner Lucio Lara from the Politburo and two of his key allies, former foreign minister Santos Onambwe and Air Force commander Henrique Carreira, were removed from the Central Committee (*FBIS*, 12 December; *WP*, 13 December).

Mass Organizations. The MPLA-PT took the lead in organizing mass support groups and front organizations for the regime even before creating constitutional assemblies. Among the most important sectors organized thus far are youth, women, trade unionists, and various militia groups. In April a delegation of the JMPLA, led by First National Secretary Domingos Bartolomeu, hosted a Soviet delegation from the All-Union Komsomol and signed a five-year accord for cooperation (*FBIS*, 15 April).

The National Union of Angolan Workers (UNTA) plays a powerful role in the political affairs of Angola, having thrown its support to the MPLA during the crucial struggle of 1974–1975. According to MPLA-PT figures, there are now 628,000 members of the UNTA. In addition, a total of 1,070,603 members belong to the Organization of Angolan Women, and the people's vigilance brigades have 320,000 men enrolled (*FBIS*, 21 March).

Domestic Affairs. The domestic realities of Angola since obtaining independence have been ten years of chaos and war. The thorough alienation of the Ovimbundu people from the Luanda regime, first through the defection of Daniel Chipenda from the MPLA-PT and then through his exclusion from the Politburo, has resulted in a loss of government control over about one-third of the country. Other parts of the country are intermittently beyond the reach of the MPLA-PT, particularly among the Bakongo people in the north near the border with Zaire.

The military battle between the MPLA-PT central government and the UNITA forces raged to new heights in 1985. With UNITA having 30,000 men under arms, the threat to MPLA-PT hegemony become more palpable, especially given UNITA's apparent ability to operate freely in the countryside through much of the country. Estimates indicate that UNITA has small military units operating in about 90 percent of the country (*WP*, 20 September).

In August and September the MPLA-PT launched an offensive against UNITA's bases with active Cuban involvement. The town of Mazongo fell to the MPLA-PT on 18 September, and the government forces then threatened the heartland of UNITA control, the towns of Mavinga and Jamba. At that point, South African military forces intervened with air power and drove back the communist offensive, with significant losses to both sides.

The economic scene remained bright only in the area of oil production, although even the secure installations in Cabinda came under attack from opposition forces during 1985. Attacks against the British diamond mines in the northeast occurred regularly, the most recent reported incident occurring in May, and transport for the coffee harvest to ports was apparently unavailable, which meant that the crops were simply not harvested (ibid.).

International Relations. The foreign policy of Angola since independence has been characterized by dependence on Cuba and the Soviet Union. The October 1976 treaty of friendship and cooperation between Moscow and Luanda, which was to be valid for twenty years and committed both sides to close cooperation between political parties, was the axis around which Angola constructed its foreign relations. The MPLA-PT's claims to be an authentic Marxist-Leninist party were confirmed by that treaty, even more so than by the cooperation agreements with Cuba signed in July 1976 and subsequently augmented. Yet the Cuban agreements have constituted equally important steps in terms of concrete cooperation. Recent estimates suggest that about 30,000 Cuban military personnel are in Angola, along with 5,000 civilian advisers and technicians. A recent estimate of Eastern bloc personnel included 900 Soviets and 1000 East Germans (*Soviet Analyst*, 25 September).

In 1985 the provision of military hardware by the Soviet Union took on increased importance, given the decision to launch all-out offensives against UNITA. A key meeting in this regard was apparently a set of tripartite (Soviet-Angolan-Cuban) talks held in Moscow on 6 March; top-level military representatives attended along with then–foreign minister Andrei Gromyko and B. N. Ponomarev of the Soviet Union (*FBIS*, 8 March). The Soviets supplied a sophisticated air defense system (radars and missiles), tanks, Mi-24 helicopter gunships, and MiG-23s; also crucial to Angolan military reach was the Soviet lengthening of the runway at Menongue in south-central Angola to handle the new advanced aircraft (*WP*, 29 September, p. A23).

It is known that the Soviets and Cubans sustained some casualties during the August–September offensive against UNITA. The destruction of aircraft produced identifiable pilot fatalities of non-Angolan origin, and the destruction of armored columns resulted in Soviet casualties (*FBIS*, 5 September). President Dos Santos visited Cuba in late October, following the failure of the offensive (ibid., 29 October).

The maintenance of these ties with other communist states and parties has resulted in a constant exchange of high-level visits. The fourth session of the Soviet-Angolan Commission for Trade, Economic, and Technical Cooperation was held in Luanda at the end of March; special emphasis was given to planning and research on construction of a hydropower station at Capanda (in an area currently beyond MPLA-PT control), construction of a fishing port, mining, and bridge reconstruction (ibid., 1 April). The signing of an Angolan-Soviet cultural/scientific exchange agreement in May specified 300 scholarships and fifteen apprenticeships of from three to six months for Angolans in Soviet schools (ibid., 24 May). In Sofia in early July, an agreement was signed between the two countries on cooperation in the field of "people's vigilance" (ibid., 11 July). Talks between the Angolan minister of foreign affairs, Afonso van Dunem Mbinda, and the Soviets took place on 7–8 August. Topics covered included "the agenda of the forthcoming 40th session of the United Nations General Assembly and the situation in the south of Africa" (ibid., 9 and 16 August). On 2 October the minister of transport and communications visited Berlin to sign an agreement with the GDR for long-term technical cooperation (ibid., 4 October).

In early September the MPLA-PT demonstrated its ability to broaden its international base when it hosted the eighth Non-Aligned Ministerial Conference in Luanda (ibid., 11 September). It was an impressive accomplishment from the Angolan point of view, both in terms of providing security and gaining publicity. In May the MPLA-PT announced the extension of a cooperation agreement with the Algerian ruling party, the National Liberation Front (FLN), after a week-long visit of Central Committee members in Algiers (ibid., 8 May).

Talks with non-Marxist countries became an important dimension of Angolan foreign relations during 1985. For example, Angola's relationship with the United States varied greatly. The year began with regular negotiations over the future of Namibia; the MPLA-PT position in those talks was that a settlement in Namibia and withdrawal of South Africa would allow it to send home all but 10,000 Cuban troops. The MPLA-PT became skeptical of U.S. intentions when UNITA hosted the formative meeting of the "Democratic International" on 2 June in Jamba, a U.S.-inspired effort to create a coalition of anticommunist resistance forces from Angola, Afghanistan, Cambodia, Nicaragua, and Laos. In July the MPLA-PT view was reinforced when the U.S. Congress repealed the Clark Amendment, thereby making possible U.S. aid to UNITA or other opposition forces. The MPLA-PT therefore broke off diplomatic contacts with the United States, and the Central Committee met on 3 August to issue a ringing denunciation (ibid., 6 August).

Relations with South Africa were poisoned considerably during the year. After the brief respite from hostility—a pause made possible by the Lusaka agreement of February 1984—mutual recriminations escalated over MPLA-PT tolerance of SWAPO raids into Namibia and South African raids into southern Angola. When a group of South African soldiers were caught attempting to damage the Cabinda oil installations on 21 May, the MPLA-PT told South Africa it would break off negotiations over Namibia (*Los Angeles Times*, 4 June). In September the South African government admitted publicly for the first time that it had been giving aid to UNITA (*FBIS*, 21 September). Despite verbal Angolan outrage, the Luanda government returned to indirect talks (through U.S. auspices) with South Africa over Namibia in December.

Richard E. Bissell
Washington, D.C.

Benin

Population. 4,015,000
Party. People's Revolutionary Party of Benin (Parti revolutionaire du Peuple du Benin; PRPB)
Founded. 1975
Membership. No data
Chairman. Mathieu Kerekou

Politburo. Elected November 1985: Mathieu Kerekou, Martin Dohou Azonhiho, Joseph Degla, Gado Girigissou, Roger Imorou Garaba, Justin Gnidehou, Sanni Mama Gomina, Romain Vilon Guezo, Vincent Guezodje, Idi Abdoulaye Malam, Simon Ifede Ogouma
Central Committee. 45 members
Status. Ruling party
Last Congress. Second, 18–24 November 1985
Last Election. 1984, all 196 members of the National Popular Assembly approved by and included on the PRPB list.
Auxiliary Organizations. Organization of the Revolutionary Youth of Benin (PJRB); Organization of the Revolutionary Women of Benin (OFRB); National Federation of Workers' Unions of Benin (UNSTB); Committees for the Defense of the Revolution (CDR)
Publications. *Andoya* (PRPB publication); *Ehuzu* (government-controlled daily)

For president and PRPB chairman Mathieu Kerekou, who has been in power since 1972 and is by far the most durable Beninese leader since independence in 1960, 1985 was a paradoxical year. He finally succeeded in purging Michel Alladaye from the PRPB Politburo and the party; Alladaye was the last survivor of the group of officers who staged the 1972 coup that brought Kerekou to power. The party congress in November appeared to solidify Kerekou's grip on power. Most of the newly elected Politburo members were more or less under his sway. However, Kerekou's and perhaps even the PRPB's control over the country was, for the first time since 1975, challenged by internal unrest coming from high school and university students. In addition, the worsening economic situation of the country appears to have the potential to strengthen Kerekou's opposition and impose on the regime a number of limitations bound to narrow its political base.

Domestic Party Affairs. In January Kerekou took a number of measures "to stamp out arbitrary arrests" by the security forces, which indicated that his control over the military and police was far from complete (*FBIS*, 23 January). Throughout the year the PRPB was preoccupied with the worsening economic situation, which was largely due to the collapsing price of oil. This, in turn, resulted in the weakening of Nigeria's economy, on which Benin depends to a decisive extent. One of the immediate results of this preoccupation was the appointment of Idi Abdoulaye Malan as technical adviser to the president on economic affairs at the beginning of April and his promotion to the Politburo after the November party congress.

Among the measures taken by the regime to cope with the economic crisis was the postponement of employment of university graduates by the government toward the end of 1984. On 10 April, when certain positions were open, they were far too few for the new graduates. In a country where the bureaucracy has always been disproportionately large and the university graduates were used to receiving government jobs, such a drastic change served to release pent-up frustrations among the youth and to revive old grievances. It also served to strengthen the influence of the extreme left, which was disenchanted with Kerekou's relatively flexible foreign and domestic economic policies. Some of the former activists of the far left involved in the 1974 student strikes—members of the General Union of the Dahomean High School and University Students (UGEED)—together with sympathizers of the exiled Communist Party of Dahomey and disgruntled members of the International League in the Defense of the Rights of People ("La Ligue"), have succeeded, directly or through their followers, in taking control over the Executive Bureau of the National University Cooperative, the leading student organization.

Student protests at the Abomey-Kalavi campus of the National University began on 21 March and were aimed at the government's unwillingness or inability to guarantee full employment for graduates. Soon the disturbances spread to the Cotonou and Porto Novo campuses, and on 27 April the government disbanded the Executive Bureau (*FBIS*, 1 May). The students immediately declared a nation-wide strike. Disturbances spread farther and by the first days of May reached the primary schools and even the nurseries, with youths rampaging throughout Cotonou, Abomey, and Porto Novo and, according to the government, engaging in "vandalism and looting" (ibid., 8 May). On 6 May, Kerekou ordered the chief of staff of the army "to check most vigorously all acts of vandalism and to get the soldiers to shoot on sight any demonstrator" and shut down all of the nation's educational institutions (ibid., 7 May). At least two students were killed (*Afrique Nouvelle*, 19–25 June, p. 6).

The government blamed the disturbances on a "handful of irresponsible and anarchist students and schoolchildren" (*FBIS*, 7 May) or on a "small political group that claims to be communist" (ibid., 8 May). Specifically, the instigators were said to be "base individuals" granted amnesty in August 1984—that is, members of the far left opposition (ibid., 7 May).

The degree to which the student riots of April and May shook the Kerekou regime was made clear in the following weeks. Kerekou needed to reassure himself of the army's loyalty in a highly tense meeting on 10 June. He then proceeded to purge the PRPB leadership. In an 11 June communiqué, the PRPB Politburo announced the dismissal of Alladaye, who had been minister of secondary and higher education, and of the president, vice president, and general secretary of the National University of Benin (UNB). In addition, nineteen "anarchist and leftist students were sacked from the UNB for blatant subversive activities" (ibid., 13 June).

The dismissal of Alladaye, who was also relieved of his posts as Politburo member, first deputy chairman of the Security and Defense Commission of the PRPB Central Committee, and suspended from the party, was far more important than the simple punishment of an incompetent minister. Alladaye was known to be very close to the Soviets and to still have supporters both in the army and among the important Fon ethnic group of Abomey and Ouidah (*Africa Confidential*, 13 July p. 7). Whether or not the regime's claim that the "anarchist and leftist" student leaders were linked with foreign powers referred obliquely to the USSR and Alladaye's links to Moscow is unclear. What is clear, however, is the renewed Beninese sympathy for China and North Korea, perhaps as a counter to the previously growing influence of Cuba and the Soviets. At any rate, Alladaye's ministerial post was taken over by Vincent Guezodje, a known hardliner and Politburo member who is very close to Kerekou and who played no role in the 1972 coup. Martin Dohou Azonhiho, formerly the second most powerful leader of the regime who was almost dismissed and relegated to the minor job of provincial governor, made a comeback after the PRPB congress and is now mentioned with equal prominence as all the other members of that body save Kerekou himself.

Regarding party membership, the congress mentioned a recruiting drive following an ideological seminar of 1984, but actual PRPB membership numbers are still uncertain. A party Institute of International Relations was envisaged at the congress and intensive training of cadres of the Foreign Ministry was suggested pending its creation (*FBIS*, 27 November).

International Relations. The order in which foreign communist parties were mentioned in Kerekou's address at the congress is highly significant for the PRPB's orientation. The Chinese and North Korean parties were mentioned first, followed by those of the USSR, Czechoslovakia, East Germany, Hungary, Poland, Romania, Bulgaria, Cuba, France, and the ruling National Liberation Front of Algeria. Moreover, Kerekou felt it necessary to "stress particularly the appreciable contribution of the PRC and the DPRK to the social and economic development of our country, the PRPB" (ibid.). It is interesting to note that the North Koreans provide Kerekou with his own personal bodyguards (*Africa Confidential*, 13 July) and that China has donated food and materials for the internal security ministry.

Relations with the Soviet Union included a parliamentary visit by Avgust Voss, the chairman of the USSR Supreme Soviet Council on Nationalities, in April, and visits by Soviet youth and journalist delegations.

On a regional basis, Benin's policies continued and expanded the trend toward the formation of a coalition of West African radical states, including Ghana, Burkina Faso, and Libya. The main expression of this trend was the quadripartite summit of 27 April in Burkina Faso that stressed the continuation of the "revolutionary solidarity" ties with Ghana in particular. Those participating included host Thomas Sankara, Jerry Rawlings of Ghana, and Libyan second-in-command Jallud.

Michael Radu
Foreign Policy Research Institute

Congo

Population. 1,798,000
Party. Congolese Party of Labor (Parti Congolaise du Travail; PCT)
Founded. 1969
Membership. ca. 9,000 (official figures)
Chairman. Denis Sassou-Ngouesso
Politburo. No data
Central Committee. 60 members
Status. Ruling and sole legal party
Last Congress. Third, 23–30 July 1984, in Brazzaville
Last Election. 1984, 95 percent, all 153 members PCT approved
Auxiliary Organizations. Congolese Trade Union Confederation (CSC); Revolutionary Union of Congolese Women; URFC); Union of Congolese Socialist Youth (UJSC)
Publications. *Mweti* (national daily, under government control); *Etumba* (weekly, organ of the PCT Central Committee); *Elikia* (quarterly, under PCT control)

The Congo, formerly known as Congo-Brazzaville, is the oldest self-proclaimed Marxist-Leninist regime in sub-Saharan Africa. What was then defined as the Marxist-Leninist "option" was made public soon after the 13–15 August 1963 events that brought to power the radical group centered around Alphonse Massemba Debat. Since then, the pattern of Congolese politics has been characterized by a steady movement to the left and by growing political and security ties with the Soviet bloc and China. (For more detail on the background of the PCT, see *YICA*, 1984, pp. 15–16.)

Party and Domestic Affairs. The PCT's Politburo called its first meeting of the year on 26 January. It dealt primarily with the political indoctrination of the army and security forces. After reiterating that "the political organs in the Popular National Army are the leading organizations of the party in the army," the group chaired by Denis Sassou-Ngouesso established political commissions that were empowered to strengthen PCT control over the military (*Mweti*, 29 January). The Politburo meeting also organized the celebrations for the sixth anniversary of the Movement of February 5th—the date of the political coup against then-president Yhombi-Opango that brought Sassou-Ngouesso to power in 1979.

Nineteen eighty-five was described as the "Year of National Overcoming Against the Perverse Effects of the Crisis" (ibid.). The "crisis" was the Congolese economic slump, due to past government policies but also aggravated by the fall in oil prices. With oil by far the largest source of export revenues and with a large number of economically unproductive state and parastate enterprises, the government was faced with serious political and economic problems.

The most serious attack against the regime of President Sassou-Ngouesso originated from students, a group that was traditionally supportive of the ruling PCT. Following a government decision on 6 November to introduce a competitive examination for high school (lycée) graduates seeking university scholarship as part of a general policy of austerity, massive student demonstrations occurred in Brazzaville. Quite clearly the government felt seriously attacked, since it decided to put the blame on "former politicians," including former president Yhombi-Opango, and on "illegal" religious sects (*FBIS*, 18 November). In fact, the student protests appear to have come from the left rather than the more conservative elements associated with Yhombi-Opango. In December the government underwent serious changes, some related to the student demonstrations (for example, changes in the Education Ministry leadership) and some to the austerity policies (for example, a reduction of the number of ministers).

Ideology. Theoretically, structurally, and functionally the PCT is a Marxist-Leninist, "vanguard" party, similar to those in Eastern Europe. However, any perceptive visitor to Brazzaville cannot fail to notice the lack of ideological interest and commitment on the part of the entire population, with the possible exception of university and high school students. Moreover, all of the essential military, government, and many party positions are filled by military officers, and of these a majority are northerners. Nevertheless, ideology and ideological purity are taken seriously by the regime and go beyond the omnipresent ideological graffiti on the walls, billboards, and streets of Brazzaville. One reason for this was pointed out by Celestin Goma-Foutou, PCT Central Committee secretary in charge of ideology and political training, who asked for renewed efforts in the ideological field to counter "repeated attacks by enemies of socialism" (*FBIS*, 11 February).

The most significant ideological event of 1985 was the joint PCT–Communist Party of the Soviet Union (CPSU) colloquium on ideology, which took place in Brazzaville in February. It was the fifth such meeting, and its main concern was, in the words of Pierre Nze, Politburo member and PCT secretary for external relations, "to exchange experience in order to achieve a better understanding of the socialist system" (ibid.). The importance given to the colloquium by the Soviets was underscored by their choice of leader of the Soviet delegation—Solodovnikov, former director of Moscow's Africa Institute, ambassador to Zambia, and prominent theoretician of Marxism-Leninism in the Third World. Solodovnikov's paper delivered in Brazzaville dealt with "Marxism-Leninism and Its Peculiarities in Developing Countries Engaged in Socialism." Goma-Foutou, the leader of the Congolese delegation spoke on "Stages of the Democratic and Popular Revolution: Facts of Theorization on the Congolese Experience" (ibid.).

Auxiliary Organizations. Like all Marxist-Leninist parties in power, the PCT directly controls all institutional forms of political or group expression in the country, with the exception of the Catholic Church. The CSC controls the trade unons; the URFC is in charge of women's activities; and the UJSC controls youth political activities, although the events mentioned above throw some doubt over its effectiveness.

International Views and Contacts. The Congo's rather heterodox ideological attitudes were demonstrated in February, almost concurrently with the Congolese-Soviet ideological colloquium, when then–planning minister Pierre Moussa visited Beijing and claimed that "we have something to learn from China's planning experience" (*FBIS*, 17 February).

A similar attempt to maintain as extensive a network of relations as possible was demonstrated by Sassou-Ngouesso at the 11 March symposium organized in Brazzaville by the URFC. After reiterating the Congo's desire to improve and expand relations—particularly economic ones—with the United States, he strongly condemned "American imperialism" and its activities in Central America.

The Congo's primary foreign interest—ideologically, politically, and economically—remains the Soviet bloc. Sassou-Ngouesso visited the German Democratic Republic (GDR) in May, in addition to Romania and Bulgaria, and has expanded the Congo's already extensive ties to the Palestine Liberation Organization (PLO). Relations with the Soviet Union also continued to expand; the Soviets contributed advice to the Congo's Five-Year Plan and they aid in training of "hundreds" of Congolese youths, offer support for twenty major development projects, and teach at a number of Congolese technical and vocational training centers (*Izvestiia*, 13 August, p. 5).

Factionalism and Opposition to the PCT. Although the Sassou-Ngouesso regime appears stable, there are certain groups both within and outside the PCT that actively challenge it. By far the most important is a loose grouping of ideological hardliners, who also happen to be northerners, subverting the president's own popular support base—the February 22 Movement (Mouvement du 22 Fevrier; M-22)—which includes Camille Bongou, Ambroise Noumazalaye, and Benoit Ngollo (see *YICA*, 1984 and 1985). All are hardline Marxists (*Africa Confidential* 26, no. 14 [3 July]: 5–6). The main external opposition, the Congolese Patriotic Movement (MPC), is itself Marxist, and largely irrelevant as well as vulnerable to regime brandishments and co-optation. Although the MPC called for pluralistic party politics in the Congo, its credibility among non-Marxists is close to nil, at least in Brazzaville. As for the Congolese Democratic Party (PDC), a free-trade and free-market group based in France, its ideas have so far remained alien to most citizens of the Congo. Factionalism within the PCT, rather than ideological or French-based opposition, seems to be the only serious challenge to the regime. The future appears to hold more of the same, or perhaps an even more Leninist hardline regime, as the alternative to Sassou-Ngouesso.

Michael Radu
Foreign Policy Research Institute

Ethiopia

Population. 34,483,000
Party. Workers' Party of Ethiopia (WPE)
Founded. 10 September 1984
Membership. 50,000
Secretary General. Mengistu Haile Mariam
Politburo. 11 full members: Mengistu Haile Mariam, Fikre-Selassie Wogderess, Fisseha Desta, Tesfaye Gebre Kidan, Berhanu Bayih, Legesse Asfaw, Addis Tedlay, Hailu Yimenu, Amanuel Amde Michael, Alenu Abebe, Shimelis Mazengia; 6 alternate members
Secretariat. 8 members: Fisseha Desta, Legesse Asfaw, Shimelis Mazengia, Fasika Sidelil, Shewandagn Belete, Wubeset Desie, Ashagre Yigletu, Embibel Ayele
Central Committee. 136 full members, 64 alternate members
Status. Ruling party
Last Congress. First, 6–10 September 1984, in Addis Ababa
Last Election. N/a
Auxiliary Organizations. All-Ethiopian Peasants' Association; Kebelles; All-Ethiopia Trade Union; Revolutionary Ethiopia's Women's Association; Revolutionary Ethiopia's Youth Association
Publications. *Serto Ader*, *Meskerem*, *Addis Zemen*, *Ethiopian Herald*, *Negarit Gazeta*

The WPE specified that its primary responsibility in 1985 was to begin drawing up a new constitution that would lead to the creation of a People's Democratic Republic of Ethiopia (PDRE). In addition, the WPE took charge of coordinating the resettlement of 1.2 million people devastated by the famine from their homes in the north to land in the south and southwest.

Leadership and Party Organization. In a speech before the third regular session of the WPE Central Committee, Mengistu Haile Mariam revealed the extent of the efforts taken by the party to prepare a draft constitution: "[A] basic draft has been prepared . . . that will be enhanced and amended in the future. Its general features incorporate 1) the political, economic, and social system of the PDRE; 2) the basic rights and obligations of citizens; 3) the structure of the government of the PDRE; 4) the formation and working process of organs of power and administration; 5) the judiciary and the attorney general; and 6) general regulations" (Addis Ababa Domestic Service [AADS], 3 September). According to the Central Committee, a constitutional commission will be charged with organizing discussions through the rubric of party structures and auxiliary organizations so that people throughout the state can participate in finalizing the constitutional strictures (*Pravda*, 6 September). The primary purpose of the constitution and the PDRE is part of a "long-term plan to construct a prosperous socialist society in our country" (AADS, 3 September).

Despite criticism from Western relief organizations that forced population shifts were taking place in an attempt to deplete support for the secessionist movements in the north, the WPE oversaw the resettlement of 510,287 families from the north to the south and southwest (ibid., 2 September). This was to be part of a larger movement of peoples that would total 1.2 million and would be completed in 1986. According to Mengistu, land, tools, and oxen had been set aside, water had been made available, and the peoples of the south had been socialized in an effort to make it easier for the new settlers (ibid.). In addition, peasant associations in the south were organized to aid those being resettled.

Organizing this vast resettlement program could not have been accomplished without the support of the Soviet Union, whose planes and trucks transported the majority of these refugees. Indeed, during an official visit to Moscow in early November, Mengistu personally thanked Mikhail Gorbachev, general secretary of the CPSU Central Committee, for the efforts of the USSR in aiding Ethiopia in its long-range efforts to deal with the famine (*Pravda*, 3 November). He went on to say that despite Western reports to the contrary, the resettlement effort was undertaken so as to provide destitute northern farmers with fertile land that had access to water. By the end of 1985 the famine had affected almost 8 million people with more than 3 million still facing starvation.

International Views, Positions, and Activities. Strenuous efforts were made by Ethiopia to strengthen and develop relations with Bulgaria and North Korea. The sixth session of the Joint Bulgarian-Ethiopian Commission for Economic, Scientific, and Technological Cooperation was held in Addis Ababa in October. Plans were drawn up for the development of irrigation projects, agricultural equipment plants, land improvement projects, and enterprises for the processing of farm produce. These plans are in addition to the 36 agro-industrial projects that are presently being designed and constructed by Bulgarian specialists (*Bulgaria Today*, no. 450; *JPRS-EPS*, 15 October). After a series of visits to Pyongyang and Addis Ababa by North Korean and Ethiopian party representatives, Mengistu visited North Korea in November. Although apparently no agreements were signed, North Korea indicated obliquely that it would look favorably on increasing its aid to Ethiopia (Korean Central News Agency, 18 November).

Relations with the USSR continued to improve. In February the Soviet Union agreed to provide Ethiopia with $124 million in loans to be used in developing irrigation projects; the same month an agreement was signed by which the USSR would provide a loan of $372 million to plan development projects (AADS, 14 February). Soon thereafter the USSR agreed to provide Ethiopia with construction equipment, clothing, and blankets that would be used by Ethiopia's Relief and Rehabilitation Commission (ibid., 16 March). In October Mikhail Sergeychik, chairman of the Soviet State Committee for Foreign Economic Relations, visited Addis Ababa and agreed to continue providing funds for the completion of the Melka Wakena hydroelectric project, which is being constructed jointly by Ethiopia, the USSR, and Czechoslovakia (ibid., 25 October). During the year trade agreements were also signed with the People's Democratic Republic of Yemen, Cuba, Egypt, and the German Democratic Republic, and diplomatic relations were reestablished with Sudan.

In the north the Tigre Popular Liberation Front (TPLF) and the Eritrean secessionists continued their battles against Ethiopia. Rebellious movements in both provinces also battled verbally with each other. In August the strategic town of Barentu in Eritrea was recaptured by Ethiopia after being held for two months by the rebels. The TPLF accused Eritrean rebels of preventing food supplies from entering Tigre in an effort to limit its political authority. Apparently the famine has caused bitterness to emerge among the rebellious groups since their popular base is being eroded by the effects of the famine and the resettlement of refugees to the south.

Peter Schwab
State University of New York
College at Purchase

Lesotho

Population. 1,512,000
Party. Communist Party of Lesotho (CPL)
Founded. 1962
Membership. No data
Chairman. R. Mataji
Secretariat. Jacob M. Kena (secretary general), John Motloheloa, Khotso Molekane
Status. Semilegal (see below)
Last Congress. Seventh, November 1984
Last Elections. September 1985
Auxiliary Organizations. International front affiliates probably auxiliary to the ruling Basotho National Party (BNP) rather than to the CPL: the Lesotho Peace and Solidarity Council (LPSC; affiliate of the World Peace Council); the Lesotho Afro-Asian People's Solidarity Committee (affiliate of the Afro-Asian People's Solidarity Organization); and apparently the Lesotho Youth Committee (probable affiliate of the World Federation of Democratic Youth)
Publication. *Mozhammokho* (Communist)

The CPL was formerly noted as having its primary support from Basotho workers in South Africa (*Political Handbook of the World*, 1982–83, p. 292). However, since the ban on its activities was "partially lifted" in 1984, it has been reported as having strength in the capital city of Maseru as well as in certain parts of southern Lesotho (*Rand Daily Mail*, 2 October 1984). The CPL is strongly pro-Soviet and anti-Chinese and, of course, opposed to the government of South Africa (ibid.; Moscow, Tass, 4 May 1982; *FBIS*, 10 May 1982).

In an article in the South African Communist Party's *The African Communist* (third quarter), CPL secretary Khotso Molekane lauded the "progressive" foreign policy of Premier Leabua Jonathan. Specifically, the BNP had established diplomatic relations with communist countries in 1983 and had earlier forged close ties with the FRELIMO government in Mozambique and the (South) African National Congress (ANC) (p. 61). Molekane characterized the major opposition parties as being to the right of the BNP and noted that the CPL's Seventh Congress had called for "a broad front of all patriotic forces of the Basotho people in opposition to South Africa's imperialist intervention" (p. 64). This was an apparent offer of support to the government against South African actions, which had reached a high point in a December 1982 invasion of Maseru in order to wipe out a group of ANC refugees residing there (p. 62). According to Molekane the congress also implicitly criticized the government's internal policy by calling for a "socialist alternative in [Lesotho's] sociopolitical development as an independent Marxist-Leninist vanguard of the working people" (p. 64).

The government did not accept the invitation. The CPL was not officially legalized in 1985, although it was allowed to continue to operate openly. In August its Maseru headquarters were raided by government security forces, and party literature found there was confiscated (Radio Johannesburg, 9 August; *FBIS*, 13 August). In September the CPL, just like the right-wing opposition forces, apparently failed to participate in the national elections; the latter groups blamed the government's bureaucratic and physical harassment for this (Johannesburg Television, 19 September; *FBIS*, 25 September). One bright spot for the CPL during the year was its acceptance as the 66th Communist Party to be represented on the editorial council of the *World Marxist Review (Problems of Peace and Socialism)*, the Prague-based, Soviet-line theoretical monthly (*WMR*, June, p. 2).

Lesotho-Soviet relations developed further with the arrival of a resident Soviet ambassador in Maseru in July; by October he was noted as having a staff of 27 (*FPI International Report*, 9 October, p. 3). The BNP-dominated LPSC also continued to prosper. The January issue of the World Peace Council's *Peace Courier* carried a story of a joint WPC-LPSC campaign against "South African aggression," and in October a low-level LPSC delegation visited the USSR as a guest of its Soviet counterpart (Radio Moscow, 17 October; *FBIS*, 18 October).

A possible balancing of such relationships might be seen, however, in the April announcement that Lesotho was trying to improve its heretofore bad relations with the traditionally pro-Chinese Pan-African Congress of South Africa (Radio Johannesburg, 3 April; *FBIS*, 4 April) and the August-September visit of King Moshoeshoe II to China. The effect may have been somewhat diminished by the announcement that these were Lesotho government, not BNP, actions (ibid.; Beijing, *Xinhua*, 31 August–2 September; *FBIS*, 6 September).

Wallace H. Spaulding
McLean, Virginia

Mozambique

Population. 13,776,000
Party. Front for the Liberation of Mozambique (Frente de Libertação de Moçambique; FRELIMO)
Founded. 1962
Membership. 110,323 (*African Communist*, 4th Quarter, 1983)
Secretary General. Samora Moisés Machel
Politburo. 11 members: Samora Moisés Machel, Marcelino dos Santos, Joaquim Alberto Chissano, Alberto Chipande, Armando Emilio Guebuza, Jorge Rebelo, Mariano de Araújo Matsinhe, Sebastião Marcos Mabote, Jacinto Soares Veloso, Mário de Graça Machungo, José Óscar Monteiro
Secretariat. 6 members: Samora Moisés Machel, Marcelino dos Santos, Joaquim Alberto Chissano, Jorge Rebelo, Armando Panquene, José Luís Cabaço
Central Committee. 118 members
Status. Ruling party
Last Congress. Fourth, 26–29 April 1983, in Maputo
Last Election. 1977; won all 226 seats in the National People's Assembly
Auxiliary Organizations. Organization of Mozambican Women (Organização da Mulher Moçambicana; OMM); Mozambique Youth Organization (OJM)
Publications. *Notícias* (daily); *O Tempo* (weekly); *Diário de Moçambique* (daily); *Domingo* (Sunday paper); *Voz da Revolução* (Central Committee organ)

FRELIMO assumed power in the southeast African country of Mozambique in 1975 after successfully waging a ten-year guerrilla war for independence from Portugal. With the collapse of Portuguese rule, FRELIMO—the only legal political party—proclaimed an independent People's Republic of Mozambique. (For additional details on the origins and background of FRELIMO, see *YICA*, 1982, p. 37.) In 1985 Mozambique's economic woes loomed larger and more unsolvable than ever for the government, and the country's armed internal opposition posed grave concerns for FRELIMO. Despite its many problems, Mozambique staged large-scale demonstrations in the capital and elsewhere on 25 June to celebrate a decade of self-government.

The year witnessed a continuation of Mozambique's problems and FRELIMO policies of the previous year. Beset by a seriously faltering economy and a worsening antigovernment insurgency in 1984, FRELIMO undertook initiatives toward the West, while maintaining its ties with the Soviet Union and preserving its Marxist party structure and control over the population. For example, Mozambican president Samor Moisés Machel met with U.S. president Ronald Reagan in Washington, D.C., for a two-hour working lunch during mid-September. Machel stated that "we seek the participation of the United States and of its private sector" in developing Mozambique's natural resources (*Washington Times*, 20 September). Afterward, Machel met with businessmen in the United States to explore ways for more American investment in Mozambique. One month later in Maputo, the Mozambican Association of Friendship and Solidarity with Soviet Peoples sponsored a ceremony to mark the 68th anniversary of the October Revolution (Maputo Domestic Service, 6 November; *FBIS*, 6 November).

Organization and Leadership. Despite a more pragmatic foreign policy of seeking Western aid and financial investment in Mozambique, FRELIMO's party structure has continued to adhere to many of the standard practices of communist organizations. Formed in 1962 from three small factions, FRELIMO appeared to be a national front organization throughout much of the independence struggle, while its political orientation moved leftward. After the Second Congress in 1968, FRELIMO's radicalization process became delineated in both the organizational structure and in its Marxian phraseology. FRELIMO moved to implement democratic centralism and a cell structure as left-wing elements consolidated control over the national front; this leftward movement was accompanied by bitter internal struggles that resulted in several murders. Eduardo Mondlane, the first president, fell victim to assassination. For six months a troika ruled after Mondlane's death until Machel emerged as both president and head of the guerrilla army.

In 1977 the Third Congress approved the Central Committee's recommendations to transform FRELIMO into a "Marxist-Leninist vanguard party." Even before this announced change, FRELIMO had already structured its organization along typical communist party lines. The congress, for example, approves the Central Committee (now some 118 members), which is to carry out its policies. As in most communist party structures, the Politburo (now with eleven members) shapes policy for FRELIMO. Most of the Politburo members also have ministerial portfolios and as such have seats on the Council of Ministers, which is the government's cabinet. Mozambique's constitution views the People's Assembly as the country's highest legislative body. Below this national organ, FRELIMO established local, district (112), and provincial (10) assemblies. The People's Assembly delegates are chosen by an elaborate, country-wide election process that is to take place every five years. However, in June the thirteenth session of the People's Assembly unanimously approved the postponement of general elections until 1986. Allowing a Standing Commission to fix the date later, the assembly reportedly gave its reasons for postponing the election of deputies as "the whole people are engaged in the great tasks, mainly the fight against famine and the armed bandits" (Maputo Domestic Service, 14 June; *FBIS*, 17 June).

Characteristic of the interlocking of party and government in communist countries, Mozambique's president is also head of the party. Constitutional provisions empower the president to appoint provincial governors and members of the Council of Ministers, among others. He can, for example, annul decisions made by the provincial assemblies. In spite of rumors of coups to replace Machel, there is no clear successor, although there is reportedly growing dissatisfaction with the government's handling of Mozambique's deepening problems. The Third Congress abolished the office of vice president. In a practice virtually unique to Mozambique, high FRELIMO officials have been dismissed from ministerial posts and sent to provincial and even district posts. In addition to administrative functions, these officials serve as first party secretaries in their regions. The practice of strong, appointed district administrators follows from the Portuguese tradition. Unlike 1984, however, there were no reported dispatching of prominent cabinet ministers to lesser offices or country posts. (For details see *YICA*, 1985, p. 17.).

Mass Organizations. During the guerrilla war against Portugal, FRELIMO appealed to various population groups, such as women and youths. As an outgrowth of these appeals as well as replication of typical communist party structures, FRELIMO established the OMM, which has as its goals the liberation of women from their traditionally low standing and enhancement of the economic and political position of women. The OMM also fulfills FRELIMO's guidelines by publicizing and implementing the party line among men as well as women. It has taken stands against child marriage, polygamy, and the bride-price. Established in 1973, the OMM is the oldest and most active of the mass organizations. The group held its fourth major gathering in November, 1984.

After the Third Congress, FRELIMO established the OJM. The OJM's charter underscored the necessity of mobilizing Mozambicans between the ages of 18 and 35. Initially, it instituted campaigns in urban areas against what it viewed as "bourgeois habits," concentrating on trendy dress, materialism, and other incorrect political behavior. In 1985 delegates from the OJM went to Luanda to meet with Angolan youth. Together they issued a communiqué in October condemning South Africa and expressing their solidarity with the African National Congress (ANC) and the Southwest People's Organization of Namibia (Luanda, ANGOP, 6 November; *FBIS*, 6 November). In order to engage workers in factories, mills, and foundries, FRELIMO set up Production Councils in 1976. Initially confined to Maputo, the Production Councils were extended beyond the capital city after the Third Congress. Their function centered on efforts to mobilize workers "in an active, collective, and conscious way in the discussion and resolution of their problems, especially in relation to production and productivity" (*Notícias*, 12 November 1976). Mass organizations for artists and journalists have not gone far beyond the planning stage. All the mass organizations have been impeded in their development by the party's need to focus on the internal war and economic plight.

The People's Forces for the Liberation of Mozambique (FPLM). With the help of the Soviet bloc, FRELIMO started converting its guerrilla forces into a conventional army, known as the FPLM. A nationwide draft kept fresh recruits coming into an army that is currently estimated at about 25,000 regular troops. At the beginning of the decolonization era, the FPLM's missions called for a defense force and a mobilizing cadre to spread the party's message. The FPLM waged a counterinsurgency campaign against widespread internal enemies, but this has not deflected its goal to modernize. Machel, who holds the military title of field marshal, stated in 1983 that by 1989 the army "must be the most modern in Africa in terms of study, combat, and production" (Maputo Domestic Service, 30 September 1983; *FBIS*, 3 October 1983).

Since the early 1980s, the FPLM has confronted a serious threat in the form of a nearly nationwide insurgency by the Mozambique National Resistance (RENAMO, formerly MNR). Formed initially by the Rhodesian Central Intelligence Organization, RENAMO came into being from disgruntled black Portuguese soldiers in the Portuguese army and anti-Marxist, former FRELIMO members. When white Rhodesia collapsed, RENAMO received support from the Republic of South Africa, which used Mozambican rebels as a counterweight to FRELIMO's policy of aiding the ANC. The ANC launched raids into South Africa from bases inside Mozambique. With South African logistical and training support, RENAMO flourished and has grown to an estimated 20,000 members, most of whom are reportedly located in Mozambique. RENAMO's sabotage has worsened the economic problems caused by the FRELIMO policies of collectivization and nationalization as well as a serious drought in the early 1980s. Maputo refuses to negotiate with RENAMO, except to discuss its capitulation and amnesty for the rebels.

Buffeted by RENAMO, the FRELIMO government has had to rely increasingly on foreign forces to support its shrinking sway in the countryside. An estimated 20,000 foreign troops, military advisers, and security police experts are in Mozambique from Zimbabwe, Cuba, the German Democratic Republic (GDR), and the Soviet Union. Mozambique's air force is headed by Major General Hama Thai, a North Vietnamese officer. The planes, primarily MiG-17s and MiG-21s, are piloted by East Germans. In the past, however, the East Germans have been largely responsible for the formation and support of Mozambique's secret police, *Serviço Nacional de Segurança Popular* (National Service for the People's Security; SNASP). In addition to its security functions, SNASP operates the country's prisons and re-education camps where hundreds are reportedly held, many of whom are detained without trial (*Amnesty International Report, 1984*, London: Amnesty International Publications, 1984, pp. 72–76). One source reported that an estimated 75,000 persons have perished in Mozambican prisons and "re-education camps" (*Washington Times*, 5 February). A U.S. Department of State report on human rights stated that "the total could add up to several thousand [prisoners] if re-education camp inmates are included." It further stated: "However, most observers believe there is a downward trend in numbers of persons incarcerated for their political beliefs" (*Country Reports on Human Rights. Report submitted to the Committee on Foreign Relations, U.S. Senate and Committee on Foreign Affairs, U.S. House of Representatives by the Department of State*, February, p. 230). In August, Zimbabwe's president, Robert Mugabe, pledged to deploy some 31,000 of his 41,000-man army inside Mozambique by the end of 1985 (*CSM*, 26 August). The government also turned to arming villagers and creating local militias to combat RENAMO's attacks.

Typical of guerrilla warfare, each side fighting in the Mozambican countryside proclaimed its own success and the other side's casualties. As one illustration, the Mozambican rebels claimed that they "had killed more than 400 Government soldiers last month" (*NYT*, 8 June). The government's FPLM maintained that it "killed 100 armed bandits, destroyed fourteen camps, and captured a significant quantity of war material in Sofala Province between January and April" (Maputo Domestic Service, 24 May; *FBIS*, 28 May). Conflicting reports aside, the war remained most serious in the northern provinces, particularly Nampula, which is largely occupied by rebel forces. The insurgency is widespread in the nearby provinces of Cabo Delgado, Niassa, and Tete, where economic activity is nearly paralyzed. Serious attacks also took place in the south, including sabotage against factories in the suburbs of the capital itself (*WP*, 6 January). Communication links with Maputo, Swaziland, and South Africa came under fire again this year, disrupting transport to and from the capital. Attacks against foreign residents continued with a number of reported cases of murder and kidnapping. The government has informed foreign diplomatic missions that it can no longer ensure the safety of their citizens; even before the official announcement, several embassies had advised their staffs not to travel outside main towns (Paris, AFP, 4 January; *FBIS*, 7 January). The government announced the capture of a significant rebel base, Casa Banana, in Gorongosa at the end of August.

Domestic Affairs. The high government personnel shuffles of 1984 did not recur this past year. Instead, the main characteristic of Mozambique's domestic policies centered on liberalization of the economy as a means to encourage agricultural and industrial recovery. Agriculture is the major focus of the country's reconstruction effort. On 13 May the Council of Ministers announced economic liberalization measures to decontrol prices on a number of foodstuffs ("Mozambique," *Quarterly Economic Review of Tanzania, Mozambique*, 2nd Quarter, p. 22). The emphasis of the new measures is to strengthen private agricultural producers and transporters and to reduce the role of state wholesale enterprises. These state intermediate structures have been held responsible for delays, waste, and corruption. Their reduction, or in some cases elimination, came about as a method to stimulate private marketing of goods. Soon afterward, increased prices for both food and export crops were announced. These upward prices had as their aim the fostering of a "commercial ethic" in the farming sector (*Notícias*, 25 May). As a result of the government pricing, one source noted more food in Maputo's bazaar as farmers found it worth the effort to bring their food to town (*CSM*, 16 July).

Food remained an item of high priority in Mozambique. According to FRELIMO officials, some 100,000 people died of starvation and disease in southern Mozambique in late 1984 and early 1985. Drought caused food shortages in the south that were not offset by supplies from the north. Northern foodstuffs were not shipped south because of the insurgency and because farmers in the north and in Malawi saw little profit in selling their produce for low prices in what they regarded as worthless Mozambican currency. The absence of consumer goods in Mozambique acted as an additional disincentive to agricultural commerce (Johannesburg Domestic Service, 9 April; *FBIS*, 10 April).

There were other acts of liberalization, such as incentives designed to expand acquisition of hard currency. To make this goal operable, the government decreed that managers of firms earning foreign exchange may be rewarded by payment of part of their salaries in hard currency. Since many of the country's necessities could only be purchased in the capital's hard currency store, officials anticipated positive results. This and other means, it was hoped, would contribute to a reduction of a flourishing black market. To rehabilitate industry, FRELIMO looked to foreign aid. The government's liberalization efforts prompted the World Bank, which Mozambique had joined in 1984, to announce a loan of $45 million mainly for industrial recovery. Economic recovery was also thought to be enhanced by the end of drought conditions in most of Mozambique this year. The repercussions of the drought, however, will be felt for years to come.

Despite moves toward a less controlled economy, the state still retains the overall responsibility for both the public and private sectors. Government planning remains central and deeply entrenched in the economic life of the country. One-third of the 1985 budget, as adopted by the People's Assembly on 13 June, is allocated to defense and security, reflecting the severity of the insurgency. After the military's appropriations, the largest budget shares went to the central and provincial administrations, education, and health ("Mozambique," p. 5). In many respects the liberalization of some aspects of the economy represented a continuation of the reforms initiated by the Fourth Congress. That congress had sought to reverse the declining economy. (For more on the Fourth Congress, see Joseph Hanlon, *Mozambique: The Revolution Under Fire*. London: Zed Books, 1984, pp. 244–51).

In December the fourteenth session of the People's Assembly opened. Finance Minister Rui Baltasar reported that the 1986 state central plan provides for "a general economic growth rate of 13 percent, which means that we will produce about 90 percent of what we produced in 1984." He pointed out that "1986 will be an extremely difficult year" (Maputo Domestic Service, 13 December; *FBIS*, 17 December). The FRELIMO president said "the state agricultural production has dropped by 35 percent in 1985." Machel attributed the reduced output to the lack of material support "in particular to the shortages in fertilizers and fuel." However, he placed high hopes on the family sector to retrieve 1985 agricultural shortfalls (Maputo Domestic Service, 13 December; *FBIS*, 18 December).

International Affairs. As in domestic affairs, Mozambique's foreign affairs policies continued the previous year's formulations. Specifically, FRELIMO tried to implement a rapprochement with its powerful neighbor, the Republic of South Africa, and a pragmatic realignment toward the West to gain private investment and foreign aid for development. At the same time it strengthened its ties with the Soviet Union, which provided military and some economic aid. The USSR not only continued to furnish nearly all Mozambique's liquid fuel requirements but also expanded its shipments to allow a small surplus for export to neighboring countries. Under a trade agreement signed in late May, the USSR was also to give during the fourth quarter of the year $11.7 million in consumer goods, including cloth, watches, and footwear, in exchange for Mozambican agricultural products. As part of its plans to stimulate farm produce, FRELIMO is importing consumer items destined for the rural areas ("Mozambique," p. 29). Speaking at the signing of the agreement, Minister of Home Trade Aranda da Silva stated: "For the Mozambican people, the friendship and solidarity of the Soviet people are nothing new" (Maputo Domestic Service, 29 May; *FBIS*, 31 May).

Most significantly, an agreement on cooperation between the Council of Mutual Economic Assistance (CMEA) and the People's Republic of Mozambique was signed in Moscow on May 17 (Tass, 17 May; *FBIS*, 20 May). Although no details were provided in the report, the agreement itself marks a departure since Mozambique had previously been excluded from membership in CMEA.

In addition to trade and aid from the Soviet Union, Mozambique and the USSR strengthened their traditional ties by visits and agreements. On 17 March, for example, Machel met in the Kremlin with General Secretary Mikhail Gorbachev of the CPSU Central Committee (*Krasnaya Zvezda*, 15 March: *FBIS*, 15 March). In April, FRELIMO's minister of planning, Mário de Graça Machungo, led a delegation to Moscow for the third meeting of the Intergovernmental Commission for Economic and Technical Cooperation and Trade. A number of documents were signed as a result of the talks. These accords aimed at strengthening economic links between the two countries, specifically in mining, transport, engineering, and fishing. The Soviet Union is to assist in the development of mining infrastructure at the Moatise coal deposits and rail lines to the port of Beira. Moscow is also to supply fishing equipment and machinery for repair of merchant ships (Tass, 19 April; *FBIS*, 23 April). In early May a Soviet delegation visited Mozambique; it was headed by I. S. Gustov, a member of the CPSU Central Committee. During this visit a plan for interparty contacts between the CPSU and FRELIMO for 1985–1986 was signed by Gustov and Joaquim Alberto Chissano, FRELIMO's secretary for external relations. It provides for party exchanges and training assistance for FRELIMO cadres (*Pravda*, 4 May; *FBIS*, 10 May).

Under the plan for party ties between the CPSU and FRELIMO, a Mozambican party delegation visited the Soviet Union "to familiarize itself with the CPSU's experience in mass agitation." FRELIMO delegates also noted the CPSU's "experience in mobilizing working people to fulfill party and government decisions." They were quoted as saying the FRELIMO "has set the aim of building a new life in the People's Republic of Mozambique" (*Pravda*, 11 October; *FBIS*, 18 October). Chissano led a party and government delegation in November to Moscow where it was greeted at the airport by Eduard Shevardnadze, minister of foreign affairs of the USSR, and other Soviet officials (*Pravda*, 5 November; *FBIS*, 5 November).

Aid from the United States increased. In 1984 Washington provided Mozambique with more emergency food assistance than any other African country—$22 million. In 1985 the amount increased threefold, bringing the tonnage of food to 150,000. Trade and technical aid totalled about $8 million. But the Reagan administration's plans to send $1.1 million in nonlethal military assistance was blocked by Congress. Five U.S. congressmen visited Mozambique in August to determine the economic situation. Machel's visit to the United States in September continued the thaw in relations between Washington and Maputo that had begun in the early 1980s. During his visit with President Reagan, the Mozambican president congratulated the U.S. administration for imposing limited sanctions on South Africa and called on it to take "further steps" to pressure Pretoria to end its apartheid policy (*WP*, 27 September).

Relations with South Africa remained problematic despite the 1984 Nkomati Accord. This nonaggression pact forbade the signatories to support insurgent groups opposed to the respective governments. Throughout 1985, FRELIMO officials accused South Africa of aiding RENAMO. Confronted by captured documents from the rebel base in Gorongosa indicating Pretoria's assistance, Foreign Minister R. F. Botha acknowledged at a briefing that South Africa had furnished aid to the Mozambican rebels. But Botha argued that only limited assistance had been supplied and termed it "humanitarian aid," denying military help (*WSJ*, 20 September). South Africa countercharged that Mozambique had also continued to aid Pretoria's enemy, the ANC, in spite of the Nkomati Accord. Attacks on South African targets near the Mozambican border cast doubt in Pretoria's mind whether Mozambique was honoring the agreement. Earlier in the year, Pretoria's deputy foreign minister, Louis Nel, had stated that it was South African policy "to help get rid of RENAMO and to work with the international community to block their supplies" (Johannesburg, SAPA, March; *FBIS*, 1 April). Subsequent revelations belied this statement. The status of the accord remained uncertain at the end of 1985 from actions by both signatory countries.

Publications. FRELIMO controls the media. Since independence FRELIMO has relied on two publications to carry its message to the Mozambican people: the daily paper *Notícias* and the weekly magazine *O Tempo*. So as to enhance the popular appeal of the print media, the government launched two more national-circulation newspapers in 1981: *Diário de Moçambique* in Beira, the country's second largest city, and the Sunday paper *Domingo*. (For more information see *YICA*, 1982, p. 41.) *Voz da Revolução*, an organ of the Central Committee, deals with Marxist theory and FRELIMO policies.

Thomas H. Henriksen
Hoover Institution

Nigeria

Population. 91,178,000
Party. Socialist Working People's Party (SWPP)
Founded. 1963 (SWPP: 1978)
Membership. No data
Secretary General. Dapo Fatogun
Politburo. 4 members: Chaika Anozie (chairman), Wahab Goodluck (deputy chairman), Hassan Sunmonu, Lasisi A. Osunde
Secretariat. No data
Central Committee. No data
Status. Proscribed
Last Congress. First, November 1978
Last Election. August/September 1983, SWPP ineligible
Auxiliary Organizations. No data
Publication. *New Horizon*

No Marxist political organization or activity was apparent in Nigeria during 1985. All political parties and formal political activity remained proscribed, and until it fell in a military coup on 27 August, the repressive government of Major General Muhammadu Buhari had even banned debate about the country's political future. During its twenty months in power, the Buhari government kept hundreds of former politicians and many prominent social critics in prison without trial. A number of former public servants and party leaders were sentenced to long prison terms for corruption. In addition, the press was severely constrained and intimidated by harsh decrees, and the activities of major interest groups, such as student and trade unions, were sharply curtailed.

In this repressive climate, communist activity and organization, if it continued to exist at all, was driven deep underground. There was no sign of activity of the SWPP, which had been the most prominent Marxist party (although too weak to gain official recognition) during the four years of the Second Republic, which fell in a military coup on 31 December 1983. In 1985 there was no evidence of SWPP presence in international Marxist gatherings or publications. The most prominent SWPP figure on the national political scene, Hassan Sunmonu, lost his major power base when his term ended as president of the sole union confederation, the Nigerian Labor Congress (NLC), and he was replaced by Alhaji Ali Chiroma.

The political climate changed dramatically on 27 August, when the Army chief of staff, Major General Ibrahim Babangida, took power in a bloodless military coup. Denouncing the repression and arrogance of the Buhari regime, Babangida immediately released from prison all journalists and dozens of politicians who had not been formally tried. He also exposed violations of human rights by the dreaded Nigerian Security Organization and promised to overhaul that body thoroughly. Making good on his pledge to eliminate the climate of fear in the country and to govern in a more liberal and accountable manner, the new military president threw open the issue of Nigeria's negotiations with the International Monetary Fund (IMF) to spirited public debate.

The new political freedom brought an outpouring of popular opposition to the proposed IMF loan, and Babangida surprised many observers by breaking off negotiations with the IMF in response at the end of the year. Although the NLC and other popular and left-wing political forces claimed victory on this issue, the left, and organized labor in particular, remained weak as a result of the continuing massive economic depression. Nigerian oil income continued to decline, after falling by more than half in three years, and the economy contracted sharply. Unable to prevent massive retrenchment of workers in the public and private sectors or to resist other severe austerity policies, the NLC lost considerable power and influence: its ultimatums against government pay cuts rang increasingly hollow by the end of the year.

Although Marxist ideology and rhetoric continued to have some appeal among students and the intelligentsia, the prospects for Marxist political organization remained bleak.

The primary source of potential popular unrest or mass mobilization continued to derive from religious fanaticism. For the fourth time in five years, violence erupted from the extremist Maitisine religious sect, whose radical, antimodernist beliefs are regarded as heretical by most Nigerian Muslims. In addition, Islamic fundamentalist sentiment appears to be growing in northern Nigeria (where the bulk of the Muslim half of Nigeria's population resides). Admiration for Ayatollah Khomeini and Moammar Khadafy is manifest among many Muslim intellectuals and students in the north.

Larry Diamond
Hoover Institution

Réunion

Population. 537,000
Party. Réunion Communist Party (Parti communiste réunionnais; PCR)
Founded. 1959
Membership. 7,000 claimed (*Témoignages*, 11 February); 2,000 estimated (*YICA*, 1982, p. xvi)
Secretary General. Paul Vergès
Politburo. 12 members: Julien Ramin; remaining members unknown
Secretariat. 6 members: Paul Vergès, Elie Hoarau, Jean-Baptiste Ponama; remaining members unknown
Central Committee. 32 members: Bruny Payet, Roger Hoarau, Daniel Lallemand, Hippolite Piot, Ary Yee Chong Tchi-Kan, Laurence Vergès, Laurent Vergès; remaining members unknown
Status. Legal
Last Congress. Fifth, 12–14 July 1980, in Le Port
Last Election. March 1985, cantonal (county) election, 31.1 percent (*Témoignages*, 18 March)
Auxiliary Organizations. Anticolonialist Front for Réunion Autonomy; Réunion Front of Autonomous Youth; Réunion Peace Committee; Réunion General Confederation of Workers (CGTR); Committee for the Rally of Réunionese Unemployed (CORC); Committee for the Rally of Réunionese Youth (CORJ); Réunion Union of Women (UFR); Réunion General Union of Workers in France (UGTRF);

Réunion General Confederation of Planters and Cattlemen (CGPER)

Publications. *Témoignages* (daily, Elie Hoarau, chief editor); *Travailleur réunionnais* (semimonthly; published by CGTR); *Combat réunionnais* (published by UGTRF)

The island of Réunion is a French overseas department and as such is an integral part of the French Republic. It is governed by a Paris-appointed commissioner (who is the senior local official), a 36-member General Council, and a 45-member Regional Assembly. It is represented in the French parliament by three deputies and three senators. The PCR, a small party that gathers most of its support from sugarcane cutters and workers in the Le Port area, was founded in Le Port in 1959, when the Réunion Federation of the French Communist Party became autonomous. The PCR advocates increased autonomy without complete independence from France.

The PCR's electoral standing improved during 1985. It garnered 31.1 percent of the vote in the March cantonal (county) election, enabling it to claim itself to be the largest single party on the island (*Témoignages*, 18 March). Although it received the largest percentage of the vote, only four of its eighteen candidates were elected (ibid., 11, 18 March). The March election allowed the PCR to continue its longstanding fight against conservative Jean-Paul Virapoullé, mayor of Saint-André since 1972. In May the PCR city councillors of Saint-André resigned, charging that Virapoullé had been elected fraudulently (ibid., 2 May). All elections in Saint-André since 1983 have been declared irregular and annulled. This election, being no exception, was officially rescheduled for 25 August. The PCR mounted a campaign for bulletins with symbols representing the parties, decentralized voting booths (which have been instituted for the March 1986 legislative elections), the use of precise addresses and of identity cards with photos, and control of voting lists by the National Institute of Statistics and Economic Studies in Réunion instead of in metropolitan France (ibid.). The PCR lost again and repeated its accusations against Virapoullé for strong-arm tatics and electoral fraud (ibid., 26 August) and demands for the government to void the election (ibid., 31 August–1 September).

In February the PCR had begun an electoral campaign to discredit the extreme-right National Front, which is led by Jean-Marie Le Pen, in preparation for the cantonal election. However, the National Front received the next highest percentage of votes, 15.91 percent (ibid., 18 March). The party continued its efforts after March to try to weaken the National Front's electoral standing for the 1986 legislative elections (ibid., 20 February).

In April French president François Mitterrand announced the institution of a proportional representation voting system to replace the majority balloting system. This was well received by the PCR, which said that proportional representation marked the end of an injustice of nearly 30 years. The new system, which takes effect for the legislative elections in 1986, virtually assures the PCR two seats in the National Assembly (ibid., 6–7 April).

In February the PCR held its first mass assembly in its history to discuss the crises facing Réunion. The 5,139 participants listened as party secretary general Paul Vergès repudiated the policies of the current socialist government, saying it was pursuing the same policies as the right had during the previous 30 years. He reiterated the necessity to review the economic and political structures of Réunion and to create conditions for its development. He announced ten measures for economic stimulation that the party would strive for: re-equilibration of economic sectors; reduction of income inequalities; maintenance of a constant franc and globalization of public credit transfers; maximization of agricultural production; continued fishing traditions; increased industrialization depending on both fishing and agriculture; control of foreign trade; encouragement of housing self-contruction; improved training programs; and associated power and guarantees and impulsion of public credits to private capital (ibid., 11 February). The party also stated its goal of reaching 10,000 members (ibid.).

Chronically poor economic conditions and unemployment remained the major problems facing Réunion and the PCR. The party continued its efforts to revitalize the economy, primarily the agricultural sector, and to stimulate employment and development. (Réunion has an agricultural economy based primarily on sugarcane, which comprises 90 percent of its exports. Its exports cover only 14 percent of its imports.) A drought for the second year in a row in the southern and western regions of the island continued to affect agricultural production. The idea of crop diversification continued to be discussed (Alan Raker, editor, *New African Yearbook, 1984–85*, IC Magazines, Ltd.).

The PCR, along with the CGTR and the CGPER, continued to lead campaigns against sugarcane plantation and factory owners and to fight for better wages. After the government decided to increase the price of a ton of cane by 4 percent instead of the desired 8 percent, the CGTR called for strikes (*Témoignages*, 24 June). The CGTR leadership declared that workers should receive at least a minimum net income of 3,500 francs per year by the end of 1985 (ibid., 29 January). The PCR press claims that 7,000 workers marched in the CGTR's 1 May parade in support of that proposal (ibid., 2 May). In another worker-related proposal, the PCR declared that it would fight to give the city's day-workers a salary scale and a degree of job security on par with their colleagues in metropolitan France (ibid., 4 January).

At over 30 percent, Réunion has the highest unemployment rate of all French overseas departments; the rate had increased 18 percent between November 1983 and November 1984 (ibid., 4 January). The CORC was founded in December 1984 in La Possession to rally the unemployed to fight for more rights, and Vergès announced in his New Year's address that the CORC would have an important function throughout 1985 in promoting unity among the unemployed (ibid., 1, 3 January). At the CGTR congress on 13–14 April in Saint-Pierre, the union leadership called for a massive demonstration on 13 May—called "île morte" (dead island)—to support the CORC's pleas for increased family and housing aid for the unemployed (ibid., 16 April). The reports in *Témoignages* of 14 May indicated that the "île morte" demonstration received a low turnout.

Mario Hoarau, president of the Regional Assembly, mayor of Saint-Leu, and a prominent PCR member, traveled to Paris in April to discuss regional cooperation projects with government officials (ibid., 29 May).

A deputy to the European Parliament (EP) since 1979, Paul Vergès again tried to sensitize the European Economic Community (EEC) to Réunion's agricultural and developmental problems during 1985. Réunion's integration into the EEC partly caused the economic crisis on the island; although Réunion's sugar economy is fully entitled to benefits of sale and price guarantees of EEC producers, it is also subject to the same obligations to production control mechanisms. Réunion sugarcane growers have not been able to mechanize and continue to hire agricultural day-laborers, and small-scale growers have gone bankrupt (*New African Yearbook, 1984–85*, p. 105). In April Vergès announced that the price of a ton of cane should be based on production costs (*Témoignages*, 5 April). In September a delegation of EP deputies from its Regional Policy and Territorial Development Committee visited the island (ibid., 16 September). The PCR has said that EEC enlargement in January 1986 to include Spain and Portugal represents a serious danger to Réunion products, especially rum (ibid., 17 April).

In his New Year's address, Vergès announced that because the U.N. General Assembly had declared 1985 the Year of Youth, the CORJ would figure prominently on the PCR's agenda. After the Youth and Student Festival of the Islands of the Indian Ocean during 16–18 May, the CORJ announced the creation of the Association of Friendship and Solidarity for Development, Employment, and Peace (ibid., 28 May). The reduction in 1984 of school lunch aid for Réunionese students continued to be a source of student unrest; violent student demonstrations in September and October delayed the opening of school for a week (*Le Monde*, 8 November).

Regarding the PCR auxiliary organizations, the UFR directing committee decentralized and created a new committee in the eastern region of the island in February (*Témoignages*, 29 January). At the CGTR congress in April, Bruny Payet was reelected secretary general and Georges Marie Lepinay became deputy secretary general (ibid., 15 April).

Party Organization and Leadership. Paul Vergès has been PCR secretary general since 1959, is a deputy to the EP, and is mayor of Le Port. He also heads the Réunion Intercommunal Syndicate for Multiple Vocations, which is a grouping of PCR communes (except Sainte-Rose) established in late 1983. He ran unsuccessfully in the March cantonal election in Saint-André against Virapoullé and did not run in the rescheduled contest in August. According to the French daily *Le Monde* (12 September 1984), Vergès's popularity has waned within the party since the European elections because he has adopted the image of a "notable" and charismatic revolutionary and because fellow PCR members have charged him with nepotism (his two sons have gained prominence within the PCR). *Le Monde*'s 8 November issue depicted him as a realistic politician who was willing to work with other parties on the island to effectively develop Réunion. With proportional representation, Vergès is assured to win a seat in the National Assembly in the 1986 legislative election.

Secretariat member (and number two in the party) Elie Hoarau serves concurrently as secretary of the Réunion Peace Committee, secretary general of the CGTR, and a member of the World Peace Council (WPC). He is also mayor of Saint-Pierre and chief editor of the party newspaper, *Témoignages*. Bruny Payet, a member of the party's Central Committee, serves concurrently as president of the Réunion Peace Committee, head of the CGTR, and first deputy mayor of Sainte-Marie. Payet is also a member of the WPC and the General Council of the World Federation of Trade Unions (WFTU). Ary Yee Chong Tchi-Kan, a member of the Central Committee, heads the youth sector of the party. Other PCR members holding elected office are Mario Hoarau, Lucet Langenier (mayor of Sainte-Suzanne), and Central Committee member Roger Hoarau (regional counselor). Other noteworthy PCR members are Laurent and Laurence Vergès, Julien Ramin (who represented the PCR at the French Communist Party's Twenty-fifth Congress in February), Daniel Lallemand, Hippolite Piot, Roland Robert (mayor of La Possession), Claude Hoarau (mayor of Saint-Louis), and Patrick Boîtard (youth leader).

Prominent leaders within the PCR auxiliary organizations are Angelo Lauret, who serves as president of the CGPER, and Isnelle Amelin, president of the UFR.

Domestic Policies and Activities. The major goals of the PCR are to achieve autonomy for Réunion from France, a more balanced economy, and redressment of inequalities between social benefits in France and on the island. It contends that policies for France cannot apply to Réunion and has emphasized the necessity for an increased number of development projects, including self-construction projects, on the island. Paul Vergès has stated that the PCR regards Réunion as a colonized country requiring a series of measures for its development that amount to decolonization (*New African Yearbook, 1984–85*, p. 106). The PCR favors independence for New Caledonia (a French territory), claiming that a people cannot be stopped en route to freedom (*Témoignages*, 9 January).

The PCR and progressive parties in the other French overseas departments met to discuss the process of self-determination; they emphasized the need for basic freedoms, elimination of electoral fraud and corruption, and the institution of proportional representation, which was introduced in April (*New African Yearbook, 1984–85*, p. 106). The PCR criticizes President Mitterrand's decentralization efforts of 1982 and 1984, saying that they do not take local particularities into account (*Témoignages*, 6 March). The PCR opposes integration of French overseas departments into the EEC and contends that the French government should pay the price of that policy (that is, freight costs from Réunion to Europe to keep Réunionese goods competitive). The PCR dedicated 1985 to the future of youth and the fight against unemployment (ibid., 1 January). As in 1983 and 1984, the PCR continued to call for the closure of the South African consulate in Saint-Denis, and the UFR continued to organize demonstrations against racism and apartheid in South Africa.

In an interview in the 8 November issue of *Le Monde*, Vergès indirectly criticized the ruling French Socialist Party. He said that while the left has assured the French their freedom to demonstrate, it has shown a lack of imagination, humility, and political will in dealing with the worsening economic situation. He also said that the Réunionese need to take up their responsibility for developing the island and not rely on more aid from metropolitan France to solve Réunion's problems. With the PCR's electoral strength, he believes the parties on Réunion will have to work with the PCR, and he favors working with those parties to overcome Réunion's difficulties. He said, however, that the many divergences between the parties and the fact that Parisian directives do not apply to Réunion impede cooperation.

International Affairs. The PCR has a strong interest in regional development in the Indian Ocean and keeps in close contact with neighboring communist parties, as well as communist parties in France and other French overseas departments. A PCR delegation led by Vergès traveled to the People's Republic of China in November to resume relations between the parties (*FBIS*, 24 November; Beijing, *Xinhua*, 24 November). The PCR opposes apartheid in South Africa, supports the liberation struggles of the Namibian people (*Témoignages*, 3 January) and the African National Congress, and endorses the actions of the Palestine Liberation Organization. It favors the creation of a zone of peace in the Indian Ocean and has repeatedly called for the removal of military, particularly nuclear, forces from the region (ibid., 12 February).

Biography. *Bruny Payet.* Payet, who is now about 60, was born into a poor family in Rivière Saint-Louis. A high school classmate of Paul Vergès, Payet at 17 accompanied Vergès to England and joined the Free French Forces in 1942. He served as a naval officer during World War II. After the war he attended the Advanced National School of Electricity and worked as an electrician until 1953, when he returned to Réunion to begin party work. He collaborated with Raymond Vergès, serving as his secretary general while he was mayor of Saint-André. He helped Vergès found the PCR in 1959 and subsequently assumed the direction of the CGTR. He has served as general counselor of Saint-Paul and of Le Port. He received the Legion of Honor in 1983 (*Témoignages*, 16–17 March).

Hilarie Slason
Arlington, Virginia

Senegal

Population. 6,755,000
Party. Independence and Labor Party (Parti de l'indépendance du travail; PIT)
Founded. 1957
Membership. No data
Secretary General. Amath Dansoko
Chairman. Seydou Cissoko
Politburo. 14 members: Seydou Cissoko, Amath Dansoko, Samba Dioulde Thiam, Maguette Thiam, Mady Danfaka, Sadio Camara, Seydou Ndongo, Semou Pathe Gueye, Makhtar Mbaye, Bouma Gaye, Mohamed Laye (names of other three not known)
Secretariat. 7 members: Seydou Cissoko, Amath Dansoko, Semou Pathe Gueye, Maguette Thiam, Samba Dioulde Thiam, Mady Danfaka, Makhtar Mbaye
Central Committee. 55 members (secretary: Semou Pathe Gueye)
Status. Legal
Last Congress. Second, 28 September–2 October 1984, in Dakar
Last Election. 1983, 0.5 percent, no seats
Auxiliary Organizations. Women's Democratic Union
Publications. *Daan Doole*, *Gestu*

Senegal's numerous Marxist parties remained weak and divided in 1985. The ruling (non-Marxist) Socialist Party (PS)—which is bitterly condemned as "bourgeois" and "parasitic" by its Marxist rivals—consolidated its dominance over Senegalese political life. The PS won 111 of 120 National Assembly seats in the 1983 elections, after lifting the restrictions on formation of political parties in 1981; it then scored a staggering sweep of all 37 municipalities and 318 rural districts in the November 1984 local elections. Those elections did little to enhance PS legitimacy, however, as they were contested by only two of the fourteen recognized opposition parties—the Democratic League/Movement for the Party of Labor (LD) and the Party for the Liberation of the People (PLP). The pro-Soviet PIT joined the electoral boycott in the final week in protest against electoral irregularities.

Out of some eight Marxist or quasi-Marxist parties, the PIT remained the one recognized by the Soviet Union and the most prominent in the international communist movement; nevertheless, it showed few signs of vitality domestically. (The LD is also close to Moscow but is not formally recognized by it). Like the previously legal communist movement from which it split in 1981—the African Independence Party (PAI)—and like the (Trotskyist) Socialist Workers Organization (OST) and most other Marxist parties, the PIT remained limited in its political support to small groups of students, intellectuals, and trade-union activists.

A more effective Marxist party, and perhaps the only one with any significant base of popular support, appears to be the And Jef/Revolutionary Movement for a New Democracy (AJ/MRDN), headed by Landing Savane, which draws its support from separatist sentiment in Casamance (*Africa Confidential*, 27 February). Casamance is an extremely underdeveloped region in southern Senegal between Gambia and Guinea-Bissau. Its half million people follow primarily African (and some Christian) faiths rather than Islam, and they believe that they have been discriminated against in the distribution of development resources.

The PLP is the only left-wing party with representation in the National Assembly. Its leader, Babacar Niang, assumed the seat to which Cheif Anta Diop, leader of the National Democratic Rally (RND), had been elected after Diop refused it in protest against election rigging. Since then the RND has virtually ceased to function and the PLP appears to have occupied its niche as the party of radical African nationalism.

The recognition of a fifteenth opposition party early in the year underscored the importance for the opposition parties of merging their political bases and resources. Thus the year saw several efforts at political cooperation and consolidation among the Marxist parties in particular. Late in January, eight opposition parties joined together to denounce the harsh austerity policies implemented by President Abdou Diouf as a condition of International Monetary Fund assistance. This coalition, which issued a joint resolution on 10 February, comprised the AJ/MRDN, PAI, LD, OST, pro-Albanian Democratic People's Union (UDP), Democratic People's Movement (MDP), Senegalese People's Party (PPS), and Communist Workers League (LCT). The OST chaired the February conference, which was held at the headquarters of the PAI (*Intercontinental Press*, 27 May).

A more significant opposition coalition emerged in July, when four Marxist parties—the LD, OST, AJ/MRDN, and (Maoist) New Democratic Union—joined with the largest opposition party, the moderate Senegalese Democratic Party (PDS), which won eight seats in the National Assembly; these five parties formed the Democratic Senegalese Alliance (ADS), chaired by O. Abdoulaye Bathily, leader of the LD. The group became the target of government harassment in August when fifteen of its supporters were arrested in an unauthorized demonstration it organized against apartheid in South Africa (*FBIS*, 3 September). On 5 September the Ministry of the Interior prohibited the ADS from all political activities until it declared itself and was recognized as a political party, stressing that political party alliances were illegal.

Although the parties of the left could conceivably become a significant opposition force if they were allowed to combine, the gravest challenge to the regime comes not from them nor from the militant trade unionists allied with them, who have been attempting (in the face of considerable government pressure) to organize a counter to the sole recognized union confederation, the National Confederation of Senegalese Workers (CNTS). Rather, the real threat to the regime comes from Islamic consciousness and mobilization. Almost 90 percent of the population is Muslim. Muslim brotherhoods and marabouts hold great sway among the people, and radical Islamic figures such as Ayatollah Khomeini and Moammar Khadafy have increasing appeal to Senegalese Muslims, especially the young. It is perhaps for this reason that the PIT has concluded, "Religion therefore is a socio-political force which the Party cannot ignore" (*African Communist*, no. 100).

The analysis and strategy of the PIT was spelled out in international publications once again by Semou Pathe Gueye, secretary of the Central Committee of the PIT. In articles in the *World Marxist Review* (April) and *African Communist* (no. 102), Gueye emphasized the need for more aggressive political organization aimed at building a "broad alliance of different classes in a *Democratic Front* of struggle" (emphasis in the original). He suggested that the middle class, in particular "the intellectual salaried workers," are at this moment, because of "their level of political awareness," best placed to lead the struggle; he also stressed the need to mobilize a mass base among the working class and peasantry, exhorting the party to "shake off the narrowness inherited from a long period of clandestine activity." Gueye denounced not only foreign domination of the Senegalese economy but also Senegal's military cooperation with France and NATO and its permission for the United States to use the air base at Thiès.

Notwithstanding its close ties to the West, Senegal also preserved its warm relations with China. The ruling PS established relations with the Chinese Communist Party (CCP) in 1979 and has since exchanged party visits at high levels. Hu Qili, a member of the Secretariat of the CCP Central Committee, visited Senegal in August. Preceding him in April on a government visit was the Chinese minister of public health. China has given Senegal extensive health assistance, and it donated ten tons of drugs and medical equipment in June.

Larry Diamond
Hoover Institution

South Africa

Population. 32,465,000
Party. South African Communist Party (SACP)
Founded. 1921
Membership. No data
General Secretary. Moses Mabhida
Leading Organs. Composition unknown
Status. Proscribed
Last Congress. Late 1984 or early 1985
Last Election. N/a
Auxiliary Organizations. None
Publications. *African Communist* (printed in the German Democratic Republic (GDR) and distributed from London); *Umsebenzi* (published clandestinely in South Africa)

Thirty-five years after the dissolution of the Communist Party of South Africa, its direct successor, the SACP, remains active in exile and clandestinely within the country. It is still linked closely with the African National Congress (ANC), South Africa's oldest and most prominent nationalist movement, which also operates illegally and in exile since its proscription 25 years ago. Buoyed by the year-long sustained upsurge of black challenge to the Nationalist government of President P. W. Botha, the SACP optimistically asserted that conditions were favorable "for the further growth of our Party, attracting to itself the most advanced and conscious sons and daughters of the working class of our country. At the same time, this organizational work as well as the practical, political, and ideological involvement of our Party with the workers in particular, will ensure the continued growth of the influence of the communist cause and enable the working class of our country to carry out its historic mission of taking power from the capitalist class and building a socialist society" (*African Communist*, no. 101, p. 6).

The SACP was formed underground within the country in 1953; this reversed the decision taken by a majority of the party's Central Committee three years earlier to disband as a formal organization. It has proudly carried on the tradition of the continent's first Marxist-Leninist party and the country's first nonracial party. (For details on the history of the South African party since 1921, see *YICA*, 1985, pp. 25, 27.)

Organization and Leadership. Late in 1984 or early in 1985, the SACP held a congress at an undisclosed location, almost certainly not in South Africa and very likely in London. In keeping with the spirit of party rules requiring secrecy—"maintaining secrecy about the existence of the Party had, in fact, been written into the new rules of membership adopted at the first illegal Party Conference, and maintained ever since" (*African Communist*, no. 100, p. 22)—no names of participants were mentioned with the exception of Moses Mabhida, who was re-elected unanimously as general secretary. Mabhida, a 62-year-old, long-time African trade unionist who joined the party in 1942 during its legal existence, had been elected to his post at the last major party gathering, an extended meeting of the Central Committee in 1979. In the period prior to his election as general secretary, he had been working full time with Umkhonto we Sizwe, a clandestine military organization dedicated to selective sabotage of government installations and communication facilities.

Mabhida represents the dwindling but still important older cadre of the party whose roots stretch back to the days of the legal Commmunist Party of South Africa. In recent years an increasing role has been taken by post-1976 recruits, whose militancy was tempered in the fire of direct challenge to the government within the country. After the congress it was reported that "a great number of delegates were young people who entered the struggle at the time of the 1976 Soweto uprising... [who] participated actively and proudly in the congress, united with veteran party members...the attendance of this vital young generation was certainly one of the highlights of our congress and it contributed to the dynamic and optimistic spirit that was prevalent throughout several days of session" (*FBIS*, 31 January). The balance between old and new members was not hinted at, nor was the party leadership named or the number of delegates given. It was merely noted that the congress was attended by "tens of delegates" (*African Communist*, no. 101, p. 51). It was also stated that the delegates "adopted a new constitution to regulate the work and functioning of the SACP" and elected a new Central Committee (ibid., p. 8).

With its membership dispersed in Europe and across the African continent, the SACP faces a difficult task of coordination between the established external leadership and the younger militants. The latter are most likely concentrated in Umkhonto we Sizwe and ANC training centers outside the country and in underground cells within South Africa. The SACP claims to be increasing in strength, "especially inside our country, drawing into its ranks outstanding working class and youth activists in particular" (ibid., p. 5). Most internal membership is probably active in the major urban centers of South Africa along the Witwatersrand, around Durban and Cape Town, and in the industrial areas of the Eastern Cape. Undoubtedly many of the SACP's activities are closely intertwined with those of the ANC.

Both within South Africa and in exile, the SACP centers much attention on the ANC, which from its foundation in 1912 has been open to Africans from across the political spectrum. Since the late 1920s, African Communists have been active within the ANC, although in the early 1930s and again in the 1940s and late 1950s, elements of the ANC membership challenged communist involvement on the intertwined grounds of the multiracialness of party membership and the extracontinental origin of its ideology. It was within this stance that the Africanist dissidents broke with the ANC in 1959 to form the Pan Africanist Congress (PAC), but the ANC leadership continued to accept Communists as full participants at all levels of the organization. In the wake of the banning of the ANC in 1960, the shared underground and exile experience of the ANC and SACP contributed to a new closeness, with lines being further blurred by the 1969 decison of the exiled ANC leadership to accept non-Africans as members. Immediately prominent non-African Communists (including Dr. Yusef Dadoo and Joe Slovo) were made members of key ANC bodies, joining prominent African SACP members who had long been active in the senior councils of the ANC.

In June the second consultative congress of the ANC decided to drop all racial qualifications for membership in the national executive; non-African Communists were thus among those elected to the new 30-member body, which also includes Mabhida and undoubtedly other African SACP members who have not publicly identified themselves. In the view of Oliver Tambo, President of the ANC, "South African Communist Party members in our ranks have learned very well to differentiate between the Communist Party's policy and the ANC's policy. They are loyal and devoted ANC members. Possibly South African Communist party members act in a different way than Communists usually do" (*Der Spiegel*, 12 August, p. 89).

In the perspective of the late Dr. Dadoo, "The ANC and the SACP personify the two complementary streams of revolutionary consciousness and revolutionary organization. They are complementary because in South Africa the struggle for national liberation insistently requires organized participation by the working class and its political vanguard, the Communist Party, and the struggle for socialism just as insistently requires a powerful movement for the freedom of the oppressed nations and races, a movement led by the ANC... The front of the fighters for the victory of the national-democratic revolution is led by the...ANC..., a vanguard movement which includes Africans, coloureds, Indians, and the most courageous, far-sighted and increasingly democratic-minded section of the white community...the South African Communist Party expresses the interests of the proletariat, which acts not only within the national-democratic front, but also carries on its own class struggle. Its goals do not conflict with the goals of the national-democratic revolution, but go beyond these, to the prospect of a radical restructuring of the society on socialist lines" (*WMR*, December 1982, pp. 18, 24).

Domestic Activities and Attitudes. Early in the year, even before the almost continuous disturbances in African townships in the Transvaal, the Eastern Cape, and previously quiet smaller rural townships, the SACP leadership was optimistic about prospects for widening the challenge to the government. "The Congress characterized the mood among the masses of the oppressed people in South Africa as one of revolt. A state of incipient civil war exists in the country... The objective and subjective factors exist for the rapid escalation of the struggle which should aim, in particular, to reduce the capacity of the regime to govern our country. The successful accomplishment of this task requires that all the masses of the oppressed people should be mobilized into struggle. In this regard, special attention should be given to the further organization and mobilization of the women and rural masses, to elevate their involvement in the struggle. It is also of vital importance that the organized detachments of our revolutionary movement, including our Party, should continue to strengthen their presence among the people, and mobilize the masses to address, in action, the question of the seizure of power" (*African Communist*, no. 101, p. 7).

In the eyes of the SACP Central Committee, growing militancy was finding expression in new forms of popular organizations, "including trade unions, community, youth, and women's organizations. The coming together of hundreds of these organizations in a united front [United Democratic Front; UDF, founded in 1983] and its united action, constitutes one of the most important advances that the democratic movement has made, and is an expression of the objective requirement of the national democratic revolution to unite all classes, strata, and national groups that are interested in the victory of the revolution...despite all its efforts, the apartheid regime has failed to expand its social base. Even the black middle strata, whom the ruling class and their state have sought to expand and bribe to come over to the side of state-monopoly capital, continue, in the main, to demonstrate that their interests would be best served by the victory of the national democratic revolution" (ibid., p. 14). Nevertheless, as Joe Slovo warned, "it is equally possible that if the people's victory is dominated by the aspirant black capitalist class or middle class, sections of the Freedom Charter could be used by them to take South Africa along the capitalist road. We must therefore work to ensure that in the present state of the struggle the working class assumes the leading and dominant role" (*ANC News Briefing*, 14 July).

With this imperative in mind, party spokesmen have continued to be concerned about "the various forms of economism, trade-union politics, and workerism which are being peddled today in a bid to divert the workers from the true road of revolution" (*African Communist*, no. 100, p. 55). In the view of the SACP Central Committee, "the organized working class has both political and economic tasks to accomplish. It must continue its work to expand, strengthen, and unify the trade-union movement in one federation" (ibid., no. 101, p. 17). Accordingly, the creation of the multiracial Confederation of South African Trade Unions (COSATU) in November, which claims a following of a half million workers (but excludes trade unions that are identified with the black consciousness movement), was welcomed. Although COSATU could not be viewed as a direct successor to the nonracial South African Congress of Trade Unions (SACTU, established in 1955), COSATU's militant endorsement of divestment, nationalization of mines, and abolition of pass laws did represent the type of trade-union unity that party spokesmen had advocated: "unity on the basis of a united front platform against the apartheid regime for the legitimate demands and needs of the workers—higher wages, improved working and health conditions in factories, mines, plants, and all employment institutions, for the democratic rights of our people, for majority rule in our country" (ibid., no. 100, p. 45). Simultaneously, the SACP contends that "the working class should not be satisfied merely to belong to trade unions, important as these are as mass organizations of the proletariat. In addition, it is in the vital interest of the working class that it strengthens the ranks of the ANC and Umkhonto we Sizwe in order to play its role in accomplishing the political and military tasks of the national democratic revolution...It is also clear that these workers must engage in struggle for a democratic South Africa fully conscious of their unique class interests, the necessity to make their imprint on the democratic revolution and to prepare the conditions for an uninterrupted advance from popular democracy to proletarian rule" (ibid., pp. 17–18). In the estimation of the Central Committee, "we have it within our power to emerge victorious sooner rather than later. The call of the day is: Unite! Mobilize! On with the Offensive for Freedom and Socialism" (ibid., p. 18).

International Views and Activities. The SACP has continued to find a source of its strength, according to the last testament of Dr. Dadoo, in "the unswerving loyalty and respect our party has for the CPSU" (ibid., no. 96, p. 20). In this vein the SACP has been unusually concerned about what it perceives as an expanding anti-Soviet climate. "Hostility, or even neutrality, towards the Soviet Union and other countries of existing socialism can only undermine the struggle for national liberation, peace, and social progress in South Africa, Africa, and the world. The enemy of our enemy is our friend, not for opportunistic reasons, but because Soviet policies have been firmly rooted in the principles of Marxism-Leninism and proletarian internationalism. Ever since 1917 the Soviet Union has shown itself to be the most consistent ally in the struggle against imperialism, for national independence, peace, and social progress. At a time when the racists and imperialists are leaving no stone unturned to destabilize the socialist bloc and destroy the monumental achievements of the October Revolution, it is the duty of all genuine revolutionaries to make it unmistakably clear that they have the correct attitude towards the Soviet Union and are ready to come to its defense" (ibid., no. 98, pp. 18–19). At the congress the SACP reiterated its support for a central Soviet goal, "the convening of a world conference of the communist movement in order further to strengthen the unity and effectiveness of this movement as well as the anti-imperialist forces as a whole" (ibid., no. 101, p. 8).

There were no reports in the party press of meetings of SACP leaders with counterparts in other communist parties, but existing links with the CPSU and its allied parties were surely maintained. In Africa, Mabhida represented the SACP at the founding congress of the Ethiopian Workers' Party. He welcomed this new addition to the Marxist-Leninist parties of Africa as "an assertion that Marxism-Leninism is as much part of the soil of Africa as marioca, cassava, or mealies"; he went on to urge that "it is therefore all the more important that the small but growing band of Marxist movements in Africa should work more closely together to spread a true understanding of socialist thinking" (ibid., no. 100, p. 78). It is probable that the SACP continued to cultivate ties with the nearly one dozen Marxist-Leninist parties on the continent with which it found affinity in the past decade.

Publications. One of the major vehicles for displaying the SACP's concern for fraternal African parties and movements has been through its quarterly publication, *African Communist*, published from its inception "in the interests of African solidarity, and as a forum for Marxist-Leninist thought throughout our Continent." At the start of the year the quarterly celebrated the production of its hundredth number; it is published in the GDR and distributed through an office in London that also sells other party publications. In line with concern articulated at the party congress "to strengthen the Party organizationally and reinforce its role not only as a constituent part of the liberation alliance headed by the African National Congress but also as the independent vanguard of the South African proletariat," the SACP has commenced production of a new underground paper, *Umsebenzi*, within South Africa. The publication of *Umsebenzi* (the Zulu/Xhosa word for worker and the title of the Communist Party of South Africa's newspaper from 1930 to 1936) is viewed as the implementation of a congress decision that "we must continuously sharpen our ideological weapons to combat backward nationalism and chauvinism in all its forms and spread an understanding of the connection between racial oppression and capitalist exploitation. The perspective of a future socialist society in South Africa must be spread with greater vigor" (ibid., no. 102, p. 16).

SACP publications produced externally and internally are complemented by those of the ANC. Independently the SACP also distributes propaganda leaflets and flyers within South Africa at political and trade-union gatherings and on occasions such as May Day.

The written word is supplemented by "Radio Freedom, Voice of the African National Congress and Umkhonto we Sizwe, the People's Army," which is broadcast several hours daily on the shortwave facilities of the state radio stations in Angola, Ethiopia, Madagascar, Tanzania, and Zambia.

Sheridan Johns
Duke University

Sudan

Population. 21,800,000
Party. Sudanese Communist Party (al-Hizb al-Shuyu'i al-Sudani; SCP)
Founded. 1946
Membership. 9,000 est.
Politburo. 6 members: Muhammad Ibrahim Nugud Mansur, Ali al-Tijani al-Tayyib Babikar (number-two leader, arrested November 1980, freed April 1985), Dr. Izz-al Din Ali Amir, Sulayman Hamid, Al-Gazuli (Jizuli) Said Uthman, Muhammad Ahmad Sulayman (Suleiman)
Secretariat. 7 members: Muhammad Ibrahim Nugud Mansur, Ali al-Tijani al-Tayyib Babikar, Dr. Izz-al Din Ali Amir, Abu al-Qasim (Gassim) Muhammad, Sulayman Hamid, Al-Gazuli Said Uthman, Muhammad Ahmad Sulayman
Central Committee. 12 members: in addition to 7 listed above, Sudi Darag, Khad(i)r Nasir, Abd-al-Majid Shakak, Hassan Gassim al-Sid (World Peace Council [WPC] Presidential Committee member and World Federation of Trade Unions [WFTU] staff member), Ibrahim Zakariya (secretary general of WFTU)
Other Prominent SCP Members. Sharif Dishoni (former party spokesperson), Ahmad Salim (member of Prague-based Editorial Council of *World Marxist Review*)
Status. Legal
Last Congress. Fourth, 31 October 1967, Khartoum
Last Election. N/a
Auxiliary Organizations. Democratic Federation of Sudanese Students (DSFS; affiliated with International Union of Students); Sudanese Youth Union; Sudan Workers' Trade Federation (SWTUF; operates with quasi-official standing); Sudanese Defenders of Peace and Democracy (presumably a WPC affiliate)
Publication. *Al-Maydan* (newspaper that reappeared in July 1985 after long-time ban)

A small group of intellectuals at Khartoum University founded the SCP in 1946. The party became a leading force in the popular struggle for Sudanese independence from Britain, which was achieved in1956. The SCP was the only political party in Sudan to oppose the military regime under General Ibrahim Abbud that seized power in November 1958 in a coup d'etat. Abbud arrested all the Sudanese Communist leaders he could locate and forced party members still at large to go underground. The Abbud regime foundered, however, because of its inability to bring the war in southern Sudan under control.

A group called Anyanya (Scorpion) launched a rebellion in the south that was aimed at securing autonomy and perhaps even secession for the region. The southerners, who constitute 25–30 percent of the country's population, are primarily black, non-Arabic-speaking Christian and animist tribes. They resented their subordination to the Muslim Arabs of the north and charged, in addition, that northern Sudan was receiving the lion's share of economic development funds.

A popular revolt and a general political strike against the Abbud regime erupted in 1964, providing the SCP an opportunity to organize workers, peasants, students, professionals, and intellectuals in the north. A parliamentary government supplanted the junta, and in 1965 some SCP officials were elected to the parliament. However, the new coalition government came to regard the Communists as a threat and denied them their parliamentary seats. Once again the SCP was forced underground.

On 25 May 1969, Colonel Jaafar Numeiri seized control of Sudan in a virtually bloodless coup. The SCP gave him its support and became the only legal party in the country. The victory of Numeiri and his SCP allies represented a triumph for the left against powerful economic interests and foreign capital in Sudan. In 1970 the SCP's popularity and prestige reached an all-time high. With a membership totaling 5,000 to 10,000, it was the strongest and best organized Communist Party in the Middle East or Africa.

The failure of Numeiri's socialist policies and Sudan's continuing reliance on Western financial support prompted the regime to move to the right. A moderate faction within the SCP accepted Numeiri's drift rightward and his plan to dissolve the SCP into his newly created Sudan Socialist Union (SSU), which was to be the country's sole political organization. The SCP's more radical faction (strongly represented by procommunist army officers) opposed Numeiri's shift, however. Leftist officers evidently masterminded an abortive 1971 coup, in the aftermath of which Numeiri outlawed the SCP and liquidated most of its leadership. (For more detail on the origins and background of the SCP, see *YICA*, 1985, pp. 33–34.)

In 1972 Numeiri managed to end the seventeen-year-old Anyanya rebellion, which had severely drained Sudan's economy and military resources. He created a Ministry of Southern Affairs to work out a plan for regional autonomy. This plan became the basis of a settlement, signed in the Ethiopian capital of Addis Ababa, that unified the three southern provinces into a single autonomous region, established a regional assembly and executive council, promised the impoverished south an economic development program and a more equitable share of the national income, and arranged for the incorporation of the Anyanya guerrilla units into the Sudanese army.

On this fundamental dispute, the SCP was the only Sudanese political party to propose regional autonomy for the south. It has advocated broad autonomy—the right of the southerners to enjoy their own religion, language, and customs—within the context of a unified, democratic Sudan. However, the SCP has also attempted to exploit the problems of the south and of sectarian politics in order to enhance its status.

Numeiri's grant of relative autonomy to the south greatly eased the country's regional tensions, but in the early 1980s violence flared anew. Some of the Anyanya had never reconciled themselves to the Addis accords and had reverted to guerrilla warfare. External developments also affected the course of events in southern Sudan.

In August 1981 Ethiopia, Libya, and the People's Democratic Republic of Yemen (PDRY) signed a tripartite pact in Aden after close consultation with the Soviet Union and Cuba. The pact was aimed at undermining pro-Western governments in the Middle East and Africa, and Sudan became a major target of this campaign. Sudanese rebels received sanctuary in camps along the Ethiopian side of the frontier, from which they launched cross-border raids into Sudan. Libya and the PDRY provided arms, training, and logistical and financial support for this effort, while Soviet and Cuban military and intelligence personnel in Ethiopia apparently played a coordinating role.

In May 1983 a southern army battalion based in

the upper Nile town of Bor mutinied against orders that would have replaced it with northerners. The orders contravened the spirit of the Addis accords, which had stipulated that military and administrative duties by northerners in the south would be minimized. When the army attacked the Bor garrison, the battalion resisted briefly and then departed to join guerrilla forces in the area. A former army commander, Colonel John Garang, also joined the guerrillas. He is a member of the Dinka, the dominant tribe in southern Sudan. By July 1983 Garang, who holds a doctorate in agronomy from Iowa State University, had organized the guerrillas into the Sudanese People's Liberation Movement (SPLM), of which he is chairman. He also serves as commander-in-chief of the SPLM's military wing, known as the Sudanese People's Liberation Army (SPLA). The SPLA, which has at least 10,000 fighters, arms and trains its recruits at facilities just across the Sudanese border in Ethiopia, receives appreciable support, and is creating a political infrastructure among its supporters inside Sudan.

A pamphlet issued by the SPLM describes it as Marxist-Leninist and as aspiring to become the "sole people's political organization" in Sudan. According to the pamphlet, the SPLA is committed to conventional as well as guerrilla warfare (Sudan News Agency, 4 March 1984). Joseph Oduho, former regional minister of southern Sudan and now head of the Political and Foreign Affairs Committee of the SPLM, announced that "the aim of our fight is the creation of a united and Socialist Sudan, which can only be achieved by a lengthy revolutionary armed struggle" (Paris, *Le Monde*, 27 April 1984).

The SPLM's stated intention to overthrow "the Khartoum regime set up by the northern and southern bourgeoisie" (*Washington Times*, 12 June 1984) and to create a unified socialist Sudan coincides with the avowed goal of the SCP. Indeed, General Omar Mohammed el-Tayeb, Sudan's former first vice president, accused the northern-based SCP of coordinating its activities with the southern-based SPLM. "The conspiracy is aimed at both southern and northern Sudan," he declared (*Intercontinental Press*, 16 April 1984, p. 196).

Garang's movement reaped a windfall when Numeiri announced in June 1983, in the aftermath of the Bor rebellion, a redivision of southern Sudan into its three constituent provinces. This cancellation of the key provision of the Addis accords was attacked by the southerners as a ploy to divide and rule their tribes. On the heels of this move came Numeiri's September 1983 announcement of the introduction of shari'a, the Islamic code of law, into Sudan. The non-Muslims of southern Sudan regarded this move as a direct assault on their Christian and tribal religions.

Still another issue exacerbated relations between northern and southern Sudan around this time. The Numeiri regime called in Western experts to develop recently discovered oil deposits in the south and to build the 217-mile Jonglei Canal to increase the flow of the White Nile. The southerners believed that these projects would deprive them of their oil and water resources, which would be diverted to the north and, in the case of oil, abroad. In February 1984 the SPLA attacked the headquarters of the Chevron company, killing three foreign oil workers and wounding seven others. Subsequent guerrilla attacks on the French engineers excavating the Jonglei Canal brought work on that project to a virtual halt. Oil exploration also appears to be at a standstill.

During a speech on 2 March 1984 to commemorate Libya's national day, Libyan leader Moammar Khadafy declared that his country was "allied with the popular revolution in the southern Sudan" (ibid.). Exactly two weeks later a Soviet-made Libyan bomber raided the Sudanese city of Omdurman, attacking—among other targets—the building that houses the radio station. Citing the raid and the growing unrest inside Sudan, which he believed to be foreign-inspired, Numeiri declared a state of emergency in the country on 29 April.

Domestic Attitudes and Activities. During its prolonged status as an illegal organization, the SCP retained considerable influence among intellectuals, students (especially at Khartoum University), railway workers, sympathizers in the armed forces, and cotton growers. The SCP amassed particular strength in the trade unions. Communist inroads also became visible among the 2–3 million refugees in Sudan. In addition, the SCP maintained links with some Sudanese refugees in Ethiopia.

In an effort to broaden its base, the SCP joined the newly formed National Salvation Front (Jabhat al-Inqaz al-Watani) in August 1984. Sudanese opposition forces in London stated that the new front consisted of the SCP, the Democratic Unionist Party (al-Hizb al-Ittihadi al-Demuqrati), the 'Umma Party (hizb al-ummah), the Popular Army for the Liberation of Sudan (al-Jaysh al-Sha'bi li Tahrir al-Sudan), and several other figures and organizations in northern and southern Sudann (Kuwait, *Al-*

Watan, 21 August 1984). The front's charter called for bringing "those gambling with the fate of the country" to task, an obvious reference to the Numeiri regime. It advocated formation of "a provisional government that rules the country for three years for the purpose of instituting basic liberties, sovereignty of law, and a free, independent and nonaligned foreign policy." The provisional government would be responsible for formulating a draft constitution based on democratic principles.

On 6 April 1985, General Abdel Rahman Siwar el-Dahab, the defense minister and commander-in-chief of the armed forces, seized power in a military coup. Numeiri, en route home from the United States, learned of his ouster during a stopover in Egypt, where he remains in exile. Siwar el-Dahab staged his coup in the midst of demonstrations and strikes protesting a rise in food prices that formed part of the austerity program worked out for Sudan by the International Monetary Fund. The new regime suspended the constitution and dissolved the National Assembly (parliament) and the SSU. Siwar el-Dahab and his fellow officers organized themselves as a fifteen-man Transitional Military Council (TMC) and pledged to return to the barracks in a year after free and fair elections. Dr. Gizzuli Daffa-Allah, head of one of the professional associations that played a key role in the street demonstrations against Numeiri, was appointed prime minister of the provisional government.

Having spent fourteen years underground, the SCP resurfaced after Numeiri's downfall and soon was legalized. Ali al-Tijani al-Tayyib Babikar, the party's number-two man, was among the political prisoners released when crowds stormed Kober prison in Khartoum. Other SCP officials, including Secretary General Muhammad Ibrahim Nugud Mansur, emerged from clandestinity; still others returned from exile. The party belonged to the National Alliance, an umbrella organization of political parties and trade and professional unions seeking to democratize Sudan. The organization comprised most of the groups that had formed the National Salvation Front, as well as others that joined after Numeiri's ouster. In an interview with the French Communist Party newspaper *L'Humanité* (summarized in *Pravda* on 27 April), Nugud stated that representatives of the SCP were participating in meetings with the TMC to discuss the creation of the provisional government and plans for elections. On 13 April, however, the SCP sent a letter to the chairman of the TMC, the leaders of the trade-union confederation, and the heads of political parties. It complained that the TMC was acting autocratically by making decisions arbitrarily and limiting the role of the National Alliance to one of "advice and recourse." The letter also accused the TMC of violating an understanding to the effect that in the interim period before elections the country would be governed in accordance with the 1956 constitution, as amended in 1964 ([clandestine] Radio of the SPLA, 11 May).

One of the first public statements by a top official of the SCP after Numeiri's ouster came from Izz-al Din Ali Amir, a member of the Secretariat. Speaking from London, he told the Kuwaiti newspaper *Al-Watan* that the party rejected any foreign intervention in Sudan, whether from the United States or from Arab countries. He called in particular for the cancellation of Sudan's mutual defense agreement with Egypt. Amir also expressed a need for self-rule on a democratic basis in southern Sudan (*Al-Watan*, 16 April).

On 21 April the Union of Sudanese Women held its first rally in fourteen years. It was addressed by Fatima Ibrahim, widow of the secretary general of the SWTUF who was executed in 1971. The SWTUF is an important SCP front. On 6 May the SCP held its first mass rally since it was proscribed. Addressing the gathering at the Khartoum University stadium, Nugud castigated the United States for alleged interference in Sudanese internal affairs and Egypt for refusing to extradite Numeiri for trial (ibid., 13 May). Nugud also emphasized the country's need to eliminate the legacy of the Numeiri regime, implement socioeconomic transformations in the interests of the working masses, strive for the democratization of sociopolitical affairs, and ensure the fundamental solution of the crisis in southern Sudan. He urged the cohesion of all "progressive" forces in pursuit of these objectives and, according to the 7 May issue of *Pravda*, "The rally showed that, despite many long years of persecution and repression, the SCP has been able to preserve its ranks and is an influential mass party in the vanguard of the struggle for the working people's interests and the national interests of the whole of Sudan."

During an interview on 19 May with *Al-Hadaf*, the organ of the Popular Front for the Liberation of Palestine, Nugud returned to the theme of Numeiri's extradition. In addition, he demanded the abrogation of the mutual defense pact binding Egypt and Sudan and denounced the alleged secret role played by Numeiri in the emigration of the Ethiopian Jews to Israel (AFP, 19 May).

On 4 July the SCP held a public rally in Omdurman. There Nugud called for a reduction of prices for food and other basic necessities to lessen the economic burdens of the Sudanese masses. He also stressed the need to abrogate various state security laws that hampered the people's (and parties') freedoms (Sudan News Agency, 5 July).

The new regime in Khartoum has made no headway in terminating the insurgency in southern Sudan. Garang has refused to recognize the legitimacy of the TMC and claims that the army has "stolen victory from the masses" and that the new government represents "Numeiryism without Numeiri" (*Intercontinental Press*, 13 May, p. 265). He has threatened to expand the insurgency to northern Sudan. Having failed to entice Garang into negotiations by offering the SPLA a post in the cabinet, Siwar el-Dahab has focused on improving Sudan's relations with Libya and Ethiopia, the SPLA's chief foreign patrons.

International Views. Libya was among the first to accord recognition to the new Sudanese government, and Libyan leader Khadafy visited the country briefly on 18 May. The Sudanese defense minister subsequently spent a week in Libya, culminating on 6 July with the signing of a military accord that provided for Libyan assistance in naval and air defense, logistics, transport, equipment, and the training of Sudanese military personnel. In return, Libya promised to close down the SPLA's radio station on its soil (the primary radio station operates out of Ethiopia), to stop furnishing financial and other support to the insurgency, and to help arrange peace talks between the Sudanese government and the rebels. Libya also promised to supply Sudan with oil and to finance a major agricultural project (*NYT*, 10 July; *U.S. News & World Report*, 22 July, p. 39).

A high-level Sudanese delegation visited Ethiopia in late April. Siwar el-Dahab met with Ethiopian strongman Mengistu Haile Mariam in July. Garang lives in exile in Ethiopia, and the SPLA operates a radio in the Ethiopian capital; Khartoum's announcement in August that a Sudanese government delegation would visit the USSR raised the question whether the Sudan would urge Moscow to stop funneling Soviet weapons from Ethiopia to the SPLA.

On 1 September, Nugud declared that the rebellion in the south could be resolved only through the formation of a broad front of political forces in Sudan—a front that he deemed a prerequisite for the solution of the country's other pressing problems as well (Sudan News Agency, 2 September). The SCP organ *Al-Maydan* stated that the widest possible unity of forces was needed to bring about the establishment of democracy (cited in *Pravda*, 21 October). Nugud elaborated on the party's position on both domestic and foreign issues during an interview with the Czechoslovakian Communist Party newspaper. Asked about the chances of creating a "united democratic front" to foster democracy in Sudan, Nugud replied:

> Such a possibility exists . . . of establishing a democratic front that would incorporate the parliament, various political parties, trade unions, social organizations, as well as mass information media. On the other hand, its members cannot comprise those forces that, although they oppose Numeiri—for example, some national bourgeois and traditional political parties—are now trying to constrain democratic development and would prefer a certain type of military government. (Prague, *Rude Pravo*, 2 August)

Responding to a question about the SCP's platform for the national elections scheduled for April 1986, Nugud stated that the hallmarks of the party's campaign would be "defending the progressive demands of the popular uprising of last April and democratic freedoms, resolving economic problems, and cutting down to the minimum the pilferage of the national wealth by imperialist circles." He cited the chief priorities in foreign policy to be a Sudan that is "nonaligned and, within our region . . . emancipated from the influence of Saudi Arabia and Egypt" (ibid.).

The SCP closely parrots the radical Arab Communist line on Middle Eastern politics. "U.S. imperialism" and the "Zionist aggression" of Israel are the villains. The Sudanese Communists also condemn moderate Arab countries, such as Egypt, for siding with the U.S.-Israeli "strategic alliance." The SCP chides the United States for its arms sales to Sudan and for making threats against Libya. The SCP reiterated those points in June 1983 during a meeting of twelve Arab communist and workers' parties (*IB*, September 1983, pp. 24–28). On 7 November 1983 the SCP joined eight other Middle Eastern and North African communist parties in issuing an appeal to "all the progressive and patriotic forces in the Arab world, and also in the camp of our people's friends" to further their unity "against U.S. imperialism, Zionism, and Arab reaction." The appeal was issued in Prague (*IB*, January 1984, p. 27).

In December 1984 the SCP participated in a gathering of world communist parties in Prague under the auspices of the journal *Problems of Peace and Socialism (World Marxist Review)*. Thcsc gatherings occur periodically (the latest was in 1981) to assess the international situation and formulate communist strategies and tactics for the coming years (*Rude Pravo*, 7 December 1984).

Marian Leighton
Defense Intelligence Agency

Zimbabwe

Population. 8,667,000
Party. Zimbabwe African National Union (ZANU)
Founded. 1963
Membership. No data
First Secretary and President. Robert G. Mugabe
Politburo. 14 members (15 seats): Robert Mugabe, Simon Muzenda (holds 2 seats), Maurice Nyagumbo, Enos Nkala, Herbert Ushewokunze, Emmerson Munangagwa, Nathan Shamuyarira, Didymus Mutasa, Dzingai Mutumbuka, Teurai Ropa Nhongo, Ernest Kadungura, Sydney Sekeremayi, Rex Nhongo, Josiah Tongamirai
Central Committee. 90 members
Status. Ruling party
Last Congress. Fifth, 8–12 August 1984
Last Election. 1985, 76 percent, 64 of 100 parliamentary seats
Auxiliary Organizations. People's Militia
Publication. *Moto* (magazine); ZANU has strong influence in all Zimbabwan media.

ZANU is the ruling party of the Republic of Zimbabwe. Though not an avowedly communist party, it professes to be Marxist in ideology. It was formed in 1963 by the African nationalist Ndabaningi Sithole after he split from Joshua Nkomo's Zimbabwe African Peoples' Union (ZAPU). Robert Mugabe, a Marxist, became ZANU secretary general under Sithole's presidency. In the late 1960s, ZANU launched a guerrilla war against the white-dominated Rhodesian government of Prime Minister Ian Smith. Much of ZANU's logistical and training support came from the People's Republic of China. After a bitter power struggle in 1974, Mugabe was elected to replace Sithole as party president. Internal leadership struggles continued, but by the time of the peace negotiations in Geneva in 1976, Mugabe had gained almost complete control. At the Geneva conference the frontline states forced Moscow-supported Nkomo and ZAPU into a Patriotic Front (PF) alliance with Mugabe and ZANU in order to present a stronger, more united opposition to the Rhodesian regime.

This fragile fabric of unity began to unravel in February 1980 when ZAPU contested the pre-independence elections as a separate party. ZANU won a stunning landslide, gaining 57 of the 100 parliamentary seats to ZAPU's 20. Mugabe emerged as prime minister when Zimbabwe achieved independence from Britain that year. ZANU's strength derives mainly from the majority Shona people, while ZAPU's support comes overwhelmingly from the Ndebele, who constitute only 18 percent of the population.

After independence, the two parties formed a coalition government, but this collapsed in early 1982 after Nkomo spurned Mugabe's call for a merger into a single party. In February of that year Mugabe sacked Nkomo from his cabinet post, along with other ZAPU ministers, accusing them of stockpiling arms in preparation for a coup. ZAPU and ZANU have since been in an adversarial relationship.

ZANU expanded its parliamentary majority to 64 seats in July 1985, the first general election since independence (*NYT*, 10 July). Sixty-one-year-old Mugabe was elected to a second five-year term as prime minister, gaining 76 percent of the vote. However, he secured very little support from the Ndebele population (*FBIS*, 12 July). ZANU's electoral victories were marred by its inability to make any inroads among the Ndebele. Thus, the nation remained deeply divided, both ethnically and geographically.

Organization and leadership. ZANU is directed by a 90-member Central Committee under the presidency of Robert Mugabe, who is also the country's prime minister and the minister of defense and of national security.

The first party congress in twenty years was convened in August 1984. It was held amid bitter political infighting based more on personality and ethnicity than on ideology. More than 6,000 delegates attended and adopted a new charter, or constitution, for the party. By its terms, the Central Committee was tripled in size to 90 members. The National Executive was abolished and replaced by a fifteen-seat Politburo. As the party's supreme executive organ, the Politburo rules the Central Committee and, ultimately, the entire country. It supervises all government ministries and agencies. In many respects it supercedes the cabinet, which has been reduced in size and authority. The Politburo's membership has been drawn from the ranks of the Central Committee by Prime Minister Mugabe and not by a body within the Central Committee. The party congress also created five standing committees that now handle broad questions of public policy and seek to turn the resolutions of the party congress into comprehensive programs. Each committee chairperson is appointed by the Politburo and holds a cabinet portfolio. Thus, real power in Zimbabwe now lies with the ZANU Politburo, although ultimate authority rests with Mugabe, serving as party head.

Mugabe's position in both government and party has been greatly strengthened and more centralized as a result of the new party structure. At the congress he was unanimously re-elected to the party leadership, with the new titles of first secretary and president. Mugabe has now begun to press for the creation of a powerful executive presidency for the government, modeled after that of Mozambique. The party congress gave him a firm mandate to transform the nation into a one-party, ZANU-controlled regime. Mugabe also reaffirmed his commitment to the establishment of a one-party socialist state based on Marxist-Leninist lines, but he has assured the population that socialist goals will be achieved "by education and persuasion, and not by imposition and compulsion" (*FBIS*, 20 July).

At the party congress, Mugabe introduced a "Leadership Code of Conduct," aimed at curbing corruption and nepotism and at instilling greater ideological discipline. It would also discourage party officials from amassing wealth in the private sector. The Marxist prime minister is concerned that too many ZANU officials are engaging in capitalistic activities inimical to the country's socialist goals. In 1985 the code was honored more in the breech, as officials simply transferred their assets to proxy owners. Others left government service for the more lucrative private sector. Consequently, the code was not vigorously enforced (*WP*, 6 June).

ZANU remains a party dominated by the Shona ethnic group, which comprises approximately 80 percent of the population. Mugabe has had little success in attracting more Ndebele, largely because of the government's brutal tactics in suppressing dissident activity in Matabeleland. The few Ndebele who serve in the government tend to be vehemently anti-ZAPU and have almost no following among their own ethnic group. The overwhelming majority of the Ndebele have remained in ZAPU, the major opposition party. ZANU's Central Committee thus continues to be dominated by Shona speakers. Key positions on the Politburo are held by Mugabe's own Zezuru clan of the Shona. Moreover, in 1985 all Ndebele were purged from the recently merged Central Intelligence Organization (CIO) and the police Special Branch, and many

Ndebele officers were prematurely retired from the national army.

ZANU recently established an ideological institute, called the Chitepo College of Marxism and Leninism. It has also begun a militia training program for local party leaders to teach them to protect themselves from guerrilla dissidents. This complements a program that has already trained more than 10,000 private citizens (*Harare*, 28 March). In addition, the ZANU youth brigades have an estimated 40,000 members, many of whom have received paramilitary training (*African Recorder*, 4–17 June).

ZANU's professed Marxism has been substantially diluted since the end of the liberation struggle and its elevation as the ruling party. Mugabe has become more cautious and pragmatic in his policies. He is committed to a mixed economy, has refrained from expropriating private property, and pays fair market prices for all government acquisitions. ZANU tolerates the white-dominated private sector because it is so vital to the economy. Whites continue to play an important, though steadily diminishing, role in public service. After the election in 1985, Mugabe sacked the highly influential, white minister of agriculture, leaving only one remaining white in the cabinet.

The country is in desperate need of foreign capital and has therefore permitted considerable foreign equity control over locally based enterprises. However, ZANU seeks greater state control and progressive expansion of the state in economic development. Toward that end, the government has purchased the major newspapers, a large bank, and a pharmaceutical company and has created a state-owned minerals marketing board. In early 1985 it announced its intention of securing majority ownership or complete control over the private flour-milling companies. Mugabe would also like to acquire white-owned farmlands that are not being utilized in order to settle more than 115,000 currently homeless families. Nevertheless, top Politburo leaders, notably the minister for political affairs, Maurice Nyagumbo, have asserted that "the private sector should be left alone to compete with the public sector...and so the state gains technology and management experience from it." (*Los Angeles Times*, 1 April).

Modest efforts to form agricultural cooperatives have been blocked by prominent civil servants who have a stake in the private sector. Other government officials have secured from the World Bank a $10 million loan to help small businesses in improving management techniques (*African Recorder*, 2–15 July). In the areas of social services and education, the government has introduced free health care for people with low incomes and free education at the primary school level. Consequently, literacy and life expectancy rates have soared. However, state agricultural, industrial, and trading schemes have been delayed because of high capital costs. The expensive guerrilla war in Matabeleland and declines in world mineral and commodity prices have caused delays in the implementation of socialist programs. This has heightened the power struggle between the fiscal conservatives, or pragmatists, and the "scientific socialist" radicals. The former remained in control of economic matters, but the radicals' influence over purely political questions continued to grow. Nevertheless, it is unlikely that Mugabe will make any direct moves against foreign business interests for fear it might further weaken the economy.

Economic conditions improved dramatically in 1985, largely as a result of good rainfall and bumper harvests of food staples and commercial export crops. African peasants brought in a record maize crop, thus lessening the country's dependence on white commercial farmers. The rural economy is again thriving (*Africa News*, 7 October) and the trade balance and balance of payments situation is greatly improved (*African Business*, September). Several hundred white families returned to Zimbabwe and resumed economic activity for the first time since independence (*Herald*, 22 October).

Domestic Affairs. Zimbabwe's population remains deeply divided over fundamental questions of power and of national purpose and direction. This is reflected in ambivalence and contradictions in economic theory, in development, and in dealings with foreign diplomats and business people. Ambiguities in policy statements cause considerable uncertainty over the future direction of government. The whites, numbering approximately 115,000, are generally against ZANU's social policies but grudgingly cooperate. They are internally divided and politically apathetic. Less than half of those eligible voted. Yet in the 1985 elections they gave Ian Smith—the intransigent former Rhodesian prime minister—and his Conservative Alliance Party fifteen of the twenty parliamentary seats reserved for whites. This worried white liberals, angered Mugabe, and further strained race relations (*NYT*, 10 July). Mugabe announced bitterly that henceforth all cabinet positions would be filled by ZANU people only (*CSM*, 9 July). However, parliament and cabinet have become less relevant as power gradually shifts to Mugabe and the ZANU Politburo.

ZANU's relations with ZAPU remained extremely tense and bitter. The number and magnitude of violent interparty clashes increased dramatically in the first part of 1985 and flared again immediately following the elections. The year witnessed a resurgence of assassinations, abductions, harassments, and arrests of ZAPU followers in Matabeleland. Six ZAPU ministers of parliament and seven Bulawayo councillors were detained for alleged support of dissidents, and Nkomo's residences were searched for firearms. Amnesty International and the Catholic Justice and Peace Commission complained of government torture of political prisoners. As elections approached, the level of violence subsided (*Economist*, 12 October), yet in the days following, ZANU women rampaged through suburban Harare ransacking the homes of ZAPU supporters (*Facts on File*, 12 July).

In October, ZAPU's leader, Nkomo, sought a resumption of the unity talks that had been broken off several years before. Later that month, ZANU and ZAPU leaders reached a general agreement on the principle of a merger (*African Recorder*, November–December). However, hardliner elements in both parties opposed compromise. The unification issue had generated considerable intraparty turmoil, and some ZAPU militants feared that a merger would be tantamount to a ZANU takeover (*CSM*, 27 September).

International Views and Positions. ZANU and the government officially adhere to a policy of nonalignment. The country was selected as venue for the 1986 summit of the Movement of Nonaligned Nations, and Mugabe was chosen as the group's chairman until 1989 (*WP*, 13 September). Looking forward to the summit, Zimbabwe has greatly strengthened its ties with communist bloc countries. In May 1985, Mugabe traveled to Romania and Yugoslavia and also established diplomatic relations with the People's Democratic Republic of Yemen (*FBIS*, 26 May). In August he visited North Korea, China (PRC), the Soviet Union, and Bulgaria (*Pravda*, 1 September; *FBIS*, 28 August). Agreements were signed for greater cooperation in the areas of education, media, and culture. The Soviets will participate in the construction of Beira's port Moatize, which will help Zimbabwe's trade through Mozambique (*Financial Times*, September). In October, Mugabe stopped off in Cuba enroute to the annual Commonwealth summit in the Bahamas (*CSM*, 22 October).

The prime minister returned to Moscow in early December with a large ZANU party and government delegation. They were guests of the CPSU Central Committee and the Council of Ministers of the USSR (*Africa Economic Digest*, 7 December). Several confidential accords were signed following meetings with Mikhail Gorbachev (*NYT*, 5 December). Coupled to these high-level meetings in various communist countries were separate visits to Moscow and other communist capitals by the Zimbabwe National Chamber of Commerce and numerous cultural and educational organizations. The Soviets, in turn, sent several cultural and trade delegations to Zimbabwe. All this seemed to point to a substantial improvement in Zimbabwan-Soviet relations, which had been strained since independence.

On the African continent, Zimbabwe enjoys especially close relations with the Marxist republics of Angola and Mozambique. In June the leaders of Zimbabwe, Tanzania, and Mozambique met in Harare to consider greater military support for Mozambique in its struggle against the guerrilla movement RENAMO (*WP*, 13 June). Zimbabwe has already deployed over 4,000 troops inside Mozambique (*African Recorder*, 16–29 July) to guard the vital 250-mile corridor to Mozambique's post of Beira. Through it passes roads, railways, and an oil pipeline to Zimbabwe. The latter carries all of Zimbabwe's gasoline and diesel fuel. By September the Zimbabwan army had shifted from defensive to conventional tactics against RENAMO in Mozambique.

Zimbabwe's relations with South Africa rapidly deteriorated in late 1985. Mugabe called for international economic sanctions against the Botha regime and accused South Africa of propagandizing Zimbabwe's population through the government-owned Radio Truth, which is beamed into turbulent Matabeleland. In return, South Africa alleged that ANC guerrillas staged landmine attacks in the northern Transvaal from bases in Zimbabwe. The government threatened to send its army into Zimbabwe in pursuit of guerrillas in the event of future incidents (*CSM*, 2 December). Nearly 90 percent of Zimbabwe's trade passes through South Africa, and that country is Zimbabwe's biggest source of raw materials and largest export market (London, *Economist Intelligence Unit* [*EIU*], 4th quarter).

Zimbabwe continues to play a leading role in the Southern Africa Development Coordination Conference (SADCC) and the eighteen-member Preferential Trade Agreement (PTA) with central and east African countries. The prime minister is still chair man of the SADCC, and a prominent Zimbabwan economist is executive secretary of the PTA. Moreover, the Reserve Bank of Zimbabwe acts as a clearinghouse in the settlement of financial accounts of PTA member states.

Zimbabwe continues to support the Southwest Africa People's Organization (SWAPO) and the efforts of Angola to defeat the antigovernment forces of UNITA. It is opposed to the Reagan administration's policy of "constructive engagement" as it pertains to South Africa. Zimbabwe is an active member of the Organization of African Unity (OAU) and supports movements aimed at establishing multiracial social governments in South Africa and Namibia.

Publications. Government control over the media continues to grow. In 1985 the editor of the influential *Sunday Mail*, who was a leading independent journalist, was replaced by a man close to Mugabe and the ZANU party line (*EIU*, 4th quarter). All the country's media organs, with the possible exception of the *Bulawayo Chronicle* in Matabeleland, are under strong ZANU editorial influence. In 1984–1985 the country strengthened its media links with the East through agreements with the Soviet, North Korean, Romanian, Bulgarian, and East German news agencies (*FBIS*, April).

Richard W. Hull
New York University

THE AMERICAS

Introduction

Fidel Castro's Cuba remains the dominant communist influence in the Americas. This was evident in Havana's continuing support for the Sandinista government in Nicaragua, which was symbolically most obvious when Castro attended the inauguration of that country's new president, Daniel Ortega, on 10 January. The major communist party event of 1985 was the conference of Latin American and Caribbean communist parties that Castro hosted in June, which issued the predictable denunciations of the United States.

The Cuban economy continued to depend on the assistance of more than $4 billion in military and economic aid and credit from the Soviet bloc. Cuba's current debt to the bloc is estimated at approximately $22 billion. Cuban documents admit a debt to the West of $3.42 billion, although outside observers estimate that it is higher. Even though Castro makes all payments on his debt, he conducted a prolonged campaign during the year to convince other Latin American countries to renounce their foreign debts altogether. The campaign did not draw much support around the continent despite the admitted magnitude of the problem of indebtedness and debt service.

The year began with some hope that U.S.-Cuban relations might be on an upswing, despite continued Cuban support for the Sandinista government in Nicaragua and the guerrillas in El Salvador and the stationing of some 44,000 troops abroad, mostly in Africa. Hopes were high for an improvement in relations because in a December 1984 agreement Cuba pledged to take back nearly 3,000 unwanted refugees from the Mariel exodus. However, Castro renounced the agreement in May when the United States began broadcasts to Cuba on Radio Martí. At the end of the year, new U.S. restrictions were imposed on Cuban officials in the United States.

Domestically there was evidence of changes taking place on the Caribbean island, most important of which were numerous shakeups in the leadership of the Cuban Communist Party and government hierarchy. This meant that some of Castro's old guard were demoted or promoted out of power, which was evidently an effort to remove incompetents from office and replace them with technocrats. Speculation continues as to Castro's health, with some convinced that he is losing his mental capacities; Fidel announced officially that his brother, Raúl, will succeed him to power.

The Sandinista government in Nicaragua became the focus of much international attention during 1985. Significant events included the inauguration of Ortega in January, the new president's trips to Mosow in March and May, and a meeting of the Mixed Commission on Cooperation between the Council on Mutual Economic Assistance and Nicaragua, which resulted in about twelve major development projects approved for the latter. In the fall, the International Court of Justice heard Nicaragua's charges that the United States was violating international law in its support of rebel activities against the Managua government. The United States refused to present its case, arguing that the court lacked jurisdiction.

Meanwhile, U.S. support for the rebel war against the Sandinista government in Nicaragua continued. After first refusing to fund the rebels, the U.S. Congress authorized $27 million in "humanitarian" aid after Ortega made one of his poorly timed trips to the Soviet Union. Anti-Sandinista rebels abroad came close to complete unity when they formed the United Nicaraguan Opposition; in June three prominent exiles assumed leadership of this umbrella organization—Adolfo Calero, Alfonso Robelo, and Arturo Cruz. The guerrilla forces, which by the end of the year numbered about 20,000, were a presence in many provinces; however, the delivery of Soviet-built Mi-24 Hind helicopter gunships kept the military balance on the side of the government. Sandinista negotiations with some of the Miskito Indians failed to reach any agreement.

The United States imposed an economic embargo against the Sandinista government in May, which eliminated 15 percent of the nation's foreign trade. On 16 October the government declared a state of emergency that cut civil and human rights to their lowest point since 1979. Relations with the orthodox church, and particularly with Miguel Cardinal Obando y Bravo, continued to worsen; by October, Interior Minister Tomás Borge was calling the cardinal "a Siamese twin of Ronald Reagan." Perhaps the most important Nicaraguan official to flee the country during 1985 was Alvaro Jose Baldizon Aviles, the chief personal investigator of rights violations for Borge. Baldizon confirmed the existence of a government hit squad and most of the rights violations reported earlier by the increasingly muzzled, independent Permanent Commission on Human Rights.

El Salvador had municipal and legislative elections in March that gave President Napoleón Duarte a good working majority in the legislature. Nevertheless, Duarte's position was weakened because of a lack of economic and social progress in addition to uncertainties concerning the eventual outcome of the ongoing civil war.

The peace talks launched between the Salvadoran government and the Farabundo Martí National Liberation Front (FMLN) guerrillas in 1984 made no progress in 1985. Instead, the year found the two sides altering their tactics. The government took a more aggressive line on the ground and in the air, killing and capturing some important leaders in addition to guerrilla fighters. The FMLN, to avoid heavy losses in bombing raids, broke down into smaller operating units and increased its activities in urban areas. This included terrorist attacks in San Salvador—including one that killed six military and business people from the United States—and kidnappings of scores of small-town officials and, in September, of Inez Durán, the president's daughter. Most of the kidnapped individuals were freed after some humiliation of the Duarte government.

While the five guerrilla groups in the FMLN tried to form a single Marxist-Leninist party, some leaders of the guerrilla political front—the Democratic Revolutionary Front (FDR)—criticized the increasing terrorism; some were said to be considering a return to the country to participate openly in the political system. The international position of the FMLN would be greatly weakened if the FDR were to split up and/or withdraw its support from the guerrillas, who still maintain close ties to Managua and assorted terrorist groups.

In Colombia a truce between the government and guerrilla forces successfully reduced conflict with the Revolutionary Armed Forces of Colombia (FARC). There was no agreement with the National Liberation Army (ELN), however, and in November the government killed the group's founder, Ricardo Lara. The truce with the M-19 guerrillas was unevenly successful until mid-year. In June the M-19 announced that it would resume fighting, and government counterinsurgency strikes took many guerrilla lives. In November the M-19 carried out the most spectacular terrorist activity of the year in Latin America, perhaps with support from the Nicaraguan government, when it stormed the Palace of Justice in Bogotá. The government refused any negotiations and stormed the palace; all 35 guerrillas were killed, as were 64 civilians, including 12 Supreme Court justices. At year's end, the government claimed that almost 90 percent of the country's estimated 10,000 guerrillas had agreed to the truce and to participate in the 1986 elections.

In Ecuador the Communist Party was a small part of a broadly based opposition front that the government systematically undermined throughout the year. The Ecuadorean government broke relations with Nicaragua in October. The Alfaro Vive! guerrilla group, formed only five years ago, gave evidence of becoming the most effective such organization in recent Ecuadorean history. Alfaro Vive! coordinates some of its activities with the M-19 in Colombia, and it suffered a setback similar to the Colombian group in August. The guerrillas kidnapped a wealthy businessman and demanded the release of prisoners, a large ransom, and safe passage to Nicaragua. Instead, government forces stormed the house; the hostage and four guerrillas were killed.

The Communist Party of Chile, once the most successful Latin American proponent of electoral politics, has changed its tactics since the coup that overthrew President Salvador Allende in 1973. During

1985 it was actively involved in political, labor, and terrorist activities in Chile, the latter with support from the Soviet Union. This involvement in bombings, as well as blackouts and sabotage, kept the Communist Party from entering broader alliances, including the Democratic Alliance formed in 1983. The Communists were excluded from the National Accord reached by many opposition groups in September.

In Peru the Communist Party remained the largest and most important group in the Union of the Revolutionary Left, the second most powerful electoral alliance in that Andean nation. This Peruvian front, which holds 26 percent of the seats in the Chamber of Deputies and 25 percent in the Senate, consists of four parties, two coalitions, and assorted smaller groups and individuals. It is the largest Marxist political group operating in any Latin American democracy. The front was weakened during the year, however, by internal rivalries and policy differences. The Maoist guerrillas of the Sendero Luminoso ("Shining Path"), which emerged in Ayacucho, remained active and now are able to undertake coordinated attacks in almost any part of the nation. The Sendero guerrillas tried to convince people not to vote in the April election that brought Alan García Pérez of the American Popular Revolutionary Alliance (APRA) to the presidency; their forms of persuasion included death threats, assassinations, bombings, roadblocks, and blackouts. During the year the death toll in the country's guerrilla war passed 6,000. The fanaticism of the group isolates it from the front and even, it would seem, from most other guerrilla groups.

Communists participated in legislatures and/or supported elected governments in other countries as well. In Costa Rica, where the democratic tradition is long-standing, the communist movement was weakened by internal dissension.

Constitutional governments were restored after years of military rule in Uruguay and Brazil. The once-powerful Communist Party of Uruguay, though technically banned, received a quarter of the votes cast for the Broad Front in November 1984—some 6 percent of the votes in the election—and actually took its seats in February 1985. The National Liberation Movement (MLN-Tupamaros) in Uruguay, now operating as a small legal group, held a convention in December and admitted all the mistakes it had made as one of the continent's most feared guerrilla movements during the late 1960s and early 1970s. In January the Brazilian Communist Party and two of its splinter groups, which were illegal at the time, took refuge in the major opposition party, which ended up electing its candidate as president.

In Guyana the unexpected death of Forbes Burnham resulted in an election in December, which found Cheddi Jagan's People's Progressive Party, now formally calling itself a Marxist-Leninist party, coming in a distant second to the People's National Congress in somewhat tainted elections.

The Communist party of the United States continued its membership drive, but by the end of the year still had a maximum of 20,000 members nationwide. Lacking any significant base of support, the party often gives its stamp of approval to "progressive" Democrats it sees as decidedly better than the Republican opposition. The Socialist Workers Party has thrown off several factions in recent years; it now has less than 1,000 members, still considerably more than any of the factions. It refuses to endorse the establishment party candidates and even denounces Jesse Jackson for attracting labor support that might otherwise go toward forming a truly revolutionary labor party.

William Ratliff
Hoover Institution

Argentina

Population. 30,708,000
Party. Communist Party of Argentina (Partido Comunista de la Argentina; PCA)
Founded. 1918
Membership. 70,000 (estimated); 200,000 (claimed)
Secretary General. Athos Fava
Politburo. 8 members: Athos Fava, Jorge Pereyra, Rubens Iscaro, Fernando Nadra, Óscar Arévalo, Irene Rodríguez, Luis Heller, Hugo Ojeda
Central Committee. 92 members, 33 alternates
Status. Legal
Last Congress. Extraordinary, 5–6 September 1983
Last Election. 1985 (parliamentary and provincial midterm elections); PCA joined with the Movement Toward Socialism (MAS) in the Front of the People (FREPU) coalition; 2 percent, no representation.
Auxiliary Organizations. Communist Youth Federation; local branch of World Peace Council; Committee in Solidarity with Nicaragua; the party effectively controls the Argentine Permanent Assembly on Human Rights.
Publications. *¿Qué Pasa?* (weekly); *Aqui y ahora* (monthly). The popular political gossip magazine, *El Periodista* (weekly), is generally regarded as controlled by party members.

In 1985 the government of President Raúl Alfonsín continued to move to a more moderate, centrist position, consolidated its electoral gains, and reaffirmed its popularity in midterm elections. The opposition Peronist party divided in two, and although repeated efforts were made to heal the breach, it appeared that the schism was permanent; the more moderate, "renovationist" list emerged as the more popular of the two at the ballot box. In spite of the fragile history of democratic institutions in Argentina, 1985 witnessed much evidence of a strong popular consensus for civilian, representative government and a decided repudiation of both left and right extremes.

This was all the more extraordinary considering the parlous economic situation, which was characterized by a mounting foreign debt ($45 billion), widespread unemployment, and a declining standard of living. A general strike called by the Peronist-led General Confederation of Labor (CGT) in May failed in its purpose to bring the country to a standstill. A drastic reordering of economic policy in June (the so-called Plan Austral) was greeted with widespread approval, in spite of the fact that the plan implemented austerity measures of the type that the International Monetary Fund had long been requesting of Argentina and that the government had firmly rejected until the end of 1984 (*YICA*, 1985, pp. 45–46). In the short term, the new policies drastically reduced inflation from its high of 2,000 percent per year to 26.8 percent by the end of 1985 and won the support of the U.S. Treasury Department, which enthusiastically joined a search for new capital to tide the Alfonsín government over its rough spots (called the Baker Plan).

Perhaps the most remarkable development of the year was the trial of former leaders of the military juntas that governed the country on a de facto basis between 1976 and 1983. At issue was the conduct of the armed forces and police during the so-called "dirty war" against an active urban guerrilla movement from 1974 to 1978, in which thousands of innocent persons were arrested, tortured, or simply "disappeared." In December, after months of testimony and arguments for both the prosecution and the defense, a federal court convicted former president Gen. Jorge R. Videla, Admiral Emilio Massera, Gen. Orlando Agosti, former president Gen. Roberto Viola, and Admiral Armando Labruschini to sentences ranging from 54 months to life. Although all but two of the convicted defendants received sentences more lenient than that demanded by the prosecution, the trials set an important precedent; never before in Latin American history had an elected government brought military predecessors to justice for state terrorism. (Former Montoneros guerrilla leader Mario Firmenich [see *YICA*, 1985, pp. 47–48] was also brought to justice at the same time, although his trial had not concluded by the end of the year.)

The trials themselves fueled a continuing debate on the rights and wrongs of subversion and antisubversive activities in parliament, the press, and on the part of human rights organizations. Defense Minister Raúl Borrás suggested at a press conference in April that the country could not forever leave open the wounds of the recent past, because "a nation cannot be based on revenge, persecution and hatred" (Argentine Press Agency [TELAM], 2 April; *FBIS*, 8 April); this was widely interpreted by the government's opponents on the left to be setting the stage for some sort of amnesty, even though Borrás had emphatically stated on the same occasion that "freedom from punishment can no longer exist in the country." When the convictions came in December, these same critics expressed disappointment at their relative lenience and at the continuing refusal of the government to order the judicial arm to reach farther down into the command structure.

A resurgence of terrorist incidents throughout the country—primarily bombings of the headquarters of both left and right parties—was attributed by the government to paramilitary groups that had functioned in the 1970s with the connivance of the ruling junta and its intelligence organizations. The failure of a federal prosecutor to obtain a writ against an alleged group of civilian and military plotters led President Alfonsín to declare a 60-day state of siege in the final days of October, when Argentines were preparing to go to the polls for the first midterm parliamentary election in twenty years. The elections themselves took place as scheduled and reaffirmed Alfonsín's Radical Civic Union party as the most popular in the country (44 percent), polling almost twice as many votes as its nearest competitor, the Justicialist, or Peronist, party (24 percent). The Radicals increased their parliamentary representation by one seat in the Chamber of Deputies to 130; the Peronists lost eight, largely to parties farther to the left and right.

As in 1983, the Communist Party had little to show for its efforts at the ballot box. Despite a well-funded campaign, it failed to elect a single deputy or member of any provincial assembly, even though it ran a joint list with the tiny, Trotskyist MAS under the label FREPU. FREPU garnered only 2 percent (350,816) of the nearly 19 million votes cast. Although the party was active in many other areas, it continued to suffer electorally from a continued division of the forces of the left.

Leadership and Party Organization. Rodolfo Ghioldi, one of the founders of the PCA and a member of the Central Committee Political Commission, died in July.

In December Secretary General Athos Fava was awarded the Order of Lenin by the Communist Party of the Soviet Union, an unusual distinction since the medal is normally reserved for chiefs of state or persons who have rendered extraordinary services to the Soviet cause. Fava was the first Argentine to receive this honor, although in previous years the Lenin Peace Prize, lower on the heirarchy of Soviet decorations, had been awarded to economist Alfredo Varela and Writer María Rosa Oliver.

A new party journal, *Aquí y ahora*, was established, as well as a new radio program, "A People in My Voice," the first party show to be broadcast over a national network.

Domestic Party Affairs. Having supported the Peronist presidential ticket in 1983 (see *YICA*, 1984, pp. 82–83), the PCA was forced to regroup ideologically in 1984 and 1985. Central Committee member Fernando Nadra told an interviewer that the new ruling party was sharply divided into "progressive" and "reactionary" sectors; he identified the former simply as "an important sector of the Radical Youth, [certain] members of the government and parliamentarians who have spoken out against the International Monetary Fund, the financial policy, and the drastic solution to the foreign debt problem" (*La Prensa*, 8 June; *JPRS*, 23 May). For his part, Secretary General Fava described the PCA's relationship to the Alfonsín government as one of conditional approval. The latter, he affirmed, required "strong political and material support on a mass scale to resist the opposition of reactionary circles, the landowning oligarchy, and North American imperialism." At the same time, he reserved the right to "tirelessly . . . criticize any decree or measure by the administration that is at variance with or harmful to the lawful interests of the working people" (Moscow, *Politischeskoe samoobrazovanie*, July 1984; *JPRS*, 8 January). For example, the party supported the general strike called by the CGT, opposed the payment of Argentina's foreign debt, and repeatedly called on the government to break relations with the International Monetary Fund.

In the articles cited above, Fava referred to the political tasks assigned by the 1983 plenum of the Central Committee, which were the need to step up labor agitation, organize work among women (who he claimed constituted 40 percent of the party's new members), and create a united front of democratic forces. The last is an old theme in PCA literature, since it has long abandoned the hope of succeeding in any frontal attack on the Peronist party or, for that matter, reabsorbing the dozens of splinter groups of the left that have departed its ranks.

Central to the PCA's efforts has been the labor movement, which remains firmly under the control of the Peronist party. In a special report to the Central Committee in April, Luis Heller outlined new organizational efforts to attract "the most advanced elements of Peronism" to the party, particularly in the larger factories, although he admitted—probably a vast understatement—that these efforts had not been sufficient "to change the balance of power." He rejected the notion of the Alfonsín government (which was seeking wage restraint as part of its austerity package) that strikes or heightened labor agitation were inherently destabilizing; "the defense of the constitutional regime," Heller noted, "must not become an end in itself, because in that case it would become a paralyzing slogan" (*¿Qué Pasa?*, 10 April; *JPRS*, 23 May).

During the election campaign, the PCA (along with other leftist groups) focused on the foreign debt almost to the exclusion of all other issues. Its official program called for a unilateral moratorium for ten years, during which neither principal nor interest would be paid to the country's creditors; this was congruent with a proposal advanced for all of Latin America by Cuban president Fidel Castro.

Auxiliary and Front Organizations. In the environment of complete political freedom that now prevails in Argentina, the PCA was able to pursue its agendas through many front organizations as well as the mass media, the universities, and the state cultural agencies, where many party members are employed. Of particular significance in this regard was Radio Belgrano, which broadcasts much Cuban and Nicaraguan propaganda, and Argentine State Television, whose treatment of major news events, such as the tenth anniversary of the fall of Saigon, elicited much shock and dismay from moderate and conservative sectors of opinion.

Of the front organizations, the Committee in Solidarity with Nicaragua and the Argentine branch of the World Peace Council were especially active. However, by bringing military leaders to trial, the government had somewhat defused the human-rights issue; hence, the organizations devoted to this matter declined in political salience. At the same time, the active assistance of the Reagan administration on debt issues has dulled the edge of traditional anti-American sentiment in Argentina, upon which the Communists and their allies have historically enjoyed something of a free ride.

International Views, Positions, and Activities. The party was at considerable pains to stress certain convergences of opinion between it and the Alfonsín government, particularly on Third World issues, opposition to U.S. intervention in Central America, and the Malvinas (Falkland Islands). With respect to the latter, Secretary General Fava urged that "the South Atlantic region . . . become a zone of peace, free of nuclear states" (*Politischeskoye Samoobrazovaniye*, July 1984; *JPRS*, 8 January). This was another way of demanding immediate British withdrawal and tying the presence of the United Kingdom there with larger NATO issues.

In January a group of 120 members of the Communist Youth Federation went to Nicaragua to assist in the coffee harvest.

A delegation from the CPA (Fava, Jorge Pereyra, Fernando Nadra, and Fanny Edelman) attended a conference on the Latin America debt convoked by Castro in Havana in March.

Rubens Iscaro, former PCA presidential candidate, and Simón Lazara, leader of the Authentic Socialist Party, attended a World Peace Council Presidential Committee Bureau meeting in Moscow in May.

The Argentine party hosted a meeting of the South American Communist Youth Organization in Buenos Aires 2–4 July. In attendance were delegates from Bolivia, Brazil, Colombia, Chile, Ecuador, Guyana, Peru, and observers from Cuba.

Relations with the Soviet Union and Other Bloc Members. In conjunction with a long-standing commercial relationship with Argentina, the Soviet Union accelerated its economic, diplomatic, and cultural activities there. The country received visits from Viktor Ivanov, Soviet deputy minister for foreign trade, in January; from Antanas Barkauskas, deputy chairman of the USSR Supreme Soviet Presidium and president of the Lithuanian Supreme Soviet, in June; and from Viktor Vol'skiy, head of the Latin American Institute of the USSR Academy of Sciences, in October. There was a perceptible increase in the number of Soviet ballet stars, concert artists, and motion pictures dispatched to Argentina, as well as the amount of all-expense-paid tours of the Soviet Union offered by the recently opened Aeroflot office in Buenos Aires.

The Soviet Union remained Argentina's most important trading partner in cereals, accounting for $1.3 billion in purchases—some 60 percent of exports. At the same time, Moscow sold Argentina only $35 million worth of goods, although contracts were signed in 1985 for the sale of machinery amounting to $80 million. A meeting of the joint Argentine-Soviet Commission in November 1984, explored the possibility of Argentina purchasing Soviet products and services for $500 million over the next five years, including railway electrification, and proposals to remodel the port of Bahia Blanca, mine coal, and construct gas pipelines (*Clarín*, 22 October; *FBIS*, 29 October). The government of Chaco province contracted for Soviet road graders, and discussions continued on the transfer of technology and assistance in mining and energy fields.

An agreement was reached with Bulgaria in October for the sale of argricultural products; Bulgaria would also market Argentine meat in Middle Eastern countries. In spite of its economic troubles at home, the Alfonsín government granted a 3-year, $600 million line of credit to Cuba and a similar concession of $50 million to Nicaragua to enable it to buy Argentine wheat.

Guillermo Ungo, leader of the FDR-FMLN guerrilla movement in El Salvador, was received with full honors by Alfonsín in April, and the president took special care to appear alongside Nicaraguan cultural minister Ernesto Cardenal on his visit in March.

Huang Hua, vice president of the National Peoples Congress of the People's Republic of China visited Argentina in June, followed by PRC premier Zhao Ziyang in November. On that occasion the latter admitted that his country had sold heavy water to Argentina for its atomic energy program (*Noticias Argentina*, 7 November; *FBIS*, 8 November).

Other Leftist Groups. The Intransigent Party, led by Oscar Alende, doubled its parliamentary representation from three to six seats in the Chamber of Deputies in the November elections, absorbing many left-wing votes that had gone to Alfonsín in 1983. It was generally thought that most of the former militants of the leftist guerrilla movements of the 1970s were active in the Intransigent Party and saw it as the proper vehicle for their future activities. While Alende admitted this might be so, he also stated that "I would [only] be concerned . . . if there were an attempt to implement those violent methods in our party. But this is not happening, nor is it going to happen" (*SOMOS*, 26 April; *JPRS*, 31 May).

Other groups on the left were hopelessly divided. Of all the parties claiming to be socialist in one form or another, only MAS, as noted above, joined the PCA's call for a united front. The Socialist Alliance, an ostensible coalition of five parties, agreed to run on one election ticket nationwide, but it was beset with internal controversy almost from the start and failed to appear on the electoral map.

Mark Falcoff
American Enterprise Institute

Bolivia

Population. 6,195,000
Party. Communist Party of Bolivia (Partido Comunista de Bolivia; PCB)
Founded. 1950
Membership. 500 (claimed)
Secretary General. Simón Reyes Rivera
Status. Legal
Last Congress. Fifth, 9–13 February; Extraordinary, 2–5 August
Last Elections. 14 July; the United Peoples' Front (FPU), the electoral coalition supported by the PCB, won 4 seats in the Chamber of Deputies.
Auxiliary Organizations. Communist Youth of Bolivia
Publications. *Unidad* (two versions)

The most important events in Bolivia during 1985 were a general election for president and congress a year ahead of schedule, an inflation rate officially reported as 14,000 percent (July 1984–July 1985), a continuing (but still unwon) struggle against cocaine production and smuggling, and two month-long general strikes. Insofar as the PCB was concerned, the most significant development was the consummation of its most serious split in more than twenty years.

The PCB was founded in 1950 by a group of young people who broke away from the country's first pro-Stalinist party, the Left Revolutionary Party (Partido de Izquierda Revolucionaria; PIR), which had collaborated with conservative governments of the 1946–1952 period. After the Bolivian National Revolution, led by the Nationalist Revolutionary Movement (Movimiento Nacionalista Revolucionario; MNR), the PCB remained a minor force in national politics and the labor movement. However, in the twenty years following the overthrow of the MNR regime in 1964, the Communists became the largest single political group in the organized labor movement and particularly among the tin-workers of the Miners' Federation (FSTMB).

During the elections of 1978, 1979, and 1980, the PCB formed part of the Popular Democratic Union (UDP), which backed the candidacy of ex-president Hernán Siles Suazo of the Left MNR (MNRI). After Siles was finally inaugurated as president in October 1982, the PCB was represented in his cabinet by two ministers, those of Mines and Labor. However, as a result of a long cabinet crisis, beginning in November 1984, the Communists finally left the government in January 1985.

Fifth Congress of the PCB. The Fifth Congress of the PCB met in La Paz on 9–13 February. Its agenda included four items: the report of the Central Committee, a programmatic thesis, revision of party statutes, and election of a new party leadership (*Unidad*, 2–8 February). The most important items were the first and last of these. The party organ, *Unidad*, reported that "more than half a thousand" delegates participated in the congress. It also maintained that "the discussion of the subjects was full and positive" (23 February–1 March).

The congress was marked by "criticism and self-criticism" of the PCB's participation in the Siles government. According to *Unidad*, the congress "indicated that the leadership of the Party did not act with the firmness and consequence necessary in applying the programmatic line of the UDP, permitting the execution of a conventional economic policy with monetarist characteristics . . . Nor did it present a responsible policy towards the productive sectors, particularly towards the state enterprise . . . It is important to note that these were the reasons which brought the PC to leave the government" (23 February–1 March).

Subsequently, it was reported that there were three tendencies in the Fifth Congress. One group apparently defended the party's behavior in the Siles government; another was highly critical of that behavior; and a third, "centrist" group was fundamentally concerned with maintaining the unity of the party (*Unidad*, 15–21 June). The principal figures in the three factions were, respectively, the longtime secretary general, Jorge Kolle Cueto; Ramiro Barrenechea, deputy and former minister of Labor under President Siles; and Simón Reyes, a leading figure in the Miners' Federation and the Bolivian Labor Central (Central Obrera Boliviana; COB).

Certain leadership changes resulted from the Fifth Congress. Reyes succeeded Kolle Cueto as secretary general, who returned to the party ranks. Several dissidents were promoted to the party leadership, and one of them, Carlos Soria Galvarro, was named editor of *Unidad*.

Split in the PCB. The Fifth Congress clearly did not settle the internal dissension in the PCB. Controversy centered on interpretations of the decisions of that meeting. It culminated with the publication of a pronouncement of the Cochabamba regional committee that was highly critical of the behavior of the "right" and "center" of the party at the Fifth Congress (*Unidad*, 15–21 June). The majority of the Central Committee responded by removing Soria from his post and expelling him from the Political Committee and the Central Committee of the party.

On 2 July, five members of the Central Committee—Soria, Ramiro Barrenechea, Fernando Fuentes, Emil Balcazar, and Carlos Ortega—set up a Provisional Political Committee and summoned an Extraordinary Congress of the party. These moves were repudiated by the majority of the Central Committee, led by Simón Reyes (*Unidad*, 6 July, and *Unidad*–Soria, ed., 6–12 July). The Soria-Barrenechea faction was to the left of the PCB led by Reyes. This was made clear by Barrenechea's statement to the effect that "the armed struggle will be appropriate in the not distant future when it is necessary to define 'the question of power' " (*Meridiano*, 15 August).

Both of the PCB factions continued to call themselves Partido Comunista de Bolivia. They also both continued to publish a newspaper entitled *Unidad*. The dissident group held its Extraordinary Congress on 2–5 August in La Paz. It discussed "the situation and strategy of power of the PCB" and elected a new Central Committee and Control Commission (*Unidad*–Soria, ed., 27 July–2 August).

The PCB and the Election. The Reyes PCB sought to organize a broad left-wing coalition for the election of 14 July. The party first sought to include several dissident factions of the Movement of the Revolutionary Left (Movimiento de Izquierda Revolucionaria; MIR), the peasant party headed by union leader Genaro Flores, and even the Revolutionary Party of the Nationalist Left, led by Juan Lechin. In the end, however, the PCB's only ally in the United Peoples' Front (FPU) was the faction of the MIR headed by Antonio Aranibar Quiroga, who became the FPU's presidential candidate. Oscar Salas Maya of the PCB was named candidate for vice president.

After the split in the PCB, the dissident faction did not overtly support the FPU. In a press conference on 2 July it called on all far-left groups to withdraw from the "fraudulent" election (*Unidad*–Soria, ed., 12–19 July). Yet an editorial in the group's periodical shortly before the election implied that it would be acceptable for its supporters to vote for the FPU or for either of two other parties on the far left. It also emphasized the need to unite a wide coalition of far-left groups after the election (*Unidad*–Soria, ed., 29 June–5 July).

The FPU coalition was not a major factor in the election. Its candidates received 38,124 votes: some 2.21 percent of the total. It did elect four members to the Chamber of Deputies (*Hoy*, 8 August).

Since no presidential candidate received a majority of the popular vote, the final decision passed to Congress. The two leading candidates were expresidents Victor Paz Estenssoro and Hugo Banzer. Simón Reyes, the first secretary of the Communist Party who had been elected a deputy, explained in the chamber why his party members cast blank ballots (*Unidad*, 10 August).

The PCB and the Labor Movement. In the September 1984 congress of the Bolivian Labor Central (COB), the PCB had suffered a severe defeat when it lost the majority of its posts in the COB executive committee. The split in the PCB during 1985 also reduced the party's labor influence, since some of its trade-union leaders were in each camp. However, the Communists continued to be a major force in the trade-union movement. Reyes continued to be a leader of both the Miners' Federation and the COB. The party reinforced its position among the miners by winning control of several local unions.

At the time of the prolonged general strike of the COB in February–March against the Siles government's austerity measures, the PCB, in spite of recently having supported such measures while still in the government, strongly supported the strike. It called upon Siles to negotiate with the COB and proclaimed that "we Communists will continue fighting for the worker and popular mobilization to culminate in a result which, preserving the unity of the trade union movement, signifies an advance in the economic and social conquests of the working masses and in the recuperation of the political initiative by the democratic, progressive and revolutionary forces." At the same time, in a meeting of the COB, Reyes strongly attacked the "adventurous" positions assumed there by Trotskyist leaders of Guillermo Lora's Revolutionary Labor Party (POR) (*Unidad*, 23–29 March).

International Relations of the PCB. The PCB continued throughout the year to be loyally associated with the pro-Soviet current in international communism. After the split in the party in July, the majority faction led by Reyes seemed to have the support of the Soviet Communist Party.

At the time of the Fifth Congress in February, the meeting had received greetings from a variety of communist parties in the Soviet camp. These included the parties of the Soviet Union, East Germany, Cuba, Vietnam, Bulgaria, Argentina, Poland, Mongolia, Romania, Afghanistan, El Salvador, Great Britain, and the United States (*Unidad*, 23 February–1 March).

In June, a delegation from the Communist Party of the USSR, headed by N. K. Dybenko, candidate member of the CPSU Central Committee, visited Bolivia. He was met at the airport by Reyes (*Pravda*, 4 June; *FBIS*, 5 June). The Soviet communist delegation met extensively with Reyes and other members of the PCB leadership, and it also visited regional and local party groups. It was received by President Siles and by Julio Garret, the president of Congress (*Pravda*, 3 June; *FBIS*, 7 June).

In November, Reyes visited the Soviet Union. The fact that he was received by Boris Ponomarev, the CPSU official charged with dealing with foreign communist parties, indicated that the Reyes faction of the PCB enjoyed the support of the Soviet party (Tass, 18 November; *FBIS*, 19 November).

However, the Soviet regime maintained relations throughout the year not only with the PCB but also with the Bolivian government. In January the USSR had offered Comibol, the Bolivian state mining company, a loan of $220 million to finance the acquisition of new equipment (Radio Illimani, 7 January; *FBIS*, 11 January). In June it was reported that the Bolivian government had decided how it wanted to spend the Soviet financial aid (*Presencia*, 7 June; *FBIS*, 18 June).

With the change of government, the Soviet Union continued its efforts to maintain good relations. Ambassador Arkadly Glukhov paid a special visit to newly inaugurated President Paz Estenssoro on 12 August (Cadena Panamericana, 12 August; *FBIS*, 13 August). Ten days later, the Supreme Soviet Presidium sent a cable of congratulations to Paz Estenssoro (*Izvestiia*, 22 August; *FBIS*, 6 September).

Other Radical Groups. Although the pro-Soviet Communists remained the largest single Marxist-Leninist element in Bolivian politics, they competed in the labor movement and elsewhere with several other groups. These included at least two factions of the MIR, a Maoist party, and several Trotskyist groups. There were also rumors during the year of the continued existence of guerrilla-oriented factions.

The faction of the MIR headed by Antonio Aranibar Quiroga allied itself with the PCB in the July elections, and Aranibar was the coalition's presidential nominee. Earlier, he had made a trip to Havana at the invitation of President Fidel Castro. The other MIR faction on the far left was that headed by a trade-union leader, Walter Delgadillo (Radio Illimani, *FBIS*, 28 May).

The Marxist-Leninist Communist Party (PCB-ML), headed by Oscar Zamora Medinacelli, which had been formed in 1964 as a Maoist offshoot of the PCB, continued to exist. It formed part of a coalition in the election, the United Revolutionary Directorate (DRU), with Juan Lechin's PRIN, the Trotskyist faction United POR (POR-U), and the Revolutionary Front of the Left (*Hoy*, 13 April). However, the PCB-ML apparently supported Paz Estenssoro in the 14 July election (*Unidad*, 22 August). A dissident faction of the PCB-ML, headed by Gilberto Bernal, was also registered for the election (*Hoy*, 23 April).

Bolivian Trotskyism, which had once been the largest element in the far left, remained splintered throughout the year. There were at least four different groups proclaiming loyalty to Trotskyism. The most significant Trotskyist faction was the Revolutionary Labor Party (POR) led by Guillermo Lora. It controlled the student federation of San Andres University in La Paz and still had influence among the miners. After calling unsuccessfully for a united-left ticket, the POR named Lora as its candidate for president in the 14 July election. He received 13,712 votes, or 0.79 percent of the total (Cadena Panamericana, *FBIS*, 16 May; *Hoy*, 8 August). The Lora POR was not affiliated with any faction of International Trotskyism.

Another faction of the POR, the so-called United POR (POR-U), was affiliated with the United Secretariat of the Fourth International. It had been formed by a merger of two other groups in 1983. Although it was registered for the 1985 election and participated in the DRU coalition, there is no information concerning the vote it received, if it actually ran candidates (*Hoy*, 23 April).

The Bolivian affiliate of the "Morenoite" faction of International Trotskyism is the Socialist Workers Party (PST), originally established as a faction of the Socialist Party of Marcelo Quiroga in the late 1970s. At the September 1984 congress of the COB, the PST had several delegates, including representatives of the Teachers' Union of Oruguo and the Factory Workers of La Paz (*Working Class Opposition*, October 1984). At the time of the COB general strike in March, the PST called upon President Siles to resign (Cadena Panamericana, *FBIS*, 15 March). The PST was registered for the 1985 election, but there is no indication as to whether it actually ran candidates or, if so, how they fared (*Hoy*, 23 April).

Finally, the tiny Trotskyist-Posadist PO (POR-TP), headed by Felix Aranda Vargas, still continued to exist as the Bolivian affiliate of the faction of International Trotskyism founded by the late J. Posadas. It also registered for the 14 July election (*Hoy*, 23 April).

Throughout the year, reports of actual or potential far-left guerrilla activity continued to surface. In July it was alleged that two meetings, in January and May, had been held in Bolivia between Bolivian far leftists and representatives of the Peruvian Shining Path and the M-19 movement of Colombia; they were to plan guerrilla activity in Bolivia (Cadena Panamericana, *FBIS*, 29 July). In October, Defense Minister Fernando Valle reported that although no guerrilla groups were then active, an organization existed to supply "logistical support" for such a movement (Spanish News Agency, *FBIS*, 24 October). In that same month some arrests of suspected guerrillas were made in Santa Cruz (Paris, AFP, *FBIS*, 21 October).

Robert J. Alexander
Rutgers University

Brazil

Population. 134,502,000

Party. Brazilian Communist Party (Partido Comunista Brasileiro; PCB); originally Communist Party of Brazil (Partido Comunista do Brasil; PCdoB), name changed in 1960.

Founded. 1922

Membership. 10,000 (Giocondo Dias in *Folha de São Paulo*, 9 June; *JPRS*, 28 June); 20,000 (*Veja*, 2 October; *FBIS*, 3 October)

Secretary General. Giocondo Dias (72 years old)
National Provisional Steering Committee (Politburo). Giocondo Dias, Hercules Correa, Givaldo Siqueira, Almir Neves, Salomão Malina (60), Teodoro Melo, Roberto Freire, Ivan Pinheiro, José Paulo Neto, Regis Frati, Paulo Elisario, Sergio Moraes
Central Committee. Reportedly will have 101 members; 66 members elected in January 1984.
Status. Legalized 9 July 1985
Last Congress. Seventh, January 1984
Last Election. 15 November 1985. Mayoral in 201 cities. PCB participated in most important cities: alone in two cities, the rest in coalitions. Exact percentages not available. Dias says PCB has 10 federal deputies, 20 in state assemblies, more than 100 councilmen in municipal assemblies, and 7 or 8 mayors (*Folha de São Paulo*, 22 May; *JPRS*, 19 June).
Publications. *Voz da Unidade*; director, João Aveline

Military rule in Brazil ended with the 15 January election of Tancredo Neves in the Electoral College; he was not only the first civilian president in 21 years but candidate of an opposition coalition supported by the PCB and two of its splinters, the Communist Party of Brazil (PCdoB; it broke away from the PCB in 1961 and was originally Maoist, now pro-Albanian) and the 8 October Revolutionary Movement (Movimento Revolucionário 8; MR-8). All were illegal at the time and took refuge in the major opposition party, the Brazilian Democratic Movement Party (PMDB). To ensure Tancredo's victory in the college, the PMDB formed the Democratic Alliance (AD) with a dissident faction of the official Social Democratic Party (PDS) calling itself the Liberal Front. AD's vice-presidential candidate, José Sarney, was former president of the PDS.

Tension mounted with Tancredo's illness just before inauguration and his subsequent death in April, but Sarney's succession proceeded smoothly. Despite his lack of liberal credentials, he has been rather well accepted by all sectors. The Workers' Party (Partido dos Trabalhadores; PT) may join Leonel Brizola's Democratic Labor Party (PDT) to renew the campaign for direct presidential elections in 1986, but the communist parties will not. The latter spent the first half of 1985 working toward legalization of their groups and the second half preparing for the November elections, which was their first legal participation since 1946. The PCB has enjoyed legal status during only two of its 63 years of existence.

Leadership and Organization. According to Secretary General Giocondo Dias, the PCB's acceptance of the plural party system and its revision of the concept of the dictatorship of the proletariat did not signify "tactical concessions" in the search for legalization: "These problems are not doctrinaire and we had to adapt the struggle for the socialist revolution to Brazilian conditions" (*Correio Braziliense*, 23 January; *JPRS*, 7 March). In a later interview, Dias said, "The Communist International was dissolved in 1943. The movement today has no central leadership . . . we have no international connections as far as organization is concerned" (*Folha de São Paulo*, 9 June; *JPRS*, 28 June).

Exceeding requirements for legalization, the so-called big party ("Partidão") established temporary regional commissions in 22 states and the Federal District, and went on to set up hundreds of municipal commissions. PCB delegates to the Supreme Electoral Court (TSE) included Deputy Roberto Freire (PMDB, Pernambuco), Carlos Alberto Muller Torres (president, PMDB regional directorate in Brasilia), Cristiano Cordeiro (last surviving PCB founder), and two former federal deputies from the 1946 Constituent Assembly. The seniority represented by Cordeiro and the former deputies will presumably be important when the TSE decides which of the two communist parties may use the hammer and sickle emblem. Former long-time secretary general Luiz Carlos Prestes remains disaffected. He supported the PDT in Rio de Janeiro in the November election and is rumored to be considering a PDT senate nomination in 1986.

Since legalization of the party, Deputy Alberto Goldmann has acted as leader of the PCB faction in congress, which also includes Roberto Freire, Fernando Santana, Nelson Wedekin, and Tidel de Lima, all elected on PMDB tickets. The status of some other PCB deputies is still ambiguous, but no deadline has been set for ending two-party membership and those exercising it will not be expelled (ibid.).

Domestic Affairs. A February meeting of the National Committee for the Legalization of the PCB approved a statement outlining the party's priorities during the transition period that will end with the promulgation of a new constitution. (The congress to be elected in November 1986 will be seated as a National Constituent Assembly.) After congratulating the PCB for its historically correct emphasis on mass mobilization as the means of ending the military dictatorship (see *YICA*, 1985, p. 51), the document stresses the need for further strengthening of the broad front and formation of a political-social pact to clear away inherited restrictive legislation and implement needed social and economic reform (*Voz da Unidade*, 23 February–1 March).

The PCB has selectively supported the present administration. It criticized recessive economic policy but applauded the limits placed on International Monetary Fund auditors in Brazil as well as Sarney's United Nations speech against no-growth debt restructuring. In the same way, it welcomed the more understanding attitude toward labor and the introduction of agrarian reform but felt that much remained to be done in both areas.

In November, for the first time in 21 years, mayors were chosen by direct election in the state capitals and in cities with state mining industries or other "national security" designations. In most cities, the newly legalized PCB supported the PMDB ticket but presented its own candidates in Recife and Belo Horizonte; it also joined a coalition in Rio de Janeiro with the new Socialist Party and the PCdoB. The votes in Rio and Belo Horizonte were small but a little better than expected. The poor performance of Roberto Freire in Recife, however, could adversely affect his chances for re-election in congress in 1986 (*Folha de São Paulo*, 17 November).

Auxiliary and Front Organizations. Among PCB priorities for the transition period was the repeal of restrictive labor legislation. This has been only partially accomplished. Although laws prohibiting national confederations of unions are still in place, the Labor Ministry officially recognizes the two existing confederations: the Congress of the Working Class (Congreso da Classe Trabalhadora; CONCLAT), supported by the PCB, PCdoB, and the PMDB, and the PT-dominated Single Labor Central (Central Unica dos Trabalhadores; CUT).

CONCLAT has carefully followed PCB precepts of "regaining organic labor unity and overcoming the CUT-CONCLAT polarization" (*Voz da Unidade*, 16 March). In this respect, CONCLAT considered the adherence this year of the giant Confederation of Industrial Workers (CNTI) doubly important, as the CNTI had been forming yet a third division of the national labor movement. Unification of the conservative CONCLAT and the aggressive, more radical CUT will not be achieved easily. Strikes have been predictably frequent throughout the country this year, but CUT and CONCLAT have carried out only one cooperative action—the 5–6 November strike in São Paulo. This was quite effective, particularly in the important automobile industry, since CONCLAT controls the São Paulo metallurgical workers union and CUT dominates the São Bernardo union in the suburban industrial belt. Neither CUT nor CONCLAT is advancing very rapidly in talks with Labor Minister Almir Pazzianotto. A former union lawyer, Pazzianotto recognizes "the debt Brazil owes to the working class" and hopes that talks will lead to a social pact the country can live with. Joaquim dos Santos Andrade, president of the São Paulo metal workers and CONCLAT coordinator, agrees with Jair Meneguelli, president of the São Bernardo union and of CUT, that a dialogue exists but there can be no talk of a social pact at present (*Latin America Weekly Report*, 1 November).

The PCB approves of the government's agrarian reform program but prefers the proposal of the National Confederation of Farmworkers (Confederacão dos Trabalhadores na Agricultura; CONTAG). CONTAG is a member of the secretariat of CONCLAT. Its importance increased substantially this year with the creation of the new Ministry for Agrarian Reform. Heretofore, CUT had taken the lead in rural organization and protest, with cooperation from the church's pastoral land committee (CPT). Resistance to agrarian reform is strong and armed conflict is increasing.

International Views. The PCB transition statement advised the new government to, among other things, "pursue a policy of non-alignment, advocate an end to the arms race, and . . . support peace and a new economic order" (*Voz da Unidade*, special supplement, March). It should expand "diplomatic, trade and cultural relations with all countries. In this respect, re-establishment of relations with Cuba is a priority . . . Implementation of this foreign policy should help to enlarge Brazil's international role and enable her to be an intermediary in the North-South dialogue" (ibid.). The international analyst of the PCB organ writes that Nicaraguan Daniel Ortega's visit for the presidential inauguration was more than "simple formality"; Brazil should show its solidarity with that incipient and embattled democracy by becoming the fifth member of Contadora (*Voz da Unidade*, 9 March).

PCdoB. The PCdoB was legalized on the same day, 9 July. The petition it had filed with the TSE was signed by the members of its own steering committee: Secretary General João Amazonas, José Duarte, Dyneas Fernández Aguiar, José Renato Rabelo, Roberto D'Olne Lustosa, Ronaldo Cavalcanti Freitas, Elza de Lima Monnerat, João Batista de Rocha Lemos, Pericles Santos de Souza, Alanir Cardoso, and Maria do Socorro Moraes Vieira. Amazonas said the PCdoB seeks "the unity of broad forces toward democracy. It does not want to be an exclusive party" and the program filed with the TSE "does not deal with the great socialist themes. It is nationalistic and democratic, anti-imperialist and antitrust in keeping with the current Brazilian situation and the period of democratic transition" (*O Estado de São Paulo*, 23 June; *FBIS*, 27 June). According to Amazonas, the party had 15,000 members in June and should increase to 40,000 after legalization. Both figures are probably inflated.

The PCdoB supported candidates of other parties in the November elections but will present its own slates in 1986. It has four federal deputies elected on PMDB tickets: Haroldo Lima (Bahia), Aurelio Peres (São Paulo), Luiz Guedes (Minas Gerais), and Aldo Arantes (Goiás). Peres said the PCdoB is "organizing the union rank and file for a prolonged struggle that will end with a central union organization, pluralist but single" (*Folha de São Paulo*, 27 January; *JPRS*, 27 March). The PCdoB publishes the newspaper *Tribuna da Luta Operaria*.

MR-8. The former guerrilla organization MR-8 emerged from a late 1960s split in the PCB. According to Secretary General Claudio Campos, the MR-8 will register as a civil body and continue to operate as a group within the PMDB. He explains that the group is comfortable in the PMDB front and feels no need for its own identity at present. MR-8 publishes the weekly *Hora do Povo* and apparently has no representation in congress.

PT. The PT grew out of the 1978–1980 labor movement in São Paulo and its radical image has sharpened as its influence expands. Luis Ignácio "Lula" da Silva is still president and Francisco Weffort is secretary general. The PT has five federal deputies: Djalma Bom, Eduardo Matarazzo Suplicy, Irma Passoni, José Genoino, and Luiz Dulci. (Three deputies—Airton Soares, Bete Mendes, and José Eudes—were expelled for disobeying party instructions to abstain in the January Electoral College vote.) In the November mayoral elections, the PT participated in 62 cities, always with its own slate. In two upsets, the PT elected its candidate in Fortaleza (capital of Ceará state) and just missed doing the same in Goiânia, against overwhelming odds. The new mayor of Fortaleza, Maria Luiza Fontenelle, has been said to have ties with the Revolutionary Communist Party (PCR; see below). Eduardo Suplicy won 19.7 percent of the vote in São Paulo, contributing to the defeat of the left-leaning PMDB candidate and hence to the election of anticommunist former president Jânio Quadros.

At the January national congress, the PT reiterated its call for direct elections at all levels and opposed the granting of constituent powers to the congress to be elected in 1986. It likewise rejected any kind of bloc "that would allow the reformist parties, the PCB and the PCdoB, to change their reformist image and coopt the popular and trade union movement into the Democratic Alliance" (*Intercontinental Press*, 18 March). A plenary session of CUT in August demanded "real" agrarian reform under the control of the workers, including much swifter implementation than the current program provides and "immediate legalization of occupied lands"; until then, CUT will continue to support occupation movements, camping, active resistance against expulsion, and squatting (*O Estado de São Paulo*, 7 August; *JPRS*, 4 October).

The PT harbors a number of extreme-left groups that have shown no desire for independent legalization. Mergers and name changes, sometimes from state to state, make it difficult to compile a definitive list. For the moment, the Trotskyist groups seem to include:

- Socialist Democracy (DS) led by economist João Machado is the largest of the Trotskyist groups. It represents the United Secretariat of the Fourth International in Brazil. DS publishes the paper *Em Tempo*, edited by Juarez Guimarães.
- Socialist Convergence, known in student circles as Socialist Youth Foundation (Alicerce da Juvemtud Socialista), is associated with the Workers International League of the Fourth International.

Susete Pavão and Eduardo Almeida Melo are members of the National Directorate.

• Freedom and Struggle (Libelu) is the youth group of the Fourth International Splinter Group or International Center for Fourth International Reconstruction. It publishes *O Trabalho*, edited by Josimar Melo.

• The Organization of the Fourth International publishes *Labor Cause (Causa Operária*; *CO*). Costa Pimentel is a journalist on the staff of *CO*.

Non-Trotskyist Marxist-Leninist groups include:

• Proletarian Democracy, a result of the fusion of the MEP (Movement for the Emancipation of the Proletariat) with part of the old AP (Popular Action) and the Red Wing (Ala Vermelha; AV), a PCdoB splinter.

• The Brazilian Revolutionary Communist Party (PCBR) apparently retains some influence in the northeast, especially Recife, but has disappeared elsewhere.

• The Revolutionary Communist Party (PCR) is a 1984 splinter of the PCdoB. It obeys the concept of an avant-garde Communist Party working toward socialism within the PT but not mixed with it. Ozeas Duarte "represents" the PRC to "the outside public"; number and identity of Central Committee members are secret (*Folha de São Paulo*, 25 August; *FBIS*, 29 August; *O Globo*, 2 June; *JPRS*, 22 July).

Carole Merten
Miami, Florida

Canada

Population. 25,399,000

Parties. Communist Party of Canada (CPC); Communist Party of Canada (Marxist-Leninist) (CPC-ML); Revolutionary Workers' League (RWL); Trotskyist League (TL); Forward Readers Group (FRG); International Socialists (IS)

Founded. CPC: 1921; CPC-ML: 1970; RWL: 1977; TL: 1975

Membership. CPC: 2,500 (estimated); CPC-ML: 500–1,000; RWL: 200

Secretary General. CPC: William Kashtan; CPC-ML: Hardial Bains; RWL: John Riddell

Central Committee. CPC: 77 members

Status. Legal

Last Congress. CPC: Twenty-sixth, 5–8 April 1985, in Toronto; CPC-ML: Fourth, 3 April 1982, in Montreal; RWL: Fifth, 27 December 1983–1 January 1984

Last Federal Election. 4 September 1984; CPC: 52 candidates, average vote 162; RWL: 5 candidates, average vote 127; no representatives

Auxiliary Organizations. CPC: Parti communiste du Quebec, Canadian Peace Congress, Conseil québecois de la paix, Association of United Ukrainian Canadians, Congress of Canadian Women, Young Communist League, Workers' Benevolent Association of Canada; CPC-ML: People's Front Against Racist and Fascist Violence, Revolutionary Trade Union Opposition, Democratic Women's Union of Canada, East Indian Defence Committee, West Indian People's Organization, Communist Youth Union of Canada (M-L), Canada-Albania Friendship Association; RWL: Young Socialist Organizing Committee, Comité de la jeunesse révolutionnaire

Publications. CPC: *Canadian Tribune*, *Pacific Tribune*, *Combat*, *Communist Viewpoint*, *Le Communiste*, *Rebel Youth*, *Jeunesse militante*, *Nouvelle revue internationale*; CPC-ML: *Marxist-Leninist*, *Le Marxiste-Leniniste*, *Voice of the Youth*, *Voice of the People*, *West Indian*, *Lok Awaz*, *Etincelle*, *RTUOC Weekly Bulletin*, *Democratic Women*, *People's Front Bulletin*, *Canadian Student*, *BC Worker*; RWL: *Socialist Voice*, *Lutte ouvrière*, *New International* (copublished with U.S. counterpart); TL: *Sparticist Canada*; IS: *Socialist Worker*

Several Marxist-Leninist parties and groups operate legally in Canada. The oldest and largest is the CPC. Since its founding in 1921, the CPC has been consistently pro-Moscow in alignment. The CPC-ML, founded in 1970, is pro-Albanian. Several Trotskyist groups exist, including the RWL, the TL, the IS, and the FRG.

In the 1984 federal election, the Conservative Party under Prime Minister Brian Mulroney won a landslide victory. The combined vote for all communist parties was in the vicinity of 0.1 percent of the vote. No candidates were elected. Communist parties have been increasingly active in municipal elections, notably in Vancouver, Winnipeg, and Toronto, and several members have won election.

Provincially two historic elections occurred. In Ontario, the 42-year-old Conservative dynasty ended when a minority Liberal government was elected. In Quebec, Premier René Levesque resigned and the nine-year rule by the separatist Parti Quebecois (PQ) ceased with the election victory of the Liberal party.

The Canadian economy continues to be mired in its worst recession since the 1930s. Unemployment remains above 10 percent, the Canadian dollar continues to fall in value, and several major banks collapsed. The federal government, along with most provincial governments, continued to attempt cutbacks in social services, wage restrictions, and freezes in the growth of the civil service. Following the 17–18 March meeting in Quebec City between President Ronald Reagan and Prime Minister Mulroney, free trade with the United States has been increasingly discussed despite the fact that Canadian opinion is divided on the issue.

The continued testing of the U.S. cruise missile, Canada's possible role in the controversial Strategic Defense Initiative (SDI), and the upgrading of the Distant Early Warning (DEW) line have generated considerable debate and acted as catalysts for the formation of the Canadian Peace Alliance, a confederation of 1,000 peace organizations.

Communist Party of Canada. Headquartered in Toronto, the CPC ran 52 candidates in the 1984 federal election and received just over 8,000 votes. It ran ten candidates in the 1985 Ontario provincial election, with an average vote of 373 (*Canadian Tribune*, 13 May). Under the label of the Parti communiste du Quebec it also ran ten candidates in the Quebec provincial election compiling 99 votes per candidate. At the Twenty-sixth Congress of the CPC held in Toronto on 5–8 April, 151 delegates and alternates attended; 47 of the delegates were trade unionists and the average age was 44 years (ibid., 15 April). The CPC set a goal of a 5 percent overall increase in membership and a 10 percent increase in subscriptions to the party newspaper (ibid., 28 January and 23 December). The weekly paper has been expanded in size from eight to twelve pages, with a new, special two-page section covering the Prairies (ibid., 27 May and 9 December). On 9–10 February the CPC annual *Communist Viewpoint* conference was attended by 175 persons (*Canadian Tribune*, 18 February). Later in the year, the Canadian Society for Ukrainian Labour Research was founded by the Association of United Ukrainian Canadians and the Workers' Benevolent Association of Canada (ibid., 11 November). It was also announced that the party's official history was now available in French (ibid., 15 April).

During the year, official delegations of the CPC went to Moscow to attend Konstantin Chernenko's funeral and the 40th anniversary of the end of World War II (ibid., 18 March and 6 May). Delegations also traveled to France and North Korea (ibid., 18 February and 30 September). CPC members were part of the 170 Canadians who attended the Moscow World Festival of Youth and Students and the twelve-member Canadian Electric Brigade that traveled to Nicaragua (ibid., 22 July). Soviet Politburo member V. Vorotnikov visited Canada and met with CPC secretary general Kashtan (ibid., 10 June).

Several prominent party figures died in 1985. The most famous were Alice Buck, wife of former CPC leader Tim Buck, and Sydney Gordon, who under the pseudonym Fils Delisle wrote a *Canadian Tribune* column from Berlin (ibid., 13 May and 24 June). After 25 years as labor columnist for the *Canadian Tribune*, William Stewart moved to

Prague as the CPC representative for the journal *World Marxist Review*. His former column and post are now held by George Hewison (ibid., 7 January).

The CPC notes that Canada, severely affected by the economic crisis, has seen an intensification of the class struggle and that united efforts are required to prevent a turn to the right. New antilabor legislation, government cutbacks in social services (for example, attempted de-indexation of old-age pensions), attacks on the universality of welfare programs, and Charter of Rights–based assaults on unions should all be opposed (ibid., 22 July and 19 August). The CPC characterizes the Conservatives as the "American party in Canada" and calls for "a people's majority outside Parliament to counter the Tory majority inside" (ibid., 28 January and 18 February). Not surprising, the CPC has been highly critical of the new Mulroney conservative government in Ottawa and depicts Mulroney as "selling out" Canada by weakening the National Energy Program and transforming the Foreign Investment Review Agency into Investment Canada. The CPC also criticizes Conservative moves toward deregulation and increased military spending. It condemns the new budget as an "attack on working people" (ibid., 2 September) and warns that the Canadian people did not turn to the political right but rather voted against the Liberals (*Communist Viewpoint*, September 1984). The CPC calls for extensive "nationalization" with "democratic control" and a reduction in the hours of work without a decline in pay as methods for economic recovery.

The CPC observes that "reformist illusions" still characterize most Canadian workers and that most progressive and socialist-minded Canadians are New Democratic Party (NDP) supporters. The CPC thus gives critical support to the NDP. The CPC welcomed the Ontario Liberal-NDP alliance that displaced the provincial conservative government, believing that it could yield some "useful reforms" (*Canadian Tribune*, 10 June). While critical of past NDP provincial governments' antilabor legislation and the NDP leadership's attempts to displace the Liberals by shifting the NDP to the right (ibid., 11 February and 8 July), the CPC calls for cooperation with the NDP, particularly in municipal politics. Accordingly, Communists have run under the label of the Committee of Progressive Electors in Toronto and Vancouver and the Labour Election Committee in Winnipeg. Some have been successful in the latter two cities.

Over the past several years the CPC has noted the gradual disintegration and final collapse of the PQ government in Quebec. The CPC suggests that Quebecois separatists who once had a "respectable petit-bourgeois and indepentiste party" now "have lost their party" (ibid., 28 January). The PQ's new leader, Jean-Marc Johnson, has turned it into a conservative reincarnation of the "union-nationale." While noting the re-emergence of the Quebec provincial NDP, the CPC nevertheless calls for a new "mass labor" party in the province.

The CPC has criticized expanded state funding to Catholic schools on the grounds that such moves will fragment the public school system (ibid., 28 January). It has also argued that neofascists have no right to free speech (ibid., 11 March). At the same time, the CPC calls for an expansion of the Charter of Rights so as to include the right to work, join unions, and receive extensive social benefits (ibid., 24 June).

In general, the CPC favors any efforts at Canadianization of the economy. The CPC points out that Canadian problems are accentuated by Canada's high degree of economic dependence on the United States (*Communist Viewpoint*, June). It noted the continued U.S. pressure to keep Canada as a "resource hinterland" and calls for limits on the export to the United States of water and hydro-electric power (ibid., March). The CPC warns that free trade will lower the Canadian standard of living, will undermine Canada's manufacturing industry, and will ultimately lead to the "absorption" of Canada into the United States (*Canadian Tribune*, 28 January and 4 February).

The recent selling of the Canadian government's crown-owned de Havilland aircraft company to the U.S. multinational Boeing Corporation has been condemned as "odious" (ibid., 9 December). The CPC calls instead for a nationalization of U.S. branch plants in Canada. The CPC also sees the conservative government's efforts to "privatize" the arts as an undesirable step to "Americanizing" Canadian culture (ibid., 4 February and 11 March). The CPC applauds the newly acquired independence of the Canadian section of the United Auto Workers union from its less "militant" U.S.-based international parent organizatin (ibid., 16 September). It characterizes this as a "coming of age" of the Canadian union movement that will shift the power to Canadian rather than internationally based unions in the Canadian Labour Congress (ibid., 18 February). The goal of a "united, independent and sovereign" union movement, the CPC believes, is "becoming a reality" (ibid., 8 April).

The CPC warns that we have entered a more

critical stage internationally due to the "deterioration" of U.S.-Soviet relations (ibid., 23 September). Under Reagan, according to the CPC, the United States has shifted to a cold-war, confrontationist policy of preparing for war and opting for a first-strike strategy (ibid., 25 March). The United States is seen as pursuing a "more muscular" foreign policy (ibid., 4 November). The U.S. aim is to achieve military superiority and foster an arms race that is designed to economically "exhaust" the communist regimes and undermine their stability. Noting that the detente of the 1970s occurred when both superpowers achieved a "rough balance" militarily (*Communist Viewpoint*, March), the CPC welcomed the Geneva summit as a means to breaking the "log-jam" in U.S.-Soviet relations (*Canadian Tribune*, 22 September). The important summit meeting between Mikhail Gorbachev and Reagan was seen as positive by the CPC in that the United States was "compelled" to declare nuclear war unwinnable and accept nuclear parity (ibid., 9 December).

The CPC suggests that world peace is, more than ever before, a priority task and observes the growing size of the peace movement. The recent addition of key Canadian labor organizations to the peace cause is welcomed. Most important, it sees the newly formed Canadian Peace Alliance as a "landmark" and "most significant event" (ibid., 11, 18 November). The CPC notes, however, that while most Canadians are pro-peace, many still hold "anti-Soviet views" and falsely see the United States and the USSR as equally responsible for the escalation of the arms race. The CPC implores that ideological differences be put aside in the peace movement (*Communist Viewpoint*, March).

The CPC reiterates its demand that cruise missile testing in Canada be halted. Such testing, it is argued, is not part of Canada's NATO obligation (*Communist Viewpoint*, March). The CPC believes that Canada should be declared a nuclear weapons–free zone and condemns previously secret military plans to store such weapons in Canada (*Canadian Tribune*, 21 January). The CPC is highly critical of plans to modernize the North American Air Defense Command (NORAD) and the DEW line. It is believed that the latter will increase U.S. military presence in Canada's north and is an "integral part" of the SDI (ibid., 4 March and 15 April). Research and deployment of SDI weaponry will, according to the CPC, militarize space, "qualitatively escalate the arms race," and perpetuate the Cold War (ibid., 7 January, 4 February, and 2 September). The CPC calls for a more independent foreign policy, for Canadian withdrawal from NATO, the NORAD, and the Defence Production Sharing Agreement, and for an end to secret military pacts with the United States (ibid., 13 May). The recent voyage of the USS *Polar Sea* into Canada's Arctic was seen as an infringement on Canadian sovereignty (ibid., 19 August). The CPC continues to express concern that the United States is intending to invade Nicaragua and praises Canada for not echoing the anti-Sandinista campaign (ibid., 13 May and 29 July).

In general, the CPC continues to echo Soviet positions in foreign affairs and reiterates the call for a convening of an international conference of communist and workers' parties. As a member of the international editorial board of the *World Marxist Review*, the CPC favors publishing only items that unite the different communist parties. It fears that printing materials on which the parties differ would transform the journal into a forum for "polemics between parties and for criticizing each other's positions" and would ultimately undermine the journal (*Communist Viewpoint*, March).

Communist Party of Canada (Marxist-Leninist). The CPC-ML, headquartered in Montreal, celebrated the fifteenth anniversary of its formation. First Secretary Hardial Bains published two books: *The Call of the Martyrs* and *The Times are a Calling*. Although the party's newspaper, *Marxist-Leninist*, continued to be published on a daily basis, its weekly edition ceased operation. The CPC-ML publishes on an irregular basis a large number of newsletters and small newspapers through a variety of front organizations. A proposed new journal, *New Literature and Ideology*, has been announced (*Canadian Student*, January).

The CPC-ML perceives that the "capitalist-revisionist crisis" has deepened and that the bourgeoisie have launched an all-out ideological attack against the workers. The CPC-ML believes that while objective conditions are ripe for revolution, subjective conditions lag. In part this is due to the working class being "confused" as to what Marxism-Leninism is (*Marxist-Leninist*, 31 March). Since there can be no third road between the dictatorship of the bourgeoisie and the dictatorship of the proletariat, the party calls on workers to reject the "class-collaborationist" schemes of "labour-aristocrats" and to reject all demands for concessions in salaries and services (ibid., 19 April and 10 May). Efforts should be made to resist the shifting of the burden of the crisis onto the backs of the working class. Instead the party's slogan is "Make the Rich Pay for the Crisis."

The party did not contest either the Ontario or Quebec provincial elections and portrayed them as "frauds" (ibid., 14, 28 June). The CPC-ML engages in "relentless ideological struggle" against "revisionism" in its many guises (for example, Khrushchevism, Titoism, Maoism, Trotskyism, Eurocommunism, and social democracy). It sees Soviet revisionism as the most dangerous form (ibid., 31 March). It stresses the importance of Marxist-Leninist "purity" as interpreted by Albania's Enver Hoxha (ibid., 21 March and 10 April). What the long-term consequence will be of Hoxha's death on the CPC-ML is unclear. In the short run, there appears to be no ideological shift. The NDP is portrayed as a bourgeois party with a "socialist mask" that, when in power, fosters "state monopoly capitalism"; it is condemned for a lack of firm resolve on the demand for Canada's withdrawal from NATO (ibid., 25 March and 26 April). The PQ is characterized as seeking to split people along "reactionary narrow nationalism and chauvinism" and as not offering a policy of real economic independence (ibid., 24, 26 June).

Increased restrictions on immigration and student visas, police harassment of minorities, and "super exploitation" of immigrants provide evidence, according to the CPC-ML, that there is a growing tendency toward fascism and state-fostered racism. Racism is portrayed as a phenomenon fostered by the rich, not the people. Canada is seen as becoming increasingly a "military-bureaucratic state machine" that is escalating its attacks on "progressive and democratic organizations." Such an intensified bourgeois offensive necessitates that the "people" militantly defend themselves against such assaults. The CPC-ML asserts that fascists and racists have no right to speak or organize (ibid., 13 March), and it has endeavored to block right-wing speaking engagements and Defence Department recruitment meetings at several universities. The CPC-ML has also organized "militant pickets" around visiting warships, military recruiting centers, and military parades (ibid., 11 April). CPC-ML militancy has frequently led to scuffles, arrests, and fines (ibid., 4 April, 19 June, and 10 July; *Canadian Student*, January). The party remains resolute in its call for "revolutionary violence" as the means for establishing a communist regime.

On the international scene, the CPC-ML sees interimperialist contradictions as sharpening and says the "imperialist" United States and the "social-imperialist" USSR are aggressive and seek to dominate the world (*Marxist-Leninist*, 12 March and 13 June). The CPC-ML dismisses disarmament talks such as the Geneva summit as "fraudulent" and a "farce." Such meetings are designed to foster a false image of peace while superpower war preparations continue (ibid., 19 March, 10 April, and 12, 13 June). According to the CPC-ML, Soviet-U.S. rivalry is rooted in the "objective basis of the imperialist system" and no amount of good will and dialogue will eliminate the contradictions between the two states (ibid., 21 March and 12 June). Thus, while diplomatic talks occur, the arms race continues unabated. Both superpowers are seen as endeavoring to intimidate smaller states into joining the "aggressive" military blocs (ibid., 4 April).

The continuing turmoil in India is, in part, explained as due to U.S.-Soviet efforts to seek domination over the subcontinent. The Indian government and ruling class are condemned for fostering communalism and persecution, particularly in the Punjab (ibid., 1 May and 7 June). The recent Air India crash is noted with regret but the use of this incident by Canadian government authorities to engender "racism" and "chauvinism" is criticized (ibid., 11, 27 June and 11 July).

Noting with dismay the Mulroney government's actions of allowing increased U.S. domination of Canada, the CPC condemns the proposed free trade as a "national betrayal" (ibid., 2 May). The CPC-ML calls on Canada to regain its sovereignty. This can be accomplished by withdrawing from NATO and the NORAD, refusing to test cruise missiles, opposing the upgrading of the northern radar installations, prohibiting any U.S. military bases in Canada's north, and saying "no" to the SDI (ibid., 19, 25, 26 March). The CPC-ML is also critical of both U.S. and Canadian imperialism in the Caribbean. Albania is held up as the only state pursuing a proper course of action, and defense of Albania is portrayed as the "touchstone of proletarian internationalism" (ibid., 4 April).

Revolutionary Workers League. The RWL belongs to the Trotskyist Fourth International. It ran a candidate in both the Ontario and Quebec provincial elections, although neither was elected. Part way through the year the RWL announced that it was undergoing "considerable reorganization" due to its "smaller" membership size and "fewer resources." The Vancouver branch was closed and all members were to be concentrated in Toronto and

Montreal (*Socialist Voice*, 8 April). The RWL's Central Committee reiterated its 1979 decision to place most members in industrial unions and favored building "pan-Canadian factions" within such unions (ibid., 8 April). The RWL called on its membership to step up its work within the Fourth International and to travel more extensively to Cuba and Nicaragua. The party's Canadian newspapers, *Socialist Voice* and *Lutte ouvrière*, were scaled down, and greater emphasis has been placed on the journal *New International*, which is copublished with its U.S. counterpart, the Socialist Workers Party. A French version, *Nouvelle Internationale*, has been inaugurated.

While the RWL acknowledged the Gauche socialiste (GS) as a "sympathizing group" and accepted "formal relations" with the Alliance for Socialist Action (ASA), it warned that "real and important differences" exist between these groups and the RWL. Nevertheless, it raised as a possibility the reunification of all within a "single, centralized and disciplined party" (ibid., 8 April). In 1985, Political Committee member Joan Newbigging died.

Although several RWL members have been expelled from the NDP, the RWL, on the whole, supports the union-based, "reformist" NDP. Nevertheless, the RWL is critical of the "pro-capitalist" NDP leadership and calls for the NDP to take a more socialist and pro-Quebec position. It eschews the electoral alliance between the Ontario NDP and Liberals (ibid., 17 June).

The RWL characterizes the new Canadian constitution as a "fraud" and decries the loss of Quebec's veto (ibid., 1 July and 25 November). It sees Quebec as an oppressed nation and, although it previously conceded some positive role for the "bourgeois nationalist" PQ, the RWL now characterizes the post-1980 period as one in which the PQ has increasingly become "anti-worker and pro-federalist" (ibid., 14 October). "Canadian imperialism" is seen to have gained from the PQ's abandonment of the goal of Quebec sovereignty (ibid., 11 February). The RWL proposes the creation of a new and labor union–based party in Quebec.

Employers and governments are portrayed as having begun a "large-scale offensive against union power," and as a result labor has suffered a "decade of take backs" (ibid., 25 March and 8 April). While calling for increased labor militancy on wage concessions, the party views the renewed stress on nationalism in union ranks as undermining international labor solidarity and in no way breaking with the pattern of class collaboration (ibid., 14 January).

According to the RWL, the danger of war is caused, not by the USSR, but by U.S. imperialism. Focusing on events in Central America, the RWL condemns U.S. "aggression" against Nicaragua (ibid., 25 March). It warns of the danger of a possible American "invasion" (ibid., 17 June). The RWL demands a withdrawal of all U.S. troops and arms from the region and criticizes Canadian complicity (ibid., 25 February). While the Nicaraguan regime is seen to have made some "mistakes" and some "social problems still persist" (ibid., February 25), it is also seen as following the sound, revolutionary path pioneered by Cuba. On the international economic front, the RWL calls for cancellation of the foreign debts of the Latin American countries and urges an economic boycott of the apartheid regime in South Africa (ibid., 2, 16 September and 28 October).

International Socialists. The International Socialists concede that in the current era workers are on the defensive and no longer "confident and militant" and that many on the left are "demoralized" (*Socialist Worker*, December). The IS thus suggests that, although it is "not possible today to build a mass socialist party," a "modest organization which is fully revolutionary" is plausible (ibid., December). Despite obstacles, a Leninist party must be built. Accordingly, the IS has called for a refocusing of its activities on the party's monthly paper (formerly *Workers' Action*, now *Socialist Worker*), bringing in new members, and building "well organized weekly branch meetings" in key cities (ibid., November).

The IS perceives the left in general to be floundering in reorganization. The IS is critical of efforts by left wingers to build a party without democratic centralism (*Socialist Worker*, December), yet paradoxically it advocates "socialism from below" (*Workers' Action*, August). It also reacts negatively to the softening of attitudes toward the "reformist" NDP. While the IS defends the NDP against the "big business parties," it nevertheless opposes the NDP's reformism (*Socialist Worker*, December). The NDP is chastised for backtracking on such important issues as access to abortion, gay rights, and an anti-NATO stance (ibid., September, November, and December). The IS is also critical of "union bureaucracies" that, it feels, have usurped power from the rank and file workers. The IS calls for resolute shop-floor action. Where necessary it advocates "militant pickets," "illegal strikes," and the use of the "mass strike" (ibid., October, November, and December). Concerned over the re-emergence of racist ideas, the IS opposes "freedom of speech" for fascists (ibid., September).

The IS supports Quebec's right to self-determination (*Workers' Action*, August). On Canadian-U.S. relations, the IS is critical of both free trade and nationalist protectionism. Instead it calls for an internationalist perspective of providing more jobs and higher wages throughout the world (*Socialist Worker*, November).

Echoing the line of the Socialist Workers Party in the United Kingdom, the IS denies the existence of successful "socialist" states elsewhere. The Soviet Union is characterized as a "totalitarian" and "state capitalist" regime that was established by the Stalinist "counterrevolution" (ibid., September). The new emphases in China on privatization and market forces are dismissed as insignificant, since China is perceived as having "never been communist" (ibid., December). While Nicaragua is praised for its opposition to U.S. imperialism, the new regime is not portrayed as socialist (ibid., September and November) since workers continue to lack freedom. Nicaragua is also criticized for failing to extend the socialist revolution beyond its border into neighboring Central American states (ibid., September). Socialism in just one country is clearly seen to be untenable. While accepting the necessity of revolution, the IS nevertheless decries "terrorist tactics." It warns that such acts only evoke more state oppression and alienate most workers (*Workers' Action*, August).

Trotskyist League. While conceding Quebec's right to independence, the TL is critical of the allegedly progressive character of Quebecois nationalism and instead favours "bi-national class unity" within Canada and joint "U.S.-Canadian working-class unity" toward a "continental socialist revolution." North America is seen as the main imperialist enemy.

Although critical of the Stalinist degeneration of the USSR caused by a parasitic leadership caste, the TL claims that the USSR still possesses the "historic gain" of its collectivized economy (ibid., September) and accordingly should be defended from attacks. The TL believes that Central America is a key realm in the defense of the USSR since the imperialists' target in domino-like fashion is first Nicaragua, then Cuba, and finally the USSR itself (ibid., September). The TL is critical of so-called Trotskyist groups that only give nominal defense of the USSR. The TL denies that the self-proclaimed Trotskyist RWL is revolutionary, noting that the RWL is unwilling to use violence and even supports the "anti-communist and pro-capitalist" NDP. The TL also condemns NDP's stress on Canadian "protectionism" (*Sparticist Canada*, April).

Believing in "permanent revolution," the TL calls for a military victory in El Salvador and urges that the "petty-bourgeois, radical nationalist" Sandinistas consolidate and complete the revolution (ibid., April). Accordingly, it calls on both Cuba and the Soviet Union to increase aid given to Nicaragua. It warns that detente is an illusion and that the United States is preparing for an invasion of Nicaragua and Cuba and gearing up its first-strike drive to war (ibid., April). The TL calls for a reforged Fourth International.

Other Publications and Groups. No copies of *Forward*, issued by the FRG, appeared in 1985. Several ex-members and the former leader of the now-defunct, Maoist Parti communiste ouvrier/ Workers Communist Party publish the magazine *Liberation*. *Gauche Socialiste* is published by former members of the Groupe Marxiste Revolutionaire; it is portrayed as a sympathetic group to the RWL. *Bulletin* is co-published by the Workers League of Canada and its U.S. counterpart, the Workers League. Most of the material is of American origin. It describes itself as a Trotskyist "revolutionary party."

Alan Whitehorn
Royal Military College of Canada

Chile

Population. 11,882,000
Party. Communist Party of Chile (Partido Comunista de Chile; CPC)
Founded. 1922
Membership. 20,000 (estimated)
Secretary General. Luís Corvalán Lepe
Politburo. 20 members (clandestine and in exile)
Secretariat. 5 members (clandestine and in exile)
Central Committee. Over 100 members (clandestine and in exile)
Status. Illegal, but operates through Popular Democratic Movement.
Last Congress. Sixteenth, June 1984, held clandestinely in Chile and simultaneously outside the country; clandestine Central Committee plenum held in January 1985.
Last Election. March 1973, 16 percent, 23 of 150 seats
Auxiliary Organizations. Communist Youth (illegal); National Trade Union Coordinating Committee (CNS; headed by a Christian Democrat); Popular Democratic Movement (MDP; includes part of the Socialist Party and the Movement of the Revolutionary Left [MIR])
Publications. *El Siglo* (clandestine)

In January the CPC held a ceremony in Santiago marking the 63rd anniversary of its founding (Radio Moscow, 22 January; *FBIS*, 24 January). Despite the past eleven years of persecution and repression, the party continues to be an active presence on the Chilean political scene. It is used by President Augusto Pinochet to justify his hold on power and to frighten the middle classes and the armed forces with the possibility of a communist takeover in the event of his departure.

The CPC has considerable powers of organization and coordination of action; through a front group, the Manuel Rodriguez Patriotic Front (FPMR), it has been able to carry out bombings, sabotage, and blackouts. The resort to violence in practice has been justified in theory by the CPC since the end of 1980, when it changed its public posture from the *via pacifica* to support for "all forms of struggle." Shortly thereafter it issued joint declarations with a left faction of the Socialist Party and with its old enemy, the radical-terrorist MIR. This marked a movement away from the historic position of the party that, prior to September 1973, had exercised a significant influence in Chilean electoral politics, even in the period 1948–1958 when it was declared illegal. In most elections the CPC received 10–16 percent of the vote, and through coalitions with the Socialist Party or the broader Popular Unity Party led by Salvador Allende in 1970–1973, it was even more influential.

Although most of its activities had been carried out clandestinely since the 1973 coup, the CPC took an active role when the anti-Pinochet protests began to emerge in 1982. Because of its support for violence, it was not asked to join the Democratic Alliance, a broad opposition coalition formed in 1983 that includes representatives ranging from the right through the Christian Democratic and Radical parties to a substantial element of the former Socialist Party. Instead, the CPC formed its own group, the MDP, which was headed by a Socialist of the leftist Almeyda wing of that party and included the MIR and other extreme left groups, but which was controlled by the Communists. Shortly thereafter the party was also instrumental in the creation of the FPMR, which was formed to carry out revolutionary actions of the type that had earlier been characteristic only of the MIR. The CPC insisted that it only supported the "Rodriguistas," who included Marxists, Christians, and young people of a more secular orientation, but it was clear that the group was supplied and directed from Moscow. The CPC is one of the most pro-Moscow parties in the world communist movement.

The CPC has had a long-standing base among organized workers, especially Chile's copper miners. The communist-dominated CUT trade-union federation was dissolved by the Pinochet government shortly after the coup. In recent years, however, the party has been able to work through the CNS to influence the National Workers Command (CNT), which has had a significant leadership role in organizing anti-Pinochet protests. The CPC thus has under its influence or control a political movement, a terrorist organization, a significant element of the trade-union movement (although the Christian Democrats and, to a lesser degree, the Socialists are also influential in labor), and organizations of the poor and shantytown dwellers such as the Popular Movement of the Poor (MPP). CPC activity is illegal and it is repressed more than most other antigovernment movements, yet it continues to function effectively and even to issue public statements and hold press conferences.

During 1985 the most visible and controversial activities of the CPC and related groups involved, on the one hand, an upsurge in violence (principally bombings and blackouts) and, on the other hand, the question of the relation of the MDP to the newly broadened opposition coalition that rallied behind the program of the Democratic Accord.

The bombings began in early January with an attack on the Sheraton Hotel. Thereafter bombs were set off at a number of banks, at the Chilean–U.S. Binational Cultural Institute, at the Carrera-Sheraton Hotel, at the offices of IBM, at the government newspaper office opposite the presidential palace, and in front of the U.S. consulate. In most cases there were no casualties, although a passing motorist was killed by the car bomb set off in front of the consulate, and two government intelligence agents died when they attempted to dismantle an underground television transmitter in a Concepción hotel room. In an interview in *El Mercurio* (9 August), Chile's most influential newspaper, the exiled head of the MIR, Andres Pascal Allende, took (dubious) credit for the Concepción killings and claimed that the MIR and the FPMR were each responsible for about half of the bombings in Chile during the current year. Chileans who study the subject attribute a larger role to the FPMR because of its closer relationship to the Soviet Union as a source of technology and supplies. (The technical capacity of the FPMR was demonstrated on 10 August when it blacked out most of the country.)

The FPMR argues that it is based on "a deeply democratic, nationalistic, patriotic, and pro–Latin American conviction" and that it favors "a broad alliance of democratic forces" (Radio Moscow, 14 November; *FBIS*, 20 November). FPMR spokesmen described the group's objective as the development of "the self-defense capabilities of the masses." The latter term was also used by the January Communist Party plenum in its discussion of violence and of the need to prepare for the "final confrontation . . . a state of generalized rebellion capable of paralyzing the country, with uprisings in the main cities" (Radio Moscow, 1 March; *FBIS*, 12 March).

In April the president of the Christian Democratic Party published an open letter to the Communists criticizing their commitment to violence "not only in declarations but through the Manuel Rodríguez Patriotic Front, an organization that has claimed responsibility for several terrorist actions"; he added, "We know that the PCCh [Partido Comunista de Chile] proposals are wrong, and even worse that they are self-defeating" (Madrid, EFE [Spanish News Agency], 18 April; *FBIS*, 25 April). The Communists replied that they did not seek civil war but "a combative and determined social mobilization" that would lead to "a rising of the masses" and "the paralyzation of the country." They proposed joint action with the Christian Democrats to overthrow the dictatorship (Paris, AFP, 30 May; *FBIS*, 31 May).

The issue of joint action became a more serious one when, under U.S. pressure, the Chilean government lifted the state of siege imposed in November 1984 that had been used to prevent public meetings, censor the press, suppress publications, and arrest, detain, or exile over 33,000 Chileans (Santiago Radio Cooperativa, 12 July; *FBIS*, 15 July). The left had held one unsuccessful protest in March, but now it was possible to do so legally. Before the first large protests took place in September, however, an important new development occurred that altered the relationship between the government and the opposition and between the MDP and the other opponents of the regime. This was the signing of the National Accord on a transition to full democracy by the leaders of the Democratic Alliance and of the two most important rightist groups, the National Party and the National Union. The accord had been developed by three well-known Chilean figures at the request of Cardinal Juan Francisco Fresno. Because of the conservative background of both Fresno and the authors of the document, it marked an important step in the consolidation of the opposition to Pinochet.

The accord called for direct elections of the president and congress, reform of the 1980 constitution, and a mixed economy with firm guarantees for private property. Parties whose "objectives, actions, and conduct" indicate that they do not respect "democracy, legality, and the rejection of violence" could be declared unconstitutional by the Constitutional Tribunal (*El Mercurio*, International Edition, 24–30 August). The document was signed by twenty of the leading political figures of Chile from eleven political parties. Significant by their absence were the leaders of two right-wing pro-Pinochet groups and the representatives of the MDP.

The Communists were thrown into disarray by the accord. They issued divergent statements on the subject and finally focused their criticism on the guarantees of property and the fact that the accord was signed by right-wing politicians who had formerly supported Pinochet. Pinochet in turn said that it was only a document signed by a few individuals who were associated with the discredited pre-1973 politics. Its significance, however, was that it provided an answer to Pinochet's claim that Chileans were obliged to choose between him and communism; it finally aligned significant sectors of the right against the regime.

At the end of March there had been a particularly brutal set of political murders involving a former leader of the Communist Party (then head of the Secondary School Teachers Association [AGECH], another communist activist, and a lawyer associated with the church-sponsored Vicariate of Solidarity. The government immediately attributed the murders to the Communists, but careful investigation by a Chilean judge and, it appears, rivalries among Chilean intelligence agencies led to the discovery of proof that the murders had been carried out by a special branch of the carabineros, or national police. When two policemen were indicted and seventeen others prohibited from leaving the country, the special unit was dissolved, the head of the carabineros was forced to resign from both his post and his membership in the ruling junta, and the government was further discredited. In a Chilean magazine it was also revealed that the teachers' union president had been the sole member of the CPC Central Committee to have survived a series of assassinations and disappearances carried out by the government in 1976 (*Hoy*, 5 August; *FBIS*, 11 September).

In September and October prominent citizens—including a number of generals—publicly announced that they were signing the National Accord. The Air Force member of the junta said favorable things about it, and it was reported that the new carabinero head was also favorable, but Pinochet's principal concern was with possible erosion of support in the army. Pinochet therefore removed the army representative in the junta who was reported to favor negotiations with the signers of the accord and replaced him with a trusted confidant. In October the Communists scored 40 percent in the first elections at the University of Chile since the lifting of the state of siege, and in November the largest antigovernment demonstration in Chilean history was held. That demonstration was called by the Democratic Alliance but it received the cooperation of the Communists through the MDP and the FPMR. The latter organization announced a 48-hour truce in its antigovernment actions, and the demonstration was remarkable in the total absence of any violence or casualties.

By the end of the year all attention was focused on 1989, when Pinochet's current term ends and when, under the 1980 constitution, the junta can nominate him or someone else for approval by a plebiscite. Chileans wonder whether Pinochet could pull it off, given his much reduced base of support. In November the United States sent a new ambassador who immediately and publicly took strong stands in favor of the return of democracy, and even conservative circles in the United States have begun to worry about a possible "Nicaraguanization" of Chile. As former Communist Senator Volodia Teitelboim indicated in an interview in December (*Cauce*, 10–16 December; *FBIS*, 20 December), if such a process should take place "the struggle would increase and move on to more important stages," and the Communists as well as the FPMR are ready.

Paul E. Sigmund
Princeton University

Colombia

Population. 29,506,000
Party. Communist Party of Colombia (Partido Comunista de Colombia; PCC)
Founded. 1930
Membership. 12,000 (estimated)
General Secretary. Gilberto Vieira
Executive Committee. 14 members
Central Committee. 80 members
Status. Legal
Last Congress. Fourteenth, 7–11 November 1984
Last Elections. 1984: municipal and state assembly, 2.0 percent; 1982: presidential, 1.2 percent; congressional, 1.2 percent, 1 of 114 senators, 3 of 199 representatives
Auxiliary Organizations. Trade Union Confederation of Workers of Colombia (CSTC); Federation of Agrarian Syndicates; Communist Youth of Colombia (JUCO), claims 2,000 members
Publications. *Voz Proletaria* (weekly), 40,000 circulation; *Margen Izquierda*, political journal; Colombian edition of *World Marxist Review*, 2,000 circulation; JUCO publishes a monthly supplement to *Voz Proletaria*

The communist movement in Colombia has undergone various transformations in both name and organization since the party's initial formation in December 1926. The PCC was publicly proclaimed on 17 July 1930. In July 1965, a schism within the PCC between pro-Soviet and pro-Chinese factions resulted in the latter's becoming the Communist Party of Colombia, Marxist-Leninist (PCC-ML). Only the PCC has legal status. It has been allowed to participate in elections under its own banner since 1972. In 1984, the PCC participated in municipal council and departmental assembly elections as the leading member of a leftist coalition called the Democratic Front, which received 2.0 percent of the total popular vote.

According to U.S. intelligence sources, the PCC has 12,000 members. Although the party contends that its ranks have increased in recent years, the 1982 and 1984 elections suggest that the party's growth has been less rapid than its leaders had hoped, especially in the larger cities. The PCC exercises only marginal influence in national affairs.

The highest party authority is the congress, convened at four-year intervals. Gilberto Vieira, the general secretary of the PCC, is 76. A major source of the party's influence is its control of the CSTC, which is reportedly Colombia's largest trade-union confederation and a member of the Soviet-front World Federation of Trade Unions. The Betancur government suspended the CSTC's legal status for six months in 1985 for its part in organizing the 20 June national strike. The CSTC's president Gustavo Osorio, and its secretary general, Angelino Garzón, are members of the PCC's Central Committee.

The PCC's youth organization, the JUCO, operates through the National Youth Coordinating Committee, where it plays an active role in promoting party policy among university and secondary school students. The JUCO held its Sixth Congress in Bogotá on 25–29 September. Its general secretary, José Anteguera, stressed the importance of the JUCO's role as an auxiliary organization of the PCC and called on regional groups in Antioquia, Bogotá, and Valle to "overcome stagnation" (*Voz Proletaria*, 3 October).

Guerrilla Warfare. Although not a serious threat to the government, guerrilla warfare has been a feature of Colombian life since the late 1940s; the current wave began in 1964. The four main guerrilla organizations are the Revolutionary Armed Forces of Colombia (FARC), long controlled by the PCC; the M-19, a guerrilla organization that began as the armed hand of the National Popular Alliance (ANAPO); the pro-Chinese People's Liberation Army (EPL), which is the guerrilla arm of the PCC-ML; and the Castroite National Liberation Army (ELN). A fifth group, the small, urban, Trotskyist-oriented Worker's Self-Defense Movement (ADO), announced in July that it would join the FARC's new political movement, Patriotic Union (FARC-UP). A sixth group, the Quintín Lamé, named after a Colombian Indian leader, is a recently formed pro-Indian guerrilla organization that operates primarily in the Cauca department. Quintín Lamé denies any formal alliance with other guerrilla organizations and claims to be neutral in the confrontation between the FARC and its dissident Ricardo Franco Front (*El Tiempo*, 10 May). While the movement maintains "good relations" with other armed groups, the Quintín Lamé asserts that its work "depends basically on the problems and needs of the Indian population" (ibid., 4 September). In September the Quintín Lamé, the Ricardo Franco Front, and the M-19 reportedly formed the United Revolutionary Directorate of Colombia (Dirección Revolucionaria Unida de Colombia; DRUC) to coordinate guerrilla activities (Spanish News Agency [EFE], 27 October). Army sources reported in November that one of Quintín Lamé's founders, Luis Angel Monroy, was killed in a skirmish in Valle (*El Tiempo*, 12 November).

Domestic peace has been a primary goal of President Belisario Betancur since he began his four-year term in August 1982. His efforts to negotiate a peaceful solution to Colombia's long-standing guerrilla problem culminated in historic truce agreements in 1984. Under the accords, the FARC agreed to a one-year cease-fire, effective 28 May, and the M-19, EPL, and ADO agreed to suspend armed activity indefinitely after 30 August 1984. Neither agreement required the guerrillas to surrender their weapons, nor did the government make any explicit commitment to withdraw troops from those areas affected by guerrilla violence.

The Revolutionary Armed Forces of Colombia. According to the FARC's principal leader, Manuel Marulanda Vélez, the movement has some 6,000 men operating on 27 fronts. Each of the FARC's rural fronts is composed of two columns, numbering about 200 men. The FARC has expanded its areas of influence in recent years to include portions of the departments of Huila, Caquetá, Tolima, Cauca, Boyacá, Santander, Antioquia, Valle, Meta, Cundinamarca, and the intendance of Arauca. The FARC's general headquarters is located at La Uribe. Jacobo Arenas is Marulanda's second-in-command: other members of the FARC's central staff are Jaime Guaraca, Alfonso Cano, and Raúl Reyes. Although Marulanda has never confirmed officially that the FARC is the armed wing of the PCC, it is widely believed that the leadership mechanisms and general policy of the FARC are determined by the PCC's bylaws, and political resolutions emitted at party congresses and plenums are presumably transmitted to the fronts through Marulanda's directives.

In March, FARC leaders announced the official emergence of its political movement, the FARC-UP, and declared that it would participate in the 1986 elections. During a meeting with the National Peace Commission at La Uribe, Jacobo Arenas spoke about the need to implement agrarian, electoral, and urban reforms and to popularly elect mayors and governors as fundamental conditions to facilitate the guerrillas' progressive participation in Colombia's institutional life (*El Tiempo*, 31 March). The FARC's platform also calls for the nationalization of banks, foreign companies, and the transport sector; an independent foreign policy "free from the influence of Yankee imperialism"; democratization of the armed forces; a civilian minister of defense; and a reduced military budget (*Vox Proletaria*, 28 February).

The FARC's general staff met with the National Peace Commission again on 28 May to commemorate the first anniversary of the signing of the cease-fire. Marulanda blamed the social conditions in Colombia for the birth of guerrilla movements and violence in general, and he warned that "if reforms are not carried out, it will be difficult for peace to last" (*El Espectador*, 29 May). He praised Betancur's peace policy and assured the government that the FARC would continue to honor the truce and cease-fire agreements during the conduct of its political campaign. In August, Marulanda announced that FARC representatives would join the national dialogue in an attempt to revitalize the peace process (EFE, 6 August).

In a letter to President Betancur in September, the FARC proposed extending the truce agreement—scheduled to end in January 1986—through 20 September 1986 "to give the government and congress time to prepare the political, economic, and social reforms provided by the La Uribe agreement and which have not yet been fulfilled" (*El Espectador*, 8 September). FARC-UP coordinator Braulio Herrera said in October that the FARC would only become a political party if the reforms were ready by 1 December. He announced that the FARC-UP would register at the Electoral Court and asked that President Betancur meet with its leaders "so that he may learn about things which he surely ignores, such as the death of 70 [FARC-UP] militants during the last four months and the military hostilities against FARC camps in Santander and Antioquia" (*Vox Proletaria*, 17 October). FARC spokesmen have stated that the FARC will dissolve "the moment there is a true democratic opening in Colombia, which will not occur until there is a political reform that juridically ends the Liberal-Conservative biparty system" (*El Tiempo*, 21 October).

FARC and Patriotic Union leaders condemned the M-19's takeover of the Palace of Justice and termed the operation a "stupid and futile genocide" (AFP, 11 November). The Patriotic Union held its first national congress in Bogotá on 14–16 November. Representatives of the Patriotic Union Front, consisting of the FARC-UP, ADO, and PCC, called for "all Colombian democrats and revolutionaries to close ranks in a broad action to strengthen the democratic opening." The congress concluded with a rally and speech by the FARC-UP's presidential candidate, Jacobo Arenas (*El Espectador*, 17 November).

Dissension within the FARC over the status of peace negotiations with the government continued in 1985. FARC spokesmen insist that the Ricardo Franco Front, which calls itself a part of the FARC, is "a gang of common bandits who deserted our organization" (*El Tiempo*, 10 May). The Ricardo Franco group's principal leader is Javier Delgado, although unconfirmed reports in late December indicated that Delgado had been relieved of his command and would be "court-martialed" by the group's new leadership (*FBIS*, 3 January 1986).

FARC fronts have been authorized to eliminate dissident groups operating in their areas. In April, the FARC occupied a Ricardo Franco camp in the central Andean range and "executed" a dissident guerrilla member (*El Siglo*, 25 April). Seven FARC dissidents were killed in northwestern Cauca in August (ibid., 13 August). The Ricardo Franco Front issued a communiqué in September stating that it had not been defeated and would not yield in the face of "the outrageous proclamations of war to the death issued by the central staff of the FARC-UP—the puppet armed branch of the PCC" (*El Tiempo*, 4 September). Despite a total of eighteen members killed during clashes with the FARC "official" sector, the Ricardo Franco Front vowed to continue its military actions at the national level against "the bourgeois Communist Party, its armed branch, and its political headquarters" (ibid., 19 September).

Domestic Attitudes and Activities. The PCC recognizes the experience of the Communist Party of the Soviet Union (CPSU) as an ideological source, but it also takes "maximum account of the national characteristics and revolutionary and democratic traditions of the Colombian people." This has enabled the party to devise its own tactics, which combine diverse forms of struggle ranging from electoral campaigns to guerrilla warfare. The documents and declarations approved by the PCC's Fourteenth Congress indicate that the strategy and tactics of the PCC will continue to be a combination of all forms of struggle. According to Vieira, "We communists want to advance by democratic means, by what we call action and the mass struggle, and not only by means of elections, which are only one part of the process." Vieira claims that the PCC has failed to become an important factor in the electoral process because of Colombia's deeply rooted bipartisan tradition. The party includes among its most urgent tasks "the struggle for reforms aimed at liquidating the exclusive monopoly of the traditional ruling parties in Colombia's political life" (*Voz Proletaria*, 28 June 1984).

The PCC defines its political line and organizes its activity on the basis of work among the masses. Party statements criticize "adventurist and terrorist practices," such as the M-19 seizure of the Palace of Justice, that militate against the unity of the masses and weaken the prospects of the popular movement. The PCC views as its principal tasks the attainment of unified activity by the working class and the repair of the 1947 split in the trade-union movement, which Vieira attributes to "agents of U.S.

imperialism supported by the local reactionary regime" (*Pravda*, 31 May 1984).

In an assessment of the national political situation, the PCC's Executive Committee declared in January that militarism impedes a true opening toward effective democracy, while class interests continue to dictate the policy directions of the traditional parties, most of Congress, and the decisive sectors of government, making them resistant to any positive change. The Executive Committee called for the demilitarization of the country and an elimination of paramilitary groups operating against the "popular movement" in order to create a new political climate. Committee members also exhorted party militants to struggle for a general amnesty, political and social reforms, an end to the state of siege, an authentic agrarian reform, and a unified labor movement (*Voz Proletaria*, 17 January).

The Central Committee elected by the party's Fourteenth Congress held its first plenary session in Bogotá on 31 March. Vieira said that the PCC welcomes the Patriotic Union's initiatives "because we can see in this project a new step toward a common front and popular unity." He denied any contradiction between the goals of the Democratic Front and the Patriotic Union, since the latter has adopted the perspective that a front must be created to link the various popular and revolutionary groups disposed to struggle for major change in Colombia (ibid., 3 April). Alberto Rojas Puyo, Central Committee member and the PCC's representative to the National Peace Commission until its reorganization in October, called the emergence of the FARC-UP "an important step toward strengthening the peace process." He noted that the name chosen points to the creation of a broad national movement (ibid.). In addition to a resolution supporting the Patriotic Union, the Central Committee endorsed the intensification of preparations for a national civic strike and solidarity with Nicaragua. The party also opened discussion on its platform and candidates for the 1986 elections.

The PCC's continued failure to recruit new members as rapidly as it would like was a major topic at the party's Eighth Organizational Conference in Bogotá on 29–31 March. Teofilo Forero said that the party has an "urgent need" to commit itself to the recruitment of militants through its participation in labor, agrarian, and popular meetings; in the government's Peace, Verification, and Dialogue commissions; and in the organization of the Patriotic Union. He also cited the party's need to adopt more modern techniques to reach the masses, to simplify its internal structure, and to revitalize activity at the cell level. In reviewing the conference's conclusions, Forero said that the PCC would continue to identify itself with popular struggles "directed against the imperialist pillage of our national resources and against the oligarchy, who resort to a state of siege to maintain their power in the face of popular protest" (*Voz Proletaria*, 3 April). In April the PCC published the first issue of a new political journal, *Margen Izquierda*, which has replaced *Documentos Políticos* and *Estudios Marxistas*.

The PCC vigorously criticized President Betancur's economic policies in 1985, which it contends "threaten national sovereignty and worsen the plight of the working masses." At a meeting of leftist organizations on 22 April, Vieira described the social and economic situation in Colombia as "explosive." He accused the government of precipitous action in agreeing to International Monetary Fund (IMF) demands and asserted that Colombia's agreement with the IMF is "unconstitutional" because "it curtails the self-determination of the country's legitimate authorities to handle the nation's economy" (ibid., 25 April).

The PCC worked to postpone the national labor strike from the first week in June to a later date in order to allow the Colombian Congress to consider a package of reforms designed to formalize the truce agreements and to enable the PCC to set up a legal framework that would allow the FARC to participate in the 1986 general elections (*Latin America Weekly Report*, 31 May). At the Patriotic Union's opening political rally, the PCC reaffirmed its support for the electoral process and spoke out against violence. Vieira said that "this is the time for action by the masses, not for senseless terrorist attacks." This view was echoed by FARC-UP coordinator Herrera, who asserted that "in spite of the snags in the peace process, there are powerful democratic reserves in Colombia" (*Cromos*, 3 June).

In an editorial condemning the M-19's seizure of the Palace of Justice, Vieira considered the takeover "totally isolated from the popular masses and the entire revolutionary movement." He claimed that the M-19 erred in choosing its target because of the Supreme Court's institutional prestige. After noting the M-19's responsibility, Vieira stated that it was also necessary to establish clearly the responsibility of the government and the military high command in the tragedy (*Voz Proletaria*, 14 November).

International Views and Positions. The PCC faithfully follows the Soviet line in its international positions. According to Vieira, the party is engaged primarily in the struggle for the emancipation of the Colombian people. However, the PCC insists that it is impossible to remain neutral in the "great international struggle" between socialism and capitalism. The party therefore "enthusiastically" supports the socialist countries and particularly the Soviet Union "because it defends genuine socialism, despite its imperfections" (*YICA*, 1985, p. 65). At the same time, the party claims that it is not dependent on Moscow, Havana, or "any foreign place," nor does it serve as the agent for the international policy of any foreign country. The PCC wants a Colombian international policy that is "independent and autonomous."

According to Vieira, Colombia is beset externally by the "threat of U.S. imperialist adventurism." Although he sees the expansionist course of U.S. aggression directed against all of Latin America, it is of special significance for Colombia "because of its proximity to Central America" (*Pravda*, 30 May 1984). Nevertheless, the PCC considers that under President Betancur there has been a shift for the better in Colombia's official stand on a number of international issues. Party statements have been highly supportive of Betancur's active participation in the organization of the Contadora group and of his efforts to improve Colombia's relations with Cuba and Nicaragua.

Political declarations approved by the Fourteenth Congress expressed "serious anxiety" over "President Reagan's aggressive military policy," the growing involvement of U.S. imperialism in El Salvador's civil war, and the undeclared war of the United States against Nicaragua.

The Maoists. The PCC-ML is firmly pro-Chinese, although recently the party has looked more toward Albania for political guidance. Its present leadership hierarchy is not clearly known. The PCC-ML has an estimated membership of one thousand. Unlike the PCC, it has not attempted to obtain legal status, and its impact in terms of national life is insignificant. Its official news organ is *Revolución*. The Marxist-Leninist League of Colombia publishes the monthly *Nueva Democracia*. PCC-ML statements are sometimes found in Chinese publications and those of pro-Chinese parties in Europe and Latin America.

The PCC-ML's guerrilla arm, the EPL, was the first to attempt a "people's war" in Latin America. The EPL has conducted only limited operations since 1975, although according to Colombian intelligence it still has an estimated 350 guerrillas organized in four fronts. The EPL operates mainly in the departments of Antioquia, Córdoba, and Meta, with urban support networks in several of the country's larger cities.

On 23 August 1984 the EPL concluded a cease-fire agreement with the government approved by the Twelfth Congress of the PCC-ML. In keeping with the national command's order to all EPL units to cease offensive military actions, there were no major skirmishes reported between EPL guerrillas and army patrols during the first six months of the year. In February the EPL's military commander, Ernesto Rojas, announced that the movement would not surrender its weapons as a precondition for participation in the 1986 elections (*FBIS*, 28 February). In April the EPL rejected the pardon under consideration by Congress and demanded "a new general amnesty with no conditions." The movement's most visible political leader, Oscar William Calvo, reiterated EPL complaints of harassment by government security organizations (*El Tiempo*, 13 April).

In July, Calvo complained that the government's peace commissions had failed to achieve anything positive. He strongly urged President Betancur to bypass intermediaries and talk directly with representatives from guerrilla groups "in order to save the peace agreements, the cease-fire, and the national dialogue from collapsing" (*El Siglo*, 5 July). On 24 July troops killed seven EPL guerrillas during an armed clash near Uraba, Antioquia (*El Espectador*, 25 July).

In an undated open letter to FARC leaders, the EPL indicated its desire to "discuss and solve the existing differences with the FARC." It accused various FARC fronts of maintaining an "unresponsive attitude" toward the EPL's appeals for guerrilla unity (*El Tiempo*, 31 August). Following a meeting in September of the government's Verification Commission, the EPL, and the FARC, the EPL accused the PCC of "trying to make us appear in the eyes of the people as opponents to the peace efforts initiated last year" and of "spreading slander against the movement which is a standard bearer in defense of Marxist-Leninist positions" (ibid., 4 September).

At a Bogotá press conference on 20 November, Calvo termed an EPL attack on the police station in

Urrao, Antioquia, as "a necessary reaction to constant military harassment." He said the attack did not signify a repudiation of the truce agreement or a resumption of the armed struggle. Calvo told newsmen that "if the government violates the agreements, we cannot just sit and do nothing." He claimed that the army's plan was to destroy the M-19, then the EPL, and finally the FARC (*FBIS*, 21 November). Calvo and two companions were shot to death later the same day by unidentified assailants.

On 29 November the EPL announced that it would no longer honor the truce agreement, charging that Calvo's death proved there were no guarantees for its members who had accepted the truce. EPL guerrillas in Antioquia ambushed an army patrol near San Pedro de Uraba on 8 December, killing seven soldiers and wounding six others (AFP, 8 December). At year's end, the EPL was still holding for ransom two U.S. engineers whom it kidnapped on 11 December at a pipeline construction site near the Venezuelan border.

The Independent Revolutionary Workers' Movement (MOIR) has aspired since 1971 to become the first mass-based Maoist party in Latin America. Its leadership and organization are independent of those of the PCC-ML. The MOIR has no military branch and has been unable to strengthen its political position in recent elections. The MOIR's general secretary is Francisco Mosquera.

The M-19. The M-19, which first appeared in January 1974 as the self-proclaimed armed branch of ANAPO, takes its name from the contested presidential election of 19 April 1970. Since 1976 the M-19 has been actively involved in Colombia's guerrilla movement, pursuing "a popular revolution of national liberation toward socialism." An estimate on the movement's size is 8,000 members (*NYT*, 9 November).

The M-19 held out for what it considered a "broader peace agreement" from that reached by the government with the FARC. For most M-19 leaders, the peace accord signed with the government on 24 August 1984 constituted an agreement to end hostilities in order to open the way to a "national dialogue." Unlike the FARC, the M-19 has lacked a consistent policy regarding the cease-fire, the national dialogue, or its political future, leading the government to complain of numerous "irregularities" in M-19's compliance with the truce. In January the M-19 reached agreement with the government on a cease-fire to end fighting in Carinto, where the army decided to prevent the M-19 from establishing armed camps similar to the communist "independent republics" of the early 1960s.

The M-19 held its first open congress on 13–17 February at Los Robles, Cauca. Alvaro Fayad was elected commander and a new general staff was appointed consisting of Fayad, Carlos Pizarro León, Antonio Navarro Wolff, and former commander Iván Marino Ospina. The M-19 proposed that a public debate be held to discuss the conditions under which it would be prepared to surrender its arms and rejoin society. Government minister Jaime Castro warned guerrilla groups that they would not be permitted to engage in political activity while armed (EFE, 23 February). M-19 spokesman Israel Santamaría responded that the M-19 would not surrender its weapons until social, economic, and political conditions change (*FBIS*, 28 February).

At a Bogotá rally in Bolívar Plaza on 15 March, the M-19 proclaimed itself a "democratic government for the people" and declared the region of Los Robles as "free Colombian territory." M-19 leaders called on the masses to support a nationwide strike and warned that if the peace process failed, the M-19 would "stop being a guerrilla movement and become an army" (*El Tiempo*, 16, 17 March).

Military sources reported several clashes between army patrols and M-19 units during April and May, principally in the Magdalena region of Valle. On 23 May, Antonio Navarro Wolff and several companions were seriously injured by a bomb explosion at a Cali restaurant (EFE, 23 May). In the face of growing M-19 presence in Cali, Defense Minister Miguel Vega Uribe warned that no guerrilla group would be allowed to maintain urban camps "to promote political proselytism." Described by the M-19 as "camps for democracy and peace," the military charged that such sites were being used as military training and recruitment centers for youths from slum sectors in Cali, Medellín, and other cities (*El Espectador*, 28 May).

In early June some 3,000 troops supported by helicopters moved against M-19 guerrillas operating in the rural areas of Magdalena and Habana. Military sources indicated that 86 rebels had been killed since April during clashes in central Valle, most of them belonging to the M-19 and its dissident faction headed by Gustavo Arias Londoño (EFE, 11 June).

Following months of increasingly tense relations between the M-19 and government authorities, Carlos Pizarro informed journalists on 21 June that the truce had been broken. He accused the government of violating the cease-fire and national dialogue agreement, and he blamed President Betancur for the failure of Congress to enact promised reforms. He announced that the M-19 would resume guerrilla activities (*El Tiempo*, 26 June). M-19 units escalated attacks on army patrols and stepped up their occupation of towns, starting with the takeover of Genova, Quindío, on 28 June, in which nineteen police agents, civilians, and rebels were killed. The army countered with a widespread offensive in the mountainous region along the Tolima-Quindío border (*FBIS*, 2 July).

By early August, Navarro Wolff and other M-19 leaders indicated a desire to re-establish talks with the government (*El Tiempo*, 5 August). General Manuel Guerrero Paz, the armed forces commander, rejected the M-19's proposal for a direct dialogue and warned that "no new talks should be held as long as the M-19 persists in acting outside the law." He described the situation as "too difficult and complex to resume the dialogue" and announced a "total war" against the M-19 (ibid., 9 August). Subsequent counterinsurgency actions inflicted heavy casualties on M-19 personnel. On 28 August military sources reported the death of Iván Marino Ospina during a shootout in Cali. In the first week of October, 32 soldiers and 24 guerrillas were killed in an ambush and clashes in Tolima, Cauca, and Valle. General Vega accused the M-19 of "preparing for war, not for peace," and said the movement was "bent on a senseless war to bathe Colombia in blood" (*El Siglo*, 2 October; EFE, 4 October). For its part, the M-19 claimed credit for the assassination attempt on Army Commander General Rafael Samudio Molina, who was wounded slightly in Bogotá on 23 October (EFE, 23 October).

In the year's most dramatic and tragic guerrilla incident, 35 M-19 guerrillas seized the Palace of Justice in Bogotá on 6 November, ostensibly to gain access to the media and compel the government to resume negotiations. In the ensuing battle to recapture the building, all 35 guerrillas (including M-19 leaders Luis Otero Cifuentes and Andrés Almarales), 64 civilians (including 12 Supreme Court justices), and 16 soldiers and police were killed.

The M-19's suicidal attack brought universal opprobrium to the movement and decimated its leadership structure. Alvaro Fayad, Carlos Pizarro, Antonio Navarro, and Gustavo Arias are the most prominent surviving members of the M-19's high command. The movement's principal units are now gathered in the Andean central mountain range. In December the M-19 announced the formation of the "Andrés Almarales Command," which will operate in Cauca (*El Tiempo*, 7 December). Military authorities in Cali imposed a curfew on 2 December as part of an operation to break up M-19 guerrilla cells, which had reportedly taken over the southwestern sector of the city (EFE, 2 December). The M-19 announced plans to intensify its activities during Christmas and threatened to stage terrorist acts in several cities, similar to the attack on a military bus in downtown Bogotá on 6 December, which killed two soldiers and wounded fourteen others (*FBIS*, 13 December).

The National Liberation Army. The ELN was formed in Santander in 1964 under the inspiration of the Cuban revolution. It undertook its first military action in January 1965. Once recognized as the largest and most militant of the guerrilla forces operating in Colombia, the ELN has never recovered from the toll exacted on its leadership and urban network by an army offensive in 1973. According to Colombian intelligence, the ELN has approximately 350 men organized in four fronts. It operates in a vast region of northeastern Colombia, in North and South Santander, Bolívar, Cauca, and Antioquia, and in the intendance of Arauca. Discounting FARC and M-19 dissidents, the ELN was the only guerrilla movement that did not sign a cease-fire agreement with the government in 1984.

In February the ELN reaffirmed that under no circumstances would it engage in a peaceful dialogue with the government. ELN spokesmen asserted that the government's peace initiatives had failed, and they justified kidnapping and extortion as "legitimate forms of political struggle" (AFP, 27 February). After a six-month lull, ELN guerrillas renewed harassment of foreign oil companies working in the eastern Llanos. Guerrillas dynamited installations at the Cano Rondón fields in Arauca where various companies have been installing exploratory wells (*Latin America Weekly Report*, 7 June). An ELN force attacked the town of El Tabor on 12 October and killed four members of the Patriotic Union. The ELN issued a statement saying it had "executed" the four Communist political leaders after a "people's court" condemned all members of the Patriotic Union for "betraying the revolutionary struggle" (AFP, 31 October).

Ricardo Lara Parada, founder and former ELN leader, was killed near his home in Barrancabermeja on 15 November. The ELN claimed credit for his death and announced that it would "execute" former members of the organization who "make wrongful use of the name of the movement for political or personal gain" (*El Tiempo*, 2 December).

On 9 December two ELN urban fronts signed a peace agreement with the National Peace Commission. Ernesto González, principal leader of the fronts that agreed to sign the truce, explained that they will join the FARC's political activities through the Patriotic Union (*El Siglo*, 11 December). Various leaders of the ELN's rural fronts reasserted on 11 December that they "will never sign truce agreements with the government" and rejected the pact signed by the urban fronts. During a news conference in Bucaramanga, the ELN reaffirmed that the "only way to reach power is with weapons" (EFE, 12 December).

Peace Prospects. It is clear that despite President Betancur's historic breakthrough in 1984, guerrilla violence in Colombia has not been eliminated. According to Colombian military sources, a total of 321 members of the armed forces and national police and 967 guerrillas have lost their lives in the eighteen months since the cease-fire agreements went into effect. In addition, some 318 peasants have been killed by either guerrillas or criminal "death squads." During the same period, 26 attacks on military bases, 84 attacks on police posts, 34 ambushes on army and police patrols, 66 attacks on villages, farms, and small towns, 71 attacks on armed forces' vehicles, and 68 attacks on banks have taken place. It was also reported that some 200 citizens were kidnapped by armed groups and common criminals over the same period (*El Siglo*, 11 December).

Confrontations between military and guerrilla forces belonging to the M-19, ELN, FARC dissidents, and Quintín Lamé intensified in the second half of the year, particularly in the departments of Tolima, Quindío, Valle, Cauca, and Antioquia. General Vega Uribe described the guerrilla situation at year's end as "very serious" and said that the armed forces would intensify their security operations to deal with "the critical situation of violence that threatens us" (*El Espectador*, 11 December).

With FARC committed, albeit tenuously, to upholding the peace process, President Betancur claims that 90 percent of Colombia's estimated 10,000 guerrillas have accepted the government's truce and will participate in the 1986 elections as a political force. There is little prospect for a resumption of the government's dialogue with the M-19, the EPL, or other guerrillas who either rejected or broke the peace agreements in 1985. The military appears firmly resolved to eradicate them.

Daniel L. Premo
Washington College

Costa Rica

Population. 2,655,000

Party. Popular Vanguard Party (Partido Vanguardia Popular; PVP). A splinter faction is the Costa Rican People's Party (Partido del Pueblo Costarricense; PPC), led by the PVP's former secretary general Manuel Mora Valverde and his brother Eduardo. Other secondary leftist parties are the Movement of the New Republic (Movimiento de la Nueva República; MNR), formerly the Revolutionary People's Movement (Movimiento Revolucionario del Pueblo; MRP), and the Costa Rican Socialist Party

(Partido Socialista Costarricense; PSC). All formed part of the leftist electoral coalition, United People (Pueblo Unido; PU), in the 1978 and 1982 elections.

Founded. PVP: 1931; PPC: 1984; MNR: 1970 (as MRP); PSC: 1972

Membership. PVP: variously estimated at 3,500 to 10,000 prior to 1984 split of PPC. Other left parties have only miniscule memberships.

President. PVP: Arnoldo Ferreto Segura (honorific post)

Secretary General. PVP: Humberto Vargas Carbonell; PPC: Manuel Mora Valverde

Undersecretary General. PVP: Oscar Madrigal; PPC: Eduardo Mora Valverde

Central Committee. PVP and PPC each have 35 members, 15 alternates

Status. Legal in all cases

Last Congress. PVP: Fifteenth, 15–16 September 1984, in San José; PPC: Fourteenth, 10–11 March 1984, in San José

Last Election. 1982 PU coalition won 3.2 percent of presidential vote, compared to 2.7 percent in 1978; elected 4 of 57 national deputies, compared to 3 in 1978.

Auxiliary Organizations. General Workers Confederation (Confederación General de Trabajadores; CGT); National Peasant Federation (Federación Campesina Nacional; FCN); Costa Rican Peace and Solidarity Council (an umbrella group made up of some 50 union and solidarity committees)

Publications. PVP: *Libertad Revolucionaria* (weekly); PPC: *Libertad* (weekly)

Left politics in Costa Rica in 1985 continued to reflect the infighting resulting from the late 1983 purge of the PVP's first and only secretary general, Manuel Mora Valverde. However, as the Mora-led faction regrouped in the rival PPC and the official PVP leadership further consolidated its hold over its own party apparatus—receiving Soviet recognition and blessing as well—a certain stability was returned to this end of the national political spectrum. This stability led to a flurry of matchmaking and rival coalition building with a view to the upcoming (February 1986) national elections. Other issues that engaged the local left during 1985 were those of U.S. policy in the region, especially military aid to Costa Rica, the Monge government's Nicaraguan policy and border clashes, the question of its own alleged military training for "subversion," and youth-oriented activities including a world youth festival in Moscow in August and the PVP youth organization's Fourth Congress in April.

Preparations for the 1986 national elections further hardened the split between the PVP and PPC; each group fielded its own coalition or "front" slate of candidates and vied for both name recognition among voters and support from the few remaining independent leaders on the left. The minor parties of the earlier left coalition—PU, MNR, and PSC—joined forces with the Mora-led PPC and several former major party progressives in forming the Patriotic Alliance (Alianza Patriótica; AP) in May 1984. However, since this vehicle did not move forward rapidly, the MNR and PSC carried out a coup of sorts in achieving the official inscription of the coalition name United People, formerly used by the united left forces in 1978 and 1982, as their own electoral banner. They clearly hoped to benefit from any possible voter confusion, and they nominated only their own candidates for deputyships. The PPC and Mora's role in the upcoming elections remains in question, but the fact that the MNR and PSC formed their own electoral coalition suggests the weakness and disarray of Mora's group. Nevertheless, the PVP considered this theft of the coalition's mantle of legitimacy to be the work of the Moras and the PPC, using the MNR and PSC as a front (*Libertad Revolucionaria*, 15–21 February).

Not to be outdone in either coalition-building or purposeful voter confusion, the PVP announced the formation of its own electoral vehicle, the Popular Democratic Union (Unión Democrática Popular; UDP) in April. The UDP was formed by the PVP and a so-called Broad Democratic Front (Frente Amplio Democrático; FAD), led by ex-PSC leader and deputy Mario Devandas Brenes. However, the PVP later named this vehicle the Patriotic Alliance for a brief period, only confusing itself with its opponents earlier and ill-fated organization, proclaiming as its presidential candidate Dr. Rodrigo Gutiérrez Sáenz, twice before the candidate of the PU for president. It remains doubtful that such slight-of-hand tactics and terminology will strengthen the position of either left faction, both seriously weakened over the past two years (*Libertad Revolucionaria*, 12–18 April, 14–20 June).

One further area of factional dispute traceable to the PVP-PPC split developed within the formerly PVP-dominated Unitary Workers Central (Central Unitaria de los Trabajadores; CUT). The PPC members of CUT called the Third Congress of the organization for 15–17 March in San José, while the PVP opposed this in favor of a November congress. The March gathering, led by Mora sympathizers within the CUT hierarchy—in particular Lenín Chacón of the PPC—called for the creation of a new name for itself, the Constitutional Congress of the Confederation of Workers of Costa Rica, perhaps in anticipation of the PVP challenge to the congress's legitimacy. The weakening of the labor movement appeared to be the only immediate outcome of yet another indulgence in left factionalism.

The official PVP leadership of Humberto Vargas Carbonell received an unmistakable sign of approval from Moscow when he was received with considerable publicity in Moscow, Prague, and Warsaw during June and July. Moreover, Vargas took an active part in the subsequent August meetings on the question of foreign debt in Havana, scoring points both with regional left figures and his own compatriots of other parties in attendance. Thus, Vargas's control of the remaining PVP party structure seems assured for the foreseeable future (*Libertad Revolucionaria*, 31 May–6 June; 9–15, 16–22 August).

Chief among the U.S. policies attacked by the left were the installation of a powerful Voice of America transmitter in northern Costa Rica in January (*FBIS*, 18 January, 2 April; *Central America Report*, 18 April), the visit of the warships USS *King* and *Iowa* in April and the USS *Luce* in August (*Libertad Revolucionaria*, 16–22 August), the arrival of U.S. military trainers in May (*FBIS*, 31 May; *Libertad Revolucionaria*, 31 May–6 June; *Inforpress Centroamericana*, 8 August), and the verbal faux pas of departing U.S. Ambassador Curtin Winsor as well as the arrival of his successor Dr. Lewis Tambs, formerly U.S. envoy in Colombia (*Libertad Revolucionaria*, 25–31 January, 1–7 March). On many of these issues the left was joined in its opposition by a broad spectrum of liberal opinion in Costa Rica, however much its aggressively pro-Nicaraguan position may have lost favor society-wide. This was perhaps most clearly revealed in the comparison of the mid-May public forum and demonstration for peace, led by major party progressives with left support as well, followed by the 31 May border incident in which two Civil Guardsmen were killed (*FBIS*, 1 August; *Inforpress Centroamericana*, 6, 13, 25 June, 6, 18 July, 8, 15 August). While the general national mood by that time had become anti-Nicaraguan, and nearly all major party leaders either condemned Nicaragua or, more appropriately, called for clarification of the facts of the matter, the PVP immediately blamed *contra* forces tolerated by the Costa Rican government for the killings, virtually absolving the Nicaraguan government of any and all blame (*FBIS*, 6, 12, 18 June).

On the perennial issue of their alleged "terrorist" or "subversive" character, the left parties counterattacked quite effectively by pointing to a rising tide of far-right activity, including for the first time in recent memory violent acts such as the stoning of the Nicaraguan embassy in San José after the May border incident and the rightist bombing of an electrical transmission line carrying power to Nicaragua. Much was made again this year of supposed Cuban or Nicaraguan military training of Costa Rican leftists. However, it has long been public knowledge that Costa Rican leftists have fought in Nicaragua, and the current round of speculation merely highlighted their potential for or alleged intent to provoke armed actions within Costa Rica, with no proof offered once again for such purposeful speculation in the press (*FBIS*, 25 March, 17 May, 23, 30 July, 2 August; *FPI International Report*, 8 May).

The question of how to deal with these charges of subversive and terrorist intent did lead to a division within the left. During May a new antiterrorist law was debated in the National Assembly, one which was supported by the two socialist deputies, Sergio Ardón (MNR) and Alvaro Montero (PSC), but opposed by PVP deputies Arnoldo Ferreto and Freddy Menéndez. Ardón moved that a commission be formed to investigate terrorist groups and acts, arguing that such a legislative commission would reveal the growing rightist threat and government complicity with *contra* forces and thus aid the cause of a left untinged by terrorist designs. The PVP deputies opposed both the idea of a commission and the subsequent proposed legislation on the grounds that in the currrent political climate these vehicles would be used by right-wing deputies and judges to persecute the left, regardless of its guilt or innocence, rather than revealing rightist groups' actions or terrorist organizations tied to these groups (*Libertad Revolucionaria*, 10–16 May; *JPRS*, 22 July).

One final area of PVP and left concern during 1985 was related to youth-oriented activities. The PVP's youth branch, the JVC, held its Fourth Congress in San José 26–28 April, with 210 national and 8 foreign delegates in attendance (*Libertad Revolucionaria*, 3–9 May). The PVP also took part in the August international youth festival in Moscow, sending four representatives, along with eight from other left parties and a total of some 60 nationwide. The participation of twelve representatives of the youth group of the ruling National Liberation Party (Partido Liberación Nacional; PLN) served as yet another pretext for the national daily, *La Nación*, to beat its anticommunist drums and undermine the position of its current major party nemesis, the PLN's presidential candidate Oscar Arias (*FBIS*, 25, 26 July).

Lowell Gudmundson
University of Oklahoma

Cuba

Population. 10,105,000
Party. Communist Party of Cuba (Partido Comunista de Cuba; PCC)
Founded. 1965
Membership. 434,143 (*WMR*, July 1981)
First Secretary. Fidel Castro Ruz
Politburo. 14 members: Fidel Castro Ruz, Raúl Castro Ruz (second secretary), Juan Almeida Bosque, Ramiro Valdés Menéndez, Guillermo García Frías, José Ramón Machado Ventura, Blas Roca Calderío, Carlos Rafael Rodríguez, Pedro Miret Prieto, Sergio del Valle Jiménez, Armando Hart Dávalos, Jorge Risquet Valdés, Julio Camacho Aguilera, Osmany Cienfuegos Gorrián; 9 alternate members.
Secretariat. 10 members: Fidel Castro Ruz, Raúl Castro Ruz, Sixto Batista Santana, Jaime Crombet Hernández-Baquero, Jorge Risquet Valdés, Lionel Soto Prieto, José Ramón Machado Ventura, Jesús Montané Oropesa, Julio Rizo Alvarez, José Ramón Balaguer
Central Committee. 148 members, 77 alternates (*Granma*, 5 April 1981)
Status. Ruling party
Last Congress. Second, 17–20 December 1981
Last Election. 1981, all 499 representatives PCC approved
Auxiliary Organizations. Union of Young Communists (Unión de Jóvenes Comunistas; UJC), Union of Cuban Pioneers (Unión de Pioneros de Cuba; UPC), Federation of Cuban Women (Federación de Mujeres Cubanas; FMC), Committees for the Defense of the Revolution (Comités de Defensa de la Revolución; CDR), Confederation of Cuban Workers (Confederación de Trabajadores de Cuba; CTC), National Association of Small Farmers (Asociación Nacional de Agricultores Pequeños; ANAP)
Publications. *Granma* (six days a week), official organ of the Central Committee; *Juventud Rebelde* (daily), organ of the UJC

The year 1985 saw the beginning of a major shakeup of government and party leadership and, possibly, of a generational turnover in the Cuban hierarchy. The government of Cuba also began 1985 with expectations for an improvement in relations with the United States, which continue to be of great importance for the country's economic and political life. At year's end, however, these relations were at a point of higher tension than at any time in the last decade, with little prospect for improvement soon.

Leadership and Party Organization. The first change in the PCC was made by the eleventh special plenary session of its Central Committee held 11

January in Havana and convened by the Politburo only a month after the tenth plenary meeting. The Central Committee "approved the proposal made by the Politburo to remove comrade Antonio Pérez Herrero from his post as alternate member of the Politburo and member of the Secretariat of the Central Commitee." This decision was made as a result of the analysis undertaken by the Politburo concerning "shortcomings and repeated errors in the fulfillment of his duties." Yet in view of "his many years of service in the party," Pérez Herrero was not stripped of his Central Committee membership (*Granma*, 10 February). Named to the Secretariat was José Ramón Balaguer, who relinquished his job as party first secretary in the Santiago de Cuba province; his current job is to oversee education, science, and sports.

To "improve the Party's work in the ideological and cultural spheres," the Central Committee named Politburo and Secretariat member Jorge Risquet Valdés as head of the Departments of Revolutionary Orientation and of Culture. The Advanced Party School became a separate department of the Central Committee and was placed under the supervision of another Politburo member, José R. Machado Ventura. The Central Committee also announced the creation of a new Department of Religious Affairs and named as its head José Felipe Corneado (ibid.). Other important party changes announced in January included the party secretary in Havana being switched to Santiago and the Havana post, vacated by Balaguer, going to Jorge Lezcano Pérez.

All these changes began a process in which older as well as incompetent party and government leaders were replaced by younger apparatchiki or technocrats. In the case of Pérez Herrero, the Central Committee removed "a group regarded as hardline and doctrinaire" (*NYT*, 3 February). For years, Pérez Herrero was in charge of the education and training of communist cadres on all levels, and his leadership and ideas were found to be "erroneous."

A few months after the ouster of Pérez Herrero, several of his friends were dismissed from high positions. Wilfredo Torres Yribar, president of the Academy of Science, was replaced by Rosa Elena Simón Negrín; Carlos Galván Vilo was removed as president of the National Institute for Sports, Physical Education, and Recreation and replaced by Conrado Martínez Corona as president, with Olympic middle-distance runner and gold medalist Alberto Juantorena as vice president; Nivaldo Herrera Sardiñas lost his job as president of the Cuban Institute of Radio and Television and was succeeded by Ismael González González.

In April, Cuba replaced two high officials in an apparent effort to revamp its failing economy. Francisco García Vals was replaced by Rodrigo García León as president of the State Finance Committee; and a communist provincial secretary, Roberto Oganda Zas, replaced Manuel Millares in the Light Industry Ministry, which supervises production of most consumer goods (*NYT*, 4 April).

Whereas party demotions and promotions were made by its Central Committee, government changes were made and announced by the Council of State of the Republic of Cuba, which heretofore has had a relatively minor role in the country's governance. The Council of State, whose president is Fidel Castro, is the organ of the National Assembly of People's Power (NAPP; elected every five years) that represents it in the periods between its two annual sessions. According to Article 87 of the Cuban Constitution, it is "the highest representative of the Cuban State." The Council of State has a president, a first vice president and five other vice presidents, a secretary, and 23 other members. (For a list of its powers, see *Granma*, 24 November.)

During the summer, the governmental shakeup continued. Politburo member Guillermo García Frías was released from his post as minister of transportation and replaced by Diocles Torralba González, a former top military commander. Antonio Rodríguez Maurell was named minister of the sugar industry, and the name of his predecessor in that key agency was not even mentioned in the announcement. Humberto Pérez González was removed from his post as vice president of the Council of Ministers and minister-president of the Central Planning Board, the agency in charge of the short- and long-range planning of the country's economy and of the execution of these plans. He was replaced by José López Moreno. The Council of State also named Raúl Cabrera Núñez as minister of construction. Most of the new appointees have been described as young technocrats (*NYT*, 2 July).

On 2 July, the twelfth plenum of the PCC's Central Committee was held. Possibly referring to changes in the party and the government, the communiqué of the session said that the plenum "analyzed the tense circumstances and great burden of work surrounding the preparations for the 3rd Congress, coinciding with other national and international tasks." In view of these tensions, the Central Committee decided to postpone the congress and hold it 4–7 February 1986 (*Granma*, 14 July).

In December Havana announced two new and important government changes. Sergio del Valle, Politburo member, left his post as public health minister and another Politburo member, Ramiro Valdés Menéndez, was replaced as interior minister by his deputy, Gen. José Abrahantes Fernández, who is also commander of Fidel Castro's personal guard. The Interior Ministry controls Cuba's internal and external police apparatus, uniformed police, and prisons, and it supervises operations of the CDR, whose strength as of October was 6,398,000 (*Granma*, 6 October). Valdés had a reputation as a hardliner in security matters and his removal was seen as an effort to "put a more humane face on the Revolution" (*Miami Herald*, 4 December). This was the second time that Valdés was removed from the Interior Ministry; the first was in 1968 when he was substituted by Sergio del Valle. Del Valle, a physician and one of the Castro Revolution veterans, moved to the Health Ministry in 1979 and Valdés was back in charge of the Interior Ministry. Now Valdés will supervise the electronics industry, according to the announcement of his dismissal. Another official replaced was Attorney General Idalberto Ladrón de Guevara, who headed the state prosecution office. His successor is Ramón de la Cruz Ochoa, formerly deputy minister of justice. In all it is believed that about 25 high-level party and government officials were replaced and perhaps ten times as many third- and fourth-level functionaries. It appears to be the most sweeping reorganization of the Castro regime in 20 years, and before the February congress more personnel shifts are expected. Although experts have not noticed any ideological change in the shakeup, it is evident that many younger, possibly better educated officials were promoted to posts of responsibility.

The Castrista Old Guard, which for more than 26 years has occupied principal posts in the party and government, has many members with limited formal education. A few of them might have acquired some executive experience, but reports from Cuba indicate that pressure has been building for years to replace them with a new generation of well-trained and educated leaders who did not participate in the Castro revolutionary struggle and who have not been able to attain top positions occupied by cronies of the Cuban president. Some observers also believe that Castro, who will be 60 in August 1986, is slowly preparing a succession to his unipersonal regime by strengthening the authority of his younger brother, Raúl. One casualty of the shakeup is Carlos Rafael Rodríguez, the 72-year-old Politburo member and vice president. Rodríguez, leader of the communist Old Guard in the Cuban regime, had been in charge of the Cuban economy—supervising central planning, banking, and most other economic ministries. Now he seems to have been removed from exercising these functions and his new duties have not been specified. Despite the changes, the Castro regime does not appear to have come to grips with a crucial issue of other communist states: the separation of government and party functions in running the country.

The Economy. The Cuban economy was affected in 1985 by continuing low prices of sugar, the country's principal export, by natural calamities, and by the perennial problems of low productivity and heavy bureaucratic control of virtually all activities. "After 26 years under Castro's leadership, Cuba's economy is nearly moribund, kept alive by a Soviet subsidy of $10 million a day," said a *Wall Street Journal* correspondent who visited Cuba in June. "A pair of shoes costs more than one third of an average monthly salary; a pair of jeans, more than half. The black market flourishes, and housing is in chronic short supply. Cuba's leading technological university has only 30 micro-computers for its 15,000 students" (*Miami Herald*, 24 June).

During most of the year, agricultural output was affected by a drought. Sugar production was 8.1 million tons, about 300,000 tons less than planned for the harvest that ended by mid-year. The 1985–1986 harvest was estimated at 7.2 million tons, half a million tons under the plan. Sugar prices on the world market, which fluctuated around 3 cents per pound, were much less than the Cuban cost of production. In November, hurricane Kate caused extensive damage to the drought-stricken farmland. Over 2.5 million acres of ripening sugar cane were destroyed or damaged. Kate was "the worst natural disaster to hit Cuba this century," according to Havana. It was reported that in seven provinces sugar cane would have to be cut and loaded by hand because the cane flattened by wind makes the use of machines practically impossible; industrial workers would have to be diverted to agriculture (*Granma*, 8 December).

The extent of the support given by the Soviet Union to the Cuban economy was recognized in a report by the Cuban National Bank prepared for the country's creditor banks. Havana disclosed that Moscow pays Cuba ten times the world price of sugar. At the same time, Cuba buys Soviet oil at prices near the world-market level, using some of it for re-export and sale for hard currency. In the document, Cuba's total debt to the West was placed at U.S. $3.42 billion. Its debt to the Soviet bloc was not mentioned but is estimated by American analysts at around U.S. $22 billion, the largest in per capita terms in Latin America. Other details mentioned in the report included reference to a decline in Cuba's trade with noncommunist countries from 22 percent in 1977–1980 to 13 percent in 1982–1984 (*NYT*, 5 June).

While Cuba has been urging other Latin countries to refuse paying their foreign debt, Havana has been paying interest on its debt to the West promptly, even though it did renegotiate payment terms. Internally, as of 1 July, the government began selling state-owned houses to their dwellers with the right to rent them, pass them to children, and obtain government loans for repairs. This small concession to market economy was done to free the government from the burden of fixing roofs and plumbing.

The new regulation enabling people to own their homes was the first change in Cuba's housing laws since 1960, the year after Castro took power. Under the 1960 law, the government seized tens of thousands of apartments and houses throughout Cuba from landlords. It permitted Cubans to retain possession of a primary residence and a vacation retreat, but title could not be transferred, and eventually the property became the state's. The government also seized houses and apartments as they were abandoned by Cubans who fled the communist system to live in other countries (ibid., 30 June).

In 1986, as a result of the failure to meet 1985 production goals for sugar and other exports, Cuba will reduce its outlays for the military and public security. According to the figures of the 1986 budget, military and security appropriations will be cut by $165 million to $1.43 billion. The report foresees growth of 3–3.5 percent for 1986, down from 4.8 percent in 1985 and 7.4 percent in 1984 (ibid., 12 December).

Cuban Armed Forces. Cuba increased its military presence abroad to 44,000. According to Western estimates, Cuba had 35,000 troops in Angola (30,000 combat troops and 5,000 advisers; Cuban troops continued to guard petroleum installations operated by American companies in Angola's Cabinda region); 5,500 in Ethiopia (2,500 combat troops and 3,000 advisers); between 2,500 and 3,500 in Nicaragua; 800 in Mozambique; 100 in Sao Tome; and 50 each in Guinea Bissau and Tanzania.

The country's military forces comprised an army with 130,000 soldiers and a 131,000 reserve; a Navy with 13,000 men and an Air Force with 18,500. Its territorial militia of 1,200,000 is to be expanded to 2 million (*Los Angeles Times*, 6 December). According to Elliot Abrams, assistant secretary of state for interamerican affairs, Cubans in Nicaragua have been moving beyond their former advisory role and participating in combat against anti-Sandinista guerrillas. The Managua government has denied that foreigners have been engaged in combat.

Foreign Relations. Cuba began the year expecting to improve relations with the United States. In December 1984, the two countries signed a wide-ranging agreement under which Havana agreed to take back 2,746 unwanted refugees from the United States, most of whom were criminals in federal prisons. On its part, the United States was to accept annually about 20,000 Cubans—families of those already in this country. The U.S. Interests Section in Havana was to be considerably expanded to process these new immigrants. U.S. and Cuban officials indicated in January that the accord could serve as a possible starting point for normalizing bilateral ties. U.S. congressmen who spoke in January with Fidel Castro said he was willing to discuss the withdrawal of Cuban troops from Africa and Nicaragua, a new antihijack pact, and the release of political prisoners in Cuba.

Cuban–U.S. relations deteriorated drastically on 20 May when the U.S.-sponsored Radio Martí, which is part of the Voice of America, began broadcasting to Cuba. Castro, in what many thought was an overreaction to the generally noncontroversial, factual programming of Radio Martí, called its inauguration a "cynical and provocative" attempt at subverting Cuba, and he suspended the December agreement. Soon, he and President Reagan traded some of their strongest insults in years. Reagan began by including Cuba in a list of five countries that he said formed a "confederation of terrorist states" run by "the strangest collection of misfits, Looney Tunes and squalid criminals since the advent of the Third Reich." Castro called Reagan "a big liar" and "a madman, an imbecile and a bum" who was "saying a bunch of stupidities and lunacies" (*NYT*, 20 August).

Cuba reportedly protested what it called "acts of arrogance perpetrated by the current U.S. administration," referring to three flights over Cuban territory in 1985 by USAF SR-71 Blackbird reconnaissance planes and six such flights since 1983.

In October the Reagan administration imposed new restrictions on the entry of Cuban officials into the United States. This action barred the entry of Cuban government and Communist Party officials unless they were coming exclusively to conduct business in the United Nations in New York or at the Cuban Interests Section in Washington. The new restriction would include officials coming into this country to make speeches or for business contacts (*NYT*, 9 October).

While Cuban–U.S. relations were deteriorating, Havana's ties with Latin America were improving. The process started with Castro's strong support for Argentina during the Falkland Islands war with Great Britain three years earlier, following which Argentina gave Cuba a $600 million loan to buy that country's products. In April, Ecuador's right-of-center president León Febres-Cordero paid a state visit to Cuba, and a month later U.N. secretary general Javier Pérez de Cuéllar also traveled to Havana. Without resuming formal ties, Colombian president Belisario Betancur reportedly often talks to Castro by telephone. Uruguay restored full relations with Cuba on 17 October and a few weeks later Peru followed suit. Brazil was also considering the reopening of a mission in Havana. In July the Latin American Parliament, an informal body of legislators from Latin American countries, overwhelmingly voted for Cuban membership. Only Paraguay and El Salvador voted no.

Possibly to ingratiate himself with Latin American governments that were confronting the problem of liquidity, Castro began an intensive campaign early in the year against the International Monetary Fund and U.S. banks; he claims that their pressure on Hemispheric countries to repay their $360 billion debt was tantamount to an "imperialist aggression." In January he forgave a $70 million debt owed Cuba by Nicaragua for construction of a sugar mill. Initially, Castro suggested that the Latin American debt should be paid to the American banks by the U.S. government, which, for that purpose, should reduce its military budget by 12 percent. Later, Castro began urging Latins to declare the debt null and void.

In July, Castro hosted a five-day conference whose theme was "The Latin American Debt Is Unpayable." About 1,200 people, mostly members of the Hemisphere's left, flew to Havana at the government's expense. No Latin country sent senior government officials to the conference despite Castro's personal invitation. On 12–14 June, before the conference, representatives of Latin American and Caribbean communist parties met in Havana to "exchange information and views on the grave economic crisis" affecting the nations of the region (*Granma*, 23 June).

Castro's relations with the newly elected president of Peru, Alan García Pérez, did not begin in a friendly fashion, although by the end of the year the differences appeared to have been smoothed over. García, in his July inauguration speech, announced his foreign debt repayment plan under which Latin countries would pay 10 percent of their export earnings. The García plan, which found wide support in the Hemisphere's leftist circles, irritated Castro, who ridiculed it publicly. Ironically, as U.S. officials pointed out, Castro's posture was somewhat hypocritical: at the time when he was urging Latin governments not to repay their debts, his own regime was renegotiating Cuba's payments for its debt.

Castro did not travel to the Soviet Union to Konstantin U. Chernenko's funeral, although the Cuban leader had met him in 1984 when he attended the funeral of Yuri A. Andropov in Moscow. His brother, Raúl, attended Chernenko's funeral instead and met the new general secretary Mikhail Gorbachev.

Visitors to Cuba. Among prominent visitors to Cuba in 1985 were: President Chaddi Bendjedid of Algeria; President Julius K. Nyerere of Tanzania, who visited Cuba for the third time since 1974; Polish Communist leader Wojciech Jaruzelski; Prime Minister Robert Mugabe of Zimbabwe; and President Kenneth Kaunda of Zambia. The African leaders are customarily taken to the Nenrik Witbooi School on the Isle of Youth where close to 12,000 African youths are studying under a Cuban full-scholarship program.

State-Church Relations. A delegation of U.S. Catholic bishops visited Cuba in January and met with Castro. Havana said that the bishops favored lifting the U.S. embargo on trade with Cuba and supported the normalization of U.S.–Cuban relations, which the Cuban bishops also endorsed. Shortly afterward, Havana said that José Corneado, the 69-year-old head of the Department of Religious Affairs of the party's Central Committee, met with a delegation of Cuban bishops and began a dialogue that continued throughout the year. Archbishop

Jaime Lucas Ortega Alamino of Havana, commenting on these contacts, said that "the situation has gotten better and I think it is going to get better" (*NYT*, 29 May). In November seven bishops met again with Vice President and Politburo member Carlos Rafael Rodríguez and Corneado, who also met separately with representatives of various protestant churches. This latter delegation was headed by the Reverend Adolfo Ham, president of the Cuban Ecumenical Council (*Granma*, 24 November). There were reports that Castro has indicated to Cuban bishops who assisted the Extraordinary Synod in Rome later in the year, that he would like Pope John Paul II to visit Cuba. Castro, educated by the Jesuits, was reported to have called the Pope a "noteworthy politician" and said that religion "is not necessarily the opiate of the people."

George Volsky
University of Miami

Dominican Republic

Population. 6,588,000
Party. Dominican Communist Party (Partido Comunista Dominicano; PCD)
Founded. 1944
Membership. 500–1,000
Secretary General. Narciso Isa Conde
Central Committee. 27 members
Status. Legal
Last Congress. Third, 15–17 March 1984
Last Election. 1982, 7.1 percent, no representation
Auxiliary Organizations. No data
Publications. *Hablan los Comunistas* (weekly)

Economic difficulties continued to affect life in the Dominican Republic. In addition, political divisionism, which for years has been a trademark of the Marxist left, spread to government and opposition parties. Although the general elections were scheduled for 16 May 1986, by the end of 1985 Dominicans still did not know who would be the presidential candidate of the ruling left-of-center Dominican Revolutionary Party (PRD).

The PRD, in office since 1978, has been split into two factions. President Salvador Jorge Blanco originally supported a faction headed by Jacobo Majluta, president of the Senate, whose bid for the party's presidential nomination is contested by the mayor of Santo Domingo, José Francisco Peña Gómez. However, Blanco later switched his endorsement to Peña Gómez.

At the same time, the PCD—the principal Marxist group—and the Socialist Bloc (Bloque Socialista; BS) have decided to enter independent presidential candidates in the May 1986 elections even though they and several other leftist groups belong to the Dominican Leftist Front (Frente de Izquierda Dominicana; FID). The remaining members of the FID might boycott the vote altogether.

The main opposition parties—the Reformist Social Christian Party (Partido Reformista Social Cristiano; PRSC) and the Dominican Liberation Party (Partido de la Liberación Dominicana; PLD)—have nominated their presidential candidates. The PRSC's slate will be headed by former president Jaoquín Balaguer and that of the PLD by another ex-president, Juan Bosch.

The rift in the ruling PRD has become so deep and bitter that Majluta has stated that he would be a presidential candidate even if he had to resign from his party and form another one should the PRD choose Peña Gómez. The partisans of the Santo Domingo mayor have clashed on the streets of the city with those of Majluta. To make the situation more complicated, there were reports that President Blanco was encouraging Peña Gómez and Majluta to fight for the nomination and defeat each other in the process, so that he, Blanco, would be asked by the party to run for re-election. There are no legal impediments for the president to do so, but in the past the PRD has been a strong opponent of presidential re-election, and during his 1982 campaign Blanco promised to abolish second term for president.

The PCD's secretary general, Narciso Isa Conde, was named the communist presidential candidate, but the BS's candidate was not immediately known. The disarray in the FID was such that two small groups, the Dominican Workers Party (Partido de Trabajadores Dominicanos; PTD) and the Anti-Imperialist Patriotic Union (Unión Patriotica Anti-Imperialista), said they would leave the alliance. There was also a possibility that in the last moment two leftist candidates would withdraw and support the presidential bid of Juan Bosch, who was known for his backing of leftist causes. But Bosch's erratic behavior and his age—he is in his 80's—were his more visible handicaps. Similarly, Joaquín Balaguer, the figurehead president under dictator Leonidas Trujillo who also served as president between 1970 and 1978, is blind. Many observers believe that the 1986 elections represent a last chance for democracy in the Dominican Republic, which they say is in peril because of the country's economic crisis and social unrest (*Los Angeles Times*, 25 August).

The country's political developments were taking place against a background of its perennial economic crisis and widespread popular discontent fueled by high unemployment, which is estimated between 25 and 30 percent, and an increase in prices of most consumer goods. At the beginning of 1985, the Dominican central bank found itself without foreign currency. Only an emergency $50 million grant from the U.S. government and Venezuela's help in deferring payments for petroleum imports averted a calamitous stoppage of all imports.

Since 1984 the Dominican government has been negotiating with the International Monetary Fund (IMF) over the conditions of interest payments on its $3 billion foreign debt. The IMF advised the government to drastically reduce imports and devalue the Dominican peso, among other economic measures. Some of these were put into effect, causing riots in various parts of the country in which almost 90 persons were killed. Although President Blanco retained most of the belt-tightening measures, among them a 48 percent rise in fuel prices, inflation in 1985 was 25 percent for the second year in a row.

A general strike on 11 February demanded a break with the IMF and the restoration of lower petroleum prices, but the government stood firm. In July, confronted with the threat of another 48-hour general strike by all the trade-union groups, President Blanco approved a raise in minimum salary, from $58 to $83 per month, and other wage increases that the Dominican Congress had passed and he had threatened to veto.

The Reagan administration was watching Dominican events with keen interest. There was concern in Washington over the economic situation in the country, which has traditionally had close ties with the United States. U.S. troops, as the main part of a force of the Organization of American States, intervened in the country in 1965 to end a civil war and, at the same time, to prevent a left-wing pro-Castro regime from taking over.

Although Marxist groups were making every effort to take advantage politically of the Dominican economic crisis, they were not succeeding either to gain strength or even to unite their fragmented and constantly quarreling ranks. Some 30 extreme-left organizations, most with a few dozen members each, continued to operate legally in the country. In all, these groups are said to have about 5,000 members. Some observers believe that the failure of the left to unite is due to two principal factors: the lack of a charismatic leader who could coalesce most Marxist factions, and the argumentative, divisive character of the country's political life in the last two decades, a reaction to the end of the bloody 30-year dictatorship of Gen. Rafael Trujillo, who was assassinated in 1961.

Leaders of the Marxist left, many of whom have held their positions for decades, have not been able to come up with any fresh ideas. The Cuban and

Soviet political and economic line, which is publicized by a few local Marxist publications, has little acceptance even among the country's leftists. The failure of the Cuban economic model is generally known to the Dominicans.

The FID, formed in 1983 in an attempt to unite all leftist factions, includes the PCD, the BS, the PTD, the Anti-Imperialist Patriotic Union, the Revolutionary Communist League (Liga Comunista Revolucionaria), and the Movement for Socialism (Movimiento pro Socialismo). The BS comprises the Socialist Party (Partido Socialista), the Socialist Workers Movement (Movimiento Socialista de Trabajadores), and the Communist Workers Nucleus (Núcleo Comunista de Trabajadores).

George Volsky
University of Miami

Ecuador

Population. 8,884,000

Party. Communist Party of Ecuador (Partido Comunista Ecuatoriano; PCE; pro-Moscow, participates in elections as part of the Frente Amplio de Izquierda coalition, FADI); Marxist-Leninist Communist Party of Ecuador (PCE-ML; pro-Beijing, participates in elections as the Movimiento Popular Democrático, MPD); Revolutionary Socialist Party of Ecuador (Partido Socialista Revolucionario; PSRE; pro-Havana, participates in elections as part of FADI).

Founded. PCE: 1928; PCE-ML: 1972; PSRE: 1962

Membership. PCE: 500; PCE-ML: 100; PSRE: 200 (all estimated)

Secretary General. PCE: René Mauge Mosquera; MPD: Jaime Hurtado (National Director)

Central Committee. PCE: Milton Jijón Saavedra, José Solís Castro, Efraín Alvarez Fiallo, Bolívar Bolanos Sánchez, Ghandi Burbano Burbano, Xavier Garaycoa Ortíz, Alfredo Castillo, Freddy Almeidau (*YICA*, 1985)

Status. Legal

Last Congress. PCE: Tenth, 27–29 November 1981, in Guayaquil

Last Election. 29 January 1984; FADI, 3.6 percent, 2 of 71 seats; MPD: 6.1 percent, 3 of 71 seats.

Auxiliary Organizations. PCE: Ecuadorean Workers' Confederation (Confederación de Trabajadores del Ecuador; CTE) comprises about 20 percent of organized workers; Ecuadorean University Students' Federation (Federación de Estudiantes Universitarios del Ecuador; FEUE); Ecuadorean Indian Federation (Federación Ecuatoriana de Indios; FEI)

Publications. PCE: *El Pueblo*; MPD: *Patria Nueva* (Director: Franciso Hidalgo)

The concerted efforts of the conservative government of President León Febres-Cordero to undermine the position of parties on the left and center proved successful in 1985. In addition to weakening the institutional role of Congress in the policymaking process, the Febres-Cordero government was able to induce a realignment of party alliances that split the majority opposition bloc in Congress and created a new progovernment ruling coalition. Opposition leaders such as Congressmen Jorge Moreno (MPD) and Efraín Alvarez Fiallo (FADI) viewed with alarm Febres-Cordero's aggrandizement of executive power and undermining of the opposition; they feared the development of a new hybrid "democratic-authoritarian" regime, one that would concentrate all effective power within the office of the presidency while maintaining a facade of constitutionality.

Opposition leaders depicted the development of an imperial presidency as the political sine qua non for the imposition of the neoliberal economic program that Febres-Cordero espoused during his 1984 presidential campaign. By the end of 1985, tentative moves toward the implementation of such a program had been taken. These included resisting dramatic wage increases, an aggressive program to attract foreign investment, and a shift in developmental priorities toward large-scale export industry and away from internally oriented import-substitution industries.

Domestic Affairs. After the slim victory of Febres-Cordero in the presidential elections of 1984, the opposition parties in Congress united to form the Frente Progresista (FP) bloc and vowed to oppose the neoliberal economic program of the new government. Joining the congressmen from the MPD and FADI in Frente Progresista were the other center-left parties: Izquierda Democrática (ID), Democracia Popular (DP), and Partido Democrata (PD) (*Hoy*, 12 July). Although not an official member of the FP, the regionally based Frente Radical Alfarista (FRA) of Guayaquil also sided with the principles espoused by the opposition majority.

The progovernment parties in Congress were grouped together as the Frente de Reconstrucción Nacional (FRN) and included the Partido Social Cristiano (PSC), the Partido Conservador Ecuatoriano (PC), the Partido Liberal Radical (PLR), and the Partido Nacionalista Revolucionario (PNR). These parties, along with the miniscule Coalicción Institucionalista Democrata, had composed the electoral coalition that supported the Febres-Cordero candidacy. While officially maintaining an independent stance, the populist party of Guayaquil, Concentración de Fuerzas Populares (CFP), informally cooperated with the progovernment forces in Congress during 1984.

Faced with a center-left opposition majority in Congress, the Febres-Cordero government engaged in an all-out campaign to undermine the unity of the opposition as well as undercut its ability to use Congress to obstruct presidential initiatives.

Confrontational-style tactics and clashes over the constitutionality of executive and legislative actions continued through the first half of 1985. By an emergency decree designed to circumvent a congressional bill, President Febres-Cordero was able to undercut the FP's efforts to raise the monthly minimum wage to S/10,000; he enacted a more moderate increase that raised the standard to S/8,500 (*Weekly Analysis of Ecuadorean Issues*, 11, 18 March). In addition to the salary controversy were conflicts over the jurisdiction of the Constitutional Tribunal and appointments to the Superintendency of Banks and the Electoral Tribunal (ibid., 4 July).

By August, the FP had crumbled under the relentless attacks. While the FADI and MPD deputies remained firmly within the ranks of the FP, desertions from other parties—such as the PD, ID, DP, and FRA—eroded the FP majority. The voting power of the congressional FP bloc was pared to 33, in contrast to the 38 votes accumulated by the FRN. The new constellation of forces was reflected in the August elections, which installed a progovernment leadership in Congress. Averroes Bucaram, leader of the CFP, was elected as the new president of Congress; Iván Castro of the FRA became vice president. With the FRN-CFP-FRA alliance in place, the government introduced bills aimed at restructuring the Supreme Court that would allow for new appointments by the progovernment majority and a freeze of that majority through a suspension of the scheduled 1986 congressional elections (ibid., 30 September). All in all, by the end of 1985 the opposition's fears of a dictatorship under the guise of constitutionality did not seem far-fetched.

Auxiliary Organizations. The CTE joined with the other major labor confederations (CEOSL and CEDOC) in organizing demonstrations against the neoliberal economic initiatives of the Febres-Cordero government. Two general strikes were organized by the umbrella association that unites the three confederations, the Frente Unitario de Trabjadores (FUT). The first 48-hour strike began on 7 January and ended in violent clashes between police and demonstrators. The second 24-hour strike was called by the FUT for 27 March. The purpose of this strike was to protest the president's veto of the FP's minimum-wage bill. Joining the FUT in demonstrations was the People's Front organization, composed of student, peasant, worker, and teacher associations (Spanish News Agency, 26 March; *FBIS*, 28 March). In addition to confrontations with the police, FUT charged the government with the use of paramilitary bands to attack demonstrators (*El Pueblo*, 29 March–4 April). These charges were in line with previous accusations made by the left that the government was actively organizing paramilitary units to intimidate the opposition. Ex-president Osvaldo Hurtado charged the government with responsibility for an attack on the headquarters of his DP party (*Weekly Analysis of Ecuadorean Issues*, 25 January).

Guerrilla Activity. The five-year-old guerrilla organization known as Alfaro Vive! (named after Ecuador's famous liberal leader of the nineteenth century) showed signs of developing into the most serious movement of its kind in contemporary Ecuadorean history. The temporary seizure of a radio station in Guayaquil was followed by a sensational escape of Alfaro guerrillas from Quito's Garcia Moreno penitentiary (AFP, 27 March; *FBIS*, 28 March; *Weekly Analysis of Ecuadorean Issues*, 6 September). The regional director of the Agrarian Reform Institute, Jose Piedra, was kidnapped and released after the guerrillas publicized their calls for agrarian reform (Voz de los Andes, 2 May; *FBIS*, 8 May). The guerrillas briefly occupied the Mexican embassy in Quito for the purpose of sending a telex message to the Contadora group protesting the breaking of diplomatic relations between the governments of Ecuador and Nicaragua (Spanish News Agency, 16 October; *FBIS*, 16 October).

The most audacious action staged by the Alfaro group was the August kidnapping of the wealthy Guayaquileño businessman, Nahím Isaías. Isaías was seized by guerrillas in his weekend home outside of Guayaquil. Police raids in search of the kidnappers produced arrests and at least two deaths. Isaías and the kidnappers were finally located by police in a house in the working-class district of La Chala. In the negotiations for the release of Isaías, the guerrillas demanded the release of imprisoned Alfaro members, $5 million ransom, and a plane to transport them to Nicaragua. President Febres-Cordero intervened, took personal control over the negotiations, and offered the guerrillas only the opportunity to surrender. When they refused, an assault on the house was ordered. Isaías and the remaining four guerrillas were killed during the assault (*Weekly Analysis of Ecuadorean Issues*, 6 September; *NYT*, 3 September).

Although opposition parties repudiated the actions of Alfaro Vive!, President Febres-Cordero intimated that the opposition leaders were soft on terrorism and were therefore creating a climate conducive to incidents such as the Isaías affair. Febres-Cordero was especially disturbed by the decision of the Constitutional Tribunal (chaired by PCE leader Edgar Ponce) to put time limits on the investigations of suspects by police. René Mauge Mosquera, secretary general of the PCE, responded by declaring that his party "rejects and condemns" terrorist acts and denouncing the government for its attempt to link the political opposition to Alfaro Vive! (*Weekly Analysis of Ecuadorean Issues*, 6 September).

There was no evidence of any link between Alfaro and the legal political opposition, but there were numerous reports of cooperation and coordination between Alfaro and Colombia's M-19 guerrilla movement. At least five Colombians were reported to be involved in the Isaías kidnapping and Colombian military sources disclosed that M-19 guerrillas were training Alfaro recruits in the Cauca region of Colombia (*Weekly Analysis of Ecuadorean Issues*, 6 September; *Washington Times*, 1 August).

International Views and Positions. President Febres-Cordero's stringent anticommunism and his commitment to neoliberal economic principles were clearly reflected in his conduct of foreign and trade policies during 1985 (*Weekly Analysis of Ecuadorean Issues*, 10 December).

Tentative moves toward improving relations with some communist-bloc countries were overshadowed by the deterioration of relations with Nicaragua and the strengthening of ties to the United States. Febres-Cordero made an unexpected trip to Cuba for talks with President Fidel Castro (*CSM*, 15 April). In a ceremony commemorating the fortieth anniversary of the establishment of diplomatic relations between the USSR and Ecuador, Undersecretary of Foreign Relations Diego Paredes declared the commitment of the Febres-Cordero administration to maintain an "open dialogue with the USSR, in order to strengthen our relations" (Voz de los Andes, 18 June; *FBIS*, 21 June). However, these gestures were accompanied by the development of closer relations with the United States. On 28 February, U.S. Secretary of State George Schultz met with Febres-Cordero and delivered an official invitation for a future meeting with President Reagan. On an unofficial trip to the United States in April, Febres-Cordero met and made public appearances with Vice President George Bush. Senator Richard G. Lugar, chair of the Senate Foreign Relations Committee, held discussions with Febres-Cordero in Quito and was reported to have been sympathetic toward channeling more aid to Ecuador (*Weekly Analysis of Ecuadorean Issues*, 21 October).

Febres-Cordero aligned his government even more closely with the Reagan administration when he broke off diplomatic relations with Nicaragua in October. The already strained relations between Quito and Managua came to a head as the Febres-Cordero government considered participation in the Contadora support group being formed by Brazil, Argentina, Uruguay, and Peru. With this question on the agenda, Febres-Cordero made remarks to the press that questioned the legitimacy of the 1984 elections in Nicaragua; he argued that violence and intimidation had produced the Sandinista electoral victory (*El Comercio*, 9 October). President Daniel Ortego of Nicaragua immediately lashed back, calling Febres-Cordero "a tool of the U.S." and accusing him of violating Ecuador's constitution because of his suspension of municipal elections. Citing Ortega's response, the Foreign Ministry of Ecuador issued an official communique severing diplomatic and consular relations with Nicaragua. In comments to the press, Foreign Minister Edgar Teran stressed that the decision was not the product of ideological or political differences with Nicaragua, but a "simple and natural response to rudeness" that could be remedied by an apology (Radio Quito, 11 October; *FBIS*, 15 October). Opposition leaders in Ecuador criticized the administration for its impulsiveness and recklessness in the handling of the incident (*Weekly Analysis of Ecuadorean Issues*, 21 October).

By the end of 1985, the Febres-Cordero government had effectively eroded the position of the opposition forces, including FADI and the MPD. Given the likely suspension of municipal and midterm congressional elections in 1986, opposition parties face the likelihood of a continued marginalization from the policymaking process. With the opposition defused, the Febres-Cordero administration is fashioning public policies based on orthodox economic formulas and a strong commitment to anticommunism.

Catherine M. Conaghan
Ohio State University

El Salvador

Population. 5,072,000

Marxist-Leninist Groups. The Farabundo Martí Front of National Liberation (Frente Farabundo Martí de Liberación Nacional; **FMLN**) is the armed Marxist-Leninist movement currently at war with government forces. It is composed of the following movements, with their leaders indicated: the Popular Liberation Forces (Fuerzas Populares de Liberación; **FPL**), Leonel González, with Dimas Rodríguez second in command; the People's Revolutionary Army (Ejército Popular Revolucionario; **ERP**), Joaquín Villalobos, with Ana Guadalupe Martínez, Ana Sonia Medina Arriola ("Mariana"), Mercedes del Carmen Letona ("Luisa"), Claudio Rabindranath Armijo ("Francisco"), Juan Ramon Medrano ("Balta"), and Jorge Melendez ("Jonas"); the Armed Forces of National Resistance (Fuerzas Armadas de Resistencia Nacional; **FARN**), Fermán Cienfuegos (real name Eduardo Sancho Casteñeda); the Communist Party of El Salvador (Partido Comunista de El Salvador; **PCES**), Shafik Jorge Handal; the Revolutionary Party of Central American Workers (Partido Revolucionario de Trabajadores de Centroamerica; **PRTC**), Robert Roca, with Jaime Miranda, Mario Gonzales ("Mario"), Ismael Dimas Aguilar ("Ulysses"), Maria Concepcion de Valladares ("Nidia Díaz"), and Fabio Castillo Figueroa. These groups participate equally in the governing body known as the United Revolutionary Directorate (Directorio Revolucionario Unificada; **DRU**).

The Political Arm. The Democratic Revolutionary Front (Frente Democrático Revolucionario; **FDR**), an umbrella group of those opposing the government and headquartered in Mexico City, includes the five DRU groups as well as the minute National Revolutionary Movement (Movimiento Nacional Revolucionario; **MNR**), a social-democratic party until 1980, and a small splinter group of the ruling Christian Democrats, the Popular Social Christian Movement (Movimiento Popular Social Cristiano; **MPSC**). The FDR has no control over the military operations of the FMLN, and its role is essentially that of a highly visible propaganda outlet for the latter, largely directed toward the Western and Third World countries (*ORBIS*, winter, pp. 9–20).

Founded. FDR: 1980

Membership. N/a

The Political-Diplomatic Commission of the FDR. Guillermo Manual Ungo (chairman; MNR), Rubén Zamora (MPSC), Fabio Castillo Figueroa (PRTC), José Napoleón Rodríguez Ruiz (FARN), Mario Aguiñada Carranza (PCES), Salvador Samayoa (FPL), Ana Guadalupe Martínez (ERP), Héctor Oqueli (MNR)

Fronts and Auxiliary Organizations. FPL: The People's Revolutionary Bloc (BPR); ERP: The Party of the Salvadoran Revolution (PRS), the Popular Leagues 28th of February (LP-28); FARN: The United People's Action Front (FAPU); PCES: The Armed Forces of Liberation (FAL), Nationalist Democratic Union (UDN); PRTC: Popular Liberation Movement (MLP)

Status. Illegal

Congresses. FPL: Seventh Revolutionary Council, August 1983; ERP-PRS: general plenum, July 1981; PCES: Seventh, April 1979

Publications. *Venceremos* (published abroad); *Senal de Libertad* (published in Mexico City); the FDR has occasional access to the FMLN-controlled Radio Farabundo Marti and Radio Venceremos. In addition, *El Rebelde* (FPL; irregular); *Farabundo Martí Weekly Informative* (FPL; for external propaganda); *Weekly Popular Combat* (FPL-BPR; published abroad); *Juan Angel Chacón Bulletin* (FPL-BPR); *Pueblo Internacional* (FARN; irregular); *Parte de Guerra* (FARN); *Voz Popular* (PCES; irregular); *Fundamentos y Perspectivas* (PCES).

Political Developments. The municipal and legislative assembly elections in El Salvador were the main political events of the year. Originally scheduled for 17 March, they were not held until 31 March. Before the elections, the conservative parties held a 36 to 24 majority in the legislature. Despite predictions to the contrary, President Napoleón Duarte's Christian Democrats succeeded in gaining 53.9 percent of the popular vote (*Los Angeles Times*, 2 April) and, for the first time ever, a majority of 33 deputies in the legislature as well as the mayoralty of San Salvador (*CSM*, 5 April). The elections also resulted in a change in the leadership of the leading conservative party, the National Republican Alliance (ARENA). Hugo Barrera, ARENA's vice presidential candidate in 1984, left the party and established his own organization; Roberto D'Aubuisson, ARENA's controversial founder and presidential contender, gave way as leader to technocrat and businessman Alfredo Cristiani. These developments increased the tensions between ARENA and its electoral ally, the National Conciliation Party (PCN).

Throughout the year, Duarte managed to enjoy a number of successes. He convinced the United States to continue its massive military, economic, and diplomatic support to El Salvador, and he obtained West European economic aid. In addition, Duarte re-established diplomatic relations with Mexico, which leveled a serious blow to the FDR political and diplomatic struggle.

Despite these successes, however, Duarte's position weakened. This was due to the government's lack of clear economic policies, which alienated businessmen, workers, and peasants; the president's growing concentration of power; the continuing uncertainty regarding the outcome of the civil war and/or government intentions concerning negotiations with the FMLN-FDR; and the manner in which the government handled the kidnapping of Duarte's daughter, Inez Duarte Durán, by the FMLN.

Militarily, the war in 1985 followed patterns established since the second half of 1984. The Salvadoran army grew more aggressive and began to search for the guerrillas rather than wait for their attacks. More effective and comprehensive anti-insurgency tactics were employed in certain areas, particularly in Chalatenango, where the return of Colonel Sigifredo Ochoa as departmental commander threatened the very existence of the FPL "liberated areas." Anti-insurgency mobilization in the war zones began timidly and included the formation of self-defense paramilitary groups. In addition, the rapidly expanding Salvadoran Air Force (from 19 to over 60 helicopters in less than eighteen months) grew much more effective and forced the FMLN to divide their units into small groups and to fight at night. These efforts were underscored by the FDR's most recent propaganda target, the "indiscriminate bombing of civilians." Finally, a large number of top-level guerrilla leaders were either killed in action (for example, commander "Arlen" of the PRTC) or captured (for example, "Nidia Díaz," top-ranking PRTC leader, and Américo Mauro Araujo Ramírez, second in command of the PCES armed branch, FAL).

On the FMLN side, the war also demonstrated changes in tactics. Most important were the decreasing size of operating units, due to the threat of air attacks during the day as well as at night, and a shift back to urban operations, which had been discontinued since late 1980. Not surprising, the two smallest FMLN members, the PCES and the PRTC, were in the forefront of the "return to the city" strategy, since their cadres are almost exclusively urban and thus not adapted to rural warfare. This new strategy resulted in the slow but steady fragmentation of the FMLN's largest regular warfare unit—ERP's "Rafael Antonio Arce Zablah Brigade" (BRAZ)—into smaller units (commandos), and the creation of PRTC's "Mardoqueo Cruz Urban Commandos" and PCES's "Pablo Castillo" Metropolitan Front. The latter two units, as well as the older, renegade "Clara Elisabeth Ramírez" Metropolitan Front (CERMF), a splinter of the FPL, may have had as many as 500 fighters and a few thousands sympathizers in San Salvador during the year. They clearly stole the headlines from the far larger forces in the countryside. From both the PCES and PRTC viewpoint (the latter is increasingly seen as infiltrated by the former), urban terrorism is a shortcut toward competition in the military realm with the far larger FPL, ERP, and FARN.

Throughout the year military operations combined large-scale army actions against guerrilla concentrations, for example, on Guazapa Hill in January, and were answered by ERP attacks against cotton plantations (*FBIS*, 23 January, pp. 3–4). While the army gained free access into most of Morazán and Chalatenango, areas previously under FMLN control, the guerrillas spilled over into some of the western departments seldom touched by the war in the past (*NYT*, 24 January). Disputed "pockets" of border territory with Honduras allowed the FMLN to retain some presence in the remote areas of Morazán and Chalatenango, while inhibiting the Salvadoran military—or the Hondurans—from reacting. For public relations reasons, both sides accepted a truce for the child vaccination campaign in January (*JPRS-LAM*, 12 February, p. 114), but afterwards the FMLN economic sabotage campaign continued, concentrating on the electric grid and the public and private transportation networks (ibid., 13 February, p. P2).

The urban operations of the FMLN and CERMF became much more intense and frequent throughout the year. Aside from spectacular terrorist actions, they also resulted in a few direct military clashes, such as that of 21 February following an attack on the PCN headquarters in downtown San Salvador (ibid., 21 February, p. P6). As a rule, however, urban terror operations involved small groups and avoided as much as possible any clash with security forces. When such attacks did occur, as in the case of the rocket attack against the National Police general headquarters on 28 March (an attempt to disrupt the coming elections), they were indiscriminate and killed more civilians than security forces (ibid., 29 March, p. P4). The headquarters of the National Police was the specific target of the BRAZ.

In the rural areas, particularly in Chalatenango, the military commanders broke with the convenient "body count" approach, and Ochoa himself proudly mentioned only small but repeated clashes with the guerrillas (ibid., 23 May, p. P4). By midyear the Salvadoran military as well as the U.S. media optimistically predicted a decisive turn in the conduct of war, in favor of the military. Such predictions, like the opposite ones at the end of 1983, seem premature. However, the military's growing effectiveness was demonstrated by the half-year casualty figures, which show that only 2,834 soldiers were killed or wounded between June 1984 and June 1985, compared to 3,108 casualties the year before. This decrease occurred despite the dramatic increase in army activities, numbers, and self-initiated operations (*NYT*, 14 July, p. 1). The March elections themselves demonstrated a decline in the FMLN's ability to disrupt or control significant areas, since 97 percent of the municipalities were able to vote (*FBIS*, 1 August, p. P5). As for guerrilla casualties, Defense Minister Vides Casanova claimed that, although there were some 11,000–

12,000 FMLN fighters in 1983, only 6,000–6,500 remained in July 1985, a figure largely accepted by external observers (ibid., 1 August, p. P7). Even from a human-rights policy viewpoint, the FMLN and the military began receiving balanced review or blame from such different groups as the Americas Watch and the Salvadoran Catholic Church. The guerrillas were blamed for forced recruitment, killing civilians in San Salvador, political assassinations, and economic sabotage (*Los Angeles Times*, 13 September). Road traffic disruptions, and particularly the destruction of private and public buses by the guerrillas, helped to decrease the already limited public support of the FMLN-FDR in the countryside. The San Salvador terror killings created an atmosphere of fear strongly disliked by all but the most committed Leninists among the civilian population, and even the Church publicly expressed its disfavor through the office of San Salvador's archbishop, Arturo Rivera y Damas.

The largest attack by FMLN forces against the Salvadoran military occurred on 10 October, when the BRAZ, led by "Jonas," attacked the Training Center of La Unión. The ERP claimed as many as 200 army casualties, while the military admitted 42 killed and 68 wounded, as against at least nine guerrillas dead (*FBIS*, 11 October, pp. P1–3).

Terrorism. Throughout the year the left has aimed attacks at individuals, whether politicians or civilians and military leaders, in San Salvador and in the countryside. The ERP in particular concentrated on local elected officials in the northern and eastern departments. Immediately after the election, scores of village and small-town mayors were kidnapped; most were Christian Democrats but some were ARENA and PCN members. The ERP killed at least three mayors, dozens of civilians, and members of the fledgling civil-defense forces. Quite clearly this kidnapping and killing of elected officials was part of the ERP's psychological campaign to show the peasants the military's inability to protect them. The attacks on civilians and civil-defense members also discouraged the population from joining army-controlled organizations or from leaving guerrilla areas. Some of the kidnapped mayors were offered release for ransom or in exchange for the growing number of FMLN cadres captured by government forces.

While the ERP conducted its rural terror campaign, terrorist activities in the capital increased sharply, with the PCES, PRTC, and CERMF the most active. On 7 March the CERMF claimed responsibility for the murder of Colonel Ricardo Aristides Cienfuegos, the army's press spokesman (*Latin America Weekly Report* [*LAWR*], 22 March, p. 2), on a tennis court in the center of the capital. Interestingly, the CERMF took "credit" in the name of the FPL, probably with the intention of forcing FPL's hand since the murder occurred only a few weeks before the fifteenth anniversary of the FPL founding (*FBIS*, 12 March, p. P1). On 23 March retired general Jose Alberto "Chele" Medrano was also gunned down in San Salvador by the CERMF, as part of the same "Long Live the Fifteen Years of Prolonged People's Warfare" terror campaign. Medrano was a former presidential candidate, a war hero of 1969, and the founder of the paramilitary organization ORDEN in the late 1960s. ORDEN was one of the major reasons that leftist guerrillas were an unsuccessful threat in El Salvador until the late 1970s and are still largely inactive in the western half of the country. The CERMF's historical revenge campaign can be traced to 8 January when a former policeman, Manuel de Jesus Flores Mateo, accused by the group of having tortured the FPL founder Salvador Cayetano Carpio, was murdered in San Salvador (ibid., 11 January, p. P3).

The CERMF actions were strictly political in origin. Their primary goals were to humiliate the government, by proving its inability to protect its own supporters, and the FMLN (particularly the FPL), by demonstrating the effectiveness of urban terror and CERMF's own loyalty to the Carpio line. As for the PCES and PRTC, both had more immediate reasons for their urban terrorist activities.

The PRTC, the smallest of the FMLN member organizations, has a long-standing preference for kidnappings to raise funds and spectacular killings to attract attention. In addition, the PRTC leadership seems to have convinced itself that the United States had a direct, decisive, and immediate role in the capture and wounding of Nidia Díaz, because a U.S. citizen was aboard the helicopter that captured her (*NYT*, 24 May); see also Nidia Díaz's statements (*FBIS*, 23 October, p. P23). As a result, on 19 June the PRTC's "Mardoqueo Cruz Urban Guerrillas" commando, led by "Ulysses," instigated the "Zona Rosa" attack in which four U.S. Marines, two American businessmen, one Chilean, one Guatemalan, and five Salvadoran civilians—none of whom was armed—were killed (ibid., 20 June, p. P1). The episode further served to alienate U.S. public opinion from the Salvadoran Communists' cause and to strengthen congressional support for the Reagan administration's Salvadoran policies. Moreover, the PRTC's name for the attack, "Yankee Aggressor, Another Vietnam Awaits You in El Salvador," also served to harden U.S. public and media opinion against the FMLN.

The PCES and their urban commandos managed the terrorist feat of the year in Central America when they kidnapped President Duarte's daughter, Inez Duarte Durán, in San Salvador on 10 September. There were a number of reasons for PCES activity in urban terrorism, most importantly the party's huge casualties against the military's offensive that resulted in the capture of some of its most prominent members—for example, Américo Mauro Araujo Ramírez. Although other FMLN groups suffered similarly significant losses—the PRTC lost "Arlen" and, temporarily, Nidia Díaz; the FPL lost Miguel Castellanos (alias "Napoleón Romero"); and the ERP lost Yaneth Samour—the PCES could least afford such losses, considering its small size in general and its minute military leadership in particular. Furthermore, the party failed in its first large-scale attempt at urban guerrilla activities, the "Mariona Fridon" jail break in July. Only thirteen "political prisoners," as opposed to 136 common criminals, escaped (*NYT*, 14 July). Also, based on the actions of FPL leader Castellanos and Nidia Díaz, revelations from Araujo can be expected.

The capture of Inez Duarte, in addition to her own controversial behavior while in captivity, forced her father to suspend his personal involvement in day-to-day affairs and to exchange his daughter and the mayors, in whom he did not seem very interested, for a large number of recently captured FMLN top cadres. The final exchange, following negotiations in Panama, involved Inez Duarte and her companion plus (solely at the army's insistence) 23 kidnapped mayors, for over 100 captured FMLN cadres.

For the Salvadoran left 1985 was a year of internal tensions and reassessments, manifest in simultaneous centrifugal and centripetal moves within the FMLN and FDR and between them. Within the FMLN the most serious problems were faced by the FPL, a group long plagued by fratricidal conflicts. On 19 April, Miguel Castellanos surrendered to the army in Zacatecoluca. As an FMLN Central Committee member, he was the highest ranking guerrilla leader to surrender in 1985. According to his statements, the conflict between various FMLN elements was approaching deadly levels and he was afraid for his life (San Salvador, *La Prensa Gráfica*, 29 April, p. 40).

The FPL appears to be divided among people like Castellanos, who are nationalists rather than Marxist-Leninists and thus resent Cuban, Nicaraguan, and Soviet control over the strategy of the FMLN (ibid.); the top leadership, which supports such external directives and works toward the amalgamation of the FMLN member groups; and the ultra-left represented by the CERMF. Established soon after the 1983 death of FPL founder Salvador Cayetano Carpio in Managua and his public condemnation by the FPL, the CERMF remains opposed to the insurrectional and broad front strategy adapted by the FMLN. Under the influence of the ERP and PCES and following the murder of Colonel Cienfuegos, the CERMF claimed that "our people are resuming the prolonged warfare strategy" first pursued by Carpio (*FBIS*, 12 March, p. P1). According to Castellanos, this is in clear contrast to the prevailing attitude of the FMLN leadership, which believes "that the armed struggle will last 2 years at most and that they will win" (ibid., 6 May, p. P6). As late as May the CERMF was still linked to the FMLN; Radio Venceremos continued to publicize their urban assassinations. By August, however, the CERMF had openly adopted the "protracted war" strategy of Carpio, conducted its first "broad revolutionary meeting" (i.e., founding congress), taken the name "Farabundo Martí" People's Liberation Forces–Prolonged People's War (Fuerzas Populares de Liberación "Farabundo Martí"–Guerra Popular Prolonged; FPL-GPP), and thus formally split with the FPL and the FMLN umbrella (ibid., 22 August, p. P4). However, not all of the FPL-GPP's urban cadres were involved in the split. Some participated with the PCES and FAL in the "Pedro Pablo Castillo" Front that kidnapped Inez Duarte in San Salvador (*Washington Times*, 19 September, p. 6A).

The Inez Duarte kidnapping illustrated the inner tensions between the FMLN and FDR, as well as the tactical disagreements among the guerrillas themselves. Following the strong support received by Duarte from such liberal or leftist luminaries as Senator Edward Kennedy, former Venezuelan president Carlos Andres Pérez, and Argentine president Raul Alfonsín, it is likely that the FMLN initially decided to deny any involvement in the kidnapping. Moreover, all evidence indicates that FDR leaders in Mexico City—Zamora and Ungo—were not informed by the FMLN, did not know of the existence of the "Pedro Pablo Castillo" Front (*Los Angeles Times*, 17 September), and have no information on the kidnapping (San Salvador, *Diario de Hoy*, 17 September, p. 15).

It is interesting that on 15 September the Pedro Castillo group claimed it was the sixth front of the FMLN (Radio Farabundo Martí, 15 September, in *FBIS*, 19 September, pp. P9–10), and three days later Ungo still maintained that the existence of the group was "speculation" (ibid., p. P5). By 2 October, however, Ungo had shifted his position and admitted that the existence of the Pedro Castillo group and its link to the FMLN was "a strong possibility," that someone "has tried to keep it secret to seek direct negotiations" with Duarte, and that "we deplore it" (Panama City, ACAN, in *FBIS*, 3 October, pp. P3–4). Even more embarrassing for Ungo was his admission that Handal, the PCES secretary general whose men abducted Inez Duarte, did not inform him of the situation at a meeting following the abduction. Moreover, Handal signed a joint letter to the PCN opposition party proposing new negotiations (ibid., 10 October, p. P5). The final humiliation of the FDR formal leadership occurred during the negotiations, whereby Inez Duarte was released in exchange for 123 guerrillas. Salvador Samayoa of the FPL and Mario Aguiñada Carranza of the PCES, who in addition are members of the FDR Political-Diplomatic Commission, led the negotiations.

The implications of the events surrounding Inez Duarte's kidnapping are extremely significant and have resulted in the complete discredit of Ungo and Zamora, Duarte's inability to obtain army support to negotiations with the FMLN-FDR, and most likely a return to the no-prisoners approach to war by the Salvadoran armed forces. The latter received an additional blow when, days after the release of Inez Duarte, the FMLN kidnapped Colonel Omar Napoleón Avalos, head of Civilian Aeronautics, and refused to release some of the kidnapped mayors included in the Inez Duarte exchange package.

Ungo's loss of credibility in the eyes of both the Salvadoran government and many of the FDR's foreign supporters, as well as the FDR's obvious inability to influence let alone "deliver" the FMLN in negotiations, further distanced the government from the guerrillas.

Prospects for Negotiations. Throughout the year the FMLN as well as the FDR voiced their willingness to negotiate a "political solution" to the war with the government. The position adopted by the FMLN demands the withdrawal of U.S. military advisers and a stop in the military's weapons acquisitions (Salvador Guerra of the FPL, in *FBIS*, 8 January, p. P10). Furthermore, as Leonel Gonzalez stated, democracy means "people's power" and the March elections were simply "part of the counterinsurgency"; the solution to the conflict should be "a full pursuit of the people's war by all Salvadorans" (ibid., 21 March, p. P6). As for Duarte's call for the "humanization" of war, Shafik Handal rejected it, claiming that "war is war, and there cannot be a war without war" and "sabotage is one of the characteristics of any people's war" (ibid., 26 July, p. P9). This position contradicts that of the civilian member parties of the FDR—the MNR and MPSC—which, in an August statement, declared that "in the past we have expressed our disapproval of specific FMLN military actions because of the consequences for the civilian population." They did, however, justify such acts as an answer to the "state terrorism" practiced by the government (San Salvador, *El Mundo*, 27 August, in *FBIS*, 30 August, p. P6). In addition, Jorge Villacorta, a member of Ungo's MNR, defined the Zona Rosa killings as "terrorist" (ibid., 26 June, p. P1). Complicating further any understanding of the FDR-FMLN position on such issues, Mario Aguiñada Carranza, the top PCES and FDR leader, still maintained that the FMLN-FDR has "agreed to make progress in the humanization of the conflict," even after the wave of assassinations in the spring (ibid., 15 May, p. P3). A few months later he was deeply involved in representing his party's kidnappers at the negotiations for the release of Inez Duarte.

On 5 July Villalobos, Handal, Leo Cabral of the FARN, Facundo Guardado of the FPL, and Miguel Mendoza of the PRTC held a press conference in Perquín. Describing the FMLN strategy, Villalobos made it clear that "political destabilization is another basic component of our plan. We seek to break the economy . . . and now, the dismembering and decomposition of their [the government's] political organization" (text in *FBIS*, 18 July, p. P6). As for negotiations, Villalobos defined the FMLN's basic demand as "the end of U.S. intervention. That is our fundamental point in the process of a negotiated solution" (ibid., p. P9). If that is the case, then there seems to be little the Salvadoran government has to negotiate with the guerrillas, as their foreign policy has already been determined. The Duarte and Avalos kidnappings demonstrated that the FMLN believes it should continue to escalate the conflict and it may win. For purely propagandistic reasons, however, the FMLN continues to speak of negotiations while also making unrealistic demands. The latest demand calls for the Salvadoran army to renounce the military draft (*FBIS*, 18 October, p. P7), even though the guerrillas forcibly draft peasants into their rank, a practice they admitted in 1984 but now deny.

The FMLN is convinced that it will win the war; therefore, negotiations are only necessary to minimize the cost of their victory. They believe that the government and the Salvadoran Constitution are illegitimate, the FMLN military force must be maintained, and the FDR and FMLN members must be included in the government. There will be no "humanization" of the war until it ends (full text in *FBIS*, 21 November, pp. P2–18). Considering the FMLN trend toward unification as a Marxist-Leninist party and the dominance of Villalobos and Handal, the chance of a change in the group's approach to negotiations is highly unlikely in the near future, unless dramatic military reverses force a reassessment.

Domestic Affairs. Throughout the year the FMLN worked on reinvigorating its internal fronts. Some are renewed versions of the older "popular organizations" of the late 1970s—for example, the National Federation of Salvadoran Workers Unions (FENASTRAS) and the United Workers' Federation of El Salvador (FUSS), both of which are taking advantage of the opening media and labor activities of the Duarte government's democratic program. Others are "human-rights" groups, such as the Committee of Mothers and Relatives of Political Prisoners and Missing and Murdered Persons in El Salvador, the Marianella Garcia Villa Committee of Relatives for Freedom of Political Prisoners and Missing People in El Salvador, the Committee of Political Prisoners of El Salvador, and the Christian Committee of Displaced People. All of these groups signed a 19 January declaration claiming that the Salvadoran people are "victims of U.S. aggression" and demanding that the Duarte government negotiate with the FMLN on FMLN conditions (*FBIS*, 29 January, pp. P6–7). In February the same human-rights groups called for resistance to the national draft, thus first making public what later became a formal FMLN demand (ibid., 14 February, pp. P8–9). At the same time, FMLN infiltration and control of student organizations, such as the General Association of Salvadoran University Students (AGEUS) and the Association of University Students (AEU), intensified during the year.

Foreign Affairs. The FDR continues to represent the Salvadoran left internationally in the West and in Latin America, while the FMLN and particularly the PCES were active in the Soviet bloc countries. Thus, Guillermo Ungo traveled to Uruguay in March for the inauguration of President Mario Sanguinetti and Héctor Oqueli visited Spain in October. However, the growing evidence of the FDR's decline and the Inez Duarte kidnapping resulted in serious blows to the international images of Ungo and especially Zamora. In August Mexico restored diplomatic ties with El Salvador, after years as the FDR's main diplomatic and political supporter. In September the Christian Democratic Organization of America, the Latin American branch of the international Christian Democratic organization, accused the FDR of being "accomplices of terror tactics" for not denouncing the kidnapping of Duarte's daughter (*FBIS*, 30 September, pp. P3–4). However, the guerrillas were endorsed by a delegation of the West German Green Party that spent one month in Morazán (*FBIS*, 14 March, p. P1). The FMLN organizations continued their close ties to Cuba, Nicaragua, and the Soviet bloc. An FMLN delegation composed of PCES members and led by Enrique Guatemala was well received in Moscow in January; another PCES group, led by Norma Guevara, visited Czechoslovakia the same month (Eastern Europe, *FBIS*, 29 January, p. D4). The PCES also received congratulations on the occasion of its 55th anniversary. The Vietnamese Communist Party's message underscored "their unswerving militant solidarity with the fraternal Salvadoran people" (Southeast Asia and the Pacific, *FBIS*, 1 April, pp. K3–4).

Events during the year also continued to demonstrate the close links between the various FMLN elements and the Soviet bloc, Cuba, and Nicaragua. Commanders Marco Antonio Grande and Adid Inglés Alvarado, who surrendered in June, both admitted that they were trained at the Leningrad University and in Cuba respectively (*FBIS*, 13 June, p. P3). Castellanos, called a "traitor" by the FPL after his surrender in April, confirmed the strategic control of Cuba and Managua over the FMLN. The most important revelations were contained in documents captured with PRTC leader Nidia Díaz on 18 April, which confirmed most of Castellanos's claims. They indicated that Ungo was upset at being left outside the decisionmaking process of the guerrillas, that the FMLN sees Duarte as its most dangerous enemy, and that in 1985 alone thirteen PRTC leaders were scheduled to attend training courses in Bulgaria, the USSR, and Vietnam. Díaz was scheduled for Hanoi (*NYT*, 21 May; *Los Angeles Times*, 25 May). In 1984 trainees were also sent to East Germany to learn the use of explosives (ibid.). The documents also support previously known information on the close ties between the FMLN and Nicaragua. In 1983 Managua threatened to cut off aid to the guerrillas as a result of the Grenada invasion, but later prepared to use the guerrillas against the *contras* in Nicaragua (ibid.), since "the defense of the Sandinista revolution is the responsibility of FMLN and the FSLN." The latter was implicitly confirmed by Shafik Handal, who stated that "our continued struggle and progress have insured the continuity of the Central American revolutionary movement. It is the contribution of the Salvadoran people and revolutionaries to the defense of Nicaragua" (Mexico City, *Asi Es*, 17 May, p. 15). The FMLN solidarity with Nicaragua was not limited to statement or strategic cooperation. On 3 May the guerrillas blew up power pilons in San Miguel "in response to the U.S. trade embargo against Nicaragua." They added that this was an "expression of solidarity and support for Nicaragua" (*FBIS*, 7 May, p. P2). The FMLN's regional involvement was further demonstrated by the presence of a Costa Rican and a Honduran among the rebels released in exchange for Inez Duarte.

Michael Radu
Foreign Policy Research Institute

Grenada

Population. 110,000
Party. Maurice Bishop Patriotic Movement (MBPM); New Jewel Movement (NJM)
Founded. MBPM: 27 May 1984; NJM: 1973
Membership. MBPM: no data (voter strength in 1984: 2,039); NJM: no data
Chairman. MBPM: Kenrick Radix; NJM: Ian St. Bernard
Status. Legal
Last Congress. MBPM: October 1985
Last Election. MBPM: 3 December 1984, 5 percent, no seats
Auxiliary Organizations. The Maurice Bishop and Martyrs of October 19, 1983, Memorial Foundation; The Grenada Foundation, Inc.; The Maurice Bishop Youth Organization (MBYO)
Publications. *The Indies Times* (weekly); *The Democrat* (biweekly)

The existence of two distinct communist parties in Grenada became apparent during 1985. Both organizations—the MBPM and the renascent NJM—represent wings of the NJM that ruled Grenada from 1979 to 1983 as the vanguard party of the People's Revolutionary Government (PRG). With most of its leaders in prison waiting trial for the 19 October 1983 murder of Maurice Bishop and other PRG officials, the NJM offers little threat to its bitter rival, the politically active MBPM.

Leadership and Party Organization. The MBPM's chief party organization, the National Representative Council, meets on an irregular basis to coordinate political activities with delegates from Grenada's six parishes. Kenrick Radix (PRG minister of industrial development, labor, and legal affairs) remains the uncontested leader of the MBPM as chairman of the party's steering committee.

Most of the party's overt activities take the form of rallies and demonstrations to commemorate events of Grenada's revolutionary period or show solidarity with Third World causes. Although the MBPM is a frequent critic of the island's governing New National Party (NNP), it is almost equally antagonistic toward the NJM. In March, MBPM official Don Rojas (former PRG press secretary now living in Prague) condemned the NJM for "lying, scandalizing, deceiving, and brutalizing tactics" that "are not the stuff of revolutionary politics." Accusing NJM leaders Bernard Coard and Selwyn Strachan of "misappropriating the ideas of Marx and Lenin," Rojas stated that Grenadians "must emulate the leadership of the Cuban revolution in accepting the objective truths that" the current NJM leadership was "responsible for the murder of Bishop . . . the overthrow of the revolution and subsequent Yankee invasion" (*Intercontinental Press*, 1 April). Radix ruled out any possibility of holding unity talks with the NJM, calling its members "radicals" and "dangerous people" (Caribbean News Agency, 19 March; *FBIS*, 21 March).

Auxiliary and Front Organizations. The MBPM has continued its extensive international ties through support groups such as the Grenada Foundation in the United States, the Organization of Grenada Nationals in Canada, and associations of leftist Grenadian exiles in Guyana, Cuba, Nicaragua, the Soviet bloc, and Great Britain. Most of the party's operating funds come from overseas support groups (Caribbean News Agency, 20 June; *FBIS*, 21 June).

The MBPM's principal domestic auxiliary organization is the Maurice Bishop and Martyrs of October 19, 1983, Memorial Foundation, founded in January 1984. During 1985, the MBYO was also launched; it has several hundred members throughout Grenada and Carriacou, most of whom are former activists from the PRG's National Youth Organization (NYO) and the original NJM's Pioneers.

International Views, Positions, and Activities. The MBPM has maintained its strong ties with the socialist bloc. Grenadian students have continued to be sent to Cuba on scholarships offered under the auspices of the Maurice Bishop and Martyrs of October 19, 1983, Memorial Foundation, joining over 70 other youths from Grenada studying in Cuba (Caribbean News Agency, 18 January; *FBIS*, 22 January). MBPM party members also attended the first Latin American Congress on Anti-Imperialist Thought, held in Managua in February (Managua Radio Sandino Network, 19 February; *FBIS*, 21 February). A twenty-person MBPM/MBYO delegation participated in the twelfth World Festival of Youth and Students held in Moscow in July and August. The delegation was led by Terry Marryshow, a Cuban-trained physician and personal favorite of Fidel Castro, whose grandfather, T. A. Marryshow, is revered as Grenada's foremost patriot. Nine of the twenty delegates resided in Grenada, whereas the remaining eleven were members of an MBYO branch among Grenadian students in Cuba (*Indies Times*, 20 July).

The MBYO also sent a delegation to a special conference on the Latin American and Caribbean debt crisis (*Diálogo Juvenil Y Estudiantil de América Latina Y El Caribe Sobre La Deuda Externa*), held in Havana 11–14 September. In a statement issued at the conference, the MBYO paid tribute to the "brilliant analyses of Comrade Fidel" regarding the debt problem and told "the Sandinista youth that the MBYO is your fellow struggler in building a new Nicaragua"—a possible reference to the continuing presence of Grenadian *brigadistas* in Nicaragua (*Indies Times*, 28 September, p. 3).

In May, Einstein Louison—Soviet-trained chief of staff of the disbanded People's Revolutionary Army (PRA)—had his passport seized by Grenadian authorities as he prepared to leave the island for a trip to Cuba, Western Europe, East Germany, and the Soviet Union. The Grenada government had pledged to restrict overseas travel of local leftists, charging that they were serving as conduits for funds from communist-bloc countries to help the MBPM regroup and prepare for "another revolution" (Caribbean News Agency, 20 June; *FBIS*, 21 June).

The MBPM has been unequivocal about its goal of seizing power again in Grenada. At a rally commemorating the sixth anniversary of the NJM's 1979 coup d'état, Radix urged a crowd of 300 supporters "to prepare themselves to regain power" and "rise again to build the revolutionary process in Grenada" (Caribbean News Agency, 20 March; *FBIS*, 21 March). The inability of Grenada's democratically elected NNP government to deal with the island's chronic economic problems is being exploited by the MBPM, especially among the disaffected youth. Referring to the October 1983 U.S. intervention, Radix said: "The Grenada events were a disaster for the left but what is clear is that the right doesn't have the solutions. We are the party of the future" (*Albuquerque Journal*, 21 July).

The New Jewel Movement. The NJM's influence on Grenadian politics is negligible. Although the party claims some 1,200 members—primarily ex-soldiers of the PRG—"in every village across Grenada," it probably has little real support beyond former Deputy Prime Minister Coard and eighteen other Stalinist members of the PRG imprisoned for the murder of Maurice Bishop and others. Ian St. Bernard, former PRG police commissioner, has served as the NJM's de facto party leader since his release from prison in August 1984. In October 1985, a fifteen-page paper written by imprisoned NJM official Leon Cornwall was presented to a conference of the U.S.-based National Congress of Black Lawyers held in Toronto. Cornwall, a former PRA officer, NJM Central Committee member, and ambassador to Cuba, had compiled the report "with considerable assistance from outside," according to Grenadian authorities. Cornwall's report on the political situation in Grenada devoted twice as much space to an attack on the MBPM as it devoted to criticism of the ruling NNP (Caribbean News Agency, 8 November; *FBIS*, 14 November).

Timothy Ashby
Heritage Foundation

Guadeloupe

Population. 333,000
Party. Communist Party of Guadeloupe (Parti Communiste Guadeloupéen; PCG)
Founded. 1944 as a section of the French Communist Party; 1958 as independent
Membership. 3,000 (estimated)
Secretary General. Guy Daninthe
Politburo. 12 members
Status. Legal
Last Congress. Eighth, 27–29 April 1984
Last Election. March 1985, partial General Council elections, 4 of 24 contested seats; leftist coalition, 24 of 42 total seats
Auxiliary Organizations. Union of Guadeloupan Communist Youth (UJCG); General Confederation of Guadeloupan Labor (CGTG); Union of Guadeloupan Women (UFG)
Publications. *L'Etincelle* (PCG; weekly); *Madras* (UFG; monthly)

The PCG found itself walking a tightrope between an increasingly militant independence movement and unintimidated supporters of the status quo. Its own position, constantly reiterated and defended, was that there must be more decentralization of power and more attention to economic and cultural development before the desired end of sovereignty could be reached. For this reason party leaders tried to focus the people's attention on employment problems, local political races, the continuing decline of agriculture, and the need for the articulation of a cultural identity. Their apparent inability to attract new members is not surprising, given the Guadeloupan suspicion of all political organizations; however, although the strength of their representation in local councils and the French parliament is much stronger than that of the Communist Party of neighboring Martinique, they are only able to make their voices heard because of their alliance with the Socialists. This alliance was confirmed by the partial cantonal elections of 10 and 17 March that sent representatives to the General Council.

Leadership and Party Organization. Guy Daninthe continued his long service as secretary general. On 12 May he organized a seminar of communist elected officials, which included a senator in the upper house of the French National Assembly who, although not a member of the PCG, is allied with it. In addition, eleven Communists and allies in the Regional Council attended along with nine members of the General Council and elected officials from six town councils.

Jean-Claude Lombin, who had been secretary general of the UJCG since 1977, ceded his position to Fred Sablon. Claude Morvan maintained his position as secretary general of the CGTG. Henri Bangou—physician, historian, mayor of Pointe-à-Pitre, and member of the political bureau—continued to take the lead in articulating the PCG's positions. He published a new book, *The Socialist Party and Decolonization*.

Domestic Party Affairs. Try as it might, the PCG could not ignore the increasingly violent independence movement. Led by the Union for the Liberation of Guadeloupe (UPLG), the nationalists took heart over events in New Caledonia, the French territory in the South Pacific where rioting forced changes just short of independence. In April the UPLG organized a conference of representatives from the overseas possessions of France in order to denounce what it called French colonialism. Representatives arrived from Réunion, Martinique, Guyana, Mayotte, and Guadeloupe. (Some other territories and departments were not represented.) Trotskyist parties in metropolitan France, such as the Revolutionary Communist League and the Communist Party Marxist-Leninist, sent representatives. The traditional Communist Party of France (PCF) and the PCG did not attend even though some of their members were invited. The Guadeloupe Communists did, however, express publicly their support for New Caledonian independence.

The PCG's position became increasingly delicate because of bomb explosions that killed innocent people, the arrest of one of its own members, and the arrest and imprisonment of George Faisans, a teacher committed to independence. The party leadership condemned the use of violence and terrorism even when this included Jocelyn Olimé, its own member caught carrying explosives in 1984. The PCG did criticize the prison sentence given to Olimé, however. In the case of Faisans, the PCG joined forces with the nationalists and supported popular action of a peaceful nature. Faisans, a member of the People's Movement for an Independent Guadeloupe (MPGI), had been imprisoned for hitting a teacher of French origin who had hit a black student. He went on a hunger strike in the French prison to which he had been sent, and in July a general strike in Guadeloupe forced his release.

The PCG stood firm in its opposition to the idea of immediate independence. The main point of the communist argument was that the independence movements were composed of the petty bourgeoisie, not the masses. According to party leaders, "independence for the sake of independence is not our policy. We want a well prepared and progressive independence which improves the material, cultural and moral situation of our people and not one which satisfies the ambitions of some leader looking for power" (*L'Etincelle*, 20 July, p. 1). This position did not satisfy the anti-independence opposition, which called the PCG traitors and liars.

The PCG had something to be happy about as a result of the March elections. The number of cantons had been increased, and 24 seats in the General Council were to be challenged out of a total of 42. The PCG backed fourteen party members and supported one ally. They and the Socialists agreed to support one another during the second round. The Communists won a total of four seats, while the Socialists won nine. Joining with other allies and the previously elected Socialists and Communists, the left counted 24 as opposed to 18 from the Gaullists and other opposition parties. The previous council—when there were only 36 representatives because of fewer cantons—had been controlled by the opposition. After the March elections, however, the Socialists and Communists agreed on a socialist candidate for president, and together they formed the executive. The cooperation between Socialists and Communists in Guadeloupe seemed much more solid than in metropolitan France.

Auxiliary Organizations. The UJCG held its Third Congress in May and elected Fred Sablon as secretary general. The UJCG also celebrated its eighteenth anniversary at the end of the year.

International Views. The PCG, like its counterpart in Martinique, remained firmly committed to Moscow, and its publication *L'Etincelle* (which celebrated its 41st anniversary) hardly let a week go by without some praise for the Russians. Party criticism of the USA was unrelenting, and its support for black majority rule in South Africa grew.

Guadeloupans attended the twelfth World Festival of Youth and Students in the USSR. Guy Daninthe spoke at the Twenty-fifth Congress of the French Communist Party. Guadeloupans hosted the fourth Conference of Unity and Solidarity of the Workers of the Caribbean, at which a Cuban presided, and they traveled to Havana in September to hear Fidel Castro call for a repudiation of foreign debts. PCG members met with Martiniquan Communists in Pointe-à-Pitre and in Paris, and delegates from Guadeloupe attended the Third Congress of the Jamaican Workers Party in December 1984.

Emmanuel Ibéné and others founded a new radio station, GAÏAC, which formally began to broadcast at the end of May. Thus the PCG had a new method to counteract what it had always considered to be unfair reporting by the most important radio stations.

Brian Weinstein
Howard University

Guatemala

Population. 8,335,000
Party. The Guatemalan Party of Labor (Partido Guatemalteco del Trabajo; PGT)
Founded. 1952
Membership. Under 500
Secretary General. Carlos Gonzáles, of largest PGT faction ("camarilla")
Leading Body. Political Commission
Status. Illegal, but eventual legalization will come under 1984 constitution.
Last Congress. Fourth, December 1969
Last Election. 1953
Auxiliary Organizations. Guatemalan Autonomous Federation of Trade Unions (FASGUA); Patriotic Youth of Labor (JPT)
Other Marxist-Leninist Organizations. Rebel Armed Forces (Fuerzas Armadas Rebeldes; FAR); Armed People's Revolutionary Organization (Organización Revolucionaria del Pueblo en Armas; ORPA); Guerrilla Army of the Poor (Ejército Guerrillero de los Pobres; EGP)
Publications. *Verdad* (irregular, primarily abroad)

A Guatemalan communist party was established by the Comintern through its Mexican, European, and American cadres in 1922. The Ubico regime wiped out the party in 1933. In September 1949, a secret Marxist-Leninist cell within the then-ruling Guatemalan political party established a new organization, which on 18 December 1952 was formally and legally named the PGT. The party is now illegal, but the 1984 constitution provides for its eventual legalization.

The most important event of 1985 in Guatemala was the orderly transition from the military regime of General Humberto Mejia Victores, who was in power since August 1983, to a freely elected civilian government controlled by the Christian Democratic Party (PDC). In the 3 November congressional electon, the PDC obtained 51 seats in the 100-member National Congress. The Christian Democrats' presidential candidate, Vinicio Cerezo Arévalo, won over 38 percent of the popular vote, by far the largest share, but was forced into a runoff election on 8 December against Jorge Carpio Nicolle of the National Center Union (UCN) with 20 percent. In the second round Cerezo won a comfortable 68.37 percent and became Guatemala's first civilian president since 1966 (*FBIS*, 10 December). At the same time, the PDC won a large majority of the mayoral races on 3 November. The only significant exception was in Guatemala City, where the party's candidate finished a poor third. Both rounds of voting were characterized by modest participation (by Latin American standards)—in the second round of the presidential election, 34.63 percent of the potential voters abstained—and by the absence of violence or fraud. For the first time in years a party of the true left, the Social Democrats, participated in the elections. They received less than 7 percent of the votes and no congressional seats.

The problems facing the incoming president and the PDC government to be installed on 14 January 1986 are staggering. Two of the most formidable are the collapsing economy and the burden of foreign debt. Apparently, these are primary reasons for the military's decision to return to the barracks.

Nevertheless, even with a strong consensus among the officer corps regarding the need for civilians to take over the government, it appears that the army will retain significant powers, both openly and in a more discreet manner. Some of Vinicio Cerezo's post-victory statements indicate a few of the problems he expects. First and foremost, Cerezo and all of the other presidential candidates have unanimously rejected the idea of putting on trial members of the armed forces or police suspected of committing human-rights abuses at the height of the anti-insurgency campaign of 1982–1983. Second, regarding the army's anti-insurgency tactics and the civilian rural patrols, Cerezo promised only a "dialogue" with the military about possible changes (ibid.). Third, Cerezo promised no amnesty for the guerrillas, only a willingness to talk to them in somewhat ambiguous terms. There is an almost universal consensus in Guatemala City that the army's main anti-insurgency program, the "poles of development" (polos de desarollo) in the highlands, will continue in one form or another. Currently they are concentrated in the department of Quiché and at Playa Grande, Acul, Chisec, and the Ixil Triangle, with some 38 interlinked villages in those four areas.

The Guatemalan army's inability—or unwillingness—to hinder or influence the elections demonstrated the shift in the balance of power between the army and the guerrilla groups. Guerrilla activity has declined throughout the country. The available evidence indicates some significant changes in the relative strength of the four major guerrilla organizations, as well as an increased level of coordination among them.

EGP, the largest organization of the violent left, was clearly the military's main victim in its offensive against the guerrillas. The EGP's strength and ability to engage in large-scale operations has been almost fatally impaired. The PGT's strength remains insignificant, although FAR, the oldest guerrilla group, appears to have regained some strength. Mostly, however, they are a nuisance rather than a threat to the government.

This year there were a smaller number of armed incidents and clashes with the military. There was also a growing perception among usually sympathetic elements in the Catholic Church and Guatemala City student and middle-class groups that the forces of the National Revolutionary Unity of Guatemala (URNG)—the umbrella organization of the Marxist-Leninist left that includes FAR, ORPA, EGP, and a faction of the PGT—is in decline. This may well explain the growing silence of the many Catholic clergy who once sympathized with the guerrillas, as well as the decision of the Mejia Victores regime to enter the campus of the San Carlos National University in search of guerrilla sympathizers in September. Finally, the Mexican government decided to relocate many of the Guatemalan refugees, a sizable number of whom are guerrilla families and supporters, from the border state of Chiapas to the interior state of Campeche, following Mejia Victores's visit to Mexico in September. The Mexican government would never have acted in this way if the URNG army had been strong.

Although none of these facts signal the end of the 23-year-old guerrilla campaign in Guatemala, it is clear that this was a decisive year for the military. It succeeded not only in pressing on and following its successes of 1984 but also in decisively cutting off the URNG from its usual base of support (Mexico and Guatemala City). More important, the military undermined the guerrillas' main political argument—that they are fighting against a military dictatorship. Vinicio Cerezo's victory seriously weakened the political ground of URNG propaganda throughout the country and among all social groups.

Guerrilla Activities. The URNG appears to have limited itself to propaganda activities abroad, rather than concentrating on military coordination or actual unification of the four groups involved. According to Gregorio López, ORPA and URNG leader, three of the four groups maintain separate and exclusive operational zones; only the PGT and its faction that belongs to the URNG, the National Leadership Nucleus, have no specific operational areas (*Latin America Regional Reports: Mexico & Central America*, 12 July, pp. 6–7). This is another indication of the party's irrelevance to the military aspects of the war. The only form of military coordination within Guatemala mentioned by López is the existence of *jefaturas* (literally "chieftainships"), which are supposed to coordinate activities on a regional basis but in fact keep other URNG groups out of the particular bailiwick of its three militarily active members (ibid.).

The army-sponsored "poles of development" program has also affected the level of guerrilla activity. According to Rolando Paiz, the civilian architect of the program, it has forced the EGP in particular to improve its behavior toward the civilian population since the majority of the poles are located in Quiché, one of the departments in which the EGP operates. In these poles, the military uses force and persuasion on civilians to get them to reject the guerrillas. In addition the military has been able to demonstrate the guerrillas' inability to protect, much less feed, their own sympathizers in "liberated areas." As a result the insurgents' largest recruiting pool, the peasantry, are turning against them.

Another important aspect of the Guatemalan insurgency that applies to all of the URNG member groups is the growing willingness to ignore the eastern half of the country and its Ladino population as an area of operations. López himself has admitted this (ibid.). Seen in the context of the Indian population's self-centered attitudes, its growing ability to participate in national politics (an Indian was vice-presidential candidate for a minor party in the November elections), and its reluctance to join causes espoused and led by Ladino intellectuals (who are the overwhelming majority of leadership in all URNG groups), it appears that the URNG's chances of reviving its sagging fortunes there are minimal at best. Furthermore, within the left itself many groups, even politically influential ones, are reluctant to join the URNG. The PGT-dominant "camarilla" faction and the newly formed People's Guerrilla Commandos (Comandos Guerrilleros del Pueblo; established in June) are examples. Both decided to encourage but not to join the URNG. The heretical People's Revolutionary Movement–Ixim (Movimiento Revolucionario del Pueblo–Ixim), a renegade group that includes the PGT "Military Commission" faction as well as dissidents from the EGP and ORPA, remains active, engaging in sporadic terrorist actions and blaming other leftist groups by attributing the "credit" to them. In this sense, the defeat of the URNG groups both militarily and politically (since the election) could turn Guatemala into a Beirut-like situation, with organized guerrilla groups forced into terrorist activities out of despair.

Mexico, the guerrillas' last source of recruits and logistical support, has begun to realize that the URNG is losing the war and that the advantages of supporting, or at least closing its eyes to the URNG's logistical network, are not worth the problems they entail. The decisions to move the Guatemalan refugees to Campeche and to invite Mejia Victores to Mexico City were not only mutually related but were linked to Mexico's Central American policies. One of these policies concerns Guatemala's neutrality, which appears to be the price paid by Mejia Victores and Vinicio Cerezo for the continuation of Mexico's oil subsidies and refugee-displacement policies aiding Guatemala.

By far the most spectacular guerrilla action of the year was the January attack on Santiago Atitlán, an important administrative and resort center in Sololá. It was carried out by ORPA's "Xavier Tambriz" front (*FBIS*, 30 January). Yet despite the attack, this author was able to travel near Santiago in November and found that fog, rather than the ORPA, was the main impediment to travel. Obviously, ORPA felt that it could not defend Santiago and therefore retreated to the hills east of Lake Atitlán.

In the San Marcos department, ORPA's second most important operational area, the guerrillas took over Radio Frontera on 12 May and broadcast propaganda for half an hour (*FBIS*, 13 May). Four days later ORPA attacked a farm in the Suchitepéquez department but was defeated, and three attackers were captured, including one with Cuban training (*Central America Report*, 14 June, p. 173). Sporadic attempts to destroy the economic infrastructure in Suchitepéquez continued during the first half of the year, with the coffee harvest the main target. Other targets of ORPA, and particularly of the FAR and EGP, were the members of the civilian patrols operating under military guidance.

The EGP, for a period the largest and most active guerrilla organization in Guatemala, continued to diminish in importance throughout the year. This was due largely to the blows it suffered in Quiché, its traditional area of operations, and to the army's anti-insurgency strategy and intensive expansion of civilian patrols. EGP's response to this reversal has been an exaggerated sense of its own importance and closer ties with Cuba, Nicaragua, and the Soviet bloc. In a document celebrating the EGP's thirteenth anniversary in January, Rolando Morán—the supreme commander of the EGP (see biography)—flatly rejected any political or negotiated solution to the insurgency, described the electoral process as "farce, more contradictions, a dead-end street," and predicted "renewed efforts and greater strength to increase the level of revolutionary action" (Mexico City, *El Día*, 21 January, p. 16). To underscore its internationalist view of revolutionary war, the EGP, unlike ORPA or FAR, named its militant fronts after such revolutionary models as Ho Chi Minh, Augusto Cesar Sandino (in Quiché), and Ernesto "Che" Guevara (in Huehuetenango) (*Los Angeles Times*, 8 June).

The municipality of Acul in Quiché, once the center of the "Ho Chi Minh" front, is now the army's showcase "pole of development," which illustrates the EGP's growing weakness. Numerous testimonies from Quiché indicate that the EGP's failure to keep their long-standing promises of protection and social and economic progress to the Indian population have turned the Indians against the guerrillas. In fact once the military proved able to feed and protect them, the Indians played an essential role in the army's success with the development poles. As an Indian from Quiché put it, "They [the EGP] said that in one or two years, we would be free . . . they said we would eat well and have cars" (*WSJ*, 20 September). Unfortunately the result, according to a sympathetic nun, was that "the guerrillas lit a fire in people . . . And then they left them to the army" (ibid.).

The EGP concentrated most of its activities, particularly attacks against army and civil patrols, in the Nebaj area in Quiché and in Huehuetenango, where proximity to the Mexican border made retreat safer. Most significant, however, was that the majority of EGP activities were defensive protection of camps and depots. On 4 April, for instance, fourteen EGP supply caches were captured by the army in the area (*Central America Report*, 26 April, p. 119). At the same time a safe house in Guatemala City was also discovered.

The latest outburst of EGP activities took place on the occasion of the November elections, again around Nebaj. Earlier, on 19 October, an EGP military engagement had resulted in the deaths of eight soldiers (including two officers) and ten guerrillas (including one EGP leader, Commander "Patricia") (*FBIS*, 23 October). Commenting on these attacks and the impact of the elections, Morán stated that "the people's struggle has been increasing" and that the new Christian Democratic government will have no power or "the military, social, economic or political capacity to try a real reformist movement that would force us to reconsider some of our proposals" (Guatemala City, *Prensa Libre*, 15 November, p. 19).

From the guerrillas' standpoint, EGP's decline was almost countered by the relatively surprising effectiveness of the FAR. In January, on the occasion of FAR's 22nd anniversary, 200 guerrillas participated in an "armed propaganda" action (that is, temporarily taking as hostages an entire village population for forcible indoctrination) in El Petén (*Central America Report*, 15 February, p. 43). This was an impressive number for an organization whose total strength had been less than 200 for years. Moreover, the first months of 1985 witnessed FAR's unending harassment of traffic on the Poptun–Santa Elena highway in El Petén, thereby blocking land communications with the departmental capital of Flores (*Prensa Libre*, 27 February).

Equally significant was FAR's ability to expand its operational areas from the remote rain forests of El Petén to the densely populated highlands and the southwest. A FAR member captured in February admitted that he was recruited from among the trade-union members at an Escuintla papermill and underwent training in Cuba, Nicaragua, and Mexico (*FBIS*, 6 March). Even the military admitted that FAR's fronts—"Feliciano Argueta," "Lucio Martinez," and "Raul Orante"—all in El Petén are well organized (ibid.). The "Tecun Uman" front in Chimaltenangon opened in 1982 and became more active in 1985, with an unsuccessful attack in February (twelve FAR members captured) and another in May. Moreover, in an escalation of its El Petén activities, FAR declared its opening of a new "Mardoqueo Guardado" front.

The most important development of FAR activities, however, was its ability to undertake operations in the departments of Escuintla (at Santa Lucia Cotzumalguapa) and Sololá (San Lucás Tolimán) (*Central America Report*, 14 June, p. 174). Further activities in Chimaltenango occurred on 16 June, at San Martin Jilotepeque, in a remote area near the border with Quiché (Guatemala City, *El Grafico*, 16 June, p. 3). Whether that clash, which left two civil patrolmen dead, was undertaken by FAR or the EGP is unclear, but it seems to indicate the beginning of open competition between the URNG guerrilla groups instead of the usual separation of operational areas.

Despite its increased activity, FAR has suffered significant reverses as well, including defections, dozens of captured members, the death in action of Commander "Ramón" (28 May in Escuintla), and the loss of numerous supply caches and training camps, particularly in El Petén. FAR attacks on oil fields failed in August and again against Texaco oil wells in September. The organization was unable to disrupt the November elections seriously, despite its attempts and statements to the effect that the newly elected government would become an open puppet of the United States (*Prensa Libre*, 21 August, p. 4). In fact, of all the URNG groups, FAR seems to have been the most actively engaged in pre-election violence. Its operations were stepped up the weeks before and after the voting.

As always, the PGT was the least active violent Marxist-Leninist group in Guatemala during the year. Its claimed bombing in January of the buildings of an Italian construction company in Santa Cruz Verapaz (Alta Verapaz department) was its most significant action (*Central America Report*, 15 February, p. 42). In fact, a FAR communique on 24 October following the guerrillas' capture of a radio station on the Mexican border in El Petén did not even mention the PGT (that is, the National Leadership Nucleus) as a member of the URNG (*Prensa Libre*, 27 October, p. 31).

FAR activities in El Petén the week before the elections reached a stage at which General Lobos Zamora, the army chief of staff, visited the area to prove that the army was in control. On 31 October the guerrillas killed a military commissioner in El Petén and staged an attack in Tecpan (Chimaltenango). Whether in conjunction with FAR or because of their common hostility toward Guatemala's first free elections in years, the EGP and ORPA also expanded their activities just prior to the balloting. ORPA's bloodiest attack was the mining of a landing strip in Suchitepéquez (24 October), which resulted in four deaths, including the Norwegian honorary consul Norman do Lind (*El Gráfico*, 24 October, p. 11).

Other Violent Activities. A number of assassinations of persons known to be hostile to the left occurred, mostly in the capital. On 31 March retired general Manuel Francisco Sosa Avila, former National Police and Navy Chief and field commander in Quiché, El Petén, and Quetzaltenango in the mid-1970s, was gunned down in Guatemala City, together with his three-year-old grandson. On 3 April six policemen were assassinated there, and on 6 July a police intelligence officer was murdered in the street. In October a congressional candidate of the center-right PCDN party was murdered in Alta Verapaz. The murder of businessman Roberto Castañeda Felice on 12 August was blamed by the government on the URNG elements, but the organization denied the accusation, claiming rather disingenuously that it "only applies (revolutionary) justice [that is, assassination] to those who are responsible for the murder and slaughter of our people . . . and not against its political and ideological enemies" (*FBIS*, 29 August). Since the PGT (all factions), the EGP, FAR, probably ORPA, and non-URNG affiliates have a presence in Guatemala City, it is almost impossible to assign responsibility for urban terrorism to any particular group.

However, the guerrillas' loss of most of their urban and rural fronts since 1982 has clearly resulted in disjointed terrorist attempts that lack a strategy or coordination with rural guerrilla or urban political campaigns. The PGT and remnants of the "Robin García" and National Committee for Labor Unity (CNUS) guerrilla fronts did try to infiltrate and change the nature of the legal demonstrations of the Guatemalan Workers Trade Union (UNSITRAGUA) on 6 September; they attacked the police, engaged in vandalism, and looted in the hope of provoking a violent confrontation. However, these tactics were not successful. UNSITRAGUA itself condemned such acts as "criminal" and distanced itself from them (*FBIS*, 9 September).

The violent left had more success with their attempts at maintaining influence at the San Carlos National University, a traditional recruiting ground and propaganda center of Leninist groups since the late 1960s. Student riots in September were led by violently Leninist, anti–United States, and anti-government elements whose heroes are Sandino, Guevara, and Luis Turcios Lima. The same elements have occasionally engaged in assassination of moderate or conservative students. The autonomy of the university prevents the police from entering its grounds and thus provides excellent pretexts for right-wing death squads to kill leftists on the campus in reprisal. On 4 September the military entered the campus briefly and claimed to have found weapons and guerrilla literature. Whether or not the student organizers of the September disturbances attempted to provoke the army into postponing or stopping the elections according to the URNG desires, rumors appeared at the time that a coup was in the making (*Washington Post*, 14 September).

The URNG demonstrated signs of tensions among its member groups throughout the year. In addition to the mentioned absence of the PGT in URNG statements made by FAR, the EGP also condemned the December 1984 statement of the umbrella group, which stated its intention of "pushing forward with greater determination the Revolutionary People's War" and clearly rejected any kind of elections (*Intercontinental Press*, 18 February, p. 79). In May the EGP defined such claims as "radical and virulent language," despite its own opposition to elections (*Central America Report*, 14 June, p. 174). All the statements made by the URNG during the year expressed support for the Sandinista regime in Nicaragua and threatened a generalization of the war if the United States invaded Nicaragua. Despite the statements, it appears that the relations between the three major military elements of the URNG—ORPA, FAR, and EGP—were far from amiable, as demonstrated by their limited coordination of actions against the electoral process, rhetorical snipings against each other, and operations in each other's domains. FAR was particularly guilty in this respect.

Other Developments. Apparently following the example of the Argentine Mothers of Plaza de Mayo, a Mutual Support Group (GAM) of relatives of "disappeared" persons was established in 1984. They engaged in repeated protests against the government and demanded information on their relatives. The most prominent action of the group, other than the demonstration in April that attracted such international leftist luminaries as Rev. Sloane Coffin, was the occupation of the Metropolitan Cathedral on the wake of the November elections. The group demanded an investigation on the fate of the disappeared, and this provided a propaganda bonus to Christian Democrat presidential candidate Vinicio Cerezo, who was asked to "mediate" between Guatemala and the government. The police largely ignored the takeover of the cathedral, and it ended without incidents.

Biography. *"Rolando Morán" (Ricardo Ramírez de León).* Ramírez-Morán is the supreme commander, political leader, and founder of the EGP in Guatemala. He was born in 1932 and, according to his own testimony, became active in politics in 1949. By the following year he was already one of the founders and leaders of a communist-led splinter of the Association of University Students, the Democratic University Front (Frente Universitario Democratico; FUD). By 1953 Ramírez-Morán led one of the organizing commissions for the Festival of Friendship for the Youth of Central America and the Caribbean, planned for the end of 1954. He had already gained organizing experience as a member of the Guatemalan delegation to the 1953 Third World Youth Festival in Bucharest, Romania.

During the fall of the Arbenz regime in 1954, Ramírez-Morán, according to his own claims, was one of the few who actually tried to fight against the Castillo Armas forces. Ultimately he had to take asylum at the embassy of Argentina, where he met another pro-Arbenz radical, Ernesto "Che" Guevara. Ramírez-Morán had been a PGT member, first of the party's youth branch and then of the party itself, since 1951. Allowed to go to Argentina, he was briefly jailed, engaged in "student movement" activities, traveled, and "read voraciously" (*Companero*, vol. 2, 1984, pp. 63–66).

Once Castro took over Cuba, Ramírez-Morán went there and "worked as a reporter for a student magazine." At the end of 1959 he returned to Guatemala and immediately began working for the PGT as a youth-branch activist.

In November 1960 Ramírez-Morán was one of the Communists who attempted unsuccessfully to join the failed coup of junior officers. Nevertheless, he was able to continue his open activities, and after the beginning of the guerrilla war, under the leadership of the 1960 military rebels, he served as the PGT guerrilla liaison. Throughout the mid-1960s he was closely associated with guerrilla leaders Marco Antonio Yon Sosa and particularly Luis Turcios Lima, who he claims "showed us the way" (ibid.).

"Together with 1,119 other compañeros," Ramírez-Morán established FAR in November 1963. He became the group's main ideologue and the author of the programmatic "Manifesto from the Sierra de las Minas." When ideological and tactical disputes resulted in the rupture between FAR and the PGT, Ramírez-Morán joined the former and left the party in 1965. Between 1963 and 1965 he was a comrade of Pablo Monsanto, the founder and main leader of FAR's present incarnation.

At the end of 1965 Ramírez-Morán left for Cuba, allegedly because of tuberculosis, and was one of the Guatemalan delegation members at the Tricontinental Conference. In 1968, following Turcios Lima's death and the defeat of FAR by the Guatemalan army, he began attracting a small group of survivors who would later return and start the guerrilla struggle again. He accomplished this through infiltration from Mexico at the beginning of 1972. A few years later, this small nucleus of less than a dozen militants became the EGP, the largest Guatemalan Marxist-Leninist guerrilla organization to this day.

During the 1960s Ramírez-Morán—using the names Ricardo Ramírez, Arnaldo Fratti, or Orlando Fernandez—became one of the most prominent theoreticians of guerrilla warfare in Latin America. He wrote the "official" (Cuban-sponsored and published) biography of Turcios Lima, contributed to Régis Debray's *Critique des Armes*, significantly influenced Roque Dalton's critique of Debray, and had François Maspero, the French leftist publisher, publish his *Lettres du Front Cuatemalteque* in 1970.

Michael Radu
Foreign Policy Research Institute, Philadelphia

Guyana

Population. 798,000
Party. People's Progressive Party (PPP); Working People's Alliance (WPA)
Founded. PPP: 1950; WPA: organized in 1973, became formal party in 1979
Membership. PPP: 100 leaders and several hundred militants above non-Marxist rank and file (estimated); WPA: 30 leaders (estimated)
General Secretary. PPP: Cheddi Jagan
Politburo. PPP, 12 members: Cheddi Jagan, Janet Jagan, Ram Karran, Feroze Mohamed, Pariag Sukhai, Clinton Collymore, Narbada Persaud, Isahak Basir, Rohit Persaud, Cyril Belgrave, Reepu Daman Persaud, Harry Persaud Nokta; WPA, 5 members: Clive Thomas, Walter Omawale, Moses Bhagwan, Eusi Kawayana, Rupert Roopnarine
Status. Legal but sometimes harassed
Last Congress. PPP: Twenty-second, 3–5 August 1985
Last Election. 9 December 1985. PPP: 45,926 votes, 16.84 percent, 8 of 53 seats in National Assembly; WPA: 4,176 votes, one seat in National Assembly.
Auxiliary Organizations. PPP: Progressive Youth Organization (PYO), Women's Progressive Organization (WPO)
Publications. PPP: *Mirror* (weekly), *Thunder* (quarterly); WPA: *Dayclean* and *Open Word* (weeklies)

On 7 August 1985 Guyanese president Linden Forbes Sampson Burnham died during a minor throat operation while in the care of two specially invited Cuban doctors. Thus ended 21 years of uninterrupted and unchallenged leadership of Guyana by the founder of the People's National Congress (PNC). Burnham was succeeded without incident by his vice president and close adviser, Desmond Hoyte. Nevertheless, Burnham's death did enhance rivalries within the PNC, particularly between Hoyte and Hamilton Green.

National elections were held on 9 December. The PNC received 228,718 votes and 42 seats in the 53-member National Assembly. The PPP took 45,926 votes and eight seats, the United Force 9,810 votes and two seats, and the WPA 4,176 votes and one seat. All parties but the PNC protested the election.

PPP delegates to the assembly will be Cheddi Jagan, Janet Jagan, Reepu Persaud, Harry Nokta, Cyril Belgrave, Clinton Collymore, Isahak Basir, and Feroze Mohamed. The WPA delegate is Eusi Kwayana. The PPP uses its presence in the assembly to publicize its policies and criticize the opposition, particularly the PNC when the budget is released in the spring.

Cheddi Jagan remained the dominant opposition voice, and the PPP claims to "occupy the centre stage of Guyana's politics" (Georgetown, *Mirror*, 31 March). However, the December election did not demonstrate the PPP's majority position in the nation. Although the election outcome was almost certainly affected by significant instances of fraud—all elections since independence in 1966 have been—there is no evidence that anything like the entire East Indian population (50 percent of the country's total), the traditional source of PPP power, turned out on the party's behalf.

Jagan and the PPP receive strong backing from the PYO and WPO. Described as a "training ground for young Communists," the PYO is a member of the Soviet-front World Federation of Democratic Youth; it is led by Navin Chandarpal. The WPO is led by Janet Jagan, Gail Teixeira, and Indra Chandarpal. Both PPP auxiliaries focus on problems of employment, education, and social issues.

A resolution adopted at the Twenty-second Congress in August stated that the PPP has now completed the sixteen-year process of transforming itself from a nationalist mass party into a disciplined Marxist-Leninist organization (*Mirror*, 11 August). The main aim of the party organization, according to Central Committee secretary Janet Jagan, is "to enhance the party's role among the population at the place of residence and work and educational institutions and in mass organisations" (*WMR*, August).

The PPP describes the current system in Guyana as "anti-working class. . . what we call bureaucratic, state, co-operative and parasitic capitalist," which has brought twenty years of "steady decline in all aspects of life." At its congress the PPP said that the PNC had "perfected a military and bureaucratic apparatus that is used primarily to bolster the government. Undemocratic methods of rule, discrimination, corruption, extravagance, and fear have been the hallmarks of PNC rule" (*Mirror*, 19 May and 11 August).

In recent years the PPP has consistently called for a "political solution" to the country's domestic crisis. The solution would be based on democracy, anti-imperialism, and a socialist orientation undertaken by a National Patriotic Front government comprising all left and democratic forces (ibid., 31 March). The PNC would be welcome to participate in the government, Cheddi Jagan has said, if it decided to practice democracy, deepen its anti-imperialism, and lay the foundations for socialism (ibid., 19 May). On 9 June the *Mirror* announced that the PPP had decided to accept an invitation from the PNC—issued in January—for dialogue. The PPP delegates were Executive Committee members Feroze Mohamed and Clement Rohee; PNC delegates were Elvin McDavid and Ranji Chandisingh, who is a former high-ranking PPP official but is now PNC general secretary (Bridgetown, CANA, 19 June; *JPRS*, 22 July). However, talks had not begun by the time of Burnham's death; the two sides reaffirmed their interest in dialogue after the PNC change of guard. The PPP stated that it is prepared to make compromises so long as they "are not matters of principle" (*Mirror*, 11 August).

The most important arena of confrontation between the PPP and the PNC is in the labor movement. The largest union in the nation is the Guyana Agricultural and General Workers' Union (GAWU), which the PPP controls through Ram Karran. In recent years it has worked closely with three smaller unions: the Clerical and Commercial Workers Union, headed by Birchmore Philadelphia; the National Association of Agricultural, Commercial, and Industrial Employees, led by Nankishore Gopaul; and the University of Guyana Staff Association, headed by WPA official Clive Thomas. The four unions, which are thought to represent about 40 percent of Guyana's workers, have long charged the 23-member Guyana Trade Union Congress (TUC) with adopting a collaborationist policy toward the PNC. Since late 1983 these four have often been joined by two, sometimes three, other small unions. In fact, since late 1984, even new TUC membership has taken some stands more critical of the government. Early in 1985 one estimate of union membership reported 50,000 workers critical of the government and only 30,000 supportive (CANA, 22 April; *FBIS*, 26 April). In mid-December the PPP and WPA urged Guyanese workers to strike and demonstrate in protest against what they charged was the fraudulent 9 December election (CANA, 16 December; *FBIS*, 17 December).

The PPP has consistently adopted international positions that parallel those of the Soviet Union. The party hosted a consultative meeting of Caribbean "communist, revolutionary, and anti-imperialist" parties after its party congress in August. At the same time, one of Jagan's greatest obstacles in trying to bring down the PNC government is the fact that the Soviet Union maintains close relations with the PNC; a CPSU delegation attended the PNC's national congress in mid-August, for example, and the Soviet media gave at least as much attention to that congress as it did to the PPP's congress several weeks earlier. In mid-December the PNC government expressed its interest in consolidating its relations with the Soviet Union, although it simultaneously showed signs of closer ties to Washington.

The WPA. Throughout 1985 the WPA promoted the practice of free and fair elections in Guyana, confident that if such were held the PNC would be removed from office. The WPA elaborated on its expectations for a fair election at home, and party leader Eusi Kwayana went to Trinidad and Tobago in May to testify before the British Parliamentary Human Rights Group and Americas Watch Committee when permission to hold hearings in Guyana was denied by the Burnham government (see Georgetown, *Dayclean*, 11 May; *Interim Report of the Joint Mission to Investigate Political Freedom in Guyana*, New York: Americas Watch, 1985).

The WPA said that the Guyanese people need to fight both the Burnham dictatorship and "old politics." The major grievances of the people during the year, the WPA claimed, were the elections, violent crime, and food shortages (*Catholic Standard*, JPRS, 1 October). Prior to Burnham's death, the party regretted that the popular struggle had not yet advanced far enough to make it possible to squeeze concessions from the government (Bridgetown, *Caribbean Contact*, June). In its statement on Burnham's death, the party pledged its continuing adherence to nonviolent political conflict. It called for an honest evaluation of Burnham's achievements in an effort to build on them and find better policies for the future (*Open Word*, 12 August).

The WPA, originally associated with a Castroite line under its late founder Walter Rodney, has now adopted less militantly Marxist-Leninist positions and drawn criticism from the PPP (*Mirror*, 24 March), although the two parties tried to work together on occasion during the year.

Meeting of Caribbean Communist, Revolutionary, and Anti-imperialist Parties. Nine parties met in Guyana on 1–2 August, immediately prior to the opening of the Twenty-second Congress of the PPP. The nine were the PPP (Guyana), People's Popular Movement (Trinidad), United People's Movement (St. Vincent), Dominica Liberation Movement (Dominica), Workers Party of Barbados (Barbados), Workers Revolutionary Movement (St. Lucia), February 25th Movement (Suriname), Frente Sandinista (Nicaragua), and Communist Party of Cuba.

The official communiqué (text in *Mirror*, 11 August) noted in particular that (1) the Reagan administration poses a growing threat to world peace; (2) the United States has imposed an unjustified trade embargo against Nicaragua and continues to finance and arm the counterrevolutionary Nicaraguan forces, thereby engaging in state terrorism; (3) the Caribbean parties support Cuba's contention that the foreign debt of the Latin American countries should be cancelled and that a new international economic order should follow the cancellation if the countries of the Third World are ever to be able to survive economically; (4) grave difficulties affect member-states of the Caribbean; (5) there has been a dissipation of the despondency that pervaded the region following the U.S. invasion of Grenada; and, (6) the parties stand firm in their solidarity with the Cuban, Nicaraguan, and Surinamese revolutions and with the freedom fighters of the FMLN-FDR of El Salvador.

William Ratliff
Hoover Institution

Haiti

Population. 5,762,000 (about one million outside Haiti)
Party. United Party of Haitian Communists (Parti Unifie des Communistes Haïtiens; PUCH)
Founded. 1934 (PUCH, 1968)
Membership. 350 (estimated; mainly outside Haiti)
Secretary General. René Théodore
Secretariat. Includes Rock Derose (in prison in Haiti).
Status. Illegal and proscribed until 1985; law passed in 1985 and announced 13 November nullified the 1969 law that provided the death penalty for persons engaged in activity labeled "communist."
Last Congress. First, 1979
Last Election. N/a
Auxiliary Organizations. No data
Publications. The newspaper *Haiti-Progrès* often publishes material reflecting PUCH point of view. René Théodore and others also address letters occasionally to other Haitian publications in the United States.

The PUCH celebrated its 50th anniversary at the end of 1984. Writers and intellectuals such as Jacques Roumain brought together Marxist study groups in 1934 to form the Communist Party of Haiti, which reorganized itself first in 1959 into the Party of National Unity of Haiti and then into the United Party of Haitian Communists in 1968. Through an article in *Pravda* (23 December 1984, p. 5) "Soviet Communists express solidarity with the courageous struggle Haitian communists are waging. . . ." Secretary General René Théodore marked the anniversary by stating party demands in January, including the "release of all political prisoners, including communists . . . freedom of movement of citizens . . . respect for the right of political parties, including the United Party of Haitian Communists, to organize and operate freely . . . respect for freedom of speech" (*Information Bulletin*, April, p. 29).

The Communists of Haiti operate underground or, more often, outside the country in Montreal, Mexico City, and Havana. In 1949 all parties were banned, and in 1969 President François Duvalier passed a law punishing with death all those involved in activities labeled "communist." On 8 June a bill was introduced to the Haitian legislature by President Jean-Claude Duvalier legalizing all parties that pledge to support the life presidency of Duvalier and that have 18,000 members, thereby excluding all opposition groups from party status.

On 13 November the minister of information announced the suppression of the death penalty for political crimes, which implicitly abolished the death penalty for communist activities. However, PUCH has wisely avoided publicizing its membership, partly because it is small and partly because it is likely they would be persecuted, no matter what the law now says. Rock Derose, who is openly identified as a member of the secretariat of the Central Committee of PUCH, is now in a Haitian prison.

The party has been characterized by friendly Haitians as a "brain without a body," meaning that its members and supporters are primarily a small group of intellectuals and writers. The masses of Haitians inside and outside Haiti are divided politically and are suspicious of most parties, above all the Communists. Furthermore, from the occasional open letters in the press, it is clear that party leadership, headed by René Théodore, spends a great deal of time on personal and petty disputes.

PUCH representatives and allies—including Gérard Pierre-Charles, the economist; Ben Dupuy, editor of *Haiti-Progrès*; and René Théodore—attended meetings in Havana, and Frank Hyppolite has been the representative of PUCH in Havana (*Haiti-Observateur*, 1–8 March, p. 1), and there are regular PUCH broadcasts over Radio Havana to Haiti. Nevertheless, the Communists of Haiti remain isolated from other movements within and outside of Haiti.

Brian Weinstein
Howard University

Honduras

Population. 4,394,000

Major Marxist-Leninist Groups. Communist Party of Honduras (Partido Comunista de Honduras; PCH), founded in 1927, crushed by 1932, and reorganized in 1954, of which Rigoberto Padilla Rush—now living in Cuba—claims to be secretary general, although Mario Sosa Navarro—probably living underground in Honduras—appears to be the actual leader; the Central American Workers' Revolutionary Party (Partido Revolucionario de Trabajadores de Centro-America–Honduras; PRTC-H), the Honduran offshoot of the PRTC established in 1976 in Costa Rica, probably led by Wilfredo Gallardo; the Morazanist Front for the Liberation of Honduras (Frente Morazanista para la Liberación de Honduras; FMLH), founded in 1969 but inactive until 1980, leadership includes Octavio Pérez (probably an alias) and "Fernando López"; the Lorenzo Zelaya Popular Revolutionary Forces (Fuerzas Populares Revolucionarios Lorenzo Zelaya; FPR-LZ), founded in 1980, leadership unknown; and the "Cinchoneros" Popular Liberation Movement (Movimiento Popular de Liberación Cinchoneros; MPL), founded in 1981, leadership unknown.

Marxist-Leninist Front. National Unified Directorate of the Honduran Revolutionary Movement (DNU-MRH), a nonfunctioning umbrella organization of the Marxist-Leninist left

Status. All are illegal.

Publications. *Vanguardia Revolucionaria* (PCH), *Lorenzo Zelaya* (FPR-LZ; irregular, published in Mexico)

The DNU-MHR was established in 1982 as an umbrella organization of the Honduran Marxist-Leninist left. In addition to the parties listed above, it includes smaller groups such as the Party of Socialist Action (Partido de Acción Socialista de Honduras; PASOH), led by Virgilio Carias. One of the Marxist-Leninist groups that does not belong to the DNU-MHR is the Communist Party of Honduras–Marxist-Leninist (Partido Comunista de Honduras–Marxista-Leninista; PCH-ML), a pro-Chinese splinter of the PCH founded in 1967 and little known even today.

For all practical purposes the DNU-MHR is largely a fictional umbrella group of Marxist-Leninist organizations that have no common program, strategy, or leadership. The PCH, which is the oldest of the participating parties, is badly divided; the PRTC-H is little more than a Cuban and Nicaraguan intelligence and subversive branch in Honduras; the Cinchoneros is a fully controlled creation of the Salvadoran Popular Revolutionary Army (ERP) and Popular Liberation Forces (FPL); and the FMLH and FPR-LZ are under joint control of Managua and the FMLN groups of El Salvador. To complicate matters further, the PCH-ML is adamantly opposed to everything the PCH stands for. Hence it supported the 22 November presidential and congressional elections, probably solely because the PCH publicly opposed them.

The split within the PCH continued throughout 1985 and was particularly evident with regard to the November elections. Mario Sosa Navarro, who opposed the elections, made it clear that his opposition—and therefore that of the internal PCH leadership—was one based on timing rather than principle (*FBIS*, 8 August, p. P9). Only a few weeks later the party urged abstention on election day; at the same time, under the signature of PCH Political Committee member Francisco Ortega, it bitterly attacked "the far-leftist group that Rigoberto Padilla leads from abroad" (ibid., 8 November, p. P9). Moreover, in a statement indicating the tension within the DNU-MHR umbrella, Ortega claimed that "we do not want alliances with him [i.e., Padilla] and a group of 15 traitors who live in the country and spend their time speaking about 'revolution' every time they get their 'salaries'" (ibid.). This seems to indicate that the official PCH line on Padilla—that he lost his position because he lives abroad and thus, according to party rules, cannot be secretary general—is not the real reason for Padilla's ouster. Ortega himself admitted the existence of fifteen internally based Padilla supporters. The primary reason for the PCH split was the factional struggle between the Padilla and Sosa Navarro groups, with the latter coming out on top for the time being.

According to the dominant Sosa Navarro faction, the "abuses" of the General Alvarez regime (or of his period of army command) could and should be investigated by the new military leadership. The declaration concluded by stating that the "Armed Forces still have time to vindicate themselves" (*FBIS*, 8 November, p. P10).

The Sosa Navarro faction of the PCH was long known as moderate, living rather comfortably in San Pedro Sula, and unlikely to be attracted by the "adventurist" (that is, violent-prone) policies advocated by Padilla. Its apparent victory over the foreign-based Padilla faction seems to preclude any serious PCH involvement in revolutionary violence in Honduras, despite rhetorical demonstrations of solidarity with the Sandinistas in Nicaragua and claims of admiration of the Castro regime (ibid.).

The only significant act of violence on the part of the Honduran Marxist-Leninist left in 1985 came from the FMLH, which bombed a discotheque in Tegucigalpa in March as a protest against the "Pine III" joint Honduran-U.S. military maneuvers; the group also tried, unsuccessfully, to kill Captain Raymond Shear of the U.S. Army Green Berets (ibid., pp. P2–3). The long-standing link between Honduran and Salvadoran revolutionary groups was once again demonstrated by the presence of a Honduran (Dr. Reyes) among the terrorists released to Havana by the government of El Salvador in exchange for President Duarte's daughter, and by repeated indications of Salvadoran guerrilla activities, with Honduran help, among the Salvadoran "refugee camps" in Honduras throughout the year.

The PCH-ML statement regarding the November elections flatly declared that the Honduran left, lacking its own instrument for electoral participation, must participate in the democratic process by supporting "progressive" candidates such as the marginal Christian-Democrats and the Innovation and Unity Party (PINU), while rejecting both the free market–oriented National Party candidate, Rafael Leonardo Callejas, and the establishment's Liberal Party champion, Azcona Hoyo (ibid., p. P6).

The Padilla faction of the PCH remains the most staunchly pro-Soviet and pro-Cuban group of the Honduran Marxist-Leninist left. Padilla demonstrated his own close ties to Moscow by publishing an article entitled "Armed Intervention on the Pretext of Countering a Mythical Threat" in the *World Marxist Review* (June, pp. 24–30). In this article Padilla invoked the name of Francisco Morazán, the father of the Honduran nation, advocated a "flexible policy of alliances" of all anti-American parties, and "rejected" factional (that is, Sosa Navarro's) actions (ibid.).

Michael Radu
Foreign Policy Research Institute

Jamaica

Population. 2,428,000
Party. Workers' Party of Jamaica (WPJ)
Founded. 1978
Membership. 50 (estimated)
Secretary General. Trevor Munroe
Leading Bodies. No data
Status. Legal
Last Congress. Third, December 1984
Last Election. 1983, WPJ boycotted.
Auxiliary Organizations. No data
Other Marxist-Leninist Groups. Jamaica Communist Party; Revolutionary Marxist League (RML)
Publications. *Struggle*

The growing deterioration of the economic and social situation in Jamaica found expression in 1972 in the victory of the democratic-socialist People's National Party (PNP), headed by Michael Manley. The PNP government remained in power until 1980, when the opposition Jamaica Labor Party (JLP) won a landslide victory and its leader, Edward Seaga, became prime minister.

In December 1983, two years before constitutionally mandated, Seaga called an election. The PNP boycotted the elections because Seaga had not brought the electoral rolls up to date, as he had promised to do before new elections were called. The result was that the JLP won all seats in Parliament.

Both the PNP and the Workers' Party of Jamaica (WPJ) agitated throughout 1984 for new elections, and during the January riots slogans such as "Seaga Out! Elections Now!" appeared on walls throughout the country. Seaga finally conceded to hold municipal elections but still refused to call a new parliamentary poll. He was probably influenced by the decline in his party's popular support shown in July by the JLP having the backing of only 25 percent of the electorate, whereas the PNP was supported by 61 percent (*Caribbean Report*, 27 September).

The economic situation continued to deteriorate throughout the year. In April it was reported that unemployment was 25 percent or more, and inflation was running at 30 percent (*WSJ*, 5 April). Bank interest rates were reported at about the same time to be 30–35 percent (Port-of-Spain, *Sunday Guardian*, 31 March).

Leadership and Organization. The WPJ has had the Moscow franchise in Jamaica. The rival Jamaica Communist Party, organized in 1975 by Chris Lawrence, did nothing of note in 1985. The WPJ grew out of the Workers' Liberation League, organized in the early 1970s by Dr. Trevor Munroe, a member of the political science department of the Jamaican branch of the University of the West Indies. It was formally established as a political party in December 1979. During the Manley era, the WPJ gave crucial support to the PNP government. It backed PNP candidates in 1980, but in June 1985 Munroe indicated that the WPJ intended to run its own candidates in 10–13 percent of the constituencies in forthcoming municipal elections (*WMR*, June).

The Third Congress of the WPJ had been held in Kingston in December 1984. Munroe subsequently gave information on the delegates. Some 32.4 percent were workers as compared to 23.1 percent in the Second Congress in 1981. The party was also apparently older: 54.3 percent of the delegates were over 30 as compared to only 22.3 percent three years earlier. He claimed that 45 percent of the delegates were "leaders" in nonparty organizations.

Munroe reported that the Third Congress saw Jamaica experiencing "a nonrevolutionary situation, with increasingly prerevolutionary elements." He added that "the overall tactical line set by the Congress was to retain the defensive against a dangerous regional and local reaction, whilst at the same time increasing our preparedness to pass over to the offensive in keeping with the possibilities of the mass movement." He noted that "the Congress directed that the struggle against sectarianism and to overcome abstract Marxism in sufficiently taking into account Jamaican and regional peculiarities was to infuse all aspects of party work" (*WMR*, June).

Domestic Attitudes and Activities. In mid-January spontaneous protests, including the mounting of barricades, broke out against the Seaga government's decree to increase fuel prices. Five people died and twenty were wounded in clashes with the police.

During these events, the WPJ issued a press release in which "it noted that its members and supporters were taking part in the roadblocks to 'maintain the people's protest'" (*Intercontinental Press*, 18 February). However, Trevor Munroe reported subsequently that "our party applied the tactics approved by the Congress, namely, to strengthen the protest activity of the masses whilst being careful not to overestimate the possibilities of specific episodes and, most of all, ensuring that the party does not become isolated from the still relatively nonrevolutionary middle-of-the-road tendency in the country. Hence, party members and supporters gave active propaganda and practical support to the road blocks, but called for their termination when the balance of forces began to change against that form of action" (*WMR*, June).

The WPJ also supported massive strikes that took place in June. Those strikes involved the country's teachers, electric power workers, and government civil servants, among others (*Caribbean Report*, 14 June, 19 July).

International Views, Positions, and Activities. The WPJ maintains more or less close relations with other pro-Soviet parties. Thus, at the December 1984 congress of the party, there were in attendance delegations from fifteen foreign communist parties, including representatives from the international information department of the Central Committee of the Soviet Communist Party (CPSU) (*Pravda*, 15 December; *FBIS*, 26 December).

WPJ relations with parties in the Caribbean area were particularly close. Thus, the Central Committee's report to the party's Third Congress declared that "we re-dedicate ourselves to the primary responsibility of the Caribbean and the Latin American people—the primary responsibility of solidarity with the Cuban Revolution, which represents the finest achievement of the Caribbean and Latin American peoples. We re-dedicate our solidarity with the embattled patriots in Central America, particularly in Nicaragua, facing imminent United States imperialist aggression" (*WMR*, June). In March the People's Progressive Party of Guyana, in turn, expressed its support for the WPJ. It publicized a protest against alleged executions of patriots by the Jamaican police (Georgetown *Mirror*, 24 March).

Of significance is that overseas pro-Moscow parties sought throughout the year to maintain contact with the PNP. Thus, a CPSU delegation led by Y. S. Znamenskly, first secretary of the Gorno-Altay CPSU Obkom, attended the PNP's 47th annual national convention (*Pravda*, 29 September; *FBIS*, 7 October).

Revolutionary Marxist League. The third and smallest Marxist-Leninist organization in Jamaica is the RML. It was organized in the late 1970s and identifies itself as Trotskyist. It is, however, aligned with the Revolutionary Socialist League in the United States, which repudiates the traditional Trotskyist position that the Soviet Union and other Soviet-bloc states remain "workers' states." In 1982 the two groups proclaimed their intention of forming an "internationalist tendency" within the Trotskyist movement. At the time of the widespread strikes in June, the RML "began a campaign demanding the government's resignation and calling for an interim government of the trade unions and other workers' organizations." It widely circulated a pamphlet and put up posters stating this position (*Torch*, 5 October–14 November).

Robert J. Alexander
Rutgers University

Martinique

Population. 327,000
Party. Martinique Communist Party (Parti Communiste Martiniquais; PCM)
Founded. 1921 (PCM, 1957)
Membership. Under 1,000
Secretary General. Armand Nicolas (60, French citizen)
Politburo. 3 members
Secretariat. 4 members
Central Committee. 33 members
Status. Legal
Last Congress. Eighth, 12–13 November 1983
Last Election. March 1985, won 2 out of 27 contested seats in General Council; total 3 of 45 seats
Auxiliary Organizations. General Confederation of Martiniquan Labor (CGTM); Martiniquan Union of Education Personnel (SMPE-CGTM); Union of Women of Martinique (Union des Femmes de la Martinique); Martiniquan Committee of Solidarity with the Peoples of the Caribbean and of Central America
Publications. *Justice* (weekly newspaper)

The PCM marked the 64th year of its existence by calling for the unification of all parties on the left for the elections to the French National Assembly in March 1986. The appeal signaled its continuing weakness, caught as it is between more conservative parties and nationalist parties. It is probably weaker now than at any time since 1957, when it transformed itself from a section of the French Communist Party (PCF) into an independent party.

Continuing economic difficulties, an unemployment rate of over 30 percent, and new signs of serious urban crime and disorder troubled the party. Under increasing pressure to join the independence movement, the PCM proclaimed its continuing commitment to decentralization, local autonomy, and "eventual" independence.

Leadership and Organization. Secretary General Armand Nicolas struggled to maintain party discipline, which had been badly shaken by defections and severe internal criticisms in 1984, and to increase party membership. On his 60th birthday, Nicolas received the Order of Friendship Among Peoples from the Soviet Union.

In preparation for the partial cantonal elections in March to choose representatives to the newly strengthened General Council, the PCM agreed with other parties on the left—such as the Socialists and the progressives of Aimé Césaire—to continue supporting each other in the runoffs. The Communists ran only nine candidates in 27 districts. It won two seats, bringing to a total of three its seats in the General Council, which has a total of 45.

Domestic Party Affairs. Unlike the PCF, the PCM expressed its satisfaction in many ways with the socialist government of France. It applauded the Socialist appointed prefect in Martinique, and it praised the Socialists for reorganizing the cantons of Martinique. Reorganization meant adding twelve new cantons in heavily populated areas to equalize the number of people represented by each member of the Regional Council. Thus, each canton now contains 8,000 to 9,000 people.

Party leadership openly announced that it would follow a pragmatic line concerning the Socialists even in the absence of Communists in the French prime minister's cabinet. If the Socialists' policies were good for Martinique, the PCM would praise and support them. Conversely, if their policies were harmful, the PCM would criticize the Socialists, according to the secretary general. In addition, the party newspaper was filled with appeals to the Socialists and the progressives to unite with the Communists for purposes of electing officials to the local assembly and other offices.

Of considerable concern to the PCM is the rise of an extreme right group, the National Front (FN), led by Jean-Marie Le Pen. They consider the FN as a sign of growing racism in France. The shooting of a young Martiniquan man and other signs of violence against blacks outraged party members who called, once again, for the unification of all forces on the left to combat what they termed racist and fascist threats to democracy in France. They calculated that almost 50 percent of all Martiniquans and persons of Martiniquan descent now live in metropolitan France.

International Views. The PCM carefully watched events in New Caledonia, a French overseas territory where an independence movement vowed to drive the French out of the Pacific. In January the Martiniquan Communists expressed their support for independence for the native Kanaks, as the New Caledonians call themselves, and held demonstrations in Fort-de-France, Martinique's capital. *Justice*, the party newspaper, ran a story in practically every issue on the movement for independence in New Caledonia.

The Martiniquan Communists also maintained their close ties with the Soviet Union and Cuba, their two most important outside links. They sent delegates to the twelfth World Festival of Youth and Students in Moscow at the end of July. A Cuban theatrical company visited Fort-de-France, and Camille Jacaria, secretary general of the communist-affiliated trade union, CGTM, attended a trade-union conference in Havana. Two members of the Politburo attended a meeting of Caribbean and Latin American communist parties in Cuba. The PCM also sent a delegation to the Twenty-fifth Congress of the PCF and to the Third Congress of the Jamaican Labor Party.

The party sent a telegram to President Reagan protesting U.S. actions against the government of Nicaragua. An exposition of photographs at party headquarters expressed PCM solidarity with the blacks of South Africa.

Brian Weinstein
Howard University

Mexico

Population. 79,700,000
Party. United Socialist Party of Mexico (Partido Socialista Unificado de México; PSUM)
Founded. 1919 (PSUM, 1981)
Membership. 40,800 (*IB*, no. 15, p. 21)
Secretary General. Pablo Gómez Alvarez
Political Commission. 21 members: Pablo Gómez Alvarez, Sabino Hernández Tellez, Gilberto Rincon Gallardo Meltiz, Manuel Stephens García, Jorge Alocer Villanueva, Rolando Cordera Campos. Ivan

García Solis, Arnaldo Martínez Verdugo, Eduardo Montes Manzano, Pablo Pascual Moncayo, Marcos Leonel Posadas Segura, Gerardo Unzueta Lorenzana, Miguel Angel Velasco Muñoz, Leopoldo Arturo Whaley Martínez, Valentín Campa Salazar, Eduardo González Ramírez, Adolfo Sánchez Rebolledo, José Woldenberg Karakowsky, Amalia García, Gustavo Adolfo Hirales, Enrique Semo

Secretariat. 7 members: Pablo Gómez Alvarez, Sabino Hernández Tellez, Gilberto Rincon Gallardo Meltiz, Manuel Stephens García, Jorge Alocer Villanueva, Jesús Sosa Castro, José Woldenberg Karakowsky

Central Committee. 74 members

Status. Legal

Last Congress. Second, 9–14 August 1983

Last Elections. 1985 midterm elections. 3.24 percent of the vote for, and 12 of 400 seats in, the Chamber of Deputies (lower house of the Mexican Congress)

Auxiliary Organizations. Youth/Student Section of the PSUM; Independent Center of Agricultural Workers and Peasants (CIOAC); Sole National Union of University Workers (SUNTU); Single Union of Workers of the Nuclear Industry

Publications. *Asi Es* (weekly, Mexico City)

The PSUM, recognized by the Soviet Union as the official party of the country, was formed in 1981 as the product of a fusion between the Mexican Communist Party (Partido Comunista Mexicano; PCM) with four smaller groups: the Popular Action Movement (Movimiento de Acción Popular; MAP); the Mexican People's Party (Partido Popular Mexicano; PPM); the Revolutionary Socialist Party (Partido Socialista Revolucionario; PSR); and the Socialist Action and Unity Movement (Movimiento de Acción y Unidad; MAUS). In 1984, however, the PSR withdrew from the PSUM in protest against its style of leadership, and in 1985 the PPM made a de facto break with the party over allegations that the group from the PCM was monopolizing all the leading positions and acting autocratically. Secretary General Gómez has not formally recognized the withdrawal of the PPM, and so the PSUM's composition, along with its membership figures, remains in flux.

The PCM was the most cohesive and well organized among the plethora of leftist parties in Mexico and the only party with a nationwide apparatus and support structure. Ideology has been less important in dividing the various leftist groups than has the emergence of strong personalities, each wanting to dominate his own organization rather than dilute his power in a cooperative venture with like-minded parties.

The PSUM held its first congress in March 1982. The conclave adopted a declaration of principles and a party program and rules. It also elected a Central Committee. After the congress, the Central Committee selected a Political Commission, which in turn chose Pablo Gómez Alvarez as the party's secretary general. The Leninist theory of "democratic centralism" was adopted as the PSUM's modus operandi (*Asi Es*, 16–22 April 1982).

In the period following the merger, the dominant PCM faction within the PSUM evidently retained its Eurocommunist orientation and was allied with the MAP, a "national socialist" and anti-Soviet group (*El Dia*, 30 June 1983). These two components of the PSUM were reportedly pitted against the other three (ibid.). The PSR had displayed a slavishly pro-Soviet tendency, supporting the USSR on the litmus tests of Poland and Afghanistan (*YICA*, 1982, p. 123), and the PPM had also backed Moscow on the Afghan issue (*YICA*, 1981, p. 91).

On 25 June 1984, an article in *Uno Mas Uno* stated: "According to Roberto Jaramillo—the most recent defector from the PSUM—the irresponsibility, charlatanism, and ambitions of the . . . PSUM have ruined leftist unity in this country and turned the PSUM into 'a weak party involved in a permanent internal struggle, a party in crisis, a party that is merely a house of cards which can be blown away.'"

During the Central Committee's sixth plenum, on 22–23 July 1984, the participants bewailed the failure to implement many of the programs set forth by the party's Second Congress; this failure was attributed to "insufficient . . . agreement on extremely important aspects of our policy" and to "the lack of participation . . . on the party's various leadership levels, but especially in . . . the Political Commission, in which outstanding leaders failed to participate because of their disagreement with the results of the Congress." The plenum noted the close connection between the party's internal struggle and its inability to accomplish its political objectives. The discussants emphasized that "our internal situation is not a quarrel among us, at least not that alone. It is a problem of a national nature" (*JPRS-LAM* 84-136, 13 December 1984, pp. 2–3, 9). Central Committee member Raymundo Cardenas declared that "with the activity being carried out by the government's PRI [Institutional Revolutionary Party] and the National Action Party [PAN; the chief opposition party], we shall be left on the sidelines completely if we don't . . . give another loud ring of the bell, so to speak . . . I maintain that those who do not do everything that should be done internally to achieve unity will be condemned by history" (ibid., p. 29).

Complementing the PSUM's efforts to structure its leadership in a manner more representative of the elements comprising it was its campaign to seek allies to contest the 1985 Mexican elections. "Unity of the left" became the PSUM's electoral battle cry.

Two major obstacles lay in the path of the PSUM's attempt to forge a broad leftist alliance. One was the law on political organizations and electoral processes (LOPPE), which stipulated that any party participating in an alliance would lose its registration with the Federal Election Commission. The other obstacle to unity involved resistance from factions within the PSUM itself, notably among former chief of the PPM Alejandro Gascon Mercado and his followers. Several of the leftist groups that the PSUM majority regarded as potential allies—for example, the Popular Socialist Party (PPS) and the Socialist Workers Party (PST)—were regarded by Gascon as virtual satellites of the ruling PRI. Moreover, Gascon objected to the PSUM's decision to support the candidates of other leftist parties in various local elections—a decision that was tantamount to "riding on the coattails of the other organizations" (*Uno Mas Uno*, 15 October 1984).

On 16–18 August 1984 in Mexico City, the PSUM held a National Organization Conference, with delegates representing some two-thirds of the party's membership. Gómez and Sabino Hernández Tellez, head of organizational affairs for the Central Committee, presided. The conference was devoted to resolving the structural and organizational problems that had plagued the PSUM since its creation. In addition, the conference aimed at providing scope for the party's components to express their views within the context of "democratic centralism" and at strengthening the party's unity and effectiveness in the face of its participation in the 1985 national elections and its avowed desire to forge a unified democratic left in the country (*Asi Es*, 31 August 1984, p. 15).

The conference issued a general resolution (published in *Asi Es*, 14 September 1984, pp. 15–20) that proclaimed the PSUM's intention of becoming a "revolutionary workers party" that would aim at "turning the Socialist alternative into a mass project . . . a political, ideological and cultural movement capable of challenging the hegemony of the forces that support and defend the current capitalist system of exploitation and domination." As a prerequisite to becoming a mass party, however, the resolution stressed the necessity of overcoming the sectarianism that was plaguing the organization.

The PSUM's organizational tasks were described in the resolution as twofold: an increase in membership and a solidification of the party structure. Every level of organization, from rank and file associations through zone, municipal, regional, and state committees to the national level, were deemed in need of strengthening. The resolution emphasized in particular the need to build up rank and file organizations in workplaces, housing centers, rural areas, agrarian communities, and ethnic enclaves. Such bodies would be designed to recruit new members into the party, direct activities in support of the party, and promote understanding of its philosophy and objectives. The expansion of political indoctrination sessions for party members and the broader dissemination of propaganda among sympathizers were also stressed.

Pointing to the importance of unity of action within the party, the resolution asserted that "the national presence of the PSUM may be firmly established only through the application of a single political line of conduct followed by the entire party on the main national issues, relating action undertaken in any region to that taken throughout the country." It emphasized that "the PSUM resolves to grow in an organized fashion throughout the country, building a structure based on the political divisions existing in Mexico."

The resolution called for more discipline within the PSUM but observed at the same time that "the debate transpiring in our rank and file concerning the role of internal democracy and the manner of exercising it points up that it is still necessary to accentuate methods and forms of participation in the drafting and daily application of PSUM policy . . . There must be respect for minority opinions . . . without this signifying any justification in avoiding compliance with accords drafted collectively and adopted by the majority."

In his report to the conference, Hernández exhorted the delegates to "make an effort to outline and develop the concept of party that has united us and that is the basis for the most important effort made in Mexico, following decades of dispersion and scattering, to achieve the cohesion of the forces of Socialist revolutionaries." He reiterated, however, that the PSUM must achieve internal unity in order to promote more effectively the nationwide unity of the left. "Practices of internal struggles leading to divisions and expulsions or alienation must be fought in the PSUM," Hernandez warned. "A serious obstacle to the construction of the PSUM would be that opinions held might turn into factions, continuing groupings with a defined structure and leadership, their own discipline and character. Their participation as such in party life would break down unity and democracy."

With regard to the upcoming Mexican elections, Hernández noted that "we participate in elections because they make it possible to measure the party's advances among the workers and the people, evaluate the effects of party speeches, increase the political influence gained by the party among workers, develop the party, influence government decisions through mobilization and achieve representation in legislatures and town councils." He went on to say that:

> Nevertheless, some problems have not been resolved. We still have not fully linked election participation with the political struggles of the masses. We have not turned the elections into a movement of general rejection of the capitalist system, of its national government and its policies. We have not clearly outlined the need to oust the current government . . . in order to build a new government. We have not presented ourselves as this country's socialist alternative . . . In order to do this, we must develop a clear conception of the election struggle as a revolutionary action permitting construction of the party in factories, on communal farms, in the schools, towns, and participation in trade unions, farm struggles, the people's movement in urban areas and culture.

During the course of his report, Hernández revealed that the PSUM had 63,212 members, of which some 48,000 had already received their credentials. About 37 percent of these were wage-earning workers, almost equally divided between industrial and agricultural workers. Farmers and peasants constituted about 29 percent of the party membership, according to Hernández's figures, and students about 10 percent. He added that women accounted for 27.5 percent of the members (*Asi Es*, 28 September 1984, pp. 15–19).

The PSUM's organizational activities and plans for participation in the national elections continued to suffer from the intraparty struggle. Gascon and 24 other Central Committee members boycotted the ninth plenum, which took place in November 1984. The plenum re-elected Gómez and the Political Commission (which was composed almost exclusively of his supporters). "It sidestepped the party's central problem, however, which is its lack of unity and the mounting discontent among national, state and local leaders over the performance of the party's secretary general . . . who is charged with being the main force behind the party's parochialism and internal repression" (*Uno Mas Uno*, 12 November 1984, p. 4). Gascon lambasted Gómez for insisting on the PCM's monopoly of the leadership and ignoring the demands of the PSUM's other components for a proportional share of the top positions. Gascon's supporters observed with irony that the PSUM was suppressing democracy internally even while it was trumpeting it in its campaign for the national elections (ibid.).

The party's infighting escalated with Gascon's charge, on 4 February, that Gómez and his supporters had seized control of PSUM conventions in several states in order to force the selection to the national electoral assembly of delegates in sympathy with their views. The task of the electoral assembly was to choose candidates for seats in the federal Chamber of Deputies. Gómez was accused of preparing to hold parallel conventions of his supporters in the states—including most of those along the Pacific coast—where Gascon's faction was predominant. Gascon's charges were contained in a six-page document that outlined "step by step, the process pursued by Gómez to take control of the entire power and of the next PSUM congressional faction in the Chamber of Deptuies" (*Uno Mas Uno*, 6 February, p. 4). The signers of the document included Manuel Stephens García, Jorge Alocer Villanueva, Pablo Pascual Moncayo, Marcos Leonel Posadas Segura, and Gustavo Adolfo Hirales, all of whom sit on the party's Political Commission. "The Radical Democratic Movement of PSUM, to which we belong, insists upon a return to democratic existence within our party, which has been violated by the trouble-making, factional positions of a leadership which has taken a stand apart from the statutory legality and the most fundamental democratic principles that should govern our party's existence," the document concluded (ibid.).

Against this backdrop of internecine warfare, the PSUM Central Committee's eleventh plenum convened on 6 February:

> taking up virtually only one topic: the charge against. . . Gómez of sponsoring antidemocracy in the election processes for delegates to the National Electoral Assembly . . . and of encouraging an atmosphere of internal violence intended to put out into the street an entire movement calling itself "democratic and radical" headed by Alejandro Gascon Mercado, so as thereby, contrary to any political price or credibility, to bolster the perpetuation of the former leadership cadres of the abolished party as a current Mexican Communist Party. (Ibid.)

A majority at the plenum voted to disavow the legality of the electoral convention held in the state of Nayarit, where Gascon has presided over the largest PSUM faction in the country. As a result of the vote, Gascon and his supporters made a de facto break with the PSUM. Gómez persisted in denying that a schism had occurred in the party, even when about 300 delegates (representing 40 percent of the total) walked out of the national electoral assembly as a gesture of loyalty to Gascon.

> With the de facto break-off by Gascon Mercado's movement, the third force of the five which created PSUM has disappeared: Heberto Castillo's PMT heeded the call for the creation of PSUM, but never joined because of differences in its leadership composition and because of the initials and the logos; Roberto Jaramillo's PSR left PSUM last year, after a series of serious accusations against the PSUM leadership. With Gascon's movement leaving, in fact, the Mexican People's Party . . . is leaving. At present, PSUM consists only of those who comprised the Mexican Communist Party and the Socialist Action and Unity Movement. (*Uno Mas Uno*, 8 February, p. 5)

Gascon delivered a parting shot at his former comrades:

> PSUM has been seized by a reformist bureaucracy capable of committing the necessary arbitrary acts, such as inflating figures or holding parallel congresses, so as to retain the privileges that will ensure them their vested interests. Arnaldo Martínez Verdugo is the brains, the gray eminence, of that closed group; Pablo Gómez is the operator. One produces and determines the ideas, and the other takes action, strikes blows and destroys. (*Proceso*, 18 February, pp. 22–25)

Aside from the PCM and the MAUS, only the MAP remained a part of the PSUM. This faction has threatened to withdraw, however, in protest over the manipulation by Gómez's cohorts of elections in various PSUM-dominated unions and other organizations. Rolando Cordera Campos, a member of the MAP who sits on the PSUM's Political Commission, accused former PCM cadres of taking over leadership positions in the Trade Union of Workers of the National Autonomous University of Mexico that previously had been reserved for MAP people. He also accused a PCM adherent of challenging the MAP's candidate for the post of technical adviser at the university's school of economics (*Uno Mas Uno*, 17 March, pp. 1, 7).

On 12 February, at the moment of the PSUM's greatest internal weakness, an electoral front was formed among five groups for the purpose of contesting the national midterm elections. The PSUM masterminded the grouping, which also included the PPS, the Mexican Workers Party (PMT), Communist Left Unity (UIC), and Socialist Current (CS). A common electoral platform was adopted, and it was agreed to field a single candidate for federal deputy in each electoral district in the country. A member of the PPS then serving as a federal deputy stated that "this is not a temporary or specialized alliance, inasmuch as the organizations are willing to give up their individuality in the future to form a single party" (*El Nacional*, 13 February, p. 2). The new front was unable to agree on more than eight joint candidates, however (*Uno Mas Uno*, 7 March, p. 4). In the meantime, several hundred Communists who had recently left the PSUM announced the creation on 24 February of the Party of the Socialist Revolution, which defined its goal as the organization and control of the country's workers and peasants (*Uno Mas Uno*, 25 February, p. 4). Gascon was perhaps the best-known leader of the new party. It was agreed that the party would contest the national elections under the emblem of the PMT.

At stake in the elections were all 400 seats in the Chamber of Deputies (of which 300 were directly contested and the other 100 divided among minority parties in proportion to their share of the vote), seven state governorships, and hundreds of mayoralties and other municipal and state offices. The ruling PRI claimed to have won 292 of the 300 seats in the direct election (down from 299 in the 1982 voting), all seven of the governors' posts, and the great majority of the other offices in the election. The main opposition party, PAN, accused the PRI of extensive vote rigging and fraud. The PAN won 38 legislative seats (down from 55 in 1982); six came from the direct election and 32 from the share allotted to the minority parties (a designation covering every party except the PRI). The PSUM was a distant third in the election; it polled 3.24 percent of the vote (down slightly from 1982) and took twelve seats (down from seventeen) in the Chamber of Deputies. The new Party of the Socialist Revolution, appearing on the ballot under the PMT's logo, won six seats. On 22 July the Mexican newspaper *Excelsior* observed that, while the PSUM would hold only twelve seats in the federal chamber, "the group's composition is one of the most solid within the presumed opposition congressional groups, in view of the accumulated experience of its proposed candidates and of the three joining under its registration who belong to allied organizations."

The PSUM's international activities have focused heavily on developments in the hemisphere. In May 1984 the PSUM sponsored a festival of solidarity with the revolutionary struggles in Central America (*Pravda*, 22 May 1984). The party gave sustained and positive media coverage to the Contadora negotiations aimed at bringing peace to Central America and reducing the U.S. military presence there.

In December 1984 the PSUM participated in a meeting of communist parties in Czechoslovakia under the auspices of the Prague-based journal *Problems of Peace and Socialism (World Marxist Review)*. Such meetings are held periodically to assess the international situation and plan future strategies and tactics.

The PSUM's fifteenth Central Committee plenum, held in November 1985, devoted itself to questions of peace and international security. It issued an appeal urging the Mexican government to maintain its nonaligned position in world affairs but to pursue an active rather than a passive neutrality. The appeal emphasized that Mexico must refuse to participate in any military alliances or blocs and must actively foster peaceful coexistence and detente. In addition, the appeal accused the United States of militarizing the Central American region and thus causing the situation there to deteriorate (*Pravda*, 26 November).

Marian Leighton
Defense Intelligence Agency

Nicaragua

Population. 3,038,000
Party. Sandinista Front of National Liberation (Frente Sandinista de Liberación Nacional; FSLN)
Founded. 1960
Membership. ca. 4,000
National Directorate. Nine members: Daniel Ortega Saavedra, Humberto Ortega Saavedra, Victor Manuel Tirado López, Tomás Borge Martínez, Bayardo Arce Castaño, Henry Ruiz Hernández, Jaime Wheelock Román, Luis Carrión Cruz, and Carlos Núñez Téllez
Executive Commission. 5 members: Daniel Ortega Saavedra (coordinator), Bayardo Arce Castaño (deputy coordinator), Humberto Ortega Saavedra, Tomás Borge Martínez, Jaime Wheelock Román

Main State Organs. The Sandinista Assembly, 105 members, is supposed to convene every year. Ordinary party affairs are handled by seven auxiliary departments: general affairs (led by Rene Núñez), organization (Lea Guido), agitation and propaganda (Carlos Fernando Chamorro), political education (Vanessa Castro Cardenal), international organizations (Julio Lopez), finance (Plutarco Cornejo), and studies of Sandinism (Flor de Maria Monterrey). The cabinet includes: Daniel Ortega Saavedra (president of the republic), Humberto Ortega Saavedra (defense), Tomás Borge Martínez (interior minister), Luis Carrión Cruz (interior deputy minister), Henry Ruiz Hernández (planning and external cooperation), Jaime Wheelock Román (agrarian reform), and Carlos Núñez Téllez (president of Constituent Assembly).
Status. Ruling party
Last Congress. August 1985, FSLN Assembly
Last Election. 4 November 1984; presidential race, 63 percent; Constituent Assembly, 61 of 96 seats
Front and Auxiliary Organizations. Sandinista Defense Committees (Comités de Defensa Sandinista; CDS), estimated membership 150,000, led by Leticia Herrera; Sandinista Youth (Juventud Sandinista 19 de Julio), led by Carlos Carrión; "Luisa Amanda Espinosa" Association of Nicaraguan Women (Asociación de Mujeres Nicaraguenses Luisa Amanda Espinosa; AMNLAE), led by Glenda Monterey; Sandinista Workers' Central (Central Sandinista de Trabajadores; CST); Farmworkers' Association (Asociación de Trabajadores del Campo; ATC)
Publications. *Barricada* (party daily, circulation 110,000); *El Nuevo Diario* (government daily, 60,000); *Nicarahuac* (ideological journal); *Segovia* (army journal); Radio Sandino and La Voz de Nicaragua are the two major radio stations.
Other Marxist Parties. Several small leftist parties include the pro-Soviet communist group formed in 1937 and known as the Nicaraguan Socialist Party (Partido Socialista de Nicaragua; PSN), secretary general, Gustavo Tablada; the Communist Party of Nicaragua (Partido Comunista de Nicaragua; PCdeN), headed by Eli Altamirano; and the Popular Action Movement–Marxist-Leninist (Movimiento de Accion Popular–Marxist-Leninist; MAP-ML). Other leftist parties include the Workers' Revolutionary Party (Partido Revolucionario de Trabajadores; PRT), led by Bonifacio Miranda, and its close ally, the Central American Unification Party (Partido de Unificacion Centro Americana; PUCA), headed by Alejandro Perez Arevalo.

The ideological, political, economic, and military trends of 1984 continued throughout 1985. The FSLN tightened its grip over all sectors of Nicaraguan life but at the same time lost large segments of public support both at home and abroad. The attempt by Mexico, Colombia, Venezuela, and Panama to negotiate a solution to the series of crises in Central America (the Contadora process) had practically collapsed by the end of the year. This was due in large part to Nicaraguan actions. The isolation of the FSLN regime continued in the West and, to a lesser but growing extent, in Latin America, as did the unremitting hostility of the Reagan administration toward Managua.

Domestically, the FSLN conflict with the Catholic Church in general and with Miguel Cardinal Obando y Bravo in particular sharpened dramatically. Toward the end of the year the opposition parties, including some Marxist-Leninist groups, appeared to have moved closer to an anti-Sandinista position. At the same time the armed opposition pushed toward at least a political and strategic unification. Sandinista attempts to sever the Atlantic coast Indian opposition from the rest of the insurgents appear to have failed.

Militarily, despite the Sandinista Popular Army's (Ejército Popular Sandinista; EPS) claims of near victory, the insurgents (generally known as *contras*, a Sandinista-coined term) have expanded their operations in the strategically vital departments of central Nicaragua and have advanced to less than 100 miles outside Managua. The regime increased and armed its military establishment and used the war as a pretext to crack down on remaining civil liberties and as an excuse for the disastrous economic situation.

Party Affairs. Although the top Sandinista leaders share the same goals, it became evident throughout the year that their personal and tactical conflicts had grown. The conflict pits the tactically flexible followers of the Ortega brothers and Jaime Wheelock against the ideological hardliners led by Interior Minister Tomás Borge Martínez and Bayardo Arce Castaño.

The most important manifestation of the division was the outcome of the August special session of the Sandinista Assembly. The Political Commission of the National Directorate, the policy and ideological center of the party led by Arce, was abolished. It was replaced by an Executive Commission, chaired by President Daniel Ortega, which included Borge and the three members of the former Political Commission: Arce, Wheelock, and Humberto Ortega. The change aimed to "place the FSLN in a better position to coordinate the basic structures of revolutionary power; to strengthen the political unity of the FSLN; to turn the auxiliary departments into instruments of effective support for the National Directorate, among others" (Managua, Radio Sandino, in *FBIS*, 6 August, p. P6). Although these goals are natural objectives for the FSLN, abolition of the Political Commission and the establishment of the Executive Commission was clearly a thinly veiled attack against the Borge faction. In the old body Borge's group held one position out of three, and in the new body it has two out of five members, but Daniel Ortega is the leader.

At the time of the Sandinista Assembly and during the following weeks a discreet but massive purge of FSLN and auxiliary organizations occurred. During the assembly meeting members were informed that they would be divided into two categories, full or alternate, and that the National Directorate may ask certain assembly members to "contribute to the discussion of particular problems" (ibid., pp. P6–7). In other words, the National Directorate became the source of power and the Sandinista assembly was formally relegated to a consultative role. The distinction between full and alternate members presents unlimited possibilities for the Sandinista factions to increase the number of their own supporters. A similar purge of a greater proportion, given the numbers involved, occurred among the CDS. According to Milagros Leyton, a member of the CDS National Executive Committee, by November active membership had declined to about 300,000 from a peak of half a million (*Los Angeles Times*, 14 November, p. 14). Such massive purges probably result from an exacerbation of intraparty fights.

Intraparty fights also influence the distribution of government and military positions, from which emerges a pattern of permanent balancing, mutual surveillance, and distrust among the FSLN factions. The pattern is best illustrated in the distribution of key positions in the vital interior and defense ministries and in army leadership. Significantly, the only ministry containing two members of the National Directorate—Borge and Luis Carrión Cruz—is the interior, which oversees the secret police, political commissars of the army, and the CDS. These members belong to opposing factions. An apparently innocuous change such as the appointment of Vanessa Castro Cardenal (Jaime Wheelock's wife) to head the FSLN political education department indicates a growing alliance between the Ortega and Wheelock-Carrión factions; however, army control remains divided among Defense Minister Humberto Ortega, Political Commissar Hugo Torres (a Borge supporter), and Chief of Staff Joaquin Cuadra Lacayo (a Wheelock supporter). Thus, factional conflicts have not yet reached a decisive stage.

According to opposition paper *La Prensa* (27 March, pp. 1, 10), the FSLN again moved decisively toward eliminating the independence of the judiciary in March when President Ortega named Alejandro Serrano Caldera, former ambassador to France, as chief justice of the Supreme Court. Under the current constitution, the appointment should have been made by the Constituent Assembly. Ortega's action appears to have shifted permanently the balance of power within the court toward pro-FSLN, Marxist-Leninist judges. Whether the *La Prensa* claim is true or not, however, is irrelevant; the Nicaraguan judiciary has been under FSLN control since 19 July 1979, when the Sandinistas came to power. In addition, the FSLN's control over the Constituent Assembly was ensured when they and a rump of the Conservative Party led by Cordoba Rivas decided that the constitution could be discussed and amended by a 60 percent majority. The FSLN membership, which totals 61, exceeds the 60 percent mark (*FBIS*, 12 March, p. P9).

Ideology. The changes in the composition and leadership of the FSLN Political Commission caused no significant ideological shift. Arce and Borge remain, with Vice President Sergio Ramírez, the most active spokesmen of the party. During the year attention focused on the civil war and its implications for the revolution's ideology. Emphasis was also placed on the indoctrination of the military and the population of Managua and the repeated attacks against the Church, by Borge in particular. In a major ideological text in *Pensamiento Propio* (Managua, June–July), Borge claimed that "the fact of the matter is that the enemy's ideological organization is both structurally and technically better than ours." Comparing the Church to the *contras*, he went on to declare, "the Church is a strong organization. Its generals, its task force chiefs, its best cadres—theological scholars, experts in the use of words—are assigned to the ideological struggle" (ibid.). Nevertheless, Borge stated that the FSLN will win the civil war because "real revolutions," those based on class struggle, are "irreversible," unless, like in Grenada, the revolutionary leaders fight among themselves (ibid.). He went on to say that the war has forced the regime to direct its attention toward the military rather than the ideological front, which is preferable, because once the war is won, "the ideological war and conspiracies will assume fundamental importance." His solution to such circumstances involves FSLN development of "counterintelligence organs" (ibid.).

Borge's references to Grenada paralleled remarks by Daniel Ortega that compared the FSLN regime in Nicaragua to the Allende regime in Chile. Both references demonstrate the importance of previous Marxist experience in Latin America to the Sandinistas. Ortega claimed that unlike the Allende regime's inability to control the media, military, and economy and thus to defend itself, "the revolution has the right and obligation to defend itself" (*FBIS*, 24 September, p. P10). Referring to the media in particular, Ortega believed it "played a key role in undermining the Popular Unity government of President Salvador Allende." In Nicaragua, however, "we are not going to be so naive as to give [the enemy] room in the news media to undermine us and destroy the revolution" (ibid.).

Human and Political Rights. These attitudes on the role and importance of the media were directly translated into continuous and largely successful attempts to silence all non–FSLN-controlled media, including newspapers of the leftist parties. Thus, in June the government suspended the sale of hard currency to purchase paper and printing materials under the pretext of an economic crisis brought about by the war and the U.S. embargo (ibid., 7 June, p. P18). The hardest hit were the weeklies, *Paso a Paso* of the Independent Liberal Party (PLI), *Avance*, and *El Popular*. Despite these economic and financial restrictions, the regime was able to start publication of *Segovia*, the magazine of the army, on 2 August.

Press censorship continued to tighten throughout the year, which even Daniel Ortega admitted. However, Minister of Culture Ernesto Cardenal denied the existence of censorship even as new censorship laws were decreed (*FBIS*, 18 October, p. P13). The Catholic newspaper, *La Iglesia*, was banned after its first issue. The Interior Ministry explained the ban as a reaction to the newspaper's "highly political" tone and its open attack on "the revolution's defense policy, particularly the mandatory military service" (ibid., p. P12). The main victim of censorship and of repeated government attacks remained the independent newspaper *La Prensa*. Among the many accusations against it was that it used U.S. Information Agency (USIA) sources for its editorials. According to Radio Sandino, the USIA is guilty of promoting terrorism, trying to "disarm people ideologically," and spreading misinformation "against the world's progressive ideas and movements" (*FBIS*, 27 September, p. P7).

Throughout the year a number of Sandinista actions attracted criticism from previously neutral or sympathetic groups abroad, for example, the New York–based Lawyers' Committee for International Human Rights. These actions included the role of the "people's courts"; the right of police to arrest and detain, for up to two years without trial, persons accused of sympathy for the insurgents; and use of psychological and physical coercion to extract confessions (*Los Angeles Times*, 5 April). In addition, the Sandinistas began subjecting the independent Permanent Human Rights Commission to censorship in November (*NYT*, 22 November). To counter accusations, the government changed the membership of its National Commission for the Promotion and Defense of Human Rights; this followed allegations by a former member that it was manipulated by the Interior Ministry. Most human rights abuses in Nicaragua are made public by the Commission for the Defense of Human Rights in Nicaragua, which is based in the United States.

Nicaragua's justice system is demonstrated by the widespread use of so-called people's courts, which are composed of largely nonprofessional judges drawn from the CDS, as well as by arbitrary gestures such as Borge's instant release of prisoners to impress foreign visitors (*WSJ*, 11 October).

On 16 October the FSLN government declared a state of emergency. It suspended most constitutional guarantees, further tightened press censorship, denied the rights of habeas corpus and public assembly and the rights to organize trade unions, strike, receive a speedy trial, and appeal sentences (text of the decree in *FBIS*, 16 October, pp. P8–9; see also *Los Angeles Times*, 16 October). President Ortega imposed the state of emergency because of the U.S.

embargo, the civil war, and the "agents of imperialism who are acting through some political parties, through some communications media or religious organizations" (ibid.).

Relations with the Catholic Church. Throughout the year, relations between the Sandinista government and the influential Catholic Church steadily deteriorated. Borge has admitted that certain anti-Church abuses have been committed (*FBIS*, 14 February, p. P18), and the regime is relentlessly hostile toward the Church in general and Cardinal Obando y Bravo in particular. However, the Sandinistas' attempts to set up an alternative to the Catholic hierarchy have failed. Fernando Cardenal, education minister and a prominent leader of the so-called popular church, was expelled from the Jesuit Order in December 1984. His brother Ernesto had previously been forced out of the Trappist Order. Only Foreign Minister Miguel d'Escoto retains his membership in the Maryknoll organizations. The Vatican gave these and Organization of American States (OAS) ambassador Edgar Parrales an ultimatum regarding their position as ministers and clergymen. Parrales resigned from the priesthood that same month. These pressures on the radical priests were begun by the Nicaraguan hierarchy. Despite the loss of their clerical status, some radical former priests contended that their faction and not the Catholic Church of Nicaragua has the support of the "masses" (see Ernesto Cardenal interview in Vienna, in *FBIS*, 11 June, pp. P17–18).

Politically, the sharpest conflict between the Church and the government resulted from the Church's support for negotiations between the FSLN and the insurgents. In a statement on 22 March the Nicaraguan Episcopal Conference called for dialogue "as the path toward conciliation," in the conviction that "violence will never solve a problem from its roots," and offered to play the role of mediator (*La Prensa*, 23–24 March, p. 1). The government has consistently rejected negotiations with the insurgents and attacked the bishops as collaborators with the revolution's enemies.

In addition to the general political disagreements between the government and the Church, two specific issues have intensified the conflict: the compulsory military service, including the drafting of seminarians, and the suppression of the Church media and radio outlets. In October and November the government forcibly drafted eleven seminarians from the southern cities of Rivas and San Juan, thus provoking sharp condemnations by the bishops. In addition, the FSLN has engaged in a pattern of expelling those foreign priests with whom it does not agree; seventeen have been expelled since 1982, and twenty more were threatened with expulsion in October (*Los Angeles Times*, 6 October). In an October statement, the Episcopal Conference declared that such actions are "a form of intimidation of the Church that, instead of lessening tensions, increases them, and makes church-state talks more difficult" (San Jose, *La Nación*, *Nicaragua Hoy* supplement, 26 October, p. 3C). In November the offices of the archibishopric of Managua came under military occupation and, as noted above, the Church's newsletter was banned at its first appearance.

Since his elevation to cardinalate in June, Obando y Bravo has come under growing attack from the regime and its sympathizers in the Church. The Sandinista-controlled Base Ecclesiastical Communities (CEB) claimed that the archbishop's elevation was "a political decision" and does not make him more important than other bishops (*FBIS*, 11 July, p. P14). Toward the end of the year Borge stated that "at least ideologically, from the viewpoint of his political pronouncements, if a Siamese twin of Ronald Reagan must be found, it is Miguel Obando. He is a political opponent of the revolution" (Madrid, *El Pais*, 26 October, p. 4).

Legal Opposition. The trend toward sharpening conflicts with the Church was paralleled by a worsening of relations between the FSLN and the legal opposition parties, including those of the far left such as the PSN and the PCdeN.

The Sandinistas' slogan for 1985 was "Unity for Peace Against the Aggression" but, except for a brief truce at the time of Daniel Ortega's inauguration in January, any internal agreements between the FSLN and the opposition steadily collapsed toward the end of the year. The Sandinistas lacked the interest to pursue the scheduled "national dialogue" talks among the FSLN, its supporters among other parties (particularly the Popular Social Christian Party [PPSC] and the Democratic Conservative Party [PDC]), the Marxist-Leninists of the PSN and PCdeN, the three major parties of the Nicaraguan Democratic Coordinator (CDN; comprising Social Christians, Liberal Constitutionalists, and Conservatives), and the Liberal Independents. The Superior Council of Private Enterprise (COSEP) is playing a growing role within the CDN and has increasingly articulated its own anti-FSLN positions. The only party to openly condemn the very notion of a national dialogue was the MAP-ML, which has assumed ultraleftist positions throughout the year. Claiming that it represents the "proletariat" of Nicaragua, MAP-ML has consistently accused the other Marxist parties of being "conciliatory" toward the bourgeoisie and has often come close to accusing them of treason. Such rhetoric has helped maintain the FSLN's self-serving image as a reasonable and mature party.

The PSN, which since 1979 had appeared to move closer to the FSLN, apparently changed course during 1985. It supported the abortive dialogue between the Church and the FSLN, based on noninterference in other's institutional affairs, and viewed the dialogue as a step toward "reestablishment of confidence and stability in Nicaragua" (*El Nuevo Diario*, 16 January).

Together with eight other parties, the PSN drafted a joint document calling for a renewal of the national dialogue, and on 20 January it co-signed a statement with the PUCA, PCdeN, PLI, PPSC, and Social Democratic Party (PSD) that condemned "intransigent attitudes" on the part of the FSLN and "deplored" its failure to engage in talks (*La Prensa*, 20 January). Then–secretary general Luis Sánchez made it clear that the PSN considers a fundamental consensus between all the legal parties vital to forestall the continued deterioration of the domestic and international situation (ibid., 23 January).

"Bureaucratic mechanisms" prevented the marginal PUCA and PRT from participating in the 1984 elections. They were then excluded from the political process. The two groups' request to be allowed to observe the debates of the National Assembly was "based on our party's firm anti-imperialist position" (*El Nuevo Diario*, 17 January) but did not succeed.

The pro-Sandinista PDC, led by Córdoba Rivas and Eduardo Molina, lost its position as the largest opposition group in the Constituent Assembly (with 14 seats). This shift followed the departure of four deputies, dissatisfied with the leadership's knee-jerk support for the Sandinistas, who joined the nine PLI deputies (*Central America Report*, 22 February, p. 55). Under the CDN umbrella, serious tensions developed throughout the year between the COSEP and the PSD on the one hand and certain elements of the PPSC on the other. The former apparently maintained close, if discreet, ties with external opposition leaders such as Arturo Cruz and Pedro Joaquin Chamorro, Jr. (ibid., 1 March).

COSEP leader Enrique Bolanos Geyer has distinguished himself among legal opposition members by articulating clear ideological grounds for opposing the Sandinistas. He compared the FSLN's Marxism-Leninism to a religion and described Nicaragua's future under the FSLN with reference to Cuba's past (*La Estrella de Panama*, 22 March, quoted in *FBIS*, 27 March, pp. P10–13).

With regard to Nicaragua's position toward the United States, the PSN and PCdeN have consistently supported the government's policies. They rejected President Reagan's peace proposal, although the PSN was prepared to accept talks with the insurgents so long as there were no preconditions—that is, so long as the revolutionary structures were not negotiable (*FBIS*, 10 April, p. P12). Eli Altamirano shared this view indirectly; he condemned the proposal but at the same time demanded an "internal solution" (ibid.).

The major dispute between the PSN and PCdeN on the one hand and the FSLN on the other appears to center around the former's fear that the Sandinistas are trying to eliminate them completely. Sánchez defined the differences with the Sandinistas as rooted in the fact that "we believe that the revolution should not become divorced from genuinely democratic principles" (ibid., 19 April, p. P17). Such accusations provoked counterattacks from both the Sandinistas and their alter egos in the PDC. The latter's Eduardo Molina accused the Marxist opposition of "opposing the FSLN." The ruling party was even more open; Borge claimed that "instead of boosting support for the attacked revolution, what those allegedly left-wing gentlemen are doing is sabotaging the revolution" (ibid., 14 November, p. P10).

So far as the leftist parties were concerned, the U.S. embargo and congressional decision to provide aid to the insurgents produced a temporary closing of ranks with the FSLN. Carlos Cuadra labeled the embargo as "aggression"; even the PLI's Juan Manuel Gutierrez defined it as "imperialist"; Tablada considered it "evil"; and Mauricio Diaz of the PPSC called it "repressive actions of punishment" (*Barricada*, 3 May). By summer's end, however, and particularly following the decree on the state of emergency, anti-U.S. consensus gave way to growing anti-FSLN unity.

The parties' reaction to the emergency varied. Dissident Conservative deputy Enrique Sotelo claimed that "the peaceful, civic struggle inside Nicaragua is over" (*NYT*, 17 October), and Tablada believed that the emergency "hurts political pluralism" (*FBIS*, 23 October, p. P18). Despite such differences of interpretation, the PPSN, PCdeN,

PRT-PUCA, PSD, PDC, and PLI signed a joint statement on 29 October, urging the lifting of the state of emergency. The statement (text in *FBIS*, 31 October, pp. P16–17) declared that the emergency, "far from contributing to overcoming the profound crisis afflicting the country, has further worsened the already difficult national situation." In addition, it was said the "the state of emergency closes the door on the civic struggle maintained by various political parties advocating a civic option" (ibid.).

The formation of a united opposition to the Sandinistas was further advanced when the CDN umbrella, PLI, PDC, PCdeN, PUCA, and PSN formed an alliance that was openly directed against the ruling FSLN (*FBIS*, 6 November, p. P11). The very composition of the new alliance indicated clearly that ideological differences between Marxist-Leninist parties and democratic or capitalist-oriented ones were unanimously seen as less important than the threat of extinction posed by the emergency. Evidently, the process of isolating the FSLN within the political spectrum of Nicaragua had reached a new height at the very moment that the insurgents had increased military pressure. To the extent that the surviving internal legal opposition decides to join forces openly with the insurgents and the exiled political leaders, the nature of the Nicaraguan civil war will change dramatically. At the same time, the collapsing economy may further erode the significant support for the FSLN among the poorer sectors of the population.

The Economy. The economic situation continued to deteriorate sharply throughout the year, which was a result of FSLN policies, conflicts with the private sector, the civil war, and the conflict with the United States. While strict censorship prevents a precise assessment of the economic situation, even the Sandinistas' admissions are enough to produce an alarming picture. Before the U.S. embargo, Nicaragua's foreign debt and trade deficit reached crisis levels. Official sources admit 50 percent inflation (*FBIS*, 26 February, p. P8), and the PSD claims that since 1979 wages have grown four times while prices have increased 40 times (*La Prensa*, 13 July). The same source claimed that Nicaragua's exports in mid-1985 were lower than before the revolution and represented less than half the value of imports; the 1979 foreign debt was $1.6 billion compared to $4.5 billion in 1985. At the beginning of the year Nicaragua stopped paying interest on the external debt. There has been no new private investment, and the black market exchange rate for the córdoba is 400 to $1, as compared to the official 10 to 1. The food situation has reached famine proportions in certain areas (*Economist*, 2 February, p. 27). In February the prices for meat, milk, and eggs—products already rationed—were doubled (*NYT*, 7 February). At the beginning of 1985 the FSLN described the economic situation in grim terms: a foreign debt of $4.352 billion (on which the interest alone was $872 million); defense expenditures equaling 40 percent of the national budget; subsidies of over 7 million córdobas; and "mistakes, vice, and corruption, which have yet to be eradicated" (Managua Domestic Service, in *FBIS*, 11 February. pp. P10–15).

In March Nicaragua became "the first country ever to fall six months behind in repaying loans to the World Bank" (*NYT*, 27 March), and the flow of foreign aid from Western countries or of foreign non-Soviet bloc loans has stopped almost completely. The impact of the insurgency had a multiple effect: the militarization of the country created labor shortages at critical times, for example, during the coffee harvest; the military budget prevented any new social or industrial investment or even the continuation of many programs; insurgent attacks against economic objectives, such as coffee and sugar plantations, destroyed part of the export crops and increased the cost of producing the rest; and political and social acts of the FSLN continued to sharpen the conflict between the government and the private sector, while continuous shortages of staple foods undermined support for the government and increased sympathy for the insurgents, particularly in rural areas.

The Insurgency. The year's important events with regard to the Nicaraguan civil war were the Reagan administration's success in obtaining congressional approval for "humanitarian aid" to the insurgents, the rapid steps toward unifying the various insurgent groups and exiled political figures, and the Sandinista failure to break the ranks of the Indian resistance on the Atlantic coast. Militarily, the picture changed rapidly throughout the year. The EPS largely succeeded in demoralizing and dislodging the guerrillas of Edén Pastora from their areas in the southern part of the country. At the end of 1984 Pastora claimed to command over 8,000 guerrillas active in the southern, central, and Atlantic regions; by April 1985, in a letter to President Reagan, he had reduced his claims to 7,000 (*FBIS*, 11 April, p. P13). Despite significant losses and even more significant desertions, Pastora continued to make implausible claims throughout the year, for example, the opening of an urban "insurrectional phase" (*FBIS*, 14 March, p. P9). In fact, the Democratic Revolutionary Alliance (ARDE) not only lost its remaining Nicaraguan large base at Sarapiqui but it also allowed Pastora to continue raising obstacles to the unity of the anti-Sandinista military forces. As late as October Pastora stated that he "did not accept an unconditional liaison with the north [i.e., with the Nicaraguan Democratic Force (FDN)] specifically because that would mean joining in the disrespect for human rights and a certain return to a Somozist past (San Jose, *La República*, 19 October).

While ARDE split politically and declined militarily, the FDN grew throughout the year. The excessive hopes for FDN's leaders never materialized—in January Indalecio Rodriquez of the political leadership predicted military victory by the end of the year (*FBIS*, 9 January, p. P18)—but the organization, effectiveness, and popular support for it expanded significantly.

The FDN military organization has operated in almost all of Nicaragua's departments—Esteli, Madriz, Nueva Segovia, Jinotega, Matagalpa, Boaco, Chontales, Zelaya, Chinandega, and Leon—and has begun penetration of Rio San Juan from Costa Rican sanctuaries. Humberto Ortega's own claims at the end of the year illustrated the intensity of the fighting. According to Ortega, the Sandinistas lost 1,143 military personnel as well as 1,560 "civilians" (many of them political cadres of the FSLN) in 1985, as opposed to 4,608 insurgents (*Economist Foreign Report*, 9 January 1986, p. 6). Moreover, the new amnesty law that "reincorporates" into society peasants from the northern region who have been "fooled by the counterrevolutionaries," was the regime's admission that the peasants indeed supported the insurgents (*Barricada*, 24 January).

The state of generalized war was most clearly described by the present chief of secret police, Omar Cabezas: "Excepting Managua, its outskirts, and Nicaragua's Pacific seaboard, where a subsidized peace exists, we are waging an open war against the . . . FDN and the . . . ARDE, counterrevolutionary groups financed by the United States, on the Atlantic seaboard, in the mountains, and in the country's north and on the borders, where the FDN and ARDE operate" (Mexico City, *Unomasuno*, 21 August, p. 12). The FDN, ARDE, Indian forces, and FARN have a generally assessed total strength of over 20,000 guerrillas armed and engaged in combat at various times.

On 2 March the first step was taken toward almost complete unity of all Nicaraguan political and military opponents of the FSLN living abroad, including Alfonso Robelo of the ARDE, Adolfo Calero of the FDN, Indian leader Steadman Fagoth Muller, Carlos Fernando Chamorro of the FARN, Arturo Cruz of the CDN, and Pedro Joaquin Chamorro (see text in *FBIS*, 4 March, pp. P8–11). In June Calero, Robelo, and Cruz assumed the joint leadership of a new umbrella organization, the Unified Nicaraguan Opposition (UNO). Simultaneously, insurgent forces reached and occupied briefly the village of Cuapa, only 160 kilometers from Managua, and a renewed increase in fighting occurred; the Defense Ministry admitted that between 15 and 21 August there were 22 clashes in the Chontales, Jinotega, and Matagalpa departments (*El Nuevo Diario*, 22 August, p. 10). During the same month the insurgents briefly captured the small town of Trinidad, less than 75 miles from Managua (*Economist*, 17 August, p. 30).

Extended use of the growing number of sophisticated Mi-24 Soviet-made helicopter gunships and better training of the newly established Irregular Warfare Battalions (BLI) by the government have enabled the regime to maintain the tactical initiative, but by the end of the year the insurgents, for the first time, succeeded in downing a Mi-24 and have continued to expand the conflict area. At year's end both sides were confident of their strength. On 20 October, Daniel Ortega claimed that "we have victory within our reach" and that "we've got them beat, got them defeated, demoralized and disjointed" (*NYT*, 21 October). In December the insurgents "proved their ability to mass troops and mount an attack in the center of the country, far from their sanctuaries across the Honduran border" (*Los Angeles Times*, 6 December).

The situation on the Atlantic coast with its indigenous Indian and Creole rebels remained different from that of other members of the armed opposition. For a time it appeared that Sandinista efforts to split Indian ranks by offering negotiations while building its own sympathetic organization would succeed. The Organization of the Miskitos of Nicaragua (Misatan), established under FSLN prodding in 1984 and led by Fornes Rabonais, proved to be little more than a ghost organization. As a result, negotiations began in Colombia at the end of 1984 between Brooklyn Rivera, leader of the Miskito organization Misurasata, and Luis Carrión Cruz.

Rivera was expelled by his own group because of the negotiations, but he was also forced to end the talks following alleged Sandinista bombings of Indian villages (*FBIS*, 5 February, p. P15). The elders of Misura, the other major Indian organization, also complained that villages were bombed by the Sandinista air force and pledged to continue fighting against Managua. The government answered these claims by accusing the Indians of attacking the army and accusing Misura of "intensifying armed clashes in the region" (Carrión quoted in *FBIS*, 1 February, p. P16). In March another Indian organization, Misurasata–Southern Indigenous Creole Communities (SICC) accused Managua's regime of being "racist, anti-Indian, and neocolonialist" (ibid., 15 March, p. P6). In May talks between Rivera and Carrión broke down, although Carrión and Borge continued to claim interest in a negotiated solution, and various proposals for autonomy of the Atlantic coast region were made throughout the year. This reshuffling of Indian leadership, as well as Rivera's being compromised by both negotiating with Managua and failing to bring results, resulted in the formation of yet another Indian organization in September. The Unity of the Nicaraguan Atlantic Coast Peoples (KISAN) included Misura and Misurasata-SICC and was headed by Wycliffe Diego and Roger German. Despite the KISAN's pledge to continue fighting, the situation at year's end remained fluid; some Indians were still interested in negotiations, some returned to their ancestral villages along the Rio Coco, and the majority cooperated with the FDN in Northern Zelaya.

International Contacts. The FSLN's foreign policy during the year attempted to retain if not expand ties with Western Europe and Japan economically and to strengthen links to the Soviet bloc, Cuba, radical Third World regimes, and a number of revolutionary and terrorist organizations from Latin America, Western Europe, and the Middle East. At the same time relations with the United States reached a new low and by December were limited to the presence of embassies in the two capitals. The imposition of a total trade embargo by the United States on 2 May practically reduced bilateral contacts to occasional visits by members of the U.S. Congress to Managua and by Nicaraguan officials to the United States in New York. Nicaragua reacted to the embargo, which eliminated the 15 percent of its external trade that was conducted with the United States, by asking for a United Nations Security Council meeting.

Throughout the year the Nicaraguan government, while consistently accusing the United States of causing the war, the economic crisis, inflation, debts, and so forth, also continued to call for renewed talks with Washington and expressed consistent but vague support for the Contadora process. The Reagan administration continued to support the insurgents publicly. In May the U.S. Congress reversed itself, following Daniel Ortega's trip to Moscow, and approved $27 million for the insurgents in "humanitarian" (that is, nonmilitary) aid. A brief meeting between presidents Ortega and Reagan in New York in October resulted in a cold exchange of minimal courtesies. While Daniel Ortega often sounded conciliatory and interested in direct talks with the United States, the general tone of the FSLN statements, particularly those of Borge and Arce, indicated the Sandinistas' deep hatred for the United States. According to Borge, "imperialism does not want justice, democracy, human rights, economic development for the poor countries" (*FBIS*, 1 November, p. P11).

Relations with West European governments continued to exist but did not expand, despite Ortega's visit to the region on return from Moscow and such exchanges as the visit of West German deputy foreign minister Alois Mertes to Managua in March.

Until the end of the year Nicaragua was the only Marxist country in the world to maintain full diplomatic relations with Taiwan, and the Nicaraguan tourist minister Herty Lewites even visited Taipei in September. Despite receiving Taiwanese aid, however, Nicaragua broke diplomatic ties with Taipei in December and started negotiations to establish ties with Beijing.

Relations with Terrorist Organizations. The issue of Nicaragua serving as a haven for international terrorism has been consistently raised by the United States. In May 1985 Italian prime minister Bettino Craxi openly addressed Daniel Ortega on the question of Red Brigade fugitives, and the issue became more widely known. The Sandinista reply to Craxi, as well as to Spanish prime minister Felipe Gonzales's inquiries about the presence of Basque Homeland and Liberty (ETA) terrorists in Managua, denied the accusations and, interestingly, demanded further information (Managua Domestic Service, 20 August; Madrid, Spanish News Agency, 19 August, in *FBIS*, 20 August, p. P5). According to the *Miami Herald*, the FSLN has "fraternal relations" with the following guerrilla and terrorist organizations: the Argentine Montoneros, the Salvadoran Popular Revolutionary Army (ERP), Baader Meinhof of West Germany, the Red Brigades, ETA, the Tupamaros of Uruguay, the Movement of the Revolutionary Left (MIR) of Chile, the M-19 of Colombia, the Tupac Amaru Revolutionary Movement (MRTA) of Peru, the Palestine Liberation Organization (PLO; which has an "embassy" in Managua), and all Central American Marxist-Leninist guerrilla groups (*Miami Herald*, reprinted in *Sandinistas Attract a Who's Who of Terrorists*, Cuban American National Foundation, Washington, D.C., 1985).

Toward the end of the year Nicaraguan involvement in arming the Colombian M-19 guerrillas, who took hostages and killed most of Colombia's Supreme Court justices in October, was made known and brought ambiguous denials from Managua. Ecuador, which broke ties with Nicaragua, also accused the latter of supporting subversive elements attacking the government in Quito.

Nicaragua's good relations with Libya were further strengthened in January, when a $15 million trade agreement was signed in Managua. The agreement allowed Nicaragua to send coffee, cotton seed, flour, and sesame to Libya in exchange for oil (*FBIS*, 17 January, p. P4). Although trade between Nicaragua and Iran—primarily meat and sugar for oil—is small, the trip to Managua by Iranian prime minister Hossein Musavi made a political impact. President Reagan treated Musavi's 22–25 January visit as another example of Sandinista flirtation with terrorism. A member of the Iranian delegation stressed that "our revolution is in solidarity with the Nicaraguan revolution . . . because our two countries are anti-imperialist and oppose U.S. intervention" (*La Prensa*, 25 January).

Relations with the Soviet Bloc. During the year Nicaragua's ties with Cuba and the rest of the Soviet bloc intensified. High-level visits included Fidel Castro's presence at Daniel Ortega's inauguration as president and the latter's two trips to Moscow—in March for the funeral of Konstantin Chernenko and in May, when he also visited Eastern Europe. In October the Mixed Commission on Cooperation between the Council on Mutual Economic Assistance (CEMA) and Nicaragua met in Managua; this resulted in agreements regarding CEMA's aid for irrigation, mining, training, and processing industries. The agreements involved about twelve major projects (*Izvestiia*, USSR, in *FBIS*, 31 October, p. BB1).

Since 1979 Soviet bloc military aid to Nicaragua has surpassed $500 million, the bulk of it in 1984 and 1985, with a slightly larger amount in economic aid (*WSJ*, 3 April, pp. 1, 27). Even before the U.S. embargo and Ortega's second trip to Moscow, Vice President Ramirez stated that the socialist countries had become Nicaragua's most important sources of aid (Mexico City, *El Dia*, in *FBIS*, 22 March, p. P15). This dependency increased after May. With Mexico and Venezuela cutting the amount of oil at subsidized prices sent to Nicaragua, the USSR has become that country's main energy supplier during the year, providing 80–90 percent of total oil imports (*NYT*, 21 May).

It was projected that 35 percent of Nicaragua's total external trade would be with the communist countries by the end of 1985. In addition to Soviet oil, imports include Soviet wheat, lard, and tractors, East German medical equipment and trucks, Bulgarian canned food, and Hungarian textiles and medicines (*Los Angeles Times*, 10 May). East Germany (GDR) is now Nicaragua's second largest Soviet bloc trading partner; $200 million in credits have been extended to Managua since 1981, mostly for the purchase of transportation equipment and machinery (*Barricada*, 29 March). In addition, the GDR sent a $5 million donation of clothes and hospital equipment in August. The same month wounded EPS soldiers began arriving in East Berlin for treatment (*FBIS*, 13 August, p. P11). Moreover, in a direct and public effort to upset the impact of the U.S. embargo, the GDR extended another $40 million line of credit in late June (ibid., 1 July, p. P22).

Relations with Cuba continued to be extremely warm throughout the year. Castro was the only prominent chief of state who attended Daniel Ortega's inauguration. There are an estimated 8,000 Cubans in Nicaragua, about half of them military personnel (*Washington Times*, 19 September). Toward the end of the year, the U.S. State Department claimed that Cuban pilots were flying combat missions against the insurgent forces, particularly on Mi-24 helicopter gunships.

Defectors from the Salvadoran Farabundo Marti National Liberation Front (FMLN), and documents captured during the year, confirmed a continued high level of Nicaraguan strategic control over the Salvadoran guerrilla insurgency (*NYT*, 21 May; *Los Angeles Times*, 25 May; see also El Salvador profile).

Michael S. Radu
Foreign Policy Research Institute

Panama

Population. 2,038,000
Party. People's Party (Partido del Pueblo; PDP)
Founded. 1930 (PDP, 1943)
Membership. Over 500
Secretary General. Rubén Darío Sousa (or Souza)
Politburo. Includes César Agusto De Leon Espinosa, Miguel Antonio Porcella Peña, Anastacio E. Rodríguez, Clito Manuel Souza Batista, Ruperto Luther Trottman
Central Committee. 26 members
Status. Legal
Last Congress. Sixth, 8–10 February 1980
Last Election. 1984, less than 3 percent, no representatives
Auxiliary Organizations. Panama Peace Committee, People's Party Youth, National Center of Workers of Panama, Union of Journalists of Panama, Federation of Panamanian Students, National Union of Democratic Women
Publications. *Unidad* (weekly)

Party Organization. The ruling body of the PDP is the National Congress, which is supposed to meet every four years. The congress elects a Central Committee, which in turn elects the Secretariat and Politburo.

During much of 1985 the PDP looked forward to its next congress, to be convened 24–27 January 1986. The party organ related the long and difficult struggle the party had waged before achieving its legality in 1981. During the years ahead, the Communists' task would be "the transformation of our party into a great Marxist-Leninist party of the masses." This party would have to "assume its role as revolutionary vanguard" in the ideological and political fronts and the anti-imperialist march into the future. In anticipation of the congress, numerous lower-level meetings were convened around the country by both the party and its youth group (*Unidad*, 27 September–3 October and 11–17, 25–31 October).

Domestic and International Policies. The year was an unsettling one for Panama. In early September Hugo Spadafora, a former official under the popular General Omar Torrijos (who died in a helicopter crash in 1981) and a declared enemy of Defense Forces commander General Manuel Antonio Noriega, was assassinated. Later that month President Nicolas Ardito Barletta was forced to resign after less than a year in office as Panama's first elected president in nearly two decades. He was succeeded by Eric Arturo Delvalle, and the military increasingly meddled in the political affairs of the country (*WSJ*, 6 December).

The PDP, with its greatest strength among university students, played only a minor role in these and other national events. However, it did comment on them, agitate in student and labor organizations, and make plans for the future.

The PDP claimed to see the hand of the United States behind the assassination of Spadafora, as it had allegedly been behind the "killing" of Torrijos and the removal of Barletta. After all, during Barletta's short tenure "North American imperialism had suffered a defeat in the united and combative actions of the masses toward the International Monetary Fund" (*Unidad*, 21–26 September).

The party repeatedly called for a "new turn" in

the country and noted the critical need for changes to come from below, not from above. The PDP repeatedly lavished praise on the late General Torrijos—he was pictured in the party organ more often than any other person except Sousa—and strove to increase their own popularity among the Panamanian people by tying themselves in with the Torrijos image of the past (see, for example, *Unidad*, 14–20 September). Panama, the party argued, is passing through "the stage of the democratic revolution of national liberation, which has as its fundamental enemy North American imperialism." This imperialism operated in Panama within the upper and some of the middle layers of society.

The revolution that the Communists support necessitates the formation of a Democratic Front of National Liberation and an alliance of the workers and peasants (*Unidad*, 4–10, 11–17 October). The program for the construction of such an organization consists of four key elements: (1) a strategy of economic development that is both anti-imperialist and democratic and will lead to national liberation; (2) support for the Panama Canal treaty signed by Torrijos and U.S. president Jimmy Carter, which assures that U.S. military bases in Panama are not used "against people fighting for their liberation" and guarantees that the canal is in Panamanian hands by the year 2000; (3) the installation of a people's democratic government incorporating the workers, peasants, and middle classes; and (4) a foreign policy based on the principles of the self-determination of peoples, diplomatic relations with all nations on the basis of mutual respect and noninvolvement in their domestic affairs, support for people fighting for their liberation, and a policy for peace and against war (*Unidad*, 4–10 October).

The PDP maintained strong support for the Sandinista government in Nicaragua, the Castro government in Cuba, and the Soviet Union (*Unidad*, 24–31 July). The Panamanian Communists argued that capitalism is in a state of crisis, that "state terrorism originates in Washington," and that all underdeveloped countries should confront the foreign debt problem jointly (*Unidad*, 7–13 September and 11–17 October; *Critica*, 28 January, in *FBIS*, 31 January).

Other Leftist Parties. Among the other leftist parties in Panama are Tendencia, which broke from the PDP in 1974, the Socialist Workers' Party (PST), and the Trotskyist Revolutionary Workers Party (PRT).

William Ratliff
Hoover Institution

Paraguay

Population. 3,722,000
Party. Paraguayan Communist Party (Partido Comunista del Paraguay; PCP)
Founded. 1928
Membership. 4,000 (estimated)
Secretary General. Julio Rojas (acting); Antonio Maidana (official) is under arrest.
Leading Bodies. No data
Status. Illegal
Last Congress. Third, 10 April 1971

Last Election. N/a
Auxiliary Organizations. No data
Publications. *Adelante* (underground weekly)

In February the minister of labor and justice, Eugenio Jacquet, announced that he was forming a special Anti-Communist Action Group that would be made up of young Colorado Party militants who would "fight against the infiltration of communism in all sectors of society." This was flattering to the PCP, which was surprised to learn that it was making so much headway toward its goal of overthrowing Alfredo Stroessner's 31-year-old dictatorship. Observers of the Paraguayan scene, however, attributed the government's new anticommunist crusade to tensions arising from increasingly evident decay in the regime and struggles inside the ruling Colorado Party, rather than to any serious threats from the Communists. Stroessner is 73, and so there has been a gathering mood of political crisis among Paraguay's elites (*Latin America Weekly Report*, 15 February).

The regime has had reason to be nervous, despite the Colorado Party's predictable landslide in the October municipal elections. Public rallies calling for democracy were held in Asunción on 17 February, 14 May, and 29 September. Organized by students, priests, and opposition-party leaders, they drew crowds of between 2,000 and 5,000, a large turnout in this capital. There were also strikes and threatened work stoppages during the year, as the government seemed incapable of controlling inflation or providing jobs for growing numbers of unemployed people. Most serious of all were signs of spreading discontent in the countryside, which had long provided the regime with a stable political base. The root of the trouble was that Paraguay's traditional agriculture, based on plentiful land and a numerous class of small, self-sufficient proprietors, was being transformed by the incursion of Brazilian colonists and multinational agribusinesses. Throughout 1985 there were more than a dozen protest incidents by landless peasants and small farmers who had lost their land through lack of a clear title; these ranged from angry village demonstrations to mass invasions of private estates that brought about clashes with government troops (*Latin America Regional Report, Southern Cone*, 11 October).

At the same time, a power struggle has been going on among the regime elites. The Colorado Party is split between "traditionalists" and "militants." The latter faction is made up of Stroessner loyalists, while the former claim to represent the Colorados' heritage from pre-Stroessner days. The militants, led by the president's private secretary, Mario Abdo Benítez, have sought to perpetuate the dominance of the palace *camarilla* by nominating Stroessner's elder son, Gustavo, an Air Force officer, to succeed him when his term expires in 1988. The traditionalists want a "party man," such as Luís M. Argaña, the president of the Supreme Court. They also have the support of General Andrés Rodríguez, the powerful commander of the First Army Corps, who has presidential ambitions of his own. Rodríguez is personally connected to Stroessner, since his son is married to Stroessner's daughter. In this tug-of-war, the military is said to be divided. Many senior officers are, like Rodríguez, involved in the illegal trade in drugs and other contraband, and therefore look to him as the man most likely to maintain their lucrative privileges. On the other hand, some junior officers would like to clean up Paraguay's rampant corruption, and they view Gustavo Stroessner as their best bet for reform. Paradoxically, this split in the Colorados' ranks may lead to the reintegration of their exiled left wing, the Movimiento Popular Colorado (MOPOCO), which is bitterly anti-Stroessner. Some MOPOCO leaders were recently allowed to return to Paraguay, but the danger of their allying with the traditionalists led to the arrest of several of them in August (*Latin America Regional Report, Southern Cone*, 6 September).

Alert to the possibilities inherent in this situation, the PCP has tried to position itself to take advantage of them. It claims to have organized many new cells, regional commissions, and sections in the underground. It also started two new front organizations in exile—the labor-based Movement of Unity and Trade Union Action in Exile and the Paraguayan Democratic Union—to compete with the National Accord coalition formed by the opposition Febrerista, Christian Democrat, MOPOCO, and Authentic Radical Liberal parties, from which the PCP is excluded. The National Accord participants, according to the PCP, "have made no progress in expanding the social composition of their coalition and stubbornly persist in their exclusive sectarian position, thereby weakening resistance to the pressure of the dictatorship and U.S. imperialism" (*IB*, February). Such comments point to the fact that, so far, there has been no parallel within Paraguay's opposition to the Marxist infiltration of the Sandinista movement that characterized the denouement of the Somoza regime in Nicaragua.

Paul H. Lewis
Tulane University

Peru

Population. 19,532,000
Party. Peruvian Communist Party (Partido Comunista Peruano; PCP)
Founded. 1930
Membership. 5,000
Secretary General. Jorge del Prado Chavez (75)
Central Committee. 15 members: Gustavo Espinoza Montesinos, Guillermo Herrera, Asunción Caballero Mendez, Jorge del Prado Chavez, Olivera Vila, Isidoro Gamarra, Roberto Rojas, Valentín Pacho Quispe, Julián Serra, Jaime Figueroa, Víctor Checa, Antonio Torres Andrade, César Alva, Carlos Bonino, Alfonso Barrantes Lingán
Status. Legal
Last Congress. Eighth Extraordinary, 27–31 January 1982
Last Election. 1984 presidential and parliamentary. The PCP has six delegates and is part of a coalition of the United Left that has 26 percent of the delegates in the Chamber of Deputies. The PCP has two senators in the coalition that has 25 percent of the representation in the Senate.
Auxiliary Organizations. Confederation of Peruvian Workers (CGTP), Peruvian Peasant Confederation (CCP)
Publications. *Unidad* (newspaper of the PCP); *El Diario Marka*, (leftist newspaper)

The PCP is the largest and most important single component of the United Left (IU) political front. The IU emerged from Peru's 1984 presidential and parliamentary elections as the second most powerful electoral alliance in the nation and the largest Marxist political movement active in any Latin American democracy. The strength of the IU was indicated in the November 1983 municipal elections when front candidates polled 30 percent of the national vote and Dr. Alfonso Barrantes Lingán captured the mayoralty of Lima. In April 1985, Barrantes ran as the IU's presidential candidate and came in second, with 21.3 percent of the vote, behind Dr. Alan García Pérez of the American Popular Revolutionary Alliance (APRA). García became president with 45.7 percent of the vote in the nine-candidate race.

The election represented an historic shift in Peru, since two-thirds of the population voted for parties advocating substantial system change. The APRA and the IU soundly defeated the center-right parties that in five years of government had produced economic collapse, had allowed widespread corruption, and had been unable to stem the tide of guerrilla terrorism and state repression. The social-democratic APRA won a clear majority in both houses of the legislature, with 32 of 60 senate seats and 107 of 180 deputy seats, and the IU elected 15 senators and 48 deputies. Outside commentators consistently remarked that Peru now had a "leftist" government. Therein lay the major dilemma for the PCP and the IU: how to define their roles vis-à-vis the new Aprista government.

Party Organization and Leadership. The IU is a conglomeration of four political parties, two coalitions, various small groups, and individuals who identify with the front. It includes the major Marxist parties in Peru with the exception of the Trotskyist groups—Ricardo Napurí's Socialist Workers Party (PST) and Hugo Blanco's Revolutionary Workers Party (PRT)—and the armed guerrilla groups, such as the Peruvian Communist Party –Sendero Luminoso (PCP–SL) and the Revolutionary Movement of Tupac Amaru (MRTA). The National Directive Committee of the IU is composed of Jorge del Prado Chavez; Enrique Bernales, head of the social-democratic Revolutionary Socialist Party (PSR); Manuel Dammert, leader of the Revolutionary Communist Party (PCR); Javier Diez Canseco, head of the Unified Mariateguista Party (PUM); Jorge Hurtado, head of the Maoist front Union of the Revolutionary Left (UNIR); and Genero Ledesma, leader of the Trotskyist Worker, Peasant, Student, and Popular Front (FOCEP). IU has been held together by ideological coincidences, electoral success, and the leadership of its elected president, Barrantes. Each of these components was undermined in 1985.

The April election prompted as much internal struggle for the IU as it produced interparty debate on national issues. The major problem was the lack of a coherent policy line. The coalition was almost split by the so-called ala dura, or hardline, represented by members of PUM, FOCEP, and UNIR's component the Peruvian Communist Party–Red Fatherland (PCP–PR). They maintained that Barrantes was too concerned with the election and not sufficiently revolutionary to articulate the popular view.

Given the IU's coalition structure and the geographic and proportional allocation of places on the IU electoral lists, each group conducted its own campaign and individual leaders consistently contradicted Barrantes. He felt that the IU's revolutionary solutions to Peru's problems were clearly distinguished from APRA's measures, but at the same time he did not want the IU linked with Sendero Luminoso, whose guerrilla warfare has ravaged the Andean countryside and increasingly threatened the urbanized areas of the coast. Carlos Malpica (UNIR) and Javier Diez Canseco (PUM), among others, had repeatedly promised that if the IU gained power, it would initiate a dialogue with Sendero and decree a political amnesty (*Resumen Semanal*, 16–22 March, p. 7). However, Barrantes said, "We will never reconcile ourselves with terrorism . . . if the others wish to look for dialogue and draw near to Sendero, they have the right to do so, but it is not the official line of IU" (ibid., 30 March–4 April, p. 3).

As a result of the political in-fighting, the IU's official plan of government was not released until 3 April. Its main points were: an immediate rise in salaries; the nationalization of private banks and major companies such as Southern Peru Copper; regionalization of government; a military involved in social action; and a reorganized police (ibid.). This plan was only slightly different from that of the APRA; the major exception was the call for nationalization. A glaring problem from the hardline perspective was the absence of a position on dialogue with Sendero Luminoso.

Discontent within the IU increased greatly after the election because critics saw Barrantes's moderate stand as responsible for the IU "defeat" and the basis for a capitulation to the APRA. In the Chamber of Deputies, the IU won 48 places with representatives in all departments except Amazonas, San Martín, and Tumbes. In Huancavelica and Moquegua, the IU is the majority party. The PCP is represented by two deputies in Junín and Lima, one in Cuzco, and one in Ica. As an electoral alliance, the IU has fifteen seats in the 1980–1985 Peruvian Senate. Of the five PCP members on the IU list for senators, the two who won seats in the preferential poll were Secretary General Jorge del Prado, who polled as the second highest individual on the list, and labor leader Valentín Pacho Quispe, who was sixth in preference.

Despite the fact that the number of IU representatives is considerably higher than in the previous government, the percentage of the vote for the IU (27 percent) was slightly lower than it was in the 1983 municipal elections (30 percent). Given the precipitous decline of the right in 1985 and repeated assurances that there would be no military veto of an IU victory, IU analysts viewed their inability to gain votes as a defeat. Even worse, critics viewed Barrantes's and IU's immediate cooperation with the APRA as "pro-Aprista opportunism."

The constitution required a second-round election between the two candidates with the most votes. However, a little more than a week after the unofficial results were in, Barrantes and the majority of the IU decided to withdraw from the run-off. They felt that the popular will was clear, the expense of another election unjustified, and the period of uncertainty only damaging to the legitimacy of the system. Furthermore, Barrantes felt that withdrawal underscored the IU's rejection of the new law that included null and blank votes as valid votes (ibid., 26 April–2 May, p. 1).

From a pragmatic perspective, del Prado and the PCP supported the withdrawal because they suspected that the right wanted the second round only to produce a defeat for the IU (*Unidad*, 20 June; *JPRS*, 15 August). The hardline disagreed; it wanted the opportunity to keep the IU in the second round and force a review of the two parties' platforms and the country's problems.

Barrantes defined the IU role as nationalist, patriotic, and constructive opposition, whereby IU members would work in parliament to pursue the people's interests but not serve in the cabinet (ibid., 6–12 September, p. 4). This stance was not sufficient for members of UNIR, who argued that "the difficulty in distinguishing between APRA and the left has damaged the popular movement" (*El Diario Marka*, 20 October; *FBIS*, 14 November). They defined the APRA as "populist, corporatist, reformist, authoritarian, and an obstacle in the advance to socialism because it represents a grand capitalist bourgeoise strategy that ignores true contradictions in society" (*Resumen Semanal*, 7–13 June, p. 3). The hardliners were concerned that participation in the parliament would cause the IU to "forget the work in the social sectors" and the "need to maintain an alternative to APRA despite coincidences" (ibid., 27 September–3 October, p. 4).

At the November plenary, the hardline faction demanded a reorganization of the National Directive Committee; Malpica wanted more power for the larger parties—PUM, PCP, and UNIR. This distinction was not accepted by others who noted that in the last election 58 percent of the vote was for the IU as a party and the remaining 42 percent was divided as follows: PUM 11 percent, PCP 8 percent, UNIR 7 percent, PSR 5 percent, and 11 percent dispersed among the independents (ibid., 18–24 October, p. 1). Despite the charges and countercharges, the IU's plenary emerged in support of Barrantes; he was still the only individual all the others could accept as a leader, and his continued assertion that "there is no possibility of confusion between Marxist IU and social democratic APRA" provided steady, if slow, guidance toward a program. Barrantes saw no weakness in accepting points of coincidence, nor did Jorge del Prado, who proposed Barrantes's re-election as head of the IU (*El Diario Marka*, 20 October; *FBIS*, 14 November). In fact, at the fourteenth plenum of the PCP, del Prado recognized that "while APRA was not consistent, it nevertheless struggled against and distanced itself from the Belaúnde government and the right wing." He explained that "to win they hoisted the banners IU unfurled" (*Unidad*, 20 June, *JPRS*, 15 August).

Although Barrantes retained his leadership, the program adopted was one that its authors hoped would define the IU as the revolutionary opposition to the APRA. It included the following points: (1) debt moratorium of five years and the formation of a debtors' club; (2) reduction of profit remissions abroad and recuperation of national property; (3) fulfillment of promises to the Unitary National Agrarian Council (CUNA); (4) labor amnesty and labor stability; (5) respect for autonomous organizations; (6) civilian supremacy over the military; (7) political amnesty; and (8) decentralization (*Resumen Semanal*, 22–28 November, p. 3).

Domestic Affairs. As the April election approached it became clear that the government party, Popular Action (AP), and the center-right in Peru would be handed a devastating defeat. AP's primary concern became to hold the elections and preserve Fernando Belaúnde Terry's place in history by overseeing the first legitimate transfer of power between two elected presidents in over forty years. Despite calls by radical parties to boycott the elections and death threats to participants, 8.2 million Peruvians went to the polls and the majority of them—workers, slum dwellers, and peasants—cast their ballots for social reform.

A smooth transition was marred somewhat by the slowness of the electoral counting, the constitutional/political debate on the necessity of a second round, an assassination attempt on the director of the National Election Jury, and charges of irregularities in the senate preferential votes. Finally, however, on 1 June Alan García Pérez was proclaimed president-elect.

The dynamic young leader heads the oldest mass party in Peru. The APRA's origins and those of the PCP stem from the radical movement in the 1920s. Yet whereas José Carlos Mariátegui, founder of the PCP, embraced a Marxist understanding of Peruvian reality, the founder of the APRA, Víctor Raúl Haya de la Torre, opted for an indo-American analysis that was nationalist, popular, and anti-imperialist but non-Marxist.

García immediately and vigorously set out to deal with Peru's economic collapse, its guerrilla conflict, and its bureaucratic corruption. He declared a "war on misery and crisis" and promised a government of "social and economic democracy of participation" to attack the "deep crisis of poverty, unproductiveness and dependence, and the negative criminal expression in response to that crisis as demonstrated by Sendero Luminoso" (*Latin America Weekly Report* [*LAWR*], 7 June, p. 8).

In his first three months in office, García initiated an economic reactivation plan that included wage increases, a devaluation of the sol, price and exchange controls, and a lowering of interest rates. This mandated control of inflation saw the monthly rate drop from an average of 10.9 percent in January–August to 3.5 percent in September. As he announced a balanced budget for 1986, he noted its emphasis on basic needs, especially the revival of the domestic agricultural sector, cuts in infrastructure projects and military expenditures, and major tax reform (*LAWR*, 6 September, p. 8).

While many of his moves were pure populist—for example, cuts in his own salary and that of congress, the sale of embassy residences, and the creation of jobs in the shantytowns through sanitation, irrigation, and reforestation projects—García also moved forward on projects that had been part of the IU's party platform. Contracts with three foreign oil companies were rescinded in August, remittances of profits were banned in September, and import restrictions were placed on products that competed with locally produced goods. Most notable, however, was his move to unilaterally restructure Peru's foreign debt of U.S. $14 million. García's position was that Peru would honor its external debt, but because its internal debt to the poor was more pressing, his government would pay only 10 percent of the nation's export earnings to service the debt. More significantly, he proposed that this be done directly with the creditors and not negotiated through the International Monetary Fund (IMF) (*Resumen Semanal*, 26 July–1 August, pp. 1–2).

On none of these points did the Peruvian left disagree with García in terms of direction; instead, differences arose over detail. The IU called for a five-year moratorium on the debt. It wanted still deeper cuts in the military budget and nationalization, not renegotiation, with foreign companies. The IU also accepted the long-discussed need to decentralize government to stem the unwieldy growth and predominance of Lima to the detriment of the provinces. It supported García's move to divide the nation into eight financial districts in which all national banks (industry, agrarian, and a new development bank) would maintain branches (*Latin America Regional Reports* [*LARR*], 4 October, p. 3).

In fact, only one of García's early initiatives was immediately rebuffed by IU adherents and that was the "social pact" designed to provide the government with some measure of labor calm as the economic readjustment took place. In 1985 the most aggressive sectors in terms of strike activity were miners, municipal workers, and public servants in general. In the manufacturing sector the economic health of business was so bad that more than one thousand firms went bankrupt. Thus, despite a domestic decline in real wages of 40 percent in four years, union leaders were reluctant to jeopardize even more jobs through strike action (*LARR*, 1 March, p. 2).

Nevertheless, the public sector was hard hit as the unrecognized Intersectorial Confederation of State Workers (CITE) carried out two major strikes. For 23 days in March, virtually all of the workers at the ministries of education, transportation, and finance were on strike with one-half of the postal workers, one-third of the employees in state enterprises, one-fourth in state agriculture, and almost all airport workers and customs officials. In June 400,000 members and sympathizers of CITE launched a 50-day action that paralyzed eighteen government ministries and state offices. In each instance the workers were demanding the fulfillment of previous agreements that the government argued were impossible to meet. Prime Minister Luís Percovich announced that state employees had received the equivalent of an 81 percent increase in six months and anything more was impossible because outgoing President Belaúnde had spent all but U.S. $250 million of the 1985 budget, which would meet only one-third of the public sector wages (*LAWR*, 12 July, p. 9).

Given this untenable situation, it was imperative that the new government reach an agreement with the unions on a way to weather the budget crisis created by the previous regime. The first step taken by García was to create a tripartite social pact between the state, workers, and business. All the union confederations signed with the exception of the procommunist CGTP. The CGTP is the largest such organization in Peru with approximately 300,000 members. The second largest is the Confederation of Peruvian Workers (CTP), which has nominal ties to the new Aprista government, and its ranks of 90,000 are expected to grow in a climate favorable to union organizing. The other two major union confederations—the Christian Democratic National Workers Union (CNT) and the Velasquista Confederation of Workers of the Peruvian Revolution (CTRP)—have memberships under 15,000 each. According to the ministry of labor, however, only 11 percent of the economically active workers in Peru belong to unions and fewer have legal collective bargaining rights (*LARR*, 1 March, p. 2).

Valentín Pacho, secretary general of the CGTP, attended the meetings of the tripartite group and recommended adherence to measures regarding price controls, agricultural development, and wage increases. He was less supportive of the labor stability legislation and he opposed the APRA's proposal to have labor disputes tried by the judiciary rather than by the ministry of labor (*Resumen Semanal*, 31 May–6 June, p. 3; Paris AFP, 18 August; *FBIS*, 19 August; *LARR*, 4 October, p. 3).

Another important politicized sector in Peru is the rural proletariat and peasantry. Today's most important agrarian organization, CUNA, came into being in response to Belaúnde's liberal policies, which encouraged imports, cut domestic prices, and dried up credit. It is comprised of 36 organizations that range from the National Agrarian Organization of prosperous dairy farmers and cattle breeders, to the National Agrarian Confederation (CNA) formed by beneficiaries and defenders of ex-president Velasco's agrarian reform, to the radical peasant union, the CCP. Given a situation in which five key products—cotton, potatoes, rice, corn, and sugar cane—are at per capita consumption levels of the 1950s and that only rice prices cover production costs, the CUNA persuaded candidates Barrantes and García to sign a commitment to restructure agriculture. The main points were (1) to encourage changes in consumption patterns to favor Peruvian produce and subsidize staples where necessary, (2) to negotiate with agro-industrial companies to reduce imports and restrict price increases, (3) to include farmers and campesinos in policymaking, and (4) to defend the agrarian reform (*LARR*, 17 May, p. 5).

The foremost concern of the PCP, the CGTP, the CNA, the CCP, and the IU in general has been that the organized unions and groups in Peru's work places, neighborhoods, and rural cooperatives maintain their autonomous identity under the Aprista government. They are watchful and cautious of any moves that they see as possible attempts to co-opt existing organizations, create parallel organizations, or mobilize previously unorganized groups. Most important, they want to ensure that "tripartite" commissions and/or schemes to include workers and peasants into decisionmaking are not corporatist and authoritarian.

International Relations. The PCP and the IU were pleased and supportive of the general direction taken by the García government in foreign relations, which was a definitive stance toward leadership in regional matters, nonalignment, and greater attention toward the Third World. President García made a dramatic bid for regional leadership that rested on a call for indo-American unity on three fronts. The first front was that of political unity, which emphasized the importance of Latin American solutions to Latin American problems. Supporting the Contadora process, García vigorously criticized the U.S. embargo on Nicaraguan goods: "We reject the interpretation that Nicaragua is part of the East-West confrontation. Nicaragua is part of Latin America and Peru will do its best to impose Latin America's presence in Nicaragua" (Managua Domestic Service, 12 July; *FBIS*, 15 July).

On the second front, economic unity, the goal was to form a common vanguard for the debtor nations of the hemisphere that collectively owe $370 million to U.S. commercial banks. While not welcomed in the United States, this move also drew fire from Cuba. Fidel Castro had previously focused on the broader dimensions of the debt issue, alleging that Latin America's debts were virtually "unpayable." But García questioned the Cuban president's right to direct any hemispheric movement because his country's foreign debt was not owed to capitalist banks. More pointedly, García took a "third position" opposing all imperialisms, including the Council for Mutual Economic Assistance as well as the IMF. Given this challenge, relations with Cuba became tense and Castro's inaugural greeting was described by political analyst Tad Szulc as "probably unmatched in the annals of diplomatic insults" (*Los Angeles Times*, 8 September, pp. 1–2). The PCP parted company with President García on this issue as well and supported the Cuban position that a debt moratorium is the proper path. Still, Peru remains the Latin American nation with the most radical position in practice; the others have renegotiated within the IMF framework.

The third front was that of regional disarmament. García made his plea in Lima and at the United Nations for the need to cut military spending if the poor, debtor nations are to revive their economies, not to mention increase their national security (*Resumen Semanal*, 20–26 September, p. 2).

Relations with the United States were mixed. Major points of contention included Peruvian attacks on U.S. foreign policy toward Central America, a unilateral declaration of debt repayment, revocation of oil company contracts, lingering negotiations on airline licensing, and protective tariff disputes. Yet, cooperation in extensive anti-drug traffic operations in the Amazon indicated a continuation of generally cordial relations.

Minor diplomatic problems also arose with the Soviet Union in regard to the Soviet fishing fleet that operates off the Peruvian coast. A commercial dispute with an intermediary company led to the seizure of the fleet and an embargo on its goods in May (ibid., 24–30 May, p. 2). Under the García government, the licenses with intermediary companies were canceled and a new agreement was signed by the State Company of Peru and the Soviet Union's Sovriblot, which allowed them to continue fishing off the Peruvian coast in return for 15 percent of the catch, an increase from 8 percent (ibid., 8–14 November, p. 5; *FBIS*, 14, 15 November). This arrangement complemented García's aim to increase local sources of food.

For the second consecutive year, the Peruvian delegation to the Soviet Union reached an advantageous accord to repay their debt with $50 million in traditional exports—such as textiles, candy, construction, footwear, fishing boats, and frozen chicken—and $150 million in nontraditional exports (*Resumen Semanal*, 23–29 March, p. 5; Lima, 30 April; *FBIS*, 1 May). In the former category was included an agreement for thirty thousand tons of sugar to help alleviate a quota reduction by the United States (*Resumen Semanal*, 10–16 May, p. 5). Similar barter agreements were reached with Yugoslavia, Romania, Hungary, and Czechoslovakia.

New trade relations with the People's Republic of China also fit the economic direction of the new government; head of the delegation Xiang Fenneng offered a $200 million line of credit for reactivating the agriculture sector. He said they would study the market for agriculture machinery, equipment tools, motorcycles, and bicycles (Paris, AFP, 17 November; *FBIS*, 19 November).

In keeping with his commitment to nonalignment, García's foreign minister Wagner went to the Luanda Non-Aligned meeting in August, discussed opening new embassies in Kenya, Zimbabwe, and Morocco, and promised that trade relations with all nations, especially the socialist world, would be increased (Paris, AFP, 26 August, 10 October; *FBIS*, 28 August, 17 October).

Terrorism. Formed in 1970 by Abimael Gúzman Reyenoso, a philosophy professor at the University of Huamanga in Ayacucho, PCP–Sendero Luminoso launched its armed struggle in May 1980 after a decade of preparation (see *YICA*, 1984, pp. 166–68; 1985, pp. 123–26). Sendero's strength is still a subject of debate as is its national and international support, but it is capable of launching coordinated, destructive attacks in almost every region of the nation. There are few signs that the Aprista government has made a real difference in stopping the bloodshed, although its approach and methods are distinctly different from the previous government.

The longer the Sendero phenomenon exists the more puzzling it is. Its fanaticism separates it from all other Peruvian parties and its juxtaposition in the revolutionary world is still unique and unfixed. The Trotskyist media argues that, although the world press describes Sendero as Communist or Marxist, it is neither. Rather, "in its program, political approach and organizational structure, Sendero Luminoso is a Stalinist formation" that identifies with Mao's prolonged people's war (*Intercontinental Press*, 18 March, p. 152). In its revolutionary struggle, Sendero claims to be in the fourth phase, "begin the great leap," with 100,000 people living under and participating in a new political order—the Organizing Committee of the New Democratic Republic of the People (*LAWR*, 5 April, p. 4).

Much of the organized left in Peru is frustrated by Sendero's ideological and armed hostility to its revolutionary program. Hugo Blanco (PRT) echoed this frustration, complaining that "PCP–SL has no perspective of participating in the working class struggles and does not do so." It participates in no mass organizations and seeks no base of support in the trade unions. It does not attempt to win working-class support or even understand its actions, "pays no attention to public opinion in its activities, issues no regular communiques, has no publications or newspaper, gives no interviews by its leaders, has no radio stations and refuses to claim or deny responsibility for any of its armed actions. It does not even issue denials of the many atrocities committed by the repressive forces attributed to Sendero Luminoso" (*Intercontinental Press*, 18 March, p. 153).

Sendero calls the IU "objective allies of reaction," and it refuses to participate in any united front with "false proletarian political parties that are really bourgeois workers parties." In fact, IU deputies and labor leaders have been targets of violent attacks. Even in the rural areas, Sendero's actions—such as mandatory production quotas, closing of "capitalist" local markets, and destruction of agricultural equipment, infrastructure, irrigation systems, and transportation—appear contrary to the peasant's interests. Blanco charges that "they treat cooperatives as though they were enemy organizations" (ibid.).

Another bone of contention is Sendero's lack of concern with an international struggle. It has made no statements on the events in Central America or anywhere else in the world. Sendero refutes the notion that no oppressed peoples can liberate themselves without agreement with one or another imperialism; thus, its target is as likely to be the Soviet Union or the People's Republic of China as it is the United States. This position is antithetical to the PCP, since they clearly define imperialism as a capitalist phenomenon.

Finally, the organized left in Peru is concerned that the government has used Sendero's activities to discredit Peru's workers' and peasants' movements. After major offensives it is more often the militant labor leader, activist student, or neighborhood dissident than the elusive terrorist who is hauled away in the police sweeps.

In 1985 the toll in Peru's guerrilla warfare passed 6,000 and there was a state of emergency in 25 provinces (seven in Ayacucho, five in Apurímac, five in Huancavelica, six in Huánuco, one in Pasco, and one in San Martín). Sendero's offensives reached their greatest intensity around the April election, the May anniversary of the initiation of their armed struggle, and the July transfer of power.

Sendero's campaign against the election included posters and signs saying "don't vote," death threats to intimidate candidates, and mutilated fingers and defaced registration cards to warn those who contemplated voting. They blocked access roads and called a 72-hour strike to frustrate election-day activity. Ten days after the election, the head of the National Election Jury was shot as he went to work, adding considerable delay in tabulating the official results and in making crucial decisions on the second round.

Selective assassination of public officials continued in May; on Sendero's anniversary, 16 May, the group carried out their largest concentrated effort in Lima in five years. Under cover of a major blackout, over twenty bombs went off all over the city. The most significant targets were the embassies of the United States, the Soviet Union, and the People's Republic of China (*Resumen Semanal*, 10–16 May, p. 3).

In June the guerrillas introduced a new weapon—the car bomb. Attacks near the Presidential Palace and the Palace of Justice produced millions of dollars of damage to ten department stores (*LAWR*, 14 June, p. 9). Occurring as they did during a state visit of President Alfonsín of Argentina, the attacks underscored the uncertainty of Lima's security and influenced many dignitaries, including Alfonsín, to cancel their attendance at President-elect García's inauguration on 28 July.

Government success against the guerrillas was mixed. The military proudly announced that several plans to thwart the election or frustrate the inauguration were uncovered by police, and two of five *senderista* cells in Lima were dismantled. Losses in the countryside proved to be heavy, since close to 90 percent of the peasant communities in the emergency zone formed active vigilante groups. In addition, clashes with military patrols brought in some major, experienced commanders. As a result guerrilla activity in Ayacucho was less frequent and less intense than in previous years (Lima, 16 March; *FBIS*, 26 March, 23 July; Paris AFP, 22 July; *Los Angeles Times*, 12 April; *Resumen Semanal*, 17–23 May, p. 1). Peasant support was seen to be declining as areas that had been "liberated" returned to government authority. In October two groups of *senderistas* surrendered to the civil guard (*Resumen Semanal*, 18–24 October, p. 2).

Overall terrorist activity did not diminish, however, as other groups also resorted to political violence. Most were minor irritants claiming one or two actions, such as the Popular Revolutionary Commandos (CRP), which surfaced in July (EFE [Spanish News Agency], 19 July; *FBIS*, 22 July). More prominent is the MRTA, which was formed in 1984 by intellectuals dissenting from the nonviolent path of the parliamentary left (see *YICA*, 1985,

p. 124). They have adopted traditional Peruvian symbols and their targets of attack are representatives of North American capitalism and government agencies. They have been careful not to harm innocent people and their image has developed as "Robin Hoods" who take from the rich (food delivery trucks) and distribute to the poor. Although they urged the people not to vote in the election, their political demands were virtually identical to those of the IU, and as the new García government made moves in this direction, the MRTA members even announced a "truce." They agreed to respect the majority vote and "take no military actions if García's administration did not attack the people" (*Resumen Semanal*, 16–22 August, p. 3). The truce lasted only three months. In November MRTA took up arms again, saying it saw no difference in the new government (Paris, AFP, 9 November; *FBIS*, 12 November).

Sendero Luminoso rejected the Apristas from the beginning: "The government intends to confuse the people with its demagoguery by reducing prices and eliminating corruption. What it really intends to do is consolidate itself in power and change present corrupt officials for others equally corrupt, but who will be at its service . . . repression is increasing" (Paris, AFP, 26 August; *FBIS*, 27 August). It also reiterated that there was no possibility of dialogue (*Resumen Semanal*, 29 November–5 December, p. 2).

The PCP and the IU have consistently condemned terrorism and all human-rights violations. They see the cause of violence rooted in social-economic stress and believe that the solution is primarily political, not military. They also agree that state repression and an increase in human-rights violations are not solely a response to the Sendero phenomenon but are also calculated to undermine the parliamentary left. The parties disagree, however, on the means to combat both guerrilla and state violence. Although social-economic development is seen as a necessity, calls for dialogue are controversial in that the underlying assumption—Sendero's willingness to participate—appears to be totally unfounded. Therefore, Barrantes and his followers agree that the best approach to diminish support for Sendero is to increase support for the government establishment, not only by social economic development but also through an entirely different counterinsurgency policy. The IU program demands that this plan should instill respect for authority by restoring civilian control, subordinating the military to civilian demands and needs, and making the judicial system worthy of respect. It also demands a general political amnesty to initiate this new approach (ibid., 22–28 November, p. 3).

President García promised to combat terrorism within the law and to suppress all who violated human rights, whether they be guerrillas or security forces. In marked contrast to the Belaúnde administration, the Apristas approach the problem as primarily a social-economic one, earmarking $6 million for emergency development projects. They have created a Peace Commission to investigate means for reconciliation and pacification. They have also paid attention to reports from domestic and foreign human-rights organizations, and García took decisive action in several cases of proven abuse.

The institutionalization of human-rights organizations grew considerably. The IU supported the creation of the National Commission for Human Rights (CONADEH) and cooperated with the United Nations and other international observers investigating the charges of forced and involuntary disappearances in the emergency zone. The IU participated on all the committees created by García and his administration with regard to human rights, including committees on human rights in both houses of Congress and the special blue-ribbon Peace Commission. Bernales (IU) called it the "conscience of the country" with the mandate to look for a national accord, examine all cases of the detained and accused, and investigate dialogue and pacification measures (ibid., 30 August–5 September, p. 2). The first report from the commission described the situation as a civil war and recommended modification of antiterrorism law, pardons for 160 IU "political prisoners," and the speedy disposition for those detained without trial for more than two years (EFE, 9 November; *FBIS*, 13 November).

García's counterinsurgency effort was also linked to a campaign against bureaucratic corruption that included the forced retirement of 303 police officers and the reorganization of the three police forces: the Peruvian Investigative Police (PIP), the Republican Guard, and the Civil Guard (Paris, AFP, 19 September; *FBIS*, 20 September). García then committed himself to reinvigorate the judiciary, which foreign committees have repeatedly called a contributing factor to human-rights violations because of its incompetent and slow process. Finally, in the new legislature, formal charges have been brought against former government ministers, supreme court justices, and ex-legislators for "neglect of duty," embezzlement, drug trafficking, influence peddling, and other abuses of power (*LARR*, 26 July, p. 4; *Resumen Semanal*, 6–12 September, p. 4; *LAWR*, 16 August, p. 3).

The rhetoric was put to the test in several ways, most significantly with the discovery of two massacres in October. García immediately ordered investigations of the massacre of 69 persons in Acconamarca and the discovery of a mass grave in Pucayacu. When satisfaction was not forthcoming, three top military officers were removed from their posts (*LAWR*, 4 October, p. 1). Critics argued that while García's tone was different—he even interviewed the survivors—he still relied on the military option. In fact, Javier Valle Riestra (APRA) resigned as chair of the Senate human-rights committee because the lieutenant in charge of the Acconamarca massacre was to be tried by a military tribunal instead of a civilian court (EFE, 9 November; *FBIS*, 1 November).

In essence, the direction of the García government is one that broadly coincides with that of the IU at this stage in their revolutionary program. The difficulty for the IU lies in maintaining support for immediate social reform without losing sight of long-term socialist goals. The moderates of the IU, the *barrantistas*, claim they have no difficulty in defining critical support for García as they pressure him to stay on the path to socialism. Yet the hardliners are concerned that since the initiative has now been taken, the IU will lose its revolutionary zeal and be co-opted by the reformists. The prospect is good that continued debate about the future of the coalition and the position of each party vis-à-vis the APRA will dominate 1986. The prospect is also good that a split between the reformist and the revolutionary Marxists will occur, similar to that of the Velasco era in which the PCP provided critical support for the government's reform efforts.

Sandra Woy-Hazleton
Miami University

Puerto Rico

Population. 3,300,520
Party. Puerto Rican Socialist Party (Partido Socialista Puertorriqueño; PSP); Puerto Rican Communist Party (Partido Comunista Puertorriqueño; PCP)
Founded. PSP: 1971; PCP: 1934
Membership. PSP: 150 (estimated); PCP: 125 (estimated)
Secretary General. PSP: vacant; PCP: Franklin Irrizarry
Leading Bodies. No data
Status. Legal
Last Congress. PSP: Second, 1979; PCP: none known
Last Elections. 1984; PSP: 0.3 percent; no representatives
Auxiliary Organizations. No data
Publications. PSP: *Claridad* (weekly)

The already insignificant political faction of the Puerto Rican Marxist left weakened even further in 1985. Federal and local law enforcement agencies dealt a heavy blow to the major leftist terrorist organization operating on the island and in the continental United States. After a seven-year investigation by the FBI, the Justice Department obtained on 23 August an eight-count indictment by a Federal Grand Jury in Hartford, Connecticut, charging seventeen Puerto Ricans with various offenses. The charges stemmed from the 12 September 1983 armed robbery of over $7 million from the Wells Fargo depot in West Hartford. According to FBI director William H. Webster, sixteen of the seventeen persons indicted were members of the Ejército Popular Boricua (EPB), or "Los Macheteros" (machete wielders). Webster described Los Macheteros as "one of the most violent clandestine groups operating in Puerto Rico . . . Among their most notorious actions claimed were the attack on a U.S. Navy bus at Sabana Seca, and the destruction of nine U.S. military aircraft at the Muñiz Air Guard Base, San Juan, as a result of which five persons were killed and numerous others wounded and injured." Among those indicted were Victor Manuel Gerene, 27, a former security guard employed by Wells Fargo who had been on the FBI's Top Ten Fugitive List, and Filiberto Ojeda Ríos, 52, who had evaded arrest for fifteen years and who, the FBI said, had been a Cuban agent for 25 years (press release of the FBI, Washington, D.C., 30 August).

The FBI also said that Gerene, after taking $7,007,151 in cash from the Wells Fargo depot, has sought refuge in Cuba and that at least some of the cash was "in the care and custody of the Cuban Government." It said that the Cuban government apparently handled the money like a banker, allowing Los Macheteros to draw what they needed to finance their activities (*Miami Herald*, 13 September). Ojeda, who was arrested in Puerto Rico and held without bail, was charged with placing bombs in hotels and bars in the tourist areas of San Juan. He is said to be the leader of the Armed Independence Revolutionary Movement (MIRA) (*NYT*, 7 September). According to law enforcement sources, the clandestine Marxist-oriented terrorist Puerto Rican groups, which advocate the island's independence, have been operating for about twenty years in Puerto Rico and various U.S. cities with a large Puerto Rican population. They have claimed responsibility for a dozen bombings in Puerto Rico, New York, and Chicago. Los Macheteros took responsibility for the 1979 machine-gunning of a Navy bus carrying enlisted personnel to a communications transmitter on the island in which two persons were killed and ten injured. That same year, Los Macheteros announced they had joined forces with two other small underground groups and with the mainland-based Armed Forces of National Liberation (Fuerzas Armadas de Liberación Nacional; FALN). In all, the terrorist groups are believed to have less than 50 members.

The majority of Puerto Rico's Marxists have been seeking independence by peaceful means. In the November 1984 election, the candidate of the Puerto Rican Independence Party (PIP), Fernando Martín, received 3.5 percent of the vote and most of it was from non-Marxist *independentistas*.

The principal Marxist group is the Puerto Rican Socialist Party, a pro-Cuban organization with some 150 members. Its leader and former secretary general, Juan Mari Bras, is a personal friend of Fidel Castro, whom he frequently visits in Havana. In 1982 the 58-year-old Mari Bras resigned his position, which he had held for many years, and the organization has been reorganizing its top leadership since. The PSP publishes the weekly newspaper *Claridad* in San Juan and advocates the establishment of Puerto Rico as a socialist state.

Equally small, with some 125 members, is the PCP, which is pro-Moscow and closely associated with the Communist Party USA. Even smaller in membership are two Trotskyist parties, the International Workers League and the Puerto Rican Socialist League. A Puerto Rican, Andrea González, was candidate for vice president of the United States on the Socialist Workers Party (SWP) ticket.

The political life of Puerto Rico continued to be centered around the competition of two principal parties: the New Progressive Party (NPP), which favors statehood for the island, and the Popular Democratic Party (PDP), which wants to maintain the present commonwealth status (also called "free associate state"). On 2 January, Rafael Hernández Colón, leader of the PDP who defeated Carlos Romero Barceló of the NPP, took over as governor of Puerto Rico. Even though Hernández Colón has long been identified as an ally of the liberal wing of the Democratic Party, his relations with the Reagan administration were friendly and businesslike.

The economy of the island, heavily dependent on federal aid, improved somewhat. Unemployment dropped to 19 percent from nearly 22 percent, and the construction and tourism sectors showed renewed strength. But agriculture continued to decline and there were doubts as to whether the tax reform law going through Congress would retain Clause 936, under which U.S. businesses opening plants in Puerto Rico are eligible for special tax benefits.

In October, in what was believed to be the greatest natural disaster in the island's history, hundreds of people died in a mud slide on the southern coast, near the city of Ponce.

George Volsky
University of Miami

Suriname

Population. 377,000
Party. 25 February Unity Movement, or Standvaste (25FM), pro-military; Revolutionary People's Party (Revolutionaire Volkspartij; RVP), pro-Cuban; Communisty Party of Suriname (KPS), pro-Albanian
Founded. 25FM: 1983; RVP: 1981; KPS: 1981
Membership. 25FM: 25,000 (claimed, but figures inflated); RVP: 100 (estimated); KPS: 25 (estimated)
Leadership. 25FM: Desire (Desi) Bouterse (chairman), Etienne Boevereen (secretary), Paul Bhagwandas (treasurer), Harvey Naarendorp (secretary general, Organizing Committee); RVP: Edward Naarendorp, Glenn Sankatshing, Lothar Boksteen; KPS: Bram Mehr was executed in 1982, current leadership unknown.
Status. Restrictions on political parties were lifted in the fall of 1985.
Last Congress. 25FM: First, 12 May 1984; KPS: First, 24 July 1981

Suriname gained independence from the Netherlands in 1975. Plagued by ethnic factionalism and governmental corruption, the country's democratically elected government was overthrown in February 1980 in a military coup that brought Lieutenant Colonel Desi Bouterse to power. Sixteen noncommissioned officers created the National Military Council (Nationale Militaire Raad; NMC) and assumed total control over the security apparatus and the government. Over the next two years, half the NMC was either jailed or killed for alleged involvement in plotting coups.

After expelling the pro-Cuban elements of the NMC in April 1980, Bouterse adopted a moderate veneer of developmentalism and appointed Henk Chin A Sen as president. After the NMC refused appeals to restore democratic rule, Chin A Sen resigned in February 1982. A series of political struggles within the military ensued and numerous coup attempts against Bouterse occurred between December 1982 and November 1983. The most dramatic event in recent Suriname history occurred on 8–9 December 1982, when at least two dozen prominent Surinamese intellectual, political, and labor leaders were executed by the military authorities; Bouterse himself participated in the episode. Always adept at maintaining power, Bouterse subsequently formed governments with the small, radical parties the Progressive Workers and Peasants Union (PALU) and the RVP. Charging the Dutch government, the U.S. Central Intelligence Agency (CIA), and Surinamese exiles with plotting to overthrow the Suriname revolution, Bouterse has maintained a permanent state of emergency for the past three years.

The 1982 developments led to the suspension of

critical economic aid from the Netherlands. The economy, which is dependent on the bauxite industry for 80 percent of its export earnings and 60 percent of the government's revenues, has severely deteriorated and foreign reserves have evaporated. Suriname's gross domestic product has fallen by one-third since 1982. Over 1,500 bauxite workers have been laid off since 1982 and another 500 layoffs are expected as the strike-plagued industry now runs at a loss for the first time in its history. Chronically stalled negotiations with the International Monetary Fund have led to demands that the massive public sector (45 percent of the workforce) be reduced, currency be devalued (up to 30 percent), and government subsidies on utilities and foodstuffs be eliminated. The government has moved to control the flourishing black market and alleviate the chronic shortage of goods by conducting raids on the smuggling rings operating on the Guyanese border and by instituting emergency rationing. This critical and worsening situation has led Bouterse to court a wide array of nontraditional aid donors and trading partners, to attempt a rapprochement with the Netherlands, and to explore barter-trade arrangements with the Soviet bloc.

These economic pressures have been translated into domestic demands for a restoration of democracy in the country. Challenged by strike actions in December 1983 and January 1984, Bouterse formed a new government headed by Willem (Wim) Udenhout, the former adviser to Prime Minister Henck Arron. This government, composed of representatives from the trade-union movement, the private sector, and the 25FM, was empowered to establish "permanent democratic structures." The military created the Denkgroep (Think Tank) from the same sectors to formulate plans for a transitional period until the establishment of a new political system.

After nearly a year of debate the Denkgroep, chaired by then–deputy prime minister Frank Leeflang, a professional soldier, announced on 5 December 1984 its plans for the democratization of the country. It proposed the creation of a 31-member National Assembly whose responsibilities would include the creation of a constitution within 27 months and the power to legislate and authorize government spending. Under a compromise formula, fourteen seats were allotted to the military, eleven to the trade unions, and six to the private sector. Initially, the influential Suriname Industries Association refused the plan and only later in 1985 joined the government. The transition phase of the plan began on 1 January with the government's appointment of the National Assembly and talks of elections in March 1987 (*NRC Handelsblad*, 26 November 1984, in *FBIS*, 4 December 1984; *NYT*, 8 December 1984; *De Volkskrant*, 6 December 1984, in *FBIS*, 13 December 1984; *Times of the Americas*, 19 December 1984).

Over objections by both the private sector and the powerful trade unions, the National Assembly was dominated by representatives of the NMC and the 25FM. Bouterse designated Ulrich Aron, director of the Tensau (Back to Suriname) Foundation and local governor of the Martowijne district, as chairman of the assembly. Jack Pinas, a trade-union leader and 25FM member, was designated vice president.

Although the army controlled fourteen seats in the assembly, only militant Marxist Charles Mijnals, a member of the NMC since the 1980 coup, is a professional soldier; the others are civilian supporters of the 25FM. Among the six delegates selected from the Association of Surinamese Manufacturers (ASFA), four were government employees. Three of the most powerful trade unions—the C-47, the Moederbond, and the CLO—were represented along with the 25FM's youth and women's wings. Even representatives from the independent trade unions were widely perceived as supporters of Bouterse. Many had been politicians in the now-defunct Nationalist Republic Party (PNR), a black nationalist organization created by Eddy Bruma, who became the principal political adviser to the sergeants who formed the NMC in 1980 (*Miami Herald*, 7 January; *NRC Handelsblad*, 31 December 1984, in *FBIS*, 8 January; *De Volkskrant*, 2 January, in *FBIS*, 8 January; *Latin America Regional Reports*, 22 February).

Domestic Party Affairs. The 25FM chaired by Bouterse was launched as a mass movement called Steadfast (Standvaste in Dutch) on 12 May 1984, the date of its First Congress. It was first suggested by Bouterse in 1983 as a way to commemorate the 1980 coup and was registered later that year as an official political party. The 25FM was conceived as replacing its predecessor, the Surinamese Revolutionary Front (SRF), which had been founded in November as a loose coalition of small, left-wing parties such as the PALU and the RVP, the trade-union movement, and the military. According to

Bouterse, this new movement aimed at greater national unity and was open to all citizens providing they shared the movement's aspirations "to create a new Surinamese citizen."

When Bouterse formally announced its formation in June 1983, he envisioned a vanguard socialist party similar to other national liberation movements. At its inaugural congress in 1984, movement leaders were appointed and seven sections were set up: youth, women, production, labor, defense, propaganda, and foreign relations. Bouterse was unanimously entrusted with leadership of the movement and proclaimed the "Defender of the Revolution" with the honorific title of commander (*Political Handbook 1984–1985*; *YICA*, 1985).

The pro-Cuban RVP headed by Edward Naarendorp, the cousin of the once powerful Bouterse aide and co-founder of the 25FM Harvey Naarendorp, chose to dissolve itself in 1983 and incorporate into the new movement. However, it still maintains a quasi-independent existence. Eight of its cadre were involved in the creation of the 25FM's militia and its leadership controls the faculty of the National University.

The more nonaligned and nationalist PALU, while retaining its trade-union function, has also effectively merged into the 25FM.

Membership in the movement is required by government employees and is said to ensure better treatment during periods of rationing. The movement's "people's militia" and the so-called anti-intervention committees have largely become dysfunctional, although there are still complaints from the private sector about extortion by party militants. The *Standvaster*, the movement's newspaper, ceased to exist in 1985 after an aborted attempt by the military to make it the nation's only newspaper. Previously banned newspapers and radio stations have since renewed operations although they are subjected to a system of prior censorship.

At a July meeting to evaluate the movement's progress, it was resolved that the 25FM should maintain monthly contact with the Council of Ministers and the National Assembly and create its own trade-union federation and farmers' organization, the Association of Suriname Agriculturists (ASA) (*Keesing's*, June; Council for the Liberation of Suriname, *Bulletin*, October; author's interviews).

After a cabinet shake-up in April that led to the withdrawal of the most powerful trade union, the C-47, from both the cabinet and the National Assembly, the assembly announced plans to complete a constitution by November 1986 (Hilversum International Service, 8 July; *FBIS*, 9 July). The commission established to draft the new constitution is to be chaired by assembly president Ulrich Aron and includes members of the 25FM, CLO, Moederbond, PALU, and ASFA. The creation of the commission came after the Suriname National Assembly approved a bill formalizing the position of Bouterse as head of government and chairman of both the Council of Ministers and the NMC (Bridgetown, Cana-Reuter, 5 August; *FBIS*, 6 August; *Keesing's*, October).

With his power formally recognized, Bouterse quietly accelerated his private discussions with the leaders of the "old" Surinamese parties: Henck Arron, the former prime minister and leader of the Suriname National Party (NPS); former opposition leader Jaggernath Lachmon of the United Reform Party (VHP); and Willy Soemita of the Javanese Farmers' Party (KTPI). Calling the talks "a dialogue of a structural nature," Bouterse lifted the five-year ban on political parties, allowing them to hold public meetings in October. Bouterse continually pressed for the amalgamation of the "old" parties, which represent over 80 percent of the population, into one large national party including the PALU and RVP. However, both Arron and Lachmon rejected the proposal and urged the military to accept a restoration of a parliamentary system of government determined by free elections. In return, the political parties would accept a permanent role for the military in Suriname's political system (*NRC Handelsblad*, 26 February, in *FBIS*, 4 March; *Latin America Regional Reports*, 10 May; *De Volkskrant*, 5 October, in *FBIS*, 16 October; Cana-Reuter, 11 October; *FBIS*, 11 October).

On 23 November the NPS, VHP, and KTPI signed an agreement with the government over a transition that would end in 1987 with the drafting of a new constitution. The agreement could theoretically open the way for a return to a parliamentary sytem within two years. However, the parties accepted the economic, educational, and political administrative order that had been established by the military in 1980. The document made no mention of general elections at a national level involving political parties. Instead, it proposed a multitiered electoral system in which deputies for a national assembly could be chosen via "people's committees and district councils." A second document included in the agreement contained a number of "discussion points" between the military and the political parties, including their possible role in the National Assembly and the Supreme Council. For their part, the political parties continue to demand general and secret elections before the transitional phase is completed. Yet Bouterse insists that his 25FM organization will remain active and that "we military will never go" (AFP, 26 November, in *FBIS*, 2 December; Paramaribo International Service, 27 November, in *FBIS*, 2 December; *Times of the Americas*, 4 December; *ANP News Bulletin*, 30 October, in *FBIS*, 29 November).

Foreign Relations. The deteriorating economic situation and the continued suspension of Dutch aid to the country in 1985 forced Suriname to diversify its international relations and tap nontraditional aid donors. The year saw Suriname strengthen its regional ties with Brazil and Colombia as well as seek assistance from radical Arab states in an attempt to break the country's diplomatic and economic isolation.

Relations with the Netherlands continued to be tenuous. After the events of December 1982, the Dutch government suspended its $1.1 billion aid package that was to continue through 1990. After two years of diplomatic silence, direct ministerial-level talks began in the summer of 1984 between the two countries to resolve their differences. According to several statements by the Dutch Ministry of Foreign Affairs, good relations were only possible if Suriname took concrete steps for the return of "democracy and the rule of law." Over the course of 1985 the Dutch frequently criticized the democratization plans of the Surinamese government for failing to meet the general expectations of free and general elections and a representative National Assembly (*Daily Gleaner*, 8 July 1984; *Times of the Americas*, 2 January; *Keesing's*, June and October).

For its part, the Suriname government opened the year demanding the cessation of Dutch humanitarian aid through private channels and calling on the Netherlands to drop its insistence on the reestablishment of a democratic order (*NRC Handelsblad*, 29 January, in *FBIS*, 5 February). Before his March meeting with Dutch foreign minister Hans Van den Broek in Brasilia, Bouterse said he was prepared to take the Netherlands to the World Court in the Hague for allegedly breaching the 1975 treaty committing the Dutch government to economic assistance to Suriname (Cana, 23 February; *FBIS*, 27 February; *Latin America Weekly Report*, 8 March).

In May Henk Heidweiler, the Surinamese ambassador to the Hague, was recalled, ostensibly for financial considerations, but not before he criticized Dutch apathy toward Suriname's gestures for improvements in relations (Cana, 23 May, in *FBIS*, 31 May; Hilversum International Service, 3 July, in *FBIS*, 5 July). After the Dutch again criticized Suriname's human-rights practices, Bouterse demanded that the Hague scale down its embassy to a charge d'affaires level until relations were normalized. The Surinamese leader criticized negative broadcasts on Radio Nederland Wreldomroep, the alleged payment of opposition leaders by the Dutch, and Holland's refusal to crack down on Bouterse's opponents (*NRC Handelsblad*, 15 July, in *FBIS*, 19 July).

After the November signing of the political agreement between the military and the leaders of the three political parties, the Dutch extended an invitation to them to discuss the possible resumption of aid. However, this new bid for a dialogue was rejected because of the exclusion of Bouterse from the proposed delegation (Bonaire Trans World Radio, 7 December, in *FBIS*, 13 December; Cana, 19 December, in *FBIS*, 23 December).

The year ended with Foreign Minister Van den Broek informing the Dutch parliament that the new agreement was a step forward but not sufficient to justify an improvement in relations (Hilversum International Service, 12 December, in *FBIS*, 13 December).

Relations between the United States and Suriname, which had soured after December 1982, continued to improve slightly. Although the U.S. Congress authorized $50,000 in International Military and Education and Training (IMET) funds for fiscal year 1986, it is unlikely that those funds will be disbursed any time soon. The renewal of additional aid in the near future is doubtful because of human-rights restrictions affecting economic assistance (*Times of the Americas*, 28 August).

The deepening relations between Brazil and Suriname remain the most crucial for the country's economic and political survival. In 1983 the Reagan administration reportedly urged the Brazilian military to pressure Bouterse to downgrade Suriname's military relations with Cuba. Washington's confirmation of CIA plans to infiltrate and destabilize Paramaribo and a summer threat by the Brazilian military to invade the country if steps were not taken to curb the Cuban influence there persuaded Bouterse to request that Havana withdraw its ambassador and sharply reduce its remaining diplomatic staff in the country (*YICA*, 1984).

In late 1984 the Dutch press published the secret minutes of the high-level meeting held at the Memre Boekoe military barracks in Paramaribo on 15 September 1983 that had triggered the final decision to substitute Brazilian for Cuban assistance. The meeting included army representatives, members of the 25FM, and the PALU and RVP, and was chaired by Prime Minister Wim Udenhout. In explaining his decision, Bouterse maintained that the Soviet Union withheld support from Suriname after December 1982 because its ambassador informed him that his country did not want to annoy the Netherlands because of the debate over the deployment of the cruise missiles. Also, according to Bouterse, the Soviets could not rationalize any substantial economic assistance to a country with such a high standard of living.

Only the Naarendorps argued against the alliance with Brazil on the grounds that the United States exerted considerable leverage over that country. Instead, they advocated a rapprochement with Holland. In dismissing the ability of both Cuba and Libya to make up the fiscal shortfall following the cutoff of Dutch aid, Bouterse told the cadres that neither country could realistically provide the needed economic and military assistance to ensure the consolidation of the Suriname revolution. Libya, he maintained, was an arms supplier of the last resort (*NRC Handelsblad*, 24 November 1984; *FBIS*, 13 December 1984).

Consequently, Brazil's military government supplied the Surinamese armed forces with at least sixteen small tanks and other military transport and provided military training programs for the army. During the Western boycott of the country, Brazil supplied vital foodstuffs and took an increased share of Suriname's bauxite exports. It also modernized the country's telephone networks (*Times of the Americas*, 28 August).

The newly elected Brazilian government continued its assistance programs to Suriname and served as a diplomatic broker to end the regime's regional and international isolation. While in Brasilia for the March inauguration of President José Sarney, Bouterse was accompanied by Surinamese chief of staff Iwan Graanogst and cabinet chief Henk Herrenberg during private talks with the presidents of Argentina, Uruguay, and Nicaragua; they also met with the foreign ministers of Libya, Colombia, and Brazil. At the request of the Brazilians, Bouterse and Van den Broek held talks about the normalization of relations. This marked the first direct contact between a Dutch minister and Bouterse since the December 1982 killings (*NRC Handelsblad*, 26 March; *FBIS*, 29 March).

During a later visit to Brasilia by Wim Udenhout, the Brazilian government granted Suriname a $20 million credit line for the purchase of Brazilian raw materials in addition to scholarships for Surinamese students and increased technical assistance in the field of agriculture. In early November President José Sarney promised sufficient assistance so that Suriname "can lay the groundwork for uninterrupted economic growth without restraint or impositions from abroad." However, Brazilian foreign minister Olavo Setubal cautioned Suriname about expecting increased economic assistance (*Folha de São Paulo*, 6 November; *FBIS*, 12 November).

After a January visit by Udenhout to Bogota, Bouterse traveled to Colombia on 21 and 22 February to confer with President Belisario Betancur, Colombian foreign minister Augusto Ramirez Ocampo, finance minister Roberto Junguito, and officials from the Central Bank. The meeting ended in the signing of a bilateral commercial and financial agreement that called for the exchange of vegetable oils and Surinamese alumina. In addition, Colombia offered a $15 million credit line to finance the purchase of industrial equipment to process rice, African palm, and sugarcane.

However, Suriname has found it difficult to meet the hard-loan requirements of the Colombian line of credit. Similar $70 million credit lines from Taiwan and $30 million from the Fiat company have gone unused, since half of these commercial arrangements are rather stringent hard loans. Thus far Suriname has only been able to buy car tires and medicines from Colombia (*ANP News Bulletin*, 30 January, in *FBIS*, 15 February; Reuter, 21 February, in *FBIS*, 25 February; Bogota Domestic Service, 23 February, in *FBIS*, 25 February; *ANP News Bulletin*, 22 August; *JPRS*, 30 September).

The Soviet Union maintains an embassy with 30 staff personnel in Paramaribo under Ambassador Igor Bubnov, a KGB officer formerly stationed in Washington, D.C. Since mid-1984 the Surinamese News Agency has disseminated Tass reports and received Soviet technical assistance. The Soviet Union has constructed radio facilities that has enabled the government to begin three short-wave broadcasts per week to Europe (*YICA*, 1985).

During 1985 the Soviet Union targeted the powerful Surinamese trade-union movement for increased influence. During the summer, two delegations of Surinamese trade unionists traveled to the

Soviet Union on a cultural exchange. On 25 September L. N. Tulkunov, chairman of the USSR's Supreme Soviet, conferred with a Surinamese delegation headed by Jack Pinas, vice president of the National Assembly and the trade-union leader charged with creating a new 25FM labor federation (*Izvestiia*, 27 September; *FBIS*, 7 October).

Although bilateral relations with Havana remain suspended, Suriname sent both official and party delegations to regional meetings organized and attended by Cuba's Communist Party. During the summer of 1984, the 25FM failed to attend the First Consultative Meeting of Anti-Imperialist Organizations of the Caribbean and Central America held in Havana. The 25FM's absence from this meeting, which included all of the region's guerrilla movements, national liberation groups, and communist parties, was considered a sign of the permanent distancing of the Bouterse regime from Castro (*Caribbean Insight*, July 1984). However, in July 1985 Suriname sent a full diplomatic delegation to the Continental Dialogue on Latin American-Caribbean Foreign Debt hosted by the Cuban premier. During the opening sessions, former prime minister Henck Arron spoke for Suriname (Havana Television Service, 20, 28 July and 2 August; *FBIS*, 31 July and 5 August).

In August the 25FM attended a meeting of regional liberation movements held in Georgetown, Guyana, and hosted by Cheddi Jagan's People's Progressive Party. The meeting included delegations from the Cuban Communist Party and the FSLN of Nicaragua. It was notable in expressing solidarity with the Cuban, Nicaraguan, and Suriname revolutions and with the FMLN of El Salvador, South Africa's ANC, and SWAPO in Namibia. The delegations unanimously approved Havana's debt policies and condemned the Reagan administration's Caribbean Basin Initiative and its support for the anti-Sandinista guerrillas (Tass, 10 August; *FBIS*, 13 August).

Since the 1983 expulsion of the Cubans, Suriname has broadened its links with Nicaragua. Discussions on normalizing relations began during Bouterse's visit to Managua for the fifth anniversary celebrations of the Nicaraguan revolution held in July 1984. There the Sandinista People's Army (EPS) rendered him military honors. Accompanied by Harvey Naarendorp, Suriname's ambassador to Mexico, and Captain Etienne Boevereen, Bouterse held extensive meetings with Daniel Ortega Saavedra and Nicaraguan foreign minister Miguel D'Escoto Brockman. Both delegations signed an agreement to establish diplomatic relations and exchange nonresident ambassadors. Ortega accepted an invitation to visit Suriname at a later date (Cana, 5 July, in *FBIS*, 6 July 1984; Managua, Radio Sandio, 18, 22 July, in *FBIS*, 19, 23 July 1984; *NRC Handelsblad*, 25 July 1984, in *FBIS*, 31 July 1984; Hilversum International Service, 25 July, in *FBIS*, 26 July 1984).

Suriname sent an official delegation to the inauguration of Nicaraguan president Ortega and vice president Sergio Ramirez Mercado. Members of 25FM reportedly remained to study the Nicaraguan National Assembly process (Radio Sandino, 5 January; *FBIS*, 7 January). In May Bouterse defended the closer links with Nicaragua, saying that they were in keeping with Suriname's "principled stand on sovereignty and noninterference" (Cana, 1 May; *FBIS*, 2 May).

Suriname's long-standing territorial claim of the Berbice Triangle section of neighboring Guyana did not deter the government from stabilizing relations with Georgetown. After Bouterse met with Guyana's president Forbes Burnham in the summer of 1984, the two countries agreed to technical exchanges between their national universities and cooperation on agricultural research. Both countries have cooperated in police and army operations to curtail the burgeoning black market and smuggling activities along the Courantyne River (Cana, 23 July 1984; *FBIS*, 24 July 1984; *Daily Gleaner*, 13 December 1984).

During the last week of January, Suriname embarked on "Operation Clean Sweep," an action carried out by military authorities to deport Guyanese immigrants back to their country. In the process, some 4,000–6,000 Guyanese immigrants were forcibly rounded up and taken to deportation centers at Fort Zeelandia and Nickerie for return to Springlands, Guyana, where Guyanese officials reprocessed their entry. Government officials maintained that the Guyanese population was responsible for the rise in crime and drug dealing in the country. The nearly 30,000 undocumented aliens, according to the government, represented a national security threat. Most observers, however, claimed that the military was reacting to the worsening economic conditions in the country (OAS, Inter-American Commission on Human Rights, *Second Report on the Human-Rights Situation in Suriname*, October; *Daily Gleaner*, 24 January; AFP, 25 January; *FBIS*, 25 January).

Suriname strengthened its relations with radical Arab states and political forces. In early February the government announced that both Palestine Liberation Organization (PLO) leader Yasir Arafat and Libyan leader Moammar Khadafy were invited to the 25 February celebration of the fifth anniversary of the 1980 coup, although they did not attend (Bonaire Trans World Radio, 1 February; *FBIS*, 4 February). The same month Iwan Graanogst visited Libya for preliminary trade talks and to arrange Bouterse's visit (*Keesing's*, June).

On 1 March, Bouterse and a delegation including Udenhout, Henk Herrenberg, and Paul Bhagwandas landed in Tripoli and were met by Libyan army major 'Abd al-Salam Jallud (*NRC Handelsblad*, 4 March; *FBIS*, 14 March). Two working groups were formed to handle financial and economic matters separately from the strictly political and military discussions. After private discussions between Khadafy and Bouterse, the two men signed a $100 million trade and aid package that included provisions for military assistance. As part of the joint economic agreements covering mining, petroleum, and agriculture, the Libyans were able to establish a People's Bureau in Paramaribo when three trade officials were finally accredited as diplomats in April (*Caribbean Insight*, April; *Latin American Regional Reports*, 10 May).

Suriname sought to assuage regional fears of a Libyan presence in the region by claiming that ties with Tripoli would not affect its relations with neighboring countries. Referring also to Suriname's closer ties with Ghana and Nicaragua, Bouterse said such links as those with Libya were part of an effort to defeat "mischievous efforts to isolate Suriname because of its revolutionary process" (Cana, 1 May; *FBIS*, 2 May). Quoting intelligence sources, American columnist Jack Anderson claimed that Khadafy wished to obtain Surinamese passports for Libyan assassination squads and Palestinian terrorist organizations and to use the country as a base to expand his influence in Latin America (*Diario Las Americas*, 18 December). Surinamese exiles reported that in a 25FM meeting Bouterse announced that fifteen Surinamese military personnel would receive special training in Libya in the fall. Apparently in an attempt to squash rumors of an increased Libyan presence in the country, Bouterse denied that large numbers of Libyans and Cubans were permitted in Suriname (Council for the Liberation of Suriname, *Bulletin*, September).

Citing press dispatches by AFP and the Palestinian press agency Wafa, opposition leaders reported in August a meeting between a Surinamese delegation and Farouk Kaddoumi, head of the political department of the PLO, and Khalil Al Wazir, commander and acting chief of staff of the Palestinian forces. They discussed "the means to strengthen the concerted struggle against Zionism and American imperialism" (ibid., August).

An Iranian delegation headed by Vice Minister of Foreign Affairs Javad Mansuri held talks in Paramaribo on the continuation of Surinamese exports of rice, prefabricated housing, and timber to Iran in exchange for oil. The late October meeting ended with an agreement by the Iranian delegation to finalize both trade and political agreements on a return visit in December (Paramaribo International Service, 30 December [as dated]; *FBIS*, 4 November).

For the fifth anniversary of the 1980 coup, North Korean (DPRK) president Kim Il-song sent Bouterse greetings, praised his government's efforts in safeguarding the revolution, and expressed the conviction that "the friendship and cooperation between the two countries will further strengthen and develop." During the celebrations, Bouterse met with the DPRK government delegation headed by the minister of labor administration, Yun So, and expressed his support for Korean reunification (Pyongyang, KCNA, 25 February; *FBIS*, 4 March).

Suriname also opened up trade relations with Czechoslovakia, signing agreements to export alumina in exchange for heavy equipment. In the fall Suriname established diplomatic relations at an ambassadorial level with Angola and in December with Zimbabwe (Bonaire Trans World Radio, 11 September; *FBIS*, 13 September; *Caribbean Insight*, January 1986).

At an intergovernmental level, Suriname assumed the chairmanship of the African, Caribbean, and Pacific (ACP) bloc of countries at the July meeting in Brussels between the ACP and the European Economic Community (EEC). Suriname was elected the chairman only after Grenada withdrew its candidacy when it failed to muster the necessary votes (Kingston Domestic Service, 1 August, in *FBIS*, 2 August; Cana, 20 July, in *FBIS*, 23 July).

In October Bouterse addressed the United Nations General Assembly on its 40th anniversary. He called for the establishment of a new international economic order, the restructuring of the United Nations to allow for Third World domination, and the support of national liberation struggles in Southern Africa and Central America. Regionally, he supported the Contadora peace process and the integration of Latin America (*NYT*, 23 October; United Nations Televison, 22 October; *FBIS*, 22 October).

Terrorist Activities. In its October report on Suriname, the Inter-American Commission on Human Rights of the Organization of American States (OAS) noted that Surinamese exiles in Holland were physically attacked, harassed, and sometimes murdered by progovernment groups and agents of the Suriname consulate in the Netherlands. According to testimony the commission received, some 20–25 persons were paid by Surinamese diplomats to harass opponents of the Bouterse regime. Over the past several years, such progovernment groups as the League of Surinamese Patriots and the Union for People's Democratic Suriname have threatened and harassed opposition groups. Exiled leaders have been murdered and opposition homes have been firebombed in Holland. On 7 March, two armed men with automatic weapons entered the antigovernment Council for the Liberation of Suriname's offices in Riswijk and mistakenly killed Dutch musicians practicing in a rented hall (OAS Inter-American Commission on Human Rights, *Second Report on the Human Rights Situation in Suriname*, 2 October).

In August opposition spokesmen announced the formation of a guard service to protect its leaders after a hit squad arrived from Brussels to assassinate exiled politicians. According to council spokesman Glenn Tjong Akiet, a former leader of the Moederbond trade union, a Surinamese hit team using diplomatic passports intended to kill former president Henk Chin A Sen and Rudolf Jankie, chairman of the Suriname Democracy and Human Rights Foundation (*Weekkrant Suriname*, 17–23 August; *JPRS*, 10 October). In Paramaribo, Bouterse summoned Dutch ambassador Dirk van Houten to assure him that the government had no designs on Chin A Sen's life since he no longer posed a security threat to the country (*ANP News Bulletin*, 16 August; *JPRS*, 23 September).

Opposition. The government's agreement to enter into negotiations with the former political parties during the summer prompted a renewal of unification talks between the four opposition groups in exile. These are the Amsterdam Popular Resistance (AVV), the Suriname Democratic Rule of Law (DROS), the Suriname Democratic Alliance (DAS), and the Council for the Liberation of Suriname (RBS). The aim of the talks was to adopt a unified strategy regarding the military's opening toward the formerly outlawed political parties (*Weekkrant Suriname*, 3–9 August; *JPRS*, 10 October).

The establishment of councillor ties between Suriname and French Guiana has hastened the end of paramilitary actions against the regime by various exiled groups. Internal political disputes still erupt violently within the Surinamese military. In March two soldiers—Oskar Kluis and John Barrow, who were accused of plotting to overthrow the government—committed suicide according to official reports. Most observers suggest that the two men were executed (*Keesing's*, June). In addition, former president Chin A Sen charged that four military men were assassinated and another 30 detained, some of them later released over a six-week period beginning in February (AFP, 3 April; *FBIS*, 10 April).

R. Bruce McColm
Freedom House

United States

Population. 239,000,000
Party. Communist Party USA (CPUSA)
Founded. 1919
Membership. 10,000–20,000
Secretary General. Gus Hall (75)
Politburo. 14 members: Gus Hall, Henry Winston (74), James Jackson (71), Charlene Mitchell (55), George Meyers (72), Jarvis Tyner, James Steele (35), Arnold Bechetti, John Pittman, Helen Winter (78), Daniel Rubin (53), Lou Diskin, Mike Zagarell (41), James West (72)
Central Committee. 83 members
Status. Legal
Last Congress. Twenty-third, 10–13 November 1983, Cleveland, Ohio
Last Election. 1984 presidential, Hall-Davis ticket, under 0.1 percent
Auxiliary Organizations. U.S. Peace Council, National Alliance Against Racist and Political Repression, Trade Unionists for Action and Democracy, Women for Racial and Economic Equality, Labor Research Association, Benjamin Rush Society
Publications. *Daily World* (Mike Zagarell, ed.), *People's World* (Carl Bloice, ed.), *Political Affairs*

The CPUSA is the oldest and largest of the numerous Marxist-Leninist parties in the United States. It was founded in 1919 and reached its height in the late 1930s, when it had nearly 100,000 members and significant influence in the labor movement and a variety of other organizations. After World War II, the party entered a long period of decline caused by the Cold War and domestic anticommunism. Its own tactics, including a decision to transform itself into an underground organization, contributed to the decline. Shaken by revelations of Stalin's crimes, most party members quit in the late 1950s. Although it has remained a marginal political movement since then, the CPUSA has made some modest gains in membership and influence in the last several years.

Leadership and Organization. Gus Hall has been the party's general secretary since 1959. Henry Winston is party chairman. Other leaders include Arnold Bechetti (national organizational secretary), Sid Taylor (treasurer), and James Jackson (secretary of the Central Committee and Politburo). James Steele, formerly head of the Young Communist League (YCL), was recently appointed legislative and political action director. Important party commissions and their chairs include George Meyers (labor), Charlene Mitchell (Afro-American affairs), Si Gerson (political action), Victor Perlo (economics), Judith LeBlanc (cadres), and Lee Dlugin (international affairs). Party leaders in key states include Jarvis Tyner (New York), Rich Nagin (Ohio), Sam Webb (Michigan), Ted Pearson (Illinois), Helvi Savola (Minnesota), and Maurice Jackson (Maryland–D.C.).

The party has made a major effort in the last several years to become more visible. Large ads in major newspapers have been used to present communist positions and party clubs have been urged to become more active. Despite a sharp decline in its national vote totals in the 1984 presidential race (35,000 compared to 45,000 four years earlier), the party has boasted of its increasing acceptance by ordinary Americans.

Party leaders have provided varying accounts of how many members are in the CPUSA. Recent figures have ranged from 10,000 to 20,000; it is likely that the lower figure is closer to the mark (*Frontline*, 28 November 1983). The party has concentrated its recruitment efforts among blacks, chicanos, and other "oppressed minorities" in recent years but does not provide information about their relative proportions among the membership.

Domestic Affairs. The CPUSA's goal has remained the creation of an antimonopoly people's party built on the foundation of a people's front against Reagan. Gus Hall insisted that the basis for such a front was unity among the trade-union movement, the black community, and the Rainbow Coalition of Jesse Jackson (Gus Hall, *Fightback II*). In spite of its desire for an independent political party, the CPUSA recognizes that most of the forces it seeks to attract remain committed to the Democratic Party; as a result it often supports "progressive" Democrats as an alternative or lesser evil. Because one of the party's major villains, Mayor Ed Koch of New York, ran for re-election on the Democratic ticket in 1985, the party ran Jarvis Tyner for mayor on a People Before Profits ticket. He received 3,319 votes out of more than one million cast.

The CPUSA has consistently opposed all of President Reagan's domestic programs and policies on the grounds that they benefit the wealthy at the expense of the vast majority of Americans. The farm crisis, the balance of trade deficit, unemployment, and plant closings have all been cited as evidence of the growing economic crisis. Hall noted that to the general crisis of world capitalism and the structural crisis of developed capitalism was now being added a new cyclical crisis of American capitalism (*Political Affairs*, January).

Auxiliary Organizations. The YCL, founded in 1983 in its new guise, has been associated with the CPUSA since the 1920s. It publishes a monthly newspaper, *Dynamic*. The YCL's chair is John Bachtell. Elena Mora is administrative secretary and Joe Simms, Bill Dennison, and Keta Miranda are vice chairs. Its biggest project in 1985 was the twelfth World Festival of Youth, sponsored by the World Federation of Democratic Youth and held in Moscow. The YCL played the major role in putting together an American delegation and gathering an impressive array of endorsers, including numerous congressmen, mayors, and public figures ranging from Andrew Young and Wilson Goode to John Kenneth Galbraith and Jesse Jackson (*New Republic*, 12–19 August).

Other party auxiliaries include the National Alliance Against Racist and Political Repression (Frank Chapman, executive director; Angela Davis, chair); the U.S. Peace Council (Michael Myerson, executive director); Women for Racial and Economic Equality (Cheryl Allen Craig, national president; Vinnie Burrows, international secretary); Labor Research Association (Joseph Harris, director; Greg Tarpinian, editor, *Labor Notes*); Trade Unionists for Action and Democracy; and the Benjamin Rush Society.

International Views, Positions, and Activities. The CPUSA is one of the most consistently pro-Soviet parties in the communist world. It reflexively defends Soviet policies and actions against the United States or critical communist regimes. In the last few years it has focused much of its effort on opposition to President Reagan's deployment of Cruise and Pershing missiles in Europe and the Strategic Defense Initiative (SDI) program. The CPUSA placed great emphasis this year on the Reagan-Gorbachev summit. Prior to the meeting, it harshly attacked the president for seeking to "sabotage" the chances for peace, charging that he was "hellbent on a policy of first-strike nuclear aggression" and suggesting that by not following the Soviet lead in banning nuclear testing, he was "setting the stage for the final end of the human race" (*Daily World*, 20 September). Hall maintained that Reagan's "last minute" proposals were a reflection of the building pressures in the United States for peace but warned that the SDI program had to be stopped (ibid., 7 November).

The CPUSA has strongly supported the Sandinista government in Nicaragua and condemned U.S. aid to the *contras*. It has been active in protests calling for U.S. divestment from South Africa. The party supports Yasir Arafat and the PLO, while maintaining that Israel has a right to exist alongside a PLO state. Although it condemns terrorism, the CPUSA has refused to accept that forces it supports engage in it. One party columnist, while denouncing the hijacking of the Achille Lauro and the murder of an American tourist, accepted the PLO's denial of responsibility and suggested that the whole affair smelled of an Israeli provocation (ibid., 11 October).

Publications. The CPUSA announced that the *Daily World*, published five times a week in New York, and the *People's World*, published weekly in San Francisco, would merge early in 1986 to create a "new, national daily working-class newspaper." It will also have a new name (ibid., 10 October).

Socialist Workers Party. The largest of several small Trotskyist parties in the United States is the Socialist Workers Party (SWP), founded in 1938. Although American laws prevent it from affiliation with the Fourth International, the SWP cooperates with that body. It publishes a weekly newspaper, the *Militant*.

American Trotskyism has undergone one of its periodic fissures in the last few years. Four groups have broken away from the SWP and formed new organizations: the Fourth Internationalist Tendency, Socialist Action, Socialist Unity, and the North Star Network. None have more than a few hundred members, and the SWP probably has less than one thousand. There are also several tiny Trotskyist sects, such as the Spartacist League and the Workers League, that have been in existence for nearly two decades.

The SWP held its 33rd convention in August with 900 delegates and guests in attendance. Jack Barnes is national secretary, and Barry Sheppard, Malik Miah, and Mary-Alice Waters are national co-chairs. Mac Warren is national organizational secretary. The party's new national committee of 50 includes 17 women, 12 blacks, and 7 Latinos. The convention declared that the party's major priority in the coming year would be participation in the antiapartheid struggle. One of the major speakers, Neo Mnumzana of the African National Congress, told the gathering that "when we fight the United States in the so-called outposts on the periphery of imperialism, we are also fighting the U.S. on behalf of your freedom" (*Militant*, 13 September).

Unlike the CPUSA, the SWP shuns any form of cooperation with capitalist parties. Not only does it strenuously oppose Democratic politicians, it also denounces people like Jesse Jackson for making the formation of a labor party more difficult. The Rainbow Coalition was simply "a wing of the Democratic Party that seeks to advance the interests of U.S. imperialism through liberal policies" and "offers a face-lift for the bosses' system" (ibid., 24 May). Mac Warren favorably contrasted the National Black Independent Political Party (NBIPP), a small group in which the SWP has some influence, to Jackson. Urging support of the NBIPP, he praised its "anticapitalist, anti-imperialist program" (ibid., 22 February).

Over the past several years the SWP has abandoned a number of traditional Trotskyist precepts, such as the doctrine of permanent revolution, while giving more support to such Marxist-Leninist regimes as Cuba and the Sandinistas in Nicaragua. The *Militant* devotes a considerable amount of space to Nicaragua and actively promotes assistance to that regime.

Although the SWP is critical of aspects of the Soviet government, it generally supports its international policies. It has attacked the "brutal methods" used by the "bureaucratic rulers of the Polish workers state" to silence its critics and criticized its trial of such dissidents as Adam Michnik (ibid., 18 January). The CPUSA has complained that "the large-scale U.S. intervention in Afghanistan" was undermining the Pakistani government and denounced the Afghan rebels as reactionary feudalists (ibid., 24 May). Similarly, the SWP supports the Vietnamese invasion of Kampuchea and denounces those fighting against it.

The SWP strenuously opposes Israel's right to exist, calling for a democratic secular state in Palestine. It has gone further than almost every other radical group in its embrace of anti-Semitism, charging that accusations of racism and anti-Semitism against Louis Farrakhan, the Black Muslim minister who called Judaism a "gutter religion," are a "frame-up." The SWP denied for months that Farrakhan had made any anti-Semitic remarks (ibid., 4, 18 October). The *Militant* reversed its view of Farrakhan in late November, accusing him of defending capitalism and "expressing anti-Semitic prejudices and religious myths" (ibid., 22 November).

The SWP's largest auxiliary is the Young Socialist Alliance (YSA). Its leaders include Peter Thierjung, national secretary and editor of *Young Socialist*, and Jackie Floyd and Laura Gerza, national co-chairs. At its twenty-fourth convention it boasted that a majority of its members were industrial workers. The YSA set its priority as developing labor opposition to U.S. policy in Central America (ibid., 1 February).

Other Marxist Parties. The Maoist movement that flourished in the mid-1970s has been decimated as a result of internal political developments in

China and alterations in Chinese and U.S. foreign policy. The Communist Party (Marxist-Leninist) has recently disbanded. The Communist Workers Party—five of whose members were killed by the Ku Klux Klan and Nazis in Greensboro, North Carolina, in 1979—changed its name in 1985 to the New Democratic Movement, abandoned Marxist-Leninist rhetoric in favor of appeals to the American revolutionary tradition, and announced that its goal was to gain control of the American Express company. Its membership and influence are insignificant. The League of Revolutionary Struggle, led by Amiri Baraka (formerly LeRoi Jones) and Carl Davidson, supports the Chinese government. The Revolutionary Communist Party, led by Bob Avakian, continues to defend the Gang of Four and Mao's policies. Both groups are very small.

The only other Marxist-Leninist group with more than a handful of members is the Workers World Party, led by Sam Marcy. Founded in 1958 after a fissure in the SWP, it has steadily moved away from Trotskyism and is strongly pro-Soviet. Its few hundred members have played an important role in recent years in building coalitions that have united a variety of radical groups; its two most successful front groups are the People's Anti-War Mobilization and the All-Peoples Congress.

Harvey Klehr
Emory University

Uruguay

Population. 2,926,000
Party. Communist Party of Uruguay (PCU)
Founded. 1920
Membership. 7,500 (estimated)
Secretary General. Rodney Arismendi
Leading Bodies. No data
Status. Legal (March)
Last Congress. Twentieth, December 1970 (National Conference, December 1985)
Last Election. November 1984; PCU ran within Frente Amplio coalition, 6 percent, no representatives.
Auxiliary Organizations. Union of Communist Youth
Publications. *La Hora*; *El Popular* (newspaper)

Constitutional government was restored in Uruguay in 1985. The November 1984 elections led to the reopening of Parliament on 15 February and the assumption of office by President Julio María Sanguinetti of the Colorado Party on 1 March. The rapid restoration of civil liberties included the release of all political prisoners, complete press freedom, and the legalization of all groups and parties banned during the twelve years of military dictatorship, including the PCU.

In the November elections, the PCU was technically still banned but was able to run under the surrogate name of Democracia Avanzada. The party did poorly, receiving only 6 percent of all the votes cast and some 25 percent of the vote of the leftist coalition known as the Frente Amplio (Broad Front). The Frente Amplio garnered 22 percent of the national vote and, like the two traditional parties (Blanco and Colorado), spent the year trying to define its positions, test the opposition, and reconstruct the alliances all but destroyed—or at least suspended—by the dictatorship.

The Frente Amplio consists principally of a social-democratic group, List 99 (Movimiento por el Gobierno del Pueblo), headed by Senator Hugo Batalla; the PCU, led by General Secretary Rodney Arismendi; the Socialist Party, led by Senator José Pedro Cardoso; a small Christian Democratic Party; and several minor leftist groups. Among the still unresolved issues confronting the Frente Amplio are the questions of internal organization and the creation of common political positions among the various groups. List 99 has argued for an executive committee based on the voting strength of the respective parties, while the PCU has pushed for the continuation of a one party–one vote system for executive-committee representation, whereby decisions taken by this body would be binding on all factions.

An even more difficult, and potentially divisive, issue confronting the left is the expected request by the ex-guerrilla movement, the Movimiento de Liberación Nacional (MLN-Tupamaros), for admission to the Frente Amplio. The Tupamaros, which was decimated by the military in the early 1970s and whose members languished in jail during the dictatorship, is now a legally functioning (albeit very small) political group that has expressed its desire to participate peacefully in the political life of the country. Tupamaros leaders, such as Raúl Sendic and Mauricio Rosencof, have indicated that the movement now wants a legal and peaceful struggle for change within the context of strengthening Uruguay's newly established democracy. The Tupamaros held a convention in late December with 1,000 in attendance. The convention discussed such issues as the errors made by the movement in the early 1970s, its current political program, and the possibility of the Tupamaros officially joining the Frente Amplio. The Christian Democratic Party has strongly indicated its objection to Tupamaros membership in the coalition on ideological grounds. Yet the more difficult problem is clearly political. The Frente Amplio may lose some of its more moderate adherents if the Tupamaros is permitted to join the coalition, although the ultimate effect would be uncertain, given the fact that under the Uruguayan constitution the next elections will not take place until 1989.

The PCU celebrated its 65th anniversary in the midst of its relegalization and the return of many of its exiled activists. Arismendi, the most prominent of the returnees, stressed the need to strengthen pluralist democracy in Uruguay. As he put it:

> Lenin used to say that each country would find its own form of Socialism, in keeping with its own national characteristics and the will of its own people. We are not copying anyone. For example, we are in favor of a democratic, anti-imperialist, and pluralist government with socialist tendencies. When we define the Broad Front as a real practical instrument by which to achieve socialism, it means that we are considering a pluralistic option. (*La Hora*, 5 March; *FBIS*, 20 March)

The PCU faced strong competition for its historical control of the union movement. The return of democracy brought with it a vigorous renewal of union activity. The new union confederation that had emerged toward the end of the dictatorship—the Plenario Intersindical de Trabajadores (PIT)—merged with the old communist-dominated Confederación Nacional de Trabajadores (CNT) into a general federation known by its anagram, PIT-CNT. Internal elections took place in dozens of unions, whereby the Communists gained a majority of union delegates but received strong competition from a coalition of social-democratic, socialist, and christian-democratic union leaders. Indeed, several key unions, including those involving bank and health workers, elected noncommunist leaders.

There were numerous strikes and work stoppages during the year. However, the government reacted with maturity and firmness in regard to labor unrest by recognizing that after twelve years of banned union activity and a 40 percent decline in real wages, Uruguay's workers needed to vent their frustrations and assuage their hunger. At the same time, the government made it clear, in word and in deed, that it will not tolerate worker sit-ins at factories, schools, or other public buildings. The labor conflicts were of concern to both the business community and the government, which employs 25 percent of the work force. President Sanguinetti and his minister of labor, Hugo Fernandez Feingold, devoted enormous time and energy in an effort to reduce labor unrest.

The PIT-CNT held a national convention in early December, during which a significant split developed. The noncommunist delegates representing some 40 percent of the congress walked out in protest over communist manipulation of the agenda for the meeting and their attempts to dominate key positions in the labor federation. This split had immediate repercussions in the Frente Amplio, since the parties in the coalition were obviously the same ones that were contesting representation and leadership roles within the labor movement.

The PCU held a National Conference (not a Party Congress) at the end of December. The conference was attended by some 2,600 party delegates and 600 representatives of the Union of Communist Youth, as well as observers from other communist parties. They debated the experience of the dictatorship, the meaning of redemocratization, and the current political, economic, and social situation in the country. Arismendi made use of this platform to indicate that he believed the split in the labor federation would be overcome by the expansion of executive committee representation and the scheduling of another National Conference for July 1986.

The restoration of democracy has been accompanied by a spate of new publications, especially from leftist parties and groups. Within the Frente Amplio the Christian Democrats publish *Aqui*, the Socialist Party publishes *Alternativa*, the faction known as IDI (Izquierda Democratica Independiente) publishes *Asamblea*, and the PCU publishes *La Hora* and its old newspaper, *El Popular*. Late in the year, List 99 announced the publication of a new magazine, *Zeta*, which will appear every 40 days.

The economy did not respond as well as the new government had hoped. An expected modest growth of 1–2 percent in fact showed a fourth consecutive yearly decline of 1–2 percent. Exports were down some 10–15 percent and inflation held to a 70 percent annual rate. The government is predicting a 2–4 percent real growth in Gross Domestic Product (GDP) for 1986 but is worried about triple digit inflation if budget deficits are not reduced.

The government's economic plan is clearly based on an export-led recovery. While not unduly optimistic in this regard for 1986, the Sanguinetti team believes that its aggressive international efforts to open new markets and its careful targeting of the 50-odd firms that are responsible for 90 percent of exports, could increase total exports some 50 percent by 1991. Exports totaled U.S. $928 million in 1984 but declined to an estimated U.S. $850 million in 1985.

The government had greater success in dealing with renegotiation of its foreign debt. Agreement was reached with the private international banking community as well as with the International Monetary Fund (IMF). The Letter of Intention signed with the IMF targeted an inflation rate of 45 percent for all of 1986. In addition, the government pledged to reduce the overall deficit from 10 percent of GDP to 5 percent by the end of the year while keeping central government expenditures at 19 percent of GDP. These figures meant that Sanguinetti strenuously opposed the increases that Parliament attached to his budget proposal. Although the government did agree to modest increases in the education and health components of the budget, the year ended with a threatened presidential partial veto of the budget that was expected to be passed in early January. The government had greater success in obtaining the passage of complicated and sensitive legislation concerning the refinancing of the internal debt. Without the resolution of this issue, there was little hope of renewed capital formation and investment.

For the first time in years, Uruguay had a dynamic foreign policy. Foreign Minister Enrique Iglesias, former head of the Economic Commission for Latin America (ECLA), used his contacts and economics background in an aggressive drive to open new markets for Uruguay. Diplomatic relations were re-established with Cuba, and trade and diplomatic delegations were sent to the Peoples' Republic of China, which still does not have diplomatic relations with Uruguay. The country also became more involved with foreign policy issues in its own hemisphere. Uruguay became a supporter of the Contadora group, successfully completed bilateral trade agreements with Argentina, and was an active participant in the Cartagena Consensus, which seeks to coordinate Latin policy concerning the debt problem.

The year ended in a near state of exhaustion for the players in the renewed game of democratic politics in Uruguay. The governing Colorado Party hoped to get a budget it could live with. The Blanco opposition, led by Wilson Ferreira Aldunate, tried to define its position between the Colorados and the left. The Frente Amplio, hurt by the split in the union movement, sought to resolve issues of internal governance. In March 1986, following summer vacation, the struggle to preserve democracy and stimulate economic recovery—all in the presence of the united and deeply reactionary armed forces—comes back to center stage.

Martin Weinstein
William Paterson College of N.J.

Venezuela

Population. 17,810,000
Party. Communist Party of Venezuela (Partido Comunista de Venezuela; PCV)
Founded. 1931
Membership. 4,000 (estimated)
Secretary General. Alonso Ojeda Olaechea
President. Jesús Faría (75)
Politburo. Reduced to seven members and three alternates. Members: Faría, Ojeda Olaechea, Pedro Ortega Díaz, Eduardo Gallegos Mancera, Radamés Larrazábal, Trino Melcan, and Silvino Varela. Alternates: Alí Morales, Luis Ciano, and José Manuel Carrasquel.
Central Committee. Increased from 53 to 65 members.
Status. Legal
Last Congress. Seventh, 24–27 October 1985
Last Election. 1983, 2.0 percent, 3 of 195 seats
Auxiliary Organizations. United Central of Venezuelan Workers (Central Unitaria de Trabajadores Venezolanos; CUTV); Communist Youth (Juventud Comunista; JC)
Publication. *Tribuna Popular* (weekly)

Economic reactivation remained illusory in 1985, becoming still more problematical as petroleum prices continued to fall. The foreign debt, unemployment, and cost of living were criticized by all opposition parties but merited special attention at the PCV's Seventh Congress.

The congress may not have laid to rest all dissension in the party, but discipline was maintained—so well, in fact, that little information is available. Hector Mujica, apparently one of the group of intellectuals demanding greater internal democracy, was not returned to the Politburo. Mujica, however, denied any differences with Jesús Faría and said he had asked to be dropped in order to devote full time to writing.

Faría stepped down after 30 years as secretary general to become president of the party, a post left vacant by Gustavo Machado's death in 1983. He was succeeded by Alonso Ojeda Olaechea, who had held the position clandestinely on two occasions during the Pérez Jiménez and Betancourt regimes. Although the old guard retained the top leadership, they did approve the formation of a National Secretariat that will presumably promote democratization and decentralization by bringing more members into activities at the national level. Another reform calls for biannual local and regional conferences. Leaders were pleased by the increased number of workers and labor directors at the congress and in the Central Committee, but this was offset by the very small increase in female members (*El Nacional*, 18–31 October).

The small PCV–dominated CUTV labor confederation has continued to offer fairly militant, if token, opposition to the government. On some issues it has even been joined by the Venezuelan Labor Confederation (CTV), which controls 90 percent of organized labor and responds to the governing Democratic Action Party (AD). The CTV agreed, for example, that the government's wage and price committee had been counterproductive, and it joined CUTV delegates in Havana in July for the Latin American debt conference. (CUTV president Hemmy Croes was murdered in early March. Police investigations point to a crime of passion, but the PCV insisted that it was political and most likely done by the CIA [ibid., 14 March]).

The PCV opposed a government proposal to reform the petroleum nationalization law, which would permit the state firm, PDVSA, to associate itself with private or public multinational petroleum corporations abroad. PCV deputy Radamés Larrazábal called it "a threat to our sovereignty and to the fixed price policies of OPEC, an invitation to corruption on a super scale, as well as unconstitutional" (ibid., 4 December). Larrazábal has likewise denounced stepped-up pressures against OPEC, noting that spot prices remained relatively stable while prices on OPEC contracts with multinationals were forced down again and again (ibid., 14 November). The PCV expects a hefty devaluation of the Bolívar as compensation for reduced local currency income from petroleum exports. This would have no effect on international payments, however, and Larrazábal expects no help from the Baker Initiative. The new U.S. plan, he feels, will increase both indebtedness and conditionality without lowering interest rates or even providing sufficient new funds to cover interest payments (ibid., 10 December).

The working papers approved by the Seventh Congress noted that the existing electoral system unfairly favors the establishment parties, but the congress nonetheless condemned voter abstention and stressed instead the need for better mass organization, particularly in industrial zones. According to the document, leftist unity remains the strategy for attaining popular power and any eventual adoption of nonpeaceful measures would depend upon greatly exacerbated social contradictions (ibid., 28 October).

Faría's opening speech to congressional delegates and guests from 22 communist and workers' parties condemned aggressive U.S. foreign policy, particularly as reflected by the occupation of Grenada and constant provocations against revolutionary Nicaragua and other Central American peoples (*Pravda*, 25 October; *FBIS*, 28 October). Greetings to the congress from the Soviet Communist Party (CPSU) echoed those concerns and went on to stress the importance of the international antiwar movement (*Pravda*, 26 October; *FBIS*, 29 October). Greetings from the Socialist Unity Party of Germany (SED) also warned of the U.S. threat to world peace and called for the unity of "all anti-imperialist and democratic forces to preserve peace" (East Berlin, *Neues Deutschland*, 24 October; *FBIS*, 30 October).

Two PCV founders died this year, Miguel Otero Silva (MOS) in August and Rodolfo Quintero in November. Otero Silva had received the Felix Varela Order from Fidel Castro in Havana just three months before his death. A MOS Internationalist Brigade was formed in the state of Falcón in October; among other things, its members will help with the coffee harvest in Nicaragua (*El Nacional*, 24 October). The Central Committee of the CPSU awarded the Order of the October Revolution to Faría on his 75th birthday (ibid., 27 June).

Movement to Socialism (Movimiento al Socialismo; MAS). Between campaigns and primaries, most of the year was spent in electing a new national directorate. Yet when it was all over, very little had changed. Pompeyo Márquez, secretary general of MAS since its split from the PCV in 1971, replaced Teodoro Petkoff as president of the party. From the same faction, Freddy Muñoz became the new secretary general. Juvencio Pulgar's candidacy represented the only real challenge to Muñoz's election; in his own words, Pulgar "received the bill" a few months later when he was relieved of his position as leader of the MAS faction in congress (*El Nacional*, 5 November). Márquez reportedly wants the presidential nomination in 1988. Pulgar was rumored to have favored an "independent friend of the MAS, such as Reinaldo Cervini" as presidential candidate (*Bohemia*, 8–14 April; *JPRS*, 15 May).

At the Sixth National Convention in June–July, delegates again defined MAS as a socialist force somewhere between the communist left and the social democracy of AD. The party structure that had been dismantled in 1984 was restored: a 45-member national directorate and an executive committee composed of the president, secretary general, and 15 members of the national directorate.

MAS considered Fidel Castro's foreign debt conference "politically inadvisable" for debtor countries. According to Anselmo Natale, the Havana meeting tended to "situate the debt problem within the framework of East-West rather than North-South conflict" where it belongs (*El Nacional*, 31 July). Earlier that month, MAS leader Eleazar Díaz Rangel had presided over the fourth congress of the Federation of Latin American Journalists (FELAP) in Havana. Foreign debt figured prominently on the agenda and FELAP urged nonpayment (ibid., 8 July). As second vice president of the senate, Pompeyo Márquez formed part of the official Venezuelan delegation to Daniel Ortega's inauguration in Managua. Until the group's activities were suspended in December, MAS supported Contadora and would have liked to see Nicaragua and all Central America removed from the terms of the East-West conflict.

MAS agreed with the need to "internationalize" PDVSA's activities but insisted on congressional approval of major contracts with other multinational corporations. Muñoz blamed government "irresponsibility" for the existing impasse in the process (ibid., 6 November). In 1984, two MAS founders—Antonio José Urbina and Germán Lairet—were named ambassadors of Venezuela in Sweden and Yugoslavia, respectively. Both had disagreements with Muñoz, and Lairet is expected to leave the party to support the 1988 re-election campaign of former President Carlos Andrés Pérez (AD) (ibid., 19 November). Petkoff recently denied that he will work for Pérez's re-election, saying that these rumors were launched to give an impression within AD of extraparty support for Pérez (ibid., 15 November).

Other Marxist Parties. The People's Electoral Movement (Movimiento Electoral del Pueblo; MEP) grew out of a 1967 AD split led by Luis Beltrán Prieto Figueroa. The aging Prieto was still president at the end of 1985, but co-founder Jesús Angel Paz Galarraga gave up his post as secretary general in 1984. He was succeeded by Adelso González Urdaneta. This deliberate effort to revitalize the party was accompanied by other reforms promoting greater internal democracy. The MEP had only four deputies in congress, but its labor sector was the strongest of the left. In the ninth congress of the CTV, the MEP retained its two seats on the executive committee and MEP political secretary César Olarte was elected secretary general of the CTV. (AD had the CTV presidency and 10 seats on the executive committee; Social Christian Party [COPEI], three seats; Democratic Republican Union [URD], one; and MAS, one. COPEI refused the post of secretary general because of differences with AD on labor policy.) González Urdaneta attended Sandinista anniversary celebrations in Managua and went on to the foreign debt conference in Havana.

The Revolutionary Left Movement (Movimiento de Izquierda Revolucionario; MIR) broke away from AD in 1960. Following a 1980 split, the Moisés Moleiro faction, representing the Marxist-Leninist position, was allowed to keep the party name. Américo Martín, founder and presidential candidate in 1978, led a social-democratic tendency that subsequently joined Guillermo García Ponce's old United Communist Vanguard (VUC) to form the New Alternative (Nueva Alternativa; NA). The NA was a vehicle for the 1983 presidential candidacy of José Vicente Rangel. Martín has since abandoned politics altogether but his theories were adopted by the MIR. The Tenth National Convention in June dropped the dictatorship of the proletariat from the party program and defined the MIR as socialist, revolutionary, and democratic. Moleiro did not give up his post as he had promised in 1984. He remained secretary general and Hector Pérez Marcano became president.

The Socialist League (Liga Socialista; LS) was the last remaining Marxist-Leninist group and little was heard from it in 1985. Secretary General Julio Escalona resigned in 1984 and the party has presumably still been headed by President Carmelo Laborit. Its one congressman, David Nieves, was the only leftist politician consulted by the press who condemned Colombian president Belisario Betancur for his handling of the M-19 guerrilla assault on the Palace of Justice in Bogotá (ibid., 8 November).

Guerrillas. The Venezuelan guerrilla group Red Flag (Bandera Roja; BR) received little publicity except for some initial suspicion of complicity in the M-19 assault of the Colombian Palace of Justice. Venezuelan interior minister Octavio Lepage said "there is no evidence" of BR participation in the attack (*Diario Las Américas*, 9 November). A Venezuelan with ties to M-19 was arrested in Bogotá in December but there was no indication that he was a BR member (*El Nacional*, 12 December). Former guerrilla leader Douglas Bravo was detained by police for an hour "by mistake" a day after the M-19 attack (ibid., 7 November).

Under incentives offered by the present administration, agricultural production registered important increases. This very necessary growth has been threatened, however, by the insecurity that is driving growers out of good lands all along the long border with Colombia. Some land invasions were fomented by the Peasant and Farmworkers' Federation (Federación Campesina) in a never very well explained prelude to elections within the federation. More worrisome was the epidemic of extortion, kidnapping, and murder of landowners, primarily by Colombian guerrillas, as well as a growing number of skirmishes between Venezuelan troops and Colombian guerrillas. Enrique Urdaneta, president of the National Cattle Raisers' Federation, said, "Producers don't dare to sleep on their own ranches . . . the lack of security is causing an exodus to the cities and robbing future generations of their training on the land" (ibid., 22 March).

Colombian guerrillas have been crossing into Venezuela not only in connection with the flourishing drug traffic within the region but also as a refuge from increasing persecution in their own country. In a letter to the Venezuelan consul in Cúcuta, the Castroite National Liberation Army (Ejército de Liberación Nacional; ELN) threatened to convert the country into a "free zone" for ELN activity unless Venezuelan authorities refrained from handing over captured guerrillas to the Colombian military. The "free zone" would be subject to "attacks against prominent Venezuelans, banks and institutions" (*Diario Las Américas*, 12 October). On 15 October an M-19 cell was dismantled in Cúcuta; the Colombian Revolutionary Armed Forces (FARC) and Popular Liberation Army (EPL) have also been present in the region but the extent of cooperation among the groups is not known.

Carole Merten
Miami, Florida

ASIA AND THE PACIFIC

Introduction

Much of continental Asia's population lives under communist rule. The communist leaders of Mongolia, North Korea, the People's Republic of China, Vietnam, Kampuchea (Cambodia), and Laos have pursued the same policies in recent years, with only minor exceptions in the case of North Korea.

Communist activity in the Philippines continued to grow on many fronts: expansion of the sphere of influence of the New People's Army; more terrorism and the deliberate assassination of civilians to sow maximum confusion and mistrust between the populace and the government; and further efforts to use "united front" tactics in the cities and metropolitan areas by allying with labor unions, students, and other anti-Marcos forces.

Elsewhere in the region communist activities merely replicated those of recent years, with minor variations that can be highlighted by classifying communist activity as follows: states with ruling Communist parties, states with legal Communist parties in opposition; and states with banned Communist parties.

States with Ruling Communist Parties. North Korea, Mongolia, the People's Republic of China, North Vietnam, Laos, and Kampuchea are regimes in which the Communist party rules supreme. North Korea's Kim Il-song, leader of the Korean Workers' Party, continued to transfer political power to his son Kim Chong-il. In 1985 the top leadership initiated a major reorganization in government and forged closer ties with the Soviet Union. All ministries under the cabinet were reorganized by combining two or more ministries under a new organ called the "commission." The party appointed new personnel to lead those new organs. It is not clear whether this widespread reorganization is related to the transfer of power to Kim Chong-il, a new streamlining effort to increase economic efficiency and control, or both.

But more important was the marked shift toward a stronger Soviet-Korean alliance. All North Korean ports are now open to Soviet ships, and several hundred vessels called there in 1985. Several squadrons of Soviet aircraft and a small naval detachment made highly publicized visits to North Korea in May and August. Soviet aircraft now fly directly over North Korean air space en route to their military bases in Vietnam, instead of flying down the Korean Straits as before. In exchange for these new benefits, the Soviets are transferring some 45 to 50 Mig-23 fighters to Pyongyang. Further, more than twenty Soviet missions visited Pyongyang in August alone to celebrate the fortieth anniversary of North Korea's liberation from Japanese rule. A stream of high-ranking Soviet officials went to Pyongyang, culminating in the arrival of Foreign Minister Shevardnadze on 9 July.

Pyongyang also conducted more discussions with Seoul than at any time since the country was divided into two states. These talks related to possible economic cooperation, cultural and people-to-people exchanges, and the staging of the 1988 Olympic Games. Red Cross officials from both sides agreed on 30 May to exchange family relatives as well as art troupes, and on 20–23 September those visitations took place. Meanwhile, Pyongyang continued to press for a meeting of the two Korean sides and the United States to resolve tensions on the peninsula. As Pyongyang inches toward an "open door" policy to encourage broad relations with nonsocialist countries, that regime is also obtaining more military aid from the Soviet Union and giving that superpower greater access to Korean ports and air space. All of these developments signaled new activity in North Korea as a transfer of power takes place within the communist leadership.

In Communist China Deng Xiaoping and his supporters completed a major administrative shuffle that represented an important move to consolidate the Chinese Communist Party's control over the country through a new generation of leaders loyal to Deng and his policies. This reshuffling of officials included the replacement of more than half of the 20 provincial party secretaries, replacing one-third of the government's 45 ministers, appointing 9 provincial governments and scores of new mayors for large cities, and replacing 131 members of the CCP's Central Committee, as well as 10 of the 29 members of the powerful Politburo. These changes meant the exodus of older party leaders and their replacement by younger members allegedly sympathetic to the reform policies of Deng.

The Beijing leadership continues its campaign to rectify the Communist party and build the "third echelon" of cadres, the younger, highly select group of leaders who will eventually replace the old party guard. So far, rectification has subjected 960,000 cadres to intense testing and screening, with approximately 60,000 purged from the party. The next stage of rectification will deal with some 13.5 million cadres who work in local organs, large enterprises, and higher education.

Deng's economic reforms remain on course, but zigs and zags still occur, with the party alternating between relaxing and tightening controls over the market and imposing limits upon personal freedoms. In late 1985 new controls were again in place to prevent a further drain upon the foreign-exchange reserve. In December another crackdown to curtail the spread of "spiritual pollution" in music and literature occurred. Earlier in the year the Central Discipline Inspection Commission had urged strong action against party officials accused of speculative activities and squandering public funds for personal gain. Such cases of party corruption are widely publicized in the press.

Deng is committed to reducing the scope of planned economy, enlarging a flexible pricing system, and tolerating a small free-market sector. He intends to create this new socialist economy gradually while purifying the ranks of the party and promoting into the top echelon those loyal and committed to his party line. These actions, however, require that personal freedoms continue to be limited and that socialist orthodoxy be upheld in the arts.

Meanwhile, North Vietnam continued to try to impose its hegemony upon Kampuchea, but without success. That war still continues. The party held its eighth plenum in June 1985 and candidly discussed the serious economic problems in the country. Party leaders condemned official corruption and ineptitude, but they have not yet agreed upon policies that would revive incentives in this drab, poor, and inefficient economy beset by severe commodity scarcity. The party seems intent upon pursuing a massive resettlement and building program to eliminate the village, downgrade provincial centers, and create 426 district agrocomplexes where around a quarter of a million souls would live, with about 25,000 farming an average 20,000 hectares of land. The party, of course, continues to recruit from the very young and submits the promising members to intensive ideological training so that they may replace those incompetent cadres who are to be jettisoned from the party.

States with Legal Communist Party Opposition. Bangladesh, India, Nepal, Sri Lanka, Japan, Australia, and New Zealand allow Communist parties to be active as long as they obey the nation's laws. Very little changed in these states with regard to Communist party activity. Factions within those Communist parties continued to quarrel; party leaders tried to expand party membership and influence events in the political arena, but without success.

In 1984 the Bangladesh Communist Party had fomented strikes and demonstrations to help the opposition parties force President Hussain Mohammed Ershad to end martial law and hold elections. In 1985 the party opted for a less active role, preferring to keep a low political profile. The Soviet Union tried to improve ties with Bangladesh, and in August A. L. Volkov, a high-ranking official from the Foreign Ministry, visited Dhaka in order to promote more trade between the two states.

Aside from India's nearly half-million Communist party (CPI) members, another quarter-million are members of the Communist Party of India–Marxist (CPM), with its stronghold in West Bengal. The CPM lost fourteen seats in the provincial parliamentary elections of 1984. In 1985 both parties continued to debate what relationship the two should establish. Factions in each criticized the other party most severely, so that ideological and tactical differences seem to be impossible to bridge.

The Nepal Communist Party is badly splintered, and its actual size is still undetermined. Key factional leaders declared they would not participate in the May 1986 government elections.

The 470,000-member Japanese Communist Party still has not been able to expand its membership to reach the half-million mark, in spite of annual campaigns to recruit new members and expand the subscribers' list of the party paper, *Akahata* (Red flag). The party convened its eleventh Central Commitee plenum in early September 1985. The chairman of the Central Committee, Miyamoto Kenji, charged the government with full responsibility for the Japan Airlines crash on 12 August in which 520 persons died, including several leaders of the JCP. He also elaborated the party's line on domestic and international issues and instructed members to mobilize more members. The party continues to attack any buildup for national defense, and it pursued a line often critical of both Moscow and Beijing.

States with Banned Communist Parties. Burma, Thailand, Malaysia, Singapore, Indonesia, the Republic of China on Taiwan, South Korea, and the Philippines have outlawed Communist parties and any activity to create groups supportive of those parties. Except for the Philippines, communist activity has been on the decline or virtually eliminated.

In Thailand the party had 12,000 armed insurgents in 1978, but by late 1985 only a few hundred remained, largely because of the massive defections that had occurred. The party's united front organization, which had tried to be active in the cities, has become virtually defunct.

In Indonesia the government executed Mohammed Munir, a member of the Political Bureau of the Central Committee of the Indochinese Communist Party (PKI). Three other leaders were also executed in July. The few PKI leaders who still survive live in China, Eastern Europe, or the Soviet Union.

The Burmese Communist Party's broadcasting station in China's Yunnan Province went off the air on 16 April, an apparent casualty of the growing rapprochement between the Burmese government and Beijing, the BCP's main backer for the last twenty years. Little is now known about the BCP, and major Chinese support for it appears to have been withdrawn.

The Philippine government states that 1,885 villages—roughly 5 percent of some 40,000—have been politicized by the New People's Army (NPA). U.S. intelligence counters that the true figure is closer to 8,000 villages—20 percent—and that the actual membership of the Communist Party of the Philippines (CPP) has doubled in the past five years. Whichever is the case, there was a steady increase in terrorism and killings of local and influential people in 1985, most of it at the hands of the NPA. The NPA strongholds are in northern Luzon and on the islands of Samar, Leyte, Negros, and Mindanao (*Times Tribune*, February 8, 1986).

At the same time, the CCP-led umbrella organization, the National Democratic Front (NDF), has greatly expanded its influence in the cities and towns. The NDF has penetrated and extended its control over such organizations as the Association of Revolutionary Workers, the Organization for Nationalist Women, the Moro Revolutionary Organization, Christians for National Liberation, the Organization of Nationalist Peasants, Nationalist Youth, and the Association of Nationalist Teachers (*FEER*, 21 November, p. 55). The economic crisis of the past three years has boosted unemployment in the cities. Spurts of inflation have further eroded purchasing power. Under these conditions, the urban associations and organizations just mentioned have been greatly infiltrated by the CCP's NDF. By fomenting strikes and public demonstrations, the NDF is driving a larger wedge between the populace and the government.

Soviet Activity in the Region. Soviet military and economic aid to Vietnam continued as in the past. The newest developments of Soviet influence in the region were an escalated use of North Korean air space and ports by the Soviet military and Moscow's transfer of more advanced jet aircraft to Pyongyang.

Ramon H. Myers
Hoover Institution

Australia

Population. 15,700,000 (*World Factbook*, July 1985)
Parties. Communist Party of Australia (CPA); Socialist Party of Australia (SPA); Communist Party of Australia–Marxist-Leninist (CPA–ML); Socialist Workers Party (SWP); Socialist Labor League (SLL); Spartacist League of Australia and New Zealand (SLANZ)
Founded. CPA: 1920; CPA–ML: 1964; SPA: 1971; SLL: 1972
Membership. CPA: 1,000; SPA: 500; CPA–ML: 300; SWP: 400; SLL: 100; SLANZ: 50
Leadership. CPA: Judy Mundey, general secretary; SPA: Peter Dudley Symon, general secretary, J. McPhillips, president; CPA–ML: Edward Fowler Hill, chairman; SWP: Jim Percy, national secretary
Status. Legal
Last Congress. CPA: Twenty-eighth, 4 November 1984; SPA: Fifth, September 1984
Last Election. 1 December 1984, negligible vote for Communist parties, no representatives elected
Publications. CPA: *Tribune* (weekly); SPA: *Socialist* (fortnightly), *The Guardian* (weekly); CPA–ML: *Vanguard* (weekly), *Australian Communist*; SWP: *Direct Action* (weekly)

Although Australia's Communist parties hold no real power in the Australian parliamentary system, these organizations—with a little over 2,000 members—exert a disproportionate influence on the Australian political scene due to their close ties with several large labor unions. Even though party membership has declined over the years, party structures have not deteriorated and activities seem to be on the upswing, at least for the Socialist Party of Australia and the Socialist Workers Party. Most important, Australian Communists seem to be taking a more pragmatic approach to politics. They are becoming involved in mainstream political parties and have infiltrated single-issue parties such as the Australian Nuclear Disarmament Party. In this way, they are succeeding in translating left-wing goals into acceptable public policy.

Communist Party of Australia (CPA). The Eurocommunist CPA, the largest Communist party in Australia, was formed in Sydney in 1920. Originally pro-Soviet, the CPA's fortunes historically have depended on events outside Australia. Feeding on the social and economic ills of the global depression, the CPA was at its height in the 1930s and 1940s, reaching a membership of 23,000 in 1945 and sending its only member to Parliament in 1944. By the late 1960s, however, the CPA's membership had fallen to less than 5,000—largely due to the Soviet invasions of Hungary in 1956 and Czechoslovakia in 1968. As a result, the CPA adopted a neutralist position during the Vietnam era and has since been critical of both Soviet and Chinese behavior, particularly in Southeast Asia.

Although the CPA is not represented in Parliament, it has a limited influence on national politics. CPA members hold high positions in several large trade unions–including Australia's largest, the Amalgamated Metal Workers and Shipwrights Union. These unions, with a combined membership of over 400,000, are generally affiliated with the ruling Australian Labor Party (ALP), and they send voting delegates to ALP national conferences. Although members of Communist parties are banned from the ALP, communist-designated union representatives form a considerable segment of the Socialist Left faction in the ALP, which sponsors left-wing resolutions at ALP conferences.

Like all Australian Communist parties, however, the CPA has found it increasingly difficult in the 1980s to maintain membership, which today stands at only 1,000 (less than 200 reside outside the Sydney and Melbourne metropolitan areas). Some former party members in Melbourne, however, have joined an organization called the Socialist Forum, which allegedly is a "halfway house" for former Communists seeking to become active in mainstream Australian politics via the Australian Labor Party (*Social Action*, September).

Socialist Party of Australia. The pro-Soviet SPA splintered from the CPA in 1971 after the CPA condemned the Soviet invasion of Czechoslovakia. In 1975, Moscow publicly recognized the SPA as the only Marxist-Leninist party in Australia. Moscow has been rewarded with SPA support for several Soviet foreign policy initiatives, including the imposition of martial law in Poland.

The SPA is the most tightly organized and active of Australia's Communist parties. For one thing, the party's effective cadre structure has maintained the SPA's ideological purity. In addition, the SPA is well supplied with funds—as evidenced by the recent publication of a new weekly, *The Guardian* (ibid.). The SPA's 500 members often serve full-time in pro-Soviet unions, Soviet-bloc friendship societies, and left-wing bookshops.

Although the expulsion of former SPA secretary Pat Clancy in 1983 cost the party its largest union connection, it remains closely tied with several smaller unions, including the 12,000-member Australian Federated Union of Locomotive Enginemen. The SPA also serves as the most active proponent of the activities in the South Pacific of the World Federation of Trade Unions (a Soviet front). It is also involved in Moscow's propaganda efforts in Australia (*Quadrant*, August).

Communist Party of Australia–Marxist-Leninist (CPA–ML). The CPA–ML, a highly doctrinaire group, split from the CPA in 1964 because its members supported Beijing in the Sino-Soviet dispute over socialist ideology and practice. Moreover, the Marxist-Leninist group disapproved of the CPA's pragmatic policy of supporting the Australian Labor Party (ALP) when ALP resolutions coincided with communist aims (*Dictionary of Australian History*, 1982). The pro-Beijing party finds its strongest support among leftist university students and teachers.

With a national membership of only 300, the CPA–ML exists on the fringes of Australian politics and has only one large union connection, the 24,000-member Building Laborers Federation (BLF). Because the BLF is such a powerful and active union, however, the CPA–ML exerts a disproportionate influence on the Australian labor movement. BLF boss Norm Gallagher has become a thorn in the side of moderates in the Australian Council of Trade Unions (ACTU; the equivalent of the AFL-CIO in the United States) because he has repeatedly called for BLF strikes with the stated purpose of breaking the ACTU's "wage accord" with the current Labor government. The strength of the BLF was recently demonstrated when nationwide strikes by the BLF forced the Victoria State Supreme Court to release Gallagher from prison and call for a retrial. Gallagher was serving a four-year sentence for receiving illegal commissions.

Other Communist Groups. Australia's other communist organizations—with less than 400 members each—include the Socialist Workers Party (SWP), the Socialist Labor League (SLL), and the Spartacist League of Australia and New Zealand (SLANZ). All have their roots in Trotskyism and espouse worldwide class revolution. They campaign domestically against uranium mining and U.S.-Australian military ties. In keeping with their ideology, the parties try to recruit industrial workers, but to date have had little success.

The SWP, the largest of these parties, broke away from the Trotskyite Fourth International in August 1985—apparently frustrated with the organization's insistence on ideological purity. The SWP has been drifting away from Trotskyism for a decade, believing that pragmatism is needed to foster revolution (*Intercontinental Press*, 23 September). Together with the SPA, the SWP supports revolutionary movements in Central America by organizing "Southern Cross Brigades" of leftist students, academics, unionists, and public servants who donate their summer holidays doing manual labor in Cuba and Nicaragua. The SWP's youth wing, "Resistance," is active on at least five Australian university campuses (working paper by Michael Danby, journalist).

The Australian Political Scene. The charismatic leader of the Australian Labor Party, Bob Hawke, has labored patiently to swing his party to the right and undercut the influence of the left. For example, he has returned four right-wing unions to the Victorian Labor Party, long recognized as the stronghold of the Socialist Left faction. In addition, by exploiting his longstanding union ties, he convinced the ACTU to abandon its anti-uranium stance and is largely responsible for the virtual absence of politically motivated strikes.

Despite Hawke's dominance of the Australian political scene, the country is facing a growing nuclear disarmament movement in which Communists play an important role. This movement led several ALP members—who were disaffected with Hawke's moderate nuclear stance—to form the Nuclear Disarmament Party (NDP) in mid-1984. The NDP received 6 percent of the popular vote in the December 1984 national elections and was threatening to become the most influential public forum for Australian leftists. The NDP, however, suffered a setback in April 1985 when the SWP badly bungled an attempt to broaden the NDP's single-issue platform to include a variety of anti-West positions. The NDP's three most prominent members—including a senator—walked out in protest and the party is now suffering from factionalism.

Joanne P. Cloud
Annandale, Virginia

Michael Morell
Arlington, Virginia

Bangladesh

Population. 101,408,000
Party. Communist Party of Bangladesh (CPB)
Founded. 1948 (as East Pakistan Communist Party, banned in 1954, re-emerged in 1971 following the establishment of Bangladesh)
Membership. 3,000
Secretary General. Muhammed Farhad
Politburo. 913 members
Secretariat. 10 members
Central Committee. 37 members
Status. Legal
Last Congress. Third, February 1980
Last Election. 1981 national election; CPB ran no candidates, though it did support candidates of other parties.
Auxiliary Organizations. Trade Union Centre, Cultural Front, Bangladesh Chatra Union, Khetmozdur Samiti
Publications. *Ekota* (in Bengali)

Bangladeshi politics in 1985, as in 1984, centered on formulating terms for parliamentary and presidential elections acceptable to both the martial law government of President Hussain Mohammed Ershad and the opposition political parties. The government's efforts to get broad political backing for an election timetable failed for the second consecutive year.

Leadership and Party Organization. The CPB, successor party to the East Pakistan Communist Party, has served as Moscow's standard-bearer in the country since its independence in 1971. The CPB has been in the opposition since the military coups of 1975. After Ershad came to power in a bloodless coup in March 1982, the CPB remained a conspicuous participant in the campaign to restore an elected government. Despite a membership of only 3,000, the CPB exercises influence out of proportion to its popular following by coordinating activities with an array of pro-Soviet political groups and front organizations. With the financial resources to hire full-time workers, the CPB and its fronts have organizational advantages absent in most other political groups in the country. These resources also enable the party to sponsor cultural events designed to build support for Marxism, the Soviet Union, and the CPB.

The most active front groups are the Mahila Parishad (for women), the Chatra Union (for students), the Krishad Samiti and Khetmozdur Samiti (for farmers), the Khelegor (for children), and the Trade Union Centre (TUC). The TUC has some strength in Dhaka, particularly among transport workers. The women's front has branches all over the country. In addition, the CPB has influence in the Bangladesh Peace Council, whose general secretary, Ali Aksad, is a member of the party's Central Committee, the "Udichi" singing society, and a theater group. Several newspapers are edited by people closely associated with the CPB.

At the top of the party hierarchy is the ten-member Politburo headed by Secretary General Muhammed Farhad. Party president Moni Singh is the party's grand old man, but he lacks real power. The Central Secretariat implements the Politburo's decisions. There is also a larger Central Committee, many of whose members lead various front groups. This arrangement ensures close cooperation between the party and its fronts.

Issues. The CPB decided to adopt a lower profile in 1985. Indeed, the Bangladeshi press suggests that it may even have argued in favor of the government's election schedule in opposition circles. For example, one popular journal reports that the CPB called the opposition of the fifteen-party alliance to the 15 April elections "adventurist" (*Holiday*, 26 July). Although most other leftist parties backed the election boycott, the press notes that CPB members, along with members of other opposition parties, ran for subdistrict posts in the May nonparty elections.

The CPB's more restrained posture may have been prompted by Soviet efforts to improve ties with Bangladesh. Soviet-Bangladeshi relations had plummeted in late 1983 with the expulsion of fourteen Soviet diplomats and the subsequent closure of the Soviet cultural center at Dhaka. The August 1985 visit of A. L. Volkov, head of the South Asia Department in the Soviet Foreign Ministry—and the first senior level Soviet official to visit in six years—suggests that Moscow wishes to iron out its outstanding differences with Dhaka. Volkov reportedly was pleased by the prospects for economic and trade cooperation, though still disappointed by Bangladeshi "negativism" regarding cooperation in cultural fields (*Holiday*, 16 August).

Bangladesh's economic ties with the USSR did improve marginally during the year. On 1 April, a Soviet export firm agreed to provide an $82 million credit to the Bangladesh Power Development Board for a fifth turbine at the Soviet-built Ghorasal Steam Power Station (*Bangladesh Observer*, 1 April). Later that month, the two countries signed their fourteenth barter trade protocol, which envisaged an exchange valued at some $60 million, somewhat higher than in 1984.

There were, however, continuing signs of Bangladeshi suspicion of the Soviet Union. Dhaka refused to issue official clearance permitting Bangladeshi participation in the Soviet-sponsored International Youth Festival held 27 July–3 August in Moscow. The Deputy Minister for Youth and Sports justified the refusal on the ground that the invitation had not gone to the government, but to the sponsoring student group (*New Nation*, 28 July). The student organizers were members of the CPB's student front. The Soviet embassy, for its part, complained publicly about alleged anti-Soviet bias in the press and the activities of the Afghan Mujahedin Solidarity Council Movement (*Holiday*, 8 February).

In contrast to the cool but correct relations between the USSR and Bangladesh, Sino-Bangladeshi ties remained very good. China continued to be a major arms supplier and an important trading partner. At year's end, Bangladesh and the PRC signed an $87 million barter protocol, the largest yet between the two countries. Ershad visited China in July with a large delegation. Chinese foreign minister Wu Zueqian arrived in Dhaka 24 December for a three-day visit, the first time a Chinese foreign minister had come to Bangladesh.

Other Communist Parties. Other than the CPB, some 30 parties claim Marxist credentials, and these tiny groups exist largely because of personal leadership. They are constantly combining and splitting. For example, the pro-Soviet Workers' Party, formed in the late 1970s by segments of two other leftist parties, split in 1985, ostensibly over the question of unification with the Revolutionary

Communist League (*Holiday*, 26 July). In fact, the split occurred because the league's two most prominent figures could not work together.

Among the more prominent pro-Soviet parties are the Samyabadi Dal, the Sramik-Krishak Samajbadi Dal, and the Labor Party. The major pro-Chinese parties are the Biplabi Communist League and a faction of the Bangladesh Workers' Party, both members of the seven-party alliance. Some of the groups, such as the Revolutionary Party of Bangladesh, stand for "equidistance" between Moscow and Beijing. A few, such as the National Awami Party (Harun) and the National Awami Party (Muzaffar), function almost as political affiliates of the CPB.

Walter K. Andersen
Arlington, Virginia

Burma

Population. 36,919,000
Party. Burmese Communist Party (BCP)
Founded. 1939
Membership. 3,000 (1979); estimated armed strength 8,000–15,000
Chairman. Thakin Ba Thein Tin
Politburo. 8 members: Thakin Ba Thein Tin, Pe Tint, Khin Maung Gyi, Myo Myint, Tin Yee, Kya Mya, Kyin Maung, Yeba Taik Aung
Central Committee. At least 20 members
Status. Illegal
Last Congress. Third, 9 September–2 October 1985; a major meeting, variously characterized as a "congress," was held in November 1979
Last Election. N/a
Auxiliary Organizations. None identified
Publications. None identified

The Burmese Communist Party's forty-sixth anniversary, the commemoration of the BCP's founding on 15 August 1939, went unheralded in 1985. Historically the anniversary has been the occasion for a major statement of the BCP's activities and a contemporary interpretation of its Marxist-Leninist-Maoist line. Over the last fifteen years, this statement has been broadcast over the Voice of the People of Burma (VOPB), a clandestine propaganda radio station operating under communist Chinese tutelage out of a base in China's Yunnan Province. This year there was no statement, since the VOPB went off the air on 16 April 1985, an apparent casualty of the growing rapprochement between the Burmese government and Beijing, the BCP's principal backer for the last twenty years.

China's own ideological reorientation and strategic need to improve relations with its Southeast Asian neighbors have dictated a drastic reduction in its ties to the BCP and its willingness to support the Burmese communist struggle. The BCP's future is largely a speculative matter, since the termination of the VOPB broadcasts has deprived external observers of the one window through which the BCP could be watched. Without the ideological pronouncements and periodic battle reports that were the substance of VOPB broadcasts any observations must, of necessity, be highly conditional. What is clear, however, is that the BCP is now in its most precarious position, cut off from both matériel and mentor. Its prospects rest not only on its ability to develop an alternative matériel base but also on its success in redeveloping an ideological line that is capable of sustaining the movement in the absence of any external direction.

As noted here last year (*YICA*, 1985, p. 162), day-to-day activities of the BCP are probably under the control of two shadowy party vice-chairmen, Thakin Pe Tint, himself a "Beijing returnee," and Khin Maung Gyi. There were no reports of their activities in 1985. It seems unlikely that either has solidified control over the party machinery or assumed Ba Thein Tin's mantle. Given the party's precarious position, particularly the critical change in its relationship with China, it seems far more likely that the BCP's center will be increasingly strained by the pull of subordinate leaders, each building his own regional freedom. In the best of days, party organizational control was weak—the geography militated against the laws of hierarchy, and the BCP's always-strapped communications capability never provided an alternative control mechanism. In these circumstances, BCP regional leaders may well become indistinguishable from the other armed groups marauding through the Golden Triangle under various flags. Lingering ideological concerns could provide the basis for a continuing BCP. Such a BCP, however, would be more a loose confederation than a well-structured communist movement. Left-wing warlordism may be the lasting legacy of these problems.

Party Internal Affairs. With the termination of VOPB the outside world has also been deprived of its one little window on the BCP's internal affairs, since it was the party's vehicle for disseminating party reports and propagandizing the party line. Even before VOPB went off the air, however, the station was largely silent on ideological matters. There was no New Year's statement broadcast this year, a statement that in the past often articulated criticism of the Burmese government and cataloged the social ills that would be the targets of BCP political action.

One suspects that whatever passes for the BCP's political bureau is probably paralyzed today as the party thinkers seek some explanation of the alienation of the BCP from its spiritual and material benefactors in China after twenty years of dedicated emulation of the Chinese line. Ever since the party congress in 1979 (*YICA*, 1981, p. 130; *YICA*, 1982, p. 170), there have been increasing signs of ideological disarray within the party as it sought on the one hand to sustain a critique of the government's "Burmese way to socialism" while on the other it tried to adjust to the political moderation and economic reform being promoted by Beijing.

Although the party's propaganda organs have been silent about the problems of apostasy, the Burmese government's *Working People's Daily* (9 July) carried an unusually pointed and long column by Sai Hso Long, a senior Shan member of the BSPP, discussing the BCP's dilemma. He wrote:

> If it suits their personal interests, the BCP even dare to betray their party. . . These BCP, for their continued existence, switched allegiance from one foreign Communist party to another. They shamelessly go to various countries seeking to follow others' leadership. . . Accepting the authority of this master and that master, the BCP's life has crumbled and they now exist without any aim or objective. . .
>
> No matter how much they try to shuffle, the BCP cannot develop from their zero existence. They do not get any support from the people and always [are] facing losses. They create plots on the run and rehearse while in hiding. However, they cannot handle their own drama.

Sai Hso Long then argued that "the BCP, who had no proper master, are now looking for a new master. They are making contacts. The master they are trying to follow is none other than a Communist Bureau formed with communist remnants from noncommunist Southeast Asian nations. A big communist country is pulling the strings of the bureau." While his observation diplomatically skips over the past role of the Chinese masters—Rangoon's etiquette has always dictated extreme circumspection in publicly alleging misdeeds by the giant to the north—it does raise the fear that the Soviets, i.e., "a big communist country," may seek to exploit the BCP's estrangement from the Chinese. With the BCP's population base primarily rooted in Burma's mountainous minorities, who are isolated geographically and culturally from Burma's heartlands, and with the party lacking any urban organization, it is, however, doubtful that the Soviets would find the BCP an easy organization to develop or one quick to assimilate a new orthodoxy.

If the party's ideological center is in disarray, there is growing evidence that away from the center economic considerations have taken precedence over political concerns. Regional party leaders have capitalized on the opportunities offered by the lucrative narcotics trade, which is now at the heart of the Shan plateau's political economy. Control over the production of the opium poppy provides a ready source of revenue to acquire arms and ammunition and to finance the alliances necessary to shore up local power. Over the past couple of years, BCP cadres have moved beyond the brokering of opium transactions and, in some areas, are operating the far more profitable morphine base and heroin base laboratories. This "economic activity" probably ensures the continuation of relatively large and well-armed BCP units in the northern and eastern Shan state, but these units over time will probably come to resemble the narcotics-trafficking warlord organization more than the disciplined, ideologically motivated insurgent force to which BCP cadres once aspired. With no unifying ideology, increasing infighting among these opium fiefdoms can be expected. Such warlordism will continue to present Rangoon with trying security problems, but they will be of a different kind and political magnitude than they were a decade ago, when China served as arms supplier and mentor of the insurgency.

The Insurgency. BCP forces have continued widespread guerrilla activity but most has been small raids, ambushes, and the episodic mining of roads and highways in the region. The VOPB carried few statistics about military engagements, but the government in March presented a report to the Pyithu Hluttdaw (National Assembly) that summarized Burmese army security operations against the BCP and other insurgent forces from 1983 to 1985. (Data from the report were published in the *Working People's Daily* and other indigenous press over the last ten days of March 1985.) According to the government report, fighting in the northern and northeast command was at about the same level as the previous year, with seven major battles and 858 engagements in the 1984–1985 period, compared with seven major battles and 805 engagements in the 1983–1984 period. Of the major 1984–1985 battles described in the report, however, four were against Kachin Independence Army forces or involved joint KIA/BCP units. The report also described an increase in engagements in the eastern command area, suggesting an expansion of BCP activity in an area historically controlled by Han and ex-Chinese Nationalist Kuomintang warlords.

Thai papers reporting later in the year also indicated "BCP insurgents" were operating along the Thai/Burmese border in the area abutting Chiang Mai Province (*Bangkok Post*, 6 August; *Bangkok World*, 23 August). This part of the border is one of the principal concentrations of heroin refining and has been the target of frequent narcotics-suppression operations by both Thai and Burmese forces. From the press reports it is unclear whether the insurgents involved were from a BCP main force or were simply ethnic insurgents who had a confederated affiliation with the BCP. Nevertheless, many observers expect to see the BCP push closer to the border to gain access to the heroin trade, the most profitable part of the Golden Triangle narcotics trade. While the financial possibilities for the BCP are certainly seductive, opening a base on the border exposes them to direct Thai as well as Burmese action. The Thais are simply not prepared to permit a communist presence on their border with the Burmese and would likely move quickly to dislodge it.

International Views and Contacts. The BCP has historically followed China's lead on the international front, echoing the Chinese on Southeast Asian matters—resisting Vietnamese hegemony—and geopolitical issues—fighting the larger hegemonists, the Soviets. As must now be clear from the preceding discussions of BCP internal affairs, the Chinese subordination of BCP interests to larger Chinese political objectives raises profound questions of the continued durability of the BCP-Chinese communist alliance. The reduction in Chinese material support for the BCP over the past few years has been gradual, generally reflecting the warming relations between Rangoon and Beijing. Despite this rapprochement, China, through the Chinese Communist Party, has kept party-to-party links with the BCP, a relationship that allowed the Chinese government to deny it was supporting the Burmese communist insurgents. This fiction has been maintained through a number of Burmese-Chinese state or "official friendly" visits; Burmese president San Yu's trip to China in October 1984 (*YICA*, 1985, p. 164) was the most recent "state" visit. Perhaps during these visits the question of Chinese support for the BCP was discussed privately, but publicly all that was ever acknowledged was the historical party-to-party relationship between the CCP and the BCP.

Ne Win's widely publicized "official friendly"

visit to China in May 1985, however, may have jeopardized the polite fiction. Ne Win was invited by Deng Xiaoping not as president or head of the Burmese state but rather as the chairman of the BSPP, a party that the Chinese have not previously given any official recognition (coverage of the visit by Xinhua was extensive; translations are in *FBIS*, 4–5 May). This reception of Ne Win in his party role by Deng Xiaoping and other Chinese party officials falls short of formal recognition of the BSPP, but as a precedent of some sort, it cannot have cheered the BCP cadres who have watched their China ties wither on many fronts.

Jon A. Wiant
U.S. Department of State

Note: The views expressed here are the author's own and do not necessarily represent those of the Department of State or the U.S. government.

China

Population. 1,041,346,000 (July 1985)
Party. Chinese Communist Party (Zhongguo gongchan dang; CCP)
Founded. 1921
Membership. Over 40 million
General Secretary. Hu Yaobang
Standing Committee of the Politburo. 5 members: Hu Yaobang, Chen Yun, Deng Xiaoping, Li Xiannian (president, People's Republic of China [PRC]; chairman, National People's Congress [NPC]), Zhao Ziyang
Politburo. 20 full members: Hu Yaobang, Chen Yun, Deng Xiaoping, Fang Yi, Hu Qiaomu, Hu Qili, Li Peng, Li Xiannian, Ni Zhifu, Peng Zhen, Qiao Shi, Tian Jiyun, Wan Li, Wu Xueqian, Xi Zhongxun, Yang Dezhi, Yang Shangkun, Yao Yilin, Yu Qiuli, Zhao Ziyang; 2 alternate members: Chen Muhua, Qin Jiwei
Secretariat. 11 members: Hu Yaobang, Chen Pixian, Deng Liqun, Hao Jianxiu, Hu Qili, Li Peng, Qiao Shi, Tian Jiyun, Wan Li, Wang Zhaoguo, Yu Qiuli
Central Military Commission. Chairman: Deng Xiaoping; permanent vice-chairman: Yang Shangkun
Central Advisory Commission. 162 members. Chairman: Deng Xiaoping; vice-chairman: Bo Yibo
Central Commission for Discipline Inspection. First secretary: Chen Yun; second secretary: Wang Heshou; permanent secretary: Han Guang
Central Committee. 210 full members and 133 alternate members (since September)
Status. Ruling party
Last Congress. Twelfth, 1–11 September 1982, in Beijing (but a rare National Conference of Party Delegates was held on 18–23 September in Beijing)
Last Election. 1981. All 3,202 candidates were CCP approved
Auxiliary Organizations. The All-China Women's Federation, led by Kang Keqing; the Communist Youth League of China (50 million members), led by Hu Jingtao; the All-China Federation of Trade Unions, led by Ni Zhifu; the People's Political Consultative Conference (CPPCC), led by Deng Yingchao

Publications. The official and most authoritative publication of the CCP is the newspaper *Renmin Ribao* (People's daily; *RMRB*), published in Beijing. The theoretical journal of the Central Committee, *Hongqi* (Red flag), is published approximately once a month. More influential in recent years, however, is *Liaowang* (Outlook), the weekly publication of Xinhua (the New China News Agency; NCNA), the official news agency of the party and government. The daily paper of the People's Liberation Army (PLA) is *Jiefangjunbao* (Liberation Army daily). The weekly *Beijing Review* (*BR*), published in English and several other languages, carries translations of important articles, editorials, and documents from these three publications and other sources. *China Daily*, the first English-language national newspaper in the PRC, began official publication in Beijing and Hong Kong on 1 June 1981. It began a New York edition in June 1983.

Domestic Affairs. This was yet another successful year for Deng Xiaoping and his reform agenda. A large number of important personnel shifts were brought about smoothly in the party, government, and military. This included the resignation, at the Fourth Plenum of the Central Committee, of 131 senior party leaders from the Central Committee, the Central Advisory Commission, and the Central Commission for Discipline Inspection. The resignations were followed by 179 promotions of younger leaders at the National Party Conference in September. These changes were reflected in the transformation of the Politburo itself, as announced at the Fifth Plenum following the party conference. More than half of the party secretaries of the 29 provinces and autonomous regions changed in the six months preceding the September party meetings. In the same period of time some 15 of the government's 45 ministers were replaced, while 9 governors were removed and many new mayors were appointed in scores of major cities, including Shanghai. In the PLA, the number of regional military commands was trimmed from 11 to 7, and 8 of the commanders were removed (*Honolulu Sunday Star-Bulletin and Advertiser*, 8 September). In the meantime, the rectification campaign concentrated on its second stage and, near year's end, was poised to move into its third and final stage. This campaign continued to be viewed as a complement to the economic and political reforms that have so transformed China since 1979. But it is not clear how effective the campaign has actually been in eliminating its principal targets.

The year began on an encouraging note for Chinese intellectuals. At the Fourth National Writers' Congress, held in Beijing from 29 December 1984 to 5 January, Hu Qili, reputed to be the likely successor to General Secretary Hu Yaobang, assured the delegates that "literary freedom is a vital part of socialist literature," and he acknowledged that "'leftist' tendencies are still an obstacle to progress" (*BR*, 14 February). Hu's speech was greeted by 33 bursts of spontaneous applause, the lengthiest lasting more than a minute (*Asiaweek*, 18 January). In contrast, when the regards of the absent party propaganda director, Deng Liqun, were conveyed to the delegates, not a single one applauded (*Asiaweek*, 8 February). As heartening as the conference was, many intellectuals remain cautious. Only a month later, the Guangdong provincial party secretary told writers to guard against corrupt capitalist thinking and to exercise freedom in such a way as to better serve socialism (*Asian Wall Street Journal* [*AWSJ*], 11 February). Also, in April Hu Yaobang made it clear that the party's journalism "is the party's mouthpiece, and. . . the mouthpiece of the people's government, which is led by the party." His remarks were taken as a corrective to the earlier assurances regarding creative freedom for writers (Beijing, *Renmin Ribao*, 14 April; *FBIS*, 15 April).

During the year schoolteachers were given a pay raise, with one billion yuan having been appropriated for distribution to ten million teachers (*BR*, 14 February). Peking University students used banned wall posters during their protest over the elimination of stipends, a dispute that was settled by means of a compromise with authorities (Peking, AFP, 15 January; *FBIS*, 15 January).

On 24 January Wan Li spoke to the Third Session of the Central Committee for Promoting Five Stresses, Four Beauties, and Three Loves. He declared that in the past three years this campaign had become a major vehicle for putting into practice the guidelines of the Twelfth Party Congress. The program, he said, was a cardinal component in the work of building socialist spiritual civilization. The campaign includes an annual "civility and courtesy month" (Beijing, Xinhua, 24 January; *FBIS*, 28 January).

On 30 January, the *China Daily* reported that the Central Discipline Inspection Commission had urged firm action against party officials who profiteer through speculative activities (exacting unauthorized high prices from consumers or squandering public funds in the name of "bonuses"), "irregularities which are reaching epidemic proportions among the party's organizations and cadres" (*FBIS*, 5 February). The commission held a meeting on 8 February, at which Wang Heshou, the commission's permanent secretary, listed some of the principal unhealthy tendencies: "party and state institutions and party and government cadres engage in commerce, run enterprises, and abuse their power by buying and reselling products for profit; prices are being raised indiscriminately in violation of policies; wages are being increased at will; bonuses and materials are being given out indiscriminately; fraud is being practiced; the practice of giving feasts is expanding in scope and rising in degree and some unhealthy newspapers are being run for profit" (Beijing, Xinhua, 8 February; *FBIS*, 11 February). As a result of an ensuing investigation during the year, almost 9,000 profit-making businesses formed by party and government departments were closed, and more than 90 percent of the 67,041 party and government officials connected with businesses reportedly severed their ties, as ordered (*WSJ*, 29 October).

Premier Zhao spoke about the replacement of the rural quota system at a New Year's party in Beijing, commenting that it was "the second major step in the reform of the rural economic structure since the introduction of the contract responsibility system with remuneration linked with output." He said the "reform is what we have hoped for but dared not carry out. Now we are able to go ahead as conditions are ripe" (ibid.; see also "Second Stage Rural Structural Reform," *BR*, 24 June). Zhao's remarks were in reference to the substance of Central Committee Document No. 1 of 1985, entitled "Ten Policies of the CPC Central Committee and State Council for Further Invigorating the Rural Economy," which was published in late March.

In February, Bo Yibo, vice-chairman of the party's Central Advisory Commission, told the Hong Kong *Ta Kung Pao* that the first stage of the party rectification campaign had been basically completed. The campaign had involved some 960,000 members in central, provincial, and municipal-level organs and the military since it was initiated in late 1983. About 13.5 million party members—about a third of the total membership—were to be involved in the second stage, which was targeted mainly at prefectural and city organs, universities, colleges, and large enterprises. The campaign, Bo said, was aimed at Cultural Revolution leaders who had seized political power, those who had vigorously supported Lin Biao and the Gang of Four, and those who had engaged in beating, smashing, and looting. He said that the party expects to expel some 40,000 members, amounting to about 0.1 percent of its membership (*FEER*, 14 February). However, only two months later, Hao Jianxu, a rapidly rising female official, said in an interview that some 60,000 had already lost their membership during the campaign (*Asiaweek*, 19 April). Her comments came several days after the Central Commission for Guiding Party Rectification had issued its Circular No. 12, requesting that all units engaged in the second-stage rectification pay attention to stressing key questions while pursuing the campaign (Beijing, Xinhua, 12 April; *FBIS*, 13 April). Three months later, Hu Qili, speaking at a seven-day meeting sponsored by the commission, said that the most fundamental guideline for party rectification at this stage "is to ensure and expedite reform, and this guideline will never vacillate" (Beijing, Xinhua, 14 July; *FBIS*, 15 July).

The *People's Daily* had earlier announced that it was compiling a book entitled *One Year of Party Rectification*, which would include the first eleven circulars issued by the Central Commission for Guiding Party Rectification during the first stage of the campaign, the commission's summation of experience in the first stage, proposals and arrangements for the second stage, and *People's Daily* editorials and commentaries on the campaign (*RMRB*, 18 January; *FBIS*, 23 January).

A speech that Hu Yaobang delivered on 19 January to 400 graduates of a high-level party training course was published on 20 Feburary. In this speech Hu candidly conceded that of the past 36 years "there are not many of these in which we could say we have done a good job. You could say we have wasted 20 years" (*NYT*, 21 February).

On 7 March, Deng Xiaoping reaffirmed to a national science conference that, despite the introduction of some private ownership, China today is building socialism with the ultimate goal of realizing communism (*BR*, 18 March). Zhao Ziyang told the same conferees that there was an urgent need to reform the country's science management (*BR*, 8 April; the Central Committee's 13 March decision on reforming science management is highlighted on pp. 19–21).

In his talk with the visiting vice-president of the Japanese Liberal Democratic Party, Susumu Nikaido, on 28 March, Deng Xiaoping called

China's economic reform a "second revolution" (*BR*, 8 April).

After severe criticism in a secret party document, Jin Deqin, the president of the Bank of China, resigned in March and was replaced by Zhao Bingde, a bank vice-president. Soon afterward, State Councillor Chen Muhua, previously minister of foreign economic relations and trade, was named president of the People's Bank of China (Beijing, Xinhua, 21 March; *FBIS*, 21 March).

The Third Session of the Sixth NPC was held in Beijing from 27 March to 10 April. There were 2,628 deputies at the opening. The session approved the Sino-British Joint Declaration on Hong Kong and a committee to draft the basic law that will govern the Hong Kong Special Administrative Region in 1997. It approved China's first inheritance law, a law on foreign economic contracts, and Premier Zhao's government work report. The Third Session of the Sixth National Committee of the CPPCC was held almost simultaneously, from 25 March to 8 April.

Zhao's report to the NPC's Third Session departed from the format of previous government reports, which had been comprehensive accounts of developments in the country and its foreign diplomacy. Zhao concentrated on the economy, pointing to an increase of 14.2 percent over the previous year in the total value of industrial and agricultural output. National income and state revenue had both risen by 12 percent, indicating a steady improvement in the nation's finances. Furthermore, 1984 had been another year of bumper harvests, with grain output rising 5.1 percent (to 407 million tons) and cotton output rising 31.1 percent. Altogether, 741 Chinese-foreign joint ventures were approved in 1984, more than the combined total of the previous five years. The foreign funds thus obtained totaled $2.6 billion, a 35.7 percent increase over the preceding year.

Zhao outlined steps taken toward economic reform and discussed how the government was to deal with the "unhealthy tendencies" that had appeared in recent months. He said the wage reforms would concentrate on eliminating irrational pay structures, so that the practice of everyone "eating from the same big pot" would be gradually abolished. By shifting to the principle of pay according to work, workers could earn more but would have to pay taxes on personal income exceeding a certain level. Reasonable disparities in wages would be allowed but that gap must not widen. As for reforming the price system, Zhao outlined future measures: readjusting the purchasing and marketing prices of grain and the purchasing price of cotton; introducing contracts for state purchases; relaxing price controls on other farm and sideline products and permitting market prices to take over; raising charges for short-distance railway transport in order to stimulate trucking and water transport; and encouraging price differences for products of different quality and bringing regional price differences into line with costs.

Zhao noted that too much currency had been issued last year and some commodity prices had risen. He promised that major steps would be taken to reform the price system and also to prevent price fluctuations. Administrative expenses would be cut by 10 percent and major purchases by work units and enterprises would be curtailed by 20 percent. Zhao also said that socialism required price stability but this did not mean a price freeze or lower living standards. Zhao emphasized that China would rely on thrift and hard work, and that it is wrong to seek blindly a high level of consumption regardless of production capacity and actual conditions (text of Zhao's report is in *BR*, 22 April).

State Planning Minister Song Ping and Finance Minister Wang Bingqian then described how the economic structure would be reformed. Growth of the economy had exceeded all plans over the previous year, and the rapidity of the increase (14.2 percent) was straining transport and energy. Thus an 8 percent growth rate should be targeted for industry and 6 percent for agriculture (excerpts of both reports in *BR*, 29 April).

Xinhua announced on 3 May that the Central Committee would soon publish, through the People's Publishing House, *The Annotated Edition of the Resolution on Certain Issues in the History of Our Party Since the Founding of the People's Republic of China*. The book has 130 annotations and more than 400,000 Chinese characters. It is said to make a "relatively accurate and systematic description, analysis, and explanation of the important theses in 'The Resolution on Certain Issues in the History of Our Party Since the Founding of the People's Republic of China' [adopted by the Sixth Plenum of the Eleventh Central Committee on 27 June 1981] by relying on an abundance of economic statistics as well as reliable materials from literary archives and by relying on the results of theoretical research" (*FBIS*, 7 May).

In May, authorities in Beijing warned hundreds of property owners along nine major city thoroughfares to convert or rent their premises for commercial purposes. Card-carrying party members were not eligible for capitalist pursuits of this kind. In fact, the *China Daily*, only a day earlier, had reported that hundreds of party members and bureaucrats in the capital were punished for engaging in commerce (*Honolulu Sunday Star-Bulletin and Advertiser*, 19 May).

In July, State Councillor Gu Mu revealed that of the fourteen coastal ports that had been opened in 1984, only four—Shanghai, Dalian, Tianjin, and Guangzhou—would continue to be promoted, while financial controls were being reimposed on the ten smaller port cities. This decision reflected a disappointing reassessment of progress in the fourteen coastal cities and the four Special Economic Zones. Only a fraction of the expected investment, technological advance and export revenues had been achieved (*Honolulu Sunday Star-Bulletin and Advertiser*, 14 July).

On 1 August, the PLA celebrated its 58th birthday "on the operating table." This medical expression is a reference to a statement of Deng Xiaoping's in 1975 regarding the need to reduce the size of the army. This long-delayed plan had been announced again by Deng only two months earlier, on 4 June, when he said that the army would be reduced by one million men, or one-fourth of its personnel, over a period of two years (*BR*, 17 June). This confirmed a remark made by Hu Yaobang on 19 April during his visit to New Zealand, which was quite a disclosure inasmuch as that decision was not formally adopted until an enlarged meeting of the Military Affairs Council met on 23 May–6 June (*FEER*, 22 August). The massive personnel reduction was complemented by other major developments. In June, eight of the eleven regional commanders either retired or were transferred, and the number of military regions was reduced from eleven to seven. By mid-September the readjustment of the leading bodies of the PLA and all the major military regions, services, and arms was said to have been completed. The average age of officers in the leading bodies of all major units has been lowered from 64.9 to 56.7 years (Beijing, *Zhongguo Xinwen She*, 18 September; *FBIS*, 19 September).

It was announced in July that the Organization Department of the Central Committee had recently sponsored two national forums—one in Zhongshan, Guangdong, and the other in Harbin, Heilongjiang—to discuss the implementation of the policy regarding intellectuals. Wang Zhaohua, deputy head of the department, said that the Organization Department should be in complete charge of the work on intellectuals, strengthening its cooperation with the United Front Work Department to do so (Beijing, Xinhua, 16 July; *FBIS*, 17 July).

In July, it was revealed that a reshuffle had taken place in the party's Propaganda Department. Controversial Deng Liqun stepped down as head of the department in favor of 54-year-old Zhu Houze. Deng Liqun remained responsible for propaganda work, however, in his capacity as secretary of the Central Committee's Secretariat (Hong Kong, *Ta Kung Pao*, 14 July; *FBIS*, 15 July).

Apart from the protest at Peking University in January, in late April the capital saw the first public protest in five years, when several hundred former "rusticated youths" staged a sit-in demonstration on the steps of the municipal party headquarters. They claimed that of the 400,000-odd youth sent to Shanxi during the Cultural Revolution, as many as 20,000 still remained there. The protesters were sternly told that the action was itself a "poisonous remnant of the Cultural Revolution." The protest was terminated before May Day celebrations took place (*Asiaweek*, 10 May). On 18 September, and again on 20 November, student protests took place on Tiananmen Square, ostensibly targeted against Japanese commercial activities in China. This atmosphere was created in part by earlier Chinese government criticism of Prime Minister Yasuhiro Nakasone's official visit in August to a shrine for Japanese war dead (*NYT*, 25 August). Similarly, commemorative articles on the fortieth anniversary of the end of World War II, recollecting Japanese atrocities, may have heightened feelings. But authorities quickly concluded that the protests were also serving as a means for calling into question the open door policy that had enabled Japan to mount such a "second occupation" of China. Posters appeared at Peking University and in pamphlets available on campus that raised questions about rising foreign influence, the highhandedness and corruption among leading party cadres and their families, and purported departures from Marxism. The government prohibited further unapproved protests, including one planned for 9 December, the fiftieth anniversary of student protests against Japanese imperialism. Instead, on that date the party sponsored a rally of 4,000 high school students who, in freezing weather on Tiananmen Square, listened to speeches in support of the open door policy (*Honolulu Star-Bulletin*, 12 December).

In May, a major effort was launched to replace China's Soviet-style educational system with one similar to Western models and to counter certain traditional pedagogical practices that still persist. This began with a major speech by Deng Xiaoping on 19 May to a national conference on education (*BR*, 10 June). Then on 29 May the Central Committee publicized its "Decision on the Reform of the Educational System" (ibid.). The purpose of the reform was to facilitate the training of needed professionals for the modernization program. The emphases were decentralized control, liberalization of requirements, and pragmatism (Wendy Lin's article from Beijing in *The Chronicle of Higher Education*, 26 June). These efforts at educational reform were further boosted with the elevation of the former Ministry of Education to a higher status as the State Education Commission (similar to the powerful State Planning and State Economic Commissions). The new commission's first director is Vice-Premier Li Peng (ibid., 11 September).

It was announced in June that China had completed its massive five-year drive to dismantle the 56,000 rural communes as the basic unit of state power and had now replaced them with more than 92,000 new local township governments (*BR*, 17 June).

The Twelfth Session of the Sixth NPC Standing Committee in September adopted regulations on identification cards for all residents sixteen and older, to be used to identify status, facilitate citizens' participation in social activities, maintain public order, and to safeguard the lawful rights of citizens (Beijing, Xinhua, 6 September; *FBIS*, 9 September).

The Fourth Plenary Session of the Twelfth Central Committee was held on 18 September, following four days of preliminary meetings. The plenum passed draft proposals on the seventh five-year plan and discussed the election of new officials to central leading organizations. Just prior to the plenum, 131 aging party veterans asked to be allowed to resign from the Central Committee, the Central Advisory Commission, and the Central Commission for Discipline Inspection. Most notable among these were Ye Jianying and Deng Yingchao (*BR*, 23 September). A few days later, it was announced that 1.1 million elderly party members had retired (*WSJ*, 20 September).

Immediately following the Fourth Plenum, from 18 to 23 September, came the extraordinary National CCP Conference of Party Delegates, with 992 delegates in attendance. The conference was supposed to facilitate the orderly transfer of power to a new generation of officials. This national conference of party delegates had only a single precedent, the party conference in 1955, convened to handle the Gao Gang-Rao Shushi purge and to discuss the five-year plan of that period. Since a party congress is composed of elected party delegates, whereas this kind of party conference comprises only invited members, this may have been a quick way to bring about personnel shifts, despite the fact that according to the party constitution only a congress can elect a new Central Committee (see, e.g., *WSJ*, 30 September). Nevertheless, the conference elected 64 new leaders to the Central Committee—29 as full members and 35 as alternates. Another 56 officials joined the Central Advisory Commission and 31 joined the Central Commission for Party Discipline Inspection. This personnel change was seen to complement the shifts that had been taking place across China in the previous nine months, which saw more than 200,000 younger, better-educated cadres given leadership responsibilities at and above the county level.

The party conference also discussed the draft of the seventh five-year plan, which will be presented in final and more detailed form to the NPC in the spring of 1986. The new plan carries forward to 1990 the development programs of Deng Xiaoping, featuring a restrained annual growth rate of 7 percent and a continued shift from direct to indirect state control of the economy. Foreign trade is hoped to increase by 40 to 50 percent, and the open door policy for foreign investment is to continue, as is an expanded use of foreign technology (*CSM*, 23 September).

In his concluding remarks to the conference, Deng Xiaoping said that the seven years since the Third Plenum of the Eleventh Central Committee in December 1978 had constituted one of the best periods the country has had since 1949. As Deng said, "We have set wrong things right." However, at the conference, Chen Yun, a more orthodox Marxist and long-tolerated party curmudgeon, gave a talk that included criticisms of Deng and his policies. Chen suggested that Deng has had too free a hand in setting policy. He also warned about the possibility of social disorder if the peasants' flight from the farms was not arrested, and he argued that the economy should continue to be based on central planning and not on market forces (*NYT*, 24 September).

Following the party conference, the Fifth Plenary Session of the Twelfth Central Committee met on 24 September. The Fifth Plenum changed the composition of the Politburo dramatically. Ten of the original 27 members were partly replaced by younger men. Although nine of the ten being replaced were or had been military men, not even one new representative from the military was added. Except for the resignation of Ye Jianying, the Politburo's Standing Committee remained the same. Five new members joined the Central Secretariat, replacing three who had resigned (*BR*, 30 September).

On 30 October, the *Guangming Daily* in Beijing published lengthy excerpts of an article from the journal *China Social Science* (issue no. 5), which re-evaluated Chen Duxiu, the principal original founder of the CCP and its first chairman. The article apparently reflected a more balanced attitude toward Chen Duxiu and a partial rehabilitation of him. Chen had been expelled from the party in 1929 for alleged mistakes in guiding the party during that difficult early period. His more favorable treatment at this juncture is consonant with the party's effort to raise the spirits and status of intellectuals. Chen had also been a prominent and highly respected intellectual during his career (*FBIS*, 4 November). Similarly, earlier in the year, Hu Yaobang had made a very positive evaluation of Hu Feng, a prominent party literary figure who had been imprisoned in 1955 for alleged counterrevolutionary statements. Hu Feng was exonerated in 1980 and passed away on 8 June (*FEER*, 27 June).

In November, Zhang Xingxiang of the State Industrial and Commercial Administration said that between 20,000 and 30,000 new free markets would be established in the next five years. This would bring the number of free markets to about 90,000 by 1990. The government sought to achieve its goal of one free market for each 30,000 to 50,000 residents in medium and large cities, and one for each 10,000 to 20,000 people in smaller cities (*San Francisco Examiner and Chronicle*, 17 November).

Vice-Premier Li Peng delivered an encouraging report on the current economic situation at the Thirteenth Session of the Sixth NPC Standing Committee on 18 November. First of all, Li said, the economy had shown sustained, balanced, and steady development in the past seven years. The total product of society, the total industrial and agricultural output value, and total national income had increased an average of 10 percent a year during the sixth five-year period. In 1982 China stopped the decline in state revenues that had occurred in the three preceding years and in fact the country had increased revenues steadily for the following three years. Second, he said, the readjustment of the structure of industry in recent years had rectified the longstanding, serious imbalances in the national economy. Third, the structural reform had ushered in a period of economic prosperity unprecedented in the PRC. Although China's arable land accounts for only 7 percent of the world's total farmland, China had satisfied the basic needs of 22 percent of the world's population in food and clothing. Fourth, Li noted, the open door policy had turned China's closed economy into an open one, enabling the country to make "fairly good achievements" in developing economic and technological cooperation with foreign countries. During the sixth five-year plan period, China's total volume of import-export trade doubled over that of the previous five years, and exports had increased more than imports. Fifth, Li said, urban and rural living standards had improved to varying degrees, compared to the record of no remarkable changes for many years.

Li Peng did take note of difficulties that were faced in the period between the fourth quarter of 1984 and the first quarter of 1985: "first, excessive growth rate for industrial production; second, oversized fixed-asset investment; and third, excessive increase in credit and consumption funds and a decrease in foreign exchange fund deposits." The principal measures taken to correct these problems were: "first, firmly controlling investment scale on fixed assets; second, checking excessive increase of consumption funds; third, gradually reducing industrial growth rates to normal level; fourth, controlling the scale of loans and issuance of currency; and fifth, intensifying supervision over foreign exchange" (Beijing, Xinhua, 18 November; *FBIS*, 19 November).

From 18 to 24 November, a national forum on theoretical work was held in Chengdu, Sichuan, by the Central Committee's Propaganda Department. This was in response to a demand from Deng Xiaoping that both new and old cadres study Marxist theory. While the new policies of economic reform and the open door were being pursued, it was "necessary to prevent corruption by capitalist thinking and to keep to a correct, socialist orientation," according to the Xinhua report of 25 November. More than one hundred persons attended the meeting (*FBIS*, 27 November).

It was reported that some two to three hundred

Uygur students staged an unprecedented antinuclear demonstration on Tiananmen Square in late December, protesting testing at Lop Nor in the Taklamakan Desert in Xinjiang Province (*Honolulu Advertiser*, 24 December).

Auxiliary and Front Organizations. This was not a particularly important year for the auxiliary and front organizations except for the convening of the Third Session of the Sixth National Committee of the CPPCC from 25 March to 8 April, almost simultaneously with the Sixth NPC's Third Session. The session heard speeches from Deng Yingchao, Fei Xiaotong, and others. More than a thousand motions were submitted. Mathematician Hua Luogeng was elected a new vice-chairman of the CPPCC National Committee. The final resolution urged members to help the government carry out China's reforms in economy, science, and education, noting that the reforms were the country's central task and that the CPPCC should make concentrated efforts to ensure its success (Beijing, Xinhua, 8 April; *FBIS*, 8 April).

Liu Yandong, 39, was elected president of the All-China Youth Federation at the Third Session of the Standing Committee of the Federation's Sixth Committee on 27 April. Liu is the first woman leader of this organization (Beijing, Xinhua, 27 April; *FBIS*, 6 May).

The Central Committee invited responsible persons from China's democratic parties, members of the All-China Federation of Industry and Commerce, leading individuals without party affiliation, and noted public figures to attend a forum from 10 to 12 September. The forum provided a briefing on the impending National Conference of Party Delegates and the accompanying Central Committee plenary sessions, and sought the participants' opinions on the personnel changes in the party's leading organs and on the draft proposal for the seventh five-year plan (Beijing, Xinhua, 12 September; *FBIS*, 13 September).

International Views and Positions. The PRC's foreign relations continued to be highlighted by the energetically pursued "open door" policy. There was much activity on all fronts: political, diplomatic, and economic. Wu Xingtang, a spokesman for the Central Committee's International Liaison Department, affirmed in early October that the resumption of Sino-Soviet party relations was still "out of the question," and that the CCP still did not have relations with the Communist parties of East Germany, Hungary, Poland, Czechoslovakia, or Bulgaria. He also made it clear that the CCP still does maintain relations with the Communist parties of Southeast Asia. He said that these relations were based on "morality," meaning that the parties express support for each other, render mutual political support, but do not afford "material conditions that may harm the relations between countries" (Hong Kong, *Ta Kung Pao*, 6 October; *FBIS*, 8 October). In November it was announced that the Chinese and Japanese Communist parties have discussed renewing their links after a break of almost twenty years. According to the Japanese, this was in response to a formal request of the CCP (Beijing, AFP, 21 November; *FBIS*, 22 November).

In July, State Councillor Gu Mu wrote an interesting article entitled "Opening to the Outside World: A Strategic Decision Reinvigorating China" as part of the commemoration of the fifth anniversary of the Beijing publication *Shijie Jingji Dabao* (in a special issue entitled "Reform Is China's Second Revolution").

In January it was announced that the NPC would send delegations to more than twenty countries (compared with four in 1984) and would host more than twenty parliamentary delegations from throughout the world (twenty in 1984) (Beijing, Xinhua, 18 January; *FBIS*, 22 January).

During the year, Hu Yaobang visited five South Pacific countries, Peng Zhen visited Japan, and Zhao Ziyang visited three West European countries. A common purpose of these trips was to study the international environment for China's economic development during the seventh five-year plan and to weigh the current economic structural reform in the "balance" of world economic development (Beijing, *Liaowang*, 30 September; *FBIS*, 21 October). Zhao Ziyang also visited several Latin American countries. Li Xiannian visited Canada and the United States.

In February it was announced that China would open 109 more cities and counties to foreign visitors, bringing the total to 257, one of the best manifestations of open door relaxation thus far. Over a million foreign tourists visited China in 1984, representing an increase of about 27 percent over 1983 (*AWSJ*, 14 February).

In March it was reported that in 1984, 160,000 Chinese had made "personal" trips out of the country and 130,000 had returned. Moreover, many who had not yet returned were individuals such as students, who remain abroad for an extended period of time. The number of border crossings for Chinese on official business in 1984 came to 550,000, up 65 percent from 1983. The number of illegal immigrants from China, principally through Hong Kong, has been rising again, however. More than 13,000 illegal immigrants in Hong Kong were returned to China in 1984, an increase of about 50 percent over 1983, although well below the ten-year peak of over 80,000 in 1980 (*CSM*, 7 March). In mid-November it was reported that since July 1984 the China Travel Service had organized more than four hundred groups, some 16,000 Chinese, to visit Hong Kong and Macao. Furthermore, beginning in March 1986 this activity of the China Travel Service was to expand to all provinces and municipalities in China. Thus far it had been conducted only from Guangdong, Fujian, Jiangsu, Zhejiang, Beijing, and Shanghai (Beijing, *Zhongguo Zinwen She*, 18 November; *FBIS*, 21 November).

In November it was announced that China had halted the drain on its foreign exchange reserves and expected levels to improve in 1986. Foreign bankers estimated that reserves stood at about $8 billion in October, down from a record $16.67 billion in September 1984 (*WSJ*, 25 November). By year's end, however, Finance Minister Wang Bingqian indicated that China's state revenues in 1986 would show a 20 percent increase, and the fiscal deficit would be eliminated after several years of deficits (*BR*, 23 December).

According to Xinhua, more than a thousand foreign businesses have opened in China since 1979. More than half are located in Beijing. The largest number, 288, are Japanese, while Americans have 125 enterprises. All local personnel must be obtained from the Foreign Enterprise Service Corporation (FESCO), the official state agency in charge of such personnel (*Parade Magazine*, 8 September).

In October, China announced formation of a third, nongovernmental, national trade and development corporation, called the China Incomic Development Corporation. Its main responsibilities are to bring smaller foreign and domestic joint-venture partners together and to provide them with investment capital and arrange for loans. The other two national-level "private corporations" are China International Trade and Investment Corporation, essentially an international finance and investment bank, and Everbright Industrial Corporation, a Hong Kong–based company that principally imports used factories and equipment (*WSJ*, 16 October).

In 1984 Beijing sold $1.66 billion in weapons, accounting for nearly 7 percent of its total export earnings. China is now the world's fifth largest arms merchant. Such exports are handled by China North Industries Corporation (Norinco), which was established by the Military Affairs Commission (*WSJ*, 17 June).

In June it was reported that China had become the principal buyer of airplanes in Asia. The Civil Aviation Administration of China (CAAC) has bought 40 new aircraft in the past two years, spending $1 billion in 1985 alone. The prospects for future purchses are very good (*WSJ*, 14 June).

China's open door policy has clearly been extended to countries with whom normal diplomatic ties do not exist or with whom there is no regular, official relationship. Indirect trade with Taiwan, for example, has increased sharply and was expected (perhaps with some direct trade) to reach $1.5 billion in 1985 (Taipei, *China Post*, 18 April; *FBIS*, 30 April). The Taiwan government, however, firmly maintains a policy of avoiding direct trade with the Chinese mainland, and appears to discourage indirect trade as well (*FBIS*, 8 July).

Similarly, the unofficial trade between China and South Korea is expected to reach $1 billion in 1985. Much of the trade is conducted through Hong Kong, although some is direct (*Korea Herald*, 10 May). Two leading Korean companies, Daewoo and Lucky-Goldstar, were completing plans in mid-year for joint ventures in Fujian (*CSM*, 10 July). In March, South Korea quickly and amicably returned to China a torpedo boat and crew that had drifted into Korean waters following an onboard gunfight. This seems to have enhanced the informal relationships between the two countries, similar to the improvement that followed the return to China of a hijacked passenger plane two years earlier. The event did not enhance Seoul's relationship with Taiwan, however (Hong Kong, *South China Morning Post*, 31 March). Seven leading Chinese nuclear scientists attended the Pacific Basin Nuclear Conference and Exhibition in Seoul in May, along with Taiwanese scientists (*FEER*, 30 May). In the meantime, China appears concerned lest North Korea gravitate too closely to the Soviet Union. Accordingly, Hu Yaobang made a secret weekend visit to North Korea's border town of Shinuiju on 5 and 6 May, meeting with both Kim Il-song and his son Kim Chong-il (*Korea Herald*, 10 May). Nevertheless, the Soviet Union does seem to have made headway in its relations with Pyongyang. The Soviets now appear to have overflight rights over North

Korea and permission to install intelligence and communications equipment in the country, in return for delivery of advanced MiG-23s. The statement on 11 September by a Chinese Foreign Ministry spokesman, who said that China was "pleased to see the development of [North Korea's] relations with the Soviet Union," was greeted with some skepticism (*FEER*, 26 September).

Although China and Indonesia still do not have diplomatic relations, the two countries agreed to direct trade amounting to $300 million during the visit of an Indonesian trade mission, the first of its kind in eighteen years. The Chinese also accepted an invitation to send a trade delegation to Indonesia (*Korea Herald*, 6 August).

Foreign Minister Wu Xueqian attended a meeting in Indonesia on 24–25 April marking the thirtieth anniversary of the historic 1955 Bandung Conference. At the meeting, Wu reaffirmed China's opposition to hegemonism and said that it will never seek spheres of influence (*BR*, 6 May). Even though relations appear to be warming somewhat between China and Indonesia, so that direct trade now takes place again, the establishment of diplomatic relations is not yet in sight. The Indonesians apparently insist on Chinese acknowledgment of complicity in the bloody 1965 coup (see, e.g., *FEER*, 23 May). However, Indonesia has specifically denied that it has asked China for such an apology. Foreign Minister Mochtar Kusumaatmadja did say that Indonesia would be satisfied with no more than a declaration that China would no longer support underground movements against Southeast Asian governments (*FEER*, 6 June). In September, however, a spokesman for the CCP's International Liaison Department expressed deep regret at the reported executions of three former Indonesian Communist Party leaders by Indonesian authorities (Beijing, Xinhua, 2 September; *FBIS*, 5 September).

Hu Yaobang made a high-profile visit (12–24 April) to the South Pacific, with stops in Australia, New Zealand, Western Samoa, Fiji, and Papua New Guinea. This was only Hu's second visit to a nonsocialist country. Hu said in Wellington that "China had no intention whatsoever of playing any military role in the South Pacific" (*BR*, 6 May). It was also in Wellington that Hu candidly revealed that China would soon reduce its troop strength by one million men (*Asiaweek*, 3 May).

Relations with Vietnam remained tense. China continued to support Kampuchean rebels against the Hanoi-installed regime in Phnom Penh. However, the truculence exhibited by Foreign Minister Wu in January, to the effect that China would administer a "second lesson" to Vietnam, was abandoned as the year wore on. Presumably, a decision was made that another military campaign would be too expensive, particularly in light of China's present military capabilities (*FEER*, 30 May). Beijing apparently became somewhat more conciliatory following Vice-Premier Li Peng's visit with General Secretary Mikhail Gorbachev in March. On 17 April, Deng Xiaoping said that some of the obstacles to improved Sino-Soviet relations could be removed by Soviet encouragement of Vietnamese troop withdrawal from Cambodia. Deng added that the Soviets could "still retain the bases provided by Vietnam." Also, in late April, Vietnamese and Chinese officials met quietly in Beijing, the first known high-level private meeting since 1979. Although the talks were supposed to be concerned with economic matters, there was speculation that these might lead to diplomatic normalization (*FEER*, 30 May). Nevertheless, the tension along the border remained quite tangible; a Chinese artillery blitz reportedly killed more than two hundred Vietnamese troops near the Laotian frontier area during the summer (*Beijing Ribao*, 4 August; Seoul, *Korea Times*, 6 August). By December, Chinese impatience was registered in an article by foreign affairs specialist Xue Mouhong, who argued that Hanoi must be pressured to move out of Kampuchea (*BR*, 23 December).

China signed a new five-year trade and economic cooperation agreement with the European Economic Community on 21 May. EEC officials expressed concern that they were still losing ground to both Japan and the United States even though trade with China had improved over the last few years (*FEER*, 6 June). China also announced two planned Eurobond issues, following its successful bond issue in Tokyo in November 1984. This decision was made despite the controversy regarding the defaulted Qing Dynasty railway bonds, which the PRC has refused to honor. The current issue is guaranteed by the China International Trust and Investment Corporation (*FEER*, 23 May).

In a simple ceremony on 27 May the Chinese deputy foreign minister, Zhou Nan, and British ambassador Sir Richard Evans exchanged instruments of ratification, bringing into formal effect the agreement of their respective countries to return Hong Kong to Chinese sovereignty in 1997 (*Asiaweek*, 7 June). Sino-British relations are prospering. British exports to China jumped 78 percent in the first quarter of 1985. Premier Zhao's week-long visit to Britain in June was a particularly warm and successful one (*FEER*, 20 June).

Relations with Japan, China's largest trading partner, continued to be excellent during the year, although marred by anti-Japanese student protests and by memories elicited at the commemoration of the end of World War II. Peng Zhen, Politburo member and chairman of the NPC Standing Committee, visited Japan in May. Peng said that the two countries now have the "best relations in more than 100 years." He also said that China was "open to all countries in the world but we put Japan, our close neighbor, first, especially Japanese businesses." Approximately a third of the foreign visitors to China are Japanese. Limited cooperation continued to manifest itself in military matters as well. In May military officials of both countries, for example, discussed "strategy, the military situation in Asia and the Soviet military buildup in the Far East" (*Honolulu Sunday Star-Bulletin and Advertiser*, 5 May; *BR*, 6 May).

Chinese student demonstrations were initially prompted by the Chinese government's protest over Prime Minister Nakasone's official visit on 15 August to the Yasukuni Shrine in Tokyo, where Japanese military casualties are commemorated as Shinto divines. Some observers have wondered, however, if the demonstrations were not being used as a pressure tactic by the Chinese to extract more favorable economic concessions from Japan. Even if this were true, however, it would probably be a mistake to underestimate the depth of Chinese feelings on a matter of such fundamental concern (*WSJ*, 11 November). In any case, once the student demonstrations revealed signs of protesting *Chinese* policies they were discouraged by authorities. The Chinese media did recall prominent Japanese atrocities during the fortieth anniversary commemorations. Remembered in a prominent publication, for example, were the more than 300,000 civilians who were killed during the 1937 "Rape of Nanking" (*BR*, 2 September) and the 3,000 Chinese who were killed in germ warfare experiments near Harbin (*Korea Times*, 10 August).

Relations with the USSR. The improved atmosphere in this relationship that began in late 1984 continued through 1985, particularly with the ascension to power of Mikhail Gorbachev. But the "three main obstacles" to normalization, as viewed by the Chinese, also remained in place. Hence, even with some improvements in diplomatic, economic, and social relations, the two largest Communist parties remain estranged.

In what may have been his last public comments on ths issue, Konstantin Chernenko, on 23 February, said that the Soviet Union attached great importance to the normalization of relations with China, and he noted that some beneficial steps had been taken in the past year toward improvement, although serious political differences still existed. He said that the Soviet Union hoped that relations would be further improved through the efforts of both sides (*FBIS*, 25 February).

Li Zewang, the new PRC ambassador extraordinary and plenipotentiary to the Soviet Union, presented his credentials in the Kremlin on 1 March (*FBIS*, 4 March).

A Chinese NPC delegation, headed by NPC member Zhang Chengxian, made an eleven-day visit to the Soviet Union in March, the first such visit in more than twenty years (*WP*, 4 March). Following the completion of the visit, Zhang termed it a "complete success" (Beijing radio, 16 March; *FBIS*, 18 March). This visit was reciprocated by a delegation from the Supreme Soviet of the Soviet Union, led by Lev Nikolayevich Tolkunov, the chairman of the Supreme Soviet, in October (Beijing, Xinhua, 10 October; *FBIS*, 11 October).

China expressed condolences on the death of Chernenko on 11 March, noting that the late Soviet leader had "expressed more than once the hope for the development of relations with China" (*FBIS*, 12 March).

Chinese leaders quickly noted that Chernenko's successor as CPSU General Secretary, Mikhail Gorbachev, appointed on 11 March, held views somewhat similar to their own on economic development, reforms, bureaucracy, and other topics (Hong Kong, *Wen Wei Po*, 13 March; *FBIS*, 13 March). Vice-Premier Li Peng headed the Chinese delegation to Chernenko's funeral. In Moscow, Li Peng met with Gorbachev on 14 March, telling the latter that China was in agreement with his 11 March expression of hope for a major improvement in Sino-Soviet relations (Moscow, 14 March; *FBIS*, 15 March). On his return to Beijing, Li Peng told journalists that the conversation with Gorbachev (which, incidentally, was not required by protocol) had been "friendly and positive and that Sino-Soviet relations would be gradually improved" (Beijing radio, 15 March; *FBIS*, 18 March). Also notable is that the Chinese media used the term "comrade" for

Gorbachev, a term long absent in Chinese references to Soviet leaders.

However, these initial expressions of optimism were dampened somewhat by more temperate comments by Deng Xiaoping and Hu Yaobang in talks with Susumu Nikaido, deputy leader of the Japanese Liberal Democratic Party, in late March. Hu assured the Japanese visitor that China "will not abandon old friends while making new friends, or sacrifice friendship with one in exchange for friendship with another." Deng said that despite the conciliatory note sounded by Gorbachev, Moscow's policy toward China had not undergone any fundamental change, and Deng reiterated the obstacles that hampered normalization of Sino-Soviet relations (Hong Kong, *South China Morning Post*, 31 March).

On 4 April, China and the Soviet Union agreed on a program of educational and research exchanges for 1985–1986. This followed an agreement earlier the same week on increased local border trade and the signature of a document on trade and transport in 1985 (Peking, Reuters, 4 April; *NYT*, 5 April).

The sixth round of Sino-Soviet "consultations" was held in Moscow from 9 to 23 April. China was represented by its special envoy and vice-minister of foreign relations, Qian Qichen (Moscow, Xinhua, 23 April; *FBIS*, 23 April). Both sides "expressed willingness to expand contacts and exchanges in the political, economic, trade, science-technology, cultural, and other fields" (Moscow radio, 24 April; *FBIS*, 29 April).

On 17 April, as noted above, Deng Xiaoping issued a strong public appeal to the Soviet Union to help persuade Vietnam to withdraw its military from Cambodia, and he suggested for the first time that China would be willing to accept the Soviet use of Cam Ranh Bay.

A Soviet delegation led by the vice-minister of foreign trade, I. T. Grishin, visited China in May (Xinhua, 30 May; *FBIS*, 31 May). In June, consular delegations of the two countries' ministries of foreign affairs held consultations in Beijing on improving and developing further consular relations (Tass, Beijing, 14 June; *FBIS*, 17 June). It was subsequently announced that China would open a consulate general in Leningrad and the Soviet Union would open one in Shanghai (*FBIS*, 21 June). On 16 June a plan for cultural cooperation for 1985 was signed in Beijing (Tass, 16 June; *FBIS*, 17 June).

The fiftieth anniversary of the death of Qu Qiubai, an early CCP member and party chairman, was commemorated in various ways in Moscow, including a 19 June soiree hosted by the Federation of Societies for Friendship and Cultural Relations with Foreign Countries and the Soviet-Chinese Friendship Society (Moscow radio, 19 June; *FBIS*, 21 June).

A television crew of the Japan Broadcasting Corporation (NHK), which visited the Sino-Soviet border in May, noted that a high school in Suifenhe again teaches the Russian language, and a daily train for passengers and freight crosses the nearby border with the Soviet Union. Also, Soviet officials were invited by the small town of 20,000 to participate in a party on the eve of May Day (Tokyo, *AWSJ*, 24 June).

On 28 June, Gorbachev, speaking at a dinner for the visiting head of Vietnam's Communist party, Le Duan, called on China to improve relations with both Moscow and Hanoi (*NYT*, 29 June). The fact that the Le Duan visit was apparently downplayed in Moscow was taken as the first clear Soviet response to Deng Xiaoping's comments of 17 April regarding Soviet assistance to Vietnam in Cambodia (*FEER*, 11 July). Two days earlier (26 June), Gorbachev, during a speech at a Ukrainian factory, said that good-neighborly cooperation between the Soviet Union and China is very possible and desirable. "I think that time has shown to both sides that none will gain from discord, and even less from unfriendliness and suspicion." He said that the Soviet side "intends to actively contribute to the complete overcoming of the negative phase in Soviet-Chinese relations which had produced many artificial overlayers" (Beijing radio, 27 June; *FBIS*, 1 July).

From 9 to 16 July, Vice-Premier Yao Yilin made an official visit to the Soviet Union, reciprocating the December 1984 visit of Ivan Arkhipov, first vice-chairman of the Council of Ministers of the Soviet Union. In Moscow, Yao signed an agreement on trade turnover and payments for 1986–1990 and an agreement on economic and technical cooperation in the construction and reconstruction of industrial installations in the PRC (Tass, Moscow, 10 July; *FBIS*, 10 July). The two agreements signed by Yao called for a doubling of bilateral trade (to $3.5 billion by 1990) and Soviet cooperation in building seven new Chinese plants and modernizing seventeen that had been built in the 1950s with Soviet help (*FEER*, 25 July).

The PRC signed a contract on 18 July to purchase 17 Soviet TU-154M passenger airplanes during the 1985–1986 period (Beijing, Xinhua, 18 July; *FBIS*, 19 July).

According to the *Xinxi Huibao*, China has decided to build a railway west of Urumqi and plans to connect it with the Soviet Central Asian Railway. When completed, this would give China its third route—"the northwest thoroughfare"—in addition to its northeast and northern routes for the shipment of goods to Europe and the Middle East (Shanghai, *Jiefang Ribao*, 28 July; *FBIS*, 7 August).

On 2 September, the China Council for the Promotion of International Trade and the USSR Chamber of Commerce and Industry signed a cooperation agreement in Moscow (Beijing, Xinhua, 3 September; *FBIS*, 3 September).

On 2 October a Soviet official indicated that Chinese and Soviet foreign ministers had agreed to exchange visits, another first since the 1960 split (Peking, Reuters, 2 October; *NYT*, 3 October).

The seventh round of consultations between China and the Soviet Union was held from 4 to 18 October in Beijing. L. F. Ilichev, special envoy and vice–foreign minister, headed the Soviet participants. The talks "proceeded in a frank, calm and business-like atmosphere." The next round of consultations is to be held in Moscow in April 1986 (Beijing, Xinhua, 20 October; *FBIS*, 21 October).

In late December, Vice-Premier Li Peng held an unexpected meeting in Moscow with Gorbachev. But only two days later the Chinese government delivered a scathing denouncement of the Soviet Union's six-year-old invasion of Afghanistan, saying that the Soviet presence in that country "seriously undermined" regional stability and constituted a threat to China. This criticism was voiced by foreign ministry spokesman Ma Yuzhen at a weekly news briefing (*Honolulu Star-Bulletin*, 25 December).

Relations with the United States. This was another year of improving U.S.-China relations, the high point of which was President Li Xiannian's visit to the United States. This improvement in relations seemed readily apparent despite a "misunderstanding" over the aborted visit of American naval vessels to China, continued stalemate over the Taiwan issue, American criticisms of China's population policy, and the threat of protectionist legislation in Washington. Trade had reached a record $6.1 billion in 1984, with China suffering a deficit of $1.5 billion. Trade was expected to increase even more in 1985.

General John Vessey, chairman of the U.S. Joint Chiefs of Staff, was the first person in this office to visit China. For a week in January he had talks with Zhao Ziyang, Defense Minister Zhang Aiping, and his opposite number, Yang Dezhi. The visit was the culmination of a process begun many months earlier, and agreement was reached in principle regarding purchase of American Phalanx guns, gas turbine engines, sonars, and torpedoes. It was also agreed that three American destroyers would visit Shanghai in April, the first such naval courtesy call by American naval vessels in 35 years (*Asiaweek*, 25 January). Although the military connection between the two countries was to deepen throughout the year, the planned naval visit was indefinitely postponed. This might be attributed to Hu Yaobang, who publicly announced that the United States had agreed that the ships would not carry nuclear arms. Whether or not Washington had given such assurances to the Chinese has not been confirmed, nor is it likely to be. Any such assurance presumably was accompanied by the expectation that the Chinese would not reveal it. Hence this affair has become an embarrassment for both parties and has been discreetly set aside for the moment (see, e.g., *FEER*, 23 May).

William Schneider, U.S. undersecretary for security assistance, science, and technology, said in March that a decision had been made to improve the administrative apparatus for approving the sale of technology to China (*Asiaweek*, 29 March). This was in response to the phenomenon of surging computer equipment sales to China in recent months and the immense backlog awaiting official U.S. approval.

Former vice–foreign minister Han Xu became the new ambassador to the United States on 21 April. Han had served as deputy head of China's liaison office in Washington from 1973 to 1979, the period just prior to normalization of diplomatic relations.

Commerce Secretary Malcolm Baldridge led a 31-member delegation to the third meeting of the U.S.-China Joint Commission on Commerce and Trade in May. Baldridge said the United States had agreed to help China evaluate its industrial modernization program. He also said that discussions with Chinese officials had removed many of the roadblocks, so that trade relations now follow a more normal trade pattern (*FEER*, 23 May). Premier Zhao expressed appreciation for American efforts to promote technological transfer to China (Beijing, Xinhua, 14 May; *FBIS*, 15 May).

Soon afterward, Washington received the support of allied nations for a proposal to exempt a large part of the technology trade with China from multilateral screening, a process that had caused long delays (*WSJ*, 4 June).

Following his visit to Canada, 80-year-old President Li Xiannian made a state visit to the United States (21 to 31 July), with stops in Washington, Chicago, Los Angeles, and Honolulu. During Li's visit, on 23 July, the controversial U.S.-China Nuclear Cooperation Agreement, initialed during President Ronald Reagan's visit to China in 1984, was signed. It took effect 90 days later, since neither house of Congress chose to reject it by a majority vote. The agreement enables American companies to compete for a share of China's multibillion-dollar civilian reactor program (Washington, D.C., Xinhua, 23 July; *FBIS*, 24 July; see U.S. Department of State, Bureau of Public Affairs, Current Policy No. 729, August 1985). Also signed were bilateral accords on education, culture, and fisheries.

Deng Xiaoping criticized the Reagan administration's Strategic Defense Initiative (SDI), describing it as a plan that would add a dangerous new dimension to the arms race between the two superpowers. Deng's remarks were made in early August in an interview with British publisher Robert Maxwell. A team from the U.S. National Security Council had been sent to Beijing in June to brief the Chinese on the SDI program (*WP*, 6 August).

During an August visit to China by a group of American senators, Senator Patrick Moynihan took to task his Chinese hosts, including Deng Xiaoping, for their record of voting overwhelmingly against the United States in the United Nations (*NYT*, 1 September).

Former president Richard Nixon made an unofficial visit to China in September, meeting with Deng Xiaoping, Hu Yaobang, and Zhao Ziyang. It was Nixon's fifth visit to China (*Honolulu Advertiser*, 6 September).

Chinese leaders were offended by the debate in the United States over China's population control policy, and were specifically concerned when this affected a source of funding. On 25 September, a Foreign Ministry spokesman criticized the U.S. Agency for International Development for issuing a statement "distorting China's population policy and falsely accusing China of practicing so-called forced abortion. The agency has also withheld, on this ground, the pledged sum of ten million U.S. dollars to the United Nations Fund for population activities." The spokesman continued, saying that the AID statement "wantonly interfered in China's internal affairs and obviously violated the important principle that the formulation and implementation of population policies is the sovereign right of each nation" (Beijing, Xinhua, 27 September; *FBIS*, 30 September).

Vice-President George Bush visited China on 13–18 October at the invitation of the Chinese government. Deng Xiaoping told Bush that the changes the latter had noted since his last visit to China in 1982 were "not big enough." "If you revisit China in three years, you will see substantial changes, for initial results will have been achieved in China's economic structural reforms in the urban areas," Deng said (Beijing, Xinhua, 15 October; *FBIS*, 15 October). Zhao Ziyang, during his meeting with Bush, asked the United States to implement the joint communiqué of 1982, regarding arms sales to Taiwan. The Taiwan issue remains the major problem in U.S.-China relations, he said (*BR*, 21 October).

Also of concern to the Chinese, as it was to other U.S. trading partners in Asia, was the threat of impending protectionist legislation in Congress. The Jenkins Bill, e.g., when passed by a large vote in the House of Representatives, drew sharp criticism from the Chinese Foreign Ministry (*Honolulu Sunday Star-Bulletin and Advertiser*, 13 October).

In November, Larry Wu-tai Chin, a former intelligence officer in the CIA's Foreign Broadcast Information Service, was arrested and held without bail on espionage and conspiracy charges. Chin had allegedly been paid more than $140,000 by the PRC's intelligence service since 1952, at which time he allegedly began selling information on the location and interrogation of Chinese prisoners of war in Korea (*Honolulu Sunday Star-Bulletin and Advertiser*, 24 November).

Stephen Uhalley, Jr.
University of Hawaii

India

Population. 762,507,000
Party. Communist Party of India (CPI); Communist Party of India–Marxist (CPM)
Membership. CPI: 478,500 (Calcutta, *Telegraph*, 26 October 1984); CPM: 271,500 (Calcutta, *Statesman*, 3 November 1982)
Secretary General. CPI: C. Rajeswara Rao; CPM: E. M. S. Namboodiripad
Politburo. CPI: Central Executive Council, 11 members; CPM: 10 members
Central Committee. CPI: National Council, 124 members; CPM, 66 members
Status. Legal
Last Congress. CPI: Twelfth, 21–28 March 1982, at Varanasi; CPM: Twelfth, 25–30 December 1985, at Calcutta
Last Election. 1984. CPI: 2.71 percent, 6 seats; CPM: 5.96 percent, 22 seats (out of 509 contested in 544-seat parliament)
Auxiliary Organizations. CPI: All-India Trade Union Congress, All-India Kisan Sabha, All-India Student Federation; CPM: Centre for Indian Trade Unions, All-India Kisan Sabha, Students Federation of India
Publications. CPI: *New Age*, *Party Life*, Indian-language dailies in Kerala, Andhra Pradesh, West Bengal, Punjab, and Manipur; CPM: *People's Democracy*, Indian-language dailies in Andhra Pradesh, Kerala, and West Bengal

Rajiv Gandhi assumed power in late 1984 at a time of escalating social tension believed by many political parties, including the communist ones, to threaten the unity of the country. Reducing this tension has been his priority concern. During 1985, Gandhi worked out a series of agreements with protest leaders that significantly reduced the level of violence.

In June, Gandhi signed a peace accord with leaders of high-caste Hindu groups who were protesting increased employment and educational quotas for historically disadvantaged castes in the state of Gujarat. A second accord was worked out with the leaders of the Sikh community who advocated increased autonomy for the state of Punjab. A third was signed in August with Assamese students who demanded the expulsion from their state of illegal Bangladeshi immigrants.

In each case, Gandhi brought the protest leaders to the bargaining table by employing conciliatory rhetoric, offering concessions, and involving himself personally in the negotiations. His popularity soared. His prestige was further buttressed by a healthy expansion of the economy and his successful visits to the USSR and the United States. Relations with Pakistan, while sometimes tense, were at least under control at the end of the year, when Gandhi and Pakistan's President Zia met to discuss their major bilateral problems.

Because of Gandhi's domestic and foreign policy successes, the opposition parties were left without a major issue to bring them closer together. Indira Gandhi's confrontational style had made her an easier rallying symbol than her son and successor. Opposition efforts to establish joint fronts collapsed after her death, and the opposition remained in disarray both during the December 1984 parliamentary elections and throughout 1985. The two major Communist parties, the pro-Moscow Communist Party of India (CPI) and the larger and more independent Communist Party of India–Marxist (CPM), tried to coordinate their activities but were a long way from close cooperation.

Even though Gandhi's Congress (I) Party had won an unprecedented victory in the 1984 parliamentary elections, the opposition, including the CPI and CPM, was unable to establish firm electoral agreements prior to the March election of one-half of India's 22 state assemblies. The Congress, though performing less well than in the 1984 parliamentary elections, won control of eight of the eleven states. The Communist parties, whose parliamentary standing declined by about 40 percent in the 1984 elections, continued their downward slide in the state polls, as well as in the September Punjab and the December Assam state assembly elections. Even where the two worked well together, as in the Punjab assembly elections, the Communists were wiped out in a state where the CPI and CPM traditionally had pockets of support. The mediocre electoral performance of both the CPI and CPM during 1985 further fueled the self-criticism that gripped both parties in the wake of the 1984 electoral debacle. The eroding membership base of their front organizations seemed to confirm the need to re-examine party tactics and policies.

The CPM. *Organization and Leadership.* The aging leadership of the CPM both at the center and in its major stronghold, West Bengal, came under unprecedented attack as a result of the party's losses in the 1984 parliamentary elections. The party's representation dropped from 36 to 22; most of the losses occurred in West Bengal. Discontent had been growing for years against the entrenched party elite, most of whom had joined the party in the 1930s. Electoral losses in 1984 and 1985 emboldened the critics to go public.

Critics of the party leadership in West Bengal argued that the CPM's eight continuous years in power had resulted in a loss of vigor, induced corruption, undermined the party's Marxist orientation, and alienated supporters. Some critics even demanded the resignation of Chief Minister Jyoti Basu and the CPM state secretary, Saroj Mukherjee. Shortly after the 1984 parliamentary elections, Mukherjee felt it necessary to query the local units regarding the desirability of the CPM remaining in the government (*Telegraph*, 13 January). Basu for his part threatened to take disciplinary action against indiscipline (*Telegraph*, 13 March). In early 1985, Mukherjee expelled 123 party workers and removed another 150 from their posts (*Hindu*, 24 May). The leadership's credibility was not strengthened by the narrow victory of the left front in the June city elections in Calcutta.

The attack against West Bengal's state establishment was led by a small group of young, ideologically centrist, activists who had been groomed by the late party secretary, Pramode Dasgupta. The most prominent of these activists were Biman Bose, Buddhadev Bhattacharya, and Anil Biswas. They advocated a re-evaluation of policy, proposing that the party concentrate more on building an independent communist movement than on seeking closer ties with the CPI or other opposition parties. To buttress the party's independence, many dissidents in West Bengal, opposing the increasingly pro-Soviet tilt of the CPM, advocated going back to the party's former policy of equidistance between the PRC and the USSR.

The party's central establishment engaged in self-criticism, noting the "uneven growth" of the front organizations and their lack of initiative, and also attacking the lack of central control over state units (*Telegraph*, 1 November). Party leaders pointed out that the CPM had been unable to expand beyond traditional regional bases in Andhra Pradesh, Kerala, West Bengal, and Tripura. Indeed, the CPM had become a regional party. Despite the rumble of discontent and the self-criticism, the party establishment at the center and in the key West Bengal unit, retained their power with only minor personnel changes. Nonetheless, the openness of the attack and the intensity of the criticism suggest that the geriatric leadership could soon face challenges to its authority unless it accommodates the younger cadre.

During 1985, the two Communist parties continued to debate what kind of relationship they wanted to establish. Although their diminished electoral support in 1984–1985 seemed to argue for closer relations, deep-seated antagonism kept cooperation at a modest level. (Party support bases lay in different parts of the country, so cooperation could only have marginally helped either party.) The vocal left of the CPM denounced the CPI as right revisionist while the potent right of the CPI preferred links with the ruling Congress (I) Party. The elderly establishments of the two parties could not forget old battles, some dating back to the party split in 1964. In mid-year, *People's Democracy* and *New Age*, official journals for the CPM and CPI, respectively, ran lengthy and vituperative articles, each party blaming the other for the split.

The two parties, nonetheless, had a formal structure for working out joint activities. The Central Coordination Committee, however, formed in 1980, did not meet until 1985—the first bilateral meeting of the two communist parties since 1978. The committee met in April and June, spending much of its time discussing the lack of cooperation in the March assembly elections. The CPI proposed coordination committees at the state level, but the CPM, the stronger party, viewed this as a veiled CPI effort to gain influence in the CPM strongholds of West Bengal and Kerala.

The CPI, for its part, was the more ardent advocate of cooperation. Commenting on the consequences of a divided Indian communist movement, Rajeswara Rao, CPI secretary general, remarked that "neither the CPI nor the CPI–M will be there if things continue as they are" (*Patriot*, 2 June). The CPI's Kerala unit openly called for a reunited Communist party. However, CPM Secretary General E. M. S. Namboodiripad in August rejected speculations of a merger, stating that they diverted attention from united work in practical fields and overlooked the ideological gulf between the two parties (*Times of India*, 28 August). Indeed, Politburo member M. Basavapunnaiah openly stated that the CPI was not even a legitimate Marxist organization (*Telegraph*, 8 July).

Issues: Domestic and Foreign. Rajiv Gandhi's first year in office was a political honeymoon, and India's Communists were caught up in the same mood of goodwill. For example, Secretary General Namboodiripad argued that the people "with some justice" perceived that Gandhi's Congress (I) Party could better preserve national unity than the divided opposition (*Statesman*, 9 January). However, the two Communist parties became increasingly critical of Gandhi as the year progressed. Gandhi's efforts to strengthen market forces in the Indian economy bothered them most. The CPM generally backed his efforts to reduce interethnic and intercaste violence. It also welcomed the Punjab peace accord, though, like most opposition parties, the CPM worried that elections might trigger renewed violence. In principle, the CPM welcomed the Assam agreement, though it opposed removal from the electoral rolls of those illegal immigrants who had crossed the border before 1972. Gandhi's decision to reconsider an increase of equal opportunity benefits in Gujarat (and elsewhere) received mixed reviews within the CPM. However, the party strongly opposed the Terrorist and Disruptive Activities (Prevention) Act, which gave the government power to arrest those it believed might engage in or assist terrorism. The CPM, like some other opposition parties, feared that the government might use the act to restrain legitimate political activity.

The party establishment's somewhat relaxed approach to Rajiv Gandhi was severely criticized in some places, including West Bengal. The West Bengal unit even passed a resolution for the Twelfth Congress in December proposing that "a revival of authoritarianism" was "inevitable" under Rajiv Gandhi (*India Today*, 31 May).

The CPM governments of Tripura and West Bengal had to worry about improving the job situation in states with relatively stagnant economies. To encourage investment, the government, disregarding its own Marxist credentials, actively sought domestic and foreign private investment and promised to put a brake on the labor unions. Its agricultural policy was equally pragmatic. Landlords were paid for expropriated property and tenant farming was permitted, though tenancy rights were protected. Chief Minister Jyoti Basu justified this nonrevolutionary approach by arguing that such policies were necessary as long as the Communists did not control the central government in New Delhi (*FEER*, 12 December).

Rajiv Gandhi's foreign policy was generally described as "progressive" and aroused less debate than some aspects of his domestic policy. At least at the national party level, the CPM continued to veer toward Soviet positions on such issues as Vietnam, Kampuchea, Afghanistan, and disarmament. However, there was disagreement with such stands at the local level. For example, a vocal youthful element in West Bengal advocated more of a balance between the PRC and the USSR. Both the CPI and the CPM supported the militant Tamil movement in Sri Lanka, which advocates an autonomous, if not independent, Tamil state in northern and eastern Sri Lanka. Some of the Tamil militants are Marxists, and the Indian press reports that Indian communist leaders occasionally meet with them.

The CPM, once deliberately aloof from the affairs of other Communist parties, sent several delegations to communist states, including three to the USSR. The visits to Moscow involved party-to-party talks, which strongly suggests that the USSR has accommodated itself to the independent CPM, the larger of the two Communist parties in India. One prominent CPM official claimed that "official" ties already existed (*Patriot*, 24 September). However, the CPSU has not announced existence of formal links, though it is possible that the Soviets might follow the example of the French Communist Party and recognize both the CPI and the CPM.

Front Groups. The party leadership severely criticized the CPM's front groups for their lack of initiative and inability to mobilize mass support. Their declining membership was a sign that something was wrong. The women's wing of the party dropped from 950,000 to 825,000. The Students Federation of India dropped from 475,000 to 390,000. The Centre for Indian Trade Unions remained stagnant at 1.7 million members, about half the size of its CPI counterpart, the All-India Trade Union Congress. The farmers' front lost some 350,000 members. Part of the problem, according to some CPM leaders, can be traced to lack of party guidance. The CPM resolved to monitor its front organizations more closely.

The CPI. *Organization and Leadership.* Self-criticism within the CPI exacerbated the differences between the minority faction, which sought to revive the old united front policy with the Congress (I) Party, and the dominant group, led by Secretary General Rao, who advocated strengthening the party's ties with the left. This controversy may have contributed to the delay of the Thirteenth Party Congress from March 1985 to February 1986.

The challenge to the establishment was led by H. K. Vyas, Mohit Sen, and M. K. Sundaram, members of the National Council. This nucleus of dissent was occasionally joined by Romesh Chandra, president of the pro-Moscow World Peace Council. At the first National Council meeting after the parliamentary elections in December 1984, this group blamed Rao's left alliance line for the poor showing and demanded that he and the entire Secretariat resign (*Indian Express*, 20 January). They circulated a pamphlet, "Lok Sabha Elections: Communist Review," which criticized existing party tactics. The dissidents argued that the parliamentary elections underscored the leadership's incorrect line, which, they claimed, was against the "mood of our people" and undermined the cause of "internationalism" (a shorthand term for Soviet foreign policy). They criticized the leadership for cooperating with opposition parties that did not understand the danger of national disintegration and were therefore not vigilant regarding dangers to national unity. The greatest bulwark of national unity, they argued, was the Congress (I) Party. As for the CPM, the document urged caution, stating that the CPI not give in to the CPM's "opportunistic policies and their one-point programme of reducing the strength of our party."

Still other dissidents took a different line from those supporting cooperation with the Congress (I) Party. Some, such as the Rajasthan unit, called for "left unity" rather than the present "left and democratic" line, arguing that many of the so-called "democratic" parties were in fact quite reactionary (*Patriot*, 20 January).

Despite attacks on his policies, Rao was never seriously threatened. The dissidents controlled approximately 15 percent of the National Conference membership. Rao was sufficiently confident of his position that he publicly announced early in the year that the CPI would continue to oppose the Congress (I) Party and would support the existing "left and democratic" line (*Telegraph*, 25 January). The CPI worked out electoral alliances with the CPM and other "democratic" parties for the eleven state assembly elections in March as well as the subsequent assembly elections in Punjab and Assam.

Issues: Domestic and Foreign. The CPI's policies on both domestic and foreign policy questions were close to those of the CPM, despite elaborate efforts by party leaders to make them sound different. India's foreign policy was defined as "progressive," while the party expressed misgivings about the increasing "embourgeoisment" of the economy under Rajiv Gandhi. Like the CPM, the CPI argued that Gandhi's liberalization program would benefit "imperialist" states and enhance the power of the "monopolists" in India (*New Age*, 18 August). Also like the CPM, it generally supported Gandhi's peace accords.

The only significant foreign policy difference between the CPI and the CPM was in their approach to Sino-Indian relations. The CPI advised the government to pursue rapprochement with great caution, while the CPM advocated closer Sino-Indian ties. During 1985, the CPI was unusually restrained concerning China, perhaps because of the resumed Sino-Soviet talks. Indeed, a delegation of CPI labor leaders led by the president of the All-India Trade Union Centre, Chaturanan Mishra, visited China in September. The Chinese Communist Party reportedly asked Mishra to inform the CPI leadership of its desire for formal party-to-party relations. Secretary General Rao opposed such ties on the grounds that the USSR and the PRC are not likely to reconcile their differences (*Indian Express*, 30 October). The right wing of the party would also have strongly resisted such a move.

Other Communist Parties. Small Communist parties exist on both the left and right of the two major Indian Communist parties. On the right is the All-India Communist Party (AICP), established by S. A. Dange, a Lenin Peace Prize recipient who bolted the CPI in 1980 in a disagreement over its decision to abandon the united front policy with the Congress Party. The AICP elicited limited support in both the 1984 parliamentary elections and the state 1985 assembly elections. Rejected by Moscow and without a coherent program, it was not able to lure disgruntled right-wing members of the CPI into its camp. To the left of the CPI and CPM are a number of small Maoist parties, often called Naxalites—a reference to a district in West Bengal where radical Communists tried to establish a base of operations in the late 1960s. Some have retained their revolutionary fervor and others have become more moderate. Some of the seventeen factions of the late Charu Mazumdar's Communist Party of India (Marxist-Leninist) moved to unite. Six of them, all but one from northeastern India, met on 19 May to establish the Communist Organization of India–Marxist-Leninist (COI–ML). The founders deliberately avoided calling themselves a party because they perceived elections as nothing more than a tactic to mobilize the people for the eventual revolution. The new organization opposed both the "individual terrorism" of the old CPI–ML and the "parliamentarism" of the two dominant Communist parties. It attacked China's efforts to build an anti-Soviet front with "U.S. imperialism"—a marked shift from the pro-Chinese orientation of its constituent units. However, the disappointment with recent Chinese foreign policy has not resulted in a counterbalancing pro-Soviet stance. The USSR is still attacked by most Marxist-Leninist groups as hegemonistic and revisionist (*Statesman*, 24 July). Kanyu Sanyal, leader of the largest constituent unit, became the COI–ML's general secretary.

Radical Maoist groups more in line with the old CPI–ML became more active in Andhra Pradesh, which, along with West Bengal, had been the center of radical communism in India. The government of Andhra Pradesh reportedly asked the federal government for troops to combat the growing danger of radical communism in the state. In 1985, the Indian press reported the death of 31 Maoists in a number of encounters with the police. Reacting to this surge in violence, the Andhra Pradesh government drafted preventive detention legislation modeled after the federal government's Terrorist and Disruptive Activities (Prevention) Act (*Times of India*, 8 October).

Walter K. Andersen
Arlington, Virginia

Indonesia

Population. 173,103,000 (*World Factbook*, May 1985)
Party. Indonesian Communist Party (Partai Komunis Indonesia; PKI)
Founded. 1920
Membership. 1,000–3,000 (estimated) in country (*World Factbook*, May 1985); 100–300 in exile
Secretary General. Pro-Moscow: Satiadjaya Sudiman; pro-Beijing: Jusuf Adjitorop
Leading Bodies. No data
Status. Illegal

Last Congress. Seventh Extraordinary, April 1962
Last Election. N/a
Front Organizations. None identifiable in Indonesia
Publications. None known in Indonesia

In 1985 the PKI celebrated some major anniversaries: 65 years since the founding of the Partai Komunis Indonesia (PKI), 40 since the establishment of the Republic of Indonesia, 30 since the Bandung Conference, and 20 since the abortive communist coup that led to the dismantling of the third largest Communist party in the world. A few party activists remained minimally visible abroad. The Indonesian government marked the anniversaries by executing several former top party leaders, dismissing some 1,700 oil workers for past ties to the party's trade union, and announcing a new campaign to selectively rehabilitate 1.7 million former Communists.

Leadership and Party Organization. Satiadjaya Sudiman, a top leader of the Communist Party of Indonesia, continued to be the most visible figure in the pro-Moscow wing. He participated in two international meetings sponsored by the *World Marxist Review* and contributed several articles to that journal during the year (see *WMR*, March, May, June, August, September).

Jusuf Adjitorop, long believed to be the leader of the pro-Beijing wing, emerged from the shadows to send condolences to the Albanian party on the death of its leader; he was identified as a member of the Politburo and secretary to the Central Committee (Albanian News Agency, 17 April; BBC, 17 April). He also signed, on behalf of the PKI, a protest condemning the execution of a former PKI leader in Indonesia. The protest appeared in the *Information Bulletin* (*IB*) of the *World Marxist Review*, not the usual outlet for statements by members of pro-Beijing Communist parties (*IB*, no. 16, p. 46).

Information about rank-and-file PKI members abroad remained fragmentary. The Indonesian Foreign Ministry said in mid-year that hundreds of PKI members lived in East European countries. On a visit to Sofia in July, the deputy speaker of the Indonesian Parliament, Harjantho Sumodisastro, appealed to the Bulgarian government to prevent Indonesian "communist remnants" living there from engaging in activities undermining the Indonesian state. An official trade mission to Eastern Europe and the USSR urged those governments not to allow any PKI members to represent Indonesia in any international meetings (Jakarta International Service, 25 July; *FBIS*, 31 July, 1 August; AFP, 1 August). Another Indonesian parliamentary leader, Dr. Suhardiman, said that young Indonesian communist cadres in Berlin continued to undermine the Indonesian government by discouraging foreign investment and preventing foreign tourists from traveling to Indonesia (*Sinar Harapan*, 13 August; *JPRS*, 12 September). After his visit to Eastern Europe, Deputy Speaker Harjantho said that some of those who had fled to socialist countries after the failed coup of 1965 were now "behaving well" by going to Indonesian embassies on 17 August to observe Indonesian independence day. In the USSR, Harjantho noted, there were seventeen such "well-behaved" former PKI members. The number of those still at large in socialist countries was unknown, but some had taken up permanent residence in bloc countries and others had been naturalized (*Merdeka*, 30 August; BBC, 13 September).

Information about the pro-Beijing wing of the party is equally murky. The vice-chairman of the parliamentary functional group faction, Dr. Suhardiman, stated that there are still 60 PKI figures in the People's Republic of China and their efforts to infiltrate into Indonesia are a serious threat (*Sinar Harapan*, 13 August; *JPRS*, 12 September). The Chinese foreign minister, Wu Xueqian, however, told reporters that the Chinese Communist Party (CCP) has had no more contacts with the PKI since the 1965 attempted coup and that China has pledged not to interfere in Indonesia's internal affairs, in line with the Bandung Principles adopted at the 1955 Asian-African Conference. Asked about PKI leaders still living in the PRC, Wu Xueqian replied: "In accordance with the PRC constitution, we allow them to stay in our country and during the last 18 years, some have died of old age, while certain others have gone to other countries" (*WP*, 26 April; *Sinar Harapan*, 24 April; BBC, 8 May). A few months later, the Indonesian foreign minister, Mochtar Kusumaatmadja, said that the PRC had confirmed that no more PKI members were hiding in China (AFP, 1 August; *FBIS*, 1 August).

There is no observable PKI organization inside Indonesia, although the Indonesian government clearly suspects that a party apparatus still remains.

Commenting on *Problems of Communism*'s identification of exiled PKI members in its March–April issue, a Jakarta broadcast called attention to party cadres who had not registered so as to have greater freedom of movement. "Those who are not in exile" must not be forgotten because it will take time for them to renounce their political beliefs after undergoing communist indoctrination for many years (BBC, 17 July). As for former or bona fide Communists in the country, the government estimates their number to be 1,459,107. There are 363 designated as "Category A," those who were involved in the rebellion; 34,718 as "Category B," those indirectly involved; and 1,424,026 as "Category C," those suspected of complicity. East Java had the highest number of detainees, 458,308, followed by Central Java with 289,750, and West Java with 218,221 (*Merdeka*, 8 June; BBC, 14 June).

In August the justice minister confirmed that Mohammed Munir, a PKI Central Committee member, had been executed in July with three other former PKI leaders. The latter three had been captured in Blitar while leading the last pocket of communist resistance. They were identified as Rustomo, former head of a PKI special bureau for East Java; Joko Untung, former head of PKI's agitprop department in East Java; and Gatot Sutarjo, also known as Gatot Lestario, former chairman of the PKI's Provisional Committee for East Java (Reuters, 19 August; *Jakarta Post*, 31 August; *JPRS*, 11, 30 September; AFP, 28 August). Two other former leaders who had been sentenced to life imprisonment, Marto Suwandi and Rewang, were released under a presidential amnesty on 17 August. Former Communists in Indonesia said that Ruslan Widjaya Sastra, head of the PKI after his five predecessors were captured or killed, and himself captured in 1968, was next in line for execution. International appeals for clemency then focused on appeals to the Indonesian government to spare his life (AFP, 30 August; *FBIS*, 30 August).

Domestic Party Affairs. The Indonesian government suspects that remnants of the PKI are seeking to re-establish the party apparatus and make common cause with other dissidents in the country. These fears were increased by calls for a united front in Indonesia issued by Satiadjaya Sudiman in the pages of *World Marxist Review*. In an article in March, "Bitter Fruits of a Capitalist Orientation," he identified "the most pressing task of the party as bringing about cooperation among all patriotic and anti-imperialist forces and the formation of a national unity front." While noting the unwillingness of some of the party's potential allies to cooperate with the PKI, he said that the party is rallying together Communists "including those who have extricated themselves from the meshes of Maoist policy" (*WMR*, March, p. 90).

In September Sudiman's article, "Taking Account of Past Experience," appeared. It described efforts to revive the party organization and referred to the many Communists prepared to continue the struggle who, "because of the divisive policy of the Maoists," are still outside the party. Sudiman wanted the party to appeal to "the national patriotic bourgeoisie, the intelligentsia, and, of course, the working people of town and countryside. These are the social groups that today constitute the foundation of the opposition actions, although often they are unfolding under the banner of Islam . . . which is legal throughout the country" (*WMR*, September, p. 51).

In late 1985 a presidential directive gave voting rights to Indonesian citizens involved in the abortive PKI coup if they could pass close scrutiny. Then came an announcement of a nationwide campaign to screen 1.7 million former Communists before the election (*Merdeka*, 10 September; BBC, 17 September; Reuters, 27 November). The 21,463 inmates of prisons all over Indonesia were to be freed or their sentences reduced (UPI, 18 August).

One of the more puzzling official actions was the simultaneous dismissal on 1 November of some 1,700 oil company employees with alleged past ties to Perbum, the long-banned, PKI-affiliated, oil workers' union. In May, the foreign and defense committee of parliament had recommended removing former PKI members from jobs in the oil and fertilizer industries because they posed a threat to strategic and vital projects. Armed forces commander General Murdani said at that time that those in low-level jobs did not have to be removed and there would be a thorough investigation before any steps were taken (AP, 28 May). In November, on the orders of the Security and Order Restoration Command (KOPKAMTIB), 960 workers were dismissed from the state-owned oil company, Pertamina, and 637 from Caltex Pacific, among others, and plans were announced for screening a number of other workers. Those dismissed, mostly blue-collar workers, were said to be former members, or relatives of former members, of Perbum. Most of the dismissed workers were men in their fifties with eighteen or more years of service in their jobs. No unrest was anticipated as a result of the firings because the companies provided the men with sizable amounts of severance pay, and state authorities had already tightened security (*Sinar Harapan*, 5 November; *FBIS*, 13 November; *WSJ*, 25 November; *Financial Times*, 6 November).

It was not clear why the government chose to remove the oil workers at that time. Interviewed in Australia, the foreign minister said the dismissals were a security problem, noting that "when things were better, perhaps they were not considered too dangerous" (Radio Australia, 14 December; BBC, 17 December). Some military officers were quoted as saying privately that KOPKAMTIB had always feared a union between the extreme left and radical Islam, and the dismissals were probably intended to weed out disgruntled Communists who could help Islamic extremists intent on sabotage of the vital oil industry (Reuters, 27 November). Executives of foreign oil companies expressed surprise that the government had waited nearly twenty years to order the alleged former Communist sympathizers fired, but there was speculation that the timing was linked to the 1987 parliamentary elections and the desire to eliminate potential troublemakers from vulnerable key industries. Other theories speculated that the move was a sweep against the left to balance the government's crackdown on Muslim extremists over the past year, or was due to fears that recently increased trade contacts with the PRC and the Soviet-bloc countries might allow agents to infiltrate the country in significant numbers (UPI, 5 November; *WSJ*, 25 November).

International Views, Positions, and Activities. Satiadjaya Sudiman took an active part in Prague at the Special Meeting of the *World Marxist Review* Editorial Council on the Fortieth Anniversary of the Victory over German Fascism and Japanese Militarism. He also participated in another international symposium under the same auspices, on "The Growing Role of the Developing Countries' Struggle for a New International Economic Order and the Communists" (*WMR*, June, p. 74). *World Marxist Review* published his vigorous condemnation of the executions of former PKI leaders (*WMR*, August, pp. 47–48).

Indonesia resumed direct trade ties with the PRC in 1985 and continued its expansion of diplomatic and trade links with countries of the Soviet bloc. President Suharto traveled to Romania and Hungary after his foreign minister's visit to Moscow in 1984 and a succession of visits by high-ranking Indonesians to Eastern Europe. In January, Foreign Minister Mokhtar said that normalization of trade relations with China should not be linked with the normalization of diplomatic relations, noting the disappointing results of Malaysia's efforts to persuade the CCP to sever relations with Communist rebels in Malaysia (Jakarta International Service, 30 January; BBC, 31 January). In May, he said normalization would have to be a gradual step-by-step process (Jakarta International Service, 30 April; *FBIS*, 2 May). General Murdani told parliament that the resumption of direct trade with China was not a threat to Indonesia's political, cultural, and economic system, although a few weeks earlier he had called on Indonesian citizens not to visit the PRC.

Many politicians reportedly criticized the resumption of direct trade, fearing China could use it to sow trouble in Indonesia. The head of the Indonesian Secret Service said that the crews of Chinese boats visiting Indonesia should be watched closely (*Merdeka*, 2 May; *FBIS*, 14, 30 May; AFP, 28 May). The directive governing the implementation of direct trade with China was signed by President Suharto on 24 July, and immediately thereafter a delegation of the Indonesian Chamber of Commerce (KADIN) was dispatched to China (AFP, 24 July; *FBIS*, 26 July). Later in the year, the National Defense Institute initiated seminars for private businessmen trading directly with Eastern-bloc countries and China to give them "a strong mental shield" against breaches of security. Major-General Subiakto, the institute's chairman, said the briefings and seminars, which included courses in the Indonesian national ideology, were intended to provide businessmen with sufficient armor to minimize the security risk to Indonesia of such trade (AFP, 11 December; *FBIS*, 12 December).

Chinese protests over the executions of former PKI leaders were somewhat belated. It was not until early September that a spokesman for the CCP expressed "deep regret at this inhuman act of the Indonesian authorities" (Xinhua, 2 September). Nevertheless, official Indonesian reaction took particular note of the CCP's protest. In general, the government viewed the numerous protest demonstrations abroad as evidence of communist activity and dispatched a parliamentary mission to convince the European Parliament to withdraw its resolution condemning the executions (*Antara*, 5 August; *JPRS*, 14 September). These protests, and especially that of the CCP, were cited by Dr. Suhardiman as the reason for having to issue a warning of infiltration of communist cadres into Indonesian agencies (*Indonesia Times*, 27 September; *FBIS*, 3 October).

The USSR made one of its rare attacks on the Indonesian government with a stinging editorial in *Pravda* condemning the execution of Mohammed Munir (*Pravda*, 12 June). The more typical Soviet statement was that of the visiting delegation headed by the deputy chairman of the USSR Council of Ministers, which reported that their talks had emphasized mutual respect for sovereignty and noninterference in each other's internal affairs (Moscow Domestic Service, 30 October; *FBIS*, 31 October). The year ended with an invitation to President Suharto to visit Moscow (Kyodo News Service, 7 December).

Jeanne S. Mintz
Washington, D.C.

Japan

Population. 120,691,000 (*Japan Times*, 31 July 1985)
Party. Japan Communist Party (Nihon Kyosanto; JCP)
Founded. 1922
Membership. 470,000 (*World Factbook*, 1985)
Central Committee Chairman. Kenji Miyamoto
Presidium Chairman. Tetsuzo Fuwa
Central Committee. 206 members
Status. Legal
Last Congress. Seventeenth, 19–25 November 1985
Last Election. December 1983, 9.43 percent, 14 of 252 in House of Councillors, 26 of 511 in House of Representatives
Auxiliary Organizations. All-Japan Student Federation, New Japan Women's Association, All-Japan Merchants' Federation, Democratic Foundation of Doctors, Japan Council of Students, Japan Peace Committee, Japan Council Against Hydrogen and Atomic Bombs
Publications. *Akahata* (Red banner), daily circulation 550,000, Sunday circulation 2,450,000, total readership, 3,000,000; *Zen'ei* (Vanguard), monthly theoretical journal; *Gekkan gakushu* (Education monthly), education and propaganda magazine; *Gikai to jichitai* (Parliament and self-government), monthly; *Bunka hyoron* (Culture review); *Sekai seiji shiryo* (International politics); *Gakusei shimbun* (Students' gazette), weekly

Party Leadership and Meetings. Kenji Miyamoto remained chairman of the Central Committee of the JCP and ranking member of the party as well as its spokesman on all major issues, in spite of his age (76 in 1985) and a brief period of hospitalization in June. His medical problem was described by the party as a benign throat polyp, and party officials said it did not constitute a health problem. Miyamoto had to be hospitalized a second time after surgery to remove the polyp, but he was active again within a few weeks (*Mainichi*, 29 June). Tetsuzo Fuwa continued to run many of the party's day-to-day activities as chairman of the Presidium.

Mitsuhiro Kaneko, chief of the Secretariat; Yoshinori Yoshioka, chairman of the Policy Commission; and Shoichi Ichikawa, director of the Party Organization Bureau, are some of the leaders of the JCP that constitute what may be called the "second echelon."

In January the JCP convened a meeting of prefectural and district committee chairpersons. At that meeting Miyamoto declared that it was the party's goal to expand its membership to 500,000—a goal that he had reiterated for a number of years. He said membership was "nearly 500,000." Miyamoto reported that only 30 percent of party members had read published reports in *Akahata*, the party newspaper, about decisions made at the last plenum. He expressed disappointment at this figure and suggested means to rectify the situation. He also set forth the party's "urgent tasks": prevention of nuclear war, the elimination of nuclear weapons, and rectifying the fall of living standards in Japan (see *Akahata*, 1 January 1985 for original statements about the "tasks").

The JCP held its Tenth Plenum (of the Sixteenth Central Committee) from 14 to 17 May at its headquarters in Tokyo. Central Committee chairman Miyamoto gave the opening address and reported on party policies and major issues. Reflecting the party's efforts to capitalize on antinuclear war and arms control sentiment and the fact that it was the fortieth anniversary of Hiroshima and Nagasaki, he gave major emphasis to the issue of nuclear weapons.

Miyamoto also detailed the party's strategy for the upcoming Tokyo metropolitan elections and discussed a conference on atomic and hydrogen weapons and work with trade unions, farmers, students, and other youth. He set a goal of 4 million *Akahata* readers. Readers, he said, had increased by 100,000 since April (but the number was probably not much, if any, larger than two or three years ago). "Consultation posts," Miyamoto said, were at a record high, distribution of the party's paper and pamphlets was becoming more efficient, and awareness of party decisions had increased (*Akahata*, 16 May). Miyamoto also spoke of relations with the Communist parties of the Soviet Union and the People's Republic of China, relations with Komeito (the Clean Government Party), party finances (which appeared to be down somewhat), and party building. He also announced that a party congress would be held in November.

The party convened its Eleventh Central Committee Plenum from 5 to 7 September. Miyamoto also addressed this meeting. He blamed the government for the Japan Airlines crash on 12 August that killed 520 people (including several JCP members), applauded the party for its success in the JCP-sponsored International Symposium held in June, and praised the work of the World Conference Against Atomic and Hydrogen Bombs. He credited the party with a victory in the Tokyo metropolitan and other local elections.

Miyamoto elaborated on the party stance on a number of domestic and international issues, relations with other political parties in Japan, and party work. He also announced "tasks" for the Seventeenth Party Congress. Presidium Chairman Fuwa proposed a draft resolution calling for a "month of mobilization" of all party members to strengthen the party prior to the congress.

From 19 to 24 November the JCP convened its Seventeenth Party Congress in Atami in Shizuoka prefecture. Miyamoto was re-elected as chairman of the Central Committee, Fuwa as chairman of the Presidium, and Kaneko as secretary general. In short, the top leadership remained unchanged. Shinichi Takahara, formerly head of the Finance and Business Bureau of the party, was elected vice-chairman of the Presidium, replacing Tomio Nishizawa (who had passed away). The Control Committee was increased in membership from eight to nineteen, "in order to promote party discipline." The Central Committee increased in size to 206 regular members plus alternates (Jiji Press, 25 November).

The party revised its platform for the third time since it was adopted in 1961. Revisions reflected the JCP's independent line, its advocacy of the total elimination of nuclear weapons, and its view that the Nakasone government is "leading the country down the path of militarism." Although the new platform in some ways toned down the JCP's opposition to "hegemonist acts of socialist countries" (because of better relations with Moscow), this tenet nevertheless remained part of the JCP's line. The JCP also held to its demand that the Soviet Union return the northern territories (small islands north of Hokkaido) to Japan (*Japan Times Weekly*, 7 December).

Notwithstanding anti-Soviet declarations in the revised platform, Moscow sent representatives to the Seventeenth JCP Congress, and relations seemed unaffected by events there. East Germany, Yugoslavia, and a number of other Communist parties were also represented at the meeting. In all, representatives from 27 foreign parties attended. A Kampuchean delegation had planned to attend, but was not granted visas because Kampuchea has no diplomatic ties with Japan.

The congress devoted considerable attention to

relations with other political parties in Japan, particularly the Japan Socialist Party (JSP). Miyamoto noted that relations with the JSP were at their "lowest ebb with no immediate prospects of a rapprochement." He alleged that the JSP's plan to form a coalition with the Nakasone government stood in the way of establishing a united front with the JCP. It was the first time that the JCP barred JSP reporters from a party congress (*Japan Times*, 7 December).

Chairman Fuwa reported on party membership and circulation of the *Akahata*. His use of the words "approaching the level of the last Congress" (in July 1982) suggests that both party membership and readership of *Akahata* may be below the 1982 estimates of 480,000 and 3 million (KDK Information, December).

Domestic Activities and Issues. The party's major issue during 1985, and the focus of much of its energies, was nuclear policy—banning nuclear weapons, nuclear protests, and opposition to the security policies of the Nakasone government. In their New Year's message, JCP leaders called for the elimination of nuclear weapons (*Japan Times*, 1 January). This emphasis can be explained by the party's long-held opposition to nuclear weapons, its reputation for antinuclear principles, and a perceived growth in public concern about nuclear war, combined with the government's efforts to increase the defense budget (at the request of the United States) and to participate in "star wars" research.

The JCP remained the only political party in Japan to oppose the U.S.-Japan Security Treaty. And it did so despite public opinion polls reflecting strong support for the treaty. The party took a strong position on defense spending, calling for decreases instead of increases (while around 75 percent of the public supported neither increases nor decreases). JCP leaders adamantly defended the "Three Non-Nuclear Principles" and charged that the Liberal Democratic Party (LDP) sought to ignore them. JCP leaders and party members in the Diet went on the attack whenever the issue of Japan's participation in research for the Strategic Defense Initiative arose. In this case, public opinion was on its side. The party's position was that SDI would be unnecessary if nuclear arms were banned (*Akahata*, 1 July). Noteworthy was the fact that the JCP's position differed from many other antiwar groups that advocated an equilibrium or a "freeze": the JCP preferred disarmament to arms control.

JCP antinuclear activities were not without problems, however. A JCP affiliate, the Japan Council Against Atomic and Hydrogen Bombs, experienced continued factionalism (or worse, a split) as a result of the purge or dismissal of two leaders of that organization by the JCP leadership. The Soviet-sponsored World Peace Council was involved in the dispute, although JCP officials denied that it forced or supported the split (*Akahata*, 2 March).

In October the JCP staged independent rallies throughout Japan on international antiwar day. At the rallies the JCP adopted resolutions against increased defense spending, the Anti-Espionage Bill, and nuclear weapons. It also called for the resignation of the Nakasone cabinet. In Tokyo the party and its affiliate organizations attracted a gathering of about 20,000—while the JSP and its associated groups attracted about ten times that number (Kyodo News Service, 22 October). In addition, the antinuclear movement seemed to be growing in large part outside party-supported organizations: a number of resolutions passed in local elections or referenda appeared to ignore the position of the JCP or any other political party (*FEER*, 18 April).

The JCP took a strong position on several other issues during 1985: the State Secrets Protection Law, the national budget, tax increases, and the breakup and privatization of the Japanese national railways. JCP leaders strongly opposed the State Secrets Protection Law on the basis that it violated individual civil rights and represented what the party called a "return of militarism" in Japan. The JCP did not oppose reducing taxes, but advocated tax relief at the lower level and "fairer" (increased) taxes for large corporations. The party charged that too much of the national budget was being devoted to defense spending and an insufficient amount was allocated to welfare, social services, and other domestic programs.

JCP leaders, however, could not agree with the other opposition parties in offering an alternative national budget. The JSP, the Democratic Socialist Party, Komeito, and the United Social Democratic Party agreed on a budget proposal and made coordinated budget proposals without JCP support. The JCP submitted separately its proposed budget, which included a tax cut and a $5.35 billion reduction in defense spending (Jiji Press, 22 February).

During the year the JCP's relations with other political parties remained strained and sometimes worsened due to rumors that the other parties might form a coalition with the LDP or form an opposition coalition that excluded the JCP. Relations with Komeito only showed signs of getting worse. In April Komeito's supporting organization, Soka

Gakkai (a Buddhist lay organization), was charged with wiretapping Chairman Miyamoto's home and was ordered to pay a solatium amounting to a little over $4,000 (Jiji Press, 23 April).

Elections. No national election was held in Japan in 1985. However, there were nationwide local elections, including the quadrennial Tokyo metropolitan election and elections for a number of city mayors.

The JCP won a small victory in the Tokyo metropolitan election, increasing its representation in the Tokyo Assembly from 16 to 19—while the JSP, the Democratic Socialist Party, and the New Liberal Club all lost seats. This placed the JCP in third position in terms of assembly representatives, after the LDP and Komeito—with 57 and 29 seats, respectively. At the same time, the JCP failed to join a coalition to elect the governor of Tokyo as it had done many times in the past (*FBIS*, 8 July). After the election—inasmuch as the JCP had not campaigned in cooperation with any other party—Presidium chairman Fuwa stated that the party had become the "real opposition party" in Japan. Miyamoto later said that the election reflected the people's disappointment in those parties that lost and was a good sign for the JCP, since the Tokyo election is generally regarded as a bellwether for future elections.

JCP candidates were also elected in Naha (the capital of Okinawa prefecture, where 50 percent of U.S. military bases are located) and Zushi (a city adjacent to the huge U.S. naval base at Yokosuka). In the Naha election the party won in cooperation with the Okinawa Socialist Mass Party, a local leftist party—defeating a candidate supported by the LDP in cooperation with other conservative parties (*World Marxist Review*, August).

The JCP lost but made a good showing in the mayoral race in Kyoto, where the party contested against the LDP, the Democratic Socialist Party, and Komeito. Miyamoto later claimed that "progressive forces" had made a "major gain" in Kyoto even though his party's candidate lost the election (*Akahata*, 9 September).

In July, Miyamoto declared that the party had suffered a decline, but that there were still 149 "progressive" local governments, where 32 million people live, in which the JCP was the ruling party (*Akahata*, 15 July). In September, Miyamoto reported that the JCP was represented in the National Diet by 41 representatives (just over 5 percent of the total), a number unchanged since 1983. He also stated that in local assemblies, despite an increase of 1.7 million votes in local elections and gains in the Tokyo Metropolitan Assembly, the increase in seats generally was less than losses due to deaths or other causes in recent years (*Akahata*, 9 September).

International Views and Activities. In July the JCP sponsored an international symposium on the "Struggle for Stopping Nuclear War and Realizing a Total Ban on and the Elimination of Nuclear Weapons." During this meeting 40 representatives of Communist and workers' parties from 27 nations participated. It was the fourth such meeting the JCP had sponsored since 1972. This gathering, however, was especially noteworthy in that it was the largest of the meetings. Previous meetings had been attended only by parties from capitalist countries; this time eight socialist (communist) countries were represented—including the Soviet Union.

Following four days of debate, participants agreed that the United States and its allies were mainly responsible for the nuclear arms race. However, the JCP also expressed the view that America's "opponent" was partly responsible. A Soviet delegate responded by charging this "supports U.S. imperialism and places the Soviet Union on par with the United States." This disagreement dampened the spirit of the conference and split delegates on an important issue. Meanwhile, the JCP failed to win much support for its view that efforts should be made in the direction of totally eliminating nuclear weapons (KDK Information, August).

The most salient change in the JCP's relations with other Communist parties and nations was its continued rapprochement with the Communist Party of the Soviet Union (CPSU) and a new and promising relationship with the Chinese Communist Party (CCP). It is, in fact, noteworthy that the JCP improved relations with both during the year. This can best be explained by the JCP's stance on nuclear weapons and the importance of the 1985 arms talks between the superpowers to both Moscow and Peking.

Better relations with the CPSU followed a partial rapprochement between the two in 1984. A week of talks were held in December 1984, after which a communiqué was issued by both parties. The communiqué, however, did not touch on the issues of Soviet "occupation" of Japanese territory, the Afghanistan invasion, Poland, or Czechoslovakia. Rather it simply called for a ban on nuclear weapons and pledges by all nations not to make a first-strike nuclear attack (see *YICA*, 1985 and 1984).

In March Presidium chairman Fuwa and Mitsuhiro Kaneko, chairman of the Secretariat, visited Moscow and conferred with General Secretary Gorbachev. The two sides discussed the December 1984 communiqué and reiterated their support for that agreement. Upon his return to Japan, Fuwa told reporters that he had invited a Soviet delegation to attend the international symposium and that Gorbachev proposed inviting a group of atomic bomb victims to the Soviet Union at some future time (*FBIS*, 18 March). The importance of the JCP visit was underscored by the fact that, besides the JCP, the Italian Communist Party was the only other nonruling party to have representatives received by the new General Secretary immediately after he assumed power.

Relations between the JCP and the CPSU continued to warm somewhat throughout the year, notwithstanding differences over nuclear weapons and the JCP's position on Soviet partial responsibility for the arms race. However, none of the really troublesome issues between the two were broached. In November Moscow dispatched a delegation, although not a high-level one, to attend the JCP's Seventeenth Party Congress.

In March the Chinese Communist Party announced that it was ready to restore relations with the JCP after nineteen years of strained relations. At the same time a CCP spokesman said that China respected the JCP for its activities on disarmament and spoke of the JCP as a "peaceloving party." He also said that the CCP had been restoring relations with Communist parties in other countries on the principle of "independence, equality, mutual respect, and nonintervention" (*FBIS*, 1 March).

In June Miyamoto said at a party meeting that there would be no "basic difficulties" in restoring relations between the two parties "if both sides stick to communist principles." He went on to say that his "communist principles" were "equivalent" to the CCP's "four principles" of peaceful coexistence, which have served as the basis for mending relations with a number of parties and nations. Miyamoto also said that he would not renew attacks on the CCP for its "hegemonistic interference" in JCP affairs during the Cultural Revolution. Some interpreted this to mean that Miyamoto had forgiven the CCP for those past actions (KDK Information, June). Shortly before, the chairman of the Chinese National People's Congress Standing Committee, Peng Zhen, visited Tokyo. At a press conference during the visit, he spoke of normalizing relations with the JCP, saying "Let's leave things connected with history to historians." He also asserted that he was "forward looking" regarding ties with the JCP (*Asahi*, 25 April).

The JCP, apparently responding to reunification efforts between the two Koreas, in April adopted a position in favor of establishing working relations with South Korea (*FBIS*, 3 April). Since 1977 JCP leaders had advocated working with the Seoul government to resolve fishing disputes and other problems, but it had never advocated direct contacts. Before the party's Seventeenth Congress JCP leaders publicly denounced the North Korean government for practicing a "barbaric form of hegemonism"—a response to North Korea's fatal shooting of a Japanese fisherman. It was the first time JCP leaders had advocated the incorporation of such a criticism of another Communist party in a resolution at a party congress (BBC, 13 November).

John F. Copper
Rhodes College

Kampuchea

Population. 6,249,000 (July 1985). Average annual growth rate is 2.1 percent.

Parties. Kampuchean (or Khmer) People's Revolutionary Party (KPRP); Party of Democratic Kampuchea (PDK)

Membership. KPRP: 7,500 (*FBIS*, 21 October 1985, p. E3); PDK: no data

Founded. The historical antecedent of both the KPRP and the PDK was the (Khmer) Kanapak Pracheachon (Khmer People's Party), founded in June 1951.

Secretary General. KPRP: Heng Samrin (b. 1934, former Khmer Rouge official and military commander); PDK: Pol Pot possibly still the dominant figure, in spite of his reported ill health and retirement.

Politburo. KPRP: 9 full and 2 candidate members—Heng Samrin (b. 1934, chairman, Council of State); Chea Sim (b. 1932, chairman, National Assembly; chairman, national council of the Kampuchean United Front for National Construction and Development); Hun Sen (b. 1951, chairman, Council of Ministers; prime minister; foreign minister; chairman, KPRP Foreign Relations Commission); Say Phuthong (b. 1925, Secretary, KPRP Central Committee; vice-chairman, Council of State; chairman, KPRP Central Control Commission); Bou Thong (b. 1938, minister of defense; vice-chairman, Council of Ministers); Chea Soth (b. 1928, minister of planning; vice-chairman, Council of Ministers); Men Sam-On* (b. 1953, chairwoman, KPRP Central Propaganda and Education Commission); Mat Ly* (b. 1925, vice-chairman, National Assembly; chairman, Kampuchean Federation of Trade Unions); Ney Pena* (first deputy minister of the interior); Chan Seng* (b. 1935, candidate member; secretary, Siem Reap-Oddar Meanchey provincial KPRP committee); Nguon Nhel* (candidate member; secretary, Phnom Penh municipal KPRP committee). PDK: no information available. *Indicates new members selected at the Fifth KPRP Party Congress in October 1985.

Secretariat. KPRP: Heng Samrin, chief; Hun Sen; Bou Thong; Men Sam-On; Ney Pena. PDK: no information available.

Control Commission of the Central Committee. KPRP: Say Phuthong, president; Chan Seng; Sim Ka; Men Sam-On; Say Chhum; Mean Sam-An; El Vansarat. PDK: No information available.

Central Committee. KPRP: 31 full and 14 candidate members—Bou Thong (b. 1938, minister of defense; vice-chairman, Council of Ministers); Chan Phin (minister of finance; minister for local and foreign trade); Chan Seng (b. 1935, secretary, Siem Reap-Oddar Meanchey provincial KPRP committee); Chay Sangyum (deputy chief, general staff of the Khmer People's Revolutionary Armed Forces [KPRAF]); Chea Chantho (candidate member); Chea Sim (b. 1932, chairman, National Assembly; chairman, national council of the Kampuchean United Front for National Construction and Defense); Chea Soth (b. 1928, minister of planning; vice-chairman, Council of Ministers); Chhay Than (candidate member; vice-minister of finance); Chheng Phon (b. 1934, candidate member; minister of information and culture); El Vansarat (vice-chairman, general political department of the KPRAF); Heng Samkai (secretary, Svay Rieng provincial KPRP committee); Heng Samrin (b. 1934, chairman, Council of State); Ho Nan (female; deputy minister, cabinet of the Council of Ministers); Hul Savoan (commander of the KPRAF fourth military region); Hun Neng (candidate member; secretary, Kompong Cham provincial KPRP committee); Hun Sen (b. 1951, chairman, Council of Ministers; prime minister; foreign minister; chairman, KPRP Foreign Relations Commission); Keo Kimyan (secretary, Battambang provincial KPRP committee); Kham Len (candidate member); Khoy Khunhuor (secretary, Preah Vihear provincial KPRP committee); Kim Yin (director general, Voice of the Cambodian People Radio); Kong Korm (b. 1951, first deputy foreign minister); Koy Buntha (b. 1952); Lak On (female; secretary, Ratanakiri provincial KPRP committee); Lim Thi (candidate member; secretary, Kandal provincial KPRP committee); Mat Ly (b. 1925, vice-chairman, National Assembly; chairman, Kampuchean Federation of Trade Unions); Mean Sam-An (female; b. 1956, chairwoman, Association of Revolutionary Women of Kampuchea); Men Sam-On (female; b. 1953, chairwoman, KPRP Central Propaganda and Education Commission); Neou Sam On (candidate member; vice-chairman, KPRP Central Organization Commission; chairman, Cambodian-Laotian Friendship Association); Ney Pena (first deputy minister of the interior); Nguon Nhel (secretary, Phnom Penh municipal KPRP committee); Pen Navuth (candidate member; minister of eduation); Rongphlam Kaysone; Ros Chhum (candidate member; deputy minister of planning); Sam Sarit (candidate member; representative, rubber plantation workers); Sam Sundoeun (b. 1951, chairman, Association of Revolutionary Youth of Kampuchea; member, commission for cultural and social affairs of the National Assembly); Sar Kheng (chief of cabinet, KPRP central committee); Say Chhum (secretary, Kompong Speu provincial KPRP committee; member, KPRP Central Control Commission); Say Phuthong (b. 1925, vice-chairman, Council of State; chairman, KPRP Central Control Commission; secretary, KPRP central committee); Say Siphon (candidate member; vice-chairman, Cambodian Federation of Trade Unions); Sim Ka (minister for control of state affairs); Som Kim Suor (female; b. 1949, editor-in-chief, *Pracheachon* semiweekly); Som Sopha (candidate member); Tea Banh (b. 1945, candidate member; minister of communications, transportation, and post); Thong Khon (candidate member; mayor of Phnom Penh); Yos Son (chairman, foreign relations commission of the KPRP central committee). PDK: no information available.

Status. The KPRP is the sole authorized political party in all areas of Kampuchea controlled by the regime in Phnom Penh. As in other Marxist states, party and government are synonymous, and KPRP leaders concurrently serve as key officials in the governing apparatus of the People's Republic of Kampuchea (PRK). The PDK is the renamed Kampuchean (or Khmer) Communist Party (KCP), the political instrumentality of the Khmer Rouge (KR), who governed Kampuchea (Cambodia) harshly from April 1975 until December 1978, when they were driven from power by the Vietnamese invasion. The KCP ostensibly was dissolved in December 1981 to make way for the KR to join in a common front with the Khmer People's National Liberation Front (KPNLF) of Son Sann and the FUNCINPEC (Front uni national pour un Cambodge indépendant, neutre, pacifique et coopératif [National United Front for an Independent, Neutral, Peaceful, and Cooperative Cambodia]) of Prince Sihanouk to oppose the continuing Vietnamese occupation of Cambodia. The KR (as represented by the PDK) remains the dominant partner in this tripartite anti-Vietnamese front, which took the name of the Coalition Government of Democratic Kampuchea (CGDK) in mid-1982. PDK authority, however, extends only to the refugee and insurgent camps that the party controls along the Thai border.

Last Congress. KPRP: The Fifth Party Congress was held in Phnom Penh on 13–16 October 1985. It was attended by 250 delegates from 22 subordinate party committees representing the provinces, municipalities, and armed forces of the PRK. The previous (Fourth) congress, attended by 162 delegates, was held in May 1981. PDK: The Third and last party congress was in Phnom Penh on 14 December 1975.

Last Election. KPRP: The last election held was for the National Assembly of the PRK in May 1981. It was single-party KPRP contest, unchallenged by any political opposition. Of 148 candidates running for office, 117 were elected. PDK: The last election held was for the People's Representational Assembly of Democratic Kampuchea on 20 March 1976. One hundred and fifty peasants, 50 workers, and 50 soldiers were elected to the body.

Auxiliary Organizations. KPRP: Cambodian Federation of Trade Unions (80,000 members); Association of Revolutionary Women of Kampuchea (1.3 million members); Association of Revolutionary Youth of Kampuchea (70,000 members); Kampuchean United Front for National Construction and Defense (KUFNCD), formerly called the Kampuchean National United Front for National Salvation (KNUFNS); PDK: no information available

Publications. KPRP: *Pracheachon* (People), semiweekly of the KPRP Central Committee, editor-in-chief Som Kim Suor; *Kongtap Padevoat*, weekly of the Khmer People's Revolutionary Armed Forces; *Phnom Penh*, weekly of the Phnom Penh municipal KPRP committee; *Kampuchea*, weekly of the KUFNCD. The official news agency is SPK (Sar-Pordamean Kampuchea), acting director Sum Mean.

Domestic Party Affairs. *KPRP.* The landmark party event of 1985 was the Fifth KPRP Congress, held in Phnom Penh in October. The event was attended by 250 participants from party committees in the provinces, cities, and armed forces (*FBIS*, 22 October, p. H4). The conference set forth a number of tasks to lend greater impetus to "the Cambodian revolution's advance." These tasks were defined as defending Cambodian independence, rebuilding the nation, improving the quality of life, and promoting community development within the context of socialism. The tasks, the congress determined, could be accomplished if the party and armed forces strove to put into practice the resolutions adopted by the delegates (ibid., p. H5). The conference in its closing sessions also adopted Kampuchea's first five-year plan, revised party statutes, and announced the new composition of the Politburo and Central Committee. The Politburo contained three new appointees; the Central Committee was enlarged from 20 to 45 full and candidate members. Of the 31 full members, 12 were new appointees and 5 were promoted from the list of candidate members announced in late 1984 (*FEER*, 31 October, p. 42). Heng Samrin was retained as general secretary of the party.

PDK. Little information is available; party dynamics are concealed from outsiders. Factional disagreements have been hinted at by the defection of several senior PDK personalities, who reportedly left the party because of its ideological rigidity (*Bangkok Post*, 8 August, p. 4; *JPRS*, *Southeast Asia* [*SEA*]-85-146, 25 September, p. 132).

Military Issues. *KPRP.* The Khmer People's Revolutionary Armed Forces (KPRAF) is the military instrument of the nation and the party, and numbers about 30,000 to 35,000 personnel. It consists of the regular army, the regional forces, and the militia. The regular army comprises about five understrength divisions (including the 4th, 196th, and 286th) and three independent brigades. Three of the divisions are deployed in blocking positions at Battambang City, Sisophon, and Treng in Battambang Province in western Cambodia (*Indochina Report*, October 1984, p. 6; *Asian Defense Journal*, August, p. 112).

Party activity in the KPRAF has aimed at building up membership in all units. In late 1984, KPRP goals were to establish a party committee in each regiment of the regional forces, and a party cell or chapter in each battalion and company at district level (*FBIS*, 30 October 1984, p. H6). By mid-1985, the KPRAF reported that a number of its regional force battalions in the districts had indeed been able to form such chapters. There was also a hint that for KPRAF personnel, membership in the KPRP might not be entirely voluntary, as cadres at all echelons were urged to spot capable military individuals and induct them expeditiously into the party (*JPRS-SEA*-85-104, 2 July, p. 69).

PDK. With the retirement of Pol Pot, the Supreme Military Commission of the NADK was reportedly disbanded, and Pol Pot himself was replaced as armed forces commander by Son Sen. At present, observers rate the NADK as the most effective guerrilla force opposing the KPRAF and the Vietnamese People's Army in Cambodia. It has about 35,000 combatants and maintains its forces separately from those of its noncommunist partners in the CGDK coalition.

Auxiliary/Front Organizations. *KPRP.* The KUFNCD concluded its fourth plenum early in the year. The conference, attended by 236 delegates, reported sharp increases in membership in the KPRP's auxiliary/front organizations. KUFNCD enrollees were reported to have risen to 100,000 from 20,000 in 1983; the youth organizations to 70,000 from 50,000 two years previously; while the Federation of Trade Union membership grew 43 percent during the same period. The Association of Revolutionary Women of Kampuchea was reported, perhaps overoptimistically, to have 1.3 million members (*Indochina Chronology*, January–March, p. 11). The KPRP considers the auxiliary/front organizations to be the breeding ground where future party cadres will be spotted, assessed, and trained for future leadership positions.

PDK. No data is available on auxiliary/front organizations. A delegation of "Democratic Kampuchean Youths" was reported to have attended an international conference in Beijing. No mention was made of the name or membership of their organization.

International Issues. *KPRP.* The presence of Vietnamese advisers in Cambodia is ubiquitous. They number about 12,000 personnel exclusive of Hanoi's military forces in the country. On the national level, there is a Vietnamese advisory mission headquarters of 600 experts accredited to Cambodia. This mission has an inner core codenamed "Cuc B" that is subdivided into an "A50" office concerned with Phnom Penh, and an "A40" office concerned with the remainder of the country. "Cuc B" and the overall Vietnamese advisory mission are reportedly subject to the Central Kampuchean Affairs Commission of the Vietnamese Communist Party (VCP) Central Committee. VCP Politburo member Le Duc Tho allegedly supervises the work of "Cuc B" with the assistance of fellow VCP Politburo member Vo Chi Cong (*Indochina Report*, October 1984, p 5).

Vietnamese advisers officially are assigned to the KPRP, but in actuality work to influence the PRK government apparatus and to make certain that Khmer officials do not diverge from the directives of Hanoi. Below the national level, Hanoi's advisory cadres are found at the province, district, and subdistrict level. They also visit Cambodian units of production and strategic hamlets (ibid., p. 6).

Because of the dominating influence of the VCP on both the KPRP and the PRK, neither the party nor the Phnom Penh government is free to pursue an independent foreign policy. KPRP and PRK pronouncements on international issues are identical to those uttered by Hanoi, which in turn echo those emanating from Moscow. The KPRP lends rhetorical support to the Soviet Union, routinely denounces China in terms identical to those heard from Hanoi, and occasionally remembers to censure the United States on specific issues such as the Strategic Defense Initiative. Soviet relations with the Phnom Penh government and the KPRP are cordial. Soviet aid is now channeled directly to the PRK, usually going through the port of Kompong Som, without recourse to Vietnam as intermediary. Delegations from the USSR and its allies prominently attended the KPRP Fifth Congress in October.

The United States does not recognize the PRK on the grounds that it was put in place by an invading Vietnamese army. However, two U.S. congressional delegations (led by Congressmen G. V. "Sonny" Montgomery and Stephen J. Solarz) visited Phnom Penh in December 1984 and held talks with KPRP and PRK officials.

PDK. The major international mentor of the PDK is China, with whom the now disbanded KCP maintained cordial relations for nearly two decades. Present Chinese involvement with the PDK is continuous, and is a function of China's fear of encirclement by the Soviet Union and its allies. Beijing is the principal supplier of armaments to the NADK in its guerrilla war against the Vietnamese. It has pushed the PDK into a fragile coalition with the noncommunist KPNLF and FUNCINPEC, and has exacted military reprisals along the Sino-Vietnamese border when Hanoi's troops have gone on the offensive in Cambodia.

The United States has eschewed any contact with the PDK, although it generally supports the KPNLF and FUNCINPEC components of the CGDK. The participation of the PDK in this coalition has precluded the global isolation that would otherwise have resulted, had the party chosen to go it alone internationally. The CGDK continues to hold Cambodia's seat in the United Nations, and is recognized by a small number of Third World countries. During the year, PDK leaders such as Khieu (Ieng) Thirith, the wife of Ieng Sary, made several trips abroad, including visits to Kenya and Japan, to gain for the CGDK (and the PDK) increased international respectability.

Russell R. Ross
Library of Congress

Korea: Democratic People's Republic of Korea

Population. 20,082,000
Party. Korean Workers' Party (Choson Nodong-dang; KWP)
Founded. 1949
Membership. 3,000,000
General Secretary. Kim Il-song
Presidium of the Politburo. 3 members: Kim Il-song (DPRK president), Kim Chong-il (Kim Il-song's son and designated successor), O Chin-u (minister of People's Armed Forces)
Politburo. 17 full members: Kim Il-song, Kim Chong-il, O Chin-u, Kang Song-san (DPRK premier), Pak Song-chol (DPRK vice-president), Yim Chun-chu (DPRK vice-president), Yi Chong-ok (DPRK vice-president), So Chol, Kim Yong-nam (DPRK deputy premier and foreign affairs minister), Ho Tam, Yon Hyong-muk (DPRK first deputy premier and chairman of the Metal and Machine Industry Commission), O Kuk-yol, Chon Mun-sop, Choe Yong-nim, Kim Hwan, Paek Hak-im, So Yun-sok; 15 alternate members: An Sung-hak (deputy premier and chairman of the Chemical and Light Industry Commission), Chon Pyong-ho, Kim Chung-nin, Kong Chin-tae, Chong Chun-ki (deputy premier), Hong Song-yong (deputy premier), Cho Se-ung, Kim Pok-sin (deputy premier and chairman of the Foreign Trade Commission), Hyun Mu-kwang (deputy premier and chairman of the Construction and Building Material Industry Commission), Kim Tu-nam, Choe Kwang (deputy premier), Yi Kun-mo, Kang Hui-won, Chong Kyong-hui, Kim Kwang-hwan
Secretariat. 9 members: Kim Il-song, Kim Chong-il, Ho Tam, Hwang Chang-yop, Ho Chong-suk, So Kwang-hui, Chae Hui-chong, Pak Nam-ki, Kim Chung-nin
Central Committee. 145 full and 103 alternate members
Status. Ruling party
Last Congress. Sixth, 10–15 October 1980, in Pyongyang
Last Election. 1982, 100 percent, all 615 candidates for the Supreme People's Assembly approved by the KWP beforehand
Subordinate and Auxiliary Organizations. Korean Social Democratic Party, Young Friends' Party of the Chondogyo Sect, General Federation of Trade Unions of Korea (2,000,000 members), League of Socialist Working Youth of Korea (2,700,000 members), Union of Agricultural Working People of Korea, Korean Democratic Women's Union, General Federation of the Unions of Literature and Arts of Korea, General Federation of Korean Workers in Industry and Technology, Korean Committee for Solidarity with the World People, Committee for the Peaceful Reunification of the Fatherland, United Democratic Fatherland Front (united front organization), Korean Writers' Union
Publications. *Nodong Sinmun* (Workers' daily), KWP daily; *Kulloja* (Workers), KWP monthly; *Minchu Choson* (Democratic Korea), organ of the Supreme People's Assembly and the cabinet; *Choson Inminkun Sinmun* (Korean People's Army news). English-language publications are the *Pyongyang Times*, *People's Korea*, and *Korea Today*, all weeklies. The Korean Central News Agency (KCNA) is the official news agency.

Leadership and Organization. As the cult of Kim Il-song and his family members (especially his son and heir-designate, Chong-il) continued unabated in 1985, the DPRK regime reiterated its official line that "Kim Il-songism" is eternal, to be carried into the next generation by the junior Kim. Great efforts were made to endow him with the stature of his father.

On 15 April the Pyongyang regime celebrated Kim Il-song's seventy-third birthday by holding various events throughout the country. One of the biggest events was the Spring Festival (the entire month of April), in which 50 foreign art troupes from five continents participated.

Two weeks before this birthday celebration, North Korea staged another round in the Kim Il-song cult campaign by holding a public rally in Pyongyang to celebrate the publication of the thousandth book written by the DPRK leader. The *Pyongyang Times*, North Korea's official English-language paper, reported on 8 May in a front-page article (titled "Great Leader President Kim Il-song's Works Abroad") that the DPRK regime had hitherto published 27 million volumes of "Kim Il-song works" in numerous foreign languages.

The 7 January issue of KWP organ *Nodong Sinmun* called upon all members of the party to renew their determination to spare no efforts to treasure and protect Kim Chong-il as the "heart of the party." As part of the ongoing campaign for "Learning Comrade Kim Chong-il's Virtue," according to North Korean radio broadcasts on 31 May, all party members were engaged in reading sessions, panel discussions, and seminars to study the junior Kim's speeches, writings, and instructions given on various occasions in the past.

Prince Norodom Sihanouk, a longtime friend of Kim Il-song, who spends each spring in Pyongyang in a traditional-style Korean palace built for him by the senior Kim, told journalists in Beijing on 9 July about the junior Kim's role: "He is now leading the country." "He deals with the party, army and other organizations that are building the country," the prince said. He described Kim Chong-il as "a good successor to his father but more mysterious" (Beijing, AFP, 9 July).

In mid-July President Kim Il-song for the first time used the phrase "Kim Chong-il era," indicating that his son's succession to power was an established fact. The senior Kim's remarks were heard on a radio program of the North Korean government-run Central Broadcasting Station (KBCS) on 12 July, which reproduced a full text of his written answers on 9 July to questions put to him by Japanese monthly magazine *Sekai* (World). (For the full text of Kim's remarks to Japan's *Sekai*, see *FBIS*, Asia and Pacific, 15 July, pp. D4–D17.)

During 1985 the following high-ranking party-government figures died: Yi Chae-hwa (60), alternate member of the Sixth KWP Central Committee; Yi Chong-nok (57), member of the Sixth KWP Central Committee and first deputy foreign affairs minister; Kim Tu-yong (72), member of the Sixth KWP Central Committee; Pak Im-tae (63), alternate member of the Sixth KWP Central Committee and former chairman of the Land and City Management Commission; and Chang Yun-pil (69), member of the Sixth KWP Central Committee and chairman of the Union of Agricultural Working People of Korea.

In late February Kim Chung-nin, alternate member of the party Politburo, who was removed from the party Secretariat and demoted from regular to alternate Politburo member on 14 February 1984, was reappointed secretary of the Party Central Committee.

In early April Party Secretary Hwang Chang-yop was transferred to a post responsible for international affairs in the party Secretariat, replacing Kim Yong-sun, who had held the position since February 1984 and disappeared from the public scene in September 1984. Before this new post, Hwang had been the secretary in charge of ideological affairs since 1980.

On 13 April, two days before his seventy-third birthday, Kim Il-song promoted a number of military generals to higher ranks through a decree issued by the Central People's Committee. Singled out for a special promotion was Armed Forces Minister O Chin-u, who had been a four-star general for a long time. O was given the title of vice marshal, militarily second only to Marshal Kim Il-song. Among those who were promoted to the rank of general (four-star general) from senior general (three-star general) were: O Kuk-yol (general chief of staff of the People's Armed Forces), Paek Hak-im (vice minister of People's Armed Forces), Kim Tu-nam (member of the Military Committee of the KWP Central Committee), Yi Ul-sol (member of the Military Committee of the KWP Central Committee), Chu To-il (member of the Military Committee of the KWP Central Committee), Kim Pong-yol (vice minister of People's Armed Forces), Kim Kwang-chin (artillery commander), and Yi Tu-ik (member of the Military Committee of the KWP Central Committee).

On the same day the Order of Kim Il-song was awarded to 28 leading personnel of the party, state, economic, and cultural organs and commanding cadres of the Korean People's Army. Among them were An Sung-hak, Chae Hui-chong, Pak Nam-ki, Kim Kwang-chin, Kang Sun-hui, Choe Chong-kun, Yi Yong-su and Chon Se-pong.

In early July Pak Su-tong replaced Pyon Chang-pok as chairman of the Union of Agricultural Working People of Korea; Yi Cha-pang became chairman of the State Science and Technology Commission, replacing Choe Chae-wu; and Kim Song-ku was appointed to head the Chemical Industry Ministry, replacing Maeng Tae-ho. In mid-August General Kim Kwang-chin was appointed vice-minister of the People's Armed Forces.

At a joint meeting of the KWP Politburo and the Central People's Committee, held on 31 September, Yon Hyong-muk was named first deputy premier of the State Administration Council, replacing Choe Yong-nim, and An Sung-hak was appointed deputy premier and chairman of the Light Industry Commission, replacing Kim Pok-sin. Paek Hak-im became minister of public security, replacing Yi Chol-pong. Kim Pok-sin was named chairman of the Foreign Trade Commission, retaining the deputy premiership. He replaced Kong Chin-tae, who became chairman of the People's Service Commission after being relieved from the posts of deputy premier and chairman of the Foreign Trade Commission. Choe Yong-nim and Kim Kwan were released from the office of deputy premier and given other duties, but the DPRK regime did not disclose what the "other duties" were.

On 19 November the DPRK reorganized the State Administration Council, which controls the agencies responsible for industrial development, and added a new deputy premier to the cabinet (Hyon Mu-kwang; thereby bringing the number of deputy premiers to nine). The reshuffle came during a joint meeting of the KWP Politburo and the Central People's Committee. The joint meeting organized the Commission of Metal and Machine Industry by merging the Ministries of Metal Industry, First Machine Industry, and Second Machine Industry; created the Commission of Chemical and Light Industry by merging the Commission of Light Industry and the Ministry of Chemical Industry; established the Commission of Construction and Building Material Industry by merging the Ministries of Construction and the Building Material Industry; set up the Commission of Extractive Industry by merging the Ministries of Mine Industry, Coal Industry, and Resource Development; and established the Commission of Transportation by merging the Ministry of Railways and the Ministry of Land and Sea Transportation.

The joint meeting made the following appointments: Yon Hyon-muk, first deputy premier and chairman of the Commission of Metal and Machine Industry; An Sung-hak, deputy premier and chairman of the Commission of Chemical and Light Industry; Hyon Mu-kwang, deputy premier and chairman of the Commission of Construction and Building Material Industry; Hong Si-hak, chairman of the Commission of Extractive Industry; Yi Kil-song, chairman of the Commission of Transportation; Kim Yun-sang, chairman of the Commission of Fisheries; Yi Chi-chan, chairman of the Commission of Power Industry; and Yi Chong-yul, minister of Public Health. Yi Yong-ik became general secretary of the Central People's Committee.

Domestic Attitudes and Activities. Kim Il-song's New Year message neither touched on the results of the second seven-year economic plan (1978–1984) nor presented a new economic plan for the coming year. In previous New Year messages, he had discussed the various economic programs. Instead, Kim concentrated on Pyongyang's policy toward South Korea and the Third World. He considered the "tripartite talks" of Washington, Seoul, and Pyongyang more important than the inter-Korean talks that began during the latter part of 1984.

As for Pyongyang's policy toward the Third World, Kim Il-song said that "south-south cooperation" would be the key policy of North Korea in 1985, recalling the fact that North Korea in 1984 helped many African countries to increase their agricultural production.

On 16 February the Central Statistical Bureau announced the results of the second seven-year economic plan (for the details of this report, see *FBIS*, Asia and Pacific, 22 February, pp. D1–D7). The announcement claimed that the gross industrial product of North Korea had increased 2.2 times over 1977. The announcement only presented figures to represent the growth rate in major industrial sectors since 1977. Remarkable increases were made, especially in mining and the metal-industrial sectors. Other achievements disclosed in the announcement were the attainment of the ten-million-ton goal for grain production set for 1984, the twofold increase over 1977 in the capacity to produce electric power, an increase of 230 percent in the machinery industry, and the electrification of more than 1,500 kilometers of railways.

Kim Il-song hinted on 29 June that there would be a third seven-year economic plan. Probably as part of its preparation for this new plan, the North Korean cabinet in November reorganized its economic industries as described above.

Radio Pyongyang said on 27 February that North Korea had started building a 46-story hotel in its capital city with Compenon Bernard Construction Company of France. Gilbert Simonet, president of the French construction company, attended a ground-breaking ceremony on 26 February. The construction was the first such project to be carried out under the new joint-venture law adopted by the DPRK government in September 1984. North Korea was reported by Radio Beijing on 12 December to have established joint-venture relations in 1985 with several Western countries in the sectors of hydroelectricity, nonferrous metals, light industry, and the service industry.

Toward the end of 1985, Pyongyang intensified its campaign to spur workers to redouble their production efforts in order to attain the economic goals for 1985. An editorial in *Nodong Sinmun* on 19 November, entitled "Mobilizing All Possible Means to Achieve the Target of the 1985 Economic Plan," said that all officials in charge of economic affairs should make the utmost effort to solve the problems that hindered attainment of the target. The editorial emphasized mining, electric power, the metal production industries, and railway transportation, saying that the fulfillment of this year's target was dependent mainly upon success in these fields.

On 24 February North Koreans throughout the country flocked to the polls to elect people's assemblies for cities, provinces, and counties. A total of 26,793 nominees were elected to the local assemblies, an increase of 2,231 delegates over the previous assemblies.

North Korea on 9 April fixed its budget for fiscal 1985 at 27,383,600,000 *won* (in North Korean currency), or an equivalent of $11.6 billion, representing an increase of 4.1 percent in revenues over the previous year and a 4.7 percent rise in spending. The budgetary action came during the three-day fourth session of the Seventh Supreme People's Assembly, which opened on 9 April in Pyongyang. The DPRK government did not disclose the percentages for various fields such as the people's economy, social welfare, and the military in relation to the total outlay.

Relations with South Korea. North Korea's relations with South Korea remained basically hostile during 1985, although this year saw the most active dialogue between Pyongyang and Seoul during their 40 years of division.

With the approach of the scheduled dates of several inter-Korean talks in 1985, Pyongyang had intensified its anti-Seoul propaganda campaign. The KCBS reported on 8 August that the "Revolutionary Party for Reunification" (RPR), which North Korea claims is operating underground in South Korea, was renamed the "Korean National Democratic Front" in a move to "support more effectively the South Korean people's antigovernment struggle." The anti-Seoul propaganda radio station, the "Voice of the Revolutionary Party for Reunification," was also renamed the "Voice of National Salvation," the KCBS said.

On 22 October an armed North Korean spy boat sailed into South Korean territorial waters off Pusan and was sunk by South Korean naval ships.

During 1985 North and South Korea continued their dialogue on such issues as economic cooperation, family reunions, joint sports ventures, and legal matters. Four rounds of economic talks, three full-dress Red Cross meetings, two preliminary meetings to discuss the possibility of holding parliamentary talks, and one round of sports talks were held at Panmunjom.

In the fall of 1985 both Pyongyang and Seoul denied rumors that an unprecedented face-to-face meeting was being arranged between South Korean president Chun Doo-hwan and North Korean leader Kim Il-song. Japan's *Yomiuri Shimbun* reported in mid-September that a senior member of the KWP Politburo, Ho Tam, was believed to have secretly visited Seoul in early September to discuss such a top-level encounter. South Korea's intelligence chief, Chang Se-dong, was rumored to have secretly traveled to Pyongyang on a similar mission in mid-September.

The North-South economic talks were held four times—on 17 May, 20 June, 18 September, and 20 November.

At the 17 May meeting (second round), which lasted almost two hours, North Korean chief delegate Yi Sung-nok proposed the establishment of a high-level joint committee for economic cooperation, to be headed by deputy prime ministers from the two sides. Under his plan, seven subcommittees would handle such areas as resource development, commodity trade, and banking. Yi expressed hope that the committee could hold its first meeting in Pyongyang in September.

South Korean chief delegate Kim Ki-hwan, however, stressed immediate work on specific tasks. He mentioned the opening of ports to each other's vessels, restoration of a North-South rail line, and creation of a joint fishing ground. Working-level meetings on the rail line should be held within a month, he said. As a first step toward trade, the South Korean chief delegate said that the South was ready to purchase 300,000 tons of anthracite coal from the North this year. South Korea has almost no energy resources of its own. The North Koreans, however, refused to discuss the South Koreans' proposal and reiterated their desire for formation of a joint committee.

During the third round of the inter-Korean economic talks held on 20 June at Panmunjom, both sides agreed in principle to study the problem of setting up a North-South joint economic cooperation committee that would be co-chaired by deputy prime minister–level officials. This agreement came after the two sides exchanged draft agreements.

North and South Korea failed to make any progress at the fourth round of economic talks held on 18 September at Panmunjom. The two sides fell short of adopting an agreement on trade and economic cooperation and the establishment of a Joint Economic Cooperation Committee. The sides only exchanged revised draft agreements without making any detailed discussions of previously agreed items on the agenda.

Major differences surfaced over how to conduct negotiations for an agreement concerning exchange of materials, economic cooperation, and the establishment of the joint committee. The Pyongyang side insisted that negotiations on the agreement be handed over to working-level officials and the main conference be permanently terminated. But the Seoul delegation proposed that the discussions on major agenda items be held during the main conference and other minor procedural matters be handled at working-level meetings.

North and South Korean delegates met on 20 November at Panmunjom for the fifth round of the inter-Korean economic talks only to agree to meet again in the same place on 20 January 1986.

The Red Cross meetings between Pyongyang and Seoul were held on 27–30 May in Seoul (eighth full-dress since July 1973), 15–19 July at Panmunjom (working-level), 22 August at Panmunjom (working-level), 26–28 August in Pyongyang (ninth full-dress), and 3–4 December in Seoul (tenth full-dress). These meetings dealt with the reunion of millions of families in both Koreas that were separated by the 1950–1953 Korean War.

North and South Korean Red Cross officials on 30 May reached a dramatic agreement to exchange "hometown visiting groups" (i.e., visits by separated family relatives) and folk-art troupes around 15 August, the fortieth anniversary of national liberation from Japanese colonial rule. The 15–19 July Red Cross meeting, however, failed to settle details such as the size of both the hometown visiting groups and the art troupes, the timing of their visits, or the sites of the visits.

A meeting of Red Cross officials from the two Koreas held at Panmunjom on 22 August agreed on three points: (1) each side's group would comprise 151 members, consisting of 50 hometown visitors, a 50-member folk-art troupe, 30 press men, and 21 supporting personnel; (2) visits would be restricted to Seoul and Pyongyang; and (3) the visits would take place from 20 to 23 September. Both sides also agreed that the visiting groups would be led by the heads of the North and South Korean Red Cross societies and that a two-hour-long art performance would be held on 21 and 22 September, simultaneously in Seoul and in Pyongyang.

Red Cross delegates from North and South Korea, each consisting of 84 members, held the ninth full-dress inter-Korean Red Cross talks in Pyongyang on 26 August. Two sessions were held on 27 and 28 August. The sessions ended only with an agreement to hold the next (tenth) full-dress talks in Seoul in early December.

On 20–23 September the two sides sent their hometown visiting groups and art troupes to Seoul and Pyongyang for the first time since the territorial division of Korea in 1945. Through this hometown visit, some members of separated families, though they were only a handful of the ten million families separated since the Korean War, were reunited briefly and tearfully.

The Seoul side, during the tenth full-dress Red Cross meeting held in Seoul on 3–4 December, proposed that hometown visiting groups be exchanged again, but the Pyongyang side rejected the idea. However, the next Red Cross meeting slated for February 1986 in Pyongyang was to take up the matter.

On 9 April Pyongyang proposed a joint meeting of parliamentarians of the two Koreas to discuss such inter-Korean political issues as a declaration of nonaggression by both sides and the withdrawal of U.S. forces from South Korea. The DPRK proposal was countered by Seoul on 3 June when the South Korean National Assembly proposed that five lawmakers from each side meet in Panmunjom sometime in July to talk about the creation of an interparliamentary committee to write a constitution for a unified Korea.

A preliminary meeting to arrange for inter-Korean parliamentary talks was held on 23 July at Panmunjom with five delegates each from Seoul and Pyongyang attending. The meeting failed to agree on an agenda for the forthcoming full-dress talks. The preliminary meeting produced no substantial results and ended with an agreement concerning only procedural matters: the next meeting would be held on 25 September and a direct telephone line would be installed between Seoul and Pyongyang.

Parliamentary delegates from the two Koreas on 25 September sat together in a second preliminary meeting at Panmunjom. At this meeting, the two sides again failed to narrow the difference in their views. The Pyongyang side again insisted on discussing the issue of a nonaggression declaration while rejecting the Seoul side's suggestion that the inter-Korean parliamentary talks should deal with the writing of a constitution for a unified Korea.

During 1985, finally, Pyongyang and Seoul met once in Switzerland to discuss joint activities in connection with the 1988 Olympics.

Ever since Seoul was chosen in 1981 as the site of the 1988 Olympics, Pyongyang had persistently waged a propaganda campaign to foil the Seoul Games, saying that Seoul was not an adequate place for hosting the Olympics. The Pyongyang regime had claimed that "a warlike atmosphere" prevailed in South Korea and that "the venture should be relocated in order to avoid boycotts by socialist countries." On 24 April 1985, furthermore, the North Korean vice–foreign affairs minister, Chon Yong-chin, said that his country would not participate in the 1988 Olympics in Seoul because its attendance would be exploited to perpetuate the separation of the divided Korean peninsula.

On 30 July Pyongyang abruptly came up with a new proposal, namely, that the 1988 Seoul Olympics should be jointly hosted by both Koreas. This proposal was announced in a special statement issued in the name of North Korean Deputy Premier Chong Chun-ki. Chong said that he made the proposal "in order to save the Olympic movement from the danger of a breakup." He said in the proposal that "if the Olympic games were to be held exclusively in one part of the divided country, socialist countries as well as nonaligned countries would boycott the games." Pyongyang's proposal also included the forming of a single team representing the two Koreas.

Pyongyang's proposal was immediately rejected by the International Olympic Committee (IOC) president, Juan Antonio Samaranch. A news dispatch from Moscow (30 July) indicated that Samaranch, during a meeting with the North Korean sports minister in Moscow, emphasized his intention to respect the Olympic charter. Samaranch reportedly rejected Pyongyang's idea that a part of the games should be organized in North Korea. Both Samaranch and the DPRK sports minister were visiting Moscow on the occasion of the twelfth annual youth festival being held there. On the same day, in Lausanne, Switzerland, IOC spokeswoman Michele Verdier was reported to have said that the games had been awarded to the South Korean Olympic Committee (NOC) under the IOC charter, specifying that all events would take place in the territory over which the NOC had jurisdiction. She was quoted as saying that if the games were to be shared with North Korea, the rules would have to be changed by a two-thirds majority of the 91-member IOC.

After the IOC position was made clear by these two officials, the DPRK continued to assert that its proposal to co-host the Seoul Olympics was most realistic. *Nodong Sinmun* on 1 August carried a special article supporting the proposal.

Delegations of the North and South Korean National Olympic Committees held talks in Lausanne from 8 to 9 October to find a way to establish a cooperative sports relationship in connection with the 1988 Olympics. The talks, sponsored by Samaranch, were held in the IOC's office in Lausanne.

The talks were deadlocked from the very beginning. North Korean chief delegate Kim Yu-sin demanded that the title of the Seoul Games should be changed to the Pyongyang-Seoul Olympics, and that all the events including the opening and closing ceremonies should be shared equally by North and South Korea. He also demanded that the telecast proceeds be shared fifty-fifty. Kim warned that Seoul would face a massive boycott by the communist countries if the games were not distributed equally across the border of the divided Korean peninsula.

Kim Chong-ha, president of the South Korean Olympic Committee, rejected Pyongyang's proposal for co-hosting the games but offered a conciliatory proposal suggesting that a few of the preliminary contests might be organized in the North Korean zone. IOC President Samaranch also reportedly suggested that such events as the volleyball and basketball preliminaries could be conducted in the North. But North Korea's Kim Yong-su disregarded this suggestion and persisted in advancing Pyongyang's proposal for co-hosting the games. The two sides agreed to meet again in Lausanne in early January 1986.

International Views and Positions. As in previous years, Pyongyang's diplomacy concentrated on the promotion of friendly relations with the nonaligned Third World. The DPRK's exchanges of visits with the outside world, aside from the Soviet Union and China, were mainly with countries on the African continent. For example, the following African heads of state visited North Korea at the invitation of Kim Il-song: Tanzanian president Julius K. Nyerere (22 August), Zimbabwean prime minister Robert G. Mugabe (28 August), Madagascan president Didier Ratsiraka (5 October), and Ethiopian president Mengistu Haile-Mariam (10 November).

According to Radio Pyongyang (6 December), African countries such as Tanzania, Guinea, Ghana, Benin, Zambia, the Central African Republic, Mozambique, Burundi, Rwanda, Bourkina Faso, and Lesotho were among the major clients of Pyongyang's aid program. Pyongyang's aid to these countries included agricultural programs, construction of pump factories and irrigation facilities, and other small-scale projects of a similar kind. North Korea has operated agricultural research centers under various names including the *Chuch'e* (Kim Il-song's ideology, meaning "self-identity" or "national identity") Agricultural Science Institutes and the Kimilsong Agricultural Research Centers. Pyongyang also operates propaganda organizations like the *Chuch'e* Idea Research Centers, the *Chuch'e* Idea Study Groups, and the Kimilsongism-Kimchongilism Research Centers. The number of such organizations was reported by the DPRK news media to have totaled 1,500 in more than 100 countries by the end of 1985.

On 23 January the DPRK established the International Training Center for Journalists in Pyongyang to foster pro–North Korean views and opinions in the Third World and to export *Chuch'e* ideology to the nonaligned, developing countries. The KCBS reported on 11 May that the opening ceremony of the first-term "International Journalist Training Course" was held on the same day at the same center. It also reported that the course was attended by more than twenty invited journalists from Asian and African countries.

On 9 January North Korea established diplomatic relations with the Ivory Coast. This action brought to 105 the number of countries with which the DPRK had established diplomatic relations. (Since 1961, the Ivory Coast has also maintained diplomatic ties with South Korea.)

Grenada severed diplomatic relations with North Korea on 24 January.

The Soviet Union and China. It became apparent during 1985 that Pyongyang has tilted toward Moscow and away from Beijing. Official exchanges between Pyongyang and Moscow were more frequent than those between Pyongyang and Beijing.

Pyongyang and Moscow grew closer, particularly in military relations. In April the Soviet Union started supplying North Korea with the MiG-23 fighter planes that Pyongyang had long requested. The DPRK will receive from 45 to 50 MiG-23 fighters by the end of 1985 (*FEER*, 26 September, 5 December; Tokyo, *Sankei Shimbun*, 7 October, 26 December). Several squadrons of Soviet air defense fighters and a small naval detachment, led by Vice-Admiral Nikolai Yasakov, first deputy commander of the Soviet Pacific Fleet, made highly publicized visits to North Korea in May and August. During 1985, Soviet military planes flew over North Korean air space en route to their military bases in Cam Ranh Bay in Vietnam—instead of flying down the Korean Straits between Korea and Japan, where the Japanese military had been monitoring the movements of Soviet aircraft and warships.

North Korean ports now receive Soviet ships. Radio Moscow on 24 October reported that Soviet ships in 1984 alone made 170 calls to North Korean ports and that Soviet use of these ports has increased. The Soviet Union's Far Eastern Maritime Company has shipped its cargo not only through

Najin, but also through Chongjin, Wonsan, and Hungnam on the east coast as well as Nampo and Haeju on the west coast of North Korea. In recent years the cargo handled at the Najin port alone amounted to about 600,000 tons annually. Since 1975 Najin port near the DPRK-USSR border has been used as a transit port for Soviet cargo bound for Vietnam.

North Korea and the Soviet Union signed two protocols in Moscow during 1985: one for scientific and technological cooperation between Pyongyang and Moscow for 1986–1990 (2 October); and another for developing trade and economic cooperation for 1986–1990 (24 December).

Pyongyang's political attitude toward Moscow has also changed. In an unprecedented gesture, Kim Il-song attended a banquet at the Soviet embassy in Pyongyang on 22 May to mark the first anniversary of Kim's Moscow visit. The DPRK leader reportedly had never visited a foreign mission in Pyongyang, except for brief calls to pay his condolences when heads of states died.

Through various mass rallies, especially those for the 15 August Liberation Day celebration, the DPRK regime openly lauded the role that the Soviet Union had played in 1945 in liberating the country from Japanese colonial rule. In August the DPRK media specifically called the Soviet Union the "liberator," a term not used for more than two decades. The North Korean people had been taught through the propaganda programs that Kim Il-song had played a decisive role in the liberation.

More than twenty Soviet missions visited Pyongyang between 10 and 17 August to participate in the anniversary celebration of North Korea's liberation. The Kremlin sent senior Politburo member Geidar Aliev to Pyongyang along with a high-level military delegation headed by the Soviet first deputy defense minister, Marshal V. I. Petrov. During a celebration banquet, Aliev was said to have offered a toast to Kim Chong-il, indicating that Moscow implicitly recognized Pyongyang's hereditary succession scheme.

From 16 to 23 April the DPRK deputy premier and foreign affairs minister, Kim Yong-nam, made an official visit to Moscow at the invitation of the Soviet government. During his stay Kim met with new Soviet leader Mikhail Gorbachev and Foreign Minister Andrei Gromyko. On 17 April North Korea and the Soviet Union concluded two (border and consular) agreements in Moscow. A Radio Pyongyang broadcast said on 19 April that Gorbachev had asked Kim to convey his "heartful regards to the respectable comrade Kim Il-song and the respectable comrade Kim Chong-il."

On 11 September the new Soviet foreign minister, Eduard Shevardnadze, met with Kim Yongnam, his North Korean counterpart, who stopped over in Moscow in his return from the eighth Ministerial Meeting of Nonaligned Nations held in Angola. Shevardnadze accepted an invitation to pay an official visit to the DPRK in early January 1986.

On 23 December North Korean Premier Kang Song-san visited Moscow at the invitation of the Soviet government. On 25 December Mikhail Gorbachev held talks with Kang at the Kremlin. Official Soviet news agency Tass gave no details of the discussions, but said that the talks covered bilateral and international questions, including Asian security.

Kang invited N. I. Ryzhkov, member of the Politburo of the CPSU and chairman of the Soviet Council of Ministers, to pay an official goodwill visit to Pyongyang at a time he thought fit. Ryzhkov apparently accepted this invitation.

China has publicly reacted to the new Pyongyang-Moscow relations with a nonchalance bordering on passivity. On 11 September a Foreign Ministry spokesman not only endorsed the improvement in Soviet–North Korean relations, but described these developments as part of Pyongyang's effort (like that of China) to develop an independent foreign policy and broaden contacts with the outside world (*WP*, 12 September). It was extremely doubtful that all Chinese officials held such a sanguine view. Some specialists on Chinese affairs believed that the Chinese were concerned about the Soviets' recently strengthened ties with North Korea and were putting the best face possible on a delicate or awkward situation. If this analysis was correct, Beijing's equanimity masked underlying anxieties about the long-term prospects for Sino–North Korean relations.

In 1985 China sent a string of delegations to Pyongyang, the most important of which was led by Beijing's rising star, Vice-Premier Li Peng. Despite Pyongyang's policy of leaning closer to Moscow, there was no sign of a basic change in the DPRK's policy of maintaining balanced relations with the two major communist powers. Indications were that North Korea remained basically friendly with China.

On 12 January a DPRK government economic mission, led by Deputy Premier Kong Chin-tae, visited China. In an hour-long talk with the visiting North Korean deputy premier on 16 January, Chinese Communist Party leader Hu Yaobang reassured the North Korean mission that the Beijing government and the Chinese people would "continue to render internationalist assistance to the DPRK within our ability." On 17 January North Korea and China concluded an agreement in Beijing to promote China's economic aid to Pyongyang. Kong thanked China for its assistance.

General Secretary Hu Yaobang made a three-day visit to North Korea from 4 to 6 May for talks with Kim Il-song and his son. Both Radio Beijing and North Korea's KCBS simultaneously said on 7 May that the visit was made at the invitation of President Kim and that both sides met at the North Korean border town of Sinuiju to discuss "important matters of mutual concern." It was reported that the two sides held three rounds of talks that lasted nearly nine hours.

The details of the talks were not revealed by either Beijing or Pyongyang. The KCBS reported on 7 May that both sides shared "identical views" on everything discussed. After returning to Beijing, Hu said: "I spoke and agreed with President Kim Il-song on a wide range of issues." According to a report from Japan's Kyodo News Service agency in Beijing on 9 May, Hu expressed China's willingness to host a direct meeting between North Korean and U.S. officials in Beijing.

Both North Korea and China marked the twenty-fourth anniversary (11 July) of the signing of the treaty of friendship, cooperation, and mutual assistance between the two countries by simultaneously holding mass rallies and diplomatic receptions.

In October Pyongyang invited more than a dozen delegations from China to mark the thirty-fifth anniversary (25 October) of Chinese participation in the Korean War. A large-scale Chinese party-government mission, led by Deputy Premier Li Peng, made a four-day official visit to North Korea to join in Pyongyang's celebration of the anniversary. Li stressed in his speech at a mass rally that the "blood relationship" between the two countries would last forever. Medals of honor were conferred on Li and other members of the Chinese party-government mission.

Japan. On 1 January Japan lifted the official sanctions it had imposed against North Korea fourteen months previously to protest the October 1983 terrorist bombing in Rangoon, Burma, that killed seventeen South Korean officials. As of New Year's Day, Japanese government officials were allowed to travel to North Korea and DPRK officials were permitted entry to Japan. Also lifted were a ban on contact between Japanese and North Korean diplomats and a ban on charter flights between Tokyo and Pyongyang. (There are no scheduled flights linking the two cities, and Japan and North Korea have no formal diplomatic relations.)

A mission of the KWP organ *Nodong Sinmun*, led by chief editor Kim Ki-nam, arrived in Tokyo on 18 April for an eight-day visit at the invitation of the Japan Socialist Party (JSP). In his meeting with the JSP leader (Chairman Masashi Ishibashi), Kim delivered President Kim Il-song's personal message and appealed for the JSP's support of Pyongyang's recent proposal for an inter-Korean parliamentary conference. (The North Korean mission received entry permits from the Japanese authorities on the condition that it would refrain from political activities during its stay in Japan.)

On 5 June a North Korean goodwill delegation, led by Kim U-chong, head of the DPRK-Japan Goodwill and Friendship Association, arrived in Tokyo at the invitation of the suprapartisan Dietmen's League for Promotion of Japan-DPRK Friendship. This delegation stayed ten days in Tokyo to hold talks with senior Diet (parliament) members of the ruling Liberal Democratic Party, as well as other Diet members, and to tour factories. (Kim U-chong is also a member of the Supreme People's Assembly, Pyongyang's parliament.)

Kim told a news conference shortly before his departure for Pyongyang that he had stressed in talks with his Japanese hosts that the two countries "should increase personal exchanges, particularly of politicians" in order to promote bilateral relations. He said that his delegation and the Dietmen's League for Promotion of Japan-DPRK Friendship had reached basic agreement that their countries should establish trade representative offices in each other's capitals and promote a "wide range" of personal exchanges. But he hastened to add that negotiations and guarantees at the government level would be necessary to facilitate these plans.

On 12 June, meanwhile, Japanese prime minister Yasuhiro Nakasone told a South Korean press corps at his official residence that his government would never negotiate unilaterally with North Korea in disregard for the intentions of the Seoul government.

A delegation of the Japan Socialist Party, led by Chief Secretary Makoto Tanabe, made a five-day visit to Pyongyang from 21 to 25 May at the invitation of the KWP. The delegation met DPRK leaders, including Kim Il-song. Pyongyang did not reveal the details of the talks except that it asked the JSP to support the North Korean position concerning the inter-Korean problem. (On 17 December, incidentally, the KWP expressed its appreciation to the JSP for supporting Pyongyang in its policies toward the Korean peninsula.)

The Korean Central News Agency said on 18 February that the Nakwon (Paradise) Department Store, which was jointly established by North Korean and Japanese firms, had opened in Pyongyang a day earlier. The store, which sells textiles, clothes, furniture, musical instruments, and foodstuffs, represented a joint venture of the DPRK-controlled Nakwon Trading Company and the Asahi Company Ltd. of Japan.

On 10 September Den Kawakatsu, chairman and president of Japan's Nankai Electric Railway Company, flew into Pyongyang for business talks at the invitation of Yi Song-nok, deputy foreign trade minister and concurrently chairman of DPRK-Asia Trade Promotion Association. In an interview in Beijing on 17 September after his return from Pyongyang, Kawakatsu said that while he was in North Korea, he and Deputy Trade Minister Yi had signed a memorandum calling for joint efforts to effect a variety of joint ventures in trade, economic, and technical fields, based on mutual equality.

The Japan Communist Party (JCP) severely criticized North Korea's ruling Communist party for practicing the cult of personality and "a barbaric form of hegemonism." The criticism came in a draft resolution that was adopted at the JCP's Seventeenth Party Congress, which started on 19 November. In the attack against the KWP, the JCP referred to the fatal shooting of a Japanese fisherman by a North Korean patrol boat in the East Sea last year. The party also said that it resolutely rejected the hegemonist attitude, in which "-ism" was added to the name of the state leader.

The United States. As an annual event since 1960, mass rallies have taken place to "swear revenge against the United States imperialists." In 1985 these rallies were held as a prelude to the start of the "Month for Anti-U.S. Joint Struggle," which stretched from 25 June (the day the Korean War began in 1950) to 27 July (the day the armistice agreement was signed in 1953).

The North Korean media quickly reacted to President Reagan's remarks linking the DPRK (along with Iran, Libya, Nicaragua, and Cuba) with an international terrorist network. *Nodong Sinmun* said on 10 July: "It is ridiculous to call us a terrorist state, for we are only engaged in a struggle against the imperialists, especially against the United States. We are only maintaining a progressive policy in an effort to support revolutionary movements in developing countries."

On 12 September *Nodong Sinmun* denied a report from Washington that said that North Korea might possibly possess chemical weapons. The report was made by the *Washington Post*, which on 9 September revealed that four major countries—the United States, the Soviet Union, France, and Iraq—were believed to possess chemical weapons, and that eleven others, including North Korea, might possibly have access to them.

The *New York Times* on 8 October carried a full-page advertisement for Kim Chong-il. The pro-Pyongyang General Association of Korean Residents in Japan placed this $33,000 advertisement praising the junior Kim.

The so-called cross-recognition of South and North Korea—the recognition of Seoul by the Soviet Union and China and of Pyongyang by the United States and Japan—was the "ultimate goal" of U.S. policy as applied to the Korean peninsula, a ranking U.S. official said on 29 April. The official, who requested anonymity, made the remark while briefing reporters on the Reagan-Chun summit in Washington in late April.

Gaston Sigur, a U.S. National Security Council adviser, said in Tokyo on 14 May that the United States firmly upheld Seoul's position on the Korean question: i.e., that the best way to reduce tensions on the Korean peninsula was through direct contacts between South and North Korea. He added that the U.S. government would never respond to any Pyongyang proposal for expanded negotiations such as the so-called tripartite talks involving Seoul, Pyongyang, and Washington, "unless substantial progress was made in direct inter-Korean dialogue."

The United States for the first time granted visas to three scholars from North Korea, who were invited to attend a nongovernmental academic conference on Asian studies at the George Washington University from 25 to 27 October. The three North Korean scholars were Choi Chin-hyok, chief of the Institute of History in the Academy of Social Sciences, Kim Chang-il, the institute's senior researcher, and Kang Ki-su, its public relations officer.

The U.S. Commerce Department said on 2 February that it had evidence that a West German businessman had illegally shipped to North Korea as many as 82 Hughes helicopters with potential military applications (*NYT*, 4 February). Theodore Wu, deputy assistant secretary for export enforcement of the Commerce Department, added that the transaction involved enough helicopters "to support a large-sized force like a regiment."

The United Nations. The Pyongyang regime in 1985 named Pak Kil-yon the North Korean ambassador to United Nations Headquarters in New York. He replaced Han Si-hae, who had held the post since November 1977.

North Korea accepted a UN invitation for representatives of observer countries to address the upcoming fortieth anniversary session of the UN General Assembly in October. On 17 October DPRK vice-president Pak Song-chul was in New York as a special envoy of President Kim Il-song. (Kim Yong-nam, deputy premier and foreign affairs minister, was also there.) Pak told a commemorative session of the UN General Assembly that separate UN membership for the two Koreas would "only lead to fixity of the division" of the Korean peninsula. "It is our stand that Korea's membership in the United Nations is not an issue of top priority today," Pak said. "Should Korea enter the United Nations, she has to enter the organization under the single name of one state, at least after the realization of north-south confederation."

On 23 October South Korea's prime minister, Lho Shin-yong, and Vice-President Pak met briefly at a diplomatic dinner given by Prime Minister Rajiv Gandhi of India. The two men briefly discussed the situation on the Korean peninsula, according to the South's semiofficial Yonhap News Agency.

Tai Sung An
Washington College

Laos

Population. 3,584,803 (1985 census)
Party. Lao People's Revolutionary Party (Phak Pasason Pativat Lao; LPRP)
Founded. 22 March 1955
Membership. More than 42,000
General Secretary. Kaysone Phomvihane (premier)
Politburo. 7 members: Kaysone Phomvihane, Nouhak Phoumsavan, Souphanouvong (president), Phoumi Vongvichit, Khamtai Siphandon, Phoun Sipaseut, Sisomphon Lovansai
Secretariat. 9 members: Kaysone Phomvihane, Nouhak Phoumsavan, Khamtai Siphandon, Phoun Sipaseut, Sisomphon Lovansai, Sali Vongkhamsao, Sisavat Keobounphan, Samon Vi-gnaket, Maichantan Sengmani
Central Committee. 47 full members, 6 alternate members (for names, see *FBIS*, 30 April 1982)
Status. Ruling and only legal party
Last Congress. Third, 27–30 April 1982, in Vientiane
Last Election. 1975, all 46 candidates were LPRP approved
Auxiliary Organizations. Lao Front for National Construction (LFNC)

Publications. *Pasason* (The people), LPRP central organ, published in Vientiane (daily). *Alun Mai* (New dawn), LPRP theoretical journal, published in Vientiane (quarterly) since March, 1,000 circulation (Radio Vientiane, 12, 13, 18 April; *FBIS*, 15, 22, 26 April). The official news agency is Khaosan Pathet Lao (Pathet Lao News Agency; KPL), established 6 January 1967.

The Lao People's Democratic Republic (LPDR) carried out a population census in March 1985. The LPDR observed a number of important anniversaries during 1985—the thirtieth anniversary of the founding of the LPRP (22 March), the twenty-fifth anniversary of diplomatic ties with the Soviet Union (7 October), and the tenth anniversary of the establishment of the LPDR (2 December). A new development since 1984 has been the appearance of articles in the Soviet press taking note of the "special relationship" among the LPDR, the People's Republic of Kampuchea, and the Socialist Republic of Vietnam (SRV)—and the steadily increasing economic integration of the three countries.

Leadership and Party Organization. No significant changes in LPRP leadership were revealed during 1985.

Domestic Party Affairs. LPRP general secretary Kaysone Phomvihane, in an article in *Nhan Dan*, claimed that the LPRP has doubled its membership since 1976 (Vietnam News Agency, 3 December; *FBIS*, 5 December). Although no new figure was revealed, Kaysone himself, in an article published earlier in the year, stated that at the time of its Second Congress in December 1972, the LPRP had 21,000 members (Vietnam News Agency, 22 March; *FBIS*, 27 March), meaning that the current total must be in excess of 42,000.

An LPRP Central Committee directive, issued on 9 April, reorganized party-military relations within the Lao People's Army. The directive spoke of introducing the single commander system, downgrading the political commissar. The new organization appeared to be similar to that used in the SRV and the Soviet Union (Radio Vientiane, 9 April; *FBIS*, 18 April).

In an important article published on the founding anniversary of the LPRP, Kaysone reviewed 30 years of the party's struggle for national independence and socialism. Writing in the Vietnamese Communist Party theoretical journal, *Tap Chi Cong San* (Kaysone is fluent in Vietnamese), he stressed the party's solidarity with, first, the Vietnamese party and, second, the CPSU. China, on the other hand, was portrayed as the past and present enemy of the Lao revolution.

Kaysone characterized the LPRP in the following manner: "The party has correctly applied Marxism-Leninism to the specific conditions of the Lao revolution, selectively learning from the experience of fraternal parties to inspire and organize the whole people to make their best efforts so that, in coordination with the strength of the militant alliance of the three Indochinese countries and international assistance and support, they can successfully fulfill the tasks of the Lao revolution, and contribute to the revolution in Indochina and the world as a whole" (VNA, 22 March; *FBIS*, 27 March).

In terms of historical interest, the article made it clear that in the view of the LPRP leadership, the decisive step on the road to victory was the signing of the Vientiane Agreement on 21 February 1973. That agreement provided for the establishment of the third coalition government in independent Laos's history and led to the "neutralization" of the towns of Vientiane and Luang Prabang. "That victory," Kaysone wrote, "marked the fundamental change in the balance of force, creating favorable conditions for achieving complete victory for the national democratic revolution in Laos" (ibid.).

Initial results of the national population census carried out in the first seven days in March were announced at a press conference in Vientiane on 15 June by Sali Vongkhamsao, chairman of the Central Population Census Guidance Committee. These results included a breakdown by male and female and by each of the sixteen provinces and Vientiane municipality (Radio Vientiane, 15 June; *FBIS*, 20 June). A further round of results was promised for the future.

The tenth anniversary celebrations on 2 December were held in a low key, with emphasis on the military, including a parade. Invitations were not extended to non-bloc journalists. Among the invited foreign dignitaries present were Le Duan (representing the VCP), Heng Samrin (the Kampuchean People's Revolutionary Party), and Yakov Petrovich Ryabov (CPSU). The anniversary provided the occasion for several interviews reviewing the accomplishments of the LPDR in various fields.

President Souphanouvong, in an interview with VNA, claimed that illiteracy had been eradicated throughout Laos by the end of 1984 (VNA, 30 November; *FBIS*, 2 December). Rice production had risen to the basic self-sufficiency level, with production amounting to 380 kg. per capita in 1985. The agricultural sector included 3,184 cooperatives, comprising nearly 50 percent of all farming families and more than 50 percent of the total farmed area. There were 45 state-run farms, and thousands of mutual aid teams had been formed, Souphanouvong said. Since 1975, 135 irrigation projects had been built or reinforced, he added.

Kaysone, in his speech on the occasion, gave a rundown of accomplishments in the economic and foreign relations areas (Radio Vientiane, 2 December; *FBIS*, 4 December).

Auxiliary Organizations. The LFNC, the party's principal mass-mobilization organization, was seldom in the news during 1985. This fact may have been connected with the preparations for the population census, which was the responsibility of another government committee.

International Views, Positions, and Activities. There were no marked changes in 1985 in the LPDR's foreign relations. General tendencies were continuing adherence to Hanoi's worldview, a spate of fulsome praise of the Soviet Union (for which the twenty-fifth anniversary of diplomatic relations provided a convenient reason), and some slight rapprochement with the United States (again, a development that was not inconsistent with Hanoi's interests).

The "special relationship" among the LPDR, the People's Republic of Kampuchea, and the SRV was prominently featured in the LPDR press and, increasingly, abroad. An editorial in the party organ *Pasason* on 23 February drew attention to the historic significance of the summit conference of leaders of the three countries that had been held in Vientiane on 22–23 February 1983 and the "various important agreements reached at the meeting" (Radio Vientiane, 23 February; *FBIS*, 11 March).

The significance of the 1983 summit conference was also underlined in an article by VCP Central Committee member Dang Thi, titled "On the Economic and Cultural Cooperation Among the Three Indochinese Countries in the New Stage" (*Tap Chi Cong San*, May; *FBIS*, 13 May). The conference, it said, marked a "new development in the relations among the three countries."

With respect to what contributions Laos might make to closer economic integration, and what form of contributions it might receive, the article argued that Laos possessed land, forests, and minerals, but, being landlocked, transport and communications were "hampered by great difficulties." Therefore scarcities existed.

The article made the interesting point that the meaning of coordinated economic strategies and planning would be manifest in the fact that "Here, national interests and international interests are woven so closely together that it is impossible to tell what is being done to assist fraternal countries and what is being done for ourselves. In this relationship, it is impossible to determine which country has to rely on the others, for all three countries must depend on one another."

For the first time, serious Soviet commentary on the issue of integrating these three countries appeared. The Soviets stressed the benefits that such a development will bring to Laos, the least developed of the three. Although considerable lip service is paid to the historic leadership provided by the Indochinese Communist Party and its successors, Vietnam's role as the chief initiator of economic integration is played down.

Writing under the title "Development of Cooperation Among the Countries of Indochina," M. Isayev and I. Ognetov noted, "The growing unity and close cooperation between the Marxist-Leninist parties of these countries—the CPV, the LPRP, and the KPRP—which exchange opinions on how to deal with the outstanding tasks in domestic and foreign policy, is the key factor contributing to the cohesion of the three countries of Indochina" (*Far Eastern Affairs* (Moscow), no. 4, 1984, p. 52). These same authors praise the role of the Communist International in promoting the "formation and activities of the Indochinese Communist Party."

The LPDR's relations with the People's Republic of China continued in 1985 to be formally correct, but at a low level of dialogue and representation. Kaysone's references to China in his 2 December speech were noticeably more moderate than in his *Tap Chi Cong San* article. In the latter, he accused the PRC of having "committed direct acts of sabotage against the Lao revolution" and claimed that at the time of the PRC's limited attack against the SRV in 1979 "the Chinese disguised as 'road builders' were ousted" from Laos. He also categorized the PRC as the enemy: "The direct and most dangerous enemy of the three countries' revolutions at this new stage is Chinese big-nation expansionism, which is colluding with the U.S. imperialists and other ultra-rightist reactionary forces to oppose the revolutions of the three Indochinese countries—a main obstacle to China's scheme of conquering all of Southeast Asia."

These are statements that Kaysone as party leader can permit himself to make to an audience composed of Vietnamese party functionaries, and they may well reflect his own beliefs. However, independent sources maintain that during 1985 there was a remarkable absence of tension in the border region between Laos and the PRC, military personnel were conspicuous by their absence, and local trade was taking place across the border. Thus, the expressions of hope for a normalization of relations between the LPDR and the PRC voiced by Kaysone as premier on 2 December may not be as far-fetched as imagined. Such a normalization, it must be understood, remains hostage to the fundamental conflict between Vietnam and China over Kampuchea.

Relations between the LPDR and Thailand remained strained and were aggravated by a series of border incidents and the absence of real negotiations on border demarcation in areas where there are conflicting claims. Relations with the United States, however, improved noticeably as a result of greater LPDR cooperation on the issue of the search for remains of U.S. servicemen missing in action in Laos. In February, one such search yielded positive results, and agreement was reached on search of a second site. In March, U.S. National Security Council staff member Richard Childress and Ann Mills Griffiths, executive director of the National League of Families of American Prisoners and Missing in Southeast Asia, visited Vientiane. In August, the MIA issue "and other matters of mutual concern" were discussed by a U.S. delegation led by Childress in Vientiane (Radio Vientiane, 28 August; *FBIS*, 29 August). In December, U.S. Assistant Secretary of State Paul Wolfowitz visited Vientiane and had talks with LPDR Foreign Minister Phoun Sipaseut about "regional problems, bilateral relations, and other issues of mutual interest" (Radio Vientiane, 16 December; *FBIS*, 16 December).

Among travels abroad by LPDR leaders during 1985, Kaysone paid a "working friendship visit" to the Soviet Union from 25 to 29 August and met Mikhail Gorbachev (Radio Vientiane, 29 August; *FBIS*, 30 August). According to Phoun Sipaseut in an interview in *Pasason*, this visit resulted in "unanimity of views between the highest leaders of our two nations" (KPL, 8 October; *FBIS*, 10 October). Kaysone also visited the SRV for national day observances (Radio Vientiane, 3 September; *FBIS*, 6 September).

Souphanouvong visited the Soviet Union for the funeral of Chernenko in March. Phoun Sipaseut represented the LPDR at the Indochinese foreign ministers' meeting in Phnom Penh on 15–16 August.

The LPDR hosted a high-level delegation of VCP leaders led by Truong Chinh in May (VNA, 27 May; *FBIS*, 29 May).

Arthur J. Dommen
Bethesda, Maryland

Malaysia and Singapore

Population. Malaysia: 15,664,000; Singapore: 2,562,000 (*World Factbook*, May 1985)
Party. Communist Party of Malaya (CPM); Communist Party of Malaysia (MCP); North Kalimantan Communist Party (NKCP)
Founded. CPM: 1930; MCP: 1983
Membership. CPM: estimated 3,000 armed insurgents on Thai side of border; estimated 300 full-time inside Peninsular Malaysia; estimated 125 in Sarawak (*World Factbook*, May 1985)
Secretary General. CPM: Chin Peng; MCP: Ah Leng; NKCP: Wen Ming-chuan
Politburo. No data
Central Committee. CPM: No data; MCP: Chang Chun (chairman), San Cheng Ming, San Sen, rest unknown
Status. Illegal
Last Congress. CPM: 1965 (last known)
Last Election. N/a
Auxiliary Organizations. CPM: Malayan People's Army (MPA), Malay Nationalist Revolutionary Party of Malaya (MNRPM), Islamic Brotherhood Party (Paperi), Malayan People's Liberation Front (MPLF), Barisan Sosialis, People's Liberation Organization (the last two based in Singapore); MCP: Malaysian People's Liberation League (MPLL)
Publications. No regular periodicals known; CPM: Voice of Malayan Democracy (VOMD), clandestine radio station broadcasting from southern China; MCP: Voice of the People of Malaysia (VOPM), clandestine radio station, location unknown

The Communist Party of Malaya (CPM) remained a voice offstage in 1985, and an infrequently heard voice at that. Its recently established rival, the Communist Party of Malaysia (MCP), was barely audible, and the level of communist guerrilla activity in the country was relatively low.

Leadership and Party Organization. There was no apparent change in the leadership of the proscribed CPM in its 55th year. Chin Peng, the party's long-time leader, remained head of the Central Committee (VOMD, 29 April; *FBIS*, 7 May). The MCP, the coalition formed in December 1983 by two breakaway factions of the CPM, the Communist Party of Malaya—Revolutionary Faction (CPM/RF) and the Communist Party of Malaya—Marxist-Leninist (CPM/M-L), appeared to be barely functioning. Official Malaysian and Thai government reports of guerrilla activities in the border areas continued to refer to camps and units of the two separate groups, the CPM/RF and the CPM/M-L. (For background on the MCP, see *YICA*, 1985, pp. 211–12.)

The North Kalimantan Communist Party (NKCP) a small affiliate of the CPM, sent a warm anniversary greeting to the CPM, referring to the "intimate friendship" between the two parties, like that "between lips and teeth." The greeting, signed by Wen Ming-chuan, chairman of the KNCP Central Committee, praised the CPM for its strict adherence to "the combination of Marxism-Leninism–Mao Zedong thought with the concrete practice of the Malayan revolution" and for its continuous leadership of "the multiracial people in various fronts" fighting to establish a coalition government comprising "all nationalities." The message referred to the "present deadlock and ups and downs" but asserted confidence in the success of its efforts "to form a broadly based united front and launch a logical, favorable, and limited struggle" (VOMD, 25 July; *FBIS*, 26 July).

In Sabah, there was some concern about security, but whether communist units were considered part of the threat was not clear. In Singapore there was no evidence of activity by the CPM, which purports to speak for Singapore, not having accepted its separation from Malaysia.

Domestic Party Activities. As an outlawed party, the CPM's activities in country can only be inferred, but its plans and aspirations are available through broadcasts on its clandestine radio. In April, commemorating the 55th anniversary of its founding, the CPM announced a series of amendments to the special program adopted by the party five years before.

Like the program adopted by the CPM immediately after the establishment of the MCP, the amended CPM program placed particular emphasis on appeals aimed at the Malay population, in an attempt to broaden party support beyond its traditional ethnic Chinese composition. In a year when the deputy prime minister was warning the electorate that if the Pan Malaysian Islamic Party (PAS) were elected to power it would withdraw the special privileges of the indigenous Malays and abolish the position of Malay as the national language (*New Straits Times*, 25 September; *FBIS*, 2 October), the CPM's new amended program was urging "respect for Malay special rights" and development of Malay education. The program stated that "Malay is the lingua franca for the people of all nationalities and the medium in relations with foreign countries," while it also called for equality for all national languages and groups. The amended program called for the creation of "a national culture with the Malay culture as its main element, the Chinese and Indian cultures as its important elements." In a section devoted to religious freedom, the statement urged protection of mosques and other places of worship and accused the Malaysian government of using religion for political purposes to oppress the masses (VOMD, 29 April; *FBIS*, 7, 9 May).

The paragraph devoted to Singapore also contained a call for protecting Malay rights and interests in that country, but there were no such recommendations in the sections devoted to Sabah and Sarawak. In Sabah, local reaction against special privileges for Malays had led to a political coalition of Christian Chinese and the local Kadazan people, which had just won control of the state government. In Sarawak, there was strife inside the long-dominant Muslim party and the non-Muslim Dayaks, many of them Christians, were stirring politically (*FEER*, 30 May, p. 36).

Fear of Islamic fundamentalism was a continuing concern of the government, a concern linked to the fear that Muslims would be exploited by dormant revolutionaries. "The communists just learn to say *salaam* and they are in your house," the deputy prime minister and home affairs minister, Musa Hitam, told foreign journalists in remarks about the dangers of religious extremism. He said that the inability to cope with change underlies both Islamic extremism and the lure of leftism (*NYT*, 18 August).

Sporadic activity by communist guerrilla forces continued throughout the year, although the number of incidents and the size of the guerrilla units involved remained low. Most of the incidents reported occurred on the Thai border, especially around Betong, where several raids in February against CPM strongholds were characterized as highly successful. In one of those raids, Thai forces captured the CPM/M-L's largest base in the area with more than 126 resident units, water and electrical systems, a training compound, and a sports field. The base reportedly had supported some 200 to 250 armed men (*Nation Review*, Bangkok, 28 February; BBC, 2 March).

A barbed-wire and chain-link fence constructed along some 35 miles of the northwestern border was believed to be relatively effective in curbing infiltration in that area by some 100 CPM/RF guerrillas. The Malaysian government planned a 15-mile brick wall in the area near Kroh in an attempt to keep 760 CPM/M-L guerrillas based in southern Thailand from infiltrating into Malaysia along jungle tracks (Reuters, 10 May). The construction of major economic projects in the northern states of Peninsular Malaysia, together with extensive operations by security forces, were also credited with greatly checking guerrilla infiltration of the country (Kuala Lumpur domestic service, 11 August; *FBIS*, 12 August). Attempts by guerrilla forces to set up bases in Kelantan and Perak were believed to have failed because of continuous operations by security forces (*New Straits Times*, 13 June; *FBIS*, 18 June). In Kelantan, however, guerrillas were still making use of the forested area near the Cameron highlands and were threatening aborigine villages (*Berita Harian*, 13 July; *FBIS*, 23 July).

In October, the chief of Malaysian defense forces noted that there were clear signs of declining communist activity and that only 200 communist terrorists were still believed to be operating in Peninsular Malaysia and 60 others in Sarawak. Nevertheless, he urged Malaysian army personnel not to be content with their joint successes with the Thai forces in the border areas "as the enemy was always waiting for the right moment to attack" (AFP, 9 October; *FBIS*, 10 October).

In August, the CPM was reported to have categorically turned down an overture from the Thai government for peace talks aimed at ending the decade-long insurgency in southern Thailand. The CPM said that it could not accept the unconditional demand for its guerrillas to surrender their arms without any guarantee of their status or knowledge about whether they would be repatriated to Malaysia. The CPM reportedly vowed to continue its struggle to achieve its ultimate aim of "liberating" Malaysia if the objective of the proposed truce talks was first to lay down its arms unconditionally (*Bangkok Post*, 23 August; *FBIS*, 23 August). There was evidence of continued activity of the military arm of the NKCP in November, when a cache of weapons, food, and medicine was found on the Indonesian border (BBC, 28 November).

While there was no evidence of communist-inspired activity in Singapore, Prime Minister Lee Kuan Yew, concerned that the revival of opposition parties would endanger the country's stability, linked his rivals to the outlawed CPM (*CSM*, 15 August).

International Views, Relations and Activities. The CPM remains a pro-Beijing party, reiterating in its anniversary statement its strict adherence to "the general truth of Marxism-Leninism–Mao Zedong's thought," combined with the concrete practice of the Malayan revolution. "Two superpowers—the United States and the Soviet Union—are stepping up their competition for world hegemony," the party's amended program states. Homage to the PRC was not as effusive as in past years, the statement noting only that "the PRC has achieved considerable success in its image and socialist development. The PRC's international influence is further expanding" (VOMD, 29 April; *FBIS*, 7, 9 May).

It was another difficult year for the pro-Chinese CPM. Although the PRC's failure to renounce unconditionally any form of support, moral or otherwise, for the CPM remained a source of concern to the Malaysian and Singapore governments, both governments nevertheless actively sought increased trade ties with the PRC. The prime ministers of both countries visited China for that purpose during the year, and both governments eased restrictions on their nationals' travel to the PRC.

Diplomatic ties between Malaysia and the PRC were established in 1974 but the relationship remained cool, and Malaysian citizens still need government permission to visit China. For some years, Malaysia had been trying to develop direct trade links with the PRC. A special confidential task force set up by the cabinet to review relations with China reportedly recommended loosening some clamps on personal contacts in China purely for business reasons. Although the government reportedly took a decision in June to ease up on visits to China, normal personal contacts, not related to business, were to continue to be closely monitored. In 1983, nearly 9,000 Malaysian Chinese had received visas to visit the PRC and in 1984 the number had risen to almost 14,000 (*FEER*, 4 July, pp. 12–14).

The contrasting political systems between Malaysia and the PRC would not prevent the two countries from forging closer ties, the Malaysian foreign minister said a few days before the prime minister's visit to China (Kuala Lumpur international service, 15 November; *FBIS*, 15 November).

The real concern of the Malaysian government over unrestricted contacts with China was expressed by Prime Minister Mahathir Mohamed at a press conference during his first official visit to the PRC in November. He said that some of Malaysia's problems come from "people who feel they can call on the might of China to support their activities, even if China disavows such interventions" (*FEER*, 5 December, pp. 29–30). In the course of that visit, the prime minister began by urging China to resolve longstanding political disputes, certain "core bilateral issues" that have impeded the overall growth of Sino-Malaysian relations (UPI, 20 November). By the end of his stay he had downgraded the issue of CCP-CPM ties to a "minor problem."

The Malaysian government claimed to be satisfied with China's assurance during its prime minister's trip to the PRC that China would not interfere in the domestic affairs of Malaysia. This statement, the Malaysian foreign minister said on his return from China, was "a slap" for the CPM, "which has all along assumed their acceptance by the superpower." The foreign minister said it was a misconception on the part of the CPM leaders to think that they always had the support of the MCP in toppling the government elected by the people. Malaysia, he said, was heartened by the assurance and would reciprocate by giving support and cooperation to China in assisting to develop the country and improve the standard of living of the people (Kuala Lumpur domestic service, 30 November; *FBIS*, 2 December).

Singapore prime minister Lee Kuan Yew, on his return from China some months earlier, had expressed optimism at having broken new ground for economic cooperation (*Straits Times*, 26 September; *FBIS*, 2 October). A second official Singapore delegation traveled to the PRC in November in furtherance of establishing improved economic ties (Xinhua, 17 November; *FBIS*, 20 November).

While Malaysian relations with the Soviet Union had been "very cool" in recent years because of the Soviets' "continuous espionage activities there" (*New Straits Times*, 16 August; *FBIS*, 21 August), Malaysia has become the USSR's most important Southeast Asian trading partner. The same deputy foreign minister who later complained of Soviet spying in Malaysia went to Moscow in May for talks on economic and technical cooperation (*FEER*, 28 November, p. 19; *Izvestiia*, 2 May; *FBIS*, 3 May). There were frequent visits to the Soviet Union and the Eastern bloc by other Malaysian officials during the year and return visits by Soviet officials, including one by a very high-ranking official shortly before the Malaysian prime minister's visit to China.

The CPM, traditionally ranged against Moscow, and barely acknowledged by the PRC, was not a participant in international communist gatherings.

Jeanne S. Mintz
Washington, D.C.

Mongolia

Population. 1,912,000 (average annual growth rate 2.7 percent, *World factbook*)
Party. Mongolian People's Revolutionary Party (MPRP)
Founded. 1921
Membership. 80,200 (*Problems of Communism*, July/August)
Secretary General. Jambyn Batmonh
Politburo. 8 members: Jambyn Batmonh (chairman, Presidium of People's Great Hural), Dumaagiyn Sodnom (premier), Bat-Ochirym Altangerel (chairman, People's Great Hural), Tumenbayaryn Ragchaa (first deputy premier), Damdiny Gombojab, Demchigiyn Molomjamts, Tserendashiyn Namsray, Bujyn Dejid; 2 candidate members: Nyamin Jagbaral (deputy chairman, Presidium of People's Great Hural), Sonomyn Lubsangombo (deputy chairman, Council of Ministers)
Secretariat. 7 members: Jambyn Batmonh, Damdiny Gombojab, Demchigiyn Molomjamts, Paavangiyn Damdin, M. Dash, Tserenpilyn Balhaajab, Tserendashiyn Namsray
Central Committee. 91 full and 71 candidate members
Status. Ruling party
Last Congress. Eighteenth, 26–31 May 1981, in Ulan Bator
Last Election. 1981, 99 pecent, all 370 seats approved by MPRP

Auxiliary Organizations. Mongolian Revolutionary Youth League (over 200,000 members), T. Narangerel, first secretary; Central Council of Mongolian Trade Unions (400,000 members), B. Lubsantseren, chairman; Committee of Mongolian Women, L. Pagmadula, chairwoman; Mongolian Pioneers Organization (MPO), C. Tserendulam, chairwoman of MPO Central Council

Publications. *Unen* (Truth), MPRP daily organ, published Tuesday–Sunday. Montsame is the official news agency.

Leadership and Party Organization. In a speech to the members of the Central Committee on 28 February, General Secretary Jambyn Batmonh discussed the party organization's role in achieving national goals, specifically those stipulated by the Eighteenth MPRP Congress. He addressed the problem of increasing quality, efficiency, and productivity to enhance economic development. Emphasis was also given to the importance of maintaining close contact with the masses and improving training and ideological education. "As the socialist construction deepens," stated Batmonh, "the vanguard role of party organizations grows and the closer the party organizations are to the working masses, the more their vanguard role is ensured" (Montsame, 28 February; *FBIS*, 1 March).

Tserendashiyn Namsray, a Politburo and Secretariat member, echoed these sentiments. Namsray noted that current statistics show party members constitute 66 percent of the leaders of local People's Hurals, 60 percent of trade union leaders, and more than 25 percent of the leaders of the Revolutionary Youth League (RYL) (*WMR*, July).

The MPRP organization, in addition to its national acitivities, remains committed to the principles of Marxism-Leninism and the worldwide communist movement. Close "fraternal" relationships are cultivated with socialist parties from other countries. The MPRP frequently expresses solidarity with these groups and shares their common goals of protecting socialism's international gains and promoting world peace.

During 1985 there were no major changes in Mongolian leadership. However, three notable appointments had been announced on 28 December 1984. Battsagan Tsiyregdzen was appointed first deputy minister of public safety, Dendebiyn Gendenpil became first deputy minister of defense, and Byaraagiyn Chimid became chief arbiter of the Mongolian People's Republic (MPR).

Domestic Affairs. Mongolia's seventh five-year plan concluded in 1985. Batmonh spoke in April to a group of top-level and local government officials regarding the remaining work necessary for the achievement of plan targets. For agriculture, he stressed some improvement in distribution of food to rural and urban areas. For production, his talk focused on the consumer goods industry and the new methods that might improve their quantity and quality.

Mongolia's domestic development primarily depends on assistance from Soviet-bloc nations. These countries arrange mutually beneficial agreements through the coordination of their national economic plans. This year, economic, scientific, technical, and cultural agreements of this sort were signed with Bulgaria, Yugoslavia, and Czechoslovakia. An agreement with Hungary was also signed to improve interaction in areas of agriculture, food, and light industry.

Czechosolovakia has been especially instrumental in developing Mongolia's mineral-resource industry through geological prospecting and mining. Establishment of a joint-venture enterprise, Mongol-Czechoslovak Metal, further coordinated this relationship. Considerable assistance has also been provided for the MPR's leather and shoe industry and the training of Mongolian students by Czechoslovak institutions and enterprises (Montsame, 4–5 July; *FBIS*, 9 July).

Mongolia remains most heavily dependent upon the USSR for economic assistance. Presently 80 percent of Mongolian trade is with the Soviets (*World Factbook*). The remaining portion is almost entirely generated with other communist countries through the Council for Mutual Economic Assistance (CMEA)—a group in which Mongolia has been a member for 23 years (*National Geographic*, February). In June, Ulan Bator, the Mongolian capital, hosted two CMEA commission meetings. The Standing Commission on Electric Power met to discuss future development of the Interconnected Electric Power Systems that benefits member states. It also considered providing assistance to Mongolia, Vietnam, and Cuba in the field of power engineering (Montsame, 8 June; *FBIS*, 11 June).

The Permanent Commission for Cooperation in the Sphere of Light Industry also met and concluded a protocol to enhance interaction in the light, woodworking, and printing industries (Montsame, 21 June; *FBIS*, 25 June). Both meetings were attended by representatives from Bulgaria, Hungary, Vietnam, Czechoslovakia, Cuba, Romania, Poland, East Germany, and the Soviet Union.

The member countries of the CMEA have also been of great help to Mongolia in the construction of a national water-management system. Again, the Soviets have played the largest role. Over the past two five-year periods extensive irrigation facilities and land-reclamation installations have been built to water crops and pastures, with the direct aid of the USSR. Soviet colleges also educated engineering specialists and technicians to support these water projects. In addition, during the past five years Hungary, Czechoslovakia, East Germany, and Romania contributed to watering installations in some of Mongolia's Gobi regions (Montsame, 8 June; *FBIS*, 11 June).

Auxiliary Organizations. In July, Moscow hosted the twelfth World Festival of Youth and Students. The convocation's motto was, "For anti-imperialist solidarity, peace, and friendship." A delegation of 540 students representing the Mongolian Revolutionary Youth League attended. T. Narangerel, first secretary of the MRYL's Central Committee, led the group. Batmonh sent his greetings to this forum, praising its purpose in fostering communication among international youths to promote peace and prosperity (Montsame, 29 July; *FBIS*, 31 July).

The sixtieth anniversary of the founding of the Mongolian Pioneers Organization (MPO) was celebrated in 1985. Political leaders met with Pioneers and schoolchildren on 9 May to celebrate the occasion. In his speech at the meeting, Batmonh lauded the organization for educating future activists in socialist principles. The pioneers responded with a pledge to work hard and follow the lead of the MPRP.

International Views and Affairs. As the Soviet Union's oldest ally, the MPR espouses views on international events that mirror those of the USSR. It considers the United States the foremost imperialist aggressor and a primary threat to world peace. In May the MPR representative at the United Nations addressed the Security Council and scathingly criticized U.S. intervention in Nicaragua. He urged the council to condemn American actions (Montsame, 11 May; *FBIS*, 17 May).

On other international issues, the MPR backs the Vietnamese, Kampuchean, and Lao peoples' fights for independence; advocates the withdrawal of U.S. troops from Korea and reunification under the Democratic People's Republic of Korea; supports Soviet assistance to Afghanistan, rejecting international accusations of encroachment or human-rights abuses; seeks closer ties with China and a solution to Sino-Soviet conflicts; believes in the constructive efforts of the nonaligned movement, struggling against imperialism; and, finally, promotes the Soviet proposal for the resolution of Middle Eastern tensions under the direction of the UN, with all parties, including the PLO, present.

Demchigiyn Molomjamts, Mongolian Politburo and Secretariat member, led a delegation to Moscow on 7 May. In turn Batmonh received Z. N. Nuriyen, deputy chairman of the Soviet Council of Ministers. On 9 May, Batmonh and Prime Minister Dumaagiyn Sodnom sent a congratulatory message to the Soviet Union to commemorate the victorious day on which "fascism and militarism" were defeated. They hailed the Russian role in securing peace for mankind and in subsequently developing the socialist world community (Montsame, 9 May; *FBIS*, 17 May). One other significant event in the Soviet-Mongol relationship was Batmonh's visit to Moscow in August. He signed a fifteen-year agreement with Mikhail S. Gorbachev on economic, scientific, and technical cooperation (*NYT*, 29 August).

Mongolia's diplomatic affairs during 1985 included the establishment of relations with the Arab Republic of Yemen (23 August), a meeting with former Canadian prime minister Pierre Trudeau (13 July), the receipt of credentials from the ambassadors of Algeria and Mali (9 July), and a meeting with the chairman of the Communist Party of Denmark, Jorgen Jensen (12 June).

Throughout the year Mongolian officials continued to promulgate their dedication to international peace and disarmament in speeches to both domestic and international audiences. They supported a larger role for the UN in preventing war and enhancing cooperation among states. Praise was bestowed upon the USSR and China for their mutual renunciation of first use of nuclear weapons. The arms talks between the USSR and the United States are considered to be extremely important for world peace. This pacific orientation was further reinforced by mention of their 1981 UN proposal which called for nonaggression in relations between Asian states, and also by references to the MPR declaration on "the rights of peoples to peace."

Colleen E. Foraker
Stanford, California

Nepal

Population. 16,996,000

Party. Nepal Communist Party (NCP), with two neutralist factions; Nepal Communist Party (Marxist-Leninist) (NCP [M-L]), with four pro-Beijing factions; Nepal Communist Party/pro-Moscow (NCP/M), with four pro-Moscow factions. A new organization, Janabadi Morcha (Democratic Front), emerged in 1985 with declared allegiance to the ideas of Che Guevara.

Founded. NCP: 1949; NCP(M-L): 1978; Janabadi Morcha: founded in 1980 as radical democratic organization, but turned Che Guevarist in 1985.

Membership. 5,000 (estimate), with pro-Chinese and neutralist factions accounting for almost 75 percent of members.

Leadership. NCP/neutralist factions—Man Mohan Adhikary, Mrs. Sahana Pradhan (Pushpa Lal's widow); NCP(M-L)/pro-Beijing factions—Radha Krishna Mainali and Mohan Chandra Adhikary, Fourth Congress: Mohan Bikram Gharti, Mashal: Nirmal Lama, Nepal Workers' and Peasants' Organization: Narayan Man Bijukchhe 'Rohit'; NCP/M (pro-Moscow factions)—Rayamajhi faction: Dr. Keshar Jung Rayamajhi, Manandhar faction: Bishnu Bahadur Manandhar, Varma faction: Krishna Raj Varma, Tulsi Lal faction: Tulsi Lal Amatya; Janabadi Morcha/Che Guevarist: Ram Raja Prasad Singh.

Politburo. No data

Secretariat. No data

Central Committee. 35 members in NCP/M (Rayamajhi faction); no data on other factions.

Status. Proscribed

Last Congress. 1961 (last pre-split congress)

Last Election. 1959, 7.5 percent, 4 of 109 seats.

Auxiliary Organizations. Neutralist: Nepal Progressive Student Union; pro-Beijing: All Nepal National Free Student Union, All Nepal National Teachers Organization; Anti-imperialist Front; pro-Moscow: Nepal National Student Federation, Nepal National Youth Federation. In addition to these organizations, pro-Beijing and neutralist communists have shadow organizations within the government-sponsored labor and peasant organizations.

Publications. Neutralist: *Naya Janabad* (New democracy) and *Nepal Patra*; NCP(M-L): *Barga Sangharsha* (Class struggle) and *Mukti-Morcha* (Liberation front); pro-Beijing: *Mashal* (Torch); NCP/M: *Samikshya Weekly* (reflects views of all pro-Soviet factions)

As the political situation in Nepal remained fluid and volatile in 1985, demands for political change were made vociferously from all segments of the populace, including some prominent retired civil servants and diplomats. The Nepali Congress (NC) continued preparation for proposed *Satyagraha* or civil disobedience, seeking an alternative to the partyless Panchayat system. The divided Communist party sought unity to push for the NC's *Satyagraha* (*FBIS*, 24 May). The NC leadership, in addition to submitting to King Birendra a petition signed by 321,463 persons asking redress of political and economic problems (*Nepal Press Digest* [*NPD*], 13 May), also gave an ultimatum to the king to restore the multiparty system or face a *Satyagraha* on 23 May (ibid., 20 May). The NC launched its *Satyagraha* as scheduled, and it continued until the terrorist bomb blasts on 20–22 June in several parts of the country. All communist groups except the pro-Beijing Mashal and pro-Moscow Rayamajhi factions participated in the NC-led movement. An estimated seven thousand rank-and-file members of both the NC and the NCP courted arrest (*FBIS*, 21 June).

Amid the chaos and confusion of *Satyagraha*, Nepal was rocked by a series of terrorist bombings in different parts of the country, including the gate of the Royal Palace, the National Panchayat, and a luxury five-star hotel. Eight persons were killed, including a member of the National Panchayat, and several others were injured (ibid., 21 June). The explosions took place the day after King Birendra flexed his muscle against the opponents of the Panchayat system in the National Panchayat by saying that it was "the bound duty" of all supporters "to counter those who seek to create an atmosphere of instability in the country by spreading unnecessary confusion about the system chosen by the people themselves in free exercise of their will" (*NYT*, 21 June; *FBIS*, 21 June). Both the NC and the NCP condemned the terrorist bombings and called off their month-long agitation for the restoration of a multiparty system (*FBIS*, 21, 24 June). The Janabadi Morcha, a staunchly antimonarchical organization led by a former member of the National Panchayat, Ram Raja Prasad Singh, claimed responsibility for the explosions (to prepare for the overthrow of King Birendra). Mr. Singh reportedly said that Latin American revolutionary Che Guevara was his idol (ibid., 12 August). The government took 1,750 persons into custody for investigation, including some Soviet-educated engineers.

Meanwhile, the national legislature adopted a tough antiterrorist law providing death sentences for persons involved in terrorism (ibid.). The government formed a tribunal to indict 101 of the 1,750 persons held in custody under this newly adopted law (ibid., 26 August). The political situation in Nepal apparently returned to normal by the time of the Dasain festival in October after the release of thousands of detainees, including senior leaders of the NC and the NCP (ibid., 16, 17 October). The mood of the political forces, both ruling and nonruling, however, remained confused and directionless. In late November, all opposition leaders except pro-Moscow Dr. Rayamajhi boycotted the nationwide Pancha convention inaugurated by King Birendra, indicating their nonparticipation in the forthcoming May 1986 Panchayat elections.

Leadership and Organization. The year 1985 saw a further split in the pro-Moscow group led by Bishnu Bahadur Manandhar, as Krishna Raj Varma, one of the two leaders in the group, broke away and held the Manandhar group responsible for the split in the anti-imperialist movement in Nepal (*NPD*, 21 January). In April 1984, Dr. Rayamajhi's group had convened its sixth conference at Patan, attended by 167 delegates from 57 districts of Nepal. The conference re-elected Dr. Rayamajhi as president of the party for the fifth term, and also formed a 75-member national assembly and a 35-member central committee. Another pro-Soviet group is led by a former communist member to the 1959–1960 parliament, Tulsi Lal Amatya. This faction occasionally rears its head by issuing statements against the government.

Another pro-Beijing group led by Narayan Man Bijukchhe 'Rohit' functions under the name Nepal Workers' and Peasants' Organization (also known as the Rohit group), and is influential in the Bhaktapur district and surrounding areas. This group differs from other Maoists in that it believes in both covert and overt strategy to achieve its objectives, and it participates in Panchayat elections. One of the National Panchayat members representing the Bhaktapur district, eight miles east from Kathmandu, is allegedly sponsored by the Rohit group.

Domestic Party Affairs. Three pro-Beijing groups—the Fourth Congress, Mashal, and the NCP (Marxist-Leninist)—agreed to promote functional unity in order to move toward a struggle against the king's feudal system (*NPD*, 4 February). The Supreme Court ordered the release of three leaders of the NCP(M-L) group, Radha Krishna Mainali, Khadga Oli, and Mod Nath Prasrit, who were serving jail sentences for their terrorist and subversive activities. They were rearrested by the government (ibid., 18 March)—an action that was denounced by such personalities as former prime minister Tanka Prasad Acharya and NC leader Krishna Prasad Bhatterai, who demanded the captives' immediate release (ibid., 8 April).

The five leftist groups among the various Communist parties—Adhikary, Amatya, Varma, Rohit, and Fourth Congress—formed a Leftist Front to organize a mass movement against the Panchayat system alongside the NC's *Satyagraha*. The front made every effort to forge unity with the NC for joint struggle, but the NC's response was negative. Meanwhile, pro-Moscow leader Tulsi Lal Amatya declared that "leftists are not a minor force, they are a force capable of acting independently" (ibid.). On the eve of the NC's *Satyagraha*, the five-group Leftist Front put forward nine demands and began its agitation. The nine demands were: (1) introduction of a multiparty system and lifting of the ban on political parties; (2) restoration of fundamental rights, such as press freedom, freedom of speech and movement, and the right to open class organizations; (3) the impartial, immediate, and unconditional release of political prisoners; (4) protection of tenancy rights and fixation of minimum wage for agricultural laborers; (5) an increase in factory workers' wages; (6) guaranteed security of service and enforcement of labor legislation; (7) price control; (8) a halt to the eviction of landless people, and (9) an increase in grants to educational institutions, reduced tuition fees, and fulfillment of the teachers' organization's demands (ibid., 20 May). All prominent leaders of the front were arrested while trying to address public meetings at several places in Kathmandu (ibid., 3 June). The Sahana group and Manandhar group, though not represented in the Leftist Front, offered their support to leftist agitation and the NC's *Satyagraha*. The Sahana group characterized the five-group front as an "unholy alliance" and tried to organize separate agitation. Mrs. Sahana Pradhan and B. B. Manandhar both were arrested while trying to address public meetings (ibid., 3, 17 June).

Meanwhile, the Marxist-Leninist group surprisingly issued a statement expressing solidarity with the anti-Panchayat struggle by the Nepali Congress as well as the Leftist Front (ibid., 10 June). The Mashal group, however, took the *Satyagraha* as NC's existentialist politics and described it as unrealistic and misleading. It emphasized a liberation struggle as the only means to end the growing oppression, injustice, tyranny, corruption, repression, and terror (ibid., 8 April). The five-group Leftist Front welcomed the Marxist-Leninist group's support for the agitation and appealed to it to take a direct and active part. The front also expressed satisfaction over the Manandhar and Sahana group's participation, albeit separately, and invited the Mashal group to follow suit (ibid., 24 June). Dr. Keshar Jung Rayamajhi's group did not participate in the agitations. Rayamajhi said in a statement that he did not believe that *Satyagraha* or any other activity that disrupts normal life in the country can bring about a multiparty system. He emphasized the need for historic compromise between partyless politics and group-based politics. He appealed to the king to hold political consultations and direct the formation of a political committee (ibid.).

The Leftist Front called off its agitation following the 20–22 June bomb explosions caused by Janabadi Morcha. The front condemned the terrorist violence and said that "a political change favorable to the people cannot be achieved by exploding a few bombs" (ibid., 1 July). The two other pro-Beijing groups—Marxist-Leninist and Mashal—announced that they would continue their struggle. The NCP(M-L) declared: "It seems that our rulers have engineered the bomb explosions with the design of generating a sympathy wave in their favor and dividing anti-Panchayat forces. We must be aware of their motives and conspiracies and carry forward our joint struggle against despotism" (ibid.). The group's leader, R. K. Mainali, issued a statement from Palpa jail saying that "terrorism cannot solve any problem. It only undermines the morale of the people" (ibid., 15 July). The Mashal group called on the people to continue their struggle against both the "white terror" unleashed by the government and the violence let loose by the terrorists. It declared, "The present government is using the bomb explosions as pretext to intensify the white terror" (ibid.).

Auxiliary and Front Organizations. The nationwide general strike launched by the Nepal National Teachers' Organization (NNTO), demanding higher salaries and other facilities (*NPD*, 7 January), lasted for six months. In March, teachers all over the country locked up their schools and marched into Kathmandu to press their demands. The government met the teachers' demonstration with heavy force, and about a thousand teachers were arrested (ibid., 18 March). In May, a front of six leftist student organizations—three factions of the All Nepal National Free Students Union, the

Nepal Democratic Student Union, the Nepal Revolutionary Student Federation, and the Nepal National Student Federation—partially united to organize a nationwide general strike (Nepal Bandh or Nepal close-out) in support of the five-month-old teachers' agitation. Demonstrations were organized in various parts of the country in protest against increased tuition and the continued detention of teachers arrested in connection with their strike. The main market of several towns in the country remained closed (ibid., 27 May). In Dharan and Hetauda, the police opened fire with blanks, fired tear-gas shells to disperse the demonstrators, and arrested several hundred students. An official source said one person was killed and 40 injured as police clashed with demonstrating students and leftist activists in several areas of Nepal. The opposition, however, maintained that 4 persons were killed and more than 80 injured (*FBIS*, 20 May). The front's decision to organize a "Kathmandu Valley Bandh" as well as mass meetings at Kathmandu and another twelve towns in Nepal between 4–9 July could not be realized, since the front called off the proposed movement following the bomb explosions. The front condemned the explosions but at the same time castigated the government for using the explosions as a pretext to loose a fresh campaign of repression against the student community (*NPD*, 1 July).

Notable Figures and Newsmakers. M. M. Adhikary, who is in his late 60s, continued to be a prime newsmaker because of his charismatic personality. It should be noted, however, that Mr. Adhikary is more popular among non-Communists, since his speeches are balanced and lack orthodox Marxist-Leninist jargon.

Chitra Krishna Tiwari
Arlington, Virginia

New Zealand

Population. 3,300,000 (*World Factbook*, July 1985)
Parties. Communist Party of New Zealand (CPNZ); Socialist Unity Party (SUP); Workers Communist League (WCL); Socialist Action League (SAL)
Founded. CPNZ: 1921; SUP: 1966; SAL: 1969; WCL: 1980.
Membership. CPNZ: 50; SUP: 100–250; others, no data
Leadership. CPNZ: Richard C. Wolfe; SUP: G. H. "Bill" Andersen, national president, George Jackson, national secretary; others, no data
Status. Legal
Last Election. July 1984, no representatives elected
Auxiliary Organizations. SUP: New Zealand–USSR Friendship Society, New Zealand Council for World Peace, Union of New Zealand Women, Young Workers' Alliance; SAL: Young Socialists
Publications. CPNZ: *People's Voice* (weekly); SUP: *New Zealand Tribune* (bimonthly), *Socialist Politics* (quarterly journal); WCL: *Unity* (monthly news sheet); SAL: *Socialist Action* (bimonthly).

Because New Zealand's Communist parties—the Communist Party of New Zealand, the Socialist Unity Party, the Workers Communist League, and the Socialist Action League—have very small memberships, they are relegated to the fringes of New Zealand politics. None of the parties are currently represented in Parliament. Nevertheless, these parties exert an influence on the New Zealand political scene. Some members hold leadership positions in large trade unions and other auxiliary organizations. In addition, other Marxists—although not members of Communist parties—hold influential positions in the ruling New Zealand Labor Party.

The Communist Party of New Zealand (CPNZ). The CPNZ is the parent of all of New Zealand's Communist parties. Founded in Wellington in 1921 in sympathy with the Leninist revolution in Russia, the CPNZ supported the Soviet Union for the next 40 years. In the mid-1960s, however, the CPNZ broke with Moscow and adopted a pro-Beijing line. Six CPNZ members who opposed this move formed the Socialist Unity Party—now the largest Communist party in New Zealand. After the fall of the Gang of Four in 1976, the CPNZ again changed its orientation and now aligns itself with Albania.

As a result of decades of factional splitting, the CPNZ now exerts almost no influence on New Zealand's political life. Membership has been reduced to approximately fifty, with most based around its Auckland headquarters. The CPNZ has never won parliamentary representation and is considered by other Communists an impotent arm of the communist movement.

The Socialist Union Party (SUP). The SUP, which maintains a high public profile, is the most influential of New Zealand's Communist parties. It is the only Communist party in New Zealand recognized by Moscow, and the SUP has sent delegations to the Soviet Union to study organizational and party activities (Tass, 20 May 1984). In 1980, the New Zealand government charged that Moscow was channeling funds to the SUP and as a result expelled the Soviet ambassador to Wellington (*Political Handbook of the World*, 1984–1985). Moscow's support of the SUP has been rewarded with SUP endorsement of the Soviet invasion of Afghanistan, Soviet proposals on disarmament, Soviet activities in Poland, and Moscow's explanation of the Korean Airline shootdown (*New Zealand Tribune*, 29 April).

Domestically, the SUP's influence results from its extensive trade union connections. SUP president Bill Andersen heads the Auckland Trades Council, the largest regional organization of trade unions in New Zealand, and sits on the National Executive of the 450,000-member New Zealand Federation of Labor (FOL). In addition, the SUP's most effective spokesman, Ken Douglas, is secretary-treasurer of the FOL and is considered one of the trade union movement's best organizers. Although he denies membership in the SUP, the president of the FOL, Jim Knox, recently accepted the chairmanship of the Asian Coordinating Committee of the World Federation of Trade Unions.

Still, the SUP suffers from serious membership problems—which even President Andersen publicly admits (*New Zealand Tribune*, 29 April). Party sympathizers are often reluctant to join the SUP because membership demands not only financial contributions but also an agreement to follow the party's rules and policies without question and to donate large amounts of time to party work. The seventh triennial conference of the SUP, held last October in Auckland, underlined the membership problem, as fewer than 30 people attended.

The Workers Communist League (WCL). The WCL has neither the membership nor the following of the SUP. The party is relatively young, having been formed in 1980 when two pro-Beijing groups that had split from the CPNZ joined forces, and its influence is confined to the Wellington area. Composed primarily of young college graduates and factory laborers, the party is active in the Wellington Trades Council and the Wellington Unemployed Workers' Union. Political causes espoused by the WCL include protests against apartheid in South Africa.

The Maoist WCL is generally considered the most radical communist group in New Zealand. Though legal, it keeps its membership and goals secret. The government's publication of a security report on the WCL in 1982, which described it as "a revolutionary communist party dedicated to the violent overthrow of the state," suggests that Wellington keeps a close watch on the party's activities.

The Socialist Action League (SAL). The SAL originated as a university movement in 1969 and is a pro-Cuban, Trotskyite group affiliated with the Fourth International. The party maintains its university ties through its association with the Young Socialists, but is attempting to broaden its appeal to older New Zealanders. Its fortnightly publication,

Socialist Action, supports a wide variety of left-wing causes, including the "revolutionary movement" in Central America. The party also denounces right-wing dictatorships in Latin America.

The New Zealand Political Scene. Communist groups in New Zealand historically have been hampered by demographics. Organization has been made difficult by New Zealand's relatively high standard of living and the high proportion of New Zealanders living in rural areas. Even industrial workers have been unwilling to risk their relatively comfortable living standards for militant strike action or ideological causes.

More important, the New Zealand Labor Party has been progressive enough to satisfy many leftists who might otherwise have joined Communist parties. Several Marxists—although not Communist party members—sit in Parliament, including Helen Clark, chairman of the government's Foreign Affairs and Defense Committee. Clark is probably the strongest member of the Labor Party's left wing, and her views influence Labor party policy. Another left-leaning Labor member of Parliament escorted 60 New Zealand youths to Beijing for a study trip late last year. The itinerary included an audience with the general secretary of the Chinese Communist Party.

Communist party leaders themselves appear to be recognizing that many of their goals can be achieved by the mainstream Labor Party. During the July 1984 parliamentary elections, won by the Labor Party, the SUP declined to enter its own candidates, instead asking its members to vote for Labor. In addition, several other communist groups, including the Socialist Action League and the Young Socialists, actively campaigned for the Labor Party (*Intercontinental Press*, 6 August 1984). The Communists have not been disappointed. The Labor government's policy forbidding port calls by nuclear-armed or nuclear-powered warships, which has caused serious discord between Wellington and its Western allies, has long been a goal of New Zealand's Communists.

Michael Morell
Arlington, Virginia

Joanne P. Cloud
Annandale, Virginia

Pakistan

Population. 99,199,000
Party. Communist Party of Pakistan (CPP)
Founded. 1948
Membership. Under 200 (estimate)
Secretary General. Ali Nazish
Status. Illegal
Last Congress. First, 1976 (clandestine)
Leading Bodies. No information available
Publications. None

The pro-Soviet Communist Party of Pakistan (CPP), banned in 1954, has never achieved a mass following. Consequently, the CPP, seeking to influence the left in Pakistan, has traditionally employed a united-front strategy. Since the imposition of martial law in 1977, when all party activities were prohibited, the minuscule CPP has had little effect on antiregime activities. The Soviet occupation of Afghanistan in 1979 strengthened the popular perception of the CPP as a tool of Soviet subversion within Pakistan.

Marxists operating outside the CPP exercise political influence in Pakistan through trade unions, student organizations, and more respectable political parties. Some politicians in the eleven-party opposition organization, the Movement for the Restoration of Democracy (MRD), claim to be Marxist, including some figures in the left wing of the Pakistan People's Party (PPP), the only party of the MRD with a mass base. Marxists do not currently pose a major threat to the government, however. They do possess the potential to exploit unrest, particularly in the three non–Punjabi-language provinces (Baluchistan, Sind, and the Northwest Frontier Province), where they appeal to regional grievances against the alleged domination of Pakistan by its most populous province, Punjab. The government of President Zia-ul Haq has expressed concern regarding subversive activities in the three minority provinces by Pakistani leftists based in Kabul and London.

During 1985, the martial-law government of President Zia moved gradually to restore a democratic system. At the end of 1984, Zia won a referendum vote that asked voters whether they supported his Islamization policies. The government's announcement of a 60 percent voter turnout, with almost 98 percent voting favorably, was charged by the MRD with being grossly inflated. Nonetheless, President Zia interpreted the outcome as a mandate for him to retain the presidency for five years.

In January, Zia announced that nonparty elections for a National Assembly and the four provincial assemblies would be held in February. Although the ban on party activities continued, Zia, to encourage participation in the elections, removed prohibitions that had prevented most former party officials from taking part in politics on any basis. However, the ban on party activities continued. The MRD, insistent that martial law be lifted prior to the poll, called for a boycott of the February elections. Zia announced that he would be satisfied if 40 percent of the electorate voted; the opposition doubted that the vote would go higher than 10 percent (*NYT*, 22 February).

In what most observers describe as a fair election, some 57 percent of eligible voters cast their ballots in the provincial contests, and 53 percent voted at the parliamentary level. Over 1,100 candidates contested the 207 National Assembly seats, and 3,600 candidates stood for the 460 provincial assembly seats. Despite the MRD boycott, some 155 candidates formerly associated with the PPP reportedly participated in the nonparty elections (*FEER*, 21 February), and about one-third of them won (*FEER*, 7 March). Zia selected Mohammad Khan Junejo, a Sindhi politician formerly associated with the Muslim League, as prime minister.

The outcome suggests that the people wanted a peaceful return to democracy but were not prepared to give a blank check to Zia. Seven of Zia's cabinet ministers, including Defense Minister Ali Ahmad Talpur, lost—as did 30 sitting members of Zia's hand-picked national legislature (*NYT*, 27 February). The MRD for its part was in a quandary as to how to respond. The elections had been fair and the turnout high. The newly elected representatives could claim the legitimacy of the ballot box. The MRD's tactics were to be conditioned by the independence granted to the new legislative bodies and by Zia's plans regarding the lifting of martial law.

Perhaps emboldened by the election results, Zia in early March announced the revival of the previously suspended 1973 constitution and the gradual removal of martial law (*Los Angeles Times*, 3 March). However, he also proposed amendments to the 1973 constitution that would greatly strengthen the president's power relative to parliament and the new prime minister. This issue was to preoccupy Zia, Junejo, and the newly elected National Assembly for the next several months. A significant minority, calling itself the Independent Parliamentary Group (IPG), opposed the changes. The MRD charged that the amendments made a mockery of democratic rule. Ghulam Mustafa Jatoi, convenor of the PPP in the absence of exiled party head Benazir Bhutto, announced a fourteen-point program for parliamentary consideration, including the restoration of the 1973 constitution and the rejection of all presidential amendments to it (Karachi, *Dawn*, 18 April).

Zia, probably concerned by the prospect of popular protests during a sensitive transition period, agreed to compromises on his proposed amendments, even though he had the necessary two-thirds vote in the National Assembly to pass the original proposals. Following negotiations between Junejo and IPG leaders, the National Assembly in October unanimously approved a modified version of the amendment bill. The new bill provided significant checks on both the prime minister and the president, with a parallel arrangement in the provinces regarding the centrally appointed governors and elected chief ministers. The bill subsequently was also passed by the indirectly elected Senate. Prime Minister Junejo stated that the bill, creating a balance between the prime minister and the president, was the first step toward lifting of martial law (Karachi Domestic Service, 17 October). (On 14 August he had promised that martial law would be lifted by the end of the year.)

In December, the National Assembly and the Senate approved the Political Parties Bill, legalizing the re-establishment of political parties. Prime Minister Junejo had earlier stated that this move would be the second step taken before martial law was lifted. On 30 December Zia told a joint sitting of the National Assembly and the Senate that martial law was lifted on that day. In addition, the state of emergency was lifted, thus removing emergency powers from the executive for the first time since 1965.

The opposition parties were thus confronted with a new and unexpected political situation. The MRD was uncertain about what tactics it should take in the new situation to mobilize public support without risking a reimposition of martial law. The MRD still holds that neither the president nor the members of the legislatures have a right to exercise power, since they were not elected in accordance with the provisions of the 1973 constitution. Nevertheless, some elements of the MRD may choose to accept the government's regulations for registering political parties and try to challenge the government within the new system. Whether Benazir Bhutto will follow the game plan remains to be seen. Last summer, she reportedly told members of her party at the end of her three-month sojourn in Pakistan that the "policy of confrontation" had failed and a new strategy was needed (Dhubai, *Khaleej Times*, 21 November).

Party Affairs. The tiny CPP generally supported the activities of the MRD. In early 1985, General Secretary Imam Ali Nazish denounced the December referendum and supported the MRD's call for a boycott of the February elections (*New Age*, 3 March). A few months later, the CPP reaffirmed the united-front line. Indeed, it advocated bringing all "anti-imperialist democratic forces" together on a "single platform" (*New Age*, 8 September). But the CPP, not a constituent member of the MRD, could exercise negligible influence on its own. Marxists outside the CPP, however, played some role among the PPP's militant left (not its dominant element) and among three leftist constituents of the MRD: the Qaumi Mahaz Azadi (QMA), the Pakistan Socialist Party (PSP), and the Pakistan Progressive Party. The general secretary of the QMA is Iqbal Haider, who also serves as an associate secretary of the MRD. The PSP is led by its veteran organizer, C. R. Aslam. The Pakistan Progressive Party, led by Azaz Nasir, takes a rigidly pro-Moscow position.

Marxists have a base among regional parties supporting greater provincial autonomy. The most important of these parties is the rural-based Sindhi Awami Tehrik (SAT), which combines Sindhi nationalism with Marxism. SAT, headed by Rasool Bux Palejo, supports an impressive array of auxiliary organizations and may have replaced the PPP as the dominant political force in the rural areas of Sind Province. In the Northwest Frontier Province, Pushtun opposition to the government finds expression in the Mazdoor Kisan Party (Workers' and Farmers' Party) led by Sardar Shaukat Ali and Fatehyab Ali Khan. Direction is provided by Afzal Bangash, an expatriate who divides his time between Kabul and Moscow.

In Baluchistan, the major political organization advocating autonomy is the Pakistan National Party, led by Ghaus Bux Bizenjo, a hereditary tribal chieftain. During the year, Bizenjo made a controversial two-month trip to Moscow, ostensibly as guest of honor at the thirteenth International Youth Festival in Moscow. On his return, he called for improved relations with the USSR (Karachi *Dawn*, 19 September). Other groups in Baluchistan that support autonomy are the Baluchistan People's Liberation Front and the Baluch Students' Organization. Both are Marxist-Leninist in orientation, although their leaders reject any ideological alignment with Moscow or Beijing. Still other prominent Baluch figures calling for autonomy are Khair Bux Marri and Ataullah Mengal. Like Bizenjo, they are hereditary chieftains. However, they are both exiles. Marri resides in Soviet-occupied Afghanistan, while Mengal operates in exile from Great Britain.

Exiled politicians in early 1985 called for a confederation of Pakistan's four provinces with virtual self-government granted to each. To this end, they established the Pushtun-Baluch-Sindhi Front in London. The moving figures behind this front are two Baluch figures, Khair Bux Marri and Ataullah Mengal, as well as such PPP figures as Mumtaz Bhutto and Hafiz Pirzada. Within Pakistan, Bizenjo expressed support for the front's program, as did Pathan nationalist Wali Khan of the leftist National Democratic Party. The CPP also backed the notion of provincial autonomy (*New Age*, 24 February).

The confederation proposal further underminded the morale of the MRD. Already divided over how to respond to the high turnout in the February assembly elections, this issue further exacerbated differences in the organization. The Punjab branches of the constituent parties, particularly the powerful Punjab branch of the PPP, were not in favor of the confederation (*FEER*, 21 March). Another divisive issue among MRD members is the question of direct talks between Pakistan and the Karmal regime in Kabul on a political resolution of the Afghan crisis. The Pakistani government at the UN-sponsored Geneva proximity talks on Afghanistan has consistently argued that it will not engage in direct talks because the Karmal regime is a puppet government kept in power by Soviet troops. Some major PPP figures, such as Benazir Bhutto and Mustafa Jatoi, have avoided expressing support for either of the controversial proposals.

The al-Zulfiqar terrorist organization, once frequently cited by the government as a major cause for subversive activities, has now faded away. It lost public sympathy in Pakistan in the wake of the 1981 hijacking of a Pakistani commercial airplane, which resulted in the murder of a Pakistani diplomat. Subsequently, Benazir Bhutto denied any organizational links with the terrorist organization established by her two brothers, Murtaza and Shahnawaz. The Afghan government and its mentors have apparently severed connections with it. In July, Shahnawaz Bhutto died under mysterious circumstances in France (*NYT*, 4 September). On 29 December a military court sentenced Murtaza Bhutto (reportedly resident in Libya and Syria) in absentia to fourteen years hard labor for engaging in violence to spread his message (Reuters, 29 December).

Some of the parties on the left may not be permitted to register under new regulations governing their re-establishment. A special parliamentary committee recommended no legal status for parties opposing Islamic ideology or the sovereignty, integrity, and security of Pakistan. In addition, "No person should form, organize, or convene a foreign-backed party or in any way be associated with such a party" (Karachi Domestic Service, 7 August). This surely means that the CPP will remain a banned party and some of the explicitly Marxist groups will almost certainly not be certified. The powerful religious right in Pakistan has already come out against their participation in politics. For example, Wazi Hussain, party secretary of the Jamaat-e-Islami, generally supportive of the government, said his group would not allow "secularists and communists to pollute the atmosphere with activities against the ideology of Pakistan" (*FEER*, 16 May).

Foreign Affairs. Relations between Pakistan and the USSR in 1985 were correct, if not particularly cordial. Both sides, however, were anxious to retain a semblance of normal relations in noncontroversial areas such as trade, economic aid, and scientific exchanges. The Soviets agreed to supply economic and technical aid to Pakistan's 1983–1988 economic plan, most notably for showcase projects such as the Karachi steel complex, completed in 1985, and the Multan thermal project begun during the year. The USSR also extended aid to the private sector of the economy for the first time. The two sides signed an agreement in September to increase commercial air traffic.

President Zia visited Moscow in mid-March to attend the funeral of Chairman Chernenko. Afterward, he told reporters that his meetings with Chairman Gorbachev and Foreign Minister Gromyko convinced him that the USSR was prepared to get tough with Pakistan because of its Afghan policy. He speculated that the USSR might try to punish Pakistan economically or might even try "some military twisting of my arm," such as "hot pursuit" or perhaps overflights (*Pakistan Times*, 8 April). Shortly before his departure from Pakistan, retiring Soviet ambassador Vitaly Smirnov claimed that Pakistan was responsible for the deaths on 26–27 April of some dozen Soviet prisoners at a camp run by Afghan resistance fighters. The Soviet prisoners died during an attempt to take over a part of the camp. On being asked if the incident would further undermine Soviet-Pakistani ties, he responded that relations were already at "an all-time low" (*FEER*, 13 June). Nonetheless, Smirnov's successor, Abdul Rakhman Khalil Ogly Vezirov, soon after told reporters that his mission was to normalize relations (*Jang*, 15 July).

The major divisive issue between the USSR and Pakistan remains the Afghan question. During the UN-sponsored talks in Geneva aimed at finding a political solution, Pakistan continued to oppose direct talks with the Karmal regime, even though both Moscow and Kabul demand such direct talks as necessary for a final political solution. Foreign Minister Sahadzada Yaqub Khan stated during the

December foreign policy debate in parliament that Pakistan would not confer legitimacy on a puppet regime rejected by a majority of its people (Karachi Domestic Service, 6 September). At the talks themselves, the major unresolved issue is a timetable for Soviet troop withdrawal.

The Soviet press periodically launches propaganda campaigns against alleged Pakistani complicity in Afghan resistance activities, probably in an effort to erode public support for the government's position. Consistent with this practice, *Pravda* on 6 June charged that Pakistan, engaged in an "undeclared war" against Afghanistan, was a base for U.S. geopolitical designs in the region. More recently, Moscow's media has tried to exploit dissensions among some of Pakistan's tribes by charging that Pakistani troops are "occupying" the legally autonomous tribal territories. Nonetheless, Foreign Minister Yazub Khan told parliament that Pakistan would continue trying to keep its differences with the USSR on Afghan questions separate from the bilateral relationship (Karachi Domestic Service, 6 September).

In sharp contrast to the suspicions and mutual recriminations that characterize Pakistani-Soviet relations, Islamabad's ties with China remain a cornerstone of Pakistan's foreign policy. China is viewed as a reliable ally that has stood by Pakistan since the 1960s. It remains a major source of military equipment. China's importance was underscored by the mid-November visit of Prime Minister Junejo to the PRC, his first overseas travel after assuming office. During that visit, the two sides agreed in principle to more than double the two-way trade from its present level of $200 million. Just prior to his trip, Junejo dedicated a PRC-built aircraft-gun factory, highlighting the important military supply relationship between the two countries (AP, 5 November). At the end of the year, Chinese warships visited Karachi (and several other Indian Ocean ports) during the first deployment of Chinese warships to the Indian Ocean since the Communists came to power.

Walter K. Andersen
Arlington, Virginia

Philippines

Population. 55,808,000
Parties. Communist Party of the Philippines, Marxist-Leninist (CPP); Philippine Communist Party (Partido Komunista ng Pilipinas; PKP)
Founded. CPP: 1968; PKP: 1930
Membership. CPP: 15,000 (estimates range from 10,000 to over 30,000); PKP: 200
Leadership. CPP: Rodolfo Salas (former student organizer), chairman; Rafael Baylosis (former university lecturer), secretary general; Antonio Zumel (former journalist), Politburo member and head of the National Democratic Front; Juanito Rivera, commander of the New People's Army (NPA); and Benito Tiamzon, Benjamin De Vera, Ignacio Capegsan, Central Committee members. PKP: Felicismo C. Macapagal, secretary general; and Alejandro Briones, Jesus Lava, Jose Lava, Merlin Magallona, Central Committee members
Status. CPP: illegal; PKP: legal
Last Congress. CPP: unknown; PKP: Eighth, 1980
Last Election. Not applicable

Auxiliary Organizations. CPP: New People's Army (NPA), National Democratic Front (NDF), May First Movement (KMU), Nationalist Youth (KM), league of Filipino Students (LFS), Youth for Nationalism and Democracy (YND), Christians for National Liberation (CNL), Nationalist Health Association (MASAPA), Nationalist Teachers' Association (KAGUMA), Union of Democratic Filipinos (KDP), Justice for Aquino–Justice for All, August 21 Movement, Association of Concerned Teachers, Ecumenical Movement for Justice and Peace, Movement of Attorneys for Brotherhood, Integrity and Nationalism; PKP: National Association of Workers (Katipunan), Democratic Youth Council of the Philippines, Philippine Committee for Development, Peace, and Solidarity (PCDPS), Association of Philippine Women Workers, Philippine Printers Union, Agricultural Workers Union

Publications. CPP: *Ang Bayan* (The nation), monthly: NPA: *Pulang Bandila* (Red flag), bimonthly (started in 1985); NDF: *Liberation*, monthly; *Taliba ng Bayan*, biweekly; *NDF-Update*, bimonthly, published in the Netherlands; *Ang Katipunan*, irregular, published in Oakland, California; PKP: *Ang Komunista*, irregular

In 1985, the Philippine communist insurgency "took a qualitative leap in importance" (Guy Sacerdoti and Philip Bowring, "Marx, Mao and Marcos," *FEER*, 21 November), which was due, in large part, to the deepening economic problems and abuses of power by the government of Ferdinand Marcos. The Marcos government was found to be "unable and unlikely to make the necessary reforms to slow or halt the insurgency"; and the Philippines had "about three years to effect fundamental reforms to head off an all-out civil war," according to a U.S. Senate Select Committee on Intelligence staff report ("The Philippines: A Situation Report," 31 October, p. 2). A U.S. Special National Intelligence Estimate, prepared by the CIA, the DIA, and the State Department, predicted that "if the present trend continues, within three to five years the NPA would be able to fight the Armed Forces of the Philippines to a stalemate and grab political power" (Nayan Chanda, "Dear Mr. President," *FEER*, 31 October).

Leadership and Organization. For the second time since World War II, a revolutionary movement is challenging government authority in the Philippines. As in the case of the Huk rebellion of the 1940s and 1950s, the current radical insurgency is rooted in poverty and injustice. It has been fueled in recent years by the combination of economic decline, political repression, and a widespread belief that the government was responsible for the assassination of Benigno Aquino, Jr.

The success of the CPP is also due to a new generation of radical nationalist leaders who acquired their political views during the 1960s, when the influential international events of the day were the Cuban revolution, Sukarno's Guided Democracy in Indonesia, the Cultural Revolution in Maoist China, and the escalation of the U.S. war in Vietnam. They have no recollection of the days of the Japanese occupation. They did not fight with the Allies in the resistance movement. They did not share in the postwar celebrations. However, they have studied and learned the lessons of the rise and fall of the postwar Huk rebellion (analyzed in *Marxism in the Philippines*, University of the Philippines, Third World Studies Center, 1984).

This has led to their development of a new radical political strategy for achieving power. The CPP, the NPA, and the NDF are developing and implementing a distinctly Philippine version of Maoist revolutionary theory. In brief, it calls for a nationalist, rural-based, protracted people's war carried out through highly self-sufficient and very decentralized guerrilla fronts combined with widespread political mobilization.

Ideology and Strategy. The NPA is a political and propaganda force as well as a fighting force. Its first objective, according to its basic document, is to help recruit and train Communist party members; second, to carry out agrarian reforms; third, to build rural bases or guerrilla fronts and to engage in armed struggle; and, fourth, to help mobilize support for the NDF.

Most NPA members are not soldiers; they are political workers, social workers, agricultural advisers, paramedics, and teachers. They work in rural barrios and poor urban centers, in factories and on plantations, in churches, and even in government offices. Accordingly, a guerrilla front is not just a military unit. It is a provisional local government. It provides a regular exchange of material benefits for political support.

The strategy is summarized in the party slogan, "centralized leadership and decentralized operations." The Central Party Committee formulates general policies and guidelines. The local committee or guerrilla front has a lot of flexibility to experiment with different tactics for implementing general policy. As a result, guerrilla fronts have been created in almost every ethnolinguistic and geographic region of the country, from Mountain Province in the North to Mindanao in the South.

Even though there have been arrests and defections from the movement, CPP and NPA membership and activities have steadily increased, by almost all accounts. This strategy of decentralized operations has a risk of deteriorating into isolated components, but there is little evidence of such a trend. To the contrary, there seems to be an effective NPA and network of communications and transportation throughout the country (Steve Lohr, "Filipino Insurgency: Out of the Rice Paddies and into the Cities," *NYT*, 3 July).

Notable journalists with the rebels include Antonio Zumel, alleged chairman of the NDF and former news editor of the defunct *Manila Chronicle*. He went underground when martial law was declared in September 1972 ("Journalist Politicians," *FEER*, 23 May). Another journalist-turned-revolutionary is Saturnino Ocampo, former assistant business editor of the *Manila Times*, whose 5 May escape from custody ended nine years of military detention. His ordeal of torture and solitary confinement became the rallying cry for numerous human-rights groups, both locally and abroad (ibid.). In an underground interview, he commented on how the country's austerity has also affected CPP finances. "The leadership of the movement are devising ways and means by which to raise funds and among these are what we call revolutionary taxation. The basic idea is to impose some taxes on the big corporations, whether foreign or local, that are exploiting the natural resources and human resources of the country, like the mining areas, logging areas that are denuding the forest, or the huge plantations in Mindanao" ("Back with the People," *FEER*, 2 January, 1986).

The NPA and CPP have "expanded heavily" into the sugar-producing regions of Negros and Panay islands and into northern Mindanao, where firefights and general strikes occur with regularity, and where even shadow governments have been formed in the hinterland villages (*Asia 1986 Yearbook*, pp. 221–22). The NPA has also begun expanding outside the mountainous province regions in northern Luzon to provinces such as Ilocos Sur to the west and Nueva Viscaya and Nueva Ecija to the east. It now also has some units in the Zambales mountains, close to the Subic naval base. Cebu, the bastion of traditional moderate political opposition factions, has also become a target for expansion (ibid.). The first "powderkeg" of the country's communist rebellion could explode on Negros Island, where CPP spokesmen predict a strategic stalemate by 1987. CPP and NPA members now enter and leave the seaport capital of Bacolod under cover and freely roam sugar-cane fields just outside city limits. Masses of unemployed peasants and workers are ripe for the rebels, many residents believe (*FBIS*, IV, 16 October).

In early 1985, several reports appeared about NPA activity in the Manila area (Lohr, *NYT*, 3 July). "Since January, Armed City Partisans launched successful operations on several towns and cities of metropolitan Manila," said the NDF's biweekly newspaper, *Taliba ng Bayan*. Guerrilla operations have included eight arms seizures, liquidation of eight policemen and military agents, and the freeing of a political prisoner. The newspaper said that the ACP would be engaged in "firearms seizures, liquidation of 'enemies of the people,' sabotage of military installations, counter-espionage, raids on military 'safe houses' and the freeing of jailed dissidents" (*FBIS*, IV, 9 August). Alexander Birondo, alleged chief of the Armed City Partisans, was wounded and captured in a shoot-out with police in Manila in June ("Philippines Steps Up Hunt for Guerrillas," *San Jose Mercury News*, 9 June). Although infiltration and operations have begun in the Manila area, rebel activities are still nowhere near the present scale of operations in Davao City, where the NPA clashes daily with government forces (Nick Williams, "Philippine Insurgents Now Targetting Cities," *Los Angeles Times*, 5 September).

In the two years since the Aquino assassination, the NPA has expanded so rapidly that it now poses a credible threat to the survival of the Philippine government. From a total force of a few thousand armed guerrillas in 1980, the NPA has grown to probably over 15,000 regulars and a larger number of part-time irregulars. NPA force estimates range from 16,500 according to the Pentagon to 32,000 according to the NPA ("Armed Wing of Communists Still Loyal to Mao's Writings," *CSM, San Francisco Examiner and Chronicle*, 1 December). These forces are fighting on as many as 60 fronts around the country including occasional company-level (200–300 men) operations. The NPA reportedly has shadow governments in 10 to 15 percent of the country's villages (Chanda, *FEER*, 31 October).

Some level of NPA activity now exists in almost all of the country's 73 provinces. The military initiative clearly rests with the NPA. It has supplied its guerrillas almost entirely with weapons captured, and occasionally purchased, from the Philippine armed forces (Senate Intelligence Committee Report, p. ii). U.S. intelligence estimates that the NPA is growing at a rate of 20 percent a year, constrained by the shortage of arms and money, not recruits (Sacerdoti and Bowring, *FEER*, 21 November).

The NPA plans to step up operations. "Guerrilla units in the most advanced NPA areas—Mindanao, for example—have already been told to launch operations at least four times a week. By 1987, the NPA aims to have 60,000 fighters in all and daily operations in their more advanced zones. They plan to attack and briefly hold major provincial towns" (Paul Quinn-Judge, "Insurgency in the Philippines Could Provoke Full-scale War Unless Growth Is Checked," *CSM*, 15 October).

In July, 26 transmission towers of the National Power Corporation in Bataan reportedly were destroyed by the NPA. The destroyed facilities were part of the distribution system of the NPC's nuclear-power plant (*FBIS*, IV, 12 July). Assassination of selected government officials continued in 1985. The governor of Surigao Del Sur, Gregorio Murillo, was shot and killed in October, reportedly by an NPA member (*FBIS*, IV, 23 October). An anticommunist mayor, Pio Diasanta of Lawaan Town, Samar, was killed in August when suspected communist guerrillas attacked a team of local officials (*FBIS*, IV, 16 August).

The NPA has reportedly organized a sea unit, Bagong Navy ng Bayan (New National Navy). Coast Guard men killed two suspected members and captured four others, including the group commander, in a seven-hour sea battle off General Santos City in November (*FBIS*, IV, 19 November).

The National Democratic Front. The NDF, the political front created and led by the Communist party, now shows some signs of developing significant support among some radical Christian groups, labor organizations, student groups, and others. The NDF's new twelve-point program was released on 1 January 1985 and has been published by the Berkeley-based Philippine Resource Center (*Philippine Report*, vol. 2, no. 2, February).

NDF influence is evident in Bayan (Nation; from Bagong Alyansang Makabayan, the New Nationalist Alliance), a legal opposition coalition founded in April 1985. Bayan grew out of the Coalition for the Restoration of Democracy, which emerged after the Aquino killing. Bayan now encompasses "elements of the Marxist Left (Church as well as CPP) plus cause-oriented groups and traditional nationalist politicians, academics and even businessmen." A conflict over leadership structure led to the departure of important supporters, including Agapito "Butz" Aquino, the brother of Benigno Aquino, and Jose Diokno, an elder statesman of Filipino nationalism (Sacerdoti and Bowring, *FEER*, 21 November).

The NDF has begun a national membership campaign to capitalize on popular discontent and to build stronger ties with other anti-Marcos groups. It claims to have over 50,000 full-time organizers at work in most of the country's provinces. It also claims constituent memberships in mass organizations of 1 million Filipinos, with a base of popular support among 10 million Filipinos.

In areas where guerrilla fronts have been established, the NDF functions as the government authority. It collects taxes, implements land reforms, organizes public works and schools, and administers "revolutionary justice." The NDF has been able to spread its anti-Marcos and anti-American views among radical opposition groups and moderate opposition groups, from rural areas to urban areas. According to Eduardo Lachica of the *Wall Street Journal*, "the left now is the best organized political movement in the Philippines" ("Manila Maneuvers: During Marcos's Illness, Speculation Intensifies on Eventual Successor," *WSJ*, 7 December 1984).

Government Response. Manila's response to the rise of the NPA has been "inept," according to the Senate Intelligence Committee Report (p. 23). Despite occasional lip service to "civic action," the government has treated the insurgency as a purely military problem. Unfortunately, the Philippine armed forces suffer from a variety of ills. The defense budget equals only 1 percent of GNP, the lowest in Southeast Asia. Shortages of supplies and equipment—trucks, aircraft, uniforms, food, fuel—are endemic. Pay is poor and medical care is often nonexistent. A disproportionate number of units are concentrated in Manila rather than sent into the field against the NPA. Equipment maintenance is inadequate and there is no logistical system worthy of the name. Morale and mobility are both low. Perhaps most important, leadership is often poor and there are no central training facilities, with the result that troops are frequently sent into the field with inadequate training. Many of the best officers and technically skilled personnel have left the armed forces to take higher-paying jobs as mercenaries with armies in the Middle East.

All these problems are magnified for the Civil Home Defense Force (CHDF), the government-sponsored local militia. Frequently, CHDF forces will throw down their arms and flee when challenged by the NPA. As a consequence, they have been a major source of weapons and ammunition for the insurgency. Ill-trained CHDF personnel are also a source of many abuses of the civilian population (see *Human Rights Situation and Militarization in the Philippines: Trends and Analysis, 1984*, report submitted to the U.N. Commission on Human Rights, Geneva, Switzerland, by the Task Force Detainees of the Philippines, February 1985; and Bob Secter, "Cardinal Accuses Philippine Military of Sadism, Urges Broad Peaceful Protests Against Marcos," *Los Angeles Times*, 3 October 1984).

The *Asia 1986 Yearbook* contrasts the "exceptionally disciplined NPA" with government-armed forces "involved in kidnappings, torture, 'salvaging' (or summary execution), intimidation of the rural population and frequent drunken binges at night with indiscriminate firing" (*Asia 1986 Yearbook*, p. 222).

Abuses perpetrated by corrupt officers and undisciplined personnel and a general breakdown of peace and order have severely shaken respect for the military and the police. Many Filipinos question the government's ability to protect them from lawless elements or to dispense justice equitably. Murder, kidnappings, torture, and lesser abuses have become commonplace occurrences in recent years. Both the armed forces and the NPA have resorted to clandestine assassination or "salvaging" as a major weapon in their struggle. Davao City has been experiencing an average of three to four killings per day, yet there has not been a murder trial in over a year. NPA killings of local government officials including mayors, police chiefs, and teachers number several hundred per year nationwide. A comparable number of salvagings may be attributed to government forces.

These and other perceived abuses have been a major factor in many Filipinos' decision to join the insurgent ranks. This is especially true of the growing number of Catholic clergy and nuns who support the Communists. Some (such as Conrado Balweg, a rebel priest and NPA commander, and even a popular Filipino folk hero to some) already play important roles in the insurgent organization. Balweg is perhaps the most widely known rebel in the Philippines. Military authorities say he is one of their most wanted fugitives, and have put an $11,000 price on his head, dead or alive. A member of the Society of the Divine Word until he joined the rebels in January 1980, Balweg is from the minority Tinggian tribe, which has been fighting government reclamation projects and a big logging company to retain its ancestral lands. When Balweg joined the Cordillera guerrillas, they had 32 fighters. By 1984, their forces in the Luzon mountain area were believed to have grown to 700. Balweg said the forces had tripled in 1984 despite a 1,000-man government military operation against them; 99 percent of the guerrilla recruits are from mountain villages ("Priest Travels with Philippine Guerrillas," AP, *San Diego Union*, 28 April).

Despite the intense pressure for reforms, President Marcos shows little indication of removing his close allies from high positions in the military or the economy (Paul Quinn-Judge, "Marcos's Top General Keeps Finger on Power," *CSM*, 4 November; "Cosmetic Changes in Philippine Military," *CSM*, 18 December 1984; and "Marcos Voices His Support for Hard-line Forces in Military," *CSM*, 28 February). However, a reform movement within the military has demanded a "cleansing" of the officer corps (Paul Quinn-Judge, "Reformers Try to 'Cleanse' Philippine Army," *CSM*, 12 July; and Marites Danguilan-Vitug, "Young Philippine Officers Press for Reform in the Military," *CSM*, 8 May).

In a statement release accompanying the 31 October report to the Senate Select Committee on Intelligence, Senator Dave Durenberger, chairman of the committee, said the Marcos government was incapable and unwilling to carry out measures necessary to restore economic growth and head off the communist insurgency, and he therefore urged Marcos to resign and make way for free and fair elections to choose the next Philippine president (Bill Keller, "A Key Senator Calls on Marcos To Step Down," *NYT*, 2 November). Shortly afterward, on 3 November, in the course of a Sunday morning news interview on American network television, Marcos announced that, despite previous assertions, he would call for an early "snap election" to demonstrate his popular support and his ability to handle the growing insurgency.

The insurgency became a major campaign issue when Marcos accused Corazon Aquino, the opposition candidate, of being "dangerously naive" about the NPA. "The communists are fighting for control of Cory Aquino," Marcos said. He feared that Mrs.

Aquino would share power with the rebels in a coalition government ("Marcos Claims If Aquino Wins Election, Philippines Will Become Asian Nicaragua," AP, *Ithaca Journal*, 21 December, p. 11). Marcos also charged that "armed communist rebels were campaigning for his rival and threatening to wipe out rural villages if residents voted for him February 7 (Criselda Yabes, "Marcos Says Armed Communist Rebels Campaigning for Aquino," AP, *Burlington Free Press*, 6 January 1986). However, an NDF party official said the elections were "largely irrelevant" to the problems of the Philippines and that the rebels "do not have a policy of disruption of the elections" (Seth Mydans, "Philippine Rebel Calls Vote Irrelevant," *NYT*, 29 December).

If elected, Corazon Aquino vowed to investigate Marcos's links to the Aquino assassination and to government corruption. She called for the eventual removal of U.S. military bases, subject to negotiation and referendum. She also said she would call for a six-month cease-fire and invite the radical insurgents to lay down their arms and pledge support to the government in exchange for the legalization of the Communist party ("Excerpts from Aquino Interview on Candidacy," *NYT*, 16 December). Former Philippines president Diosdado Macapagal also proposed that the CPP and NDF be legalized to bring them "into the democratic political mainstream" of the country (*FBIS*, IV, 5 September).

Soviet Interests. The Soviet Union, so far as is known, provides no support for the CPP. Two recent U.S. Senate studies both concluded that "there is no convincing evidence" of any outside support for the Philippine communists" (*The Situation in the Philippines*, staff report prepared for the Committee on Foreign Relations of the U.S. Senate [Washington, D.C.: Government Printing Office, October 1984]; and the Senate Intelligence Committee Report). Another observer, however, finds that "the Soviet hand in the Communist Party of the Philippines" has long been evident and "Moscow has been quite active since the Aquino assassination in strengthening links to the CPP and New People's Army" (Leif Rosenberger, "Philippine Communism and the Soviet Union," *Survey* 29 [Spring 1985], pp. 113–45). According to the CPP, in early 1985, Moscow offered substantial military aid to communist insurgents, but the offer was rejected out of hand for a variety of practical and ideological reasons. Party officials were opposed to Soviet expansionism in Afghanistan and Cambodia; they also feared it might precipitate U.S. intervention. The problems of smuggling in the arms would be almost insurmountable, party sources said (Paul Quinn-Judge, "Filipino Marxist Rebels Spurn Offer of Arms from Moscow," *CSM*, *San Francisco Examiner*, 1 December).

Soviet-Philippine government relations have gradually improved along with the expansion of trade and cultural ties. Originally, Soviet-Philippine trade consisted primarily of Soviet purchases of Philippine coconut oil and sugar. The Soviets have made several proposals for increasing bilateral trade, incuding Soviet construction of a cement factory, low-cost housing units, and a fruit-canning factory; and joint ventures in pharmaceuticals, copper smelting, and oil exploration. The major project of Soviet-Philippine economic cooperation is a proposed joint venture for a cement plant on Semirara Island, which would have an annual capacity of 1 million tons at a cost of $250 million. The Soviets would also like to develop coal deposits to provide power for the plant. The Philippines would provide partial payment for the project with manufactured goods, such as clothing, and agricultural exports. The Philippines enjoys an expanding trade surplus with the Soviet Union. Although Philippine-Soviet trade has been steadily growing, it is still only a small percentage of total Philippine foreign trade.

Nonetheless, there is considerable potential for expanding Philippine-Soviet trade, especially through Japanese firms. Negotiations are now under way to use Filipino workers on Japanese-Soviet development projects in Siberia. If these negotiations are successful, it would be the first time a capitalist country has sent guest workers to the Soviet Union (*Kyodo*, 7 August, p. 5; *FBIS*, IV, 7 August). There have been a number of attempts to broaden Philippine-Soviet trade through trade fairs, expositions, seminars for businessmen, and the like. The Soviet and Philippine chambers of commerce have signed agreements to exchange information and arrange visits of businessmen (*Ecotass*, 10 June).

Another important factor in Philippine-Soviet relations is the personal diplomacy of Imelda Marcos. She has been active in organizing ballet performances, art exhibits, national day celebrations, and other cultural exchanges. The Philippine First Lady has made seven visits to Moscow since 1972. The most recent was in October 1985, where she received assurances that the Soviets would not meddle in Philippine affairs (Seth Mydans, "Marcos's Soviet Card Is Played by His Wife," *NYT*, 8 November). She has also held talks with the Soviet ambassador, Yuri Sholmov, on expanding barter trade (Quezon City, Maharlika broadcasting system, 11 April; *FBIS*, IV, 12 April).

In terms of security affairs, Moscow has generally supported Marcos and his martial-law government. Apart from some criticism of American military bases, the Soviet government has cultivated cordial relations with the Marcos government. President Marcos has pledged that he will not permit the United States to use the Clark or Subic bases to mount an attack on Indochina, where the Soviets have their largest overseas naval base at Cam Ranh Bay in Vietnam (George McT. Kahin, "Forget Philippine Bases," *NYT*, 6 November).

U.S. Interests. Throughout 1985, the United States made several efforts to urge the Marcos government to make major reforms in order to prevent a guerrilla victory and to preserve Philippine-American ties (Eduardo Lachica, "Pressuring Manila: U.S. Is Pushing Marcos To Curb His Cronies And Prepare Successors," *WSJ*, 5 January; "U.S. Will Insist on Major Policy Changes in Philippines as Price for Continued Aid," *WSJ*, 11 March; and Don Oberdorfer, "U.S. Official Urges 'Basic Changes' in Philippine Military," *WP*, 23 February). Assistant Secretary of Defense Richard L. Armitage estimated that "if present trends continued, the Communist insurgency could reach a strategic stalemate with the Philippine Armed Forces in three to five years" (Seth Mydans, "U.S. Worries About Security of Big Bases in Philippines," *NYT*, 28 October).

Clark Air Force Base and Subic Bay Naval Base are the most visible manifestations of the U.S. presence in the Philippines. NPA propaganda has focused on the bases as symbols of the "Marcos-U.S. dictatorship" and an affront to Philippine sovereignty. The bases are located in an area of active NPA activity and perimeter security is poor at both sites. Recently, an NPA unit was detected inside Subic only a mile from an ammunition depot. NPA leaders boast that they can walk on and off Clark and Subic at will. As yet, however, there has been no effort by the NPA to target either the bases or U.S. personnel (Senate Intelligence Committee Report).

The bases agreement comes up from review in 1989 and for possible renegotiation in 1991. In anticipation of the continued polarization of Philippine politics and the renegotiation of the bases agreement, U.S. officials have begun to make detailed contingency plans to relocate navy and air force units from the Philippines to Guam, Okinawa, and other Pacific locations (Bill Keller, "U.S. Plan to Quit Manila Bases Reported," *NYT*, 25 January 1986). The United States also leased 18,000 acres on the Marianas islands of Tinian and Saipan for possible replacement of Philippine facilities. The Pentagon also began considering hiring shipyards in Singapore and South Korea to replace Philippine facilities (George Wee, DPA, "U.S. May Move Asian Operations to Singapore," *Burlington Free Press*, 10 December; and Bryan Brumley, AP, "U.S. Lines Up Alternatives to Bases in Philippines," *Burlington Free Press*, 19 January 1986).

David Rosenberg
Middlebury College

Sri Lanka

Population. 16,206,000
Party. Communist Party of Sri Lanka (CPSL)
Founded. 1943
Membership. 5,000–6,000 (estimate)
Secretary General. Kattorge P. Silva
Politburo. 11 members, including K. P. Silva (secretary general) and Pieter Keuneman (president)
Central Committee. 50 members
Status. Legal
Last Congress. Twelfth, 27–29 January 1984
Last Election. 1977, 1.9 percent, 1 of 168 representatives
Auxiliary Organizations. Ceylon Federation of Trade Unions, Youth League, Women's Organization
Publications. *Aththa* (major newspaper, editor H. G. S. Ratnaweera), *Mawbima*, *Deshabimani*, *Forward* (journal)

The pro-Moscow CPSL was once a coalition partner in the 1970–1977 United Front government of former prime minister Sirimavo Bandaranaike's social-democratic Sri Lanka Freedom Party (SLFP). Since then it has been part of the divided opposition to the conservative United National Party (UNP) government. The CPSL was briefly banned in 1983 for alleged complicity in communal violence.

Leadership and Party Organization. There have been no significant changes in the party. It remains committed to uniting the "progressive" forces and is currently allied with the Trotskyist Lanka Sama Samaja Party (LSSP) and the Sri Lanka People's Party (SLPP), which broke away from the SLFP and is led by Mrs. Bandaranaike's son-in-law. In assessing the effectiveness of party work, a CPSL Politburo alternate member, Raja Collure, asserted that the development of this cooperation among leftist parties in the past year had helped to intensify "the popular struggle." It has also become important, he said, to resolve the question of cooperation with the SLFP (*WMR*, September).

Collure argued that the most important criteria of the success of party work are not always such things as membership growth and electoral successes (ibid.). Recent data on party strength are not available, but Collure's comments might indicate that membership has been stagnant or may even have declined after the overwhelming leftist losses in the 1977 election.

Despite its policy of alliance, the CPSL must maintain its identity, according to Collure, and it seeks to keep the people informed of its own positions. One method is through the CPSL's daily newspaper, *Aththa* (Truth), which was twenty years old in late 1984. The paper's editor, H. G. S. Ratnaweera, marked the anniversary by recalling the struggle to break the monopoly of the "capitalist" newspapers. *Aththa* had survived a number of closures and continues to expose the UNP government's "lies and corruption" (*WMR*, February).

Domestic Party Affairs. Domestically, the overwhelming concern in Sri Lanka again this year was the ethnic crisis involving the Sinhalese majority and Tamil minority. The young Tamil extremists seeking a separate state in northern Sri Lanka intensified their guerrilla campaign. The All-Party Conference that had been called by the government to find a solution ended in December 1984 without success. The government began to take a harder line early in the year, condemning the militants as terrorists and rejecting any talks with those advocating separatism.

On 15 February the CPSL, LSSP, and SLPP issued a joint statement in *Forward* urging a political solution. Much of the statement blamed the UNP government and its policies for producing a situation in which the country's unity was "in serious jeopardy." The government allegedly had not seriously sought a just settlement. "Virtual martial law" prevailed in large areas of the north and east. Government forces had followed Israeli and British advice, resulting in "widespread and senseless killing, arbitrary mass arrests . . . and severe hardships for the uninvolved civilian populations." The UNP was charged with a campaign of confrontation against India, endangering Sri Lanka's security and disrupting traditional good-neighborly relations. The statement also warned that the UNP's efforts toward militarization in unaffected parts of the country, such as creation of defense committees, could ultimately be aimed at all opposition to the UNP, including the working class and trade unions. The statement, however, did contain some criticism of the Tamil extremists: the three parties opposed "any efforts to seek a solution to the ethnic crisis through terrorism, either by the state or by individuals or political groups" (*WMR Information Bulletin*, May).

The statement went on to affirm that any viable settlement should be based on the principles of the unity of Sri Lanka and, within this framework, substantial devolution of many currently centralized powers and functions. The three parties supported an "immediate ceasefire by the government and the armed youth groups" and called for efforts toward direct negotiations between the government and all Tamil groups (ibid.).

The UNP did not comment directly on the statement. The prime minister did remark sometime later, however, that the Communist party, the LSSP, and the SLPP "are working toward peace in the country and not trying to stir the people" (Colombo radio, *FBIS*, 17 June).

As the Tamil extremists escalated their antigovernment campaign, about a half-dozen of the more than 30 separatist splinters appeared to constitute the major groups. The Liberation Tigers of Tamil Ealam (LTTE) remains the most militant and, along with the Tamil Ealam Liberation Organization, seems responsible for most of the violence. The People's Liberation Organization of Tamil Ealam, on the other hand, is closer to the major moderate Tamil party, the Tamil United Liberation Front, and more willing to work toward a political settlement. All the groups have claimed to be socialist and/or Marxist. Their equipment includes Soviet weapons, but also equipment of Western, Indian, and Pakistani manufacture. There has been no reliable evidence of significant foreign communist links (*FEER*, 21 February; *Economist*, 13 April).

The Tamil attacks gradually spread to the south and east from the northern Jaffna peninsula and began to affect more civilians. In one attack in May, claimed by the LTTE, nearly a hundred Sinhalese were killed. On the other side were instances of excesses by the security forces. President J. R. Jayewardene stated in May that he would not hesitate to impose martial law if necessary. Colvin R. de Silva of the LSSP speculated that military rule or a civilian dictatorship relying on the army seemed inevitable. The CPSL's Pieter Keuneman, however, thought that the talk of martial law might just be a threat (*FEER*, 27 June).

In the deteriorating situation, with the numbers of refugees either within Sri Lanka or fleeing to India growing into tens of thousands, the Sri Lankan government began to explore with India ways of halting the violence and resuming political talks. In early June President Jayewardene visited New Delhi and agreed with India's prime minister Rajiv Gandhi that every effort would be made to rapidly restore normalcy in the north.

A three-month ceasefire was announced on 18 June, the first in more than two years of fighting. Following the ceasefire India arranged talks in Bhutan between the UNP and the Tamil separatists. Negotiations in July and August produced no breakthrough. A government proposal was reported in September to include some concessions that would require a constitutional amendment likely to be opposed by Mrs. Bandaranaike's SLFP. The Communist party and its alliance partners, however, would probably support the government. They had warned, referring to the SLFP, that "those who shout 'war' are recklessly indifferent" to the present dangers (*FEER*, 12 September). As political efforts continued, violence nevertheless began to escalate again as the year ended.

Auxiliary/Front Organizations. Although the ethnic crisis was dominant, students and youth were involved in protesting changes to the university structure. In January the government passed controversial legislation that would encourage private fee-levying institutions of higher learning. Fear that this will erode Sri Lanka's traditional system of free education provoked protests from students backed by all opposition political parties. Students were arrested, censorship was imposed on this issue, and the country's largest university was closed for a time. In a letter to President Jayewardene the CPSL, LSSP, and SLPP charged the legislation was a major departure from the existing system and would only benefit the rich. The propaganda organs of the Communist party, which has strong support on the campuses, were quite active, as was the banned Janatha Vimukthi Peramuna, the extreme leftist organization responsible for the 1971 insurgency (*FEER*, 28 March).

International Views, Positions, and Activities. The Sri Lankan government's close ties with China were marked by a visit from the Chinese foreign minister in January, during which he opposed any division of Sri Lanka (Colombo radio, 25 January; *FBIS*, 28 January). On the other hand, official relations with the Soviet Union remain correct. Commenting on the ethnic issue, the Soviet ambassador stated in Colombo that it was an "internal matter" and the Soviet Union would not interfere in internal affairs (Colombo *Sun*, 9 May; *FBIS*, 20 May). The USSR sent a congratulatory telegram on Sri Lanka's independence anniversary, and Sri Lanka's president sent condolences following Chernenko's death. The two countries also signed a cultural and scientific exchange protocol later in the year. The USSR, nevertheless, continued publicizing activities surrounding the new U.S. Voice of America transmitter in Sri Lanka, quoting local media reports that the station would provide "a good front for a secret U.S. communications center and Navy eavesdropping post in the Indian Ocean" (*Izvestiia*, 20 February; *FBIS*, 25 February).

The CPSL for its part sent a delegation to the USSR in June, headed by Politburo member S. Sudasinghe. The delegation praised Soviet policies and noted the "great significance of the CPSU's experience in resolving [its]. . . nationalities question" (*Pravda*, 12 July; *FBIS*, 16 July). In a commentary on the fortieth anniversary of the victory over Germany and Japan, Pieter Keuneman lauded Soviet sacrifices and praised the USSR's actions in avoiding another global war (*WMR*, May). In August the CPSL member of parliament, Sarath Mutteguwegama, visited Italy and met with PCI officials.

Barbara Reid
Charlottesville, Virginia

Thailand

Population. 52,700,000
Party. Communist Party of Thailand (CPT)
Founded. 1942
Membership. 1,000
Secretary General. No data (Virat Angkhathavorn, most active leader)
Leading Bodies. No data
Status. Illegal
Last Congress. Fifth, February 1984, clandestine (reported only by Thai government, no announcement by party)

Last Election. N/A
Auxiliary Organizations. No data
Publications. None

Leadership and Party Organization. Current leaders are Virat Angkhathavorn, Thong Chaemsi, and Comrade Khap (true name unknown). The controller of party finances and perhaps the most influential of these three is Virat, who has lived in the PRC since 1979. No information is available on the other members of the Politburo or the Central Committee.

There is a paucity of information about the party's current leadership. As for regional committee leaders, the South Regional Committee is under the overall supervision of Sin Toemlin, a member of the Central Committee. The Secretary of the South Regional Committee is Huang Chaichumkhun. The CPT work areas in the south recently have been reorganized as the Chumphon-Ranong-Surat Thani work area, the Nakhon Si Thammarat-Surat Thani work area, the Phangnga-Krabi-Surat Thani work area, the Nakhon Si Thammarat-Trang-Phatthalung-Krabi work area, and the Phatthalung-Trang-Songkhla-Satun work area. (*Bangkok World*, 18 January; *FBIS*, 23 January).

Domestic Developments. The defection of CPT insurgents to the government continued in 1985, but these defections no longer captured the public interest (*Bangkok Post*, 18 April; *FBIS*, 19 April). This was due in part to the fact that defections, including large-scale defections, have become so commonplace in recent years. Also, there now are few CPT insurgents remaining in the forests. In late October the Internal Security Operations (ISOC) reported that between 465 and 620 armed CPT insurgents were still operating in Thailand: between 250 and 340 were in the south, 85 to 115 in the northeast, 80 to 110 in the north, and 50 to 55 in the central plains (*Bangkok Post*, 25 October; *FBIS*, 25 October). The guerrillas are split into very small bands with the capability of conducting only small-scale, sporadic attacks.

In point of fact, these guerrilla remnants seem to have been increasingly preoccupied with political activities rather than armed struggle. Gen. Arthit Kamlang-ek, supreme commander and commander in chief of the army, stated that small insurgent groups have begun to focus on establishing personal contact with the local population in order to criticize government shortcomings and engage in general agitation (Bangkok Domestic Service, 13 May; *FBIS*, 16 May).

Thai authorities fear that former insurgents and CPT cadres other than the armed insurgents are active in big cities, particularly Bangkok. For instance, Interior Minister Sitthi Chirarot indicated that he suspected the CPT may be trying to establish some sort of operational system in Bangkok. And he seemed to imply that some former insurgents who defected and now work as advisors to government agencies may be involved in this activity (*Bangkok World*, 7 August; *FBIS*, 8 August).

Of the 22 people arrested in 1983 for violation of Thailand's Anti-Communist Act, eight were released in 1985. The military prosecutors deemed the evidence insufficient to prosecute (a decision that reportedly disappointed some senior police officers in the Special Branch). Seven arrestees were ordered to undergo up to six months of reindoctrination. One defendant, Preecha Piemphongsarn (a university lecturer), was placed on probation and was not required to attend reindoctrination classes. Thus only six of the defendants are still under detention and facing trial. The most notable of these is Phirun Chartvanitkun, a former student activist who is accused, among other things, of being a member of the CPT Central Committee (*FEER*, 25 April).

The CPT continued its efforts to re-enlist some of its defectors, especially persons who had been in leadership positions. For example, Gen. Banchop Bunnak, Chief of Staff of ISOC, reported that officials of CPT committees (presumably, provincial committees and the Northeast Regional Committee) met in early March with leaders of small armed insurgent bands in Udon Thani, Chaiyaphum, and Khon Kaen provinces to map out a means of persuading former senior CPT members to rejoin the movement (Bangkok Domestic Service, 8 April; *FBIS*, 10 April). That such efforts were made elsewhere in Thailand, with at least some success, is attested by the arrest in late October of Li Chong. Li Chong, who was arrested in Chawang District of Nakhon Si Thammarat Province on the grounds that he was surveying the area for the CPT, was reportedly a leading CPT insurgent until he defected five years ago. He is also the father-in-law of Wirot Chongchit, reputedly one of those responsible for supervising provincial-level insurgents in Nakhon Si Thammarat and the provinces of Surat Thani, Trang, and Krabi (*Bangkok Post*, 1 November; *FBIS*, 5 November).

The faction of the CPT that broke away toward the end of the 1970s has been and still is popularly referred to as the Pak Mai (New Party). In 1985 Thai authorities called it by other names as well. Colonel Yingrot Chotiphimai, deputy chief of staff of the Third Army Region, used the name New Siam Party to describe this faction (*Matichon*, 23 August; *FBIS*, 29 August). Gen. Chawalit Yongchaiyut, assistant chief of staff of the army, called it the Green Star communist movement—a reference to the Pathet Lao–style uniforms worn by this faction, which use green stars as shoulder flashes or sewn on berets and forage caps (*FEER*, 11 August).

It is not clear whether this group is yet organized as a separate communist party or whether it is still a movement that thinks of itself as a dissident faction within the CPT, though it appears to be moving in the direction of the former. Nor is it clear who leads this group. It is widely believed to be Bunyen Worthong, a former member of the Socialist Party and elected member of the National Assembly. However, General Chawalit claimed that Bunyen has only about ten followers with him in Vientiane, Laos (*Siam Rat*, 12 July; *FBIS*, 17 July). If this is true, then Bunyen may not lead Pak Mai. Furthermore, a Thai intelligence source claimed that the leader of the Green Star movement is Comrade S. Narong (*Bangkok World*, 8 June; *FBIS*, 11 June). Still another report claimed that Pak Mai is under the leadership of Prasit Taphiantong (*Lak Thai*, 11 July; *FBIS*, 26 July). It is conceivable, of course, that the latter two names are those of the same person.

The Pak Mai, which is supported by Vietnam, Laos, and the Soviet Union, reportedly has about five hundred armed members (*Matichon*, 23 August; *FBIS*, 29 August). None are now based in Thailand; they are all based in Laos. Approximately three hundred of them are based at a forward command, established in late August in the Laotian town of Phiang, of Sayaboury Province. According to informed Thai sources, this forward command is aimed at facilitating the infiltration of Pak Mai members into the upper northern Thai provinces of Chiang Rai, Phayao, Nan, Uttaradit, Phitsanulok, Petchabun, and Loei. These men were particularly active in Nan in September, mainly in the neighborhood of three villages that lie along the border and are claimed by both Thailand and Laos (*The Nation*, 20 September; *FBIS*, 20 September). Other members of the Pak Mai are based in Laotian territory opposite northeastern Thailand, and they infiltrate the provinces of Udon Thani, Nong Kai, Roi Et, Khon Kaen, Nakhon Phanom, and Sakon Nakhon (*Lak Thai*, 11 July; *FBIS*, 26 July). Some have also been reported in Mukdaharn and Surin provinces.

Pak Mai members enter Thailand in teams of three to twelve persons and remain there for short periods of time, returning to Laos after completing their missions (*Nation Review*, 21 April; *FBIS*, 22 April). Since Pak Mai has not yet reached the armed phase of its struggle, these teams avoid armed conflict with Thai security forces and instead concentrate on indoctrination of villagers, organization (creating village committees), recruitment, and the gathering of intelligence. Those villagers who are recruited as potential insurgents are taken to Laos for guerrilla and political training. A district officer in Mukdaharn claimed that Pak Mai agents had contacted some CPT defectors there in an effort to recruit them. But this assertion is questionable, because one former CPT provincial committee member indicated that, before defecting to the government, he had sent an emissary to Vientiane to ascertain the Laotian authorities' attitude toward cooperation with those insurgents who were disenchanted with CPT leadership and its reverses. The emissary learned that the Laotians regarded the top CPT leadership as their enemies. Although they sympathized with lower ranking CPT cadres, they were not inclined to trust them (*FEER*, 11 August).

Armed insurgents of the Communist Party of Malaya (CPM) and its offshoot, the Communist Party of Malaysia (MCP), continued to operate from forest camps located near the Thai-Malaysian border. Thai military authorities estimated that, as of late May, there were between 1,460 and 1,630 of these insurgents in the border area (*Bangkok Post*, 23 May). The great majority are based in Thailand. Most are ethnic Chinese, but some are Malays. Some came from Malaysia, while others were recruited from among the local citizenry of rural and urban border areas in Thailand.

As in recent years, Thai security forces aggressively sought to discover and capture camps belonging to these guerrillas. They encountered considerable success in this regard. For example, in May security forces seized and destroyed a sizable camp in Yala Province. It contained approximately one hundred shelters with corrugated iron roofs, six meeting halls, three schools and libraries, firing ranges, tunnels, outdoor basketball courts, weapons, food supplies, and a large number of documents. Four smaller satellite camps nearby were also taken (Bangkok Domestic Service, 13 May; *FBIS*, 16 May). Other camps were also captured during the year. Some of these seizures resulted in casualties among the security forces. In one operation, twenty-one soldiers were injured, mostly by landmine explosions (*Bangkok World*, 18 June; *FBIS*, 19 June). However, as senior Malaysian military officers pointed out, only a few guerrillas are killed when Thai security forces overrun CPM camps (*FEER*, 16 May).

The Thai government plans to build roads into some of the captured camps, to be completed by 1987. The camps may eventually be converted into tourist attractions, as were some captured camps of the CPT in the north. Also, large tracts of nearby land will be set aside for future farming. And the government officially announced that it would transfer such farming land to CPM defectors and, eventually, grant Thai citizenship to those among them who are not from Thailand. But if the guerrillas refuse to defect, the government promised to distribute this land to local villagers (*Bangkok Post*, 23 May).

While Thai and Malaysian security forces have cooperated for some time with respect to acting against communist insurgents along the border, the Malaysians have failed to take actions against Thai Muslim separatist insurgents, who often use Malaysian territory for their sanctuaries. In early 1985, however, a senior Malaysian army officer indicated indirectly that the threat the Muslim separatists pose to Thailand also affects the security of Malaysia. Furthermore, there were indications that Malaysian authorities are becoming somewhat more cooperative in dealing with separatists who operate from Malaysian territory (Bangkok Domestic Service, 7 April; *FBIS*, 10 April).

On two occasions in August, members of a small band of what were believed to be Burmese Communist Party (BCP) guerrillas intruded into Chiang Mai Province in northern Thailand. The guerrillas burned down a small village and clashed with troopers from the Thai Border Patrol Police (BPP). Two BPP troopers were killed on the first occasion, while two BCP guerrillas were killed the second time (*Bangkok World*, 14 August; *FBIS*, 14 August).

Auxiliary Organizations. No information is available on auxiliary and front organizations. Those that existed in earlier years appear to have disintegrated. Massive defections from the CCPDF, including the 1983 defection of Udom Srisuwan, chairman of the CCPDF and member of the CPT Politburo, left that front organization leaderless and without significance. It may no longer exist, since no reference to it appears to have been made in 1985.

International Views and Positions. The CPT continued to be oriented toward the People's Republic of China, whereas the Pak Mai faction continued to be oriented toward the Soviet Union, Vietnam, and its Laotian client. The Thai government continued to view Vietnam, especially the 160,000 Vietnamese troops in Kampuchea and 40,000 Vietnamese troops in Laos, as a threat to its security. It also supported the resistance forces of the Coalition Government of Democratic Kampuchea. Thailand continued to work for Vietnamese withdrawal from Kampuchea through joint diplomatic efforts of the Association of Southeast Asian Nations (ASEAN), and relied on the promise of American military assistance and Chinese military intervention should Vietnam attack Thailand. Finally, the government continued to view the USSR with suspicion, particularly with respect to possible Soviet efforts to extend their influence in Thailand. As evidence of the latter, Thailand reacted cautiously to recent Soviet efforts to expand trade with Thailand (*FEER*, 21 November).

M. Ladd Thomas
Northern Illinois University

Vietnam

Population. 60,492,000
Party. Vietnamese Communist Party (Dang Cong San Vietnam; VCP)
Founded. 1930 (as Indochinese Communist Party)
Membership. 1,750,000 (December 1985 estimate); 20 percent women (est.); ethnically, almost entirely Vietnamese; average age in mid-40s; 40 percent *ban co* (poor peasant); 25 percent peasant; 15 percent proletariat; 20 percent other
General Secretary. Le Duan (b. 1908)
Politburo. 16 members: Le Duan (b. 1908), Truong Chinh (b. 1909), Pham Van Dong (b. 1908), Pham Hung (b. 1912), Le Duc Tho (b. 1910), Sen. Gen. Van Tien Dung (b. 1917), To Huu (b. 1920), Vo Chi Cong (b. 1912), Vo Van Kiet (b. 1922), Do Muoi (b. 1917), Le Duc Anh (b. 1910?), Nguyen Duc Tam (b. 1920), Sen. Gen. Chu Huy Man (b. 1920), Nguyen Van Linh (b. 1915), Nguyen Co Thach (b. 1920), Dong Sy Nguyen (b. 1920?)
Secretariat. 10 members: Le Duan, Le Duc Tho, Vo Chi Cong, Nguyen Duc Tam, Nguyen Lam, Le Quang Dao, Hoang Tung, Nguyen Thanh Binh, Tran Kien, Tran Xuan Bach
Central Committee. 116 full and 36 alternate members
Status. Ruling party
Last Congress. Fifth, 27–31 March 1982, in Hanoi
Last Election. 1981, for Seventh National Assembly, 97.96 percent, 496 of 614, with all candidates VCP endorsed
Auxiliary Organizations. Fatherland Front (Huynh Tan Phat, president); Ho Chi Minh Communist Youth Union (Vu Mao, secretary general)
Publications. *Nhan Dan* (The people), VCP daily; *Tap Chi Cong San* (Communist review), VCP theoretical monthly; *Quan Doi Nhan Dan* (People's army), army newspaper

The year 1985 was a relatively uneventful one for the Vietnamese Communist Party (VCP) and the society it guides. Unlike many of the postwar years of the past decade there were no highly traumatic events. For the most part the party and the general population focused collective attention on the mundane but still vital effort to raise Vietnam's abysmal standard of living. The war in Kampuchea remained what it had long become, a protracted conflict with little hope of early resolution. The cold war with China continued more or less unabated. Vietnam remained isolated in the region, surrounded by essentially hostile neighbors. The relationship with the USSR continued to deepen. None of this differed greatly from previous years.

Probably the most important event of the year was the party's Eighth Plenum in June, which issued orders to renew the attack on the country's vast array of economic problems. The world's attention returned to Vietnam briefly in April, with the tenth anniversary of the fall of Saigon and the end of the Vietnam War, an event with symbolic meaning but little else.

Leadership and Party Organizations. There was no overtly significant change during the year in either party leadership or organizational structure. The top leadership, clearly now a gerontocracy, did not face up to the fact of its mortality by announcing plans for eventual transfer of political power. The average age of Politburo members was 70; for the Central Committee the average age, although not precisely known, is estimated to be in the mid-60s. The party organization itself struggled to polish its image, badly tarnished compared to wartime days, when its reputation bordered on the omnipotent and omniscient.

Nguyen Van Linh, ousted from the Politburo three years earlier, appeared back on its roster without fanfare or even formal announcement. In midyear Hanoi newspapers, noting his various activities—chiefly involving the party and the southern economy—began listing him as a Politburo member. Probably his reappointment is a gesture of deference by the top leadership to southern party factions, among whom feelings of northern discrimination have been high since Linh and several other key southern officials were removed by the Fifth Congress.

Leadership continued to be collective among the sixteen men of the Politburo, with the "inner circle" holding what amounted to a monopoly of political control. The circle includes Party Secretary Le Duan as primus inter pares; Prime Minister Pham Van Dong; PAVN Sen. Gen. Van Tien Dung; Party theoretician Truong Chinh; security chief Pham Hung; and the Party cadre whip, Le Duc Tho. Throughout the year there were rumors that the Tho faction was in deep political trouble because of difficulties in the south attributable to Le Duc Tho's brother, Mai Chi Tho, the party's security chief and a major figure in Ho Chi Minh City. Nothing to substantiate these rumors had appeared as of year's end.

During the year death claimed Nguyen Duy Trinh, 75, former foreign minister who had been out of government since the early 1980s; Xuan Thuy, 73, SRV diplomat best known abroad for his work at the 1963 Geneva Conference on Laos and at the Paris talks in the late 1960s; Central Committee member Nguyen Duc Thuan, president of the Vietnam General Confederation of Trade Unions; and former Central Committee member Lt. Gen. Tran Quy Hai, believed to have been killed in action in Kampuchea.

Party official Hoang Tung told a *Pravda* correspondent in mid-January that the Sixth Party Congress would be held sometime in 1986. Late in the year there were other indications from Hanoi that the congress was being scheduled for the spring of 1986. As has been the case in the past with rumors on impending congresses, the reports were accompanied by speculation that major leadership changes were being planned in the Politburo and Central Committee and a generational transfer of power would occur.

Domestic Party Affairs. By far the most important event of 1985 for the party rank and file was the Eighth Plenum (of the Fifth Congress) that met in Hanoi in mid-June, a session almost entirely devoted to economic matters. Out of it came Plenum Resolution Eight which, together with three earlier Plenum resolutions, currently forms the operative guidelines for the party, the society, and the country. The three documents are the Fifth Congress's Seventh Plenum Resolution (December 1984), the Sixth Plenum Resolution (July 1984), and the seminal Sixth Plenum Resolution of the Fourth Congress (September 1979). All of these are devoted almost entirely to the economic sector—principally to the short-run problem of getting the economic machine in gear and secondarily to the longer-range problem of economic development and nation building. The Ninth Plenum (Fifth Congress) met in mid-December 1985 to review progress ordered earlier. It broke no new ground in terms of instruction or economic direction.

Most of the new look in Vietnamese economic problem-solving was set down by the Sixth Plenum in 1979. What has been added since, particularly by the Eighth Plenum in June 1985, is specific guidance, often experimental or based on the application of recently learned lessons. It has been a slow, painful, and to date not entirely successful, effort. Progress has been made, however, particularly in achieving increased food production.

Resolution Eight set in motion a sustained party/state drive against the perceived major evils and shortcomings in the economic system, three of which drew major attention: institutional inefficiency (called "bureaucratism"), featherbedding and other economic practices that drag down productivity (called "subsidization"), and a host of administrative and bookkeeping arrangements that must be abolished and replaced by "modern socialist accounting and business methods." At root is the question of incentive, specifically in this case what is labeled pejoratively as "economic equalitarianism." Virtually abandoned in Vietnam is the once holy Marxist writ of "from each according to his ability, to each according to his need." This "equalitarianism in wages," Resolution Eight declares, causes farm and factory personnel staffs to increase steadily regardless of work load, makes it impossible to encourage worker skills or to reward those who by their demonstration of talent and diligence make the greatest economic contribution. The "socialist capitalism" (or experimental Marxism), which has found favor in China and Eastern Europe, has long been anathema to the dominant party faction in Hanoi. The issue, chiefly applicable to agriculture, has long been how best to grow more rice, whether through moral exhortation (i.e., ideological appeal) or pragmatically, by offering specific material incentives. Taken at face value the Eighth Plenum Resolution indicates the leadership is moving boldly away from ideology in the economic sector. However, as has been seen in the past, well-intentioned policy often never gets off the drafting board because it is not translated into the necessary operational instructions or is sabotaged by party ideologues.

The party views economic problems as partially an administrative or technical challenge—which requires developing economic institutions, supplying policy mechanisms, and providing sufficient numbers of trained economic cadres and technicians—and partially as a challenge to the party to assert and maintain centrality in all economic activity by offering effective, meaningful leadership and ideological guidance. In practice, apparently deliberately, the two elements—overhauling the mechanisms of the economy and keeping economic decisionmaking and policies doctrinally pure—are intricately intermixed. The overall purpose, it is clear, is less a matter of serving ideology than ensuring that the party remains the focal point of all economic activity.

It was a year of anniversaries for the party, many of them decennial and thus of importance in a Confucian culture. The observances emphasized the centrality of the party in Vietnam's history and present policymaking. In 1985 these included the tenth anniversary of victory in the Vietnam War and the subsequent unification of North and South Vietnam; the fortieth anniversary of the establishment of the Democratic Republic of Vietnam and the August Revolution; the fifty-fifth anniversary of the founding of the party; the ninety-fifth anniversary of the birth of Ho Chi Minh and the 700th anniversary of the 1285 Vietnamese victory over the invading Mongols. At the party's anniversary celebration on 3 February in Hanoi, party spokesman Hoang Tung listed the party's "five historic achievements: the seizure of power in 1945, defeat of French colonialism, defeat of U.S. imperialism, defeat of the February 1979 Chinese invasion, and abolition of oppression and exploitation in Vietnam."

The party continued to press forward with its massive restructuring plan for Vietnamese society, commonly called the "district building program." A high-level week-long conference was held in mid-January in Hanoi, at which a new institution was unveiled, the Party-State District Building Committee, which appears to be supervised by Politburo member To Huu. The district building plan is a vastly ambitious long-range development program (social as well as economic) that seeks to end the village in Vietnam and downgrade provincial centers. It envisions a population concentrated in some 426 district agro-complexes averaging about 200,000 members, with about 25,000 being farm workers who will cultivate an average of 20,000 hectares per district.

Under the goad of the Eighth Plenum Resolution, the party apparat intensified efforts to improve the quality of party cadres and rank-and-file membership, recruiting young, promising members in large numbers and weeding out the incompetent cadres and over-the-hill members. The turnover obviously was high, judged by reports at the provincial level of new member inductions—but whether this left a net gain was not clear since the official size of the party was not announced during the year. It is believed to be about 1.7 million, about the same as 1984, although possibly membership turnover during 1985 was as high as 20 percent.

The party launched a major emulation and motivation campaign early in the year against "negative phenomena": a catchall term meaning anything that "lowers the quality of socialist life." The problem has been of long standing, but apparently the party feels it has worsened in the past several years. The campaign was launched at a party cadre conference at the end of 1984, chaired by Pham Hung, the security chief. In his report he listed five negative phenomena: a negative attitude by workers and farmers ("indolent, careless, fraudulent"); a general negative attitude toward socialist property ("theft, misappropriation, and 'internal distribution'"—the latter being collusion among production and commune officials to acquire needed raw materials or to sell a portion of production outside of state channels); "smuggling, financial speculation, bribery, 'palm greasing,' loaning money at high interest rates"; "violating collective ownership rights of the people," which seems chiefly to mean setting a bad example for the young by exploiting the profitability of one's position for personal benefit or the benefit of the local work unit; and "inferior lifestyle, decadence, pursuit of material passions, and low pleasures." It is clear that some of this behavior is indeed antisocial, but also that much of it is simply the individual or work unit attempting to cope with an impossible economic situation. Interestingly, the party treats the matter as a social, not a legal, problem.

However, harsher measures were also taken. In early January Vietnam executed three men convicted of espionage after a trial of 21 men, all of whom were convicted. Five originally received death sentences. Two were commuted to life imprisonment after an appeal from France, including alleged ring leader Mai Van Hanh, whom Paris recognized as a French national. The five were accused of belonging to the United Front of Patriotic Forces for the Liberation of Vietnam, a resistance group in southern Vietnam supported by China and Thailand. The French Foreign Ministry and the National Assembly president expressed "grief and indignation" at the executions.

International Views, Positions, and Activities. Vietnam's situation internationally changed very little during 1985. With the USSR, it maintained an intimate and steadily deepening relationship based on dependency and, on Moscow's part, perceived opportunities. The cold war with China continued. The hostile relationship seemed early in the year to be improving slightly, but it turned ugly again at year's end. In Vietnam's dealings with ASEAN and the rest of the region there were intimations of improvement, but little actual change in the present semihostile relationship.

As for the rest of the socialist world (except Cuba) and most of the nonsocialist world (except India), Vietnam conducted strictly nominal relations. With the United States, clear progress was made on one outstanding matter, the resolution of the casualties issue, but the full meaning of that development was not apparent at year's end.

The focal point of Hanoi's external relations continued to be Cambodia. Virtually all of its separate bilateral relationships in one way or another directly impinged on the fact that Vietnam is bogged down in a protracted conflict in Cambodia from which it would like to extricate itself (under certain favorable conditions) but is unable to do so.

There was a good deal of diplomatic intercourse between Vietnam and the ASEAN countries over the Cambodian issue, led by Indonesia. On both sides the exchanges were partly exploratory and partly jockeying for position. Nothing significant came of this during the year. Vietnam is trapped in Cambodia at the moment with no feasible way to withdraw and differences within ASEAN (particularly between Indonesia and Thailand) limited offers to Hanoi.

Early in the year there was considerable speculation, especially in Thailand, that China was about to alter its basic position with respect to Cambodia in order to strike a deal either with the USSR or Hanoi, to the detriment of the resistance in Cambodia. Speculation was fueled by Beijing's lack of reaction to Hanoi's major January offensive against the resistance camps along the Thai-Cambodian border (unlike previous years, when there had been both rhetoric and noisy Sino-Soviet border activity). Beijing denied any change of policy and as the year progressed doubts about China began to evaporate. In late December 1985, possibly in anticipation of another Vietnamese dry-season offensive in Cambodia, there was a sharp increase in border conflicts initiated by the Chinese, particularly in the Ha Tuyen region. Artillery barrages reached as high as 80,000 shells a day, according to the Vietnamese.

It was a busy year along the Hanoi-Moscow axis with missions back and forth, some important, most chiefly ceremonial. Perhaps the most important trip was Party Secretary Le Duan's trip to Moscow in June for sessions with the CPSU's new general secretary, Mikhail Gorbachev. Discussions reportedly turned almost entirely on economic matters. Scattered reports out of Hanoi during the year tended to suggest that the Vietnamese leaders have taken careful measure of new USSR leader Gorbachev and do not particularly like what they see. Some in Hanoi reportedly are wondering whether Vietnam may have another Nikita Khrushchev on its hands, that is, a Soviet leader with no sense of empathy for Vietnam's past record or present problems and determination to serve his own priorities. But there was at year's end no particular reason not to believe that the present relationship will continue at least as long as Vietnamese dependency and Soviet opportunism.

In what was an abrupt change of policy, Hanoi officials during 1985 announced they would settle the resolution of the casualties issue with the United States in a two-year time period. Such a forthcoming gesture had not been previously seen. In promising without conditions to deliver in two years what the United States had been prepared to negotiate and presumably pay for, the move was a radical change in Hanoi's past negotiational technique. The move could be explained as a determined effort by Hanoi to establish a base for new and improved relations with the United States, or it could be interpreted as an isolated move, simply a decision (possibly forced by the professional military men in the Politburo) to end the unseemly traffic in dead bodies and get the MIA issue off the table once and for all.

Biography. *Senior General Van Tien Dung.* General Dung is the army's top military figure since the retirement of General Vo Nguyen Giap. For virtually his entire career he has been number two, serving in the shadow of his mentor and superior. Apparently the secondary position has never been a burden. Those who have known Dung over the years say he is of easy temperament, modest ego, an unimaginative mind, and a bland personality, and he has always deferred to General Giap. During much of his military career he was considered to be a "mobilizer" rather than a strategist, and in fact until quite late most of his assignments were administrative, not operational. He embraced early, and apparently without reservation, all the military doctrine and principles set down by General Giap.

Although he has written extensively, and is second only to General Giap in prolificness, General Dung's works show little original thought. Most are either interpretations or restatements of the Giap military doctrine or narrow technical discussions of specific military problems. During the Vietnam War he was considered to be a "hard-liner" in that he stood against political settlement of the war. He was also regarded as pro-Moscow although in reality this probably meant only that he was acceptable to the USSR because he showed no clear affinity for China.

His continuing interest, and apparently assignment, from the earliest days has been strategic intelligence and the high-level supervision of intelligence-collection activities.

Van Tien Dung was born in 1917 in Co Nhue village of Tu Liem district (Ha Dong Province), one of seven children in a middle-peasant family. Thus he has a less bourgeois background than most of his contemporaries in the Politburo and PAVN (People's Army of Vietnam) high command.

At 16, with about six years of schooling, he went to work. In 1938 he was employed by the Cu Chung Textile Mill in Hanoi, where he quickly became active in a front organization called the Worker's League, which was composed of 26 trade unions organized by trade. In the same year he joined the Indochinese Communist Party.

During the Viet Minh War, Dung moved steadily into ever more important assignments: "Politburo representative" in the newly formed DRV Ministry of Defense (1945); deputy secretary of the original Central Party Military Committee (1946); commanding officer of the 320th Division (1950–1951), one of five such commanders; military commander and political commissar of the Third Military Region (1952); PAVN chief of staff and PAVN political commissar (1953); delegate to the Regional (Trung-Gia) Armistice Negotiations (1954); and then representative to the International Control Commission (1955–1956). This last assignment took him to Saigon, where he allegedly arranged for the storage of arms caches for use later in the decade.

In the period between wars he continued as PAVN chief of staff. He held other state posts: National Defense Council (1960), National Assembly delegate (Ha Bac Province) in the fifth and later legislatures, and various party positions. He became a Central Committee alternate member in 1951 and a full member in 1960. He was made an alternate member of the Politburo in 1960 and a full member in 1972. Much of his day-to-day work during the early 1960s dealt with PAVN troop morale and loyalty, and he supervised the army's various indoctrination programs and institutions.

During the early years of the Vietnam War he and General Giap divided the highest-level military duties. Giap concentrated on the war in the South, while Dung handled northern air defenses, logistic operations (chiefly Ho Chi Minh Trail and sea infiltration), and the war in Laos. General Dung assumed a field command in 1971 and largely directed the 1972 Easter campaign that was able to seize and hold much of Quang Tri Province in northern South Vietnam. And he is generally credited with being the architect of the final battle of the war, what is called the Ho Chi Minh campaign.

Throughout he has climbed the hierarchy steadily: major general (then called brigadier general) in 1947; lieutenant general in 1954; colonel general in 1959; and senior general in 1974.

As General Giap faded into semiretirement after the war, General Dung gradually assumed full control of PAVN. Under his overall supervision PAVN invaded Kampuchea in December 1978 and then defended Vietnam against the retaliatory invasion by China in February of 1979.

General Dung became Minister of Defense in February 1980, a promotion that cynical Vietnamese emigres put down as a "reward" for the fact that PAVN's performance in Kampuchea as well as against China was inferior to what it had been during the Vietnam War.

General Dung has been married twice and has at least two children: a son, and a daughter married to a PAVN air force fighter pilot. His second wife, Nguyen Thi Ky (also known as Thanh Toe), is an important party official, an agitprop cadre during her early years and now a lecturer at Hanoi University.

His major work is his memoir account of the last battle of the Vietnam War, *Great Spring Victory*, a document remarkable for its candor and personalized treatment.

Douglas Pike
University of California, Berkeley

EASTERN EUROPE AND THE SOVIET UNION

Introduction

In the introduction to last year's report, we wrote: "Until a new, long-term leader takes power, Soviet politics and, of necessity, world politics will be in a state of uncertainty and flux." That leader, Mikhail Gorbachev, has now assumed power, and the year 1985 was one of significant, and at times spectacular, change in Soviet politics.

The Soviet Union. It may have been a near thing. Persistent reports have reached the West that, following Konstantin Chernenko's death on 10 March, Grigori Romanov attempted a coup against Chernenko's presumed successor, Mikhail Gorbachev, by nominating a rival candidate, Moscow party boss Viktor Grishin, for the post of general secretary. Gorbachev reportedly prevailed over Romanov's nominee by a single vote in the Politburo; a vigorous intervention by Andrei Gromyko, who nominated Gorbachev, may have proved decisive. Be that as it may, once installed, Gorbachev moved decisively to consolidate his victory. By year's end, both Romanov and Grishin (as well as Prime Minister Tikhonov) had lost their posts in the Politburo. The failed coup, assuming it occurred, may in fact have helped Gorbachev to accumulate power rapidly.

Western analysts have noted that, while Gorbachev made loud and at times threatening noises about the condition of the Soviet economy, and while he undertook major initiatives such as the much-touted antialcoholism campaign, the new Soviet leader was in fact cautious in matters of policy during the first nine months of his power. In the sphere of the economy, for example, he was careful to limit himself to advocating "within-system" reforms far less bold than current practices in Hungary and China. The draft of the party program published in *Pravda* in October is noteworthy for its blandness. The reason for such caution on Gorbachev's part is self-evident: he had to get his own men into positions of power before he could contemplate major policy initiatives. In pursuing this goal, he was greatly helped by the fact that the Twenty-seventh Party Congress was scheduled to meet less than a year from the date of his accession. This gave Gorbachev a target at which to aim and served to legitimize rapid turnover in the ranks of party and state cadres.

A kaleidoscope of new faces and recycled old faces bewildered Western analysts still accustomed to Brezhnev's "stability of cadres": a new prime minister, Nikolai Ryzhkov; a new president, Andrei Gromyko; a new party secretary for ideology, Egor Ligachev; a new foreign minister, Eduard Shevardnadze. Four new full members of the Politburo were appointed: Ligachev, Ryzhkov, Shevardnadze, and KGB chieftain Chebrikov (the first two bypassed the traditional candidate stage of Politburo membership). There was a new head of Gosplan, Nikolai Talyzin, and a new party boss of Moscow, Boris Yeltsin. There were new party secretaries: Lev Zaikov and Viktor Nikonov. Throughout the Soviet system, men in their seventies were being replaced by men in their fifties and early sixties. The generational changeover, commenced under Andropov and then put on hold by Chernenko, picked up speed and momentum.

While many of the new men—for example, Egor Ligachev and Nikolai Ryzhkov—can best be described as Gorbachev allies, some outright Gorbachev clients, such as the new secretary for party cadres, Georgi Razumovsky, and a new first deputy prime minister, Vsevolod Murakhovsky, were also being moved into place. Especially in the sphere of the troubled Soviet economy, it proved relatively easy for Gorbachev to shoulder aside aging Brezhnev holdovers, such as Gosplan head Nikolai Baibakov, and to install clients and allies in their place. Outside the economic sphere, however, more resourcefulness was called for. Entrenched bureaucrats like Viktor Grishin had to be removed with a hoe and trowel; Grishin could be jettisoned only after a relentless barrage of Aesopian criticism on the pages of *Pravda* and *Sovetskaia Rossiia*. By year's end, it appeared that Gorbachev was likely to have a tractable Central Committee to work with at the Twenty-seventh Party Congress.

Dusko Doder has pointed out that the principal reason Gorbachev was able to move so swiftly in the replacement of cadres was that Andropov had done much of the preparatory work for him. In fact, it was Andropov who brought into the Politburo most of the men who presumably supported Gorbachev against Grishin: Aliev, Vorotnikov, Solomentsev. And it was Andropov who inserted into the Secretariat the men who were to become Gorbachev's close allies, Ligachev and Ryzhkov. Without Andropov's personnel initiatives, it would have taken Gorbachev considerably longer to consolidate his power.

What kind of man is the new general secretary? Analysts have taken note of his voluntarism, his propensity for calculated risks, his populist leanings. In light of such characteristics, some have chosen to compare him to Nikita Khrushchev, like Gorbachev the son of a *muzhik*. But the differences between the two leaders can be as striking as the similarities: Gorbachev has a much better education, is far more of a technocrat, and is almost certainly a more skillful politician. Moreover, to the extent that it can be discerned, his political agenda appears to be quite different from that of Khrushchev.

Western observers were understandably interested in learning what the leadership change portended in the sphere of Soviet foreign policy. While it was aesthetically pleasing to see a healthy, presentable Soviet leader, flanked by a presentable wife, they tended to worry over Gorbachev's obviously strong character and "iron teeth," as Gromyko put it in his nominating speech. There was also Gorbachev's disquieting admiration for Stalin as a strong Soviet leader. Since Gorbachev was veiling much of his foreign policy, however, at least until the party congress, it proved impossible to discern its outlines with any certainty. It did seem clear that Gorbachev sought to emulate Andropov's "multipolar" approach to foreign affairs, but it also seemed clear that, unlike Andropov, he favored the revival of some form of détente. As Henry Rowen has written, such a tack made good sense: "They [Gorbachev and his colleagues] must be powerfully attracted to a policy line which would attempt to combine the weakening of U.S. defense efforts, further divide the West politically, and achieve gains in technology and investment. Such a policy amounts to a revival of détente, one especially oriented to Western Europe but also Japan and the United States and China" ("Gorbachev's Choices," unpublished manuscript). Finally, it is important to note that Gorbachev appeared determined to prosecute the war in Afghanistan, though sporadic interest was expressed in a negotiated settlement.

In domestic affairs, observers thought that they saw signs of an incipient Gorbachev "thaw," reminiscent of Khrushchev's tumultuous liberalizations. Valentin Rasputin's controversial Russian nationalist and environmentalist novel, *The Fire*, was published in *Nash sovremennik*; Elem Klimov's film *Agony* (English title: *Rasputin*), which had been shelved for a decade, was released; and Yevgeny Yevtushenko made a dramatic speech at the December congress of Russian writers in which he attempted to resurface the political agenda of the Khrushchev "thaw." Significantly, Yevtushenko's speech was greeted by prolonged applause on the part of the assembled delegates.

Gorbachev's treatment of the nationalities issue was another subject being watched with interest both in the Soviet Union and in the West. Andropov had been a determined enemy of the Russian nationalists; under Chernenko, the "Russian party" had regained lost ground. A proposed controversial project to divert water from the Ob-Irtysh river system of Siberia to the republics of Central Asia placed the Central Asian and Russian nationalist "lobbies" in direct conflict. At first it seemed that the Central Asians had won; on 5 June the USSR minister of land reclamation announced that the Soviet Union was going ahead with the project. A fierce counterattack on the part of the Russian nationalists followed, and in January 1986, unofficial word reached the West that the project had been abandoned.

Now that the generational changeover in the Soviet leadership has occurred, it is incumbent upon analysts to elucidate its meaning. In what ways do the new leaders differ from the gerontocrats they have replaced? Alexander Shtromas believes that the advent of the new men could signify the beginning of systemic change in the Soviet Union (see his essay in a four-volume compendium, edited by Shtromas, and to appear in 1986, entitled *The Prospects for Transformation in the Soviet Union*). Building upon insights contained in Milovan Djilas's *Unperfect Society*, Shtromas sees Soviet "technocrats" as locked in a fierce struggle—one that they are winning—with a fading generation of "partocrats" (a term coined by A. Avtorkhanov): elderly, ill-educated men of humble origins, "the notorious promotees of Stalin." Due to the growing complexity of the Soviet economy and to what the Soviets call the "scientific and technical revolution," the partocrats have become increasingly superfluous in the Soviet system, their only true skills being in the realm of party-apparat intrigue. It is the partocrats who are especially wedded to the ideology of Marxism-Leninism, "the ideology which endows them with unchecked absolute power and provides the only basis for its legitimation."

The technocrats, who are led by the "all-round technocrat" Gorbachev, are people "who possess universally applicable skills and whose livelihood depends on the successful application of those skills." They are, consequently, less wedded to the ideology of Marxism-Leninism than the partocrats and are more prepared to contemplate extrasystemic change. Shtromas stresses that, unlike the partocrats, the technocrats do not belong to a single generational cohort. Hence the aging Andrei Gromyko, a man said to admire efficiency and competence, could in some senses be considered a technocrat. If we are in fact seeing the beginning of the emergence of a "post-Soviet government," that government will, Shtromas predicts, almost certainly be "technocratic in character and [Russian] nationalist in ideology."

Shtromas's suggestive schema is obviously in need of refinement. As Seweryn Bialer noted in a book published in 1980: "The *apparatchiki* of today [Shtromas's partocrats] are technocrats regardless of the generation from which they come. . . What is important with regard to the new generation [i.e., Gorbachev's generation] is, first, that the 'technocratic' elements of its background are clearly more pronounced than in the past generation; and, second, that most of the key social characteristics provide a cumulative reinforcement in a direction away from past generations" (*Stalin's Successors*, 1980, pp. 123–24). Gorbachev, Ryzhkov, and their colleagues are considerably *more* technocratic in orientation than were their predecessors, and that fact could have important political consequences.

Recent émigré Fridrikh Neznansky believes that under Gorbachev we may be seeing "the beginning of the dismantling of the Soviet totalitarian system" (from his 16 September seminar at the Hoover Institution, and *An Emigre Reports* [Delphic Associates, October 1985]). Gorbachev is declaring war on the Brezhnev nomenklatura and is listening carefully to academic specialists like Tatyana Zaslavskaya and Abel Aganbegyan. The new role of the KGB in the Soviet system, a role dating from the Andropov interlude, is also noteworthy: "The KGB is not simply a political police anymore. It has a highly skilled professional personnel, and has direct access to the expertise of strategic institutions and R&D establishments." The KGB now dominates both the army and the defense–heavy industry complex. It is no accident, Neznansky feels, that the full membership of the Politburo presently contains three police generals–Aliev, Chebrikov, and Shevardnadze—but no army generals. The other two ruling strata, in Neznansky's schema, are the technocrats and the Central Committee apparatus, both of which are Gorbachev fiefdoms.

Neznansky's schema and Shtromas's are essentially compatible. The KGB and the Central Committee apparatus have both become increasingly technocratic in orientation. The coup d'état carried out by Andropov against the partocrats in 1982 has served to speed up history and could in fact pave the way for eventual systemic change. The approaching Twenty-seventh Party Congress, which may rival the Twentieth Party Congress in significance, ought to provide important clues. As Peter Reddaway has noted: "It now seems possible that. . . the vast, lumbering Soviet Union may start to change its course" ("Waiting for Gorbachev," *New York Review of Books*, 10 October).

Eastern Europe. Eastern Europe's military alliance system, the Warsaw Treaty Organization, in May received unanimous renewal for twenty years, with an additional decade of automatic extension after that. Pact defense ministers convened during early December in East Berlin. As usual, their communiqué revealed nothing. It spoke of decisions on "practical questions regarding activities of member state armed forces." That same month, two new defense ministers were appointed: one in East Germany and the other in Romania.

The Council for Mutual Economic Assistance (CMEA) convened twice at the prime minister level, most probably because of severe problems in almost all member countries. The basic foundations for a joint program of scientific and technical progress through the year 2000 were agreed upon at a two-day meeting in Moscow during mid-December. Gorbachev's predecessors also had attempted to place their imprint on the CMEA, e.g., Khrushchev's "international division of labor" (1962) and Brezhnev's "complex program" (1971). The latest document commits the organization to double bloc productivity over the next fifteen years, with the use of the latest available technology.

Albania has not been a de facto member of either the Warsaw Pact or the CMEA since 1961. It formally announced withdrawal seven years later, i.e., after the Soviet invasion of Czechoslovakia. Albanian Communists buried their first leader, Enver Hoxha, in April. The transition took place without incident, and heir-apparent Ramiz Alia has continued his predecessor's policies. Improved relations brought several West European delegations to Tirana, although treatment of Albanians living in Kosovo Province, Yugoslavia, restricted contacts with the government at Belgrade.

Another kind of ethnic issue involved Bulgaria, where the Turkish minority was being forced to adopt Slavic names and to stop speaking its native language in public. Officially the communist regime claims that ancestors of the Turks had been converted by force to Islam and, hence, their descendants were reverting voluntarily to the original Bulgarian heritage. The USSR ambassador to Sofia criticized "little brother's" deterioration in economic conditions in a local interview that must have embarrassed party/state leader Todor Zhivkov.

In Czechoslovakia, regime spokesmen attacked market-oriented concepts after communist leader Gustáv Husák had conferred with Gorbachev in Moscow and pledged continuation of the domestic hard line. Almost half of all foreign trade is with the USSR. Despite antireligious propaganda and repression, the 1,100th anniversary of St. Methodius's death attracted 100,000 faithful to one Mass and 150,000 others to a second. The Charter '77 human-rights activists issued around thirty documents, one-third more than in the previous year. However, the regime is stable, with five Soviet divisions "temporarily" stationed in the country since 1968.

In the so-called German Democratic Republic (GDR), the number of USSR divisions totals twenty. Three local Politburo members were replaced, including the rival of communist chief Erich Honecker, which paves the way for heir-apparent Egon Krenz to become the next party leader. A domestic austerity policy in five years has made the GDR into the most efficient economy within the bloc. However if East Berlin is to repay its ruble debt to Moscow in full by 1990, the annual trade surplus must be doubled. There also remains $3.4 billion of hard currency borrowed from the West.

The ruling Communists in Hungary continue cautious support for the New Economic Mechanism, again endorsed at the March party congress, even though NEM has problems, and four Soviet divisions have remained in the country since 1956. Although more than one candidate ran from each constituency during the June national elections, the Patriotic People's Front won 99.3 percent of the vote. None of this, of course, means genuine pluralism. The $9 billion hard-currency debt makes for a heavy repayment schedule and an estimated 10 to 20 percent of the population lives in poverty. As of January 1986, all citizens will register only four times instead of six at local police stations to obtain new identity cards: at ages 14, 20, 35, and 50. János Kádár, in power since 1956, still cannot trust the people.

The situation in Poland resembles that of Hungary after the 1956 revolt or Czechoslovakia after the 1968 Soviet military occupation. Although three USSR divisions are stationed in the country, the local military junta leader, General Wojciech Jaruzelski, had been ordered to use Polish forces to occupy the country under martial law, proclaimed in December 1981. This same man, four years later, announced that "normalization" had brought an end to organized opposition. Yet only 127,000 members of the ruling Communist party live in Warsaw. National elections in October officially brought out 78.8 percent of the voters (according to the underground Solidarity movement, the true figure was 66 percent), and the clandestine weekly *Tygodnik Mazowsza* has a current circulation of 15,000 copies. Authorities admit to holding more than 300 political prisoners in jails. They also have begun direct attacks upon the Roman Catholic Church.

Only in Romania, though its economy is the weakest of the region, does the "cult of personality" continue. Official figures showed that just 2.3 percent of the electorate voted against the regime's slate in March. However, reports of peasant riots came out at year's end. Nicolae Ceaușescu pursued a policy of rotating appointments in both government and the Communist party. His wife has emerged as second in command, although their son Nicu actually may become heir-apparent if the father lives long enough. Although differing from the USSR on some foreign policy issues, Romania's trade with its eastern neighbor rose by 17 percent during 1985.

Five years after the death of Josip Broz Tito, a crisis faces Yugoslavia. Both Tito and the system are blamed for the economic deterioration. Problems appear insurmountable, with inflation officially at 100 percent and the foreign hard-currency debt above $23 billion. The ruling League of Communists lost 75,000 members, mostly blue-collar workers, during November alone. The ethnic Albanians, some 77 percent of the population of Kosovo Province, continue to demand genuine autonomy and a substantial rise in living standards. Yugoslavia remains an associate member of the CMEA, although it never joined the Warsaw Pact. This latter condition allows authorities in Belgrade to proclaim nonalignment and receive loans as well as rescheduling of debts in the West.

John B. Dunlop
Richard F. Staar
Hoover Institution

Albania

Population. 2,968,000
Party. Albanian Party of Labor (Partia e Punës e Shqipërisë; APL)
Founded. 8 November 1941
Membership. 122,600 as of November 1981; 22,363 candidate members. Workers and peasants 66 percent, office workers/intellectuals 34 percent; women, 30 percent of full and 40 percent of candidate members
First Secretary. Ramiz Alia
Politburo. Currently, 10 full members (three vacancies have not been filled): Ramiz Alia (president of the Republic), Adil Çarçani (prime minister), Hajredin Çeliku (minister of mines and industry), Lenka Çuko, Hekuran Isai, Pali Mishka, Manush Myftiu (deputy premier), Rita Marko, Simon Stefani, Muho Asllani; 5 candidate members: Foto Çami, Besnik Bekteshi, Llambi Gjegprifti, Qirjako Mihali (deputy premier), Prokop Mura (minister of defense)
Secretariat. 6 members: Ramiz Alia, Foto Çami (elected after Hoxha's death), Vangjel Çerrava, Lenka Çuko, Hekuran Isai, Simon Stefani
Central Committee. 76 full members, 39 candidate members. Currently there are five vacancies in the Central Committee membership and one vacancy in the alternate membership.
Status. Ruling party
Last Congress. Eighth, 1–8 November 1981, in Tirana
Last Parliamentary Elections. 1982, all 250 candidates of Democratic Front. Only one ballot cast against the front's candidates.
Auxiliary Organizations. Albanian Democratic Front, Ramiz Alia, deputy chairman; Central Council of

Trade Unions (UTUA), some 610,000 members as of 1984, Sotir Koçallari, chairman; Union of Labor Youth of Albania (ULYA), Mehmet Elezi, first secretary, approximate membership 500,000; Women's Union of Albania (WUA), Lumturi Rexha, chairwoman; Albanian War Veterans, Shefqet Peçi, chairman; Albanian Defense of Peace Committee, Musaraj Shefqet, chairman

Main State Organs. Council of Ministers (20 members). The People's Assembly (250 members) is constitutionally the leading body of the state, but in reality it rubberstamps decisions reached by the party's Politburo or Central Committee.

Publications. *Zeri i Popullit*, daily organ of the APL Central Committee; *Rruga ë Partisë*, monthly theoretical journal, organ of the Central Committee of the APL; *Bashkimi*, daily organ of the Democratic Front; *Puna*, weekly organ of the UTUA; *10 Korik* and *Lluftetari*, biweekly organs of the Ministry of Defense; *Nendori*, monthly organ of the Albanian Writers and Artists League; *Laiko Vema*, organ of the Greek minority. The Albanian Telegraphic Agency (ATA) is the official state news agency.

The creation of the Albanian Communist Party was initiated by Marshal Tito of Yugoslavia, on Comintern instructions. The party was founded on 8 November 1941 in Tirana with two Yugoslav emissaries, Miladin Popović and Dušan Mungoša, serving as Tito's representatives. A total of fifteen individuals, claiming to represent established communist organizations in the cities of Korçë, Shkodër, and Tirana, assembled at a private home in the old city of the capital under the watchful eyes of the two Montenegrins Popović and Mungoša. The meeting united the three existing groups or factions under a single "national" leadership. Enver Hoxha, a teacher of the French language, was elected provisional secretary of the Albanian Communist Party.

The dominant element of the Albanian communist movement during the interwar period had been the Korçë group, which traced its origins to 1931 and bore the influence of Comintern operatives Lazar Fundo and Ali Kelmendi. Two tinsmiths from Korçë, Pilo Peristeri and Koçi Xoxe, had founded the communist cell *Puna* in 1931 and established close links with the Greek Communist Party. Peristeri sponsored the admission of Hoxha to the group and was rewarded with high positions in postliberation Albania. Currently, he serves as chairman of the Central Committee control commission.

A second significant group of Albanian Communists had been functioning in a disorganized manner since the mid-1920s in the Gheg city of Shkodër and, due to its proximity, had maintained close relations with Yugoslav and Austrian Communists. The Shkodër group was led by the prominent Albanian intellectual, Zejfula Maleshova, who had the distinction of being one of the first victims of Enver Hoxha's permanent purge.

Elements of the Shkodër and Korçë groups, along with the Tirana youth organization *Zjari* (under Hoxha's influence since 1936 and under his total control by 1941), formed the Albanian Communist Party after a series of meetings, many of which were devoted to selection of a "unifying leader." Hoxha was chosen as the most promising under the circumstances, but the Yugoslavs distrusted his obvious bourgeois habits, acquired during his studies in France. Upon the creation of the Communist party, the Yugoslav emissaries instructed their Albanian colleagues to form armed units and commence resistance against the foreign enemy. For the duration of the war and until the Tito-Stalin break, the Albanian Communist Party was under Yugoslav control. At its first regular congress (1 November 1948), the name of the party was changed to the Albanian Party of Labor (APL), and Enver Hoxha was elected its first secretary, a post he held until his death on 11 April 1985.

That first APL congress legitimized the break with Yugoslavia, exposed the plots of "Xoxe and other Titoites," and unleashed the harshest form of "class struggle" known in communist annals. Koçi Xoxe, the Yugoslav protégé, and hundreds of his followers were executed, while others were given harsh and lengthy prison terms.

Instability in the highest ranks was a permanent characteristic of the APL under the leadership of Hoxha, manifested in the form of sweeping purges at all levels. After 1941, five major purges were undertaken and carefully orchestrated by Enver Hoxha and his ephemeral associates. A total of 47 party leaders who had reached the rank of Central Committee member (two-thirds of whom were full or alternate members of the Politburo) have been purged since 1941. The latest "house cleaning" involved Mehmet Shehu (prime minister for 28 years), sixteen members of his cabinet, hundreds of his followers, and members of his family. Shehu was accused of being a triple agent by simultaneously working for the CIA, KGB, and the Yugoslav UDBA. Historically, the Albanian purges followed the Stalinist script closely: first purge the "enemies," then purge the purgers for "excessive zeal" in purging the enemies, but never admit error or rehabilitate anyone. Hoxha apparently had a perennial fear of his own instruments of oppression, security and military, if we are to judge from the fate that has befallen their leaders; with the exception of Hoxha himself, all defense and interior ministers since 1948 have been politically, and in several cases physically, eliminated.

The death of Enver Hoxha on 11 April 1985 dominated the state and party agenda for the remainder of the year. Suffering from multiple maladies, Hoxha died in Tirana at age 77 (*NYT*, 12 April). The medical bulletin, signed by eight Albanian specialists and professors of medicine, traced his health problems to diabetes, first diagnosed in 1948 (ATA, 11 April). In 1972 and again in 1973 Hoxha suffered serious heart disorders punctuated with irregular heartbeat and insufficiency, as well as "ischemic insult of the brain with transitional nemiparesis" (ibid.). The immediate cause of death was attributed to "ventricular fibrillations and irreversible consequences in brain and kidneys."

Obviously Hoxha had serious health problems, as reported on numerous occasions during the past few years (*YICA*, 1985; *NYT*, 11 November 1984), suggesting that substantial elements of power had been gradually delegated to other leaders. Ramiz Alia was the main beneficiary of Hoxha's health problems, once his main competitor, Mehmet Shehu, was executed (*NYT*, 5 March).

On 13 April, the eleventh plenum of the Central Committee was called into session to elect a successor to Hoxha. Prime Minister Adil Çarçani, a technocrat from Hoxha's hometown and deputy to Shehu, nominated Alia for the post of first secretary. In his introductory remarks, Çarçani repeatedly stated that Alia was Hoxha's as well as the Central Committee's choice (*Zeri i Popullit*, 14 April). Also present at the meeting was the widow of Hoxha, Nexhmije, to affirm the decision as in accord with the late secretary's wish.

In a manner suggesting "continuity" of the isolationist policies of Hoxha, his funeral was treated as a private Albanian affair. The arrangements committee (headed by Alia and consisting of the entire Politburo and Hoxha's wartime comrades who had survived the purges), declined all foreign offers to send delegations to attend the last rites of the last Stalinist (ATA, 14 April; *FBIS*, 15 April). The Foreign Ministry thanked all those who attempted to go to Tirana, but politely declined their offer as being "incompatible with the practices of our state." The only exception to the rule was a special invitation to the Greek communist war hero, Manolis Glezos, with whom Hoxha had established a personal friendship. A Greek military helicopter delivered Glezos to the Kakavia crosspoint to be picked up by an Albanian-driven car. After the funeral, Glezos met with Alia and other Albanian leaders who indicated a desire for further improvement in relations between the two countries (*Ta Nea*, 16 April). Condolences from the Soviet Union were rejected outright, while Chinese expressions of sympathy were acknowledged with appreciation (*WP*, 13 April). Following established policies, instructions were given to overseas missions not to accept representatives from "the USSR, U.S., South Korea, Israel, and South Africa" to sign condolence books opened in Albanian embassies (*Vienna TV Service*, 15 April; *FBIS*, 16 April).

The death of Hoxha did not signify any major changes in the party's hierarchy. Instead, numerous indications and pronouncements suggest a continuation of Hoxhaism without Hoxha and an unrelenting effort to retain intact his personality cult.

Upon his death, the eleventh Central Committee plenum decided to honor his memory by renaming Tirana University the "Enver Hoxha University," and the Durres port became "Enver Hoxha Durres Port." Appropriate monuments in the cities of Korçë, Gjirocaster, and Tirana were decided upon, and the Pioneer organization was renamed "Enver's Pioneers." In a subsequent meeting of the Central Committee, more specific instructions were given to carry out the decisions of the eleventh plenum. On 15 October a high-level commission, headed by Alia and including Hoxha's wife, was called into session and decided to build a museum in Tirana to highlight Hoxha's "achievements as leader of the armed forces, chairman of the Democratic Front, and first secretary of the Party" (*Zeri i Popullit*, 15 October). The museum and other monuments are to be built by "voluntary work" and mass participation, according to the official announcement.

The death of Enver Hoxha did not seem to have seriously affected the pattern of party life or the country's foreign policy. In fact, all party organs and state leaders went to extraordinary lengths to emphasize continuity of policies and to invoke Hoxha's wisdom in criticizing shortcomings among party cadres that negatively affected discipline during the past several years, namely, foreign influences, careless selection of cadres, and lack of zeal in party work (*Zeri i Popullit*, 29 June).

As in previous years, party organs were rather blunt about the reappearance of "liberal sectarian and other negative attitudes" among party members. In many party organizations members are selected with "little concern for their class origin" and in some cases, even offspring of *Balli Kombetar* members (a wartime right-wing organization) have been admitted to the party ranks (*Rruga ë Partisë*, March, pp. 45–53). The same issue notes not only laxity in the selection of members but outright nepotism among local party leaders. A call for better control of the selection process apparently did not have the desired results since, according to the same theoretical journal, there is an alarming tendency among party members to "ignore party meetings and party work." The party organizations of the Kolonje, Vlorë, Fier, and Permet districts (all located in Tosk territory) were singled out for sloppy practices and inadequate verification of a candidate's background.

In an effort of the post-Hoxha leadership to cling to the old policies, the principles of self-reliance and austerity were emphasized in all public commentaries following Hoxha's death. A sharp criticism of the "enemies of socialism, the imperialists, revisionists, and assorted reactionaries" was evident in *Zeri i Popullit* and other party organs prior to and after Hoxha's death. On the other hand, a resentment of Western characterizations of Albania as "isolated" was also apparent in various publications. The isolation accusation, according to Albanian propaganda organs, is a misinterpretation of the determination to "close our gates to invasion through enslaving credits, through tourists and agents, and through the decadent culture of degeneration" (*Rruga ë Partisë*, October, pp. 10–17; *Bashkimi*, 8 November; *FBIS*, 26 November).

Internal Party Affairs. The election of Ramiz Alia as first secretary by the eleventh plenum (13 April) confirmed the expectation of analysts and scholars of Albanian affairs and assures a continuity of the relatively isolationist policies initiated by Hoxha (*YICA*, 1985, p. 252; *NYT*, 5 October). With Shehu out of the way, Alia assumed the top party post without any overt difficulties from the late prime minister's strongholds, i.e., the state apparatus and security organs. Whether the peaceful coexistence between the Gheg party chief and the Tosk-dominated military and security forces will continue remains to be seen. Thus far, there have been no major changes in the party hierarchy or the cabinet, and Alia has been slow to claim for himself titles and positions held by his predecessor. This suggests that the preemptive elimination of the Shehu faction during 1981–1982 was related to Hoxha's obsession to leave a "militant ideologue" as his successor, but one who would not challenge his place in Albanian history (*Frankfurter Allgemeine Zeitung*, 15 April; *JPRS*, 23 May). The reluctance of Alia to move boldly to fill positions held by Hoxha (such as the chairmanship of the Democratic Front and chief of the armed forces) may also be related to efforts by other party strongmen to recast (or even challenge) his leadership style.

Although there is general agreement that Alia was hand-picked by Hoxha as the individual most likely to pursue a militant brand of Marxism-Leninism and a foreign policy based on self-reliance (*WP*, 14 April), there are some indications of a "lowering of ideological stridency" in pronouncements coming out of Tirana and some signs of pragmatism in the foreign policy area (*Sunday Times*, 9 June; *Daily Telegraph*, 10 June).

Following the initial mourning period, which caused the cancellations of May Day and national day parades in Tirana (*Zeri i Popullit*, 2 May, 27 November), two individuals have increased their visibility in public and party affairs: Foto Çami and Hoxha's widow, Nexhmije. Çami is the other beneficiary of Hoxha's death. The twelfth plenum, which met to discuss serious economic problems, elevated him to the position of secretary of the Central Committee. His old position, as party chief of Tirana, was given to one of his protégés, Piro Kondi (ATA, 9 July; *FBIS*, 10 July). On the occasion of his sixtieth birthday, Çami was awarded the "Order of Freedom First Class," a distinct honor for a newcomer to the Secretariat of the party (ATA, 5 October; *FBIS*, 7 October). During the award ceremonies, attended by the entire Politburo, members of the Central Committee, the cabinet, and Hoxha's widow, Çami was warmly praised for his contribution to building socialism in Albania. Alia and other speakers noted with approval his work "in the party and his faithful implementation of Hoxha's teachings" (ibid.). The depiction of Çami as continuing Hoxha's work lasted for most of the year and may have been a counter to Nexhmije Hoxha's expanded party role. In mid-October, with the active participation of Alia, Hoxha's widow, mass organizations, and regional and local party groups, an "Enver Hoxha Week" was proclaimed to commemorate the late leader and to "scientifically study his contribution to Marxism-Leninism." In this activity, Çami played a most active role. He was the keynote speaker at a conference organized by the Institute of Marxism-Leninism, headed by Nexhmije Hoxha, and the Military Academy (*Zeri i Popullit*, 11 October). His speech, which covers two entire pages of *Zeri i Popullit*, lavished praise on Hoxha but omitted attacks by name on the "enemies of the party" who always had been a favorite target during Hoxha's lifetime. The closest Çami came to attacking "party enemies" (i.e., Shehu, Xoxe, Jakova, and so on) was to say that the late secretary had been "severe and stern with enemies, provocateurs, the sinister people of counterrevolution" and that Hoxha's position always "enraged the enemies, from Nazi-Fascists to their local stooges, from Anglo-Americans to Ballists and Zogists, from Yugoslav Titoites to their camouflaged agents in the front ranks of the party" (ATA, 16 October; *FBIS*, 17 October). Çami, who has been alternate Politburo member and Tirana party chief, was introduced to the gathering as "professor" and member of the Academy of Sciences, in an apparent effort to highlight his scientific and intellectual credentials.

Nexhmije Hoxha, too, has been active in party and mass organization affairs. She accompanied Alia to celebrations of her late husband's birthday in Gjirocastër. She actively participated in the work of the commission, chaired by Alia, to carry out the decision of the eleventh plenum to properly honor the memory of her husband (ATA, 11 October; *FBIS*, 14 October). More important, Madame Hoxha was a prominent participant in state and parliamentary affairs and in the work of mass organizations for women, youth, and Pioneers (ATA, 22 October; *FBIS*, 22 October; ATA, 1 December; *FBIS*, 4 December).

The noticeable promotion of Çami by party organs and his frequent appearance in activities of mass organizations and the military parallels efforts by Alia to develop his own personality cult and to establish himself firmly in power. A tendency to be especially solicitous of Nexhmije Hoxha has characterized many of Alia's activities and public appearances since April.

Upon assumption of power, Alia reaffirmed his intention to continue the Hoxha policies without "wavering" and to "build socialism by depending only on our own means." *Zeri i Popullit* published several articles by prominent commentators, emphasizing this "line" (*Zeri i Popullit*, 23 April). In a major speech before the monument of martyrs, and in commemoration of VE Day, Alia repeated the same theme and paid homage to the 28,000 Albanians killed during the war against the Axis powers. The "continuity" theme dominated Alia's VE Day speech (ATA, 6 May; *FBIS*, 7 May). But it also included evidence of continuity of gradual efforts to expand relations with the West. Thus, in a telling manner, an Albanian delegation was dispatched to Austria to participate in ceremonies at Mauthausen concentration camp, where Albanians were executed by the Nazis during World War II (ibid.). The Albanian press devoted considerable space to underscoring the significance of VE Day and the role played by the democratic forces (*Zeri i Popullit*, 7 May).

In a manner reminiscent of Western politicians in search of votes, Alia visited most regions of the country to assure his compatriots of his intention to follow "Hoxha's example" and perhaps to expand his own links with the grassroots. In early May, accompanied by Politburo member Pali Mishka, he visited the Vlore-Drashovica region, where he spoke of the need to fulfill production tasks in agriculture and to retain a high level of party discipline (ATA, 14 May; *FBIS*, 15 May). In the monotonous manner that has characterized Albanian rhetoric since 1948, Alia implored his listeners to fulfill the agricultural plan and strongly implied that failure to do so could affect Albania's foreign trade. In June, he visited the oil-producing areas of Patos, Fier, and the "City of Stalin," where he noted, with obvious concern, deficiencies in fulfilling the oil production quota (ATA, 13 June; *FBIS*, 14 June; *WSJ*, 12 June). However, his major foreign policy speech was delivered during a visit to Korçë (a city close to the Greek border), where he sought to put to rest any notions of dramatic changes in foreign policy or ideology (*Zeri i Popullit*, 28 August). Alia made special reference to Hoxha's desire to improve relations with Athens and pointed to the late secretary's book (published posthumously), *Two Friendly Peoples*. He singled out Turkey, Greece, and Italy as examples of countries with which relations have improved dramatically and with "good prospects for further improvement." Yugoslavia, on the other hand, was criticized for maintaining an anti-Albanian policy and for oppressing the Kosovo Albanians.

In the characteristic way of post-1981 Albanian foreign policy, Alia reiterated known clichés and expressed his annoyance with those who deliberately make the wrong assumptions about the direction of his country's foreign relations. Contacts with the West were termed "normal political and diplomatic acts of our independent and sovereign state" and "those who interpret these acts as *opening up* of

Albania or as *tendencies* to get closer to one side or another are wasting their time. Albania neither *opens* nor *closes* her borders," Alia stated (*Zeri i Popullit*, 28 August).

All high-ranking party leaders led activities in various parts of the country to honor Hoxha's birthday. Alia visited Hoxha's birthplace (Gjirocastër), as stated above, accompanied by Madame Hoxha and Deputy Premier Manush Myftiu (ATA, 12 October; *FBIS*, 21 October). On October 17, Alia was decorated with the medal of a "Hero of Socialist Labor" in honor of his sixtieth birthday (*Zeri i Popullit*, 18 October) and, in early December, the first volume of his works (since assumption of the top party post) was published (ATA, 3 December; *FBIS*, 4 December). Although Alia visited most parts of the country following Hoxha's death in an apparent effort to popularize his image, the Hoxha legacy remained the rallying point for party members and mass organizations, making the emergence of an "Alia cult" rather difficult. Several volumes of the late secretary's works were published posthumously (the collected works now stand at 47 volumes). On the occasion of the 44th anniversary of the founding of the Albanian Youth Organization, two volumes by Hoxha, titled *On Youth*, were also issued. Thus even in death Hoxha continues to eclipse any attempt by Alia to promote his own Marxist-Leninist credentials. Besides the theoretical and heavily paternalistic *On Youth*, two other Hoxha books, with a heavy nationalistic content, were published in 1985 (one of them posthumously). The first is a self-justifying and one-sided account of the process of seizure of power by the Albanian Communist Party, called *Laying the Foundations of New Albania*. In it, Hoxha takes liberties with historical facts, "explains" the problems he had with "party enemies," and justifies their elimination. It is an important historical source, significant for its omissions and distortions. It is worth noting that in this book Hoxha makes no mention of any serious role by Alia in the 1940s but derides the "contributions" of Shehu and Xoxe in the formative years of the postwar Albanian state (*JPRS*, 11 January).

The *Two Friendly Peoples*, published posthumously, deals with Greek-Albanian relations and upon its Greek-language publication caused a diplomatic controversy. Former president of the Republic of Greece and academician Constantine Tsatsos was quoted in the work as saying that only some small organizations persist in referring to violation of the rights of the Greek minority in Albania. Tsatsos sharply denied ever making such comments to the Albanian ambassador in Athens, Xenophon Nushi (Hoxha's source), and he reiterated that "this matter remains a national issue" (*Kathimerini*, 6 August). In the process of his denial, President Tsatsos questioned Hoxha's motives and the integrity of the Albanian ambassador to Athens. It seems likely, therefore, that the persistence of the Hoxha personality cult will overshadow Alia's attempts to take control of all state and party structures and may increase his reluctance to attempt any changes in the party and state structures or to tamper with old idols and myths.

With the exception of the Çami elevation and promotion of Piro Kondi to the important post of Tirana party chief, no other changes have been announced in Albania. The Central Committee continues to function, with several vacancies created by the elimination of Shehu and his friends, and so does the Politburo.

Party life at the lower regional levels continued throughout the year in the same monotonous vein, with occasional sharp criticisms of low morale, lack of discipline, and reappearance of "sectarian, liberal, conservative, and other unsocialist attitudes" (*Rruga ë Partisë*, November, pp. 48–58).

Of particular concern to the party organizations (as reflected in major articles) is the behavior of youth and the creeping reappearance of harmful attitudes. Mehmet Elezi, first secretary of the ULYA and member of the Central Committee, noted "antisocialist" attitudes toward property, manifestations of liberalism and conservativism, and remnants of religion (ibid.). In an earlier article on the same subject, Elezi recommended the revival of social control groups to supervise youth behavior, particularly in the regions of "Tirana, Durrës, Vlore, Shkodër, and Sarande, where there are beaches" and where youth attire may offend puritan spirits (*Rruga ë Partisë*, July, pp. 69–80). Failure closely to supervise youth behavior, according to Elezi, "suffices for long hair and tight trousers to seek citizenship rights" in Albania.

Party-Military Relations. Ramiz Alia has not made any overt move to expand his control and impose his personality on the Albanian military. After all, his military credentials are rather thin—and his name rarely appeared in pre-Shehu accounts of the war against the occupiers and domestic class opponents. Nevertheless, he attended a number of activities celebrating the fortieth anniversary of the creation of the Albanian navy, accompanied by high-level party officials and military chiefs. In a major speech at Durres, Alia gave credit for creation of the Albanian navy to Enver Hoxha and repeated clichés about the armed forces being a "weapon in the hands of the dictatorship of the proletariat" (*Zeri i Popullit*, 14 August). However, the main festivities related to the creation of the Albanian People's Army (10 July) were presided over by Foto Çami, who was flanked by the chief of the defense staff, General Kiço Mustaqi, and the minister of defense, Prokop Mura. This address by Çami was also characterized by the absence of personal attacks against "party enemies" and sharp criticism of all revisionists (ATA, 10 July; *FBIS*, 11 July). The Vlore naval festivities were attended by numerous party officials, but the main address there was given by General Mustaqi (ATA, 16 August; *FBIS*, 26 August). Criticism of poor party work in the military characteristic of previous years, was repeated by Mehmet Elezi (Rruga ë Partisë, no. 3). The siege mentality that has characterized Albanian life since 1948 continued (*Financial Times*, 16 August; *Vradyni*, 19 June).

Auxiliary and Mass Organizations. In a routine and repetitive manner, all auxiliary organizations were implored to "turn their grief" from the loss of Hoxha into "strength for the fulfillment of the party's tasks." The general council of the Democratic Front held a joint meeting in Tirana with the Committee of War Veterans to celebrate the anniversary of the defeat of Germany (ATA, 9 May; *FBIS*, 13 May). The entire membership of the party's Politburo participated in the gathering. The proceedings were opened by Shefqet Peçi, chairman of the Albanian War Veterans, but the main speech was given by Prokop Mura, minister of defense. In October, the council of the Democratic Front was again called into session to discuss tasks related to the "intensification of the revolutionary movement and methods to implement the teachings of Enver Hoxha" (ATA, 2 October; *FBIS*, 8 October). Alia, who participated in the proceedings as deputy chairman of the front, spoke briefly. The keynote address was given by Xhorxhi Robo, secretary general of the Democratic Front and former ambassador to China.

The founding of the trade union movement was celebrated in the "City of Stalin" (Koçova) earlier in the year. Sotir Koçallari, chairman of UTUA, presided over the festivities and implored the workers to fulfill the quota in oil and gas production (ATA, 12 Feburary; *FBIS*, 13 February). A plenum of the UTUA Central Committee was held in Tirana to discuss ways of implementing resolutions reached in a major conference of "innovators" held at Shkodër (*Rruga ë Partisë*, October, pp. 18–27) and to put into effect instructions of the twelfth plenum of the APL Central Committee, which had as its central theme "austerity" (ATA, 22 November; *FBIS*, 25 November). Several overseas trips by UTUA representatives were undertaken in 1985, including a visit led by the editor in chief of *Puna*, Namik Dokle, to attend Equador's General Workers' Union conference (ATA, 1 December; *FBIS*, 4 December).

The founding of the "Anti-Fascist Women's Union," predecessor of WUA, was celebrated in the city of Berat. Nexhmije Hoxha presided over the festivities, accompanied by the chairman of the organization, Lumturi Rexha (ATA, 5 November; *FBIS*, 6 November). Madame Hoxha, who has emerged as a prominent political factor, also presided over the renaming of the Pioneer Organization to "Enver's Pioneers." On several occasions she wrote about Hoxha's success in "leaving a party clean of enemies" and her hope that it will stay that way (Radio Free Europe–Radio Liberty, *RAD Background Report*, 21 May).

In October, Madame Hoxha presided over a conference on "talented youth," organized by ULYA and its chairman, Mehmet Elezi (ATA, 22 October; *FBIS*, 23 October). This conference, which was attended by Foto Çami and other party officials, was used as a forum to attack foreign influences among the youth. The antisocial tendencies of youth came under severe criticism by the first secretary of ULYA in a series of articles in *Zeri i Popullit* and *Rruga ë Partisë* (July). The decline in youth discipline is severe, if we are to judge from the tone of the Elezi diatribes. Even during the mourning period for the death of Hoxha "destruction of property and other criminal acts" took place, according to ULYA's first secretary. Apparently the work ethic of the Albanian youth and their attitude toward socialist order declined significantly during 1985, and this was attributed by Elezi to "foreign influences" coming via the airwaves (*RAD Background Report*, 26 August). Problems afflicting youth morality and discipline have extended into the party ranks and the military. Party members, too, have come under severe attack for permitting alien ideas to infiltrate their ranks and for careless supervision of youth organizations and production enterprises (*Rruga ë Partisë*, March, pp. 45–53).

Domestic Affairs. Domestic politics in the post-Hoxha era were still dominated by the late secretary's personality cult and the usual efforts by party leaders, including Alia, to exploit Hoxha's memory in order to move the people and mass organizations to shore up the economy. With the exception of foreign policy, an area that Alia sought to "clarify" by emphasizing continuity, a state of uncertainty seems to prevail in all other facets of public life. The first secretary, who made a strong impression when he delivered the funeral oration, has since appeared to waver and has projected a "typical politician" image since he assumed the top post. Although Alia seems to behave as a typical politician with inadequate (or nonexistent) charisma to fill Hoxha's shoes, Foto Çami, formerly Tirana party chief (elevated to the Secretariat), appears more assertive and in some respects bold in his appearance.

A potentially important factor in Albanian domestic politics could very well be Hoxha's widow, Nexhmije. Since 15 April, when she placed an Albanian flag in Hoxha's bier "on behalf of the Kosovo Albanians," she has made numerous appearances at mass, party, and state activities and has been prominently mentioned in the press. In a telling fashion, she reminded crypto-enemies of Alia that "Enver Hoxha has left a party clean of enemies, an ideologically and politically molded and organizationally strong party" (ibid.). Further, she affirmed "comrade Enver's" great faith in Alia as a "capable, brave, mature leader with the necessary determination to lead the country toward the full construction of socialism" (ibid.). In a country known for its Muslim chauvinistic values (despite progress made by women), Alia does not look forceful when the widow of his predecessor behaves as his mentor. The fact that Alia did not make any changes in the cabinet, despite persistent economic failures, suggests a weakness on his part and a possible revival of factionalism.

Social and Economic Issues. The Albanian political leadership and party organizations showed an intense interest in problems affecting youth during 1985. A pervasive concern of the old guard was the perceptible intrusion of the blue jeans culture into their puritanical society. This concern dominated the political agenda of youth organizations and local party activists. The Albanian population is the youngest in Europe. More than half of it is under 22 years old, while the percentage of the population over 60 accounts for a mere 7.7 percent (ATA, 1 November; *FBIS*, 4 November). This phenomenon suggests an obvious generation gap with potentially serious political consequences.

Population growth is hailed by party and state officials as proof of their correct social policies and improvement in living standards. Yet growth in the work force has reached a level that makes it difficult for industry or agriculture to absorb. Although the Albanian government deliberately employs two-thirds of the work force in agriculture, finding suitable employment for the new entrants seems to have strained the economic capabilities of the country (Euro-Parliament, *Document PE.-226*; 13 May, p. 4). Employment of the young, who increasingly refuse to work in farm cooperatives, occupied the attention of the party's theoretical journal on several occasions. One issue all but admitted that Albania may very well have an unemployment problem on its hands. As the journal stated, "due to certain factors, the problems of full employment of new forces are becoming more acute and complicated" (*Rruga ë Partisë*, February; *FBIS*, 21 March).

Youth employment, work attitudes, and rebelliousness were the subject of a February seminar organized by the education department of the APL Central Committee and the Institute of Marxist-Leninist Studies, whose director is Madame Hoxha. The conference aimed at finding ways to "reach the youth" and to make room for them in the economic and political system. The same subject and concerns occupied the spring plenum of the ULYA central committee. Subsequent to the May plenum, which was attended by several Politburo members, Elezi wrote a series of hard-hitting articles on the need for a closer relationship between party and youth organizations to control foreign cultural intrusions. In his view, party organizations had to intensify their vigilance, particularly in the armed forces, where "youth organizations are the only social organizations available" (*Rruga ë Partisë*, March, p. 53). One way to improve party-youth relations, according to Elezi, is for party members to cease displaying excessive "self-importance, pretending that they know everything, and it is only what we say and what we decide that is important" (ibid.).

In addition, there were also troublesome signs of worker alienation, a phenomenon that has been pointed out by officials on numerous occasions during the past two years but seems to have intensified during 1985 (*YICA*, 1985, p. 259). In many production centers, mostly in the northern regions and the

Tirana district, absenteeism caused 235,000 workdays lost during the first six months of 1985 alone (*Zeri i Popullit*, 21 August). Approximately 1,500 workers per day fail to show up for work, according to the party organ, and they are responsible for low productivity in various enterprises. Absenteeism has spawned other social maladies, also alluded to in the past: nepotism, favoritism, bribery in issuing medical certificates, and careless managerial control of workers' activities outside the enterprise. Two boroughs within Tirana and several medical clinics were cited as violators of socialist discipline along with the districts of Kruje, Durrës, and Kavaje (ibid.).

The Albanian economy suffered a number of setbacks and nonfulfillment of quotas in 1985, repeating similar problems of previous years. Although most districts reported fulfillment of the plan for the first three months, there were indications that several key sectors of the economy fell short of their goals by the end of 1985 (ATA, 5 February; *FBIS*, 5 March).

The 1985 plan envisioned increase in overall industrial production of 6.2 percent and in agriculture 17.7 percent. Exports were to be boosted by 16.8 percent, domestic retail trade by 4 percent, services and construction by 5.3 percent and 2.5 percent, respectively. Key industries, gas and oil as well as agriculture, apparently did not perform well, which affected the above indices.

Some of the causes for nonfulfillment of plans in agriculture (the final account is not yet in) were attributed to the severe winter that Albania suffered, particularly in the northern regions, where at least 68 lost their lives due to ferocious snowstorms (ATA, 6 March; *FBIS*, 7 March). However, Niko Gjizari, chairman of the State Planning Commission, also pointed to sloppy local planning and inadequate involvement in enterprise control by financial institutions (*Zeri i Popullit*, 23 July).

The "central control" theme was emphasized by Alia at the beginning of the fiscal year, which in Albania coincides with the calendar year (ATA, 3 January; *FBIS*, 2 January). Alia set the tone for greater control and "thrift" in January 1985 and chided those who suffer from "gigantomania" and keep asking for new machinery when most of the old remains idle. "Thrift, comprehensive education, organizational and control work" were offered as remedies for the ailing economy by Alia (ibid.).

By mid-1985, it appears that the economic woes of Albania had increased to the point that a major press campaign was inaugurated to instill a spirit of thrift in all enterprises and to revive a sense of pride in the work force by exploiting the memory of Enver Hoxha.

On 17 July a major conference (with the cumbersome theme, "Let Us Have a Stronger Austerity Regimen Through the Frontal Realization of the Plan in All of Its Indices") was called in Tirana by the Institute for Economic Planning of the State Planning Commission (ATA, 18 July; *FBIS*, 19 July). A total of 23 papers were read, all of which had "thrift" as their central theme. A subsequent editorial in *Zeri i Popullit* cited numerous examples of failure to fulfill the state plan and singled out the districts of Mirdite and Tropoja for serious shortcomings. (Note: these were the districts most severely affected by bad weather.) Certain important industries, like chrome, chrome processing, gas and oil production, and agriculture were criticized on several occasions (*Rruga ë Partisë*, June; *FBIS*, 26 July). The June issue of the party's theoretical journal takes to task financial institutions for not using the "financial tools" of reward and denial to achieve higher productivity (ibid.).

The 1985 state budget, in support of economic growth projected at the beginning of the year, allocated essentially the same funds as in the previous year (9.2 billion lek), but increased revenues by 6 percent above the 1984 income. Approximately 60 percent of the increase was to be secured by savings (thus, the thrift campaign) and reduction in costs of materials (*Zeri i Popullit*, 26 December 1984; *FBIS*, 3 January). The defense budget was substantially increased as compared to 1984, and, according to Western accounts, the growth was related to an ongoing program of forced modernization. Not including the budget of *Sigurimi* (security) and the Interior Ministry, the 1985 defense budget stood at 1.7 billion lek, as compared to 1.01 billion for 1984. A rough breakdown of expenditures allocated 52.5 percent for capital investment, 26.8 percent for sociocultural measures, and 10.9 percent for defense. Self-reliance continued to be the basic policy, and Alia took special pride in affirming Albania's ability to produce 95 percent of spare parts domestically and to employ a work force of 60,000 Albanians with higher education and 270,000 with middle-level education (*Rruga ë Partisë*, October, p. 19).

Foreign Policy. Albania has continued the policy of guarded expansion in relations with the West, without any indication that its anti-Soviet rhetoric and position has changed appreciably. Noticeable growth in relations with Italy, France, and contacts with West Germany (a country with which Albania has no diplomatic relations) underscore what Albanian officials have termed an "active, not passive foreign policy" (*Rruga ë Partisë*, June, p. 18). During 1985, Tirana played host to the first high-level French diplomatic delegation headed by Deputy Foreign Minister Jean-Michel Baylet (10–12 September), who was accompanied by a large multiethnic group interested in doing business with Albania (*NYT*, 25 October; AFP, 12 September; *FBIS*, 12 September). More important, a delegation from West Germany, led by George von Wandenfels, state secretary of the Bavarian Ministry of Economics, visited Tirana in September and optimistically predicted that Albanian-German relations will soon be established (*Süddeutsche Zeitung*, 19 September; *FBIS*, 25 September). The West German delegation was received by Deputy Premier Manush Myftiu and was given a tour of a chrome processing plant (UPI, 11 November). Chrome is a mineral that the German auto industry has been eyeing for years, and it is Albania's chief export. On the occasion of von Wandenfels's visit, the Albanians went out of their way to praise the virtues of Bavaria's prime minister, Franz Josef Strauss, who had paid an unofficial visit to Albania in August 1984 (*RAD Background Report*, 15 November). Despite the absence of diplomatic relations, trade between the two countries has followed an upswing during the past three years (approximately 34 million dollars). The FRG delegation pointedly stated that its visit was related to the projected Albanian five-year plan (1986–1990), suggesting that Tirana will calculate Western trade and technology as an integral part of development (ibid.). Supportive of this trend is also the fact that a Japanese trade delegation visited Tirana and discussed matters related to efficiency and productivity (ATA, 17 July; *FBIS*, 18 July).

There have been no dramatic changes in Albanian attacks against "modern revisionism" and the "Soviet social imperialists." In Albanian ideological jargon the Soviet leaders are guilty of serious theoretical and political errors and have degenerated to the level of another imperialist power (ATA, 12 March; *FBIS*, 13 March).

Alia's major post-Hoxha foreign policy address, occasionally contradicted by other leaders, was given in the city of Korçë on 26 August. It was characterized by its milder than usual tone, a "pragmatic approach toward the West, a firm anti-Soviet platform, and an emphasis on Albania's desire for good relations with Greece, Italy, and Turkey" (*Zeri i Popullit*, 27 August). There was no letup in Alia's criticism of Yugoslavia, who in the eyes of Tirana officials is oppressing Kosovo's Albanian minority and "pursues an anti-Albanian policy" (*Zeri i Popullit*, 27 February, 3 April, 26 July). However, more telling than rhetoric has been practice. High-level Albanian delegations participated in major international conferences and Foreign Minister Reiz Malile seemed to be one of the busiest participants in the UN's celebration of its fortieth anniversary. Malile held private talks with sixteen leaders of foreign delegations, including those of Greece, Nicaragua, Turkey, Italy, Vietnam, and Austria (*Zeri i Popullit*, 29 September, 4 October).

Madame Vito Kapo, widow of the late theoretician Hysni Kapo and the minister of light industry, attended the Nairobi UN conference on the "Decade of the Woman," where she used the opportunity to attack both superpowers and praised her country's successful social policies (ATA, 21 July; *FBIS*, 22 July). Themi Thomai, minister of agriculture, represented Albania in the twenty-third session of the FAO general conference in Rome and was received by her Italian counterpart and other officials (ATA, 18 November; *FBIS*, 19 November).

Broadening of Western Contacts. The year 1985 was characterized by what can be described as a quantitative and qualitative growth in Albania's relations with the West—a trend that was in motion prior to Hoxha's death and continued afterward. West Germany, France, Austria, and Italy have been singled out as states with which Albania "desires improvement in relations." French-Albanian contacts resulted in a scientific and cultural exchange agreement, signed in Paris on 9 May, which coincided with the opening of a Paris trade fair where Albanian products were exhibited (ATA, 7 May; *FBIS*, 9 May; ATA, 10 May; *FBIS*, 12 May). In June a trade protocol was signed between France and Albania, covering exchanges for the 1985–1986 period (ATA, 11 June; *FBIS*, 12 June). These "normal" contacts culminated with the visit of the French deputy foreign minister in September, which resulted in the establishment of a joint trade commission charged with the task of "studying ways to expand trade" (AFP, 12 September; *FBIS*, 13 September).

Italy is developing into one of Albania's key Western partners. High-level contacts, visits by "friends of Albania," and warm exchanges of messages increased during 1985. In May the Italian-speaking prime minister, Adil Çarçani, sent a special message to Bettino Craxi expressing a desire for broader relations with Italy (ATA, 8 May; *FBIS*, 9 May). It was the first major foreign policy move following Hoxha's death. Italy responded immediately by dispatching the Italian undersecretary for foreign affairs, Bruno Corti, to Tirana. He was welcomed at the airport by his counterpart, Sokrat Pliaka, and had lengthy talks with Prime Minister Çarçani (ATA, 16 May; *FBIS*, 20 May). In a press release prior to Corti's departure, the Italian Foreign Ministry characterized the dialogue with Tirana as being of "great interest to all the Western nations who can communicate with Albania through Italy" (ANSA, 15 May; *FBIS*, 16 May). This cryptic comment fueled speculations that Rome was also serving as a link between Washington and Tirana.

A complicating factor in Albanian-Italian relations has been unplanned and unexpected: six members of an Albanian family sought asylum in the Italian embassy in Tirana and embassy officials refused to turn them over to local authorities (ATA, 12 December; *FBIS*, 23 December). The Ministry of the Interior characterized the six as "individuals compromised by antistate activities in the service of a foreign country" (ibid.). The matter remained unresolved by the end of the year and several Italian newspapers have asked Bettino Craxi to intervene and prevent the return of the Moisi Popa (a Catholic) family to Albanian authorities. Sigurimi charged the elder Popa with spying and collaborating with the fascists during the war.

Albanian negotiations with Great Britain aimed at establishing diplomatic relations have been held in Paris and London during the past year, and all indications are that a silent partner in this talk was the United States (*Financial Times*, 16 August). No serious issues separate the two countries. In fact only two matters need be resolved before relations can be established: the return of Albanian gold held in England (worth approximately 39 million dollars) and payment by Albania of damages for two British destroyers sunk by mines in the channel of Corfu (*Daily Telegraph*, 10 June; *Sunday Times*, 9 June). Alia's speech in Korçë put no special conditions on establishment of relations with Britain and West Germany, leaving open the suggestion that a compromise is possible (*Zeri i Popullit*, 27 August; *CSM*, 26 August).

Turkey continued to show its "interest" in Albanian affairs, with several visits by government officials and cultural delegations. In February, Minister of State Mustafa Tinaz Titiz visited Tirana to sign a trade protocol. He was received by Alia in his capacity as president of the republic and by Prime Minister Çarçani. In a lengthy news story, *Zeri i Popullit* extensively quoted Turkish officials on the problems of the Turkish minority in Bulgaria (ATA, 28 January; *FBIS*, 5 February). The Turkish national day reception in Tirana was attended by three Albanian cabinet members (usually an undersecretary attends East European receptions), and the outgoing Turkish ambassador was received by Ramiz Alia (ATA, 30 October; *FBIS*, 1 November; ATA, 6 November; *FBIS*, 7 November). In December, a Turkish university delegation visited Tirana in the context of Turkish-Albanian cultural relations and was given a tour of the southern part of the country (ATA, 8 December; *FBIS*, 9 December). Relations with Austria, Switzerland, Finland, and Denmark continued as in previous years. A scientific and cultural protocol was signed with Denmark and Shane Korbeçi, minister of foreign trade, led an Albanian delegation to Helsinki for trade talks (ATA, 23 August; *FBIS*, 26 August; ATA, 18 November; *FBIS*, 19 November).

Third World contacts and visits maintained pace with previous years, but it is obvious from a quantitative analysis of Albanian activities that Tirana has shifted its attention to Western European countries, with emphasis on Italy, France, Greece, and Turkey.

Yugoslavia. Relations with Belgrade followed the schizophrenic pattern of the past four years, i.e., good economic relations and a pragmatic approach to most aspects of state-to-state relations, coupled with intense nationalistic rhetoric from both sides. The year commenced with the conclusion of an overland transportation agreement and the completion of the Yugoslav part of the rail link that will facilitate Albanian trade with Western Europe (ATA, 8 February; *FBIS*, 13 February). A trade protocol signed at Tirana in November envisioned a volume of 125 million dollars in exchange from each side, which is an increase over the previous year. Furthermore, the agreement projects trade between the two countries for the period of the eighth Albanian five-year plan to reach the level of 680 million dollars (Tanjug, 16 November; *FBIS*, 21 November). In late November, talks were completed in Tirana to put into operation the rail link that the two sides have built. Service is to commence during 1986 (Tanjug, 23 November; *FBIS*, 25 November).

While commercial relations continued with some noticeable improvements, the verbal attacks from Tirana against "modern revisionism" and against the Yugoslav leadership continued unabated. *Zeri i Popullit* took offense at Yugoslav accounts of "splits" in the Albanian leadership (*Zeri i Popullit*, 27 February). An editorial in *Zeri i Popullit* sharply attacked Milka Planinc, who prior to her visit to Washington criticized the isolationist policies of the Albanian leadership (ATA, 22 May; *FBIS*, 23 May). Alia's foreign policy address in Korçë, however, repeated Tirana's desire for improved relations with Yugoslavia, but placed blame on Belgrade for the deterioration, which was traced to the Kosovo problem and what Tirana terms "harsh treatment of Albanians in Kosovo and Macedonia" (*Zeri i Popullit*, 19 November).

The post-Hoxha leadership has made it clear that it will continue to demand better treatment for the Albanian minority in Yugoslavia and will function as the center of Albanian nationalism. Symbolic of this attitude was the placement of an Albanian flag "on the heart of Enver on behalf of the Albanians of Kosovo, before his coffin was lowered in the ground by his widow, Nexhmije" (ATA, 15 April; *FBIS*, 16 April).

Greece. Relations between Greece and Albania continued to improve and in some areas expanded during 1985, despite the technical existence of a state of war between the two countries.

The year commenced with the well-publicized opening of the border crossing at Kakavia (*NYT*, 20 January; *Pravda*, 25 January), where a selected group of 2,000 Greek Communists and leftists and a similarly chosen Albanian group "celebrated" the establishment of an overland link between the two neighboring countries. Alternate foreign minister and mastermind of Greece's procommunist foreign policy, Karolos Papoulias, represented Greece in the festivities, and through his party's local organizations made sure that no critics of the Albanian regime or human-rights advocates were present (*Kathimerini*, 13 January; *NYT*, 20 January). But as soon as "the ribbon-cutting, anthem-playing, and speech-making had ended, the borders were closed, indicating that the crosspoint will be used only for official traffic" (*NYT*, 20 January).

Cultural and trade protocols between the two countries were signed covering the 1985–1986 period (ATA, 9 March; *FBIS*, 11 March). Several technical agreements regulating water distribution of border rivers (ATA, 27 November; *FBIS*, 3 December) and maintenance of border markings were carried out (ATA, 9 July; *FBIS*, 10 July). Trade with Greece is expected to double during the 1986 period, to approximately 80 million dollars (*The Economist*, 20 April).

The Albanian press and government officials followed domestic Greek developments with keen interest in 1985. Prime Minister Çarçani warmly congratulated Andreas Papandreou on his electoral victory and foresaw better relations with Athens (*Zeri i Popullit*, 4 June). But in a commentary following the June elections that same newspaper also reminded Papandreou of his promise to close down the American bases (ATA, 6 June; *FBIS*, 7 June).

Tirana expressed its annoyance with the perpetuation of the state of war between the two countries and has been pressing Athens to take the necessary legislative steps to terminate it. As far as Albania is concerned, this nonexistent war is a "ghost, an offspring of a delirium," maintained by meddlers in Mediterranean affairs (ATA, 16 December; *FBIS*, 19 December). Despite the technicality, however, and following the Papoulias visit to Tirana (*YICA*, 1985, p. 260), the two countries have increased contacts during 1985 and a number of Greek-Albanian Communists and old people were permitted, for the first time, to visit relatives in Greece.

As in previous years, the thorny issue of human-rights violations in general and of the Greek minority in particular interfered with further improvement of Greek-Albanian relations. In May, the Europarliament discussed the possibility of EEC-Albanian trade relations on the initiative of a Greek deputy, but the issue was shelved (despite the fact that the discussants thought it would be desirable). Other Greek representatives objected to such arrangements until improvements in the human rights of the Albanian people and the Greek minority are made by the Albanian government (Europarliament, *Document PE:95.226*, 13 May). Similarly, on 27 August, the UN Human Rights Commission, on the initiative of several human-rights organizations (including the nongovernmental organization, the International Federation for the Protection of the Rights of Ethnic, Linguistic, and Religious Minorities), adopted a resolution condemning Albania for constant violation of basic human rights (UN press release HR/1764). Such international pressures and the accounts of escapees regarding the conditions of the Greek minority have negatively affected further growth in relations.

A promising factor in Greek-Albanian relations has been the establishment of high-level contacts between the universities of Athens, Ioannina, and Tirana. Dr. Aleks Buda, president of the Albanian Academy of Sciences, and several other Albanian scholars visited Greece at the invitation of Buda's Greek counterpart (ATA, 6 December; *FBIS*, 9 December).

Eastern Europe. Relations with the East European states continued at the same low level and with the same pragmatic approach used in 1984. Albanian commentary kept referring to these nations as "vassals" of Moscow and denounced the renewal of the Warsaw Pact as continuation of "the enslavement of the peoples of its members" (*Zeri i Popullit*, 28 April). The Albanian press published all condolences coming from East European heads of state, and all were answered by Ramiz Alia in his capacity as president. With the exception of maverick Romania, all East European diplomatic delegations in Tirana remain at the chargé d'affaires level.

Trade protocols were signed with all East European states, as well as with North Korea, Vietnam, and Cuba. The Bulgarian trade agreement was signed in Sofia on 4 December. During the same week, several commentaries on "progress made" in Albanian agriculture were published in various Bulgarian sources. They originated in Albania, where the correspondent of the *Otechestven Front* (Fatherland Front), Lubomir Koralov, spent a week as guest of the Albanian government (*FBIS*, 25 November). As in previous years, the Albanian press gave wide coverage to the "anniversary of the Soviet occupation" of Czechoslovakia (*Zeri i Popullit*, 21 August). And again a high-level delegation from Vietnam, headed by the president of the assembly, Nguyen Huu Tho (ATA, 22 March; *FBIS*, 26 March), was given red carpet treatment in Tirana.

The USSR. Hoxha's death did not alter Albanian attitudes or policy toward the Soviet Union. The successor to the last Stalinist rejected outright the expression of Soviet condolences, and once again declared Albania's determination "not to have any relations with the two superpowers" (*WP*, 13 April). This did not deter the Soviet leadership from repeating feelers to "resolve issues" with Tirana and to repeat Gorbachev's offer to that end made in Sofia during 1984 (*Pravda*, 10 September 1984). Since Hoxha's death, Soviet media coverage of Albania has increased noticeably and maintained a positive tone. The Soviet press invariably emphasized the theme "that relations with Tirana are abnormal" (*Izvestiia*, 25 May), and expressed approval for Albanian initiatives in foreign affairs, such as the opening of the Kakavia border crossing with Greece (*Pravda*, 25 January). Throughout the year and with no noticeable difference between the pre- and post-Hoxha era, the Albanian press continued its ideological attacks against Moscow and took particular pleasure in reporting its problems in Afganistan (*Zeri i Popullit*, 12 June). Tirana denounced the Geneva summit meeting as an opportunity for the "superpowers to hatch up dangerous plots against the interests of peoples of sovereign countries" and dismissed Gorbachev as another revisionist (*Zeri i Popullit*, 24 November). A "false alarm" report that the Soviet news agency Tass had appointed a correspondent to Tirana was denied in a peculiar way by the Albanian government. The story, which originally appeared in the Soviet magazine *Zhurnalism* and was repeated by the Yugoslavs (Tanjug, 16 October; *FBIS*, 16 October), was dismissed by Albania as a "new anti-Albanian intrigue of Tanjug" (PSRA, UN Mission, press release, 17 October). Peculiarly, the ATA announcement did not directly deny the story, but repeated the fact that Albania "does not have any kind of relations, political, economic, cultural, or any other kind with the Soviet Union" (ibid.).

On the occasion of the Albanian national day, *Pravda* published a major editorial praising the contribution of Albania to socialism and expressing the hope that "with goodwill, all issues between the two countries could be resolved" (*Financial Times*, 29 November). But Muhamed Kaplani and Reiz Malile's speeches at the UN left little room for improvement in relations with Moscow (PSRA, UN Mission, speech by Reiz Malile, 30 September). The only possibility, of course, would be dramatic changes in the top Albanian leadership, which are not out of the question.

The United States. American-Albanian relations remained frozen during 1985, with one noticeable exception: Albanian officials have turned their attention to Albanian ethnics living in the United States, and important leaders of that community were invited (and appropriately entertained) by Albanian officials both in New York and in Tirana. Reiz Malile gave a reception in "honor of Albanian-Americans" (a traditional affair for him), and the editor of the Albanian-American newspaper *Liria* was invited to Tirana and received by Rita Marko and other Albanian officials (ATA, 18 June; *FBIS*, 18 June). But while Albanians friendly toward Tirana were visiting there, the press kept up its anti-imperialist barrage against President Reagan, whom it continues to present as a warmonger, and against the American presence in the Mediterranean, depicted as a threat to peace (ATA, 20 November; *FBIS*, 21 November; *Zeri i Popullit*, 24 November).

China. Relations with China seem to have stabilized during 1985 and reflected a pragmatic tone on both sides. Chinese condolences on Hoxha's death were published along with Alia's response (*Zeri i Popullit*, 14 April). More important, a trade agreement between the two countries, covering a five-year period (the duration of the new state plan) instead of one year, was signed in Peking (ATA, 5 December; *FBIS*, 5 December). This suggests that Albanian-Chinese relations are on a more stable basis and confirms a new pattern in Albanian trade practices from single year to multiyear agreements.

International Party Contacts. The death of Enver Hoxha and the extended mourning period was not conducive for party visits to Albania. Manolis Glezos, a wartime hero who defended Hoxha in his break with Khrushchev, was the sole foreign communist guest at the first secretary's funeral (*Ta Nea*, 16 April). Twenty-seven "Marxist-Leninist" parties expressed their condolences to the Albanian Party of Labor. The first secretary of the Brazilian Communist Party, Rao Amazonas, sent a warm message to Hoxha's widow. A Portuguese Communist Party delegation was received in Tirana by Alia and Çami jointly (ATA, 22 August; *FBIS*, 23 August) and an Algerian delegation, representing the majority party in parliament, was also welcomed in Tirana (ATA, 17 October; *FBIS*, 23 October).

Nikolaos A. Stavrou
Howard University

Bulgaria

Population. 8,980,000 (BTA, 31 December 1984; *FBIS*, 4 January)

Party. Bulgarian Communist Party (Bulgarska komunisticheska partiya; BCP)

Founded. Bulgarian Social Democratic Party founded in 1891; split into Broad and Narrow factions in 1903; the Narrow Socialists became the BCP and joined the Comintern in 1919.

Membership. Over 912,000 (*Pravda*, 20 July); 32.1 percent women (*Pravda*, 20 July). Bulgaria no longer publishes data on ethnic minorities; ethnic Turks and Gypsies, the two largest minority groups, are believed to be underrepresented in the party in proportion to their numbers in the general population. In 1981 11.4 percent of the party membership was under 30 years of age (*Otchet na Tsentralniya komitet na BKP pred XII kongres*, Sofia, 1981, pp. 112–13); 44.0 percent of the members are classified as industrial workers (*Pravda*, 20 July).

Secretary General. Todor Khristov Zhivkov (b. 1911)

Politburo. 11 full members: Todor Zhivkov (chairman, State Council), Chudomir Alexandrov (b. 1936, first deputy prime minister), Milko Balev (b. 1920, member, State Council), Todor Bozhinov

(b. 1931, deputy prime minister; minister of energy and raw material resources), Ognyan Doynov (b. 1935, minister of machine building and electronics), Dobri Dzhurov (b. 1916, minister of national defense), Grisha Filipov (b. 1919, prime minister), Pencho Kubadinski (b. 1918, member, State Council; chairman, Fatherland Front), Petur Mladenov (b. 1936, minister of foreign affairs), Stanko Todorov (b. 1920, chairman, National Assembly), Yordan Yotov (b. 1920, editor-in-chief, *Rabotnichesko delo*); 7 candidate members: Georgi Atanasov (b. 1933), Stanish Bonev (b. 1932), Petur Dyulgerov (b. 1929, chairman, Central Council of Trade Unions), Andrey Lukanov (b. 1938, deputy prime minister), Grigor Stoichkov (b. 1926, deputy prime minister, minister of construction, territorial structure, and architecture), Dimitur Stoyanov (b. 1928, minister of internal affairs), Georgi Yordanov (b. 1931, chairman, Committee on Culture)

Secretariat. 8 members: Georgi Atanasov, Milko Balev, Ognyan Doynov, Emil Khristov (b. 1924, member, State Council), Stoyan Mikhailov (b. 1930), Dimitur Stanishev (b. 1924), Vasil Tsanov (b. 1922), Kiril Zarev (b. 1926)

Central Committee. 191 full and 138 candidate members

Status. Ruling party

Last Congress. Twelfth, 31 March–4 April 1981, in Sofia; next congress scheduled for April 1986

Last Election. 7 June 1981. All candidates run on ticket of Fatherland Front, an umbrella organization (4.4 million members) comprising most mass organizations. Fatherland Front candidates received 99.9 percent of votes cast. Of the National Assembly's 400 members, 271 belong to the BCP and 99 to the Agrarian Union; 30 are unaffiliated (some 20 of these are Komsomols). The Bulgarian Agrarian National Union (BANU, 120,000 members) formally shares power with the BCP; holds 4 of the 29 seats on the State Council and the ministries of justice, public health, communications, and forestry; and fills about one-sixth of the people's council seats. BANU leader Petur Tanchev's post as first deputy chairman of the State Council makes him Todor Zhivkov's nominal successor as head of state.

Auxiliary organizations. Central Council of Trade Unions (CCTU, about 4 million members), led by Petur Dyulgerov; Dimitrov Communist Youth League (Komsomol, 1.5 million members), led by Stanka Shopova; Civil Defense Organization (750,000 members), led by Col. Gen. Tencho Papazov, provides training in paramilitary tactics and disaster relief; Committee on Bulgarian Women (30,000 members), led by Elena Lagadinova, no real significance

Publications. *Rabotnichesko delo* (*RD*; Workers' cause), BCP daily, edited by Yordan Yotov; *Partien zhivot* (Party life), BCP monthly; *Novo vreme* (New time), BCP theoretical journal; *Otechestven front* (Fatherland front), front daily; *Durzhaven vestnik* (State newspaper), contains texts of laws and decrees. Bulgarska telegrafna agentsiya (BTA) is the official news agency.

This has been a difficult year for Bulgaria. Adverse weather contributed to a poor harvest that exacerbated economic problems, causing the regime to raise the prices of basic commodities sharply late in the year. The government's effort to force the country's Turkish minority to profess a Bulgarian ethnic identity and adopt Bulgarian names provoked internal resistance and brought unfavorable international attention. Moreover, Bulgaria's normally smooth relations with the Soviet Union seemed to worsen as Gorbachev consolidated his power in the USSR. In Rome the trial of Sergei Antonov for allegedly participating in the attempted assassination of Pope John Paul II also focused attention on the "Bulgarian connection" to international terrorism.

Leadership and Party Organization. A *Pravda* (20 July) article on fraternal parties reported that, since the BCP's Twelfth Congress in 1981, party membership has grown from 825,876 to over 912,000. The percentage of women increased from 29.7 to 32.1, and that of industrial workers from 42.7 to 44.0. Of the approximately 87,000 new members admitted since 1981, 41 percent were women, 53 percent industrial workers, and 70 percent were under 30 years of age. Almost 23 percent had completed higher education, and an additional 68 percent had finished secondary school or were continuing their studies at a higher level.

No changes took place in either the Politburo or Secretariat. The most important governmental change came in October when Stanish Bonev, a candidate member of the Politburo, was removed as chairman of the State Planning Commission and as deputy chairman of the Council of Ministers in connection with his "transfer to other work" (BTA, 18 October; *FBIS*, 21 October). Bonev's new position was not announced, and he retained, for the time being, his Politburo position. The most immediately obvious reason for his dismissal as head of the State Planning Commission, a post he had held since July 1982, was the difficult economic situation. Indeed, shortly afterward *Rabotnichesko delo* (*RD*) sharply criticized Bulgaria's economic planning "on all levels." But there was also speculation that the chief factor was Soviet displeasure over the slow pace of reaching an agreement coordinating Bulgarian and Soviet economic plans for the 1986–1990 period. The timing of Bonev's dismissal—on the eve of Mikhail Gorbachev's visit to Sofia—gave strength to this rumor (*RFE, Situation Report*, 7 November, item 3).

Bonev was replaced by Ivan Iliev, a professor of economics who had held the chairmanship of the commission from 1973 to 1975. Born in 1925, Iliev had held a number of positions in the party and government related to economic affairs. Since October 1983 he had functioned as a personal aide to Todor Zhivkov (BTA, 19 October; *FBIS*, 21 October).

During the year the party launched a new campaign against bureaucratism and dishonesty. Organized around the theme of further developing democratic centralism, the press and party spokesmen denounced the practice of stage-managing meetings and conferences so that they are addressed only by the leaders and "those who are not sparing with their praise" (*RD*, 14 October; *FBIS*, 23 October). Criticism was also devoted to the tendency of party functionaries to deal with problems simply by holding meetings and discussions and writing memoranda. This was described as "pressing the gas pedal without engaging the gears," and party cadres were told that they should involve themselves more directly in practical activities (*RD*, 16 September; *FBIS*, 18 September). Several officials were reprimanded or punished for abusing their positions for personal gain. Svetozlar Georgiev, a former deputy chairman of the National Agroindustrial Union's executive committee, was prosecuted for using state materials and labor in the construction of his villa. Similar charges were leveled against Dimitur Gradev, director of the Center for Propaganda, Information, and Press Relations of the Committee on Culture (and against other middle-level officials in several ministries). Embezzlement was the charge against Kostadin Batalov, the general director of Interhotels, who also "turned many of his subordinates to crime," and Dimitur Nikolov, chairman of the Bulgarian Soccer Federation, who took "a large amount of foreign currency" (*RD*, 23 September; *FBIS*, 27 September). It was not clear whether this campaign was inspired by domestic causes or was simply an effort to emulate the drive against corruption undertaken by Gorbachev in the USSR.

Domestic Affairs. At its sessions on 16 and 17 May, the National Assembly dissolved one of the "superministries" that had been set up in January 1984 (see *YICA*, 1984, p. 266). The former Ministry of Energy and Raw Material Resources was replaced by three smaller ministries dealing with supplies, metallurgy, and energy. Since the combined ministry had been established, Bulgaria had experienced severe shortages in power supply and the metallurgical sector had failed to meet its plan targets. Politburo member Todor Bozhinov, who headed the superministry, was appointed to head the new Ministry of Supplies, clearly a blow to his prestige. Toncho Chakarov, 52, a mechanical engineer who had held a number of positions related to technological affairs, was named minister of metallurgy. Nikola Todoriev was appointed minister of energy, a position he had held before the 1984 consolidation. Todoriev was released from his position as chairman of the State Committee on Scientific and Technological Progress, and it was expected that this body would be disbanded, since Zhivkov had described it as "too far removed from the implementation of science in practical affairs" in an address to a BCP plenum in February (*RD*, 15 February; *FBIS*, 25 February). Later in the year, however, a new chairman was appointed, and it appeared that the committee would continue. The new chairman was Stoian Markov, 43, an electronics engineer and member of the BCP Central Committee (*RFE, Situation Report*, 7 November, item 3).

Economy. The January report on the fulfillment of the 1984 plan was generally optimistic. It claimed an increase in "domestic net material product" of 4.6 percent, substantially better than the 3.8 percent called for. This increase was credited entirely to improved labor productivity, which was said to have increased by 5.5 percent in the nonagricultural sectors. Industrial production rose 4.5 percent against a target of 5.0 percent, and shortfalls were admitted in some key sectors: rolled sheet iron, cement, cellulose, and paper, among others. Substantial improvements in the quality of production were also claimed. Products given the highest quality rating of "world level" were said to have increased by 34.3 percent, to become 19.1 percent of total production. The latter figure was 3.1 percent above that called for in the plan.

Agricultural production was reported to have increased by 6.8 percent against a plan target of 3.1 percent, but this was against the background of a very poor performance in 1983. Foreign trade turnover grew by 8.3 percent. The Soviet Union remained Bulgaria's largest trading partner, accounting for 57.5 percent of the total. The other CMEA countries accounted for an additional 18.9 percent. The plan also reported an increase in real per capita income of 2.7 percent (*RD*, 30 January; *FBIS*, 5 February; *RFE, Situation Report*, 15 February, item 2).

The current year, however, brought a number of setbacks, so that Zhivkov described 1985 in a speech to the East-West Economic Forum in September as "a year of hard trials" (*RD*, 29 September; *FBIS*, 3 October). The coldest winter in over a century stopped traffic along the Danube and froze the Sea of Azov, disrupting imports of Soviet coal, upon which Bulgaria depends for the generation of thermoelectric power. Bulgaria's own lignite mining operations were halted by the freezing of the open-face pits. The government introduced energy rationing, which led to darkened and unheated apartments, offices, and schools, and disrupted the production and distribution of industrial goods. In a televised report to the country, Energy Minister Nikola Todoriev blamed the hardships on the exceedingly cold winter, earlier droughts that had lowered water levels and so reduced hydroelectric output, wasteful consumption habits on the part of consumers and industry, and "managerial errors" that had delayed the opening of new facilities and operated existing ones inefficiently (*NYT*, 9 June; *RFE, Situation Report*, 28 March, item 2).

According to the report on the first quarter's plan fulfillment, sharp decreases occurred. Examples given included the production of phosphates, only 73.9 percent of the first quarter of 1984's production; soda ash, 70.5 percent; cement, 46.1 percent; railroad carriages, 27.5 percent; and harvesters, 20.4 percent. To make up for these shortfalls a meeting of the Council of Ministers called for an intensification of effort and the reintroduction of the six-day week (*RFE, Situation Report*, 24 May, item 3). Late in the year the press claimed that these efforts had been for the most part successful, and that they guaranteed the fulfillment of the 1985 plan (*RD*, 28 October; *FBIS*, 1 November).

Problems in agriculture mounted as the country suffered a severe summer drought that also led to shortages of drinking water. On 15 September the Council of Ministers announced a series of drastic price increases on a number of commodities and services. The price of electricity was raised 58 percent for industrial and 41 percent for private consumption. The price of gasoline was raised by 35 percent, and heating oil went up 33 percent. The cost of drinking water was increased 264 percent for industrial consumption and 66 percent for private users. The price of telephone calls also increased, as did the prices of a number of imported and luxury goods, including chocolates and cigarettes. The council also announced that liquor would become "considerably more expensive" and that its availability would be reduced. In justifying these increases, a spokesman for the Ministry of Finance stated that Bulgaria could generate electricity sufficient for its needs if industry and the population would adopt better methods of conservation. The low cost of electricity, he argued, had encouraged wasteful patterns of consumption. He also stated that the increase in the prices of commodities not directly related to energy was intended more accurately to reflect their real costs. He added that much of the increased revenue would be used by the state to develop new water resources (*RD*, 16 September; *FBIS*, 20 September; *RFE, Situation Report*, 7 October, item 1). To alleviate the impact of these price increases on the poorest citizens, the council raised the minimum monthly wage from 110 to 120 *leva* and announced that certain categories of workers with wages close to the minimum would receive a monthly increase of five *leva* (Sofia Domestic Service, 19 September; *FBIS*, 20 September).

Zhivkov delivered a major address on the country's economic future to a BCP plenum on 12–13 February. Its central theme was the need for drastic improvements in the country's level of science and technology. Zhivkov bluntly described several problem areas. The New Economic Mechanism (NEM), which was supposed to be in effect for the entire economy by 1 January 1985 has not had the expected effects and is in need of substantial revision. Too many managers prefer "bureaucratic centralism" to democratic centralism, and remain too far removed from real economic processes. And the pricing system within the CMEA has had an "unfortunate" impact on the economy. Zhivkov did not speak further about Bulgaria's problems with the CMEA, but with regard to the other issues he called for "considerable changes" in the functions and organization of the State Planning Commission to make it more responsible for scientific and technological innovation. He also called for improvements in education, suggesting the possibility of creating a large technological university to increase the number of highly qualified graduates in fields that are presently understaffed (*RD*, 15 February; *FBIS*, 25 February; *RFE*, Background Report, 18 April).

One undeniably bright spot in the Bulgarian economy was the performance of private plots in agriculture. A report in the farming newspaper *Kooperativno selo* stated that in 1984 these plots were responsible for 41 percent of the country's production of fruit, 35 percent of its vegetables, 39 percent of its meat, 30 percent of its milk, and 54 percent of its eggs. The paper warned against attributing these successes to the factor of private ownership, stressing that it was through state policies that private plots were aided with supplies of seed, livestock, and fertilizers from the agroindustrial complexes (*RFE, Situation Report*, 24 May, item 4).

Minorities. During the early months of the year it became apparent that the government had launched a major effort to convert the country's ethnic Turks into Bulgarians, and that this effort involved some degree of violence. Measures against the Turkish population, estimated to number about 800,000, included the abandonment of Turkish-language publications and radio broadcasts and the requirement that Turks adopt Bulgarian names. When these policies began to attract unfavorable international attention, the regime defended them with the argument that the "so-called" ethnic Turks were in fact the descendants of Bulgarians who had been forcibly converted to Islam and given Turkic or Arabic names during the centuries of Ottoman rule. These people were now "spontaneously reclaiming their Bulgarian heritage." At the same time reports circulated that several bombings that occurred last year (see *YICA*, 1985, p. 266) had been the work of ethnic Turks fighting against the campaign of forced Bulgarization. There were also reports that in areas with a concentration of ethnic Turks government violence and local resistance had cost the lives of as many as three hundred people. The Bulgarian government denied these reports and organized several news conferences that included appearances by individuals who had reportedly been killed. Not all such individuals were produced by the government, and the closing of certain areas to foreign journalists in January and February lent credence to the reports of unrest (*RFE, Situation Report*, 30 January, item 1, and 15 February, item 1; *NYT*, 19 May, 8 December).

During February and March senior party officials visited districts with the largest concentrations of ethnic Turks to impress the national policy on local officials. These leaders denied the existence of a Turkish minority and attributed the spate of name-changing to a revival of the Bulgarian national spirit. Prime Minister Grisha Filipov, in a tour of the Kurdzhali District, called for the transformation of the region into a "citadel of the Bulgarian spirit." Party Secretary Dimitur Stanishev, in the Blagoevgrad region, stated that there would be no emigration and no negotiations on this issue with Turkey. Most ominous of all, Politburo member Stanko Todorov told a meeting in Sliven that those who were not content with life in Bulgaria would be assured of emigration in three to four hours, "not to Turkey, but to other areas of Bulgaria, where they can live more calmly and will find their happiness." This seemed to be a warning of forced resettlement or could refer to the deportation of some Turks to Belene, the infamous concentration camp of the Stalinist era, which had been reported in the Western press (*NYT*, 8 December; *RFE, Situation Report*, 28 March, item 1).

Bulgaria's drive to assimilate its Turkish minority is a sharp departure from the policy that had been followed since the early 1960s. In the past the government boasted of its enlightened efforts to assure the Turkish population cultural autonomy—allowing Turkish-language publications, theatrical presentations, and other cultural events, and reserving places in higher education for members of the Turkish minority. The reasons for the change were not entirely clear. One Yugoslav source attributed it to the discovery of an underground organization among the Turks that was planning for the secession of Turkish-inhabited areas (*JPRS*, 1 April). A more likely cause, however, is the fear of growing nationalist sentiment among the ethnic Turks in a time of heightened feeling among Muslims worldwide. It is also possible that the authorities believe that the high birth rate among the ethnic Turks has been making them entirely too large a minority. Early in the year the government announced that a census would be held in December, and it is expected to report that the entire population is Bulgarian (*The Economist*, 2 February, 2 March; *Sofia News*, 11 December).

Culture and Education. A March issue of *Puls*, the literary weekly published by the Komsomol, contained a poem that spelled out the phrase "Down with Todor Zhivkov" with the first letter of each line. Attributed to the poet Margarita Petkova, who denied authorship, the poem had the earmarks of a literary prank and was perhaps intended to embarrass the journal's staff. As soon as the phrase was noticed by the authorities, unsold issues of the journal were withdrawn and copies in libraries and reading rooms were confiscated. No one on the journal's staff was immediately punished (*RFE, Situation Report*, 1 August, item 2).

After the match for the national soccer championship between Levski Spartak, representing the Ministry of Internal Affairs, and Central, representing the Ministry of Defense, ended in a prolonged and brutal brawl, the government announced a drastic reconstruction of the sport. Attributing the violence to the vast amount of money that had been wagered on the game and to the general air of corruption that has been characteristic of the sport in Bulgaria, the authorities disbanded all clubs associated with government agencies. Several officials and players were fined or banned from the sport, and a new governing body, the Bulgarian Soccer Union, was set up to raise the moral level of the game (*RFE, Situation Report*, 6 March, item 3; 1 August, item 3).

The Ministry of Education launched a drive to restore discipline in the country's high schools. Responding to complaints that students ignored dress codes, avoided difficult subjects, smoked, and abused alcohol, authorities established a curfew of 9 P.M. for those eighteen and under, banned them from theaters and restaurants serving alcohol, and made school uniforms obligatory. Parents were also criticized for not keeping their children occupied and for encouraging them to study arts and humanities rather than needed technical subjects (*WP*, 11 November).

Auxiliary Organizations. Last year the Fatherland Front established the National Front for Peace and Solidarity (NFPS) to channel contributions from citizens, public organizations, and enterprises to individuals or groups fighting against militarism and imperialism (see *YICA*, 1985, p. 270). Celebrating the organization's first anniversary, its executive secretary, Georgi Petkov, who is also a secretary for the Fatherland Front's National Council, reported that it had rendered assistance in Lebanon, Afghanistan, Cambodia, Ethiopia, and South Yemen. He added that the NFPS and its parent Fatherland Front also have organized training courses dealing with industry, agriculture, and "problems of cultural revolution" for guests from other countries, mentioning specifically the region of Latin America (*RFE, Situation Report*, 15 February, item 3).

Petur Tanchev, head of the Bulgarian Agrarian National Union, led a delegation to Mexico as the guest of the National Peasants' Confederation. He met with President de la Madrid, after which the usual statements in favor of peace and disarmament were issued (BTA, 30 August; *FBIS*, 1 September).

International Affairs. World attention continued to be focused on the "Bulgarian connection," the alleged complicity of Bulgarian agents in the 1981 attempt on the life of Pope John Paul II. In November 1982 Italian authorities arrested Sergei Ivanov Antonov, head of Bulgaria's Balkan Airline office in Rome and allegedly a state security agent. Two officials of the Bulgarian embassy in Rome, Todor Aivazov and Maj. Zhelyo Vasilev, who were also sought by Italian authorities, had previously returned to Bulgaria. In October 1984 formal indictments were handed down charging the three Bulgarians and four Turkish nationals with conspiracy to assassinate a head of state (See *YICA*, 1983, p. 256, 1984, pp. 306–7, and 1985, p. 270).

Labeled the "trial of the century" by journalists, proceedings against Antonov and the other defendants began in May. The investigatory phase ended on 21 December with the interrogation of Aivazov and Vasilev in Sofia, for which the Bulgarian government had given its permission. More than one hundred court sessions and the interrogation of over fifty witnesses produced a body of direct and circumstantial evidence linking would-be assassin Mehmet Ali Agca to a network of Turkish terrorists, but failed to produce convincing corroboration of Bulgarian involvement. As from the beginning, the case for a Bulgarian connection continued to rest on the testimony of Agca, whose credibility was first undermined by contradictory versions of the story that he gave after his arrest and during previous investigations. Nor was confidence in his evidence much raised when, during his first appearance on the stand, he claimed to be Jesus Christ reincarnated. In later sessions he also asserted that he was "an angel in human form," and he offered to tell prosecutors whatever story they would prefer. Despite the intense investigation no witness was found who had ever heard any of the Bulgarian defendants speak English, the language in which Agca said the conspiracy was planned, nor could any trace be found of the $1.8 million that Agca claimed to have received from the Bulgarians. Defense and prosecution attorneys were scheduled to make their concluding presentations in January 1986, with a verdict expected in February (*RFE, Situation Report*, 1 August, item 1; *NYT*, 27 May; *WP*, 29 December).

Bulgarian spokesmen described the trial as a CIA-inspired attempt to discredit the socialist camp. These charges received increased attention when Giovanni Pandico, a Neapolitan gangster who had been in prison with Agca, testified that Agca had been briefed by a high-ranking officer from Italian military intelligence. A separate investigation of this charge was begun by Italian authorities who found Pandico a less-than-credible witness, and the case was dropped "for lack of evidence" (*WP*, 19 December).

The Soviet Union. There were signs that the beginning of the Gorbachev era saw strains developing in the normally smooth relations between Bulgaria and the USSR. In an interview published in the Bulgarian weekly *Pogled*, the Soviet ambassador, Leonid Grekov, revealed that Gorbachev had told Zhivkov that "the roots of our friendship are deep and strong, but the tree must be watered and nurtured in order to bear fruit." The implication of this statement seemed to be that Bulgaria cannot depend on past services and fulsome rhetoric in praise of Moscow, but must demonstrate its continued usefulness in practical ways. Grekov criticized the quality of goods that Bulgaria exports to the USSR and the low level of labor discipline demonstrated by Bulgarian workers. He added that the Bulgarian working class is much less an urban proletariat than its Soviet counterpart, and that many Bulgarian workers maintain houses and gardens in the countryside, leading them to look upon their factory jobs as a period of rest following their agricultural labors. Grekov also had many favorable comments on Bulgaria and its relations with the USSR, but the unusually frank negative statements naturally became the focus of attention (*RFE, Situation Report*, 2 September, item 1a).

Zhivkov visited the USSR for Chernenko's funeral and stopped in Moscow again in June on his return from the Far East. On the second occasion he was received by Gorbachev, and the two leaders signed an agreement on "the development of economic and technological and scientific cooperation for the period up to the year 2000." Zhivkov was also awarded an Order of Lenin, his fourth, apparently in belated recognition of the fortieth anniversary of the Bulgarian socialist regime, which took place last year. There were rumors that difficult negotiations had taken place during the preparation of the economic agreement. Bulgaria sought guarantees of more substantial supplies of energy and support for the modernization of its production facilities, while the USSR complained that Bulgaria dumped too many low-quality products on the Soviet market. Later in the year there were reports that the agreement was already undergoing revision. It was also rumored that Soviet displeasure with Bulgaria's lack of cooperation had been the reason for Stanish Bonev's dismissal as head of the State Planning Commission (*RFE, Situation Report*, 29 June, item 1, and 7 November, items 1, 2).

Gorbachev attended the Warsaw Pact summit meeting in Sofia during 21–23 October and then stayed an extra day for a "friendly visit." In his public speech Gorbachev stated that he and Zhivkov had briefed each other in a comradely way and had exchanged opinions without avoiding the "sharp edges." Observers also noted that while Gorbachev had words of praise for Bulgaria and its people, he said little or nothing about Zhivkov personally. He did, however, invite Zhivkov to pay an official friendly visit to the USSR (*Pravda*, 24 October; *RFE, Situation Report*, 7 November, item 2).

Other East European and Balkan Countries. Turkish president Kenan Evren sent a message to Zhivkov in mid-January protesting the Bulgarian government's treatment of its Turkish minority. In February the Turkish ambassador to Sofia was recalled "for consultations," and he addressed a closed session of parliament devoted to events in Bulgaria. President Evren postponed indefinitely a planned visit to Sofia, and several other contacts were also canceled. Meanwhile the Turkish press began to condemn the atrocities and outrages directed against the Bulgarian Turks, and several anti-Bulgarian demonstrations were held. Bulgarian spokesmen denied the charges of persecution, refused to admit that there was any question to negotiate with the Turks, and accused the Turks of attempting to use the Muslim population of Bulgaria to undermine Bulgarian security. Balkanturist, the Bulgarian tourist agency, canceled the reservations of Turkish visitors, and there were reports that Turkish trucks were harassed during their passage through Bulgaria. Bulgaria organized a vigorous protest that included a number of letters from Bulgarian Muslims and clergy denying that persecutions were taking place and stating that the adoption of Bulgarian names was voluntary and spontaneous. One of these referred to Turkey's less-than-perfect record with regard to the Kurds and other minorites and concluded. "It makes no sense to peep in the yard next door when your own barn is on fire" (*Sofia News*, 4 December; *RFE, Situation Report*, 30 January, item 1, 6 March, item 1, 28 March, item 1, and 29 June, items 2, 3).

Bulgarian-Yugoslav relations continued to reflect the improvement that followed the visit of Prime Minister Milka Planinc to Bulgaria last year. The Yugoslav press did object to Bulgarian persecution of the Turkish minority, but owing to Yugoslavia's own problems with its Albanian Muslim minority, the issue was not heavily emphasized. The Yugoslav press also objected to the way in which the Bulgarian state celebrated the 1,100th anniversary of the death of St. Methodius. The Bulgarians were accused of treating Saints Cyril and Methodius as Bulgarians rather than Macedonians (*RFE, Yugoslavia, Situation Report*, 22 April, item 8).

Although Bulgaria's relations with Albania have not been close, the Bulgarian press took the occasion of the fortieth anniversary of the establishment of diplomatic relations between the two countries to call for "full normalization" and the further development of economic cooperation (*RD*, 17 November; *FBIS*, 18 November).

Bulgaria's relations with Greece have been especially cordial since the victory of Andreas Papandreou's Pan-Hellenic Socialist Movement. Zhivkov visited Athens during 22–24 July and was very warmly received there by the Greek prime minister. The two leaders expressed agreement on most international issues and described the relations between their countries as "a model for states with differing social systems." Their talks emphasized the expansion of economic cooperation, particularly in the field of joint activities (*RD*, 23, 25 July; *FBIS*, 25, 30 July).

The Third World. Zhivkov paid an official visit to Syria during 27–30 April. He held several talks with President Hafiz al-Asad, after which a treaty was signed dealing with economic, scientific, and technical cooperation through 2005. Zhivkov and al-Asad expressed "similar, even identical" views on the international situation and expressed their belief that the new agreements would lead to a "qualitative improvement" in Bulgarian-Syrian relations. (Damascus Domestic Service, 30 April; *FBIS*, 1, 6 May; *RD*, 2 May).

Bulgaria was visited by Libya's foreign minister, who brought a message from Moammar Khadafy for Zhivkov. There was some speculation that this concerned the situation of the ethnic Turks in Bulgaria, but if so, no mention of this subject was made public. After the minister's meeting with Zhivkov, ratification documents for previous agreements were exchanged and a new protocol covering cooperation during the 1985–1989 period was signed (*RD*, 7 July; *FBIS*, 10 July).

Bulgaria continued to pursue an active policy toward Africa. Robert Mugabe, prime minister of Zimbabwe, visited Bulgaria during 31 August–1 September. He met with Zhivkov to discuss ways to improve bilateral relations and to exchange views of the international situation. With regard to the latter, there appeared to be little agreement except in their mutual condemnation of apartheid in South Africa (BTA, 31 August; *FBIS*, 3 September).

Zhivkov led a Bulgarian delegation to Japan during 23–29 May to open the Bulgarian exhibition at "Expo 85." In recent years Zhivkov has expressed the desire that Bulgaria become the "Japan of the Balkans," and during his stay he met with several leading industrialists and businessmen in addition to his official reception by the emperor. Bulgaria has cultivated economic relations with Japanese firms and has established at least two joint ventures: Fanuc-Machinex, which services the automatic machines and robots supplied to Eastern Europe by Fujitsu-Fanuc and provides engineering services in machine building and electronics; and Sofia-Mitsukoshi, which will design and construct department stores and depots for consumer goods (*RFE, Background Report*, 10 April). From Japan, Zhivkov went to North Korea (29 May–2 June) and to Mongolia (2–4 June). In both countries he signed agreements calling for the expansion of trade and cultural cooperation (*RFE, Situation Report*, 29 June, item 1).

Daniel Ortega, president of Nicaragua, made a brief visit to Bulgaria during 2–3 May. He met with Zhivkov and was the subject of a popular rally organized to express solidarity with the Sandinista movement. Before his departure a protocol was signed dealing with expanded economic cooperation and the establishment of joint projects in Nicaragua (Sofia Domestic Service, 3 May; *FBIS*, 6 May).

Western Europe and the United States. West Germany is Bulgaria's largest trading partner among the Western nations. Last year, reacting to strong Soviet pressure, Zhivkov suddenly canceled a scheduled visit to Bonn (see *YICA*, 1985, p. 273). In the spring, Hans Dietrich Genscher, West Germany's foreign minister, held meetings with Zhivkov and his Bulgarian counterpart, Petur Mladenov. Although Genscher differed with his Bulgarian hosts over the Federal Republic's participation in the Strategic Defense Initiative, he spoke favorably on the development of relations with Bulgaria, particularly in the area of trade, whose value surpassed $700 million in 1985. He added that both sides would like to see Zhivkov's visit to Bonn rescheduled (BTA, 8 March; *FBIS*, 11 March).

Mauno Koivisto, president of Finland, was in Bulgaria from 23 to 25 April, meeting with Zhivkov. The two leaders praised the expansion of trade that had already occurred and called for it to reach a still higher level (Sofia Domestic Service, 25 April; *FBIS*, 26 April).

On 1 April the U.S. Department of State issued a statement of concern about the oppression of the Turkish minority in Bulgaria. Calling it a "gunpoint program," Assistant Secretary of State Elliott Abrams referred to reports of "several hundred" casualties. Through its embassy the Bulgarian government called these charges "fabricated and ungrounded" (*Los Angeles Times*, 2 April). In January, American officials broke off talks with Bulgaria on cooperation in the struggle against international narcotics traffic. According to a report issued by the American embassy, Bulgarian authorities had a history of recalcitrance in moving against known drug traffickers resident in or passing through the country. Bulgarian spokesmen denied these charges, and stated that no Bulgarian citizen or vehicle has ever been caught anywhere smuggling drugs. They attributed the breakoff of discussions with the United States to "political reasons" on the American side (*NYT*, 7 February; *RFE, Situation Report*, 15 February, item 1). In an agreement between the Bulgarian Basketball Association and the NBA that "transcended politics and ideological differences," Bulgarian basketball star Georgi Glouchkov was sent to play for the Phoenix Suns. In addition to receiving half of Glouchkov's salary and a cash payment, the Bulgarian Association will send the Bulgarian national team for training in the United States (*WP*, 18 November).

The Bulgarian press welcomed the summit meeting between Reagan and Gorbachev, expressing the hope that it would lead to a substantial reduction in world tensions. Later reports were less enthusiastic, referring to the summit's lack of concrete achievements.

John D. Bell
University of Maryland Baltimore County

Czechoslovakia

Population. 15,503,000
Party. Communist Party of Czechoslovakia (Komunistická strana Československa; KSČ)
Founded. 1921
Membership. 1,650,000 (Moscow, *Pravda*, 6 December 1985)
Secretary General. Gustáv Husák

Presidium. 11 full members: Vasil Bil'ák, Petr Colotka (deputy prime minister), Karel Hoffman (chairman, Revolutionary Trade Union Movement), Gustáv Husák (president of the republic), Alois Indra (chairman, Federal Assembly), Miloš Jakeš, Antonín Kapek, Josef Kempný, Josef Korčák (deputy prime minister), Jozef Lenárt, Lubomír Štrougal (federal prime minister); 3 candidate members: Jan Fojtík, Josef Haman, Miloslav Hruškovič

Secretariat. 10 full members: Gustáv Husák, Mikula Beno, Vasil Bil'ák, Jan Fojtík, Josef Haman, Josef Havlín, Miloš Jakeš, Josef Kempný, František Pitra, Jindřich Poledník; 2 members-at-large: Zdeněk Hoření, Marie Kabrhelová

Control and Auditing Commission. Jaroslav Hajn, chairman

Central Committee. 123 full and 55 candidate members

Status. Ruling party

Last Congress. Sixteenth, 6–10 April 1981, in Prague; next scheduled for 1986

Slovak Party. Communist Party of Slovakia (Komunistická strana Slovenska; KSS); membership: 400,000 full and candidate members; Josef Lenárt, first secretary; Presidium: 11 members; Central Committee: 91 full and 31 candidate members

Last Election. 1981, 99.0 percent, all 350 National Front candidates; 66 percent of seats reserved for KSČ candidates

Auxiliary Organizations. Revolutionary Trade Union Movement (Tenth Congress, April 1982), Cooperative Farmers' Union, Socialist Youth Union (Third Congress, October 1982), Union for Collaboration with the Army, Czechoslovak Union of Women, Union of Fighters for Peace

Main State Organs. The executive body is the federal government, which is subordinate to the 350-member Federal Assembly, composed of the Chamber of the People (200 members) and the Chamber of the Nations (150 members). The assembly, however, merely rubber-stamps all decisions made by the KSČ Presidium and Central Committee.

Publications. *Rudé právo*, KSČ daily; *Pravda* (Bratislava), KSS daily; *Tribuna*, Czech-language ideological weekly; *Predvoj*, Slovak-language ideological weekly; *Život strany*, fortnightly journal devoted to administrative and organizational questions; *Práce* (Czech) and *Práca* (Slovak), Trade Union Movement dailies; *Mladá fronta* (Czech) and *Smena* (Slovak) Socialist Youth Union dailies; *Tvorba*, weekly devoted to domestic and international politics; *Nová mysl*, theoretical monthly. Československá tisková kancelář (ČETEKA) is the official news agency.

The KSČ developed from the left wing of the Czechoslovak Social Democratic Party, having co-opted several radical socialist and leftist groups. It was constituted in Prague and admitted to the Communist International the same year. Its membership in the Comintern, however, was an uneasy one until in 1929 the so-called bolshevization process was completed and a leadership of unqualified obedience to the Soviet Union assumed control. During the First Czechoslovak Republic (1918–1939), the KSČ enjoyed legal status, but it was banned after the Munich Agreement. After the war, it emerged as the strongest party in the postwar elections of 1946, although it did not poll a majority of votes. In February 1948, the KSČ seized all power in a coup d'etat and transformed Czechoslovakia into a communist party-state of the Soviet type. The departure from Stalinist practices started later in Czechoslovakia than in other countries of Central and Eastern Europe, but it led to a daring liberalization experiment known as the Prague Spring of 1968. A Soviet-led military intervention by five Warsaw Pact countries in August of the same year ended the democratization course and imposed on Czechoslovakia the policies of so-called normalization—a return to unreserved subordination to the will of the Soviet Union and the emulation of the Soviet example in all areas of social life.

Party Internal Affairs. Among the most important tasks during 1985 was preparation for the Seventeenth KSČ Congress that will open on 24 March 1986, preceded by the Fifteenth Slovak Congress to begin on 13 March 1986. The KSČ will discuss the eighth five-year plan (1986–1990) and economic prospects through the year 2000. This was revealed after a session of the Central Committee (*Rudé právo*, 19 June; Radio Bratislava, 21 June). No other major issues seem to have been mentioned, although several important questions remain: how to achieve better performance without substantial changes in the mode of the economy; the need to appoint, or at least designate, a successor to frequently ailing Secretary General Gustáv Husák;

relations with the new leadership in the Kremlin under Mikhail Gorbachev. Husák told the Central Committee that the KSČ would not "take any road . . . that would weaken the party's leading role" (*Rudé právo*, 20 June). Party Presidium resolutions adopted throughout the year exhibited the same cautious attitude (Radio Prague, 5 March; *Rudé právo*, 22 October). The party press took great pains to warn against experiments with pluralism, inspired by other bloc countries, such as Hungary (*Tribuna*, 23 January; *Nová mysl*, no. 5, April; Bratislava, *Pravda*, 11 June). The seventeenth anniversary of the USSR military intervention in August 1968 provided a special opportunity to denounce all ideas deviating from the Soviet-imposed orthodoxy (*Rudé právo*, 21 August).

The size of the party changed little in 1985. According to a Soviet report, the KSČ had 1,650,000 members at the end of the year. This represents a modest increase of 1.6 percent, compared with the 1984 total of 1,623,000. Since the Sixteenth Congress (1981), a total of 241,245 new members have been admitted to the party; about 60 percent of them were workers (Moscow, *Pravda*, 6 December).

Domestic Affairs. The fortieth anniversaries of the Yalta Conference and the end of German occupation were celebrated by Czechoslovakia in full agreement with the official Soviet position on the historical significance of these two events. As for Yalta, the media stressed the lesson which that summit had taught about "possible collaboration of countries with differing economic systems" and "joint efforts of different social systems against aggression and for peace and international security" (Radio Prague, 3 February). The commitment made by the USSR at Yalta to respect the right to self-determination of the nations in Central and Eastern Europe was either passed over in silence or mentioned only in connection with polemics against Western commentators who were accused of "falsification of history" (*Rudé právo*, 25 January).

The anniversary of the liberation in May followed closely upon the 115th anniversary of Lenin's birth. The Czechoslovak media tried to put these two events into a quasi-causal relationship, arguing that transformation of Czechoslovakia into a communist party-state of the Soviet type had been the logical and only possible outcome of the historical forces operating in Europe since the 1917 revolution and, thus, represented a culmination of Czech and Slovak national aspirations (Czechoslovak television, 22 April; *Rudé právo*, 4 April; Radio Prague, 27 April). Some even affirmed that the 1969 imposition by the USSR of the Husák leadership and the "normalization" course had been comparable to the liberation of Czechoslovakia (Radio Prague, 17 April). Speeches of party leaders at the anniversary festivities echoed these views (Radio Hvězda, 8 May; Radio Prague, 9 May). On 9 May, Husák proclaimed an amnesty that was more lenient toward common criminals than perpetrators of alleged "crimes against the state"—usually political dissenters and cultural dissidents (Radio Hvězda, 8 May).

The year 1985 also brought re-election of KSČ Secretary General Gustáv Husák to a third term as president of the republic (*Rudé právo*, 22 May). This man already has eclipsed former party leader Antonín Novotný (1957–1968), whom he had bitterly criticized for what he himself has been doing since 1975: namely, occupying the top posts in both the party and the government. There occurred two other changes during 1985. General Martin Dzúr was relieved, for reasons of health, of his duties as minister of defense, which he had carried out for almost two decades. He was succeeded by Colonel-General Milan Václavík (Radio Prague, 11 January). Following an official communiqué, federal Minister of Finance Leopold Lér resigned, also ostensibly for health reasons (*Rudé právo*, 5 October). It was a public secret, however, that his resignation had been forced. Lér's "health problem" was alcoholism, and he supposedly was involved in a major corruption scandal that had implicated several top officials in the customs service (*The Guardian*, 18 October; *Financial Times*, 21 October).

Alcoholism continued to cause serious concern among the decisionmakers. According to official statistics, per capita consumption of alcohol has been on the rise since the 1960s, increasing by about 30 percent since then. This rate has been especially high in Slovakia. More than half of all murders have been committed in a state of drunkenness (Bratislava, *Práca*, 29 July). The regime launched a systematic campaign against alcohol abuse (*Nové slovo*, 11 July; *Smena*, 16 August). It deplored the fact that the working class, the supposed vanguard of socialism, indulges most in these excesses (*Rudé právo*, 9, 24 August).

The party was also dissatisfied with the level of class consciousness among workers and criticized their inability to relate to what is called the "socialist intelligentsia." This has been an interesting development, since until recently party spokesmen had criticized the intelligentsia for its unwillingness to relate to the working class, and it continues to be found wanting in this respect (Bratislava, *Pravda*, 5 February). Allegiance to "real socialism" also seems to be found unsatisfactory on the part of ethnic minorities in Czechoslovakia. The most frequent source of problems in recent times has been the Hungarians in southern Slovakia. The gravity of such problems lies not only in the fact that Hungarians constitute by far the largest minority (585,000 people, or almost 4 percent of the entire population); troubled relations between the Slovaks and the Hungarians have also adversely affected relations between Czechoslovakia and Hungary.

The recent improvement of economic conditions in Hungary and a certain relaxation of the political climate there have impressed Czechoslovak citizens of Hungarian origin, who cannot help making comparisons with their relatives south of the Danube. Although the Hungarian minority always has been treated with much more consideration in Czechoslovakia than, for example, in Romania, there have been some grounds for complaint. These grievances often blend with the general dissatisfaction felt by all Czechoslovak inhabitants who do not share in power and privilege. The Hungarian ethnic group is just more likely to blame its minority status rather than the prevailing socioeconomic order in which the Communist party rules subject to orders from the Soviet Union (see the selection of documents published in *Irodalmi Ujság*, Paris, September/October). Conversely, the communist regime has been prone to interpret the manifestations of ethnic discontent as signs of "antistate and antisocialist attitudes" (Bratislava, *Pravda*, 17 March). In recent years, some spokesmen for the Hungarian minority have attempted to air their grievances both through official channels and unofficially, but they have had to face repression and persecution (*YICA*, 1984, p. 314; *YICA*, 1985, pp. 276–77). The most prominent among them, Miklós Duray, had been detained for over one year, but he was released in connection with the liberation anniversary amnesty in May. His arrest in 1984 had led to a protest from the Charter '77 group as well as from individual Czech and Slovak dissidents (*YICA*, 1985, p. 282).

It appears that the party will no longer be able to disregard the ethnic minorities, any more than it can ignore the deterioration in the natural environment that it had preferred to overlook in the past. Czechoslovakia shares this latter problem with all developed industrial nations. Environmental protection has not amounted to much more than a few token gestures and some rhetoric. The chairman of the national council for the Czech Socialist Republic, Josef Kempný, announced in 1985 that expenditure for the purpose of solving ecological problems would double between 1986 and 1990 (Radio Prague, 13 March). According to another official source, degradation of the natural environment should "be halted by the end of the 1980s and, by the year 2000, conditions that had prevailed in the 1960s should be restored" (ČETEKA, 22 February). It was characteristic of the new sensitivity to environmental issues among political decision-makers when Czechoslovak diplomats and media responded with lengthy polemics to a suggestion in a West German daily (*FAZ*, 6 April) that the thermal springs in Karlovy Vary might be contaminated by waste from the nearby Sokolov coal mines. The Czechoslovak press attaché in Bonn and the party ideological organ vehemently denounced the report as "pure fabrication" (*FAZ*, 20 May; *Tribuna*, no. 27, 3 July).

Economy. The overall performance of the economy during the five-year plan that ended in 1985 was on the whole rather mediocre. Only since 1984 had there been a certain improvement, insofar as national income grew by about 3 percent; during the first three years, there had been no growth and even a decline (*Statistical Yearbook*, 1984). Following the mid-year economic report, industrial output in the first six months of 1985 exceeded target figures by about 0.8 percent. First deputy chairman of the State Planning Commission, Václav Vertelar, commented that this increase had been only quantitative; no progress was marked in the area of what is called "intensification of production," i.e., "better efficiency at lower cost, securing greater returns on available inputs" (*Hospodářské noviny*, no. 27, 19 July). The failure of intensification efforts was deplored a few weeks later in an editorial that concluded, on the basis of most recent statistics, that the "extensive" (instead of "intensive") mode of economic growth remained dominant (*Rudé právo*, 12 September). Earlier responses of planners to the problems of a stagnating economy, especially the cuts in capital investment, had been blamed on "insufficient fixed capital formation," which in turn rendered intensification of production even more difficult (Radio Hvézda, 13 January). Informed observers saw in this concern about the quality of production a sign of support, at least in certain party quarters, for a more reform-minded approach to the problems of the economy (Radio Free Europe–

Radio Liberty [RFE/RL], *Situation Report on Czechoslovakia*, no. 16, 10 October), despite the fact that Secretary General Husák in his program statement at a Central Committee meeting had said explicitly that the party "will not take the road of any of the market-oriented concepts" (Radio Prague, 19 June). Whether the persisting difficulties will eventually bring a change of heart remains to be seen.

One of the principal reasons why the economy kept exhibiting an extensive character in 1985 was the growth of energy consumption, which was out of proportion to the general economic development (Radio Prague, 26 July). Energy supplies were able to keep pace with the growing demand but a considerable portion of resources had to be committed to this purpose. Only a more rapid construction of nuclear plants can alleviate the consequences of the country's dependence on conventional energy forms: heavy pollution from coal and an adverse balance of payments due to imports of oil. The production capacity of Czechoslovak nuclear reactors increased in 1984 by an impressive 31,800 megawatts, although original projections of 430,000 megawatts by the year 1990 had to be revised down to 368,000 megawatts (International Atomic Energy Agency, *Annual Report*, 6 August). On the other hand, technological development and change generated new problems of their own.

Confronted with the dwindling scope of employment opportunities in the smokestack industries, steel, and coal, and faced with the consequences of automation in other sectors, the party has had to redefine the so-called right to work, hitherto an indisputable component of the system of social guarantees. It became evident that full employment could be maintained only at the cost of efficiency and quality; it appeared impossible to assure every individual employment for life in the area of his or her choice. The emerging dilemma is embarrassing (*Sociologický časopis*, no. 2). The ever-increasing problem, especially for the young, of securing an occupation commensurate with skills and providing an adequate income has complicated the previous simplistic expectation of a constantly rising standard of living for the entire population (*CSM*, 6 November). The difficulty has been aggravated by rising prices, outpacing the growth of wages, for certain highly desired staple products. Party economists attributed this discrepancy to the fact that productivity has lagged behind earnings. They pointed out that management in most industrial enterprises had preferred to manipulate prices for products of the plan target figures rather than to guide the workers to higher productivity (*Rudé právo*, 7 January; Radio Prague, 22 May; *Hospodářské noviny*, no. 25, 21 June; Bratislava, *Pravda*, 10 September).

Some party analysts felt that the private sector in agriculture, i.e., individual farmers and members of agricultural cooperatives producing on their own plots for the free market, enjoyed an unjustified advantage, because they were allowed to sell their produce for as much as they chose. This privilege was believed by some to be incompatible with socialist principles, and voices were heard calling for a limitation on private farmers in fixing prices (Bratislava, *Pravda*, 18 March). On this point, however, opinion appeared to be divided. Some believed that any restriction would harm the whole nation, since private farmers and owners of plots, although they controlled only a fraction of the land, produced a significant amount of food, without which serious shortages of basic foodstuffs would occur (*Rolnícke noviny*, 6 July). Supporters of restrictive measures countered the objection by claiming that current practices of farmers constituted "violations of socialist legality, ethics, and discipline" (Bratislava, *Pravda*, 1 November). This debate indicated that the idea of "socialist market relations," condemned by the party in the wake of the 1968 postinvasion "normalization," had not been altogether forgotten.

Armed Forces. The role of Czechoslovakia as a member and an important arsenal of the Warsaw Pact placed an increasing strain on the country's resources. Defense spending rose by 4.5 percent from the 1984 budget, which had allocated 7.6 percent to military outlays (Radio Prague, 11 December 1984). Officially published figures subsume all "military-related expenditure" under one item, including maintenance of police, militia, and border guards. Even though the latter costs are considerable, the total military budget remains inordinately large for a country of Czechoslovakia's size. At the end of the 1970s it ranked twenty-fifth among 133 surveyed in a UN comparative study (*Facts on File*, 1979). The burden of these expenses may have appeared disquieting to the communist leaders themselves, as some comments made during the debate about nuclear arms reduction would indicate. Regime sources imputed to the United States and its NATO allies the intention to "either gain military superiority or exhaust the Warsaw Pact countries economically by means of a military buildup" (*Historie a vojenství*, no. 5, 1984). Despite these apprehensions, the party seemed determined further to strengthen and develop its armed forces. Among the top party ideologists, it was emphasized that "every fundamental national economic measure must be viewed from the military point of view, even today, in a time of peace"—in other words, the military had priority over the needs of the population (*Nová mysl*, no. 1, January). Even assuming that this order of priorities is widely accepted, the upkeep and modernization of the vast military machine is not likely to occur without problems. A serious difficulty had been created through disruption and decimation of the professional corps after the 1968 Soviet invasion, when about 52 percent of personnel under 30 years of age left the ranks of the army. Subsequently 11,000 career officers were dismissed. Informed observers estimated that it was only in 1982 that the Czechoslovak army began to recover (RFE/RL, *Situation Report on Czechoslovakia*, 11 January). The true combat value of the Czechoslovak armed forces, especially their dependability from the Soviet point of view, is difficult to assess. There seems to be no reason to doubt the unqualified loyalty to Moscow on the part of the present party leadership; the morale of the population at large may be a completely different question. Maintenance of Soviet garrisons in Czechoslovakia, seventeen years after the 1968 military intervention, indicated the limits of Moscow's trust.

On the whole, however, the USSR military presence has kept a rather low profile. A unit of the Danube fleet, on a voyage in honor of the Soviet victory in World War II, visited Bratislava (Radio Prague, 7 April). The departing commander of the Warsaw Pact forces, attached to the Czechoslovak Defense Ministry, Colonel-General Ivan Voloshin, paid a farewell visit to President Husák at the same time he received Voloshin's successor, Colonel-General Nikolai Zotov (Radio Prague, 5 September). About a week later, Soviet chief of staff Sergei Akhromeev met with Husák at the Prague Castle for a "comradely and friendly conversation about questions of mutual cooperation by the fraternal armies of the two countries" (Radio Prague, 13 September). Earlier, the Czechoslovak army and air force had organized joint military exercises in Bohemia with the aim of practicing "coordination between various branches of the armed forces" (Radio Prague, 3 May).

Culture, Youth, and Religion. Relations between state and religious groups remained uneasy and tense. The Catholic church, by far the largest denomination in the country, continued to be the main target of antireligious propaganda and administrative harassment, although the regime occasionally showed harshness toward other churches as well. Nevertheless, the religiosity of the population, still strong after almost four decades of communist rule, was persuasively documented in the course of the year. It asserted itself most clearly during commemoration of the 1,100th anniversary of the death of St. Methodius (one of the evangelizers of the Slavs), preparations for which started in February. Party leaders viewed the festivities, which had the blessing and official support of Pope John Paul II, with great apprehension, yet they did not directly oppose them. They took particular exception to the emphasis that the pope in his message to Czechoslovak Catholics placed on the significance of St. Methodius's work for the cultural union of the peoples of Western and Eastern Europe; they felt that this position challenged the communist demand for an unconditional alignment of Central and East European states with the Soviet Union (Bratislava, *Pravda*, 23 January; *Večerní Praha*, 19 February). The organizers of the festivities anticipated more governmental interference as the day of the opening approached. Comments in the communist press deprecating the St. Methodius tradition sparked a protest letter from the Catholic primate, František Cardinal Tomášek, who addressed his remarks to the party ideological weekly, *Tribuna*. The primate also complained officially to Husák about government instructions to police and state security organs to closely supervise all people associated with the commemoration ceremonies (RFE/RL, *Situation Report on Czechoslovakia*, no. 7, 19 April).

Another deliberate obstacle raised by the regime was its refusal to award visas to primates of the Catholic Church from England, France, West Germany, and Austria, under the pretext that the anniversary of St. Methodius's death was a "purely internal Czechoslovak matter" (Radio Hvězda, 10 July). Only the representative of the Vatican, Agostino Cardinal Casaroli, was allowed to travel to Czechoslovakia. He used this opportunity to visit Husák. Their talks officially were described as "frank and businesslike," reaffirming "interest in continuing contacts and seeking a solution to outstanding issues in bilateral relations between Prague and the Vatican" (Radio Prague, 5 July).

Shortly before the beginning of festivities at Velehrad in southeastern Moravia, the site of St. Methodius's mission in the ninth century, the sixth

All-Christian Peace Assembly was held at Prague, attended by about 600 delegates from 97 countries. The timing of this assembly was hardly unintentional; obviously, its purpose was to demonstrate to the world that the communist regime did not oppose cooperation with Christians, provided it developed on communist terms (Radio Hvězda, 2 July). Party apprehensions that the Methodius anniversary would show the world a country at variance with the official image—of a nation freed from "religious superstition," rejecting all ties to the West, and enthusiastically embracing "real socialism"—proved in the end to be well founded. The festivities became a demonstration of Christian faith of hitherto unseen dimensions. No fewer than 150,000 believers came to Velehrad from all parts of the country. They gave a warm welcome to papal envoy Casaroli and demanded that John Paul II be invited to Czechoslovakia, an idea the communist rulers had rejected from the beginning (*NYT*, 8 July). Another 100,000 pilgrims participated in St. Methodius celebrations held simultaneously at the old church in Levoča, in eastern Slovakia (Associated Press, 7 July). Later in the year, the annual pilgrimage to the basilica at Šaštín, in the southwestern corner of Slovakia, attracted 40,000 participants, although in previous years no more than a few thousand had attended (United Press International, 26 September). This upsurge in religious activity alarmed the regime and the media, both domestic and international, and called for more aggressive atheistic propaganda (*Učitelské noviny*, no. 32, 12 September; *WMR*, no. 9, September; Radio Prague, 19 October).

Some Western observers speculated that the experience of these religious festivities might make the regime more amenable to a modus vivendi with the Catholic Church and Christians in general (RFE correspondent from Rome, 10 July). A fundamental change in the party leaders' attitude would be needed if something of this kind were to be achieved. There were no signs of such change; rather, the opposite seemed to be true. Czechoslovak courts imposed stiff sentences on the members of the Evangelical Church of the Czech Brethren, who had been sending Bibles to the Soviet Union, and on young Catholics who were importing liturgical objects from Poland (*WSJ*, 24 July). A written record of a police interview with a teacher who was dismissed from her position for "persisting in idealistic views and appearing unable to educate young people in the spirit of Marxism-Leninism" circulated as a *samizdat* publication in Slovakia. The document revealed that authorities had promised a special premium to teachers who persuaded students to withdraw from religious education at schools (*Deutsche Tagespost*, 11–12 October). The regime also continued to support its subservient organization of Catholic clergy, *Pacem in Terris*, which the church does not recognize. The organization held its third congress in Prague. It was attended by some four hundred participants. The primate, Cardinal Tomášek, stayed away from the gathering; the pope did not respond to the delegates' plea for his blessing (Radio Prague, 4 February; Reuters, 5 February). The federal deputy prime minister, Matej Lúcan, announced some concessions to Catholics in his speech at the congress: a large number of Bibles would be reprinted, and the number of students admitted to Catholic seminaries would be increased (*Rudé právo*, 7 February).

The regime's major concern in its struggle with the churches has been the impact of religion upon young people. It appeared, however, that there were also other forces competing with the official ideology for the minds and hearts of the young. On several occasions, party spokesmen and media complained that the values of Czechoslovak youth left a good deal to be desired, that they are "still permeated with petty bourgeois ideas that repeatedly assert themselves" (Party Secretary Josef Havlin in *Rudé právo*, 16 February). These deficiencies were often blamed upon "the activity of the main centers of ideological subversion, directed against the socialist countries." It was pointed out that "the experience of the crisis-ridden development in our country during 1968–69, as well as the recent events in Poland, sufficiently confirm that if educational influence on youth is underestimated, some young people can yield to the influence of anticommunist machinery" (Bratislava, *Pravda*, 16 April). According to party commentators, "many [enterprise] managers and teachers fail to see manifestations of hostile ideologies, which are the consumer orientation of certain pupils and students, toleration of certain tendencies in their attraction to decadent Western culture, reflected among other things in the decoration of rooms in hostels and dormitories, in clothing styles, and in the behavior of pupils and students in public" (*Život strany*, no. 28, 19 February).

Consumerism on the whole is viewed as a particularly dangerous attitude. For many Czechoslovaks, it was argued, the main object of life has become money. This, according to various surveys undertaken by the Institute of Public Opinion, is especially true about the 20- to 40-year-old population (*Rudé právo*, 15 February). The regime tried to revive the interest of young people on the occasion of the sixth Spartakiad, held in Prague. (The Spartacus Games continue the tradition of the prewar, communist-controlled Federation of Proletarian Gymnastics, but at the same time are supposed to replace the more deeply rooted tradition of the "Sokol" [Falcon] national gymnastic organization.) Over 175,000 gymnasts participated and were observed by more than 600,000 people. President Husák, in his speech at the games, stressed that the Spartakiad had "spontaneously demonstrated their optimism, confidence in the future, love of the socialist fatherland, and support for the party's policy" (Radio Hvězda, 29 June).

Another opportunity for recruiting active support from the young came at the twelfth World Festival of Youth and Students that opened in Moscow on 25 July. More than 2,000 delegates from Czechoslovakia took part. It was preceded by a preparatory meeting organized by the Czechoslovak Socialist Youth Union in Prague, under the slogan "Youth and Students for Peace—Opinions and Experience 1985." About eighty youth organizations from 46 countries participated in this meeting (*Tribuna*, no. 30, 24 July).

Dissidence. The civil rights defense group known as Charter '77 was named to remind the communist regime of the obligations it had assumed by signing the Helsinki charter. In 1985 a new trio of spokesmen for the group emerged: Jiří Dienstbier, Eva Kantůrková, and Petruška Šustrová. The group issued two documents explaining its mission, method of operation, and achievements. Almost immediately, police organs detained seven Charter activists for questioning. Those apprehended refused to answer on grounds that the documents were not illegal; they were released after 48 hours (Reuters from Prague, 4, 6 January). Communist authorities continued to subject Charter activists to restrictions and harassment throughout the year. Ladislav Lis, whom the International Federation of Human Rights had nominated deputy president and permanent representative at the regional secretariat of the UN in Vienna, was placed under "protective supervision," which seriously limited his freedom of movement (Report of VONS, Committee for the Defense of the Unjustly Persecuted, 1 January). When British foreign secretary Geoffrey Howe came to Prague, Jiří S. Hájek, a Charter member of long standing and a former foreign affairs minister in the Dubček cabinet, was ordered to remain in the countryside for the duration of the visit (Rome, ANSA, in English, 10 April).

Among documents distributed by Charter '77, an earlier piece dealing with persecution of religious orders attracted special attention (Charter Document 21, 12 December 1984). It had been prepared by a group of religious personalities, at the request of the Charter spokesmen. The document concluded that, if all police and judicial repression of religious organizations were discontinued, "normal, that is humane and just, conditions would be restored." This was an obvious allusion to the term "normalization," frequently used by the communist rulers since the 1968 military intervention. In a subsequent document, the Charter group pleaded for a European political settlement that would be conciliatory and beneficial for all (Charter Document 5, 11 March). A later declaration, published on the anniversary of the defeat of Nazi Germany in World War II, and in the form of an open letter to President Husák and Prime Minister Lubomír Štrougal, urged a "change of social climate" in order to correct alarming trends in the development of human relations. During the forty years that had elapsed since the armistice in May 1945, the letter stated, Czechoslovakia "began to lose, and continues to lose, the appreciation of its citizens as their true and inalienable home . . . Discrimination, privilege, and injustice have spread and become intrinsic to social life" (Charter Document 9, 26 April). The group also remembered the seventeenth anniversary of the Soviet-led military intervention, and issued yet another document on the tenth anniversary of the Helsinki Final Act (Charter Document 19, 23 July). Regime media found these reminders uncomfortable and argued that "the policy of peaceful coexistence of the two opposing systems . . . was never related to the field of their opposing ideology. In the ideological struggle, there is no way to come to an integration" (Bratislava, *Pravda*, 25 July).

Charter '77 returned to the same theme before the opening of the Helsinki European Forum, held at Budapest from 15 October to 23 November. It addressed the gathering in a letter summing up the difficult situation for culture in contemporary Czechoslovakia. This letter had been cosigned by several prominent Czech and Slovak artists and writers, among them the Nobel Prize laureate, Jaroslav Seifert (who died at the turn of the year). It stated that political power in Czechoslovakia waged "a comprehensive attack on the very spiritual integrity and identity of two nations with a long cultural tradition" and called upon the European Forum to "remind the Czechoslovak government of the obligations that the Helsinki Final Act entails" (Hamburg, *Die Welt*, 27 September). This letter drew considerable attention from Western intellectual and cultural circles, as did a letter sent earlier by Czech playwright and Charter '77 member Václav Havel. Havel wrote to General Jaruzelski on behalf of three leading defendants in the trial of Solidarity activists in Gdansk (AFP from Prague, 27 May). He was invited by French prime minister Laurent Fabius to participate in an international meeting on human rights in Paris, part of the celebrations of the impending 200th anniversary of the French Revolution and the 1789 Declaration of Human Rights. Although the French foreign minister himself interceded for Havel in talks with his Czechoslovak counterpart, Bohuslav Chňoupek, during a visit to Prague, Havel was absent from the Paris gathering. It seemed, however, that it was not only the reluctance of the communist authorities that prevented him from participating; Havel may have feared that his trip would enable the regime to deny him the right to return, as it did in the case of Czech writer Pavel Kohout (Reuters from Prague, 29 May).

Another interesting initiative by Czechoslovak dissidents was a joint letter of protest against nuclear armament and international tension, signed by women from England, West Germany, East Germany, Italy, and Czechoslovakia; unlike the officially organized "peace demonstrations" of Communist parties and their front organizations, this protest was delivered to all nuclear powers, including those in the Soviet Union, and in Czechoslovakia it was endorsed exclusively by women who belonged to the Charter '77 group (*Informace o Chartě*, 7 March). According to information from dissident sources, a number of persons added their signature to the basic Charter declaration of 1977, so that the total number of the members is now estimated to be about 1,200 (Charter Document 10, 20 May).

Foreign Affairs. One of the most significant events was the first official contact between Gustáv Husák and the new Soviet leader, Mikhail Gorbachev. By coincidence, Husák's trip to Moscow followed only a few days after his re-election as president of the republic, so that both Gorbachev and Husák were somewhat "new" in their roles when they met. Husák's visit received wide Soviet coverage, extolling his merits and "international proletarian solidarity" (Moscow, *Pravda*, 30 May, 1 June). Since it is uncertain what the present KSČ leadership can expect from Gorbachev, it is difficult to assess the importance of this meeting for future Czechoslovak party policies. Earlier in the year, a Soviet parliamentary delegation traveled to Prague; Federal Assembly chairman Alois Indra was its host (Moscow, *Pravda*, 23 May).

Among other guests from the countries of the Soviet bloc, East German Premier Willi Stoph visited in May, and a delegation from the People's Great Hural (national assembly) of Mongolia visited Prague in October. A special governmental delegation led by the federal deputy prime minister, Matej Lúčan, arrived in Cuba to attend the Days of Czechoslovak Culture (Radio Prague, 1 May). That same month, the minister of foreign affairs, Bohuslav Chňoupek, paid an "official friendly visit" to the People's Democratic Republic of Yemen. The ČETEKA press release on this occasion recalled previous contacts between President Husák and his previous Yemeni counterpart, Ali Nasir Muhammad (ČETEKA in English, 18 April). ČETEKA of course could not anticipate that in less than a year, Muhammad would be a refugee in the Sudan, and Czechoslovak as well as Soviet diplomats would have to seek escape, their lives threatened by the actions of yet another group of "true Marxist-Leninists." Relations with the Middle East region were reflected also in the visit by the Libyan foreign minister (Radio Prague, 11 July) and in the signing of a friendship treaty between Czechoslovakia and Syria (Radio Prague, 16 October). Another official visitor from the developing world was the chairman of the government of the Socialist Republic of the Union of Burma, U Maung Maung Kha, who met with Prime Minister Lubomír Štrougal (*Rudé právo*, 20 November).

The most important diplomatic contacts were those with the West. In fact, Czechoslovakia hosted prominent politicians from practically all major West European countries. (A stopover in Czechoslovakia by U.S. Secretary of State George Shultz during his trip to southeastern Europe was not arranged, however—probably due to fear by the government and its Soviet advisers that such a visit might elicit too enthusiastic a response from the Czechoslovak population.) The British foreign secretary, Sir Geoffrey Howe, came for a short official visit to Prague. It was the first such visit after an interval of almost twenty years. In his talks with Czechoslovak officials, Howe emphasized "the features of civilized life," i.e., the human rights underwritten by the Helsinki Agreement (BBC, *Current Affairs Research and Information Report*, 11 April). The following month, the minister of foreign affairs, Bohuslav Chňoupek, traveled to Vienna for talks with Austrian officials. Relations with Austria had become rather strained because of unresolved issues: the ecological threat to Austria from new nuclear energy projects close to its border; brutal measures against refugees trying to escape from Czechoslovakia; and rejection of visas for Austrian clergymen invited to the St. Methodius anniversary celebrations. Chňoupek, while in Vienna, also met with the foreign affairs minister from the Federal Republic of Germany, Hans-Dietrich Gentscher (Radio Bratislava, 15 May). Later in the same month, the French foreign minister, Roland Dumas, came to Prague for an official visit; not unlike Great Britain, almost twenty years had passed since the last visit of a high-level French official. Dumas also made indirect but critical references to the unsatisfactory record of the Czechoslovak government in matters of human rights (ČETEKA in English, 24 May; AFP from Prague, 24 May). Dumas's talks with Czechoslovak officials could not dissipate the mistrust and indignation accumulated in France since the beginning of the Soviet-inspired "normalization" in Czechoslovakia; the once cordial relationship between the two countries was almost at the freezing point. As the end of the year neared, yet another important visitor arrived in Prague: Willy Brandt, chairman of the socialist party of Germany (SPD) and former federal chancellor. Brandt held talks with Czechoslovak leaders during his three-day visit to the country. The fate of dissidents appeared on the agenda. Brandt characterized the talks as "significant and useful" (DPA, 7 November); according to the Czechoslovak media, the visit "reflected the current political priorities of both the KSČ and the SPD" (Radio Hvězda, 10 November).

Foreign Trade and the Foreign Debt. Foreign trade is heavily oriented toward the Soviet bloc. During recent years, Czechoslovakia's dependence on exchanges with these countries further increased. The most rapid growth occurred in relations with the USSR; of the 72 percent of goods and services exchanged with CMEA members, about 44 percent were with the USSR, while in 1980 it had been only 35 percent. The proportion of trade with hard-currency countries declined more slowly in 1985; it is likely that further reduction will not be sought because it could threaten the balance of foreign payments (*Statistical Yearbook*, 1984; *Statistické Přehledy*, 1985).

The foreign debt in convertible currencies is relatively low; it compares favorably with the situation of other CMEA countries, especially Poland. According to a statement by the chairman of the state bank, Jan Stejskal, the debt with all countries, but especially with the hard-currency area, had been declining since 1982 (ČETEKA in English, 22 January). It is uncertain, however, whether this precarious balance can be maintained; much will depend on the volume of oil imports and the price of oil. The country must import almost 90 percent of its oil, chiefly from the Soviet Union.

As in previous years, Czechoslovakia participated actively in the plans aiming at coordination of production among CMEA members. These plans are part of an ambitious long-term operation known as the international socialist division of labor. Prime Minister Štrougal reiterated Czechoslovakia's determination to promote this goal (*WMR*, no. 1, January). The coordination appeared particularly urgent in electronics, because there is likely to be a dramatic rise in the demand for hardware as well as software due to the inevitable computerization of entire production sectors (Presidium member and secretary Miloš Jakeš, on Czechoslovak television, 14 March). These questions were discussed at the fortieth session of the CMEA held at Warsaw (*Rudé právo*, 5 July).

Among the bilateral negotiations and agreements, those with the CMEA countries predominated. Romanian Vice-Premier Nicolae Constantin signed a protocol on economic cooperation with Czechoslovakia in Prague in July (Agerpress in English, 11 July). Talks on economic coordination with East Germany took place at Prague (Radio Prague, 24 January). The Cuban foreign trade minister, Ricardo Cabrisas Ruiz, met with his Czechoslovak colleague Bohumil Urban (Radio Bratislava, 18 January). The federal finance minister, Leopold Lér, conducted negotiations about economic and financial cooperation with Cuba (Radio Prague, 22 January). The volume of trade with China increased considerably (Radio Prague, 23 January). A mixed Czechoslovak-Nicaraguan commission for economic cooperation prepared a trade protocol that was signed at Prague (ibid., 18 January). A protocol on exchange of goods was also signed with Spain (*Rudé právo*, 12 July).

International Party Contacts. The Communist Party of Czechoslovakia continued to present the image of a model Soviet satellite, as it had done since the process of "normalization" began in 1968. Comments on the change in the leadership at the Kremlin strictly followed the same line. The central party daily added: "Our party, too, is undergoing the process of preparing for its next congress. That is why the creative theoretical and practical effort with which the CPSU so energetically approaches the elaboration of issues of the comprehensive perfection of developed socialism, is of such significance for us, too" (*Rudé právo*, 18 March). It was interesting to note that in this context the editor used the term "developed socialism" instead of the generally accepted "real socialism." Whatever the reasons for his choice of terminology, this "developed socialism"—in the USSR as well as in Czechoslovakia and elsewhere—has to face a host of specific problems. The lack of consensus about the concrete forms for its implementation especially seemed to worry KSČ leaders.

Secretary General Husák stated in his opening address to the Central Committee that the time had come for a new consultation on this subject among all communists. "We are convinced," said Husák, "that the unity and togetherness of the movement would be enhanced—as we emphasized at our Sixteenth Congress—by the convocation of an international conference of Communist and workers' parties" (*Rudé právo*, 19 June). It remains to be seen to what extent his enthusiasm for a new world summit is shared by other Communist parties. Some appear to be definitely opposed to any and all such ventures. This is true especially about Yugoslavia, which was a target of criticism from the KSČ for its independent stance. Czechoslovak Communists consider that to be tantamount to taking sides with "the ideological foes of socialism." On the occasion of the fortieth anniversary of the allied victory over Nazi Germany, the KSČ press accused the Yugoslav media of deliberately distorting historical facts: a Yugoslav commentator had stated that the USSR had been co-responsible for the outbreak of World War II and that the USSR was an aggressive state in search of world rule (*Tribuna*, no. 12, 20 March).

However, other European Communist parties also came under fire. In a long article on the theme of communist unity, Ivan Hlívka, member of the international section of the KSČ Central Committee, severely criticized some West European "fraternal" parties, especially those adhering to the doctrine labeled by the accepted term of "Eurocommunism," i.e., the Communist parties of Spain and France. He argued that "any relaxation in the cooperation of all Communist parties in the international field would be harmful to every one of us." The questions of international relations, he claimed, must be approached "not from the positions of toothless pacifism, barren objectivism, and unprincipled compromise with the class enemy, but from clear-cut class positions" (*Rudé právo*, 21 June).

International contacts at the party level included a visit by the first secretary from the Communist Party of Iraq, Aziz Muhammad (*Rudé právo*, 23 March); participation by the KSČ in the congress of the Communist Party of France in Paris in February (Radio Prague, 6 February); a visit by a delegation from the Communist Party of France (*Rudé právo*, 4 November); and a number of visits by lesser echelons, as well as goodwill trips by Czechoslovak officials to the meetings of other Communist parties abroad.

Zdeněk Suda
University of Pittsburgh

Germany: German Democratic Republic

Population. 16,701,000
Party. Socialist Unity Party of Germany (*Sozialistische Einheitspartei Deutschlands*; SED)
Founded. 1918 (SED, 1946)
Membership. 2,194,585 members, 98,704 candidates (*Neues Deutschland* [*ND*], 9 January 1986); 66.3 percent male, 33.7 percent female (1981); 58.1 percent workers, 4.8 percent peasants and cooperative farmers, 22.3 percent intelligentsia, 14.8 percent other (1984) (Cologne, *DDR Handbuch*, 1985)
General Secretary. Erich Honecker (73)
Politburo. 18 full members: Erich Honecker (chairman, State Council), Hermann Axen (69), Horst Dohlus (60), Werner Felfe (57; member, State Council), Kurt Hager (73; member, State Council), Joachim Herrmann (57), Werner Jarowinsky (58), Günther Kleiber (54; deputy chairman, Council of Ministers [deputy premier]), Egon Krenz (48; deputy chairman, State Council), Werner Krolikowski (57; first deputy chairman, Council of Ministers [first deputy premier]), Erich Mielke (78; minister of state security), Günter Mittag (59; deputy chairman, State Council), Erich Mückenberger (75; member, presidium of People's Chamber), Alfred Neumann (76; first deputy chairman, Council of Ministers [first deputy premier]), Günter Schabowski (56; first secretary, Berlin regional party executive), Horst Sindermann (70; member, State Council; President, presidium of People's Chamber), Willi Stoph (71; chairman, Council of Ministers [premier]; deputy chairman, State Council), Harry Tisch (58; member, State Council; chairman, Free German Trade Union Federation); 7 candidate members: Werner Eberlein (66; first secretary, Magdeburg regional party executive), Ingeborg Lange (58), Siegfried Lorenz (55; first secretary, Karl Marx Stadt regional party executive), Gerhard Müller (54; member, State Council), Margaret Müller (54; member, State Council), Gerhard Schürer (64; chairman, State Planning Commission), Werner Walde (59; first secretary, Cottbus regional party executive)
Secretariat. 10 members: Erich Honecker, Hermann Axen (international relations), Horst Dohlus (party organs), Werner Felfe (agriculture), Kurt Hager (culture and science), Joachim Herrmann (agitation and propaganda), Werner Jarowinsky (church affairs, trade, and supply), Egon Krenz (security affairs, youth, and sports), Ingeborg Lange (women's affairs), Günter Mittag (economics)
Central Committee. 156 full and 51 candidate members (1981)
Status. Ruling party
Last Congress. Tenth, 11–16 April 1981
Last Election. 1981, 99.9 percent, all 500 seats National Front
Auxiliary Organizations. Free German Trade Union Confederaton (FDGB), 9.1 million members, led by Harry Tisch; Free German Youth (FDJ), 2.3 million members, led by Eberhard Aurich; Democratic Women's League of Germany (DFB), 1.4 million members, led by Ilse Thiele; Society for German-Soviet Friendship (DSF), 6.0 million members, led by Kurt Thieme
Publications. *Neues Deutschland*, official SED daily, Herbert Naumann, editor-in-chief; *Einheit*, SED theoretical monthly; *Neuer Weg*, SED organizational monthly; *Junge Welt*, FDJ daily; *Tribüne*, FDGB daily; *Horizont*, foreign policy monthly. The official news agency is the Allgemeiner Deutscher Nachrichtendienst (ADN).

The SED is probably the best functioning, certainly in economic terms the most successful, of the Communist parties of Eastern Europe. In 1985 it remained active in foreign affairs and appeared at least to be coping with developments within East German society. The uncharacteristic conflict in relations with Moscow that became apparent in 1984 persisted, however, and the potentially more profound problem of generational change in the SED leadership loomed ever closer.

Leadership and Party Organization. The aging of the SED leadership overshadowed other party concerns in 1985, despite the rhetorical attention given to the fortieth anniversary of the end of World War II and to preparation for the Eleventh SED Congress in June 1986. The apparent illness of a key younger leader, economics tsar Günter Mittag, underlined the vulnerability of the leadership earlier in the year. Mittag continued to keep a limited public schedule after having virtually dropped from sight in late 1984. His trip to West Germany in April demonstrated his ability to carry on, however. Subsequent travels and more frequent public appearances throughout the year confirmed his recovery from the reported amputation of part of his right leg due to complications of diabetes (*Bild Zeitung*, 19 April; *FBIS*, 23, 24 April; ADN, 23 April).

Although the 20–21 June Central Committee plenum apparently did nothing more dramatic than set 17–21 April 1986 for the date of the Eleventh SED Congress, the early part of the year nonetheless saw moves suggesting that Egon Krenz was consolidating his position as heir presumptive to Honecker. As early as February, the announcement of shifts in the FDJ central council hinted at what later became clear, that Krenz was positioning himself to become heir apparent. Wolfgang Herger, 50, chief of the Central Committee youth department, was made chief of the security department, and FDJ secretary Gerd Schulz, 38, took over the youth department. Both men are relatively young, and presumably are close to Krenz, particularly since both assumed their previous positions while Krenz led the FDJ. Against this background, the occasional public appearances of Krenz's predecessor on the Politburo, Paul Verner, only underscored the power of the younger man (*ND*, 16–17 February, 9 May; *FBIS*, 22 February, 16 April; DPA, 15 April).

Krenz's influence was further strengthened by the major shifts in Politburo membership made at the Central Committee plenum on 22–23 November. Politburo and Secretariat members Herbert Häber, 55, and Konrad Naumann, 57, were released from their duties "on health grounds" (ADN, 22 November; *FBIS*, 25 November). Naumann's political decline continued days later, when the Berlin regional (Bezirk) party executive replaced him as its first secretary, "in accordance with the recommendation of the Central Committee," by Politburo member Günter Schabowski, 56. East German radio reported that Honecker attended the session, and the report omitted any mention of thanks or appreciation for Naumann's work. Schabowski was replaced as editor-in-chief of *Neues Deutschland* by his first deputy, Herbert Naumann, 56 (GDR Domestic Service, 25 November; *FBIS*, 26 November).

Häber's departure from the heights of the SED may have been partly for reasons of health, but Naumann's was clearly political. Häber was last noticed in public on 18 August, and his former deputy in charge of the Central Committee department of international politics and economics, Günter Rettner, was listed as chief of the department in early November (ADN, 18 August; *FBIS*, 19 August, 7 November; *ND*, 5 November; DPA, 6 November). Naumann, on the other hand, had long been viewed as a potential rival to Krenz to succeed Honecker, and reputedly was belligerently critical even of Honecker's limited tolerance toward intellectual and artistic dissidents, the churches, the autonomous peace movement, and exit applicants. One account suggests that Naumann precipitated his own downfall by openly challenging Honecker's church policy, particularly church involvement with draft resisters, at a 24 September meeting of the Politburo. The same publication, however, later ran an account that emphasized Naumann's drunken incivility to a group of academics and his personal abuse of Honecker in November (*Der Spiegel*, 18 November, 9 December; *FBIS*, 19 November, 10 December).

Naumann's ouster probably sprang from all the causes mentioned as well as others, but the departure of Häber at the same time supports the notion that the Politburo conflict of 24 September was the proximate cause. Illness alone, even to the point of incompetence, has never been a reason for removing leaders in the SED: witness, for instance, the case of Albert Norden. (The 1983 retirement of Paul Verner is not to the contrary, because it served Honecker's purpose of advancing Krenz politically.) Häber's departure may have been distantly related to the GDR-Soviet difficulties of August–September 1984 over his specialty, intra-German relations, but pursuit of intra-German dialogue clearly remains SED policy. The *Spiegel* account of the 24 September fracas, more pertinently, names as Naumann's partner in the attack the Politburo member most likely interested in Häber's departure, international relations secretary Hermann Axen. Axen has in fact been particularly active this year in Häber's bailiwick, after languishing somewhat during the intra-German maneuverings of 1983–1984 (ADN, 19 June; *FBIS*, 20 June). Thus Häber's departure may have been the price paid to Axen for Honecker's purge of Naumann, a price not due unless Axen were allied with Naumann in the precipitating events.

If the *Spiegel* account of the 24 September Politburo meeting is at all accurate, Honecker's counterattack was blessed by fortune in that the other Politburo member named as joining Axen and Naumann, Defense Minister Heinz Hoffmann, 75, died less than two weeks after Naumann's fall (*NYT*, 3 December). Honecker immediately elevated Heinz Kessler, 65, a long-time colleague, into the position from his post of chief of the armed forces' main political administration (ADN, 3 December; *FBIS*, 3 December). Egon Krenz's funeral eulogy for Hoffmann was a comprehensive attempt to lay any remaining intraparty conflict to rest with him, citing Hoffmann's devotion to the leadership under Honecker, his alleged youthful efforts for cooperation with the noncommunist left, and his advocacy of (Honecker's) policy "to wage a constructive dialogue for a coalition of common sense and realism" against nuclear war (GDR Domestic Service, 6 December; *FBIS*, 9 December).

The November Central Committee plenum, in addition to ousting Häber and Naumann, added three names to the list of Politburo candidate members: Werner Eberlein, Siegfried Lorenz, and Gerhard Müller. All three lead regional party organizations, and Lorenz and Müller are relatively young among SED leaders. Eberlein may have the virtue of being a known quantity to the Soviets in that he grew up in the USSR while Hitler was in power, although his father is said to have been a victim of Stalin (*ND*, 23–24 November; *FBIS*, 26 November; Berlin, *Namen und Daten*, 1982). Lorenz, a youth affairs functionary for 25 years, probably has good relations with Krenz, adding to the impression that the November Politburo changes probably have strengthened Krenz's position (*ND*, 23–24 November; *FBIS*, 26 November).

Party preparations for the Eleventh Congress got into full swing with a review of the membership similar to the last exchange of party documents, carried out prior to the Tenth Congress of 1981. The so-called trustful individual talks with SED members led directly to the expulsion of only 3,787 party members, although another 430 refused the interviews, 1,359 withdrew from membership, and another 3,107 cases were held over for further consideration. Even the total of these categories, however, 8,743 party members, amounts to less than 0.4 percent of total membership (*ND*, 17 October; *JPRS*, 10 December). The implied stability in the party rank and file, despite leadership changes, apparently was unbroken in the rounds of party elections and conferences, including numerous speaking appearances by Politburo members, that ran from 14 October through 14 December (*ND*, 14 October, 25 November, 2 December; *FBIS*, 16 October, 3 December).

These auguries of a well-orchestrated and uncontentious congress, however, left open at year's end the question of the SED's preparedness for generational change. Hoffmann died days after his seventy-fifth birthday, an anniversary that Erich Mückenberger also passed this year. Erich Mielke is older, as is Alfred Neumann. Honecker, though apparently in excellent health, is 73. As if to underscore the situation, Deputy Defense Minister Werner Fleissner, 63, died less than a month after Hoffmann (ADN, 30 December; *FBIS*, 31 December).

Domestic Affairs. *Social and Political Affairs.* The year began with several dozen East Germans still being sheltered in West German embassies, mainly in Prague but also in Warsaw, in hopes of permission to emigrate to West Germany. All reportedly had returned to the GDR by 15 January, with the promise of East German lawyer (and Honecker confidant) Wolfgang Vogel that they would escape punishment and their emigration applications would be processed in due course. Vogel warned against further attempts, however, claiming that his authority to make such promises was at an end and would not be renewed (DPA, 15 January; *FBIS*, 16 January). Nevertheless, the situation recurred on a small scale in August, when a woman and child took refuge in the Prague embassy, with a similar result and a similar warning (DPA, 9 August; *FBIS*, 13 August).

The East German regime continued to react to emigration pressure with its traditional arsenal of economic and social pressures (*Die Welt*, 1 March;

Deutschland Archiv, December 1984). It also unleashed an unusual spate of antiemigration propaganda, however, devoting the entire front page of *Neues Deutschland* to the bogus claim that 20,000 former GDR residents now in West Germany wanted to return (*NYT*, 9 March). This was an unprecedented, even if tacit, public admission of the seriousness of the emigration problem. After the limited revival in August of the Prague escape route and West German publicity over the arrival of some of the earlier Prague sit-ins, *Neues Deutschland* attempted to make much of West German controls at the intra-German border (DPA, 27 August; *FBIS*, 27 August, 20 September; *ND*, 14–15 September). Legal emigration in 1985 totaled 22,000, far short of the 1984 level but well ahead of the average for 1961–1983 (DPA, 27 December).

The mute evidence of dissatisfaction with East German conditions provided by those attempting to vote with their feet was complemented by testimony from recent emigrants, including children of the East German elite (*Die Welt*, 6–8 December 1984; *JPRS*, 15–19 February). At the other extreme, Western human rights organizations in November estimated the number of political prisoners in the GDR between 5,000 and 7,000 (DPA, 14, 30 November).

East German attempts to hold down emigration by imposing a virtual ban on contacts with the West were highlighted by West German reports that as many as 3 million GDR residents might be affected. The bans reportedly apply to many people in the police, military, and security organs; officials of the SED and mass organizations; and to industrial management personnel and those with access to scientific and technical information. Prohibited contacts include not only visits but mail and telephone calls, including those with relatives in the West (DPA, 18 July; *FBIS*, 19 July). Honecker's statements at the fall Leipzig trade fair that such bans would be applied less broadly seemed to augur little more than a slight fine-tuning of the policy (DPA, 2 September).

The continued status of security concerns within the regime was perhaps best shown by the celebration in February of the thirty-fifth anniversary of the Ministry for State Security (*Ministerium für Staatssicherheit*; MfS). Honecker, speaking at the ceremony in East Berlin marking the event, seemed to credit the MfS with significant responsibilities in virtually every sphere of East German life, with particular emphasis on the promotion of "militant spirit. . . discipline, [and] courage" within the party (ADN, 6 February; *FBIS*, 7 February).

The tense and ambivalent relationship between the East German regime and the Protestant churches seemed early in the year to be improving. Honecker's 11 February meeting with Bishop Johannes Hempel, chairman of the Protestant Church Federation (*Bund Evangelischer Kirchen*; BEK), was only the second such occasion, the first having been in 1978. The official account of the meeting predictably emphasized the church's commitment to peace, highlighting the fortieth anniversary of the end of World War II. Some weeks earlier, former Protestant chairman Bishop Werner Krusche had demonstrated another reason for official tolerance of the churches when, on West German radio, he criticized those who sought refuge at the West German embassy in Prague (DPA, 23 December 1984). Nevertheless, Hempel apparently also brought up human rights and discrimination against Christian believers in his talk with Honecker (ADN, 11 February; *FBIS*, 12 February). Hempel later said he had been promised that high-level church-state talks would continue, but he warned against illusions that such talks would bring dramatic improvements for GDR Christians (Vatican City International Service, 18 February; *FBIS*, 19 February).

Hempel and West German bishop Edward Lohse in March signed a statement for peace on the fortieth anniversary of the end of World War II, which presumably gratified East Berlin in its emphasis on disarmament, explicitly giving peace priority over all else, including German unity (DPA, 18 March). Succeeding months, however, brought demands for greater travel opportunities at a June church meeting in Greifswald, and a statement by the Protestant bishops on the tenth anniversary of the Helsinki Final Act that called for more contacts between East and West German individuals (*Die Welt*, 24 June; BBC Caris, 29 July). Equally notable, the full text of the statement was published in *Neues Deutschland* (*ND*, 1 August). Then, in September, the BEK synod in Dresden took up the theme of "deficits" in human rights, particularly with respect to travel opportunities and conscientious objection to military service and premilitary training (*Radio Free Europe/Radio Liberty* [*RFE/RL*] *Research*, 4 October). This reportedly was the occasion for a major debate over church policy within the SED leadership. The ouster of Konrad Naumann later in the year may have signaled the continued validity of

Honecker's relatively tolerant church policy, but a further Honecker-Hempel meeting that had been planned apparently fell victim to the controversy (*Der Spiegel*, 18 November).

As of year's end, the Protestant churches seemed to be holding to their concerns, as they carried out the annual Ten Days of Peace program across the GDR. The event's 1985 theme, "Peace Comes from Justice," lent itself to further expression of human rights criticisms, but left open how the church would relate its policy criticisms to individual or collective action by believers (*RFE/RL Research*, 21 November). In late summer, for instance, conflict reportedly surfaced between pacifist theological students and the universities over mandatory Marxism-Leninism courses, FDJ activities, and other issues, but the church hierarchy seems to have taken no position (DPA, 10 August).

The East German regime's acceptance of a more distant relationship with the country's relatively small Catholic community was highlighted by Honecker's audience with the pope in April during his trip to Rome. The chairman of the conference of Catholic bishops in the GDR, Joachim Cardinal Meissner, demonstrated the church's continued disdain for compromise with the regime in a sermon the preceding month. Addressing the consequences of World War II, Cardinal Meissner strongly deplored the division of Germany (*RFE/RL Research*, 22 April).

The unofficial peace movement, suffering from the emigration and deportation of most of its leaders, was largely dormant in 1985, and seemed to retreat to the cover of the church peace activities that had nourished it initially. Church-connected peace activists were particularly prominent in the notable autonomous action of the year, a letter calling for, among other measures, the withdrawal of foreign troops from both German states. It was presented to the U.S. embassy in East Berlin and, showing that intra-German peace connections persist, to the Soviet embassy in Bonn in early May (DPA, 6 May; *FBIS*, 8 May). The regime is concerned with activists remaining in the GDR, however, as shown by the news in January that pacifist Rolf Schoalike had been sentenced to seven years' imprisonment (*L'Unità*, 11 January; *FBIS*, 16 January).

There was activism in East Germany during the year over at least one other set of issues, those connected with the environment. Environmental questions were prominent at the Protestant church–sponsored peace workshop in East Berlin in June, and indeed most environmental activism seems to occur under some church auspices (ARD Television, 30 June). The regime has responded with a new series of directives on environmental practices, but even their complete fulfillment probably would not solve East Germany's critical environmental problems. The fulfillment of those directives, moreover, remains subject to doubt in view of the country's reliance on brown coal and its need to direct investment to other areas than pollution control. Nevertheless, the SED has maneuvered itself out of the ideological problem of defining environmental problems as impossible, so that there is at least theoretical scope for accommodation (*RFE/RL Research*, 16 August). At the same time, East German propaganda has not neglected the ongoing environmental discussions with officials of West Germany and other countries. Political as well as economic considerations still appear to take precedence, however, as the West German press discovered late in the year that the GDR was attempting to condition an intra-German agreement to clean up the Elbe on Bonn's agreement to recognize the center, rather than the eastern shore, of the river as the intra-German boundary(DPA, 26 December; *FBIS*, 27 December).

Economic Affairs. The East German regime claimed strong economic performance again in 1985. According to the Politburo report delivered to the Central Committee meeting in November, produced national income through October grew by 4.5 percent over the previous year. Ninety percent of this increase was attributed to higher labor productivity, which rose 8 percent in the industrial sector. Net industrial output increased by 8.6 percent, and the net money income of the population rose by 3.5 percent. Agricultural successes also were recorded, including a grain harvest of 11.6 million tons, an increase over the previous year's record performance (*ND*, 23–24 November; *FBIS*, 10 December).

More dramatically, the GDR's international financial position continued to improve in 1985. Its success in international credit markets in 1984 continued, with several placements in the hundreds of millions of dollars being arranged by multinational banking consortia. East German hard currency reserves ballooned to over $5 billion (*CSM*, 25 July).

As if to underscore East Germany's leading position, significant attention began to be paid to the organization and management of the GDR economy, particularly the large industrial agglomerations called *Kombinate*. Soviet leader Gorbachev cited the East German record with approval more than once, and GDR leader Honecker praised the Kombinat system at length in a *Pravda* article on the occasion of the thirty-sixth anniversary of the GDR's founding in October. The East German leadership also laid stress on a Politburo decision that sought closer cooperation between scientific and technical research efforts and the industrial enterprises (*Pravda*, 7 October; *FBIS*, 10 October).

The major economic planning activity of the year, however, the coordination of five-year trade plans for 1986–1990 with the Soviet Union and other CMEA partners, augured less well for the GDR's economic future. It was Mittag, the secretary for economics of the SED Central Committee, who, on behalf of his CMEA colleagues, thanked Soviet leader Gorbachev for the "frank conversation" in which Gorbachev had stressed the need for further "socialist economic integration in the light of today's raised requirements and the complicated international situation" (Tass, 21 May). The GDR's announcement of the protocol on plan coordination with the Soviets was particularly detailed, not least as to the quantities of raw materials and fuels East Germany was to receive. None of the foreseen raw materials and fuels deliveries was claimed to be an increase, however, in contrast to the increases in deliveries to the Soviets, such as a 40 percent increase in the consumer goods sector (*ND*, 1 November; *FBIS*, 8 November).

There was also trouble in the energy sector as winter weather taxed fuel supplies, particularly brown coal, and there were repeated hints that the vaunted economic management system required constant maintenance. Emergency drafts of workers from the army and other sources were put to work in the coal mines early in the year to minimize shortages, and the Politburo report to the Central Committee plenum in June suggested that the situation had required Honecker's daily attention (ZDF Television, 21 February; *ND*, 21 June; *FBIS*, 10 July). Honecker's talk with the regional (Bezirk) and local (Kreis) party secretaries in February and the November Politburo report contained half-veiled criticisms of several sectors (ADN, 1 February; *FBIS*, 6 February).

Looming over the whole economic scene, moreover, was the critical long-term question of investment in new and improved plant and equipment. Although GDR economic plans foresaw a renewal of capital investment, and Western businessmen anticipated that East German hard currency reserves would be used in part to pay for new orders, little had materialized by year's end. It remained particularly doubtful whether Soviet economic demands would leave the GDR enough margin for badly needed modernization (*CSM*, 25 July; *Financial Times*, 19 December).

Foreign Policy. *Intra-German Relations.* SED relations with the other German state began the year on a difficult note. The September 1984 postponement—presumably at Soviet behest—of Honecker's trip to Bonn had been followed by increased East German contributions to bloc propaganda against revanchism and by ostentatious attention by the SED to leaders of the West German opposition, the social democrats (*NYT*, 18 February). The publication in *Neues Deutschland* of a catalogue defining East German citizenship virtually wiped out speculation that a modus vivendi on that issue could be found (*ND*, 30 January; *FBIS*, 12 February).

The occasion of Soviet leader Chernenko's funeral, however, witnessed a meeting between Honecker and West German chancellor Helmut Kohl of more than two hours, which established a pattern in intra-German relations of carrying on despite the odds and the setbacks that had lasted most of the year. The brief joint statement from that Moscow meeting put both sides on record as favoring the development of good bilateral relations, in spite of the "frank atmosphere" of the conversation. East German rhetoric during the rest of the year often returned to the statement's endorsement of "the inviolability of borders and respect for the territorial integrity of all European states," in effect a rebuttal to revanchism charges from the Soviets and other bloc partners (ADN, 12 March; *FBIS*, 13 March). The SED itself joined the chorus when it felt it had to, however, as when Kohl attended an expellees' meeting on Whitsunday (*ND*, 17 June; *FBIS*, 19 June).

Hints of progress in such areas as environmental cooperation, the long-discussed bilateral cultural agreement, and youth exchanges were discussed in Bonn following the Kohl-Honecker meeting, but real advances seemed stalled (*Die Welt*, 20 March). Prominent SED figures continued to criticize the Kohl government over its attitudes toward the fortieth anniversary of the end of World War II, as well as its failure to reject the U.S. Strategic Defense Initiative.

The 8 May anniversary in fact threatened to

sharpen differences between the Germanys, but as the actual celebrations unfolded, the SED and the Soviets seemed to pull their hardest punches. The diffuse and relatively low-level participation by East German and Soviet figures in each other's observances—Honecker was in Moscow just before, rather than on, 8 May, and he did not speak at the main rally in East Berlin—served to ease the strain of the occasion in the intra-German sphere (ADN, 4, 5, 7 May; *FBIS*, 6, 8 May). Bonn also showed some sangfroid in avoiding panic over the possibility that the SED might be ready to bypass the intra-German connection, a prospect raised by such events as Honecker's trip to Italy.

The SED was also cooperating with the West German SPD to play a brighter tune in counterpoint to its dealings with the Kohl government. This echo of the common front strategy apparently irritated official Bonn, and such ventures as the SED-SPD proposal for a central European zone free of chemical weapons clearly were intended to put pressure on the governing coalition and to exploit divisions in West German society, in the best SED/CPSU wedge-driving style. The SED-SPD relationship nonetheless complemented regular intra-German relations, providing circumstances in which positive intentions could be expressed and helping to sustain the impression of SED goodwill. Thus, even in February, when SED international relations secretary Axen visited Bonn for an early round of the chemical weapons talks, he also met with Foreign Minister Genscher and Chancellery Minister Schäuble (DPA, 1 March; *FBIS*, 4 March). Chairman of the SPD Willy Brandt talked with Honecker in East Berlin in September, a meeting handled too much like a state visit for official West German tastes, but nevertheless it offered promises and hints of improvements in intra-German travel and other humanitarian areas that Bonn had long sought (DPA, 20 September; *FBIS*, 23 September). With the stream of SPD visitors, including party Bundestag leader Vogel in May and Minister-President (later chancellor candidate) Rau in April, Honecker consistently dealt with real intra-German issues and not merely with the possibilities for a hypothetical SPD government (DPA, 16 May; *FBIS*, 17 May).

By the time of the SED-SPD chemical weapons proposal on 19 June, moreover, 8 May apparently was long enough past that official intra-German undertakings were again in train. On 5 July, East Berlin and Bonn renewed for five years the intra-German swing credit, at a raised level of 850 million marks (DPA, 5 July; *FBIS*, 8 July). It became known at the same time that East Germany would take measures against the stream of Tamil asylum seekers entering West Berlin from Sri Lanka via East Berlin's Schoenefeld airport. Talks on environmental cooperation also took on new impetus. Perhaps most significant, later news implied that in its measures to stop the flow of Sri Lankans, the SED had the cooperation of the Soviet airline Aeroflot (DPA, 3, 5, 18 July; *FBIS*, 5, 9, 19 July).

These developments and the prospect that the postponed visit to Bonn of Volkskammer president Sindermann might occur in September appear to have been more than enough to keep the relationship on course despite a spate of spy scandals. These included the defection in August of West German counterintelligence chief Hans-Joachim Tiedge and several lesser figures, several espionage-related West German arrests, and the defection of an East German diplomat in Buenos Aires. Chancellor Kohl felt compelled to note the gap the spy cases revealed between the promise and the reality of good neighborly relations, but at the opening of the Leipzig trade fair on 1 September both Honecker and West German leaders including Franz Josef Strauss spoke of preventing the cases from disturbing intra-German relations. Honecker indicated that the removal of antipersonnel mines from the intra-German border would be completed (BBC Caris, 30 August, 4 September).

By late September, Honecker was promising Willy Brandt some relaxation in the granting of permission for East Germans to visit relatives in the West. Press speculation was also building that Honecker himself might reschedule his trip to Bonn before year's end (DPA, 20 September: *FBIS*, 23 September).

The Geneva meeting between President Reagan and General Secretary Gorbachev in November fostered further speculation over a Honecker visit, focusing increasingly on December or January. As the year drew to a close without confirmation of the visit, however, it began to appear that hopes of recovering the heady intra-German atmosphere of mid-1984 were doomed. The news that the bilateral cultural agreement was finally ready to be vetted by both sides preparatory to signature only confirmed that intra-German relations had far to go by showing how far they had come during 1985 (DPA, 4 December; *FBIS*, 5 December).

For the SED, half a loaf and promises for the future seemed to be the best that could be achieved. For the near term, having apparently been unable to secure Soviet acquiescence to the symbolically important Honecker trip, a period of lesser official bilateral efforts such as cultural and environmental cooperation agreements seemed in prospect. The approach of the CPSU and SED congresses and election campaigns in West Germany seemed to preclude a Honecker visit to Bonn in 1986 but, regardless of the outcome of that election, the SED-SPD relationship promised to remain important as a tool for defending intra-German relations against the swings of superpower relations.

Westpolitik. Probably the most dramatic aspect of East German foreign policy in 1985 was that of relations with NATO countries other than West Germany. The substance of East Berlin's existing and foreseeable ties to these countries and its agreements with them, particularly in the economic arena, hardly approached the complexity and density of its relations with Bonn, but were driven by several purposes apart from improving the respective bilateral relationships. Among these purposes were certainly Honecker's personal prestige and the general level of recognition and political weight accorded the traditionally insecure East German state.

Probably equally important, however, was the effect of this Westpolitik on the triangular relations between East Berlin, Bonn, and Moscow. Relations with other Western countries strengthened GDR arguments that its activities, and those of the other Eastern "small states," were valuable to the Soviets. At the same time, these relationships provided a backdrop that probably made its relations with Bonn stand out less in Soviet eyes. It also strengthened the East German hand vis-à-vis the Kohl government to have other, at least potentially remunerative, Western interlocutors (*RFE/RL Research*, 9 May, 2 July).

The major events of the year under this heading were Honecker's trips to Italy in April and to Greece in October, repaying visits to East Berlin by prime ministers Craxi and Papandreou the previous year. The visit to Rome was particularly notable as the first by an East German leader to a NATO capital, and also as the occasion of the first papal audience for an East German chief. Hardly less important, however, were the visits to East Berlin by UK foreign secretary Sir Geoffrey Howe in early April and by French prime minister Laurent Fabius in June. The latter was the first visit to East Berlin by a government chief from one of the three Western allies with rights in West Berlin.

Honecker made a show of SED reasonableness and flexibility, particularly during his Italian trip and the Howe visit. In an interview with Italian journalists prior to his trip, Honecker asserted his continued interest in visiting Bonn and in improving intra-German relations generally (*ND*, 20–21 April; *FBIS*, 23 April). Honecker's conversation with the pope reportedly included inquiries by the pontiff on religious freedom and human rights under SED rule. Foreign Secretary Howe made pointed comments on human rights during his East Berlin visit, and his milder remarks were even carried in *Neues Deutschland* (*RFE/RL Research*, 9 May; *ND*, 10 April). The East Germans were not above insulting their guests, however, as when they embarrassed the French by having Defense Minister Hoffmann appear in dress uniform at a dinner for Fabius in East Berlin, which the Western allies maintain is still a demilitarized city except for the occupying Allied and Soviet troops (*Le Monde*, 12 June; *FBIS*, 14 June).

The SED's attention to Soviet sensitivities was particularly evident during Honecker's Rome and Athens visits. Both of his hosts were socialists, putting Honecker firmly in support of USSR efforts to cultivate left-wing opinion in Western Europe. The high-level figures who accompanied him were probably the ones most acceptable to the Soviets: SED Economics Secretary Mittag in both cases, International Relations Secretary Axen to Rome, and heir-presumptive Krenz to Athens. Most important, disarmament themes played a strong role in Honecker's discussions, particularly with the Greek prime minister. Papandreou went so far as to declare establishment of nuclear-free zones in Europe, the main point of contact in Greek–East German relations (ADN, 8 October; *FBIS*, 10 October).

Third World. The GDR continued cultivating selected Third World countries in 1985. Nicaragua and Cuba, Syria and Libya, and Ethiopia and Angola seemed to be the most prominent East German partners in their respective regions.

Central America loomed largest among SED Third World interests this year. Heir-presumptive Krenz led an East German delegation to the inauguration of Daniel Ortega as Nicaragua's president in January, and Ortega made a return visit to East Berlin in May (ADN, 11 January, 9–11 May; *FBIS*, 15 January, 10, 13 May). There were numerous exchanges of party and ministerial visits during the year, punctuated by announcements of various forms of East German assistance, including a supplemental $40 million credit in June and a hospital completed in July (Managua Radio, 26 June; GDR Domestic Service, 23 July; *FBIS*, 24 July). The GDR also continued to treat wounded Nicaraguans in East Germany and in October renewed economic cooperation agreements with Managua (Managua Radio, 9 August, 31 October). A Sandinista official participated in a December symposium on cadre training at the Karl Marx SED college, suggesting strong links between the two parties in this traditional area of East German expertise (*ND*, 10 December).

East German relations with Cuba were highlighted by Raúl Castro's visit to East Berlin in April and the coordination of five-year economic plans, completed in June (Tass, 8 April; *FBIS*, 9 April, 1 July; ADN, 28 June). SED culture chief Hager visited Cuba in December to open a brewery (ADN, 22–25 December; *FBIS*, 26, 27 December).

In the Middle East, Honecker saw fit to address both Syrian leader Assad and Libyan strongman Khadafy as "comrade," pledging stronger SED cooperation (*ND*, 22 January, 31 August; *FBIS*, 24 January). Syria and the GDR exchanged military delegations during the year, with the East German air force commander visiting Syria in September and the naval commander in November (ADN, 25 September, 9 November; *FBIS*, 26 September, 14 November). Syrian prime minister Al-Kassam spent several days in East Berlin during October, meeting Honecker as well as Stoph (ADN, 29 October–1 November; *FBIS*, 30 October–4 November). Public contacts with Libya were lower-level and less publicized, but rumors of East German involvement in protecting Khadafy were persistent enough to provoke at least one vehement Libyan denial (*La Repubblica*, 16 October). East Germany also continued its strong rhetorical support for Yassir Arafat and the PLO, and Defense Minister Hoffman's reception of the PLO deputy commander in chief in late August suggested more tangible links as well (ADN, 30 August).

Ethiopia and Angola continued to be major East German interests in Africa, with Mozambique apparently less so. Ethiopian leader Mengistu visited East Berlin in late 1984, and an agreement on cooperation between the SED and his Workers' Party was signed (ADN, 20–21 December; *FBIS*, 21, 27 December). East German air crews received credit from one Ethiopian official for staffing much of the food relief airlift in that country (Vienna, *Volksstimme*, 24 February). Politburo member Harry Tisch brought drought aid in February, and at least two significant Ethiopian party delegations visited the GDR during the year (ADN, 3 February, 28 July, 30 October; *FBIS*, 5 February, 30 July, 31 October).

Relations with Angola led to attendance by SED Politburo member Werner Krolikowski at the Angolan party convention in December (ADN, 1 December). Earlier in the year, a major Angolan delegation had visited its SED counterparts (Luanda radio, 18 April). Arrangements for employing Angolans in the GDR were renewed during the year, and a long-term agreement on economic and scientific-technical cooperation was signed in October (Luanda radio, 31 March, 2 October).

Mozambique, by contrast, seemed less close to East Germany, since the major visitor there during the year was a deputy prime minister and minister for science and technology, Herbert Weiz, who signed an agreement between the two ruling parties in his capacity as SED Central Committee member (ADN, 27 June; *FBIS*, 28 June). Krolikowski did, however, meet with Mozambican leader Machel while at the Angolan party congress (ADN, 1 December). The claimed death of another East German at the hands of Mozambican rebels and the signing of bilateral economic and science and technology cooperation agreements in October also testified to continuing ties between the parties and countries (AFP, 11 September; ADN, 18 October; *FBIS*, 21 October).

International Party Relations. SED contacts with other Communist parties in 1985 continued to be dominated by relations with the CPSU. These were characterized by differences of emphasis that suggested continuing disagreement over intra-German relations and by a wider controversy over the role of "small states" in international, particularly East-West, relations. These difficulties were offset, however, as the year went on, by the GDR's increasing—and probably largely sincere—support of Moscow's innovations in disarmament policy and the glimmerings of better U.S.-Soviet relations. Major events of the year included the Chernenko funeral, celebrations of the anniversary of the end of World War II in Europe, renewal of the Warsaw Treaty Organization, and the Gorbachev-Reagan meeting in Geneva, with top-level Warsaw pact meetings the month before and immediately after it.

The group meeting Gorbachev granted the East European leaders at Chernenko's funeral was, if correct, hardly enough to quiet their uncertainties about his position and his attitude toward them (*ND*, 14 March). It also required Honecker to make his conversation with Polish party chief Jaruzelski the protocolary as well as political counterweight to his meeting with West German chancellor Helmut Kohl (*ND*, 13 March; *FBIS*, 13 March). The first major Soviet–East German bilateral meeting after Gorbachev's accession was a week later, through the apparently perdurable Foreign Minister Gromyko, whom GDR foreign minister Fischer met in Moscow. Their communiqué struck out at the bogey of West German revanchism, albeit not stridently enough to overshadow the Honecker-Kohl meeting completely (*Izvestiia*, 21 March; *FBIS*, 21 March). Nevertheless, rhetoric critical of right-wing political groups in West Germany, though seldom naming Chancellor Kohl, seemed to be part of the obeisance required of the SED in the preparations for 8 May. Following extension of the Warsaw Treaty on 26 April and the anniversary of the end of World War II in Europe, the pressure for demonstrations of SED loyalty seemed to ease (ADN, 25–27 April; *FBIS*, 26–30 April).

Honecker's stay in the Soviet Union during 4–5 May probably was not all he had wanted in terms of prestige and protocol, but on balance was positive. Its brevity and Honecker's sharing of the spotlight with West German and West Berlin communist leaders Herbert Mies and Horst Schmitt made the visit pale in comparison to the bilateral visit only two years earlier (ADN, 5 May; *FBIS*, 6 May). The SED leader did meet with Gorbachev, however, and the conversation revealed an appropriate unanimity of views (ADN, 5 May; Tass, 5 May; *FBIS*, 6 May). *Neues Deutschland* editorialized afterward over East German support of the Soviet Union and the honor paid during Honecker's visit to the SED's antifascist heritage (*ND*, 7 May; *FBIS*, 9 May). Moreover, sharing responsibility with Mies and Schmitt for representing unswerving loyalty to that tradition probably reduced the pressure on Honecker.

After Honecker's trip to Moscow, the actual 8 May celebrations in both capitals were, from the SED point of view, less onerous than they might have been. The Soviets were represented in East Berlin for the festivities by no greater personage than candidate Politburo member and culture minister Piotr Demichev (Tass, 6 May; *FBIS*, 6 May). Demichev, moreover, after a 6–8 May stay in East Germany, returned almost immediately for the annual Soviet culture days (13–20 May), diluting the impact of his presence on 8 May (East Berlin radio, 13 May; *FBIS*, 14, 23 May; *Pravda*, 22 May). The SED delegation in Moscow on 8 May comprised International Relations Secretary Axen, FDJ head Aurich, and Bezirk first secretaries (later Politburo candidate members) Eberlein and Lorenz.

At the 8 May ceremonies in East Berlin, Sindermann spoke rather than Honecker, and his and Demichev's remarks were relatively mild (*Izvestiia*, 9 May; *FBIS*, 14 May). The most strident note out of East Berlin during this period, in terms of the differences over East-West policy that most burdened the SED's relations with Moscow, came from CPSU Politburo member Grishin on 14 May (Tass, 14 May). This and the *Pravda* article of the following month, signed by O. Vladimirov, seemed to be the high-water mark of the Soviet need for reassertions of SED fealty (*Pravda*, 21 June). By year's end, Grishin had lost his position as the CPSU's Moscow area chief.

The Vladimirov article sharply criticized the idea that smaller Warsaw Pact states had individual roles to play in socialist strategy toward the West. This concept had been advanced by both East Germany and Hungary, whose press organs had at times seemed to form a mutual admiration society (*ND*, 4 March; *FBIS*, 8 March). Both ignored the *Pravda* piece at the time of its publication, and by August were again practicing reciprocal congratulations over foreign policy, particularly toward the West (*ND*, 9 August; *RFE/RL Research*, 23 August).

As the Soviets tried to add momentum to their disarmament initiatives, the question arose whether pact unity would take on greater priority for them, possibly stifling Hungarian and East German freedom of action. At the Honecker-Kádár summit on 29 October, indeed, there was no hint of dissatisfaction with the positions taken at the preceding Warsaw Pact summit in Sofia (ADN, 29 October; Tass, 29 October; *FBIS*, 30 October). The declaration of the Sofia summit, however, contained language that must have gone far to satisfy concerns in Budapest and East Berlin:

> Now more than ever before active collaboration is needed among all states and all forces that advocate the normalization of the international situation . . . it is entirely possible to achieve a return to détente . . . Right now it is vitally necessary on [the basis of the Helsinki Final Act] to deepen the political dialogue among the European countries in various forms and at various levels in the interests of improving the situation on the continent and strengthening mutual trust. The states represented at the [Sofia] conference

> express readiness to seek new forms of economic, scientific, and technical cooperation with the West European countries on the basis of equal rights and mutual advantage (Moscow, *Selskaia zhizn*, 24 October).

The SED also had a real interest (apart from any Soviet pressure to conform and given the domestic and West German peace activism of 1982–1984) in supporting initiatives that portrayed the East as the more accommodating party in disarmament negotiations. In any event, after the Gorbachev-Reagan meeting and the Warsaw Pact summit, the SED ignored whatever pressure it had felt, at least to the extent of continuing to proclaim an SED role in East-West relations. "We see our concrete contribution toward a turn for the better [in the international situation]," said the Politburo report to the November Central Committee plenum, "in the active policy of constructive dialogue that is producing tangible results." Erich Honecker, the report said later, "has done and is doing great, internationally recognized work in order to make relations between states stable and trustful" (*ND*, 23–24 November; *FBIS*, 10 December).

In addition to his meeting with Hungarian leader Kádár in October, Honecker met personally in 1985 with all other Warsaw Pact leaders except Bulgarian Todor Zhivkov. In addition to their March meeting in Moscow and the several multilateral meetings they attended, Honecker and Polish party leader Jaruzelski met again in Warsaw on 16 December. They signed a long-term agreement on scientific and technical cooperation, and in their communiqué criticized revanchism as a danger to peace without naming West Germany (*ND*, 17 December). Honecker met Czechoslovak leader Husák in East Berlin on 26 November, a meeting remarkable more for its occurrence than its content because the two leaders had not met in a bilateral context in over two years (ADN, 26 November; *FBIS*, 27 November). Any tension between the two countries that might have arisen had seemed to be dissipating at mid-year when Prague endorsed the chemical weapons agreement between the SED and the SPD, which later led to a joint GDR-Czechoslovak initiative toward Bonn (Bratislava, *Pravda*, 3 July). Honecker also received Romanian chief Ceauşescu for an extended visit in May, repaying Honecker's attendance at the Romanian party congress in 1984, and accompanied the Romanian on a visit to Erfurt (ADN, 28–30 May; *FBIS*, 29, 30 May, 4 June). Bulgaria had to settle for a visit from Premier Stoph in October, which still served to underscore the high level of activity within the Warsaw Pact that characterized the year (ADN, 16 October).

Honecker, however, made a significant foray into the communist world outside Warsaw Pact limits in his official visit to Yugoslavia in October, accompanied by Krenz and Mittag. The meetings apparently broke little new ground, as the communiqué stressed bilateral economic relations and international disarmament, but Honecker's travel in the country and the attendance of perhaps his two most powerful subalterns gave the trip some impact (ADN, 2 October; *FBIS*, 2 October).

It was also an important year for East German relations with the second communist power in the world, China. Although formal relations between the SED and the Chinese party apparently remained suspended, party figures exchanged visits in their government roles, and there were hints of movement toward the resumption of party ties. The highlights of the year were the visit in May of Chinese vice-premier Li Peng to East Berlin, where he was received by Honecker; the reciprocating visit in July of deputy premier and Politburo candidate member Schürer to Beijing, where he signed a long-term bilateral trade agreement and was received by party leader Hu Yaobang; deputy premier and Politburo member Kleiber's visit to China in October; and the visit to China by Volkskammer president and senior Politburo member Sindermann in December (ADN, 20 May, 10, 15 July, 28 October, 16 December; *FBIS*, 21 May).

The SED, in elevating the dialogue to the Politburo level, particularly with so senior a figure as Sindermann, drew ahead of its four Warsaw Pact counterparts who had followed Moscow's lead in breaking with Beijing (Romania was the exception). Nevertheless, the SED's actions were strictly within the precedents being set in relations between the Chinese party and the CPSU. It was also notable that the Chinese press was slightly more restrained than the East German one in describing bilateral meetings such as that between Hu and Schürer, suggesting that the Chinese were being careful to avoid making trouble in Moscow for their SED guests (Xinhua, 10 July). Sindermann apparently made stops in Moscow en route to and from Beijing (*Izvestiia*, 22 December). Sindermann also, however, made the provocative comment while in China that all Communist parties should find "their own paths to progress" (Xinhua, 16 December; *RFE/RL Research*, 8 January 1986).

Hints of accommodation between the SED and the Chinese party, in addition to the Sindermann visit itself, included several references to officials of the other side as "comrade," most recently by Sindermann in reference to Wang Renzhong, who had led a Chinese parliamentary visit to East Germany, and by the entire Chinese state leadership in addressing Honecker, Stoph, and Sindermann on the East German national day (ADN, 14 December; *ND*, 8 October). More dramatically, the Sindermann visit apparently gave rise to rumors that Honecker himself might visit China in 1986 (*WP*, 20 December; *Kyodo*, 14 December). If the visit materializes, Honecker will be the first Warsaw Pact leader other than Ceauşescu to visit China since the 1960s, unless Gorbachev or Gromyko precedes him.

John Payne
Washington, D.C.

Hungary

Population. 10,645,000

Party. Hungarian Socialist Workers' Party (Magyar Szocialista Munkáspárt; HSWP)

Founded. 1918 (HSWP, 1956)

Membership. 870,992 (13th HSWP Congress Report, 1985); women 30.5 percent; average age 46.9; active and retired industrial workers (including foremen) 42.6 percent of the membership; active and retired collective farm workers and supervisors 7.8 percent; active and retired intellectuals and white-collar workers 42.4 percent; other occupations 7.2 percent; 80.3 percent of members have joined the party since the 1956 revolution.

General Secretary. János Kádár (73, worker)

Politburo. 13 members: György Aczél (68, intellectual); Sándor Gáspár (68, worker); Károly Grósz (55, worker); Csaba Hámori (37, technical intelligentsia); Ferenc Havasi (56, worker); János Kádár; György Lázár (61, technical intelligentsia); Pál Losonczi (66, farmer); László Maróthy (43, technical intelligentsia); Károly Németh (63, worker); Miklós Óvári (60, educator); István Sarlós (64, educator); István Szabó (61, farmer)

Secretariat. 8 members: János Kádár (general secretary); Károly Németh (deputy general secretary); János Berecz (54); Ferenc Havasi; István Horváth (50, jurist); Miklós Óvári; Lénárd Pál (59, scientist); Mátyás Szürös (52)

Central Committee. 105 full members (listed in *JPRS*, 17 May 1985)

Status. Ruling party

Last Congress. Thirteenth, 25–28 March 1985

Last Election. June 1985; 387 seats (35 national list, 352 multicandidate constituencies); approximately 70 percent of deputies are party members.

Auxiliary Organizations. Patriotic People's Front (PPF), secretary-general, Imre Pozsgay; Communist Youth League (913,000 members), first secretary, Csaba Hámori; National Council of Trade Unions (NCTU) (4,399,000 members), chairman, Sándor Gáspár; National Council of Hungarian Women, chairman, Mrs. Lajos Duschek; National Peace Council

Main State Organs. Presidential Council, chairman, Pál Losonczi; Council of Ministers, chairman, György Lázár

Publications. *Népszabadság* (People's freedom), HSWP daily, deputy editor, Péter Rényi; *Társadalmi Szemle* (Social review), HSWP theoretical monthly, editor, Valéria Benke; *Pártélet* (Party life), HSWP organizational monthly; *Magyar Hirlap*, government daily; *Magyar Nemzet*, PPF daily; *Népszava*, NCTU daily. The official news agency is Magyar Távirati Iroda (MTI).

The Hungarian Section of the Russian Communist Party (Bolshevik) was founded in Moscow in March 1918 by Béla Kun (1886–1939) and a few other Hungarian prisoners of war. The Communist Party of Hungary came into being in Budapest in November 1918. Kun was the dominant figure in the communist-left socialist coalition that proclaimed the Hungarian Soviet Republic on the collapse of Mihály Károlyi's liberal-democratic regime. The red dictatorship lasted from March to August 1919.

During the interwar period, the party functioned as a faction-ridden movement in domestic illegality and in exile. The underground membership numbered in the hundreds. With the Soviet occupation at the end of World War II, the Hungarian Communist Party (HCP) re-emerged as a member of the provisional government. Kun had lost his life in Stalin's purges, and the party was led by Mátyás Rákosi (1892–1971). Although the HCP won no more than 17 percent of the vote in the relatively free 1945 elections, it continued to exercise a disproportionate influence in the coalition government. Thanks largely to Soviet-backed coercive tactics, the HCP gained effective control of the country in 1947. In 1948, it absorbed left-wing social democrats into the newly named Hungarian Workers' Party.

Rákosi's Stalinist zeal was exemplified by the show trial of József Cardinal Mindszenty and the liquidation of alleged Titoist László Rajk. The New Course of 1954–1955 offered some relief from economic mismanagement and totalitarian terror; inspired by some of Stalin's successors, it was led in Hungary by the moderate Communist Imre Nagy (1896–1958). De-Stalinization undermined the party's authority and unity, and the replacement of Rákosi by Ernö Gerö (1898–1980) could not halt the rising tide of popular opposition. Following the outbreak of revolution on 23 October 1956, Imre Nagy became prime minister for the second time and eventually headed a multiparty government that withdrew Hungary from the Warsaw Pact. On 25 October, János Kádár (1912–) became leader of the renamed party, the HSWP. The Nagy government was overthrown by the armed intervention of the Soviet Union on 4 November.

Since the end of the revolution, the HSWP has ruled unchallenged as the sole political party, firmly aligned with the Soviet Union. After an initial phase of repression that culminated in the final collectivization of agriculture (1959–1960), Kádár's rule came to be marked by his conciliatory "alliance policy" and by pragmatic reforms, most notably the New Economic Mechanism launched in 1968.

Party Affairs. The party statutes prescribe the convening of a congress every five years, and accordingly the party held its Thirteenth Congress in 1985. The congressional guidelines, issued 1 December 1984 (in *Népszabadság*), stressed continuity in the party's policies while noting shortcomings with respect to the standard of living, culture, and ideology. A regular congressional complaint reiterated in the guidelines was the formalistic and bureaucratic style of party work and slackness in party discipline. A noteworthy new element in the guidelines was reference to the justified demands of Hungarian minorities abroad for language and cultural rights. The guidelines asserted the need for higher political, moral, and professional qualifications for leading positions in state and economic administration and urged that these posts be filled by open competition.

The guidelines were submitted for debate within the party and in public forums in the months leading up to the congress. Concurrently, party elections took place from the level of the basic unit upward. In the party committee elections over 30 percent of secretaries and 43 percent of ordinary members were elected for the first time; in 4–5 percent of the cases there were multiple nominations. The report on these elections noted a growing concentration of party work on economic problems, to the detriment of ideological agitprop (*Népszabadság*, 2 February).

Nine hundred and thirty-five delegates were elected to the party congress, which was held on 25–28 March. The Central Committee's report had been previously distributed to the delegates, and Kádár contributed only supplementary comments at the congress (*Népszabadság*, 25 March). The report acknowledged that not all of the objectives of the Twelfth Congress had been achieved and urged the continuation of the party's basic policies with greater vigor and consistency. With regard to foreign affairs, the report confirmed that a sound relationship with the Soviet Union was a fundamental national interest of Hungary, and it blamed "extreme imperialist circles" in the United States for international tensions. The reference to cooperation with other communist states included China (although the Chinese Communist Party was not invited to send delegates to the congress, it did send a message of greetings).

The party's alliance policy, which aims to encompass all Hungarians, needed to be reinforced to cope with the social consequences of economic stresses and international tensions. The consolidation of socialism required firm measures against its opponents as well as improvement in the representative function of trade unions, the ideological work of the Communist Youth League, and the mobilization of mass support by the Patriotic People's Front. A relevant measure in the expansion of socialist democracy was the new electoral law requiring multiple candidacies. The report deplored the rise in the crime rate and the decline in the total population of Hungary. It denounced "bourgeois nationalism" but affirmed the language and cultural rights of ethnic minorities in Hungary—and of Hungarian minorities in other countries.

With regard to the economy, difficulties in adjusting to unfavorable external changes were noted. The national product had to be expanded at a faster rate, and domestic consumption constrained, to restore equilibrium. More efficient management and technological innovation would be needed to meet the next five-year plan's target of a 14–17 percent increase in national income. The party was committed not only to full employment but also to an efficient deployment of the labor force. The congress, in sum, anticipated fine tuning rather than major changes in economic policy. At the same time, the seriousness of the country's economic problems was addressed by several speakers. Kádár recognized that in the course of "five difficult years" the decline in the standard of living had been felt most acutely by pensioners (some 20 percent of the population) and by young people, and that special measures were needed to assist young families with housing and child allowances.

As at earlier congresses, the Central Committee reported that most Hungarians were content with socialism but that many were indifferent or hostile to Marxism, entertained illusions about the superiority of capitalism, and displayed nationalism. The usual remedy of better ideological education was recommended; ideological weaknesses in literature and the arts had to be overcome by a stronger assertion of the leading role of the party.

The party's own effectiveness was also questioned in the report, with reference made to some "political uncertainty." Improvement was needed both in democratic debate and in the disciplined implementation of policy. The report of the Central Control Committee, delivered by András Gyenes, also reflected on the party's weaknesses. Since the previous congress some 3.4 percent of the membership (28,739 members) had been disciplined and 0.9 percent (7,639) expelled. In addition, 2 percent of the memberships (17,591) were cancelled and another 2.2 percent (19,188) left the party voluntarily. The congressional resolution warned that the party had to rid itself of members whose performance was inadequate.

Between the two congresses the party's membership enjoyed a net growth of 7.3 percent, to 870,992 on 1 January 1985. The proportion of women rose from 28.3 to 30.5 percent. The proportion of industrial and farm workers was higher among new recruits than in the overall membership, and the report expressed general satisfaction with the party's composition except for recruitment difficulties among youth and certain intellectual strata.

Károly Grósz, the new Budapest party secretary and Politburo member, also spoke on the first day of the congress, addressing housing and other problems in the capital as well as the financial difficulties of the technical intelligentsia. On the second day, Prime Minister György Lázár delivered a grim and self-critical address on the state of the economy, the failure to improve productivity, and the consequent price increases and reduction in investments. He insisted that new approaches to economic management and greater income differentiation were both necessary and consistent with socialist principles. The party's chief economic spokesman, Ferenc Havasi, also addressed the problem of social tensions arising from economic problems. He noted that the current concept of socialism was "rooted in generally well-intentioned revolutionary illusions" that needed to be revised; socialism still could not guarantee steady and balanced economic development or escape the impact of the capitalist crisis, nor could it be free of nationalism. Speaking about culture, the veteran György Aczél attacked the growing criticism of Hungary's socialist achievements from both liberal and dogmatic perspectives and called for a more balanced and realistic application of Marxist ideology in education. This was needed to overcome the pervasive ideological uncertainty induced by a multiplicity of partial reforms. He also reflected the party's growing concern with historical and literary depictions of the Stalinist period of the 1950s, accounts that he said were sometimes biased in concentrating solely on negative features.

The Soviet party delegation was led by CPSU Politburo member Grigori Romanov, who commended the HSWP's achievements but emphasized the need for economic integration and political unity of the communist states. He warned against Western political pressure coming in the wake of East-West trade (Tass, 26 March; *FBIS*, 26 March).

On the third day of the congress, the union leader Sándor Gáspár criticized price increases and stressed the need for union involvement in policymaking, but he also endorsed the party's general economic orientation. The executive head of the PPF, Imre Pozsgay, praised constructive church-state relations and the PPF's role as a defender of consumer interests. He also deplored the nationalistic tendencies in certain countries with respect to ethnic minorities and called for the application of the appropriate Leninist principles.

Kádár's traditional closing speech emphasized the importance of party activism and ideological preparedness and the need for more outspoken defense of socialist ideals and achievements. He urged greater stress on superior management, worker training, and wage incentives for a stronger economy, and observed that Western credits were purely commercial matters, i.e., free of political contamination. Reflecting on the controversial second and third economies, Kádár observed (to applause) that workers should earn enough from their main job to live on. "Unearned" income should not be tolerated, and the new enterprise work partnerships should be better supervised to prevent irregularities.

Kádár also referred to the minority issue, citing as an objective the language rights of Hungarians abroad. The matter thus received unprecedented attention at this congress (Szeged University students sent to the congress an open letter requesting discussion of the grievances of the Hungarian minorities in Romania and Czechoslovakia; *Die Welt*, 2 April).

Elections to leading positions were conducted in closed session on 28 March. Kádár was re-elected with the new title of general secretary (previously, he had been first secretary). The change was congruent with Soviet practice, presumably designed to reflect his great prestige and seniority. Károly Németh, a veteran Kádár loyalist and de facto deputy, was elected to the new post of deputy general secretary. It is expected that the aging Kádár will delegate more of his duties to Németh.

The membership of the Secretariat was raised from seven to eight. Aczél, hitherto the party's most powerful cultural boss, was dropped, as was military expert Mihály Korom. Newly appointed were János Berecz (54), a foreign affairs specialist who had been editor-in-chief of *Népszabadság* (and who was also elected chairman of the Central Committee's agitprop department); Dr. István Horváth (50), formerly minister of the interior; and Dr. Lénárd Pál (59), a nuclear physicist and chairman of the National Technical Development Committee, who also became chairman of the Central Committee's educational policy working group. The other Secretariat members are (in addition to Kádár and Németh) Ferenc Havasi, who continues as head of the Central Committee's economic policy department and also became head of the cooperative policy working group; Miklós Óvári, who became head of the Central Committee's bureau; and Mátyás Szürös, the foreign affairs spokesman.

Three of the Politburo's thirteen members were replaced: Valéria Benke, Mihály Korom, and Lajos Méhes (the short-lived secretary general of the NCTU). Newly elected were Károly Grósz (55), first secretary of the Budapest party committee; Csaba Hámori (37), first secretary of the Communist Youth League; and István Szabó (61), chairman of the National Council of Producers' Cooperatives. The re-elected members of the Politburo are Kádár, Gáspár, Aczél (also head of the party's Social Sciences Institute), Havasi, Lázár, Óvári, Pál Losonczi (the head of state), László Maróthy (a deputy premier), and István Sarlós, the new chairman of the National Assembly.

These personnel changes did not significantly alter the political profile of the leading bodies. The outgoing Benke and Korom were generally considered to be conservative. The incoming Horváth is a hard-line law enforcer, while Grósz is an ambitious careerist with good organizational ability and a penchant for tough oratory. In a February speech, Grósz had caused a stir by alluding to an article asking where those responsible for the Rákosi (Stalinist) era were, and responding defiantly "Look no further: we are here" (*Népszabadság*, 14 February). In a subsequent interview he explained that he, like other survivors, was responsible for both good and bad aspects of the 1950s. Grósz also stated that there was no urgent need for political reform; that there was insufficient private initiative and income differentiation; and that it was less the private and more the state and cooperative sectors that were centers of corruption and bribery (*Nin*, 7 April; *Radio Free Europe Research*, 16 May).

The congress elected a new Central Committee of 105 members (compared to 127 in 1980); twenty-six were new members. Thirty-four Central Committee members hold office in the HSWP, 33 in government and administration, 11 in mass organizations, and 13 in economic production management.

The congress approved other personnel changes in the central apparatus. Géza Kotai was named head of the Central Committee's foreign affairs department, replacing Gyula Horn, who was appointed state secretary for foreign affairs. István Petrovszki became head of the party and mass organizations department instead of Tibor Baranyai, who was made secretary general of the NCTU. The new head of the cultural affairs department is Katalin Radics, replacing Dr. Pál Tetényi, who was appointed chairman of the National Technical Development Committee.

Government and Elections. On 6 December 1984 the Presidential Council made several new appointments to the Council of Ministers. Named deputy prime ministers were Lajos Czinege (60), who had been defense minister since 1960; Judith Csehák (44), a physician and a secretary of the NCTU; and László Maróthy (42), formerly first secretary of the Budapest party committee. Appointed defense minister was Colonel General István Oláh (58), former chief of staff. The new minister of health is Dr. László Medve (56). When István Horváth was appointed to the HSWP Secretariat, he was replaced as interior minister by Police Lieutenant General János Kamara. Party veteran Antal Apró (71) retired as chairman of the National Assembly and was succeeded by István Sarlós (64), formerly a deputy prime minister.

Apart from the HSWP congress, the main political events of 1985 were parliamentary and local council elections. In accordance with the new electoral law, nomination meetings began 15 April to select a minimum of two candidates for each parliamentary and council seat. All qualified voters could make a nomination, and nominees receiving at least one-third of the openly cast votes at two successive nomination meetings would become candidates for election—as long as they pledged in writing to uphold the electoral program of the PPF, the party's principal mass-mobilizing agent. In addition, a national list of 35 candidates chosen by the PPF would run unopposed and be voted on, individually, by all electors. Of these candidates, 16 represented the HSWP and mass organizations (including Kádár, Lázár, Gáspár, Hámori, Havasi, Losonczi, Németh, Óvári, Sarlós, and István Szabó); 6 came from the clergy; 4 from the national minorities; 5 were leading artists and intellectuals; and 4 were senior retired officials. Twenty-three of them were current members of parliament.

Several outspoken critics of the regime tried for nominations. The prominent dissident László Rajk managed to receive over one-third of the votes at the first meeting in Budapest's fifth district. The second meeting was packed with party loyalists, and his candidacy failed to receive confirmation. Another dissident, Gáspár Miklós Tamás, also did not win nomination. The regime clearly hoped that the nomination meetings would endorse the two "official" nominees of the PPF, and some two thousand complaints were registered regarding irregularities and pressure on non-PPF sponsored candidates to withdraw. Some 152 names were proposed spontaneously at the meetings, and 71 of these received sufficient support to be candidates in the parliamentary race. In 19 cases the spontaneous nominees displaced PPF nominees. At the local council nomination meetings, some 3,549 candidates were spontaneously nominated, and in some instances neither of the PPF nominees received endorsement. At the end of the nomination process 762 candidates stood for 352 parliamentary seats, and 87,334 for 42,500 local council seats. Only 77 of the parliamentary candidates were workers and 4 others were peasants.

This first experience with open nominations occasioned some alarm in official circles. Sarlós observed ruefully that it had been a mistake to expect that only supporters of PPF policies would turn up at the nomination meetings. However, the PPF's secretary general, Imre Pozsgay, observed that "for years there has been voting in Hungary; now there will be an election" (Radio Budapest, 20 May; *RFE Research*, 5 and 21 June).

On 8 June, the first round of elections, 93.9 percent of eligible voters turned out (compared to a reported turnout of 97 percent in 1980). The first round filled 310 of the 352 parliamentary seats. In 42 constituencies no candidate received over 50 percent of the vote, necessitating new nomination meetings and runoff elections. The number of invalid votes (5.4 percent) and negative votes (1.2 percent of valid votes) was larger than in previous elections. Close to 10 percent of eligible voters either abstained or cast invalid or negative votes. Of the 71 spontaneously nominated candidates, 25 were elected. Only 98 of the 172 incumbents running for election were re-elected. Seventy-seven percent of the first-round winners were party members. The majority of the winners received less than 60 percent of the vote. (Candidates receiving at least 25 percent of the vote were declared "alternate deputies.") One notable upset was the defeat of the former prime minister, Jenö Fock. In the uncontested national list election, the valid positive vote ranged from 99.1 to 99.2 percent, except for the case of Sándor Gáspár, who got only 98.8 percent.

A second round of elections was held on 22 June for 41 parliamentary and 848 local council seats, following new nomination meetings. In this round, a simple plurality of votes was sufficient to secure election, and 20 of the elected candidates were not PPF nominees, bringing the total of non-PPF parliamentary deputies to 45.

The Patriotic People's Front officially judged the new electoral law to be a success and the elections a referendum that had endorsed the PPF program. It voiced confidence that elected deputies who had not been nominated by the PPF would abide by their pledge to support the official program (*RFE Research*, 21 June). *Pravda* (12 June) construed the elections as a demonstration of support for socialism and socialist solidarity. In its final report on the elections, the PPF National Council observed that very few young people had participated in the nomination meetings; that there had been "more widespread hostility toward the so-called spontaneous nominations and suggestions by residents than was desirable"; and that 6 of the 2,000 complaints received were well founded. The PPF also warned that "democracy must not be confused with licentiousness," and indeed the dissidents' attempts to take advantage of the new electoral system may well prompt modification before the 1990 elections (Radio Budapest, 12 July; *FBIS*, 16 July).

Trade Unions. On 4 March Lajos Méhes was replaced as secretary general of the National Council of Trade Unions (NCTU) by Tibor Baranyai (55), who had been deputy head since 1972 and then head of the Central Committee's party and mass organizations department. In a significant redefinition of authority, NCTU chairman Sándor Gáspár became the effective executive head of the organization, with the secretary general relegated to the role of deputy. Gáspár thus regained the power he had enjoyed as NCTU secretary general between 1957 and 1983.

The regime's disposition to democratize elections in all spheres was displayed in the decision of the NCTU at its April session to have shop stewards elected by secret ballot, with the possibility of multiple nominations. Previously the leadership had nominated candidates for all trade union posts, and only union committees, audit committees, and delegates had been elected directly. Now both nominating committees and individual members can propose candidates for all trade union posts, and over 50 percent of the votes cast will validate a nomination. The trade union elections will be completed by 31 March 1986 and followed by the twenty-fifth congress of the NCTU.

Economic Affairs. Most economic indicators showed improved performance in 1984. Per capita real income rose by 1 percent versus the planned zero growth, and a positive trade balance was registered for the first time in three years. "Socialist" investment fell 6–7 percent below the planned level. Agricultural production met both domestic consumption and export targets and represents the main long-term achievement of Hungarian economic policy; it has been estimated that Hungarian agriculture produces enough food for twice the country's population (*Financial Times*, 14 May).

Nevertheless, the Hungarian economy and particularly its industrial sector are marked by chronic inefficiency and low productivity, and Hungary remains in the bottom third of European countries in per capita gross domestic product. The 1985 state budget projected a reduced deficit, a rise in foreign debt servicing from 9.49 to 12.56 percent of budget expenditures, and an increase of 7 percent in both average wages and consumer prices. Substantial price increases were announced in January for foodstuffs (9–29 percent), heating fuels (18–30 percent), urban transport (55–60 percent), newspapers and periodicals (25–30 percent), and other items. The official rationale was the higher cost of imports and the need to further reduce consumer price subsidies. In partial compensation, pensions and other social welfare allowances were also increased. A related measure was an increase in fertilizer and machinery prices that raised agricultural production costs by 4–5 percent and was accompanied by higher procurement prices.

Partial results indicate that the economy's performance worsened in 1985. Industrial production lagged far behind the planned rate of growth, investments fell below even the 1984 level, and, regarding trade, a substantial deficit materialized in the nonsocialist sector instead of the projected surplus (Radio Budapest, 7 August; *FBIS*, 8 August; Radio Budapest, 15 October; *FBIS*, 16 October). In a report to the National Assembly, Prime Minister Lázár acknowledged the failure to increase industrial production and observed that the servicing and repayment of the foreign debt consumed 2.5 to 3 percent of national income. Remedial measures would include official support for innovative entrepreneurial models, new forms of enterprise management, household plots, and auxiliary farming; more wage differentiation linked to productivity; and more progressive taxation (*Népszabadság*, 11 October). The Central Committee at its 12 November meeting approved the targets for the seventh five-year plan (1986–1990). These include an average annual increase of 3 percent in national income and of 1 percent in real wages.

The progressive deterioration in Hungary's terms of trade only aggravated the problems of an economy beset by low industrial labor productivity and technological backwardness. A leading Hungarian economist, Ivan T. Berend, gave one striking example: whereas in 1972 Hungary paid the equivalent of 800 Ikarus buses (a major export item) for one million tons of Soviet oil, in 1984 the price was the equivalent of 4,000 buses (*International Herald Tribune*, 18 June). In 1984, 53 percent of Hungary's trade was with the socialist countries, 32 percent with the Soviet Union alone; 35 percent of trade was with the advanced capitalist countries, and 12 percent with the developing countries. Oil, natural gas, coal, and electricity account for 47 percent of the imports from the Soviet Union. Government spokesmen assert the necessity of greater socialist economic integration, but Hungarian representatives at the fortieth session of the CMEA, held in Warsaw during June, argued (along with the East Germans) that the country needed to buy Western technology to escape its economic doldrums. In its pursuit of Western markets and know-how, the regime is reaching for innovative solutions. A new joint venture announced in January involved the creation by West German and Hungarian partners of a new cosmetics firm, in which the former hold 51 percent of the shares.

Hungarian reforms in the direction of a socialist market economy have drawn much international attention. The regime has promulgated various measures to foster private initiative and provide a legal framework for small-scale entrepreneurship. These measures alter only marginally the statist character of the economy; 98 percent of the means of production are public property, and 96 percent of the labor force is employed in the socialist sector, which accounts for 95 percent of the national product. Since 1982, when the relevant law was passed, some 35,000 small private enterprises and contractual ventures have materialized employing 350,000 people (*Magyar Hirlap*, 30 April). Of these, the "economic work collectives" have been the most controversial, for they allow groups of workers (up to thirty, although the actual average is five) to operate independent production units in their enterprises outside of normal working hours. Their productivity is reported to be 30–50 percent higher than during regular work time, and earnings are 2.5 to 3 times higher on an hourly basis. Some 90 percent of the members in the economic work collectives have kept their full-time jobs as well. The trade unions and the heavy industry sector in particular have shown some hostility to these new ventures (which do not have to set up trade union committees), claiming that they draw off the worker's energy from his principal job and that they widen income differentials. One official response has been the imposition of a special tax on the small enterprises, reducing their net income by some 10–12 percent (Budapest Television, 29 January; *FBIS*, 31 January).

When the members of these private enterprises are added to the 150,000 private farmers and shopkeepers, it appears that 10 percent of the labor force earns all or part of its income outside the socialist sector. In addition to this "second economy," there exists a "third economy": the illegal provision of goods and services, which is estimated to generate at least 20 percent of total personal income as unreported earnings. The economic and social aspects of these activities provoke much expert and public debate. It is generally recognized that wage-earners are driven to legal and illegal second employment by the recent decline in real wages (*Magyar Nemzet*, 9 March; *RFE Research*, 6 April).

The government is proceeding to increase the autonomy and internal democracy of enterprises in both the industrial and agricultural sectors, hoping that this will improve productivity. The new system of enterprise democracy, to be phased in over two years beginning 1 January 1985, provides for three distinct models. Enterprises in key industries and those providing public services will remain under the authority of a ministry, and their managers will continue to be centrally appointed, although some may acquire a managerial council with limited terms of reference. This model will apply to 20–25 percent of enterprises, totaling about 35 percent of the labor force. Smaller enterprises employing 300 to 500 workers are given the option of electing, directly or indirectly, their management; candidates will have to demonstrate their political reliability. In the third model, enterprises may choose to be run by enterprise councils, which will select the managers and exercise certain managerial rights. The councils will consist in equal parts of elected workers and of the manager and his appointees; the party, the Communist Youth League, and the trade unions are required actively to participate in the operation of this model. The early stage in the implementation of this new system has been marked by some confusion in party ranks and by delays and uncertainty in the enterprises. In some industries the managers, after preliminary classification, have asked to rejoin the presumably more secure embrace of ministerial authority (*Népszabadság*, 20 May).

In the agricultural sector, workers in producers' cooperatives have been free to elect their managers and to opt for a wage system that rewards productivity. The self-governing model was extended to state farms as well in 1985, by way of enterprise councils or delegate or membership meetings. These councils and meetings will elect the manager by secret ballot. The state farms are to gain greater operating autonomy, while remaining under the ultimate control of the Ministry for Agriculture and Food; a National Association of State Farms has been set up to coordinate their activities.

A law on dishonest business practices, enacted to take effect 1 January 1986, is designed to protect consumers by prohibiting unfair competition.

Social and Cultural Affairs. The creation of socialist man remains an elusive goal. A survey of the political attitudes of students at the Budapest Technical University found widespread disenchantment with politics, and a "conscious ideological commitment to socialism" only among 15–20 percent of the respondents (*Felsöoktatási Szemle*, November 1984; *RFE Research*, 29 December 1984). Seventy-five percent saw little progress toward democracy in Hungary, while 40 percent felt that the existing political system did not provide adequate means for expression of the popular will. A majority expressed reservations about CMEA's benefit to Hungary; about the effectiveness of the media in reporting, particularly on Soviet affairs (the remedial function of foreign broadcasts was noted); and about the possibility for improvement in the situation of Hungarian minorities in neighboring countries. The majority of students condemned materialism and corruption, expressed little interest in religion, noted the persistence of social stratification, was dissatisfied with ideological education and the activities of the Communist Youth League, and felt that an engineer did not need to be a convinced Marxist.

Partly in response to such attitudes, the regime is reforming the teaching of Marxism-Leninism in all schools and universities to include the critical analysis of bourgeois philosophical trends and contemporary capitalism. It is also introducing a new course in postsecondary institutions on Hungarian history since World War II (*Népszabadság*, 6 February).

The cultural intelligentsia is a key source of political tension. The party's Educational Working Group has forcefully reasserted the need for cultural output committed to socialist values and has criticized artists and writers for neglecting these goals in favor of national values and interests (*Kritika*, October 1984; *RFE Research*, 8 March). Much of the controversy revolves around the fate of the Hungarian minorities, a problem that the regime has belatedly acknowledged, notably at the party congress as well as in academic research. Sándor Csoóri, a prominent writer and leading figure in the neopopulist intellectual movement, was blacklisted for having written that the single-party system fails to protect minority rights. The critique appeared in his introduction to Slovak-Hungarian dissident Miklós Duray's book *Kutyaszorító* (In a bind), published in New York. Several leading members of the Writers' Union, including István Csurka, threatened to resign in protest. In November 1984 the economist György Krassó, 52, was placed under strict police surveillance for unauthorized publishing activities; twelve leading dissidents protested in a petition to the preparatory meeting of the European Cultural Forum, and close to 300 people signed a petition on 14 December 1984 protesting police harassment of the opposition figures. In January poet Gáspár Nagy was forced to resign from the Writers' Union for having written and published a poem honoring Imre Nagy, who had been prime minister during the 1956 revolution and was subscquently executed and buried in a secret place. The police also have been harassing members of the Catholic "basic communities" and seizing their publications. Copies of an illegal translation of a book about Raoul Wallenberg were confiscated. In December 1984, members of a punk rock band were jailed for singing allegedly anticommunist songs. A peaceful march of young people took place in Budapest on 15 March, the traditional national holiday commemorating the 1848 revolution, which is not officially recognized by the regime. In the summer some 45 intellectuals of various tendencies met for two days at a secretly organized gathering in Monor, near Budapest, to debate issues ranging from the Hungarian minorities to alcoholism. Dissident intellectuals also organized a counterconference to coincide with the opening of the European Cultural Forum (see below).

The authorities have responded to these manifestations of dissent and social unrest with various preventive measures. Interior Minister István Horváth warned in no uncertain terms that there were limits to the regime's tolerance (*Népszabadság*, 2 March). A new decree gives police the power to search on suspicion of a breach of regulations (*Magyar Közlöny*, 21 November 1984). Stiffer penalties, including corrective labor, are to be imposed for vagrancy—which encompasses people without regular employment who earn a living from extralegal pursuits. Another new decree of the Interior Ministry gives the police authority to take "coercive measures" against residents over the age of 16 whose behavior regularly endangers the internal order; the measure aims to prevent the commission of criminal acts, and penalties range from police supervision to banishment for a maximum of two years from the regular place of residence (*Magyar Közlöny*, 20 July; *JPRS*, 13 September). Although dissident intellectuals receive the most public attention, the majority of those charged with "incitement" are in fact workers. In a television interview, union leader Sándor Gáspár attributed the slackening in labor discipline to irritation with price increases and widening disparities in income (Budapest Television, 9 October; *FBIS*, 15 October).

Measures to further recognize the special problems of ethnic minorities in Hungary are linked to the more overt manifestation of dissatisfaction with the fate of Hungarian minorities abroad. The Academic Society for the Propagation of Knowledge has established a National Council of Nationalities to assist in the education of ethnic groups. In May the PPF set up an advisory National Gypsy Council. The close to 400,000-strong gypsy community in Hungary has high birth and crime rates and is subject to widespread prejudice.

Foreign Affairs. In foreign policy, Hungary faithfully follows the Soviet Union's lead with regard to disarmament and other East-West issues. At the same time the regime tries to foster orderly diplomatic and commercial relations with both East and West. The party's foreign affairs spokesman, Mátyás Szürös, has acknowledged that "certain doubts persist concerning the independence and efficiency of Hungarian foreign policy." He observed that because of historical, geopolitical, and economic factors Hungary was not self-sufficient and the country pursued a socialist foreign policy with national characteristics (*Külpolitika*, 4; *FBIS*, 17 October).

On 8 May, at the Human Rights Conference in Ottawa (an offshoot of the CSCE Madrid review), Hungarian spokesmen denounced nationalism and the forced assimilation of ethnic minorities. Hungary, they noted, was particularly concerned about minority rights because of the large Hungarian communities living in neighboring countries, who should serve as a bridge for friendship and cooperation. Hungary supported two Yugoslav resolutions on national minority rights at the conference, which concluded with no consensus on any issue (*RFE Research*, 21 June).

The European Cultural Forum, another offshoot of the Madrid review, brought together delegations from the 35 Helsinki Final Act signatories in Budapest during 15 October–25 November. The Hungarian hosts were intent on presenting a favorable image of the country, focusing the conference on noncontroversial themes, and preventing disturbances by excluding unauthorized participants. The forum nevertheless opened amid controversy regarding the plan of the International Federation of Helsinki Monitoring Groups to hold an independent cultural symposium with the participation of dissident intellectuals. The authorities prevented the meeting from taking place as scheduled in a Budapest hotel, prompting Western protests. The symposium was reconvened without official interference in a private residence, where intellectuals from many countries discussed issues ranging from censorship to the problems of Hungarian minorities. Hungarian dissidents also delivered to Western delegates a statement describing restrictions on cultural freedom in Hungary.

At the official forum, several Hungarian and Western participants addressed the problems of national minorities and the cultural oppression of Hungarian minorities in Eastern Europe (*RFE Research*, 27 November). Hungary, East Germany, Poland, and the Soviet Union sponsored a draft proposal on "guarantees of the exercise of cultural rights by national minorities." The eight hundred delegates discussed a multitude of cultural topics, but the conference ended without any formal agreement; even an innocuous Hungarian compromise resolution was vetoed by Romania.

Despite Hungary's official endorsement of Soviet positions on major political issues, Hungarian-American relations are relatively positive. Kenneth Adelman, director of the U.S. Arms Control and Disarmament Agency, passed through Budapest in January to brief the Hungarians on the American approach to disarmament. In the course of a "private" visit (30 January–9 February) to the United States, Politburo member Ferenc Havasi met President Reagan, Vice-President Bush, Secretary of State Shultz, and trade officials, as well as businessmen. U.S.-Hungarian trade has more than doubled since 1979, and in 1984 Hungary enjoyed its first surplus. In June President Reagan recommended extension of Hungary's most-favored-nation status, noting Budapest's relatively constructive approach to emigration. Secretary of State Shultz visited Budapest on 16 December.

Anglo-Hungarian relations also have been evolving favorably. Foreign Minister Péter Várkonyi visited London during 5–7 March in quest of more intensive bilateral contacts and trade, and he met with Prime Minister Thatcher. Labour Party leader Neil Kinnock went to Hungary in May. Positive assessments of bilateral relations also issued from General Secretary Kádár's visit to Britain during 31 October–1 November.

Frequent high-level contacts continued between Budapest and Vienna, including Prime Minister Lázár's fifth visit to Austria on 21–23 February. Austria is Hungary's second Western trading partner after West Germany, and cooperation extends to many spheres. In May, agreement was reached on establishment of a joint German-language radio station in Hungary to serve the large number of German-speaking visitors. Hungary also plans to link its cable-television network to a West German–Austrian–Swiss satellite TV program and other Austrian programs. Secretariat member János Berecz commented that it would be senseless to prohibit reception of the growing number of satellite TV programs, even though these were instruments in the ideological struggle (*Népszabadság*, 11 May).

West German foreign minister Hans-Dietrich Genscher visited Budapest during 23–25 June and met with Kádár as well as church leaders. Bilateral relations were deemed constructive, notably in the area of trade and economic cooperation. At the invitation of the HSWP Central Committee, SPD chairman Willy Brandt went to Budapest on 27 June, and SPD vice-chairman Hans-Jochen Vogel visited in July. Other foreign contacts include the official visit of Finnish prime minister Kalevi Sorsa during 9–11 December 1984, which confirmed the traditionally friendly relations and the favorable development of trade since a 1974 agreement; a visit by Norwegian prime minister Kaare Willoch from 17 to 19 January; Várkonyi's visit to Algeria during 27–30 April; and Prime Minister Lázár's trip to Japan during 17–20 September, which produced agreement on expansion of trade and on a second joint enterprise. Defense Minister István Oláh led a military delegation to Kuwait and India in late October.

Hungary became in April the first Warsaw Pact state to join two affiliates of the World Bank, the International Finance Corporation and the International Development Association. The purpose was to facilitate Hungary's participation in Third World development projects.

Communist Relations. The economic problems of Hungary and the Soviet bloc appear to be the single most important issue in Hungarian-Soviet relations. Soviet party leader Mikhail Gorbachev sent his hearty congratulations to Kádár on the latter's election as general secretary, and *Pravda* reported favorably on the HSWP congress and the party's innovative approach to economic difficulties (*Pravda*, 30 March; *RFE Research*, 27 April). Immediately after the congress, Prime Minister Lázár led a delegation including Havasi and other economic specialists to Moscow. Their principal purpose was to conclude an agreement on a "long-term program to the year 2000 for development of economic and scientific-technological cooperation" (*Magyar Hirlap*, 1 June). The program encompasses collaboration in the utilization of microelectronics, automated production, nuclear energy, and biotechnology; production specialization; Hungarian participation in the "reorganization and technical renewal of the food industry and agricultural enterprises of the USSR"; and, in general, trade expansion and the "multilateral intertwining of the national economies."

Kádár met Gorbachev at Chernenko's funeral in February and at the Warsaw Pact extension ceremonies in April. He also made a "working visit" to Moscow on 24 September; the resulting communiqué expressed satisfaction with bilateral relations and agreement on foreign policy questions. Kádár was accompanied by Central Committee department head Géza Kotai, who reported subsequently that the Hungarian economic reforms were regarded positively in Moscow (MTI, 4 October; *RFE Research*, 14 October). On 23 September, CPSU Central Committee secretary Viktor Nikonov led a delegation of the Supreme Soviet to Hungary and praised the unique features of Hungarian agriculture (*Izvestia*, 25 September; *RFE Research*, 14 October). Other Hungarian visits to the Soviet Union included that of a military delegation led by Defense Minister Oláh during 11–15 June; of Foreign Minister Várkonyi in early July; of Berecz to attend the World Youth Festival and hold talks with CPSU Central Committee secretary Boris Ponomarev in late July; and of Szürös on 31 July to discuss urgent questions of cooperation with Ponomarev.

With regard to the discussions on extension of the Warsaw Treaty, Deputy Foreign Minister István Roska noted that this required the reconciliation of the members' different interests but that these particular interests were fully compatible with the common goal of building socialism and that all pact members respected the principle of nonintervention in each other's affairs (*Népszava*, 2 March). His remarks were reprinted in *Neues Deutschland* on 5 March. At its 29 April session, the HSWP Central Committee approved extension of the Warsaw Treaty, noting that it was necessitated by the existence of NATO and of dangers threatening peace; the Warsaw Pact proposal for simultaneous dissolution of the two alliances was still valid, said the communiqué (Radio Budapest, 29 April; *FBIS*, 30 April).

There had been "no significant change" in Hungarian-Romanian relations, reported Szürös in a Radio Budapest interview on 14 November (*RFE Research*, 27 November). These relations could be much better, he said, with the greatest difficulties being in "direct human contacts and their cultivation." The Hungarian minority in Romania officially numbers 1,770,000, or some 7.8 percent of the population (*RFE Research*, 14 November), although unofficial estimates are higher. It shares in the general economic distress of the Romanian population but is also the target of special repressive and discriminatory measures that have brought international criticism on the Ceauşescu regime. The HSWP's message of greeting to the Romanian party congress (19–22 November 1984) included a reference to the Hungarian minority and the desirability of facilitating its contacts with Hungary (*Népszabadság*, 20 November 1984; *RFE Research*, 29 December 1984). Coincidentally, the Hungarian press published favorable commentary on the more conciliatory approach to the Hungarians taken in the early postwar period by the Petru Groza regime (*Magyar Hirlap*, 22 November 1984).

Foreign Minister Várkonyi met Ceauşescu and Romanian Foreign Minister Stefan Andrei in Bucharest during January. Szürös subsequently observed that "serious concerns and tensions" occasionally arose in Hungarian-Romanian relations; he reported that the Romanians had closed their consulate in Debrecen in December 1984, ostensibly for economic reasons (Radio Budapest, 13 February; *RFE Research*, 16 May). Romanian Prime Minister Constantin Dacalescu paid an official visit to Budapest during 23–24 April, and it was reported in Budapest (but not in Bucharest) that Kádár and Lázár had referred to the potentially positive function of national minorities in friendly relations and to Hungary's willingness to expand bilateral relations on the basis of past agreements, notably the Kádár-Ceauşescu accord concluded at Debrecen in 1977 (Radio Budapest, 24 April; *RFE Research*, 16 May). The official communiqué made no reference to the minority issue. The Hungarian media have reported on Romanian Radio's abolition of regional Hungarian programs and dismissal of their staffs (*RFE Research*, 21 June). Romanian authorities have also taken measures to prevent reception of Hungarian television programs in Transylvania. The Romanian regime's measures to isolate the Hungarian minority and reduce its cultural and educational facilities in the Hungarian language, the brutal treatment of minority intellectuals, and harassment at border crossings all have inflamed popular opinion in Hungary, but officials in Budapest profess impotence.

Hungarian relations with the rigid Husák regime are also marked by certain tensions. Here, too, the minority issue has come to the fore. Close to 600,000 Hungarians, some 11 percent of the population, live in Slovakia, and the alleged inadequacy of their educational and cultural facilities has sparked both domestic and foreign criticism. The rearrest in May 1984 of a prominent minority spokesman, Miklós Duray, was denounced by dissident intellectuals in Hungary, who formed a "Duray Committee" to pursue the cause. A joint Czechoslovak-Hungarian project, the partially completed Gabcikovo-Nagymaros hydroelectric dam on the Danube, prompted widespread protest in Hungary over potential ecological damage, but after much hesitation the government has decided to proceed with its completion (*Népszabadság*, 16 August). At the conclusion of party and state leader Gústav Husák's working visit to Budapest on 27 November 1984, the official communiqué expressed satisfaction with expanding trade relations (Czechoslovakia is Hungary's fourth largest trading partner, after the Soviet Union, West Germany, and East Germany) and called for "consistent enforcement of Lenin's nationalities policy" (*Népszabadság*, 28 November 1984). Kádár paid a return visit to Husák on 30 September.

The Hungarian press has been reporting favorably on economic reforms in the People's Republic of China, some of which indeed bear a similarity to the Hungarian model (*Magyar Hirlap*, 5 February). Although there are still no interparty relations, diplomatic and commercial contacts have multiplied. Chinese Vice-Premier Li Peng visited Budapest from 27 May to 1 June and had a "cordial and friendly" meeting with Németh. Trade missions have been exchanged, and a trade agreement and industrial production cooperation agreement were signed in June.

Interparty contacts included a visit in early May by the Nicaraguan Sandinista leader Daniel Ortega, who was given assurances of solidarity and support; and the signing of a cooperation agreement between the HSWP and the Arab Socialist Ba'ath party of Syria in June.

Bennett Kovrig
University of Toronto

Poland

Population. 37,100,000
Party. Polish United Workers' Party (Polska Zjednoczona Partia Robotnicza; PZPR)
Founded. 1948
Membership. 2,112,000 members and candidate members (*TL*, 13 June 1985)
First Secretary. Army Gen. Wojciech Jaruzelski
Politburo. 13 full members: Wojciech Jaruzelski, Kazimierz Barcikowski, Tadeusz Czechowicz, Jozef Czyrek, Zofia Grzyb, Stanislaw Kalkus, Hieronim Kubiak, Zbigniew Messner, Stanislaw Opalko, Tadeusz Porebski, Jerzy Romanik, Albin Siwak, Marian Wozniak; 6 candidate members: Stanislaw Bejger, Jan Glowczyk, Czeslaw Kiszczak, Wlodzimierz Mokrzyszczak, Marian Orzechowski, Florian Siwicki
Secretariat. 8 members: Henryk Bednarski, Jozef Czyrek, Jan Glowczyk, Zbigniew Michalek, Wlodzimierz Mokrzyszczak, Marian Orzechowski, Tadeusz Porebski, Waldemar Swirgon
Central Committee. 200 full and 70 candidate membrs
Status. Ruling party
Last Congress. Extraordinary Ninth, 14–20 July 1981, in Warsaw
Last Election. 1985, the regime claimed that 78.81 percent of Poles had voted; an independent estimate indicates that not more than 60 percent voted

Publications. *Trybuna ludu* (*TL*), party daily; *Nowe drogi* and *Ideologia i polityka*, party monthlies; *Zycie partii*, fortnightly party organ; *Zolnierz wolnosci*, army daily. Polska Agencja Prasowa (PAP) is the official news agency.

In December 1981, when the Polish military staged a coup d'état to preclude free elections, it promised a rapid return to socioeconomic development. This return allegedly was to facilitate political reforms that would provide an opportunity for citizens to participate in decisionmaking. It would also lead to a general economic restructuring to halt the trend toward irrational and wasteful use of resources, low productivity, and numerous other deficiencies. The military dictatorship committed itself to an economic course that would prevent yet another cycle of "crisis, reform, and stagnation"; build modern industry; and ensure stabilized social progress. The new program claimed a rational foundation that advocated practical solutions to all social and economic inadequacies.

Poland indeed is a society in transition: it appears to be rapidly degenerating into a Third World country. The economic reform of 1982–1984 has not changed the emphasis on heavy industry, which consumes excessive amounts of fuel and raw materials. This highly centralized economy, essentially a Stalinist system, has already triggered several crises and is likely to produce another. Poland is locked into the Soviet-dominated system, enforced by CMEA, whose international constraints make comprehensive economic reform impossible.

Also, the regime headed by General Jaruzelski has yet to offer political concessions to its people. Political power is centralized in the hands of the ruling elite, whose primary interest is staying in power rather than changing the system. According to the members of the "Poland 2000" committee, the country can look forward to nothing other than a "general national catastrophe." The population is apathetic, its standard of living continues to decline, life expectancy is declining, severe ecological problems continue, and the ruling Communist party has no program to avert a social catastrophe. This was the ambience of Polish politics in 1985.

The Ruling Party. Succession of a dynamic leader in the Kremlin has ended a relatively lengthy period of interregnum in Moscow. Preoccupied with their own internal problems, the Soviet Communists had shown an unprecedented tolerance toward Solidarity and the four-year-long process of "normalization" in Poland. General Jaruzelski's dialogues with the Roman Catholic Church, amnesty for the leaders of Solidarity, and unorthodox economic reforms, including an enormous growth of the private sector, were in sharp contrast with the practices of the Hungarian and Czechoslovak leaderships after the 1956 and 1968 revolts. Lack of a strong and clear policy direction from the USSR created favorable conditions for Poland's rulers to practice political restraint.

Gorbachev's accession ended five years of decentralization within the Soviet bloc. When Jaruzelski and the new Soviet leader met in April 1985, Poland reportedly was told to complete "normalization" by the end of the year. Gorbachev has given priority to synchronizing Soviet domestic and foreign policies, including termination of political "voluntarism" in Eastern Europe. Political decisions of the communist leadership in Poland reflect a high degree of pressure from Moscow, and consequently a return at least in part to ideological orthodoxy at the cost of political flexibility and realism.

In the past year, discussion of such themes as "Polish socialism" and "socialist pluralism" has almost disappeared from the press in Poland. Officially sanctioned topics include the antinational and anticommunist operations of the political underground; the Leninist concept of a worker-peasant alliance; ideological confrontation; the individual and his responsibilities to the "socialist" nation; fundamental principles of Marxist-Leninist teachings about the party; conditions for building "socialism"; peaceful coexistence; the Polish-Soviet alliance, a guarantee of Poland's independence; and the threat to world peace from policies of the United States, with its "imperialist goals and neocolonial tactics." Consequently, the political cleavage between the people and its rulers increased during 1985, and harsh criticism was voiced by individuals, social groups, and the Roman Catholic Church.

Party activities were concentrated around five Central Committee plenums, each focusing on a selected issue of national importance. The eighteenth session that met on 21–22 December 1984 was devoted primarily to implementation of the economic plan for 1985. Another theme concerned the fortieth anniversary of the incorporation of the so-called Oder-Neisse territories into Poland.

Economic problems were of paramount importance and were a source of political instability. In recent years it has become fashionable to discuss economic equilibrium, that is, a rough balance between supply and demand. This is not a new problem in the Polish economy, and response in the past involved sudden and substantial price increases for basic commodities. This crude and socially provocative tool triggered several major political shocks that had threatened the stability of the communist regime. There is nothing new in Jaruzelski's strategy of restoring economic equilibrium and restricting inflation. It continues to rely on price increases and austerity. However, the regime has a better understanding of the strong relationship between the social situation in the country and its economic problems. For this reason, the party is extremely sensitive to social moods and seeks acceptance of unpopular economic solutions before implementing them. This approach enables the party to test popular reaction and, if necessary, reduce the rate of price increase (or delay increases for several months). It also creates the impression that unpopular issues are being subjected to broad social consultation.

Besides the economic problems that complicate recovery, the country has entered an era when the labor force is exceptionally small and the numbers in pre- and postproductive ages are growing rapidly. During 1985, employment increased by only 37,000 while persons of preproduction age grew by approximately 140,000 and of postproduction age by 110,000 (*TL*, 11–12 December 1984).

This situation is further complicated by the necessity to direct almost all gains into the reproductive sphere, particularly education and health care. There is, in effect, no practical possibility of increasing employment in production. In addition, larger supplies of raw materials and energy were not expected to exceed 1.5 percent. The days of an extended economy are over, and the eighteenth plenum informed the public that growth in the coming years will be modest, if it occurs at all (*Zycie gospodarcze*, 6 January).

In short, the party acknowledged the existence of "objective difficulties," such as limited raw-material resources, excessive indebtedness, an unfavorable balance of trade, manpower shortages, lack of disciplined labor, and a high birthrate. It recommended the importation of labor-saving technology (automation); labor discipline; an end to "barbaric wastefulness" in the use of buildings, machinery, and transportation; and an increase in exports. This effort, frequently referred to as the "rationalization movement," is expected to guide the Polish economy between 1986 and 1990 (*FBIS, Eastern Europe* [*EEU*]-84-248, vol. 2, 24 December 1984).

Despite its admission that the roots of Poland's crises are internal and predominantly the product of inefficient centralized planning and management, the eighteenth plenum blamed the United States and certain other Western countries. It estimated that in 1984 losses due to economic restrictions had increased by nearly $3 billion and had passed the $15 billion mark (*TL*, 22 December 1984). As a countermeasure, the plenum recommended increasing economic, scientific, and technical cooperation with bloc countries, especially the USSR. This economic "reorientation" was regarded as a strategic move toward conditions for stable development over the next fifteen to twenty years. It should guarantee supplies of raw materials and energy as well as export markets. In practice, this means that the 1984 Long-Term Agreement on Economic, Scientific, and Technological Cooperation with the Soviet Union provides Moscow with politicoeconomic controls that define the main direction of Polish economic development and organically link the two economies.

In its lopsided position on industrial development and heavy industry in particular, the eighteenth plenum paid no more than lip service to consumer-oriented industries, services, housing construction, and agriculture. A relatively good crop and fairly healthy agriculture over the past three years undoubtedly have contributed to this negligent attitude, despite the continuing need to import grain and fodder in the millions of tons. Also, in an attempt to deceive the public, the plenum's analysis of economic problems was conducted without any reference to statistical data or other basic facts. The brief concluding resolution commented that "further progress was made in 1984" and that the "upward trends in production acquired a permanent character" (Warsaw Domestic Service, 22 December 1984; *FBIS*, *EEU*-24-248, vol. 2, 24 December 1984).

The basic purpose of the nineteenth plenum, on 13–14 May 1985, was to demonstrate how the internal situation had stabilized. The party felt confident enough to address the most assertive group in Poland, the intelligentsia. Internal emigration and the general apathy of intellectuals had become negative factors, hampering scientific-technological development. The regime realized that a solution to the country's economic and social problems will be impossible without active involvement of the most creative group within society.

Ninety-five percent of Poland's intellectual cadres have been educated during the past 40 years. Numerically, the intelligentsia is the third largest social group; approximately 3 million strong, it includes 350,000 engineers and about 1 million technicians employed by industry and the faculty and staff of 89 university-type educational institutions, 73 research institutes at the Polish Academy of Sciences, 122 scientific research centers at various universities, and 141 research and development units and central laboratories (*TL*, 10 May). The artistic community now has about 45,000 members, and some 70,000 individuals work in cultural institutions. The journalistic community totals about 9,000 people; the number of doctors and dentists approaches 100,000; and there are 140,000 people employed in central and local government. Another 527,000 are employed by various educational institutions, including 56,000 academics at 89 state universities (ibid.).

At the nineteenth plenum, the party appealed to intellectuals by promising a long-term program for development of Polish culture, including significant investments in visual media and book production. It also promised to establish a Central Research Fund (ibid.). The regime committed itself to raising the standard of living of Polish intellectuals, with better research and scientific equipment, access to scientific literature, and contacts in the international arena. In 1985 Poland allocated 2 percent of its national income to scientific research and development, and the nineteenth plenum recommended an increase to 3.5 percent by 1990.

On the other hand, the party delineated strict limits to creative and innovative work. First, intellectuals must base their activities on the theoretical-methodological principles of Marxism-Leninism and must display "patriotic attitudes" rather than "antisocialist political" ones that stimulate "reactionary slogans from distant historical periods." Intellectuals would be permitted to work only if they were "allied" with the working class, i.e., the party and its ideology. Specifically, the party threatened to suppress any manifestation of "ideological disorientation," "cosmopolitan gazing to the West," division into "we—the intelligentsia, and you—the party," and attempts to follow "mobility and petit bourgeois models" (Warsaw Domestic Service, 14 May; *FBIS*, *EEU*-85-094, vol. 1, 15 May).

Second, the party demanded immediate and active intellectual cooperation in "strengthening the state and promoting the process of socialist democracy." "Distrust and hesitation should be transformed into civic commitment," reads a resolution of the nineteenth plenum (*TL*, 17 May). The intellectuals as a group would be rehabilitated and forgiven for their support of Solidarity, provided they promoted the interests of the communist state. The party, however, did not request that the intellectuals commit themselves to the official ideology. The resolution stated that "no matter what views and philosophy he or she professes, everyone who reliably fulfills his duties and respects the law" would be allowed to carry out professional duties (ibid.).

The Central Committee met again on 12–13 June at its twentieth plenum, devoted to the "Problems of Raising the Effectiveness of Party Political-Organizational Activity." This meeting signaled a hardening of the political line, a result of Soviet pressure and the apparent failure of economic and social reforms. The Jaruzelski team had gradually drifted toward neo-Stalinism.

In the name of "self-purification" and ideological strengthening of party ranks, the twentieth plenum found it necessary to promote discipline, a militant attitude, and ideological ardor. Every member of the party was instructed to combat political apathy and "alien hostile ideology" to assure an appropriate standing for Marxism-Leninism and to guarantee the "socialist" transformation of Polish society. Principles of political pluralism were decisively rejected on the grounds that Marxism-Leninism is not simply one of many philosophies, but the only "scientific" socioeconomic philosophy (*TL*, 13 June). Speeches clearly indicated a return to narrow-minded orthodoxy, opposition to any kind of reform, and aggressive penetration and domination of all aspects of social life (*Rzeczpospolita*, 17 June).

Indirectly, the plenum endorsed a "better than expert" cadre policy and recommended appointments of individuals who were ideologically reliable, "forward-looking and dedicated to the party's program." With special apprehensiveness, the cadre situation was summarized in professional communities and universities "in which power was taken over by people unfriendly" to the party or by those whose attitude was "incorrect" (ibid.). In the opinion of the plenum, the party should initiate a campaign to mobilize all party members according to the principles of domestic "socialism" and thereby mobilize society to counter the "destructive influence and designs of forces and people who are our adversaries, adversaries of the socialist state" (*TL*, 13 June).

The twentieth plenum showed that Jaruzelski and other leaders were aware of the party's ideological weakness and realized that the period of relative political tolerance in the name of "class alliance" and national reconciliation had come to an end. Obviously, the ruling group concluded that a liberal policy had failed to rally society behind the regime and that the more drastic measures originally recommended by the hard-liners were mandatory to revitalize Polish society. As usual, the Communists turned to the old and discredited tools of Stalinism to increase their effectiveness. In the past, such a return to orthodoxy had always been followed by riots and demonstrations. The most immediate effect of the shift was that the party became more isolated in a social and political sense. The aim of the twentieth plenum was clearly the tightening of political control, in order to intimidate society.

This political militancy of Jaruzelski reflected his inability to activate society into the "political realism" in which people accept the communist system regardless of personal political convictions. His new approach was an attempt to build political consensus on a geostrategic necessity that leaves the people with no alternative but to follow the Soviet-like system. Such regional fatalism was employed in December 1981 to justify the imposition of martial law, and its logic included the argument that the only way for Poland to exist as a nominally independent state was to remain communist-ruled: therefore, it was patriotic to support the regime. Additionally, the party made it clear that no real liberalization or improvement in the living standard will be possible without public support for the current system.

The entire political strategy of Jaruzelski is founded on the misconception that a benevolent approach to opposition will inspire the nation to accept and follow him, even without the two-way national dialogue he pledged four years ago. Frustrated by lack of popular support and by intimidation from Moscow, Jaruzelski escaped into the realm of irrelevant ideological evangelizing, which precluded the reconciliation with the people that is necessary to overcome the crisis. Equally detrimental to internal stability and development was the shift toward communist fundamentalism, which reduced Poland's room to maneuver in both domestic and international affairs.

The only positive effect of the current preoccupation with ideological matters is the party's disengagement from daily political-administrative affairs. At the twenty-first plenum on 3 August, it was agreed in principle to give more voice to the government, including parliament (the Sejm). It is still too early to determine whether this move was only cosmetic. The party is interested in a division of responsibilities that would allow it to be the umpire of the communist system, while the government would be directly responsible for management of political and economic affairs.

On the pretense of enhancing "social parliamentarianism," Jaruzelski implied that his regime is the rightful heir to Solidarity (before its "deviation contrary to socialism"), and he appealed to the nation to support the elections "despite bitterness, various sore points, reservations, and doubts, and to refrain from participating in adventurist actions, rejection of antistate slogans, and choose the path of calm, work, and observance of law." Calling the democratic opposition a "pathological example of political madness," while at the same time competing with the underground for influence, Jaruzelski described the Sejm as a sovereign body representing the entire nation. The Sejm was credited with implementing such reforms as the people's council and regional self-government, employees' self-management in state enterprises, the law to counter alcoholism and prevent drug addiction, and so on (*TL*, 6 August).

Considerable emphasis was given to the democratic characteristics of the Sejm: its openness, representation of major groups within society, professionalism, expertise, and control over allocation of funds. At the same time, Jaruzelski reassured voters that the party would not assume supremacy over the Sejm, but would limit its leading role in representative organs to votes controlled by deputies who are members of the ruling party. It should be noted that the existing electoral law guarantees Communists at least a majority in the Sejm; party members occupy about 70 percent of seats at present.

Finally, the plenum defined the Sejm as a platform where the foundation could be laid for a hardworking economy and a higher standard of living, and where protection of the natural environment and social welfare issues would be discussed and solutions worked out, giving the people a chance to make their own choice. In the resolution concluding the twenty-first plenum, the party declared its commitment to improving democratic methods of government and promoting the role of the Sejm as the main instrument of national agreement (*TL*, 5 August).

It should be noted that this plenum was not the first occasion when the party expressed confidence in the political awareness of the people and adopted a resolution based on the consolidation and expansion of democracy. Since it is unlikely that the regime will risk liberalization before the economic crisis has been overcome, it seems safe to assume that realistic opportunities for a broader popular participation in governing are still far away, and the government, including the Sejm, will continue to be nothing more than a transmission belt between party and people.

Another piece of evidence pointing to the propagandistic nature of the twenty-first plenum is its apparent contradiction with conclusions advanced by the previous plenum, which had explicitly directed the party to staff key positions with trusted members of the *nomenklatura*. As he has done many times before, Jaruzelski applied a strategy of soft rhetoric combined with tough and determined action.

The last plenum of the year, the twenty-second, met on 5 and 11 November. Instead of contributing new ideas, it evaluated results of the national election held on 13 October and came to the conclusion that not only was the base of national accord broadening, but the election results had proven that social and political normalization and stabilization were permanent (*TL*, 6, 12 November 1985).

To sum up, the principal tasks of the party in 1985 were to create a facade of stability, recovery, democratization, ideological revival, and patriotic support for the regime. The actual strength of domestic opposition had been assessed independently by several government-sponsored and private groups, but their conclusions were ignored or discredited. While the party did indeed gain power, it practiced the art of self-deception and self-admiration, a political strategy adopted by two previous leaders, Wladyslaw Gomulka and Edward Gierek, on the eve of national revolts.

General Jaruzelski seems to be overly concerned with the Communist party, which he is trying to pattern after the principles of a military organization. So far he has been quite successful in reorganizing and strengthening the party, although he appears to assume that its reconstruction is synonymous with "normalization" of social and economic life. He has not yet saved Poland from the crisis, but gradually and consistently he has changed the style of party work and modified its profile. His party no longer consists of fat, opportunistic, and self-serving bureaucrats. Its distinctive feature is its accordance with the Leninist principle of a central group of militant individuals who place quality above quantity and perceive their primary duty as leading the way.

The party has been consolidating ideologically and organizationally. It has expelled more than 1 million members since 1980, and the purge continues. Members accused of violating party discipline and ideological unity, or bad management, or just laxity, are immediately expelled. On the average, several thousand per month are lost, which is regarded as a normal, if not a positive, sign. In order to form a militant frame of mind, the party consistently refers to its "combat readiness," "moral-political cohesion," "the struggle on the socioeconomic front," and similar slogans. It has overcome the traditional inertia and evolved into a lean, aggressive, and dedicated organization.

At the same time, however, Jaruzelski's program of dealing with the socioeconomic crisis has lacked clarity of purpose and determination in design and implementation. His reforms have failed. Instead of seeking alternatives and compromising with the opposition, he is applying to society the strategy he used to regenerate the party. He is tightening the screws in the hope that repressive measures will lead to social accord and general social consensus.

The Church. It is not a new phenomenon in Poland that consolidation of communist authority almost automatically has brought a negative effect to state-church relations. The party becomes more assertive, arrogant, and jealous of the church's political power, which is founded on the voluntary and spontaneous support of approximately 90 percent of the population. A secret poll conducted in Poland by the authorities indicated that 97 percent of the working class identifies itself as Catholic. When in trouble, the party is quick to approach the church and form a partnership to preserve social peace. When the regime concludes that it can rule alone, however, the partnership is dissolved, and the church is accused of political activism. This pattern of state-church relations started in 1945 and has been repeated several times in the four decades of post–World War II history.

Cooperation with the church has been a temporary, tactical exigency practiced by the communist state to consolidate its own power. Averse to pluralism and partnership, the Communists are never honest about sharing instruments of power, and the elimination of religion is the ultimate goal of communism.

Present polarization between the state and church has all the characteristics of the traditional pattern, with one important exception. For the first time since 1945, the church appears to welcome differences with the regime and is using confrontation cautiously to challenge the legitimacy of the communist system. This is a significant change from the earlier policy of acceptance and cooperation with communist power.

The primate, Jozef Cardinal Glemp, is regarded by the Poles as soft on communism. He described state-church relations as "peaceful coexistence," the lowest grade of social living together (Vienna Domestic Service, 13 March 1984; *FBIS*, *EEU*-84-053, 14 March 1984). The ideological rift between state and church is deep and, according to the church, it can no longer be bridged. The cardinal has ruled out reconciliation with the state, expressing hope that coexistence will not "exclude dialogue," but even if it does, the church should "fulfill [its] mission independently of the existing social system" (ibid.).

Marxist-Christian incompatibility is the essence of Poland's liberation theology. Its roots are in the Gospel of Jesus Christ, a message of freedom and a force for freedom from subjugation based on sin. Logically, the church advocates liberation from the numerous restrictions imposed by Marxism in ideological, economic, social, and political life. This subjugation makes it impossible for people to live in accordance with their dignity and to enjoy such basic human rights as freedom, justice, and love that are the gifts of God bequeathed to mankind without any conditions. Civil law, in consequence, has to support natural human rights, giving the church the right to propagate faith without constraints, including a right to pronounce moral judgments on issues concerning politics (Jozef Cardinal Glemp in his sermon on 21 August, Vatican City International Service; *FBIS*, *EEU*-85-168, 29 August). According to the church, the communist state in Poland is the embodiment of evil. Communism is a system "based on the notion of force" and professes materialistic views that exclude God. The exclusion of God results in the exclusion of basic human rights, a reduction of man to a subhuman, animal-like attachment to place of work. Government authorities, according to the cardinal, are actively engaged in "efforts to erase . . . the values that are most important, those connected with belief in God," and the political strategy of communism is to "postpone the final confrontation" with the church (*WP*, 27 August). Historically, it is the ambition of any communist system to eliminate all ideological and political alternatives to socialism, and, consequently, permanent accommodation between a communist state and the church is impossible. Social peace depends on respect for human rights, and that is something the communist authorities are inherently unable to provide anywhere, unless genuine national reconciliation were possible.

The church is guided by the assumption that the desire of people for liberation has become one of the fundamental phenomena of our epoch. Individuals have lost patience with passively endured exploitation, the inhuman burden of poverty, and the moral collapse of the state. Life in a communist state is a humiliation, a condition that justifies resistance against the regime.

The Polish government is presented by the church as lacking internal legitimacy. It has external legitimacy owing to the preponderance of Soviet power, but the people have no political organization representing their interests. The assumption that there is no Polish state has developed a crusading spirit among the clergy and has prompted the church to a policy of social intervention parallel with the state or even superseding the state. Poland, in the opinion of the church, has entered a period closely resembling the partitions at the end of the eighteenth century or the beginnings of Stalinism in 1948. Under such circumstances, patriotism is no longer linked to the authorities, and the church should lead the nation (*Tygodnik powszechny*, 10 March).

The official view expressed by the regime is that coexistence and cooperation between state and church is fully possible and even necessary. According to this view, the church has been slow to adapt to "socialism," but the meeting of Christianity and socialism is already unprecedented in scale and scope, with Polish patriotism providing the common denominator for both. Moreover, there are numerous areas where state and church activities overlap and positive joint action would be beneficial to society, since "socialist" values converge with certain religious values. The church is welcome to carry out its mission within the state; however, it should unconditionally recognize the supremacy of the state and refrain from involvement in politics, say the Communists (*Trybuna robotnicza*, 17 May).

The state, in effect, is asking the church for help in carrying out its socioeconomic functions. The church is asked to popularize a model patriotism that identifies national interest with communism and alliance with the USSR, strengthening observance of the law and consolidation of the system, as well as combating demoralization, alcoholism, and drug abuse. The authorities would like to exploit, for their own benefit, the enormous popularity and prestige of the church, while excluding Catholics from participation in the political life of the country. Like any other social organization, the party is striving to convert the church into an instrument of its domination.

Thus far, it has been impossible to determine "what is God's and what is Caesar's" in communist Poland. First of all, the authorities refuse to grant the Roman Catholic Church a special place, despite the fact that 95 percent of the population claim to be Catholic and about 80 percent attend church regularly. The authorities would like to reduce the Roman Catholic Church to the same role as that played by 34 smaller religious communities in Poland, which together represent less than 3 percent of the population. The church is accused of political ambitions, attempting to bring capitalism back to Poland, a "counterrevolutionary" attitude, and lack of tolerance for alternative views, including atheism.

The communist state is alarmed by the extent of church penetration into public life, by its degree of involvement outside the religious sphere, and by its judgment over official actions. Relations between those two institutions are presented as "correct," but in reality communist authorities already have adopted a roll-back approach to the activities of the church, insisting that they should be limited by the principles defined in the constitution (*Rzeczpospolita*, 26–27 January).

Written by communist authorities, the constitution provides for strict separation of state and church and speaks in favor of atheism, including atheistic education. Thus it provides the regime with legal grounds for discrimination against religion. A "confidential" document prepared for the Council of Ministers, and recently smuggled to the West, stressed the church's "unacceptable" presence in public life and concluded that the influence of religion should be eliminated outside the churches. Particularly annoying to the authorities is "religious proselytism" in universities, schools, businesses, artistic and intellectual circles, and health services, concludes the government (*Le Figaro*, 9 April).

Several attacks on the church in general, the pope, and selected priests appeared in the Polish press, despite the January trial of Father Jerzy Popieluszko's murderers. Tendentious reporting, selective presentation of facts, and flagrant abuse of the law by internal security forces are manifestations of a propaganda campaign, which, on the pretext of condemning militant priests, aims at the elimination of the church's social influence. The party and the church are again on a collision course.

The unprecedented public trial and conviction of the secret police officers who killed Father Popieluszko (their prison terms ranged from 14 to 25 years), have not improved relations with the church. Actually, during the trial an attempt was made to discredit the church, its bishops, and priests, and to equate the victim with his murderers. During the trial, Father Popieluszko was frequently depicted as an agent of counterrevolution and an advocate of terrorist methods to overthrow the political system. Some bishops were vilified as "Nazi collaborators," and, in general, the church was blamed for promoting antistate activities. In a concurrent trial, to further discredit the church, two priests were accused of attempted manslaughter (*Radio Free Europe Research, Poland*, 5 February).

The trial was no more than a cover-up, since it did not reveal who had ordered the priest's death (*NYT*, 9 February). In perspective, the entire affair was exploited by Jaruzelski to attack the church, purge the secret police, and outmaneuver hardliners within the party. In October, the underground press in Poland published Father Popieluszko's diary. It revealed that as early as December 1982, two years before his murder, he was being intimidated, shadowed, accused of possessing a submachine gun, threatened with 21 years in prison, and his apartment was bombed. When intimidation failed, he was murdered on 19 October 1984, just a few days after he noted in his diary: "I will not live to be old" (Paris AFP in English; *FBIS*, *EEU*-85-208, vol. 2, no. 208, 28 October 1985).

The trial of Father Popieluszko's killers has not ended police brutality in Poland; numerous incidents were reported in 1985. Because of its similarity to the Popieluszko case, the best publicized incident was the attack upon and torture of a young priest, Tadeusz Zalewski, in his home over Easter weekend (*Los Angeles Times*, 11 April). Other incidents involved beatings of Solidarity members, intellectuals, and American and French tourists and diplomats, but no arrests of their assailants have been announced.

Deterioration of state-church relations was evident in the substantial hardening of the Vatican's attitude toward Warsaw. In June, Foreign Minister Stefan Olszewski met with Pope John Paul II in Rome. The audience was unusually brief, and the pope rejected the Polish government's plan for the normalization of diplomatic relations with the Holy See. Instead of discussing international issues, the conversation focused on the violation of human rights in Poland, and the pope indicated his unwillingness to deal with Polish authorities as long as the repressions continued (BBC Report, no. 100/85, 24 June).

Equally unproductive was the state church summit between Cardinal Glemp and General Jaruzelski. Following the meeting, the government spokesman, Jerzy Urban, announced that the "state-church dialogue is in progress," but without any "change" in attitudes. The bishops, however, issued a strongly worded communiqué, condemning the government's violation of human rights. Repressions are now a daily tool in controlling society, and martial law continues to operate on the legislative level.

Tension between state and church reached its highest point during the fall when Jozef Cardinal Glemp traveled through the United States in September, speaking freely about the domestic situation. One month later, the church refused to support the parliamentary elections on 13 October. By keeping its distance from politics, the church voiced displeasure with Jaruzelski's policy of separation between state and church, concluding that if the state wants separation, it should be complete separation, detrimental to the state. The authorities responded with another condemnation of the church and suspension of mutual talks. Relations were officially described as "businesslike," and it was said there was no necessity to "rush" with dialogue (*Kultura*, 16 October). The government was anxious to have active church support in the elections, whose purpose was to legitimize post–martial law politics. Only the church could bestow credibility on the elections; without its support, the regime would be nothing more than an unelected Soviet-sponsored government.

Internal Affairs. Officially, Jaruzelski's carrot-and-stick policy is called the "line of agreement and the line of struggle," implying that the government is prepared to negotiate and compromise on any issue, including political questions, provided that no attempt is made to weaken the communist system or to destroy its legal order. Four years after the imposition of martial law, the regime has yet to demonstrate a willingness to conclude a single agreement with society. Instead, it is aggressively pursuing a "line of struggle," slowly and systematically waging war against every political, social, and professional group in Poland.

Jaruzelski's strategy and tactics closely resemble the process of Stalinization of the late 1940s and early 1950s. Besides the undeclared war against the church, the regime continues to struggle against Solidarity, intellectuals, students, and even its own trade unions. In effect, its opponents are primarily workers and intellectuals, approximately 75 percent of society. Most of the remaining 25 percent are found in the police force, the armed forces, and the party. Tragic economic conditions force the regime's numerous, but unarmed, opposition to display apathy and resignation, yet aggravation of repression may soon trigger an explosion of anger. So far, disapproval of Jaruzelski's actions is reflected in passive resignation, an attitude that precludes the possibility of overcoming the acute economic crisis.

The regime is armed with nightsticks and bullets, while the opposition fights with ideas. One of the legacies of Solidarity is that people continue to express their opinions. The real Poland is not that of the Communist party, the Sejm, and industry. It lives in an underground as active as that which existed under the Nazi occupation. The network of clandestine activities includes education in politics, history, and philosophy; a subterranean economy; and, above all, an extensive system of unofficial publications. Some of the best known Polish writers, soldiers, and artists contribute to the underground culture, which prints about 1,000 bulletins, 50 books, and several monthly or quarterly magazines per year. The system is remarkably efficient; this literature finds its way into the majority of Polish households. A great number of people are reached via lectures, and politically embarrassing plays are shown under the protective wing of the churches, as well as through the weekly "Masses for the Fatherland" (*NYT*, 4 August). The most successful illegal publishing house, NOVA, edited and produced 30 titles and sold 150,000 volumes in just nine months. As a NOVA activist explained, "For police, there are just too many people involved. More than a publishing house, we are a kind of social movement." NOVA is financially independent, generating enough income to pay royalties and salaries and to support families of jailed activists (*WP*, 27 September).

"Clandestine newspapers . . . will not overthrow General Jaruzelski's regime," concludes *Le Monde* (12 December 1984), although they nurture independent debate and information. The opposition is promoting political education so that it will be prepared when internal and external conditions improve.

Equally important is the contribution made by the Catholic press, which includes 31 papers, with a total circulation of over 1 million copies (*Tygodnik powszechny*, 20 January). Poles continue to be well informed about domestic and international affairs, a situation that is, perhaps, the greatest achievement of underground Solidarity. Despite arrests that include members of the editorial staff of a Catholic newspaper, head of the CDN (To Be Continued) publishing house, and seven retired army officers who published illegal materials (Paris AFP, 20 August; *FBIS*, *EEU*-85-162, vol. 2, 21 August), this form of underground activity continues to flourish in response to the steady increase in demand for uncensored information.

Attempts to erase Solidarity have not yet succeeded. The illegal union has organized several small strikes, threatened a national strike to prevent another increase in food prices, and staged a number of public demonstrations (*Los Angeles Times*, 2 May, 27 July). Although the social base of Solidarity has not been undermined, people in Poland, knowing that the regime is insensitive to social pressure, appear to be less inclined to participate in public demonstrations for fear of political and economic reprisals. According to a government survey of public opinion, active membership in Solidarity declined from 28 percent in March to 20.2 percent in June and July. Between 1983 and 1985, the segment of the population that was anticommunist and antiregime dropped from 8 percent to 5 percent. However, 64 percent of the population, although politically inactive, voiced definitely negative views about the system in Poland and its ability to improve the situation (*WP*, 11 August).

A conservative swing was evident in the official inclination to crack down and subdue any manifestations of independence. Under these adverse political conditions, magnified by sullen and pessimistic social attitudes, the principal task of Solidarity is just to survive. So far its extinction has not been possible. The police have been successful in stopping public protests and, perhaps, in preventing the emergence of new opposition groups, but they have been unable to destroy the links between Solidarity activists inside and outside the country, as well as the links binding the union with the church. Opposition to the regime is in relatively good shape. Banning the union did not lead to its collapse, but its future depends on whether it will now develop a realistic political platform. For years after the imposition of martial law, the union was on the defensive without producing any spectacular victories. On the other hand, in the words of Lech Walesa, "almost 100 percent of the people signed up to our concepts" (*WSJ*, 21 June).

The regime, whose power is founded on the police and army, has not achieved any of its socioeconomic objectives. In this respect, the long-term evolutionary program of change advanced by Solidarity is succeeding. Without national dialogue, without a minimum agreement with the nation, the Polish government cannot govern, and in the area of economics, "We are going from a crisis to a catastrophe," concludes Walesa. "People aren't dying on the street or starving, but we are threatened with going backward. It is hard for someone who is used to a car to switch back to a scythe. We call it Mongolization" (ibid.).

In essence, the situation in Poland is such that the regime has no legitimacy or credibility and is unable to implement a program of economic reform. The opposition has legitimacy and credibility, but it does not have the power to move the country ahead, and neither side is willing to employ large-scale violence, which would threaten Poland's existence as a state. It is a situation national in scope, creating a stalemate whose final outcome depends upon future developments in the international arena. Unless the communist-ruled states, and the Soviet Union in particular, find a solution to their economic problems, the evolutionary strategy of underground Solidarity has a realistic chance of succeeding. Already it has been effective in blocking the road to complete totalitarianism.

Lech Walesa, the 1983 Nobel Peace Prize laureate, seems to be enjoying immunity from arrest, but this preferential treatment does not extend to other Solidarity leaders. Infuriated by the Solidarity-led protest against proposed increases in food prices, the regime prepared a bogus "political trial" of three prominent Polish dissidents—Adam Michnik, a historian; Bogdan Lis, an engineer; and Wladyslaw Frasyniuk, a bus driver. Not only did underground Solidarity succeed in having the price increases delayed, but it issued a damaging economic report that discredited the effectiveness of economic reforms and criticized growing socioeconomic stratification. The report went on to estimate that the average real income is at the 1946 level, and it asked for an explanation of the price increase after four consecutive years of high agricultural output (*NYT*, 26 February).

To avoid giving the impression of having surrendered to Solidarity's demands, the government claimed that it had backed down over price increases because of pressure from the new post-Solidarity unions. It went on to explain that, in any case, the price increase of 25 to 73 percent for items like butter, flour, and sugar, and a 12 to 13 percent increase overall (*NYT*, 5 March), would be imposed gradually over a period of four months. These particular increases were painful, since they coincided with a doubling in rents, soon followed by increases in the cost of electricity, gas, coal, and gasoline. It is estimated that, since 1981, prices have gone up by 500 percent, or 150 percent more than wages (*Los Angeles Times*, 3 July). According to the government, these price increases are necessary for the "rationalization of the economy" program to end heavy subsidies on food. According to Solidarity, the increases were caused by the growth in Poland's exports to the Soviet Union. At the same time, the regime blocked the already-agreed-upon distribution of aid to Polish farmers administered by the church.

Consistent with Jaruzelski's habit of blundering into repression, his regime announced that it had begun an investigation into such illegal activities as inciting public unrest and the role of the underground union, at a time when his own economic practices were in question. On 13 February, the three trade unionists mentioned above were arrested and charged with conspiracy to organize an illegal "protest action in the form of a 15-minute strike on 28 February" (International Press, 8 July). The government move drew a line between permissible and impermissible action.

The three defendants were held in custody until their trial, which began at the end of May and continued for two weeks. On 14 June, the court gave prison terms to Frasyniuk, a "political recidivist" with "counterrevolutionary" tendencies (six years), Michnik (two-and-a-half years), and Bogdan Lis (two years) (*NYT*, 15 June). The *Economist* (8 June) called the trial a "political operetta" that included expelling the defendants from the courtroom and "silencing" them as well as their lawyers. Michnik described the court proceedings as follows:

> President [Judge] Zieniuk's methods were classic, and well known for having been used by Hitlerite and Stalinist justice: they take us back to an era when verdicts were delivered by bandits wearing judges' robes. The novelty of the Gdansk trial was in breaking with appearances, SB agents [secret police officials] being the only ones admitted to the main body of the courtroom. Lawyers were submitted to body searches and the minutes of the trial were falsified. Even Hitler allowed foreign observers to attend such trials, and Stalin did too, but only when the trials had been well-prepared and the accused pleaded guilty (Paris, AFP, 19 June; *FBIS*, *EEU*-85-119, vol. 2, 20 June).

More than 10,000 Poles, including Lech Walesa, signed a petition calling for release of the three Solidarity leaders, and voices of protest came from the United States and Western Europe. Nothing could stop Jaruzelski, whose record shows an active willingness to intensify repression. Police brutality included numerous incidents, one of which involved killing a student who was being questioned by the police. Nearly 15,000 persons attended his funeral in Olsztyn (Paris AFP, 6 October; *FBIS*, *EEU*-216-85, vol. 2, no. 216, 7 November).

Legal abuse in Poland is on a scale unprecedented since Stalinism. Citizens are obliged to work and can be imprisoned or sent to compulsory work without trial, while the police are authorized to use weapons for control of civil unrest, whether in pursuit of suspected citizens or of those who threaten them with "dangerous objects" (BBC, 2 January). Close resemblance to practices from the Nazi and Stalinist eras are self-evident.

Controversy over price increases focused attention on the communist-controlled unions, since they joined Solidarity in protesting against the regime. The new unions claim 5 million members, that is, one-third of Poland's labor force, or half of Solidarity prior to martial law—but 20 percent (1 million) of them are retirees, and many have been bribed into joining. The situation resembles the traditional "transmission belt" between the party and the workers' organization envisioned by Lenin, promoting production goals instead of bread-and-butter issues. Alfred Miodowicz, leader of the official union, denounced the February price increase, but his organization has no power to oppose the regime (*Economist*, 19 January; and *Radio Free Europe Research*, vol. 10, no. 13, 29 March).

Academic freedom in Poland has been the most striking legacy of Solidarity. In May 1982, when the government hoped that its commitment to liberalization would bring popular support for the ideas of socialism, a liberal law on higher education allowed for self-government in such matters as student affairs and curricula. Universities became oases of freedom and of opposition against an increasingly repressive regime, and courses in Marxism-Leninism were dropped. In the opinion of the party, universities became "bridgeheads for the destabilization of social life, and for training new cadres of conspirators" (*Chronicle of Higher Education*, 17 July).

First indications that the academic community had been selected as the next target of the authorities surfaced at the end of April, when Professor Bronislaw Gieremek, a medieval historian and leading member of the Club of Catholic Intellectuals, lost his job at the Polish Academy of Science. This eminent scholar was one of Lech Walesa's advisers during Solidarity's heyday and one of five opposition leaders who, in March 1985, met with Sir Geoffrey Howe, Britain's foreign secretary, during his visit to Poland (ibid., 15 May).

In the summer of 1985, the regime proposed an amendment to the 1982 education law. Henceforth it would: (1) eliminate tenure, and academic faculties would be hired on short-term contracts; (2) drop elections for university rectors and deans; (3) create new, single, and unified student organizations; and (4) replace all "self-governing committees" with students belonging to party-appointed organizations (ibid., 24, 31 July).

The amendment adopted by the Sejm provided a compromise that, on the one hand, dropped or modified the above-mentioned changes, which would have converted institutions of higher education into an extension of the Communist party; on the other hand, it drastically curtailed the academic freedom and political autonomy of universities. Under the new law, the Ministry of Science and Higher Education is authorized to fire or suspend faculty and expel or suspend students suspected of anticommunist activities. Student organizations have been curbed and state-sponsored youth organizations were given a decisive voice in student affairs; all university employees, faculty, and staff are required to take an oath of loyalty to the regime and its ideology. Failure to do so or violation of the oath may result in automatic dismissal.

Even a watered-down version of the amendment represents a return to the administrative procedure that gives the party a deciding voice in selecting faculty and developing academic curricula. The amendment was condemned by both faculties and students, who organized several demonstrations. Wojciech Mazurski, head of student government at Warsaw University, stated that "pluralism of views and opinions has been revoked"; and the declaration adopted by student leaders, representing 10 major institutions of higher education, recommended that students ignore parliamentary elections in October (*NYT*, 30 July). Mass purges at universities began at the end of the year, when 30 presidents and deans were suddenly fired from the Warsaw and Gdansk polytechnics and Poznan University. Charges included absence of "control of the political situation," the presence of Solidarity pamphlets, and lack of participation by students in national elections (*Le Figaro*, 3 December; *FBIS*, *EEU*-85-235, 6 December). At the beginning of December, about 70 administrators and scholars lost their jobs (*WP*, 8 December). In many cases, the firings were carried out without public explanation, just on the advice of the party organization.

Given the single-ballot nature of communist elections, the only relevant issue is how many citizens are willing to cast their vote. The new election law, adopted on 29 May, was designed to lure votes by offering a choice of one of two candidates for a seat in the Sejm (Article 61.1, *Dziennik ustaw*, no. 6, 8 June), so far the most democratic innovation in any communist-ruled state. However, in addition to a list of candidates attached to a constituency, one of whom voters had a right to choose, there was another "national list" of 50 candidates who were elected automatically. This list included Jaruzelski, Henryk Jablonski (president of the Council of State), and other members of the Politburo and government.

The political purpose of these parliamentary elections was to bring an end to the process of "normalization," begun with martial law in December 1981. It was to certify good political health to Moscow, testifying that the opposition had ceased to be effective and Poland no longer was the weakest link in world communism. Giving voters a choice between two candidates was intended to persuade them that elections are meaningful and thus active participation in society could make a difference.

The authorities had been seeking to convince the nation that boycotting the elections would be a political mistake. However, the episcopate was the first to adopt a "neutral" attitude. The church had not explicitly called for a boycott, yet, following its principle of political noninvolvement, it said that it would abstain from the parliamentary elections, as it had done in June 1984 during municipal elections. The underground Solidarity, students, and some professional organizations advocated the boycott as a form of national protest against the regime and, consequently, the "duty of all patriots" (Paris AFP,

12 August; *FBIS*, *EEU*-85-178, vol. 2, 13 September). The "Appeal of the 100" prominent individuals endorsed the idea, because the state was "in a deep economic crisis, with unsolved social and political problems, a state with political prisoners and police tyranny." Cardinal Glemp stated that he had "no intention of voting" and left for Rome during the time of elections (*FBIS*, *EEU*-85-129, vol. 2, 16 September).

Preparations for the elections involved a heavy propaganda campaign as well as arrests and intimidation of any opposition. After the elections, the regime claimed that 78.86 percent of those eligible had voted, that is, almost 4 percent more than in the June 1984 municipal elections, when, according to the government, almost 75 percent had voted. An independent estimate showed that not more than 60 percent had voted, a number in line with the 57 percent de facto participation in 1984. Once again, Jaruzelski's fabricated popular support did not indicate that his determination to govern with an iron hand had changed. He united the army, the secret service, and the party into single units, thus creating a highly organized and discipined superstructure capable of perfecting monopolistic control and the application of power. "The only message being conveyed to the people is that of force," concludes Bronislaw Gieremek (quoted in *La Repubblica*, 15 October; *FBIS*, *EEU*-85-204, 22 October).

With the new Sejm elected, significant changes in the government were made. Henryk Jablonski was removed from his post as titular president and that office was taken over by Jaruzelski, who resigned as prime minister. Zbigniew Messner, an economist previously responsible for implementing economic reforms, took that position. Stefan Olszowski, the leading hard-liner with direct connections in Moscow, was removed from his post as foreign minister and member of the Politburo and was replaced by a Soviet-trained historian and ideologist, Marian Orzechowski. Mieczyslaw Rakowski, a leading liberal and reformer who in 1980–1981 assumed the role of mediator between the government and Solidarity, was moved from deputy premier to deputy Sejm speaker.

The political implications of those changes are not yet clear, but there is no indication that Jaruzelski is losing power. He may have decided to distance himself from daily politics in order to prepare for the 1986 party congress. The balance of power in the Politburo is now decisively on the side of the hard-liners, with the outcome of the congress and Jaruzelski's market-oriented economic program uncertain (*NYT*, 7, 10 November; *Los Angeles Times*, 7, 13 November). It should be noted that the most conservative pro-Soviet individuals in the party have survived both Solidarity and martial law, and it would be logical to speculate that, with Solidarity gone, they are preparing for the final assault.

Thus, Poland has drifted away from its liberal hopes into a Czechoslovak-style, post-1968 "normalization." If political patterns resemble neo-Stalinism, major economic trends continue to favor Hungarian pragmatism.

The Economy. In 1985, the economy showed a slight recovery. Industrial production rose 2.7 percent, lower than the expected 4 percent. The five-year-old economic crisis is not over yet, and it is not likely that the country will ever make a full recovery without Western credits. Under favorable conditions, Poland should regain the 1978 level by 1990. Some argue that Poland will not be able to get back on its feet until the end of this century. Among the latter are Western bankers, who appear reluctant to extend new credits unless the regime becomes serious about economic reforms (*Economist*, 25 May).

So far, Poland has not been able to stop the dangerous price-wage spiral that is weakening the economy, eroding social morale and the value of work. The standard of living is declining, and the economic measures employed by the government have no permanent impact on halting inflation or improving the economy.

Price increases in 1985 came in three waves, between 1 March and 1 May, when the government abolished the rationing of flour and cereal products. However, basic prices went up by 12 to 13 percent, which was translated into a 15 to 70 percent increase for the consumer. The retail cost of coal and coke also went up from 20 to 30 percent. Relatively minor, and indirect, cash compensation (on the average, 6 percent) and social benefits were provided to offset the social consequences of the increase (*TL*, 2–3 May).

Soon after this increase was put into effect, the price of several widely consumed types of meat, meat products, and fish went up 10 to 15 percent. This midsummer increase did not include measures intended to soften its impact on the poor (Warsaw Television Service, 24 June; *FBIS*, *EEU*-85-122, 25 June). The third wave came in the fall, when the cost of energy went up 25 percent.

Documentation by both Solidarity and Western economists shows that the food price increases do not reduce the budget deficits, because of fast-growing subsidies in heavy industry. The latter are estimated to range above 50 percent, with an almost 30 percent increase in the government bureaucracy in just two years, 1982 to 1984. Also, it is almost impossible to reduce the demand for food—meat in particular. The average family is entitled to purchase only five and a half pounds, including bones, of various categories of meat per month, and is spending over 50 percent of its income for food. There is, consequently, hardly any room left for reduction in consumption or increase in spending. Lack of equilibrium between supply and demand is due to the shortage of manufactured goods and an oversupply of money among the privileged, i.e., members of the ruling elite and private entrepreneurs (*WSJ*, 17 April; *NYT*, 2 July).

The economy is not handicapped by the people's desire to eat, but by centrally controlled, inefficient, and alien interests in heavy industry. Jaruzelski's "rationalization" of economic programs by improving managerial and organizational efficiency, enforcing labor discipline, introducing a realistic pricing system, and promoting technological progress has produced only minor and probably short-lived results. Free-market mechanisms introduced in some industries are already on a collision course with the government bureaucracy and employees who had been promised higher wages for better productivity. As suggested by the Sejm economic report, "the positive effects of the reform may soon turn out to be weaker and weaker" (*WP*, 24 September).

Economic problems are magnified by Poland's demographic situation, characterized by a large growth in population. It is expected that the population will rise by 2.8 million before the year 2000, to a total of 40 million inhabitants. This trend is parallel with the increase of over 1 million (to 5.2 million) in the number of children of elementary-school age; a similar increase in population in the retirement-age group; and a catastrophic spread of disease, alcoholism, drug addiction, and smoking (*TL*, 22 January).

The regime's commitment to the "politics of economic reform" has not changed, but it is aware of "weakening the efficiency of the machinery of economic reform." More independence of state enterprises, greater efficiency, reduction of costs, saving of materials, and improvement of quality is urged (ibid., 1 August); however, in 1985, no concrete steps toward increased decentralization were taken.

Actually, the government has only limited control over its national economy. The 1984 agreement with the USSR made Poland a ward of Moscow. The Soviets have acquired firm control over the Polish economy via the long-term program for development of economic cooperation up to the year 2000. The USSR demands investments in Siberia for the continued supply of raw materials, including oil and gas. The Soviets have guaranteed to supply Poland with 13 million tons of oil and 2 million tons of oil products annually until 1990. This means that Moscow has agreed to meet only 48 percent of Polish oil imports, whereas 16 million tons, or 52 percent, must be imported from outside the bloc, primarily Libya. The proportion of Western imports is expected to grow and reach 23 million tons by the year 2000 (Warsaw, PAP, 20 March; *FBIS*, *EEU*-85-055, 21 March).

In practice, this means that Poland has to use her own hard currency to manufacture products exported to the Soviet Union and then is paid in rubles. Moscow is now expecting to receive quality products, which limits Poland's ability to export to the West. The Soviets imposed on Warsaw a comprehensive system of coordinating the latter's national need with Soviet needs, stressing, in particular, the development of joint enterprises, where, in exchange for long-term deliveries, Poland builds "turnkey" factories in the USSR (Radio Warsaw, PAP, 22 January; *FBIS*, *EEU*-85-015, 23 January), boosting her contribution to the Warsaw Pact.

Polish exports to the USSR include machine tools, building and road-building equipment, agricultural products, telecommunications equipment, and electrical and electronics equipment, i.e., products from industries built and supported with hard currency. In effect, Warsaw is using its own resources to save Soviet hard currency. This practice is known from the 1970s, when Polish ships exported to the USSR were equipped with expensive navigational gear purchased in Western Europe. Poland is to provide Moscow with credits of about 900 billion zloty, or $10 billion, over the next fifteen years. As Zdzislaw Rurarz, a former Polish ambassador to Japan, explains: "This development represents a sharp reversal of the practices of the recent past, when beginning in 1980 the USSR provided Poland with credit. Not only is this era over, but the roles have now been reversed" (*WSJ*, 19 June). Polish imports from the USSR in 1985 amounted to 6.4 billion rubles, exceeding exports by 1.2 billion (*Rzeczpospolita*, 23 April) and creating a total accumulated balance of payments deficit of over 5 billion rubles; that comes on top of a $26.8

billion Western debt that continues to burden the economy.

In 1985 Poland again succeeded in having its Western debt rescheduled, postponing payments of approximately $3 billion per year until 1990. It can earn about $6 billion in exports, but the country has to spend $4.5 billion on basic imports, leaving a $1.5 billion surplus, still the same amount short of meeting financial obligations to the West in the event that no deferment with Western creditors is possible (*NYT*, 10 September). Under conditions of the June agreement with the Club of Paris, a group of seventeen Western government creditors, Poland has to pay $1.3 billion in that year's interest. It should be noted, however, that Poland's ability to earn hard currency declined by $140 million in 1985, owing to the poor quality of her goods, deterioration in equipment, and Japanese competition (*Los Angeles Times*, 24 March). Also, Poland was not extended any new credit by the West since, without a fundamental change in its economic strategy, it would be like "pouring money down a rat hole," noted a Western diplomat (*WSJ*, 19 April).

The exchange rate of the Polish zloty has been devalued again to stimulate exports. At the beginning of the year, the zloty went down 12.2 percent against the dollar (from 123 to 138 zloty) and 6.9 percent against the exportable ruble (from 72 to 77 zloty). The total devaluation since January 1982 amounts to 72.5 percent against the dollar and 13.2 percent against the ruble. The real decline in the value of the zloty, measured by the black-market value of the dollar, is substantially higher (*Radio Free Europe Research*, 19 May). The government has also provided tax relief from 20 to 50 percent for companies investing in exports, in addition to interest-free loans and preferences in the supply of raw materials. Foreign trade agencies have become companies, whose shareholders are employees as well as the state (Warsaw Domestic Service, 16 November; *FBIS*, *EEU*-85-223, 19 November). This last step demonstrates Warsaw's inclination to adopt the Hungarian model.

Despite opposition from the new labor union, which objects to the excessive wealth displayed by the foreign-owned Polonia firms operating in Poland, the regime continues to encourage development of those companies that technically are owned by people of Polish descent who are active in industry or trade. It is generally known that the Polonia firms are owned and controlled by well-to-do Poles who, via someone living abroad, may invest hard currency in the national economy. These small-scale enterprises have exports valued at $23 million (7 million rubles) annually, and they provide many goods for the domestic market (Warsaw Domestic Service, 7 June; *FBIS*, *EEU*-85-113, 12 June).

There are now approximately 650 Polonia firms that employ about 100,000 persons. They are regarded as models for the changing behavior of workers, who are paid according to their productivity. The average employee is paid about 50 percent more on engagement than in the socialist sector of the economy but is expected to produce much more than a worker employed by the government. Foreign owners of Polonia may take abroad 50 percent of their gross hard currency profits, and the government is now contemplating the expansion of this Polonia experiment to include foreign investors without national ties (*NYT*, 22 April).

Poland was expected to rejoin the International Monetary Fund and World Bank in 1985. The United States, which controls 20 percent of the vote in those organizations, dropped its objections to Polish membership in December 1984 following the release of political prisoners. At the end of 1985 negotiations were still underway. It is expected that soon Poland will become the 149th member, entitled to borrow over $1 billion (*NYT*, 25 October).

One of the important aspects of Poland's foreign trade is its relations with other communist-ruled countries, particularly East Germany and Hungary. A dynamic development of trade with two of the most highly industrialized bloc states indicates some degree of political autonomy from the USSR. Poland signed new trade agreements with those governments, extending free trade from 15 to 25 percent and giving some degree of balance to its economic relations with the Soviet Union.

In conclusion, for every positive trend in the Polish economy, there is a negative development. The regime has stabilized the economy and achieved a modest growth of 2.5 percent that may continue for several years. The standard of living, however, continues to decline, and structural changes or reorganization of Poland's economy have just begun. The future of this process is dependent on the outcome of the party congress scheduled for February 1986. The future is unclear because of the government's unwillingness to compromise with the nation. It appears to be confident in the effectiveness of its oppressive measures, forgetting that the political militancy of the party always has triggered strikes and revolts. Without a political solution that would take into account the wishes and aspirations of the Poles, the economic situation will not improve and the country will follow the pattern of socioeconomic decline that prevails in the entire communist-governed world. The most simple logic would show the present rulers of Poland that it is entirely unrealistic to expect construction of an "advanced socialist party" with the help of a population that is at least 80 percent Catholic and unwilling to contribute political support or work on behalf of the regime. In recent years, the government of General Jaruzelski has frequently appealed to the political realism of the Poles. There is hardly any reason to doubt the common sense and self-restraint of the Polish people. One questions, however, the government's ability to learn from historical experience and draw conclusions from past events. The bomb is ticking, and the main issue, according to Jacek Kuron, a leading dissident and member of Solidarity, is whether "forces will appear in the government willing to prevent this catastrophe" (*Los Angeles Times*, 15 September).

Foreign Affairs. Since the end of Stalinism in 1956, the foreign policy of the Polish regime has never been more subservient to Moscow. Two consistent themes dominated Poland's foreign policy statements in 1985. First, there was unending glorification of the USSR and humiliating expressions of gratitude for Soviet help. Second were the stubborn and irrational attacks on the United States, and on President Reagan in particular, implying that Washington alone is the source of tension in the world today and the principal cause of the political and economic troubles in Poland. The Sejm adopted a resolution on foreign affairs that stressed the significance of the Soviet Union in the strengthening of peace and stability in Europe and the world. The United States, however, was charged with "aggressive strategy," "global anticommunism," and "interference in Poland's international affairs" (Warsaw, PAP, 15 March; *FBIS*, *EEU*-85-053, 19 March).

The most important international event affecting Poland was the death of Chernenko and the selection of Gorbachev as CPSU general secretary. The Poles knew immediately that this young and energetic Soviet leader would not tolerate chaos in the communist bloc and would assert tough leadership to strengthen his own power in the domestic arena and with the West. New emphasis on intrabloc discipline soon became apparent on the occasion of the twenty-year extension of the Warsaw Pact. This treaty of friendship, cooperation, and mutual assistance was originally signed on 14 May 1955, and was extended for 10 years. The extension for twenty years shows that the Soviets intend to acquire long-term control over Eastern Europe. As noted by Western observers, this latest extension was imposed by Moscow despite some opposition in Warsaw, and in an arbitrary manner described by a Polish official as "fixed" (*Le Figaro*, 27–28 April). Soviet priorities, at the present time, are to stop the Strategic Defense Initiative, since Moscow is unable to keep up the new arms race, and to return to détente in order to channel Western technology and credits to the East. This policy involves a considerable risk to the stability of the bloc, vulnerable to the ideas of democracy, since the Soviets traditionally counter the relaxation of international tension with repressive policies at home. Warsaw followed the Soviet example; economic experiments directed toward free-market methods were balanced with political practices resembling the early 1950s.

Celebration of the fortieth anniversary of the Nazi defeat became another occasion to flatter Moscow. Polish media and government statements focused their attention on the Soviet contribution to this victory, neglecting the Western allies and Poland's own role. As a young Polish writer pointed out, "The only statistics I have heard in the last few days is that 600,000 Russians were killed in Poland. But has anyone mentioned that out of 30 million Poles before the war, six million were killed, three million of them Jews, that Poland supplied the fourth largest army to the Allies after the Soviet Union, the United States, and Britain, and that Polish soldiers suffered four times as many losses as did the French?" Another Pole observed that "Poland was the first victim of the war . . . and the first victim of the peace" (quoted in *NYT*, 10 May), a reference to the 1945 Yalta agreement.

The Soviet approach to Poland in 1985 was unusually cool and high-handed. Following the 27 April meeting between Jaruzelski and Gorbachev, the joint Polish-Soviet statement omitted the customary expression of Moscow's confidence in the Polish leadership. Instead, the USSR "reiterated its unchanging solidarity with the struggle of the Polish United Workers' Party and Poland's working people for fully overcoming the effects of the crisis, for stability, and for strengthening the position of socialism." The Polish leader failed to receive personal endorsement from Gorbachev; the Soviets neither promised to restrain Poland's hard-liners nor offered any assistance to ease economic difficulties. On the contrary, Western diplomats believe that Moscow was pressing Poland to invest heavily in the modernization of its army (*Los Angeles Times*, 28 April; *NYT*, 29 April).

Poland was visited by numerous trade delegations from the Soviet Union, developing long-range ties between the two economies. This process began in December 1984, when 118 Polish research centers were linked to 138 Soviet institutions (Warsaw, PAP, 11 December 1984; *FBIS*, *EEU*-84-241, 13 December 1984), and it continued throughout the year. All major industries have been subordinated to their Soviet counterparts, and the next five-year plan (1986–1990) has been entirely integrated with the needs of the USSR economy. Neo-Stalinism is also evident in Poland's economic relations with Moscow.

Also, as in the period of Stalinism, the Polish regime no longer is inclined to balance its involvement with the East with independent ties in the West, especially the United States. Sensing strong pressure from Moscow and disappointed with the slow and cautious American response to normalization, the government in Warsaw concluded that it had nothing to lose by anti-American campaigns, with consequent deterioration in relations. Polish authorities expelled the U.S. military attaché. Later, two diplomats and four tourists accused of provoking public disorder were also expelled (*TL*, 26 February; *Los Angeles Times*, 3 May). American reaction involved the expulsion of four Polish diplomats, and Secretary of State Shultz refused to meet with General Jaruzelski during his New York visit to address the United Nations (*NYT*, 1 September).

The UN exposure was expected to boost Jaruzelski's prestige at home just before the parliamentary elections and to encourage the United States to lift economic sanctions against Poland. When U.S. officials refused to meet Jaruzelski, he decided to show his contempt by flying from Havana to New York and delivering a speech highly critical of the United States. In New York, he was met only by David Rockefeller; Zbigniew Brzezinski, President Carter's national security adviser; and Lawrence Eagleburger, former deputy secretary of state, who discussed the possibility of providing $300 million in help from the Rockefeller Foundation to private farmers in Poland (*NYT*, 26 September).

Also unproductive was Cardinal Glemp's visit to several American cities, including Washington. Coming just before Jaruzelski, the primate described sanctions as "unjust toward the Polish nation" and "of great damage to the Polish people." Specifically, the cardinal was soliciting funds for the agricultural foundation and received a $10 million pledge from the U.S. government in addition to an unknown amount of support from the Roman Catholic Church in America and private citizens (*WP*, 26 September). The Polish government has not yet agreed to establish the foundation, first proposed in 1982. The church already has secured $28 million for the pilot project, and the authorities appear to be tempted by the prospect of large sums of hard currency, although apprehensive of the political impact this church-sponsored organization would have (*Radio Free Europe Research*, 1 October). But the regime is even more alarmed with the establishment of the Solidarity fund in the United States. The advisory board to this organization includes Senator Bill Bradley and Congressman Jack Kemp, and its purpose is to aid members of Solidarity in Poland and abroad (Warsaw Domestic Service, 21 November; *FBIS*, *EEU*-85-227, 25 November).

By and large Poland continues to be politically isolated in the international arena despite visits of some prominent West European politicians and several trips by General Jaruzelski and ex–foreign minister Stefan Olszowski. Visits by West Europeans were based on a two-level approach to Poland. On the one hand, the Westerners would meet with Polish officials and, on the other, with representatives of Poland's cultural and political life who are independent or opposed to the regime. In several cases, however, the Polish government imposed restrictions on the movement of Western diplomats, who indicated that they would like to meet with representatives of Solidarity, the church, members of Poland's social and cultural community—or perhaps lay flowers at the grave of Father Popieluszko. Three West European foreign ministers—Leo Tindemans of Belgium, Fernando Moran of Spain, and Peter Barzy of Ireland—"postponed" their planned visits (BBC Reports, nos. 12 and 17, June). Only Willy Brandt, chairman of West Germany's Social Democratic Party, rejected Walesa's invitation to lay flowers at the memorial at Westerplatte, near Gdansk, where World War II began on 1 September 1939. Both Brandt and Walesa are Nobel Peace Prize laureates, and, according to Walesa, such a Polish-German ceremony would have fostered "better understanding between the two nations." Brandt turned down the invitation because his itinerary did not provide for a stop in Gdansk (Hamburg OPA, 18 November; *FBIS*, *EEU*-85-223, 19 November), but he met with Cardinal Glemp, focusing attention on the issue of human rights.

Another exception involved French president

François Mitterrand's decision to meet with General Jaruzelski on the latter's way to North Africa. Mitterrand argued that the visit would foster human rights in Poland and that he would be ready to meet with Walesa at any time. Prime Minister Laurent Fabius dissociated himself from the president, declaring publicly that he was "troubled" by the meeting (*WP*, 10 December).

In Warsaw, however, Mitterrand's visit was hailed as a great international success for Jaruzelski and a return to normal French-Polish relations. The Polish media never admitted that he had been invited to the presidential palace by the Poles themselves, stressing instead that the talks were useful and resembled the French-Soviet summit in October of last year (Warsaw Domestic Service, 8 December; *FBIS*, *EEU*-85, 9 December).

As far as international activities are concerned, the Polish regime has devoted considerable attention to Third World states. In its relations with the less developed countries, Poland is driven by such economic motives as the possibility of buying large amounts of raw materials. Jaruzelski visited India, Cuba, Libya, Algeria, and Tunisia, where he concluded various economic agreements.

There was some hope that Israel and Poland would restore diplomatic relations severed by most Soviet bloc states after the 1967 Middle East war. These speculations were produced by a meeting between the Polish and Israeli foreign ministers during the opening of the UN General Assembly, but so far no progress has been reported (*WP*, 20 October).

Poland, in conclusion, has scored a few points and lost a few opportunities without any significant change in its isolation or the prevailing view that the Polish regime does not represent the majority of its nation. The Soviet-American summit in Geneva did not bring any improvement in the international standing of Poland. The regime of General Jaruzelski is an international outcast, pushed aside by its Soviet masters, ignored by Western leaders, tolerated by the countries of the Third World, and hated by its own people. Despite this internal and external ostracism, the rulers of Poland show no inclination to make the most elementary political moves, namely to open a dialogue with the nation they have conquered and rule by force.

Arthur R. Rachwald
U.S. Naval Academy

The author is grateful to Ensign Elizabeth M. McGinn, U.S. Navy, for help in collecting and organizing the research material for this profile.

Romania

Population. 22,772,000
Party. Romanian Communist Party (Partidul Comunist Român; PCR)
Founded. 1921
Membership. 3,500,000 (*WMR*, July 1985)
General Secretary. Nicolae Ceauşescu
Political Executive Committee (PEC). 22 full members; 8 of whom belong to the Permanent Bureau: Nicolae Ceauşescu (president of the republic), Emil Bobu (chairman, Council on Problems of Economic and Social Organization), Elena Ceauşescu (first deputy prime minister), Constantin Dăscălescu (prime minister), Manea Mănescu (vice-president of the republic), Gheorghe Oprea (first deputy prime

minister), Gheorghe Rădulescu (vice-president of the State Council), Ilie Verdeţ (former prime minister, in October appointed minister of mines); other full members: Iosif Banc, Virgil Cazacu, Lina Ciobanu (chairwoman, Central Council of the General Union of Romanian Trade Unions), Ion Coman, Nicolae Constantin (deputy prime minister), Ion Dincă (first deputy prime minister), Miu Dobrescu (chairman, PCR Central Collegium), Ludovic Fazekas (deputy prime minister), Alexandrina Găinuşe (deputy prime minister), Paul Niculescu, Constantin Olteanu (first secretary of the Bucharest PCR Municipality Committee), Gheorghe Pană (in December appointed minister of food industry and farm produce acquisition), Ion Păţan (minister of light industry), Dumitru Popescu (rector of the "Ştefan Gheorghiu" PCR Academy); 25 alternate members: Ştefan Andrei (until November foreign minister; in December appointed chairman, Council of Workers' Control and Economic and Social Activities), Ştefan Bîrlea (chairman, State Planning Committee), Nicu Ceauşescu, Leonard Constantin, Gheorghe David (minister of agriculture), Marin Enache, Petru Enache (vice-president of the State Council), Mihai Gere, Maria Ghiţulică, Nicolae Giosan (chairman, Grand National Assembly), Suzana Gâdea (chairwoman, Council of Socialist Culture and Education), Nicolae Mihalache, Ioachim Moga, Ana Mureşan (minister of domestic trade), Elena Nae, Marin Nedelcu, Cornel Pacoste, Tudor Postelnicu (head of the State Security Department), Ion Radu, Ion Stoian, Gheorghe Stoica, Iosif Szasz (vice-chairman, Grand National Assembly), Ion Totu (deputy prime minister), Ion Ursu (first vice-chairman, National Council of Science and Technology), Richard Winter (minister of wood industry and building materials)

Secretariat. 11 members: Nicolae Ceauşescu, Ştefan Andrei, Iosif Banc, Emil Bobu, Ion Coman, Silviu Curticeanu, Petru Enache, Maria Ghiţulică, Cornel Pacoste, Constantin Radu, Ion Stoian

Central Committee. 265 full and 181 alternate members

Last Congress. Thirteenth, 19–22 November 1984, in Bucharest; next congress scheduled for 1989

Last Election. 17 March; of the record number of 15,733,060 registered voters, 15,732,095 (97.8 percent) cast their votes for candidates of the Socialist Democracy and Unity Front (SDUF), while 356,573 (2.3 percent) voted against them (which is 125,962 more than in 1980). Next elections scheduled for 1990.

Auxiliary Organizations. Union of Communist Youth (UTC, 4 million members), Nicu Ceauşescu, first secretary; General Union of Romanian Trade Unions (7 million members), Lina Ciobanu, chairwoman of the Central Council; National Council of Women, Ana Mureşan, chairwoman; Councils of Working People of Hungarian and German Nationalities, Mihai Gere and Eduard Eisenburger, respective presidents; Socialist Democracy and Unity Front (SDUF), Nicolae Ceauşescu, chairman, Manea Mănescu, first vice-chairman, Tamara Maria Dobrin, chairwoman of the Executive Bureau

Publications. *Scînteia*, Ion Mitran, editor-in-chief, PCR daily (except Monday); *Era Socialistă*, PCR theoretical and political biweekly; *România Liberă*, SDUF daily (except Sunday); *Lumea*, foreign affairs weekly; *Revista Economică*, economic weekly. Agerpress is the official news agency.

The Romanian Communist Party (PCR) was founded on 8 May 1921, in Bucharest, as a section of the Communist International. It operated legally until April 1924, when it was outlawed by the Liberal government then in power. After its delegalization, some of its members continued to operate underground in Romania, while others formed an external leadership center in Moscow. Throughout all its clandestine years, the PCR demonstrated a total and unconditional subordination to Comintern headquarters. Primarily composed of militants belonging to ethnic minorities, the PCR failed to understand and endorse Romanian national aspirations. It was therefore perceived as an alien political force, deeply and consistently attached to the expansionist interests of the Soviet Union. Following the occupation of the country by the Soviet Army, the PCR played an increasingly influential role. It was instrumental in the neutralization of traditional political parties and engineered the destruction of the Romanian parliamentary system. The establishment of a left-wing government led by fellow traveler Petru Groza on 6 March 1945 as well as the electoral farce in November 1946 facilitated the task of Romanian Communists. The PCR was committed to implementation of a so-called people's democracy, which was only another name for repressive dictatorship. Internecine struggles within the party leadership resulted in the elimination of the Muscovite faction headed by Ana Pauker and Vasile Luca (May–June 1952) and the triumph of "national" Communists grouped around Gheorghe

Gheorghiu-Dej. The PCR was extremely active in the anti-Yugoslav campaign that followed the Cominform resolution in June 1948. The headquarters of the Cominform journal *For a Lasting Peace, For People's Democracy* was moved from Belgrade to Bucharest, and all Romanian leaders joined in the propaganda war against Yugoslavia. Nicolae Ceauşescu's political career was marked by his association with Gheorghiu-Dej. He had been directly involved with various purges, including the anti-intellectual campaigns of 1957–1958. He also benefited by elimination from the Politburo in June 1957 of a powerful rival, Miron Constantinescu. At the First Congress of the Romanian Workers' Party (Partidul Muncitoresc Român; PMR) in 1948, Ceauşescu was elected a member of the Central Committee. At the Second Congress in 1955, he became a member of the Politburo and a national secretary. Under Gheorghiu-Dej, the PCR opposed any attempt at liberalization and carried out a drastic Stalinist program of industrialization. Forced collectivization of agriculture and incessant persecution of intellectuals enabled the ruling elite of the PCR to gain absolute control over the country. Gheorghiu-Dej and his comrades resented Khrushchev's calls for de-Stalinization as well as Soviet hegemonistic behavior within the Warsaw Pact and CMEA. A statement regarding the position of the PCR on relations between socialist countries was published in April 1964. This declaration emphasized national values and deplored attempts to violate the principles of equality and independence. Nicolae Ceauşescu succeeded to the PCR leadership in March 1965 and intensified Dej's politics of economic autonomy vis-à-vis the Soviet Union. After a simulacrum of liberalization between 1965 and 1971, the regime reasserted its Stalinist legacy both in socioeconomic and cultural policy. No genuine reform developed in Romania, and ideological orthodoxy maintained its upper hand over all intellectual life. Certain independent foreign policy initiatives have been continuously invoked in order to justify the internal repression. An unprecedented cult of personality, with almost religious overtones, has characterized Ceauşescu's authoritarian leadership.

A dogmatic approach to economic realities and the refusal to encourage any form of market mechanisms generated serious difficulties during the late 1970s and early 1980s. The working class is increasingly discontented with low salaries and food shortages, while the "new agricultural revolution" has failed to improve living standards in the rural areas. Unfavorable international economic conditions and the intransigent commitment to bureaucratic centralism dramatically worsened socioeconomic conditions in Romania. Ceauşescu's decision to pay off all foreign debts by 1990 resulted in a draconian program of austerity that severely affected the life of the whole population. An increasing estrangement between the party leadership and the working class has been accompanied by an amazing concentration of power into the hands of the president's family. Persistent rumors circulated in 1985 concerning a deterioration in the health of the general secretary, and there were speculations regarding preparation of a dynastic succession. National apathy and all-pervading distress are phenomena increasingly noticed by all foreign observers. As the energy crisis continued for the second year, Western diplomats say that the government's response took on a desperate air. In September, Ceauşescu spoke of deporting pensioners from the cities to the countryside (*NYT*, 15 December). There is a general feeling in Romania that a solution has to be found to the growing political and economic crisis for which Ceauşescu is held principally responsible.

Leadership and Organization. In the documents of the Central Committee plenum, held during 26–27 March, there are detailed statistics on the numerical strength and social composition of the party. According to these statistics, on 31 December 1984 the PCR had nearly 3,500,000 members. At present the proportion of Communists adds up to over 22 percent of the adult population and to almost 33 percent of the working population. Among PCR members, 55.67 percent are workers, 15.67 percent peasants, 20.65 percent intellectuals or white-collar workers, and 8 percent pensioners or housewives. In 1984 the PCR admitted 132,000 new members. Of these 65.26 percent were workers, 15.56 percent peasants, and 19.18 percent intellectuals. Of this group 77 percent came from the Union of Communist Youth. The number of women in the PCR reached 1,126,000 by the close of 1984, and the proportion among the nation's female population in the party rose to 32.5 percent. More than half of the members admitted in 1984 were women. Party organizations are increasingly promoting women to leadership positions. Of those elected in 1984 to party organs, they comprise 38.3 percent as compared to 32 percent in 1979. During the same period the proportion of women among party functionaries rose from 16.5 to 25.7 percent. At the end of 1984, the party structure included 40 counties and the Bucharest municipality; 55 other municipalities; 188 towns and 2,705 communal organizations; 6,344 party units led by committees in enterprises, institutions, agricultural units; 72,735 basic organizations; and 12,964 party groups (*Scînteia*, 3, 5 April).

The Ceauşescu cult of personality intensified, particularly on such occasions as his birthday (26 January), the twentieth anniversary of his election as general secretary (26 March), and the twentieth anniversary of the Ninth PCR Congress (24 July). As usual, odes and hymns were produced by sycophantic writers celebrating the alleged "genius" of the general secretary. The party's propaganda apparatus mobilized itself in order to foster Ceauşescu's image as the "architect of Romania's independence," while an avalanche of ideological articles promoted the myth of him as an original Marxist-Leninist thinker. During a meeting of the Political Executive Committee on 26 March, prime minister Dăscălescu indulged in unrestrained adulatory remarks. Paying homage to the celebration of two decades since Ceauşescu's election as head of the party, Dăscălescu glorified the leader's role in both domestic and foreign policy. According to him, Romania's president made crucial contributions toward "solving the great problems of the contemporary world, developing a climate of international peace, security and collaboration, and the setting up of a juster and better world on our planet" (*JPRS*, 22 April). A special Central Committee plenum was devoted on 24 July to the anniversary of twenty years since the Ninth PCR Congress and Ceauşescu's election as general secretary. No reference was made to his predecessor, and all speakers competed in expressing their admiration for the man whom they described as the creator of a new era in Romania's history. Once again, Dăscălescu outdid himself in voicing unlimited respect and veneration for the "heroic helmsman of the national destiny." That speech was a masterpiece of flattering rhetoric, impregnated with servile epithets and excessive hyperbole. With regard to Ceauşescu's merits, both Dăscălescu and Manea Mănescu, who presented the party's tribute to the general secretary, found it necessary to extol his unequaled intellectual force: "as a unique personality who opposes ideological dogmas and taboos, Nicolae Ceauşescu has ensured throughout these glorious years a never-ending source of ideas and concepts for the overall theoretical and practical activity of our party and state, thus permanently establishing his name as founder of a new, socialist country" (*Scînteia*, 25 July). The pages of all publications as well as the radio and TV broadcasts were flooded with grotesque Byzantine metaphors glorifying "the brilliant founder of the historical period that bears his name." The climax of the whole anniversary show was reached during a solemn session of the Romanian Academy, when Ceauşescu was elected as its honorary president. Ironically, these festivities coincided with persistent rumors concerning the aggravation of a presumed serious illness (*Los Angeles Times*, 20 July; *FBIS*, 23 July). Foreign media increasingly tend to depict Ceauşescu as the "sick man of communism," and speculations came out that alluded to a potential military reaction against the general secretary's erratic rule (London, *Economist*, 26 October). The ouster of General Constantin Olteanu in December seems to confirm the president's suspicions about a presumed lack of loyalty on the part of some military men.

Another beneficiary of the personality cult is Elena Ceauşescu, the general secretary's wife, who is widely perceived as the real deputy leader of the party. She is not only a first deputy prime minister and chairwoman of the National Council for Science and Technology, but also the head of the party's Commission for Cadres. This last position enables Mrs. Ceauşescu to oversee all organizational activities and promote to influential places people directly associated with the presidential clan. The dynastic scenario imagined by the Ceauşescus is bound to be fulfilled not only on the basis of consanguinity, but also through the promotion of cadres originally from Scorniceşti (the president's birthplace) and from Olt County (to which Scorniceşti belongs). Elena Ceauşescu's alleged contribution to the development of Romanian science was stridently emphasized during the first Science and Education Congress held in Bucharest during 28–29 November (*Scînteia*, 29 November). She is also mainly responsible for the promotion of certain women to top party functions, including the national party Secretariat. Alexandrina Găinuşe, Maria Ghiţulică, Lina Ciobanu, and other high-ranking women owe their current positions directly to Mrs. Ceauşescu and represent a potential power base for her.

Another peculiar Romanian development consists of the spectacular rise to political prominence of Nicu Ceauşescu, the couple's youngest son. Born in September 1951, Nicu was elected first secretary of the UTC and de facto minister of youth affairs in December 1983. His activities, both as UTC leader and chairman of the United Nations Commission for the International Year of Youth, were regularly covered by the Romanian media. At the Thirteenth RCP Congress in November 1984 Nicu was voted a candidate-member of the Political Executive Committee. His wife, Poliana Cristescu, was elected to full membership on the Central Committee. At the Twelfth UTC Congress in May, Nicu was retained as first secretary, while his wife kept her positions as a secretary and member of the UTC Central Committee Bureau (*Scînteia*, 19 May). It seems that Nicolae Ceauşescu, who started his career as a UTC leader, is intent upon grooming his son for the succession. The election of Cornel Pacoste as a national party secretary on 13 November illustrates Nicu's growing influence (*FBIS*, 13 November). Pacoste is former secretary of the Bucharest Party University Center, a position in which he had been able to collaborate in the early 1970s with Nicu, then a young student leader. Like Ştefan Andrei and Ştefan Bîrlea, Pacoste is a construction engineer turned into a professional apparatchik. They all graduated from the same institute in Bucharest and have maintained close interpersonal relations. Furthermore, Pacoste worked for some years as Andrei's deputy at the Foreign Affairs Ministry, before becoming first secretary of the Timiş County party committee. The presence of both Andrei and Pacoste in the Secretariat suggests configuration of a pressure group closely linked to Nicu. The UTC first secretary sees his main duty as mobilizing Romanian youth for fulfillment of the objectives established by the party leadership. Directly involved in proliferation of the so-called "national building sites of the youth," Nicu obediently follows his father's instructions concerning the tightening of discipline within the UTC. Militarized labor and simulated enthusiasm cannot conceal the total lack of appeal of party slogans, which are perceived as outdated Stalinist clichés. A national building site inauguration was attended on 4 June by Nicu and Vasile Bărbulescu (first secretary of the Olt County party committee) at Frunzaru-Olt in southern Romania (*FBIS*, 5 June). Bărbulescu is himself a member of the presidential clan, being married to one of Ceauşescu's sisters. As for Nicu, besides various trips abroad (USSR, Austria, Japan, Spain, GDR), he played host in Bucharest to the World Conference of National Committees for the International Youth Year (*FBIS*, 5 September).

Other members of the family have been placed in key party and government positions: Lieutenant General Ilie Ceauşescu, the president's brother, remains deputy minister of national defense and secretary for the Higher Political Council of the Armed Forces. Another brother, Nicolae A. Ceauşescu, is chief of the cadres department of the Internal Affairs Ministry. A third brother, Ion Ceauşescu, is first vice-chairman of the State Planning Commission and a de facto member of the government. Without being related to the ruling family, Manea Mănescu and Ilie Verdeţ, both former prime ministers under Nicolae Ceauşescu, have long been associated with the general secretary. Ilie Verdeţ lost his membership in the Secretariat when he was appointed minister of mines (*FBIS*, 13 November). As a result of the same "cadre rotation," Ştefan Andrei was replaced as foreign minister and elected a national party secretary. The new foreign minister, Ilie Văduva, is former rector of the Bucharest Academy of Economic Sciences and had been active for many years in the propaganda apparatus of the Bucharest party committee. He then became a vice-chairman of the Grand National Assembly, while maintaining his teaching position. According to foreign correspondents, there were rumors in Bucharest that Ceauşescu had decided to appoint a new foreign minister, the almost anonymous Ilie Văduva, with the aim of eventually replacing him with his son Nicu (ibid.). On 17 December, the defense minister, Colonel General Constantin Olteanu, was relieved of his duties. His successor was the former first deputy and chief of staff, Colonel General Vasile Milea. During a meeting of a high-level military group, Ceauşescu announced that General Olteanu would transfer to party activity (*FBIS*, 24 December). As a result of another major reshuffle, Marin Enache was named minister of metallurgy in place of Neculai Agachi; Gheorghe Pană became head of the newly created Ministry of Food Industry and Farm Produce Acquisition, losing his influential position as first secretary of the Bucharest party committee (*NYT*, 18 December). He was replaced by General Olteanu (*FBIS*, 23 December).

There is no doubt that all these measures are bound to consolidate the power of the hegemonic group and strengthen Ceauşescu's control over the apparatus. The consequence of permanent "cadre rotation" is an increasing feeling of insecurity among members of the *nomenklatura*, who can hardly anticipate the eccentric wishes of the general secretary. There is no coherent and consistent party line in contemporary Romania, except the often contradictory "indications" of the president.

Ceauşescu's behavior has become alarmingly unpredictable, with dramatic consequences in all areas of human existence, from the economy to cultural life. General confusion and despairing powerlessness are the price the party bureaucrats pay in order to maintain their privileges during these times of dynastic twilight.

Domestic Affairs. It is difficult to distinguish the Romanian government from the party. Ceauşescu has favored the unification of some offices and mixed party-government bodies (e.g., the Central Council of Workers' Control and Economic and Social Activities) that would coordinate PCR decisions with government legislation. All deputies elected to the Grand National Assembly on 17 March were candidates of the SDUF. Agerpress reported that in Ceauşescu's district in Bucharest, all of those eligible (73,027) had voted, including Romanians living abroad at the time of the elections, which resulted in unanimity for the general secretary (Radio Free Europe, Romanian Situation Report, *RFE SR*, 9 April). The most significant aspect of this election was publication of figures that indicated the largest percentage of votes ever cast against the regime (2.27 percent of the electorate or 356,573 people—compared with a 0.14 percent opposition in 1965 and 1.50 percent in 1980) (*FBIS*, 25 March). The antigovernment vote was stronger in areas where ethnic minorities (Germans and Hungarians) live. In the central town of Sibiu, which has a large German population, some 6.8 percent of the vote went against government candidates. In nearby Brasov, the opposition totaled 5.77 percent (ibid.). Problems with the national minorities arose during the candidates' nomination campaign. On 17 March, Radio Budapest complained that "nationality candidates were running as a rule in areas not populated by national minorities. For example, Deszö Szilágyi, editor-in-chief of the Bucharest-based Hungarian-language daily *Elöre*, was nominated in a Moldavian district [Rădăuţi]" (*RFE SR*, 14 May). With regard to the ethnic composition of the new parliament, it is striking that, while the number of seats remains the same as in 1980 (369), the number of Hungarian-nationality deputies has declined from 29 to 27 (ibid.). As mentioned, the electoral campaign coincided with festivities meant to celebrate two decades since Ceauşescu's election as party head. On 27 March, a plenum of the PCR Central Committee and a plenum of the SDUF National Council decided separately to propose to the Grand National Assembly that Ceauşescu be re-elected president of the republic. On 29 March, at the first session of its ninth legislature, parliament unanimously supported re-election of the head of state (*FBIS*, 29 March). The doyen of the legislature, Ion Popescu-Puţuri, described Ceauşescu as the "most prominent personality in Romania's history." Sash and scepter had been handed over to Ceauşescu by Nicolae Giosan, president of the GNA, who praised "the heroic deeds of the homeland's bravest man" (*RFE SR*, 14 May). As for the leader himself, it seems that he was far from embarrassed by this orgy of eulogies. In a speech to the Central Committee plenum on 27 March, the general secretary indulged in remarks concerning his boundless commitment to the revolutionary ideals of the people: "As far as I am concerned, as a son of my people and as a faithful soldier of the party for more than 50 years now, I have done all I can to serve the cause of social and national liberation, the cause of progress, democracy, and socialism in Romania. And from the moment in which the party entrusted to me the high position of general secretary I have had no rest. Day and night, I could say, my thoughts have focused on how I can best serve the cause of the people and the party and on what action has to be taken to achieve optimally the wonderful ideals of socialist and communist society on Romanian soil" (*Scînteia*, 28 March). This was only a reassertion of Ceauşescu's frequent call for national unity centered on his own person. Mass organizations have been mobilized to endorse this identification of the party with the person of the general secretary, and all congresses and forums in Romania have been dominated by slogans celebrating the "most beloved son of the nation." On 8 February, the third SDUF congress ended in Bucharest with Ceauşescu re-elected as chairman (*FBIS*, 11 February). On 7 March he addressed the National Women's Conference, and his speech was repeatedly interrupted by loud cheers and long chants of "Ceauşescu and the people!" (*FBIS*, 12 March). On 16 May, he took the floor during the Youth Forum, which grouped delegates to the twelfth UTC congress and the conferences of the Union of Communist Students' Associations, the Pioneers, and the Fatherland's Falcons (*Scînteia*, 17 May). Another opportunity for him to reiterate the basic propaganda themes was the First Science and Education Congress, where he emphasized the principle of communist education and the necessity to intensify the struggle for the "fashioning of the new man, with high revolutionary and communist awareness" (*Scînteia*, 29 November).

Economy. The economic situation continued to deteriorate during 1985. Romania has the advantage of being Eastern Europe's only sizable oil and gas producer, besides having large deposits of coal. Gigantomania and lack of realism have resulted in a perpetual crisis of the Romanian economy. Mismanagement and miscalculations created a state of general stagnation, including those areas where the regime had hoped to reach high performance. Originally, Romanian planners expected oil production to climb during the 1970s and pressed ahead with oil refineries and chemical, steel, and aluminum plants. But after peaking at 14.7 million metric tons in 1976, oil output dropped to 11.5 million tons by 1980 and has remained near that level since (*NYT*, 15 December). Coal production has not met the optimistic figures imagined by party economists, and the rate of growth of natural gas, significant in the 1970s, slowed in the early 1980s. Energy shortages have become an endemic problem of the economy. The official press has conceded that some factories are working at 20 to 30 percent capacity, aggravating the shortage of food and goods. In the fall, former prime minister Ilie Verdeţ replaced Marin Ştefanache as minister of mines (*Scînteia*, 19 October). After last year's tragic winter, there were unconfirmed reports that hundreds of elderly people and small children had perished throughout the country as temperatures in many apartment buildings sank to between 32 and 40 degrees Farenheit and the use of portable electric heaters was banned (*Los Angeles Times*, 19 October). Draconian measures have been adopted by the regime in order to avert power shortages. Although industry suffered in the energy crisis, the public was most affected by the power cuts. To enforce austere regulations, authorities introduced vigilante teams to inform on violators. Domestic consumption of electricity now accounts for only 7 percent of national output, compared with 27 percent in Hungary and 19 percent in Bulgaria (*WSJ*, 10 April). In October, the PEC adopted emergency measures, which included establishment of military commands at major electric generating stations. The PEC decided to dismiss the minister of electric energy and the deputy prime minister who had responsibility for that sector. In agreement with the presidential decree signed by Ceauşescu, the PEC decided to introduce a militarized work regime in the power sector (*FBIS*, 21 October). In his speech to the Central Committee plenum on 13 November, Ceauşescu dealt with some of the most dramatic economic problems. Once again he made reference to the decision to repay the foreign debt of $12 billion by 1990: "if we take into account solely the balance of our foreign debt—considering that an important sum of money is also due to us—this balance amounts to some $4 billion, a sum that no longer poses particular problems and permits us to pay off our foreign debts completely and in a relatively short period of time" (*Scînteia*, 15 November). In the meantime, Ceauşescu rebuffed any attempt at developing private economic initiative: "We must reject with great determination certain ideas that can be heard here and there. It is true these are not heard in our country, but I cannot say that there are no people with such ideas in our country; I can only say that they do not voice their opinions regarding a certain reduced role and importance of the common property of working people and regarding the stimulation, in one form or another, of certain forms of private property. Such tendencies and ideas are completely at variance with socialist principles" (*FBIS*, 26 November). Responsibility for the grim economic situation was attributed by the general secretary to certain unnamed party activists who allegedly disregarded instructions and directives of the party leadership. Allusions were made to members of the Central Committee and the PEC who have not taken all necessary measures to ensure implementation of party and state decisions at their workplace. This discourse sounded like an ultimatum to all those dissatisfied party leaders who presumably dared express minimal reservations concerning the unrealistic decisions imposed by Ceauşescu: "I personally have always known that to be a member of the Central Committee or the Political Executive Committee, to be a minister or hold some other leading position, means great responsibility and it means to act with even greater determination and exactingness to implement decisions and not to accept any infringement or violation of the state's laws and the party's decisions" (ibid.).

The agricultural crisis was discussed during a plenum of the Romanian Council of Agriculture held in Bucharest during May. Ceauşescu attended on the last day (31 May) and expressed displeasure at several suggestions made in the meeting before his arrival, especially one that advocated "better material incentives" for farmers through higher prices for food products (*Scînteia*, 1 June). In his speech the general secretary blamed Romanians for not taking an active interest in farming the land: "some prefer to stay in offices, others even in pubs or on the edge of a ditch, instead of going out and using the hoe to weed as always was done" (*RFE SR*, 17 July). Ceauşescu expressed discontent with the present result of the mechanization process and the shortcomings in the supply of fertilizers. According to the central plan for the agricultural sector, a cereal output of 29,650,000 tons had been envisaged for 1985, although the previous year, under good conditions for agriculture, the total harvest had been only 23,600,000 tons (ibid.). The abortive "New Agricultural Revolution" has resulted in increased food shortages. This situation became worse because of the recent rerouting of produce from the domestic market to export markets, in order to pay for the country's rigid industrialization program. Estimates of how much farm produce is actually exported vary; some go as high as 50 percent of the entire food output (*RFE SR*, 1 October).

Foreign Debt. According to Romanian finance minister Petre Gigea the country enjoyed a favorable balance of foreign trade in 1984 and was able to repay a major part of its external debt (*Scînteia*, 19 June). On the other hand, it seems that the combination of an unusually hard winter and permanent economic incompetence on the part of the party leadership led to serious economic failures that have damaged the country's export capabilities and affected its resources of hard currency (*RFE SR*, 13 August). Over the first six months of 1985, marketable industrial production increased by only 5 percent compared with the planned 7.5 percent (ibid.). Another obstacle had been the need to import an additional million tons of oil from the Soviet Union because of the harsh winter conditions. Romania paid for this by exporting to the USSR high-quality goods that could have earned $200,000,000 on Western markets (Bucharest, Reuters, 21 June). The country negotiated a short-term loan in May from a consortium of four Western banks (*Financial Times*, 19 June). It is not difficult to notice that this agreement and other similar Romanian approaches suggest a reassessment of Ceauşescu's policy of refusing to borrow from Western banks and seeking to promote financial autarky (ibid.).

Destruction of Old Bucharest. Despite widespread protest at home and abroad, the large-scale demolition of Bucharest's center continued unabated. Ceauşescu seems intent on putting his mark on the city in order to fulfill his Pharaonic dreams. At least ten churches, three synagogues, and many other buildings of historic and architectural significance have been bulldozed or dynamited to make way for mammoth buildings to house the offices of the Central Committee and the government. According to the chief architect of Bucharest, the idea of constructing a new center for the capital belongs to the general secretary himself (*NYT*, 6 October). The "Ceauşescu epoch" has thus to be immortalized through huge monuments that will glorify the initiatives of the post-1965 leadership. Prominent intellectuals expressed their revolt against these anticultural operations, but the general secretary remains unaffected. The destruction of old Bucharest was also mentioned in connection with the extension of most-favored-nation status for Romania when former U.S. ambassador to Bucharest, David Funderburk, declared that "a regime that turns bibles into toilet paper, that bulldozes churches. . . does not deserve most-favored-nation treaty status" (*RFE SR*, 13 August).

Religious Repression. The regime intensified its campaign against religious beliefs and practices. Articles condemning "church militants" regularly have appeared in the official press. People bringing bibles or other religious publications into the country without authorization are arrested and fined (*RFE SR*, 13 August). The scandal of the recycled bibles was brought to the attention of the U.S. Congress and shed a new light on the real situation of human rights in Romania. According to Congressman Robert Dornan, some 20,000 bibles donated in the 1970s by the World Reformed Alliance to the Transylvanian Magyar Reformed Church with the permission of Bucharest were diverted to a mill in Braila, as the label on the rolls indicated, for recycling into toilet paper. The high-quality Western paper and ink, however, resisted the smashing, and the biblical words were easily legible in the creases (*WSJ*, 14 June; RFE *Background Report* [*RFE BR*], 30 August). As a result of external pressures on the Romanian government, Orthodox priest Gheorghe Calciu, a main defender of religious values and a victim of continuous communist persecution, was allowed to emigrate to the West (BBC *CARIS Report*, 24 July). In 1979 Father Calciu had been imprisoned for his views and only as a result of Western pressure was he released in August 1984. He then survived under house arrest but continued to write texts critical of the abuses and crimes committed by the regime. New arrests and trials of evangelical Christians symbolized the government's decision to thwart religious sects and annihilate their militants. Romanian authorities' opposition to evangelical communities that attempt to construct or extend church buildings further eroded the country's credibility in terms of its human rights record. Restrictions on Roman Catholic churches were mentioned on several occasions by Vatican representatives (*RFE BR*, 30 August).

Intellectual Dissent. Despite the existence of a permanent chorus of well-paid professional zealots, the regime failed to suppress all forms of cultural dissent. Among those who dared to challenge ideological orthodoxy and political autocracy, poet and journalist Dorin Tudoran has been particularly articulate and courageous. He is the author of a poignant essay, "On the Condition of the Romanian Intellectual," one of the few attempts to elaborate a psychosociological profile of the contemporary Romanian intellectual class and its ethical ambivalence (*RFE SR*, 2 November 1984). In early 1981, Tudoran resigned from the council of the Writers' Union, protesting constant and brutal party interference in the internal running of the union. Later he handed in his party membership card and resigned completely from the Writers' Union. Totally stripped of work, banned from publication, and a victim of permanent threats, Tudoran had no other solution but to apply for emigration. In two open letters to Ceauşescu, he stressed the "profound incompatibility" between his notions of civic liberties and cultural freedom and the regime's totalitarian practices (*RFE SR*, 26 June). In his political texts, which belong to the best tradition of Romanian democratic thought, Tudoran described the Solidarity movement in Poland as a major source of inspiration for all those who refuse to comply with tyranny. Furthermore, in February he cosigned an appeal by the Transylvanian Hungarian poet Géza Szöcs proposing establishment under United Nations auspices of an international body concerned with the problems of ethnic minorities in all countries of the world (ibid.). Giving in to Western public opinion pressures, the authorities eventually allowed Tudoran to emigrate to the United States (BBC, *CARIS Report*, 24 July). Other writers voiced their distress and disgust with present conditions, making use of unequivocal parables and pungent metaphors. Augustin Buzura published essays on the paranoiac mentality of dictators (*RFE SR*, 22 February), Ana Blandiana wrote a cycle of poems deploring the people's resignation to the current situation (*RFE SR*, 8 February), and even the court-poet Adrian Paunescu expressed disenchantment and pessimism (ibid., 10 January).

Minorities. In a radio interview, Hungarian Socialist Workers' Party national secretary Mátyás Szürös admitted that "from time to time serious concerns and tension arise in Hungarian-Romanian relations, which we would not like to dramatize" but would instead like "to solve in a spirit of friendship and mutual respect and understanding" (*RFE BR*, 27 November). The treatment of the Hungarian ethnic minority in Romania is a matter of concern both for Hungarian leaders and critical intellectuals. It is thus significant that several moving appeals on behalf of poet Geza Szöcs were released during an unofficial cultural forum in Budapest.

Meanwhile, during the official CSCE Cultural Forum, which opened in Budapest on 15 October, many speakers incriminated Ceauşescu's regime for persecution of the Hungarian minority. A month later Marton Klein, a department head in the Ministry of Foreign Affairs, condemned what he called "the oppression of 3,000,000 Hungarians in neighboring countries" (ibid.). Members of a literary circle formed among young ethnic German writers were interrogated and even mishandled by Romanian security police (*RFE SR*, 29 October). The regime is less inclined than ever to tolerate cultural diversity and/or ideological pluralism, and ethnic minorities have bitterly experienced the effects of what Ceauşescu calls "the Marxist-Leninist solution to the national problem."

Foreign Affairs. As in previous years, Romania maintained a highly personalized style in its foreign policy. Almost all initiatives are presented by official propaganda as expressing the general secretary's "creative approach to international issues." The main source of pride for the regime, Romania's alleged independence in international affairs, is increasingly questioned and a realignment with other Warsaw Pact countries may be required by Moscow as a price for economic support.

Communist Regimes. Romania is a member of the Council for Mutual Economic Assistance (CMEA) and the Warsaw Treaty Organization (WTO). Relations with neighboring Bulgaria, Yugoslavia, Hungary, and the Soviet Union are considered by Ceauşescu as fundamental in defining the country's foreign policy. Romania was the first Eastern bloc country to address the issue of renewing the Warsaw Pact Treaty in November

1984. At the Central Committee plenum during 26 and 27 March, Ceauşescu asked for authorization to sign the pact (*RFE SR*, 30 May). On 11 May, the PEC approved the WTO extension protocol. In January, prime minister Dăscălescu traveled to Moscow and negotiated long-term economic cooperation between the two countries. Gorbachev's election as general secretary of the CPSU was the occasion for resuming these negotiations. On 18 March, Dăscălescu again flew to Moscow accompanied by Ion Stoian, party secretary for foreign affairs; Ştefan Andrei, minister of foreign affairs; and Ştefan Bîrlea, chairman of the state planning council (*Scînteia*, 17–20 March). At the CMEA meeting, held in Warsaw during June, Dăscălescu was outspoken in indicating what he considered the shortcomings of this economic organization (*Scînteia*, 27 June; *RFE SR*, 11 September). He complained that the costs and benefits for countries taking part in multilateral investment schemes were frequently unspecified. He also complained about the prices for farm products and about the general price-setting mechanism within the CMEA. While the meeting was going on, Foreign Minister Ştefan Andrei had talks in Brussels aiming to improve Romania's relations with the European Economic Community. Theoretical statements published in Romania expressed the party's opposition to the Brezhnev Doctrine: "There are theories. . . that the old traditional principles of international relations have 'lost' their relevance for relations between socialist states. . . A thorough analysis of the relations between these countries clearly proves that such theses are far from consonant with the [goal] of the building of a new type of relationship between socialist states" (*Era Socialistă*, 25 February). In the party's view, underestimation of national interests can generate tensions and crises. "Supranational assimilation" was rejected by Romanian ideologues as leading to growing economic disparities (*Era Socialistă*, 25 September, 10 October). Ceauşescu attended the Warsaw Pact summit in Sofia during 22 and 23 October. Later, after the Reagan-Gorbachev meeting at Geneva, Ceauşescu was among the Warsaw Pact leaders summoned by the Soviet general secretary to the briefing session in Prague. Reflecting Ceauşescu's view, the party concluded that the Geneva summit had led to a series of positive results and that "under the current very grave international situation [it] was a very important fact" (*FBIS*, 9 December). Contacts were intensified with other communist-ruled countries. In May a party-state delegation led by Ceauşescu visited East Germany. In February, Romania had received the visit of president of the Socialist Federated Republic of Yugoslavia, Veselin Djuranović. According to the communiqué, "special attention was given to economic collaboration and its development in the future, particularly as concerns cooperation in production and production specialization, the growth of trade, the permanent expansion of economic exchanges in the border area" (*FBIS*, 6 February). A delegation from the League of Communists of Yugoslavia (LCY), headed by Stanislav Stojanović, executive secretary of its presidium, visited Bucharest toward the end of the year (*FBIS*, 10 December). A new visit by Nicolae and Elena Ceauşescu to Yugoslavia that same month, as well as visits to Bulgaria, emphasized Romania's interest in developing cooperation with other Balkan countries. In November talks were held at Bucharest with Polish party and state leader, General Wojciech Jaruzelski. In his luncheon toast, Ceauşescu declared that Romania and Poland "shared stances on the fundamental problems" (*FBIS*, 27 November). That same month, Bulgarian prime minister Grisha Filipov paid a visit and held talks with Ceauşescu and Dăscălescu (*FBIS*, 26 November). In December, Bulgarian leader Todor Zhivkov visited Bucharest (*Scînteia*, 21–24 December). Invited by Ceauşescu, Czechoslovakia's party and state leader, Gustáv Husák, came for a "working visit" in December. The official communiqué stated that, on the fundamental problems of world political life, Romania and Czechoslovakia shared "identical or very close stances" (*FBIS*, 13 December). Hungarian foreign minister Péter Várkonyi paid an official visit during 21 and 22 January. It failed to solve the controversial issues in Romanian-Hungarian relations, and the joint communiqué was a clear sign of disharmony (*RFE SR*, 8 February). Ceauşescu was not able to reach his main objective: an invitation from János Kádár to visit Hungary. His last official visit to Hungary was in 1967. Hungarian leaders established as a precondition an improvement in the lot of the Hungarian minority in Romania.

Ceauşescu also visited China, where he held talks with Deng Xiaoping and other Chinese leaders (*FBIS*, 18 October). Earlier, he stopped in North Korea and met Kim Il-song (ibid., 16 October). This was his fifth visit to communist-ruled Asian countries in twenty years.

Balkan Contacts. On his way back from a visit to the Soviet Union, Greek prime minister Andreas

Papandreou stopped in Bucharest to discuss with Ceaușescu the idea of a Balkan summit (*RFE SR*, 22 February). In June, Turkish president Kenan Evren paid an official three-day visit. He expressed his skeptical view of transforming the Balkans into a nuclear-free zone. He seemed interested, however, in using Romanian roads and even the Danube–Black Sea Canal for truck and passenger transit in order to bypass Bulgaria. According to Turkish press reports, Evren confided to Ceaușescu his disappointment with Bulgarian leader Todor Zhivkov over his handling of the Turkish minority question (*RFE SR*, 13 August; *Scînteia*, 12 June).

Third World Relations. Romania was visited by chief of state and chairman of the Congolese Labor Party, Denis Sassou-Nguesso in May (*FBIS*, 29 May). Prime minister Dăscălescu made an Asian tour and stopped in Thailand, Singapore, Malaysia, Burma, and Indonesia (*RFE SR*, 26 June). In July Ceaușescu held talks in Bucharest with president Agatha Barbara from Malta (*JPRS*, 15 August). An article published in *România Liberă* on 31 August emphasized Romania's interest in developing close ties with nonaligned countries (*FBIS*, 6 September) and justified Romanian participation, as an invited guest, at the ministerial conference of nonaligned countries in Luanda, Angola, during September. Talks were held in Bucharest during September between Nicolae Ceaușescu and Burkina Faso president, Captain Thomas Sankara (*JPRS*, 3 October).

Middle East. On 15 Feburary Yasir Arafat, chairman of the PLO, was received by Ceaușescu. On 21 February the Romanian leader had talks with Israeli prime minister Shimon Peres, also in Bucharest. According to the Romanian press, Ceaușescu emphasized how important it was now to increase political and diplomatic efforts in order to achieve a just and durable peace. The press offered a laconic description of Peres' reaction and no communiqué was issued (*RFE SR*, 9 April; *Scînteia*, 22, 23 Feburary). In an interview with the Israeli daily *Jerusalem Post* (*Scînteia*, 1 March), Ceaușescu insisted that Israel had to improve its relations with the Soviet Union, China, and other states as well as renounce its current policy. At the beginning of March, Ceaușescu had a strained meeting with Libyan leader Moammar Khadafy in Tripoli. In a toast at a dinner, Khadafy reproached Romania for its relationship with Israel, threatening that this position would have "consequences" for its relations with Arab countries (*RFE SR*, 25 March). Ceaușescu has developed close personal contacts with King Hussein of Jordan and Egyptian president Mubarak.

Western Contacts. Ceaușescu also visited Canada (*FBIS*, 23–25 April), where he tried to establish and develop areas of economic cooperation. King Juan Carlos of Spain came to Romania in June and held talks with Ceaușescu. Two months later, the Romanian president received Franz Josef Strauss, chairman of the Christian Democratic Union and minister-president of Bavaria (*FBIS*, 12 August). One of the most important Western contacts, with far-reaching effects upon Romania's foreign policy, was the visit paid to Bucharest by U.S. Secretary of State George P. Shultz (*NYT*, 15, 16 December). According to Western observers, Romanian leaders tended to regard the secretary of state's visit as a confirmation of their country's special ties to the United States. Their expectations were not met by Mr. Shultz's outspoken criticism of Romania's human rights record. Because of the permanent harassment of some Christian sects, the U.S. secretary of state warned Ceaușescu that the country was in jeopardy of losing its tariff preferences (*NYT*, 19 December). The lavish cult of personality surrounding the Romanian president and the harsh repression of dissent have been deplored by West European countries (*NYT*, 20 December).

International Party Contacts. In February, a message was sent by the PCR to the Fifth Congress of the Bolivian Communist Party. That same month Ceaușescu received Giancarlo Pajetta, national Secretariat member of the Italian Communist Party (*FBIS*, 12 February). Dumitru Popescu, a member of the PEC, attended the Twenty-fifth Congress of the French Communist Party and was received by Georges Marchais (ibid.). Ceaușescu met with Gerardo Iglesias, general secretary of the Commu nist Party of Spain. The communiqué emphasized the close ties between the two parties and advocated "each party's right to self-reliantly work out its policy, revolutionary tactics and strategy, in concordance with the specific historical, social, and national conditions in which it carried out its activity" (*FBIS*, 26 June). A delegation of the Ba'th Arab Socialist Party visited Romania between 19 and 26 July (*FBIS*, 29 July). On 8 July, Ceaușescu met Jørgen Jensen, chairman of the Danish Communist Party. At the end of November, Ceaușescu received

Hans Kleven, chairman of the Communist Party of Norway (*FBIS*, 2 December).

It has become increasingly clear that Romania is nearly at a crisis stage in the second half of this decade. The country has been confronted with growing economic problems that the arbitrariness of the ruling family's decisions can only exacerbate. Self-congratulatory proclamations and frenzied exhortations have ceased to persuade anyone, while the cult of personality engineered by the Ceauşescu clan is experienced by the Romanian people as a most depressing nightmare. Sooner or later the PCR will understand the political risks involved with this situation and embark on a different strategy, more attuned to the needs and aspirations of those it pretends to represent.

Vladimir Tismaneanu
Foreign Policy Research Institute, Philadelphia

Union of Soviet Socialist Republics

Population. 276,300,000 (*Izvestiia*, 5 February)
Party. Communist Party of the Soviet Union (Kommunisticheskaia Partiia Sovetskogo Soiuza; CPSU)
Founded. 1898 (CPSU, 1952)
Membership. 18.5 million (*Pravda*, 4 June 1984); 44.1 percent workers; 12.4 percent peasants; 43.5 percent technical intelligentsia, professionals, administrators, and servicemen; women, 27.6 percent of all party members, 33 percent of candidates; estimated total membership as of 1 January 1986, 19 million
General Secretary. Mikhail S. Gorbachev
Politburo. (Unless otherwise indicated, nationality is Russian; first date given is year of birth, second date is year of election to present Politburo rank) 11 full members: Mikhail S. Gorbachev (b. 1931, e. 1980), Geidar A. Aliev, Azerbaijani (b. 1923, e. 1982, first deputy chairman [first deputy prime minister], Council of Ministers), Viktor M. Chebrikov, Ukrainian (b. 1923, e. 1985, chairman, Committee for State Security [KGB]), Andrei A. Gromyko (b. 1909, e. 1973, chairman of the Presidium [president], Supreme Soviet), Dinmukhamed A. Kunaev, Kazakh (b. 1912, e. 1971, first secretary, Kazakh Central Committee), Egor K. Ligachev (b. 1920, e. 1985), Nikolai I. Ryzhkov (b. 1929, e. 1985, chairman [prime minister], Council of Ministers), Vladimir V. Shcherbitsky, Ukrainian (b. 1918, e. 1971, first secretary, Ukrainian Central Committee), Eduard A. Shevardnadze, Georgian (b. 1928, e. 1985, foreign minister), Mikhail S. Solomentsev (b. 1913, e. 1983, chairman, Party Control Committee), Vitali I. Vorotnikov (b. 1926, e. 1983, chairman, Russian Soviet Federated Socialist Republic [RSFSR] Council of Ministers); 6 candidate members: Piotr N. Demichev (b. 1918, e. 1964, minister of culture), Vladimir I. Dolgikh (b. 1924, e. 1982), Vasili V. Kuznetsov (b. 1901, e. 1977, first deputy chairman, Presidium of the USSR Supreme Soviet), Boris N. Ponomarev (b. 1905, e. 1972), Sergei L. Sokolov (b. 1911, e. 1985, minister of defense), Nikolai V. Talyzin (b. 1929, e. 1985, first deputy chairman [first deputy prime minister], Council of Ministers)
Secretariat. 9 members (* indicates members of Politburo): *Mikhail S. Gorbachev (general secretary), *Egor K. Ligachev (ideology and personnel), *Vladimir I. Dolgikh (heavy industry), Boris N. Ponomarev (international affairs), Ivan V. Kapitonov (b. 1915, light industry), Viktor P. Nikonov

(b. 1929, agriculture), Konstantin V. Rusakov (b. 1909, ruling communist parties), Lev N. Zaikov (b. 1923, defense industry), Mikhail V. Zimianin (b. 1914, Belorussian, culture)

Central Committee. 319 full and 151 candidate members elected at Twenty-sixth CPSU Congress; approximately 290 active full members as of 1 January 1986. Central Committee apparatus is organized under 24 departments; key department heads include Boris N. Ponomarev (international), Nikolai I. Savinkin (b. 1913, administrative organs), Vladimir A. Karlov (b. 1914, agriculture), Nikolai E. Kruchina (b. 1928, administration of affairs), Klavdii M. Bogolyubov (b. 1909, general), Georgi P. Razumovsky (b. 1936, party organizational work [cadres]).

Status. Ruling and only legal party

Last Congress. Twenty-sixth, 23 February–4 March 1981, in Moscow; next congress scheduled for February 1986

Last Election. Supreme Soviet, 4 March 1984; more than 99.9 percent of vote for CPSU-backed candidates, all 1,500 of whom were elected; 71.4 percent of elected candidates were CPSU members.

Defense Council. The inner circle of the leadership concerned with national security affairs; only the chairman is publicly identified. Chairman: Mikhail S. Gorbachev; probable members, as of 1 January 1986: Andrei A. Gromyko, Nikolai I. Ryzhkov, Egor K. Ligachev, Marshal Sergei L. Sokolov; probable associates: Viktor M. Chebrikov, Marshal Sergei F. Akhromeyev (b. 1923), chief of staff and first deputy minister of defense

Government. 110 members of Council of Ministers. 115 members confirmed by Supreme Soviet April 1984, including three first deputy chairmen (first deputy prime ministers), ten deputy chairmen (deputy prime ministers), 63 ministers, and 22 chairmen of state committees. An additional first deputy chairman was named 1 November 1985 and five ministries were abolished 22 November 1985. Key members of government not identified above: Vsevolod S. Murakhovsky (b. 1926, Ukrainian, first deputy chairman, Council of Ministers, and chairman, State Committee for the Agroindustrial Complex), Guri I. Marchuk (b. 1925, Ukrainian, deputy chairman for science and technology, Council of Ministers), Vitali V. Fedorchuk (b. 1918, Ukrainian, minister of internal affairs), Yakov P. Ryabov (b. 1928, deputy chairman for international economic affairs, Council of Ministers), Mikhail S. Smirtyukov (b. 1909, administrator of affairs)

Auxiliary Organizations. Communist Youth League (Kommunisticheskii Soiuz Molodezhi; Komsomol), 42 million members, led by Viktor M. Mishin (b. 1943); All-Union Central Council of Trade Unions (AUCCTU), 132 million members, led by Stepan A. Shalayev (b. 1929); Voluntary Society for the Promotion of the Army, Air Force, and Navy (DOSAAF), led by Georgi M. Egorov, more than 65 million members; Union of Soviet Societies for Friendship and Cultural Relations with Foreign Countries

Publications. Main CPSU organs are the daily newspaper *Pravda* (circulation more than 11 million), the theoretical and ideological journal *Kommunist* (appearing 18 times a year, with a circulation over 1 million), and the semimonthly *Partinaia zhizn*, a journal of internal party affairs and organizational matters (circulation more than 1.16 million). *Kommunist vooruzhennikh sil* is the party theoretical journal for the armed forces, and *Agitator* is the same for party propagandists; both appear twice a month. The Komsomol has a newspaper, *Komsomolskaia pravda* (6 days a week), and a monthly theoretical journal, *Molodaia gvardiia*. Each USSR republic prints similar party newspapers in local languages and usually also in Russian. Specialized publications issued under supervision of the CPSU Central Committee include the newspapers *Sovetskaia Rossiia*, *Selskaia zhizn*, *Sotsialisticheskaia industriia*, *Sovetskaia kultura*, and *Ekonomicheskaia gazeta* and the journal *Politicheskoe samoobrazovanie*. Tass is the official news agency.

The USSR experienced a period of unprecedented instability in its top leadership during the first half of the 1980s. Only four men had served as full-term leaders of the country over the 64 years between 1917 and 1982; four general secretaries appeared in rapid succession in the course of 52 months between November 1982 and March 1985. This rapid turnover was the legacy of Brezhnev's "stability of cadres" policy, which had inhibited the rise of relatively young, experienced political leaders. Meanwhile, the regime was plagued by severe domestic problems: pervasive corruption, widespread alcoholism, low labor productivity, and a widening technological gap vis-à-vis the developed capitalist economies. Cohesion of the Soviet bloc was precarious and Moscow's drive for "restructuring of international relations" in the Third World had run out of steam. The breakdown of détente and the thrusts of Western rearmament had further worsened the USSR's position in the world "correlation of forces." Selection of the aged, ailing Konstantin Chernenko as general secretary of the CPSU in February 1984 seemed to confirm the impression of a stagnant, immobilized political system.

Against this background of disarray, Mikhail Gorbachev assumed the reins of leadership upon the death of Chernenko in March 1985. The new general secretary's rapid assumption of authority was stunning as he projected an image of vigorous and more open leadership. Derailing opponents and installing his own men in a flurry of personnel changes, he revived Yuri Andropov's drives for stricter discipline and better economic performance. Surprisingly, Gorbachev took personal command of foreign policy and pursued an activist course featuring a wide range of initiatives designed to improve the USSR's world position. The new leadership's dramatic first year was climaxed by Gorbachev's impressive performance at the November Geneva summit, which probably strengthened his domestic position on the eve of the Twenty-seventh CPSU Congress.

Despite the whirlwind early pace, at year's end enormous obstacles remained in the way of Gorbachev's drive to get the USSR moving again. The manifold "contradictions of socialism," rather candidly admitted during the Soviets' "Time of Troubles," 1982–1985, continued to challenge a new generation that had long awaited its chance to lead the system.

Leadership and Party Organization. In the early weeks of 1985, the Kremlin did a reprise of the Andropov death watch a year earlier. Chernenko had missed the Red Square funeral ceremonies for Defense Minister Dimitri Ustinov in late December and, after a TV appearance on 27 December, disappeared from public view for two months. In January, the Warsaw Pact summit meeting set for Sofia was postponed, presumably due to Chernenko's ill health (*WP*, 15 Janaury) and Soviet officials reportedly told Western visitors that the general secretary was ailing (*NYT*, 22 January).

An official statement indicated that Chernenko had addressed a Politburo meeting in early February (Tass, 7 February) but Western observers were skeptical, particularly since the statement followed by one day the first public confirmation of the leader's illness, by *Pravda* editor Viktor Afanasyev in a live interview with Italian state television (*WP*, 8 February). In late February, an obviously frail Chernenko appeared on television twice within five days, supposedly casting his ballot in the RSFSR Supreme Soviet elections and accepting his credentials as a deputy. However, Moscow party chief Viktor Grishin appeared both times with Chernenko and the two men were evidently wearing the same suits and ties during the second telecast as for the first; moreover, the background walls and curtains were identical for the two newscast scenes. Western observers concluded that this was a single ineptly staged propping up of the failing leader in his hospital room, with slight changes of scenery to give plausibility to the claim that he had been able to vote at a polling station (ABC News, 28 February; *WP*, 1 March; *NYT*, 1 March).

Chernenko died on the evening of 10 March. An autopsy report signed by the chief Kremlin physician, Dr. Evgeny Chazov, and nine other doctors cited heart failure traceable to emphysema as the cause of death; Chernenko was also said to have suffered from chronic hepatitis and cirrhosis (*NYT*, 12 March). The Politburo reportedly met during the night of 10 March to select Mikhail Gorbachev as the new general secretary, and the choice was duly ratified by the Central Committee on the following day (*Pravda*, 12 March).

The hierarchy moved with almost unseemly haste to confirm the succession: Gorbachev was formally installed as the new leader almost immediately after the first announcement of Chernenko's death. Chernenko was largely ignored by the Soviet media over the next few days as maximum attention was concentrated upon Gorbachev; moreover, the funeral rites for Chernenko were extremely perfunctory.

The circumstances surrounding the transition suggested that Gorbachev had been selected well in advance. However, reports surfaced in Moscow of a last-ditch effort, spearheaded by Grigori Romanov, to install Moscow party chief Viktor Grishin as interim leader. According to these reports, it was claimed that Chernenko had indicated Grishin as his choice, a claim allegedly disputed by Foreign Minister Andrei Gromyko. A subsequent "inside" story from the Moscow rumor mill indicated that Gorbachev had been elected by a 5-4 secret ballot of the full Politburo present in Moscow on 10 March; this supposedly accounted for the rush to confirm Gorbachev, at the insistence of senior hierarch Gromyko (*WP*, 1 November). *Pravda* reported on 25 December that Boris N. Eltsin (b. 1931), a secretary of the Central Committee, had replaced Grishin as first secretary of the Moscow City Party Committee.

Whatever the validity of these reports, two aspects of the succession drama were unquestionable. First, the old Brezhnevites and the hordes of office holders who had benefited from the "stability of cadres" policy could not have been happy with the choice. Second, Gorbachev acted from the first moment of his accession like a man with a clear mandate to rejuvenate the Soviet system. And the new leader left no doubt that he would pursue policies similar to those initiated by Yuri Andropov during his brief tenure as general secretary: Gorbachev's first two speeches featured clarion Andropovian calls for discipline and efficiency.

In his speech to the extraordinary plenary meeting of the Central Committee on 11 March, Gorbachev emphasized the economic tasks that lay ahead: "We face the job of making a decisive breakthrough in placing our national economy on a footing of intensive development. We must, we are duty bound, to attain in a very brief period the most advanced positions in science and technology, the highest world level in the productivity of social labor" (*Pravda*, 12 March).

The new leader was even more blunt in his eulogy at the Chernenko funeral rites: "The development of the initiative and creative endeavor of the masses, strict observance of law and order, consolidation of labor, state, and party discipline will continue to remain in the center of attention. We will support, encourage, and elevate in all ways those who by deed, practical results, rather than by words, show their honest and conscientious attitude toward civic duty" (*NYT*, 14 March).

Much more impressive than Gorbachev's confident bearing and firm postulation of systemic goals was his rapid takeover of key levers of command. Soviet history demonstrates that it is not policy preferences but control of the flow of personnel that undergirds the authority of the general secretary, and Gorbachev, in the weeks following his accession, moved more quickly than any previous Soviet leader to establish his personal ascendancy over the mammoth regime bureaucracy.

The Central Committee, at its April plenum, elevated to full Politburo membership three Gorbachev supporters who had risen from obscurity to high positions during the tenure of Yuri Andropov. Promoted from candidate membership was Viktor Chebrikov, 61, head of the KGB. Bypassing the candidate stage, party secretaries Egor Ligachev, 64, and Nikolai Ryzhkov, 55, were elected directly to full Politburo membership. Marshal Sergei Sokolov, 73, named in December 1984 to succeed Dimitri Ustinov as defense minister, was elected as a candidate member of the Politburo (*Pravda*, 24 April).

Remarkably, there had been a total absence of uniformed figures atop the Lenin Mausoleum during the Chernenko rites (*NYT*, 14 March), evoking speculation that the military leaders were unhappy with Gorbachev's selection or, alternatively, that the marshals were big losers in the succession sweepstakes. The simultaneous rise of Chebrikov to full Politburo membership and limitation of Sokolov to candidate status lent some support to the view that the KGB had overtaken the military in Kremlin influence and, in some quarters, Chebrikov's promotion was viewed as a payoff for police support in the succession.

Ligachev and Ryzhkov were both closely identified with Gorbachev, having served under his direct supervision in the Central Committee Secretariat, and they were known as strong advocates of the Andropov-Gorbachev policy line. The April plenum apparently left Gorbachev with a solid majority of supporters on the Politburo. His hold on the Secretariat was also strengthened with the selection of Viktor P. Nikonov, 56, to fill Gorbachev's former post of party secretary for agriculture (*Pravda*, 24 April). Nikonov, minister of agriculture of the Russian Republic since 1983, was first secretary of Mari *obkom* from 1965 to 1979, and USSR deputy minister of agriculture from 1979 to 1983.

The impact of these moves upon the upper levels of the hierarchy was soon apparent. Gorbachev's presumed main rival, Grigori Romanov, disappeared from public view after 9 May, missing the general secretary's highly publicized visit to Leningrad and an important Warsaw Pact meeting. Romanov was reportedly on vacation, but Western observers noted that it was a strange time for him to go on leave and, as his "vacation" approached the two-month mark, his exit from leadership ranks seemed a likely prospect.

When the Central Committee met on 1 July, Romanov was summarily dismissed from both his Politburo and Secretariat positions, although his departure was couched in the usual "at his own request" language (ibid., 2 July). The often stormy career of the abrasive 62-year-old Leningrader thus apparently had come to an inglorious end. The principal reason for Romanov's dismissal was probably his hostility toward Gorbachev. However, there were reports that Romanov was undergoing treatment for acute alcoholism (*Radio Liberty Research*, 1 July). Health reasons were cited in the announcement of Romanov's resignation and such a problem, quite consistent with his previous reputation, would have been incompatible with the abstemiousness demanded by the virtual teetotaler Gorbachev.

The July plenum also promoted Georgian party leader Eduard A. Shevardnadze, 57, to full Politburo membership (*Pravda*, 2 July). The full significance of this move became apparent on the following day when Shevardnadze was named foreign minister, replacing Andrei Gromyko, who moved up to the Soviet presidency (see below). Shevardnadze, in his thirteen years as party boss in Georgia, gained a reputation as an inveterate foe of corruption and as one of the Soviet Union's more innovative administrators. He had been an enthusiastic executor of experimental reforms in agricultural organization under Gorbachev's direction and reportedly owed his leadership post in Georgia largely to the backing of Gorbachev's patron Andropov.

Two new members of the Central Committee Secretariat were named at the July meeting. Lev N. Zaikov, 62, Leningrad *obkom* first secretary, and Boris N. Eltsin, 54, head of the Central Committee Construction Department since April 1985, were the new appointees. Zaikov was manager of a military-oriented high-tech government corporation in Leningrad until 1976, when he became that city's mayor. He served in that post until 1983, when he succeeded Romanov as Leningrad province party chief. Given his background, it seemed probable that he was now succeeding Romanov again, assuming the latter's yielded responsibility for the defense industry (*NYT*, 2 July). Eltsin, a protégé of former Politburo stalwart Andrei Kirilenko, was first secretary of Sverdlovsk *obkom* from 1976 to April 1985. The selection of Eltsin, two major promotions for Nikolai Ryzhkov, and the continued high visibility of deputy premier Yakov Ryabov during the year indicated that Gorbachev was successfully pursuing a gambit initiated by Andropov, that of coopting the "organizational tail" of the fallen hierarch Kirilenko.

Another Gorbachev ally, Nikolai V. Talyzin, was elected a candidate member of the Politburo at the October plenum (*Pravda*, 16 October), following his appointment as first deputy premier. The Gorbachev-Talyzin connection had first become apparent in 1984, when Talyzin was elected a Supreme Soviet deputy representing Krasnodar *krai*, a region controlled by the Andropov-Gorbachev "reformist" wing of the party.

When Ligachev moved up to full Politburo rank and assumed the ideology portfolio in the Secretariat, a replacement was needed for the job of overseeing party personnel. The new head of the Organizational Party Work Department of the Central Committee was Georgi P. Razumovsky, 49, first secretary of Krasnodar *krai* since 1983 (Radio Moscow, 3 June; *Radio Liberty Research*, 4 June). In 1982–1983 Razumovsky had served as head of the Agroindustrial Complex of the USSR Council of Ministers, in which post he worked closely with then party agriculture secretary Gorbachev, who probably was responsible for tapping him to be Vitali Vorotnikov's successor as Krasnodar regional secretary in 1983.

As impressive as Gorbachev's rapid takeover at the top was, perhaps even more significant was the spate of replacements in lower echelons. Twenty additional regional secretaries were replaced between January and July (some of whom were promoted). More than 30 percent of the Brezhnev appointees in the regional posts had been replaced since November 1982 and the process of personnel turnover was almost certain to accelerate as Gorbachev consolidated his power position. Since most of the regional secretaries qualify automatically for Central Committee membership, the widespread changes promised considerable alteration in the composition of the Central Committee at the Twenty-seventh CPSU Congress. Preparation of the slate of candidates for Central Committee membership presumably would be in the hands of Gorbachev's deputies: the party's number two man, Ligachev, and cadres secretary Razumovsky.

One indication of a strategy of "packing" cadre ranks with Gorbachev devotees was the large number of recent appointees with backgrounds in agriculture to the Central Committee apparat. However, among the new regional secretaries whose dates of birth were available, the average age was 53, against an average age of 59 for Brezhnev appointees still in office, possibly indicating some difficulty in finding younger qualified officials (*Radio Liberty Research*, 20 June). It might also suggest that Gorbachev, like Brezhnev, will tend to rely upon men of his own generation. Most of the recent appointees, particularly those above regional level, were born between 1920 and 1935, thus raising the possibility of a new phase of "immobilism" for party hopefuls under the age of 50.

The most prominent of the new regional appointees was Yuri F. Solovyev, 60, named to succeed Zaikov as Leningrad *obkom* first secretary (*Pravda*, 9 July). Solovyev served as Leningrad *obkom* second secretary, 1975–1978, as Leningrad *gorkom* first secretary, 1978–1983, then as USSR minister of industrial construction until his reassignment to Leningrad.

An important transfer was that of Aleksandr A. Khomyakov, 53, who moved from Tambov *oblast* to the first secretaryship of Saratov *obkom* upon the appointment of incumbent Vladimir K. Gusev to a first deputy premiership of the Russian Republic (ibid., 12 April).

The first major personnel change after Gorbachev's assumption of the first secretaryship was the retirement of 70-year-old Ivan P. Bespalov as first secretary of the industrial Kirov region and his replacement by Vadim V. Bakatin, a former first secretary of the Kirov *obkom* party committee and a CPSU inspector at the time of his new appointment (ibid., 24 March). Other appointees in major regional posts were drawn from the Central Committee apparat and had worked under Gorbachev's supervision during his tenure as CPSU "second secretary." These included I. K. Polozkov, Razumovsky's successor in Krasnodar *krai*, a section head in the Central Committee's department (ibid., 4 June); M. A. Knyazyuk, successor to Vladimir G. Klyuev (see below) in Ivanovo *oblast*, an inspector of the Central Committee (ibid., 16 July); Nikolai S. Ermakov, new first secretary of Kemerovo *obkom*, first deputy head of the Central Committee's heavy industry department (ibid., 13 April); Yuri V. Petrov, Eltsin's successor in Sverdlovsk, deptuy head of the Central Committee's cadres department (ibid., 20 April); and Valentin A. Kuptov, new secretary of Vologda *obkom*, an inspector of the CPSU Central Committee (ibid., 21 July). Longtime Tula province first secretary Ivan K. Yunak, 67, was replaced by Yuri I. Litvintsev, another CPSU Central Committee inspector (ibid., 6 August).

The pattern continued with the naming of I. S. Boldyrev, a former secretary of the Stavropol *krai* party committee and more recently a CPSU Central Committee inspector, as successor in the Stavropol regional post to Vsevolod Murakhovsky, who was appointed as a USSR first deputy premier (ibid., 5 November). And when Turdakun U. Usubaliev, 66, retired as first secretary of the Kirgiz party, he was succeeded by another Central Committee inspector, A. M. Masaliev, former first secretary of the Issyk-Kul province party committee (*Izvestiia*, 2 November; *Pravda*, 2 November).

G. I. Revenko, deputy head of the CPSU Central Committee Department of Party Organizational Work, formerly second secretary of the Kiev *obkom*, was named first secretary in Kiev province upon the retirement of longtime incumbent Vladimir M. Tsybulko, 61 (*Pravda*, 2 November).

Moldavia, long a Chernenko stronghold, was particularly hard hit by the Gorbachev purge. Y. P. Kalenik and B. N. Savochko were dismissed as members of the Central Committee bureau and were succeeded by Vladimir F. Semenyov as secretary for industry and Mircha I. Snegur as secretary for agriculture (*Sovetskaia Moldavia*, 1 June). In Uzbekistan, where party chief Inamzhon B. Usmankhodzhaev appeared to be firmly in Gorbachev's corner, two new party secretaries were appointed, Vladimir P. Anishchev for industry and Khabibulla A. Shagazatov for construction (*Radio Liberty Research*, 30 July).

In Latvia, where party first secretary Boris K. Pugo, a former KGB official, was notably active in the anticorruption campaign, several changes were made in the apparat's top ranks. Anatoly V. Gorbunov, 43, head of the Latvian party Department of Administrative Organs, was promoted to party secretary for ideology (*Sovetskaia Latvia*, 29 March). Gorbunov was succeeded in his former post by N. J. Usin. A. E. Ikaunieks was dismissed as a Central Committee secretary and replaced by K. I. Njuska. A. J. Gruduis was named head of the Central Committee Department of Research and Educational Institutions (ibid., 19 May). Arnold Klaucens moved from head of the Department of Light Industry and Consumer Goods to first secretary of the Riga city party committee (ibid., 26 June). P. J. Strautmais was dismissed from the Central Committee Bureau and replaced by A. P. Klautsen (ibid., 29 September).

Yuri P. Kochetov, 53, a CPSU Central Committee inspector, was named second secretary of the Armenian party, replacing Gennadi N. Andreyev, 49, appointed as ambassador to Ethiopia (*Pravda*, 13 April).

When Eduard A. Shevardnadze moved to Moscow as USSR minister of foreign affairs, Dzhumber I. Patiastivili, 46, Central Committee secretary for agriculture, was promoted to first secretary of the Georgian party (*Zaria vostoka*, 7 July).

A major personnel change in Kazakhstan demonstrated that generational turnover was not the only consideration involved in personnel shuffling. Kenes M. Aukhadiev, 47, chairman of the Youth Commission of the USSR Council of Nationalities, was relieved of his duties as first secretary of Alma Ata province "in connection with his transfer to work in the economy" and was replaced by M. S. Mendybayev, chairman of the Kustanai province Soviet Executive Committee (*Pravda*, 25 August).

Restaffing of the departments of the Central Committee, initiated by Andropov, continued apace. New department heads included Arkady I. Volsky, a former aide to the general secretary, as head of the Machine Building Department, and Nikolai A. Stashenkov, the former deputy head of the Trade and Consumer Services Department (*Radio Liberty Research*, 30 July). Stashenkov's new post was not specified but was probably that of head of the Trade and Consumer Services Department. There were persistent reports that Leonid M. Zamyatin, perhaps the most obnoxious of all Soviet officials in the eyes of Western correspondents, would be fired and that his entire International Information Department would be scrapped (Paris, AFP, 20 June; *FBIS*, 21 June). However, such rumors had also surfaced during the tenure of Yuri Andropov and, in November, Zamyatin was still on the job as briefer of Western journalists at the Geneva summit.

Perhaps the most significant appointment in the Central Committee was that of Aleksandr N. Iakovlev, 61, as head of the Propaganda Department (*Pravda*, 22 July). Iakovlev, longtime ambassador to Canada, had served as Gorbachev's host during his visit to that country in 1983 and had been director of the Institute of World Economics and International Relations of the USSR Academy of Sciences since 1984. His appointment demonstrated the extent of Gorbachev's determination to have his own men in key positions. Iakovlev's predecessor, Boris I. Stukalin, 62, as a Suslov protégé and Andropov appointee, seemed immune to the purge. Nevertheless, Iakovlev, a Gorbachev favorite, displaced him, and Stukalin was consigned to the diplomatic "dumping ground" in the relatively unimportant post of ambassador to Austria (ibid.).

An editorial in *Pravda* a week after Gorbachev's accession indicated that the purge might extend to the lowest ranks of the party. The editorial, entitled "Raising Exactingness," called for the elimination of all manifestations of "showy behavior, empty words, boastfulness, and irresponsibility" (ibid., 18 March; *Radio Liberty Research*, 22 March). The editorial highly praised an innovation recently introduced in the Georgian party, the "report and character assessment" (*kharakteristika*), which involves evaluation of party members not by their superiors but by their peers.

The negative thrust of Gorbachev's campaign to revive party vigor and discipline was supplemented by positive calls for sacrifice and commitment to regime goals. Making a "populist" appeal for support over the heads of officials (similar to the approach of Nikita Khrushchev), Gorbachev mixed with the masses in highly publicized visits to factories and other workplaces in Leningrad, Kiev, Moscow, and the Tyumen province oil fields (*NYT*, 17 April; *Pravda*, 19 May, 27 June, 5–6 September; *Izvestiia*, 7 September).

During the final weeks of the year, party officials at all levels were busy with preparations for the Twenty-seventh CPSU Congress, scheduled to convene in Moscow on 25 February 1986. As usual, much attention was concentrated upon the outlines of the new five-year plan but perhaps even more important was consideration of the new party program, to supplant the one approved at the Twenty-second CPSU Congress in 1961. The earlier document, filled with grandiose and subsequently embarrassing projections at the insistence of Nikita Khrushchev, was shelved in 1983 by Yuri Andropov, who commissioned the drafting of a new long-range program. The draft of the new program, approved at the October plenum of the Central Committee, avoided commitment to spectacular goals concerning the march toward communism. The new program promises to meet consumer demands "more fully," but the only areas in which full consumer satisfaction is promised are those of construction material, sanitary supplies, and gardening tools and supplies (*Literaturnaia gazeta*, 30 October). If the consumer sector is somewhat slighted, other areas, such as high-tech, are not; economic planning for the fifteen-year period from 1985 to 2000 calls for a doubling of the USSR's productive capacity.

Government. Restaffing of the governmental as well as the party apparat was clearly high on Gorbachev's agenda, and sharp public criticisms of various ministries were accompanied by forced retirements of veteran officeholders. Less than two weeks after Gorbachev's election, Piotr S. Neporozhny, 74, minister of power and electrification for 22 years, retired "for health reasons" and was replaced by Anatoly I. Mayorets, 55, minister of the electrical equipment industry (Tass, 23 March; *CSM*, 25 March). The change came one week after a front-page *Pravda* article sharply criticizing the power ministry.

A similar fate befell Ivan P. Kazanets, 67, USSR minister of ferrous metallurgy since 1965. Kazanets retired in July as did Nikolai N. Tarasov, 73, USSR minister of light industry since 1965 (Tass, 6 July). Both ministries had been under heavy fire for inadequate performance. Kazanets's successor was Serafim V. Kolpakov, who moved up from first deputy minister. The light industry post was filled by Vladimir G. Klyuev, 61, first secretary of Ivanovo *obkom* since 1972, with a career background in the textile industry.

Viktor S. Fedorov, 73, retired as minister of the petroleum refining and petrochemical industry and was replaced by his deputy, Nikolai V. Lemayev, 56. Nikolai S. Patolichev, 77, retired as minister of foreign trade "for reasons of health" and was succeeded by Boris I. Aristov, 60, a deputy foreign minister since June 1983. Other new appointees included Gennadi A. Iagodin, 58, former rector of the Mendeleev Chemical-Technical Institute in Moscow, as USSR minister of higher and secondary specialized education (*Izvestiia*, 17 July); Arkady N. Shchepetilnikov, 55, minister of industrial construction of the Ukraine, as USSR minister for that economic sector; Sergei F. Voyenushkin, 56, USSR minister of the construction industry, after filling the corresponding post in the RSFSR (ibid.); and Gennadi P. Voronovsky, USSR minister of the electrical equipment industry, and Vladimir A. Brezhnev, USSR minister of transport construction, who both rose from first deputy rank in their ministries (ibid., 8 May).

These changes presumably dealt a considerable jolt to the stultified governmental bureaucracy, but shuffles at the top of the system attracted much more attention. The July Supreme Soviet session produced a major surprise.

It had been widely expected that Gorbachev would assume the Soviet presidency at the July meeting. Instead, the post went to Foreign Minister Andrei A. Gromyko, who yielded both the foreign ministry and a first deputy premiership upon his election as chairman of the Supreme Soviet presidium. Gorbachev, who in April 1984 had nominated Chernenko for the presidency, citing foreign policy considerations as compelling the combination of party leadership and head of state, put forward Gromyko's name at the July session, asserting that he was unable to take the position due to his pressing responsibilities for the party's domestic program (*Pravda*, 3 July).

Gromyko had reportedly been the prime mover behind Gorbachev's assumption of power and had apparently emerged as the number two man in the regime. In these circumstances, the "promotion" was a rather startling "kick upstairs" for the veteran diplomat. Most observers concluded that Gorbachev intended to take personal control of foreign policy. In any case, the shift of Gromyko meant the end of an era, following his record 28 years as USSR foreign minister, during which he had put his own indelible stamp on the conduct of Soviet diplomacy. Perhaps as a sop, Gromyko was accorded a protocol rank ahead of the prime minister, in defiance of the conventional order, at the November Bolshevik Revolution anniversary celebration (ABC News, 7 November).

Even more surprising was the identity of Gromyko's successor. Chosen as new foreign minister was Georgian party leader Eduard Shevardnadze (*Pravda*, 3 July), who had no foreign policy experience whatsoever except as head of delegation on several junkets. Shevardnadze was possibly selected in part because his style was compatible with Gorbachev's desire for a more open and public relations–oriented conduct of foreign affairs and, indeed, the new foreign minister subsequently brought a more cordial personal tone to Soviet diplomacy, especially in relations with the United States.

The long-expected retirement of the 80-year-old prime minister, Nikolai A. Tikhonov, a Brezhnev crony, finally came in September. After Gorbachev had passed up the presidency, many Western observers had predicted that he would assume the premiership, combining the top party and government posts as had Stalin and Khrushchev. Should he not do so, the leading contenders for the premiership were expected to be first deputy premier Geidar A. Aliev or RSFSR prime minister Vitali I. Vorotnikov. Instead, the position went to party secretary Nikolai I. Ryzhkov (*Izvestiia*, 28 September; *Pravda*, 28 September).

Ryzhkov appeared to be the prototypical technocrat in the mold obviously favored by Gorbachev. Following service as head of the Sverdlovsk

Uralmash complex, first deputy minister of heavy and transport machinery, and first deputy head of Gosplan, Ryzhkov was named as a CPSU Central Committee secretary at the behest of Yuri Andropov in November 1982. Subsequently, as head of the new Economics Department of the Central Committee, he had become the principal figure on the party side in supervision of the economy and, in April 1985, had received the unusual distinction of direct election to full Politburo membership without passing through candidate status (see above).

An official with a similar technocratic background, Nikolai V. Talyzin, 56, was chosen as new head of Gosplan, replacing Brezhnev appointee Nikolai K. Baibakov, 74, who had filled the position for twenty years (*Izvestiia*, 16 October). Baibakov was an obvious candidate for a Gorbachev purge, since he had engaged in a debate in the public press with Yuri Andropov in 1983 over questions of economic reform (see *YICA*, 1984, pp. 382–83). Talyzin's career profile includes fifteen years in the communications ministry, the last five (1975–1980) as minister, and five years as deputy premier in charge of CMEA affairs (1980–1985). Upon his assumption of the Gosplan post, Talyzin was also promoted to first deputy prime minister. This double appointment seemed a clear signal of Gorbachev's intention to upgrade Gosplan and downgrade the governmental ministries (see below).

Talyzin's position as USSR representative to CMEA was taken by deputy premier Aleksei K. Antonov (*Pravda*, 4 November). Antonov's old deputy premier slot was filled by Ivan S. Silaev, 55, who moved up from the post of minister of aviation (Tass, 3 November; AP, 4 November).

Nothing else demonstrated so clearly Gorbachev's hold on power as did the next appointment of a first deputy premier. A protégé of Gorbachev and his successor in the Stavropol kraikom party first secretaryship, Vsevolod S. Murakhovsky, 59, was named first deputy chairman of the Council of Ministers at the beginning of November (*Pravda*, 2 November; *Izvestiia*, 3 November). Murakhovsky's appointment coincided with the retirement of Ziya N. Nuriev, 70, as deputy premier (*Pravda*, 2 November) and signaled an upgrading for the governmental supervisor of the agroindustrial complex comparable to the enhanced status for the head of Gosplan. Murakhovsky was the first regional secretary to move directly to such a high government post since Frol Kozlov in 1957. The pace of Gorbachev's takeover was indicated by the fact that Brezhnev had required nearly twelve years to install Tikhonov, his hometown crony, in a first deputy premiership, while Gorbachev had required less than eight months for a similar appointive coup.

The November session of the Supreme Soviet featured a report by Gorbachev on the Geneva summit, approval of the new five-year plan, and confirmation of Ryzhkov, Talyzin, and Murakhovsky (*Izvestiia*, 27, 28 November; *Pravda*, 27, 28 November).

The Soviet military leadership also experienced a shakeup, amid indications that the marshals were not entirely pleased with the Gorbachev succession (see above). General Aleksei A. Epishev, 77, a close associate of Brezhnev who had served as head of the Main Political Administration of the Armed Forces since 1962, was replaced by Colonel-General Aleksei D. Lizichev, 57, who had been serving as chief political commissar of Soviet forces in Germany (*Krasnaia zvezda*, 20 July). General Piotr G. Lushev, commander of the Moscow Military District, displaced General Mikhail M. Zaitsev as commander in chief of Soviet forces in Germany (East Berlin, ADN, 19 July; *FBIS*, 22 July). General Yuri P. Maksimov was appointed as a deputy minister of defense and probably replaced Marshal Vladimir F. Tolubko, whose retirement was announced, as commander in chief of strategic missile forces (*Radio Liberty Research*, 30 July).

A report appeared in the Western press in July suggesting that Marshal Nikolai V. Ogarkov, 67, had replaced Marshal Viktor G. Kulikov, 64, as USSR first deputy minister of defense and commander in chief of Warsaw Pact forces (*WP*, 18 July). The Soviet Defense Ministry issued official denials of the report (London, *Daily Telegragh*, 20 July; AP, 25 July). After Ogarkov was abruptly supplanted as first deputy minister of defense and chief of staff in September 1984 by Marshal Sergei L. Sokolov, it was generally assumed that he had been demoted in a most summary manner. However, by mid-1985, many Western military analysts concluded that Ogarkov had been reassigned in September 1984 to organize a western theater of operations and upgrade the organizational readiness for war of Soviet and allied forces (*Radio Liberty Research*, 24 July). Soviet officialdom seemed reluctant to clear up the mystery surrounding the controversial Ogarkov and, at year's end, his exact position in the military hierarchy remained unclear.

Domestic Affairs. Gorbachev inherited a plethora of seemingly intractable domestic problems and confronted the primary conundrum of reform, the delicate balance required for reinvigoration of the system without sacrifice of central political control. Most of the problems revolved around the economy: low productivity, declining growth rate, a lengthening technological lag vis-à-vis the developed capitalist countries, low capacity for innovation, endemic inefficiency and corruption, and the continuing inability of the Soviet Union to feed itself.

There had been some hints during the interim Chernenko leadership that the USSR under Gorbachev would pursue decentralization of the economy and move to some extent toward free market operations. However, once in power, Gorbachev proceeded cautiously for a time on reorganization and appeared set against experimentation along the line of the new Chinese and Hungarian models. Ending its hesitation, in October and November the leadership moved boldly, initiating major structural changes in economic organization. Meanwhile, the drive against corruption that had marked the brief Andropov era was resumed with vigor and tough measures were introduced to curb alcoholism, viewed as the main cause of the labor force's high rate of absenteeism.

The main aim of the new powerholders appeared to be the conveying of an image of forceful leadership on all fronts, to convince the Soviet public that "business as usual" would not be tolerated. None of Gorbachev's words or actions during his first ten months in power indicated the slightest tendency toward domestic liberalization, although the new leader's open, "populist" style did signal a different approach to the masses. Previous policies concerning human rights and the subordinate nationalities remained unchanged. In the realm of ideology, attention centered on the continuing redefinition of the concept of "developed socialism" and the drafting of the CPSU program to be adopted at the Twenty-seventh Congress.

Economy. The Soviet economy had continued in the doldrums during 1984. Reported growth in national income was 2.6 percent, against a U.S. rise in GNP of 6.9 percent (*Pravda*, 26 January; *Time*, 25 March). The grain harvest was an estimated 170 million tons, down from 195 million in 1983 (AP, 17 January). The Central Statistical Administration's annual report indicated particular problems in the petroleum industry, which failed to fulfill the 1984 plan and was below 1983 levels in both production volume and labor productivity. According to the report, 613 million tons of petroleum were extracted in 1984, three million tons less than in 1983 and well below the target of 624 million tons. Coal production dropped from 716 to 712 million tons but natural gas output was up to 587 billion cubic meters against a goal of 578, a sharp rise from 536 billion in 1983. The fruit and vegetable and microbiological industries fell short of planned targets (*Pravda*, 26 January).

There were indications that the general economic situation worsened in the early months of 1985. An official commentary in February reported a failure in some areas to implement measures for the increase in production of grain and other products and blamed "the inactiveness and sometimes irresponsibility of farm leaders" for 1984 grain crop losses (*Izvestiia*, 14 February). The RSFSR Council of Ministers reported in March that industrial output in the Russian Republic fell by 1.5 percent from the previous year's figures in the first two months of the year. The report also cited shortcomings in railroad and road transport and noted that the volume of consumer services was below planned targets, particularly in the countryside (*Sovetskaia Rossiia*, 20 March). In April, Gorbachev was critical of first-quarter plan results, attributing failure largely to "poor organization, sometimes complacency, and in some places the lack of a sense of responsibility" (*NYT*, 8 April).

The construction industry continued to draw heavier fire than most others. An expanded session of the collegium of the USSR Ministry of Construction in January reported that the ministry "has grave shortcomings in the organization and management of construction and is weakly exploiting the large reserves available" (Moscow Domestic Service, 14 January; *FBIS*, 17 January). Gorbachev's initial response to the critical state of the construction industry was to call Boris N. Eltsin from the Sverdlovsk *obkom* first secretaryship to take over, in April, as head of the Central Committee Construction Department. In July, Eltsin was promoted to Central Committee secretary, presumably with continuing responsibility for the construction industry (see above).

Many other changes in key industrial posts followed, but it was clear that a new managerial team would not alone correct the chronic disarray of the economy. Since Andropov's accession in 1982, a wide-ranging debate among Soviet economists had pointed to deep-seated structural problems in the economy, some of the analyses corresponding rather closely to those proffered by Western experts. Gorbachev's earlier statements had positioned him among the "reformers" but the specific contours of his reform program were not immediately evident.

In the first weeks of his leadership, the new general secretary concentrated upon the Soviet Union's technological lag and the need for greater work discipline. Both points were emphasized in his acceptance speech at the March Central Committee plenum: "We should, we are bound to attain within the briefest period the most advanced scientific and technical positions, the highest world level in the productivity of social labor" (*Pravda*, 12 March).

Echoing the new leader's call for harder work, a *Pravda* front-page editorial (20 March) advocated the "strengthening of organization, order, and discipline in all spheres of production and management" to turn the economy "onto the path of intensive development." Another article on the same day noted the urgency of economic reform, pointing to experiments in the Ukraine giving factory managers greater independence from central planning authorities. "The current economic situation simply does not allow us to mark time," the article said (*Literaturnaia gazeta*, 20 March). These exhortations followed more disappointing news on the economy. Statistics for the first two months showed oil and coal production down from the same period of 1984, a drop in industrial production growth from 5.6 percent to 3.7 percent, and a decline in labor productivity growth from 5.4 percent to 1.3 percent (*Los Angeles Times*, 21 March).

In his speech at the April Central Committee plenum, Gorbachev called for "revolutionary changes" in the economy. Goals set out by the general secretary included less rigid economic planning, more independence for Soviet enterprises, improved management techniques, increased emphasis on consumer products and service industries, and a retooling of the economy to install advanced technology (*Wall Street Journal*, 24 April). Two days after Gorbachev's speech, Stepan Sitaryan, a deputy head of Gosplan, offered some specific proposals designed for carrying out the general secretary's broad ideas on the economy. These included new incentive bonuses for efficient workers, greater freedom for managers to make production and investment decisions, limited profit sharing for workers in efficient enterprises, incentives to reduce excess use of labor, and use of price changes to encourage innovation (ibid., 26 April).

Hopes that the "reform" movement would take a free-market turn were jolted in June by Gorbachev's two closest associates on the party secretariat. In a speech to graduates of the Academy of Social Sciences, Egor Ligachev said that needed changes in the economy will take place "in the framework of scientific socialism without any diversions in the direction of a market economy." Similar sentiments were voiced by Nikolai Ryzhkov in an address at the national economics academy (*Pravda*, 29 June).

Gorbachev himself continued to be hazy on the specifics of structural redesign of the economy. A lengthy speech by the general secretary at a high-level meeting on science policy sponsored by the Central Committee on 11 June maintained the pattern of a call for revolutionary change while avoiding a detailed blueprint. However, Gorbachev's three major speeches to date seemed to indicate an intention to maintain a hierarchical, centrally administered economic system but to streamline the hierarchy, reducing the detailed control powers of the ministries and providing more scope for initiative at the enterprise level (*Radio Liberty Research*, 17 June).

Two authoritative articles in June citing leading advocates of reform pointed toward possible solutions for the reorganization problem. Tatyana Zaslavskaya, author of the celebrated 1983 Novosibirsk report, called in an interview for a strengthening of central planning and a concurrent devolution of authority to individual enterprises (*Izvestiia*, 1 June). This seemed in line both with the limited experimentation begun under Andropov and with Gorbachev's current thinking. In his 11 June speech, the general secretary hinted at the creation of superministries to render industrial sectors less unwieldy and foster more detailed decisions by groups of enterprises. This was a far cry from radical decentralization; Gorbachev suggested that these ministries should have more control over their industries, not that industries should be more independent (*Wall Street Journal*, 12 June).

An article by Aleksandr Chekalin entitled "Incentives to Development" favorably quoted B. P. Kurashvili of the Soviet Academy of Sciences, an advocate of Hungarian-style reform, on the need for "regulative management," which would avoid formal plan targets and use "economic methods" to encourage the production of new output and halt the production of obsolete products. According to Chekalin, "once the opportunities for the upper echelons to exercise direct leadership over production are reduced, it will not be necessary to keep the present oversized management apparatus" or "to have as many narrowly specialized ministries as today" (*Pravda*, 17 June). While a restructuring of the ministerial apparat was compatible with Gorbachev's public statements, it seemed highly unlikely that he would countenance the sort of drastic market reform advocated by the controversial Kurashvili, particularly in view of the speeches by Ligachev and Ryzhkov and his own praise for the wartime command economy under Stalin, at the May VE Day anniversary celebration (ibid., 9 May).

While the debate continued, Gorbachev rejected the first draft of the new five-year plan, a direct slap at premier Tikhonov and Gosplan head Baibakov (*NYT*, 12 June), both of whom would leave their posts within four months.

The mid-year economic report offered scant evidence of a turnaround in the economy. The petroleum, coal, ferrous metallurgy, chemical, mineral fertilizer, timber and paper, and construction materials industries were all short of planned targets (*Ekonomicheskaia gazeta*, no. 33, 12 August). Similar results were reported for the third quarter (*Izvestiia*, 4 November).

A Central Committee resolution in August on the limited economic reform begun by Andropov pronounced the experiment a success, noting the acceleration of scientific-technical progress, improvement in the quality of output, and effective use of "economic levers" (*Pravda*, 4 August). However, past experience indicates that concentration upon a few industries makes relatively easy the achievement of set goals, while producing complications for related economic sectors. Moreover, there seemed to be a general awareness of the very real risks entailed in generalization of any economic reform, and it was certain that any major overhaul would be resisted by the entrenched governmental bureaucracy.

A clearer indication on Gorbachev's reorganization plans came in October. The naming of Nikolai V. Talyzin as head of Gosplan, his promotion to first deputy premier (*Izvestiia*, 15 October), and his election as a candidate member of the Politburo (*Pravda*, 16 October), pointed toward a major new role for the state planning commission and a lessening of the decisionmaking power of the individual ministries.

There were some early indications that the USSR faced another bad year on the farms. At the end of August, it was reported that crops had been late in ripening in a number of regions and that harvesting of grain in the Russian Republic was running behind the 1984 pace (*Sovetskaia Rossiia*, 30 August; *FBIS*, 11 September). In October, the CPSU Central Committee openly criticized eight ministries for failure to help develop supplemental agricultural production (Beijing, Xinhua, 25 October; *FBIS*, 25 October).

In a major speech in Tselinograd in September, delivered to party and management personnel from the Virgin Lands area, Gorbachev called for a doubling of the increase in meat production during the period 1986–1990 as compared with 1981–1985. He said that measures were being considered to increase the independence of state and collective farms, but there was no suggestion of important changes in agricultural policy or organization (*Radio Liberty Research*, 12 September). Indeed, one puzzling aspect of Gorbachev's performance during much of the year, in view of his background and the severity of the farm problem, was the relative inattention to agriculture as compared with other economic sectors.

But Gorbachev had evidently been quietly nurturing his plans for this economic sector. In early November, his protégé Vsevolod Murakhovsky was appointed as first deputy premier with responsibility for agriculture (see above). Three weeks later, Gorbachev took his most dramatic step to date in the effort to revitalize the economy. Murakhovsky was named head of a new agency, the State Committee for the Agroindustrial Complex, which was assigned full authority over the production and processing of agricultural products. At the same time, five ministries—Agriculture, Fruit and Vegetable Industry, Rural Construction, Meat and Dairy Industry, and Food Industry—were abolished (*Izvestiia*, 23 November). The consolidation of authority in the agricultural sector indicated that Gorbachev had firmly committed himself to the "superministries" option. It seemed likely that the reorganization of agriculture would serve as a general model, leading to abolition of many ministries and the creation of other superagencies designed to streamline management of the economy (*NYT*, 23 November).

The "Comprehensive Program for the Development of Consumer Goods, 1986–2000," unveiled in October, promised more housing and consumer goods, improvement in product quality, and upgrading of services (*Pravda*, 9 October). However, when the specific targets called for in the plan are set against the overall goal posited by Gorbachev of a doubling of the nation's total production by the year 2000, it appears that consumer satisfaction is not at the top of the new leadership's list of priorities.

Campaigns against alcoholism and corruption. Alcoholism has long been regarded as the leading reason for absenteeism and poor work performance in the economy, as well as a major factor in the decline of life expectancy of males from 67 to 62 in the last twenty years (*WP*, 17 May). After Gorbachev assumed the general secretaryship, police crackdowns on public drunkenness were reported in various parts of the country and, in May, a wide-ranging program to combat alcohol abuse was introduced.

The drinking age was raised from 18 to 21; the opening of liquor stores on working days was set at 2 P.M., three hours later than before; a gradual reduction in the production of vodka and other strong beverages was to start in 1986; and the sale of barmatukha, a sweet and potent fruit wine, was to be banned completely by 1988. Stiff penalties will be imposed for public drunkenness and drunken drivers will be fined 100 rubles and lose their driving licenses for three years (Tass, 16 May; *Pravda*, 17 May).

A full-scale press campaign against alcoholism was mounted to support the new measures, and leading public organizations, particularly the trade unions and the Komsomol, were enlisted in the drive. Liquor vanished from Moscow's prestigious clubs and the Kremlin stopped the serving of hard liquor at official banquets (*WP*, 1 June).

The campaign against corruption initiated by Yuri Andropov had not stopped, but it had slowed considerably during the tenure of Konstantin Chernenko as general secretary. Gorbachev promised a revived campaign in his first speech as party leader (*Pravda*, 12 March). The press emphasized the need for *poriadok* (order) and reported numerous cases of prosecutions of lawbreakers. In late March, a Kiev accountant named Dubchak was executed by firing squad for embezzlement in the dairy supplies industry (London, *The Economist*, 30 March). The renewed anticorruption drive was presented as an essential aspect of the projected revitalization of the society, being coupled in the press with the debate on ways to "intensify" the economy (*NYT*, 26 March; *Pravda*, 13 July).

Dismissals for "misdeeds" were reported in Ufa, and a public housing scandal was aired in Volgograd; the city party secretary, the mayor, and other officials were dismissed in Bratsk for "gross abuse of their positions" (*Pravda*, 25 March). A critical report on Yaroslavl noted that state losses from embezzlement in 1984 rose by 42 percent over the previous year (*Sotsialisticheskaia industriia*, 25 March).

The anticorruption drive gathered steam as Gorbachev moved to consolidate his power position. The Party Control Committee, restored to its assigned watchdog function under the vigorous direction of Mikhail Solomentsev, played a leading role. In April, the Party Control Committee expelled from the party three officials in the Kalmyk ASSR charged with corrupt activities (*Pravda*, 6 April) and, in August, the committee supervised punishment of a number of officials in Perm *gorkom* for failure to enforce the new regulations against drunkenness and alcoholism (Moscow Television Service, 5 August; *FBIS*, 6 August).

Several officials in the railway industry were sentenced to long terms by a Leningrad court for bribe-taking (Moscow Domestic Service, 16 July; *FBIS*, 17 July). In Georgia, new party leader Dzhunbar Patiashvili served notice that the anticorruption efforts of Eduard Shevardnadze would be maintained. In August, it was reported that minister of local industry Tengiz P. Geleishvili and newspaper editor O. D. Ioseliani had been dismissed for corruption (*Zaria vostoka*, 31 August).

Two union-republic leaders reportedly close to Gorbachev added to their reputations as tough opponents of corruption. Boris K. Pugo, 49, had carried out a considerable purge in Latvia since his installation as first secretary of the union-republic party in April 1984. In March, a plenum of the Latvian party's Central Committee noted satisfactory results and a continuation of the anticorruption drive (*Cina*, 29 March). In Uzbekistan, first secretary Inamzhon Usmankhodzhaev, 55, continued his ruthless drive to clean up the union-republic in accord with Moscow's directives. In August, deputy premier Akram R. Khodzhayev was fired "for shortcomings in his work and for abusing his post to solve housing problems of members of his family" (Tass, 3 August; *NYT*, 4 August).

Dissent. A major event was the release of Elena Bonner, wife of Andrei Sakharov and a leading spirit of the democratic movement, to seek medical treatment in the West. Bonner arrived in Rome on 2 December; she was to receive treatment for eye problems in Italy and then go to the United States for consultations with heart specialists. Sakharov has been restricted to the closed city of Gorky since

1980 and his wife was exiled to Gorky in 1984. Bonner refused to talk to Western newsmen, saying that this was a condition for her permission to travel and return to the Soviet Union (AP, 2 December). However, members of her family reported that Sakharov was in failing health and had been subjected to forced feeding during his hunger strike to secure permission for Bonner to obtain medical treatment in the West (ABC News, 2 December).

The approval of Bonner's travel permit obviously was a sop to Western public opinion on the eve of the Geneva summit. Prior to the summit, in discussions of the Sakharov case, Soviet officials omitted the usual references to the dissident leader's possession of state secrets, raising hopes that he might be allowed to emigrate. There was also speculation that an increase in Jewish emigration might be permitted, both to further the "spirit of Geneva" and to enhance prospects for Soviet participation in the Mideast peace process. However, aside from permission for a number of Soviet spouses to be reunited with their mates in the West (*NYT*, 20 November), there was no evidence of any "thaw" in domestic control policies.

During his early months as party leader, Gorbachev, indeed, provided no hints whatsoever suggesting general liberalization on this front. But organized domestic dissent was not a problem compelling Gorbachev's attention; the relentless KGB campaign over two decades had eliminated virtually all overt dissent. When Gorbachev assumed the leadership, only three organizations created on the basis of the Helsinki Final Act remained active, each with a handful of members: the Action Group for the Defense of the Rights of Invalids, the Catholic Committee for the Defense of the Rights of Believers in Lithuania, and the Georgian Helsinki Group (*Radio Liberty Research*, 30 July).

The Soviet record on human rights remained a sore spot in relations with the West, and national and religious discontent continued to be troublesome for the Kremlin although these were not major immediate problems for the new leadership. Lithuania, with its large Catholic population and intense nationalism, was still a potential powder keg. Three members of a family of Georgian dissidents trying to emigrate demonstrated outside the Interior Ministry's visa office in Tbilisi in January (Paris, AFP, 22 January; *FBIS*, 23 January). Eight issues of the *samizdat* periodical *Chronicle of the Catholic Church of Ukraine* reached the West just as Foreign Minister Gromyko met with Pope John Paul II for talks, which reportedly included discussions on the plight of the Ukrainian Catholic Church (*CSM*, 1 March; *Radio Liberty Research*, 8 March).

The Soviet press reported in July a recantation by one of the better known Ukrainian political prisoners, Yuri Shukhevych-Berezynskyi, who allegedly denounced "Ukrainian nationalism" in a letter to the editor (*Visti z Ukrainy*, Kiev, no. 28, 1985; *Radio Liberty Research*, 23 July).

The trial of Vladimir Brodsky resumed in Moscow in August, after a July adjournment apparently aimed to avoid adverse publicity during the World Peace Festival. Brodsky, a 34-year-old physician, had been a leading activist for Jewish emigration and a prominent figure in the Unofficial Group to Establish Trust Between the USA and USSR. The group, set up in 1982, has campaigned for nuclear disarmament in East and West (BBC, 15 August).

The continuing harsh domestic political climate was emphasized by the arrest, at the end of 1984, of the historian Anton Antonov-Ovseyenko, 64, a survivor of Stalin's concentration camps and author of *The Time of Stalin*, widely acclaimed upon its publication in the West in 1981 (Vienna, *Die Presse*, 21 January; *FBIS*, 23 January). Antonov-Ovseyenko was reportedly being held in the Lefortovo KGB prison.

Ideology. Between 1982 and 1984, Soviet theorists had engaged in a remarkable debate on the "contradictions of socialism," sparked by Yuri Andropov's statements re-evaluating "developed socialism." This concept had been advanced during the Brezhnev era to denote an allegedly high level of social development attained by the Soviet Union. In Andropov's view, the USSR had not progressed nearly so far as claimed during the Brezhnev years, and giant strides in productivity and technology were required to move the society along the path of "developed socialism." If the Brezhnevian claims of social advance were exaggerated, the projections in the party program adopted at the Twenty-second CPSU Congress seemed positively ludicrous, and Andropov had commissioned a rewriting of the program. This work was completed in 1985. In the process of revision, the theoretical retooling was strongly influenced by practical questions of labor discipline and economic reform and by the political struggle between the Andropov-Gorbachev "reformists" and the entrenched old guard.

An article by Konstantin Chernenko at the end of 1984 set the tone for the continuing discussion of "developed socialism." Chernenko spoke of "developed socialism" as "a historically long period" and said that the two major tasks for the foreseeable future were the raising of the efficiency of production and the further inculcation of socialist values (*Kommunist*, no. 18, December 1984). Two weeks after Chernenko's authoritative statement, *Pravda* editor Viktor Afanasyev penned a commentary on the article that spotlighted the "disproportions, shortfalls, contradictions" of "developed socialism." According to Afanasyev, Soviet social development is still characterized by "many objective difficulties" and by "shortcomings and unresolved tasks arising from subjective factors." To meet these problems, Afanasyev called for "fundamentally new, truly revolutionary technical and technological solutions" and for improvement in the "economic machinery and the entire system of management" (*Pravda*, 11 January).

One day after publication of Afanasyev's article, a front-page *Pravda* editorial took up Chernenko's theme of ideological indoctrination, stressing the importance of an effective integrated counterpropaganda system to cope with a claimed Western ideological offensive. The editorial denounced capitalist propaganda that "extols 'living standards,' views, and values alien to us, exalts individualism, inflames private ownership instincts, and fans religious and nationalist sentiments" (ibid., 12 January). Another *Pravda* front-page editorial five days later commented further on the Chernenko article. The editorial cautioned that in the period of developed socialism "we cannot be allowed to set ourselves attractive but unattainable goals," and maintained that a "qualitative advance in the entire national economy is imperative" (ibid., 17 January). One day later, *Pravda* continued its elaboration of Chernenko's position on developed socialism with an editorial, "The Party and the Deepening of Socialist Democracy." The editorial stressed that "our socialist democratism is incompatible with anarchic arbitrariness and attempts to counterpose citizens' rights and freedoms to duties, and democracy to discipline" (ibid., 18 January).

The most extreme revision of the Brezhnevian view of developed socialism was put forward in a February front-page editorial in *Izvestiia* (13 February). Against earlier claims that Soviet society was well along in this historic stage of development, the editorial stated bluntly that "today our country is at the beginning of the stage of developed socialism."

Following Gorbachev's assumption of power, the press placed even greater emphasis upon the necessity for economic reform and modernization in discussions of the concept of developed socialism and the forthcoming party program. Typical was a May article by Professor G. Volkov, which noted that the USSR "has entered the stage of developed socialism." This period, said Volkov, "is relatively long and, within its framework, we have to resolve impressive economic, social, and political tasks. It is necessary, above all," Volkov maintained, "to cardinally rearm and modernize the material and technical base of society in accordance with the latest achievements of science and technology" and "to achieve a sharp rise in the level of productive forces and labor productivity" (*Pravda*, 27 May).

When the long-awaited draft of the new party program was finally released in October, the document appeared to be relatively sanitized and innocuous, as compared with the controversial 1961 version. The draft carefully avoided any explicit admission of a recent downturn in the world correlation of forces, which had been implied in statements by authoritative regime spokesmen during 1983 and 1984, or of a retrogression in Soviet social development, which had been implied in the debate over the "contradictions of socialism." Mostly, the draft featured standard formulas and stock slogans. There were, however, some notable points of interest.

The draft program said that the USSR had entered the stage of developed socialism and acknowledged that much work remained in economic development to complete this phase. The concept of "party and state of the entire people" was retained and a brief reference indicated that the reversal of the Marxian concept of "division of labor," spearheaded by Institute of Marxism-Leninism director Anatoly Egorov in the 1970s, was still accepted. The program spoke of the "definitive overcoming of vestiges of the old division of labor" at the "highest phase of communist formation," but not of abolition of the division of labor as projected by Marx. The "withering away of the state" was declared subject to achievement of the "necessary socioeconomic and ideological prerequisites" and "existence of the appropriate international conditions."

Criticism was aimed at the Brezhnev leadership for "unfavorable tendencies" in the 1970s and early 1980s. The program called for further struggle against bourgeois ideology, confirmed the approach of socialist realism in the arts, stressed the growth of the party's leading role in Soviet society, and upheld "proletarian internationalism," i.e., subordination to Moscow, as the guiding principle of relations with communist and workers' parties. The references to improvement in the work of cadres hinted at the possibility of a purge of the ranks (*Pravda*, 26 October; *FBIS*, 28 October; *Literaturnaia gazeta*, 30 October).

The cautious rehabilitation of Stalin continued. A May article by literary critic Konstantin Priima was highly laudatory of Stalin (*Sovetskaia Rossiia*, 19 May; *Radio Liberty Research*, 29 May) and appeared eleven days after Gorbachev's favorable reference to Stalin's wartime role in the VE Day anniversary speech to veterans (*NYT*, 9 May). However, the draft party program did not mention Stalin in its commentary on the Great Patriotic War and did castigate Stalinism when it spoke of the party's work "to eliminate the consequences of the personality cult and deviations from Lenin's norms of party and state leadership and to rectify errors of a subjectivist, voluntarist nature" (*Pravda*, 26 October). Negative comments about Stalin were also contained in published extracts from the memoirs of the late Soviet president, Anastas Mikoyan; the dictator was said to have been directly responsible for the USSR being taken by surprise when Germany attacked in 1941 (*Voprosy istorii KPSS*, no. 12, December).

Auxiliary and Front Organizations. The All-Union Central Council of Trade Unions (AUCCTU), which had been subjected to a widespread purge of officials in 1983–1984 (see *YICA*, 1985, p. 349), continued under heavy fire in 1985. AUCCTU head Stepan A. Shalaev, a Chernenko protégé, engaged in a "self-criticism" performance on Moscow television in May, admitting that "until recently, many trade union organizations were taking a conciliatory attitude toward cases of drunkenness" (Moscow Television Service, 23 May; *FBIS*, 24 May).

Shalaev promised that the trade unions would take an active role in strengthening discipline and combating alcoholism. The prevailing political currents were obvious in his designation of the "labor discipline guaranteed by the collective" movement pioneered in Sverdlovsk *oblast* as a model for the unions. Sverdlovsk, long a fiefdom of Andrei Kirilenko, has more recently been a key bastion of the Andropov-Gorbachev "organizational tail."

The Communist Youth League (Komsomol), assigned a major supportive role in the discipline and antialcoholism campaigns, provided some exemplary victims in the wholesale purge of officials. A plenum of the organization's central committee on 2 November fired A. N. Kolyakin, the chief Komsomol ideologist, from his post and expelled him from the All-Union Komsomol central committee "for having compromised himself." A. B. Chesnokov and V. M. Tankeev were removed from the Komsomol central committee "for instances of drunkenness and violation of labor discipline" (*Komsomolskaia pravda*, 3 November; *Radio Liberty Research*, 7 November).

The annual prizes of the USSR Union of Journalists also served as a barometer of the political weather in Moscow. The Voronskiy Prizes for the best works in international journalism were awarded to Anatoly Gromyko, son of Andrei and director of the Africa Institute of the USSR Academy of Sciences; Vladimir Lomeiko, head of the Press Department of the USSR Ministry of Foreign Affairs, for the book *New Thinking in the Nuclear Age*; Aleksandr Iakovlev, director of the Institute of World Economics and International Relations of the USSR Academy of Sciences (appointed in July as head of the CPSU Central Committee Propaganda Department), for the book *From Truman to Reagan*; and Kurt Bachmann, member of the Presidium of the German Communist Party "for articles exposing the designs of West German imperialism" (Moscow Television Service, 4 May; *FBIS*, 6 May).

The Presidium of the World Peace Council met in Moscow, 22–25 March, to discuss the "most urgent problems of the acute international situation." The session was attended by 400 "activists of the antiwar movement," including leaders or members of 21 communist parties, 25 "revolutionary democratic" parties, 8 social democratic parties, and major trade unions of North America and Western Europe (Moscow Television Service, 6 April; *FBIS*, 15 April).

The twelfth World Youth Festival, a week-long gathering to demonstrate "anti-imperialist solidarity, peace, and friendship," opened in Moscow on 27 July with 20,000 delegates from 150 countries. General Secretary Gorbachev delivered a welcoming address at the opening ceremony, which was also attended by the other ten Moscow-based Politburo members. Massive security measures were in force, with document checks reported as far away as 100 miles from the capital. Tass criticized a U.S. State Department report that said the festival is part of the Soviet effort to influence the world's youth against Western democracies (AP, 28 July).

International Views, Positions, and Activities. Soviet activities in the international arena during the year displayed the same dominant features as efforts on the domestic front: wide-ranging attempts to reverse unfavorable trends of the early 1980s and the vigorous leadership of newly installed General Secretary Gorbachev.

The general situation confronting the new leader was rather bleak. Following the Soviets' failure to halt installation of modernized NATO missiles in 1983, "star wars" had become the *bête noire* of Moscow's world policy in 1984. As the Reagan administration proceeded with plans for the Strategic Defense Initiative (SDI), Konstantin Chernenko, long an outspoken advocate of détente, had evidently taken the lead in September 1984 in directing the Soviets back to the bargaining table. However, the physical debility of Chernenko and uncertainty concerning the succession did nothing to dispel the general impression of drift and indecisiveness in Moscow's external relations. Moreover, in the resumed arms talks, neither side appeared amenable to any significant compromise.

Another major headache for the new leader was a deteriorating situation in the Third World. In all of the major areas where the USSR had scored major gains in the 1970s in the Third World "restructuring of international relations"—Nicaragua, Angola, Ethiopia, Afghanistan, and Southeast Asia—ruling clients or allies of the USSR were seriously challenged by anti-Soviet forces. "Restructuring" in the Third World had slowed to a halt and, given the continued hostility between Moscow and Washington, the whole "two-track" policy of the Brezhnev era, which had combined détente with Soviet freedom of action in regard to "national liberation movements," had unraveled.

The election of Mikhail Gorbachev as general secretary of the CPSU in March left Western statesmen both hopeful and wary. The new leader had created a favorable impression during his visits to Canada and Britain in 1983–1984 but resolution of the long-running succession crisis promised to make the Soviet Union a more formidable adversary. Two assumptions concerning the new leadership were almost universally held: first, the need to concentrate upon domestic problems would impose some inhibitions upon the USSR's world role; second, in view of Gorbachev's inexperience in international affairs, Andrei Gromyko would continue to dominate foreign policy. Gorbachev would shortly confound these expectations.

Launching an unprecedented public relations blitz designed to influence world, especially Western, public opinion, Gorbachev sought to restore sagging Soviet prestige via diplomacy and propaganda. And in July he made a stunning move, elevating Gromyko to the USSR presidency and installing Georgian party leader Shevardnadze, untested in world affairs, as foreign minister. Subsequently, it was clear that Gorbachev had taken effective personal control of foreign policy.

While questions of the strategic balance retained the highest priority, Gorbachev appeared to adopt a strategy adumbrated during the brief tenure of Yuri Andropov, one placing less emphasis upon relations with the United States. In contrast to the failed "two-track" policy, which had linked Soviet-American détente with gains in the Third World, Gorbachev evidently concentrated upon Western Europe and peripheral areas stretching from Egypt to Japan, apparently hoping to end the USSR's relative isolation and to foreclose the potential of a feared geographical "encirclement."

Diplomatic overtures and pressures vis-à-vis Western Europe evoked Washington's concern but had a limited initial payoff for Moscow. At year's end, Britain had agreed to join in the development of a space defense, and West Germany was about to climb aboard the SDI bandwagon. Despite lavish Soviet blandishments, the Netherlands parliament voted to go ahead with missile deployment, although reservations attached to the Dutch approval threatened to render this a Pyrrhic victory for NATO. In the borderlands between the two camps, there was some easing of tensions, particularly in relations with China and Japan, but fundamental issues remained unresolved.

Overshadowing this apparent reorientation of Soviet strategy, the November Geneva summit was the cynosure of world attention as Gorbachev and U.S. president Ronald Reagan met for the first time. The two leaders appeared to establish a cordial personal relationship and, ignoring their expert aides, held lengthy talks à deux. The atmospherics generated by these private discussions provided the most impressive feature of the conference, which yielded only agreements on cultural exchanges and other minor matters and instructions to negotiators to accelerate arms control talks without any directive resolving the thorny issues between the two sides. The talks seemed to strengthen the domestic and bloc political positions of both leaders and there was some subsequent easing of tensions, reflected in the reception of a U.S. trade mission to Moscow in December. But the basic points of contention between the superpowers had not been altered.

Gorbachev's first ten months in power had resulted in some reassertion of Soviet initiative in world affairs. However, the changes wrought by the new leader's activism thus far appeared to represent variations of style more than of substance.

U.S.-Soviet Relations. At the outset of the year, Soviet commentators set out the major theme of subsequent dealings between the superpowers. Valentin Falin said that U.S. insistence on "star wars" could stall any talks (*Izvestiia*, 3 January) and Yuri Kornilov asserted that a race in space weapons would "give an impetus to the arms race in other areas" (Tass, 3 January; *WP*, 4 January).

Against the backdrop of apparently adamant positions on both sides, Foreign Minister Gromyko and U.S. Secretary of State Shultz met in Geneva on 7–8 January. The tone of the meeting was reportedly cordial, and agreement was reached on resumption of arms talks, with the date and place of negotiations to be set "within one month" (AP, 9 January). Commenting on the news from Geneva, President Reagan said there were no preconditions for the talks but insisted that the United States would go ahead with research on a space defense. He also denied that SDI would be used as a bargaining chip (*NYT*, 10 January).

The opening of the talks was set for 12 March in Geneva. Prior to the resumption of negotiations, a new issue clouded U.S.-Soviet relations. A report issued on 1 February in Washington accused the USSR of "a clear violation" of the 1972 antiballistic missile (ABM) treaty. The official Soviet response was given at the end of the month by foreign ministry spokesman Vladimir Lomeiko, who called the charges "slanderous" but did not comment on the report's assertion that a new radar system under construction in central Siberia is "almost certainly" designed for ABM purposes (*WP*, 28 February). Earlier, a Soviet press release had hinted that prospects for an arms control accord would be improved if the United States ignored violations of existing agreements; such charges, according to the statement, did not contribute to a "favorable atmosphere" for the upcoming talks (Tass, 13 February; *Wall Street Journal*, 14 February).

The propaganda offensive against SDI escalated as the date for resumption of talks approached. On a visit to Spain, Gromyko said that the possibility of nuclear war is "no exaggeration" if the arms race is allowed to "erupt in space." However, Gromyko also held out a carrot: "Once 'Star Wars' projects are abandoned, the possibilities will be open for a reduction, even a drastic reduction, of strategic weapons and medium-range nuclear arms" (*WP*, 2 March). Col. Gen. Nikolai F. Chervov, who accompanied Politburo member Vladimir Shcherbitsky on a visit to the United States, warned in Washington that the USSR will "develop and perfect strategic offensive arms" rather than negotiate reductions if the United States continues its missile defense research program (ibid., 6 March).

The talks in Geneva began as scheduled on 12 March despite the death two days earlier of CPSU General Secretary Chernenko. Significantly, Soviet chief delegate Viktor P. Karpov said that he had received his instructions from Gorbachev, indicating that the latter had been in charge in Moscow during Chernenko's terminal illness (*Los Angeles Times*, 13 March).

Meanwhile, the 1980s ritual of expression of sanguine hopes upon installation of a new Soviet leader was played out in Moscow. Both Vice-President George Bush, who headed the U.S. delegation at Chernenko's funeral, and Secretary of State Shultz professed to be favorably impressed with Gorbachev. Bush conveyed an invitation for a summit meeting from President Reagan and said that he believed "we can move forward with progress" (*NYT*, 14 March). Shultz said that Reagan is ready to work with the Soviets for a more constructive relationship "across the board" (AP, 16 March).

The mild euphoria generated by the conversations in Moscow was promptly dissipated by the slaying of American liaison team member Maj. Arthur D. Nicholson by a Soviet sentry in East Germany on 24 March. The Soviets claimed that Nicholson was shot in a restricted area; however, Ambassador Anatoly Dobrynin met with Shultz on the matter, as did Soviet military commanders in Germany with their American counterparts. The Reagan administration made clear from the outset that the incident would not be allowed to interfere with the thawing of U.S.-Soviet relations (AP, 31 March).

While Washington and Moscow traded verbal thrusts over the incident, the Soviet military newspaper published two articles sharply critical of the training of USSR troops in East Germany (*Krasnaia zvezda*, 2, 3 April). A week later, East European diplomats were quoted in Bonn as saying that the Soviet soldier who shot Major Nicholson would be disciplined (Paris, AFP, 11 April; *FBIS*,

11 April). The U.S. State Department announced on 16 April that the Soviet military had agreed not to use force or weapons against the U.S. military team in East Germany; the U.S. demand for an apology and compensation was sidestepped by referring the matter "to higher authority" (*Los Angeles Times*, 17 April). However, on 23 April, the USSR denied that it had agreed to such renunciation of force or to consider compensation for Major Nicholson's family (Tass, 23 April). On 26 April, the United States expelled a Soviet military attaché (*NYT*, 27 April), and Moscow and Washington traded further verbal blasts as the confrontation proceeded to an inconclusive fadeout.

Another meeting between Shultz and Gromyko was scheduled for May in Vienna (Tass, 10 April; *FBIS*, 11 April) as Gorbachev assumed an increasingly prominent public role in Soviet foreign policy. The new leader met with an American congressional delegation headed by House Speaker Thomas P. O'Neill (*Pravda*, 11 April) one day after a meeting between Gromyko and foreign minister of the Netherlands, Hans van der Broek (*CSM*, 9 April). The visits followed the revival of antinuclear protests in several European countries, and these events coincided with the latest salvo in the Soviet "peace" offensive. In a major statement on foreign policy, Gorbachev announced a moratorium on deployment of Soviet missiles aimed at Europe and proposed a mutual freeze on middle-range missile deployment in Europe and a suspension of space weapons research while arms talks continue in Geneva (*Pravda*, 8 April). U.S. national security adviser Robert McFarlane said that the proposed moratorium would give the Soviets a considerable advantage and rejected it as illusory and "disappointing" (*CSM*, 10 April).

With negotiations stalemated due to the essentially uncompromising stances of both sides, Soviet-American relations increasingly took on the appearance of a public relations battle, with West European public opinion the main target. In his speech at the April plenum of the Central Committee, Gorbachev accused the United States of striving for military domination of the world (*Pravda*, 24 April) but followed this with a message to Soviet and American veterans gathered in Torgau to commemorate the 1945 linkup of forces, suggesting the wartime alliance as a model for current cooperation (*Los Angeles Times*, 26 April). Reagan's controversial visit to Bitburg cemetery in May provided an opening for Soviet propaganda, for the Moscow media utilized the incident to depict a U.S. linkage with fascism and "revanchism" (*Pravda*, 11 May; *NYT*, 4, 10, 11 May).

Defense Minister Marshal Sergei Sokolov, in an early May interview, called "star wars" a greater threat to peace than the atomic bomb and said that the United States had sought military superiority over the Soviet Union since the end of World War II (*Krasnaia zvezda*, 5 May). A similar view was expressed in Gorbachev's hard-line, "anti-imperialist" speech to Soviet war veterans on the VE Day anniversary (*Pravda*, 9 April).

In the following week, Shultz and Gromyko met in Vienna, with no apparent progress in resolving the arms deadlock, although both sides described the talks as "useful" (Reuters, 15 May). When Reagan dispatched Commerce Secretary Malcolm Baldridge to Moscow with a letter proposing increased trade, Gorbachev responded that the USSR wanted "stable relations" with the United States and blamed the "unsatisfactory state of Soviet-U.S. trade and economic links" on the "policy of discrimination conducted by the U.S. administration" and American attempts to use trade "as a method of political pressure" against the USSR (*Krasnaia zvezda*, 21 May; *FBIS*, 21 May).

The second round of negotiations opened in Geneva on 30 May, with no signs of impending agreement (*WP*, 30, 31 May).

American industrialist Armand Hammer reported after a meeting with Gorbachev in June that the Soviet leader was cool toward the idea of a summit (*Los Angeles Times*, 18 June), but in early July the two countries agreed upon the place and date of the summit. The scheduling of the meeting coincided with the appointment of Eduard Shevardnadze to succeed Gromyko as USSR foreign minister (see above). The switch in leadership of the Smolensk Square establishment marked a decided turning point in Soviet diplomacy. Not only did it mean the end of Gromyko's long reign over the diplomatic apparatus; it brought an open, public relations–oriented style to the Soviet foreign office not seen since the tenure of Maksim Litvinov in the 1930s. The personal touch of Shevardnadze was soon evident in more cordial relations with the United States.

The change in tone was first apparent at the July observance in Helsinki of the tenth anniversary of the accords on European security and cooperation (CSCE). Shevardnadze and Shultz displayed unusual conviviality, and their private meeting reportedly yielded progress on setting the summit agenda (*NYT*, 31 July). In his speech to the conference,

Shevardnadze called for a joint effort to ease tensions and improve the international political climate (*Pravda*, 31 July).

Despite the improved atmosphere, the superpowers continued their verbal sparring as they lurched toward the summit. Gorbachev announced a five-month moratorium on nuclear testing (ibid., 30 July) and called on the United States to follow suit. The Soviet press cited favorable foreign reaction to the moratorium (*Izvestiia*, 31 July), but Shultz denounced it as a publicity stunt (*NYT*, 31 July). A U.S. State Department spokesman said that the proposal did not provide for effective verification procedures (*WP*, 31 July). Meanwhile, the Soviets spurned a U.S. invitation to send observers to the next nuclear test in Nevada (Tass, 30 July; AP, 31 July).

Some flexibility was evident in the reported decision to allow Western experts to inspect two Soviet nuclear reactors. However, Western observers saw this as another public relations gesture, designed to improve the Soviet image at the August conference in Geneva to review the 1970 nuclear nonproliferation treaty (*NYT*, 12 August). When the conference met, the Soviets unveiled a proposal for a "star peace" international space agency (UPI, 20 August). As the Soviets continued their vehement opposition to U.S. plans for a space-based missile defense, an influential military journal reported that the USSR had been working on its own "star wars" program since 1964 (*International Defense Review*, August).

During the two months preceding the summit, Moscow and Washington traded proposals and maintained the public relations game. Shevardnadze met with Reagan at the White House and tendered an offer to cut nuclear arms by 50 percent in exchange for U.S. curbs on SDI (*NYT*, 30 September). The United States countered with a plan for missile reduction independent of space defense. In his October speech to the French parliament, Gorbachev suggested for the first time that an agreement on intermediate-range missiles could be reached "outside of direct connection with the problem of space and strategic arms" (ibid., 8 October). This was followed by a Soviet proposal at the Geneva talks for a temporary freeze on intermediate-range missiles to separate those weapons from strategic missile and space arms (*WP*, 24 October).

Many Western observers saw the Soviets as ahead on points in the pre-summit jockeying. The Reagan administration sought to blunt the Soviet propaganda offensive by focus on the USSR's role in regional conflicts, Moscow's human rights record, and alleged violations of previous agreements. In his weekly radio address on 12 October, Reagan charged that as many as ten thousand Soviet scientists and engineers were working on the USSR version of SDI and said that the construction of the radar complex near Krasnoyarsk was an "out-and-out violation" of the 1972 ABM treaty (AP, 13 October). The Soviets indicated willingness to halt the Siberian radar construction if the United States would forego modernization of two advanced radar stations, a feeler promptly rebuffed by Washington (*Wall Street Journal*, 1 November). Meanwhile, Soviet ire was aroused by apparently aborted proposals in Washington to interpret the ABM treaty as compatible with "star wars" testing (*NYT*, 3 November).

One positive note was the signing in Tokyo of an agreement on air safety by the United States, the USSR, and Japan (AP, 8 October). The pact was an American precondition for restoration of civil aviation ties between the United States and USSR; Soviet-American technical talks in Moscow in October prepared the way for a subsequent agreement on restoration of airline service between the two countries. But the usual irritants in Soviet-American relations, and some unusual ones, diverted attention from major issues during the pre-summit period.

The International Press Institute in London reported in August that the Soviet press had stepped up attacks on Western correspondents since Gorbachev's election as general secretary. Continuing Soviet harassment of Western reporters was highlighted by an incident in Leningrad, involving a two-day seizure of journalistic materials belonging to the *Christian Science Monitor*'s Moscow correspondent, Gary Thatcher (*CSM*, 12 August). More serious was the State Department's protest over alleged Soviet use of a possibly cancer-causing chemical to track the movements of American diplomats and identify people with whom they come in contact (*Wall Street Journal*, 22 August).

A Soviet sailor jumped ship near New Orleans on 24 October and was twice returned to his ship, as U.S. immigration officials apparently badly bungled the case. The incident set off a confrontation between the Reagan administration and irate members of Congress, led by North Carolina Senator Jesse Helms (Republican), but the U.S. foreign policy establishment was obviously disinclined to invite trouble with the Soviets at this critical juncture. When a federal judge ruled against a petition by groups that questioned Miroslav Medvid's "voluntary" statement that he wished to return to the USSR, his ship, the *Marshal Konev*, was allowed to sail for home with Medvid aboard (*NYT*, 26–30 October).

While the U.S. administration coped with the aftermath of the Medvid case, suspending two immigration officials for inept handling of the affair, a more startling "defection" story broke. Vitali Yurchenko, a major official in the KGB who had defected in Rome on 1 August and had been trumpeted by the CIA as a prize catch, showed up at the Soviet embassy in Washington on 2 November. Before returning to the USSR, he held a press conference in which he claimed that he had been kidnapped and drugged by the CIA (ibid., 2, 5–7 November). Western observers were unsure whether Yurchenko was a genuine redefector or a KGB plant, but in any case, the incident produced considerable embarrassment for the U.S. Central Intelligence Agency.

The attempted redefection of a Soviet soldier in Kabul in the same week brought a direct Soviet-American confrontation that had to be resolved at the highest levels. When the soldier sought asylum in the U.S. embassy in the Afghan capital, the Soviets cut off power to the compound and surrounded the embassy with troops pending return of the defector, who was described by American officials as "puzzled and tired" (AP, 3–5 November).

One further incident on the eve of the summit threatened to poison the atmosphere in Geneva. When Reagan arrived in the Swiss city, he was greeted with news of the leak of a letter from Defense Secretary Caspar Weinberger (who had not been invited to accompany the president) warning Reagan against the acceptance of Soviet positions (*WP*, 18 November). Some Western journalists speculated that the leak was an effort by hard-liners to sabotage any potential Soviet-American "deal," but administration officials dismissed the matter as unimportant.

Two major surprises marked the negotiations in Geneva on 19–21 November, the first U.S.-Soviet summit meeting since 1979. First, the two sides agreed to a news blackout while the conference was in progress, leaving the horde of assembled journalists so bereft of hard news that they began interviewing each other. Second, starting with an informal fireside chat, the two leaders assumed personal command and spent much of the time in lengthy conversations without the presence of their expert advisers. The two highly personable leaders apparently established a rapport that softened somewhat the rough edges of the superpower relationship (*NYT*, 22 November).

On the major issues, no agreement was reached and, indeed, none had been expected. SDI and the missile balance in Europe remained areas of sharp disagreement, as did the regional conflicts involving the superpowers' clients and allies (*WP*, 22 November). However, it was agreed to "accelerate" arms control negotiations set to resume on 16 January in Geneva, and to hold two further summit meetings, one in the United States in the summer of 1986, to be followed by another in the Soviet Union in 1987 (*NYT*, 22 November).

The summit yielded a number of accords on less controversial matters. The U.S.-USSR-Japan agreement on air safety was endorsed, and arrangements were made for negotiations on resumption of commercial air travel between the United States and the USSR. Two agreements were signed on cultural exchanges, and it was agreed that the United States will open a consulate in Kiev and the Soviet Union will open one in New York. An agreement was signed on the transfer of technology and "basic knowledge" relating to solar energy, and both sides said they favor a prohibition on chemical weapons. Finally, the two countries reaffirmed commitment to the nuclear nonproliferation treaty (AP, 21 November).

In a 90-minute press conference following the summit's closing ceremony, Gorbachev said that the talks were "to a certain extent productive" but warned that "all restraint will be blown to the wind" unless the United States compromises on "star wars" (*NYT*, 22 November). In a televised report to the U.S. Congress, Reagan called the meeting "constructive" and said that "while we still have a long way to go, we're at least heading in the right direction" (AP, 21 November).

One evident result of the conference was strengthening of the domestic and bloc political positions of both leaders. Gorbachev became even more of a star attraction for the Soviet media and was warmly received when he reported on the summit results to Warsaw Pact leaders in Prague (*NYT*, 23 November). Reagan drew much favorable comment when he reported on the summit to several allied leaders gathered in Brussels (ibid., 22 November), and at home his favorable rating in the public opinion polls rose to unprecedented heights. The summit was clearly reassuring for nervous U.S. allies and did serve to lower somewhat the temperature of superpower relations.

In December, Gorbachev offered to let American inspectors visit Soviet underground nuclear test sites, provided the United States would accept a moratorium on further tests. The White House promptly rejected such a link, at least for the present (AP, 19 December). A *Pravda* editorial (19 December) warned that the Soviets' unilateral moratorium, due to expire 1 January, would be extended only if the United States joined it. U.S. officials maintained that the proposed freeze was one-sided, since the Soviets had already concluded their testing program.

A less frosty atmosphere was evident when U.S. Commerce Secretary Baldridge returned to Moscow in December for trade talks, heading a delegation of four hundred American business executives. Baldridge said that his department will begin an "active official trade-promotion program" in the Soviet Union but cautioned that trade will not grow without a political thaw (AP, 9 December). Gorbachev spoke in favor of increased trade with the United States but, after a private meeting with Baldridge, said at a dinner for the American businessmen that economic ties will not improve until the United States removes "political obstacles" (UPI, 10 December).

The problem of Soviet espionage against the West, highlighted by spy scandals in Western Europe and the United States during the year, was certain to be unaffected by the "Spirit of Geneva." On 12 December, the State Department announced that about a hundred Soviet citizens working at the U.S. embassy in Moscow will be replaced by Americans to counter a "hostile intelligence threat" (AP, 12 December).

The superpowers traded bitter words about Afghanistan during the last week of the year but did agree on an unprecedented exchange of New Year's greetings. It was announced that President Reagan would speak to the people of the Soviet Union via radio and television and that General Secretary Gorbachev would deliver a similar message to the American people (AP, 27 December).

Western Europe. Following the near-total diplomatic isolation of the Soviet Union during the closing days of Andropov's tenure and the concentration of the relatively weak Chernenko leadership on relations with the United States, Moscow revived its hopes of splitting the NATO alliance by pressuring West European countries to move away from allegiance to Washington. Soviet need for Western technology and trade was one consideration, but much more important was the regional correlation of forces in Europe. Moscow stepped up its offensive against the deployment of modernized NATO missiles, but the Soviet leaders seemed even more concerned about West European attitudes toward, and possible participation in, American development of "star wars."

On the trade front, Gorbachev called in May for economic cooperation between the Council for Mutual Economic Assistance (CMEA) and the European Economic Community (EEC) (Reuters, 30 May). This was followed in June by an invitation from CMEA officials for the EEC to join exploratory trade talks in Moscow (ibid., 14 June). Earlier, French and Soviet trade officials had held extensive talks in Paris on economic links (see below). By the end of the year, Gorbachev apparently had become more pessimistic about the possibilities for an early upgrading of economic relations with the West. He told Commerce Secretary Baldridge that, while he favored improved trade relations with other parts of the world, his first priority was increased trade within the CMEA bloc (UPI, 10 December).

In regard to the major strategic issues, the Soviets displayed under Gorbachev a new interest in, and finesse in addressing, Western public opinion. From his public appearances during the Chernenko funeral rites to his post-summit press conference in Geneva, Gorbachev consistently sought to sway the European public against U.S. policies. One preferred tactic for pressuring West European governments was close collaboration of all "peace forces," including cooperation between communist and socialist parties. However, as continued Soviet disgruntlement over the 1981–1984 PCF-Socialist coalition in France made clear, any approval by Moscow of "popular fronts" was contingent upon the stance of target groups in regard to the USSR's international policies.

The Federal Republic of Germany, as the economic and strategic hinge of the Western alliance, remained the Soviets' number one target, despite abysmal failures to weaken FRG ties to NATO in 1983–1984. One constant theme was Soviet opposition to West German participation in "star wars." Varied Soviet pressures on this matter were to no avail; much to Moscow's dismay, at year's end the FRG was preparing to follow Britain in agreeing to participate in SDI development.

During the last weeks of Chernenko's tenure, Moscow maintained a harsh tone toward the Bonn regime. Reports of conversations between the FRG

Defense Ministry and West German industrial leaders on possible participation in the development of space weapons evoked a sharp denunciation from Soviet analyst Oleg Shirokov, who charged that "revanchist sentiments" were prevalent in leading circles of the FRG and maintained that the West German army was already the strongest in Western Europe (Tass, 14 February; *FBIS*, 15 February).

The Chernenko funeral rites brought an apparent mellowing in USSR-FRG relations. Gorbachev's conversation with FRG Chancellor Helmut Kohl was reportedly cordial and the Soviets even tolerated a friendly meeting between Kohl and East German leader Erich Honecker (*NYT*, 16 March). However, relations between Moscow and Bonn quickly turned sour. Moscow predictably denounced a statement by Kohl in the Bundestag defending SDI (Tass, 19 April; *FBIS*, 22 April), and the Soviets strongly criticized West German media coverage of a visit to Bonn by a parliamentary delegation led by Central Committee secretary Mikhail V. Zimianin (Tass, 27 April; *Radio Liberty Research*, 25 June).

The Easter peace marches in Western Europe had disappointingly low turnouts, but an estimated 300,000 to 400,000 had turned out in West Germany (*CSM*, 9 April). Gorbachev's moratorium announcement had presumably been aimed mainly at the Western peace groups, and the May visit to Moscow by West German Social Democratic Party chairman Willy Brandt (Tass, 27 May) was not likely to further improved relations with the Kohl government. Following Brandt's visit, the Politburo issued a statement calling for expansion of "the interaction of all forces interested in safeguarding and consolidating peace" and for the development of contacts between the CPSU and socialist parties (ibid., 30 May).

By May, the Soviet leadership had evidently written off any prospects for direct influence upon the Kohl government and subsequent Bonn-Moscow relations were clouded by the fresh Soviet hard line toward East bloc cohesion, with particular emphasis upon the German Democratic Republic. Moscow could perhaps derive some comfort from apparent discord within the Kohl government over SDI. While Chancellor Kohl's Christian Democrats supported SDI research, Foreign Minister Hans-Dietrich Genscher and other Free Democrats demanded new negotiations with the United States. In December, amid reports of an imminent formal enlistment by the FRG for U.S.-sponsored space defense research, Genscher said that there would be "minimal participation" on the part of West German industry (UPI, 15 December).

While "star wars" was given priority in the Soviet "peace" offensive, pressures to disrupt Western nuclear rearmament continued. On a visit to Rome in February, Gromyko warned Italy and other Western nations of their "responsibility" for permitting deployment of the new American missiles, while also calling upon the Italians to oppose "takeoff of the arms race toward outer space" (*Los Angeles Times*, 27 February). Belgian Foreign Minister Leo Tindemans, in Moscow for Chernenko's funeral, was warned by Gorbachev about the "consequences" of Euromissile deployment, and Foreign Minister Hans van den Broek of the Netherlands experienced an apparently similar rough session with Gromyko, in Moscow on 10 April (*Radio Liberty Research*, 25 June).

The French government, under President François Mitterrand, has been perhaps the most consistent West European critic of Soviet policies, both domestic and foreign. That stance was unchanged during the year, although high-level contacts between the two governments were cordial.

On the economic front, Renault abandoned a project to build an engine plant in the USSR when studies showed that its costs would not be offset by Soviet orders for equipment and machine tools (*Wall Street Journal*, 6 March). A Soviet trade delegation encountered tough bargaining in Paris, and the climate of negotiations was not helped by press disclosures about the effects of Soviet industrial espionage in France (Paris, *Le Monde*, 2 April; UPI, 2 April; *Radio Liberty Research*, 12 April).

Stepan V. Chervonenko, head of the Cadres Abroad Department of the CPSU Central Committee, led a parliamentary delegation to France in June. Chervonenko conferred with Mitterrand and Foreign Minister Roland Dumas on questions of the arms race and bilateral relations. The Soviet report on the meetings expressed "satisfaction on the whole" with recent Soviet-French relations (Tass, 26 June; *FBIS*, 3 July). A week after the Chervonenko visit, Moscow announced that Gorbachev had accepted an invitation from Mitterrand to visit France in October (Tass, 3 July; *FBIS*, 3 July).

As the "star wars" controversy continued, the French government pursued its own original line on the issue. Mitterrand opposed U.S. development of space weapons on grounds that it would weaken American commitment to Western Europe's defense (ABC News, 2 October). On other major issues, France was adamantly opposed to Moscow's positions. When the two leaders met in Paris on 2–5 October, the French president was politically vulnerable at home due to the Greenpeace bombing scandal, and he was in no position to work any compromises with Gorbachev, even if he had been so disposed. Mitterrand was rigidly correct in his reception of Gorbachev and results of the conference were predictably inconclusive (*NYT*, 6 October). The Paris visit did give the Soviet leader another opportunity to pursue his public relations campaign, directed at the Western public. Gorbachev and his wife, Raisa Maksimovna, enhanced their image as the "Gucci Comrade" stars of the Western media (ABC News, 5 October). However, the official meeting with Mitterrand was overshadowed by street demonstrations against Gorbachev prior to his arrival (prohibited by the French government during the visit) and by a challenge on the USSR's human rights record from Paris mayor and Gaullist leader Jacques Chirac (Paris, AFP, 3 October; *FBIS*, 3 October).

The Soviets could derive some comfort from France's continuing independence in foreign affairs, as Mitterrand boycotted both the October presummit meeting of Western leaders (*CSM*, 2 October) and the post-summit session in Brussels (*NYT*, 22 October).

Moscow seemed to place higher hopes on relations with Italy, having singled out that country for the role of sympathetic intermediary between East and West (*Radio Liberty Research*, 28 May) and a strategically important target for Soviet pressures against the installation of Euromissiles. Italian premier Bettino Craxi was welcomed to Moscow with much fanfare in late May. Gorbachev used the occasion to renew Yuri Andropov's offer to reduce the number of Soviet medium-range missiles in Europe to the combined total of such French and British weapons, with the offer conditional upon a NATO agreement to remove the Euromissiles and U.S. cessation of SDI research (Tass, 29 May; *WP*, 30 May).

The talks with Craxi, which mainly dealt with questions of the arms race, were described by the Soviets as "thorough and businesslike" (*Pravda*, 30 May). Craxi said that he was "satisfied" with the talks and "convinced of the peaceful intentions of the Soviet Union." Craxi added that he understood the Soviet concern that SDI would upset the "existing balance of forces" (Tass, 29 May; *FBIS*, 30 May).

Although Craxi maintained cordial relations with the Soviets, there was no ensuing slippage in Italy's commitments to NATO, even after the *Achille Lauro* affair seriously strained relations between Washington and Rome, due to the Craxi government's release of the alleged mastermind of the hijacking.

With Soviet initiatives elsewhere registering dubious results, the leadership apparently concluded by the autumn that the last best hope for a breakthrough in the "peace" offensive was the Netherlands. The culmination of a sustained diplomatic and propaganda effort to sway the Dutch government on the Euromissile issue came in September. It was reported that the Soviets were moving missiles to provide technical compliance with the Dutch demand that the SS-20 count revert to the June 1984 total of 378: a Dutch condition for refusal of U.S. cruise missiles at the time of the scheduled 1 November decision (*Los Angeles Times*, 26 September). Despite a wide range of positive and negative pressures from Moscow, the parliament of the Netherlands approved acceptance of the cruise missiles. However, the outcome was not a total loss for Moscow, since a political condition for the favorable vote was a renunciation by the Netherlands of other responsibilities in NATO's contingency planning (*NYT*, 2 November).

The tone of relations with Britain had warmed a bit, largely due to the friendly personal exchanges between Gorbachev and Prime Minister Margaret Thatcher during his 1984 London visit and at the time of the Chernenko rites. However, early in Gorbachev's tenure, Soviet-British relations plunged back to their former dismal state. When Britain expelled five Soviet diplomats for spying in April, the two countries engaged in a virtually unprecedented exchange of mutual expulsions, a diplomatic struggle finally won on points by the Soviets but at considerable hazard to future relations with the United Kingdom (London, *Times*, 25 April; Tass, 27, 28 April; *NYT*, 25 April, 1 May).

Soviet espionage also continued to produce frictions in relations with Belgium. Vladimir Makeev, a member of the Soviet trade mission in Brussels, was expelled in July for spying. The latest episode followed the May 1984 expulsion of the first secretary of the Soviet embassy in Brussels and two other Soviet nationals for attempting to obtain confidential NATO documents (Paris, AFP, 19 July; *FBIS*, 19 July).

Intrusions by the Soviets in northern waters continued to trouble relations with key Scandinavian countries. In July, the USSR officially apologized to Norway for an incident in the Barents Sea when a

Soviet navy vessel cut seismological cable from a Norwegian research ship (Paris, AFP, 18 July; *FBIS*, 19 July). In November, a political crisis for Prime Minister Olaf Palme's Socialist government in Sweden was triggered by charges from a senior naval officer, Captain Hans von Hofsten, that the Palme government had ignored repeated violations of Swedish territorial waters by Soviet submarines (UPI, 11 November).

The naval encounters and controversies came on the heels of a more serious incident. The defense ministries of Norway and Finland reported on 2 January that a Soviet cruise missile had flown over the countries on 28 December 1984. Norwegian and Finnish officials reported on 4 January that the USSR had apologized for the mishap. The errant missile was found near Lake Inari on 30 January and was subsequently returned to the USSR (*NYT*, 3, 5, 31 January).

Eastern Europe. The new leadership appeared to be heavily committed to the rallying of a united front in the bloc as a necessary precondition for the success of foreign policy initiatives elsewhere. Evidence of bloc incohesion in the early 1980s had coincided with an apparent downturn for the Soviets in the global correlation of forces. Major efforts had been devoted to bringing East European regimes into line during 1984, with Gorbachev playing a major role, and this continued to be the major thrust of Soviet policy toward the region in 1985. Moreover, there were indications that the USSR was demanding increased assistance from the allies in the resolution of its own economic problems.

Moscow's new emphasis upon the bloc was evident in the unusual number of meetings. Three Warsaw Pact summits were held during the year. The April meeting in Warsaw renewed the Warsaw Pact for ten years and endorsed USSR positions on major international issues, particularly matters of arms control (*NYT*, 27 April). Meeting in Sofia in October, the Warsaw Pact leaders ratified Gorbachev's stance on East-West issues as preparations were being completed for the November Geneva conference (*WP*, 22, 23 October). Following the Geneva superpower conclave, the Warsaw Pact leaders reassembled in Prague to hear and approve Gorbachev's report on his talks with President Reagan (*Pravda*, 23 November).

A tentative détente between Bonn and East Berlin had been brutally squelched in 1984, and Moscow continued to keep a close watch on the East Germans during 1985. The friendly meeting between Chancellor Helmut Kohl and GDR leader Erich Honecker in Moscow on the occasion of Chernenko's funeral (see above) had raised hopes for a more flexible Soviet stance on contacts between the two Germanys. However, in May, amid violent Soviet attacks on West German "revanchism," Honecker journeyed to Moscow, where he reasserted East Berlin's opposition to German reunification (*Los Angeles Times*, 6 May). Moreover, Moscow party boss and Politburo member Viktor V. Grishin and Minister of Culture Piotr N. Demichev, in East Germany for VE Day observances, remained for several days of conversations with GDR officials, apparently to emphasize Moscow's hard line on German questions (*Radio Liberty Research*, 25 June).

Close watch was also kept over Poland, which remained potentially explosive. While in Warsaw for the Warsaw Treaty Organization summit in April, Gorbachev publicly expressed "solidarity" with the leadership of Gen. Wojciech Jaruzelski (*NYT*, 28 April). This was followed in June by a visit of the chairman of the CPSU Party Control Committee, Mikhail Solomentsev—evidently a troubleshooting mission to check on conditions in Poland (Reuters, 17 June).

The Hungarian economic experiment has figured prominently in Moscow debates on reform of Soviet economy. When Politburo member Grigori Romanov's mission to Budapest in March emphasized economic matters (*Pravda*, 28 March), speculation increased concerning at least partial adoption of the Hungarian model. However, by the time of Gorbachev's September visit to Budapest (Budapest Domestic Service, 25 September; *FBIS*, 27 September), such expectations had been rather conclusively dashed.

Relations with Yugoslavia remained mostly cool and correct. Politburo member and RSFSR premier Vitali Vorotnikov visited Belgrade in March for talks described by the Soviet media as having been held in an "exceptionally warm atmosphere" (Tass, 7 March; *FBIS*, 8 March).

In view of the historical connection between Soviet-Yugoslav relations and those between Belgrade and Tirana, a November article, "Albania's Liberation Day," by commentator N. Yurchenko, attracted some interest. The article spoke glowingly of Soviet friendship for the Albanian people and recounted approvingly the 1959 pact between the two countries. However, the article's emphasis upon "proletarian internationalism" hinted that any renewal of Albanian adhesion to the bloc would be strictly on Moscow's terms (*Pravda*, 28 November).

The general approach of the new leadership to the bloc countries seemed to be clearly articulated in an authoritative article published in June. The article by O. Vladimirov (believed to be a pseudonym for Oleg Rakhmanin, deputy head of the Central Committee department for relations with ruling Communist parties) violently attacked "revisionism," "national communism," and "anti-Sovietism" within the socialist community; defended orthodoxy in social organization (implicitly criticizing economic innovation such as the Hungarian experiment); and blasted attempts of "small countries" to mediate in East-West relations (ibid., 21 June). The article represented a rather explicit call for greater subordination to Moscow and rejection of "liberalism" at home and abroad.

Meanwhile, Moscow stepped up its drive for economic integration of the bloc and put in motion measures to utilize East European resources more fully for Soviet benefit. It was announced in June that all Soviet government ministries had been instructed to plan on "fuller" cooperation with East European trading partners "to solve major national economic problems" (ibid., 15 June). Such enhanced "cooperation" was clearly designed to tap the scientific and technological resources of Eastern Europe to a growing degree. Moreover, the terms of trade were tilting against the other CMEA countries. In 1984–1985, the USSR demanded growing amounts of high-quality machinery, modern consumer goods, processed food, and advanced technology in exchange for smaller quantities of oil and induced the other countries to subsidize major new Soviet projects for the development of natural gas and iron ore resources, in addition to ongoing nuclear power projects (*Los Angeles Times*, 25 August).

Afghanistan. The Soviets stepped up their already heavy commitment to suppression of rebel forces in Afghanistan, and there were indications of a preference for total military victory to take the issue of the USSR's intervention out of the diplomatic arena, where it produced complications with many countries, both East and West. Moreoever, there were signs that Soviet forces had dug in for an indefinite stay, if necessary, in the country.

In the winter of 1984–1985, Soviet forces, now reportedly numbering 115,000, actively engaged guerrilla forces (in contrast to previous winters, when Soviet troops had generally stayed in barracks). The Soviet army had reportedly taken over the fighting in Afghanistan completely and had moved a considerable force close to the eastern border with Pakistan in a campaign to cut rebel supply lines from that country (*San Francisco Examiner and Chronicle*, 10 February).

The vulnerable Soviet propaganda position on Afghanistan was demonstrated anew in late February, when a United Nations report accused USSR forces in the country of a "deliberate policy" of bombarding villages, destroying food supplies, massacring civilians, and disregarding the Geneva Convention (*CSM*, 1 March). In March, rebel sources reported that Soviet atrocities were continuing. According to the report, Soviet troops in March burned more than a dozen remote villages and killed most of their inhabitants (*WP*, 30 March).

Adverse publicity from such reports and continuing condemnation of the intervention by countries outside the bloc did nothing to deter Soviet activities inside Afghanistan. Soviet involvement intensified during the year, with the expansion of seven major air bases and stepped-up antiguerrilla action on the ground. Autumn operations in the Panjshir Valley involved as many as 10,000 troops, led by airborne forces and air assault troops carried in helicopters (*NYT*, 3 November).

The tough Soviet stance on Afghanistan was also apparent on the diplomatic front. During a meeting with Pakistan's President Zia ul-Haq in Moscow during the Chernenko rites, Gorbachev issued a thinly veiled warning that the USSR might foment trouble inside Pakistan if support for the insurgency continued. The official Soviet report on the meeting noted that "aggressive actions" against the Kabul regime "cannot but affect in the most negative way Soviet-Pakistani relations" (Tass, 14 March).

Alongside the generally obdurate approach, the Soviets continued to hold out the possibility for a negotiated settlement. Whether this was mainly designed for propaganda effect or represented a Soviet search for a highly favorable settlement was uncertain. In November, a UN mediator resumed talks in Geneva with the Afghan and Pakistani foreign ministers. Meanwhile, Afghan forces were reportedly back in action; army troops and secret police had allegedly killed more than a thousand guerrillas in the southern section of the country (UPI, 16 December).

Peripheral Areas. Even during the 1970s, when the Soviets boasted of a progressively more favorable world correlation of forces and depicted a developing political-strategic "encirclement" of capitalism, Moscow had often displayed nervousness concerning the possibility of a specifically geographical "encirclement" of the USSR by hostile countries. Yuri Andropov had made tentative moves to deal with this problem from the outset of his tenure, but his terminal illness and the diplomatic disasters of the failed antimissile campaign and the destruction of a Korean Air Lines jetliner had blunted this thrust of Soviet policy. Under Chernenko, the concentration upon superpower relations had overshadowed this goal, but it remained on the back burner, to be revived by Gorbachev.

The strategy involved was quite transparent. The Soviets sought to influence countries from the eastern Mediterranean to the Sea of Japan, in order to draw them further away from the American orbit and closer to Moscow. By reducing threats and underlying hostility in these borderlands between the two camps, the Soviets could banish the nightmare of a geographical encirclement, and any diplomatic successes here would bolster the USSR's position in the global correlation vis-à-vis the United States. It was unclear how far the Soviets would go in pursuit of this aim, but optimal execution of the policy could provide the cutting edge for a new overall strategy to replace the defunct "two-track" approach of the 1970s.

Near and Middle East. In the eastern Mediterranean area, the Soviets continued their drive to restore "normal" relations with Egypt, paid court to often-prickly ally Syria, and reaffirmed support for the PLO. However, the most intriguing aspect of Soviet policy in the region was a limited thaw in Moscow's relations with Israel. In May, the Soviet press published a VE anniversary message from Israel's president, Chaim Herzog (*Izvestiia*, 13 May) and publicized the establishment in Israel of a Public Committee to Celebrate the Victory over Fascist Germany (*Pravda*, 13 May). It was reported in July that ambassadors of the two countries had met in Paris to discuss the possibility of restoration of normal diplomatic relations (*CSM*, 23 July). Reestablishment of diplomatic links, as a precondition for Soviet participation in the Mideast peace process, apparently remained a possibility at the end of the year. In September, it was reported that, starting in October, Israeli tourists would be allowed to visit the Soviet Union. Meanwhile, there were indications that the Soviets might be moving toward an easing of Jewish emigration, along with a new stance of treating this as a Soviet-Israeli issue rather than a Soviet-U.S. one (*Los Angeles Times*, 1 October).

The many-sided campaign to expand Soviet influence in the turbulent region received a jolt when the USSR found itself in the unusual position of terrorist victim. In late September, four Soviet officials were kidnapped in Beirut (*CSM*, 1 October); this crisis was ultimately more or less resolved after a reported Syrian intervention in the matter. However, according to a report that surfaced in December, the KGB had taken a direct hand in the matter, abducting twelve Lebanese extremists and killing one of them after the murder of one of the Soviet hostages. The KGB had secured release of the remaining three Soviets by threatening to kill the Lebanese "one by one" (London, *Daily Mail*, 12 December).

The USSR continued its attempts to forge stronger economic links with Turkey; trade between the two countries was scheduled to double during the year (*Radio Liberty Research*, 21 December 1984). Much more attention was devoted to Greece, which had tilted toward Moscow since the government of Premier Andreas Papandreou came to power in October 1981. Papandreou was welcomed in February to Moscow, where he spoke of "our corresponding views on many international issues" and attended the signing of several minor agreements (*NYT*, 13 February; *Pravda*, 14 February). The Soviet-Greek rapprochement apparently survived disclosures concerning Soviet activities in Greece that resulted from the defection of Sergei Bokhan, first secretary of the Soviet embassy in Athens and reportedly the deputy chief of the KGB *rezidentura* in Greece (*Washington Times*, 27 June). Although the rhetorical drift of the leftist government in Athens was highly gratifying to Moscow, Papandreou's plan to withdraw from NATO had been abandoned, and the dismantling of U.S. bases in Greece had been postponed until 1989 (*Radio Liberty Research*, 11 February). On the Soviet side, restraints were imposed by Moscow's unwillingness to take sides in Greece's conflict with Turkey over Cyprus (*NYT*, 13 February).

Further east, Moscow attempted to forge closer ties with Iraq, evidently no longer constrained by any hopes of patching up battered relations with Iran. Teheran had been virtually written off for its "anti-Soviet line" in an authoritative P. Nadezhdin commentary in the first week of March (*Pravda*, 6 March). In June, the Iraqi minister of industry and mineral resources visited Moscow for talks on trade and economic cooperation. In December, Iraqi president Saddam Hussein was welcomed to Moscow for talks with Gorbachev, Gromyko, and Shevardnadze. Hussein and Gromyko issued a call for a negotiated end to the five-year-old war between Iran and Iraq (Tass, 16 December; UPI, 16 December).

India. Much more crucial than any of these initiatives was Soviet diplomacy toward the three major countries in East Asia. Soviet-Indian ties had been somewhat jeopardized in late 1984 by the assassination of Prime Minister Indira Gandhi and the selection of her son, Rajiv Gandhi, as the new Indian leader. Gandhi was known to be much more favorably disposed toward the United States than his mother had been. When a Soviet spy scandal broke in January, relations between Moscow and New Delhi seemed to be at their lowest point in the decade. Thirteen Indians were arrested in the espionage case and a Soviet diplomat, allegedly a member of the KGB, was expelled (AFP, 7 February).

Moscow went all out to repair the damage and influence the new Indian leadership. Particular attention was devoted to Gandhi when he attended the Chernenko funeral. Agreements for cooperation on prospecting for oil in India and radio and television exchange were signed in Delhi on 27–29 March (Tass, 27 March; Moscow Domestic Service, 29 March; *FBIS*, 1 April). Indian Defense Minister P. V. Narasimha Rao was welcomed in March to Moscow, where he conferred with Defense Minister Marshal Sergei Sokolov; Mikhail Sergeichik, chairman of the State Committee on Foreign Economic Relations; and other officials (Tass, 31 March, 1 April; *FBIS*, 1 April).

Prime Minister Gandhi was accorded an exceptionally warm welcome when he returned to Moscow in May. Agreements were signed on trade, scientific, and technical cooperation for the period 1985–2000 (Moscow Domestic Service, 22 May; *FBIS*, 22 May). Gorbachev, playing host to the Indian leader, returned to the theme of the Indian Ocean as a "zone of peace" and also revived the idea of an Asian security conference (Tass, 21 May; *Radio Liberty Research*, 25 June).

Following the Gandhi visit, Moscow continued to push the recharging of the old Delhi connection. Consultations between Soviet and Indian diplomats took place in Delhi in August on the agenda for the fortieth UN General Assembly session and on the question of a "zone of peace" in the Indian Ocean (Tass, 7 August; *FBIS*, 8 August). Seeking to soften the major irritant in recent Soviet-Indian relations, the Soviets backed the meeting of a joint Indian-Afghan commission in August to deal with questions of economic, technical, and cultural cooperation (*Pravda*, 7 August). Gandhi warmly received a Soviet delegation, headed by Temirbek Koshoiev, which was in India for celebration of the fourteenth anniversary of the Soviet-Indian friendship treaty and the thirty-eighth anniversary of India's independence (Tass, 22 August; *FBIS*, 26 August). Despite all these favorable signs, less Indian dependence upon the USSR in the future seemed likely, due to the developing détente between India and Pakistan.

China. Sino-Soviet relations, strained by the abrupt postponement of first deputy premier Ivan Arkhipov's scheduled May 1984 visit to Beijing (apparently in response to President Reagan's visit to China), had eased somewhat when Arkhipov finally appeared in the PRC capital in December 1984 for the signing of several trade agreements. However, the last weeks of Chernenko's leadership were mostly marked by discord, featuring angry press exchanges over the issues of Afghanistan and Kampuchea (*Izvestiia*, 24 January, 14 February; Xinhua, 16 February, 12 March). Beijing also spurned the Soviet proposal for a world conference of communist parties (*Radio Liberty Research*, 3 April).

A change in tone was evident immediately upon Gorbachev's assumption of the Soviet leadership. Chinese party leader Hu Yaobang dispatched a message of congratulations to Gorbachev, who told PRC vice-premier Li Peng, head of the Chinese delegation at Chernenko's funeral, that "we would like a serious improvement in relations with the Chinese People's Republic and believe that, given reciprocity, this is quite possible" (*Pravda*, 15 March). In his first speech as Soviet leader, Gorbachev had expressed his hope for improved relations with China. The PRC responded favorably; Chinese Politburo member Peng Zhen, visiting the Soviet embassy in Beijing to sign a book of condolences, said that "we too cherish the same hope" (*NYT*, 13 March).

These conciliatory gestures were not followed by any significant alteration of positions on the three basic issues separating the two countries—Afghanistan, Kampuchea, and the Soviet military presence on China's borders. However, Soviet media attacks on Beijing for its stance on Afghanistan were suspended and some Asian officials noted an apparent slight softening in China's opposition to the Soviet military involvement in Afghanistan. In late March, the Chinese announced that a sixth round of talks aimed at improving bilateral relations had been scheduled for 9 April in Moscow (*CSM*, 31 March). One negative note was sounded by Hu Yaobang, who was quoted as saying that restoration of party-to-party relations with Moscow "is not possible at present" (UPI, 28 March).

The mild thaw in relations spurred a flurry of minor agreements between the USSR and the PRC. In the first week of April, agreements were signed on increased local border trade, on trade and transport in 1985, and on educational and research exchanges for 1985–1986 (Reuters, 4 April). The two countries agreed in June on plans for cultural cooperation in 1985 (Tass, 16 June; *FBIS*, 17 June) and the opening of consulates in Leningrad and Shanghai (Budapest Domestic Service, 25 June; *FBIS*, 26 June). The lessening of tensions with the USSR was probably a contributing factor in the PRC's June decision to reduce the size of the Chinese armed forces by one million men over the next two years (Moscow Television, 25 June; *FBIS*, 26 June).

In his speech to workers in Kiev on 26 June, Gorbachev said that neighborly cooperation between the Soviet Union and China "is very possible and desirable" (*Pravda*, 27 June). This conciliatory gesture was followed two days later by the reception in Moscow of Vietnamese leader Le Duan, who was promised the continuing "reliable support" of the USSR (ibid., 29 June). Even so, Le Duan's visit was marked by a noticeable coolness on the Soviet side (see below). Continuing the emphasis on relatively noncontroversial economic matters, PRC vice-premier Yao Yilin was welcomed to Moscow in July for trade talks. Agreements were signed on mutual goods deliveries to the year 1990 and on Soviet participation in the construction and reconstruction of industrial installations in the PRC (ibid., 12 July).

In August, Foreign Minister Shevardnadze met with Ambassador L. Zewang; the two men expressed agreement on the aim of normalizing relations between the USSR and the PRC (Tass, 23 August; *FBIS*, 26 August). At the same time, the PRC made a significant gesture symbolizing the altered political climate: broadcast of Russian-language lessons, suspended in 1966, was resumed by Beijing Radio (Moscow Radio, 22 August; *FBIS*, 26 August).

Shevardnadze met in September with Foreign Minister Wu Xueqian at the UN's fall meeting in New York. The two foreign ministers agreed to exchange visits, the first such meetings since the split between the two countries in the early 1960s (Reuters, 2 October; *NYT*, 3 October).

The overall scorecard for the year showed a marked improvement in the atmosphere of Sino-Soviet relations but no perceptible alteration by either side of positions on long-standing major issues.

Japan. The late 1984 visit of Politburo member Dinmukhamed Kunaev to Japan was followed by several cordial exchanges between the two countries in 1985. With tensions rising between Tokyo and Washington over economic issues, the Soviet leadership apparently concluded that amelioration of the long-hostile relations between the USSR and Japan was a distinct possibility.

One indication of a thaw was Tokyo's hosting of talks on air safety in the northern Pacific, which yielded an agreement signed by the United States, the USSR, and Japan (AP, 8 October).

The capstone of Soviet efforts vis-à-vis Tokyo was the November announcement that Foreign Minister Shevardnadze would visit Tokyo in January 1986. At the same time, Japan's prime minister, Yasuhiro Nakasone, lauded the meeting of Gorbachev and Reagan in Geneva and drew important implications for Soviet-Japanese relations. "If the United States and Soviet Union can do that much," he said, "then it's time to improve Japan-Soviet relations" (AP, 28 November). However, Nakasone insisted throughout the year that there would be no compromise on the Japanese demand for return of the territories lost to the Soviet Union at the end of World War II.

The USSR had not achieved major breakthroughs in the "borderlands" target areas during the year. However, the Soviet leadership could be reasonably satisfied with the results of its activist diplomacy. The temperature of relations with a number of countries previously hostile or cool toward Moscow had been raised, and the USSR had vigorously reasserted its role as a superpower with farflung interests.

Third World and National Liberation Movements. Reverses suffered by Soviet clients in the Third World had been a considerable embarrassment during the first half of the decade; indeed, these regional setbacks had been a factor in the apparent downturn for the USSR in the global correlation of forces. The general thrust of Soviet policy under the new Gorbachev leadership—holding the line against the United States while placing increased emphasis on Western Europe and the "borderlands"—seemed to imply some downgrading of Third World "restructuring," at least for the short run, as did the overwhelming concentration on revival of the domestic economy. On the other hand, Moscow could not entirely discount revolutionary movements in the Third World, especially those that held power and were in trouble. The unexpected turnabout in critical areas rankled, and the USSR's superpower status required at least a potential presence in all parts of the world. Further, given the stagnation, both social and ideological, at home, the Soviets' claim to be a "progressive" force in the world rested heavily on a connection with revolutionary movements in the undeveloped countries. Perhaps most important, the Soviets could not ignore the potential for future gains in areas such as Africa and Latin America that were likely to become more unstable over the next decade.

These varied considerations no doubt influenced Gorbachev's first pronouncement on revolutionary forces in the Third World following his election as general secretary. In his acceptance speech to the Central Committee, he reaffirmed Soviet support for national liberation movements: "The Soviet Union has always supported the struggle of peoples for liberation from colonial oppression. And today our sympathies go out to the countries of Asia, Africa, and Latin America that are following the road of consolidating independence and social renovation. For us, they are friends and partners in the struggle for a durable peace, for better and just relations between peoples" (Tass, 11 March).

This reaffirmation was notably less emphatic than previous Soviet pronouncements, particularly that of Leonid Brezhnev at the Twenty-sixth CPSU Congress, which pledged the USSR to pursue "the consolidation of the alliance of world socialism and the national liberation movement" (*Pravda*, 24 February 1981).

Seemingly scotching the idea of a lower priority for Third World concerns, Gorbachev at the time of the Chernenko funeral rites delivered his sharp warning to Pakistan's Zia on Afghanistan (see above) and provided strong rhetorical support for the Sandinista regime in Nicaragua. However, Afghanistan appeared to be a special case. A contiguous socialist country allied to Moscow, its civil war could be considered a bloc matter. Moreover, as the year wore on, it became increasingly clear that Moscow did not intend (and probably also lacked the resources for) an immediate general offensive in the Third World, although diplomatic contacts were stepped up enormously over the last four months of 1985. Rather, relations with particular regimes and movements appeared to be governed by their connection with the major thrusts of Soviet policy, by regional strategic considerations, and by the need to maintain linkage with "national liberation" forces for possible future utilization.

A continuing problem was Cuba. Relations with Havana had been strained at least since the U.S. invasion of Grenada in 1982; the Soviets and Fidel Castro had held sharply differing views on the coup that triggered the American intervention. The rift had widened in March 1984 when, reportedly against Castro's advice, Soviet leader Chernenko had refused to allow a Soviet naval flotilla to approach Nicaraguan waters following the damaging of a Soviet tanker by a mine at the entrance to Puerto Sandino harbor. Apparently as a protest against Soviet policy on Nicaragua, Castro failed to attend the funeral of Konstantin Chernenko, sending his brother Raúl instead; Fidel had been present at the rites for Brezhnev and Andropov. To make his point unmistakably clear, Castro also failed to sign the book of condolences at the Soviet embassy in Havana (*WP*, 24 March).

Perhaps partially as a reaction to Havana's alienation, Gorbachev warmly welcomed Nicaraguan leader Daniel Ortega to Moscow in April and promised continuing Soviet economic and diplomatic support (*Pravda*, 30 April). This led to a predictable backlash from some Democratic members of the U.S. Congress who had previously opposed American aid to the Nicaraguan *contras*.

When Washington imposed economic sanctions against the Sandinista regime, Moscow agreed to provide Nicaragua with most of its oil requirements, a considerable concession in view of the USSR's inability to fully supply the petroleum needs of the allies in its base bloc (*NYT*, 21 May). Subsequently, the Soviet Union reportedly increased arms shipments to Nicaragua significantly, transferring them through Cuba (*WP*, 5 November).

In another area that had witnessed some slowdown on "restructuring" in the early 1980s, the Soviets made one move to consolidate regional gains. The Soviet deputy foreign minister, Mikhail Kapitsa, led a major Soviet diplomatic effort to persuade ASEAN countries to accept Hanoi's formula for a settlement of the Cambodian question (*NYT*, 8 April; *Radio Liberty Research*, 25 June).

However, the visit of Vietnamese leader Le Duan to Moscow in June pointed up some tensions in the Soviet-Vietnamese relationship.

Following an unusually perfunctory welcome by Politburo member Egor Ligachev at the Moscow International Airport, Le Duan met with Gorbachev in the Kremlin on 28 June (*Pravda*, 29 June). Gorbachev reaffirmed Moscow's support for Vietnamese objectives in Indochina and accepted an invitation to visit the Democratic Republic of Vietnam at an unspecified date. The Soviets also extended a new five-year commitment for credits and agreed to reschedule the DRV's debt to the USSR (ibid., 1 July). However, the Soviet media gave most emphasis to the passage in the joint declaration calling for "normalization of the relations of the Soviet Union and the DRV with the PRC" (Tass, 30 June); this was the first time that the Vietnamese had formally endorsed the process of Sino-Soviet normalization. Moreover, Le Duan was obliged to admit that Vietnam had fallen short on economic matters. The DRV, which receives annual subsidies from the USSR estimated to exceed a value of $1 billion, promised to "make the greatest possible effort to fulfill its commitments for the delivery of goods to the USSR" (ibid.).

The meeting with Le Duan came just as Moscow was accelerating the rapprochement with China (see above). Moscow appeared unwilling to accept Beijing's proffered terms for a settlement in Southeast Asia—acceptance of the Soviet military presence in Cam Ranh Bay in return for withdrawal of Vietnamese troops from Cambodia. Nevertheless, as one diplomat assessed the outcome of Le Duan's visit, "it was a clear signal to Beijing that Moscow has no intention of allowing relations with Hanoi to stand in the way of Sino-Soviet normalization" (*FEER*, 11 July).

Moscow also moved to cement relations with two Marxist regimes whose connections with the USSR had featured some frictions in recent years. A delegation from Angola, headed by M. A. Rodriques and A. dos Santos Franca (members of the Politburo of the Popular Movement for the Liberation of Angola), visited Moscow in March for talks that yielded a declaration of support for Angola's policies vis-à-vis South Africa (*Pravda*, 8 March). Gorbachev conferred with Mengistu Haile Mariam during the Ethiopian leader's twelve-day autumn visit to the Soviet Union (*Izvestiia*, 12 November).

Three weeks later, Zimbabwe's leader, Robert Mugabe, visited Moscow and pledged "eternal friendship" with the USSR. However, the visit pointed up Soviet caution toward early risky commitments in Third World trouble spots, as Mugabe left Moscow without firm assurance of military aid from the USSR in Zimbabwe's struggle with the Union of South Africa (UPI, 4 December).

Probably aiming to exert pressure for USSR participation in the Mideast peace process, the Soviets gave an exceptionally warm welcome to Libya's Moammar Khadafy, a difficult and often embarrassing ally, on his October visit to Moscow. *Pravda* (10 October) printed a front-page photograph and biography of Khadafy, and he was featured prominently on the main evening television news program. His talk with Gorbachev was described as having taken place in a "warm and friendly atmosphere" (*Pravda*, 16 October), and a long-term agreement on scientific, technical, and trade cooperation was signed (Tass, 14 October; *FBIS*, 15 October). Although the joint communiqué condemned Israel and strongly supported Palestinian liberation (*Pravda*, 16 October), the visit came only a week after a Gorbachev statement supporting Israel's right to exist within secure frontiers (*Los Angeles Times*, 11 October).

Results of Soviet overtures toward a number of "bourgeois" and non-Marxist regimes in the Third World were mixed. Deputy premier Yakov P. Ryabov, the highest Soviet official to visit Indonesia in twenty years, arrived in Jakarta in October to negotiate an aid agreement on hospital construction (*FEER*, 17 October). However, Indonesia turned down a Soviet offer of a $180 million loan to build three hospitals.

The busy Ryabov journeyed next to Kuala Lumpur, where he discussed the sale of Soviet cargo helicopters to Malaysia. Soviet trade with Saudi Arabia increased 16 percent during the first half of the year, and diplomatic relations were established with Oman and the United Arab Emirates. However, a Soviet trade delegation met a cool reception in Thailand in October and during the summer all Soviet diplomats were expelled from Liberia (*NYT*, 8 December).

International Party Contacts. As the new leadership launched its wide-ranging diplomatic offensive to restore positions lost during the lengthy succession crisis, relations with other communist and "revolutionary" parties attracted much less attention. However, the CPSU continued to pursue the goals of the Andropov and Chernenko years in its dealings with other parties and achieved no overall amelioration of the problems long associated with those relationships.

In Eastern Europe, the CPSU sought to cement ties in the fractious bloc and generate support for Soviet policy toward NATO. Elsewhere, interparty relations were dominated by Soviet efforts to add punch to the various "peace" campaigns, to stanch the hemorrhaging of Soviet strength in regional correlations of forces, and to restore some measure of unity to the world movement. As usual, the CPSU apparat under party secretary Boris Ponomarev displayed a high degree of flexibility in interparty relations, but the pronounced emphasis on "proletarian internationalism" in the draft CPSU program (*Pravda*, 26 October) offered little hope for Moscow's future toleration of diversity in the world communist movement.

There were indications, however, that even the most loyal parties were unwilling to countenance the idea of a restoration of a monolithic movement under Moscow's leadership. Most revealing in this respect was the January meeting of fourteen communist parties in Nicosia, Cyprus. The meeting was attended by representatives of the Communist parties of Afghanistan, Bahrain, Cyprus, Egypt, Ethiopia, Greece, Iran, Iraq, Israel, Jordan, Palestine, Syria, Saudi Arabia, and Turkey (ibid., 22 January). All of these are "orthodox," Moscow-oriented parties; nevertheless, while the conference endorsed Soviet positions on most world issues, there was no mention of the CPSU's project, launched in 1980 and supported by two international meetings of Communist parties in 1984, for a world conference of parties, presumably under Moscow's leadership (*Radio Free Europe Research*, 25 January).

The year 1984 had featured serious strains in the East European bloc over questions of East-West relations. During 1985, Moscow attempted to present at least a facade of unity on these and other matters. The first meeting of Warsaw Pact leaders since 1983 was scheduled for Sofia in January but had to be postponed due to the illness of General Secretary Chernenko (*NYT*, 14 January). In March, new CPSU leader Mikhail Gorbachev conferred with most of the Warsaw Pact party leaders who were in Moscow for Chernenko's funeral (ibid., 13, 14 March).

The bloc leaders assembled for their rescheduled summit in Warsaw in late April, with Polish party chief General Jaruzelski as host. The conclave renewed the Warsaw Pact for ten years and endorsed Moscow's positions on East-West issues (*Los Angeles Times*, 26 April; *NYT*, 27 April). Heading the other delegations were party leaders Todor Zhivkov of Bulgaria, Gústav Husák of Czechoslovakia, Erich Honecker of East Germany, János Kádár of Hungary, and Nicolae Ceauşescu of Romania. In addition to Gorbachev, the Soviet delegation included Politburo members Nikolai Tikhonov and Andrei Gromyko, Politburo candidate member Marshal Sergei Sokolov, and the Central Committee secretary for relations with ruling Communist parties, Konstantin Rusakov.

The bloc leaders met again in October in Sofia (*WP*, 22, 23 October) to endorse Soviet arms control proposals, and in November in Prague to hear a report by Gorbachev on the Geneva summit and to reaffirm their support for Moscow's positions on fundamental East-West issues (*Pravda*, 23 November; *NYT*, 23 November).

Politburo member Vitali I. Vorotnikov visited Belgrade in March for talks with the chairman of the LCY Presidium, Ali Šukrija, and other officials. The talks dealt with "the further development of relations" between the CPSU and the League of Communists of Yugoslavia and with "questions of present-day international relations"; the Soviet media reported an "exceptionally warm atmosphere" during the visit (Tass and Moscow Domestic Service, 7 March; *FBIS*, 8 March).

The Soviet leadership's desire for enhanced bloc cohesion and subordination to Moscow's policies was evident in relations with major East European parties. Erich Honecker visited Moscow in May and reaffirmed his opposition to a reunified Germany (*Los Angeles Times*, 6 May). CPSU Politburo member Viktor V. Grishin and candidate member Piotr N. Demichev took part in VE Day ceremonies in East Germany and remained in the country for several days to confer with German party officials (*Radio Liberty Research*, 25 June).

Grigori V. Romanov, Central Committee secretary and Politburo member, headed the CPSU delegation at the Thirteenth Congress of the Hungarian Communist party, held in Budapest in March. The Soviet press report on Romanov's meetings with Hungarian party leader János Kádár and other officials devoted major attention to matters of economic integration (*Pravda*, 28 March). CPSU Central Committee secretary Ponomarev met in Moscow in July with Mátyás Szürös, secretary of the Hungarian party for international affairs and interparty relations (ibid., 2 August, 5 August).

Gorbachev traveled to Budapest in September for talks with Kádár, said to have been held in a "comradely atmosphere" (Budapest Domestic Service, 25 September; *FBIS*, 27 September).

A delegation headed by Boris K. Pugo, first secretary of the Latvian party, visited Poland in April at the invitation of the Szczecin provincial party committee (*Sovetskaia Latvia*, 30 April; *FBIS*, 17 May). In June, chairman of the CPSU Party Control Committee, Mikhail S. Solomentsev, visited Poland to confer with party leaders and to check on conditions in the country (Reuters, 17 June).

French Communist party leader Georges Marchais met informally with Gorbachev in the Crimea in August and then attended a formal interparty session in the Kremlin on 2 September. Present at the Kremlin talks were Gorbachev and Vadim Zagladin, deputy head of the International Department, and Marchais and French Politburo member Maxime Gremetz. The official communiqué emphasized the opposition of both parties to American plans for "star wars" and carefully avoided any criticism of French president François Mitterrand, Gorbachev's host for an October meeting in Paris (Tass, 3 September; *FBIS*, 4 September; Paris, *L'Humanité*, 4 September). However, there were some indications of friction, with the Soviets reportedly critical of earlier (1981–1984) PCF participation in France's governing coalition (*Radio Free Europe Research*, 9 September).

One party that has consistently adhered to the Moscow line and echoed the Soviet view of "proletarian internationalism" is that of Austria. As a consequence, the CPSU has accorded the Austrian Communist party recognition out of all proportion to its size and importance. In April, a CPSU delegation led by Gennadi F. Sizov, chairman of the Central Auditing Commission, participated in the Austrian party's celebration of the fortieth anniversary of the liberation of Austria and thirtieth anniversary of the signing of the Austrian State Treaty (Tass, 17 April; *FBIS*, 18 April).

The CPSU continued to display concern about the split in the Finnish Communist Party (SKP). Deputy head of the International Department, Vitali Shaposhnikov, visited Helsinki in February for talks with SKP chairman Arvo Aalto and other leaders of the Finnish party. The talks reportedly dealt with the continuing struggle of the SKP majority against the dissident Taistoite splinter group (Helsinki International Service, 2 February; *Svenska Dagbladet*, Stockholm, 3 February; *FBIS*, 5, 7 February).

Continuing support for the puppet regime in Kabul was emphasized by the CPSU's participation in the January celebration of the twentieth anniversary of the Afghan Communist Party (PDPA). The CPSU delegation was headed by Uzbek party first secretary Inamzhon B. Usmankhodzhaev, who presented a message of greetings from the CPSU Central Committee to PDPA leader Babrak Karmal (*Krasnaia zvezda*, 11 January).

One of Mikhail Gorbachev's first major moves as general secretary was to welcome Nicaragua's Daniel Ortega to Moscow and pledge additional aid to the Sandinistas (Tass, 29 April).

Another ruling party under attack from anti-Soviet forces received moral support during a March visit. A delegation from Angola headed by M. A. Rodriques (Politburo member of the MPLA and interior minister of the People's Republic of Angola) and A. dos Santos Franca (MPLA Politburo member and chief of the Angolan armed forces) joined a Cuban delegation led by J. Riquet Valdes (Cuban Politburo and Secretariat member) for discussions in Moscow on the situation in southwestern Africa. Andrei Gromyko, Boris Ponomarev, Defense Minister Sokolov, and Oleg Rakhmanin, first deputy head of the Central Committee department for liaison with ruling parties, represented the Soviet party and state. Moscow had demonstrated some recent uneasiness over MPLA policy toward Pretoria, but the meeting communiqué fully endorsed Angolan positions and denounced South Africa's "aggression and indirect aggression" (*Pravda*, 8 March).

Mengistu Haile Mariam, general secretary of the Workers' Party of Ethiopia, visited the Soviet Union from 31 October to 1 November and conferred with Gorbachev and other top party and government officials (*Izvestiia*, 12 November).

A delegation of the Congolese Labor Party (PCT), headed by Central Committee secretary J.-J. N. Mvouenze, conferred with CPSU officials in Moscow and the Ukraine (ibid., 30 May).

The CPSU also sought to strengthen ties with the Iraqi Communist party. A delegation of the Iraqi party, led by first secretary Aziz Muhammad, was welcomed to Moscow in July for "comradely" talks with Boris Ponomarev and Karen Brutents, deputy head of the International Department (Moscow Domestic Service, 20 July; *FBIS*, 22 July).

The overriding Soviet interest in rallying Communist parties against American arms policies was demonstrated by the participation of Y. A. Krasin, prorector of the CPSU Academy of Sciences, in a theoretical conference of the Communist Party of Canada. The theme was "Imperialism—The Source of War Danger" (*Pravda*, 8 February; *FBIS*, 14 February).

The anti-U.S. thrust of CPSU relations with other parties was also evident in the visit of Japanese Communist Party (JCP) chairman Kenji Miyamoto to Moscow at the end of 1984. The CPSU and JCP effected a limited rapprochement, but opposition to American nuclear policies was the only area of agreement. Long-standing issues of contention between the two parties, such as the "lost territories," Poland, and Afghanistan, were not mentioned in the joint communiqué (*Radio Free Europe Research*, 9 January).

Three other Far Eastern delegations visited Moscow in January en route from the inauguration of Daniel Ortega as president of Nicaragua. The delegations were led by Pak Song-chol, member of the Politburo of the Korean Workers' Party; Chu Huy Man, member of Vietnam's Politburo; and deputy chairman of the Mongolian People's Great Hural, Gurragchaa (*Izvestiia*, 19 January; *FBIS*, 23 January).

An important meeting was held in the Kremlin on 28 June between a Vietnamese delegation led by the Communist Party of Vietnam's general secretary, Le Duan, and a Soviet team including CPSU leader Gorbachev (see above).

A close associate of Gorbachev, Tadzhik party second secretary Yuri P. Belov, led the CPSU delegation at the Twenty-second Congress of the People's Progressive Party of Guyana (Tass, 30 July; *FBIS*, 1 August).

Biographies. *Mikhail Sergeevich Gorbachev.* Born 2 March 1931 in Stavropol *krai*, Gorbachev is Russian and the son of a farmer. He worked at a machine tractor station in Stavropol *krai* during his teenage years and was admitted to Moscow State University in 1950. He became a member of the Communist Party of the Soviet Union in 1952 and was active in the Komsomol at the university, from which he graduated in 1955 with a degree in law. Returning to his native region after graduation, he pursued correspondence studies in agronomy and was awarded his second degree by the Stavropol agricultural institute.

Gorbachev worked as first secretary of the Stavropol city party Komsomol committee (1956–1958), second and then first secretary of the Stavropol regional Komsomol committee (1958–1962), first secretary of the Stavropol city CPSU committee (1962–1968), and second secretary of the Stavropol *krai* CPSU committee (1968–1970). In 1970, at the age of 39, he advanced to the party first secretaryship of Stavropol *krai*, one of the more important regional posts in the Soviet Union.

Elected a member of the CPSU Central Committee at the Twenty-fourth Congress in 1971, Gorbachev first attained recognition at the all-union level in 1974 when he was named head of the Youth Affairs Commission of the USSR Supreme Soviet Council of the Union.

Gorbachev made a reputation in Stavropol as an effective administrator, particularly during the record harvest year of 1978, but his political ascent was largely due to the patronage of Politburo members Mikhail Suslov, Fedor Kulakov, and Yuri Andropov. Following Kulakov's death in 1978, Gorbachev was selected as his successor in the position of CPSU Central Committee secretary for agriculture.

Despite a string of poor harvests, Gorbachev's political stock in Moscow rose steadily. Elected a candidate member of the Politburo in November 1979, he was promoted to full membership on 21 October 1980. He also served as chairman of the Legislative Proposals Commission of the Council of the Union from 1979 to 1984.

During the tenure of Andropov as CPSU first secretary, Gorbachev became the leader's closest associate in the Secretariat and assumed general direction of the economy and responsibility for personnel matters.

When Andropov died in February 1984, Gorbachev was passed over for the top post but was soon recognized as Konstantin Chernenko's chief deputy and heir apparent. An indication of his enhanced status was his election as chairman of the Council of the Union's Foreign Affairs Commission, a post usually reserved for the second ranking figure in the party. Upon the death of Chernenko, Gorbachev was elected on 11 March 1985 as general secretary of the CPSU Central Committee.

Prior to his assumption of the general secretaryship, Gorbachev had travel experiences in the West rare for a leading Soviet politician. He vacationed with his wife in France and Italy and led CPSU delegations to Belgium (1972), West Germany (1975), France (1976), Canada (1983), and Italy and Great Britain (1984). (Sources: Borys Lewytzkyi and Juliusz Stroynowski, eds., *Who's*

Who in the Socialist Countries, Munich, 1978, p. 188; *Pravda*, 28 November 1979; *Radio Liberty Research*, 29 June 1983; *Pravda*, 12 March; *NYT*, 12 March).

Egor Kuzmich Ligachev. Born in 1920, a Russian, Egor Ligachev became a member of the CPSU in 1944. Trained as an aircraft engineer, he graduated from the Moscow Aviation Institute in 1943 and from the Party Higher School of the CPSU Central Committee in 1951. After several years of work in industry and the Komsomol, Ligachev was assigned to full-time party organizational work in 1949, subsequently rising to the position of secretary of the Novosibirsk *oblast* party committee. In 1961, he was transferred to the RSFSR office of the CPSU Central Committee, serving first as deputy head of the Department of Agitation and Propaganda, then as deputy head (for industry) of the Department of Party Organs.

Selected as first secretary of the Tomsk *oblast* party committee in 1965, Ligachev gained a reputation as a hard-driving foe of corruption and inefficiency, attracting the favorable attention of Yuri Andropov. In the summer of 1983, Andropov installed Ligachev as head of the Cadres Department of the CPSU Central Committee. At the December 1983 plenum, Ligachev was named a secretary of the CPSU Central Committee.

Ligachev was elected as a full member of the Politburo in April 1985, bypassing the usual candidate status. He soon emerged as the number two party official, assuming responsibility for ideology and foreign affairs in the Secretariat, in addition to supervision of personnel. At the July session of the USSR Supreme Soviet, he was elected as Gorbachev's successor in the chairmanship of the Council of the Union Foreign Affairs Commission.

Elected as a candidate member of the CPSU Central Committee in 1966, Ligachev was promoted to full membership in 1976. He has been a deputy to the USSR Supreme Soviet (seventh through eleventh) and the Russian Republic Supreme Soviet. (Sources: Borys Lewytzkyi and Juliusz Stroynowski, eds., *Who's Who in the Socialist Countries*, Munich, 1978, p. 356; *Pravda*, 27 December 1983; *NYT*, 27 December 1983; *Radio Liberty Research*, 9 September 1983; *Pravda*, 24 April, 3 July).

Vsevolod Serafimovich Murakhovsky. Born in 1926, a Ukrainian, Vsevolod Murakhovsky graduated from Stavropol Teacher Training Institute. His tour of army duty, 1944–1950, included service in World War II. In the 1950s, he held a teaching post, then worked in the Komsomol and, from 1957 to 1965, was a party and Soviet official in Stavropol *krai*. In 1965, he was named first secretary of the Kislovodsk city party committee.

From 1970 to 1974, Murakhovsky served as first secretary of the Stavropol city party committee and, in 1974–1975, as a secretary of the Stavropol *krai* party committee. In the latter two posts, he was under the direct supervision of Stavropol regional secretary Mikhail Gorbachev. From 1975 to 1978, Murakhovsky filled the post of first secretary of the Karachaevo-Cherkess province party committee. When Gorbachev moved to Moscow in 1978 to become CPSU Central Committee secretary for agriculture, Murakhovsky succeeded him in the Stavropol *krai* first secretaryship and served in that post until his 2 November 1985 appointment as first deputy chairman of the USSR Council of Ministers. On 22 November, Murakhovsky was appointed to an additional post, that of chairman of a new agency, the State Committee for thc Agroindustrial Complex.

Murakhovsky has been a member of the CPSU Central Committee since 1981 and a deputy of the USSR Supreme Soviet since 1979. He holds the award of Hero of Socialist Labor. (Sources: *Pravda*, 5 December 1978; *Izvestiia*, 3, 23 November).

Nikolai Ivanovich Ryzhkov. Born in 1929, a Russian, Nikolai Ryzhkov joined the CPSU in 1956 and is a graduate of the S. M. Kirov Urals Polytechnical Institute in Sverdlovsk. Starting in 1950, he was successively shift foreman, bay superintendent, shop superintendent, chief welder, deputy director, and chief engineer of the S. Ordzhonikidze Urals Heavy Machinery Plant in Sverdlovsk. In 1970, he became director of this plant and later general manager of the Uralmash (Urals Heavy Machinery Plant) Production Association.

In 1975, Ryzhkov was called to Moscow as USSR first deputy minister of heavy and transport machinery and, in 1979, was promoted to the position of first deputy head of the USSR State Planning Committee (Gosplan).

Ryzhkov was one of the first appointees to assume high office after the accession of Yuri Andropov. Named a secretary of the Central Committee in November 1982, he also was made head of the new Economics Department and soon became the principal figure on the party side in direction of the economy.

In April 1985, Ryzhkov was elected as a member of the ruling Politburo, bypassing the usual candidate status. Upon the retirement of premier Nikolai Tikhonov in September 1985, he was named as chairman of the USSR Council of Ministers.

Ryzhkov has been a member of the CPSU Central Committee since 1981 and has been a deputy to the USSR Supreme Soviet (ninth through eleventh) and the Russian Republic Supreme Soviet. He has been awarded two USSR State Prizes. (Sources: *Pravda*, 24 April; *Izvestiia*, 24 April, 28 September).

Eduard Amvrosievich Shevardnadze. Born 25 January 1928, a Georgian, Eduard Shevardnadze is the son of a teacher. He became a member of the CPSU at the age of 20, while still a student, and later graduated from the local party school and the Kutaisi Teachers College, where he studied history.

He became a member of the Georgian Supreme Soviet in 1959 and worked in the Komsomol from 1959 to 1961. From 1961 to 1964 he served as first secretary of Pervomaiskii *raion* party committee in Tbilisi. In 1964, Shevardnadze switched to police work, becoming first deputy minister of the Georgian Ministry for the Maintenance of Public Order. A year later, he was promoted to minister, a job he held for seven years (the title was changed to minister of internal affairs in 1969).

In the wake of corruption scandals in the republic, Shevardnadze displaced Vasili P. Mzhavanadze as first secretary of the Georgian party in 1972, reportedly with the backing of USSR KGB chief Yuri Andropov. He was elected a member of the CPSU Central Committee at the Twenty-sixth Party Congress in 1976 and two years later was named a candidate member of the CPSU Central Committee Politburo, apparently as a reward for his success in directing the Georgian economy and for his relentless campaign against black marketing and other illegal activities in the republic.

Shevardnadze was promoted to full Politburo membership at the Central Committee plenum of 1 July 1985. One day later, he was named as USSR foreign minister, succeeding Andrei Gromyko, who was elected as chairman of the USSR Supreme Soviet Presidium.

Shevardnadze has been a deputy to the USSR Supreme Soviet since 1974 and is a recipient of the Hero of Socialist Labor award. (Sources: Borys Lewytzkyi and Juliusz Stroynowski, eds., *Who's Who in the Socialist Countries*, Munich, 1978, p. 553; *Pravda*, 2 July; *Izvestiia*, 3 July).

Nikolai Vladimirovich Talyzin. Born in 1929, a Russian, Nikolai Talyzin is a graduate of the Communications and Electrical Engineering Institute in Moscow and holds a Doctorate of Technology and the rank of professor. From 1954 to 1975, he was successively an engineer, a head designer, a senior research associate, and the deputy director of a research institute.

Between 1965 and 1975, Talyzin served as deputy minister, then as first deputy minister, of the USSR Ministry of Communications. In 1975, he was named as minister of communications, serving in that post until his October 1980 appointments as deputy chairman of the USSR Council of Ministers and as USSR representative to the Council for Mutual Economic Assistance (CMEA).

Talyzin was appointed chairman of the USSR State Planning Committee (Gosplan) and promoted to first deputy chairman of the USSR Council of Ministers on 14 October 1985. On the following day, the CPSU Central Committee elected him as a candidate member of the Politburo.

Talyzin was elected a candidate member of the Central Committee by the Twenty-fifth CPSU Congress in 1976 and a full member by the Twenty-sixth CPSU Congress in 1981. He has served as a member of the USSR Supreme Soviet, representing Krasnodar *krai* in the Council of the Union since 1984, and has been awarded the Order of Lenin and the Order of the Red Banner. (Sources: Borys Lewytzkyi and Juliusz Stroynowski, eds., *Who's Who in the Socialist Countries*, Munich, 1978, p. 613, *Pravda*, 7 March 1984, *Izvestiia*, 7 March 1984; *Izvestiia*, 16 October).

R. Judson Mitchell
University of New Orleans

Yugoslavia

Population. 23,137,000

Party. League of Communists of Yugoslavia (Savez komunista Jugoslavije; LCY). The LCY is the only political party in the Socialist Federal Republic of Yugoslavia (SFRY). However, there are party organizations in each of the six republics and two autonomous provinces, as well as within the Yugoslav armed forces (JNA).

Founded. April 1919, as the Socialist Workers' Party of Yugoslavia; disbanded and replaced by the Communist Party of Yugoslavia (CPY) in June 1920. The CPY took the name League of Communists of Yugoslavia at the Sixth Party Congress in November 1952.

Membership. 2,188,943 (Tanjug, 19 March; *FBIS*, 20 March).

President of the Presidium. Vidoje Žarković, 58, Montenegrin (elected for a one-year term in June 1985)

Secretary of the Presidium. Dimče Belovski, 62, Macedonian (serving the second half of a two-year term). In 1982 three executive secretaries were appointed (with the provision that more could be added as needed): Trpe Jakovlevski, Vlado Janzić, and Marko Lolić.

Presidium. 23 members representing the republics, autonomous provinces, and the LCY organization in the Yugoslav armed forces. Fourteen members of Presidium hold that job between party congresses. However, there are nine ex officio members who take part in Presidium meetings by virtue of their positions as presidents of their own territorial League of Communists (LC) or as head of the JNA party organization. Since these presidencies rotate on different schedules, on either a one- or two-year basis, the makeup of the ex officio members can change within any given year. The 14 core members include Slovenia: Mitja Ribičič, Milan Kučan; Croatia: Juri Bilić, Dušan Dragosavac; Bosnia-Herzegovina: Nikola Stojanović, Franjo Herljević; Montenegro: Vidoje Žarković, Miljan Radović; Macedonia: Dimče Belovski, Kiro Hadži-Vasilev; Serbia: Dragoslav Marković, Dobrivoje Vidić; Kosovo: Ali Šukrija; Vojvodina: Petar Matić. The 9 ex officio members (October 1985) are Slovenia: Andrej Marinc; Croatia: Mika Špiljak; Bosnia-Herzgovina: Mato Andrić; Montenegro: Marko Orlandić; Macedonia: Tome Bukleski; Serbia: Ivan Stambolić; Kosovo: Svetislav Dolasević; Vojvodina: Boško Krunić; and General Georgije Jovičić, representing the LCY in the JNA.

Central Committee. 165 members: 20 from each republic, 15 for each of the two autonomous provinces, and 15 for the army's party organization

Status. Ruling party

Last Congress. Twelfth, 26–29 June 1982. Thirteenth Congress scheduled for June 1986.

Last Elections. 1982. The Yugoslav parliament has two chambers; a 220-member Federal Chamber and an 88-member Chamber of Republics and Provinces. Elections are conducted by the Socialist Alliance of the Working People of Yugoslavia via a complex delegate system. In May 1985 Ilijaz Kurtesi was elected president of the SFRY Assembly.

Auxiliary Organizations. The Socialist Alliance of the Working People of Yugoslavia (Socijalistički savez radnog naroda Jugoslavije; SAWPY) is an umbrella mass organization that includes all major political/social organizations as well as individuals. SAWPY provides the political machinery for conducting elections and mirrors the tensions reflected in the LCY itself. There is also the Confederation of Trade Unions of Yugoslavia (Savez sindikata Jugoslavije; CTUY), and the League of Socialist Youth of Yugoslavia (Savez socijalističke omladine Jugoslavije; LSYY).

Governmental Bodies. An 8-member collective state presidency was elected in May 1984 for five-year terms. The president and vice-president serve for one year and these positions rotate among the membership. In May 1985 Radovan Vlajković, 62 (Vojvodina) became president of the SFRY; Sinan Hasani, 62 (Kosovo) became vice-president. Other members of the presidency are: Slovenia, Stane Dolanc; Croatia, Josip Vrhovec; Bosnia-Herzegovina, Branko Mikulić; Montenegro, Veselin Djuranović (president for the first four-and-a-half months of 1985); Macedonia, Lazar Mojsov; and Serbia, Mikola Ljubičić. Vidoje Žarković meets with the presidency as an ex officio member in his capacity as head of the LCY Presidium. There is also an administrative secretary general of the presidency, Muhamed Berberović. Day-to-day government is in the hands of a 29-member Federal Executive Council elected for four years and headed by Prime Minister Milka Planinc (to be replaced by Branko Mikulić in May 1986). There are three vice-premiers: Borislav Srebić, Mijat Šuković, and Janez Zemljarič. Among the most important federal secretaries are Raif Dizdarević, foreign affairs; Admiral Branko Mamula, defense; Dobroslav Ćulafić, internal affairs; and Vlado Klemenčič, finance.

Publications. Main publications of the LCY are *Komunist* (weekly) and *Socijalizam* (monthly); SAWPY's main publication is *Borba*, a daily newspaper with Belgrade and Zagreb editions. Other major dailies include *Politika*, *Večernje novosti*, *Politika ekspres* (Belgrade), *Večernji list*, *Vjesnik* (Zagreb), *Delo* (Ljubljana), and *Oslobodjenje* (Sarajevo). Prominent weeklies are *NIN* (*Nedeljne informativne novine*, Belgrade) and *Danas* (Zagreb). Among the boldest of the youth newspapers is the occasionally banned Belgrade weekly, *Student*; much controversial religious material appears in the biweekly Catholic journal, *Glas koncila* (Zagreb). Tanjug is the official news agency.

Five years ago the godfather of Yugoslav communism, Josip Broz Tito, died. During 1985 the forecasts that without him Yugoslavia would fall apart continued (*WP*, 8 August). Given the complicated nature of post-Tito political solutions, Western and Yugoslav observers alike might be excused for wondering whether the country, or at least the League of Communists of Yugoslavia (LCY), had not inadvertently "withered away." For Yugoslavia is ruled by a rotating collective leadership chosen on the basis of "national" (ethnic) and territorial/bureaucratic criteria. This elaborate quota system is unique among ruling Communist parties. Some continuity at the top is provided by staggered rotation schedules. For example, members of the state collective presidency were elected for five-year terms in May 1984, while the next LCY Presidium will be chosen at the Thirteenth Party Congress in 1986. This is reinforced by the informal, often criticized, practice of "horizontal rotation," whereby political leaders at all levels play musical chairs with high-ranking party, state, and government posts. Although this undeniably violates the intent of Tito's initiative on "collective work" (November 1978), it does assure ongoing political experience, if not agreement, at the top of the party/state hierarchies.

The current political structure of Yugoslavia stems from the confederal principles retained in the 1974 constitution, which recognizes the "sovereign rights" of the nations of Yugoslavia. Thus, with the exception of defense, foreign policy, and an increasingly mythical "united market," the powers of the Yugoslav federal center have devolved back to its component parts: the six republics and two autonomous provinces. Virtually by default, the LCY has been reduced to an arena for achieving agreement among increasingly powerful republic and provincial political actors; a consequence that escaped notice during Tito's lifetime due to his personal authority. But with his passing, the centrifugal tendencies of the manner in which Tito stage-managed his own succession have become ever more obvious.

Nonetheless, the "Titoist solution" was ratified at the Twelfth LCY Congress in June 1982, including (1) federalization of the LCY into nine parts (republic, province, and army party organizations); (2) interrepublican consensus as the standard basis for federal decisonmaking; and (3) republic/province and ethnic keys applied to most political jobs at all levels. Whatever the problems with these principles, the 1982 "Congress of Continuity" could not agree on an alternative. Thus, the search for consensus became institutionalized at the highest level of the party and has continued to proliferate in federal structures and procedural rules. The ongoing efforts of Yugoslav politicians to find an acceptable substitute for Tito's charismatic leadership, while they jump on and off the political merry-go-round of collective leadership, can only be understood within this political reality.

Leadership and Party Organization. In 1985 the LCY leadership continued on a treadmill of agonizing reappraisal and self-criticism in its efforts to apply the "Titoist solution" reaffirmed by the Twelfth Party Congress. This is a chicken-and-egg problem, including an admitted lack of party unity and disagreement about the direction of needed political reform, further undermining the party's leading role (*Nova Makedonija*, 1 January; *FBIS*, 10 January). As the year opened, some 70,000 basic party organizations were dutifully considering the LCY Presidium's draft resolution of June 1984, criticizing the relationship between central party organs and the republic/province organizations (*Politika*, 13–15 July 1984). Secretary of the Presidium Dimče Belovski's denial of conflict between the Presidium and the LCY Central Committee notwithstanding (*Politika*, 12 September 1984), the latter appeared to have passed its responsibility to the lower party level due to dissatisfaction with the draft. As Spiro Galović (a member of the Serbian presidium who sits on the LCY Central Committee) subsequently admitted, "real disagreements" existed although they were cloaked in jargon (*Danas*, 22 January).

At the Sixteenth Session of the LCY Central Committee on 5 and 6 March, that body returned to the Presidium's draft in light of the eight-month public debate. The plenum adopted a resolution on "Implementation of the Leading Role and Consolidation of the Ideological and Action Unity of the LCY" (Tanjug, 9 March; *FBIS*, 13 March) that essentially adhered to the original version. For all its frankness in admitting that the top party bodies were as much a part of the problem as of the solution (*Večernje novosti*, 6 March), the plenum again postponed the decision of "what is to be done" with the promise that the Central Committee "will establish and formulate a program for analyzing and resolving the most important, outstanding, and topical issues" of socioeconomic and political development.

That March resolution emphasized the principle of democratic centralism, stressing that this organizing principle must apply equally to all party organizations, not just to relations within the republic and province parties. The national parties in turn exhibited a "less binding attitude" toward decisions of the Central Committee (ibid.; *FBIS*, 13 March). However, although the March plenum reached new levels of critical debate, it did not offer concrete guidelines for overcoming the degeneration of democratic centralism into "sterile repetitions of exactly the same resolutions, lack of adherence to these resolutions in practice, and the evasion of democratic debate" (*Komunist*, 13 April 1984). By mid-year, Presidium member Ali Šukrija warned against different interpretations of democratic centralism, sometimes amounting to "a process of endless agreement and discussion that obligates nobody" (*Politika*, 29 July; *FBIS*, 8 August). And at its 30 July plenum the Central Committee threatened to expel party members who refused to fall in line behind its policies, including its own members and those of the Presidium (*Verčernji list*, 3–4 August; *Radio Free Europe* [*RFE*] *Research*, 3 September).

Nonetheless, given the 30–31 October plenary session of the Central Committee, which adopted a resolution on the pros and cons of Yugoslav federalism, it appears that differences of views on the nature of relations within the federation continued to raise "doubts" about where the Yugoslav federation was heading and the policy of the LCY itself (Tanjug, 2 November; *FBIS*, 13 November). The strengthening of the Central Committee as the highest party organ between congresses, emphasized at the June 1982 congress, was evident in the resolution's somewhat contradictory description of the tasks of the CC and its Presidium. The Central Committee was to "take the initiative" in tackling difficulties in decisionmaking and "harmonization" of republic/province interests. Conversely, the LCY Presidium was in charge of the "ideopolitical questions of implementing relations" within the Yugoslav federal system, thereby affirming the positions of the Central Committee.

This is certainly not the original Leninist version of democratic centralism; nor does it resemble the practice of other communist political systems, where central committees are largely ratifying institutions for party policies that come down from their politburos. While it might be going too far to say that Yugoslav democratic centralism became unrecognizable, on a day-to-day basis the concept appeared increasingly relegated to an instrument of implementation as opposed to an organizing principle. This flowed logically from a commitment to consensus as a decisionmaking procedure in which agreements among republics and provinces were "harmonized" by means of compromises and political tradeoffs. Thus, unity of the League of Communists existed only in the most general terms and had to be renegotiated, sometimes recreated, on every specific issue.

Throughout 1985 some rank-and-file party

members, discouraged by LCY performance and the lack of any solution to the country's overwhelming economic difficulties, voted with their feet. Attention to this problem sharpened with an unprecedented case: all 70 members in an LCY basic organization at a pump and filter factory in Tesanj, Bosnia-Herzegovina, turned in their party cards (*Danas*, 29 January; *JPRS*, 12 February). By mid-1985 some 20,800 individuals reportedly had left the party (*Borba*, 9 October; *FBIS*, 23 October). Even the number of Communists in the army suffered attrition, due to difficulties in the "socioeconomic situation" (*Narodna armija*, 20 June; *FBIS*, 28 June).

Yet despite the frustrating search for an elusive unity at the top of the party and creeping political apathy in the ranks, the machinery put in place by the Twelfth Congress creaked along. Rotation schedules were observed, and on 25 June Belgrade television showed Vidoje Žarković assuming his seat as president of the LCY Presidium, next to party secretary Dimče Belovski (*JPRS*, 28 August).

Domestic Affairs. Yugoslav domestic politics during 1985 were a function of the imperatives imposed by debt-servicing obligations on a foreign debt of roughly $19 billion. Although the need to implement the 1983 Economic Stabilization Program (see *YICA*, 1985, p. 368) remained the official priority, struggle continued over who would make the necessary sacrifices. In principle, there was agreement with Prime Minister Milka Planinc's insistence on market-oriented economic reform. In fact, an entrenched opposition, consisting of those asked to pay the price in power, privileges, and money, resisted the move toward "market socialism," much as had been the case during the earlier economic reforms of 1961 and 1965.

Consequently, discussion turned to the need for political reform as a necessary step on the road to economic recovery. It was not a new topic. Indeed, no sooner had the delegates to the Twelfth Congress packed their bags than Professor Najdan Pašić, a Central Committee member from Serbia, addressed a "Letter to the LCY Presidium" calling for reform of the political system to overcome the "parcelization" of power, which in his view prevented effective policymaking and paralyzed the party (*Politika*, 29 September 1982). Pašić's call for limited recentralization expressed Serbian frustration with federalization of Yugoslav institutions. In November 1984 that frustration took the form of concrete recommendations by the Serbian Central Committee for change in the areas of self-management, cadres policy, and relations between Serbia and the autonomous provinces of Kosovo and Vojvodina (*Borba*, 26 November 1984). As might have been expected, the Serbian initiative was not welcomed by political leaders in Kosovo and Vojvodina. Head of the Priština party, Azem Vlasi, made clear that in his view the prerogatives of the autonomous provinces were "a social reality that one must recognize" (*Danas*, 15 January). Nor did Slovene and Croat leaders appreciate the proposal to recentralize the main party organ by changing the voting procedure for the LCY Central Committee so that its members would be chosen at the LCY congress and not by their republic/province parties (*NIN*, 30 December 1984; *Komunist*, 12 December 1984).

Thus, throughout 1985 a political tug-of-war went on between those committed to federalization, who viewed political reform as improving on but not fundamentally changing the "Titoist solution," and Serbian reformers intent on reversing the federalization of Serbia if not of all Yugoslavia. This dynamic was particularly complicated, because the Serbian position linked recentralization and restrictions on decisionmaking by interrepublic consensus with support for economic reforms, which are typically favored by the more developed republics of Slovenia and Croatia. Hence, Slovene and Croat policymakers resisted the Serbian preference for packaging economic and political reform and rejected a linking of economic stabilization to change in the political system.

Not surprisingly, given the depth of disagreement about the direction of political change, most major decisions were postponed. However, the 16 March plenum of the Central Committee did take a step forward on the issue of elections by insisting on the need for multiple candidates at all levels, including candidates for the "most responsible" offices in the League of Communists (Tanjug, 9 March; *FBIS*, 13 March). This call for multiple candidates reflected dissatisfaction with the scope for participation in the "delegation system" and with the qualifications of those holding party/government posts. The intent was both democratization and better educated/qualified policymakers. As with every effort to improve the political process, it led to an attempt to turn the multiple-candidate issue into a wedge for comprehensive reform (*Danas*, 21 May; *JPRS*, 26 August).

Unresolved debate swirled on applying such an election procedure to the highest party levels

(*Borba*, 26 April; *FBIS*, 6 May). And at least in Serbia the final decision on whether to have one or more candidates was left to basic party organizations and communal conferences (*Politika*, 23 August; *FBIS*, 30 August). Although it is true that multiple candidates would not prevent creeping bureaucratization, inhibiting the performance of whoever was elected (*Borba*, 14–15 September; *FBIS*, 26 September), the outcome in terms of the 1986 election can be seen as a test of the Yugoslav leadership's ability to orchestrate incremental political reform.

By mid-summer, substantial political energy focused on preparations for the Thirteenth LCY Party Congress in 1986. Some objections were raised to platform drafting as a form of avoidance behavior in which "much time will be unnecessarily lost" (*Danas*, 6 August; *FBIS*, 19 August). But the process rolled forward, involving some 260 expert consultants as well as the members of the LCY Central Committee. They produced a 140-page document that LCY Presidium president Vidoje Žarković admitted mirrored the contradictions and lack of clarity of the country's political life (Tanjug, 30 July; *FBIS*, 31 July). Questions remained regarding foreign exchange, planning, and the monetary, banking, and taxation systems. Logically, the draft reflected the fact that as yet positions had not been "harmonized" on the future development of the economic/political system, and the promised critical analysis of the functioning of the political system had not been completed. According to a Zagreb weekly, the end product was "like a loaf of Swiss cheese, huge and full of holes" (*Danas*, 6 August).

It remains to be seen how the cross-cutting cleavages emerging among confederal forces (those who are firmly committed to interrepublic consensus-achieving procedures; Serbian market-oriented recentralizers; and an amorphous group of ideological conservatives including veterans, members of the revolutionary generation, and some of the current military elite) will influence political options in the potentially tension-filled months before the June 1986 congress. For the time being what may be seen as party/army partnership steering the post-Tito ship of state has held firm, despite strains introduced by charges that the army favored "abstract unitarism," a euphemism for centralism (Tanjug, 5 March; *FBIS*, 8 March). A particularly sharp exchange occurred between the Slovene Youth Organization's paper *Mladina* (7, 14 March) and the army weekly *Narodna armija* (14 March; *RFE Research*, 28 March).

In general, civilian party leaders appeared to be sensitive to the issue of the military budget (Tanjug, 13 November; *FBIS*, 14 November), while military spokesmen within the party maintained a consistent voice for efficiency in action and more responsibility. General Bruno Vuletić complained to the eighteenth Central Committee plenum, in the name of the party organization of the armed forces, that he had heard "many fine speeches" that did not tell him "anything concrete about what we should do" (*Večernje novosti*, 19–20 July; *RFE Research*, 12 August). He called for accountability for failures, "to find out who really works effectively." Such views were by no means unique to military members of the top party bodies. Moreover, in light of the Polish experience with martial law, Yugoslav leaders are unlikely to ignore the warning signal of the armed forces' impatience with the erratic progress of economic stabilization and the "futile discussions, incessant repetition of generalizations, and constant insistence on differences" (as a former defense minister and member of the SFRY collective presidency, Nikola Ljubičic, put it) (Tanjug, 7 September; *FBIS*, 10 September).

Although military coups do tend to occur when civilian legitimacy vanishes, neither the LCY nor the armed forces gave signs of having reached a dead end during 1985. Indeed, the reaction of the army weekly to the draft platform for the Thirteenth LCY Congress, which said it was lacking in "concreteness and clarity" (*Narodna armija*, 8 August; *FBIS*, 19 August), was considerably milder than the *Danas* coverage. Having been routinely involved in the effort to achieve economic stabilization at the highest levels, it was unlikely that Yugoslav military leaders harbored a "secret plan" to save the economy or aspired to become surgeons on the Yugoslav body politic. As with everything else in this political drama, maintaining the present civil-military balance beyond 1985 depends on economic variables, at best only partly within the control of Yugoslav political actors.

The Economy. The year 1985 repeated a by now standard scenario. As the Yugoslav economy staggered, the International Monetary Fund (IMF) and Western bankers again stepped in with $300 million in IMF standby credit (*NYT*, 30 April). The IMF credit came at the cost of yet another austerity program, approved by the Yugoslav parliament on 14 March, that virtually ended government subsidies and price controls. This cure for the economy brought with it an inflation officially admitted to be

80 percent (*Borba*, 16 October; *FBIS*, 1 November), and unofficially estimated at 100 percent (*RFE Research*, 14 November).

Although not as pessimistic as the 130 percent inflation predicted by Miloš Minić at the February 1984 Central Committee session, the pressure of 80 percent or more inflation combined with 15 percent unemployment—said to be the highest in Europe (*NYT*, 19 May)—translated into an almost insupportable burden for housewives. According to reports at the 30 and 31 October LCY Central Committee plenum, only 5 percent of Yugoslav households earned enough to balance their family budgets, some 76 percent barely got by, and an estimated 19 percent did without or sank into debt. Among the most hopeless economically were the elderly living on fixed pensions, 60 percent of whom received about 10,000 dinars (roughly $40) a month. Some areas were worse off: unemployment in Kosovo was estimated at 30 percent (*NIN*, 5 May), while in Macedonia 70 percent of workers earned less than the average monthly wage of 29,500 dinars (about $100) (*Večernje novosti*, 31 October; *RFE Research*, 14 November).

At this level of economic hardship, there was understandable concern about the political consequences. Zorka Šekulić, Central Committee member from Serbia, said bluntly that the present circumstances had not so much "shaken" workers' confidence in the regime as "completely destroyed" it (ibid.). This realistic worry about political unrest in the face of further belt-tightening, combined with improvement in some other economic indicators, undoubtedly facilitated Yugoslavia's rescheduling of negotiations with some fifteen Western governments and the state of Kuwait. That agreement deferred about $700 million, 90 percent of Yugoslavia's debt principal due between 1 January 1985 and 15 May 1986, for a period of nine years, with a four-year grace period (Tanjug, 24 May; *FBIS*, 28 May). Discussions continued on the rescheduling of another $3.6 billion of debts with 600 commercial banks and $1.5 billion owed to other governments (Tanjug, 15 October; *FBIS*, 17 October). The hope was to reduce the amount of foreign exchange that the Yugoslavs must set aside for debt-servicing from the current 40 percent to 25 percent; thereby returning to what Finance Minister Vlado Klemenčič described to the annual conference of the World Bank and IMF in Seoul, Korea, as "business as usual" (*Danas*, 15 October; *FBIS*, 17 October).

In 1984 Yugoslavia had achieved a balance-of-payments surplus with foreign countries of $750 million. Its foreign-exchange reserves had increased to $2.4 billion. Economic data for the first nine months of 1985 showed industrial production up by 2.4 percent above the 1984 figure, with a 7 percent increase in exports (*Borba*, 16 October; *FBIS*, 1 November). Regardless of the extent to which these trends continue, further refinancing will likely be needed to give the Yugoslav economy breathing space.

As important as such continued access to convertible currencies is, however, the basic issue for the Yugoslav economy in 1985 had as much to do with distribution as accumulation of foreign currencies. Conflict over foreign currency earnings, which acted as a catalyst for the 1971 Zagreb student strike, did not end with Tito's minicultural revolution against Communists in Croatia and elsewhere who were "nationalistically minded." Emotions run high, and the issue has resisted all efforts to achieve interrepublic consensus. In July, two foreign currency laws that failed to obtain the required two-thirds majority in the Chamber of Republics and Autonomous Provinces were "temporarily" passed by the state presidency to increase the share of foreign currency going to the central government (*Vjesnik*, 26–27 July; *RFE Research*, 12 August).

The incident served as a reminder of the power of the state presidency to override republic/province deadlocks via emergency decrees issued by an enlarged body including the LCY secretary, the president of the Assembly, the prime minister, foreign minister, interior minister, and minister for defense. This is a procedure that allows government to function at the expense of bypassing participatory institutions and strengthening the Federal Executive Council. Its use was one sign of what may be a shift in the balance of power within the post-Tito political system. Government rather than party decision-making bodies are assuming a de facto "leading role," the rhetoric of Central Committee plenums notwithstanding. If the depth of disagreement concerning the proposed law on planning continues (Tanjug, 26 July; *RFE Research*, 12 August), that too may wind up on the state presidency's agenda.

Another indicator of the times could be seen in the intensified dismay expressed by economists and sociologists at the state of the economy and society. The year opened with a conference of some two hundred academics discussing "The Crisis in the Yugoslav Economic System." The conference for the most part strongly supported market-oriented reforms, most especially the need to get the party out of the economy at all levels (*Politika*, 22 February; *RFE Research*, 1 March). Conversely, sociologists at a conference on "Sociology and Social Reality" warned that more market socialism without political moves to soften the human impact and growing inequalities might well backfire, causing those working in the socialist sector of society to "reconsider" their ideological values (*Večernje novosti*, 8 April; *RFE Research*, 22 April).

This raised a question that has been assiduously avoided by politicians who have assumed that the answer to economic and political reform in post-Tito Yugoslavia is more, or "real," self-management: what if the answer is not more, but less, self-management? As Dr. Miroslav Živković put it, "The Yugoslav self-management system is not a remedy for our crisis, and it is an illusion to believe that" (*Večernje novosti*, 16 April; *RFE Research*, 22 April). He recommended full-fledged social democracy as an alternative. But at least throughout 1985 self-management remained the founding myth of post-Tito Yugoslavia, and political/economic reforms, cosmetic or real, were legitimized within the framework of self-managing socialism.

This is not to say that all myths remained unshaken. As the fifth anniversary of Tito's death approached, his personality cult had become tarnished. Still controversial, to some almost heretical, a form of de-Titoization was nevertheless taking place (*Vjesnik*, 21 April; *RFE Research*, 28 May). The charges against Tito ranged from realistic criticism of the economic plight inherited by his successors to exaggerated rumors that cast doubt even on the break with Stalin in 1948 (*NYT*, 29 November). It was much too soon to tell whether a more balanced approach would come out of these conflicting interpretations of Tito's legacy, thus allowing Yugoslav politicians the option of evaluating the "Titoist solution" apart from his legend.

Dissent. At one end of the spectrum, dissent in Yugoslavia in 1985 was rather clearly a matter of definition. Disagreement raged on the problem of defining political crimes (*Danas*, 19 February; *JPRS*, 31 May) and distinguishing "intellectual counterrevolution" from permissible ideological diversity (*Borba*, 2–3 February; *JPRS*, 30 April). Much of the controversy centered on the fate of the "Belgrade six," those six Serbian intellectuals charged with "antistate" activity for participating in a discussion group. Meeting on 20 April 1984 in the apartment of Milovan Djilas—Yugoslavia's most internationally renowned dissident—the group heard his views on the country's highly sensitive "national" question (*YICA*, 1985, p. 371).

Of the 28 persons swept up in a security raid on the meeting, most, Djilas included, were released. Faced with a flood of embarrassing international and domestic protest, in February the charges against three of the six were lessened to "hostile propaganda," and they received from one- to two-year sentences. Proceedings were dropped against a fourth defendant, and separate trials were ordered for the remaining two (*CSM*, 8 February). Speculation that the arrests had been intended to undermine the Serbian party's credibility in its drive for recentralization (*RFE Research*, 12 February) made the Serbian leadership obviously uncomfortable. Rather than intimidating dissidents, creating scapegoats of the "Belgrade six" had dramatically expanded criticism. The six became celebrities at home and abroad. Spiro Galović, a member of the Serbian Communist party presidency, referred to their "undeserved fame," acquired in his view "only because we made a mistake. . . due perhaps to the oversensitivity of officials in authority who find subversion everywhere" (*NYT*, 19 November). In the summer, charges against radio technician Dragomir Olujić were dropped during his appeal; the sentences of Miodrag Milić and Milan Nikolić were reduced to 18 and 8 months, respectively. Milić continued his appeal to the federal court, while Nikolić was granted until 31 December to continue his work on a sociological study for the Institute of Agricultural Economics.

When it came to "nationalist" crimes in the Albanian-dominated autonomous province of Kosovo, however, judicial moderation ended. A Prizren district court sentenced an unemployed villager and his minor accomplice to three years in prison/reform school for "conspiring to carry out enemy activity" by setting up a group of "Marxist-Leninists" to write "enemy slogans, [wrecking]. . . Yugoslavia's brotherhood and unity" (Tanjug, 5 April; *FBIS*, 10 April). Amnesty International announced that it was adopting over 200 Yugoslav "prisoners of conscience" serving sentences averaging six-and-a-half years, some as much as 15 years. The human-rights organization urged the Yugoslav government to stop using "hostile propaganda" laws for purposes of political oppression (Amnesty International news release, 28 May).

Notwithstanding such international appeals, trials of ethnic Albanians continued in Kosovo, many facing long sentences if convicted. Some of these cases stemmed from manifestations of more violent, unambiguous acts of dissent such as the 10,532 fires reportedly set by Albanian nationalists in 1984 at a cost of 123 dead, 519 injured, and some 5.7 billion dinars in damage (Report to the SFRY Federal Assembly, *Borba*, 31 May; *FBIS*, 6 June). In connection with these figures, the Federal Secretariat for Internal Affairs announced that there were 14.7 percent fewer such incidents of arson than in 1983, but that explosions in the workplace were up 12.7 percent—totaling 221 explosions in which 47 persons were killed and 161 injured. The report went on to complain that the program for modernizing the Secretariat for Internal Affairs had stagnated for lack of resources and that the secretariat's performance was hampered by outdated information systems (*FBIS*, 6 June).

Serb and Montenegrin emigration from Kosovo continued although, according to Dr. Kurtes Salihu, that process was gradually being turned around. The member of the Kosovo LC presidium cited evidence that 47 Serbian and Montenegrin families returned in 1984, compared to a previous two-year outflow of 1,529 families (Tanjug, 17 June; *FBIS*, 18 June). Among the more inflammatory incidents was the much-disputed mutilation of Djordje Martinović, a 56-year-old part-time Serbian farmer who claimed that he had been attacked in the fields and subjected to a Turkish torture by masked Albanians; Kosovo police authorities insist that he subsequently confessed to injuring himself in an act of attempted sexual self-gratification (*Economist*, 15 June). Transferred to a Belgrade hospital, Martinović promptly reversed his confession. An investigating commission was appointed. But no matter what that commission concludes, the damage has been done in terms of intensified Serbian backlash and deepened bitterness on the side of Albanian Kosovars (*WP*, 8 August).

In Croatia eleven people were tried for planting explosives, scheming toward an independent Croatia, and maintaining connections with Ustašha terrorist organizations in West Germany (*NYT*, 9 April).

As with "hostile" intellectual activity, religious dissent was as much a function of official "oversensitivity" as intent. Given the ideologically embarrassing, if economically rewarding, "miracle" of Medjugoje—a village in the Mostar diocese where visions of the Virgin Mary reportedly appeared regularly to six young Yugoslavs during 1981—and the heterogeneous nature of the religious population of Bosnia-Herzegovina, it was not surprising that authorities in that republic were particularly on their guard. One Bosnian Catholic priest was reportedly sentenced to prison for asking in a sermon why young people preferred church to Communist party meetings (*Economist*, 9 February). Another Catholic friar, Branko Jurić, received 40 days in jail for "insulting Tito's memory while hearing confessions" (*Politika*, 14 May; *RFE Research*, 28 May).

On balance, the authorities' fears of a religious revival under conditions of increasing economic hardship and political alienation appeared more substantial than the actual "nationalistic deviations" for which they castigated the Catholic hierarchy, Serbian Orthodox clergy, and Muslim religious leaders. Throughout the year a steady stream of criticism signaled official nervousness, which undoubtedly escalated when Jakov Blažević (public prosecutor in the trial of Catholic archbishop Aloysius Stepinac in 1946 for alleged war crimes) made known his current opinion that there would have been no trial had the archbishop not been "politically narrow-minded" (*Polet*, 8, 15 February; *RFE Research*, 28 March).

The ideological commission of the Montenegrin party found "extremist members" in all three religious communities, but "hostile activity" especially in the Catholic and Islamic sectors (*Politika*, 2 February; *RFE Research*, 28 March). The postponed construction of a mosque at Zagreb had its counterpart in the continual delays on the part of the Serbian authorities before granting permission to build the Serbian Orthodox St. Sava Cathedral (*Večernje novosti*, 1 March). The continuous sniping against presumed clerical bastions of nationalism simultaneously drained political energies and created abroad a sometimes exaggerated image of paranoid Yugoslav policymakers.

Finally, the most potentially serious form of dissent was worker dissatisfaction, expressed in strikes and absenteeism. Some 341 work stoppages took place during the first half of 1985, almost double that for the comparable period in 1984 (Belgrade Domestic Radio, 24 September; *FBIS*, 26 September). For the most part these strikes protested low wages and poor economic conditions as well as discontent with increased administrative salaries. In addition, growing absenteeism cut deeper into productivity among workers who did not actually strike; a statement of "hidden dissatisfaction that can neither be controlled nor directed" (*Intervju*, 24 May).

Auxiliary Organizations. The issues that preoccupied the umbrella political organization, the Socialist Alliance of the Working People of Yugoslavia (SAWPY), were essentially the same problems that plagued the LCY. Thus, the year began with a report to the SAWPY Federal Conference Presidium by Vice-President Janez Zemljarič on implementation of the socioeconomic development resolution (Tanjug, 14 January; *FBIS*, 16 January). On one level, this session was informational, briefing SAWPY leaders on the state of negotiations with the IMF and sixteen creditor countries. On another, it was designed to begin mobilizing the necessary machinery to cushion the blow of yet another painful austerity program.

Much of the discussion centered on already escalating prices, emphasizing federal responsibility for (1) curbing associated labor organizations that ignore price controls, and (2) keeping the public better informed on the reasons for price increases. However, considerable dissatisfaction also was expressed concerning the disparity between some 300 existing laws and 1,000 regulations and the actual results in terms of environmental protection. Criticism centered on the officials responsible for cleaning up the Sava River and on loopholes stemming from lack of a unified approach, i.e., the fact that environmental pollution is a republic/province function. The general thrust of these comments was that protection of the human environment must be incorporated into the medium- and long-term development plans currently under discussion.

The Kosovo SAWPY focused its efforts on containing "nationalist/irredentist" activity and slowing the emigration of Serbs and Montenegrins from the province. At a session of the provincial conference, President Abdulah Hodža seemed cautiously optimistic about the security situation. He stressed the relationship between political stability and increasing economic cooperation between organizations of associated labor in Kosovo and such organizations in the rest of the country, especially Serbia, noting that 98 agreements had been signed (Tanjug, 26 June; *FBIS*, 27 June). Representatives from SAWPY organizations in Serbia, Vojvodina, and Macedonia also took part in the Kosovo conference meeting.

A substantial amount of SAWPY political energies, at the federal and republic/province levels alike, of necessity was devoted to preparing for the upcoming elections. Here the confused guidelines on how many candidates should in fact run for each post had practical repercussions. As Bogdan Tankošić, a member of the Vojvodina SAWPY presidium, put it, "guesswork" on the issue of several candidates distracted public attention from "the essence of the delegate elections," which in his view required bringing "young and expert forces into the self-managing currents of political work," and electing "those who are successful in their work," honest, knowledgeable, and diligent (*Borba*, 26 August; *FBIS*, 30 August).

During 1985 the Confederation of Trade Unions of Yugoslavia (CTUY) did not make much progress in defining its role vis-à-vis self-management organizations, enterprise managers, and its party patrons. Given the rising number of strikes, trade unions found themselves in an increasingly awkward position as representatives of workers visibly unhappy with their share of the economic pie and disillusioned with self-managing solutions. Local union leaders who resolved their identity crisis by organizing the strikes themselves reportedly lost their union posts and were sometimes expelled from the party. The basic dilemma for unions remained: did they represent the workers' needs to the LCY, or did they represent the party's needs to the workers? There appeared to be some effort to mobilize Tito's memory on the side of protecting workers from officials who "become bureaucrats" (*Borba*, 24 January; *RFE Research*, 1 March).

Finally, at the ninth congress of the Writers' Association of Yugoslavia in Novi Sad, prominent authors from all parts of the country attacked the "verbal crime" clause in the penal code and the "dogmatism preached by communist bureaucrats" (*Vjesnik*, 21 April; *RFE Research*, 28 May). Although the core demand was for greater cultural freedom, i.e., improvement in their own working conditions, the writers also warned of the dangers of both "unitarism" and "separatist nationalism." Meanwhile, fallout from the Croatian White Book, banned in Belgrade for criticizing cultural developments in Yugoslavia and most especially in Serbia (*Verčernje novosti*, 29 June 1984; *RFE Research*, 28 May), continued in the form of heated polemics. Slovene writer Ciril Zlobec was elected president of the association for the coming year.

International Views, Positions, and Activities. In foreign policy Yugoslavia reasserted the "lasting validity and vitality" of nonalignment, despite increasingly difficult international conditions (Tanjug, 19 April; *FBIS*, 22 April). Foreign

Secretary Raif Dizdarević took part in the Nonaligned Movement Coordinating Bureau's 19–21 April meeting in Delhi on the issue of Namibia. During that session, the Yugoslav foreign secretary reportedly held bilateral talks with high-ranking officials from India, Nicaragua, Botswana, Tanzania, Zimbabwe, Algeria, and Angola. Commitment to nonalignment also topped the list in a major review covering 40 years of Yugoslav foreign policy that went on to emphasize the universal nature of détente, rejection of a bipolar international system, and the need for democratization of international relations (Tanjug, 18 November; *FBIS*, 18 November).

Yet economic difficulties undeniably had had an adverse impact on the economic dimension of Yugoslavia's nonaligned activities. Exports to developing countries dropped 14 percent in 1984; imports from the Third World decreased 3 percent. The target of increasing such trade to 26 percent of the total during the current five-year period was not achieved, and it hovered at an estimated 17 percent (*Politika*, 25 March; *FBIS*, 15 April). At the same time, the imperatives of economic stabilization led to demands for reduction of official travel (Tanjug, 27 April; *JPRS*, 3 June).

In February, Yugoslavia and Iran signed a trade agreement totaling $700 million for 1985, some $100 million more than in 1984, according to the Iranian news agency (*WSJ*, 11 February). Contacts with other such countries in 1985 balanced between exchanging views on the agenda of the coming conference of nonaligned foreign ministers in Luanda, Angola, and exploring economic options (with less concrete results). Yugoslav-Algerian talks emphasized the need to upgrade economic cooperation and to give such issues priority at the Luanda meeting (Tanjug, 25 March; *FBIS*, 27 March). At the conclusion of Guyana president Forbes Burnham's visit to Yugoslavia a communiqué was issued that criticized superpower rivalry, called for a resumption of the North-South dialogue, stressed the need for a conference on money and financing of development, and "paid particular attention" to economic projects in Guyana in which Yugoslavia was participating, including the possibility of future participation in Guyanese hydroelectric projects (Tanjug, 20 April; *JPRS*, 17 May).

When the foreign minister of Malta visited, the emphasis was on the nonaligned ministerial conference, the crisis in the Mediterranean, and "fresh efforts" to promote economic cooperation (Tanjug, 27 July; *FBIS*, 2 August). Also during July, Prime Minister Planinc met with the Libyan People's Congress leader in Belgrade for a comprehensive discussion of issues concerning bilateral cooperation and problems of international relations. Federal Secretary for Foreign Trade Milenko Bojanić scheduled economic talks with Burma, Sri Lanka, and India in conjunction with his participation in a New Delhi ministerial-level conference of developing countries to discuss improving their global terms of trade (Tanjug, 17 July; *FBIS*, 18 July).

Notwithstanding the seriousness of their own economic crisis, Yugoslav humanitarian organizations sent another five tons of food to Ethiopia and some 660 kilograms of medication to Mali during January. This continued the previous pattern of contributions, which totaled some 7,700 tons of food in 1984 (Tanjug, 17 January; *FBIS*, 18 January).

The tenth anniversary of the Helsinki Conference on Security and Cooperation in Europe gave the Yugoslavs an opportunity to reiterate the relevance of nonaligned principles for European politics. Foreign Minister Dizdarević called the Helsinki Final Act a "star moment of détente," thereby underlining the Yugoslav position that détente requires democratization of international relations as well as superpower dialogue. He also took the occasion to emphasize the role played by neutral and nonaligned countries as the builders of bridges for European cooperation (*Politika*, 31 July; *FBIS*, 6 August).

In reality, networking among European neutral and nonaligned countries declined somewhat in 1985 under pressure of Yugoslavia's deepening economic crisis. Of necessity, multilateral and bilateral negotiations with the West focused primarily on the need to alleviate the impact of debt-servicing obligations. This involved exploring trade possibilities between Yugoslavia and the European Free Trade Association (EFTA), multiple sessions of the EEC Council for Cooperation with Yugoslavia, and increased interest in Yugoslav participation in the "Eureka Program" launched by French President François Mitterrand in 1984, whereby some seventeen European countries engage in joint civilian technological development to help them compete more effectively with the United States and Japan (Tanjug, 13 November; *FBIS*, 14 November).

West German Foreign Minister Hans Dietrich Genscher visited Belgrade during 31 January–1 February for a round of talks that focused on the Yugoslav need to reschedule Western debts and the country's unfavorable balance of trade with the FRG. Also discussed were the problems of some

400,000 Yugoslavs living in West Germany, the sensitive issue of terrorist activities on the part of Yugoslav exiles and inappropriate retaliation tactics by the Yugoslav secret police (UDBA), and the growing number of West German tourists (*RFE Research*, 12 February). In April, Minister of Foreign Trade Milenko Bojanić went to Bonn for four days to continue discussions of the trade deficit with the Federal Republic and the needs of Yugoslav guest workers. These visits culminated in Chancellor Helmut Kohl's June meetings with top Yugoslav leaders at Belgrade and Ljubljana (the capital of Slovenia). Kohl "positively assessed" Yugoslav progress on the economic stabilization front and complimented the "constructive role" of the neutral and nonaligned nations in contributing to European cooperation. Both sides agreed to tackle the problem of Yugoslav émigré extremist groups in a spirit of "mutual trust" (Tanjug, 6 June; *FBIS*, 7 June).

Meanwhile, some progress was also made in reducing Yugoslavia's third largest trading deficit, with Austria. Talks on financial cooperation between the two countries resulted in a bilateral trade protocol favorable to the Yugoslavs (Tanjug, 12 April; *FBIS*, 16 April).

Economic issues were at the top of the agenda during Prime Minister Milka Planinc's trip to Washington, where she met with President Reagan, Secretary of State George Shultz, Chairman of the Federal Reserve Board Paul A. Volcker, Commerce Secretary Malcolm Baldrige, and officials of the IMF and World Bank. Shultz stressed "strong continuing support" for Yugoslavia's stabilization program and promised "constructive assistance" (*NYT*, 31 May), but he was not forthcoming about specifics. Despite considerable annoyance in Congress at Yugoslavia's refusal to extradite the alleged mastermind of the *Achille Lauro* hijacking, Abdul Abbas (*WSJ*, 23 October), and Shultz's outspoken remarks on the need for international cooperation to combat terrorism (*NYT*, 18 December), the U.S. secretary of state reaffirmed Washington's commitment during his December visit to Belgrade.

Belgrade's long-standing support for the Palestine Liberation Organization (PLO) and other "national liberation movements" not in Washington's good graces has been a continual source of tension in U.S.-Yugoslav relations. But the bottom line for American policymakers has been that, with all its quirks, a nonaligned Yugoslavia is preferable to the alternative. The difficulty of translating U.S. economic power into influence over any aspect of Yugoslav politics from human rights to general foreign policy is that exercise of such influence strengthens forces already hostile to the "Western financial circles" that dictate prolonged austerity. Western bankers will not be better off if those who favor default instead of debt rescheduling take over.

Although nonalignment remained a top foreign policy priority and the Yugoslavs still insisted that foreign troops withdraw from Afghanistan (Tanjug, 12 November; *FBIS*, 18 November), the imperatives of debt-servicing made economic nonalignment more difficult to maintain with or without unwelcome political pressures. By 1985 the CMEA countries accounted for some 40 percent of the country's foreign trade, and Yugoslavs were participating in 135 multilateral projects in the Eastern bloc (Tanjug, 11 January; *FBIS*, 14 January). Still more worrisome from the point of view of many Yugoslavs and Westerners was the country's increasing economic dependence on the USSR. The Soviet Union was Yugoslavia's single largest trading partner. Commodity exchange for the 1981–1984 period totaled $24.4 billion. It was assumed that the $32 billion target for the current five-year planning period would be achieved by the end of the year (Tanjug, 21 May; *FBIS*, 22 May).

Yet another long-term protocol was signed at the conclusion to the twenty-third session of the Soviet-Yugoslav Intergovernmental Committee on Economic, Scientific, and Technical Cooperation; the committee projected a $40 billion trade turnover for the 1986–1990 period (Tanjug, 19 June; *FBIS*, 20 June). Moreover, a substantial part of that trade was in oil imports, which increased due to the negative impact of the Iran-Iraq war on other Yugoslav sources of supply. Initially policymakers attempted to deal with this problem by rationing gasoline, but in line with IMF austerity prescriptions that ended in 1985; the impact on oil imports is as yet unclear.

On the Soviet side there appeared to be some effort to take advantage of the decentralized Yugoslav political system by establishing direct relations with individual republics. Soviet Politburo member V. I. Vorotnikov discussed economic cooperation in Serbia and Montenegro during March, and later in the spring a delegation of the CPSU Auditing Commission visited Serbia (Tanjug, 21 May; *FBIS*, 22 May).

Perhaps in part to counter the political implications of these economic realities, Belgrade media strongly attacked what was seen as a deliberate Soviet attempt to downgrade Yugoslavia's "authentic revolution" to the level of "resistance movements or areas ruled by local quislings," i.e., Romania,

Hungary, and Bulgaria (*Borba*, 10 January; *RFE Research*, 24 January). After Mikhail Gorbachev took over as general secretary, some attempt was made to calm Yugoslav sensitivities in this regard. In an interview with the Yugoslav party weekly, the editor of the CPSU daily *Pravda*, Viktor Afanas'ev, pointed out that his newspaper had not been involved in any such "anti-Yugoslav activities" and stressed that among the people he knew there was a high opinion of the Yugoslav liberation struggle (*Komunist*, 5 April; *RFE Research*, 22 April). Either this was not explicit enough or perhaps not at the desired political level, for within days of the *Komunist* interview, another Yugoslav daily printed an attack on Soviet historiography concerning the Yugoslav partisans (*Politika*, 11 April).

Notwithstanding these polemics, state relations between Yugoslavia and the Soviet Union remained cordial. Prime Minister Planinc balanced her trip to Washington at the end of May with a visit to Moscow in July, where she reminded her Soviet hosts that the spirit of the 1955 Belgrade Declaration and the 1956 Moscow Statement, recognizing Yugoslavia's "separate road" to socialism, was "irreplaceable" in Soviet-Yugoslav relations (Tanjug, 4 July; *FBIS*, 9 July). Although neither Gorbachev nor Soviet Prime Minister Nikolai Tikhonov referred to these documents in their remarks, a major article in *Pravda* was devoted to the thirtieth anniversary of the Belgrade Declaration, in which what might be called a Gorbachev strategy toward the maverick Yugoslavia could be discerned (*Pravda*, 1 June; *FBIS*, 7 June).

The *Pravda* article recognized the importance of "specific features of development of individual countries" in building socialism. At the same time it pointed out that the Belgrade Declaration recognized the importance of "the teachings of Marx, Engels, and Lenin, creatively applied" along the road to socialism; and the writer stressed that Soviet-Yugoslav relations are built "on class foundations." Although "specific features of development" and "creatively applied" may be considered loopholes, that interpretation potentially allowed for substantially increased pressure to conform to Soviet-defined "Leninism," a far cry from the political guidelines in place in post-Tito Yugoslavia. In short, the USSR left open the option of being more or less flexible in ideological/political terms.

Given that the new CPSU draft program omitted the 1961 program's attacks on Yugoslav "revisionist deviations" and scaled down Moscow's own objectives from building communism to "perfecting Soviet socialism," Yugoslav commentators were cautiously optimistic that in the future the Soviet approach might be "more tolerant, more acceptable for future exchanges of opinion" (*Politika*, 26 October; *FBIS*, 19 November). Whether that optimism was warranted or wishful thinking, as with the Yugoslav response to Khrushchev's outmaneuvering of the "antiparty" group in June 1957, remains to be seen. Meanwhile Soviet deputy defense minister A. N. Yefimov appeared in Belgrade on an official visit that implied collaboration might be moving into the military arena (*Krasnaia zvezda*, 19 November; *FBIS*, 25 November).

In terms of relations with Yugoslavia's East European neighbors, polemics on the festering Macedonian question rose to new heights. There were claims of Bulgarian collaboration with Croatian exiles intent on destroying Yugoslavia (*Vjesnik*, 14 April; *RFE Research*, 22 April). Subsequently, Belgrade commentator Milo Djukić accused Bulgarian generals of trying to intimidate Yugoslavia with the threat of Warsaw Pact forces coming to Bulgaria's assistance in regaining its terra irredenta (*Večernje novosti*, 19 October; *RFE Research*, 14 November). Such charges escalated the debate from political to strategic concerns. Protest continued against Bulgarian "denationalization" of the country's Turkish and Macedonian minorities. Sofia's appeals to Yugoslav Macedonians to declare themselves ethnic Bulgarians continued to fuel speculation that Bulgaria is setting the stage for territorial claims against Yugoslav Macedonia (*Danas*, 15 October). The number of anti-Yugoslav books coming from Bulgarian publishing houses for display at the Moscow book fair did not escape attention.

Yet in 1985 Yugoslav-Bulgarian relations had an almost schizophrenic dimension. Even as the war of words raged over Macedonian identity and territory, economic contacts revived. By August, Yugoslav-Bulgarian trade reached $160 million with a balance of payments favorable to the Yugoslav side. Further increases were written into the Bulgarian five-year plan (*Vjesnik*, 17 October). In November the chairman of the Bulgarian Council of Ministers paid an "official, friendly" visit to Yugoslavia to exchange views on bilateral cooperation at the highest level (Tanjug, 12 November; *FBIS*, 14 November).

Meanwhile, the death of Enver Hoxha, first secretary of the Albanian Workers' Party, produced a lull in the long-standing dispute over the situation of the Albanian population in Kosovo. The Yugoslav media greeted Hoxha's passing as "the death of the last Stalinist" (*Večernje novosti*, 12 April; *RFE Research*, 22 April), and Yugoslav state president Veselin Djuranović sent the new first secretary, Ramiz Alia, a telegram of condolences (*Politika*, 12 April; *JPRS*, 8 May). The Yugoslavs clearly intended to take advantage of the situation to improve relations if possible. However, in light of what many Yugoslavs saw as Tirana's subversive support of nationalist-sparked violence in Kosovo, there were also warnings against overly optimistic assessments of the new chapter in Albanian politics. Speaking to a meeting of the Priština party committee, Svetislav Dolasević reminded his audience that, even without Hoxha, Stalinism had deep roots in Albania, hostile propaganda still came from Tirana, and at best gradual change could be expected (Priština Radio, 22 April; *FBIS*, 24 April).

Nonetheless, as with Bulgaria, efforts were made to decouple nationalist polemics from economic issues. An Albanian delegation visited Belgrade following agreement to establish a railway linking the two countries, while a Yugoslav trade team traveled to Tirana for a meeting of the Yugoslav-Albanian trade commission, with an eye to increasing trade turnover from $90 million in 1984 to $120 million in 1985 (Tanjug, 24 May; *RFE Research*, 3 June).

Less contentious ethnic and economic issues were on the agenda during Djuranović's meeting with Romanian President Ceauşescu and other high-ranking Romanian officials. On his return, the SFRY president reported that he had discussed the situation of Serbs and Croats in Romania as well as that of the Romanian minority in Yugoslavia. In evaluating these talks, the Yugoslav president pointed to the foreign policy dimension, i.e., the need for greater public involvement to halt the arms race and achieve universal détente, with particular emphasis on the role of nonaligned countries in solving the most important international problems (Tanjug, 13 February; *FBIS*, 14 February).

Relations with Poland improved or perhaps "normalized" with the visit of the first secretary of the Polish United Workers' Party, General Wojciech Jaruzelski, to Belgrade in July. The communiqué issued at the conclusion of the talks provided an interesting mix of economic and political information. Trade between Yugoslavia and Poland was predicted to increase 60 percent over the next five-year period, with the signing of a trade protocol that called for a $5 billion trade turnover from 1986 to 1990. There was a pledge of regular political meetings at the highest level. The call for expanded contacts between SAWPY and the Polish Patriotic Movement for National Renewal (PRON)—Jaruzelski's own effort at building a popular front—indicated a potentially different level for exchange of experience. Moreover, both sides stressed the importance of the nonaligned movement as "an independent global factor," a formulation not at all typical in Yugoslavia's communiqués with its East European neighbors (Tanjug, 10 July; *FBIS*, 11 July).

LCY presidium member Dragoslav Marković headed a delegation to the Hungarian Socialist Workers' Party's Thirteenth Congress (Tanjug, 24 March; *FBIS*, 25 March). Trade grew between the two countries, with industrial products accounting for some 40 percent of goods exchanged. Yugoslav predictions called for a total trade turnover of some $4.6 billion by 1990, an estimated 58 percent increase over the current five-year period (Tanjug, 26 June; *FBIS*, 27 June).

Conversely, relations with the countries of Soviet-style "real socialism" did not lead to particularly positive results. Talks were held with East German first deputy foreign minister, Dr. Herbert Krolikowski, "within the framework of regular political consultations" (Tanjug, 11 April; *FBIS*, 12 April). Contacts with Czechoslovakia were conspicuously lacking.

On balance, activity was relatively limited in the intracommunist arena. Upon reflection, the Yugoslavs turned down the Argentine Communist Party's call for a world communist conference to deal "with the problems of human civilization, the threat of nuclear war, and the struggle for peace." In doing so the LCY presidium reiterated that Yugoslavia does not object to such multilateral meetings if "they are open, public, and do not adopt binding documents" (Tanjug, 7 February; *FBIS*, 8 February). But in its opinion, the struggle for peace progresses better if Communist parties do not shut themselves off from "other progressive and democratic parties in the world." The Yugoslav reply also expressed concern that such a conference would deepen existing disagreements and lead to unnecessary confrontation among the parties attending.

Bilateral meetings did occur. In February, Presidium member Vidoje Žarković led a Yugoslav delegation to Paris for the Twenty-fifth Congress of the French Communist Party; delegations of the LCY and the Greek Communist party met in Athens; and high-level talks were held with the

Japanese Communists in Belgrade (Tanjug, 15 February; *JPRS*, 19 March).

Dobroslav Čulafić, the federal secretary for internal affairs, met in Beijing with the general secretary of the Chinese Communist Party, Hu Yaobang, and Premier Zhao Ziyang as well as his counterparts in the Chinese security services (Tanjug, 9 October; *FBIS*, 9 October). Republic officials also participated in the search for markets. For example, an eight-member economic and educational delegation representing the Republic of Macedonia's executive council and the Committee for Economic Relations with Foreign Countries spent a week in February visiting Jiangxi Province in China at the invitation of the province's department for the promotion of foreign economic relations.

Biographies. *Vidoje Žarković.* President of the LCY Presidium from June 1985 to June 1986, Montenegrin, born June 1927. Žarković was educated at the Higher Military Academy, Djuro Djaković Higher School of Politics and Faculty of Political Science. He has close connections with the military, took part in the partisan war of liberation during 1941–1945 and held responsible staff posts with the JNA after the war. He has served in numerous high-ranking party and government posts in Montenegro, including secretary of the Montenegrin central commitee and president of the executive council of Montenegro. Member of the LCY Presidium, 1974– ; also a member of the SFRY presidency, 1974–1984. Žarković served as vice-president of the SFRY twice: in 1976–1977 and again in 1983–1984. With Velko Milatović's resignation, he became one of Montenegro's representatives on the LCY Presidium. (Source: *International Who's Who*, 1985–1986.)

Radovan Vlajković. President of the SFRY collective presidency, May 1985–May 1986. Born in 1922, Vlajković is a Serb by nationality. He fought with partisan forces during the Yugoslav national liberation struggle, receiving the 1941 partisan commemoration medal. He joined the Communist Party of Yugoslavia in 1943. Vlajković held responsible party/government and trade union positions in Vojvodina for many years, serving as a member of the Vojvodina provincial committee from 1949 to 1969. From 1974 to 1981 he was president of the presidency of Vojvodina and an ex officio member of the presidency of Serbia. In 1981 he was elected to the SFRY presidency, where he is currently serving his second term. He is married with two children. (Sources: Tanjug, 13 May; *FBIS*, 14 May; *International Who's Who*, 1985–1986.)

Milka Planinc. Prime minister. Croatian, born in 1922. Planinc was educated at the Higher School of Administration. She joined the Communist Youth League in 1941 and the Communist Party of Yugoslavia in 1944. She was a commisar with partisan forces during the national liberation struggle and after the war held a series of increasingly responsible party/government posts in Croatia. A member of the Croatian LC presidium since 1964, she became president of the Croatian LC after the traumatic events of 1970–1971, when Tito purged the Croatian leadership for being "nationalistically minded." She was re-elected in 1977; she became prime minister of Yugoslavia in 1982. Milka Planinc is a mother and grandmother. (Sources: *International Who's Who*, 1985–1986; *NYT*, 18 May.)

Robin Alison Remington
University of Missouri–Columbia

Council for Mutual Economic Assistance

The year 1985 was marked by continued CMEA stress on integration and coordination as well as calls for dynamic socioeconomic development based on more rapid scientific and technical progress. The fortieth CMEA session did not produce any dramatic changes, as it considered the 1986–1990 economic plans; the forty-first adopted an ambitious fifteen-year scientific and technical program.

While publicly proclaiming unity, sovereignty, equality, and cooperation among CMEA members, Soviet primacy had not lessened; equality continued to be a pious wish, and cooperation appeared elusive. Prospects for reform appeared poor within the command economy concept. Overall development and external policies of the East European regimes faced definite limitations and a bleak future.

Between CMEA Sessions. Neither radical change nor lasting solutions resulted, and the seemingly endemic problems have continued. The non-Soviet members, traditionally far from being mirror-images of the USSR, nevertheless have had the latter as their basic economic model. Through the CMEA management mechanism and intertwined bilateral arrangements, the members are inescapably tied to Moscow and to one another, with the result that a degree of uniformity prevails.

Early in 1985 the CMEA planning committee met in Prague to discuss economic integration during the 1986–1990 period, consider the comprehensive and more intensive utilization of new sources of energy on a long-term basis, and coordinate investment (*Rudé právo*, 9 January). Participants were mindful that economic planning is considered "vital" by Moscow and must be conducted with a "socialist orientation." Hosting the meeting, Prime Minister Lubomír Štrougal said that strengthening technical and economic independence of CMEA is a "strategic issue" because of political and economic pressures from the West: "We must oppose this discriminatory policy with a united, coordinated trade and economic policy" (ibid.).

Between the thirty-ninth and fortieth sessions of CMEA, members were required to implement strategies established at the Moscow economic summit, including cooperation and economic integration. They were to improve coordination of national economic plans, extend the links between enterprises, exchange scientific achievements, and strengthen production and scientific/technical cooperation (*Survey of CMEA Activities*, Moscow CMEA Secretariat, 1985).

Planners in the science and technology sector were faced with an uneven development of their economies and the need to coordinate capital investment. In February, a Committee on Cooperation in Engineering was established for ensuring multilateral cooperation and raising the quality of products to world levels. Emphasis was given to agreements on industrial robots and microprocessors. In the power, fuel, and raw materials sectors, members sought to extend coordination in surveying and prospecting for oil and gas. Coordination of interconnected electric power systems continued.

At its 113th meeting, the Executive Committee approved long-term development of the power industry through the year 2000 (communiqué in ibid., pp. 35–36), although efficiency and reliability needed improvement. The joint use of coal deposits near Lublin, Poland, was considered. The participants initiated a draft agreement on codeveloping the West Siberian natural gas field at Yamburg and constructing the 4,607 kilometer "Progress" gas pipeline to the western border of the USSR. Coordination continued in agriculture to improve food supplies and extend agreements on specialization.

The CMEA Secretariat claimed that foreign trade among members continued to develop successfully. However, discussions were held to improve the methodology of internal pricing by member states, and proposals were considered on the interrelation of domestic prices and prices on world commodity markets (ibid., pp. 4–10).

The Fortieth CMEA Session. Held at Warsaw during 25–27 June, under the chairmanship of Prime Minister Wojciech Jaruzelski, this meeting was "designed to share initial experiences on implementation of strategic decisions reached by the 1984 economic summit in Moscow, spot reserves, and map out specific roads and main directions for deepening economic cooperation" (Radio Moscow, 24 June; *FBIS*, 25 June). Participants included heads or deputy heads of government from the ten member states. A Yugoslav representative, B. Srebrić, took part in the session's work. Observers came from Angola, Afghanistan, South Yemen, Laos, Mozambique, Ethiopia, Mexico, and Nicaragua.

USSR premier Nikolai Tikhonov accused the West of stepping up activities toward "weakening socialism economically and breaking up the unity among fraternal countries. This makes it incumbent on us . . . to unite our efforts . . . to strengthen the economic might of our community" (*Izvestiia*, 26 June; *FBIS*, 27 June). The lengthy communiqué three days later devoted considerable space to denouncing the West. The situation in the developed capitalist countries, it said, is "unstable and crisis-ridden, which is adversely affecting international economic cooperation." Nevertheless, this did not prevent those assembled from advocating an expansion of trade and economic links, including a proposal for establishing relations between CMEA and the European Economic Community (EEC).

Coordination of the five-year (1986–1990) national economic plans had not materialized. The communiqué only claimed "progress" and noted the growing role of economic, scientific, and technical cooperation in boosting the efficiency of social production. Cited as important was the implementation of the main directions in the long-term strategy for economic development (*Pravda*, 29 June; *FBIS*, 1 July).

The communiqué also stated that, during 1984, aggregate national income rose by 3.6 percent and real per capita income by 2.6 percent; aggregate industrial production by 4.4 percent and aggregate agricultural production by 3.0 percent. Total foreign trade turnover increased by 9.7 percent, and rose within CMEA itself by 10.6 percent. The session drew particular attention to the need to coordinate member states' scientific-technical production more closely.

At a press conference, the host country's permanent representative at CMEA, Deputy Premier Janusz Obodowski, went beyond the Aesopian language of the communiqué and statements of party leaders, acknowledging that "the results cannot be evaluated as satisfactory," a conclusion that included the five-year plans and intrabloc trade. As to economic integration, he said that all countries agreed it was too slow (PAP, 28 June; *FBIS*, 1 July). The deputy premier referred to members' long-range coordination of growth guidelines up to 1995 and beyond, but cited the 1986–1990 five-year period "as time for switching their economies to intensive growth factors." Some 130 agreements on production specialization and coproduction were to be signed or extended by year's end (ibid.).

The comprehensive program of scientific-technical development during the next ten to fifteen years is to be accelerated. The program, which will receive approval at the 1986 CMEA session, was described by Premier Tikhonov as of "prime importance," designed for transition to new generations of machines and modern technologies. He said it must have specific targets and completion schedules (*Izvestiia*, 26 June). Czechoslovak Premier Štrougal lamented the inadequate application of scientific-technical knowledge and also urged appropriate action (Radio Prague, 25 June; *FBIS*, 26 June).

No strides were visible on direct links between enterprises. The Soviet Union had inaugurated these in 1984 between its own factories and plants in Eastern Europe to facilitate intrabloc development. In an interview after the CMEA session, Štrougal admitted that industrial "enterprises are not adequately interested and stimulated to enter into direction relations" (Radio Prague, 27 June; *FBIS*, 28 June).

Other representatives expressed criticism of the existing situation in CMEA. Tikhonov voiced dissatisfaction with the coordination of the national economic plans, deliveries of foodstuffs and consumer goods, and modernization of food and light industries (ibid.). Other Czechoslovak officials pointed to the unsatisfactory preparations of their own five-year plan. Romania's prime minister, Constantin Dăscălescu, was perhaps the most outspoken. He reminded the gathering that plan coordination had not been completed, specifically in energy and raw materials, an area of particular importance to his country. He favored more cooperative production in industries where Romania has capabilities. Dăscălescu's reference to democratic principles seemed to reflect concerns about Soviet domination (Radio Free Europe [RFE], *Romanian SR/13*, 11 September).

In the "rationalization program of production inputs," various members feared they might suffer from CMEA's division of labor. Agriculture and food were conspicuously ignored in the communiqué. Hungarian and Romanian representatives indicated concern with pricing. Hungarian premier György Lázár expressed regret that, after many years of negotiations, no agreement had been reached on conditions (i.e., higher prices) to stimulate production and exchange of agricultural products among members (*MTI*, 25 June).

The Forty-first CMEA Session. This extraordinary meeting, on 17–18 December, took place in Moscow. It adopted a fifteen-year "Comprehensive Program for Scientific and Technical Progress." The initiative for this complex undertaking came from the Kremlin, and the Soviet Union pledged to carry the burden for its implementation. The program had been mandated by the 1984 Moscow economic summit (see *YICA*, 1985, p. 374) and was prepared by the Executive Committee meeting in Moscow during 18–19 November.

In welcoming the delegates, Gorbachev said that realization of socialism and "technological independence from and invulnerability to pressure and blackmail on the part of imperialism" depend on success in the scientific and technological revolution. He declared that the CPSU "regards the implementation of the program as a political task of paramount importance," and "directs Soviet communists and economic managers toward the most vigorous participation in the joint work of scientific institutions and enterprises" (Tass, 17 December).

It was clear that the stress would be on integration—the long-standing bête noire of certain East European regimes—of CMEA economies, especially in science and technology, to bridge the East-West technology gap. As the participants began their session, they were reminded by their Soviet host of the dangers of diverging from unity (recalling the crises in Hungary, Czechoslovakia, and Poland), and were told that factors uniting them were stronger than their differences (Reuters, 17 December).

The new Soviet premier, Nikolai Ryzhkov, chaired the session and acknowledged difficulties in preparing the program: "It is perfectly obvious that this was not an easy task and involved the adoption of responsible and complex decisions." Externally, he charged, the Western countries are "waging technological warfare against the socialist world with the help of embargoes, bans, and various types of restrictions" (*Izvestiia*, 18 December; *FBIS*, 18 December).

The other nine CMEA members supported the Soviet program, although with varying degrees of enthusiasm. The Hungarian premier cited those areas in which targets coincided—for example, electronics, mini- and microcomputers, medical instruments, and computerization of agriculture—and stressed the increasing role of nuclear energy. Lázár also raised problems of implementation, including the shared financial burden and importance of supervision (*MTI*, 17 December).

The Polish prime minister, Zbigniew Messner, stressed the importance of effective implementation. He charged that results had not matched the "huge intellectual potential" of CMEA and enumerated areas of weakness: no agreement on policy, repetitive research, insufficient cooperation in manufacture of high-quality apparatuses, and poor exchange of information. "We are all suffering from a lack of funds," Messner admitted, and "we must find the funds for progress even if it means postponing other tasks." He proposed a special joint fund to be established by the members (*Trybuna ludu*, 17 December; *FBIS*, 31 December).

The brief communiqué said the CMEA members had "agreed to take all the necessary steps to ensure organizational, legal, economic, and other conditions for the timely implementation of the program." Toward these ends, the session adopted a general agreement on multilateral cooperation in designated fields (*Pravda*, 19 December; *FBIS*, 19 December).

The program is designed to develop into a system of interconnected agreements that would form a basis for scientific and technical coordination and, in some spheres, a single scientific and technological policy for CMEA. Its adoption was viewed as "a landmark event for the entire world community" (Moscow, *New Times*, no. 52, December). Members proclaimed intensification of production on the basis of acceleration of scientific and technological progress. Accordingly, they agreed to coordinate efforts to create and utilize new types of machines and technology in five priority areas: electronics, automation, nuclear power, new materials and technologies, and biotechnology. They set "a truly revolutionary task" to double productivity by the year 2000, which would strengthen their competitive position with capitalism. The human factor—the "decisive factor in all changes"—will be "galvanized" for this effort (*Pravda*, 19 December).

Immediate attention was to be given to the priority areas designated in the program. The 1986–1990 five-year plans would be amended as required, with necessary material and financial resources made available. Members pledged to develop "direct relations between enterprises" and to establish joint scientific, technical, and production associations. Financing would come from national funds, credit facilities of CMEA banks, and joint funds. Heretofore, relations or "links" had existed on a government-to-government basis, largely in trade, with serious shortcomings.

According to an *Izvestiia* editorial (21 December), about 700 scientific organizations were to be involved in the implementation of the program. Alexei Antonov, deputy premier and Soviet permanent representative to CMEA, said that samples of new output and technology should be appearing within three years (*Izvestiia*, 25 December). Moscow needs East European machinery and other products, which closer coordination between five-year plans and the new program may provide.

Drafted and adopted while the session was in progress were major multilateral agreements for automated design systems, optical fiber technology, and the formation of the "Interrobot" scientific-production association to coordinate automation. The early convocation of the session itself reflected the "urgency of all-round acceleration of the scientific and technological program" (*New Times*, no. 52, December) to produce results quickly, contrary to CMEA's tradition of bureaucratic lethargy.

While all countries signed and endorsed the program, receptivity fluctuated—from Czech and Bulgarian alacrity through Polish, Hungarian, and GDR moderation, to Romanian reservations. Ceauşescu considered it "highly important" but indicated that 1986–1990 plan coordination had not been attained, and he was not satisfied with the way problems were being jointly solved. He emphasized Romania's special interest in problems relating to energy, raw materials, and the development of new technology, with power generation the central question (Agerpres, 27 December).

All bloc countries are vitally interested in and concerned with energy, although for different reasons. As seen above, nuclear energy received priority attention in the program, and one official—Vyacheslav Sychev, the CMEA secretary—said that the capacity of nuclear power plants would double in the next five years (Radio Moscow, 20 December; *FBIS*, 23 December). Although the organization as a whole has been developing nuclear energy, distribution is uneven. Shortages plague some countries, Romania most of all, causing reliance on USSR sources. The latter's interest in expansion of nuclear energy facilities is to conserve its own oil and gas. Reliance on Soviet oil has contributed to Kremlin control over Eastern Europe and has served as a lever for adoption of the program. On the other hand, certain sectors of economies in these client states are more advanced than those of the metropole—e.g., Czechoslovakia, East Germany, and Hungary in electronics and machinery—and thus are valuable to the USSR.

Prospects for EEC-CMEA Accord. The *Christian Science Monitor* (7 August) aptly characterized the long-running discussions with the European Economic Community as follows: "The world's two largest economic blocs have resumed their on-again, off-again flirtation across the East-West ideological divide." Indeed, the history of attempts to establish links between these two organizations is a prism of East-West relations over the past 25 years. Nikita Khrushchev visualized a "possibility" for cooperation and Leonid Brezhnev demanded EEC recognition of CMEA, but then he invaded Afghanistan, abruptly halting the discussions that had started in 1972.

However, CMEA's overtures to EEC have gained momentum recently, spurred by Gorbachev in a comment to Italian premier Bettino Craxi in May. This was followed by a formal letter of 14 June from CMEA secretary Sychev to EEC Commission president Jacques Delors, marking the resumption of talks after five years. At that time, the major difficulties were CMEA's proposal for a basic trade agreement and formation of a joint committee with competence over relations between the EEC and members of CMEA. The commission has been opposed to both demands. The communiqué after the fortieth CMEA session confirmed the proposal for relations between the two organizations (*Pravda*, 29 June). The EEC response was to study the Eastern proposal, which called for a joint declaration of policy to govern relations, and for establishment of official contacts.

Commissioner Willy de Clercq, head of external relations and trade negotiations, reflected the EEC position in a 29 July letter to Sychev. The communication indicated readiness to resume discussions and requested details and clarification of the proposal. Moreover, the EEC would be opposed to any change in its relations with individual members of CMEA. It has certain arrangements with Bulgaria, Czechoslovakia, Hungary, and Poland involving steel and textiles. The importance of bilateralism lies in the fact that CMEA has no common trade policy and, unlike EEC, no authority to negotiate on behalf of its individual members and no common tariffs or quotas. Moreover, EEC trade with CMEA is relatively unimportant, consisting of less than 10 percent of its turnover with nonmember countries.

On 9 October, the EEC received a draft joint declaration from CMEA "to establish official relations. . . within their respective fields of competence" and stressing an increase in trade (AFP, 9 October; *FBIS*, 10 October). Short of trade, an EEC-CMEA agreement would be quite limited but could work in environmental concerns, economic forecasts, statistics, and industrial standards. This indicated that, if the EEC would agree to a joint declaration, the individual members of CMEA would be permitted to negotiate separate trade agreements with the EEC, a concession described as an "opportunity that EEC foreign ministers should not pass up" (*Financial Times*, 21 October).

At the invitation of the USSR Supreme Soviet, a delegation from the socialist group in the European Parliament visited Moscow during 16–23 December for discussions on improving relations, including those between EEC and CMEA. This was the first delegation officially invited, although it did not represent the EEC. Soviet officials expressed their desire to give recognition to EEC, establish parliamentary links, and undertake joint scientific and technological projects, including the West European "Eureka" project, as part of the just-adopted CMEA program (DPA, AFP, *FBIS*, 20 December; and London, Press Association, 22 December).

On 18 December the commission endorsed a two-track proposal for establishment of EEC-CMEA relations, namely, a joint declaration stating that bilateral relations with individual CMEA members would be pursued. The proposal will be submitted to EEC members probably in early 1986.

Energy and East-West Trade. The performance of the Soviet Union and the six East European countries' economies has had an effect on their trade with the West. After showing a remarkable increase in their trade balance from $1.0 billion (1982), to $2.2 billion (1983), to $6.0 billion (1984), the CMEA's balance plunged to a negative $400 million during the first half of 1985, according to the UN Economic Commission for Europe Report (Geneva, 1985). The East European states showed a favorable balance of $1.3 billion in 1985, but the USSR had an unfavorable one of $1.7 billion. Non-Soviet exports to the West rose by 8 percent and 16 percent in 1983 and 1984, respectively, then fell off sharply in 1985. The Economic Commission's forecast was for modest growth and a continued narrowing of the trade deficit vis-à-vis the West.

The East European reduction of exports to the West in the first half of 1985 was small compared with the Soviet decline of 14 percent. Among the industrial countries, West Europe receives about 90 percent of Soviet-bloc exports. East European imports from the West increased by 4 percent over the first half of 1984 but food imports decreased, whereas food imports were responsible for the bulk of the 9 percent increase in Soviet imports during January–June (ibid.). Problems germane to the whole area include overconsumption of energy and raw materials, decreasing hard currency export, and the technology gap with the West. To improve their economies, CMEA members require restructuring of their industrial base and modernization of industry. For the latter, they need Western high technology, but many of the materials are on the CoCom (Coordinating Committee for Multilateral Security Controls) list (*Financial Times East European Markets*, 13 December).

Energy—basically oil—has played a major role in the economies, including East-West trade, of the CMEA countries. The fall in sales of fuel and petroleum products accounted for a good portion of the total reduction in exports to Western hard-currency countries. The large increase in the Soviet hard-currency debt during the year can be attributed largely to the decline of oil exports, which amounted to about two-thirds of 1984 earnings. Petroleum and petroleum products are of importance as export items to Eastern Europe as well. However, because of problems with its oil production, Moscow's shipments to its client states have been decreasing, as have those from the Middle East. The official January–November industrial performance statistics showed that petroleum industry plan fulfillment reached 96 percent, and production volume was only 97 percent compared with the same period in 1984. Labor productivity was 94 percent, the only category reported below 101 percent (*Ekonomicheskaia gazeta*, no. 51). This shortfall will certainly contribute to CMEA's internal energy—and possibly political—problems and will reduce the earnings of hard currency, which is needed to purchase grain and high technology. Moscow continued to be the primary energy supplier to its CMEA allies while providing substantial subsidies (*YICA*, 1985, pp. 380–81; *YICA*, 1984, pp. 412–14; John M. Kramer, "Soviet-CMEA Energy Links," *Problems of Communism*, July–August 1985, pp. 32–47).

Reductions of Soviet oil deliveries to the CMEA allies were modest compared with the decrease in exports to the West. Nevertheless, East European countries, especially Romania, Bulgaria, and Poland, experienced energy difficulties. Romania was faced with an energy problem of crisis proportions and critical shortages of electricity due to the country's modest energy supplies and its overambitious industrial consumption (RFE, *Romanian SR/1*, 17 December). This necessitated extraordinary measures, calling on the population to exhibit "civic spirit" by conserving energy in households (*Scinteia*, 4 December; *FBIS*, 24 December) and assigning military officers to direct certain power plants. Despite Ceauşescu's declaration of a "state of emergency and military work regime," the problem lies deeper than energy, for the emergency was a reflection of the difficulties in the Romanian economy (*Magyarország*, 27 October; *FBIS*, 7 November).

Bulgaria also faced energy problems. Despite indications of an increase in net production, Sofia's power industry was showing a decrease. Prices for electricity were boosted by some 40 percent for households and 58 percent for industry, and the price of gasoline, already high, increased 35 percent. Adverse weather contributed to the energy problem, but the fundamental difficulty was due to shortages of Soviet oil. Moscow is the sole supplier of oil to Bulgaria, and its supplies were insufficient. The USSR ambassador reportedly said that the Bulgarians should channel high-quality goods to Moscow, implying they were being sent to the West in preference to the Soviet Union (*Times*, 26 November).

A reporter asked why there was a coal shortage in Poland. One reason was insufficient transport, which was having a serious effect on the steel industry. In addition, with a shortage of modern equipment, most unloading was being performed manually. An important contributing factor was the neglect of Poland's economic infrastructure. In a word, "anything that has not been earmarked directly for export and for earning dollars has been put on the back burner" (ibid., 27 November). Coal joined shortages of electricity and oil, the latter the result of inadequate Soviet supplies. The Poles faced rationing of oil and a 20 and 30 percent increase in oil prices as winter set in.

An additional reason for the energy plight in the East European countries is the disregard for CMEA's regulations governing energy consumption. The Hungarian representative at the January meeting of the executive committee, Deputy Prime Minister Jozsef Marjai, whose country is not faced with a critical shortage yet, "demanded with particular emphasis" strict adherence to regulations (Radio Budapest, 15 January; *FBIS*, 16 January).

Conservation is needed, but it requires implementation. New investments include the 4,607 kilometer gas pipeline from Siberia, only now beginning construction. Nuclear power has been assigned top priority, but numerous problems will have to be overcome. Development of synthetic fuels is lagging. A turn to OPEC oil can be only temporary. Thus, the East European reliance on Soviet energy is clearly established, and Moscow's largesse will depend on each country's political loyalty and support for USSR foreign policy ("Inside Comecon: A Survey," *Economist*, 20 April). What would really help would be a fundamental change of the system, precisely what the Kremlin will not allow to take place.

John J. Karch
Vienna, Austria

Warsaw Treaty Organization

The Warsaw Treaty Organization (WTO), established 14 May 1955 for twenty years by the present seven members and Albania, was automatically extended in 1975 for another ten years. Albania withdrew in 1968, following the WTO invasion of Czechoslovakia. In 1985 the pact was renewed for another twenty years. The USSR exercises control through the WTO mechanism, bilateral treaties, and its military forces in East Germany, Czechoslovakia, Hungary, and Poland, as well as through other levers. The U.S.-Soviet summit was followed by Gorbachev's briefing of WTO leaders in Prague. USSR control, although exercised in a more conciliatory environment, was clearly in evidence. Certain East European leaders expressed concern over the degree of Soviet domination, continued interference in their internal affairs, and the unsatisfactory state of intrabloc consultations.

Military Developments. The highly mobile SS-20 intermediate-range missiles have three warheads each, the majority targeted against Western Europe. By year's end the number of SS-20s had increased to 441, with 1,323 warheads.

On 12 December Gorbachev told Louis Mermaz, head of the French National Assembly, that the Soviet Union had completed dismantling of some SS-20 installations, as Gorbachev had promised during his Paris visit. It is important to bear in mind that no SS-20 missiles or launchers were actually destroyed by this dismantling of stationary structures.

No significant changes appear to have occurred in either military personnel or armaments/equipment of the non-Soviet WTO members. Bulgaria showed a small increase in air force personnel; Czechoslovakia became the first to obtain the SU-25 Frogfoot close-support aircraft; East Germany increased its Parchim missile corvettes, doubled its MiG-23 numbers, and received some SU-22s; Hungary obtained SS-22s. Changes in Poland and Romania have been insignificant, attributed to their economic situation (International Institute for Strategic Studies, *The Military Balance, 1985–1986*, p. 17).

Warsaw Pact Renewal. At a summit meeting in Warsaw, the communist leaders of the WTO formally approved a twenty-year extension of the Treaty of Friendship, Cooperation, and Mutual Assistance. The communiqué reflected Soviet policies and stressed the "great importance" of the pact. It restated a well-known provision for the simultaneous dissolution of NATO and the WTO. The communiqué ignored the MBFR (Mutual Balanced Force Reductions) negotiations, concerned since 1973 with lowering conventional armed forces of the two alliances (*Pravda*, 27 April; *FBIS*, 29 April). A NATO-WTO dissolution would result in Soviet predominance in Europe and has been rejected by the West.

The WTO extension was hailed by all signatories and their controlled media. *Krasnaia zvezda* (28 April; *FBIS*, 30 May) said that for 30 years the pact "has reliably served the development and consolidation of its members" and that the extension "was dictated by the need to safeguard the allied countries' security and their close collaboration in international affairs." *Rudé právo* (29 April), seemingly oblivious to the WTO invasion in 1968, said that "during the past 30 years the Warsaw Pact has represented a reliable guarantee of the security, sovereignty, and peaceful development of its member-states."

One original member of WTO, Albania, denounced the extension as "an act which runs counter to the interests of the peoples of the member countries of this military pact as well as to the interests of the other European peoples and the peace, security, and the real lowering of tension in our continent." It recalled the 1968 aggression against Czechoslovakia and the "hegemonic interests" of the Soviet Union that dominate the Warsaw Pact, citing the "occupation" of Afghanistan as proof of this policy (ATA, 28 April; *FBIS*, 20 April).

Political Consultative Committee. After several postponements the highest WTO governing body, the Political Consultative Committee (PCC), met in Sofia during 21–23 October. (The previous meeting at Prague in January 1983 had been presided over by Yuri Andropov.) The two-day PCC conference in 1985 appears to have been largely a public affairs event, with a show of bloc cohesion in support of Soviet foreign policy to influence world public opinion before the Geneva summit.

The lengthy communiqué, largely a litany of known bloc positions on foreign affairs and arms control, placed the blame on "imperialism, first of all the United States," for increased tension and the threat of war. The PCC supported the USSR's proposal to ban space-strike weapons, cut U.S. and Soviet nuclear weapons 50 percent, and hold talks on the "mutual non-use of armed forces, non-increase and reduction of military expenditures, and the freezing of Europe from chemical weapons" (*New Times*, no. 45).

In a new provision, the WTO members "suggest[ed] that the numerical strength of the armed forces of the U.S.S.R. and the U.S.A., including those outside their territories, should be frozen as of January 1, 1986" (ibid.). While NATO did not issue an official comment, a spokesman said that "any Warsaw Pact proposal would be carefully examined provided it is received at the negotiating table and includes provisions for adequate verification." The official referred to the ongoing MBFR forum in Vienna, where mutual and balanced force reductions are being negotiated with verification measures (telephone interview, 24 October).

Interesting were provisions and exclusions to placate the East Europeans, such as the absence of language about the primacy of the Soviet Union, the Brezhnev Doctrine, or socialist internationalism. The communiqué cited "closer solidarity and cohesion of the socialist countries" and "Marxist-Leninist world outlook" as being particularly important. WTO members pledged to "consistently pursue the policy of enhancing the effectiveness of mutual cooperation in all fields on the basis of a well-balanced combination of their national and international interests."

One analysis suggested that the substitute wording for "socialist internationalism" seemed like a "rewording of the same idea"; that Gorbachev "conceded a point" to the Hungarians, East Germans, and Romanians; and on balance "one cannot overlook a certain measure of tolerance" by the new Soviet leadership (Radio Free Europe, *RAD Background Report* 128, 18 November).

The Post-Geneva WTO Summit. Following the Geneva summit, President Reagan briefed NATO in Brussels and Gorbachev briefed the WTO leaders in Prague. Moscow's partners were vitally interested in how the Geneva summit would affect their relations, not only with the Soviet Union but also with the West—collectively and individually (see RFE Research, *RAD Background Report* 135, 26 November, and 140, 6 December). Their joint Prague statement was positive, and pact members hailed Gorbachev's briefing. While all supported the Soviet "constructive position" at Geneva, they exhibited subtle differences in their assessment of the summit. East Germany and Hungary were the most enthusiastic, Romania the least.

Hungarian officials and media reflected the idea that improved East-West relations would increase possibilities for closer inter-European activities. Gyula Horn, director of the international relations department in the Ministry of Foreign Affairs, appearing on Budapest television, said that the summit had "achieved results that go beyond expectations (*FBIS*, 22 November).

East German leader Honecker viewed the results as "encouraging" (ADN, 22 November), while Ceauşescu said in Bucharest that "fundamental questions are still unresolved" (Agerpres, 28 November). Different opinions appeared even within individual countries—Prague's *Rudé právo* (22 November) and Bratislava's *Pravda* (22 and 23 November) reflected promising and pessimistic impressions, respectively.

Moscow's temperate rhetoric had a moderating effect on its allies, including Czechoslovakia, which had been vociferous in its denunciations of West German "revanchism" and critical of East Germany's flirtation with the Federal Republic. After Husák visited Honecker, their communiqué contained no reference to "revanchism"; instead, it supposed an expansion of East-West relations (*Neues Deutschland*, 27 November).

Intensive diplomatic activity and media proliferation followed Geneva, with U.S. officials briefing East Europeans and the Soviets Western governments. USSR deputy foreign minister

Georgi Kornienko briefed French president François Mitterrand. General Jaruzelski traveled from Warsaw to Paris, a visit that reportedly broke an "important barrier" (London, *Times*, 18 December), and Kádár went to London.

The United States countered with Secretary of State George Shultz's visits to Bucharest, Budapest, and Belgrade. Shultz discussed a range of subjects, including human rights and trade as well as East-West relations. His trip was annoying to Moscow and some of its allies. Tass (7 December) cited the Helsinki Final Act of 1975 on the "inviolability" of borders and complained of U.S. "policy directed at distorting the actual state of affairs." Other media charged Shultz with interfering in the internal affairs of WTO countries. And some—for example, Hungary—presented a more factual account (Budapest Radio, 19 December; *FBIS*, 20 December).

Military Exercises. The utility of maneuvers is well established—from training cycles in national forces to combined Soviet–East European war games—and they have been adequately cited previously. With draftees constituting between 60 and 75 percent of pact forces, training is of utmost importance. Joint exercises are assigned a special role. Problems remain persistent and the "low level" of combat readiness has been publicly criticized (*Krasnaia zvezda*, 2 and 5 April).

Over the years, the WTO record of notifications has been unsatisfactory. During 1985, only the following major exercises were announced: 25-day notice by Czechoslovakia of 25,000-man ground/air maneuvers with Soviet forces during 25–31 May, no observers invited; 23-day notice by East Germany of 25,000-man ground/air war games with Soviet troops during 6–14 July; and 21-day notice by the USSR of a 25,000-man ground/air exercise, "Kavkaz 85" (Caucasus 85), conducted during 15–21 July. Western observers to "Kavkaz 85" were invited from Greece, Turkey, Italy, Spain, Portugal, Malta, Cyprus, and Yugoslavia. Of these, only Greece, Turkey, and Italy sent observers. WTO officers are normally invited to annual NATO maneuvers in Germany.

There were, of course, other exercises and maneuvers. An East German–Polish–Soviet command post exercise for staffs was conducted during February. Fording a water hazard under winter conditions was cited as "particularly impressive." The "high combat readiness" of the forces was witnessed by Polish and East German defense ministers; Marshal Viktor Kulikov, commander-in-chief of the pact; and General Mikhail Zaitsev, commander of Soviet forces in Germany (ADN, 8 February; *FBIS*, 11 February).

The Czech-Soviet maneuvers cited above included the Soviet Central Group of Forces and Czechoslovak army and involved various types of ground and air forces that practiced coordination among units (*Pravda*, 3 May). The troops were said to have demonstrated not only skills but their "profound understanding of the complexity of the present-day international situation." According to Moscow's *Pravda* (26 May), their coordinated and precise actions attested to the "resolve" of the WTO armies to "steadfastly defend socialism and peace in a single formation." During the exercises, pact units "successfully defeated" an enemy air landing and counterattack. The games involved a forced crossing of a river (Radio Prague, 28 May; *FBIS*, 29 May).

A joint tactical-operational exercise, "Danube 85," was held during 24 June–5 July in Hungary by staffs and units of the host country, Czechoslovakia, and the Soviet Union. The war games were said to involve 23,000 troops. The scenario included defense of an enemy air and land attack, then counterattack, across the Danube (MTI, 25 June). Reuters (5 July) cited official reports that the maneuvers involved both conventional weapons and simulated weapons of mass destruction.

The Group of Soviet Forces in Germany and the East German army held a joint exercise during 6–14 July. The aim, involving ground/air force units with a total of more than 25,000 troops, was to master the interaction of different arms of the service (Tass, 14 June; *Pravda*, 15 June).

The military exercise "Kavkaz 85," cited above, was held during 15–21 July in the Transcaucasian Military District. The exercise involved ground and air force units, totaling some 25,000 personnel. The assigned task was to rehearse collaboration between different categories of troops (*Izvestiia*, 25 June). The exercise commander said that "Exercises of such a scale provide ample opportunity for working up methods and skills of cooperation among different fighting services and arms . . . improving the personnel's combat proficiency, and perfecting forms and methods of party-political work" (Moscow, *Soviet Military Review*, no. 10). A feature of the exercises was operations on mountainous and semidesert terrain.

Long, intensive preparations were made for the "Druzhba 85" (Friendship 85) joint military exercises between 4 and 10 September. The exercises involved Polish, East German, and Soviet commands, staffs, and units, and took place along the Baltic coast of Poland. Successes in defense, delaying actions, and the organizing of offensive sallies in complicated operational and tactical situations proved that "the soldiers of the fraternal armies are tough, can endure hardships, and are able to handle their equipment in a masterly manner" (*Zolnierz wolnosci*, 9 September; *FBIS*, 12 September).

Considering the Helsinki Final Act, some WTO notifications lacked adequate information, and observers have been invited to fewer than one-third of the maneuvers. In 1984, at the Conference on Disarmament in Europe (CDE), the West proposed as a confidence-building measure the exchange of an annual calendar of military maneuvers with pertinent information. On 4 October 1985, the USSR accepted the Western initiative but included an unacceptable precondition: to provide information on independent air and naval activities. Moscow is keenly aware of the NATO position, and the Soviet counterproposal goes beyond the CDE mandate.

The MBFR Negotiations. The twelfth anniversary of the negotiations on Mutual and Balanced Force Reductions (MBFR) in Central Europe occurred on 30 October 1985. These unique multilateral talks, conducted by twelve NATO and seven WTO countries, center on reductions of conventional forces and associated or verification measures in the areas of the Federal Republic of Germany, the Benelux countries, East Germany, Poland, and Czechoslovakia. In addition to indigenous forces, those forces of the United States, Canada, Great Britain, and the Soviet Union in the reductions area are affected as well.

Over the years, while limited progress has been made, two major problems have blocked progress: the so-called "data barrier" and verification measures. While both sides had agreed to establishing parity at 900,000 ground and air forces, including up to 700,000 ground forces, there are more than 200,000 troops in the area not admitted by the East.

On 14 February, the WTO tabled a modest proposal: within one year, the United States and the USSR would withdraw 13,000 and 20,000 ground troops, respectively, together with their armaments; temporary exit observation points would be established in addition to the use of national technical means (satellites); U.S.-Soviet reductions would be followed by a two-year no-increase commitment on forces and armaments in Central Europe on both an alliance and a national basis; and the sides would continue negotiations (*MBFR Press Transcript*, 14 February).

NATO welcomed the East's proposal, made ten months after the 19 April 1984 Western initiative, and said it would give careful consideration to the proposal while seeking further clarification and details (ibid., 21 February). The West also singled out WTO deficiencies, including silence on military forces in the reductions area and adequate verification measures (ibid., 20 June). Moreover, NATO emphasized that its draft treaty of 1982 and the initiative of April 1984 were still on the negotiating table (ibid., 31 October).

The West repeatedly attempted to engage the East in meaningful discussions—for example, on verification—but there was a striking absence of any constructive response from the WTO, which continued to promote its own proposal, inject propaganda, and criticize the NATO negotiators for "delaying tactics" (ibid., 10 October, 7, 21 November). The East, in effect, demanded that the West first accept its draft in principle, but the West rejected this precondition.

Over the years the stalemate has been caused by the East's unyielding position on data (that is, the number of WTO forces in the area of reductions) and verification measures. In order to make progress, the West has offered several compromise proposals. NATO, in a departure from its requirement since the negotiations began, abandoned its insistence on prior agreement on force levels—before initial reductions and a no-increase commitment were made. The West accepted as a framework, with modifications, the East's "Basic Provisions" of 14 February. The features of the new Western proposal included: (1) a reduction of 5,000 U.S. and 11,500 Soviet troops within one year—figures commensurate with the existing ratio of U.S.-Soviet ground forces in the reduction area; (2) a collective NATO-WTO and U.S.-Soviet three-year no-increase commitment on forces in the reductions area, to go into effect immediately after initial reductions are completed; and (3) a package of associated measures to ensure verification, including on-site inspections, exchange of information, and permanent exit/entry points. While the East would include the reduction of armaments, the Western proposal leaves the disposition of armaments of withdrawn troops to the discretion of each side (ibid., 5 December).

The West considers its latest proposal imaginative and a major step toward progress, but it anticipates much bargaining ahead. The East's immediate response was that while the proposal would be "carefully studied," it appeared to be of "dubious content" and "does not give cause for optimism." The Soviet spokesman reiterated the WTO position on including armaments and criticized NATO for its alleged "excessively inflated verification measures" (ibid., 5 December).

Subsequently, at a Moscow press conference, the USSR representative to the negotiations, while acknowledging the Western step as "constructive" and "positive" and in line with the U.S.-Soviet summit, criticized the proposal and pointed to its "drawbacks"—that is, the absence of arms reductions and verification measures "widened so much as to become unacceptable" (Tass, 17 December). Still, as the year ended, the popular view was one of cautious optimism.

Differences Within the WTO. References to sovereignty (Article 8 of the treaty) and needs for greater unity and combat readiness by pact officials and media attest to persistent problems within the alliance, including historical and current differences among members over nationalism, economic development, relations with the West, and amount of contributions to WTO. With the change of leadership in Moscow, speculation regarding the degree of Soviet control over Eastern Europe has continued. The countries causing the most excitement were Hungary, Romania, and East Germany. For the USSR, the question of greater latitude for its allies was not only ideological but political, economic, and practical as well.

East-West, notably U.S.-Soviet, relations affect the East European countries directly. With the deployment of U.S. missiles in Western Europe, the USSR imposed nuclear weapons on East Germany and Czechoslovakia—the intermediate SS-22s and short-range SS-21s. The latter is a mobile tactical missile with a range of 120 kilometers (75 miles) and can be equipped with a conventional, chemical, or nuclear warhead, while the former has a range of 900 kilometers. Both countries had expressed unhappiness over this burden and others have voiced regret; all acknowledged the necessity, however.

A year after the dramatic cancellation in September 1984 of Erich Honecker's announced visit to West Germany, speculation about a visit before the year's end was reported. It is important to recall that East Germany has been a loyal pro-Soviet, perhaps the most loyal, member of the alliance. However, it has shifted perceptibly in its "Westpolitik," especially toward a closer and more active inter-German relationship: enough to invite strong USSR displeasure. The visit would have occurred during a period of heightened Soviet denunciations of German "revanchism."

Whatever other lessons were served, certainly Moscow's authority and discipline over perhaps the most important WTO ally were reconfirmed. With twenty divisions and 380,000 Soviet military personnel on East German soil, and 174,000 well-trained East German soldiers—possibly the most effective of all East European forces—Moscow can least afford any disaffection there and can be expected to counter it immediately and decisively.

East German officials were careful to point out that Honecker's visit had only been "postponed." He did hold discussions with Chancellor Helmut Kohl in Moscow after Chernenko's funeral on 12 March. Honecker stated that East Germany wants "good-neighborly and normal relations between both German states in line with the principles of the peaceful coexistence of states with different social systems" (*Neues Deutschland*, 25 June). In a New Year's message, he said that "safeguarding peace" is the most important aspect of inter-German relations, and rationalized his Westpolitik as a way to promote "the constructive peace proposals of the Soviet Union, our Republic, and other countries of the socialist community" (ADN, 31 December).

Budapest's expanding relations with the West continued, to the discomfort of Moscow and Prague, but with support from East Berlin and Bucharest. Kádár, citing "historic heritage," stressed that "Hungary had regained national independence and state sovereignty, steadily follows its own road, and builds a socialist society" (MTI, 2 November). A deputy foreign minister pointed to differences among WTO members: as they are "independent and sovereign states," they "respect without exception the principle of noninterference in each other's internal affairs" (*Népszava*; 2 March; *FBIS*, 5 March).

On 25 September, Kádár held discussions with Gorbachev. In their communiqué the two leaders declared their intention to deepen Soviet-Hungarian relations "on the basis of the principles of Marxism-Leninism and socialist internationalism," to develop more effective bilateral trade, and to enhance economic integration within CMEA (Tass, 25 September). Thus, officially at least, the Hungarian leadership reaffirmed its loyal membership in both the WTO and CMEA.

In November, Kádár made his first visit to Great

Britain. The London *Times* (4 November) noted that "Mr. Kádár has not deviated one inch from the common Warsaw Pact position and it is obviously quite unrealistic to expect him to do so in the future." However, the article continued, the intensity of Anglo-Hungarian diplomacy is justified by Britain's long-term policy toward Eastern Europe, "to encourage programs toward more economic diversity, social pluralism and political democracy." It is a policy of "differentiation."

Romania has been frequently portrayed as the most independent-minded of the East European WTO members. This neighbor of the USSR has no Soviet troops, participates only in joint pact air and naval exercises, does not allow such exercises on its own territory, and has frozen its defense spending. Ceauşescu announced that two years ago Romania had decided not to increase its military spending and favored WTO countries making unilateral decisions to reduce defense budgets by 10–15 percent annually (Agerpress, 17 May). In fact, due to its calamitous economic situation, Bucharest announced a budget cut for 1986 (Reuters, 19 December). In April, Ceauşescu had favored a shorter extension period for the Warsaw Pact (Agerpress, 22 May).

On the other hand, Romania continued its membership in the WTO, readily signed the extension to strengthen "collaboration and friendship with the socialist countries" (Agerpres, 22 May), and supported the Soviet Union on ideological and major international issues. At the December conference of command party secretaries in Bucharest, Ceauşescu stressed that "the ideological activitiy of our parties and countries must take a more firm, offensive line, promptly unmasking bourgeois propaganda" (Agerpres, 19 December).

By year's end, several trends within the WTO were apparent. Military and economic integration continued. Soviet control and leadership, if not always discipline, were firmly established. The Pact's extension, basically unchanged, reflected Moscow's position, despite Romanian (and possibly Polish and Hungarian) preferences for a shorter duration.

Serious intrabloc problems plague the WTO. At the conference of party secretaries, Ceauşescu felt obliged again to call for the strengthening of collaboration among the parties "on the basis of the principles of full equality and noninterference in domestic affairs" (Agerpres, 19 December). How far individual members will be allowed to follow their particular domestic and/or foreign policies under Gorbachev remains to be seen. At least Moscow pays lip service to diversity within the alliance but strongly criticizes its allies for excessive national interests (*Pravda*, 21 June).

John J. Karch
Vienna, Austria

International Communist Organizations

WORLD MARXIST REVIEW

This Soviet-controlled international communist theoretical monthly is the only permanent institutional symbol of unity for the world's pro-Soviet and independent Communist parties (see *YICA*, 1984, pp. 426–27, for a full treatment of this subject). The year 1985 saw first a Communist Party of Lesotho representative added to the magazine's editorial council, bringing the total of such parties to 66, and then another added from the Yemen Socialist Party, the first representative from a technically noncommunist party. For this reason, the August issue stated: "On the Editorial Board and Editorial Council of *Problems of Peace and Socialism/World Marxist Review* are the representatives of parties of the following countries:"—whereas previously these were said to be "representatives of *Communist and workers'* parties" (italics added) (*WMR*, July, p. 2, and August p. 2).

The Yemen Socialist Party is a "vanguard" revolutionary democratic party according to the Soviets, meaning that it has distinguished itself from other parties of "socialist orientation" (simple revolutionary democratic parties) by having opted for "scientific socialism" (i.e., Soviet-style communism) and "proletarian internationalism" (i.e., unswerving support for the USSR). (See *Problems of Communism*, April 1982, pp. 77–82.) Still, such parties lack the ideological development and organizational discipline to be fully communist (ibid.).

Others noted in this "vanguard" category are the parties ruling Afghanistan, Angola, Benin, the Congo, Ethiopia, Mozambique, and, by implication, Kampuchea (see *Voprosy istorii*, April 1982, pp. 55–67). All eight of these parties sent delegates to the November 1981 conference on the work of the magazine, and all but Mozambique's FRELIMO attended the one in December 1984 (*WMR*, January 1982, p. 5, and January 1985, p. 2). It is expected that at least some of them will follow the Yemeni party's lead in joining the *Review*'s editorial council.

FRONT ORGANIZATIONS

Control and Coordination. The international Soviet-line communist fronts operating since World War II are counterparts of organizations established by the Comintern after World War I. Their function today is the same as that of the interwar organizations: to unite Communists with those of other political persuasions to support and thereby lend strength and respectability to USSR foreign policy objectives. Moscow's control over the fronts is evidenced by their faithful adherence to the Soviet policy line as well as by the withdrawal patterns of member organizations (certain pro-Western groups withdrew after the Cold War began, Yugoslav-affiliated ones left following the Stalin-Tito break, and Chinese and Albanian representatives departed as the Sino-Soviet split developed).

The Communist Party of the Soviet Union (CPSU) is said to control the fronts through its International Department (ID), presumably through USSR citizens serving as full-time Secretariat members at front headquarters (U.S. Congress, *The CIA and the Media*, 1978, p. 574). This is the case in seven fronts: the World Peace Council (WPC), the World Federation of Trade Unions (WFTU), the Women's International Democratic Federation (WIDF), the Afro-Asian Peoples' Solidarity Organization (AAPSO), the International Organization of Journalists (IOJ), the Christian Peace Conference (CPC), and the International Association of Democratic Lawyers (IADL). Past experience indicates that it may be the Soviet vice-presidents who exercise this function in the three other major front organizations: the International Union of Students (IUS), the World Federation of Democratic Youth (WFDY), and the World Federation of Scientific Workers (WFSW) (*YICA*, 1981, p. 455).

In addition to CPSU control of each front through the ID and headquarters personnel, coordination of front activity appears to be managed by the WPC. This makes sense because the Soviets consider the "peace movement" the most important joint action by the "anti-imperialist" forces and the most important of the movements "based on common specific objectives of professional interests"—that is, the front organizations (Moscow, *Kommunist*, no. 17, November 1972, p. 103, no. 3, February 1974, p. 101; see also *Problems of Communism*, November–December 1982, pp. 43–56). The nearly 250 positions on the WPC presidential committee include, in addition to ID deputy chief Vitali S. Shaposhnikov, one or two of the top leaders from each of the ten fronts just mentioned (except for the IADL) (see WPC, *List of Members, 1983–1986* [Helsinki], pp. 7–33, 167). The fact that the Asian Buddhist Conference for Peace (ABCP) has two presidential committee members, along with the obviously important WFTU, WIDF, WFDY, and AAPSO, means that it too might be one of the major organizations in this category (ibid., p. 31). Still another method of coordination consists of consultative meetings among the representatives of the various fronts themselves. These have taken place at least once a year since 1982 and twice a year since 1984. The 1985 meetings were held in Helsinki in April and in Havana in October. The latter meeting was presumably hosted by the Havana-headquartered Organization of Solidarity with the Peoples of Africa, Asia, and Latin America (OSPAAL) and was attended by representatives from just ten other such organizations (*CPC Information*, 1 November). It appears, then, that OSPAAL might be considered yet another major front (see *YICA*, 1985, p. 388, for earlier mention of

OSPAAL's possibly growing importance). OSPAAL does, of course, have representation on the WPC presidential committee.

Techniques and Emphases. Front activity during 1985 was characterized by a lower profile on the part of major worldwide front leaders and a concurrent effort to publicize individuals not previously notable in the front effort—all in an apparent attempt to produce enhanced credibility. This could be seen in the WPC's "no to star wars" appeal, which dealt with the primary front theme of the year, at least outside Latin America (see New Delhi, *New Age*, 31 March; Prague, *Flashes from the Trade Unions*, 18 October). The appeal, which portrayed the Strategic Defense Initiative (SDI) as offensive rather than defensive and an attempt to extend the arms race into outer space, was carried in the *International Herald Tribune* (Paris) on 5 July. It was signed by 36 personalities, only one of whom was identified with the WPC (its president, Romesh Chandra), and only 7 others with national peace committee affiliates. Yet 13 were WPC vice-presidents (among the top 40 members of the organization), 5 were additional members of the presidential committee (see above), and 6 were members of the WPC itself (WPC, *List of Members*; *New Perspectives*, no. 5). This left 11 with no apparent WPC affiliation, which, together with the downplaying of the other signatories' connections, made the appeal look like an independent undertaking. "No to star wars" had been published earlier as a document at the March meeting of the presidential committee (Helsinki, *Peace Courier*, no. 4, p. 1) in Moscow. That meeting stressed participation "by representatives from a wide spectrum of peace and antiwar groupings" (ibid., p. 10). The document was also endorsed by the meeting of thirteen major communist front organizations held in Helsinki (IUS, Prague, *Secretariat Reports*, no. 4, April).

The same downplaying of traditional WPC leaders could be seen in preparations for the next "World Congress Devoted to the International Year of Peace" (to be held at Copenhagen in October 1986). By the time of the June–July preparatory meeting, it appeared that World Federalist president Hermod Lannung (Denmark) would be its chairman (Aarhus, *Morgenavisen/Jyllands-Posten*, 12 December). Lannung is a member of the Radical Liberal Party and a traditional pacifist with no direct WPC connection. He is, however, a vice-president of the International Liaison Forum of Peace Forces (ILFPF), an extension of the WPC, whose president is also Romesh Chandra. The forum, however, appears more innocuous due to involvement of relatively "clean" persons in its leadership (*YICA*, 1984, p. 429). The last WPC-sponsored "World Congress for Peace and Life, Against Nuclear War," in June 1983 at Prague, had another ILFPF vice-president, Canadian Edyth Ballantyne of the Women's International League for Peace and Freedom, as a co-chairman. Ballantyne shared the chairmanship with Chandra and Czech WPC vice-president Tomas Travnicek (Radio Prague, 26 June 1983; *FBIS*, 27 June 1983). Lannung as sole chairman, then, would clearly be an advantage in masking Soviet/communist involvement, though he did let slip to a newspaper reporter that the initiative for the forthcoming world congress had come from "rather East European–oriented" individuals (Copenhagen, *Information*, 31 December). As for any possible ILFPF deviation from the general front line, its "Vienna Dialogue" in January gave appropriate emphasis to opposing the "militarization of space." It also sponsored an "International Dialogue" specifically devoted to this subject in Geneva in June. Three persons involved in the congress preparations under Lannung were Mikis Theodorakis (Greece), Luis Echeverria (Mexico), and Francisco da Costa Gomes (Portugal), all WPC vice-presidents who had signed the aforementioned "No to star wars" appeal.

The "International Peace Conference on the Pacific and Asian Regions," held in Sydney during 24–27 October, was handled somewhat differently, but still involved a masking process. It was technically sponsored by a "broad Australian Preparatory Committee" rather than by the WPC itself. The conference was presided over by Ernest Boatswain, and John Benson served as its secretary; but the fact that both are members of the WPC presidential committee was not mentioned (*Peace Courier*, no. 12, p. 6). Romesh Chandra, however, was cited as the WPC president when he made the conference's closing address. There had been other regionally oriented meetings involving the WPC during the early September–early November time frame (Buenos Aires, 3–6 September; Guayaquil, 21–23 October; Athens, 1–3 November), but the one in Sydney was the only one that had been mentioned in the organization's *Peace Courier* by the end of the year. Perhaps it was the success of the meeting in enlisting "clean" participants (Deputy

Prime Minister Bowen, Sydney's Mayor Sutherland, and President Crean of the Australian Council of Trade Unions) that prompted the publicity. Perhaps it was the perceived opportunity to build on gains made in neighboring, "nuclear-free" New Zealand (also currently under a Labour Government) that made it so important. In this connection, the conference expressed its "strong support for New Zealand's peace initiatives and the example and leadership the New Zealand government and people have given the world peace movement" (ibid.). Predictably, "star wars" was criticized and Soviet peace initiatives were applauded in Sydney (ibid.).

In the trade union field, this same sort of deception took place during the year; only here it was the WFTU that ostensibly took a back seat. A "Conference of Asian and Pacific Trade Union Centers on Development and the New International Economic Order" (key front themes for the Third World—see *YICA*, 1985, p. 389) was hosted in February at New Delhi not by the WFTU per se but by its Indian affiliate, the All-India Trade Union Congress (AITUC). Participation by affiliates of the basically socialist International Confederation of Free Trade Unions (ICFTU) and the basically Christian World Confederation of Labor (WCL) was stressed, even though these unions were submerged in a WFTU-affiliated majority (*Flashes from the Trade Unions*, 1 March). Most significant on this point, the new Asian and Oceanic Trade Unions Coordinating Committee set up by this meeting had the head of the New Zealand Federation of Labor (NZFOL), John Knox, as president, and former WFTU secretary K. G. Srivastava (India) as secretary (ibid.). (Presumably the latter was to be the "full-timer" at the committee's New Delhi headquarters.) Though Knox's union is an ICFTU affiliate, he is a known leftist; e.g., he served on the WPC during 1980–1983 and signed the 1985 "no to star wars" appeal. WFTU secretary general Ibrahim Zakariya (Sudan) did serve on the presidium of the New Delhi conference. Its emphases on peace, "unity of action," and opposition to transnational corporations were similar to those of the WFTU general council meeting at Moscow, which boasted the participation of over a hundred representatives from non-WFTU-affiliated organizations (*Flashes from the Trade Unions*, 18 October).

Similarly, a new International Mineworkers Organization (IMO) was established in September, with non-WFTU leader Arthur Scargill (UK) as president and ex-WFTU official Alain Simon (France) as secretary general. The latter had been secretary general of the now-defunct WFTU Trade Union International (TUI) of Miners and Energy Workers, whose unions have joined the IMO. A similar "balance" was shown at the vice-presidential level, with Mikhail A. Sibreny (USSR) "offsetting" Barry Swain (Australia). Scargill, however, has been characterized as a "Marxist" and Swain as a "radical leftist" by the anti-communist Western press (e.g., *Washington Times*, 24 September). Here again, the widely touted blending of pro-Soviet and pro-Western groups in this nearly four-million-member, Paris-centered organization appears to be primarily weighted toward the East. Scargill had taken his National Union of Miners out of the Western-oriented Mineworkers International Organization in 1983. This example of "trade union unity" might well be repeated in fields other than mining, if the WFTU-TUIs involved can find enough radical unions within their ICFTU- and/or WCL-affiliated counterparts.

Having a radical but non-WFTU president from the "White Commonwealth" (where WFTU per se has never been strong), and a person with a past history of WFTU involvement as secretary or "working head," is a pattern that was followed by the International Trade Union Committee for Peace and Disarmament ("Dublin Committee") when it was set up in 1982. Dublin Committee president James Milne, also president of the ICFTU-affiliated Scottish Trades Union Congress, has been involved in leftist affairs; e.g., in 1975, he was described as an outright Communist, he has been a WPC member since 1983, and he was one of those non-WFTU members who attended the WFTU general council meeting in Moscow (*Times*, 15 April; *List of Members*, p. 85; London, *Morning Star*, 8 October). Dublin Committee secretary Brian Price (UK) apparently continued on as a WFTU official, making the situation only slightly different from the two cases just cited. In light of all this, it is not surprising that the Dublin Committee held an Asian regional session in New Delhi just after the aforementioned conference of Trade Union Centers met there, and it claimed that many of the same persons attended (*Flashes from the Trade Unions*, 8 March).

Again, the worldwide fronts per se took a back seat in a series of six Havana conferences during June–September. Fidel Castro enunciated a regional variation on the New International Economic Order (NIEO) for the delegates, stating that Latin

American governments could not possibly pay all their foreign debts, that they should not make any more payments on principal or interest, that they should form a "united front" on this issue and otherwise coordinate their economic policies, and that the creditor nations should reimburse the banks involved with monies saved by a 10 to 12 percent cut in defense expenditures. This last point gave an implicitly pro-Soviet flavor to the campaign, since any such cutback in defense expenditures would most likely hit new programs hardest. In the United States this would primarily be "star wars," but might also stop completion of the emplacement of intermediate-range missiles in Western Europe—opposition to which was the major front theme of 1983–1984. Fidel Castro took the lead here, which does not appear to be much of a "masking" until one remembers that the audience is a Latin American one. The Cuban leader is likely to have more credibility and respect with this group than is a worldwide international front organization well known to be dominated by the Soviets.

The key statement of this program appears to have been Castro's 21 March interview with Mexico City's *Excelsior*, for excerpts were replayed by Moscow's Tass on 28 March and appeared in the international communist *Information Bulletin* (Prague, no. 13/85) and in the WPC's *New Perspectives* (no. 4) in July. The subject of debt repayment had also been taken up by Latin American regional front meetings in June: the Trade Union Unity Committee of Central America in Managua, the Latin American Continental Students Organization in Bogota and Santiago de Cuba, and the Latin American University Professionals in Quito. (The latter two are directly represented on the WPC, while the first is represented indirectly through its parent organization, the Permanent Congress of Trade Union Unity of Latin America (CPUSTAL) (*List of Members*, p. 168; *New Perspectives*, no. 4, July). Nonrepayment had also been a key point of a statement issued in Havana on 31 May by the leaders of two more regional fronts, the AAPSO and the Organization of Solidarity with the Peoples of Africa, Asia, and Latin America (again, both represented on the WPC).

The conferences at Havana most spectacularly pushed the campaign against debt repayment, however. These were openly dominated by Castro, who attended most of the sessions, formally addressed them, gave press conferences in connection with them, and informally mixed with the delegates during session recesses. Even though the first two of these conferences had not been called primarily to discuss the debt issue (they were meetings of regional fronts for other specified purposes), Castro's presence ensured that this idea would be paramount (see Havana, *Granma* daily, 6 June; and *Granma* weekly, 14 July). *Granma* weekly (16 June, 14 and 28 July, 11 August, and 22 and 29 September) reported that the following conferences were held in Havana in 1985:

1. Meeting on Situation in Latin America, 3–7 June, sponsored by the Continental Front of Women (FCM); over 200 delegates; host Vilma Espin de Castro
2. Fourth (organizational) Congress, 5–8 July, sponsored by the Federation of Latin American Journalists (FELAP); over 140 delegates; host Ernesto Vera
3. Latin American Trade Union Conference on the New International Economic Order and Foreign Debt, 15–18 July, sponsored by the Central Organization of Cuban Workers (CTC); approximately 330 delegates; host Roberto Veiga
4. Meeting on the External Debt of Latin America and the Caribbean (for political and other "personalities"), 30 July–3 August, apparently sponsored by the Cuban Foreign Ministry; over 1,200 delegates; host Carlos Rafael Rodriguez
5. Latin American Youth and Student Dialogue on the Foreign Debt, 11–14 September, sponsored by various Cuban youth organizations; approximately 600 delegates; host Carlos Lage
6. Latin American Press Forum on the Regional Financial Crisis, 17–19 September, sponsored by Prensa Latina; approximately 120 delegates; host Pedro Margolles

Several things should be noted here. Though Espin, Vera, and Veiga hosted the first three of these meetings in their capacities as leaders of the Cuban national affiliates of the pertinent fronts, they are also vice-presidents of the WIDF, the IOJ, and the WFTU, respectively (*Granma* weekly, 16 June, 14 and 28 July; *YICA*, 1984, pp. 429, 430, 432). Although three session chairmen at the trade union meeting were WFTU officers and two chairmen of the "personalities" meeting were associated with the WPC, they were introduced in their national capacities only (*Granma* weekly, 28 July; Tenth WFTU Congress, *Appeal and Resolutions*, pp. 50–57; *Granma* daily, 4 August; *List of Members*, pp. 10, 57). Similarly, Cuban IOJ vice-president Vera (see above) participated in the press forum in his national capacity (*Granma* daily, 18 September). It was only in the youth meeting that session chairmen were publicized in their international front capacities (in this case, IUS Salvadoran secretary Victor Paredes and WFDY Argentinian vice-president Jore Prigoshin [*Granma* daily, 14, 16 September]). On the other hand, those associated with moderate or even conservative organizations were also given prominent roles and their political orientation was stressed (e.g., Cesar Olarte of the Workers of Central Venezuela at the trade union meeting; ex-president of Colombia, Alfonso Lopez Michelson, at the "personalities" one; and Jorge Cahue of Venezuela's *Elite* magazine at the press forum (*Granma* weekly, 28 July, 11 August, and 29 September). Certain categories of persons were sometimes played up to give the meeting "balance," most notably Christian and Indian leaders at the youth conference (*Granma* daily, 13, 14, and 16 September). All in all, the series of Havana meetings had a rather broad-based appearance (actually coming close to reality at the "personalities" meeting [*Granma* weekly, 11 August]).

Castro was polite toward, and even laudatory of, those who propounded solutions to the debt problem diametrically opposed to his own (most dramatically, Ecuadoran presidential representative Julio Emanuel at the "personalities" meeting (*Neue Zürcher Zeitung*, 16 August). Castro has been most correct and conventional in his dealings with Cuba's Western creditors (ibid.). The Soviets, while publicizing the debt solution (see above), crediting the Havana conferences with "arousing enormous interest," and praising Castro for influencing Third World leaders on the subject (*Izvestiia*, 21 November), nevertheless also favorably publicized the efforts of Latin American governments to settle the debt problem along less radical lines (e.g., Moscow, *New Times*, no. 41, October, pp. 20–24). Reaction of the worldwide fronts included the WFTU's endorsement of the "Havana Appeal" that emerged from the trade union meeting. The appeal called for annulment *or* a moratorium *or* immediate suspension of payments *or* indefinite postponement of payment—essentially a "no-payment-now" solution, consonant with Castro's proposal. The WFTV also endorsed the day of Latin American trade union rallies, demonstrations, and strikes in support of the appeal (*Granma* daily, 18 October; *Flashes from the Trade Unions*, 8 November) and the IOJ's suggestion that individual debtor nations renegotiate their loans (Prague, *Democratic Journalist*, September, p. 5). It would seem, then, that the whole effort from the communist/front side was directed more toward mobilizing Latin American opinion against the United States, its allies, and their alleged international financial tools (the World Bank and the IMF) than toward reaching any practical solution to the problem.

Setbacks. An article by Soviet Peace Committee secretary Grigori Lokshin described the "harm" done the peace movement by the "lying and damaging concept of 'equal responsibility of both superpowers' for the arms race and for the threat of war." He also lamented the linking of the peace movement to the campaign for civil liberties in Eastern Europe and the recognition of "unofficial" peace movements in that area (*Today's Peace Movement—A Few Problems and Perspectives* [Vienna: International Institute for Peace, 1985], pp. 23–26). These elements, in fact, constitute the program of European Nuclear Disarmament (END), and it was END's decision to invite "unofficial" peace movements to its fourth Amsterdam Convention that was cited for the refusal of the official Soviet-bloc peace organizations to attend (statement by Soviet WPC secretary Tair Tairov in *Disarmament Campaigns* [The Hague, July–August, p. 8]. (See *YICA*, 1985, p. 389, for the trouble "equal responsibility" supporters gave Soviet-bloc delegates attending END's 1984 convention at Perugia.) Nevertheless, END announced at the 1985 meeting that, although it had failed to prevent deployment of Pershing II and cruise missiles in Western Europe, it would now try to prevail upon the peoples of that area to refrain from cooperating in the "star wars" program (London, *Times*, 8 July); an interesting statement for a nonaligned organization, when one remembers that its original purpose was the main front objective for 1983–1984 and its present goal coincides with front objectives for 1985.

If the 27 July–3 August Twelfth World Youth Festival in Moscow was intended to make new friends for the Soviet cause, it actually seems to have failed. Though admittedly initiated by the WFDY and IUS, this largest front meeting of the year (20,000 foreign and 2,000 Soviet delegates) attempted to project the image of a pluralistic, broad-based consensus for Soviet views (New York, *Political Affairs*, October, p. 16; *Novosti*, 19 July, in Radio Free Europe/Radio Liberty [RFE/RL] 282/85, 2 September). Both the Yugoslavs and the Democratic Youth Committee of Europe openly criticized the USSR for dominating the festival RFE/RL 282/85, 2 September). Many foreign delegates were critical of the fact that they had either been prevented from bringing literature to Moscow or had not been allowed to distribute what slipped through (RFE/RL 376/85, 12 November), even though they had earlier been assured by festival authorities that they could do so (BBC, CARIS Report, no. 99/85, 24 June). Then there were objections by various national groups, e.g., the West Germans complained because of initial recognition for a separate West Berlin delegation, contrary to previous agreement (Richmond, England, *Soviet Analyst*, 7 August, p. 2). Most important, there was anger that Russian interpreters omitted criticism of USSR policies in their translation of speeches (RFE/RL 376-85, 12 November).

When Sweden's Katrina Larsson found her criticisms of Soviet policy in Afghanistan excised from the translation, this caused a furor (Radio Stockholm, 30 July; *FBIS*, 31 July; Kingston, *Daily Gleaner*, 25 August). It was reported that some 60 persons (including Communists) from Norway, Great Britain, the Netherlands, Belgium, and Italy, as well as Sweden, criticized the USSR on this point (ibid.; RFE/RL/ 376-85. 12 November).

The Soviet press appeared to have given the festival only moderate praise, stating that it had furthered the unification of youth against the "aggressive policies of imperialism" (RFE/RL 282/85, 2 September). More significant, at its 2 November plenum one of the Komsomol's secretaries complained about the ineffectiveness of "certain" Soviet youth in debating with their foreign contemporaries at the festival and alluded to the Afghan issue in this context (RFE/RL 376/85, 12 November). Some observers cited such events as contributing to the subsequent dismissal of Aleksandr Kolyakin as Komsomol ideological secretary (ibid.).

Personnel. In the WPC, where Romesh Chandra (India) remains president and Frank Swift (UK) appears not to have been replaced as executive secretary, the following were noted during 1985: as new vice-presidents, Orlando Fundora Lopez (Cuba) and Rubens Iscaro (Argentina); as new secretaries, Kvetoslav Ondracek (Czechoslovakia) and Djanghir Atamali (the second one from the USSR) (*New Perspectives*, no. 5, pp. 1–2). Sandor Gaspar (Hungary) and Ibrahim Zakariya (Sudan) continue as WFTU president and secretary general, respectively; just as Freda Brown (Australia) and Mirjam Vire-Tuominen (Finland) remain for the WIDF. Cesar Navarro (Chile), Abd-al-Basit Musa (Sudan), and Francisco Moya (Cuba) are new WFDY vice-presidents, while new secretaries include Vladimir Johannes (Czechoslovakia) and Henrik Andersen (Denmark). WFDY secretary Joe Sims (United States) has left his position, apparently without having been replaced, while the organization continues under the leadership of president Walid Masri (Lebanon) and secretary general Vilmos Cservény (Hungary), as reported in *WFDY News* (Budapest, no. 10, p. 4).

Ahmad Hamrush (Egypt) was not confirmed in the AAPSO presidency, and Nuri Abd-al-Razzaq Husayn now serves as acting president as well as secretary general (*YICA*, 1985, p. 390; Radio Addis Ababa, 11 October; *FBIS*, 16 October). Abd-al-Muhammad Wahhab al-Zintani (Libya) and Vital Valla (Congo) were newly noted as AAPSO vice-presidents during 1985 (*Pravda*, 21 January; *6 Congrès de L'OSPAA*, n. d., p. 168). The IUS, led by President Miroslav Stepan (Czechoslovakia) and secretary general Georgios Michaelides (Cyprus) has a new vice-president in the person of Sergey Chelnokov (USSR) and two newly noted secretaries: Philip Gardner (United States) and Victor Paredes (El Salvador) (Prague, *World Trade Union Movement*, no. 11, p. 53; Prague, *World Student News*, no. 1, p. 27; *Granma* daily, 14 September). WFSW secretary general John Dutton (UK) died, and has been replaced by Reginald Bird (UK); O. M. Nefedov (USSR) is the new vice-president of the organization; and Jean-Marie Legay (France) remains as president (*Flashes from the Trade Unions*, 17 May, 30 August; Budapest, *Népszabadság*, 5 November). President Kaarle Nordenstreng (Finland) and secretary general Jiri Kubka (Czechoslovakia) still hold the top posts in the IOJ, while Lodongiin Tudev (Mongolia) and Manuel Tome (Mozambique) are new vice-presidents of that organization (Prague, *Democratic Journalist*, nos. 7–8, p. 2).

The sixth July All-Christian Peace Assembly left in place the three top leaders of the CPC: president Károly Tóth (Hungary), continuation committee chairman Filaret of Kiev and Galicia (USSR), and secretary general Lubomir Mirejobskiy (Czechoslovakia), with Georgi Goncharev (USSR) and Christoph Schmauch (United States) added to incumbent Alfred Christian Rosa (Sri Lanka) as the three deputy general secretaries (Prague, *CPC Information*, 12 July). New CPC vice-presidents are

Metropolitan Pankriti of Stan Zagora (Bulgaria), Alexei S. Buyevski (USSR), Hans Joaquim Oeffler (FRG), and Alice Wimer (United States) (ibid., 2 September, 2 October, 19 November). The IADL remains under the leadership of president Joe Nordmann (France) and secretary general Amar Bentumi (Algeria), while the Ulan Bator–based ABCP is led by president (Khambo Lama) Kharkhuu Gaadan and secretary general Ch. Jugder, both of Mongolia (*List of Members*, p. 105). OSPAAL apparently remains under the presidency of Susumu Ozaki (Japan), but Rene Anillo Capote (Cuba) appears to be its new secretary general (*New Perspectives*, no. 6, p. 2).

Wallace Spaulding
McLean, Virginia

THE MIDDLE EAST

Introduction

During 1985 Middle Eastern political dynamics remained dominated by the Iran-Iraq war, the continuing civil war in Lebanon, unsuccessful attempts to move forward in resolution of the Palestinian problem, and the mounting impact of OPEC disability. Beneath this surface, most of the region's societies continued to be pressured by Iran's fundamentalism, which was given new impetus by Israel's withdrawal from much of southern Lebanon, since this was seen as a Shia triumph greatly influenced by Ayatollah Khomeini's fervor. The embattled status of Iran's communist Tudeh Party exemplified the tenacious but peripheral role in these events generally played by Middle Eastern communist and allied parties.

Khomeini's rigid crackdown on the Tudeh continued; despite Tudeh calls (via clandestine radio from Baku) for a "liberation front" of the left, the party was ostracized by the main opposition group of fifteen parties and individuals as well as by striking industrial workers who strongly denied links to leftist parties. Khomeini's efforts to neutralize even remnant Tudeh sympathy included establishing a noncommunist leftist party to replace the Tudeh and appointing a leftist ayatollah as state public prosecutor to reduce his chances as a presidential candidate.

Soviet pleas for leniency toward the jailed Tudeh members are apparently seen by Khomeini as potential for leverage in reducing the supply of Soviet weapons to Iraq. Yet the escalated shipments of advanced Soviet weapons to Iraq during 1985 showed the uselessness of the Tudeh members as significant pawns. In fact, Soviet pressures on Iran escalated, presumably to induce negotiations to end the war. Khomeini remained as adamant on this issue as on the necessity for Soviet withdrawal from Afghanistan. Soviet technicians were withdrawn from two power plants under construction. Persian language broadcasts from Baku switched during the year from criticizing those around Khomeini to direct and vitriolic attacks against "the fascist theocratic regime" and called for "all methods of struggle, including popular armed resistance" (*FBIS*, 7, 15 May). Coupled with thinly veiled direct appeals to Iranian Baluch, Kurd, Azerbaijan, and other minorities, this pointed Soviet pressure may represent not only a desire to end the war with Iraq but also longer-term efforts toward a more docile and less evangelical post-Khomeini regime.

In neighboring Afghanistan the Soviets coped with the sixth year of unsuccessful efforts to pacify a national rebellion against their presence and the ruling Marxist Democratic Party of Afghanistan (PDPA). The PDPA's thin hold on power is almost completely dependent on Moscow's forces throughout Afghanistan. There is no evidence that the PDPA could survive as a party or as a government without determined in-country Soviet military support. Party reorganization during the year showed factional and personality disputes as well as the increasing power of the secret police, KHAD, which is controlled by the dominant Parcham faction. With the rival Khalq faction predominating in the armed forces, regime efforts to create reliable military cadres to combat the nationwide mujahideen insurgency remain frustrated. Not only are defections to the mujahideen frequent and wholesale, but ideological and ethnic divisions weaken loyalty to the PDPA regime, whose mandate for the most part is confined to the none-too-secure capital city of Kabul. During 1985 the Afghan Air Force, considered by the PDPA as the most loyal service branch, was beset with major incidents of sabotage and defection. Similarly, an elite commando brigade, considered one of the Afghan army's best units, was decimated during the summer parachute drop into the Panjshir Valley.

Despite these formidable impediments, Moscow's strategy apparently remained one of buying time. The strategy seems to postulate a gradual demoralization of those portions of the Afghan population that have not fled to Pakistan or Iran. Starvation and more direct forms of genocide can support conventional policy instruments. Although there is evidence that far from all indoctrinated young Afghans returning from training in the USSR are loyal converts, Soviet policy seems to anticipate a long struggle if necessary (*Afghanistan: Six Years of Soviet Occupation*, U.S. Department of State, December).

Like its Tudeh counterpart, the Iraqi Communist Party remains illegal, with isolated remnants fighting beside Kurdish guerrillas in the north and with a handful of leaders active on the international communist scene thanks to Syrian sanctuary. Soviet efforts to heal the Iraq-Syria split again failed in 1985 as Iraq spurned Moscow's offer to help reopen the trans-Syrian oil pipeline. The Soviets can only view Iraqi development of alternate pipeline systems—which would go through Turkey, Jordan, and Saudi Arabia—as potentially weakening elements in a postwar USSR-Iraq relationship. The Soviet position in both Iraq and Syria rests on urgent military supply requirements. Reliable ideological links are absent.

In the rest of the Persian Gulf area, the Soviets could see scant progress for the small, mostly expatriate communist parties of Saudi Arabia and Bahrain; however, diplomatic relations were opened with the United Arab Emirates (UAE) and Oman. Coupled with long-standing ties with Kuwait, these breakthroughs made a kind of circle around the Arabian peninsula. This evolution without doubt hastened the day when Saudi Arabia, long the main target, will follow. Among the many reasons prompting the strongly pro-West Omani sultan and the UAE rulers to establish relations with the USSR is their political desire to dim the silhouette of their relationship with the United States. This relationship has become an increasing political liability due to U.S. congressional refusal to approve weapons sales to Saudi Arabia, Kuwait, and Jordan and due to the decline of the U.S. image as an evenhanded Middle East peace broker. The Arab gulf states also see Soviet support for Iraq not only as a military prop against Iranian forces but as a strange-bedfellow ally against the revolutionary fury of fundamentalist Shia Islam. Some Soviet role in bringing the war to an end seems inevitable. There is the hope that Soviet leverage might be sufficient to restrain Baghdad from spreading the war across the gulf. Finally, the gulf states, although competitors with the USSR in oil exports, hope that a closer dialogue may somehow assist in stabilizing prices.

As a presumed beneficiary of expanded Soviet representation on the Arabian peninsula, the People's Democratic Republic of Yemen (PDRY) ruling Socialist Party continued to obtain increasing financial and diplomatic support from its moderate Arab neighbors. Yet the return of hardline Marxist ideologue 'Abd al-Fattah Isma'il from exile in Moscow, and his reinstatement in an expanded Politburo with several supporters, signaled the revival of old schisms in the party. While these schisms superficially relate to Marxist ideological issues, they are actually rooted more in leadership personality conflict and tribal rivalries. Given the thinness of Marxist ideological penetration throughout the PDRY as a whole, therefore, these schisms bear the potential for major and long-lasting conflict.

In the new wave of Lebanon's factional warfare following the Israeli withdrawal from much of southern Lebanon in April, the Lebanese Communist Party continued to support Lebanon's pro-Syrian, leftist coalition. As successive ceasefire and conciliation efforts fail, the more moderate leaders tend to lose ground in favor of radical and extremist elements. Given the dominance of religious and familial loyalties, however, the small Lebanese Communist Party, which is heavily Greek Orthodox, and the Organization of Communist Action in Lebanon, which is predominantly Shia Muslim, appear incapable of major expansion of influence. Israel's Communist Party remains similarly confined to an almost exclusive Arab membership except at the topmost level. The party's fraternal inclusion in the twelfth International Youth and Student Festival during July in Moscow was marred when the Libyan delegation withdrew to protest their presence.

Jordan continued its mild relaxation toward the Communist Party of Jordan as part of an effort to improve relations with the USSR for many of the same reasons as the Arab gulf states. In addition, Jordan hopes for Soviet influence to moderate Syrian potential as a wrecker of peace negotiations over the West Bank and Palestinian issues. Keeping the Soviet door ajar in anticipation of the U.S. congressional turndown of its requested air-defense package, Jordan offered to train Soviet Muslim students and mosque preachers, to facilitate Soviet pilgrimage travel via Jordan, and to accept Soviet Russian teachers at Yarmuk University.

The Syrian Communist Party continued to play the role of an essentially docile instrument of the Syrian leadership, following the Moscow line, except where President Hafiz al-Asad, in fear of a PLO deal with Jordan that would exclude Syria, has supported PLO dissidents. Also in defiance of Moscow's will, Asad continues his support for Iran and refuses to mend fences with Iraq. Egypt's highly splintered communist movement, in contrast to its Syrian counterpart, continues sporadic activity that invites quick government repression. Many Egyptian Communist Party members remain imprisoned and other groups, such as the Armed Communist Organization, were subject to arrest and heavy prison terms for possessing arms and ammunition and distributing subversive literature.

In Algeria the communist Socialist Vanguard Party (PAGS) remained without legal status and focused efforts on trying to penetrate mass labor and youth organizations of the ruling FLN party. No evidence appeared that the PAGS met with success in the Algerian environment of general hostility to Communists. Algeria has been exploring major arms purchases in the West during the year, a development that threatens what in the past has been almost a Soviet monopoly. The Soviet naval chief and deputy defense minister, Admiral Sergeoi Gorshkov, visited Algeria early in 1985 in what appeared to be an effort to retain the Soviet sales program.

In Tunisia, troubling economic developments and political ferment related to President Habib Bourguiba's ill health created openings for the Tunisian Communist Party to join with other opposition groups in order to end its marginal status in Tunisian politics. Declining oil and phosphate income, coupled with Libyan expulsion of over 30,000 Tunisian workers in September, has sharply increased opposition activity, particularly by religious fundamentalists. Israeli bombing of the Palestinian Liberation Organization headquarters shook Tunisian-American relations profoundly, particularly among the military, where the event provided a strong lever to those opposing the traditional reliance on the U.S. defense umbrella and on U.S. equipment and training.

James H. Noyes
Hoover Institution

Afghanistan

Population. 14,792,000 (estimated)

Party. People's Democratic Party of Afghanistan (Jamiyat-e-Demokrati Khalq-e-Afghanistan, literally Democratic Party of the Afghanistan Masses; PDPA). The party's two wings, Parcham (Banner) and Khalq (Masses), remain locked in fierce rivalry.

Founded. 1965

Membership. Officially more than 140,000 members and candidate members (*Pravda*, 15 September). In previous years, candidate members comprised about half the claimed total, a ratio that presumably remains unchanged. Actual numbers may be as much as half of the claimed figure.

Secretary General. Babrak Karmal

Politburo. 9 members: Babrak Karmal, Sultan Ali Keshtmand (prime minister of the Democratic Republic of Afghanistan [DRA]), Najibullah (sometimes Najib, ex-chief of the State Information Service [KhAD]), Nur Ahmad Nur (Revolutionary Council Presidium member), Ghulam Dastigir Panjsheri, Maj. Gen. Mohammed Rafi (deputy prime minister), Dr. Anahita Ratebzad (Presidium member and head of the Peace, Solidarity, and Friendship Organization and of the Democratic Women's Organization of Afghanistan [DWOA]), Mohammed Aslam Watanjar (minister of communications), Dr. Saleh Mohammed Zeary (Presidium member); 4 alternate members: Mahmoud Baryalai (a leading party theoretician and half-brother of Babrak), Abdul Zaher Razmjo (secretary, Kabul city committee), Lt. Gen. Nazar Mohammad (minister of defense), Suleiman Laeq (minister of tribes and nationalities)

Secretariat. 8 members: Babrak Karmal, Mahmoud Baryalai, Dr. Niaz Mohammed Mohmand, Nur Ahmad Nur, Dr. Saleh Mohammed Zeary, Lt. Gen. Mohammed Yaseen Sadeqi (army chief of political affairs), Mir Saheb Karwal (administrator of Central Zone), Najibullah. (Of those listed above, only Nazar Mohammad, Watanjar, and Zeary are believed to have been associated with the Khalq faction at one time or another, and none are known to have taken part in the traditional heavy infighting with Parchamis; all other Secretariat and Politburo members and alternates are known or assumed to be associated with Parcham.)

Central Committee. 53 identified full members, 27 identified alternates (*YICA*, 1985, p. 144; *Kabul New Times* [*KNT*], 3 July 1983); Ghulam Faruq Yaqubi (director of KhAD) promoted to full member and Saifullah (Kabul police chief) named candidate member in 1985 (Radio Kabul, 21 November; *FBIS*, 22 November).

Status. Ruling party

Last Congress. First, 1 January 1965, in Kabul; National Conference, 14–15 March 1982.

Last Election. Local council elections, the first of any kind under the PDPA, held August–December in Kabul and a few provincial locations.

Auxiliary Organizations. National Fatherland Front (NFF) (claims 700,000 members) (Radio Kabul, 27 March; *FBIS*, 3 April), Abdul Rahim Hatef, chairman (*FBIS*, 7 May), replacing Saleh Mohammed Zeary; Central Council of Trade Unions (claims 200,000 members) (ibid.), Abdus Sattar Pordeli, president; Democratic Youth Organization of Afghanistan (DYOA; claims 152,000 members) (Radio Kabul, 12 August; *FBIS*, 13 August), Farid Mazdak, first secretary (ibid.); Peace, Solidarity, and Friendship Organization, Dr. Anahita Ratebzad, chair; Democratic Women's Organization of Afghanistan (DWOA; claims 40,000 members), Dr. Anahita Ratebzad, chair (ibid., 27 March); Pioneers (claims 85,000 members) (*KNT*, 29 October 1984); Council of Religious Scholars and Clergy; Council of Tribal Elders; Economic Advisory Council; peasants cooperatives; "groups for the defense of the revolution." In all, "more than 16 social organizations [participate] in all revolutionary transformations" (ibid., 1 September 1984; Radio Kabul, 28 May; *FBIS*, 29 May, number raised from 15 to 16). Like the party figures, the actual number of front members is probably a fraction of official claims.

Publications. *Haqiqat-e-Enqelabe Saur* (The Saur Revolution's truth), Central Committee daily organ, claims daily circulation of 80,000; *Haqiqat-e-Sarbaz* (The soldier's truth); *Dehqan* (Peasant); *Darafsh-e-Diavanan* (The banner of youth), a daily in Pushtu and Dari; *Kar* (Labor); *Kabul New Times*, English-language daily; *Storai* (Story), DYOA monthly; *Peshahang* (Pioneer), Pioneer monthly. Total claimed newspaper circulation exceeded 500,000. The DRA produces occasional white papers and other documents on the situation in Afghanistan (Radio Kabul, 7 March; *FBIS*, 8 March). In 1984 it claimed to have eleven national newspapers and periodicals, eighteen provincial newspapers of the party, and 42 periodicals "which cater to a diversity of audiences" (*WMR*, January 1984). The regime is expanding radio and television broadcasts, such as the new television transmission facility near Ghazni (Radio Kabul, 3 February; *FBIS*, 7 February). The official news agency is Bakhtar.

In 1967, two years after its founding, the PDPA split into opposing Parcham and Khalq wings. Both kept the PDPA name and both were loyal to Moscow, but each maintained a separate organization and recruitment program. Khalq, led by Nur Mohammed Taraki, the PDPA's founder, depended for support on the relatively poor rural intelligentsia and recruited almost solely among the Pushtuns, the dominant (55 percent) Afghan ethnic group. Parcham, less numerous but more broadly representative ethnically, was urban oriented and appealed to a wealthier group of educated Afghans. It was led by

Babrak Karmal, son of an Afghan general. Both groups focused their initial recruitment efforts on intellectuals, media employees, and especially teachers. When Mohammed Daoud overthrew the Afghan monarchy in 1973, the Parchamis at first collaborated with him, but the Khalqis remained in opposition and began an intensive clandestine recruitment effort among the military, which led to the PDPA coup that was to follow five years later.

Under Soviet pressure, Parcham and Khalq formally reunited in mid-1977, and their combined strength was enough to overthrow Daoud and inaugurate the DRA in April 1978. They almost immediately fissioned again, however, and Taraki sent the most prominent Parchamis into diplomatic exile as ambassadors and jailed or demoted most of those who remained in Afghanistan. When a Parchami plot to unseat Taraki was discovered in the summer of 1978, the ambassadors were recalled but disobeyed the order and fled into exile in Eastern Europe.

Meanwhile, popular resistance to Khalq's rigorous Marxist-Leninist rule grew rapidly and soon threatened to topple the new regime in spite of massive Soviet military aid. In September 1979 the Soviets attempted to force another artificial reconciliation between Parcham and Khalq, but their plan to place all the blame for the schism on Taraki's deputy, Hafizullah Amin, backfired when Amin himself seized power and murdered Taraki. Amin, however, could not pacify his rebellious people, and on 27 December 1979, Soviet troops invaded, shot Amin, and restored the Parchamis to power. Babrak (he affects the surname Karmal, "friend of labor" and an anagram of "Kremlin," for political purposes) became the new leader and tried to heal the breach with the Khalqis on the one side and the Afghan population on the other. In neither effort was he successful, and the regime maintained a tenuous hold on power only in a few main Afghan towns during daylight hours, thanks to a Soviet presence that slowly swelled from 85,000 combat troops in 1980 to about 115,000–120,000 by the end of 1985 (U.S. Department of State [DoS], *Afghan Resistance and Soviet Occupation: A Five Year Summary*, Special Report No. 118, December 1984; DoS, *Afghanistan: Six Years of Soviet Occupation*, Special Report No. 135, December 1985; *YICA*, 1980–1984).

Since the Soviet invasion, the PDPA has not technically been a communist or even a "socialist" (in the Soviet lexicon) party but has been the ruling and only permissible party in a country undergoing the "national democratic stage of revolution." Indeed, Karmal claimed that Afghanistan is "still in the preliminary phases" of that stage (Radio Kabul, 24 October; *FBIS*, 28 October). Unlike the avowedly socialist PDPA ideologues of 1978–1979, party spokesmen since the invasion have gone through contortions to avoid using the terms "socialist" and "socialism" in referring to Afghanistan. Socialism has not even been held out as an eventual goal to domestic audiences. In 1985 party and regime statements continued to avoid mention of Marxist goals, but the party's continuing claim that its rule is "revolution," identification with the USSR, and use of Marxist-Leninist rhetoric such as "proletarian internationalism" and "democratic centralism" clearly illustrate its Marxist character (Anthony Arnold, *Afghanistan's Two Party Communism*; *YICA*, 1980–1984).

Party Developments. This was an important year for the PDPA. It opened with the celebration of the party's twentieth anniversary. By the end of 1985, however, the role of the party had diminished, since an incentive to "broaden" the base of the regime led to the inclusion of nonparty members at the highest levels of government since the 1978 coup. Despite these efforts, the Afghan regime remains unpopular and ineffective, with little prospect of standing on its own. Neither party nor regime performance and efforts to build legitimacy or a political base progressed significantly in 1985.

The PDPA marked its twentieth anniversary in January with major celebrations in Kabul. The festivities had been heavily promoted in advance by the regime but were put off for a week without explanation. The postponement may have been due to a security alert, caused by resistance attacks the previous week (AFP, 30 December 1984; *FBIS*, 2 January). The highest ranking Soviet present at the celebrations was Usmankhodzhayev, first secretary of the Communist Party of Uzbekistan. The only member of a ruling party politburo present was from Poland. The Communist parties of Germany and Denmark were the only Westerners. Nicaraguan Sandinistas, Iranian, Saudi, and Syrian Communists, and Syrian Ba'thists were among other representatives (Radio Kabul, 8 January; *FBIS*, 9 January).

After the celebrations, party affairs appeared to become secondary to the question of regime performance. Attention was focused on nonparty functions such as the Loya Jirga (the traditional grand assembly of Afghan tribal leaders) and elections, although these were dominated in both leadership and number by party figures. Aside from the "legitimacy" campaign, the Soviets and their Afghan clients were apparently devoted more to building regime institutions than to expanding the political base of the party. The secret police (KhAD) continued to be coddled and expanded. A new push was made to build local militias to fight the mujahidin (holy warriors); at the same time, the regime pursued the traditional Kabul strategy of buying the loyalty of the tribes, especially in the areas bordering Pakistan and Iran.

The shift in emphasis was reflected in Soviet treatment of the Afghan party and regime and of the leadership. Moscow's greetings on the seventh anniversary of the Saur (April) Revolution were less positive than in previous years and appeared to downgrade the status of the PDPA (*Pravda*, 27 April). References to the "leading role" of the PDPA, the Soviet Communist Party's "revolutionary solidarity" with Afghanistan, and the "social progress" achieved by the DRA were dropped. This phraseology in previous years had signaled that Moscow considered the PDPA among the world's "progressive" parties.

Continuing Soviet dissatisfaction with Karmal was apparent when he was accorded low-level treatment on a May visit to Moscow (Bakhtar, 10 May, *FBIS*, 10 May). It was his first state visit since a trip to Mongolia in July 1983. Karmal went from the USSR to Poland, where he also received a low-key reception (Radio Kabul, 19 May, *FBIS* Eastern Europe, 20 May). His second trip to Moscow, ostensibly for medical treatment, was downplayed, and the congratulatory message on Afghanistan's national day was similarly downbeat (*Pravda*, 19 August).

Throughout 1985 the party was riven by factional strife, which frequently—although perhaps not so often as in previous years—burst into violence. Karmal told the sixteenth party plenum that "the fundamental criteria for promotion ought to be . . . the capability to accept unity and steel like discipline" (Radio Kabul, 22 November; *FBIS*, 4 December). The most serious reported incident was a September gunbattle between army adherents of the rival Khalq and Parcham factions at the Arg palace in Kabul (DoS, *Afghanistan: Six Years*).

Khalq is currently led by Interior Minister Gulabzoi, who controls the regular police and was promoted (along with Nazar Mohammad and several other regime officials) this year to major general (Radio Kabul, 26 April; *FBIS*, 30 April). Parcham adherents probably constitute no more than 40 percent of the PDPA. Regime and party changes in 1985 appear to have shifted the balance of power still farther away from Khalq.

Factional differences probably contributed to a major regime personnel change, announced on 3 June, when Najibullah Masir replaced Mohammed Ismail Danesh as minister of mines and industries. Danesh, a Khalqi, then took up respectable political exile as Afghanistan's ambassador to Libya. Three new appointments were announced the same day, all with the rank of minister. Abdulbasir Ranjbar was named head of the central bank, Mohammed Daoud Kauian was named director general of the official Bakhtar News Agency, and Abdul Qadr Ashna, director of the State Committee for Culture, was elevated to Cabinet status. Ashna is a reputed Parchami; the other new ministers are likely to have similar affiliations (Radio Kabul, 3 June; *FBIS*, 4 June).

Despite much discussion of the party's role, Karmal probably best conveyed his view of party primacy in a speech to the (ostensibly ruling) Revolutionary Council at its first meeting of the Afghan year: "No important political and organizational question can be solved by the state organ without the party guidelines." Since "the state apparatus is there to implement policy," there is a "need for complete obedience by the state apparatus to party policy" (Radio Kabul, 26 September; *FBIS*, 8 October).

Leadership and Party Organization. Rumors of the impending replacement of Karmal surfaced several times during the year, especially in connection with his trips abroad. Potential successors mentioned included ex-KhAD chief Najibullah, Defense Minister Nazar Mohammad (AFP, 12 February; *FBIS*, 12 February), and Prime Minister Sultan Ali Keshtmand, an able administrator and party loyalist who is hampered by being a Hazara, Afghanistan's lowest-status ethnic group. Another party leader, Nur Ahmad Nur, spent two years in Moscow for a training course and returned to Kabul, apparently for good, in September (Bakhtar, 15 October; *FBIS*, 15 October). However, no PDPA member would attract support for the regime from the resistance. Thus, at year's end, Karmal remained in power and seemed likely to be retained by the Soviets.

At the opening session of the sixteenth plenum of the PDPA Central Committee on 21 November, a party reshuffle was announced, the first such change in three years. Ghulam Dastigir Panjsheri was dropped from the Politburo, and Danesh and former defense minister Abdul Qader—a key figure in the 1978 coup—were replaced as alternate or candidate members. Radio Kabul (21 November; *FBIS*, 22 November) announced that Qader and Panjsheri asked to be removed because of illness, but there is no evidence that they suffer from any physical infirmity; for Qader it was the end of a long political slide downward. Defense Minister Nazar Mohammad and Tribal Affairs Minister Suleiman Laeq were named as candidate members of the Politburo. Najibullah was named secretary of the PDPA Central Committee. He has apparently been given authority over the army and police security service (Sarandoy), both of which are predominantly Khalqi. This fulfilled a pledge he made at KhAD's fifth anniversary that "KhAD would be the front-runner in joint efforts with the Army and Sarandoy" (Radio Kabul, 11 February; *FBIS*, 12 February). The position of KhAD was further improved by the promotion of Najibullah's deputy, Ghulam Faruq Yaqubi, from candidate member of the Central Committee to full member. Saifullah, Kabul city Sarandoy commander and a possible Gulabzoi protégé, was also appointed candidate member of the Central Committee. On 5 December, Radio Kabul announced that Yaqubi had been named as the new director of KhAD (*FBIS*, 6 December).

PDPA claimed that membership grew throughout the year, although inconsistencies among the numbers reinforce doubts about the claims. In January, Karmal announced at the twentieth anniversary celebrations that there were 120,000 party members (30 percent workers, peasants, and tradesmen) and noted that 32,000 had joined in the year ending March 1984 (Radio Kabul, 10 January; *FBIS*, 14 January). In a July speech Karmal claimed that 134,000 members were organized in party ranks (Radio Kabul, 6 July; *FBIS*, 8 July). He said that 34,000 probationary members had been accepted in the Afghan year ending 20 March, of whom 45 percent were workers, peasants and craftsmen and about 50 percent members of the DYOA. *Pravda* reported that 9,500 Kabul residents joined the PDPA the previous year (27 April, p. 5; *FBIS*, 1 May).

In the July speech, which had been billed as a comprehensive report on the composition of the PDPA and the consolidation of the party and its leadership role, Karmal "seriously criticized" party committees and organs on recruitment. He insisted that the party accept more "leading and aware representatives" and soldiers of worker, peasant, and craftsman origin, as well as progressive intellectuals, lecturers, teachers, students, members of the DYOA, women, and other workers. He demanded increased training for party members, including literacy, especially during the period of probationary membership; this was an admission of the high illiteracy rate among current recruits. Karmal called for the enhancement of political awareness of members, especially of the new ones, citing "immoral defects, carelessness, obstinacy, arrogance, law breaking, cruelty towards people, and indifference towards people" (Radio Kabul, 6 July; *FBIS*, 8 July).

Auxiliary and Front Activities. The National Fatherland Front (NFF) is charged with bringing together various regime front organizations. It claimed up to 2,663 domestic councils in 1985 (Radio Kabul, 6 December; *FBIS*, 9 December). The NFF was used by the PDPA as its primary instrument for the assimilation of Afghanistan's clergy. In late 1984 it claimed that 600 participants attended a nationwide assembly of mullahs, or ulema (*WMR*, February, p. 53). This function was absorbed by the government in 1985 with the formation of the Ministry of Islamic Affairs.

In March, high-level party figure Saleh Mohammed Zeary was replaced as NFF chairman by Abdul Rahim Hatef (or Hatefi Pashto), a Pathan tribal elder who served in Afghanistan's parliament during the monarchy. Hatef has had high visibility as a domestic and international spokesman (Bakhtar, 4 August; *FBIS*, 5 August) and was named to head the Loya Jirga. Although not a party member, Hatef has increasingly sounded like one (Radio Kabul, 14 August; *FBIS*, 16 August) and as a result has added little to the regime's appeal.

The NFF is used to handle defectors from the resistance. There were several important defectors from the mujahidin in 1985, of which Asmatullah Muslim Achakzai was the best known. According to PDPA Central Committee member and NFF deputy chairman Bareq Shafii, "Those who have repented sincerely . . . are admitted to the NFF; the only condition of membership is not to be hostile to the new Afghanistan" (*WMR*, February, p. 53).

The Union of Writers of the DRA (UWD) is fairly marginal in a country where the illiteracy rate is over 90 percent. However, its existence may indicate the direction in which the regime, continually boasting of massive expansion of literacy, wishes to move the country. At its fourth plenum, the UWD was admonished to promote the literature of the frontier tribes and nationalities. Abdullah Spantgar, head of the publicity, extension, and education department of the PDPA Central Committee, exhorted the writers to become acquainted "with the language of the people." The UWD plenum resolved that "the present-day literature of Afghanistan is an effective way for disseminating new thoughts among the masses" (Bakhtar, 26 July; *FBIS*, 26 July). The performance of the UWD was probably disappointing to the party, however; Ghulam Dastigir Panjsheri, its director, was dropped from the Politburo in the November reshuffle.

Efforts to expand the DYOA may have been dramatically set back because of the apparently increasing need to draw on youth cadres for paramilitary activities and even to fill vacancies in the military. This security role was highlighted at the thirteenth plenum in December by a parade of DYOA volunteers in border-force uniforms and by the presence of newly appointed security chief Najibullah, Defense Minister Nazar Mohammad, and Mohammed Yaseen Sadeqi, the chief political commissar of the army. They were named in the 17 December Radio Kabul report (*FBIS*, 18 December); Farid Mazdak, still DYOA first secretary, then spoke on the role of youth in the "broadening" campaign. Radio Kabul hinted at serious disputes, perhaps factional, within the DYOA by a reference to "organizational issues on a series of changes in the composition of the DYOA Central Committee."

The DWOA also celebrated its twentieth anniversary in 1985, on 22 October. In tune with the regime's approach at the time, Karmal addressed his congratulatory remarks to "the women of various tribes and nationalities." He urged them to consolidate their links with "women living in the remote areas" (Radio Kabul, 23 October; *FBIS*, 24 October). What little support gained for the party's efforts to improve the status of women has come more from the West than from home, where female participation has been limited.

The DRA Peace, Solidarity, and Friendship Organization is the group responsible for "unofficial" contacts abroad. Its chair, Dr. Anahita Ratebzad (who is also head of DWOA), traveled extensively overseas and attended a Cairo meeting of the Afro-Asian Peoples Solidarity Organization (AAPSO), a Third World/international front group (Radio Kabul, 26 January; *FBIS*, 28 January).

The regime has also tried to develop the militia in areas both within and outside of regime control. In September Karmal told the jirga of border tribes that "over 25,000 combatants are serving in the battalions of the border militia and the units of the local forces" (Radio Kabul, 14 September; *FBIS*, 19 September). The government offers arms, money, and protection in return for a pledge to keep the mujahidin out of the village's territory. This approach, used by Kabul rulers for centuries, has succeeded in obtaining some adherents, although there are no recorded instances of militia fighting the mujahidin. In fact, some groups have taken the government booty and then gone over to the resistance.

Domestic Affairs. The DRA remains essentially a city-state that has military outposts in the hinterland and a secure civilian presence only in Kabul and a few other towns. Both Herat and Kandahar, the second and third largest towns in the country, are substantially in resistance hands. More than two-thirds of Afghanistan's population and an even greater proportion of its territory are out of regime control. Many Afghans cooperate with the regime for their livelihood (government workers' wages were increased by 18.7 percent and allowances by 29 afghanis per day [Radio Kabul, 13 May; *FBIS*, 14 May]); for leadership, however, the Afghan people continue to reject anyone perceived as cooperating with the regime or the Soviets. This apparent irreconcilability has so far stymied any hope of political compromise.

With little prospect of improved party performance or appeal, Kabul has intensified efforts to construct a facade of legitimacy for the regime through a series of public initiatives. Kabul's political initiative may have been packaged more for international than domestic consumption. Indeed, the prominent play given to these so far unsuccessful exercises in the Soviet press suggests that they may be as much intended to legitimize the war to an audience in the USSR as to any other.

On 12 April Kabul announced that it would call a Loya Jirga; on 13 April it announced that elections for Jirga representatives had already been held in 13 of the 29 provinces. By 20 April the elections were pronounced complete, and it was only then that the 23 April meeting date was announced. Such hurried scheduling suggests not only security concerns but also that the Jirga was convoked with little popular participation, perhaps dictated out of external concerns.

The Loya Jirga was historically used by Afghan kings and by the prerevolution republican government to validate a transfer of power or to gain public approval of a specific new policy of major significance. In the 1980 *Fundamental Principles of the Democratic Republic of Afghanistan*, which serves as an interim constitution, the Loya Jirga is defined as the "highest organ of state power" (Arnold, *Afghanistan's Two Party Communism*, p. 123). Neither the Karmal regime nor the preinvasion Khalq government had previously convoked a Loya Jirga, although lower level jirgas had been held. Kabul claimed that the Jirga created a "qualitatively new political situation" (Radio Kabul, 27 May; *FBIS*, 30 May). In reality, this sham Loya Jirga devalues for at least several years a device that could ultimately have been used to help genuinely legitimize the regime.

A high percentage of the 2,000 Jirga participants were regime functionaries, from the military or KhAD, or members of the PDPA or its front organizations. The "independent" delegates were paid well for attending: reportedly 20,000 afghanis per delegate, and up to 50,000 for those who agreed to speak in the televised sessions. One of these was the regime's prize defector, Asmatullah Muslim Achakzai, a former mujahidin commander.

The party and regime now derive their claim to legitimacy from the Proclamation of the Jirga (Radio Kabul, 26 April; *FBIS*, 26 April):

> The PDPA . . . is the leading and directing force of the society and state in Afghanistan . . . The home and foreign policies of the Government of the DRA formulated after the victory of the April [Saur] Revolution and its new evolutionary phase as reflected in the fundamental lines of the revolutionary tasks of the DRA, program of action of the PDPA, fundamental principles of the DRA, decrees of the DRA Revolutionary Council, and the other authoritative documents of the party and state are hereby endorsed and approved.

The resistance responded quickly. At a press conference in Peshawar, a group of party leaders from both then-existing coalitions strongly condemned the meeting, threatening vengeance on the participants. Resistance threats were not idle. A domestic flight carrying delegates to Kabul was reportedly shot down on 15 April (Tokyo, KYODO, 24 April; *FBIS*, 24 April). A number of delegates were reported killed in the aftermath of the Loya Jirga. At least two reportedly had their hands cut off, the Islamic punishment for theft (DoS, *Afghanistan: Six Years*).

In August the regime's initiative was renewed in the same unconvincing manner when local council elections were announced the day before they were to begin. In Kabul the "election" process was simple: a smattering of district residents were assembled—some unwillingly—at a meeting hall; candidates, usually one per seat, were introduced only moments before the vote; and voting meant raising hands under the watchful eyes of KhAD agents. The regime announced that 150,000 Kabul residents participated, which would have been about 90 percent of eligible voters (Radio Kabul, 22 August; *FBIS*, 22 August). However unconvincing, these were the first elections since 1978 (*WSJ*, 12 August, p. 1). *Pravda* called it "the first democratic elections in the history of Afghanistan" (11 August). Within a week there were reports of council members killed by the mujahidin. Nevertheless, council meetings were reportedly being held by the end of August. The regime announced plans to hold similar elections around the country, but by the end of the year they had taken place in only a few places outside Kabul (DoS, *Afghanistan: Six Years*).

The regime once again focused on the frontier in a 17 September jirga of the Pathan and Baluch tribes, whose territories span the borders with Pakistan and, in the case of the Baluch, with Iran. This time a somewhat higher proportion of the approximately 3,700 delegates were actually from the tribes. Asmatullah Muslim Achakzai was elected to the presidium of the jirga (Bakhtar, 15 September; *FBIS*, 16 September), and delegates were reportedly again paid well to attend. Cash payments were probably supplemented by arms, in the traditional manner of government-tribal relations. The weapons were reportedly for use in defending the frontiers and presumably also in tribal lands across the border. The regime has probably gained few long-term adherents as a result of these subventions.

At the end of September, speaking before the first session of the Revolutionary Council of the Afghan year, Karmal admitted that the last six months had been "full of difficulties" for the party and the government. While highlighting the recent political events, he took care to point out discipline problems in the armed forces, abuse of authority, nepotism, corruption in the bureaucracy, and "unrealistic, unobjective, and incomplete information" (Radio Kabul, 26 September; *FBIS*, 8 October).

In a crucial speech delivered to an extraordinary session of the Revolutionary Council on 9 November, Karmal presented the blueprint for an ideological shift toward pragmatism. Invoking Leninist phraseology (certifying no departure from the ultimate goal of communism), he outlined "ten theses" that defined the effort to broaden the social bases of the revolution. They set out what Karmal called the "tasks of the revolution" and the means for expansion of the regime's political bases and "attraction of sociopolitical allies" (Radio Kabul, 9 November; *FBIS*, 12 November). A brief summary follows:

(1) "Our main aim is to establish conditions in the country under which all national questions could be solved . . . in a peaceful way . . . without resorting to arms." The social backwardness of the total majority of the people means a long struggle. The party has made "mistakes, deviations, and serious errors" and must avoid leftist-extremist deviations, adventurism, and "infantile disorder."

(2) All political allies belonging to various strata of the society must be recruited to all organs of state power and administration. This is to be accomplished by "broadening the composition of leading state organs—that is, the Revolutionary Council and the DRA Council of Ministers—to include the credible representatives of the people who can reflect interests of various strata and groups . . . Authority will not be monopolized by the PDPA."

(3) Workers, peasants, and artisans are the pillars of the revolution. The private sector should be encouraged to increase consumer agricultural products. State farms will be established only on virgin lands.

(4) National traders and industrial capitalists are vital for economic development. Their representative institutions will be strengthened and opportunities in light industries enhanced so that they can recover their initial expenditures in a short time.

(5) The creation of other organizations that manifest the interests of intellectuals will not be blocked.

(6) Tribal self-rule is recognized and the border Pushtun and Baluch tribes will be provided with socioeconomic and cultural assistance. Traditional customs of assembly will be respected, but "we believe these assemblies will actively cooperate with state organs."

(7) The NFF should be expanded but other organizations should also be allowed if they are not against the gains of the Saur Revolution, are ready to cooperate with the NFF and the security organs, and do not struggle against the regime.

(8) The DRA observes and supports Islam.

(9) There should be a consolidation of all the armed forces. As soon as foreign intervention has been cut and its nonrecurrence has been safely guaranteed, the limited contingent of Soviet forces will leave.

(10) The DRA's foreign policy is one of "active nonalignment" and friendship with neighboring countries.

Tass responded with praise less than two hours after Kabul broadcast the speech on 9 November, a sign that Moscow had cleared the initiative (*FBIS*, 12 November). Karmal subsequently presented the theses to the sixteenth plenum of the PDPA Central Committee. He again declared that "the principal duty of the revolution is the broadening of its effectiveness on the masses and the gaining of friends" (Radio Kabul, 22 November; *FBIS*, 4 December). While asserting that the party remains "the organizing and leading force of our society," he acknowledged internal opposition and threatened that "those who do not obey the party decisions . . . have no place in the party. We do not intend to retreat from this decision."

In an effort to convince those outside Kabul of the seriousness of the initiative, on 11 November Karmal paid a one-day visit to the city of Kunduz in northern Afghanistan. Accompanied by the head of KhAD and the ministers of interior and defense, it was his first trip to the provinces in more than two years (Radio Kabul, 12 November; *FBIS*, 13 November). Later that week, Prime Minister Keshtmand reportedly made an equally rare one-day trip to Herat (Radio Kabul, 14 November; *FBIS*, 15 November).

On 26 December the regime announced the appointment of a number of purportedly "nonparty" figures. Sayed Amanoddin Amin was named a vice chairman of the Council of Ministers. This made eight holders of that rank, which is considered the equivalent of deputy prime minister. Amin is a technocrat who previously served the DRA as a deputy minister and chairman of the Economic Advisory Council. Other appointees also held important regime positions. Even their "nonparty" designations may be suspect, however. Abdul Hamid

Mobarez, named deputy education minister, was described by Radio Kabul on 26 December as a former head of the Afghan-Soviet Friendship Society (*FBIS*, 27 December). Participants with such past associations, whether party members or not, bring little credibility to the regime. In an interview with a Pakistani paper, Karmal denied that he had any intention of "broadening" the government far enough to include moderate elements of the resistance (Radio Kabul, 13 October; *FBIS*, 18 October).

Throughout 1985 combat became more intense, even during the customary winter lull. Casualties increased on both sides and among civilians as well. Soviet forces were more aggressive and launched operations in all parts of the country. Unable to eliminate growing concentrations of the mujahidin, the Soviets focused on disrupting resistance movement and supply. Resistance activity was widespread; many Soviet/regime garrisons came under attack during the year. The pace of fighting escalated in the summer as the mujahidin took the offensive. Forced to respond in order to prevent major losses, Soviet forces directly counterattacked or launched large-scale counteroffensives.

The Soviets adjusted their numbers, weapons, and tactics to compensate for the greater capabilities of the mujahidin and the decreasing effectiveness of the Afghan armed forces. The energetic General Mikhail Zaitsev was named overall commander of the Soviet effort in Afghanistan. Soviet troop strength in Afghanistan increased by a few thousand in 1985 to about 120,000. They are supported by an estimated 30,000 additional troops in the Central Asian republics north of Afghanistan. New Soviet tactics included reprisals against civilians to intimidate and deny food and other support to the mujahidin, and use of Spetsnaz paratroops.

The increased operations contributed to a higher casualty rate as well as increasing aircraft losses. Estimates vary, and the official figures are on the lower end of the scale. The U.S. government estimates that the total number of Soviet casualties in Afghanistan since 1979 is over 30,000, including more than 10,000 killed. In addition, the Soviets and Afghans together have lost nearly 800 aircraft to the mujahidin since the invasion (DoS, *Afghanistan: Six Years*).

Soviet forces in Afghanistan continue to suffer morale problems. Alcoholism, drug abuse, and disease—particularly dysentery and hepatitis—are rampant. Soviet soldiers have sold military supplies to pay for liquor and drugs, including heroin (Arthur Bonner, "Afghanistan's Other Front: A World of Drugs," *NYT*, 2 November). Increased combat involving Soviet troops has meant increased reprisals on the civilian population, which the resistance has tried to curb.

The effectiveness of the Afghan military continued to deteriorate, notwithstanding Soviet efforts to reverse the trend. Despite the December 1984 appointment of a Khalqi, Nazar Mohammad, to run the Ministry of Defense, performance by its largely Khalqi officer corps remained under par. Many enlisted men, mostly press-ganged conscripts, prefer not to fight the mujahidin. They frequently desert, and the resistance generally sends them back home or absorbs them into its ranks. The DRA military is a major source of arms and ammunition for the resistance.

"Bringing the ranks of the military up to full strength," Karmal told the fifteenth Central Committee plenum, is a task "that cannot be delayed" (Radio Kabul, 27 March; *FBIS*, 3 April). On 5 January the Politburo announced that those who "volunteer" for the army would have to serve only two rather than the three years normally required of conscripts (Radio Kabul, 5 January; *FBIS*, 7 January). In reality, many conscripts have been forced to serve beyond their required term—a major source of disaffection within the army. Four years of duty is required from those stationed in Kabul. In order to legitimize conscription by press-gang, the regime decreed that anyone between the ages of 18 and 38 who had not yet served would be liable for immediate induction.

The Afghan Air Force, previously considered the most loyal service, was wracked by defection and sabotage. In June about twenty Afghan fighter planes were destroyed by sabotage at Shindand Air Base near the Iranian border. It was the largest loss of aircraft in any single incident of the war. The saboteurs were unhappy over the disciplining of pilots who dropped their bombs in the desert instead of on a village. In July, DRA Air Force personnel defected to Pakistan with two Afghan Mi-25 (Mi-24D) export-version HIND helicopter gunships. These were the first HINDs to slip out of the control of the Soviets or their allies (DoS, *Afghanistan: Six Years*). The DRA demanded their return, claiming they were lost (Radio Kabul, 14 July; *FBIS*, 15 July).

KhAD has grown steadily and is now almost as large as the army. It is overseen closely by the Soviet secret intelligence (KGB) and other Eastern bloc security forces, and it continues to acquire a reputation for brutality and torture. By offering good salaries to those with few alternative prospects, KhAD has had some success in recruiting and keeping young, uneducated, urban males. These recruits have little or no ideological commitment but, having burnt their bridges to the rest of Afghan society, become loyal to the organization. Most KhAD cadres are based in Kabul, but KhAD operates all over the country and abroad.

Better armed and trained, and increasingly professionalized, the mujahidin were able to take the initiative in the fighting. Many fighting groups displayed increased cooperation. Improved resistance air defense, still composed primarily of heavy machine guns but increasingly supplemented by surface-to-air missiles, have blunted the impact of Soviet air power and forced the Soviets to adopt countermeasures. Arms supplies come from captured equipment and a variety of other sources, but the mujahidin are apparently stockpiling a large quantity of arms as insurance against cutoffs or future shortages (Stuart Auerbach, "Afghan Rebels Say They Hide Arms," *WP*, 21 July).

The merger of two coalitions—the seven-party "fundamentalist" and three-party "moderate" alliances—was announced on 16 May in Peshawar. The new alliance kept the same name—Islamic Unity of Afghan Mujahidin—that had been used by both coalitions. It is represented by a single spokesman, a position that rotates among the party leaders. Decisions are by consensus among the seven leaders. While it has not yet meant genuine Afghan unity, progress in developing the alliance has been relatively swift. Alliance unity has been maintained and the role of the spokesman respected by the other delegates, which is no small accomplishment for parties that in the past regularly fought each other. The major focus of the alliance thus far has been promoting the international political role of the resistance; for example, it has demanded Afghanistan's seat at the United Nations and other international representation. The alliance may eventually prove to be the most significant political development in the resistance since the Soviet invasion (DoS, *Afghanistan: Six Years*).

Much of the fighting in 1985, as in previous years, took place near the Pakistan border. In May the Soviets began to move 10,000 troops up the Kunar Valley to relieve the Afghan garrison at Barikot, which had been periodically under siege since 1978 (Radio Jeddah, 6 June; *FBIS*, 7 June). The Soviet operation was motivated partly by the failure of a smaller column to push through to Barikot earlier in the year. Shortly after reaching Barikot, the main Soviet force withdrew from the Kunar. The mujahidin quickly returned and re-established the siege of that garrison.

In the Panjsher Valley, the resistance gained a major victory and forced the Soviets to react. For the first time in the war, the resistance was able to take an important regime garrison. In June, Panjsher commander Ahmed Shah Masood's troops overcame a number of outposts, then overran Peshghor, an Afghan garrison established by the Soviets after the massive Panjsher offensive of 1984. The Soviets responded hastily, in contrast to their customary well-planned operational style. By the end of July, with over 10,000 troops in the Panjsher, the Soviets went on the offensive. They retook Peshghor but suffered heavy casualties. The mujahidin captured nearly 600 prisoners at Peshghor, including a number of Soviets and DRA officers, and they killed an Afghan general (Radio Kabul, 28 June; Radio Hong Kong, 29 June; AFP, 2 July; *FBIS*, 1 and 3 July). Many of these prisoners died when Soviet troops attacked the encampment where they were being held (AFP, 22 July; *FBIS*, 23 July).

In late summer the heavy fighting shifted south to Paktia province, on the Pakistan border. Five thousand mujahidin drawn from several parties joined forces to attack the Afghan garrison at Khost. It was the largest offensive operation ever mounted by the resistance. As many as half the outposts around Khost fell to the mujahidin. The Soviets were able to relieve the garrison by air but several attempts to send a convoy, including one with over 5,000 troops, failed to break through. Although DRA troops mounted a counteroffensive from Khost, the town remained under siege. Casualties were high on each side in some of the bloodiest fighting of the war (AFP, 3 September; *FBIS*, 4 September).

Kabul, the capital, has more than doubled in population to about 2 million since the invasion. By the end of the year it had a nightly curfew, check points, and gun and tank emplacements on all access routes. The Soviets have devoted extensive resources to maintaining security in Kabul—their minimum tactical goal in Afghanistan—particularly on symbolic occasions or during major regime meetings. During these internationally visible events as many as 60,000 Soviet or Afghan military and police personnel were deployed in the capital. Nevertheless, the mujahidin were usually able to cause some disruption, including some harassing fire at the site of the Loya Jirga. Security in Kabul deteriorated over the summer, when the resistance launched a series of fierce and apparently coordinated attacks. The Soviet Embassy compound in the western suburbs was hit, reportedly killing several Soviet guards. Attacks on the Soviet Embassy became so frequent that the Soviets installed a rocket launcher battery in the compound to return the fire (DoS, *Afghanistan: Six Years*).

In most of the rest of Afghanistan as well, resistance activity was higher than in 1984. The regime has all but abandoned the Kandahar bazaar. On 4 September resistance forces downed a civilian aircraft near Kandahar with a surface-to-air missile (Radio Kabul, 9 September; *FBIS*, 10 September). The government and the Soviets remained at the airport and were periodically attacked. In March the mujahidin attacked the Kajakai Dam, which had been built with U.S. assistance before the 1978 coup. It was the heaviest fighting of the war in the southeast. Although the Soviets have relatively better control over Afghanistan's breadbasket in the north, the resistance remained active there. There were several attacks on the pipeline that carries Afghanistan's natural gas to the Soviet Union, and the resistance occasionally made claims of forays into the USSR itself. The resistance in the north received a major setback when its most important commander was killed by a mine. Both sides were particularly active in western Afghanistan. The resistance in Herat, which operates as a coalition of several parties, began to rid the city of its minimal regime presence. The Soviets were reportedly forced to call in reinforcements directly from bases in the USSR but were able to regain nominal daytime control of the city. In central Afghanistan, Iranian-supported Shia groups such as Nasr and Sepah-e-Pasdaran vanquished the traditional Shia parties and moved to establish an Islamic republic in the Hazarajat.

The war has caused significant damage to the Afghan economy, which is one of the world's poorest. The resistance has disrupted the functioning of Afghanistan's small industrial sector, which even before 1978 was mostly state-owned. In January Karmal charged that the resistance had caused over 350 billion afghanis worth of damage and had destroyed over 1,800 school buildings, 31 hospitals, hundreds of trucks, and hundreds of electricity pilons (Radio Kabul, 11 January; *FBIS*, 15 January). The Soviets and the regime, largely in the course of fighting, have caused some disruption in agriculture.

Nevertheless, there is considerable evidence that the economy continues to function in much of the country. Neither the government nor the resistance has tried significantly to disrupt nonwar-related commerce, out of concern that the population might turn against the side that reduces the standard of living. Agricultural production reached prewar levels in 1985. The regime claimed wheat crops of 2,850,000 tons (Bakhtar, 24 October; *FBIS*, 25 October). Although regime figures on the economy are highly questionable, *Pravda* reported a Karmal statement that since the revolution the state sector's share of the national economy had grown by 20 percent, workers' wages increased by one-third, and 320,000 families received land under the land reform (12 August, p. 4; *FBIS*, 15 August). In the year ending in March, however, only 6,000 families received land (Radio Kabul, 29 March; *FBIS*, 4 April), a sign that the regime had greatly cut back on redistribution.

International Views, Positions, and Activities. In his speech to the Central Committee during the twentieth anniversary celebrations, Karmal asserted that "Today the DRA was officially recognized by 80 states. The PDPA has links with 103 fraternal communist, workers, revolutionary and democratic parties, progressive organizations and movements from among whom it has regular and all around relations with 52 organizations" (Radio Kabul, 11 January; *FBIS*, 15 January). By April, in his speech to the Loya Jirga, Karmal claimed links with 135 parties and national liberation movements (Radio Kabul, 23 April; *FBIS*, 1 May).

The PDPA attended the second conference of communist and workers' parties of the Eastern Mediterrranean, the Near and Middle East, and the Red Sea, held in Nicosia in January. Afghanistan was not mentioned in the proceedings, however (*IB*, April, p. 6). The regime continued to toe the Soviet line on international issues; it constantly repeated the Soviet position on "peace" and "disarmament" and offered revolutionary solidarity to the Sandinistas (Radio Kabul, 19 July; *FBIS*, 19 July).

This year marked the twenty-fifth anniversary of the Afghan-Soviet Friendship Society (*Pravda*, 13

February, p. 4; *FBIS*, 14 February). Because the PDPA is totally dependent on Soviet military support for its continued existence, the party has no independent voice. PDPA foreign policy is a reflection of Soviet foreign policy, but even domestic political decisions are often largely dictated by Soviet advisers, who are present in all ministries. As a result, the determinants and consequences of Soviet Afghanistan policy and any changes over time deserve close examination.

Both politically and militarily, the Soviets appear to have settled in for a long but limited war in Afghanistan. They have permitted moderate increases over the years of their total commitment of troops. They have also made extensive adjustments in tactics, equipment, and types of units deployed, as mujahidin effectiveness has steadily increased. The Soviet Union has acted in the short-term to preserve security in the capital and a few provincial centers, to protect its supply lines, and to prevent the resistance from growing too strong or threatening these secure zones. This defensive stance allows the pursuit of longer-term political goals of wearing down the Afghan people's will to resist, stabilizing the government in Kabul, and developing loyal followers in the army, the government, and the party who will be capable of running the country.

There was no evidence of enthusiastic popular support in the USSR for the military effort in Afghanistan. Although there was no widespread opposition, during 1985 there were increasing signs of discontent. There have been public demonstrations against service in Afghanistan, Armenia, Georgia, Ukraine, and other republics. Draft evasion appears to have increased, prompting Soviet authorities to issue new laws punishing those who fail to register. Samizdat (opposition literature) criticism has expanded, including both negative reports from Afghanistan veterans and open expressions of sympathy for the mujahidin by Crimean Tatar leaders. Complaints about the war have become more frequent and open and are implicitly acknowledged by coverage in the Soviet press. Unofficial polls conducted by human-rights activists in the Soviet Union showed a decline in support for the war effort.

In an obvious effort to generate more support, the Soviet media have significantly expanded their coverage of the fighting. In 1985 the war was a regular feature on Soviet television news. Combat fatalities were reported more frequently, decorations for heroism were played up, and special reports on men fighting in Afghanistan were carried in their hometown newspapers. Not all the coverage was upbeat: Soviet spokesmen have said that the fighting is "intensifying," a clear indication that Moscow is preparing its own people for a long struggle. In Geneva a Soviet spokesman publicly admitted to a sharp increase in casualties in Afghanistan during the year (DoS, *Afghanistan: Six Years*).

The Soviets appeared to be particularly sensitive about those soldiers who could be considered missing in action. Press coverage of prisoners or defectors was avoided when possible. A few Soviets have defected to the resistance; some of them even fought alongside the mujahidin. According to press interviews, Soviet defectors often convert to Islam and go by Muslim names. Some of the defectors had been in trouble before they left Soviet lines, and they stayed with the mujahidin rather than face severe punishment, perhaps death, should they return (Arthur Bonner, "3 Defectors, Turned Afghan, Fight Holy War," *NYT*, 1 November, p. 1). In addition, various resistance groups held Soviet prisoners, generally in secure base areas inside Afghanistan. The international press reported twelve Soviet soldiers killed in an explosion at the Badaber/Mattani camp in Pakistan (Radio Kabul, 7 May; *FBIS*, 8 May). The incident was reported in the Soviet media only after the news reached the Soviet Union from international news sources.

Nevertheless, Afghanistan appears to be a path to promotion for Soviet officers at all levels. Perhaps 50,000–60,000 officers have served in Afghanistan, which is a wealth of combat experience. As the Soviet media looks for heroes, it usually turns to captains and majors commanding companies and battalions. Often they leave Afghanistan with a promotion, decorations, and a place at a higher military academy or a more senior command.

For senior Soviet officers, Afghanistan has meant the most prestigious decorations, party rank, and highest military posts. Southern Theater of Military Operations (TMO) chief Sergei Sokolov became the defense minister. In 1985 his immediate subordinate, General Lushov, who was former commander of the Central Asian Military District (MD), became head of the Group of Soviet Forces Germany (GFSG). General Maximov, head of the Turkestan MD, was named head of the Strategic Rocket Forces and deputy defense minister, after an otherwise lackluster career. Army general Mikhail

Zaitsev, former head of GFSG, was put in charge of the Afghan effort as chief of the Southern TMO.

Sovietization of the Afghan economy continued. In 1984 Soviet-Afghan trade was up slightly, totaling about $1.1 billion, which was about 70–80 percent of total Afghan trade. Radio Kabul claimed that total trade increased about one-third over 1983, citing a Tass figure of 900 million rubles (26 February; *FBIS*, 27 February). Trade was in approximate balance as Afghan natural gas continued to be pumped to the Soviet Union despite occasional resistance disruption. Ariana Afghan Airlines, which had received equipment, training and operations assistance from the West, was merged into the Soviet-oriented domestic airline Bakhtar, displacing Western influence. As part of the transition, Ariana sold its single DC-10 jetliner (DoS, *Afghanistan: Six Years*).

In 1984 the Soviets pledged over $300 million in new aid and disbursed over $400 million in commodities and new project aid. In February 1985 an agreement was signed granting major additional project credits. The USSR has provided Afghanistan with assistance unprecedented in Soviet relations with Third World countries, including about two-thirds of its total program of grants, long payment terms for credits, and commodity support—even wheat, which the Soviet Union must import itself. Prime Minister Keshtmand told a Bulgarian paper that "92 percent of all credits have been granted to us by [the Council for Mutual Economic Assistance] CMEA and 72 percent of them have been granted by the USSR" (Rabotnichesko Delo, 31 December; *FBIS* South Asia, 4 January 1986).

An economic and technical cooperation agreement was signed in Moscow on 11 March. Under its framework the USSR granted a soft loan of 168 million rubles for the DRA's five-year plan, partly to repair power transmission lines and electricity substations in Kabul (Bakhtar, 18 March; *FBIS*, 18 March). Those facilities had been destroyed in 1984 by the resistance.

Much of the Soviet largess has been designed to support the military effort, particularly aid-financed expenditures on transportation infrastructure. Radio Kabul, reporting the fourth meeting of the Afghan-Soviet Cooperation Commission, indicated that in the year ending in March, the Soviet Union helped in more than 57 projects, including anti-avalanche facilities on the Salang Highway (17 June; *FBIS*, 18 June). In addition, a major portion of the commodity credit appears to have been for war-related material (such as trucks or petroleum) for the Afghan armed forces. East European aid, traditionally a fraction of Soviet aid, dropped to $12 million in new commitments in 1984, which is the latest figure available.

The effort to educate and influence Afghanistan's youth has been an important element in the Soviet long-term program to pacify and Sovietize Afghanistan. To rule the country in the future, the Soviets need to develop at least a small cadre that can succeed to the leadership of the DRA. The greatest constraint on these efforts is the lack of physical control over most of the population.

A major component in the long-term program has been Kabul's literacy campaign. Karmal claimed that 400,000 Afghans were enrolled in 20,000 literacy courses and that since 1978 over one million have become literate (Bakhtar, 8 September; *FBIS*, 9 September). The Soviets have encouraged universal and compulsory education in the areas they control. In the schools, the study of Islam and Western languages has largely been replaced with Marxist ideology and Russian study. As many as one-third of Afghanistan's teachers and school administrators may be Soviet or bloc nationals, while most of the rest are PDPA members. In February language teachers from France and West Germany were expelled, ending 60 years of educational cooperation with these countries.

An important part of the strategy is to send Afghans to the USSR for training. However, returning students vary greatly in their loyalty to the regime or to the Soviets. Adults are sometimes more hostile to the Marxists after a stay in the USSR; the Soviets have therefore brought young children aged ten or younger north for extended periods—sometimes for ten years or more. Many of these children have been orphans of regime or party personnel. Up to 2,000 children a year may be involved in this program (Bakhtar, 25 March; Paul Trottier, "Soviet Influence on Afghan Youth," U.S. Department of State, Special Report No. 139).

In his opening speech to the newly elected Pakistani National Assembly on 23 March, President General Mohammed Zia ul-Haq stressed Pakistan's continuing and long-term commitment to the Afghan people (Radio Pakistan, 23 March; *FBIS*, 25 March). Although Pakistan has remained subject to continuing Soviet/DRA pressure along the border, it appears that there is a broad consensus in favor of the government's efforts to resolve the

Afghan crisis. There were over 200 DRA/Soviet violations of Pakistani airspace and more than 25 instances of shelling of Pakistani territory (DoS, *Afghanistan: Six Years*).

Relations between Iran and the DRA remained cool throughout 1985, following a distinct downturn between the two countries in 1984. Relations were complicated by Kabul's hosting the Iranian Tudeh and Fedayeen-ye Khalq (majority) parties (Radio Kabul, 8 January, 9 February; *FBIS*, 9 January, 11 February). Iran complained of periodic border violations during the course of the year. In June Ayatollah Montazari, Khomeini's heir apparent, encouraged several Afghan Shia resistance groups to stop fighting amongst themselves and concentrate on fighting the Soviets.

Mahmoud Baryalai—Politburo alternate member, Babrak's relative, and one of the DRA's most peripatetic officials—repaid the Syrian gesture at the twentieth PDPA anniversary celebration by visiting Damascus. In a joint communiqué, Syria declared its solidarity with Afghanistan "under the leadership of the PDPA," and both sides covered standard Soviet international positions (Radio Kabul, 14 May; *FBIS*, 15 May). In December Baryalai met with Indian prime minister Rajiv Gandhi in New Delhi; Baryalai then went on to Bombay, where he met with Khan Abdul Wali Khan, leader of Pakistan's mostly Pushtun National Democratic Party, and Wali's father Abdul Ghaffar Khan, both long-time DRA contacts (Bakhtar, 31 December; Radio Kabul, 15 January 1986; *FBIS*, 31 December 1985, 16 January 1986).

India continued to call for an end to foreign intervention and interference in Afghanistan. In line with its policy of support for a political solution, New Delhi has maintained good relations with the DRA, including the provision of various forms of aid (*Pravda*, 11 August, p. 5; *FBIS*, 15 August). Bali Ram Baghat, later to be named Indian foreign minister, led a congress party delegation to the January PDPA anniversary celebrations (Radio Kabul, 8 January; *FBIS*, 9 January). In April, Indian foreign secretary Bhandari made an official visit to Kabul and met with Karmal. Bhandari told Indian radio on 13 April that he thought his visit was a success (*FBIS*, 15 April). A joint statement at the end of the visit expressed support for the U.N. negotiations and concern at increasing militarization of the region. DRA foreign minister Shah Mohammad Dost later paid a return visit to Delhi and negotiated an increase in the Indian program of assistance to the DRA. In 1985 India voted against the release of the Ermacora report in the U.N. Human Rights Commission and once again abstained on the UNGA resolution calling for the withdrawal of foreign troops from Afghanistan.

High-level members of both Indian communist parties (CPI and CPI-M) visited Kabul in 1985; both parties attended the anniversary celebrations. Raj Bahadur Gohr of the CPI led a delegation to Afghanistan in October (Bakhtar, 15 October; *FBIS*, 15 October); CPI-M Politburo member S. Mukerjee visited Kabul in October, when he met with Karmal, Hatef, Sarwar Mangal, and Baryalai (Bakhtar, 23 October; *FBIS*, 24 October).

A war of words raged for most of the year between the DRA and the People's Republic of China (Bakhtar, 4 April; *FBIS*, 11 April; Mary Lee, "Two-Way Street for Arms," *Far Eastern Economic Review*, 12 December). In a letter from the PDPA Central Committee to the Communist Party of China Central Committee, the DRA condemned Chinese support for the Afghan resistance; this set off a media dispute that went on for much of the year. The letter charged that Chinese aid included multiple rocket launchers, heavy machine guns, antitank rockets, half a million rounds of ammunition, and training both in Pakistan and in the Chinese province of Xinjiang (Radio Kabul, 30 January; *FBIS*, 31 January). The charges were replayed in the Soviet media (Tass, 7 February; *FBIS*, 8 February). On 21 February the official Chinese *People's Daily* called the DRA charges slander and stated that Soviet actions in Afghanistan represent a threat to Chinese security (Renmin Ribao, p. 3; *FBIS*, 25 February).

U.N. efforts to negotiate a settlement have resulted in six rounds of indirect talks since 1982, all held in Geneva. Negotiations have been led by the U.N. under secretary general for special political affairs, Diego Cordovez. Cordovez shuttles between delegations from Pakistan and Afghanistan, officially informing Iran of the discussions while unofficially informing the Soviets. Three rounds of indirect talks were held in Geneva during 1985: 20–25 June; 27–30 August; and 16–20 December. All parties reported progress at the June session. Cordovez described the talks as "fruitful," and the United Nations reported agreement on three of four proposed accords. The first dealt with noninterference in Afghanistan's affairs; the second encompassed international guarantees of a final settlement; and the third governed the voluntary return of the refugees. Discussion of a fourth agreement, however—which would have dealt with the key issue of a Soviet troop withdrawal and the interrelationship between that document and the other three documents—was blocked in August when Afghanistan demanded direct negotiations with Pakistan instead of the "proximity" format (Radio Kabul, 13 October; *FBIS*, 18 October). In December the sixth round of talks focused on discussion of a timetable for Soviet withdrawal, but Afghanistan refused to discuss it except in direct talks. The round was suspended and scheduled to resume in March 1986 after a Cordovez shuttle between the capitals. In the absence of an agreed settlement, Pakistan has maintained its refusal to negotiate directly with the Karmal regime (DoS, *Afghanistan: Six Years*).

In December the United Nations voted to condemn the violations of human rights in Afghanistan. The resolution was based on a report submitted by the U.N. Human Rights Commission's special rapporteur, Austrian legislator, and law professor Felix Ermacora. Ermacora found massive and systematic violation of human rights in Afghanistan. He noted that "since the April [Saur] Revolution, the internal human-rights situation has deteriorated as a result of the absence of popular participation in the choice and administration of government." Ermacora recommended the initiation of a process of political normalization, specifically including the constitution of a Loya Jirga (*Situation of Human Rights in Afghanistan*, Report of the Economic and Social Council, United Nations General Assembly document A/40/843, 5 November).

Soviet and Afghan media efforts have not been exclusively focused on their own people. Soviet and Afghan external propaganda was primarily directed at undermining the bases of international support for the resistance and was often keyed to U.S.-Soviet relations or meetings of multilateral bodies. For example, the broadening of the Kabul regime was announced shortly before the Geneva summit between Ronald Reagan and Mikhail Gorbachev.

This correspondence was particularly apparent in regard to human rights. The DRA began to implement, on paper, some of Ermacora's recommendations at the same time that the DRA and the Soviet representative to the U.N. Human Rights Commission were heaping invective on the Austrian (Radio Kabul, 18 March; *FBIS*, 19 March). The DRA staged its unconvincing version of the Loya Jirga barely a month after Ermacora's original report was released in March. In December, just before the United Nations voted for the first time to criticize the human-rights situation in Afghanistan, Kabul media began to produce numerous stories of mujahidin atrocities that were sometimes aided by "foreign advisers." Yet Karmal, in a letter to U.N. secretary general Perez de Cuellar proclaiming the regime's observance of U.N. conventions, as much as admitted the violations. He claimed that measures "had been taken or were in the process of being taken in the DRA toward achieving progress in safeguarding human rights" (Radio Kabul, 9 December; *FBIS*, 13 December).

Soviet concern with foreign media coverage led the Soviet ambassador to Pakistan, Vitaly Smirnov, to complain about foreign correspondents accompanying the mujahidin. He threatened that Western reporters entering the war zone could meet a grim fate. Not long after, *Arizona Republic* correspondent Charles Thornton became the first American known to be killed inside Afghanistan since the Soviet invasion. Thornton was traveling by truck north of Kandahar in the company of some fifteen Afghans when the group was ambushed by a Soviet/DRA unit.

The carefully orchestrated twelfth World Festival of Youth and Students, held in Moscow from 27 July–3 August, was disrupted by protests by several delegations against the Soviet occupation of Afghanistan. Swedish delegate Katarina Larsson, who was working in Afghanistan at the time of the invasion, spoke of a growing solidarity movement for Afghanistan. She said that protests would increase "until the last Russian soldier has left Afghanistan." Soviet interpreters disrupted her presentation and censored her references to Soviet aggression (U.S. Department of State, Foreign Affairs Note, 5 December). In his "election eve" speech, Karmal said that the criticism at the conference was "condemned" (Radio Kabul, 12 August; *FBIS*, 13 August).

The Afghan resistance was also invoked at a meeting in Angola among anticommunist guerrilla groups. The meeting, which formed a loose alliance called the Democratic International, was sponsored by Citizens for America (AFP, 6 June; *FBIS*, 6 June). However, the Afghan participant, Colonel Ghulam Wardak, was apparently not an authorized representative of any significant resistance group. Since the mujahidin emphasize the Islamic character of their movement, which they consider separate and distinct from other insurgencies, the Angola meeting was used by Kabul to discredit the mujahidin (Bakhtar, 9 June; *FBIS*, 10 June).

Kabul continued to condemn what it calls the

U.S. "undeclared war" on Afghanistan, which was clearly its foremost foreign policy concern. The United States continued to make Afghanistan an issue in its relations with the Soviet Union. U.S.-Soviet talks in June reportedly provided little more than an exchange of views. In December, Deputy Secretary of State John Whitehead announced that the U.S. government was willing to serve as a guarantor of a peace settlement in Afghanistan that would include a withdrawal of Soviet troops. This offer was officially made in a letter to Soviet secretary general Mikhail Gorbachev (David K. Shipler, "U.S. Offers to Act as a Guarantor of an Agreement on Afghanistan," *NYT*, 14 December, p. 1).

Although it has generated increasing atmospherics about its "flexibility" on Afghanistan, Moscow has given little indication of a readiness to abandon the PDPA to an unsupported fate. It continues to support the concept of a political settlement applying "around Afghanistan," which will maintain and legitimize the client regime in Kabul. The Soviets support the continuation of the U.N.-sponsored, indirect negotiations in Geneva but maintain that a withdrawal can be negotiated only bilaterally between Moscow and Kabul.

Craig Karp
U.S. Department of State

The views and opinions expressed here are those of the author and do not necessarily represent those of the Department of State.

Algeria

Population. 22,025,000
Party. Socialist Vanguard Party (Parti de l'avant-garde socialiste; PAGS)
Founded. 1920 (PAGS, 1966)
Membership. 450 (estimated)
Secretary General. Sadiq Hadjeres
Leading Bodies. No data
Status. Illegal
Last Congress. Sixth, February 1952
Last Election. N/a
Auxiliary organizatons. No data
Publications. *Sawt al-Sha'b* (Voice of the people), issued clandestinely at infrequent intervals.

The Algerian Communist Party (Parti communiste algérien; PCA) was founded in 1920 as an extension of the French Communist Party. It has existed independently since October 1936. Although the PCA participated in the nationalist struggle against France, it was proscribed in November 1962, only four months after Algerian independence. In 1964, dissident left-wing elements of the legal National Liberation Front (FLN) joined with Communists from the outlawed PCA to form the Popular Resistance Organization. In January 1966, this group was renamed the Socialist Vanguard Party. The party has not held a congress since 1952. Barely tolerated by the Algerian government, the PAGS is recognized in the communist world as the official Algerian communist party.

Leadership and Party Organization. Sadiq Hadjeres is first secretary of the party. Although the precise membership of the PAGS Politburo and Secretariat is not known publicly, other prominent members of the party in recent years are believed to include Larbi Bukhali, a former party secretary general, Bashir Hadj 'Ali, Ahmad Karim, and 'Ali Malki. Both Hadjeres and Malki have contributed to the *World Marxist Review* and the *Information Bulletin* on behalf of the PAGS. Malki is on the editorial council of the *World Marxist Review* and contributed to its May issue.

Party Views, Positions, and Activities. The PAGS generally has viewed the regime of President Chadli Benjedid, which has ruled Algeria since early 1979, as opportunist and reformist compared with the more militant regime of Houari Boumediene (1965–1978) (see *YICA*, 1983, p. 5). Operating in a hostile political climate and without legal standing, the PAGS prudently opted to maintain a low profile during 1985. The party did not take any public positions of note on either domestic or international issues. Instead, the PAGS continued to focus its energies on the mass organizations of the ruling FLN. PAGS members worked to gain influence among the leadership of the National Union of Algerian Youth, and the party maintained its efforts to place cells in factories to compete with the units of the General Union of Algerian Workers, the government-sanctioned labor union.

State Relations with the Soviet Union. In 1985, Algeria continued its pattern of exchanging high-level visits with the Soviet Union. In March, Cherif Massaadia, a leading official of the FLN, headed a large Algerian delegation to the funeral of Soviet president Konstantin Chernenko. While in Moscow, the Algerian delegation held political talks with a Soviet delegation headed by Boris N. Ponomarev, candidate member of the Politburo and secretary of the CPSU Central Committee (*El Moudjahid* in French, 15–16 March; *FBIS*, 21 March). The following month, a top-level Algerian military delegation made a working visit of several days' duration to the Soviet Union (Algiers Domestic Service in French, 24 April; *FBIS*, 25 April). In July, Soviet vice minister of foreign affairs Ryzhov visited Algiers as part of the regular consultations between the two countries (Algerian Press Service in English, 17 July; *FBIS*, 19 July). That same month, Colonel Abdelmadgid Cherif, commander of the Algerian Navy, made an official visit to Moscow at the invitation of admiral of the Soviet fleet and Deputy Defense Minister S. G. Gorshkov (Moscow, *Krasnaya Zvezda*, 31 July; *FBIS*, 5 August). The highlight of these visits came in August, when Algerian prime minister Abdelhamid Brahimi went to Moscow for a meeting with Soviet prime minister Nikolay Tikhonov to discuss bilateral relations (*FBIS*, 13 August). Finally, in October, a Soviet parliamentary delegation visited Algeria for talks with leaders of the Algerian National People's Assembly. This visit coincided with that of a Soviet energy delegation led by Vladimir Chirskow, the minister of construction of petroleum and gas industry enterprises (Algerian Press Service in Arabic, 21 October; *FBIS*, 25 October).

In addition to Algeria's relations with the Soviet Union, the Benjedid regime also received visits during 1985 from high officials and party delegations of a number of other communist countries, including Hungary, Poland, Bulgaria, and the People's Republic of China. Official Algerian delegations made visits to Albania, Bulgaria, Yugoslavia, and the People's Republic of China.

John Damis
Portland State University

Bahrain

Population. 427,000
Party. Bahrain National Liberation Front (NLF/B)
Founded. 1955
Membership. Unknown but believed negligible
Chairman. Yusuf al-Hassan al-Ajajai
Governing Committee. (incomplete) Aziz Ahmad Mudhawi, Aziz Mahmud, Jasim Muhammad, Abdallah 'Ali al-Rashid, Ahmad Ibrahim Muhammad al-Thawadi, Yusuf al-Hassan (alternate member only)
Status. Illegal
Last Congress. Unknown
Last Election. N/a
Auxiliary Organizations. Bahrain Democratic Youth Union (affiliated with the World Federation of Democratic Youth), National Union of Bahraini Students (affiliated with the International Union of Students), Women's Organization of the NLF/B (affiliated with the Women's International Democratic Federation), Bahrain Workers' Union.
Publications. No data

In an article in the February *World Marxist Review*, the NLF/B's Yusuf al-Hassan stresses the efforts of his organization to "consolidate the unity of the patriotic forces and to mobilize them in defense of democratic rights and constitutional freedom." He thus enunciates the line of the organization to press for "bourgeois freedoms" without any hint of resort to violence. The other revealing statement in the article vis-à-vis Bahrain is al-Hassan's notation that "we have been trying to enable the working people to set up legalized organizations" (*WMR*, February), which is possibly a reference to the shadowy Bahrain Workers' Union.

The NLF/B has continued to participate in meetings where it was the only group not officially characterized as a communist party: the eight communist and workers parties of the Arab East met in Damascus in February, and ten Arab communist parties met 10 June at an unknown location (*IB*, 10/85, p. 31, and 17/85, p. 40). The NLF/B also met with the fellow "revolutionary democratic" parties of Afghanistan and Ethiopia and eleven communist parties in the second conference of communist and workers' parties of the Eastern Mediterranean, the Near and Middle East, and Red Sea held in Nicosia in January (*IB*, 7/85, p. 13). The Soviets still categorize the NLF/B as "revolutionary democratic," a category of Marxist or semi-Marxist groupings that fall short of full-fledged communist parties because of shortcomings in areas such as ideology and organizational discipline (*Socialism: Theory and Practice*, Moscow, August 1983, p. 118).

The January conference voiced the major Soviet propaganda themes by denouncing the U.S. "star wars" plans and Pershing II and cruise missiles in Western Europe; it then turned to pertinent regional issues such as the removal of "imperialist fleets, forces, and bases from the region of the [Persian] Gulf, the Red Sea, and the Arabian Peninsula" and the "oppressive measures" undertaken by the states of the Gulf Cooperation Council (*IB*, 7/85, pp. 14, 18, 20). These latter two themes had been prominent in NLF/B propaganda in 1984 as well, and a third theme—that the Persian Gulf states should establish diplomatic relations with the Soviet bloc—was taken up by the aforementioned June party meeting (*IB*, 17/85, p. 46).

The NLF/B itself, rather than the Bahrain Peace and Solidarity Organization, has continued to be the country's affiliate of the World Peace Council (WPC), the most important of the Soviet-line international front organizations. When the WPC's *List of Members, 1983–1986* became available in early 1985, Bahrain was represented only by NLF/B chairman Yusuf al-Hassan al-Ajajai and Abdallah 'Ali al-Rashid. It is not known what happened to the other thirteen Bahrainis who served on the WPC during 1980–1983.

The Lebanese Communist Party's daily *Al Nida* noted on 27 October that the NLF/B, as well as its purported ally, the Popular Front for the Liberation of Bahrain, had representatives stationed in Damascus. This means that either or both might have headquarters in that city.

Wallace H. Spaulding
McLean, Virginia

Egypt

Population. 48,305,000
Party. Egyptian Communist Party (al-Hizb al-Shuyu'i al-Misri; ECP)
Founded. 1921; revived in 1975
Membership. 500 (estimated)
Secretary General. (Apparently) Farid Mujahid
Politburo. Michel Kamil (chief of foreign relations), Najib Kamil (representative to the *WMR*); other names unknown
Secretariat. No data
Central Committee. Farid Mujahid, Yusuf Darwish; other names unknown
Status. Proscribed
Last Congress. Second, early 1985 (possibly 1984)
Last Election. N/a
Auxiliary Organizations. No data
Publications. Circulars under the heading *al-Wa'i* (Consciousness) and leaflets; *al-Yasar al-Arabi* (The Arab Left; published by Egyptian Communists in Paris).

The communist movement in Egypt dates back to the formation in 1921 in Alexandria of the Egyptian Socialist Party (al-Hizb al-Ishtiraki al-Misri) by Joseph Rosenthal and some former members of a more diverse group founded in Cairo the year before. With its name soon changed to the Egyptian Communist Party, it was admitted to the Comintern in 1923. Suppression by the authorities started almost immediately and has continued sporadically ever since.

The movement has also been beset by factionalism. It virtually disappeared during the 1920s and 1930s. Numerous communist factions emerged during the early 1940s, and the two largest groups combined to form the Mouvement démocratique de libération nationale (MDLN) in 1947. This group also splintered, with the formation of a Unified Egyptian Communist Party in 1958. Soon, additional splintering meant that no one faction was important enough to be singled out for international recognition. At least two groups heeded Soviet instructions to cooperate with "progressive" single-party regimes by dissolving themselves in return for a commitment by the Egyptian government to tolerate individual Communists. Many of the latter occupied important positions in the Arab Socialist Union (ASU) and the mass media. But with President Anwar al-Sadat's shift to the right during the 1970s, a new ECP emerged in 1975.

The Egyptian communist movement remains as splintered as ever. Besides the ECP, several groups—including the Revolutionary Current, the Egyptian Communist Party–8 January, the Egyptian Communist Workers' Party, the Popular Movement, and the Armed Communist Organization—have surfaced during recent years. All indications point to the relative insignificance of such groups in comparison with the threat to the regime potentially posed by non-Marxist, particularly militant religious, movements.

In January the State Supreme Security Court sentenced six members of the Armed Communist Organization who were arrested in 1984 on charges of procuring explosives and ammunition. Three were sentenced to five years in prison; the others to three years. Ten others were found innocent (Cairo, MENA, 10 January; *FBIS*, 11 January).

Later that month, 26 persons were arrested on charges of membership in two heretofore unmentioned groups, the Egyptian Communist Party–Congress Faction and a Trotskyist communist organization called the Revolutionary Communist League. Most of the people arrested were professionals and students. They were accused of distributing antireligious pamphlets and materials explaining techniques of armed struggle and of making weapons (Cairo, MENA, 22 January; *FBIS*, 23 January) and calling for demonstrations and strikes (*NYT*, 20 January; Reugers). The prosecutor demanded sentences of fifteen years at hard labor (*Intercontinental Press*, 1 April, 8 July).

On 30 July, 27 people were arrested on charges of establishing an underground communist group called the Revolutionary Progressive Party, whose goal was to overthrow the government (Kuwait, *al-Ra'y al-'amm*, 1 August; *FBIS*, 5 August).

Leadership and Party Organization. Little is known about the ECP's leadership and organization. Few party officials have been mentioned in available publications; official statements by ECP leaders published abroad are mostly anonymous. The name most often mentioned is Politburo member Michel Kamil, obviously because of his position as the party's chief of foreign relations. All indications point to the typical pattern of "democratic centralism," albeit in a rudimentary form resulting from the group's small membership and clandestine character.

Domestic Party Affairs. The Central Committee of the ECP held a plenary meeting, presumably during the early part of the year. This was described as the "first plenary meeting since the party's second congress." (Since the previous plenary session had met in January 1984, one can infer that the Second Congress met in 1984 or 1985, but there is no other available information to confirm this.) In accordance with instructions from the Central Committee, the Politburo drew up a statement of the issues dealt with at the plenary session (*IB*, July, p. 35).

This statement emphasized that "the political, economic, and social crisis in the country is worsening and deepening," with "the working masses' situation . . . steadily deteriorating" and "the dependent big bourgeoisie . . . feverishly enriching itself." It pointed to signs that "discontent and revolutionary sentiments are growing" and that "the class struggle is sharpening." Various actions by workers, students, and others during the previous year were pointed to, a "growing struggle" that "has upset the government's plans, albeit partially and temporarily, to retreat" on such issues as the cancellation of subsidies and increases in prices. The statement called for the party to play the "leading role in every battle linked with national, economic, social, and democratic development" (ibid., pp. 35–36). The regime was condemned for its repressive and antidemocratic actions and for "placing the country's property in the hands of transnational monopolies." While the desirability of making use of divisiveness within the "dominant big bourgeoisie" was endorsed, it was emphasized that such differences were merely "secondary contradictions" (ibid., p. 37).

Many members of the ECP are in prison or are repeatedly arrested and retried.

Auxiliary and Front Organizations. Little information has come to light about any auxiliary organizations of the ECP. Under present conditions it seems safe to assume that children's and youth organizations do not exist. In the past, the party was actively concerned with organizing primarily students and workers.

Much more important than the ECP or any other

communist organization is the broad, legal leftist opposition front, the National Progressive Unionist Party (NPUP), whose secretary general is longtime Marxist Khalid Muhyi al-Din. (For a biography of Muhyi al-Din, see *YICA*, 1984, pp. 20–21.) Its deputy secretary general is Rif'at al-Sa'id. Some of the members of the NPUP (organized in 1976 when President Sadat first permitted the formation of leftist and rightist opposition groups) are Marxists, while others are Nasserites or other opponents of the nonsocialist, pro-Western direction of the regime. The NPUP publishes the weekly newspaper *al-Ahali* (edited by Muhyi al-Din), which has a large circulation. Before 1980 the party had three seats in the People's Assembly. In the 1984 elections it got 3.8 percent of the total vote, but application of an 8 percent rule prevented it from getting any seats in the newly adopted proportional representation system. However, a prominent member of the NPUP was among the ten additional members appointed by President Husni Mubarak—but not as a member of his party, which had rejected the election's legality (*NYT*, 20 June 1984; AP).

The second National Congress of the NPUP met 27–28 June in Cairo, with about 750 delegates attending (Joel Beinin, "Egypt's Left Opposition Party Holds Second Congress," *Merip Reports*, Washington, September, p. 29). The report of the secretary general, which was approved by the congress, stressed the necessity of preventing further economic hardship among the lower and middle classes. It called for resisting sectarian conflict, economic dependency, and "parasitical capitalism" (as opposed to the "national bourgeoisie," which is viewed in positive terms). Although the members of the congress were divided on this matter, a majority voted to approve the agreement of 11 February between King Hussein of Jordan and Chairman Yasir Arafat of the Palestine Liberation Organization (ibid.). (For analyses of the NPUP programs and activities in previous years, see Bertus Hendriks, "Egypt's Elections, Mubarak's Bind," *Merip Reports*, January, pp. 11–18 and "The Legal Left in Egypt," *Arab Studies Quarterly*, Belmont, Mass., summer 1983, pp. 260–275.)

International Views, Positions, and Activities. The ECP participated in the second conference of communist and workers' parties of the Eastern Mediterranean, the Near and Middle East, and the Red Sea, which was held in Nicosia in January to discuss regional matters (*IB*, April, p. 6). The ECP was also one of eight communist and workers' parties of the Arab East represented at a meeting in Damascus in February to discuss "the dangers latent in" the agreement between King Hussein and Chairman Arafat and "the significance of the forced withdrawal of the Israeli invaders from Saida [Sidon, Lebanon]" (*IB*, May, p. 27). Representatives of ten communist and workers' parties of Arab countries, including the ECP, met—apparently in June and in a place that was not announced—to deal with the situation in the Arab region (*IB*, September, p. 26).

Politburo member Michel Kamil met with Secretary General Abdullah al-Ahmar of the Ba'th Party and with Syrian minister of information Yasin Rajjuh in Damascus in February (Damascus Domestic Service, 23 February; *FBIS*, 26 February). An interview with Kamil—who mentioned that "we. . . make a point of coming to Damascus regularly"—was published in the Damascus newspaper *al-Ba'th* on 1 March (*FBIS*, 8 March). A joint statement of the ECP and the Syrian Communist Party was issued in March, apparently in Damascus (*Pravda*, 7 March; *FBIS*, 8 March). Delegations of the ECP and the Lebanese Communist Party issued a joint statement in Damascus later in the same month (*al-Safir*, Beirut, 13 March; *FBIS*, 15 March).

The statement adopted by the plenary meeting described the Egyptian regime as "submitting to Washington's wishes and in an effort to please it. . . making endless concessions," especially in invigorating "the process of normalizing relations with the Israeli enemy." It deplored the continuing "linkage of the Egyptian army with the NATO bloc" and asserted that "some members of the armed forces high command are becoming direct champions of the economic interests of arms-producing Western monopolies." The discovery of mines in the Red Sea was described as "staged" and "used to build up the NATO military presence." While noting the regime's re-establishment of diplomatic relations with the Soviet Union (in 1984) and the recent conditional endorsement of an international conference on the Middle East, "the essence of the policy of dependence on U.S. imperialism" was said to be unaffected (*IB*, July, pp. 36–37).

Statements adopted at the regional conference in which the ECP participated dealt with virtually every trouble spot in the world, putting all the blame on "imperialism and especially U.S. imperialism" (*IB*, April, p. 6). The "principled policy" of the Soviet Union in "averting the danger of war, strengthening peace and saving humanity from a nuclear holocaust" was praised (*IB*, September, p. 30). The continuation of the war between Iran and Iraq was deplored, as was the violation of human rights in both countries. "Arab reaction" was repeatedly singled out. Arafat's agreement with Hussein was described as "open[ing] the way to capitulationist liquidationalist methods of resolving the Palestine problem" (*IB*, September, p. 27). There were calls for full withdrawal by Israel from territories occupied since 1967; the overthrow of the Numayri regime in the Sudan, successes in the People's Democratic Republic of Yemen and Afghanistan, and victories against Israel in Lebanon were hailed. One statement declared support for "Syria's anti-imperialist and anti-Zionist national patriotic course and its opposition to U.S. diktat and the capitulationist plans" (ibid.).

Glenn E. Perry
Indiana State University

Iran

Population. 45,191,000 (does not take into account the impact of the Iran-Iraq war).
Party. Communist Party of Iran (Tudeh Party)
Founded. 1941 (dissolved May 1983)
Membership. 1,000–2,000 hardcore members; 15,000–20,000 sympathizers
Secretary General. Nurredin Kianuri (imprisoned)
Leading Bodies. No data
Status. Illegal
Last Congress. 1965
Last Election. N/a
Auxiliary Organizations. No data
Publications. *Rahe Tudeh* (Tudeh path), *Mardom*; both published in Europe; party statements are broadcast over the National Voice of Iran, thought to be located in the USSR, and the Voice of the Toilers of Iran, thought to be located in Kabul or Aden.

Domestic Affairs. The crackdown on the Tudeh Party—the Ayatollah Khomeini's other "Satan"—continued in 1985. The effectiveness of the Khomeini regime's anti–Tudeh Party campaign (as well as campaigns against other leftist parties) was manifested by two reports. First, the Tudeh Party reportedly resorted to terrorist action when three of its members attempted to hijack an Iranian aircraft. Such actions by the Tudeh Party were expected to trigger ruthless treatment of their incarcerated members and supporters by the Islamic Republic (*Iran Press Digest* IV, no. 3 [15 January]: 5). According to a second report, the striking industrial workers in Teheran and other cities, whose leftist sympathy is a matter of long-standing tradition, stated that the initiation of a strike and work slowdown was a decision taken entirely on their own; it had no relationship with the leftist political parties (Radio Nejat-e Iran in Persian, 27 January).

In an apparent move to uproot the Tudeh Party on a permanent basis, several high-ranking Islamic Republic officials—including Ali Akbar Hashemi

Rafsanjani, the speaker of the Iranian Majlis, and some former Tudeh members—were purportedly involved in establishing a leftist party to replace the Tudeh Party. The former Tudeh members were reportedly returning to their government posts and closely cooperating with the "religious Tudehis." The latter group was also expected to introduce Hojjat ol-Islam Musavi Khoiniha as a candidate for the presidency of Iran. Khoiniha, known as the "Red Hojjat ol-Islam" and a former go-between of the Tudeh Party and the Islamic Republic, supported the continuation of the war with Iraq, the exportation of Islamic revolution, and reliance on terroristic activities. However, by appointing him as the state public prosecutor, Khomeini neutralized Khoiniha's chances of running for president (Radio Nejat-e Iran in Persian, 28 May; Radio Iran in Persian, 17 June; Free Voice of Iran in Persian, 8 July).

The worsening plight of the Tudeh Party in 1985 was dramatized by the refusal of the Iranian National Council of Resistance—an umbrella body composed of fifteen organizations and personalities opposing the Khomeini regime—to cooperate with the Tudeh Party. Massoud Rajavi, the chairman of this council, stated that "they are not independent" (*Madrid El Pais* in Spanish, 24 May, p. 6; *London Morning Star* in English, 13 August, p. 3). The founder of the Tudeh Party, Iraj Iskandari, died in Berlin (*FBIS*, 14 May); its current leader, Nureddin Kianuri, remains in jail in Iran.

Foreign Relations. As the anti-Tudeh campaign of the Islamic Republic continued, so did the Tudeh Party's endeavors to seek respite. A delegation of the party headed by Babrak Amir-Khosravi and Freydoun Azarnour was received by Maxime Gremetz, a French Politburo member and secretary of the CPSU Central Committee, and by Jacques Fath of the foreign policy section. The Iranian delegation reiterated its complaints of the previous years of the alleged continued internal repression and human-rights violation by the Islamic Republic. The delegation also pointed out that the Tudeh Party was a special target of repressive policies: a large number of its members were arrested and fifteen of them were condemned to death by the government (National Voice of Iran in Persian, 22 February). Gremetz repeated the Soviet Communist Party's claim of solidarity with the Iranian Communist Party and all the Communists who were being repressed (*L'Humanité*, 22 December 1984, p. 9). Through its diplomatic contacts, the Soviet Union continued to press for the rescinding of execution orders of those activists condemned, the release of those imprisoned, and the easing of the severe crackdown on Tudeh members (Radio Nejat-e Iran in Persian, 16 February; *JPRS*, 24 May, p. 146).

In return, the Iranian government wanted the Soviet Union to stop supplying Iraq with military equipment. As the tide of the protracted Iran-Iraq war continued to turn noticeably in favor of Iraq, Iran was expected to continue its crackdown on the Tudeh Party as a minor bargaining chip vis-à-vis the Soviet Union. In fact, the Islamic Republic's decision to mount a heavy-handed campaign against the Tudeh Party was reportedly taken "mainly as a consequence of the USSR's decision in late 1982 to resume arms sales to Iraq" (Michael J. Dixon, "The Soviet Union and the Middle East," *The Soviet Union in the Third World, 1980–1985: An Imperial Burden Or Political Asset?* [Report Prepared for the House Committee on Foreign Affairs by the Congressional Research Service], 23 September, p. 158). In 1985, however, the Soviet Union clearly favored Iraq in this war. The Soviet flip-flop of the previous years on this issue—the USSR first favored Iraq, then stopped military supplies to Iraq in order to win political favor with Iran, and then again sided with Iraq—not only significantly strained Soviet-Iraqi friendship but also resulted in the Iraqi decision to diversify its military supply by turning to France. Given the high stakes attached by the Soviet Union to its military ties with Iraq, it was clear that the Soviets were more willing to sacrifice the Tudeh Party than jeopardize their friendship treaty with Iraq.

Finding an increasingly hostile environment in Iran, a large number of Tudeh members were reportedly residing in Afghanistan. Their Iran-related activities were limited to seeking solidarity with the clandestine communist parties of the neighboring countries and criticizing the alleged brutal treatment of their imprisoned compatriots by the Islamic Republic (*Iran Press Digest* IV, no. 8 [19 February]: 8. See also National Voice of Iran in Persian, 18 February, 7 June; *FBIS*, 22 February; Radio of Iranian Toilers in Persian, 20 April; *USSR International Affairs Middle East and North Africa*, 21 June).

Toward the end of 1985, the Tudeh Party "was a dead issue," according to Donald A. Robert, State Department specialist in Persian Gulf affairs. Many of its infiltrators in the Iranian armed forces were arrested, a number of its leaders were in jail, and others were living in exile in Eastern Europe and Afghanistan. The Islamic Republic threatened to execute the jailed Tudeh leaders in November, on the anniversary of the Russian Revolution, but the Soviet Union persuaded Iran to postpone their trials at least temporarily. This Iranian decision seems to indicate that the Tudeh Party continues to serve as a minor pawn in the power politics between Iran, the USSR, and Iraq.

Mohammed E. Ahrari
East Carolina University

Iraq

Population. 15,507,000
Party. Iraqi Communist Party (ICP)
Founded. 1934
Membership. No data
First Secretary. Aziz Muhammad (61, Kurdish, worker)
Politburo. (incomplete) Zaki Khayri (74, Arab/Kurdish, journalist), Fakhri Karim
Secretariat. No data
Central Committee. (incomplete) Amir Abdallah (61, Arab, lawyer), Mukarram Talabani (60, Kurdish, lawyer), Kadhim Habib, Hamid Majid Musa
Status. Illegal
Last Congress. Third, 4–6 May 1976
Last Election. N/a
Auxiliary Organizations. No data
Publications. *Tariq al-Sha'b* (People's road), clandestine; *Iraqi Letter*, issue no. 1, March 1985

The ICP is now in its sixth decade of existence. During more than a half-century of activity, it has experienced power, influence, and—more often—the contrary experience of being battered and repressed. Its present circumstances are of the latter sort. ICP cadres continue to fight the Ba'thist regime of Saddam Husayn; its leaders are mostly in exile. Data on its current organizational structure is unavailable, and only part of the membership of its leading bodies has been identified. Three of the persons listed above have come into notice since the mid-1970s, an indication that a new generation of leaders is taking over the party.

The war with Iran dominated Iraqi politics, economics, and society in 1985 as it has for the previous four years. No major change on the battle lines took place; they continue to run roughly along the international boundary. Iran occupies some areas of Iraqi territory in the Kurdish-populated north; Iraq holds some militarily advantageous positions on Iranian soil on the central and southern fronts. In the only major ground battle of the year, Iranian forces reached the Baghdad-Basrah highway on the southern front in March but were driven back with heavy loss of life. In other areas, Iraq has had the better of Iran, due in part to ample military supplies from the USSR and European arms exporters. Although strapped for foreign currency, it has managed to pay some of its bills for these and other essential imports and to reschedule other debts. Iraq increased its own oil export capacity toward the end of 1985, and its repeated air attacks on Iran's main export terminal have driven Iran to initiate construction of pipelines to safer ports farther down the Persian Gulf (*NYT*, 30 December).

Domestic Affairs. The political leadership's preoccupation with the war, and the support demanded of all Iraqis under its control, is the framework within which the ICP must operate. The ICP continues to oppose the war and work for the downfall of what it calls "the dictatorial regime of Iraq" (*IB*, April, p. 8). ICP activity is centered in the northern and eastern mountain areas where the population is Kurdish, primarily in a strip 200 km long and 25 km wide along the Turkish-Iraqi border from Zakho to the Barzan area (*The Middle East*, September, p. 11). The ICP is but one, and by no means the largest, of the guerrilla forces operating in the Kurdish area.

The scale and effectiveness of the guerrilla warfare in which the ICP participates is not possible to estimate with precision. It is severe enough to require the Iraqi government to station sizable forces in the northern provinces. The Ba'th government has also agreed that Turkish forces may cross the border to pursue Turkish Kurds who take refuge among their Iraqi comrades. Baghdad does not expect Turkish forces to discriminate between Iraqi and Turkish Kurds. The ICP and the Turkish Communist Party have demanded an end to invasion by Turkish troops because "these aggressive actions and the immoral agreement undercut both countries' sovereignty . . . and create a threat to peace in this region and throughout the world" (*WMR*, April, p. 126). The damage inflicted by the Turks in 1983 and the threat of further intervention have instilled caution among the Communists' allies in the Kurdish Democratic Party (KDP). KDP chairman Mas'ud Barzani admitted, "We do not want to create an international incident [that is, invite Turkish intervention] by blowing up the pipeline" that sends Iraqi oil through Turkey to the Mediterranean (*The Middle East*, September, p. 11). The KDP, the ICP, and the Socialist Party of Kurdistan remain the dominant groups in the National Democratic Front (NDF) formed in 1980 (see *YICA*, 1982, p. 24). Four small groups have since joined this front, but the goal of a single front of all antiregime forces continues to elude the ICP. The major organizations outside the NDF are the Patriotic Union of Kurdistan, which tried and failed through 1984 to reach agreement on autonomy with Baghdad and resumed guerrilla warfare in 1985 (Paris, AFP, 8 May; *FBIS*, 9 May and 4, 5 June), and the Muslim organization for Islamic revolution in Iraq.

There are indications that the Islamic Republic of Iran's support for guerrilla movements is changing. Radio Teheran began stressing the Islamic nature of certain Iraqi movements, referring to "Iraqi Kurdish Hezbollahi Peshmerga" (Party of God Fighters) (Radio Teheran, 1 August; *FBIS*, 2, 6, 7 August). According to a Kuwait newspaper, Iran asked the Kurdish movement to "dissolve their organizations and hand in their arms in some small areas" where they would be replaced by Hezbollahi fighters (*al-Watan*, 31 October; *FBIS*, 4 November). This approach fits with the Islamic Republic's primary interest of advancing its version of an Islamic state. The Kurdish organizations are seeking something quite different—that is, Kurdish autonomy in an Iraqi secular republic. The ICP is reacting against Iranian efforts to disarm its guerrillas (ibid.).

Al-Watan also reports that guerrilla groups are approaching the Iraqi government to explore the possibility of an accommodation. As of the end of the year, no informattion bearing on the ICP's views on such a change in policy had come to light. In September, the ICP declared the Communists' fight against the regime to be "inextricably linked" to achieving peace between Iraq and Iran (*L'Humanité*, 18 September; *FBIS*, 26 September). A joint statement by leadership delegations of the Iranian Tudeh Party and the ICP called for ending the war and establishing "a just democratic peace with no annexations whatsoever, on the basis of respect for the two countries' state borders at the start of the war, each people's national sovereignty over its territory, and endorsing each people's right to determine the socio-political system they desire" (*Iraqi Letter*, no. 1, March, p. 3).

Foreign Relations. Although the ICP is severely hampered in domestic activity by the Ba'thist regime, its representatives are active in international communist affairs. The party participated in the second conference of communist and workers' parties in Nicosia in January, which brought together more than a dozen parties from Afghanistan, the Arab world, and the Red Sea region (*IB*, April, p. 6). The ICP joined with seven other Arab communist parties to protest the February accord between Yasir Arafat and Jordan's King Hussein that "infringes on the Palestinian people's right to create their own independent national state and denies the PLO the right to act as the sole legitimate representative of the Palestinians" (*IB*, May, p. 27).

First Secretary Aziz Muhammad is reported to have had talks with representatives of the Czech Communist Party (Radio Prague, 22 March; *JPRS*, 9 April) and the Polish ZPR (Radio Warsaw, 25 May; *JPRS*, 19 July). He met the secretary of the CPSU Central Committee, B. N. Ponomarev, and K. N. Brutents of the International Department in the summer (*Pravda*, 21 July, cited in *The Soviet Union and the Middle East* [*SUME*] X, no. 7). An ICP Central Committee member participated in an international research group of the *WMR*, whose report included the following: "Various regional conflicts. . .divert public opinion of the national liberation zone nations from the need to invigorate the struggle against the threat of (thermonuclear) war. In most cases these conflicts are the product of imperialist provocation. A most tragic confirmation of this is the Iranian-Iraqi conflict" (*WMR*, April, p. 90).

This contrast is striking between the good state-to-state relations between the USSR and Iraq and the harsh treatment that the latter directs at the ICP. Soviet-Iraqi ties bring no benefit to Iraqi Communists. The USSR is, with France, the principal source of Iraq's military supplies. It extends economic assistance in such areas as petroleum, irrigation, and construction. The fifteenth session of the permanent Soviet-Iraqi commission on economic and scientific cooperation met in Moscow in June (*Pravda*, 15 June; *FBIS*, 19 June). Commentators in the Soviet press "betrayed a more pro-Iraqi stance in midyear," pointing out that "Iran's pursuit of war until victory only played into the hands of Zionism and imperialism" (*SUME* X, nos. 8 and 9, p. 16).

Soviet efforts to repair the rupture between Iraq and Syria surfaced again in 1985. President Saddam Husayn received E. M. Primakov, head of the Institute of Oriental Studies (ibid.; *Izvestiia*, 2 September). Primakov later spoke of the desirability of a Syrian-Iraqi rapprochement at a time when a committee formed at the Arab states' Casablanca summit was making efforts—so far unsuccessful—to lessen tensions between Baghdad and Damascus (*Izvestiia*, 28 October; *SUME* X, p. 17). The ICP did not figure in these efforts; it and other Iraqi opposition groups look to Syria for support in their antiregime efforts.

Three Iraqi leaders visited Moscow during the year. Foreign Minister Tariq Aziz held discussions with Andrey Gromyko "centered on questions concerning the armed conflict between Iraq and Iran" (*Pravda*, 31 March; *FBIS*, 1 April). He visited again in May. First Deputy Prime Minister Taha Yasin Ramadan went to Moscow early in the year. These contacts were capped by President Husayn's two-day working visit to the Soviet capital in mid-December, his first time in the USSR since becoming president in 1979. The discussions, which included a meeting between Husayn and Gorbachev, appear to have concerned arms supplies and the Iraq-Iran conflict (*WP*, 17 December; *Middle East Economic Digest*, 21 December, p. 10).

John F. Devlin
Swarthmore, Pennsylvania

Israel

Population. 4,255,000 (September 1985, Israeli Central Bureau of Statistics [*Jerusalem Post*, international edition, 22–28 September]), apparently including East Jerusalem

Party. Communist Party of Israel (CPI); also called New Communist List (Rashima Kommunistit Hadasha; RAKAH)

Founded. 1922
Membership. 1,500 (estimated)
Secretary General. Meir Vilner (member of the Knesset [parliament]; age: 67)
Politburo. 9 members: David (Uzi) Burnstein, Benjamin Gonen, Wolf Erlich, Emile Habibi, David Khenin, Ruth Lublitz, Emile Tu'ma (deceased in 1985), Tawfiq Tubi (deputy secretary general and member of the Knesset), Meir Vilner; 4 alternates
Secretariat. 7 members, including Zahi Kharkabi, Salibi Khamis, David Khenin, Jamal Musa, Tawfiq Tubi, Meir Vilner
Central Committee. 31 members, 5 candidates
Status. Legal
Last Congress. Twentieth, 4–7 December 1985
Last Election. 23 July 1984, 3.4 percent of the vote (with Democratic Front for Peace and Equality [DFPE]), 4 seats (for DFPE), total number of seats in the legislature: 120 (Source: *Jerusalem Post*, international edition, 5–11 August 1984).
Auxiliary Organizations. Young Communist League, Young Pioneers
Publications. *al-Ittihad* (editor: Emile Habibi); *Zo Ha-Derekh* (editor: Meir Vilner); *al-Jadid* (editor: Samih al-Qasim); *Information Bulletin, Communist Party of Israel*

The communist movement in Palestine began in 1920. Two years later, a Palestine Communist Party (Palestinische kommunistische Partei; PKP) was established; it joined the Comintern in 1924. Following the periodic appearance of factional divisions, the PKP split along ethnic lines in 1943, with the Arab breakaway faction called the League for National Liberation. In October 1948, with the new state of Israel gaining control of most of Palestine, the two groups reunited to form the Israeli Communist Party (Miflaga Kommunistit Isra'elit; MAKI).

The movement split again in 1965, partly along ethnic lines. The RAKAH—pro-Moscow, strongly anti-Zionist, and primarily Arab in membership, though with many Jewish leaders—soon eclipsed the almost completely Jewish and increasingly moderate MAKI. The latter's disappearance by the late 1970s left RAKAH (a name that is still used) as the undisputed communist party of Israel and internationally recognized successor to the pre-1965 communist organizations. With Arab nationalist parties not permitted (although the joint Arab-Jewish Progressive List for Peace [PLP] emerged in 1984 to espouse the cause of Palestinian self-determination and thus to compete for the Arab vote), RAKAH has served mainly as an outlet for the grievances of the Arab (Palestinian) minority. Almost all of the party's vote—85 percent, according to a recent conservative estimate (Mark Segal, "A Powderkeg Within," *Jerusalem Post*, international edition, 27 October–2 November)—comes from the Arab population (the CPI-dominated DFPE got about 50 percent of the Arab vote in 1977, 38 percent in 1981, and 34 percent in 1984). The DFPE has dominated most Arab town councils since the 1970s.

Leadership and Party Organization. The organization of the CPI is typical of communist parties in general. The congress normally meets at four-year intervals and chooses members of the Central Committee, the Central Control Commission, the Presidium, and the Secretariat. There are also regional committees, local branches, and cells (the latter based both on residence and place of work). According to Eli Reches, an Israeli specialist on the Arabs in Israel, no political party in the state is as well organized as the CPI, giving it an important advantage in its rivalry with the PLP for Arab votes (ibid.).

Although perhaps 80 percent of the members of the CPI are Arabs, Jews predominate in the top party organs. In recent years, the Jewish secretary general has been balanced by an Arab deputy secretary general. Although the party has been noted as a nearly unique arena of Arab-Jewish amity, there are reports of dissatisfaction on the part of the Arabs, who are numerically predominant in lower level positions but scarce at the top, a situation whose continuation is said to result from Soviet "orders" (ibid.).

Domestic Party Affairs. The Twentieth Congress of the CPI met in Haifa 4–7 December. Apparently as a move aimed at promoting improved relations with the USSR, President Chaim Herzog addressed the congress—the first time a president of the state had participated in a CPI congress

(Jidda, *Saudi Gazette*, 6 December; AP). The twenty-eighth plenary session of the Central Committee—in which the Central Control Commission also participated—met in May with Muhammad Nafa presiding and set the date for the congress (*IB*, September, p. 20). A meeting of the Politburo was reported in March (*IB*, June, p. 41).

The Communists won 4.1 percent of the vote in the Histadrut (General Confederation of Labor) elections on 13 May, slightly more than the 3.9 percent they received in the previous election, held in 1981 (*NYT*, 15 May).

Members of the CPI were also active on university campuses. Arab students at Haifa University engaged in demonstrations and strikes following the suspension of two members of the Arab Student Committee on charges of involvement in violence. The Communists have long had unchallenged control of the 11-member Arab Student Committee but recently lost two seats to the PLP and two seats to the Arab nationalist Sons of the Village. The committee, which points to growing anti-Arab racism as the cause of unrest, has ended its former relationship with the university's Arab-Jewish Center (Washington, *Chronicle of Higher Education*, 27 March). Deputy Secretary General Tawfiq Tubi, together with Muhammad Mi'ari of the PLP and members of Arab town councils in Galilee, participated in the demonstrations (*Jerusalem Post*, international edition, 17–23 March).

Rallies were held in Rahat (in the Negev) and in Sakhnin (in Galilee) in celebration of the tenth annual Day of the Land on 30 March. The rallies in Israel proper, at which speakers called for Palestinian self-determination and cessation of restrictions on the Bedouin of the Negev, were described as "relatively quiet," but security forces shot an Arab boy in one demonstration in the occupied West Bank (*Jerusalem Post*, international edition, 1–6 April). It has been argued that the Day of the Land inside Israel—in which RAKAH has always played the leading role now increasingly demonstrates not merely specific grievances but is a protest against the basic Jewish character of the state (Moshe Sharon, "What Israeli Arabs Are Thinking," *Jerusalem Post*, international edition, 1–6 April).

In the April issue of *World Marxist Review*, Assistant Secretary General (and Knesset member) Tubi analyzed the role of the Communists in the Knesset. He pictured a situation in which "everything possible is done to hamper CPI activities by invoking anti-democratic administrative regulations" and in which there is discrimination against Communists who want to enter the government service, as well as exclusion from important committees. Yet he asserted that, despite the "limited influence" of "the parliamentary form of struggle," his party "attaches great importance to it as a part of its general activity." He pointed to situations in which the CPI had led movements that later gained broader support, particularly opposition to the war in Lebanon, or in which it had been able to cooperate effectively with the Labor Alignment when the latter was out of power. Tubi even boasted that "the support our faction gave him" in the Knesset was what enabled Herzog to be elected president. Tubi singled out his party's role in "resisting the right-wing extremists" like Rabbi Meir Kahane, who was consequently stripped of his parliamentary immunity in December 1984 (*WMR*, April, p. 67).

The plenary session in May stressed its support for workers who were said to be struggling against the closure of a factory and called on the Histadrut to mobilize its members on this issue (*IB*, September, pp. 20–21).

Knesset member Tawfiq Zayyad, who is also the communist mayor of Nazareth, Israel's largest Arab town, joined other Arab mayors to participate in demonstrations in Nazareth in December. The major emphasis was to protest discrimination against Arab villages and towns in the allotment of government funds. Other issues included the confiscation of Arab land and the government's demolition of Arab houses that are built illegally, according to Zayyad, only because of unreasonable delays by the Ministry of the Interior to approve municipal plans (Terre Haute, Ind., *Tribune-Star*, 22 December; AP).

Auxiliary and Front Organizations. The CPI dominates the DFPE, which includes two noncommunist partners: the Black Panthers (an Afro-Asian or Oriental, Jewish group protesting discrimination by Jews of European origin) and the Arab Local Council Heads. Aside from the one member of the Black Panthers included in the DFPE delegation in the Knesset, there was formerly (1977–1981) a representative of the Arab Local Council Heads. The fifth member of the list in the 1984 election represented the same group. The DFPE is also organized on the local level, particularly in Arab towns and villages.

The CPI sponsors the active Young Pioneers, the Young Communist League, the Israeli Committee Against the War in Lebanon, and the Committee for the Defense of Arab Land. It also participates in the

Democratic Women's Movement, the Israel-USSR Friendship Movement, the Israeli Association of Anti-Fascist Fighters and Victims of Nazism, and, as noted above, the Arab Student Committee.

International Views, Positions, and Activities. Representatives of the CPI participated in the second conference of communist and workers' parties of the region of the Eastern Mediterranean, the Near and Middle East, and the Red Sea, which was held in Nicosia in January. The statement adopted by the conference specifically reaffirmed the participants' solidarity with the CPI and the DFPE (*IB*, April, p. 7).

A CPI delegation led by Central Committee member Yeshua Irga visited Bulgaria in June in accordance with the protocol for cooperation with the Bulgarian Communist Party (BCP). The delegation and BCP leaders discussed matters relating to further cooperation (Sofia, BTA, 18 June; *FBIS*, 19 June). Politburo member David (Sasha) Khenin also met with BCP leaders in Sofia in July (Sofia, BTA, 2 July; *FBIS*, 23 July). Libya withdrew from participation in the twelfth international youth and student festival, held in Moscow in July, because the CPI—"the Zionist Communist Party"—was also invited (Tripoli, JANA, 7 July; *FBIS*, 9 July). In October an Israeli delegation, which included Deputy Secretay General Tubi as well as Knesset members representing the Labor Alignment, Mapam, and the National Religious Party, visited Moscow as guests of the Soviet Peace Committee (Jerusalem Domestic Service, 8 October; *FBIS*, 9 October). Delegations from fifteen countries, including the USSR (led by Nikolai Nenashev, editor of *Sovyetskaya Rossiya*), attended the meeting of the party congress in December.

According to Tubi, the DFPE considers "that the paramount problem is the issue of war and peace." He reiterated his party's call for full withdrawal of Israeli troops from the territories occupied in 1967, for the creation of a Palestinian state in the West Bank and Gaza Strip, and for security for all countries in the area, "including Israel and the future Palestinian state" (*WMR*, April, p. 65). The need for a peace conference in which the Palestine Liberation Organization (PLO) would participate is also recurrently stressed. The government was accused of "providing cover" for terrorism committed by Israeli settlers in the occupied areas (*WMR*, September, p. 21).

Much attention was also given to Lebanon. A Politburo statement condemned the Israeli army's "war crimes and crimes against humanity" and demanded "immediate and unconditional withdrawal" (*IB*, June, p. 41). A statement of the Central Committee condemned "the bloody attack of the Amal [Shiite] organization" on Palestinians and called on Syria to stop such attacks (*IB*, September, p. 20); this is the kind of forthright language that is totally missing in multilateral statements of communist parties that include the Syrian Communist Party. Vilner introduced a motion in the Knesset in June calling for a commission of inquiry into the Lebanon war; this and three similar motions presented by non-DFPE deputies were defeated by a vote of 37 to 15, with 22 members abstaining (*Jerusalem Post*, international edition, 2–8 June).

Central Committee member Ibrahim Malik called for a "rebuff" of "attempts at any form of Israeli involvement in the diabolical Star Wars conspiracy." He condemned the "military-industrial interests that hold the reins of power in Israel today" for "their narrow class self-interest and blind anti-Sovietism" (*WMR*, August, pp. 115–116). CPI positions on situations throughout the world invariably parallel Soviet positions, but—aside from declarations jointly issued with representatives of other communist parties—all available statements during the year tended to avoid issues not specifically related to the immediate region.

Other Marxist Groups. For information on the Israeli Socialist Organization (Matzpen) and groups that have broken away from it, including the Revolutionary Communist League, see *YICA*, 1982, p. 29, and 1984, p. 33.

PALESTINE COMMUNIST PARTY

Population. Over 4,500,000 (estimated) Palestinians, including 900,000 in the West Bank (including East Jerusalem); 500,000 in the Gaza Strip; 600,000 in Israel; and 1.4 million in Jordan (East Bank) (estimates)

Party. Palestinian Communist Party (al-Hizb al-Shuyu'i al-Filastini; PCP)

Founded. 1982

Membership. 200 (estimated)
Secretary General. (Presumably) Bashir al-Barghuti (journalist)
Politburo. Sulayman al-Najjab, Na'im Abbas al-Ashhab, others not known
Secretariat. No data
Central Committee. Dhamin Awdah, Mahir al-Sharif, Sulayman al-Nashshab, Ali Ahmad, Mahmud al-Rawwaq, Na'im Abbas al-Ashhab, Mahmud Abu-Shamas, others not known
Status. Illegal, but tolerated to a large degree in Israeli-occupied areas
Last Congress. First, 1984
Last Election. N/a
Auxiliary Organizations. Progressive Workers' Bloc (PWB)
Publications. *Al-Tali'ah* (The vanguard; edited by Bashir al-Barghuti)

The roots of the communist movement among Palestinians in the Israeli-occupied West Bank and Gaza Strip and among those in Diaspora may be traced to the pre-1948 Palestine Communist Party (see the profile on Israel) and particularly to the post-1943 breakaway faction, the League for National Liberation, as well as to the Communist Party of Jordan (CPJ). According to Na'im Abbas al-Ashhab, a member of the PCP Politburo, one remnant of the League for National Liberation evolved into the Gaza Strip Palestinian Communist Party in 1953. Other Palestinians joined communist parties in the various Arab countries in which they resided, particularly the CPJ. In 1974, the section of the CPJ in the West Bank became the West Bank Communist Organization; with the addition of members from the Gaza Strip, the group became the West Bank and Gaza Strip Palestinian Communist Organization (PCO). Also, members of the CPJ in Lebanon became the Palestinian Communist Organization (PCO) in Lebanon (*WMR*, February 1983).

With the approval of the CPJ, the PCP was organized in February 1982. The party was to include Communists in the Gaza Strip and the West Bank, members of the PCO in Lebanon, and all Palestinian members of the CPJ except for those living in Jordan, that is, the East Bank.

Leadership and Party Organization. Relatively little is known about the organization of the PCP. Politburo member Ashhab related that the "First (constituent) Congress" was announced two years after the party's founding, which presumably means during 1984 (*WMR*, September 1984). Earlier reports that a founding congress was held in 1982 and chose a secretary general possibly referred to an unofficial meeting. The congress adopted a program and rules for the party and "elected its governing bodies" (ibid.), presumably the Politburo, Secretariat, and Central Committee. Several non-PCP sources refer to Bashir al-Barghuti as the party's "leader" (he had previously been described the same way in relationship to the West Bank and Gaza Strip PCO), but there is no evidence that he is necessarily secretary general.

Ashhab made several claims about the composition and procedures of the First Congress and the makeup of the party. The debate on "material put up for discussion" was "serious and responsible," and the atmosphere was "genuine democratic." Also, most of the delegates were young, "a natural reflection" of the fact that the PCP's "member's average age [was] about 24 years," and "a high proportion of the Congress participants were of proletarian origin . . . due to the fact that many of the Communists are workers—almost 50 percent." The "established norms of representation" required that "one delegate [be] elected from 30 working class party members, and one from 50 members from other social strata" (*WMR*, September 1984).

Domestic Party and Intra-Palestinian Affairs. Ashhab said that his party is distinguished—apparently in contrast to other components of the Palestinian national movement—by the fact "that it works primarily in the occupied territories where the main front of the struggle against the aggressors is in progress." He maintained that this, together with "our party's internationalism," has enabled it to make "an important contribution to the Palestinian national movement" (*Pravda*, 20 August; FBIS, 29 August).

The party is illegal in the occupied territories, but while concern for security sometimes leads to crackdowns (and there have been reports of individuals arrested at times for possessing communist literature), it is in fact generally tolerated. Barghuti, who was once imprisoned by the Jordanians, now edits the weekly party newspaper, *al-Tali'ah*, in East Jerusalem. There were reports in the past of another PCP newspaper, *al-Watan* (The Homeland), presumably published outside the occupied territories. PCP statements are also disseminated by the Communist Party of Israel (CPI) press, particularly by *al-Ittihad*.

Similarly, a leading Communist and labor leader, George Hazboun, was dismissed from his position as deputy mayor of Bethlehem in 1983 and subjected to town arrest in 1984. He was released in September, but the military authorities extended the overall restrictions for an additional six months in 1985 (Washington, *Palestine Perspective*, May, p. 14).

The PCP is not represented in the Palestine National Council (PNC), the Executive Committee, or other organs of the Palestine Liberation Organization (PLO), which is an umbrella group for the main organizations in the Palestinian national movement. However, the PCP was active during 1984 in the Democratic Alliance, which also included the Popular Front for the Liberation of Palestine (PFLP), the Democratic Front for the Liberation of Palestine (DFLP), and the smaller Palestine Liberation Front. The Democratic Alliance took an intermediate position in the conflict between PLO chairman Yasir Arafat and the Syrian-backed National Alliance. According to the Aden agreement worked out by the Democratic Alliance and Arafat's supporters in June 1984 (see *YICA*, 1985, pp. 420–421), the PCP was to be represented in the PNC, thus giving it full recognition within the Palestinian movement (Michael C. Hudson, "The Palestinians after Lebanon," *Current History*, Philadelphia, January, p. 20). However, the National Alliance rejected the Aden agreement. When the Seventeenth Palestine National Congress finally met in Amman in November 1984, the PCP and its allies in the Democratic Alliance did not participate. (For further analysis, see Naseer Aruri, "The PLO and the Jordan Option," *Merip Reports*, Washington, March–April, pp. 3–7.) Yet three seats on the fourteen-member Executive Committee were left vacant, possibly to be filled later by groups that boycotted the session, presumably including the PCP ("Palestine Liberation Organization," *Background Brief*, Foreign and Commonwealth Office, London, February, p. 6).

The PCP repeatedly condemned the 11 February agreement between King Hussein and Chairman Arafat. Ashhab maintained that "imperialism and Zionism. . . have seen favorable opportunities for themselves in the agreement" (*Pravda*, 20 August; *FBIS*, 29 August). However, while the PFLP joined pro-Syrian factions to form the National Palestinian Salvation Front to oppose the 11 February agreement, neither the DFLP nor the PCP did so (Paris, Radio Monte Carlo, 27 March; *FBIS*, 28 March). In early July a representative of the PFLP said that, although the Salvation Front was the "leadership of the Palestinian people until we guarantee the unity of the PLO on its anti-imperialist line," his organization was nevertheless "in daily contact with" the DFLP and the PCP (*Merip Reports*, July–August, p. 16). On 4 June, at a time of increasing Palestinian solidarity against the (Shiite Lebanese) Amal militia's attacks on Palestinian camps, the PCP joined with the PFLP and supporters of Arafat to issue an appeal for the closing of ranks (*NYT*, 6 June).

While the PCP has consistently opposed the "rejectionist" position in favor of a peace conference that would result in Israel's full withdrawal from the occupied territories and establishment of a Palestinian state alongside Israel, it also deplores "capitulationism." Ashhab spoke of the withdrawal of Palestinian fighters from Beirut in 1982 as having resulted in "pessimism among a certain section of the Palestinian bourgeoisie" and "the gradual limitation and narrowing of PLO links with progressive-patriotic movements"; this, in turn, resulted in the organization having "become a prisoner of relations with certain right-wing regimes." He called "right-wing Arab forces" the main "threat to Palestinian independence" (*Pravda*, 20 August; *FBIS*, 29 August).

Auxiliary and Front Organizations. There is little information on auxiliary organizations, but PCO or PCP involvement with labor, student, and professional groups has been reported in the past. Ashhab spoke of "voluntary labor committees, which operate in all areas of the occupied territories, provide assistance for peasants whose land has been taken away," and "have formed detachments of patriotically minded doctors to provide medical aid." He added that "trade unions, creative associations, and public organizations such as unions of students, senior pupils, women, and so forth are active" (ibid.).

In effect, the PLO is a government-in-exile. Its supporters and its leadership span the political spectrum. Its dominant component, Fatah (headed by Arafat), might in a sense be called a "united front" since it avoids ideology in favor of pursuing a national cause. It contains some Marxists but is dominated by centrists (or even conservatives) like Arafat. The Syrian-backed dissidents also range from Marxists to rightists. Small groups like the PFLP and the DFLP that have had minimal representation on PLO organs are Marxist but are not considered to be "communist."

The Palestine National Front was organized in 1973 as an alliance of Communists and others in the occupied territories. It gained some importance for a while but withered before the end of the decade (see *YICA*, 1985, p. 421).

The Progressive Workers' Bloc (PWB), which is closely tied to the PCP, dominated the General Federation of Trade Unions (GFTU) in the West Bank even before the Israeli occupation began in 1967. The PWB's hegemony was threatened during the late 1970s and the early 1980s by the emergence of increasingly important groups associated with the PFLP, the DFLP, Fatah, and the pro-Syrian Sa'iqah. This led (in 1981) to the formation of a rival GFTU by the Fatah-backed Workers' Youth Movement. The DFLP-backed Workers' Unity Bloc (WUB) and the PWB continued to compete for control of the original GFTU, with the PWB resisting the admission of new unions because of a fear of losing control (Joost R. Hiltermann, "The Emerging Trade Union Movement in the West Bank," *Merip Reports*, October–December, pp. 29–30). Yet as the Israelis have detained, imprisoned, or deported leading members of the WUB since July, the PWB was again able to reassert its primacy in elections for the (original) GFTU executive committee on 6 September (ibid., p. 31).

International Views, Positions, and Activities. The PCP was represented at the second conference of communist and workers' parties of the region of the Eastern Mediterranean, the Near and Middle East, and the Red Sea, which met in Nicosia in January (*IB*, April, p. 6), at a meeting of eight communist and workers' parties of the Arab East held in Damascus in February (*IB*, May, p. 27), and at a meeting of communist and workers' parties of Arab countries (apparently in June and at a place that was not announced) (*IB*, September, p. 26). The PCP participated in the joint statements issued at each conference (for some passages from these declarations, see the profile on Egypt in this edition of *YICA*).

Politburo member Najjab, together with several other Palestinian leaders, were guests in Moscow of the Soviet Committee of Afro-Asian Solidarity in November 1984 (Jerusalem, *The Soviet Union and the Middle East* 9, no. 11 [1984]: 5). Asshab visited Bulgaria in February (Sofia, BTA, 28 February; *FBIS*, 1 March). He also headed a PCP delegation to Moscow in May (Moscow Television Service, 22 May; *FBIS*, 23 May). An article by Ashhab was published in *Pravda* on 20 August (*FBIS*, 29 August).

Party statements emphasized the Palestine question and the relationship of the Arab world to it. A few statements dealt with broader international matters, particularly those by PCP leaders on visits to socialist countries or in joint statements with other communist parties. All such statements closely paralleled Soviet positions, and Soviet policies were hailed in glowing terms. Thus one statement "spoke of the constant historic importance of the Soviet people's triumph over Hitlerite nazism . . . and their unwavering struggle against the threat of war" (Moscow International Service, 23 May; *FBIS*, 24 May). Responsibility for the "ongoing aggravation of the situation in the Middle East" was laid at the feet of "Israel's ruling circles, most actively backed by the U.S., which persists in their aggression against the Arab countries and peoples" (Sofia, BTA, 28 February; *FBIS*, 1 March). Ashhab expressed gratitude "to the Israeli democratic forces, primarily the fraternal Communist Party of Israel" (*Pravda*, 20 August; *FBIS*, 29 August).

Glenn E. Perry
Indiana State University

Jordan

Population. 2,794,000 (excluding the West Bank and East Jerusalem)
Party. Communist Party of Jordan (al-Hizb al-Shuyu'i al-Urduni; CPJ)
Founded. 1951
Membership. Accurate estimate not available
Secretary General. Fa'ik (Fa'iq) Warrad
Leading Bodies. No data
Status. Proscribed
Last Congress. Second, December 1983
Last Election. N/a
Auxiliary Organizations. None
Publications. *Al-Jamahīr*, *al-Haqīqa*

After the partition of Palestine, the League for National Liberation (the communist party of undivided Palestine since 1943) changed the party's name in June 1951 to the Communist Party of Jordan. The Central Committee headed by Fu'ad Nassar opposed the annexation of eastern Palestine (renamed the West Bank) by King Abdullah, and it called for the establishment of an independent Palestinian state in accordance with the U.N. General Assembly resolution 181 (II) of 29 November 1947.

The CPJ entered the Jordanian parliamentary election campaign of 1951 under the name of the Popular Front, and three of its candidates were elected. It campaigned on a practical platform that called for legalizing political parties and trade unions, land reform, and industrialization in order to provide employment.

The Partisans for Peace also provided an outlet for the CPJ, which attracted establishment figures and nationalists. In addition to its official organ, *al-Muqawamah al-Sha'biyah* (Popular Resistance), the CPJ issued two others in 1952: *al-Jabha* (The Front) and *al-Raye* (Opinion).

The government clamped down by sentencing the CPJ's secretary general, Fu'ad Nassar, to ten years' rigorous imprisonment in December 1951. Two years later it amended the Law to Combat Communism, making any association with party activities illegal and punishable by a jail sentence ranging from three to fifteen years. Despite these restrictions the CPJ entered the 1954 parliamentary campaign under the name of the National Front, organized mass demonstrations against the Baghdad Pact, and together with nationalist parties helped create the atmosphere in which Jordan terminated the 1948 Anglo-Jordanian Treaty in 1956. The CPJ polled 13 percent of the vote in the 1956 elections and was the first Communist Party in the Arab East to be represented in the cabinet. A subsequent all-out offensive by King Hussein's army, backed by the Eisenhower administration, led to the ouster of the cabinet, imposition of martial law, dissolution of the parliament, and imprisonment of communist deputies and hundreds of Communists, most of whom served until the general amnesty of April 1965.

During the 1960s, the CPJ aligned itself with Egypt and Syria in accordance with the prevailing Soviet policy of cooperation with the national bourgeois regimes in the Third World. The party benefited from the decision of the Jordanian government to exchange full diplomatic relations with the Soviet Union in August 1963, but it continued to function clandestinely.

The party's 1964 program called for rapid industrialization, social welfare legislation, and a nonaligned foreign policy for Jordan. It endorsed the first Arab summit meeting of January 1964 and the creation of the Palestine Liberation Organization (PLO). But when its new official organ *al-Taqaddum* (Progress) published a front-page article that considered Arab solidarity a positive trend and regarded Jordan as progressive, an internal party rift ensued. Elements responsible were purged as right-wing deviationists.

Party Internal Affairs. Following a congress of the CPJ in 1970 in Amman, an internal rift in the party produced a faction led by Fahmi Salfiti and Rushdi Shahin. This left-wing faction operates under the name of the Communist Party of Jordan–Leninist Cadre and publishes the newspaper *al-Haqīqa* (Truth—not to be confused with the journal of the same name published by the CPJ).

The CPJ became involved in PLO politics after the 1967 Israeli occupation, and until the formation of the Palestine Communist Party (PCP) in 1982, its work centered on the West Bank.

The 1970 CPJ congress established the Ansar militia to contribute to armed Palestinian resistance against Israeli occupation. Two years later Nassar was elected to the Palestine National Council (PNC). In 1974, the CPJ published a transitional plan that influenced the posture of the Democratic Front for the Liberation of Palestine (DFLP) and ultimately the PNC decision to struggle for the establishment of an independent Palestinian state.

In late December 1981, the CPJ's Central Committee decided to authorize the Palestine Communist Organization (PCO)—the leading component of the Palestine National Front (PNF) in the occupied West Bank and Gaza—to prepare for the establishment of an independent Palestinian communist party (*IB*, March 1982). The PCP, which continued the work of PNF underground, was established on 10 February 1982 (*WMR*, February).

Domestic Attitudes and Activities. The CPJ leaders have consistently denounced the Jordanian regime for following a "course aimed at suppressing democracy and civil rights and liberties" (*IB*, April). In the first half of October 1984, the Central Committee of the CPJ held an enlarged plenary meeting and adopted resolutions against what it described as a reign of terror in Jordan. It called on "the popular masses and on all National patriotic forces to close their ranks and continue the struggle to end the policy of terror and persecution and ensure healthy and democratic operation of the parliament which will enable the people to exercise their basic rights and freedoms" (*IB*, April). The resolutions also decried the economic crises manifested in "a drop in production, a decrease of national income. . . an increase in the deficit of the trade balance and the balance of payments." Jordan is described as a consumerist society dominated by a parasitical bourgeoisie that relies on remittances from the Persian Gulf and by a bureaucratic bourgeoisie that creates state enterprises. The tensions between these two, as well as the growing number of indigenous and foreign laborers deprived of the benefits of social legislation and trade unionism, provide the CPJ with the opportunity to mobilize support among workers, students, women, and the youth. Jordanian Communists are represented in the General Secretariat of the Alignment of Popular and Trade Union Forces as well as in the newly established Committee of Political Parties and Organizations. The program of the CPJ congress of December 1983 called on the party membership to work for the formation of a "broad national democratic front of workers, peasants, members of the petty and national bourgeoisie and revolutionary intellectuals in order to bring about national democratic rule" (see Fa'ik Warrad's article in *WMR*, July 1984). An article in CPJ's *al-Haqīqa* stated that in countries like Jordan, where "power is still in the hands of domestic reaction tied economically, politically and socially to imperialism, it is necessary to form a broad national front comprising all progressive democratic forces. The purpose of this front is to fight for final deliverance from imperialist dependence and achieve a higher level of social development with due regard to prevailing socio-economic conditions" (*IB*, March).

Together with seven communist and workers' parties of the Arab East, the CPJ issued a statement in reaction to the Framework of Common Action signed by King Hussein and Yasir Arafat on 11 February. The statement considered this Amman agreement in the context of attempts by the United States "to establish fully its domination over the Arab countries. . . in order to attain a 'Strategic Consensus' and turn the region into a base of aggression against national liberation movements and the Soviet Union." In addition, the agreement "infringes on the Palestinian people's right to create their own independent national state and denies the PLO the right to act as the sole legitimate representative of the Palestinians" (*IB*, May). The signatories of the statement condemned the agreement and called for "a fight to foil it, [and] expressed spiritual solidarity with the opposition to it displayed by the patriotic Palestinian masses, organizations and leaders on and outside the occupied territories."

Auxiliary and Mass Organizations. Jordan's all-out offensive against the PLO in September 1970 and Israel's de facto annexation of the West Bank and Gaza Strip spawned the indigenous nonviolent resistance, under the banner of the PNF, *inside* the West Bank. Organized in August 1973, the PNF attracted a broad nationalist coalition reminiscent of the 1950s. The PNF organized against land expropriation and publicized various grievances under the 1949 Geneva Conventions in the Israeli Parliament through the Israeli Communist Party (RAKAH). It urged Arab businessmen not to pay taxes to the occupation authorities and organized mass demonstrations against Israeli expulsion of Palestinian leaders from the occupied territories. Israel clamped down on the PNF in April 1974 and placed many of its leaders under administrative detention.

International Activities and Attitudes. An October 1983 article by Izhaq al-Khatib, member of the CPJ Politburo, describes the party's goal as national democratic rule—that is, the establishment of a "new system, breaking with imperialism, and opting explicitly for a policy of close relations with the Arab national liberation movement, the Palestinian revolution, and of course the world revolutionary movement and the Soviet Union" (*WMR*, October 1983). The program of the congress of December 1983 recognized serious difficulties facing the Arab national liberation movement, which it attributed to the "abandonment of radical positions by the majority of patriotic Arab regimes" and the inability of the petty-bourgeois regimes to preserve gains made in the 1960s. The congress concluded that the Arab national liberation movement had entered a "new stage... characterized by the manifestly inadequate ability of the petty bourgeoisie to continue leading" that movement, and that a new leadership is taking shape in the form of "an alliance between the parties of the working class and revolutionary democrats."

During 1984, however, the CPJ began to distinguish between various Arab and Third World countries on the basis of the "degree of social development" attained by each country. In countries such as the People's Democratic Republic of Yemen and Ethiopia, the "national democratic revolution has achieved a reasonably high level of development." These countries thus formed "vanguard parties guided by the theory of Scientific Socialism, Marxism-Leninism." In countries such as Jordan and Saudi Arabia, however, where the "national and revolutionary forces are crushed and persecuted," it has been necessary to form a broad coalition of nationalist and leftist parties. Khatib's article concludes by stating that "the experience of Arab and some other developing countries has shown that the petty bourgeoisie is often unable to accomplish the tasks of the national democratic revolution and advance it to the stage of transition to socialism. The parties of the working class must therefore assume the chief role at precisely this stage" in order to build socialism (*IB*, March).

The CPJ joined a number of communist and workers' parties from West Asia and the East Mediterranean—including Afghanistan, Cyprus, Israel, Bahrain, Greece, Saudi Arabia, Turkey, Syria, Ethiopia, Iran, Egypt, Iraq, Cyprus, and the PCP—at a conference held in Nicosia in January. The declaration of that meeting expressed great concern that "the developments internationally as also in the region are rapidly acquiring an exceptionally dangerous character." It gave a catalog of significant events since the group's last meeting in 1981: for example, "the U.S.-Israeli aggression against Lebanon... the U.S. aggression against Grenada... the aggressive activities against Nicaragua and El Salvador... the threats against Cuba... the imperialist military build-up in the Gulf and the Indian Ocean... the developing of nuclear weapons by the reactionary regimes of South Africa, Israel and Pakistan" and "other U.S. escalations," including President Reagan's "star wars" plan (*IB*, April). The participants called for "an international conference of Communist and workers parties to promote joint action against the imperialist threat; for detente and peace are necessary and timely."

Government restrictions on the CPJ have been relaxed in view of improved relations with the USSR. A Jordanian-USSR Friendship Society sponsors an annual cultural event celebrating Jordanian-USSR Friendship Week (*FBIS*, 18 April 1984), and the society's chairman, Bahjat Talhouni, a former prime minister and presently a Senate member, visited Moscow on 25 September to participate in the celebrations marking the 60th anniversary of establishing the Union of Soviet Societies For Friendship and Cultural Relations with Foreign Countries (*FBIS*, 25 September).

Cultural cooperaton between the two countries has taken great leaps in recent years. During 1985, a Soviet delegation led by the secretary of the USSR Union of Writers at the Presidium of the Soviet Committee for Solidarity with Asian and African Countries visited Jordan and met with the minister of culture. Another visit was made by the USSR State Institution Workers Union delegation (*FBIS*, 4 April). A Soviet delegation led by the chairman of the Spiritual Administration of Muslims of Central Asia and Kazakhstan visited Jordan and met with Jordan's minister of religious affairs. They discussed Jordan's offer to train Soviet Muslim students and Soviet mosque preachers, to print works of Soviet Muslim scholars, and to facilitate travel of Soviet pilgrims via Jordan (*FBIS*, 3 May). Supreme Soviet Presidium member Mikhail Kondakov also visited Jordan and signed a cultural agreement for a student exchange program and for the exchange of art and cultural exhibitions (*FBIS*, 5 September). Another agreement between Yarmuk University and the Soviet Technical Corporation provides the university with Soviet staff to teach Russian during the academic year 1985–1986 (*FBIS*, 12 September). Perhaps more significant is the new air defense network deal between the USSR and Jordan, which, according to Jordan's commander-in-chief, constituted a "qualitative leap in preparation and training" *FBIS*, 6 January).

Naseer H. Aruri
Southeastern Massachusetts University

Lebanon

Population. 2,619,000
Party. Lebanese Communist Party (al-Hizb al-Shuyu'i al-Lubnani; LCP); Organization of Communist Action in Lebanon (OCAL)
Founded. LCP: 1924; OCAL: 1970
Membership. LCP: 14,000–16,000 (claimed); LCP: 5,000, OCAL: 2,000 (author's estimates)
Secretary General. LCP: George Hawi; OCAL: Muhsin Ibrahim
Politburo. LCP, 11 members
Central Committee. LCP, 24 members
Status. Legal
Last Congress. LCP: Fourth, 1979; OCAL: First, 1971
Last Elections. 1972, no representation
Auxiliary Organizations. LCP: Communist Labor Organization; World Peace Council in Lebanon; and a number of labor and student unions and movements
Publications. *Al-Nida* (The call) daily; *al-Akhbar* (The news) weekly; *al-Tariq* (The road) quarterly

The LCP was established in October 1924 as the Lebanese People's Party (al-Hizb al-Sha'b al-Lubani). During the French mandate over Syria and Lebanon (1920–1946), the LCP recruited members in both of these countries, but the Syrian element dominated the party despite its name.

The LCP was banned from 1939 to 1970, when, along with several other leftist organizations, it was granted legal status by the Lebanese government. Despite LCP's lack of legal recognition prior to 1970, it was tolerated and often participated in Lebanese parliamentary elections. On the eve of Lebanon's civil war of 1975–1976, the LCP entered the leftist, Muslim-dominated Front for Progressive Parties and National Forces (FFPNF), later known as the Lebanese National Movement (LNM).

Both the LCP and OCAL have participated in Lebanon's civil war and continue to play active roles in the country's political affairs. Traditionally, the communist appeal in Lebanon was largely confined to the Orthodox Christians, particularly the Greek Orthodox community, which provided the bulk of LCP's leaders and followers. The factional character of the LCP hindered communist efforts to attract a following among other Lebanese religious groups. Since the party's legalization, however, Shia Muslims have become increasingly visible in the LCP.

Leadership and Organization. George Hawi has served as the LCP's secretary general since 1979, and Muhsin Ibrahim has led the OCAL since its foundation in 1970.

The Congress, theoretically the highest organ of the LCP, is supposed to convene every four years; however, the LCP has held only four congresses since 1924. Authority is vested in the 24-member Central Committee, which in turn elects the 11-member Politburo. (For a listing of Central Committee members, see *YICA*, 1981, p. 14.)

The LCP maintains a well-organized and centrally controlled network of local cells, which are, in turn, organized into districts and regions. Both the LCP and OCAL maintain well-armed "self-defense" paramilitary units that participate actively in street battles and other "military operations," mainly against the Christian/rightist Lebanese Forces.

Domestic Views and Activities. The LCP continued to denounce the United States, Israel, rightists/Christians, and "Arab reactionary forces" for the continuation of political anarchy and sectarian violence in Lebanon. To ensure the triumph of the "national liberation revolution" in Lebanon, the LCP stressed the necessity of stepping up the "popular armed struggle for liberating" the remaining parts of Israeli-occupied southern Lebanon (*IB*, February). As a basis for resolving the Lebanese crisis, the LCP called for adherence to the following principles originally put forward by an enlarged plenary meeting of the party's Central Committee in February 1984: the affirmation of Lebanon's Arab character; the complete removal of confessionalism; the radical reform of the parliamentary system; the reform of Lebanon's constitution; the close cooperation of the executive authority, including the army, with "fraternal Syria first and foremost"; and radical socioeconomic transformation "to lessen dependence on international monopolies" and "to prevent the ruin of the working class and rural workers" (*IB*, May 1984).

In its circulars and public statements, the LCP continued to call for "lawful national rights" of the Palestinians in Lebanon and elsewhere and asserted that the only way to regain these rights "is not through bargaining with the hostile imperialist, Zionist and reactionary forces, but through escalating the armed struggle against the Zionist enemy and adopting clear and decisive stances against imperialism and its agents, and against all capitulationist and liquidationist plans" (Beirut, *al-Safir*, 9 January; *FBIS*, 10 January). During an enlarged plenary meeting of the Central Committee of the LCP in March, the party condemned "U.S. links with the right wing extremist forces" in Lebanon and called for "strengthening the unit of all patriotic forces against the Zionists, fascists, reactionaries and imperialism." The plenary meeting also pointed out the "deepening friendship of Lebanon with the Soviet Union" (Tass, 24 March; *FBIS*, 25 March).

Throughout the year, Lebanon's Communists continued to engage in armed clashes against Christian Maronite forces along with other leftist/Muslim groups. The LCP militiamen played a very active part, especially in suicidal operations, against Israeli forces prior to their withdrawal from most of southern Lebanon in April (*Pravda*, 8 June; *FBIS*, 11 June). Both the LCP and OCAL maintained close contact with various leftist Lebanese and Palestinian groups and remained unswerving in their support of Lebanon's pro-Syrian and leftist coalition. The alliance between the LCP and the Druze-dominated Progressive Socialist Party (PSP) was further strengthened when a Lebanese National Democratic Front was formed in Beirut in October to consolidate the leftist gains that followed Israel's unilateral withdrawal from Lebanon.

Despite efforts to solidify "fraternal" ties between the Communists and other Lebanese "progressive forces," persistent problems continued to mark these ties. In late July and again in October street clashes occurred between LCP members and gunmen of the Shia Amal Movement, who had come to dominate West Beirut (*FBIS*, 30 July, 1 November). Armed clashes were also reported in October between the Communists and the Sunni Islamic Unification Movement in Tripoli (*FBIS*, 3 October).

International Views and Contacts. The LCP remains a strong and consistent supporter of the

Soviet Union. It calls for the "intensification of the struggle for liberation and progress" and for national sovereignty in Lebanon and elsewhere in the Arab world "on the basis of the permanent and multifaceted support given by the Soviet Union and the socialist bloc countries" (*al-Safir*, 9 January; *FBIS*, 10 January). According to Hawi, the LCP is determined "to continue in the front ranks of Arab national liberation movement, acting in alliance with vanguard forces of Palestinian revolution, with Syria, Democratic Yemen, Libya, Algeria and other progressive forces" in the region. The party also reaffirmed its "unswerving desire to remain true to the traditions of alliance with the CPSU" (*IB*, February).

The LCP condemned the Camp David "deal" and subsequent U.S. proposals to settle the Arab-Israeli conflict. It maintains that the achievement of a lasting and just settlement of the conflict requires the withdrawal of Israel from all Arab territories occupied in 1967. The LCP also calls for an international peace conference, including representatives from the USSR, to settle the Middle East crisis. It condemns the "rightist deviation by the Arafat group" and calls for "the development of Palestinian national struggle in the right direction...on the basis of decisive enmity to imperialism, Zionism and reaction" (*FBIS*, 10 January).

During the year the LCP maintained extensive official contacts with Communist Party officials from the USSR and Eastern Europe. Frequent meetings also occurred with other communist and workers' parties in the Arab world, especially with the Syrian Communist Party. Nabil Abd al-Samad, an LCP Politburo member, visited Sofia on 21 January and held talks with Dimitur Stanishev of the Bulgarian Communist Party (BCP) on the situation in the Middle East and Lebanon. They discussed "measures for strengthening and expanding relations" between the two parties (Radio Sofia, 21 January; *FBIS*, 25 January). On 16 March Hawi visited Moscow and met with Boris Ponomarev, a CPSU Politburo candidate member. They noted the unanimity of views between the two parties and confirmed their aspiration for further development of fraternal ties between them (*Pravda*, 16 March; *FBIS*, 18 March). Abd al-Karim Murawah, an LCP Politburo member, also visited Moscow on 12 May in conjunction with a conference of the Soviet Committee for Afro-Asian Solidarity. In mid-June Hawi held discussions in Prague with Vasil Bilak, a Presidium member of the Czechoslovakian party's Central Committee; they called for "further development of cooperation between the two parties and stressed the necessity for a united program of patriotic and progressive forces against the aggressive plans of imperialism, reaction, and Zionism" (Radio Prague Domestic Service, 14 June; *FBIS*, 18 June). On 28 August Hawi met Milko Balev and Dimitur Stanishev of the BCP in Varna and expressed mutual support and solidarity on international and communistic issues. The two parties also confirmed their support for the PLO unity "on an anti-imperialist basis" and called for a lasting peace in the Middle East (Sofia, BTA, 28 August; *FBIS*, 29 August). Nadim Abd al-Samad visited Romania on 11 November and met with Miu Dobrescu, member of the Executive Political Committee of the Romanian Communist Party. The two sides discussed international, regional Middle Eastern, and Lebanese developments and expressed their solidarity and readiness to expand interparty relations and cooperation between the two parties (Bucharest Agerpress in English, 11 November; *FBIS*, 13 November).

Publications. The principal LCP publications are the Arabic-language daily newspaper *al-Nida*, the weekly *al-Akhbar*, and the quarterly *al-Tariq*. The party also publishes the weekly *Kanch* (The Call) in the Armenian language. They contain articles on Lebanese political and socioeconomic issues, international and Arab politics, and Marxist-Leninist ideology. These organs often disseminate the news of illegal communist parties in the Middle East, although in recent years their publication or distribution has been disrupted because of the prevailing insecurity in Beirut. Both the LCP and OCAL also publish booklets and pamphlets.

OCAL. The precursor of the OCAL was the now-defunct Arab Nationalist Movement (ANM) founded by George Habash in 1954. When the ANM began to split into various groups after the 1967 Arab-Israeli war, Muhsin Ibrahim and his colleagues established the Organization of Lebanese Socialists (OLS) in 1969. In May 1970 the OLS merged with the smaller Organization of Socialist Lebanon and a few dissident Communists to form the OCAL. This newly established "revolutionary" organization held its first congress in 1971, elected a Politburo, and designated Ibrahim its secretary general. At present, Fawwaz Tarabulsi acts as the assistant secretary general.

Like the LCP, the OCAL is an active member of Lebanon's leftist Muslim coalition. Its members are mostly students, ex-students, and other young working-class people. Shia Muslims are heavily represented in the ranks of the OCAL.

During the Lebanese civil war and its aftermath the OCAL played an active role in frontal attacks against the Phalangists and Lebanese Forces, fighting alongside the PSP and other leftists. The membership of OCAL in the leftist Muslim coalition, however, has not prevented the organization from engaging in occasional street battles against the Shia Amal Movement, especially in West Beirut (*FBIS*, 23 March 1984). The OCAL maintains close ties with the Democratic Front for the Liberation of Palestine and other leftist Palestinian commando groups. Aside from West Beirut, the organization also maintains a presence in the northern Lebanese city of Tripoli.

Initially, the OCAL was critical of the LCP and charged that it had become rigid and was not genuinely Marxist (*Arab World Weekly*, 15 May 1971). The OCAL also sided with China in the Sino-Soviet conflict. Since the mid-1970s, however, it has moderated its views and moved closer to the LCP. Interviewed in August 1977, Fawwaz Tarabulsi asserted that "our policies have been very close, at times even identical" (*Merip Reports*, October 1977). In May 1984 an agreement was reached between the LCP and OCAL "to intensify the communist military presence through the two organizations and to set up additional positions along the contact lines" (Radio Free Lebanon, 28 May 1984; *FBIS*, 1 June 1984). The OCAL also maintains close contacts with party and state officials in the People's Democratic Republic of Yemen.

Like the LCP, the OCAL denounces "various U.S. plots" against Arab national liberation movements, especially against the Palestinians. The organization also condemns "Arab reactionary circles," "capitulationists," and the "U.S.-Zionist alliance" in their efforts to "liquidate the Palestinian issues and eliminate the PLO's presence in the area" (*al-Safir*, 10 May; *FBIS*, 13 May). The OCAL emphasizes the military training of its members and supports and prepares them for "armed struggle" and "mass political action" in Lebanon. It also emphasizes the necessity of party work in labor unions and student organizations.

Auxiliary Organizations. A number of other Lebanese communist and communist-dominated organizations have been mentioned in the news media from time to time; among these, the more significant seem to be the Communist Labor Organization, the Organization of Arab Communists, the Revolutionary Communist Party (Trotskyist), the Lebanese Communist Union, the World Peace Council in Lebanon, and various "Friendship Committees" with East European countries.

Nikola B. Schahgaldian
The Rand Corporation

(Note: Views expressed in this article are those of the author and should not be construed to represent the position of the Rand Corporation or its research sponsors.)

Morocco

Population. 24,258,000
Party. Party of Progress and Socialism (Parti du progrès et du socialisme; PPS)
Founded. 1943 (PPS, 1974)
Membership. 2,000 (estimated)

Secretary General. 'Ali Yata
Politburo. 12 members: 'Ali Yata, Ismail Alaoui, Mohamed Ben Bella, Abdeslem Bourquia, Mohamed Rifi Chouaib, Abdelmajid Douieb, Omar El Fassi, Thami Khyari, Abdallah Layachi, Simon Lévy, Mohamed Moucharik, Abdelwahed Souhail
Secretariat. 4 members: 'Ali Yata, Mohamed Rifi Chouaib, Omar El Fassi, Mohamed Moucharik
Central Committee. 65 members
Status. Legal
Last Congress. Third, 25–27 March 1983, in Casablanca
Last Election. 14 September 1984, 2.3 percent, 2 of 306 seats
Auxiliary Organizations. No data
Publications. *Al Bayane* (daily), French and Arabic editions

The Moroccan Communist Party (Parti communiste marocain), founded in 1943 as a branch of the French Communist Party, was banned by the French protectorate in 1952. After three years of open operations in independent Morocco, it was again banned in 1959. Renamed the Party of Progress and Socialism, it was granted legal status in 1974. In the 1976 municipal elections, the party won thirteen seats on the city council of Casablanca. The PPS participated in the Moroccan national elections in the spring of 1977 and won one seat in parliament. In the last municipal elections, held in June 1983, the PPS won only two seats on the Casablanca city council. In Morocco's last parliamentary elections, held in September 1984, the PPS won two seats in parliament and is currently represented by 'Ali Yata and Ismail Alaoui.

Leadership and Party Organization. The PPS Third National Congress, held in March 1983, re-elected 'Ali Yata as secretary general of the party. The congress re-elected 50 of the 57 members of the Central Committee elected by the party's Second National Congress in 1979 and elected fifteen new members. The 1983 congress elected a twelve-member Politburo, all of whom were on the thirteen-member Politburo elected in 1979. At the conclusion of the Third National Congress, the Central Committee reduced the party Secretariat from seven to four members. (For details of the Third Congress, see *YICA*, 1984, pp. 45–46.)

Domestic Party Affairs. The PPS Central Committee held a regular plenum in Casablanca on 19 February. At this plenum Secretary General 'Ali Yata stated that Morocco's social and economic crisis had worsened. Yata expressed serious concern over the government's measures to weaken the state sector of the Moroccan economy through denationalization and the transfer of productive enterprises to private ownership. He stressed the party's determination to continue safeguarding the vital interests of the Moroccan working class. Yata called for the democratization of the country's political situation and made special note of the need to strengthen the PPS's ties with the masses and to enhance the party's impact on the social, economic, and political life of Morocco (Moscow, Tass in English, 19 February; *FBIS*, 22 February).

International Views, Positions, and Activities. At the Central Committee's regular plenum, 'Ali Yata stated that the present international situation was characterized by a "heightened aggressiveness of U.S. imperialism." In Yata's view, the Reagan administration is trying to change the balance of forces that has taken shape in the world and achieve military superiority over the Soviet Union. He cited the continued U.S. deployment of new nuclear missiles in Western Europe and pursuit of the Strategic Defense Initiative. Yata argued that the aggressive nature of imperialism manifests itself most clearly in the Middle East, where Israel and its allies are trying to break the Palestinian resistance movement and impose on the peoples of the region "capitulatory agreements modelled after the Camp David deal" (ibid.).

In August, Yata visited the People's Republic of China, where he met with General Secretary Hu Yaobang. At this meeting, held in Beijing on 10 August, the PPS and the Communist Party of China agreed to resume bilateral ties after an interruption of twenty years (Beijing, *Xinhua* in English, 10 August; *FBIS*, 12 August).

John Damis
Portland State University

Saudi Arabia

Population. 11,152,000
Party. Communist Party of Saudi Arabia (CPSA)
Founded. 1975
Membership. Unknown but believed negligible
Secretary General. Mahdi Habib
Other Spokesmen Noted Since 1979. Abd-al-Rahman Salih, Salim Hamid, Hamad al-Mubarak, Abu Abdallah
Status. Illegal
Last Congress. Second, August 1984
Last Election. N/a
Auxiliary Organizations. Saudi Peace and Solidarity Committee (affiliate of the World Peace Concil and, apparently, of the Afro-Asian Peoples' Solidarity Organization), Saudi Democratic Youth (affiliate of the World Federation of Democratic Youth), Federation of Saudi Arabian Workers (associate member of the World Federation of Trade Unions)
Publications. Apparently exist, but titles unknown (see *YICA*, 1984, p. 55)

Several statements published during the first half of 1985 served to illustrate current CPSA thinking. Both Secretary General Mahdi Habib in the January *World Marxist Review* (*WMR*) and Hamad al-Mubarak in a June issue of *Information Bulletin* (*IB*) call for a broad united front of workers, peasants, the petit bourgeoisie, and part of the "national bourgeoisie" (Habib adds bedouins and "revolutionary intellectuals" as well) to replace the present Saudi regime with a "national democratic" one.

There was a divergence between these two articles, however. Habib applauded both major events of November 1979—the seizure of the main mosque in Mecca and the uprising in the Eastern Province—as together constituting "the biggest and most powerful action ever launched in our country against absolute rule and its patron, U.S. imperialism" (*WMR*, January, p. 40). On the other hand, al-Mubarak characterized only the second action as being "progressive" and stated that the group seizing the mosque was essentially "reactionary," although he gave it credit for having helped spark the Eastern Province revolt (*IB*, 11/85, p. 57). Al-Mubarak went on to cite the oil workers as "the vanguard of the working class in Saudi Arabia" and noted that as largely Eastern Province Shiites they suffer religious discrimination (ibid., pp. 56–57). It is presumably from among this group that the Federation of Saudi Arabian Workers, admitted to the World Federation of Trade Unions in April, is drawn (see *World Trade Union Movement*, No. 6, p. 2). Al-Mubarak also expressed the hope that the Socialist Labor Party, which had been "hard hit" by the government and "not recovered since," would make a comeback since it had been the CPSA's "main ally" (*IB*, 11/85, pp. 57–58).

The CPSA participated in three major regional Arab communist meetings during the year: the second conference of communist and workers' parties of the Eastern Mediterranean, the Near and Middle East, and the Red Sea held in Nicosia in January; the meeting of eight communist and workers' parties of the Arab East held in Damascus in February; and the conference of ten Arab communist parties held at an unspecified location in June. The January conference voiced the major Soviet propaganda themes by denouncing the U.S. "star wars" plans and Pershing II and cruise missile deployment in

Western Europe; it then turned to the Middle East and called for "the withdrawal of imperialist fleets, forces, and bases from the region of the [Persian] Gulf, the Red Sea, and the Arabian Peninsula." The conference also condemned the Saudi government indirectly in citing the Gulf Cooperation Council as serving "imperialist" interests and directly for its "human-rights violations" (*IB*, 7/85, pp. 13–14, 20). The February meeting concerned itself almost solely with the Palestinian and Lebanese situations, particularly criticizing the Arafat-Hussein accords (*IB*, 10/85, pp. 27–31). The document of the June conference condemned the "Baghdad-Riyadh axis" as an element of "Arab reaction" and also chastised the Saudi government for not having established "diplomatic and political relations with the Soviet Union and the socialist community countries" (*IB*, 17/85, pp. 44, 46).

The Lebanese Communist Party's daily *Al Nida* noted on 27 October that the CPSA had one or more representatives stationed in Damascus, opening the possibility that party headquarters may be in that city.

Wallace H. Spaulding
McLean, Virginia

Syria

Population. 10,535,000
Party. Syrian Communist Party (al-Hizb al-Shuyu'i al-Suri; SCP)
Founded. 1924 (as a separate party in 1944)
Membership. 5,000 (estimated)
Secretary General. Khalid Bakhdash (73); deputy secretary general: Yusuf Faysal
Politburo. Khalid Bakhdash, Yusuf Faysal, Ibrahim Bakri, Khalid Hammami, Maurice Salibi, Umar Siba'i, Daniel Ni'mah, Zuhayr Abd al-Sammad, Ramu Farkha (not necessarily complete or up-to-date)
Secretariat. No data
Central Committee. Nabih Rushaydat, Muhammad Khabbad, Issa Khuri, other names unknown
Status. Component of the ruling National Progressive Front (NPF)
Last Congress. Fifth, May 1980
Last Election. 1981, 0.78 percent, no representation
Auxiliary Organizations. No data
Publications. *Nidal al-Sha'b*

The Party of the Lebanese People, founded in 1924, was one of several Marxist or quasi-Marxist groups that appeared in Syria and Lebanon during the early 1920s. It united with two other factions in 1925 to form the Communist Party of Syria and Lebanon (CPSL). The Syrian and Lebanese parties separated in 1944, soon after the two countries were officially declared independent, but maintained close ties with each other. The CPSL and the subsequent Syrian Communist Party (SCP) underwent alternate periods of toleration or legality and of suppression. The SCP often emphasized nationalism and reform and played down revolutionary ideology. It gained a considerable following and a membership that may have reached 10,000 by 1945. The party became quite influential during 1954–1958 but suffered a serious blow with the creation of the United Arab Republic and the subsequent suppression. Seemingly no longer a serious threat and following a foreign policy that often paralleled that of the

Ba'thist regime, it gained a quasi-legal status after 1966 and finally joined the Ba'th-dominated NPF in 1972.

The Syrian communist movement has undergone several schisms in recent years. Riyad al-Turk, who was chosen secretary general of one breakaway group in 1974, has been imprisoned without trial since 1980 and is said to have been "severely tortured" because of his opposition to intervention in Lebanon ("Keeping an Eye on Syrian Torture," interview with Curt Goering of Amnesty International, *Insight*, Washington, 23 September, p. 14). Yusuf Murad, a former member of the SCP Central Committee, formed another group, the Base Organization, in 1980. There is no recent information on this group.

Leadership and Party Organization. Little is known about the dynamics of the SCP's leadership except that Secretary General Khalid Bakhdash has long been the dominant figure. There have been some divisions among the top leadership; for example, Politburo member Daniel Ni'mah (now a representative of the SCP on the Central Command of the NPF) broke with the party temporarily during the early 1970s.

The SCP is organized like other communist parties. The Fifth Congress met in 1980. It has a Central Committee, a Secretariat, and a Politburo. A session of the Politburo was reported in November (*Pravda*, 17 November; *FBIS*, 19 November).

Domestic Party Affairs. In a statement supporting the nomination of President Hafiz al-Asad for another seven-year term (approved, without opposition, in a referendum on 10 February), Bakhdash called on "the country's working people to vote for his candidacy." Although emphasizing Asad's international role, Bakhdash noted that the president "has also played an important part in deepening the process of socioeconomic transformation in the country, strengthening the state sector, implementing cultural changes, and developing education" (*Pravda*, 2 February; *FBIS*, 5 February). However, other statements—though camouflaged by praise for the regime's foreign policies—demonstrated misgivings about the domestic economic situation. Thus, in a speech to the Arab Socialist Renaissance (Ba'th) Party regional (that is, Syrian) congress in January, Bakhdash called for "a more consistent democratic policy" in order to "make for a healthier national economy and help reveal all abuses, corruption and avoidable losses and improve the functioning of the state (public) sector of the economy" (*IB*, May, p. 30). The SCP Politburo was slightly more specific in its statement in November, which "expressed concern at the prevailing situation in the economic and social spheres and the rising cost of living" and spoke of "the need to eliminate negative phenomena which affect the situation of the working class and all strata of working people and which threaten the democratic gains, undermine Syria's national anti-imperialist, anti-Zionist course, and run counter to the interests of social progress" (*Pravda*, 17 November; *FBIS*, 19 November).

Auxiliary and Front Organizations. Little information on auxiliary organizations is available. The SCP probably participates in such groups as the Arab-Soviet Friendship Society, the Syrian Committee for Solidarity with Asian and African Countries, the National Council of Peace Partisans in Syria, and the Syrian-Bulgarian Friendship Society.

The present Syrian regime is officially based on the NPF, which includes the SCP, the Arab Socialist Union, the Socialist Union, and the Arab Socialist Party, in addition to the dominant Ba'th Party, which is non-Marxist. This does not mean that the SCP has any significant influence but rather that it has for the time being more or less abandoned revolutionism in favor of the comforts of a largely formal role in the personalistic dictatorship, which is garbed as a party regime. The quiet role as the regime's partner also conforms to the wishes of the USSR, whose foreign policy Syria tends to parallel in many respects. Exceptions are recent Syrian support for dissident elements in the Palestine Liberation Organization (PLO), Damascus's conflict with Iraq, and its support for Iran in the Iraqi-Iranian war.

The importance of the NPF continued to be proclaimed. President Asad mentioned the need to broaden the experience of the front in his address to the Ba'th congress (*Pravda*, 17 April; *FBIS*, 19 April). Bakhdash told the congress that the long-time Ba'thist-Communist cooperation "has been sealed with the blood of our comrades and yours" and that the unity was stronger "than ever before." Seemingly expressing dissatisfaction, he stated that the front should "not proceed as a top-level alignment. Its organization should operate among the people in urban neighborhoods, the countryside and factories" (*IB*, May, pp. 29–30). In an article entitled "A Historic Call," Bakhdash recalled the "indelible impression" made on him by his participation at age 23 in the Seventh Congress of the

Comintern, after which his "party corrected its tactics" and henceforth followed "a flexible line" in working with the "national bourgeoisie and its parties" when they demonstrated an anticolonialist attitude even "in the slightest way"—an idea that he proclaimed also "to be valid today" (*WMR*, August, pp. 50–51).

Soviet-Syrian cooperation continued on a large scale during the year. Massive quantities of up-to-date Soviet weapons, particularly surface-to-air missiles, have been provided to Syria since 1982. However, many of the Soviet advisers were withdrawn during 1985, and the missiles are no longer operated by Soviet personnel (*Jerusalem Post*, international edition, 12–18 May; *Washington Post*, 29 April). Syria has more recently acquired Soviet-built naval vessels (*NYT*, 16 December). In October, Syrian defense minister Mustafa Talas claimed that Damascus has a guarantee from Moscow to provide nuclear weapons if needed to deter Israel (Abu Dhabi, *al-Ittihad*, 4 October; *FBIS*, 7 October). The two countries have been bound to each other by a treaty of friendship and cooperation since 1980.

Numerous exchanges of visits occurred during the year between delegations of Syrian state and Ba'th Party officials and delegations of state and Communist Party officials from the USSR, Bulgaria, Romania, Czechoslovakia, Poland, North Korea, Hungary, Vietnam, Yugoslavia, and Mongolia. President Asad visited Moscow in June and conducted talks with General Secretary Mikhail Gorbachev. Asad also visited Czechoslovakia in October for talks with Secretary General Gustav Husak, and a treaty of friendship and cooperation was signed. A Soviet delegation headed by Karen Brutents, deputy chief of the CPSU Central Committee International Department met with Asad in Damascus during November. Asad met with a delegation of the Lebanese Communist Party Politburo in July. Abdullah al-Ahmar, deputy secretary general of the Ba'th Party, met with an Italian Communist Party official in July and with an Egyptian Communist party leader in February.

Yet Syrian-Soviet cooperation is hardly the result of the official existence of the "national front" government in Damascus. Its basis is purely pragmatic, not ideological. Informed observers seem to be unanimous in rejecting the idea that Syria is a Soviet satellite (see Richard B. Parker, "Syria Isn't a Servant of the Soviets," *Wall Street Journal*, 16 October).

International Views, Positions, and Activities. The SCP was represented at the second conference of communist and workers' parties of the region of the Eastern Mediterranean, Near and Middle East, and the Red Sea, held in Nicosia in January (*IB*, April, p. 4). It was one of eight parties represented at a meeting of communist and workers' parties of the Arab East, held in Damascus in February (*IB*, May, p. 27), and one of ten at a meeting of communist and workers' parties of Arab countries held in an undisclosed place, apparently in June (*IB*, September, p. 26). A report by Damascus Domestic Service on 4 August concerning the reaction of Arab communist and workers' parties to a proposal by the king of Morocco implied that another meeting had recently been held (*FBIS*, 5 August). Ramu Farkha, a member of the SCP Politburo, signed a cooperation protocol with the People's Democratic Party of Afghanistan in January in Kabul (Kabul Domestic Service, 9 January; *FBIS*, 10 January). Representatives of the SCP and the Egyptian Communist Party issued a joint statement in March in Damascus, where the meeting apparently took place (*Pravda*, 7 March; *FBIS*, 8 March). No other reports of international contacts during the year were available.

SCP leaders' statements alluded to the USSR in laudatory terms. According to Politburo member Daniel Ni'mah, "The USSR since the first days of its existence has been a sincere friend of the Arab peoples, and has invariably supported in every way their struggle for independence and social progress" (Tass, 23 October; *FBIS*, 24 October). Bakhdash wrote that "the Soviet Union and other socialist community countries constitute the main force which prevents U.S. imperialism and NATO from realizing their schemes by stepping up the danger of war" and expressed "support" for the "peace initiative of the USSR" (*WMR*, August, p. 51). President Asad was praised for Syria's "increasingly active role in the Arab national liberation movement" and for the "strengthening of friendly Soviet-Syrian relations" (*Pravda*, 2 February; *FBIS*, 5 February). Ni'mah, referring to the kidnapping of Soviet diplomats in Beirut, expressed his indignation "that such a dirty anti-Soviet provocation could take place on the soil of an Arab state" (Tass, 23 October; *FBIS*, 24 October).

Bakhdash called for "the extrication of our economic relations from the meshes of the international capitalist market" and "better economic relations with socialist countries" (*IB*, May, p. 30). Other than condemnation of "recent . . . armed clashes in Palestinian camps in Beirut" (*IB*, September, p. 27) in joint statements with other communist parties, this was the only available example of criticism, however tacit, of Syrian foreign policy. (For other joint statements see the profile on Egypt in this edition of *YICA*.)

Numerous statements dealt with current developments in the region. The SCP and the Egyptian Communist Party joined in describing the accord between King Hussein and Yasir Arafat as "the prelude for concluding a separate deal between Israel and Jordan with the aim of relinquishing the Palestinian people's right to establish their independent national state" (Damascus, SANA, 2 March; *FBIS*, 5 March). Israel's "barbarous raid" on Tunis, "the hijacking of an Egyptian civilian plane by the U.S. military, the campaign of repression and deportation of Arabs from the West Bank . . . and Washington's new conspiracies against Libya" were cited as U.S. state terrorism (Tass, 14 November; *FBIS*, 15 November).

Glenn E. Perry
Indiana State University

Tunisia

Population. 7,352,000
Party. Tunisian Communist Party (Parti communiste tuisien; PCT)
Founded. 1934
Membership. 2,000 (estimated); PCT claims 4,000
Secretary General. Muhammad Harmel
Politburo. 6 members: Muhammad Harmel, Muhammad al-Nafa'a, 'Abd al-Hamid ben Mustafa, Hisham Sakik, 'Abd al-Majid Tariki, Salah al-Hajji
Secretariat. 3 members: Muhammad Harmel, Muhammad al-Nafa'a, 'Abd al-Hamid ben Mustafa
Central Committee. 12 members
Status. Legal
Last Congress. Eighth, February 1981, in Tunis
Last Election. 1981, 0.78 percent (official figure), 15-20 percent (PCT claims), 5 percent (estimated), no representation
Auxiliary Organizations. Tunisian Communist Youth
Publications. *Al-Tariq al Jadid* (The new path), weekly

The Tunisian Communist Party was founded in 1920 as a branch of the French Communist Party and became independent in 1934. The banning of the PCT in 1963 formalized a single-party state under the direction of the Destourian Socialist Party (PSD). In July 1981, the government lifted the ban on the PCT, ending the party's eighteen-year period of clandestine existence. The PCT was the only opposition party allowed to operate openly from July 1981 to November 1983, when President Habib Bourguiba legalized two other opposition parties (see *YICA*, 1984, p. 70).

Leadership and Party Organization. The PCT's Eighth Congress (February 1981) re-elected Muhammad Harmel as secretary general and elected a three-member Secretariat, a six-member Politburo, and a twelve-member Central Committee. Politburo and Secretariat member Muhammad al-Nafa'a contributed an article to the April issue of the *World Marxist Review*.

Domestic Party Affairs. During 1985, the PCT made a concerted effort to meet and coordinate with other Tunisian opposition groups. These other groups included not only the Movement of Democratic Socialists—the major opposition force in Tunisia—but also the less powerful Movement of Popular Unity and the Movement of the Islamic Tendency. The PCT stressed that it was the first group to militate for the broadest possible alliance of all social and political forces within the country. The party's stated objective in backing a unified opposition was to obtain a large consensus among its various elements and to end the passivity of the opposition and its marginal position in the Tunisian political system (Tunis, *Réalités*, 22 February).

The Tunisian opposition shared a sense of deep disillusion about the government's ability to deal successfully with an assortment of growing social and economic problems. Wages in Tunisia have been frozen for two years to make up for declining oil and phosphate income. Barely half of the country's young people who enter the job market each year are able to find jobs (*NYT*, 27 September). The sense of disillusion led the PCT to join the other opposition parties in boycotting the municipal elections in April.

On specific issues the PCT called on the government to establish effective control over prices, increase the population's purchasing power, and run a campaign against corruption. In addition, the party called for an end to all impingements on the principle of pluralism; for guarantees of the independence and unity of the trade union movement and strict compliance with the agreement concluded between the labor movement and the government; and for the lifting of all restrictions on civil and personal freedoms (*WMR*, April). When the government repressed the major Tunisian labor union—the General Union of Tunisian Workers (UGTT)—during the fall, the party's weekly Arabic newspaper, *Al-Tariq al-Jadid*, came out repeatedly in support of the UGTT. The PCT accused the government of trying to restore the control of the ruling PSD over the labor movement with the objective of setting up new labor unions that would carry out decisions of capitalists and suggestions of the World Bank (*Al-Tariq al-Jadid*, 30 November and 7 December). This support of the UGTT led to the seizure of three issues of the party newspaper in November–December.

International Views, Positions, and Activities. In a declaration issued on 30 May, the PCT called for the unity of the Palestinian movement. The party condemned the attacks in Lebanon by Amal militia, backed by Syria, against Palestinian resistance forces (*Réalités*, 14 June). In an article in the 30 March edition of *Al-Tariq al-Jadid*, the party sharply criticized the governments of Saudi Arabia and the Persian Gulf sheikdoms for proposing a private university in Tunisia; such a university would benefit only the rich and would propagate conservative thinking in Tunisia. As a result of this article, the government suspended the party newspaper for three months.

Along with other opposition groups, the PCT backed the government in its dispute with neighboring Libya over the sudden expulsion of more than 30,000 Tunisians in September. The party condemned the Libyan action as a revengeful measure (*Al-Tariq al-Jadid*, 14 September). The PCT also criticized Tunisia's military cooperation with the United States. The party complained about the silence that surrounded the official visit of the Tunisian minister of defense to the United States in November for a meeting with Secretary of Defense Caspar Weinberger (ibid., 23 November).

In September, Muhammad Harmel made a short visit to Bulgaria at the invitation of the Bulgarian Communist Party. Harmel was received by President Bevkov of Bulgaria, who expressed his solidarity with the PCT (ibid., 14 September).

John Damis
Portland State University

Yemen: People's Democratic Republic of Yemen

Population. 2,211,000
Party. Yemen Socialist Party (YSP)
Founded. 1978
Membership. 26,000 (claimed)
Secretary General. 'Ali Nasir Muhammad al-Hasani
Politburo. 13 members
Central Committee. 47 members
Status. Ruling party
Last Congress. Third, 11–16 October 1985
Last Election. 1978; all candidates YSP approved

Since independence, the People's Democratic Republic of Yemen (PDRY, also known as South Yemen or, as preferred by its government, Democratic Yemen) has pursued a path of "scientific socialism" in domestic policy and close alignment with the Soviet Union and other Eastern bloc countries in foreign affairs. The National Liberation Front (NLF), which had waged the guerrilla campaign against the British, took charge at independence. Its successor organization, the YSP, remains the only legal party in the state. The relatively moderate wing of the NLF suffered a major setback at the hands of the radicals in 1969 and its leaders were imprisoned or forced into exile by 1971.

In 1978, the ultraradical wing of the YSP under the leadership of hardline ideologue 'Abd al-Fattah Isma'il seized control after a bloody battle. But bitterness over this power struggle, Isma'il's extreme dependence on the Soviet bloc, his willingness to send PDRY troops to fight in the Horn of Africa, his strong-arm style of governing, and dire economic straits all combined to Isma'il's downfall, and he was forced into exile in Moscow two years later. His successor, 'Ali Nasir Muhammad al-Hasani, assumed all three key positions: president of the state, head of the party, and prime minister of the government. He resigned the last post in 1985.

The constitution (adopted in 1970) specifies that the Supreme People's Council (SPC) is the highest authority. Elections to the council were first held in 1978, and members are elected for five-year terms. The SPC elects the president and eleven to seventeen members of the Presidium, to which is delegated the SPC's authority when the latter is not in session. The SPC also elects the prime minister, his cabinet, and the members of the Supreme Court.

As in other socialist states, real power rests within the party. During the 1970s, several efforts were made to transform the ruling NLF into a true Marxist organization, and several other small legal parties were incorporated into it. Among these was a local communist party, the Popular Democratic Union, founded in Aden in 1961 but never a serious challenger to the NLF for power. The first general congress of the YSP was held in October 1972, after the moderates were defeated, and another congress was held in October 1980, following the ouster of the ultraradical faction. At that time, a new Central

Committee (the permanent authority of the party when the party congress is not in session) was elected, and the committee proceeded to select a new Politburo of five members that clearly reflected the predominant position of Muhammad al-Hasani.

In May 1984, Muhammad al-Hasani's position was challenged during meetings of the SPC Presidium and the YSP Central Committee. He was strongly criticized for ideological deviation, and the return of his predecessor, 'Abd al-Fattah Isma'il, was demanded. In addition, a prominent supporter of Isma'il was named to the cabinet while four of his followers were added to the Politburo. Further changes occurred in February, when the Central Committee elevated a candidate member of the Politburo to full member status and added a new member, which swelled the Politburo's ranks to eleven. At the same time, Isma'il, who had apparently returned to Aden from Moscow in late 1984, was given a minor party post. Albeit disturbing, these developments by themselves did not decisively indicate that Muhammad al-Hasani's position had eroded.

The convening of the Third Congress of the YSP in October marked significant changes in party politics. Although Muhammad al-Hasani retained his title of secretary general, the Politburo was expanded to thirteen full members and one candidate; Isma'il was one of the two new members. Other notable Politburo members included former defense minister and Isma'il supporter 'Ali 'Antar, current defense minister Salih Muslih Qasim (also regarded as a prominent Muhammad al-Hasani opponent), 'Ali and Abu Bakr Ba Dhib (leaders of the Popular Democratic Union), Prime Minister Haydar al-'Attas, and Foreign Minister 'Abd al-'Aziz al-Dali'. These changes appear to have weakened Muhammad al-Hasani's power considerably.

In international affairs, relations with the Yemen Arab Republic (YAR, also known as North Yemen) remained good. The various unity committees made up of representatives from both Yemens continued their work throughout the year. Real prospects for unity in the near future remain negligible, however. The rapprochement with Oman, with whom the PDRY came close to engaging in hostilities in the 1970s, proceeded apace and the two countries agreed to exchange ambassadors in the near future.

Since independence, the PDRY's closest ties have been with the Eastern bloc. Although the 1979 treaty of friendship with the Soviet Union was signed by the previous president, ties to the USSR remain close. Muhammad al-Hasani attended the funeral of Konstantin Chernenko in Moscow in March and presented his condolences to Mikhail Gorbachev. Several Yemeni delegations visited Moscow and Aden played host to visits by a number of Soviet officials. Karen Brutents, the deputy chief of the CPSU Central Committee's International Department, visited Aden in April, where he gave a lecture at the Ba Dhib Institute for Scientific Socialism and discussed aspects for cooperation between this institute and the Institute for Social Sciences of the CPSU Central Committee. Visits were exchanged with other East European countries as well as the People's Republic of China, which hosted the PDRY foreign minister in March, whose talks with the Chinese foreign minister were said to produce identical or similar views on major international issues.

The PDRY has maintained close relations with radical movements in the Middle East. Its leaders sought to mediate in the Palestine Liberation Organization split between Yasir Arafat's Fatah and several anti-Arafat Marxist factions, with which the NLF has had historically close ties. George Habash, founder of the Popular Front for the Liberation of Palestine (PFLP), was welcomed publicly by President Muhammad al-Hasani at the opening session of the YSP congress in October. Delegations from the Lebanese and Portuguese communist parties also visited Aden in 1985.

The PDRY armed forces have been equipped almost entirely by the Soviet Union. By 1985 Aden had received over $2 billion in Soviet military deliveries, and about 1,000 Soviet, East European, and Cuban military advisers were estimated to be in the PDRY. The USSR makes regular use of Aden's port as an anchorage for its naval vessels, for delivery of military and economic aid, and for the shipment of cargo to Ethiopia and other parts of Africa. Aden International Airport and al-Anad airfield are used for naval reconnaissance operations in the Arabian Sea, and the Soviets operate a radio transmitting and receiving system in the country.

The Soviet Union is also the PDRY's largest creditor; Aden's debt to Moscow amounts to 80 percent of its GNP. More than 1,000 Soviet experts are involved in PDRY development projects, as are experts from Eastern Europe and Cuba. Recent meetings of the joint Soviet-PDRY economic committee have resulted in a new loan of 384 million rubles (January) and additional technical assistance for dam building and land reclamation (May). In addition, the PDRY minister of industry signed a new agreement for economic and technical cooperation on his visit to Moscow in January; an economic protocol was signed in Aden in May; and an agricultural agreement was reached in July. The joint Czechoslovak-PDRY economic committee was also active during the year and the Czechoslovak foreign minister went to Aden in April.

J. E. Peterson
Washington, D.C.

WESTERN EUROPE

Introduction

The euphoric welcome with which Western Europe's communist parties greeted the electoral victory resulting from the coalition between the French Socialists and the French Communists in 1981 prompted the *World Marxist Review* to conclude one year later that "the ideas advanced by Europe's communists meet the innermost interests of people" (November, 1983).

In 1983 and 1984, however, the cohesion of Western Europe's communist parties began to deteriorate and, while they fared moderately well at the polls, debates within many of the parties emerged that focused primarily on their future direction. In 1984 the French Communist Party resigned from the coalition government—and in so doing gave up four cabinet posts—to become an opponent of François Mitterand's Socialist Party. In Italy in 1984, party leadership changed hands for the first time since 1972 following the death of Enrico Berlinguer, and his successor has been unable to design a clear program for the future. In Spain intense party factionalism produced a split in 1984, which at the end of 1985 threatened to result in three separate communist parties. Indeed, party rifts and divisions of varying degree have increased each year since the remarkable coalition victory of the communist and socialist parties of France in 1981.

The reasons for these developments emerged more clearly in 1985 than at any time in the past, and they were succinctly expressed by the two surviving members of the Unity Convention of July 1920 that brought the Communist Party of Great Britain into existence. Writing in 1985 about the seriousness of the rift within the British Communist Party, the authors contend it is not "accidental that one of the successes of the Eurocommunists has been the attempted introduction of anti-Sovietism into the peace movement" and conclude that "Eurocommunism today is the revisionism of yesterday." The two authors, who support the policies of the Soviet Communist Party (CPSU) and reject Eurocommunism, also offer a solution: "The situation is crying out for the determined leadership which only a Communist Party united on the principles of Marxism-Leninism can give" (Andrew Rothstein and Robin Page Arnot, "The British Communist Party and Eurocommunism," *Political Affairs*, London, October, pp. 23–28).

What is remarkable about this analysis is that it could apply to almost half of Western Europe's communist parties. Thus, what was considered by many to be a challenge to the West in France in 1981, has become in a manner of speaking—as regards the allegiances of the communist parties of Western Europe to themselves or to the CPSU—a "challenge to the East" (see Kevin Devlin, "The Decline of Eurocommunism: Downhill from the Summit," RAD Background Report/60, 13 April 1984). Rife with divisiveness and struggles for control, the communist parties enjoyed, in 1984, "little prospect of gaining the popular credibility and trust that they need to become more than minority forces" (ibid.). How this challenge would be resolved remained unclear throughout 1985. By the end of the year none of Western Europe's communist parties had recorded electoral success. The decline had not only continued, it was dramatic. In all seven national elections held in Western Europe during the year, the communist parties received fewer votes in each election than in the previous one; in Belgium the Communist Party lost its parliamentary representation entirely.

Common to all of the parties, with perhaps the exception of Italy, was an absence of programs designed to offer solutions to such problems as inflation, unemployment, lagging industrial productivity, and the costs of social welfare programs. The absence of viable solutions has not increased confidence in Communist Party programs but has produced frustration and contributed to the internal party strife that intensified during 1985.

It is ironic that this process has been underway since the French Communist Party entered the French government in 1981. Initially, similar success was forecast for other communist parties in Western Europe, but it failed to materialize. By 1983 it had become clear that the "class struggle" was a question of what constitutes sound economic policy as opposed to the promises of a better life through ideology. At the end of 1984, solutions to Europe's economic problems did not lend themselves to self-serving rhetoric consisting of communist party assertions that the future of Western Europe would depend on "the cohesion of the working class, unity of action of the political parties representing it, and joint efforts to bar reaction, defend democratic achievements and open new prospects for social progress" (*WMR*, November 1982).

By the end of 1985 further erosion and open party divisions had produced a malaise among Western Europe's communist parties, which, if not irreversible, was of a serious nature. The dilemma in which they found themselves was especially well described by Aleksandr Zinoviev, who had been expelled from the USSR in 1978:

> If the Western Communists want to survive and to continue to have any influence over the masses, they are doomed to repudiate Marxist ideology. Their future, if they are to have a future, is in any case bleak indeed. They must either follow the dictates of Moscow or break up. There is no other choice: they must be either pro-Soviet or anti-Soviet. (Kevin Devlin, "Zinoviev Sees Bleak Future for Western Communist Parties," RAD Background Report/61, 2 July)

Zinoviev concluded that to survive as parties advocating viable alternatives within a democratic political structure they must "reject communist ideology" because it "no longer reflects the interests of the working class." He continued that "the defenders of communism in the West are no longer the workers but the intellectuals and state officials." He cited specific developments in France since Mitterand's election in 1981, concluding that the Communist Party there, as elsewhere in Western Europe, confronted a paradox: "They must change their ideology and their slogans; otherwise they have no future. In France, for example, it is the Socialist Party that has realized communist programs in practice" (ibid.).

The conflict to which Zinoviev referred was well illustrated by two different cases during the year. The first was the comments by General Secretary Alessandro Natta of the Italian Communist Party at the special plenum of the CPSU Central Committee held in March that dealt with foreign relations. Natta concluded that the world was "going through difficult times," which was "the fault of the imperialist circles... That is why it is so important that the Soviet Union has countered the aggressive plans of imperialism with its peaceful foreign policy." The general secretary of the Portuguese Communist Party reiterated Natta's views and stressed that the USSR "has once again reaffirmed that its foreign policy course is directed toward relaxation of international tension and against the arms race unleashed by the United States, and toward maintaining and consolidating peace on earth... In their indefatigable struggle for peace and for a better future for mankind, the Soviet people may always count on the support of the Communists and all the working people of Portugal" (*FBIS*, USSR International Affairs, 29 March). It is precisely this latter kind of propaganda that places the credibility of Western Europe's communist parties in question. The parroting of Soviet foreign policy declarations does not generate confidence in an independence and objectivity of judgment that responsible political parties must demonstrate to potential voters.

The second case illustrating Zineviev's point took place three months later, when eighteen of Western Europe's communist parties met in June in Paris "to permit the free interchange of opinions and ideas without the desire or claim that differences would be hidden" (*L'Humanité*, 22 June). In its editorial about the meeting, the French Communist Party journal *L'Humanité* described the views expressed as the reflection of "a concept of bilateral and multilateral relations based on mutual respect, independence, strict equality in rights, noninterference, and the recognition of the right to differ, even to go separate ways" (ibid.). The editorial went one step further, however, and asserted that "the meeting was possible because there is no longer an international, nor European center of leadership. This is true only of the Communists.

All other parties, of both the right and the left, are tied to supranational interests and are disturbed by our diversity which sticks to realities" (ibid.).

While these latter assertions were patently absurd, they were also representative of the seriousness of the dilemma. If Western Europe's major communist parties return to becoming closely allied with the USSR and the CPSU, their motives and methods will therefore be suspect. The lack of respect their counterparts in Eastern Europe and the Soviet Union show for democratic principles and procedures will affect their credibility and they will stand little chance of gaining power through the democratic electoral process.

If, however, moderate elements within the parties assume control and support the Eurocommunist principles of independence for individual parties, commitment to a democratic road to socialism, rejection of rigid Marxist and Leninist principles, opposition to Marxist dogma that asserts a single "correct" view about the nature of society, and socialism in nationalist colors, their parties may eventually lose their communist character to varying degrees, and they may find themselves competing against Western Europe's much stronger socialist and labor parties, such as those in France, Germany, Italy, Great Britain, the Netherlands, and Scandinavia. At the same time their motives would also remain suspect, for they "were formed and developed under the influence of the Soviet model that they now explicitly reject" (see Kevin Devlin, "Eurocommunism Revisited: A View From Down Under," RAD Background Report/69, 30 April 1984).

The significance of this situation in practice is analyzed well by Bernie Taft of the Australian Communist Party in an article on Eurocommunism published in the *Australian Left Review* in 1983:

> There remains in the public mind a degree of suspicion about the genuine nature of democratic commitment given by [Euro]communist parties, about the character of their relationship to the Soviet Union, and about the ultimate certainty (sic) of their independence.
>
> There is a fear, based on experience in (sic) the history of the communist movement, that, once in power, they may try to make sure that they remain in power, despite the commitments to pluralism that they may have now. (ibid.)

Whichever road Western Europe's communist parties take in 1986 will be dismal and difficult. The views and positions taken on domestic and foreign policy issues during 1985 did not produce the electoral success the parties sought, and there is no reason to assume that the struggle between those supporting the CPSU and those supporting independent paths to socialism will be resolved in 1986. Only the Italian Communist Party appears to be conducting an orchestrated effort to appeal to the voters. In so doing, it is employing a new term, "Euroleft," in an effort to erase the doubts and eliminate the dilemmas associated with "Eurocommunism." It is in this regard that the party's parliamentary leader, Giorgio Napolitano, emphasizes that "the communist parties can only go forward in the context of a European left. . . For many years I have been convinced that the old differences between the communist and the socialist movements are not sustainable" (James M. Markham, "Sharp Decline By Communists in West Europe," *NYT*, 3 February 1986).

If Napolitano's conclusion is correct, he is nevertheless describing a process that will require years to develop. In the meantime Jean Ellenstein of the French Communist Party has concluded that the decline of West European communist parties is "an irreversible regression. . . this is a fatal cancer" (ibid.).

It will not be possible to determine whether Napolitano or Ellenstein are correct in 1986; the horizon is too short. However, the conclusions of both raise a question the communist parties have thus far failed to address; namely, where are the struggling classes they seek to represent? Annie Kriegel, a former member of the French Communist Party, states the case explicitly: "The Communists can do nothing if the working class disappears. . . The Communists lose their social base; they are left hanging in the air" (ibid.). Yet Napolitano recognizes that the communist parties are not necessarily condemned to disappearance: "I think that to avoid the danger of decline it is necessary to think in terms of the left and less in terms of communist politics. . . We cannot be obsessed with 'the defense of our own identity.' We cannot just be a party of preachers and oppositionists" (ibid.).

In the short term the decision to adopt this course carries with it great risk. But in the long term, in the view of Luciano Pellicano, editor of the Italian Socialist Party's theortetical journal, *Mondoperaio*, "At the end of this century or the beginning of the next we will have a union of the left" (ibid.). The activities of Western Europe's communist parties for the remainder of the decade will have a major impact on the course they will be following at the end of this century. Prudent observers should bear in mind that whatever course these parties follow, wisdom acquired from historical experience dictates careful analysis of their activities.

In 1985, 13 of Western Europe's 23 parties were represented in their respective parliaments: those of Cyprus, Finland, France, Greece, Iceland, Italy, Luxembourg, the Netherlands, Portugal, San Marino, Spain, Sweden, and Switzerland. Party members held no cabinet posts for the second consecutive year. Seven national elections were held during the year in Western Europe (one election was held in 1984 and ten in 1983). They took place in Belgium, Cyprus, Greece, Norway, Portugal, Sweden, and West Berlin. The Italian Communist Party remains the strongest in Western Europe, holding slightly less than one-third of the parliamentary seats (31.43 percent; 198 of 630 seats). Of the remaining parties with legislative representation, Cyprus had the highest percentage of seats (26.8 percent), followed by San Marino (25 percent), Iceland (16.66 percent), Portugal (15.2 percent), Finland (13.5 percent), France (8.96 percent), and Sweden (5.44 percent). The remaining parties held between 4.33 percent (Greece) and 0.5 percent (Switzerland) of their respective parliamentary seats.

The views and positions of the French Communist Party (PCF) provide an excellent illustration of the problems confronting the communist parties of Western Europe. Following the election of François Mitterand in 1981 as the result of a coalition between the French Socialist (PS) and Communist parties, the PCF was given four ministerial posts in the cabinet: civil service and administrative reform, health, transport, and vocational training. These appointments were made on the basis of an agreement between both parties that required the PCF to pledge "entire solidarity" at all levels of government. In 1981 the CPSU endorsed this development as "an historic event for France and all Western Europe" (London, *Guardian*, 5 July 1981). The results of the French election meant, according to French political analyst Jean François Revel, that "Marxism had won" and "government by ideology" had returned to France (*Public Opinion*, August/September 1981).

The coalition of Communists and Socialists that had produced electoral victory, however, did not develop harmoniously once it assumed the responsibility for governing France. The domestic policies of Mitterand's government were soon characterized by devaluation of the French franc, inflation, nationalization of major French banks and industry, and changes in tax policy aimed at a small minority, based on a rationale that was punitive by design and has proved to be economically unsound. In addition, the growth of Soviet military power and its conduct of its foreign affairs have consistently elicited criticism from the French government.

Since 1981 the PCF, as a participant in the Mitterand government, has faced an increasingly frustrating political dilemma: that of remaining a loyal member of the PS-led government while maintaining sufficient independence from that party to preserve its own position as a separate and viable force on the left. During 1983 the PCF shared massive electoral losses with the PS in French municipal elections. At the same time, however, the party continued to maintain its own views on a variety of controversial issues, even if these positions conflicted with official government policy.

The PCF was reluctant to return to a self-imposed political isolation that would leave the PS as the only large governing force on the left and perhaps erode even further the PCF's narrowing base of popularity. At the same time, the PCF did not wish to be held accountable in the eyes of its constituents for the failure of the PS/PCF coalition to fulfill the promises made in 1981. Thus, when President Mitterand dismissed the Mauroy cabinet and appointed Laurent Fabius as the new prime minister in July 1984, the PCF took this opportunity to withdraw from the cabinet, enter the opposition, and in effect terminate the "Union of the Left."

During the remainder of 1984 and throughout 1985 the effects of socialist economic policies produced a major revision of Mitterand's approach to solving the problems of the French economy and resulted in a policy of economic austerity with an emphasis on private enterprise and competition. The goal, according to Prime Minister Fabius, "is to forge a large party—some call it Social Democratic—able to obtain 30 percent to 40 percent of the vote" (Nicholas Bray, "French Socialists, Losing Support, Edging Away From Marxist Roots," *WSJ*, 13 December).

These developments firmly placed the PCF in the role of severe critic of the PS and generated considerable frustration within the party. The PCF's withdrawal from the coalition unleashed a long-building and lively internal debate that broached questions of major importance—for example, Georges Marchais's ability to direct the party—as well as fundamental debate concerning the PCF's image, direction, and capacity for self-criticism. Party dissidents, or "renovators," challenged the party leaders to explain the rejection of "Unity of the Left" and to permit an open debate on the party's recent experience and future. Reform-minded critics defined the salient issues of debate as: the PCF's relationship with the PS before, during, and after its participation in the Mauroy cabinets; the leadership's responsibility for the party's demoralizing slump from over 20 percent to just over 11 percent of the vote in a period of three years (1981 to 1984); the party's relationship with the Soviet Union and other communist countries; and reform of the rule of democratic centralism.

At the party's Twenty-fifth Congress, held in February, the Union of the Left was formally abandoned, marking a return to the traditional identity of the party. At the congress Marchais and his supporters in the PCF's Politburo moved to justify their retreat from leftist unity and to isolate dissent in the party. Although party control rests firmly with Marchais, the party itself does not face an encouraging future. In cantonal elections held in March the PCF was unable to garner more than 12.6 percent of the vote. Indeed, results of an opinion poll taken during the year indicated that only 15 percent looked to the PCF as a party "of the future," while a 60-percent majority considered it a party "of the past" (News From France, 15 February).

The Spanish Communist Party (PCE) has enjoyed legal status since 1977 and, until 1981, was the leading proponent of Eurocommunism under the leadership of Santiago Carrillo. His successor in 1982 was Gerardo Iglesias (then 37 years old), who continues to serve as secretary general of the party. During 1983 and 1984 Iglesias devoted a major effort to heal internal party disputes and to establish the PCE as a major actor in Spanish politics. These efforts continued throughout 1985 but did not meet with success.

The Spanish communist movement is the most deeply divided in Europe; it is split into two rival parties espousing markedly different ideological positions. The cause of the dispute is the same as that producing party divisions elsewhere among Western Europe's communist parties; namely, a struggle between those members favoring close association with Moscow and those seeking to follow an independent, or Eurocommunist, path. The seriousness of this division was exacerbated by the negligible influence the party continues to exert on the domestic and foreign policies of Spain. The PCE retains its representation in the Spanish Cortes (parliament) with only 4 seats, following the loss of 19 of its 23 seats in the 1982 national election.

Party factionalism was intensified by Carrillo's public attacks on the ability of Iglesias to lead the party and included boycotting PCE conferences and the organization of a platform for a "party within the party." As a consequence, the PCE Central Committee expelled Carrillo and eighteen of his supporters from the Central and Executive committees in April and relieved the former party leader of his responsibility as PCE spokesman in the Cortes.

A major issue of contention was Iglesias's proposed strategy of unity of action, or "convergence," designed to produce a coalition of the PCE and other leftist groups to oppose the governing Spanish Socialist Workers' Party (PSOE). Carrillo's position emphasized, on the contrary, "revolutionary orthodoxy" and confrontation with the government. Iglesias's response was an admonishment directed to his predecessor that the PCE was not to serve as a "boxing ring" or as "personal property," and he justified the disciplinary measures taken against Carrillo as necessary to preserve party unity. This difference of opinion concerning proper party strategy produced a new division in October when the Ministry of the interior announced the formal registration of the Marxist-Revolutionary Spanish Communist Party (PCD-MR). By the end of the year Carrillo had convened a "national assembly" to elect a board (it was not described as a central committee) whose ostensible purpose was to generate support for "communist unity." The creation of this new group, while not yet resulting in an active party at the year's end, nonetheless added a third communist party to the PCE and the PC (which had been formed in January 1984 by pro-Soviet dissidents who had resigned or been expelled from the PCE; the PC is led by Ignacio Gallego, a member of the PCE Executive Committee for nearly thirty years).

The consequences of this dissension were clearly evident in several areas. Party membership, which was estimated at 240,000 in 1977, was claimed to be 86,000 in 1985. In addition, the party was unsuccessful in generating a broad electoral alliance, the rationale for which had been condemned by Carrillo. Throughout the year the PCE criticized the Spanish government's domestic policies as "antisocial" and "essentially right-wing." Its foreign policy positions also reflected critical views, which focused on opposition to Spain's membership in NATO and the Strategic Defense Initiative and on support of the peace movement.

At the end of the year the PCE remained deeply divided. It had not been able to find solutions for its internal difficulties, and in turn was unable to establish the unity of action sought by Iglesias. At the beginning of 1986, during which national elections are to be held, it appeared unlikely that the party would be able to heal its rifts successfully. Thus, the party is likely to remain divided and may be expected to exert little significant impact on Spanish political life for the foreseeable future.

Since 1961 Alvaro Cunhal has led the Portuguese Communist Party (PCP). Pro-Soviet in orientation, the party claims a membership in excess of 200,000 and at the end of 1984 held 44 of 250 parliamentary seats. The past year, however, did not see the party gather increasing electoral support. During the first half of 1985 the PCP pressed President Antonio Eanes to call new elections, with the expressed hope of replacing the cabinet with a "democratic government of national salvation" that would include members of the PCP. The national elections of October resulted in a loss of eight seats for the PCP. The government, headed by Prime Minister Mario Soares of the Socialist Party, was defeated and lost almost half of its seats in the National Assembly. The newly elected prime minister, Anibal Silva of the Social Democratic Party (PSD), formed a cabinet entirely of his own party, which had won only a third of the parliamentary seats. PCP chairman Cunhal concluded that the weak position of the new government served to strengthen support for the proposal of the PCP that endorsed "democratic government of national salvation." Cunhal therefore concluded that Angelo Veloso, a member of the PCP Central Committee, would pose a serious challenge to Mario Soares's candidacy for the presidency in elections scheduled for early 1986. The hopes of the PCP notwithstanding, it appeared at the end of the year that the party could not look forward to exercising a decisive role in Portuguese political life in 1986.

In Cyprus, Greece, Malta, San Marino, and Turkey the weakness of the respective communist parties did not result in significant activity affecting the conduct of domestic or foreign policy. In San Marino the party (CPSM) occupies 15 of 60 parliamentary seats and participates in that country's coalition government. In Malta the Communist Party (CPM) was founded in 1969. The party exerts little impact on political life and did not participate in the most recent national election (1981). During the year, however, it did announce its intention to enter the next elections, scheduled tentatively for early 1987. As in past years the CPM continued to maintain extensive party contacts with representatives from communist parties throughout Europe, which may reflect a special interest in Maltese affairs within the international communist movement. The Communist Party in Turkey remains proscribed, and as such is the only communist party in this position in Western Europe.

The Communist Party of Cyprus (AKEL) continues to draw its primary support from the Greek Cypriot majority, which comprises approximately 80 percent of the island's estimated population of 670,000. The party claims a membership of approximately 14,000, and until the 1985 parliamentary elections it was the strongest political party, although it is proscribed in the so-called Turkish Republic of Northern Cyprus. National elections held in December saw the AKEL receive 27.4 percent of the vote and slip to the position of the third strongest party on Cyprus. These election results reflected voter concern with a dispute that lasted most of the year. At the end of 1984 Cyprus president Spyros Kyprianou terminated the alliance of his party (Democratic Party; DIKO) with the AKEL. During the past year, therefore, AKEL was a strident critic of Kyprianou and advocated presidential elections. This pressure resulted in the dissolution of the House of Representatives in October and the ensuing parliamentary elections. As a result of the weakness shown by the AKEL, the party was not in a strong position at the end of the year and this situation will certainly be a major topic for discussion at the party's next congress scheduled for 1986.

In Greece the party remains split into pro-Soviet and Eurocommunist factions. The pro-Soviet faction (KKE) is represented in the Greek parliament with 13 of 300 seats (1985); KKE membership is estimated at 42,000. During the military government in Greece (1967–1974) the KKE split into two factions. The Eurocommunist faction, known as KKE-Interior, retains little of its Marxist-Leninist background and has adopted an increasingly independent and moderate position. As a consequence of national elections held in June, the KKE-Interior is represented in the Greek parliament with one seat; it received 1.8 percent of the vote.

The domestic and foreign policy positions endorsed by the KKE have generally paralleled those of the governing Panhellenic Socialist Movement (PASOK), lead by Andreas Papandreou. During the 1985 electoral campaign, however, the KKE sought to garner enough votes to deprive the PASOK of a majority. This effort was not successful. The KKE received 9.9 percent of the vote and retained the same number of parliamentary seats it had won in 1981, and the PASOK received 45.8 percent of the vote and 161 seats, ten more than the 151 required for a majority. Thus, the remainder of the year the KKE remained critical of Papandreou's leadership, but did join the PASOK in electing Khristos Sartzetakis as president of the republic, replacing the more moderate K. Karamanlis. At the end of the year it seemed clear that the KKE would continue to remain critical of the government's domestic and foreign policies but would stop short of participating in an effort to defeat the PASOK at the polls. It is, however, certain to concentrate on gaining support in the municipal elections scheduled for October 1986.

The Communist Party of Great Britain (CPGB) has been plagued with declining support for many years, and its membership is at its lowest point since World War II. In Great Britain's last general election held in June 1983, the party's 35 candidates polled only 11,598 votes. It has not been represented in the House of Commons since 1950; Lord Milford is the sole CPGB member of the House of Lords. The conflict between the Eurocommunist leadership and the pro-Stalinist faction intensified in 1985 and resulted in a special party congress held in May. The congress drew public attention to the struggle for control of the party newspaper, *Morning Star*. The result was the expulsion of eighteen pro-Stalinists from the party's Executive Committee, but the newspaper remains in control of the pro-Stalinist faction who assert that "Eurocommunism today is the revisionism of yesterday" (*Political Affairs*, October).

The CPGB continues to hold a strong position in the trade-union movement, however, and two members continue to be represented on the General Council of the Trades Union Congress (TUC): Mick McGahey of the National Union of Mineworkers and Ken Gill of the Technical and Supervisory Section of the Amalgamated Union of Engineering Workers. Gill became chairman of the TUC in September. The new year is likely to see renewed argument between the party's two factions but is unlikely to produce a split within the party. In Ireland the Communist Party (CPI) exerts little influence on political life and is not represented in parliament, although it does participate in local and national elections. The principal issue receiving CPI attention is advocacy of a single, united socialist Ireland, and the party therefore urges unity among Protestants and Catholics.

The communist parties of Belgium, Denmark, the Netherlands, and Luxembourg did not exercise significant influence in the political affairs of their respective countries during the year. The party in Luxembourg (CPL) continued to hold 2 of 64 parliamentary seats gained in the national election of 1984. Party leadership remains in the hands of the Urbany family, and the party is strongly pro-Soviet. Thus, the CPL's domestic and foreign policy views emphasize "social equality" and the peace movement.

The insignificant role played by the Communist Party of Denmark (DKP) during 1984 continued in 1985. Currently weaker than at any time since World War II, the DKP received only 23,085 votes (0.7 percent) in the last parliamentary election in January 1984. It has not been represented in parliament since 1979, when its vote fell below the 2 percent minimum required for proportional representation. For 25 years the DKP has had to compete with other Marxist parties to the left of the Social Democratic Party. In the past fifteen years these various leftist parties have normally attracted an eighth of the national vote. In 1984 they collectively polled 14.9 percent, but the DKP share continued to plummet. Public opinion polls in 1985 gave the leftist bloc nearly 20 percent without renewed support for the DKP. Major party concerns in 1985 were directed toward advocating increased state control over the economy and an expansion of power in labor unions. In the area of foreign affairs the party has continued to focus on the importance of the peace movement and nuclear disarmament.

In Belgium the Communist Party (PCB) claims a membership of 10,000 with a population of almost 10 million. In national elections held in October the PCB received only 1.2 percent of the vote and lost its 2 parliamentary seats (in 1981 the PCB received 2.3 percent and won 2 of 212 seats). Thus, the PCB was without representation in the Belgian parliament for the first time since 1925. The party's electoral losses reflect the difficulty that the party has encountered in adapting to the regionalization of Belgian politics and in articulating themes that are both distinctive and relevant to the electorate. In 1982 the party adopted a federal structure at its Twenty-fourth Congress, but neither the establishment of separate regional organizations in Flanders, Wallonia, and Brussels nor the adoption of a Eurocommunist position have proved sufficient to arrest the party's decline. In the wake of the 1985 election losses, differences between Flemish Communists concerned with Eurocommunist themes and Wallonians concerned with socioeconomic issues and the decline of their region are likely to emerge at the 1986 national congress and the regional congresses that will follow it.

In the Nordic countries of Iceland, Norway, Sweden, and Finland the communist parties did not record significant political activity. The Communist Party of Iceland (AB), following the dissolution of a coalition government in 1983 in which the AB held the cabinet posts of finance, industry, and social and health affairs, has remained in the opposition. While it is now the largest opposition party with 10 of 60 parliamentary seats, the new coalition government of the Progressive and the Independence parties jointly holds 37 seats. Although economic problems dominated Iceland's political agenda during the year, the party was unable to generate public support for its views and in public opinion polls declined in popularity to almost 10 percent, well below the level of support recorded for the AB in 1983 elections. The AB is aware of its weakness as reflected in the debates and reports of the party's November congress. Whether party leader Svavar Gestsson can provide the leadership for reform remains an open question that must be addressed in 1986.

In Norway the Communist Party (NKP) remains staunchly pro-Soviet. Its membership and popularity dwindled when Reidar Larsen and several other leading figures left the party in 1975 and established the Socialist Left Party (SV). The impact this decision has exerted on the communist movement in Norway was most recently underscored by the outcome of the parliamentary elections held in September. The NKP received 0.2 percent of the vote (1981: 0.3 percent) and has no parliamentary representation; the SV received 5.4 percent of the vote and holds 6 of 157 parliamentary seats. Despite party differences both the NKP and the SV endorse "unity of action" among parties of the left. Nonetheless, the NKP remains one of the weakest parties in Europe, and the outcome of the national elections clearly suggests that the party is far overshadowed by other parties of the left. Internally the party continues to face a serious rift between those members favoring close association with Moscow and those advocating an independent position. This debate has adversely affected the ability to attract new members, but more important it reflects similar debates taking place within other communist parties in Western Europe. One of the consequences is a loss of credibility and the resultant inability of the NKP to play an important role in Norwegian political life.

The Left Party Communists (VPK) in Sweden captured 5.4 percent of the vote in national elections held in September and holds 19 of 349 parliamentary seats. While the party claimed victory, the outcome represented a decline in popularity since the previous elections in 1982, when it captured 5.6 percent of the vote and 20 parliamentary seats. As a consequence, the leadership of party secretary Bo Hammar became the subject of increasing criticism, and he was replaced by Kenneth Kvist at the Twenty-seventh Congress held in January 1985. As the year ended the VPK remained allied with the Social Democrats under the leadership of Olof Palme. Although the social Democrats lost 7 of their 166 seats, the combined total with VPK's 19 seats produced a majority of 178 seats, sufficient to allow Palme's party to retain slender control of the 349 member parliament. What kind of strength the party will enjoy in 1986 is unclear, but it has announced an effort to gain new members as one of its major priorities.

The factional strife that characterizes the internal affairs of the Finnish Communist Party (SKP), as well as its relations with its electoral front, the Finnish People's Democratic League (SKDL), continued throughout the year. The division focuses on what kind of a party the SKP should be. The differences hardened during the 1970s, when the more moderate and majority wing of the party was part of the governing coalition between 1975 and 1982. Tension between the two wings sharpened further when the veteran and moderate leader of the SKP, Aarne Saarinen, gave up the party leadership in 1982 and was succeeded by Juoko Kajonoja. The latter promised to unify the two wings of the party, but his rigid adherence to the CPSU had the opposite effect.

In 1983 the SKP suffered the sharpest electoral defeat in its history: in 1958 the SKP had been represented by 50 seats in parliament, but in 1983 the number was reduced from 35 to 27 and its percentage of the vote fell to 14 percent. During 1984 the divisiveness continued, with the moderate wing represented by new SKP chairman Arvo Aalto and the Stalinist wing by Taisto Sinisalo. The rift developed into a complete split in 1985. At an extraordinary party congress held in March, Aalto and his wing urged adoption of a party program of "Socialism with a Finnish Face," but the congress was boycotted by the Stalinist wing. In the autumn the SKP delivered an ultimatum to the Stalinist minority to dismantle its party organization or face expulsion. By the end of the year the wing led by Sinisalo had been expelled, but a new party had not yet been formally constituted. Thus, 1986 promised a continuation of the division.

The communist parties of Austria (KPO) and Switzerland (PdAS) play minimal roles in the political affairs of their respective countries. The KPO is without representation in the Austrian parliament and received 0.66 percent of the vote in the most recent national election (1983). The party continued its endorsement of "the struggle for peace and social progress" and participated in municipal elections held in four of Austria's provinces with minor electoral gains. Similarly, the activity of the PdAS in Switzerland was quiescent, and the party recorded significant electoral losses in cantonal and municipal elections; for example, the PdAS lost all of its eight seats on the city council of Lausanne in October. The PdAS, strongly pro-Soviet, holds only 1 of 200 Swiss parliamentary seats. It is unlikely that either party will generate increased support among their respective electorates in 1986, since they both operate in countries in which appeals to the "proletariat" and "working class unity" are not popular.

In West Berlin the Communist Party was formally established in 1969 as the Socialist Unity Party of West Berlin (SEW); it exercises no significant influence on political life in the city. It is without representation in the city's parliament. The party claims membership of approximately 4,500. In the last municipal election on 10 March, the SEW received 7,713 votes, which amounted to 0.6 percent (1981: 0.7 percent). In the future it is unlikely that the city's population will find the SEW's views and positions, which mirror those of the German Democratic Republic (GDR), any more appealing than in the past. The SEW competes for electoral support with numerous leftist groups, none of which attract support from a population living in a city divided by the Berlin Wall and separated from the GDR by mine fields.

In the Federal Republic of Germany (FRG) the Communist Party (DKP) is not represented in the West German parliament and garnered only 0.2 percent of the vote in the last election (1983). The party claims its membership exceeds 10,000; it is pro-Soviet in orientation and its organizational apparatus is highly structured. Party headquarters are located in Düsseldorf, where the offices of the German Trade Unions Alliance (DGB) are also located. In September, however, the DKP opened an office in the West German capital of Bonn with ceremonies attended by the Soviet ambassador and by the permanent representative from the GDR. The views and positions of the DKP reflect those taken by the CPSU. Throughout the year party chairman Herbert Mies underscored at every opportunity the importance of the peace movement and opposition to the "militarization of space" and the Strategic Defense Initiative. Calls for unity of action in the form of "democratic election alliances" were directed especially at trade-union members and members of the Social Democratic Party of Germany (SPD). The party's efforts to achieve unity of action did not produce impressive results in state elections. The party's focus on the peace movement, however, suggests that it will devote a major effort during 1986 to achieving "unity" in this specific area. The party's progress in this regard will almost certainly be a major subject of discussion at the DKP's Eighth Congress scheduled for May 1986 in Hamburg.

Dennis L. Bark
Hoover Institution

Austria

Population. 7,540,000
Party. Communist Party of Austria (Kommunistische Partei Österreichs; KPO)
Founded. 3 November 1918
Membership. 12,000 (reported by Vienna, *Profil*, 7 November 1983)
Party Chairman. Franz Muhri (b. 1924)
Politburo. 12 members: Michael Graber, Franz Hager, Anton Hofer, Hans Kalt (secretary of Central Committee), Gustav Loistl, Franz Muhri, Otto Podolsky (Vienna party secretary), Karl Reiter, Erwin Scharf, Irma Schwager, Walter Silbermayr, Ernst Wimmer
Secretariat. 3 members: Hans Kalt, Karl Reiter, Walter Silbermayr
Central Committee. 64 members
Status. Legal
Last Congress. Twenty-fifth, 13–15 January 1984, in Vienna
Last Election. Federal, 24 April 1983, 0.66 percent, no representation
Publications. *Volksstimme* (People's voice; Michael Graber, editor), KPO daily organ, Vienna; *Weg und Ziel* (Path and goal; Erwin Scharf, editor), KPO theoretical monthly, Vienna

This was not a particularly active year for the KPO. It was the year following the Twenty-fifth Congress, and there was only one provincial election. Most remarkable, if anything, was a greater than usual number of Austrian contributions to *World Marxist Review* (*WMR*) and an above-average number of international party contacts.

The provincial election took place on 6 October in the prosperous and industrial province of Upper Austria. The KPO polled 0.7 percent of the vote, a slight advance over the 0.6 percent vote in 1979 (*Wiener Zeitung*, 8 October). The consequences of the 1945–1955 Russian occupation of the relatively poor Mühlviertel region can still be detected: the communist vote there was slightly above 2 percent (*Oberösterreichisches Tagblatt*, 7 October). Municipal elections were held in four provinces. First came Carinthia on 17 March. In the capital, Klagenfurt, the KPO vote was nearly cut in half, from 1.5 percent in 1979 to 0.8 percent. The sole communist success was in the small border town of Arnoldstein, where the party increased its vote share from 5.3 to 8.0 percent and doubled its representation from one to two seats (*Presse*, 18 March). One week later, on 24 March, municipal elections were held in Styria. Here the KPO showed slight gains; over the election of 1980 it increased its total number of municipal seats from 14 to 21, out of a total of more than 7,000 (*Wiener Zeitung*, 26 March). Lower Austria held municipal elections on 14 April, in which the KPO polled 0.8 percent, the same vote share as in 1980 (*Presse*, 15 April). The last municipal election, in Upper Austria, was held along with the provincial election of 6 October. The KPO went up from 0.5 percent in 1979 to 0.7 percent and gained one seat (from zero) in the provincial capital, Linz (*Wiener Zeitung*, 8 October). The most important shop-steward election was held at the VOEST-Alpine, Austria's leading nationalized steel plant, on 7 February. At the time, little was known of VOEST's financial difficulties, which burst into the news in November. In February, the KPO obtained 6.4 percent of the vote and raised its contingent from two to three (*Wiener Zeitung*, 8 February).

Domestic Affairs. The year brought pronouncements on one past and four current domestic problems, involving three articles in *WMR* and three members of the Politburo. The February issue of *WMR* published an article by Bruno Furch, the KPO member of the *WMR* editorial council (pp. 41–46). The author dealt with his escape from Austria in 1938, his fight in the Spanish Civil War, and his imprisonment in Hitler's concentration camps of Dachau and Flossenbürg. The article gives an interesting account of survival in Dachau, basing it on good luck and faith, which he finds in Communists as well as in Christians.

Michael Graber, the *Volksstimme* editor, wrote a January article in *WMR* on the working-class movement (pp. 90–97). The article presents a socioeconomic analysis of postwar Austria. Neutrality, nationalization, and tourism are credited with having given Austria a special and privileged status in the capitalist world. Yet, Graber writes, this status has been eroded in the last decade which has led, among other things, to the doubling of unemployment to 5 percent. Graber ends by exhorting workers and intellectuals to unite in the KPO "in the struggle for peace and social progress" (p. 96).

The June issue of *WMR* contains an article by Rosmarie Atzenhofer (member of the KPO Economic Policy Department) and Politburo member Walter Silbermayr (pp. 92–99). The authors ascribe Austria's postwar nationalization to the lack of capital at the time. They also blame Austria's social partnership and the role within it of the Socialist Party for having stifled any role the nationalized industries, which employ 400,000 people, might have played in furthering the interests of Austria's working class.

On 19 and 20 February, the Central Committee of the KPO met in Vienna. The meeting's main theme was internal policy. Franz Muhri's report to the meeting appeared in the May issue of *WMR*'s *Information Bulletin* (*IB*) (pp. 9–11). Much of Muhri's report is an attack on the Austrian Freedom Party, which since 1983 has been the Socialist Party's coalition partner. Muhri attacks the Freedom Party's claim of liberalization and calls it neofascist; as proof he adduces the formal reception of the war criminal Walter Reder by the Freedom Party defense minister, Friedhelm Frischenschlager. Muhri considers struggling against the Reder-Frischenschlager crisis to be one of the KPO's main tests; the others are the struggle for the environment, readiness for a possible early federal election (that is, prior to 1987), and the struggle for peace.

A final issue with domestic implication is the export control law passed, according to *Volksstimme* (10 August), under U.S. pressure. *Volksstimme* wonders how the Austrian government proposes to protect Austrian firms against U.S. "blackmail," which demands that Austrian importers of restricted-export U.S. goods be trustworthy in regard to the U.S. Department of Commerce.

International Affairs. Three pieces on international affairs by Austrians were published in *WMR* and *IB*. In the August 1984 issue of *WMR* (pp. 48–50), Politburo member Ernst Wimmer wrote "In the Thick of Anti-War Actions." His main point was that the Austrian peace movement has grown despite the Socialist and People's Party moves to force Austrian Communists out of the movement. The January *IB* contains a resolution of the 22–23 October 1984 Vienna meeting of the KPO's Central Committee (p. 7). The Central Committee attacks the Austrian government's decision to spend billions on the purchases of new interceptor fighters at a time when every schilling is needed "for the creation of jobs, social security, environmental protection and culture." Finally, in the July issue of *WMR*, Ernst Wimmer attacks these movements, including the Austrian Alternative Movement, for trying to deflect from the class struggle by establishing a third force (pp. 36–44).

On 17 October 1984, *Volksstimme* attacked the anti-Sandinista CIA manual. The same paper, on 26 October, contained a Muhri speech on "U.S. Pressure on Austria" and editorial comment on a *Kurier* report that CIA agents made frequent visits to Austrian high-technology firms. *Volksstimme* of 9 June reported that Muhri attacked Defense Minister Frischenschlager's claim that guided missiles with a limited range were not banned by the State Treaty of 1955. On 29 October, the paper also reported that Politburo member Irma Schwager welcomed Soviet proposals for ending the arms race.

International Party Contacts. The period November 1984 to October 1985 was an active one for the KPO's international contacts. In November 1984, a KPO delegation led by Politburo member Karl Reiter visited the German Democratic Republic. A meeting between Reiter and the German Socialist Unity Party Central Committee member Horst Dohlus resulted in a solidarity statement focusing on the NATO nuclear threat (ADN, 13 November).

The new year began with a Moscow visit by Muhri and Hans Steiner, chairman of the KPO International Department. The high point of the visit was the presentation to Franz Muhri of the Order of the October Revolution by candidate CPSU Politburo member Kuznetsov (Moscow Domestic Service, 15 January).

February was an active travel month for Muhri. In Bratislava he met Vasil Bilak, secretary of the Czechoslovakian Communist Party Central Committee. During the solidarity meeting, Muhri was presented with the Order of Friendship (Prague Domestic Service, February). Muhri also met with Todor Zhivkov in Sofia and was awarded the "People's Republic of Bulgaria" First Class Order (Sofia Domestic Service, 25 February).

The March issue of *WMR* ran a topical dialogue between Austrian Politburo member Erwin Scharf and Hans Kleven, chairman of the Communist Party of Norway (pp. 33–37). They exchanged views and agreed completely on the role of small communist parties in democratic systems.

In May and June there were two KPO contacts with the CPSU. Andrei Gromyko, then still foreign minister of the USSR, used an official visit to Vienna to have a "comradely, friendly" talk with Muhri on 17 May (*Pravda*, 18 May). In June, a Vienna City Committee delegation, led by Vienna KPO chairman Otto Podolsky, visited Moscow (*Moskovskaya Pravda*, 15 June).

Delegates of "Capitalist Europe's" communist parties met in Paris on 12 and 13 June. The KPO was among the eighteen parties represented. Austrian neutrality was among the many topics discussed (*L'Humanité*, 22 June).

On 16 and 17 October, the Socialist International held a disarmament conference in Vienna. B. N. Ponomarev, the head of the CPSU delegation, met with Muhri, Scharf, and Steiner on 18 October (*Volksstimme*, 19 October). On 19 October the same three men met wtih Zhu Liang, vice director of the Central International Liaison Department of the Chinese Communist Party Central Committee. On this meeting, Beijing *Xinhua* reported: "The Chinese Communist Party and the Austrian Communist Party have decided to strengthen their friendly relations and exchange visits" (20 October). The 22 October *Volksstimme* report differed somewhat: "The talks were held in a frank, comradely manner. On some essential questions, however, the sides held different views. Nonetheless, the resumption of contacts and talks was assessed by both sides as useful, and the restoration (sic) between the parties was welcomed."

Frederick C. Engelmann
University of Alberta

Belgium

Population. 9,856,000

Party. Belgian Communist Party (Parti communiste de Belgique; Kommunistische Partij van Belgie; PCB/KPB)

Founded. 1921

Membership. 10,000 (estimated)

Leadership. President: Louis van Geyt; vice president and president of the French-speaking council: Claude Renard; vice president and president of the Dutch-speaking council: Jef Turf

Politburo. 14 members: Pierre Beauvois, Marcel Couteau, Jan Debrouwere, Filip Delmotte, Robert Dussart, Roel Jacobs, Ludo Loose, Jacques Moins, Jacques Nagels, Claude Renard, Jef Turf, Louis van Geyt, Jules Vercaigne, Jack Withages

Central Committee. 72 full members: 37 in the French-language wing; 35 in the Dutch-language wing
Status. Legal
Last Congress. Twenty-fourth, March and December 1982 (two stages)
Last Election. 1985, 1.2 percent, no representation (*Keesings Historisch Archief*, 31 October)
Auxiliary Organizations. Communist Youth of Belgium, Union of Belgian Pioneers, National Union of Communist Students
Publications. *Le Drapeau rouge*, daily party organ in French; *De Rode Vann*, Dutch-language weekly (circulation 14,500 and 11,000 respectively); *Les Cahiers communistes*, PCB monthly ideological review; *Vlaams Marxistisch Tijdschrift*, KBP quarterly

The PCB/KPB is an insignificant force in Belgian politics. In decline for most of the postwar period, the PCB/KPB dropped from 2.3 percent of the vote in 1981 to 1.2 percent in the 13 October parliamentary elections. As a result, the party lost its two seats in the Chamber of Deputies and its one seat in the Senate. This left the PCB/KPB without representation in the Belgian parliament for the first time since 1925.

The PCB/KPB's losses reflect the difficulty that the party has had in adapting to the regionalization of Belgian politics and articulating themes that are both distinctive and relevant to the electorate. In contrast to other Belgian parties, the PCB/KPB retained a unitary party organization until 1982, when it adopted a federal structure. However, neither the establishment of separate regional organizations nor the adoption of a Eurocommunist line were sufficient to arrest the party's decline. In the 1985 election campaign, the party stressed its opposition to the deployment of cruise missiles and to the austerity measures imposed by Wilfried Martens' center-right cabinet (composed of Liberals and Christian Democrats). Yet neither this nor the PCB/KPB's claim to be the only remaining national party in Belgium were of much help in the election.

Despite the prominence of the cruise missile issue earlier in the year, the election campaign focused on the economy and the record of the Martens cabinet, which had been in office since 1981 (*NYT*, 14 October). In economically depressed Wallonia (the French-speaking region), a stronghold of the left, the opposition Wallonian Socialists (Parti Socialiste, PS) were able to maintain their electoral strength by capitalizing on the decline of the coal and steel industries. In the more prosperous Flemish-speaking region, dominated by the Christian Democrats, the Flemish Socialists (Socialistische Partij, SP) and the greens (AGALEV) were more successful in exploiting the peace and environmental issues. In both regions, Communists failed to make any gains vis à vis the Socialists and were outpolled by the environmentally minded greens, who won 3.7 percent in Flanders and 2.5 percent in Wallonia (*Keesings Historisch Archief*, 31 October). PCB/KPB pleas that voters support parties committed not only to a change of government but also a change in policy went unheeded. At the same time, the activities of the Fighting Communist Cells (CCC), a terrorist organization that claimed responsibility for more than twenty bomb attacks in Belgium in 1985 (*NYT*, 6 December), worked to the disadvantage of the PCB/KPB and the reasonable image it sought to cultivate. Unrelated to the PCB/KPB, the CCC is alleged to have links to Direct Action in France and the Red Army faction in Germany (*FBIS*, 1 May).

Leadership and Party Organization. Until 1982, the PCB/KPB maintained a unitary structure. Following its Twenty-fourth Congress, however, the PCB/KPB adopted a federal structure and established distinct Flemish, Wallonian, and Brussels regional organizations; these were interposed between local federations and the national structures of the party. Yet in contrast to other Belgian parties, in which previous federally defined structures had already given way to separate Flemish and Francophone parties, the PCB/KPB retained its national party organization—including a Politburo, Central Committee, and Secretariat—capable of speaking for the party as a whole. Regional congresses are to meet every two years, and the national party congress will meet at four-year intervals (*Statuts du Parti Communiste de Belgique*, 1982).

The purpose of the reorganization was to take account of the growing divergence between the Flemish and Wallonian wings of the party and to bring the party structure into line with the growing regionalization of Belgian politics (*YICA*, 1984, 1985). The creation of distinct regional organizations was intended to allow the party to speak more effectively on regional and "communitarian" issues and allow regional organizations to tailor their appeals and analyses to the specific problems of their regions. At the same time, maintenance of a national party structure was to enable the party to pursue a coherent line and seek national solutions to national problems (Interview with Roel Jacobs, *WMR*, January).

Because the federal structure of the PCB/KPB is relatively new, it is difficult to predict how it will work in practice. In the first regional congresses, held in 1983 and 1984, the Wallonian and Flemish organizations explored different themes. The Wallonian organization emphasized traditional socioeconomic themes, and the electorally weaker Flemish organization concentrated on the possibility of alliances with other parties and groups on the left (*YICA*, 1985). However, in the 1985 election campaign, the PCB/KPB emphasized a common opposition to the domestic and foreign policies of the Martens government. Nevertheless, particularly in the wake of the election losses, previous differences between Flemish Communists and Walloonians are likely to emerge at the 1986 national congress and the regional congresses that will follow it.

Party leadership remained stable in 1985, but changes may occur in 1986 as a result of the election defeat.

Domestic Affairs. The PCB/KPB was preoccupied with a number of domestic problems, including the election campaign and the need to distinguish itself from the increasingly active CCC. Claiming responsibility for a large number of bombings, including attacks on NATO pipelines and explosions at banks and the Belgian employers association, the CCC characterized itself in a communiqué to *Le Soir* and Belgian radio and television as an "authentically Marxist-Leninist radical, offensive alternative in the class struggle" and proclaimed its intention of attacking those parts of the economic sector linked with armaments, the military apparatus, and the political power of the bourgeois state (*FBIS*, 14 May). Committed to a Eurocommunist line, the PCB/KPB disassociated itself from the CCC. The PCB/KPB argued that the CCC was discredited in the eyes of the public and that its provocations were having a negative effect; for example, security forces were taking advantage of the disarray to associate violent extremism with the parliamentary left. Terrorist attacks provided an excuse to strengthen the repressive apparatus of the state and intimidate pacifists, political refugees, and others on the left. As a result, workers were the primary victims of terrorism (*Le Drapeau rouge*, 3 May and 6 June).

In the election campaign, the PCB/KPB had stressed not only its opposition to the deployment of the cruise missile (the Belgian government decided to proceed with deployment in March; 16 of the 48 missiles were in place shortly thereafter), but also emphasized its opposition to the austerity program of the Martens government. The PCB/KPB argued that austerity measures were not only eroding the guarantees of the welfare state but widening the gap between the rich and the poor. These developments could be stopped by rallying an alliance of progressive forces committed not only to a change of coalition but also to changes in policy. Enjoining voters to measure parties against their promises and to support parties willing to mobilize workers in support of radical changes, the PCB/KPB demanded the creation of new jobs to ease unemployment, a minimum income of 20,000 Belgian francs, a reduction in the work week to 32 hours (without any financial sacrifice by workers), a more complete federalism, and the immediate removal of the 16 cruise missiles already deployed. In addition to stimulating growth by encouraging construction and expanding public services, the government was to encourage community ownership of energy, defense, telecommunications, and credit industries and promote regionally based recovery programs.

In Flanders, the PCB/KPB emphasized the importance of replacing the Flemish regional government's commitment to a third industrial revolution by a recovery and reconversion plan emphasizing socially useful, high-value, energy-saving, and import-substituting production. The introduction of new technology was to be combined with measures to preserve employment. In Wallonia, the PCB/KPB stressed the viability of the region's steel industry, which had been severely curtailed under successive European Economic Community steel plans, and the need for an industrial policy to ensure the recovery and rejuvenation of the region's industrial base. The PCB/KPB argued that its proposals could be financed within existing means by eliminating tax fraud, curtailing tax concessions, ending the flight of capital, and shifting the brunt of taxation to higher incomes and capital intensive industries (*Programma van de Kommunistische Partij, Parlementsverkiezingen 13 oktober 1985*).

Stressing the importance of mobilizing workers, youth, and women, the PCB/KPB continued to regard itself as an important element in a potential majority committed to break with neoliberal economic policies and an independent foreign policy (*Le Soir*, 6 June). However, despite the PCB/KPB's continued call for alliances with progressive forces—the peace movement was often cited as an example—the PCB/KPB remained isolated from other parties. In Wallonia the party argued that it was an important "antidote" to the alliance between the Wallonian Socialists and the Socialist Trade Union Federation (FGTB), both of whom were too oriented toward negotiations and too willing to compromise. According to the Communists, the Socialists were dominated by their right wing; as a result, the Communists were the only remaining representative of the regional left of the 1960s (*Le Soir*, 20 September). In Flanders, the party expressed reservations about the Socialists and was critical of AGALEV for its failure to take consequential stands on economic issues (*Programma van de Kommunistische Partij*).

Auxiliary Organizations. Aside from the organizations mentioned above, the PCB/KPB has few auxiliary or front organizations. There are no direct links to either the Socialist or Christian Democratic trade-union federations.

Foreign Positions and Activities. The PCB/KPB takes a Eurocommunist position in foreign policy. Vehemently opposed to the deployment of cruise missiles and the militarization of space, the party has stressed the importance of mutual disengagement between East and West. In its election program, the PCB/KPB argued that small states can play a special role in promoting disarmament (*Programma van de Kommunistische Partij*). In the past the PCB/KPB has been critical of Soviet intervention in Poland and Afghanistan (*YICA*, 1981).

In 1985 the PCB/KPB maintained a variety of foreign contacts. In January it discussed the deployment of cruise missiles and other international issues with a delegation from the Dutch Communist Party (Tass, 30 January; *FBIS*, 30 January). In addition, a delegation to Moscow led by Politburo member Pierre Beauvois explored the introduction of computers in the Soviet economy (Tass, 30 January; *FBIS*, 31 January). In February, party president Louis van Geyt and Politburo member Jan Debrouwere explored international issues with Soviet leaders, including Mikhail Gorbachev and Central Committee secretary Boris Ponomarev (Tass, 13 January; *FBIS*, 14 February). Other contacts included a visit by a Czechoslovakian Communist Party delegation (Prague Domestic Service, 20 February; *FBIS*, 20 February) and discussions in Beijing between Jacques Moins, Rosine Lewin (member of the Central Committee), and Hu Quli (member of the Secretariat of the Chinese Communist Party). Both sides expressed satisfaction with their relations, which had been re-established in 1983 (*Xinhua*, 22 July; *FBIS*, 23 July). The PCB/KPB also took part in an informal meeting of West European communist parties held in Paris. No communiqué was issued following that meeting (*JPRS*, 7 August).

Steven B. Wolinetz
Memorial University of Newfoundland

Cyprus

Population. 670,000 (80 percent Greek; 18 percent Turkish) (estimated)
Party. Progressive Party of the Working People (Anorthotikon Komma Ergazomenou Laou; AKEL)
Founded. 1922 (AKEL, 1941)
Membership. 14,000 (*WMR*, October 1982); 67 percent industrial workers and employees, 20 percent

peasants and middle class, 24 percent women, 30 percent under 30 years old; 80 percent from Greek Cypriot community

General Secretary. Ezekias Papaioannou

Politburo. 13 members: Ezekias Papaioannou, Andreas Fandis, Dinos Konstantinou, G. Katsouridhis, Khambis Mikhailidhis, Andreas Ziartidhis, Khristos Petas, Kiriakos Khristou, Mikhail Poumbouris, G. Khristodoulidhis, A. Mikhailidhis. G. Sophokles, Dhonis Kristofinis

Secretariat. 3 members: Ezekias Papaoiannou, Andreas Fandis (deputy general secretary), Dinos Konstantinou (organizing secretary)

Status. Legal

Last Congress. Fifteenth, 13–15 May 1982

Last Election. 1985, 27.4 percent, 15 of 56 seats

Auxiliary Organizations. Pan-Cypriot Workers' Federation (PEO), 45,000 members, Andreas Ziartidhis, general secretary; United Democratic Youth Organization (EDON), 14,000 members; Confederation of Women's Organizations; Pan-Cyprian Peace Council; Pan-Cyprian Federation of Students and Young Professionals; Union of Greek Cypriots in England, 1,200 members (considered London branch of AKEL); Pan-Cypriot National Organization of Secondary Students; Cypriot Farmers' Union

Publications. *Kharavyi* (Dawn), AKEL daily and largest newspaper in Cyprus; *Demokratia*, AKEL weekly; *Neo Kairoi* (New Times), AKEL magazine; *Ergatiko Vima* (Workers' Stride), PEO weekly; *Neolaia* (Youth), EDON weekly

The original Communist Party of Cyprus (Kommonistikon Komma Kiprou) was secretly founded in 1922 by Greek Cypriot cadres trained in mainland Greece. Four years later the party openly held its first congress, after the island had become a British crown colony. Outlawed in 1933, the party thrived as an underground movement until 1944, when it resurfaced as the AKEL. All political parties were proscribed in 1955 during the insurgency against the British led by the Greek Cypriot paramilitary group known as EOKA. The AKEL leaders chose not to take up arms in that anticolonial campaign and later rationalized their inaction as "a nonviolent alternative to EOKA terrorism in the independence struggle." This peaceful tactic may have been a serious miscalculation, however, because the AKEL is still criticized by some disaffected leftists for not participating in that armed struggle. Since the establishment of the Republic of Cyprus in 1960, the AKEL has enjoyed legal status and has consistently been the island's best organized political party. Until the 1985 parliamentary elections, the AKEL had also won the largest plurality of votes in all previous elections, but the Communists slipped to third place after the latest tally.

The AKEL claims it is "a people's party of Greek and Turkish working people" (*WMR*, September 1979). Although the AKEL is officially banned in the northern sector of the island, which has been named the Turkish Republic of Northern Cyprus (TRNC) since its declaration of independence in 1983, the Communists have not stopped entreating the Turkish Cypriot minority population. One goal of the AKEL is to have "the patriotic front... include, as is done in the free territory, Turkish Cypriots (Marxists and members of progressive democratic groups living in the occupied areas)" (ibid., October 1982). Communist fronts do exist in the Turkish Cypriot part of the island, and some of their representatives attended the World Conference on Peace and Life Against Nuclear War held in Prague in 1983 (*Kharavyi*, 22 June 1983). The left-wing Republican Turkish Party (CTP), which was founded in 1970, operates openly in the TRNC and publishes most of the AKEL statements in its party newspaper, *Yeni Duzen* (New Order). In the June elections in the TRNC, the CTP gathered 21.3 percent of the vote and won 12 of the 50 seats in the new National Assembly.

Leadership and Organization. The AKEL is reputed to be a tightly controlled apparatus, structured along the principle of democratic centralism. Its highest body is the Congress, convened once every four years; the next one is to be held in 1986. The three-member Secretariat runs its day-to-day operations and a thirteen-member Politburo is AKEL's policymaking body. There was reportedly a rare disagreement in the AKEL leadership in 1984 over the party's attitude toward President Spyros Kyprianou and the "democratic cooperation" with the president's Democratic Party (DIKO). The controversy arose over whether the 30-month-old Minimum Program between the AKEL and DIKO should be renounced by the Communists. The president settled the apparent dispute in the AKEL ranks when he himself terminated his party's alliance with the Communists in December 1984. One year later, the AKEL charged that Kyprianou had ended the Minimum Program at the written request of U.S. president Reagan. In addition, the AKEL charged Kyprianou with having made a secret agreement with President Reagan to grant facilities at Larnaca airport "to the USA . . . for intervention against the people of our neighbor, Lebanon." At the same time, the Cypriot president was accused of allowing the United States to construct a "spy radio station in Nicosia" (ibid., 6 December). Thus the AKEL leaders have made a tactical shift from "the tolerance and support" that they once gave the government to their current role of "responsible and constructive opposition." As a result, the AKEL will lose such benefits as the appointment of party members to government posts and the promotion of leftists in the governmental machinery. Consequently, it came as no surprise in February that the AKEL joined the right-wing Democratic Rally Party (DISI) in censuring Kyprianou in the parliament and calling for early presidential elections (*Economist*, 2 March).

Replacement of the gerontocracy that now rules the party will be a concern for the AKEL as the current leaders grow older in their secure career positions. It is this same leadership that has repeatedly delivered a third of the Cypriot electorate to the Communists for the past 25 years until the December elections. How the AKEL has maintained its strength over the years can be explained by the fact that the party offers tangible rewards for loyalty—for example, free higher education, medical care, and holiday visits to Eastern Europe. Still, the party leaders are "grey men in grey suits, with grey hair and grey ideas" (*Economist*, 16 November). General Secretary Papaioannou was born in 1908 and has held that office since 1949; the average age of the other leaders is over 65 years. Slavishly faithful to the Moscow line, the party has nonetheless "played the parliamentary game in Eurocommunistic style; but it has not joined the Eurocommunists in criticising Soviet actions and policies" (ibid.). Perhaps that may explain why the AKEL has never been able to increase its one-third share and why they may now be on the decline for future elections.

Currently, the AKEL attaches special importance to recruiting and educating young people. Thus, the party "sees to it that comrades receive proper Marxist-Leninist training" (*WMR*, October 1982). The important youth front, EDON, has a membership of "factory workers, peasants, white-collar workers, and high school graduates between the ages of 14 and 30 . . . and it works in close cooperation with AKEL" (ibid., April 1984). At the Fifteenth Congress in May 1982, the leadership hailed its "great success in the organizational sector" and in recruitment of "new members from all strata of the people of Cyprus." Since the previous congress, party membership increased by 2,479 to its present strength of "nearly 14,000 members" (*Kharavyi*, 30 May 1982). At the Fifteenth Congress, the AKEL also emphasized its propaganda work "among the masses," so as to take the offensive on the ideological and political fronts and expose imperialist and reactionary schemes more effectively (*WMR*, July).

Each fall the AKEL holds a "fundraising drive to provide money for the party's normal activities" and to demonstrate "a symbolic expression of mass support." Additional operating capital is generated "from activities under the indirect but tight control of the party in . . . branches of . . . production and distribution of goods (cooperatives, retail stores, financial enterprises, tourist agencies, export/import businesses)." As a consequence of these commercial endeavors, the AKEL has "probably become the major employer on the island" (Athens, *Andi*, 16 January 1981). The two best-known communist-controlled businesses are the Popular Distiller's Company of Limassol, which produces wines and brandies for the domestic market and export, and the People's Coffee Grinding Company in Nicosia. Moreover, the communist-controlled labor union, PEO, is the strongest in Cyprus and its members work in virtually every phase of the island's economy. In the TRNC, the strong Confederation of Revolutionary Labor Unions (Dev-Is) is considered left wing, but its direct relationship with the PEO and the AKEL is not clearly established.

Domestic Affairs. The breakdown of the unification talks between the Greek and Turkish Cypriots in January was the single event that dominated domestic affairs in Cyprus for the entire year. Four days of talks in New York under sponsorship of the United Nations brought President Kyprianou face-to-face with the TRNC president, Rauf Denktash, for their first meeting in over six years. The gaps between the two sides had been greatly narrowed by the negotiating skills of U.N. secretary general Perez de Cuellar, who had previously shuttled between the two sides during months of "proximity talks." The framework that had been agreed on broadly provided for a reunited, federal republic with a Greek president and a Turkish vice president, along with separate legislative bodies. In turn, the Turks would retain 29 percent of their occupied territory and return 8 percent to the Greek Cypriots. However, three issues remained unresolved: which territories would be returned; who would guarantee the island's independence; and when the 18,000 mainland Turkish troops would leave the island. Denktash came to the meeting to sign the draft agreement and not to bargain further at that time. Kyprianou, on the other hand, said that the outstanding issues must be resolved before he would sign. Thus, for the four days the two leaders "engaged in a dialogue of the deaf," leading to the inevitable collapse of the talks (*CSM*, 22 January).

Subsequently the AKEL Politburo issued a statement that "the Secretary General [Perez de Cuellar's] documents contained nothing whose acceptance would have prevented the future discussion of... any detail of the pending special problems" (Nicosia Domestic Service, 30 January). The statement criticized both the Greek and Turkish Cypriot leaders for the failure of the talks, but also placed "blame on the Americans and on other NATO imperialist quarters" (ibid.). In his reply, Kyprianou stated that accepting the documents as presented "would certainly commit our side, particularly on very substantive issues, and would have a most unfavorable impact on our ability to negotiate" (ibid., 31 January). He concluded that the positions the Communists had taken in their statement "are enough to justify the decision to suspend cooperation between DIKO and AKEL." The Politburo responded by saying that "the breaking up of the domestic front has been caused and is being caused by the president's wrong actions" and not by the AKEL's criticism of these actions (*Kharavyi*, 3 February). Papaioannou took the last shot by saying that "it appears that Kyprianou is not yet conscious of the fact that as a result of his own action in renouncing the vast majority of those who voted for him, he is now a minority president" (ibid., 8 February). Despite an appeal from the Holy Synod, which was read in all the island's churches, for "the people to differentiate between party interests and national interests," the battlelines for the year ahead had already been drawn.

On 22 February the two extremes of Cypriot politics, the AKEL and the DISI led by Glafkos Clerides, joined in a vote of censure that blamed Kyprianou for the failure of the intercommunal talks in New York. Both parties held about one-third of the seats in the parliament, while Kyprianou's party, DIKO, held only one-fifth of the seats. Despite this setback, the president declared that according to the constitution he was not answerable to parliament and would not resign his office nor call for "collective decisionmaking." DIKO followers noted that the AKEL had usually referred to Clerides's party as "black fascism" and that now the two parties made strange bed-fellows. Papaioannou explained the reason for the AKEL vote as merely expedient, "since essentially the resolution introduced by DISI contained the basic points of our own resolution [and would help] the will of the House to be expressed more strongly" (ibid., 24 February). On 29 March the House of Representatives passed an AKEL-sponsored decision that criticized the president's failure to respond to the resolution of 22 February; if the president still could not comply with the resolution, then he should call early presidential elections as required by the republic's constitution. Kyprianou immediately referred the constitutional question to the Supreme Court, which the AKEL noted was correct and "in accordance with established legal procedures" (Nicosia Domestic Service, 6 April). In June the Supreme Court upheld Kyprianou's separation of powers position that the decision could not be promulgated and therefore was not binding on the president (ibid., 10 June). Kyprianou promised that he "will continue his efforts to find ways to restore unity within the domestic front," and would maintain his "dialogue" with all political elements in Cyprus. Still not satisfied, Papaioannou later reaffirmed that the AKEL "has no confidence in Kyprianou and that it would never support him for president again" (*Kharavyi*, 6 July).

Unable to make any headway with the president, the AKEL Central Committee proposed in October that the House of Representatives be dissolved, that early parliamentary elections be called for December, and that Kyprianou should call for early presidential elections, since he has "full blame for the fragmentation of our home front and the intensification of our domestic political crisis" (Nicosia Domestic Service, 8 October). The DISI representatives joined in the demand for early elections, and even Kyprianou's forces agreed that the time had come for parliamentary—but not presidential—elections. Accordingly, the House of Representatives dissolved itself on 31 October and set the new election date as 8 December. Throughout the five-week campaign, the AKEL endured the expected criticism by DIKO for its tactical support of the party of its arch-enemy, Clerides's DISI. The head of the PEO, Andreas Ziartidhis, claimed that while it was true that a "coincidence of views exists between AKEL and DISI," it would "never wipe out our ideological and class differences." He noted that the DISI would ask for the "bourgeois class" vote, while the AKEL would seek that of the working class, and that the DISI "will be our main opponent in the upcoming House elections" (*O Fileytheros*, 11 November). The statement was prophetic, but it failed to take into account the surprising strength that the DIKO would show despite Kyprianou's problems during the past year.

The total number of seats in the Greek Cypriot House was raised from 35 to 56, and the six electoral districts still included Famagusta and Kyrenia, which are now part of the TRNC. For counting the votes, the government used a system that it called "reinforced proportional representation," which means that the parties may share allotted seats only after they have achieved a certain minimum voting support. The DISI led the polls in December with 33.6 percent of the vote and nineteen seats; the DIKO received 27.7 percent and sixteen seats; the AKEL garnered 27.4 percent and fifteen seats; and the socialist EDEK followed with 11.1 percent and six seats. Voter participation reached a high of 95 percent of all registered voters (Embassy of Cyprus, Washington News Release, 10 December).

The election results were a setback for the AKEL. The usual Communist one-third of the votes was cut down by five percentage points and proportionally the AKEL lost seats from the previous election. Even the socialist party, EDEK, improved its vote from 8 percent to 11, and this produced a surprise in the first meeting of the House of Representatives. The sixteen DIKO members apparently took orders from the president to throw their support behind the EDEK leader, Vasso Lyssarides, to elect him the president of the House, which is a largely ceremonial post. Nonetheless, this may be a signal that Kyprianou, who has always been comfortable with left-wing alliances, may be looking toward the backing of the socialists in the next presidential elections in 1988. Finally, the Communists and the leading DISI failed to produce the two-thirds majority coalition as they had expected. They had hoped to use this number of seats to amend the constitution to force the president to resign if the majority of parliament called for it. By the strong showing of his party, Kyprianou felt vindicated; more important, he escaped the proverbial "bullet" for another two years. He lauded his party's "great success," for it showed that it "will make a common handling and unity of spirit on our national issues possible" (Nicosia Domestic Service, 9 December). AKEL's Papaioannou pointed out that his party "waged a difficult campaign under very adverse circumstances" while struggling "against unbridled demagogy from all sides." He promised to continue AKEL's "fight inside and outside the House of Representatives to save Cyprus" and continue "to defend the people's gains and to improve their standard of living" (ibid.).

Foreign Positions and Activities. The deputy general secretary of the AKEL, Andreas Fandis, wrote a long and significant article, "The Lie About Communism's 'Aggressiveness,'" in which he claimed that this concept "was put in circulation by the propaganda machine of imperialist countries, especially Britain and the United States" (*WMR*, July). He pointed out that vast regions of the globe are declared "as zones of vital interests to the U.S." This U.S. policy is directed toward "raising barriers to social and anti-imperialistic changes in developing countries" and it includes "plans for the extension of NATO activities in the South Atlantic, the setting up of new military political alignments, the formation of a strike force in the Caribbean, and an increased military presence in the Middle East." In order to "resist the strategy of imperialism," AKEL "invariably stresses the importance of propagating the Marxist-Leninist world-view, preserving the purity of our ideology, and defending it against all attacks or distortions from the right or 'left.'" As a result "communists are gaining ground among the people," which is "a tremendous contribution to the future of humanity" (ibid.).

Specifically, the AKEL termed the U.S. actions against Nicaragua as "inhuman and unjust." It accused the "U.S. superpower" of resorting "to gangster tactics and piracy in order to destroy a small country whose only objective is to independently form its own future" (*Kharavyi*, 4 May). Concerning the Middle East, the party newspaper claimed that the United States, using the excuse of the TWA airplane hijacking and the hostages being held in Beirut, "is now preparing for a new military presence in Lebanon." Citing that the United States had previously used "facilities" on Cyprus for past invasions, the writer warned Cyprus "not to become involved in such plans in any way, shape, or form." Since Cyprus "is a nonaligned country and its position is on the side of struggling people," the republic should not encourage "cunning, imperialist plots directed against neighboring and friendly people" (ibid., 27 June). Throughout the year, the AKEL charged that the United States had "acquired bases on the territories occupied by the Turkish troops" in Cyprus, as part of a design for using the bases "against the Soviet Union and against other friendly countries." Finally a warning to the Cypriot population was issued: "Only politically naive people can cherish delusions regarding the clearly enslaving role of U.S.-NATO imperialism in Cyprus" (ibid., 13 July).

In anticipation of the Reagan-Gorbachev meeting in November, Papaioannou noted that this will be a "definite step toward the cause of peace." The international situation remains "tense" because "Pentagon imperialist circles headed by Reagan not only react negatively to the repeated peaceful actions and proposals, but they also increase their armaments and expand their warlike plans." Strong pressure from "the American people and all the other peoples of the earth" is what the Communists think is needed "if the U.S. imperialists are to change their inflammatory, warlike policy." Papaioannou concluded that "this is why it is the supreme duty of the entire world to wholeheartedly support the struggle for peace and the struggle to prevent a nuclear holocaust." Thus, the best way for Cyprus to contribute to this lofty goal "is to be independent, sovereign, territorially integral, federal, united, nonaligned, and demilitarized" (ibid., 13 September).

International Party Contacts. The second conference of communist and workers' parties of the region of the eastern Mediterranean, the Near and Middle East, and the Red Sea was convened in Nicosia in January. It was attended by representatives of more than seventeen countries, which was more than had registered for the first conference four years earlier. The theme of the meeting was that "the developments internationally as also in the region are rapidly acquiring an exceptionally dangerous character" (*IB*, April). In the final declaration, the conferees emphasized that "the one solely responsible for this cold war turn in international relations is imperialism and especially U.S. imperialism." Such international gatherings are warmly welcomed by the leaders of the AKEL, since they help maintain the extensive relations that the Cypriot Communists enjoy with both ruling and other nonruling communist parties.

In June a delegation of the Communist Party of the Soviet Union (CPSU) visited Cyprus for what has become an annual event at the invitation of the AKEL. Their joint statement stressed "Soviet support for the U.N. secretary general's efforts toward a viable and just solution of the Cyprus issue through negotiations between the two communities on the basis of the U.N. resolutions" (Nicosia Domestic Service, 17 May). In July a delegation of 150 young Cypriots went to Moscow to participate in the World Youth and Student Festival (ibid., 24 July). During the same month, Papaioannou led a delegation to Moscow to meet with the Politburo of the CPSU Central Committee. After a "warm comradely" meeting the two parties declared their commitment to "developing mutually beneficial links between the USSR and the Republic of Cyprus . . . and consolidating the truly fraternal relations that have taken shape between the Soviet and Cypriot Communists" (*Pravda*, 30 July). A spokesman for the Republic of Cyprus commented favorably on that communiqué by saying: "this affirmation is proof of the Soviet Union's consistent support for the just Cypriot cause" (Nicosia Domestic Service, 31 July). Before returning to Cyprus, Papaioannou also stopped off in Bulgaria to discuss the Cyprus issue with the BCP general secretary, Todor Zhivkov. The two leaders "unreservedly condemned . . . the illegal Turkish Cypriot state and all the secessionist actions of the Turkish leaders" (ibid., 19 August).

The AKEL sent greetings to János Kádár on his re-election as general secretary of the Hungarian Socialist Workers' Party and wished him "further success in constructing your developed socialist society, peace and happiness" (*Kharavyi*, 4 April). A similar message was sent to Gustáv Husák and the Czechoslovakian Communist Party on the occasion of the 40th anniversary of the Red Army's liberation of Czechoslovakia from "fascist occupation" (ibid., 8 May). On the 68th anniversary of the October Revolution, the AKEL dutifully sent greetings to General Secretary Gorbachev and the Soviet Union—"a champion of freedom, justice, and peace" (ibid., 7 November).

T. W. Adams
Washington, D.C.

Denmark

Population. 5,109,000
Party. Communist Party of Denmark (Danmarks Kommunistiske Parti; DKP)
Founded. 1919
Membership. 10,000 (estimated, actual number probably lower)
Chairman. Jørgen Jensen
Secretary General. Poul Emanuel
Executive Committee. 16 members: Jørgen Jensen, Ib Nørlund (vice chairman), Poul Emanuel, Jan Andersen, Villy Fulgsang, Margit Hansen, Bernard Jeune, Gunnar Kanstrup, Kurt Kristensen, Dan Lundstrup, Freddy Madsen, Jørgen Madsen, Anette Nielsen, Bo Rosschou, Ole Sohn, Ingmar Wagner
Central Committee. 51 members, 15 candidate members
Status. Legal
Last Congress. Twenty-seventh, 12–15 May 1983; next congress scheduled for 1986
Last Election. 10 January 1984, 0.7 percent, no representation
Auxiliary Organization. Communist Youth of Denmark (Danmarks Kommunistiske Ungdom; DKU), Ole Sørensen, chairman; Communist Students of Denmark (Danmarks Kommunistiske Studenter; KOMM.S.), Mette Gjerløv, chair
Publications. *Land og Folk* (Nation and People; Gunnar Kanstrup, editor; daily circulation 13,000 weekdays and 16,000 weekends), *Tiden-Verden Rund* (Times Around the World; theoretical monthly), *Fremad* (Forward; monthly)

Although 1985 had its dramatic moments for Danish politics, the DKP spent another year in the political wilderness. Currently weaker than at any time since World War II, the DKP received a scant 23,085 votes in the last parliamentary elections in January 1984. The DKP has not been represented in parliament since October 1979, when its vote fell below the 2 percent minimum required for proportional representation in the Folketing (parliament). The November local elections demonstrated the continuing weakness of the DKP.

The political balance in parliament remains precarious, but the coalition government of conservative Prime Minister Poul Schlüter navigated another year without elections. The 1984 elections had been the country's seventh in less than thirteen years. For a decade after the destabilizing elections of December 1973, parties of the extreme left and right had controlled between a quarter and a third of the parliamentary seats, making it difficult for the more moderate parties to govern effectively. Schlüter's current four-party coalition majority depends on the Radical Liberals (a center-left reformist party) and the nonsocialist representatives from the Faeroe Islands and Greenland. This complex coalition has kept the opposition—led by the reformist Social Democratic Party (SDP)—at bay on domestic issues. The successful agreement in June of an outline for tax reform, after more than a decade of discussion, reflects SDP acceptance of the coalition's continuing viability. On foreign and security policy issues, however, the SDP can count on the Radical Liberals and the two leftist parties to challenge the government. Thus far Schlüter has chosen not to make foreign and security policy issues matters of confidence.

For 25 years the DKP has had to compete with other Marxist parties to the left of the SDP. In the past fifteen years, these leftist parties have typically attracted an eighth of the national vote. In 1984 they collectively polled 14.9 percent, but the DKP share continued to plummet. Public opinion polls in 1985 gave the leftist bloc up to nearly twenty percent without renewed support for the DKP. Until recently the SDP was also losing voters to the leftist parties, but 1985 polls suggest that this trend may be over. The independent Marxist Socialist People's Party (Socialistiske Folkeparti; SF) has advanced notably during the past eight years. It doubled its support in the 1981 parliamentary elections and held on to these gains in 1984. It advanced further in the November local elections. The third leftist party with significant support is the Left Socialist Party (Venstresocialisterne; VS), a contentious assembly of former student radicals (from the 1960s) that holds on to a base of support from students and public employees (as does the SF). The VS has five Folketing seats.

Less important are three small sects: the moribund Communist Workers' Party (Kommunistisk Arbejderparti; KAP), a "Maoist" relic that has unsuccessfully sought a closer relationship with the VS and did not run in the 1984 elections; the International Socialist Workers' Party (Internationalen Socialistisk Arbejderparti; SAP), the Danish branch of the Trotskyist Fourth International, which received 2,200 votes in 1984; and the most recent leftist group, the Marxist-Leninist Party (Marxistisk-Leninistisk Parti; MLP), whose pro-Albania line attracted fewer than 1,000 votes in January 1984. Two new parties, the Greens (De Grønne) and the Humanist Party (Humanisterne) were entered on the ballot by the Interior Ministry in recent months. Although they may not be strictly Marxist parties, they are likely to appeal to some of the same voters.

Leadership and Organization. Through good times and bad, the DKP internal organization and leadership changes little. Despite the party's decline under his leadership, Jørgen Jensen was reconfirmed as chairman of the DKP's Twenty-seventh Congress in May 1983. Jensen, a former activist and leader of a Metalworkers' Union local, succeeded to the party chairmanship in 1977 and is a veteran of more than 30 years in the DKP. Ib Nørlund, the party's number-two man and chief theoretician, has been in his post for decades. The same is true for the party's secretary (administrative director) Poul Emanuel. There have been periodic challenges to the party leadership from within, and these were quite vociferous in 1983. Such efforts at change are inevitably in vain, as the challengers are forced to leave the party by exclusion or resignation, usually accompanied by a barrage of calumny. Efforts in 1985 by the chief of the Seamen's Union, Preben Møller Hansen, who was expelled from the DKP several years ago, to increase communication between the DKP and his faction the Common Course Club (Fælles Kurs Klub; FKK) were repulsed by the Communist leadership (*Politiken Weekly*, 12 December).

The party's highest authority is the triennial congress. The Central Committee is elected at the congress, and it, in turn, elects the party's Executive Committee (Politburo), chairman, secretary, and other posts. Despite the attendance of some 453 delegates at the 1983 congress, the DKP functions fully in the Leninist model of a self-perpetuating elite. In recent years the Central Committee has met from four to six times annually. During noncongress years, the party holds an annual meeting. Such meetings, typically held in the early autumn, reaffirm the general party goals as set at the congress and are occasions for the party to use media coverage to make known its views on domestic and foreign affairs. Despite the party's weak position, media coverage is surprisingly good.

The DKP does not encourage discussion of internal organization or leadership, but hints of changes occasionally appear in the noncommunist press. A leftist newspaper ran an extensive interview with DKP Executive Committee member Jan Andersen, who emerged as a prominent leader of the large labor protests of March and April. Andersen is a local foreman in the Copenhagen section of the Metalworkers' Union and active in the Shop Stewards' Movement, which has regularly challenged the national trade-union leadership during the past decade. His emphasis on utilizing the labor movement and the unrest of many trade unionists suggests future DKP strategy. Andersen was quick to deny insinuations that the strikes and protests were engineered by the DKP. Some believe that Andersen could emerge as the next leader of the DKP when and if Jensen decides to step down (*Information*, 18 April; *JPRS*, 12 June).

The DKU is the DKP's largest affiliate; at the Twenty-seventh Congress its leadership stressed two areas of activity: support for radical trade-union factions appealing to apprentices and young workers; and mobilization and influence over young participants in the various peace organizations. The DKU has not been successful in either area. The KOMM.S. overlaps with the DKU, but concentrates its efforts on university students. Communists have periodically held high posts in the Danish National Students' Council (Danske Studerendes Fællesrad; DSF), but the DSF's influence has declined in recent years. KOMM.S. maintains some organizational autonomy and has its own publications, *Røde Blade* (Red Leaves) and *Spartakus*, and its own meetings (Sixth Congress, October 1982).

Although the DKP has policies regarding the self-governing territories of Greenland and the Faeroe Islands, it does not have organizations in either. There was an attempt to form an autonomous Faeroe Communist Party in 1975 and later years, but it apparently failed. Neither of the leftist parties active in Greenland has ties to the DKP.

Domestic Affairs. The economic recovery evident in 1984 continued in 1985, though at a more modest pace. The Gross Domestic Product grew at an annual rate of about 2 percent, and the rate of inflation fell below 5 percent, the lowest level in more than a decade. The two main economic problems remained the high level of unemployment, which nevertheless fell to 9 percent, and the balance of payment deficit, which worsened to about 20 billion kroner (approximately U.S. $1.8 billion). In regular statements (principally in *Land og Folk*), the DKP denounced nearly all governmental policies. The most controversial issue was the legislated settlement of the national collective-bargaining agreements in March. When union-employer talks seemed stalemated, the Schlüter government passed an act restricting wage increases to 2 percent for the first year and 1.75 percent for the second year. Provisions for public employees were even lower. Compulsory savings were instituted for above-average incomes, and there were tax increases for businesses. Employees are due an hour reduction in the work week in 1987. As these provisions were even more restrictive than those proposed by the Employers Association, there was considerable outrage. For days the country faced demonstrations and strikes, including a demonstration of more than 100,000 in front of parliament. Communists were prominent in these protests (*Nordisk Kontakt*, nos. 6, 7). By mid-April things returned to normal, although public opinion polls reflected a surge in support for the opposition parties.

The DKP's domestic program is spelled out in the manifesto adopted at the Twenty-seventh Congress, *The Denmark We Want*, and the action program *Our Answer*. More recent statements adjust these provisions to current issues. Among the measures desired by the DKP are: establishment of new public enterprises; nationalization of all banks and financial institutions; close state control of investment, including reductions in interest on public bonds; supervision of the cooperative movement, agriculture, and fisheries; and, finally, the perennial DKP proposal to reduce the workweek to 35 hours, restrict overtime, extend various leaves, and other measures with no reduction in real wages. These last goals are common to all of the socialist parties, although the SDP sees them as the gradual fruits of free collective bargaining.

Although labor relations and economic policy were major DKP concerns in 1985, the DKP has little formal influence over major trade unions, most of which are affiliated with the SDP. As noted, however, Communists are active in union locals, and compared to electoral politics, it is an area of some DKP strength. Communists have been especially visible in the metalworkers', typographers', and maritime unions. Although Jan Andersen was able to revive the radical Shop Stewards' Movement, that group has normally been rejected by democratic unions.

The labor unrest of the spring did not yield any lasting direct support for the DKP in regular public opinion polls. The DKP failed a more important test in the November municipal and county elections. In total votes DKP candidates collected only 1.1 percent nationwide, although individual DKP members were elected to city and county councils mainly in the larger urban areas. The SDP gained significantly, but the largest advance was scored by the SF, which nearly doubled its vote. SF candidate Charlotte Amundsen was nearly elected mayor of Copenhagen instead of veteran SDP mayor Egon Weiderkamp. Elsewhere the DKP was outpolled also by the VS (whose support declined) and even the Greens (2.6 percent) (*Politiken Weekly*, 21 November).

Foreign Affairs. Although the DKP has little effect on Danish foreign policy, the international political situation has always had a direct impact on status of the DKP. Increased East-West tensions, such as the Cold War of the late 1940s and the waning detente in the late 1970s, capped by the Soviet invasion of Afghanistan in 1979, spelled domestic disaster for the DKP. Few West European communist parties have been more steadfastly loyal to the foreign policy line of the Soviet Union than the DKP. On the other hand, the DKP has cleverly exploited international issues such as the continuing unpopularity of Danish membership in the European Economic Community (EEC) and the strong revival of the peace movement over the issue of intermediate-range nuclear missiles in Europe. Through front organizations, the DKP has been able to promote positions that would attract little attention under the DKP label.

Several foreign policy issues important to the DKP were prominent on the Danish political agenda during the past year. A security policy survey composed by senior diplomat Peter Dyvig was released in December 1984 and discussed at length during the winter. In part the report was requested by senior SDP leaders who found their party increasingly divided on security policy matters. A security policy survey by nonpartisan civil servants might depoliticize the security policy debate and, at the very least, would cool the discussion within the SDP. The Dyvig report emphasized the obligations arising from NATO membership. Danish defense rested on both NATO deterrence and credibility of outside reinforcements in the event of war. Although all of the unilateral and multilateral measures taken in the past decade to reduce European tensions have enjoyed broad support within Denmark, current proposals for such measures as a Nordic and Central European nuclear-free zone require considerable elaboration and clarification (Denmark, Foreign Ministry, *Denmark's Security Policy Situation in the 1980s* [Dyvig report]).

All of the leftist parties reject such caution, not least the DKP, for whom Danish withdrawal from NATO has always been the most important foreign policy priority. Because all leftist parties share a similar opposition to Danish NATO and EEC memberships, the DKP position is not significant as such. It has relied on dedicated individuals to exert influence on its behalf. Central Committee member Jens Peter Bonde is a leading figure in the broadly based Popular Movement Against the EEC (Folkebevægelsen mod EF), sits as one of its four members in the European Parliament, and edits its weekly paper, *Det ny Notat* (The New Notice). At the Popular Movement's annual convention, Bonde accused Foreign Minister Ellemann-Jensen of weakening Denmark's right to veto unfavorable EEC decisions. This was vehemently denied by the foreign minister (*Politiken Weekly*, 3 October). Another Communist, Anker Schjerning, has been similarly prominent in the peace movement.

The Dyvig report did not keep foreign affairs off the political agenda for long. In May an SDP motion opposing U.S. Strategic Defense Initiative research was introduced in parliament and passed with the governmental parties abstaining. Again in November another SDP motion reiterating Danish opposition to new nuclear weapons in either Eastern or Western Europe was adopted (*Nordisk Kontakt*, nos. 10, 15).

The DKP's distinction is its complete and unswaying support of every aspect of Soviet foreign policy. The final communiqué from the 1985 party meeting in Odense reiterated this total support and brought the DKP line up-to-date with recent Soviet disarmament proposals (Tass, 14 October). Previously the DKP had been careful to emphasize its support for a *Nordic* as opposed to a *Baltic* nuclear-free zone. The latter would of course require participation by Warsaw Pact nations (*Land og Folk*, 15 January; *JPRS*, 11 March).

International Party Contacts. The DKP leadership maintains close ties with other pro-Moscow communist parties, especially those in Eastern Europe. Delegations from all of the Warsaw Pact countries regularly attend DKP congresses. DKP leaders are also ardent travelers to foreign communist meetings and countries. During 1985 top DKP figures visited Outer Mongolia, Bulgaria, and the Soviet Union, and they attended a large gathering of West European communist parties in Paris. In 1984 Chairman Jensen had visited Afghanistan and certified to Soviet good intentions there.

The Mongolian and Bulgarian visits in June and July confirmed the DKP's support for Moscow's closest allies (MONTSAME, 12 June; *JPRS*, 18 June and 23 July; BTA, 3 July). Multilateral contacts with eighteen other West European communist parties occurred in more cosmopolitan surroundings at the June meeting in Paris. Reports emphasized interparty communications, but beyond reflections on the common crisis of capitalist states and the need for European workers to perceive their common problems, the Paris conference did not result in resolutions (*L'Humanité*, 22 June; *JPRS*, 7 August).

The visit of top DKP leaders to Moscow in October was probably more decisive in its consensus. Chairman Jensen and Vice Chairman Nørlund led the group that was received by CPSU Central Committee officials led by Politburo member Ponomarev. The final reports emphasized the identity of views between the two parties with particular emphasis on international issues and Soviet proposals for arms reductions (*Pravda*, 28 October; *JPRS*, 29 October).

Other Marxist/Leftist Groups. The DKP is only one of several left-wing parties currently active in Danish politics. The SF is by far the most powerful of these groups, and it continued to gain strength in 1985. Originally a splinter from the DKP (in 1958), the SF steadily gained ground despite a decade of internal splits and electoral setbacks between 1968 and 1977. Ever since it won its first parliamentary representation in 1960, the SF has sought to push the SDP leftward. In 1966–1967 and 1971–1973, SF votes kept the Social Democrats in power. The first experiment in formal SF-SDP collaboration (the co-called Red Cabinet) ended when the SF's left wing split off to form the VS party. In 1973, several right-wing Social Democrats abandoned their party to form the Center Democrats. Following the SF's advance in December 1981, it appeared that another effort would be made at collaboration. Since both parties were still short of a parliamentary majority, and since the VS would not cooperate, Anker Jørgensen's government required support from the Radical Liberals and possibly others. This baroque constellation collapsed ten months later. Despite these disasters and fundamental disagreements between the SF and the SDP, the press continues to speculate on SF-SDP relations. Both are, of course, in the opposition, but while the SF thrives on the sidelines, Social Democrats out of power are an unhappy lot.

The SF program is decidedly socialist, pacifist, and Marxian, but it emphasizes Danish values and rejects foreign socialist models. The SF is explicitly non-Leninist in both its internal party governance and its attitudes toward Danish parliamentary democracy. Its feuds and schisms now past, the SF thrives under the experienced leadership of its veteran chairman, Gert Petersen, and is the natural alternative to dissatisfied SDP and other leftist voters.

At the annual party meeting in Ålborg (3–5 May), Chairman Petersen reiterated the SF's willingness to cooperate with the SDP in defeating the Schlüter government and replacing it with an SDP minority cabinet, with which the SF would pragmatically negotiate a common domestic program. Petersen admitted that foreign and security policy differences were too great to permit a formal coalition. The SDP continues to ignore such overtures, and it failed in November 1984 to support a SF proposal to require a referendum on the government's cutbacks in unemployment insurance. Ironically, the two parties have voted together on foreign and security policy motions, although only on those more moderate measures put forward by the SDP (*Nordisk Kontakt*, no. 16, 1984, and no. 9).

The SF remains firmly committed to its opposition to Danish membership in NATO and the EEC. In May, Gert Petersen denounced the government's "slavish loyalty" to the Reagan administration's defense plans, including the Strategic Defense Initiative, which Petersen claimed was opposed by a public opinion majority in both Europe and the United States (ibid., no. 7). Such positions may limit the SF's current domestic political influence, but they are also the source of much SF popularity. Despite some fluctuation, opinion polls showed substantial advances in SF support. Unlike previous advances, these gains have not come primarily from SDP ranks; probably the SF is now gathering additional support at the expense of the DKP, VS, and other leftist groups.

The SF continues to broaden its base of support even within the labor unions despite its "white collar/public employee" image. The SF has informal but close ties to analogous parties in Norway and Sweden and looser ties to the Italian Communist Party. It is increasingly clear that the SF is more than a protest party, although dissatisfaction with the DKP and the SDP have accounted for some of its support. It is a haven for activists and voters committed to a "soft" Danish Marxism and democratic-socialist solutions without reference to or apologies for less fortunate experiments elsewhere.

The VS is much weaker, and its current decline in support was reflected in the November local elections as well as in regular opinion polls throughout the year. With five parliamentary seats, a number of municipal and county council seats, and even a magistrate (deputy mayor) post in Copenhagen, the VS remains a visible but marginal element. The party's more moderate leaders have expelled the so-called Leninists, and at the party's Fourteenth Congress in May a resolution was adopted guaranteeing human and democratic rights to all, including bourgeois opponents. Some had suggested earlier that on the "road to socialism" some of these rights might have to be temporarily suspended. The 170 delegates denounced bourgeois (that is, current Danish) democracy as an illusion. After several years of debate the VS clarified its position on Afghanistan, a source of considerable internecine strife (*Information*, 8 February; *JPRS*, 26 March). Soviet intervention could only be accepted if it were in support of genuinely strong internal forces and if there were no alternatives (*Nordisk Kontakt*, no. 9). Another controversial policy was discussed: the party's rule requiring "rotation" after seven years in a salaried office. This rule had already forced several effective VS leaders from parliament and now threatened its colorful magistrate in Copenhagen, Villo Sigurdsson (*Aktuelt*, 6 January; *JPRS*, 14 March). The change was defeated, and Sigurdsson's term has expired, although the VS continues to hold on to the position.

There are at least three additional leftist groups participating in Danish elections. The SAP has only minimal support, but its newspaper, *Klassekampen* (Class Struggle), is well informed on Danish leftist politics as well as the international Trotskyist movement. The SDP expelled three Trotskyists in August with an eye to problems in the British Labour Party with such factions (*Berlingske Tidende*, 14 August; *JPRS*, 24 September).

The Albanian perspective dominates the miniscule Marxist-Leninist Party, which was not allowed to appear on the ballot with its confusing full name: Communist Party of Denmark/Marxist-Leninist. The MLP publishes a newspaper, *Arbejderen* (Worker) and a theoretical journal, *Partets Vej* (The Party's Way). Its program is similar to other extreme leftist groups.

The KAP is the oldest of the extreme leftist sects, dating back to the student uprisings of 1968. Under its veteran leader, Copenhagen University historian Benito Scocozza, the KAP seeks to keep alive a "Maoist" tradition even as China's own policies have changed dramatically in the past decade. The KAP's overtures to other parties, such as the VS, have thus far been rejected (Ib Garodkin, *Håndbog i Dansk Politik, 1985*, 7th ed., Præstø: Mjølner, 1985).

Danish electoral laws make it possible to run nationally for parliament with only about 20,000 signatures. Danes willingly sign such petitions. A major incentive to undertake even a hopeless parliamentary campaign is the free and generous radio and television time allowed all parties. Most such media access is in the form of rigorous questioning by professional journalists. Inexperienced party spokesmen can find the procedure devastating. Nevertheless, Danish political flora is as varied and often as colorful as the Tivoli Gardens in June.

Eric S. Einhorn
University of Massachusetts at Amherst

Finland

Population. 4,894,000
Party. Finnish Communist Party (Suomen Kommunistinen Puolue; SKP); runs as the Finnish People's Democratic League (Suomen Kansan Demokraattinen Liitto; SKDL) in parliamentary elections.
Founded. 1918
Membership. 50,000 (claimed); 28,000–34,000 (other estimates)
Chairman. Arvo Aalto
Secretary General. Esko Vainionpaa
Politburo. 9 members: Arvo Aalto, Aarno Aitamurto, Helja Tammisola (deputy chairman), Erkki Kauppila, Arvo Kamppainen, Mirja Ylitalo, Timo Laaksonen, Olavi Haeninen, Esko Vainionpaa
Central Committee. 50 full and 15 alternate members
Status. Legal

Last Congress. Twentieth, 24–26 May 1984, in Helsinki; an Extraordinary Congress was held on 23 March 1985.
Last Election. 1983, 14 percent, 27 of 200 seats
Auxiliary Organizations. Finnish Democratic Youth League; Women's Organization
Publications. *Kansan Uitset* (daily); *Tiedonantaja* (daily), Stalinist; *Folktidningen* (Swedish-language weekly), all three published in Helsinki

The SKP became Finland's largest party after World War II. Unlike other European communist parties, the SKP has been part of the government coalition for some lengthy periods, from 1944 to 1948 and, with some interruptions, from 1966 to 1982. The party continued to win over twenty percent of the vote, but significant ideological differences surfaced within the party while it was in the ranks of the opposition in the 1960s. The differences became hardened during the 1970s, to the extent that the more moderate, majority wing of the party was part of the governing coalition between 1975 and 1982, while the Stalinist, pro-Soviet minority was in opposition. The tensions between the two wings of the party sharpened further when the veteran moderate leader of the SKP, Aarne Saarinen, gave up the party leadership in 1982 and was succeeded as chairman by Juoko Kajonoja. The latter promised to unify the two wings of the party, but his rigid adherence to the Kremlin line had the opposite effect.

In 1983 the SKP (and its electoral front, the SKDL) suffered the sharpest electoral defeat in its history. In 1958 the SKP had the largest group in the parliament with 50 deputies; in 1983, the number was reduced from 35 to 27, the fourth largest parliamentary group. Its percentage of the vote fell to 14 percent, also the lowest ever (the high point was 23.5 percent in 1948). This was partly due to the increasing appeal of the Social Democrats and, to a lesser extent, the new Green Party to onetime communist voters. Many voters were also alienated by the sharp, open differences between the two wings of the party and the perceived heavy-handed interference of the Soviets in SKP affairs.

The Twentieth Congress on 24–26 May 1984 was a highly contentious one, which highlighted the deepening split between the moderate wing, led by the newly elected chairman, Arvo Aalto, and the Stalinist wing, headed by Taisto Sinisalo. The hardliners were offered three of the eleven places on the Politburo and 15 of the 50 seats on the Central Committee, but they turned down the offer. Thus, the entire Politburo and Central Committee were composed of moderates. In the crucial vote that led to this state of affairs, the moderates beat the Stalinists, 183 to 163 votes.

Leadership and Organization. This could well turn out to be a watershed year in the history of the SKP. It was the year that the Stalinist wing, for all intents and purposes, was read out of the party by the majority faction. The Stalinist wing had called for an Extraordinary Congress after the severe setbacks it suffered in the 1984 party congress, yet when the congress was actually held on 23 March, it was boycotted by the Stalinists. In the meantime, Aalto and his colleagues had been orchestrating for some time what would take place at the special congress.

After the 1984 congress, the moderate wing set in motion a system by which seven new district organizations would be established parallel to those eight districts that were controlled by the Sinisalo faction. When the North Karelia district organization was set up in Joensuu on 20 January, it became the seventh and last parallel district established by the majority in a minority-controlled area. New districts had previously been set up by the moderates at Uusimaa, Varsinaid-Suomi, Pirkanmaa, South Haeme, Southeast Finland, and North Sovo (Helsinki International Service, 20 January). At the time of the 1984 congress, the Aalto wing controlled nine districts, and the Sinisalo wing, eight. Thus, by establishing seven new parallel districts, a 9-to-8 moderate-wing margin became a 16-to-8 moderate margin.

At the March Extraordinary Congress, Aalto announced a new slogan that he hoped would help the Communists again become a significant electoral force. He called for "socialism with a Finnish face," which reminded many of Alexander Dubcek's plea in Czechoslovakia in 1968 for "socialism with a human face." The *Economist* on 6 April commented that "the special congress was meant to reunite the party, but not by reconciliation . . . The majority presented the so-called Stalinist minority with an ultimatum: accept the decisions taken by the majority, or be excluded." The minority, which did not attend the congress, refused.

The special congress did not throw out members of the Stalinist faction, but it did set in motion a process by which party cards would be exchanged. Members of the hardline faction could therefore formally transfer their allegiance to the moderate wing of the SKP. It was made clear at the congress that anyone who decided not to work within the party on Aalto's terms would exclude himself from the SKP (*Hufvudstadsbladet*, 6 May). One of the major decisions made at the special congress was to give the Central Committee the right to expel Stalinist district organizations. Previously, this had been a decision that only a party congress could make. The hardliners claimed that this was an illegal move and asked Helsinki local courts to bring suit against the leaders of the majority wing (Paris, AFP, 25 March). The Swedish-language (moderate) communist weekly, *Hufvudstadsbladet*, on 27 March described the congress as an "undramatic event," because of the absence of the boycotting hardliners, but went on to say that "the absence of surface drama must not, however, mislead one into concluding that it was not a straightforward dramatic turning point in the party's conflict-filled history."

The congress also voted to install Esko Vainionpaa as secretary general. He replaced Aarno Aitamurto, who resigned. Working under Aalto, Vainionpaa is concerned primarily with taking care of the organizational machinery and the party's financial affairs (*Suomen Kuvalehti*, 29 March). A week after the special congress, Vainionpaa suggested in an interview that it was theoretically possible for the hardline group to remain in the SKDL electoral front, but in actual practice this seemed impossible. He said that he had not observed any indications from the Sinisalo wing that it was prepared for reconciliation. He said that the party leadership was willing to negotiate, but only if the following conditions were met: the eight minority districts would cease resisting the decisions of the congress in their newspaper, *Tiedonantaja*, and the districts would fully implement decisions taken by the SKP (*Hufvudstadsbladet*, 5 April).

As might be expected, the Stalinist faction reacted sharply to the decisions of the Extraordinary Congress. On 24 April, *Tedonantaja* editorialized: "Is there a communist party even left in Finland? Many members and friends of the Finnish Communist Party asked this question as the situation in the party continued deteriorating. The Finnish Communist Party still exists in Finland, though its current right-wing leadership is trying to liquidate it as a communist party. This work of destruction cannot go on forever without destroying the Communist Party."

On 13 September the other shoe dropped. The SKP Central Committee gave an ultimatum to the Stalinist minority to dismantle its party organization or face expulsion. The Central Committee sent a letter to the eight district organizations run by the hardliners, telling them to cease operations, to stop publication of *Tiedonantaja*, and to accept all decisions of the Central Committee. The SKP leadership went on to say that if the Sinisalo wing did not accept all of these conditions, no minority candidates would be included on the official party electoral lists in the general elections of March 1987 (Paris, AFP, 13 September).

The leadership of the SKP gave the minority one month to carry out the ultimatum. The Sinisalo faction refused to accede, however, and so on 13 October the SKP Central Committee formally expelled the eight district organizations controlled by the hardliners. Further, individual members in those districts were told that they would be struck off the party rolls if they did not join the mainstream organization within the next few weeks (*Economist*, 19 October). The expelled district organizations met in mid-October in Lahti in what they referred to as the "October gathering." An official delegation for the Communist Party of the Soviet Union (CPSU) attended. Sinisalo was cautious about calling for a new party; for the time being, the line was that the minority wing represented the true SKP and that the other group was abandoning socialist principles (Helsinki International Service, 20 October). The minority group released a statement saying that "by splitting the SKP, the aim is to replace the party by a nationalist and semi–social democratic organization. Thus, the way is open to a move by the right in Finland and for an assault on the treaty of friendship, cooperation and mutual assistance with the USSR" (ibid., 14 October).

Thus, Finland joined other West European countries in which the political landscape included at least two communist parties: a larger Eurocommunist-type party and a smaller hardline party. There has been considerable speculation that what was once the largest political party in Finland will be decimated in the next election. Stockholm's *Svenska Dagbladet* speculated on 22 October that the SKP is "in the process of sinking back to the level where the Nordic countries' communists generally find themselves, that is, under the 10 percent barrier." In fact, a public opinion poll carried out by Taloustutkimus for *APU* magazine indicated that in July the support for the communist electoral front dropped from the 14 percent it received in the 1983 election to 12.5 percent (Helsinki Domestic Service, 17 July).

Auxiliary and Front Organizations. The split between the two wings of the SKP has raised troubling questions for the SKDL. How well can the SKDL function with two warring communist groups? It was originally composed of members of the SKP as well as left-wing Socialists and Social Democrats who could not accept the Social Democratic line of that time. Now, only one-fifth of the SKDL's membership is Communist, but the majority of officers are members of the SKP. This fact led Eric Alenius at the SKDL party congress on 12–13 February to ask for equal treatment for Socialists and Communists. There seems to be little doubt, however, that the SKDL will continue to be communist-dominated. A major crisis facing the SKDL was the replacement of Kalevi Kivisto as chairman of the party. Kivisto, widely respected beyond party lines, was appointed by president Mauno Koivisto to be governor of the province of Keski-Suomi (Central Finland). When Kivisto resigned, *Suomen Kuvalehti* commented on 9 August that "there was nobody even in sight" to replace "the charismatic chairman."

Finally, at the fourteenth league convention on 26 May, the SKDL voted for 47-year-old Esko Helle, a first-term member of the parliament and a dentist, to be chairman. The vote was 161 to 31, the 31 votes going to Pirkko Turpeinan, a candidate put up by the Stalinist wing of the SKP. The new league board has eight SKP majority members, five socialists, and one minority representative.

In early November the SKDL expelled six minority SKP districts. The executive board explained that the districts were "continuing activity which is contrary to the goals of the SKDL and are building up a new rival organization which aims at weakening the SKDL" (Helsinki International Service, 6 November).

The split within the SKP also affected the communist youth movement, the Finnish Democratic Youth League (SDNL). There was much acrimony between the two factions, and the majority group took complete control at the SDNL congress held in Jyvaskyla over Easter (*Helsingen Sanomat*, 9 April).

SKP Domestic and Foreign Positions. In a speech in Kemi on 23 February, Aalto suggested more cooperation with the Social Democrats. He said that the bourgeoisie was doing well and the left wing suffering a decline; only the combined forces of the workers' movement could turn that situation around. He suggested that one of the major recommendations of the left wing—one that would win back support—would be to shorten the work week (ibid., 24 February). This call was made throughout the year by the SKP and SKDL; suggestions have ranged between 30 and 35 hours.

The SKP has also attempted to win back some of the Green Party vote by taking strong environmental positions. On the foreign front, the SKP made a number of statements calling for a Nordic nuclear-free zone and a halt to the nuclear arms race (Helsinki International Service, 21 August). The SKP Politburo on several occasions has condemned the Finnish government for not being strong enough in its measures against South Africa. The Politburo has said that criticism is not enough; complete severance of diplomatic and economic ties is required (ibid., 16 October).

Relations with the Soviet Union. As is well known, the proximity of the Soviet giant has had a constraining effect on decisionmakers both within the Finnish government and within the SKP. One of the most striking phenomena of 1985 is the extent to which the Aalto wing of the SKP has rejected the attempts on the part of the CPSU to influence SKP policy—and the extent to which the Soviets have tried to influence events in the SKP. On 13 September, when the majority leadership of the SKP was meeting to discuss policy toward the minority faction, the CPSU Central Committee sent a quite unambiguous message, stating its belief that "a split in the SKP will cause irreparable damage to the friendship between the parties and between our countries" (Helsinki Domestic Service, 13 September). Leningrad party leader Anatoliy Dumachev repeated the same warning in Lahti, Finland, at a 20 October meeting of the eight minority district committees that had been expelled (Paris, AFP, 21 October). In June, *Pravda* had criticized both the SKDL and the SKP leaders' preparations for the 1987 elections; the editorial questioned Vainionpaa's position that the Stalinists would not be on the electoral lists and that he, Vainionpaa, "was getting ready for an election defeat" (*Helsingen Sanomat*, 19 June).

Despite the acrimonious statements emanating from Moscow regarding the SKP, official statements from the Soviets regarding visits by President Koivisto and other Finnish officials and by a delegation from the Center Party seemed to be positive. Although Soviet statements had said that the situation in the SKP might harm relations between the Soviet and Finnish governments, the subject was not mentioned when Koivisto became the first Western head of state to be received by Mikhail Gorbachev since he assumed the leadership position in the Soviet Union (*Economist*, 19 October).

International Party Contacts. Aalto visited French Communist Party first secretary Georges Marchais in mid-June. They issued a joint statement that indicated a "new view" of party relations. The communiqué stated that "relations between the two communist parties are based on a free choice of strategy, independence, equal rights and mutual respect" (*Helsingen Sanomat*, 21 June). Before the Aalto-Marchais meeting, the SKP participated in a meeting of West European communist parties on 12–13 June that focused on "the crisis, analysis, and actions of communist parties in each country" (Paris, *L'Humanité*, 22 June).

Aalto visited the Hungarian Communist Party leader, János Kádár, while "vacationing" in Hungary. The two leaders agreed "that the process of detente begun in Helsinki must continue, and that the traditionally good and multifaceted Hungarian-Finnish relations contribute to the European cooperation" (Budapest Domestic Service, 3 October).

Peter Grothe
Monterey Institute of International Studies

France

Population. 55,094,000
Party. French Communist Party (Parti communiste française; PCF)
Founded. 1920
Membership. 610,000 (*L'Humanité*, 2 November 1984)
General Secretary. Georges Marchais
Politburo. 22 members: Georges Marchais, Charles Fiterman (propaganda and communication), Jean-Claude Gayssot (party organization), Maxime Gremetz (foreign affairs), André Lajoinie (president of the communist group in the National Assembly), Paul Laurent (liaison with party federations), Gisèle Moreau (women's activities and family politics), Gaston Plissonnier (coordination of the work of the Politburo and Secretariat), Gustave Ansart (president of the Central Commission of Political Control), Mireille Bertrand (urbanism, environment, consumption, associations), Claude Billard (party activity in business and immigration), Pierre Blotin (education of Communists), Guy Hermier (intellectual, cultural, educational, and university affairs), Philippe Herzog (economy), Francette Lazard (director of the Marxist Research Institute), René Le Guen (science, research, and technology), Roland Leroy, René Piquet (president of the French communist group in the European Parliament), Claude Poperen (health and social security, retirement), Madeleine Vincent (local communities, elections), Henri Krasucki (secretary of the General Confederation of Labor), Louis Viannet (Mail Workers Federation)

Secretariat. 7 members: Maxime Gremetz, Jean-Claude Gayssot, André Lajoinie, Paul Laurent, Gisèle Moreau, Gaston Plissonnier, Charles Fiterman
Central Committee. 145 members
Status. Legal
Last Congress. Twenty-fifth, 6–10 February 1985; next congress planned for 1990
Last Election. 1981, 16.2 percent, 44 of 491 seats
Auxiliary Organizations. General Confederation of Labor (CGT); World Peace Council; Movement of Communist Youth of France (MCJF); Committee for the Defense of Freedom in France and the World; Association of Communist and Republican Representatives
Publications. *L'Humanité*, Paris, Roland Leroy, director, daily national organ; *L'Echo du centre*, Limoges, daily; *Liberté*, Lille, daily; *La Marseillaise*, Marseille, daily; *L'Humanité-Dimanche*, Paris, weekly; *Révolution*, Guy Hermier, director, weekly publication of the Central Committee; *La Terre*, weekly; *Cahiers du communisme*, monthly theoretical journal; *Europe*, literary journal; *Economie et politique*, economic journal; 5 journals published by the Marxist Research Institute; 4 monthly magazines; other periodicals on sports, children's themes, etc., and books on political, economic, and social topics published by Editions Sociales, the PCF publishing house in Paris.

The PCF's decision in 1984 to abandon its junior partnership in the government headed by President François Mitterrand's Socialist Party (PS) unleashed a long-building and lively internal debate. This debate broached important questions about the leadership's fitness to direct the party and, more fundamental, about the PCF's image, direction, and capacity for self-criticism. Party dissidents, or "renovators," challenged General Secretary Georges Marchais to explain the leadership's reversal on "Unity of the Left" and to permit an open debate on the party's recent experience and future. Reform-minded critics defined the salient issues of debate as: the PCF's relationship with the PS before, during, and after its participation in the Mauroy cabinets; the leadership's responsibility for the party's demoralizing slump from over 20 percent to just over 11 percent of the vote; the party's relationship with the Soviet Union and other communist countries; and reform of the rule of democratic centralism. Marchais and the majority hardliners in the PCF's Politburo moved to justify their retreat from leftist unity and to isolate dissent in the party. Local elections, meanwhile, yielded fresh evidence of the PCF's decline, and, by year's end, party leaders braced for their most profound test in five years in the National Assembly elections, set for 16 March 1986.

Leadership and Internal Affairs. The time up to the party's Twenty-fifth Congress on 6–10 February featured above all a series of embarrassing votes on the leadership's draft resolution. Although it at first appeared that the draft would slide easily past critics in the Central Committee, six members abstained at the CC's late October 1984 plenum. Especially disturbing, however, from the point of view of the majority in the Central Committee, was that dissident federations of the Haute-Vienne, Corse-du-Sud, and Haute-Alpes issued ringing rejections of the draft at subsequent federal conferences. In the powerful Haute-Vienne conference—one of the few remaining departments where the PCF was able to muster over 20 percent of the vote in the spring 1984 European Parliament elections—a leading renovator and former vocational-training minister, Marcel Rigout, engineered the defeat of the leadership's wording and added sweeping amendments that embodied familiar dissent themes. These included reconsideration of relations with socialist countries and reform of democratic centralism, all of which delivered a sharp rebuke to Marchais (*Libération*, 29 January).

Unprecedented dissent arose in almost a third of the PCF's federation meetings, where over 1,000 amendments to the draft resolution were adopted (from almost 4,000 reported from section assemblies). This was a surprising phenomenon, considering that the pyramidal electoral process—from cell to section to federation—usually diluted grassroots defiance of the leadership's draft (*Libération*, 22 and 29 January). The leadership's anxiety over the level of dissent in the federal conferences was such that it reportedly considered dissolving the Meurthe-et-Moselle federation (*Le Monde*, 12 January). Votes for the draft dropped well below 70 percent in several federal conferences and passed with hardly 50 percent in others—and, in many, passed only by dint of substantive amendments.

Despite dissent in the federations, it was clear early on that Marchais and party hardliners—prominent among them, *L'Humanité* director

Roland Leroy and Central Committee secretary Gaston Plissonnier—enjoyed broad majority support among the militants; in mid-January *L'Humanité* touted 90 percent approval in 30 federal conferences, 7 percent having disapproved and only 3 percent abstaining (21 January; *Le Monde*, 23 January). In the midst of these preparations, majority hardliners in the Politburo declared their "total solidarity" with Marchais, and, in a thinly veiled claim that renovators had played into the hands of capitalists, they blasted anticommunist elements who had "for months past" indulged in "brainwashing operations" against the rank and file (*L'Humanité*, 16 January).

Notwithstanding its virtual declaration of a counteroffensive against faltering reform, the PCF leadership permitted a few leading dissidents a voice in *L'Humanité*'s "discussion tribune" section—always, to be sure, followed by a barrage of replies that mirrored the leadership's line. The most important expression of dissent in this forum came from Pierre Juquin, the increasingly marginalized leader of the reform group in the Central Committee, who theoretically still held his position as party spokesman but whose functions as PCF propaganda chief has been transferred to ex-minister Charles Fiterman. In contrast to the leadership's characterization of a betrayed party on the rebound, Juquin cataloged the PCF's creeping debilitation, noting especially its command of "only 6.2 percent of registered voters (the lowest level in 60 years), an aging electorate, greatly reduced membership, falling subscriptions, an endangered press that is read less and less, a reduced member activity, and loss of identity and credibility." Juquin disparaged simplistic theories that blamed the party's marginalization on a dearth of awareness in the masses and charged the outgoing leadership with self-serving amnesia of its own mistakes and responsibility. He framed the seminal questions facing the congress in dissident terms: "Why and how was the leadership wrong? Who decides that it is now right?" (*L'Humanité*, 10 January).

Preparations for the Twenty-fifth Congress also witnessed an escalation of attacks by Marchais on the government, presumably to underscore a prominent theme in the draft resolution—that Mitterrand had sold out his governing agreement with the PCF, had turned on the interests of the working class, had adopted the agenda of the right, and had thereby forced Marchais to finally abandon the pretense of leftist unity. Soon after PCF's withdrawal from the government it had decided to focus responsibility for the rupture on the PS, to retreat from cooperation with the Socialists in the 1985 cantonal elections, to vote against the government's budget, to adopt an anti-PS resolution in October 1984, and to launch a series of personal attacks on Mitterrand—not the least of which was Marchais's condemnation of Mitterrand's "cult of personality" (*L'Humanité*, 1 November 1984; *Le Monde*, 13 September, 3 November, and 20 December, 1984; *FBIS*, 9 November 1984). In mid-January Marchais accused the government of swelling the ranks of the needy by its policies and reiterated the by-then familiar theme of no "submission to the crisis" (*L'Humanité*, 10 January; *Le Monde*, 12 January).

When the congress finally convened at the sports arena in the working-class Parisian suburb of Saint-Ouen, most delegates and observers were unsure how the leadership would respond to the challenge posed by the obviously outnumbered "renovators." Part of the answer came when Marchais made clear that Juquin and others would be allowed to speak but that the majority intended to dismiss their complaints—especially those about democratic centralism and the Soviet "model"—as opening the door to factionalism and the "social-democratization" of the party. Juquin and Félix Damette (professor and senator from Corsica) warned of duplicating the damage caused to the PCF in the past by silencing internal dissent, of "rapidly deteriorating" relations with the electorate, and of the fallacies inherent in the PCF's constant reference to an "outside model." These warnings reportedly drew applause from a surprising third of the congress (*L'Humanité*, 8 February; UPI, 9 February). Marchais and a succession of antireform speakers—including former transport minister Fiterman (at one time thought to sympathize with the dissidents) and Politburo hardliners André Lajoinie and Paul Laurent—ignored much of the substance of the dissenting opinions. Marchais's five-hour speech laid all blame for the party's decline on the Socialists' refusal to adhere to the joint program signed on the eve of the left's victory in 1981. He thus formally abandoned the party's alliance with the Socialists and, with it, the PCF's 25-year-old strategy of gaining power through a united left (*WP*, 7 February; Reuter, 7 February; *NYT*, 11 February; *JPRS*, 6 February).

Fiterman, meanwhile, blasted those—including ultra-hardliner and ex-Politburo member Jeannette Thorez-Vermeersch—who had criticized the leadership's decision to participate in the Socialist-led government after 1981. He argued that participation had been "an experiment we could not pass up" and seconded Marchais's views on PS responsibility for the experiment's failure. Fiterman was once considered Marchais's second in command, but now he is apparently one of several contenders (including Lajoinie and Jean-Claude Gayssot) to succeed the 64-year-old general secretary. At the congress Fiterman pledged to promote the leadership's new plan for a "mass popular movement" without the Socialists in a thousand meetings across the country (UPI, 8 February).

In adopting the draft resolution and re-electing Marchais to another term, the congress ratified the leadership's decision to brush aside all but a handful of the federation amendments (156 of 1,080 were adopted) (*L'Humanité*, 11 February).

To no one's surprise, Juquin lost his position as official spokesman and was unceremoniously ousted from the Politburo, where no dissenter remained. In a move that Marchais trumpeted as indicative of the party's self-confidence and deference to internal debate, Juquin, Rigout, and Damette retained their seats on the Central Committee. Marchais's characterization rang hollow, however, to those renovators who were purged, including powerful federation officials such as François Asensi, Helène Constans, Marc Zamichei, Yvan Tricart, Alain Amicabile, and Daniel Lacroix. Guy Hermier, chief of the Bouches-du-Rhône federation, director of the Central Committee's theoretical journal, *Révolution*, and widely suspected of harboring reformist views, retained his place on the Politburo, however. Gayssot—who, together with Gisèle Moreau, had reportedly endeared himself to hardliners by enforcing discipline in some wavering federations—rose to the Secretariat; this promotion has encouraged speculation that he, rather than Fiterman, is heir apparent to Marchais. Claude Billard entered the Politburo in place of long-time stalwart Jean Colpin, who committed suicide in January and left behind an *adieux* ending with the words "Vive le 25e congrès" (*Le Point*, 24 February).

Domestic Affairs. The PCF's continued marginalization was cast into bold relief by the results of the bienniel cantonal elections, held on 10 and 17 March. After their humiliating performance in elections for the European Parliament in 1984, party bosses had argued in part that militants were notoriously reluctant to mobilize for elections that had little national importance; when a "real vote" was in the offing, the party faithful would certainly turn out to give the PCF better than the 11.3 percent it received in the euroelections. More important, Marchais and others had blamed their defeat on working-class abstentions, which they credited to general discontent with the leftist government, in which the PCF was punished by association (*NYT*, 19 June 1984; *L'Humanité*, 28 June 1984; *FBIS*, 13 July 1984). Now, however, the cantonal elections provided a contest of undeniable domestic importance that was certain to mobilize voters across the political spectrum. It was, moreover, the first test of voter reaction to the PCF's withdrawal from the government.

Results of the cantonals dovetailed nicely with well-publicized projections of voter intentions for the 1986 legislative elections. Forswearing cooperation with Socialists on the second round, communist candidates polled 12.6 percent of the first-round vote, while their former partners of the PS garnered a somewhat disappointing 25.6 percent (*Le Monde*, 13 March). The PCF's campaign strategy emphasized a mixture of anti-Socialist themes and nonstop efforts to publicize reports of informal local electoral arrangements between the racist National Front (FN) and the neo-Gaullist Rally for the Republic (RPR) party. Jean-Marie Le Pen's FN collected only 8.8 percent on first ballot; some early forecasts had predicted an FN turnout equal to that of the PCF. The Communists' decline of voter strength evinced in previous by-elections and in the euroelections undoubtedly troubled the leadership, but evidence that the party had fallen to about equal status with the extreme right fringe poured salt in the wounds. Although the PCF performance in the overall cantonal voting failed to justify the leadership's argument that the party would do better in "real elections," it could at least take some consolation from two results of the final round: the PCF's 12.6 percent outdistanced the FN's poorer-than-expected showing of almost 9 percent, and the Socialists suffered another serious reverse of at least equal proportions to that of the Communists (*Le Monde*, 12 and 19 March).

No amount of glee at FN and PS misfortune, however, could disguise the fact that cantonal voting only confirmed the PCF's sagging voter appeal. This lesson was doubtless the catalyst to the leadership's redoubled advocacy of changes in the French voting system. PCF leaders supported a switch to proportional representation. Mitterrand, who had promised proportional representation in his presidential campaign, frequently reiterated his devotion to the concept as "more democratic" than the simple majority system. Promises seem to have landed on the back burner, however, until leftist election reverses—beginning with the municipal elections of March 1983—raised speculation in both PS and PCF circles that a proportional voting system could recoup lost voting strength and cushion the left against future losses (*Economist*, 3 November 1984; *WP*, 4 April; La Représentation proportinnelle, *Pouvoirs*, 32 [entire issue]).

Mitterrand introduced proportional representation in April. This abolished France's single-member districts and winner-take-all two-round elections in favor of voting for departmental party lists. According to Mitterrand's reform, seats in the National Assembly will be distributed on the basis of each list's proportion of the total departmental vote; a minimum of 5 percent would be necessary to get one seat. The National Assembly was enlarged to 577 seats, and—although each department was guaranteed at least two seats—all representation was reapportioned to take account of population shifts (*NYT*, 4 April; *WP*, 4 April).

PCF leaders had pressed hard for proportional voting, particularly when they were partners in the leftist coalition; Marchais and others had often warned that the left faced a catastrophe in the 1986 legislative elections without it (*NYT*, 20 March). The Communists, however, had wanted proportional representation on the basis of national lists, presumably because regional lists of any sort would dilute the party's national strength, since communist votes are concentrated heavily in a few departments (*Le Monde*, 12 and 19 March). Yet computer simulations, carried out before and after Mitterrand's announcement of reform, showed that the party would probably do far better in forthcoming legislative elections with any form of proportional representation than it would with the old system. For example, one projection (*Le Point*, 2 September) gave the PCF between 11 and 12 percent of the vote and 43 to 45 seats in the National Assembly, whereas another well publicized, pre-reform projection, based on the simple majority system, predicted the PCF would win only about 26 seats. Other simulations had the party falling as low as 12 or 15 seats (*Le Point*, 15 October 1984; *Economist*, 3 November 1984). Conservatives of all stripes condemned the move as a trick to resurrect the left's sinking political fortunes, and it hardly measured up to the PCF's preferred plan. (*Le Point* projections of October 1984 indicated that full national proportional representation would have given Communists 62 seats.) However, leftist leaders accepted Mitterrand's plan as the best they could get. When conservatives later moved in the National Assembly to put the government's proposal to a referendum, Communists voted with the PS against the motion: 329 to 160 (Paris Domestic Service, 24 April).

PCF labor policy took a dramatic turn in early June—totally in keeping with the dual strategy of "resistance to the crisis" and hostility to the Socialist government—when party militants fought with police in the streets of the communist-controlled Paris suburb of Ivry-sur-Seine. Communist municipal employees occupied an SKF factory in that red-belt municipality and thus bolstered a small force of workers from the communist-dominated CGT who had occupied the plant some weeks earlier. The occupiers dared police to dislodge them, and Prime Minister Fabius quickly took up the challenge. The resulting rock-throwing slugfest caused numerous injuries on both sides and underscored how successfully the PCF had led its remaining militants back to the ghetto (*Economist*, 15 June).

Press reports of the Ivry incident speculate that the PCF took action itself to stiffen the resolve of the CGT to act more aggressively in initiating strikes and other labor disturbances. Throughout the year, however, CGT job actions proved spectacularly unsuccessful, generating questions about the diminished strength and will of France's largest and historically most militant trade union. To curb government expenditures and make state-owned industries more competitive, Mitterrand and Fabius announced the reduction of 60,000 of the 207,000 jobs in France's nationalized industries. CGT leader and PCF Politburo member Henri Krasucki declared the union's immediate hostility to the plan and vowed unremitting labor protests. Focusing its opposition on the heavily unionized Renault auto giant, the CGT tried and failed to sustain plant occupations and work stoppages. Other strike efforts sputtered as well, each time focusing national attention on the union's apparent impotence. The CGT's Forty-second Congress, held in November, heard the customary calls to action—a national "day of action" was declared for December 4—but without much conviction (*Economist*, 15 June; *NYT*, 25 October; *CSM*, 8 April; Dow Jones Wire Service, 23 October; Reuter, 16 October and 23 November; *Le Monde*, 30 November).

The last weeks of 1985 saw the PCF gearing up for the legislative elections but still in or near the bottom of most voter preference polls. Party spokesmen continued throughout the last half of the year to cudgel the PS for its alleged abandonment of the left's agenda; Marchais's report to the 25 June plenum (*Pravda*, 26 June) and Claude Cabanes's editorial in *L'Humanité* of 27 April were notable for the strength of their attacks on the PS record. The Central Committee's election policy statement of 20–21 May showed clearly that the party's election strategy would be to declare war on the Socialists and loot the PS of disgruntled constituents (*L'Humanité*, 22 May and 9 October; *JPRS*, 5 September). Attacks on the Socialists became so much a part of PCF election campaign that Marchais found himself charged with propagating a conservative victory just to avenge himself on the PS—a charge that he denied in a November radio interview (*L'Humanité*, 18 November). Election preparations coincided also with new evidence that the party had failed to crush dissent at the Twenty-fifth Congress, notably the publication of Pierre Juquin's rebuttal to the majority resolution, which renewed dissident attacks on the leadership—only now more stridently—and which reportedly infuriated Marchais (Reuter, 19 November).

Defense and Security Issues. The PCF, meanwhile, continued its campaign against the U.S. Strategic Defense Initiative (SDI) in 1985, but it found little opportunity to bludgeon the Socialists with anti-SDI rhetoric. Mitterrand's rejectionist stand, forcefully underscored at the Bonn economic summit, left the PCF for the most part to comment on British and possible West German acquiescence to the program (*L'Humanité*, 6 April; *Pravda*, 6 February).

Gremetz's annual report on the party's view of France's role in the world (*Cahiers du communisme*, July–August, pp. 72–87) played variations on the theme that Socialists had once encouraged high hopes in the world but had lately caused only disillusionment. Party leaders and journalists also criticized the Milan Executive Committee summit and France's Eureka program as politically and militarily dangerous steps toward supernationality (*L'Humanité*, 1 July).

War remembrances, usually an occasion for PCF chestpuffing, were marred by an ugly controversy over a television documentary that questioned the party's self-sacrifice and heroic role in the Resistance. "Terrorists in Retirement" alleged that the PCF had knowingly sacrificed one of its most aggressive but largely Jewish and "foreign" resistance bands to the Nazis at the end of the war so that the party could portray itself as "purely French" afterwards. The flap that broke out focused on PCF efforts to prevent the film from being aired on France's state-run television. Network executives at first appeared to cave in to communist pressure, but after a groundswell of protest in favor of its presentation Mitterrand intervened personally to order the broadcast (*WSJ*, 17 June).

The sinking of the Greenpeace ecology ship *Rainbow Warrior* in New Zealand touched off a national scandal that shook the government, ending in the resignation of Defense Minister Hernu and contributing significantly to the deepening mood of pessimism that had reportedly overtaken the PS. Communists made every effort to embarrass the government further; PCF jibes customarily focused on the culpability of the political authorities, as opposed to mere soldiers and agents (*L'Humanité*, 20 August and 27 September).

International Activities. The party congress brought a large number of visits from leaders of other communist parties. Mitterrand's decision to resume dialogue with Moscow and the eventual exchange of visits also prompted new Soviet general secretary Mikhail Gorbachev to pay an official visit to the PCF at the time of his state visit to France. The congress attracted delegations from all foreign communist parties, except Albania, and the PCF took special pains to mark that fact by staging a large international rally on 9 February. Party foreign affairs chief Maxime Gremetz presided; Marchais sat between heads of Chinese and Soviet delegations, with Vietnam's Le Duc Tho only a few seats away. Soviet Politburo member Mikhail Solomentsev stressed in his speech that the Geneva dialogue between Moscow and Washington was influenced by other nuclear powers such as France (Reuter, 9 February).

Little more than a month after the congress, Soviet leader Chernenko died. Marchais, however, did not travel to the funeral, pleading that the second round of the cantonals required his presence in France but vowing that he would meet with Gorbachev (*L'Humanité*, 15 March).

Soon after the cantonals, the party leadership entertained visits from Nicaraguan president Daniel Ortega and Argentine party chief Athos Fava, and Marchais dispatched an MCJF group to Peking and a letter of congratulations to Sam Nujoma, chairman of the South-West African People's Organization, noting the party's 25th anniversary (*L'Humanité*, 19 April and 7, 14 May; *FBIS*, 16 March). Post-congress meetings with the Nicaraguans emphasized the U.S.-*contra* threat to the regime; later, PCF officials announced the formation and dispatch of a 76-member "Solidarity Brigade" to Managua, composed mostly of young Communists from several PCF-controlled cities (*L'Humanité*, 27 June). French and Italian parties held a joint conference in mid-April that highlighted their commitment to disarmament (*FBIS*, 11 April). Party chiefs also received Finnish and Iranian party leaders (*L'Humanité*, 20 June and 22 December).

Vacations and official visits took PCF functionaries and leaders to Managua, Sofia, Budapest, Warsaw, East Berlin, Pyongyang, and Moscow. Gremetz also visited New Caledonia to demonstrate PCF solidarity with the Kanak movement for independence (ibid., 8, 14, and 24 January). A mid-June meeting of European communist parties fizzled, but PCF leaders joined those who tried to salvage its public image by touting "richness in diversity" (ibid., 4, 13, and 20 July; *JPRS*, 3 July; AFP, 14 June). Marchais saw few noncommunist world leaders; Indian leader Rajiv Gandhi proved an exception (*L'Humanité*, 8 June).

The finale of the year's international activity came in the exchange of visits between Marchais and Gorbachev, although the obvious reason for Gorbachev's travel to France was to discuss arms-control issues with Mitterrand and to telegraph Soviet positions for the Geneva summit with President Reagan. Marchais led a large delegation to Moscow in early September (though he was actually there earlier and stayed for five weeks, reportedly for treatment of his heart ailment); he met with Gorbachev on 2 September and issued a strained joint communiqué on the 4th that papered over frictions that reportedly characterized the talks (*Radio Free Europe/Radio Liberty*, 9 September). In anticipation of the Soviet leader's visit to Paris in October, *L'Humanité* devoted lavish space to the Gorbachev style and its impact on the "changing USSR" (1 October; Tass, 3 September; *FBIS*, 12 September and 4 October; UPI, 15 September). The Soviet leader reciprocated, paying equally special attention to PCF leaders during his visit by participating in several party-sponsored functions.

In December the visit of Polish leader Jaruzelski—at Mitterrand's invitation—provoked an avalanche of criticism from across the noncommunist political spectrum, but PCF leaders moved quickly to support the idea, publicly applauding it as advancing international peace and East-West dialogue.

Edward A. Allen
Washington, D.C.

Germany: Federal Republic of Germany

Population. 59,250,000
Party. German Communist Party (Deutsche Kommunistische Partei; DKP)
Founded. 1968
Membership. 50,482 (claimed); 44,500 (Federal Security Service; BVS)
Chairman. Herbert Mies
Presidium. 19 members: Herbert Mies, Hermann Gautier, Jupp Angenfort, Kurt Bachmann, Irmgard Bobrzik, Martha Buschmann, Werner Cieslak, Heinz Czymek, Gerd Deumlich, Kurt Fritsch, Wolf-

gang Gehrcke, Willi Gerns, Dieter Keller, Georg Polikeit, Rolf Priemer, Brigit Radow, Karl-Heinz Schröder, Werner Sturmann, Ellen Weber

Secretariat. 13 members: Herbert Mies, Hermann Gautier, Vera Aschenbach, Jupp Angenfort, Werner Cieslak, Gerd Deumlich, Kurt Fritsch, Willi Gerns, Marianne Konze, Josef Mayer, Fritz Noll, Karl-Heinz Schröder, Wilhelm Spengler

Executive. 91 members

Status. Legal

Last Congress. Seventh, 6–8 January 1984, in Nuremberg

Last Election. 1983, 0.2 percent, no representation

Auxiliary Organizations. Socialist German Workers Youth (Sozialistische Deutsche Arbeiter Jugend; SDAJ), ca. 15,000 members, Brigit Radow, chair; Marxist Student Union–Spartakus (Marxistischer Studentenbund; MSB-Spartakus), ca. 4,000 members (MSB-Spartakus claims 6,5000), Harms, chair; Young Pioneers (Junge Pioniere; JP), ca. 4,000 members, Gerd Hertel, chair

Publications. *Unsere Zeit* (Our Time), Düsseldorf, DKP daily organ, circulation ca. 25,000, weekend edition ca. 48,000, Monday edition discontinued; *elan—Das Jugendmagazin*, SDAJ monthly organ, circulation ca. 30,000; *rote blätter* (Red Pages), MSB-Spartakus monthly organ, circulation ca. 18,000; *pionier* (Pioneer), JP monthly organ

The pro-Soviet DKP is the successor organization of the Communist Party of Germany (Kommunistische Partei Deutschlands; KPD), which was founded on 31 December 1918. The KPD was the third largest political party in the Weimar Republic. During the Hitler regime, the party was outlawed and became an ineffective underground party with most of its leaders either in exile or imprisoned. Following World War II, the KPD was reactivated in the Allied occupation zones. In the Soviet-occupied zone, the Soviet Military Administration forced the merger of the KPD and the Social Democratic Party of Germany (Sozialdemokratische Partei Deutschlands; SPD). The merger was achieved at the "unification congress" of the two parties in April 1946. The "new" party adopted the name Socialist Unity Party of Germany (Sozialistische Einheitspartei Deutschlands; SED).

In the first national elections in the Federal Republic of Germany (FRG) in 1949, the KPD received 5.7 percent of the vote and fifteen seats in the Bundestag. In the next elections in 1953, the KPD vote decreased to 2.2 percent, below the 5 percent required by German election law for representation in the federal legislature. In August 1956, the Federal Constitutional Court outlawed the KPD for pursuing unconstitutional objectives. The KPD continued its activities as an underground party, led by Max Reimann, who resided in East Berlin. Substantial financial and operational support from the SED did not prevent the underground KPD from losing most of its members.

In September 1968 the DKP was founded as a concession from Chancellor Willy Brandt to Leonid Brezhnev. Most of the "new" party leaders had been officials in the illegal KPD, which at that time had shrunk to about 7,000 members. In 1971 the Federal Security Service (BVS) stated that the DKP, which openly stresses it is a party of the international communist movement and the only legitimate heir to the KPD, was the successor of the outlawed party.

According to the annual report of the BVS, there were two orthodox communist organizations (membership 44,500) at the end of 1984, with 13 affiliated organizations (28,000) and 50 organizations influenced by Communists (71,000). In addition there were 19 basic organizations of the dogmatic New Left (3,100) with 12 affiliated organizations (900) and 13 organizations in which these groups exerted some influence (2,700), as well as 53 undogmatic organizations of the New Left (5,100). After deducting for membership in more than one organization and children's groups, the BVS concluded that membership in these left-extremist organizations totaled 73,700 and membership in organizations influenced by these groups 55,300 (Bundesministerium des Innern, *Verfassungsschutzbericht, 1984*, Bonn, August, p. 19).

The BVS estimates that the membership in left-extremist organizations of foreigners (mostly "guest workers") at the end of 1984 was 81,650 (orthodox communist organizations: 59,650; organizations of the New Left: 22,000) (ibid., pp. 179–80).

Leadership and Organization. The fifth session of the DKP Executive in Düsseldorf (23–24 March) elected four additional members (Heinz Czymek, Wolfgang Gehrcke, Dieter Keller, and

Brigit Radow, who is chair of the SDAJ) to the party's Presidium. All of them were already members of the Executive. New members of the Secretariat are Marianne Konze, charged with women's affairs, and Fritz Noll, assigned to public relations. This session of the Executive also determined the main efforts for the next (eighth) party congress, scheduled for 2–4 May 1986 in Hamburg. These efforts are the termination of the "right-wing" government, disarmament, job creation, social rights, and strengthening of the DKP. Party chairman Herbert Mies emphasized the continuing support of the peace movement and the necessity of the communist alliance policy, which is primarily directed at the members of the SPD and trade unions. He stated that the opportunities for "unity of actions" has increased, especially within the trade unions and factories (*Deutscher Informations–Dienst [DID]*, 1 June, pp. 4–5).

The seventh session of the DKP Executive (26–27 October) was primarily concerned with issues of the "peace policy," the peace movement, the experience with the "Thälmann Appeal" for getting additional party members, and further preparations for the forthcoming party congress. Again the priorities of the DKP were support for the peace movement, the struggle against the "militarization of space," the alliance policy, the intensification of the extraparliamentary struggle, the further development of broad "democratic election alliances," and the support of the Peace List (an election coalition promoted by the DKP). Emphasis was given to the political-ideological schooling of party members and sympathizers (*DID*, 2 October, pp. 10–11).

On 5 September the DKP Executive opened an office in the center of Bonn. This event was attended by representatives of various affiliated organizations, Peace List, members of the peace movement, Soviet ambassador to the FRG Semyonov, and permanent representative from the German Democratic Republic, Moldt (*Frankfurter Allgemeine Zeitung [FAZ]*, 7 September). The DKP headquarters remain in Düsseldorf because the main office of the German Trade Unions Alliance (DGB) is located in that city. The new office in Bonn houses the departments of international affairs, alliance policies, and federal and *Land* elections. One of its main functions is contact with the news media in the nation's capital. The office is headed by Knickrehm, a member of the DKP Executive who has been pursuing alliance policy and is also a leader of the Peace List (*FAZ*, 25 June).

The SED provides substantial financial support to the DKP. The "West Department" of the SED Central Committee, headed by Herbert Häber, is in charge of supervision and control of the DKP. In 1984 the name of the West Department was changed for reason of disguise to "Department of International Politics and Economics" with about 200 staff members. SED district organizations are assigned the task of assisting specific DKP county organizations. Every year the leaderships of the SED and DKP prepare an overall plan of activities. About 300 teachers are employed at the SED party school "Franz Mehring" in East Berlin, which is exclusively for the training of DKP members and costs the SED several million marks. About 300 Communists from the FRG attend this "cadre school" every year, some of them in courses lasting up to twelve months. To date about 4,000 DKP members have been through this school (*FAZ*, 26 August). The DKP has received about 60 million marks annually from the SED by way of a network of communist-owned economic enterprises in the FRG. The financial support covers the DKP's costs for its large staff, ideological schooling facilities and programs, propaganda material, mass rallies, election campaigns, and the financing of DKP-affiliated and communist-influenced organizations. Additional expenses covered by the SED are the ambitious delegation program, holidays, and sick-leave vacations of DKP functionaries in the German Democratic Republic (GDR). No other communist party in a Western country is as dependent and as strictly controlled by a foreign party as the DKP is by the SED. Membership contributions, which average 15 marks per month, and voluntary contributions constitute a relatively small part of the party's financial needs. A new financial source are the election funds that the Peace List received from the government on the basis of the votes obtained in the last election. The DKP demanded hundreds of thousand marks from the Peace List for the election support given by the party (*Verfassungsschutz*, p. 37).

In addition to the SED's Franz Mehring school, DKP and SDAJ members attend the Institute for Social Sciences of the CPSU Central Committee in Moscow, the Free German Youth (FDJ) college "Wilhelm Pieck" in the GDR, and the college of the Komsomol (the youth organization of the CPSU) in the Soviet Union.

The DKP's political-ideological educational program is under the direction of DKP Executive member Dr. Robert Steigerwald, who is in the department of theory and Marxist education. Twice a month the party organizations conduct "education evenings" about Marxism-Leninism and revolutionary strategy and tactics. The Marxist Factory Workers' Schools, organized at county level, are also open to noncommunists. Subjects taught there deal with Marxism-Leninism. The DKP's "Karl Liebknecht" school in Leverkusen (featuring dormitories) taught about 900 party members in some 40 courses of one or two weeks duration. Subjects included work among the unemployed, the peace movement, and the women's movement (ibid., p. 36).

The DKP increased its publishing activities. The *Deutsche Volkszeitung/die tat* (German People's Newspaper/the deed; about 30,000 copies), published by the communist-controlled Röderberg Verlag in Frankfurt, started the quarterly *Illustrierte Volkszeitung* (Illustrated People's Paper). The first issue dealt with the 40th anniversary of the end of World War II. The financing came from advertisements placed by East German commercial firms, the Soviet airline Aeroflot, and the Soviet tourist bureau Intourist. The direct-mail venture Volksversand (People's Mail Order House) was also founded under the Röderberg Verlag's name by the thirteen DKP-influenced book and magazine publishers and film and travel enterprises. A 68-page catalog "media revue" contains 331 titles. All the participating publishers and bookstores belong to the DKP-led Association of Socialist and Democratic Publishers and Book Dealers (*DID*, May, pp. 15–16).

The SDAJ is the largest of the DKP-affiliated organizations with about 15,000 members organized in about 1,000 groups. The majority of the SDAJ functionaries and about 40 percent of the members belong to the party. Its chair is Brigit Radow, who is also a member of the DKP Presidium. She was elected at the Eighth Federal Congress of the SDAJ (15–16 December 1984), held in Bottrop. Of the 757 delegates, 70.2 percent were members of trade unions, 25.3 percent were active participants in the peace movement, and 14.5 percent held functions in schools or vocational schools. The SDAJ refers to the DKP as the revolutionary party of the working class and fights together with the party for a "socialist Federal Republic of Germany" (*radical info*, no. 1, p. 5).

Ideological schooling of the SDAJ members takes place in educational evenings of SDAJ group organizations and in one-week courses at the Youth Education Center Burg Wahrburg. The official SDAJ organs are the monthly *elan—Das Jugendmagazin* (about 30,000 copies) and the monthly *Jugenpolitische Blätter* (Youth Political Pages; about 2,000 copies). *Elan* also publishes the monthly *elan Artikeldienst für Betriebs-, Lehrlings-, Stadtteil- und Schülerzeitungen* (elan Article Service for Factory, Apprentice, City Area, and Student Newspapers), which helps the preparation of hundreds of local papers. Four editions of the soldiers' newspaper *Rührt Euch* (At Ease) were published by soldiers in cooperation with *elan* editors. The SDAJ maintained numerous contacts with communist fraternal youth organizations in the GDR and other countries. For years the SDAJ provided the treasurer for the World League of Democratic Youth and actively participated in the preparation for the twelfth World Festival of Youth and Students, held in Moscow on 27 July–3 August (*Verfassungsschutz*, pp. 41–42).

The Young Pioneers–Socialist Children's Organization (JP) has a membership of about 4,000. Its chair, Gerd Hertel, who is a member of the SDAJ Executive, was elected at the Fifth Federal Conference of the JP on 2–3 March in Dortmund. Many of the other JP functionaries are members of the DKP or SDAJ. The conference was attended by more than 450 delegates, including representatives from communist children's and youth organizations from the GDR and other countries as well as representatives from embassies of socialist countries. The JP leaders emphasized the close relationship of the JP with the DKP and the organization's commitment to socialism in the Soviet style (*Innere Sicherheit*, no. 2 [3 May]: 10). The JP Executive publishes the monthly *Pionierleiter-Info* (Pioneer Leader Info) and the children's newspaper *pionier*. The JP kept up its contacts with children's organizations in the socialist countries and belongs to the world children's organization CIMEA, a subsidiary of the Soviet-controlled World League of Democratic Youth (*Verfassungsschutz*, p. 43). As in previous years, the DKP and JP organized children's vacations in the GDR. Edeltraud Schönfeld, JP deputy chair, declared that these vacations include "peace demonstrations" and "solidarity meetings" and that children should be taught that those in power in the FRG are responsible for fascism and war (*Innere Sicherheit*, no. 3 [28 June]: 9).

Another DKP-affiliated organization is the MSB-Spartakus. Its chair, Harms, was elected at the Ninth Federal Congress (5–6 October) in Bochum. The congress was attended by 388 delegates and numerous domestic and foreign guests. The DKP was represented by Presidium members Hermann Gautier and Willi Gerns. Among the guests were high functionaries from the Leninist Komsomol and FDJ as well as from the Marxist-controlled South-West African People's Organization (SWAPO) and Libyan and Palestinian students' organizations. The Jusos (Young Socialist) University Groups, the Socialist University League (SHB), the permanent coalition partner of the MSB-Spartakus, and the Green Party were among the guests. The Jusos (the official youth organization of the SPD) has been in a coalition with the MSB-Spartakus and the SHB in over 80 percent of the students' governments on German universities. The Social Democratic minister for the environment of the Saarland, Jo Leinen, sent greetings to the MSB-Spartakus congress and wished it success, especially in its work for students' rights and disarmament (*FAZ*, 7 October; *Deutschland-Union-Dienst*, 17 October, p. 3).

The congress decided to utilize the universities in order to assist Soviet foreign policy and to fight the coalition government in Bonn. It declared its opposition to any research undertaken in connection with the U.S. Strategic Defense Initiative and called for a "University Peace Week" in November. The SPD's renewed relations with the CPSU found great approval, but the communist students wanted proof that the SPD would not return to the old course of former chancellor Helmut Schmidt (*FAZ*, 7 October). *Röte blätter* is the central organ of the MSB-Spartakus. A membership newspaper, *Klartext* (Clear Text), was published for the first time in 1984 (*Verfassungsschutz*, p. 44).

In order to mobilize as many citizens as possible for DKP objectives, such as the fight against the U.S. medium-range nuclear weapons, the party has the support of about 50 organizations and initiatives (action groups) that outwardly appear to be independent organizations but are in fact strongly influenced by the Communists. The majority of the members of these organizations are not DKP members; key positions, however, especially in the organizational sector (secretariats), are held by Communists. The less the target groups recognize communist influence, the more effective the organization. Almost all of the larger organizations belong to Soviet-directed front groups. A good example is the FRG-Cuba Friendship Society. The society claims 3,400 members. Klaus Thüsing of the SPD was confirmed as chair and Fritz Noll, member of the DKP Executive, as vice chair at the last federal conference in December 1984 (*DID*, 11 January). The real work of the organization is done by DKP members (*Verfassungsschutz*, pp. 44–45). Among the more important organizations are the Association of Victims of the Nazi Regime/League of Antifascists (VVN/BdA; 13,000 members), the German Peace Union (DFU; 1,000 members), the Committee for Peace, Disarmament, and Cooperation (KFAZ), the German Peace Society/United War Resisters (DFG/VK; 18,500 members), the Democratic Women's Initiative (DFI), the Association of Democratic Jurists (VDJ), and the Anti-imperialist Solidarity Committee for Africa, Asia, and Latin America (ASK).

The ASK forms the framework for "anti-imperialist alliances" of Communists with democrats in solidarity actions on behalf of Chile and Nicaragua and for the "liberation movements" in South Africa (ibid., pp. 45–52). The DFG/VK, which is the largest of the DKP-influenced organizations and has the largest number of noncommunists in its ranks, held its Fifth Federal Congress (1–3 March) in Münster-Hiltrup. The main efforts of the DFG/VK are directed to encourage resistance to military service and to support the peace movement (*DID*, 1 June, pp. 5–6). The DFU celebrated its 25th anniversary at the end of April in Bremen and re-elected its Directorate (*DID*, May, pp. 10–11).

Domestic Attitudes and Activities. *Land* elections were held in the Saarland on 10 March. The DKP received 2,334 votes (0.3 percent) compared with 3,703 votes (0.5 percent) in 1980. On the same day, local elections were held in Hesse, where the DKP obtained 10,761 votes (0.4 percent) compared with 15,825 votes (0.5 percent) in 1981 (*FAZ*, 12 March). The Peace List participated in the *Land* elections in Rhineland-Westphalia on 12 May and received 61,745 votes (0.64 percent) (*FAZ*, 14 May). More than half of the members of the Federal Executive of the Peace List are DKP members (*FAZ*, 5 November).

In 1985 the DKP intensified the party's alliance policy, which is directed at Social Democrats, trade unionists, Greens, and members of the peace movement. The "unity of actions" made considerable progress (*DID*, August, pp. 16–17; *FAZ*, 5 August). The DKP alliance policy is intended to provide the party with a mass basis and to increase its influence far beyond its electoral potential. To achieve this objective, the DKP pursues two forms of alliances. "The unity of actions of the working class" refers to the collaboration with Social Democrats, trade unionists, and workers not affiliated with any party. The "broad antimonopolistic alliance (people's front)" is directed against "monopoly capitalism" (including "imperialism"). It builds upon the "unity of actions" and includes collaboration with intellectuals and bourgeois elements. The Communists do not demand the leadership in alliances; however, according to them, their "ideological superiority" places them de facto in control, as has been observed in practically all cases (*Verfassungsschutz*, pp. 52–53). For example, the DKP-controlled Institute for Marxist Studies and Research (IMSF) held a conference at the University of Frankfurt (17–18 March), attended by about 1,000 scientists, trade unionists, factory stewards, teachers, students, and politicians of democratic parties. The subject of the conference was "Intelligentsia, Intellectuals, and the Labor Movement in Western Europe." The director of the IMSF, Dr. Heinz Jung, noted the increased opportunities of alliances between working class and intelligentsia (*Innere Sicherheit*, no. 2 [3 May]: 10).

An important forum for the communist alliance policy is the weekly *Deutsche Volkszeitung/die tat*. The number of Communists among the seventeen members of the editorial staff has increased to three-fourths (*Verfassungsschutz*, pp. 52–53).

The DKP pursued the "unity of action from above," that is, addressing its offer to work together directly to the SPD leadership. For example, the DKP invited the SPD Executive to celebrate together with the Communists the 40th anniversary of the end of World War II on 8 May (*DID*, 3 March, p. 6). The attitude of the DKP has changed dramatically since the SPD became an opposition party and pledged to remove the U.S. medium-range missiles if it formed the next federal government. The fact that a number of SPD members hold leading positions in DKP-influenced organizations, such as the KFAZ and the various friendship societies with socialist countries, is a visible success of the alliance policy. The SHB, asserting that 70 percent of its members belong to the SPD, has practiced "unity of action" with the MSB-Spartakus for many years and strongly advocates an alliance of SPD and DKP (*Verfassungsschutz*, pp. 53–54).

The communist efforts to create "unity of action from below," that is, proposing collaboration on specific issues to the SPD members and followers of the peace movement, also proved successful. Social Democrats, trade unionists, Greens, and peace activists participated in many events organized by communist-influenced organizations such as the "Easter Marches" in various cities in the FRG. These peace demonstrations were prepared by the DFU and KFAZ and featured speakers from the DKP, SPD, and DGB (*DID*, 30 March, pp. 13–27).

Trade unions remained a priority target for communist infiltration. About two-thirds of all DKP members belong to trade unions. Communists succeeded in occupying a number of leading positions, especially at land and district levels. Communist trade-union officials are of considerable influence in the Printers' Trade Union and in the Trade Union Education and Science. The work of the DKP within the trade unions is facilitated by the monthly *Nachrichten zur Wirtschafts- und Sozialpolitik* (News About Economics and Social Policies; more than 7,000 copies). This publication is intended primarily for union officials. Its publishers are three high-ranking DKP officials, one former DFU official, and the former chair of the Printers' Trade Union, Leonhard Mahlein (SPD). The editorial office consists of four DKP members (*Verfassungsschutz*, pp. 54–55).

The sixth session of the DKP Executive in June decided to utilize the "action week" of the DGB—to be held 14–20 October to protest mass unemployment and dismantling of social benefits—for communist propaganda purposes. The DKP planned a 5 October Workers' Congress in Cologne, where the tactical directions for the "action week" were to be given to party officials (*FAZ*, 27 June). The party established "peace initiatives" in factories, which had the task of adding communist policy objectives to those of the DGB, such as the rejection of any participation of the FRG in the U.S. Strategic Defense Initiative. The politicization of the trade unions in favor of the political left is a visible indicator of the effective influence of left extremists. The DGB's "action week" and the protest strikes on 10 December of about 350,000 workers, as reported by the Metal Workers' Union, are examples of the anti–coalition government policy of the DGB (*FAZ*, 11 December).

The "Cologne Advice to the Peace Movement" Conference (16–17 June) demanded the "clear rejection of the militarization of space" and also asked for the support of the DGB's "action week" (*Die Welt*, 15 July). The conference was organized by the coordination committee of the peace movement in order to prepare a new common platform for the peace actions in the fall. The official organ of the

DKP, *Unsere Zeit*, published on 20 June the new platform, which called for the stopping and dismantling of the U.S. Pershing II missiles and for the continuation of the campaign against NATO. The Action Conference of the Peace Movement was scheduled for 14–15 December to plan the program of the peace movement for 1986–1987, with special attention to the forthcoming federal elections in January 1987. The KFAZ organized three seminars in preparation for this conference to be held in Cologne and Hannover on 30 November and in Frankfurt on 1 December (*DID*, 1 November, p. 3).

On 19 January the DKP started its yearly "Week of the DKP" with the traditional "Lenin-Liebknecht-Luxemburg Meeting" in Velbert. It was attended by about 1,000 persons, among them delegations from the CPSU and SED (*Innere Sicherheit*, no. 1 [20 March]: 3–4). The VVN/BdA, DFG/VK, and KFAZ were among the organizations calling for an "International Counter-Summit" on 2 May in Bonn to protest the Economic Summit of the leading Western industrialized countries and Japan (*DID*, 22 April, pp. 4–5). The DKP and its affiliated organizations participated in various demonstrations marked by violence, such as the counterdemonstration against a meeting of the right-wing National Democratic Party of Germany (NPD) in Frankfurt (*FAZ*, 2 October). The SDAJ assisted the party in its activities, especially in mobilizing other youth organizations and in the preparatory committee for the twelfth World Festival of Youth and Students in Moscow. The SDAJ encouraged draftees to follow their call to serve in the military and to join the *Arbeitskreis Demokratischer Soldaten* (Working Group of Democratic Soldiers; ADS) or to participate in the numerous Soldiers' Initiatives (*Verfassungsschutz*, p. 64).

International Views and Party Contacts. The foreign policy statements of DKP officials are substantially the same as those made by Moscow and East Berlin. The party supports the Soviet "peace policy" and calls for the withdrawal of U.S. nuclear weapons from Europe. The DKP strongly endorses the SPD's intensification of contacts with ruling communist parties in Eastern Europe and approved the SPD-SED appeal to make Europe a region free of chemical warfare weapons.

Contacts were maintained with many fraternal communist parties, especially with those of the Soviet Union and GDR. Harry Tisch, member of the SED Central Committee and chairman of the East German trade unions (FDGB), visited the headquarters of the DKP and conferred with party chairman Herbert Mies (East Berlin, ADN, 31 May; *FBIS*, 3 June). A DKP delegation headed by Jupp Angenfort, member of the DKP Secretariat and Executive, visited East Berlin and met with SED Politburo member Egon Kranz (*DID*, 1 November, p. 2). A CPSU delegation led by A. N. Balandin, member of the CPSU Central Committee, participated in the DKP's Lenin-Liebknecht-Luxemburg Meeting on 19 January (*Pravda*, 26 January; *FBIS*, 31 January).

Mies and Karl-Heinz Schröder, member of the DKP Presidium, were received by V. V. Zagladin, first deputy head of the International Department of the CPSU Central Committee, on 18 March (Tass, March; *FBIS*, 19 March). Mies was also seen by Mikhail Gorbachev, secretary general of the CPSU Central Committee, on 5 May. Gorbachev praised the contribution of German antifascists to the struggle against Nazism and war. He emphasized the indestructible solidarity of the CPSU and DKP (*Pravda*, 6 May; *FBIS*, 6 May). Mies addressed a meeting devoted to opening the memorial museum to German antifascists in Krasnogorsk on 5 May (*Moscow TV*, 5 May; *FBIS*, 6 May). A DKP delegation headed by Kurt Fritsch, member of the DKP Presidium, visited Volgograd and Moscow and was received by Boris Ponomarev, member of the CPSU Central Committee, and V. V. Zagladin (*Moscow TV*, 31 May; *FBIS*, 5 June). A DKP delegation headed by K. Shimek visited the Soviet Union between 1–8 November and held talks at the CPSU Central Committee International Section (*Pravda*, 9 November; *FBIS*, 13 November). Josef Weber, member of the DFU Directorate and organizer of the "Krefeld Appeal" (a widely propagandized collection of signatures against the implementation of the NATO double-track decision), received the International Lenin Prize (*Innere Sicherheit*, no. 3 [28 June]: 9). V. V. Zagladin met with Mies in Düsseldorf on 11 November (Tass, 11 November; *FBIS*, 12 November).

The DKP attempted to improve the Soviet image in the FRG by sponsoring a "Week of Real Socialism—Information from a New World—the Soviet Union Today" (4–16 November). In more than 100 events, numerous Soviet politicians, journalists, writers, artists, actors, and representatives of youth and women's organizations were listed as speakers or performers (*DID*, 2 October, p. 11).

Contacts were also maintained with communist parties of other socialist countries. On 24–27 April a delegation of the Communist Party of Czechoslovakia visited the DKP headquarters (*Pravda*, 29 April; *JPRS-EPS*, 85-060, 24 May). Kim Il-song, general secretary of the Central Committee of the Workers' Party of Korea, met with Mies in Pyongyang on 25 August (Pyongyang, KCNA, 25 August; *FBIS*, 29 August). The DKP participated in the meeting of West European communist parties in Paris on 12–13 June (*L'Humanité*, 22 June) and in a July symposium of communist parties in Tokyo, organized by the Japanese Communist Party (*DID*, August, p. 12).

The DKP, SDAJ, and MSB-Spartakus founded the Volunteer Brigade–Carlos Fonseca (the name of a co-founder of the FSLN) in support of the Sandinista regime. The brigade collected 2.3 million marks and delivered a printing press to Managua on 25 March (*DID*, August, p. 11). The DKP maintains friendly relations with Toni Seedat, leader of the African National Congress (ANC) office in Bonn (ibid., p. 15).

Other Leftist Groups. In addition to the orthodox Communists, a number of small parties and associations characterized by their independence from Moscow, numerous initiatives, and revolutionary organizations of the New Left remained active during 1985. All of these organizations want the destruction of the political and social order of the FRG; many of them openly advocate the use of violence to overthrow and destroy the existing state, which would be replaced either by the dictatorship of the proletariat or by different models of a "free society." Some of the autonomous anarchist groups employed terrorist actions, including arson and bombings (*Verfassungsschutz*, p. 84).

The ever-changing organizations and splinter groups pursued different revolutionary concepts but shared a rejection of the pro-Soviet orthodox Communists, who were considered "revisionists." The New Left comprises various dogmatic Marxist-Leninists, Trotskyists, anarchists, "autonomists," and antidogmatic social revolutionaries. The membership of the Marxist-Leninist organizations (K-groups) continued to decline. Currently they have about 3,100 members in their basic organizations and 900 members in their affiliated groups. Some of the K-groups collaborated on specific objectives, for example, the anti–Economic Summit demonstrations in May, and attempted to create the "unity of revolutionary socialists." Membership in the antidogmatic groups (about 55 groups were identified) continued to increase slightly, from 4,900 to 5,100 (*Verfassungsschutz*, pp. 19, 84–85). The autonomous and anarchist groups were mainly responsible for violence against the state, and they frequently formed the militant core of the protest movement directed against the United States, NATO, and the "imperialist preparation for war." Some of the autonomous groups came close to the position of the anti-imperialist groups of the terrorists and were engaged in violent action against "West German and U.S. imperialism" (ibid., p. 85). The alternative newspapers served the antidogmatic New Left to exchange information. Many of these papers printed appeals and statements of left-extremists (ibid., p. 88).

The dogmatic New Left included four K-groups. Two of them—the Marxist-Leninist Party of Germany (Marxistische-Leninistische Partei Deutschlands; MLPD) and the Communist Party of Germany, Marxist-Leninist (Kommunistische Partei Deutschlands, Marxistisch-Leninistisch; KPD; formerly known as the KPD-ML)—consider themselves to be the "revolutionary party of the working class" and participated in some elections with devastating results. The other two groups—the League of West German Communists (Bund Westdeutscher Kommunisten; BWK) and the Communist League (Kommunistischer Bund; KB)—lost some of their members but were able to maintain organizational units in most of the federal *Länder*. The "Group Z," which split in 1979 from the KB, joined the Green Party and former functionaries of this group occupy leadership positions in the Green Party at federal and *Land* levels.

The Communist League of West Germany (Kommunistischer Bund Westdeutschlands; KBW), once the largest of the K-groups and with the best finances, decided on 16 February at a meeting in Frankfurt to dissolve itself as a political organization. Its substantial assets, estimated at some 9 million marks and consisting of houses in Frankfurt, Hamburg, Berlin, a printing plant, and a publishing house, were transferred to a newly formed organization called "Association" (Hamburg, DPA, 16 February; *FBIS*, 18 February).

The MLPD is presently the strongest of the K-groups and was able to increase its membership from 1,000 to 1,100. The chairman of the MLPD is Stefan Engel. The party is organized in eleven districts with more than 80 local groups. Its official organ, the weekly *Rote Fahne*, has a circulation of about 10,000 copies. The MLPD considers the DKP to be the main representative of modern "revisionism." Its three affiliated organizations together have about 350 members and are considered ineffective by the party: the Revolutionary Youth Association of Germany (RJVD), organ *Rebell*; the Marxist-Leninist Pupils' and Students' Association (MLSV), organ *Roter Pfeil*; and the Marxist-Leninist League of Intellectuals (MLBI).

The pro-Albanian KPD has about 400 members. Its chairman is Horst-Dieter Koch. Former chairman and long-time left-extremist activist Ernst Aust died in August. The KPD's official organ, *Roter Morgen*, has about 1,600 subscribers (*FAZ*, 28 August). Its affiliated organizations are the Communist Youth of Germany (KJD) with about 150 members, organ *Roter Rebell*, and the Communist Students (KS), organ *Zwischenruf links* (Catcall Left). The Revolutionary Trade Union Opposition (RGO), organ *RGO-Nachrichten* (RGO-News), lost about three-fourths of its members and currently has only about 300 members. Also the membership of the People's Front against Reaction, Fascism, and War (Volksfront) went down from about 1,500 to about 1,300. The KPD continued its efforts to unite the "revolutionary socialists" in one organization. Talks about unification were held with the BWK, groups of the anarcho-syndicalist Free Workers' Union (FAU) from Hamburg and Heidelberg, the Marxist-Leninist group New Main Side Theory (Neue Hauptseite Theorie; NHT), and the Trotskyist Group International Marxists (GIM) (*Verfassungsschutz*, pp. 90–91). The *Rote Hilfe* (Red Help), a KPD-affiliated organization, played a leading part in the preparation for the demonstrations against the Economic Summit in Bonn in May (*DID*, May, pp. 12–13). An "action alliance" against the Economic Summit was formed on 2 March in Bonn at a meeting called by the Federal Conference of Independent Peace Groups (BuF) and by representatives of autonomous groups: the KPD, KB, GIM, Green party, Democratic Socialists (a left-wing group that split from the SPD), local peace initiatives, anti–nuclear power plant movement (Anti-AKW Bewegung), and Central America Solidarity committees. It was decided to undertake informative and disruptive action throughout the FRG against the summit (*DID*, 22 April, pp. 10–11). The BuF also took the initiative in the beginning of October to organize a coordinating committee for the anti-NATO congress to be held in the spring of 1986. This alliance consists of BuF initiatives, GIM, KPD, KB, the Working Group Against Nuclear Energy–Göttingen, the No Peace with NATO/Out of NATO initiative, KJD, Green–Alternative List (GAL) Hamburg, Committee Anti-NATO, Federal Association of Citizens' Initiatives Protection of the Environment (BBU), and the Peace List (*DID*, 1 October, p. 7). The KPD, RGO, MLPD, and GIM called for support actions during the DGB's "action week" in October (*DID*, September, pp. 14–15).

The BWK, founded in 1980 as the result of a split of the KBW, has about 400 members, organized in groups in seven *Länder*. The official biweekly, *Politische Berichte*, has about 1,500 copies and its other biweekly, *Nachrichtenhefte*, has an edition of 1,200. Its affiliated Communist University Groups are of no significance (*Verfassungsschutz*, p. 91).

The KB, with about 400 members (200 of which are in Hamburg), lost further influence within the New Left. Its monthly publication *Arbeiterkampf* has a circulation of about 5,000 copies. The KB encouraged its members in Hamburg to join the GAL (ibid., p. 93).

The Workers' League for the Reconstruction of the KPD (AB) retained its membership of about 300, primarily in Bavaria and Rhineland-Westphalia. Its most important area of activity remained the work in trade unions and factories. It strongly supported the campaigns of the DGB. The KB's organ *Kommunistische Arbeiterzeitung* (*KAZ*) appeared irregularly. Its affiliated student organization Communist University League (KHB) was active only in cities of southern Germany (ibid.).

The thirteen Trotskyist groups, some of them with only regional organizations, have an unchanged membership of about 700. They advocate "permanent revolution" and "dictatorship of the proletariat" in the form of a "council system." They are opposed to the "decadent bureaucracy" in the socialist states. The GIM, the German section of the Fourth International (associated with the United Secretariat in Brussels), has about 250 members. Its biweekly, *was tun*, has an edition of 2,300. Its affiliated Revolutionary Socialist Youth (RSJ) has about 150 members in sixteen local groups (ibid., pp. 93–94). The League of Socialist Workers (BSA) is the German section of the International Committee of the Fourth International in London. It has, together with its youth organization Socialist Youth League (SJB), about 150 members. The SJB held its annual conference in Essen on 16–17 November (*DID*, September, p. 8; *Verfassungsschutz*, p. 94).

The Marxist Group (MG) is a Marxist-Leninist cadre party marked by a hierarchical structure, strict discipline, intense indoctrination, and secrecy. Its membership increased from 1,300 to 1,500 and consists mostly of students and academics. It has several thousand organized sympathizers. The MG believes that trained agitators must incite a class-conscious proletariat to carry on the class struggle. It publishes the monthly *MSZ-Gegen die Kosten der Freiheit, Marxistische Zeitung* (8,000 copies), the *Marxistische Arbeiterzeitung* (appears at irregular intervals), the *Marxistische Hochschulzeitung* (14,000 copies), and the *Marxistische Schulzeitung*. MG followers participated in numerous demonstrations, interrupted meetings of other political organizations, and held many, often well attended, public discussions (*Verfassungsschutz*, pp. 95, 97).

The objective of the Socialist Buro (SB) is to provide initiatives for revolutionary change of society. Its activities consisted primarily in publishing the monthly *links-Sozialistische Zeitung* (5,000 copies), the monthly *express-Zeitung für Sozialistische Betriebs- und Gewerkschaftsarbeit* (3,000 copies), and the quarterly *widersprüche*, a magazine dealing with educational, health, and social affairs (3,000 copies) (ibid., p. 95).

Various anarchist organizations were active in 1985. There was disagreement among these groups about the most appropriate organizational structure (small groups, federations, or syndicates), the form of the future society (commune or council system), and the means to reach their objectives (nonviolent or violent actions). All groups agreed that all "repressive institutions," including the state, must be eliminated (ibid., p. 97).

The anarcho-syndicalist FAU has about 150 members organized in nineteen local groups and contacts. The FAU is a member of the International Workers' Association (IAA). It considers itself a "militant, revolutionary trade-union movement" and fights for a "free society" through "resistance" in the factories and eventually through the "revolutionary general strike" and "social revolution." The FAU's organ is *direkte aktion*. A number of independent oppositional FAU groups emerged in several cities. The Free Workers' Union/Students (FAUST) joined the FAU group in Heidelberg (ibid., p. 97).

The Violence-free Action Groups–Grass Roots Movement has about 900 members operating in about 80 groups and collectives. The voice for these anarchists is the Federation of Violence-free Action Groups (FöGA). The FöGA propagates a nonviolent revolution and the replacement of the power of the state with the power of the grass roots. The monthly periodical *grasswurzelrevolution* prints about 4,000 copies (ibid., p. 98).

The autonomous anarchist groups follow different anarchistic concepts. Their followers are mostly young people and number several thousand. Most groups are small, loosely organized, and short lived. Some of them propagate an "autonomous communism," others fight "U.S. and West German imperialism." Several of the "autonomous anti-imperialists" resorted to terrorist actions, military sabotage, and arson (ibid., pp. 98–99).

The actions committed by left-extremists of all shades of the New Left against the German military and Allied forces stationed in the FRG numbered several hundred. U.S. forces and military installations were the most frequent targets of blockades, human chains, torch-light parades, and violent actions. The campaign against ammunition transports for the U.S. forces was continued. The Committee Against Trains Carrying Bombs (Bremen; KgB), a local alliance of independent antiwar groups, was the initiator of the campaign (ibid., pp. 100, 102).

Members of the New Left took part in international solidarity actions. The government of Nicaragua was a favored objective. Participation in the Workers' Brigade in Nicaragua was considered part of the anti-imperialist struggle (ibid., p. 109).

The year witnessed many terrorist attacks committed by outright terrorist organizations. These attacks were directed primarily against German and Allied military installations and also against industrial and commercial enterprises connected with the "military establishment." As of the beginning of September, there had been some 180 arson and bombing attacks (*FAZ*, 19 September). Among these terrorist actions was the murder of Dr. Ernt Zimmermann, a German industrialist, by the Red Army Faction (RAF) (*NYT*, 2 February). The same organization was responsible for the murder of a U.S. soldier, and the bombings of a PX on the U.S. air base in Wiesbaden and of U.S. air defense bases in Germany (Hamburg, DPA, 27 August; *FBIS*, 28 August; *WP*, 7 September). Other terrorist attacks were committed by the Revolutionary Cells (RZ) and antidogmatic "autonomous" groups.

The RAF was able to replace some of its apprehended members with recruits from the large group of sympathizers and thus to maintain its hard core of about twenty (*Newsweek*, 19 August, pp. 39–40). An RAF sympathizers' meeting in Karlsruhe on 26 January was attended by about 1,800 persons, some of them with masked faces. They called for a coalition of the RAF and resistance movement in order to form a terrorist action front of Western Europe (*Innere Sicherheit*, no. 2 [3 May]: 37). The *Tageszeitung* (*TAZ*) published on 4 February a solidarity appeal with the RAF that was endorsed by Spanish and Italian communist organizations, the GAL Zürich, and the Swiss Central America Committee (ibid., p. 36). The RAF formed an alliance, the Political-Military Front Western Europe, with the French terrorist group Action Directe for the purpose of coordinating their attacks against NATO facilities. It is believed that the Belgian Fighting Communist Cells (CCC), which claimed responsibility for a series of explosions at military installations in Belgium, is part of the front (*NYT*, 2 February).

The RZ comprises left-extremist groups with their roots in the mid-1970s. It is responsible for several terrorist attacks against military installations, businesses, and prominent individuals (*Los Angeles Times*, 9 March). It is claimed that members of the RZ travel from all over Germany in order to participate in demonstrations and frequently succeed in turning the events into violence (*FAZ*, 2 October).

The Jusos and other youth, student, and women's organizations affiliated with the SPD are usually not perceived as left-radical organizations. However, they share many objectives with the extreme left and have increasingly participated in "unity of actions" with Communists and other leftists. Their anti-NATO and anti–U.S. policies and their support of Moscow's "peace plans" provide the basis for increased cooperation.

WEST BERLIN

Population. 1,870,000
Party. Socialist Unity Party of West Berlin (Sozialistische Einheitspartei Westberlins; SEW)
Membership. 4,500
Chairman. Horst Schmitt
Politburo. 17 members: Dietmar Ahrens, Uwe Doering, Helga Dolinski, Detlef Fendt, Klaus Feske, Harry Flichtbeil, Margot Granowski, Heinz Grünberg, Klaus-Dieter Heiser, Volker June, Inge Kopp, Jörg Kuhle, Hans Mahle, Margot Mrozinski, Monika Sieveking, Erich Ziegler, Horst Schmitt
Secretariat. 7 members: Dietmar Ahrens, Klaus Feske, Harry Flichtbeil, Margot Granowski, Inge Kopp, Herwig Kurzendorfer, Horst Schmitt
Executive. 65 members
Status. Legal
Last Congress. Seventh, 25–27 May 1984, in West Berlin
Last Election. 1985, 0.6 percent, no representation
Auxiliary Organizations. Socialist Youth League Karl Liebknecht (Sozialistischer Jugendverband Karl Liebknecht; SJ Karl Liebknecht), ca. 550 members; Young Pioneers (Junge Pioniere; JP), ca. 250 members; SEW–University Groups, ca. 400 members
Publications. *Die Wahrheit* (The Truth), SEW daily organ, circulation ca. 13,000

West Berlin is still under "Allied occupation" by the forces of the United States, Britain, and France. The 1971 Quadripartite Agreement concerning Berlin confirmed its special status, based on previous agreements in 1944 and 1945, declaring that the former German capital is not part of the FRG. Although the 1971 agreement was meant to cover the area of Greater Berlin, the Soviet-occupied eastern sector of the city has been declared the capital of the GDR. The Western allies have encouraged the FRG to maintain close ties with West Berlin, and West Berlin is represented in the federal parliament by nonvoting deputies.

Berlin's special status made it possible for the SED to set up a subsidiary in West Berlin. In 1959 an "independent" organizational structure was introduced for the West Berlin section of the SED. In 1962 the party was renamed the Socialist Unity Party of Germany–West Berlin; in 1969 the present designation was introduced in order to make the party appear a genuine, indigenous political party.

The SEW, like the DKP, is a pro-Soviet party and depends financially on the SED. Its statements are identical with the ideological and political views of the East German and Soviet parties. SEW membership is about 4,500. In the 10 March elections for the city's House of Representatives, the SEW obtained 7,713 votes, or 0.6 percent, compared with 0.7 percent in 1981.

Among the affiliated organizations of the SEW

are the SJ Karl Liebknecht, with about 800 members, 250 of them children in the JP. The SEW-University Groups have about 400 members and the SEW-influenced Action Group of Democrats and Socialists about 500 members. Other SEW-led organizations include the Democratic Women's League Berlin (about 600 members), the Society for German-Soviet Friendship (about 500 members), and the West Berlin organization of the Victims of the Nazi Regime/League of Antifascists (about 500 members).

The SEW maintained contacts with the international communist movement by means of mutual visits, especially with the SED. SEW chairman Horst Schmitt met with Mikhail Gorbachev in Moscow on 5 May and delivered an address at a meeting devoted to opening the memorial museum to German antifascists in Krasnogorsk (*Pravda*, 6 May; *FBIS*, 6 May; *Moscow TV*, 5 May; *FBIS*, 6 May). The SEW participated in a meeting of communist parties of capitalist Europe in Paris on 12–13 June (*L'Humanité*, 22 June). Nicolas Ceauşescu, secretary general of the Romanian Communist Party, received a delegation from the SEW, led by Politburo member Margot Granowski (Bucharest, AGERPRESS, 14 November; *FBIS*, 15 November). On his 60th birthday Schmitt received the Lenin Order from the Presidium of the Soviet Union and the Karl Marx Order from Erich Honecker, chairman of the State Council of the GDR (*FAZ*, 5 September). Schmitt also received the People's Republic of Bulgaria First Class Order for his promotion of fraternal relations between the Bulgarian Communist Party and the SEW (Sofia, BTA, 2 September; *JPRS-EPS*, 85-096, 19 September).

The SJ Karl Liebknecht played an influential role in the founding of the preparatory committee of West Berlin for the twelfth World Festival of Youth and Students in Moscow (*Verfassungsschutz*, p. 40).

Many New Left and left-extremist groups operate in West Berlin. The problem posed by house occupations was successfully handled by the city's government and therefore no longer provided opportunities for militant elements. However, they turned many demonstrations and rallies into violent confrontations with the authorities. Terrorists were also active in West Berlin.

Eric Waldman
University of Calgary

Great Britain

Population. 56,437,000
Party. Communist Party of Great Britain (CPGB)
Founded. 1920
Membership. Under 16,000
General Secretary. Gordon McLennan
Political Committee. No data
Executive Committee. 45 members
Status. Legal
Last Congress. Special, 18–20 May 1985
Last Election. June 1983, 0.03 percent, no representation

Auxiliary Organizations. Young Communist League (YCL); Liaison Committee for the Defence of Trade Unions (LCDTU)

Publications. *Morning Star*, *Marxism Today*, *Communist Focus*, *Challenge*, *Spark*, *Our History Journal*, *Economic Bulletin*, *Medicine in Society*, *Education Today and Tomorrow*, *Seven Days*

The CPGB is a recognized political party and contests both local and national elections. It does not, however, operate in Northern Ireland, which it does not recognize as British territory. The party has had no members in the House of Commons since 1950, but it has one member, Lord Milford, in the non-elected House of Lords.

Leadership and Party Organization. The CPGB is divided into four divisions: the National Congress; the Executive Committee and its departments; districts; and local and factory branches. Constitutionally, the biennial National Congress is the party's supreme authority and, except in unusual periods such as at the present time, it rubber-stamps the decisions of the Political Committee. Responsibility for overseeing the party's activities rests with the 45-member Executive Committee, which is elected by the National Congress and meets every two months. The Executive Committee comprises members of special committees, fulltime departmental heads, and the sixteen members of the Political Committee, the party's innermost controlling conclave.

Party leaders remain deeply preoccupied with the continuing decline in support for the party. Electorally the party is so battered that it does not now even contest as many seats as formerly. Membership is at its lowest point since World War II, and only some 50 percent of the less than 16,000 have actually paid their fees. The decline in electoral support was most graphically illustrated in Britain's last general elections in June 1983, when the party's 35 candidates polled only 11,598 votes.

However, the poor showing of the CPGB at the polls belies the party's strength in the trade-union movement and in influencing opinion. Although the party does not control any individual trade union, it is represented on most union executive committees and has played a major role in most government-union confrontations of recent years. The CPGB's success is partly attributable to low turnouts in most union elections, to the fact that it is the only party seeking to control the outcome of these elections, and to its close interest in industrial affairs, which ensures support from workers who might not support other aspects of the party's program. There are two members of the CPGB on the General Council of the Trades Union Congress (TUC): Mick McGahey of the National Union of Mineworkers (NUM) and Ken Gill of the Technical and Supervisory Section of the Amalgamated Union of Engineering Workers. In addition, CPGB ideas exercise a considerable influence on other trade-union executives and on several Labour Party members of parliament.

Domestic Affairs. The long-standing conflict between the Eurocommunist leadership and the Stalinist hardline minority continued to intensify in 1985. The party was in an obvious crisis that had been building for some years. It centers on the dispute between the party's Executive Committee and its chief theoretical journal, *Marxism Today*, on the one hand, and the *Morning Star* on the other. The *Morning Star*, although nationally recognized as the party's daily newspaper, is technically owned by the communist but separate People's Press Printing Society (PPPS). Throughout 1985 the PPPS continued to be in the hands of Stalinist opponents of the Executive Committee's Eurocommunist policies. The *Morning Star* group was bitterly opposed to the leadership's criticisms, muted though they were, of the Soviet Union and to the transformation of *Marxism Today* into a popular, broad-based magazine.

The course of intensifying intraparty conflict in 1985 was established in January when a special Executive Committee meeting on 13 January expelled Tony Chater and David Whitfield as party members. Chater was editor and Whitfield assistant editor of the *Morning Star* and both are hardline Stalinists. The Executive Committee also announced at the same time that it had decided to press the struggle to a climax at a special party congress, which it called for 18–20 May in order to discuss and act on the growing dispute.

The Special Congress included 251 delegates. A large majority strongly supported the Executive Committee's Eurocommunist views. The main focus of the meeting was the Executive's draft resolution, which unequivocally condemned the Stalinists and their control over the *Morning Star*. The resolution said that the party was in deep crisis and blamed the troubles entirely on the "minority," which it accused of holding narrow and sectarian attitudes that were opposed to the key concepts of the party's document, "The British Road to Socialism." More specifically, the resolution accused the Stalinist faction of reducing issues of all kinds simply to class and thereby distorting the relationship that should exist between the labor movement and other social forces and movements.

The congress was predictably acrimonious even though firmly in the hands of the Eurocommunists. More than 650 amendments to the draft resolution were offered, many of which attacked the Executive Committee's leadership. But the Executive held the clear majority and defeated repeated challenges by wide margins, exceeding more than 70 percent on most votes. Moreover, the congress strongly endorsed the Executive's earlier decisions; it expelled eighteen Stalinists and, in voting for seats on the new Executive, defeated all of the candidates who supported the *Morning Star*.

The Executive Committee's victory at the congress provoked a quick response from the Stalinists. Three weeks later, in mid-June, the Stalinists decisively defeated the Executive's slate in annual elections for the management committee of the *Morning Star*. The CPGB was particularly angered by the *Morning Star*'s refusal to print the names of its nominees for the management committee until after the election. The *Morning Star* further exacerbated the conflict by publishing a barrage of gloating commentary and letters about the management election, citing the Stalinist victory as a popular rebuff to the Executive and its party congress. In response, a few days after the *Morning Star* election, the Executive Committee announced that it intended to establish a new weekly newspaper because "for the first time for over half a century there is no longer a daily paper in Britain which can be relied upon to present the policies of the Communist party." That paper, *Seven Days*, began publication on 24 October.

On 31 October the Stalinists replied again. Its organization within the party, the Communist Campaign Group (CCG) held a meeting to denounce the party's leadership. The CCG announced the publication of a booklet outlining its position, "The Crisis in the Communist Party and the Way Forward." The booklet calls on Communists to stay within the party and to fight. "If this means expulsion or any other form of discipline then the policy of the Communist Campaign Group is to urge comrades to refuse to recognise or accept such disciplinary measures." Mike Hicks, the CCG's chairman, added in a followup press conference that there was no question of the group organizing a split. Instead, the CCG would attempt to mobilize what he described as the majority of party members, whom he insisted stood with the group. As part of this effort, it was announced that the CCG would publish a new theoretical journal because it was felt that *Marxism Today*, which is controlled by the Eurocommunist leadership, was not providing a "Communist perspective but was tamely supporting Neil Kinnock."

Domestically, the CPGB's main efforts continue to be centered on the union movement and especially on the aftermath of the miners' strike, which ended in early March. The Communists had vigorously supported the strike. After its bitter end, the party just as vigorously took up a defense of the NUM's leadership and its conduct of the strike. The party was especially supportive of Arthur Scargill, the NUM president who is not a member of the CPGB. Although both factions of the party applauded Scargill's leadership, the Stalinist faction through the *Morning Star* was the more enthusiastic. Scargill made trips to Moscow, which produced financial as well as moral support for his leadership and, as a consequence, caused him to become an inflammatory figure on the British political scene. From the perspective of the internal party split, it is important that his leadership colleagues within the NUM, Mick McGahey and George Bolton, are party members and that McGahey continues as a primary spokesman for the Eurocommunist leadership. By the end of 1985 there were signs of change in party support for Scargill. As he faced an increasing challenge from a new right-wing breakaway mining union, the Eurocommunist faction was becoming more critical of his leadership; it seemed possible that Scargill might become another source of Eurocommunist disagreement with the Stalinist faction.

Other areas of CPGB activity within the union movement included strong support for the continuing National Union of Teachers dispute. The party also continued to oppose the Thatcher government's ongoing legislative program that has been incrementally raising requirements for union leadership accountability, particularly about strike actions. The CPGB continued to enjoy the incumbency of two of its members on the General Council of the TUC. One of them, Ken Gill, became TUC chairman for the year beginning in September. Although Gill's position is more prestigious than powerful and is earned as much by seniority as for other reasons, it does carry important visibility rarely gained by CPGB members.

The CPGB continued to support demonstrations objecting to most aspects of government policy, including the proposed abolition of the larger metropolitan councils, rate capping of big spending councils, and the deepening crisis between the Thatcher government and the Liverpool council. The party was also in the forefront of militant demands and protests concerning the increasingly conflictual issue of unemployment in the country. The party continued to be an active supporter of the Committee for Nuclear Disarmament and vigorously opposed the deployment of cruise missiles in Britain. The CPGB supports unilateral nuclear disarmament by the United Kingdom, which it presses on the Labour Party and Neil Kinnock at every opportunity. In 1985 this issue was coupled with strong opposition to the U.S. Strategic Defense Initiative, which was just as vigorously opposed by the Soviet Union.

Auxiliary Organizations. CPGB activity in industry centers on its approximately 200 workplace branches. Its umbrella organization is the LCDTU. Although the CPGB is riven by internal dispute, its trade-union structure can still command considerable support from prominent trade-union leaders.

The YCL, with only about 500 members, is close to collapse.

The party retains a number of financial interests including Central Books, Lawrence and Wishart Publishers, Farleigh Press, London Caledonian Printers, Rodell Properties, the Labour Research Department, and the Marx Memorial Library.

International Views and Activities. Although the CPGB leadership is regarded as revisionist by its own dissident hardline faction, there are in fact few areas where the CPGB is anything less than unstinting in its support of the Soviet Union. The party is still critical of the Soviet invasions of Afghanistan and Czechoslovakia. However, on most issues the party is staunchly pro-Soviet. The CPGB favors arms reduction talks with the USSR and opposes the deployment of cruise and Pershing missiles in Europe and the development of U.S. space weapons. The party campaigns for British withdrawal from NATO and the European Economic Community. The party is critical of Israel and seeks to promote the recognition of the Palestine Liberation Organization.

In 1985, Gordon McLennan represented the CPGB at the funeral of Soviet leader Chernenko. While in Moscow, McLennan met with two senior Soviet officials, B. N. Ponomarev and A. S. Chernayayev. Both the Eurocommunist majority leadership and the Soviet dissident faction supported the Soviet Union in its row with the British government over the series of expulsions that began on the British side.

Other Marxist Groups. Besides the CPGB, several small, mainly Trotskyist groups are also active. Although some of these groups were growing swiftly in the 1970s, their memberships are now waning. This is probably partly attributable to the adoption by the Labour Party of left policies, which has encouraged extremists to join the Labour Party itself rather than some of the fringe revolutionary groups.

Probably the most important of the Trotskyist groups is Militant Tendency, which derives its name from its paper of the same name. Militant Tendency claims to be merely a loose tendency of opinion within the Labour Party, but there is no doubt that Militant Tendency possesses its own distinctive organization and for some years has been pursuing a policy of "entryism" (the tactic of penetrating the larger, more moderate Labour Party). Militant Tendency controls about 50 Labour Party constituencies. In 1985 there were signs of a possible split within Militant Tendency over the role of Liverpool deputy leader Derek Hatton, who is a leader in the fight with the Thatcher government.

The other significant Trotskyist organizations are the Socialist Workers' Party (SWP) and the Workers' Revolutionary Party (WRP). The SWP has been particularly active in single-issue campaigns, notably the anti-unemployment campaign. It also gave active support to striking miners' families but in fact enjoys little support in the coalmining industry. The WRP's activities are more secretive but are known to center in the engineering, mining, theater, and automobile industries. It focuses attention on the young and has set up six Youth Training Centres, which are in fact more concerned with recruitment. In late October the WRP expelled its former leader, Gerry Healy. The party's newspaper, *News Line*, said it had expelled Healy, who had been a leading figure for 50 years, because he had "established non-communist and bureaucratic relations inside the party."

Gerald Dorfman
Hoover Institution

Greece

Population. 9,966,000
Party. Communist Party of Greece (Kommunistikon Komma Ellados; KKE)
Founded. 1921
Membership. 42,000 (estimated)
Secretary General. Kharilaos Florakis
Politburo. 9 full members: Kharilaos Florakis, Nikos Kaloudhis, Grigoris Farakos, Kostas Tsolakis, Roula Kourkoulou, Loula Logara, Dimitris Gondikas, Andonis Ambatielos, Dimitris Sarlis; 2 candidate members: Takis Mamatsis, Orestis Kolozov
Status. Legal
Last Congress. Eleventh, 15–18 December 1982, in Athens
Last Election. June 1985, 9.9 percent, 13 of 300 seats
Auxiliary Organization. Communist Youth of Greece (KNE)
Publications. *Rizospastis*, daily; *Kommunistiki Epitheorisi* (*KOMEP*), monthly theoretical review

During the military dictatorship (1967–1974), the KKE split into two factions. The pro-Moscow faction, initially known as KKE-Exterior, has now become the official KKE. The other faction, still known as KKE-Interior, retains little of its Marxist-Leninist background and has shifted to an increasingly independent and moderate line. Its influence remains limited mostly to leftist intellectuals. After a rather impressive showing in the 1984 election of deputies for the European Parliament (3.4 percent), KKE-Interior received only 1.8 percent in the parliamentary election of 2 June 1985 and one seat in the 300-seat legislature.

In the June 1985 parliamentary election, KKE received 9.9 percent, as compared to 10.9 in the previous (1981) election. The party had made some gains in the 1982 municipal elections when KKE-sponsored candidates received approximately 20 percent of the total vote. As predicted at the time this did not signify a permanent shift; the 1982 apparent rise was mostly due to the appeal of local candidates or the support given KKE candidates by Panhellenic Socialist Movement (PASOK) supporters and KKE-Interior followers.

During the 1985 electoral campaign for the national legislature, the KKE attacked both the governing PASOK and the right-center New Democratic Party (NDP). Its basic objective was to win enough seats in the legislature to deprive both major parties of a self-sufficient majority, thereby emerging as the king-maker. This hope did not materialize, however; PASOK received 45.8 percent and 161 seats in the legislature, ten more than the 151 needed for a clear majority.

With the support of the governing PASOK, a Marxist-oriented, anti-American, and anti-NATO point of view has made significant inroads in Greek public opinion.

Leadership and Organization. The KKE is well financed and is organized along traditional communist party patterns, with cells in factories and other places of work and with local organizations in city neighborhoods and villages. Major cities such as Athens have city committees and Communist Base organizations that coordinate the activities of the neighborhood party organizations. The party has branch organizations in the various industries, public enterprises, major utilities, and trades. It also has auxiliary party organizations within the labor unions and a strong representation in the General Confederation of Greek Workers

(GSEE). The party congress is statutorily convened every four years but this requirement has not been observed consistently. A Central Committee elected by the congress normally meets every six months. The actual power, however, resides with the Politburo. In addition to the secretary general, Kharilaos Florakis, the most influential members in the Politburo are Andonis Ambatielos, Nikos Kaloudhis, and Grigoris Farakos. The party's youth organization, KNE, is very active and has considerable influence in the universities and trade unions.

The structure of the KKE-Interior is much less elaborate and does not have the cohesion and discipline of that of the KKE. The KKE-Interior revised its organizational design during the year in order to accommodate the elevation of Leonidas Kyrkos, its most articulate and respected leader, without removing its secretary, Yiannis Banias. Kyrkos was given the newly created post of party chairman. He is now generally recognized as the party's leader.

Views and Positions. The year opened with clear signs that the KKE policy of relative cooperation with the PASOK government was being replaced by a policy of carefully orchestrated and controlled confrontation. One issue of contention was the incomes policy of the Papandreou government. An effort to tighten the rise in monetary incomes for workers and employees caused a serious rift in the leadership of the GSEE. Within the GSEE governing council, representatives of the Panhellenic Militant Workers Trade Union Movement (PASKE; affiliated with PASOK) came into serious conflict with the United Antidictatorial Labor Movement–Cooperative (ESAK-S; related to KKE) and the Antidictatorial Labor Front (AEM; related to KKE-Interior). PASKE had a majority in the council and so prevailed. The KKE used the opportunity to distance itself from the PASOK economic policies and to come out in favor of continuing increases in wages and salaries and other benefits.

Another issue that caused a rift with PASOK was the electoral system enacted by the legislature in January. The system, a version of proportional representation, was designed to benefit whichever of the two major parties (PASOK or NDP) came first in the next parliamentary election. The KKE favored a simple proportional system that would leave neither of the major parties a clear majority, in which case the KKE would hold the key for the formation of a PASOK cabinet. Such support, of course, would not be given without significant trade-offs. The electoral system enacted in January made such an eventuality unlikely.

A third issue was the re-election of K. Karamanlis to the presidency of the republic. Prime Minister Andreas Papandreou had intimated that he favored the re-election of Karamanlis, although many in his party—especially those farther to the left—were unhappy about his choice. The KKE, too, openly opposed Karamanlis's re-election. However, with the NDP support for Karamanlis, the KKE opposition to a PASOK proposal for the re-election of Karamanlis would have no effect in the legislature, where a minimum of 180 votes was required. This issue was suddenly moot when on 9 March Papandreou accepted the view of the left-wing militants in his party leadership and nominated Khristos Sartzetakis, a jurist, as the party's candidate for president. Sartzetakis was elected with the support of the KKE deputies in the legislature.

A fourth issue was Greece's membership in NATO and the European Economic Community (EEC). In the past, PASOK's coolness toward these two entities had been more or less in line with the KKE's traditional opposition. In 1985 PASOK gradually shifted toward a more moderate line, while KKE remained adamant in its objection to both.

For the first half of the year, the KKE and KKE-Interior focused their attention on the electoral contest. The KKE in particular attacked PASOK for its alleged failure to push forward the *Alaghi* ("Change," a code word used by PASOK and the left in lieu of "socialist transformation"). The KKE called for "genuine change," meaning change along more Marxist-Leninist lines, and promoted the slogan "there can be no genuine change without the KKE." The slogan implied that only strong support for KKE at the polls, which would inevitably cut into the PASOK vote, would allow the KKE to act as king-maker after the election and force on PASOK the socialist policies favored by the left. The KKE also turned against the KKE-Interior, which it accused of creating confusion among the voters and diverting from the KKE votes needed for the role envisioned by the party. The KKE-Interior responded in kind by accusing the KKE of blind subservience to foreign powers.

Following the election and its unimpressive showing, the KKE chose a low profile. Its hope to play the role of king-maker had been frustrated, but it still had a strong card in its influence within the trade-union movement. When the Papandreou government announced in November a series of strict economic measures to cope with a $3 billion deficit in the balance of payments and with the effects of its heavy external borrowing during the previous four years, the KKE found a new cause to reinforce its image as the "workers' party." In party statements and the editorials of *Rizospastis*, the KKE leadership attacked the economic measures as "antilabor" and called for their abolition. Partly with KKE instigation, strikes were called almost daily; the 17 November annual celebration of the "Polytakhnion uprising" against the Papadopoulos dictatorship in November 1973 was turned by the KKE into a strident attack against the economic policies of the Papandreou government.

The KKE did not limit its opposition to economic measures. It also turned against the apparent rapprochement of the PASOK government with the Western allies, including the United States. Papandreou, faced with serious economic problems, was abandoning the anti-American and anti-Western attitudes that had made him the darling of the left in previous years. However, as the year came to an end, it was becoming increasingly evident that the KKE's opposition was more for appearance's sake. The KKE could not afford to adopt a truly hostile policy against the PASOK government and use its influence in the trade unions to topple the government. If Papandreou fell, the possibility of having the right wing return to power could not be ruled out. Whatever its disagreements with the current government, the KKE was much better off with PASOK in power. The KKE leadership thus chose a policy designed to consolidate its influence with the trade unions and channel public discontent from the economic measures in a more leftist and militant direction. The KKE policy was assisted by dissension within the PASOK trade unionists. The leadership of the GSEE was split; those in the council who opposed the economic measures had taken over, only to be replaced by a court-appointed group associated with PASOK and supportive of the government.

As the economic measures result in higher prices and lower incomes for workers, the KKE is bound to focus on public discontent and try to pick up support. This may lead to some communist gains in the municipal elections scheduled for October 1986.

On international issues, KKE's views and positions remained fairly constant during the year. The party faithfully echoes the views emanating from Moscow on any given issue. Regarding Cyprus, the KKE has taken a position at sharp variance from that of PASOK. The KKE criticized the rejection of the plan prepared by U.N. secretary general Javier Pérez de Cuellar on Cyprus. The plan was rejected by Cyprus president Spyros Kyprianou in January, on the advice of Papandreou. It appears that the Soviet Union favors a settlement that would terminate the existence of the Turk-Cypriot "state" in the northern part of the island, which is occupied by Turkish troops, and result in a nonaligned, demilitarized Cyprus.

In late November, the KKE attacked the Papandreou government for its participation in the revision of the Treaty of Rome, which was designed to increase the cooperation among the EEC members. On other issues, such as opposition to the installation of medium-range missiles in Europe or the Strategic Defense Initiative, the KKE and PASOK are in basic agreement.

Domestic Activities. The party centered its activities in four major areas: the maintenance and strengthening of its influence in the trade-union movement and among students; the election of the new president; the electoral campaign for the 2 June parliamentary election; and the opposition to the government's austerity economic measures.

In September the KNE held its annual youth festival with the usual fanfare. The festival was well organized and was attended by several delegations from foreign communist parties. In November the KNE played an active but also divisive role in the celebration of the "Polytakhnion uprising." The communist left used the occasion to attack the PASOK government for its economic measures, in contrast to previous years when PASOK and the KKE cooperated.

In early March, a Soviet delegation visited Athens to present a special award, given by the USSR presidium of the Supreme Soviet, to the Greek-Soviet Society.

Although the KKE has dissassociated itself in recent years from acts of violence and terrorism in Greece, several extremist groups of a Marxist orientation have engaged in a series of terrorist activities including assassinations, bombings, riots, and arson. There is no evidence that the KKE is in any way involved. However, its "anticapitalist," anti-American, and anti-Western rhetoric inevitably provides the ideological justification for the activities of the extremist groups.

International Contacts. The KKE was less active in its international contacts and especially in the travels of its leaders abroad, in part due to the preoccupation of the party leadership with the election of the Greek president, the parliamentary election, and the government's economic measures. On the occasion of the new year, the KKE sent greetings to its sister parties in Cuba and Afghanistan and to the Sandinistas in Nicaragua. In March a Polish delegation came to Athens and met with KKE leaders Florakis and Farakos. In June, a KKE delegation participated in the Paris meeting of West European communist parties. In July, Florakis received Socialist Unity Party of Germany (SED) Politburo member Guenter Schabowski in Athens. Later the same month, Florakis met Bulgarian president Todor Zhivkov during the latter's official visit to Greece for talks with Papandreou.

KKE-Interior leaders met with a Communist League of Yugoslavia delegation in February. In July a delegation led by K. Gavroglou, a member of the KKE-Interior Executive Bureau, visited the People's Republic of China.

Other Marxist-Leninist Organizations. The Revolutionary Communist Party of Greece (EKKE), which publishes the weekly tabloid *I Laiki*, has a miniscule public following as shown by the last election, when its candidates received a small fraction of one percent. Its revolutionary messages, however, appear very often on posters in Athens. Other small groups include the Organization of Communist Internationalists of Greece, which is a member of the Fourth International and publishes *Ergatiki Pali*; the Organization of Communists Marxist-Leninist, which publishes *Epanastasi*; and "17 November," which has claimed responsibility for several terrorist activities since 1976. There are also certain groups of anarchist-leftists who have established their control over an Athens area known as Exarkhia.

D. G. Kousoulas
Howard University

Iceland

Population. 241,000
Party. People's Alliance (Althydubandalagid; AB)
Founded. 1968
Membership. 3,000 (estimated)
Chairman. Svavar Gestsson
Executive Committee. 10 members: Svavar Gestsson, Kristin Olafsdottir (deputy chair), Ludvik Josephsson, Helgi Gudmundsson (secretary), Margret Frimannsdottir (treasurer), Olafur Ragnar Grimsson; others unknown
Central Committee. 70 members, 20 deputies
Status. Legal
Last Congress. 7–10 November 1985
Last Election. 1983, 17.3 percent, 10 of 60 seats
Auxiliary Organization. Organization of Base Opponents (OBO; organizes peace demonstrations against U.S.-NATO bases)
Publications. *Thjodviljinn* (daily), Reykjavik; *Verkamadhurinn* (weekly), Akureyri; *Mjolnir* (weekly), Siglufjördhur

The AB is the successor to a line of leftist parties dating back to 1930, when the Icelandic Communist Party (Kommunistaflokkur Islands) was established by a left-wing splinter from the Labor Party. In 1938 the Social Democratic Party (SDP) broke from the Labor Party and joined with the Communists to create a new party, the United People's Party–Socialist Party (Sameiningar flokkur althydu–Socialista flokkurinn; UPP-SP). Although its ideology was based on "scientific socialism–Marxism," the UPP-SP had no organizational ties to Moscow. Its first goal was support for complete Icelandic independence from Denmark. By the time this was achieved in 1944, the UPP-SP was accepted as a responsible democratic leftist party, and it had participated in governing coalitions. In 1956 the UPP-SP formed an electoral alliance with other small leftist and neutralist groups, and the coalition became known as the People's Alliance. In 1968 the UPP-SP dissolved itself into the AB, which then became the current pragmatic Marxist party. It has participated regularly in coalition governments, most recently joining the Progressive Party (agrarian liberal) in a coalition headed by the late maverick Gunnar Thoroddsen, who was formerly of the moderate-conservative Independence Party (IP). The Thoroddsen government resigned following the April 1983 parliamentary elections, which had resulted in losses for all of the constituent parties. The AB held three cabinet posts: social and health affairs (Svavar Gestsson); finance (Ragnar Arnalds); and industry (Hjorleifur Guttormsson). It is now the largest opposition party.

AB's 1983 electoral setback stemmed from the severe economic recession of 1981–1983 and hyperinflation that reached an unprecedented 159 percent annual rate at the time of the elections. In May 1983 Steingrimur Hermansson formed a new majority coalition government of the Progressive Party and the ID. The new government enjoys a substantial parliamentary majority: 37 out of 60 seats.

Austerity measures were sharpened. The inflation rate declined throughout 1984, but so did real income. A wave of labor unrest erupted, and the government's income policy collapsed. Currency devaluation and rising unemployment promised an economically grim 1985. The government's popularity plunged along with the national economy. The AB has not gained from the dissatisfaction; of the four parties now comprising the opposition, only the reformist SDP and the Women's Party (Samtök um kvennalista) experienced notable gains. Jon Baldvin Hannibalsson, the dynamic new leader of the SDP, has attracted broad public support. A Gallup poll in February showed the SDP at 20.5 percent with the AB down to 10.8 percent—a severe decline from the 1983 elections. The Social Democratic Federation (SDF), a split from the SDP, also declined to 6.0 percent, while the Women's Party, an amalgam of generally leftist feminists, reached 11.2 percent.

In Iceland, too, it may be darkest just before the dawn. The Icelandic economy is notoriously volatile, and in 1985 significant improvements became apparent. The GNP grew in 1984 by an unexpected 2.5 percent and by another estimated 2 percent in 1985. The cost of living was expected to increase by 33 percent but would be matched by wage increases. Iceland's remarkably low level of unemployment would again fall below 1 percent (Central Bank of Iceland, *Economic Statistics Quarterly* 6, no. 4 [November]). The government's policies, aided by improved fish catches and international developments, were beginning to work.

Leadership and Organization. Electoral and popularity declines stimulated discontent within the AB, which was visible in the party's press and at its meetings. There was substantial criticism of Svavar Gestsson's leadership. Some blamed this on personality clashes between Gestsson and Asmundur Stefansson, chairman of the powerful Icelandic Federation of Labor (ASI). An internal AB report characterized the party as a stagnant, boring, undemocratic, male-dominated guardian of the status quo and a failure in defending the interests of wage earners (*News of Iceland*, June and October).

Such problems were hashed out at the party's congress in Reykjavik on 7–10 November. Despite continuing criticism, Gestsson was re-elected to the chairmanship. Kristin Olafsdottir was elected deputy chair as Vilborg Hardardottir chose not to seek re-election. Despite the vigorous and open party debate, one of the current leadership's harshest critics, former chair Olafur Ragnar Grimsson, was elected chair of the party's Executive Committee (*Nordisk Kontakt*, no. 15). Clearly the AB continues to prefer pluralist rather than Leninist party governance.

Domestic Affairs. As suggested above, Iceland's recent economic turmoil continued to dominate the political agenda in 1985. Iceland has long suffered from extraordinarily high inflation rates, and the Hermansson government's initiatives in labor relations and income policy (that is, the suspension of wage indexation) collapsed in 1984. The AB opposed such measures, but it reacted to labor-union demands rather than initiate them. The inflationary settlements of 1984 placed harsher demands on fiscal policy in 1985. High interest rates and austerity measures continued, and the government was deeply pessimistic at the start of the year. Foreign indebtedness (equal to 60 percent of the GNP) and interest payment costs (equal to 25 percent of export earnings) gave an exceedingly narrow scope to national economic policy. The government's next economic package was announced in February. It emphasized increased housing construction, tax reform, and, in particular, sharper enforcement of tax rules. Speaking for his party, Gestsson enounced the continuing prohibitions on wage indexation and doubted that the government's policies would end the fall in real wages (ibid., no. 4). The government did in fact repeal the prohibition in June.

The AB is well represented in the leadership of the powerful ASI. The IP is the only other party with significant union strength despite its non-socialist program. Not only is the ASI chair Stefansson an AB activist, but the party deliberately seeks to support labor's demands. After the labor victories in 1984, the moderates seemed to prevail. An unexpected pay agreement in May between the ASI and the Employers' Confederation promised reasonable wage increases for the rest of 1985. The government would be likely to apply the same rates to public employees. In October, however, a strike by the air hostesses of the economically important national airline (Icelandair) became a symbol of wage-earner discontent and the activism of Icelandic women. After a stalemate in bargaining, the government decided to end the walkout by legislation. The AB led the parliamentary protests against this intervention and was joined by the other leftist parties except for the SDP. President Vigdis Finnbogadottir almost precipitated a political and constitutional crisis when she delayed signing the law. The Icelandic president normally remains aloof from partisan issues. The president provided considerable drama in her unprecedented intervention, and the minister of transport nearly resigned (ibid., no. 14).

The dramatic decline in popular support of the AB became itself a focus for Icelandic political discussions. Iceland has long been remarkable in the Nordic region for the impotence of its Social Democratic Party and the strength of the principal party of the Marxist left. In the 1970s the SDP doubled its support to 22 percent of the vote in 1978, yet a change in leadership and disappointing performance sent the party's support plunging. Its recovery under the dynamic new leadership of Hannibalsson, together with the decline of the SDF, suggests the possibility of a significant shift to the center within Iceland's divided opposition. Such a development could severely reduce the influence of the AB (*Morgunbladid*, 31 January; *JPRS*, 12 April). Much will depend on the fate of the government's economic policies, such as new tax increases and reforms (substituting a value-added tax for the current sales tax and reducing personal income taxes). The AB opposes further burdens on wage earners, but it has not put forward a coherent alternative plan (*Nordisk Kontakt*, no. 15).

Foreign Affairs. Three issues consistently comprise the Icelandic foreign policy agenda: the NATO bases at Keflavik and elsewhere on the island; trade relations with its principal export markets; and national economic control of resources on shore and in adjacent waters. The first issue has traditionally been the main source of controversy. It would be only a slight exaggeration to suggest that without the related issues of the Keflavik bases and NATO membership, the AB would scarcely be the force it has been in Icelandic politics during the past 35 years. By participating in several governing coalitions over the decades, the AB has sought first to eliminate and later to modify the terms of Icelandic NATO membership. In 1978 the AB joined a coalition without making the elimination of the bases a precondition. It later sought the right to veto any plans for changing their status, and on two occasions the terms for the bases have been changed with the Icelandic role increased. The most recent polls on the defense question in 1983 indicated 80 percent support for NATO membership and 64 percent of the public in favor of U.S.-Icelandic defense agreements (*News from Iceland*, May, p. 15).

Iceland maintains no armed forces as such (its coast guard is lightly armed), and 3,000 U.S. troops at Keflavik and elsewhere provide the country's defense force (confusingly referred to as the "Icelandic Defense Force"). As a member of NATO, however, Iceland does participate in the alliance's political processes. Foreign Minister Hallgrimsson (IP) announced the establishment in 1985 of a new Division of Defense Affairs within the Foreign Ministry to deal with security matters. Iceland has become more active within NATO, and the Netherlands commenced negotiations on using the Keflavik base for some of its antisubmarine operations (ibid., April and June).

Recognizing the depth of public support for current defense arrangements, the AB has recently tried to separate NATO membership from the bases issue. Even within the AB some commentators have admitted the necessity of maintaining a European balance of power and the growing importance of the bases given Soviet naval expansion. The AB has turned more directly to issues popular among leftist forces in Europe and the Nordic countries: for example, the removal of nuclear weapons from Europe's NATO arsenal and the establishment of regional nuclear-free zones. The impetus for this new line came in part from the publication by William Arkin (a U.S. defense critic) of purported U.S. plans to disperse nuclear weapons in time of crisis to bases not normally possessing such weapons. Iceland was named as such a place. U.S. secretary of state George Schultz stopped in Iceland in December 1984 following a NATO meeting to explain that such contingency plans had not been approved by the president. An Icelandic debate erupted and further negotiations between Foreign Minister Hallgrimsson and U.S. State Department officials occurred in March. Hallgrimsson stated his satisfaction that all elements of the U.S.-Icelandic agreements were being observed and that Iceland was fully aware of all activities on the bases (ibid., March).

Another irritant in U.S.-Icelandic relations was the loss in 1984 by an Icelandic shipping line of lucrative freight contracts supplying the U.S. forces. A new American concern, "Rainbow Navigation" invoked the obscure Cargo Preference Act of 1904, which requires that U.S. defense goods be shipped on American flag ships if possible. Aware that economic advantages smooth the way for the NATO bases, the U.S. Defense Department sought to return the business to Icelandic ships. Icelanders threatened to invoke their own protectionist legislation (for example, banning the importation of fresh meat) if the American rules were not changed. Initially U.S. courts have upheld the legislation, but the act contains provisions for a presidential override when demanded by "the national interest" (ibid., October).

The AB failed to gain much advantage from the debate, since by December 1984 all parliamentary parties had supported a motion reiterating Icelandic opposition to the stationing of nuclear weapons on her territory and urging investigation of possible Icelandic participation in a Nordic nuclear-free zone (*Nordisk Kontakt*, no. 2). All of the opposition parties urged a stronger unconditional prohibition of nuclear weapons, but the measure was not adopted. In addition, the opposition (less the SDP) unsuccessfully proposed a measure in late 1985 against the U.S. Strategic Defense Initiative. In the debates, AB defense spokesman Hjorleifur Guttormsson called the foreign minister's reassurances insufficient (ibid., no. 15).

Thus the AB has opted for a vague "peace" and "antinuclear" line. Some balance was struck by the party's questioning of diplomatic activity in Iceland with reference to the excessive size of the Soviet embassy. Icelandic-Soviet relations are primarily commercial. For years Iceland has exported substantial quantities of fish products in exchange for Soviet petroleum products. This important agreement was expanded and renewed for another five years in April (*Morgunbladid*, 18 April; *JPRS*, 5 June).

Despite the nuclear weapons controversy and the military cargoes case, U.S.-Icelandic relations remain warm. Plans have proceeded for modernization of two large radar installations in eastern Iceland, and the United States remains Iceland's largest overseas market. In addition, more than 1,000 Icelanders work at the NATO installations.

International Party Contacts. The AB and its predecessors have always remained aloof from the international communist movement. It has tended to identify more closely with democratic socialist parties, particularly those with strong leftist and pacifist positions. It interacts informally but regularly with the Socialist Left Party of Norway and the Socialist People's Party of Denmark; the annual sessions and regular committee meetings of the interparliamentary Nordic Council provide such opportunities. At the 1983 AB congress, there were calls for more regular relationships with similar parties, at least in the other Nordic countries. Although chairman Gestsson stated that such contacts were permissible under existing party rules, others claimed that prohibitions had been enforced and that the party was hurt by a xenophobic image (*Morgunbladid*, 22 November 1983).

Other Marxist and Leftist Groups. Icelandic communism has always been pluralistic, and the AB continues that tradition. Hence the country has had relatively few small Marxist sects, which are common in most other Western countries. Nevertheless, there have been some, most notably a

Maoist group—the Communist Union (CU)—formed in 1971. It peaked at 200 members and contained Trotskyist elements who had been active earlier. It has gone through numerous schisms and name changes. In 1985 the fifteen remaining CU members decided by a one-vote majority to disband, since their group had become "a hindrance to socialist operations in other areas" (*News from Iceland*, May).

The small SDF, a splinter from the SDP in the early 1980s, continued to grope for an identity and program after the death of one of their leaders in 1984. The SDF failure to capitalize on their parliamentary position (4 seats and 7.3 percent of the vote in 1983), as well as leadership changes, have helped the SDP's dramatic political recovery.

In sum, the passionate and personal style of Icelandic politics remains very evident in the AB. Radical in program but often pragmatic in practice, xenophobic by habit but cosmopolitan in spirit, the AB remains a colorful but not currently influential element. Having lost its place in the government in 1983 was a setback, but the revival of the SDP under Jon Baldvin Hannibalsson's dynamic leadership could be a disaster for the AB. The AB is aware of its own weakness as reflected in the debates and reports at the party's November congress. Whether Gestsson can provide the leadership for reform remains an open question. Elements in the AB advocate a "common front" of all left-of-center parties. AB policies have been modified to encourage such developments. Such an alliance is unlikely so long as the SDP advances and the AB and and SDF decline. Predicting Icelandic political alliances is notoriously hazardous, yet if the current AB leadership does not soon improve the party's prospects, it could face disaster.

Eric S. Einhorn
University of Massachusetts at Amherst

Ireland

Population. 3,590,000
Party. Communist Party of Ireland (CPI)
Founded. 1933
Membership. 500 (estimated)
Chairman. James Stewart
National Political Committee. Includes Michael O'Riordan, Andrew Barr, Sean Nolan, Tom Redmond, Edwina Stewart, Eddie Glackin
Status. Legal
Last Congress. Eighteenth, 14–15 May 1982, in Dublin
Last Election. 1982, no representation
Auxiliary Organization. Connolly Youth Movement
Publications. *Irish Socialist*, *Irish Workers' Voice*, *Unity*, *Irish Bulletin*

The CPI was founded in 1921, when the Socialist Party of Ireland expelled moderates and decided to join the Comintern. During the Civil War the party became largely irrelevant and virtually disappeared, although very small communist cells remained intact. The CPI was refounded in June 1933, the date the Communists now adopt as the founding date of their party.

The party organization was badly disrupted during World War II because of the neutrality of the

South and the belligerent status of the North. In 1948, the Communists in the south founded the Irish Workers' Party and those in the North the Communist Party of Northern Ireland. At a specially convened "unity congress" held in Belfast on 15 March 1970, the two groups reunited.

The CPI is a recognized political party on both sides of the border and contests both local and national elections. It has, however, no significant support and no elected representatives.

Leadership and Organization. The CPI is divided into two geographical branches, north and south, corresponding to the political division of the country. In theory the Congress is the supreme constitutional authority of the party but in practice it tends to serve as a rubber stamp for the national executive. The innermost controlling conclave is the National Political Committee. Such little support as the CPI enjoys tends to be based in Dublin and Belfast.

Domestic Affairs. The continuing political division of the country remained the main issue in 1985. The CPI views the United Kingdom as an imperialist power that gains economically from holding Ireland in a subordinate position. While continuing to advocate the creation of a single, united socialist Ireland, the party remains opposed to the use of violence and denounces the use of force by armed gangs on either side of the communal divide. For example, it was particularly vehement in its denunciation of the Provisional IRA's bombing of the Grand Hotel in Brighton in 1984, which nearly killed several members of the British Cabinet including Prime Minister Margaret Thatcher herself.

The party believes Irish unification can be achieved only through bodies promoting working-class solidarity and thus overcoming the communal divide between Protestants and Catholics. Executive Committee member Michael Morrissey put the CPI view succinctly: "As long as the working class is divided along religious or other lines, the exploiting classes will dominate the political stage and Ireland will remain subordinate to imperialism."

International Views and Activities. The CPI is quite untouched by the phenomenon of Eurocommunism and remains staunchly pro-Soviet. Indeed, in a country where there are several larger Marxist groups in operation, perhaps the distinctive feature of CPI attitudes is simple pro-Sovietism. The party is strongly anti-American and denounces U.S. policy in Central America, the Middle East, and elsewhere. It favors arms-reduction talks in Europe and opposes the deployment of cruise and Pershing missiles and President Reagan's Strategic Defense Initiative.

The party also remains hostile to the European Economic Community, which it regards as a device for drawing Ireland into NATO planning.

A CPI delegation led by its secretary general, James Stewart, visited the Soviet Union from 13–20 January. The delegation had extensive conversations with a number of members of the CPSU Central Committee, led by Boris Ponomarev. The talks were described as friendly and included discussions about international relations, the world communist movements, and CPI-CPSU relations.

Gerald Dorfman
Hoover Institution

Italy

Population. 57,149,000
Party. Italian Communist Party (Partito Comunista Italiano; PCI)
Founded. 1921
Membership. 1,588,376 (claimed, *L'Unita*, 9 November)
Secretary General. Alessandro Natta
Secretariat. 9 members
Directorate. 33 members
Central Control Commission. 57 members; Paolo Bufalini, chair
Central Committee. 180 members
Status. Legal
Last Congress. Sixteenth, 2–6 March 1983, in Milan
Last Election. 1983, 29.9 percent, 198 seats in the 630-seat lower house and 107 of 315 seats in the Senate; election for the European Parliament, June 1984, 33.3 percent, 27 seats
Auxiliary Organizations. Communist Youth Federation (FGCI)
Publications. *L'Unità,* official daily, Emanuele Macaluso, editor, Romano Ledda, co-editor; *Rinascita*, weekly, Giuseppe Chiarante, editor; *Critica Marxista*, theoretical journal, Aldo Tortorella, editor; *Politica ed Economia*; *Riforma della Scuola*; *Democrazia e Diritto*; *Donne e Politica*; *Studi Storici*; *Nuova Rivista Internazionale*

The PCI was established in 1921 when a radical faction of the Italian Socialist Party (PSI) led by Amedeo Bordiga, Antonio Gramsci, and Palmiro Togliatti seceded from the PSI. Declared illegal under the fascist regime, the PCI went underground and the party headquarters were moved abroad. It reappeared on the Italian scene in 1944 and participated in governmental coalitions in the early postwar years. Excluded from office at the national level in 1947, the party has remained in opposition since then except for a brief period (summer 1976–January 1979) when it became part of a governmental coalition but without holding cabinet posts. At the local government level, the PCI has been in power in a large number of municipalities, especially in the regions of Emilia-Romagna, Tuscany, and Umbria.

Party Organization and Leadership. At the end of the annual membership drive in October 1985, the PCI organization office announced that there had been a loss of some 50,000 members as compared to 1984, when membership had reached 1,619,000 (*L'Unità*, 1 November 1984). This was the eighth consecutive year the party had posted a decline. Moreover, the loss recorded in 1985 was nearly twice as large as the one in 1984 (41,000 in 1982; 38,000 in 1983; 16,000 in 1984) (*L'Unità*, 20 January). The membership figures released by the party indicated that after the growth of the early 1970s, membership had peaked in 1977 with 1.8 million members and had declined since then. Analysis of the trend by party headquarters attributed this erosion to the low level of recruitment among young people. New members were added to the roster in numbers insufficient to compensate for the losses (ibid.).

Analysis of the composition of the membership showed that members under 30 and particularly in the 18–24 age group were severely underrepresented. Party members over 60 years of age represented close to 30 percent of the total, and the proportion has been increasing (ibid.). The aging of the membership—one-third of the members enrolled before 1954—was said to be particularly acute in some regions, where "members over 80 are more numerous than those between 18 and 24" (ibid.). The inability to keep newly recruited people within the ranks was said to be another reason for the decline. PCI official Fabio Mussi explained: "We have severe problems with young people . . . the surge of the young generations toward the party of the mid-1970s is now receding" (*NYT*, 24 January).

In February the Twenty-third National Conference of the FGCI convened in Naples. The focus of the conference was on how to restructure the organization, which had undergone a severe crisis in recent years. Membership of the FGCI numbers approximately 45,000 and includes students, junior employees, apprentices, and jobless youths. At the conference, FGCI secretary Marco Fumagalli recommended that the organization acquire a "new look" and "should no longer be a youth organization of the Italian Communist Party." He said that the new body should attempt to reflect the wishes and aspirations of the young people and contribute to the task of "defining a new socialist ideology" (*Xinhua*, 22 February).

The young Communists were not the only ones contemplating changes. A lively debate also took place in the party during the year. In July the party Directorate announced that Secretary General Alessandro Natta would shortly propose to the Central Committee and the Central Control Commission the convening of a national congress by the spring of 1986. "Changes in the national and international situations," it was argued, "require in-depth analysis and deliberation on the experience of recent years, on political prospects and on party matters. They require open debate and decisions at the congress level" (*L'Unità*, 12 July). The Central Committee would have to decide "the form of the debate, [and] what kind of document or documents are to be submitted for debate" (ibid.).

A wide-ranging discussion soon began that focused on internal party rules and decisionmaking procedures. Some members of the Central Committee argued for "democratic centralism." Napoleone Colajanni, an economist member of the Central Committee, stated in a dispute with Secretariat member Adalberto Minucci that party mechanisms were unable to provide guidance and direction. He argued that "the situation cannot change unless . . . there is a full realization that excessive centralization deprives the party of the contribution of forces that can be very useful in analysis and decisionmaking . . . Freedom of expression within the party is not of much use if it remains uninfluential. It is necessary to find new ways to make decisions" (*L'Unità*, 11 July). Colajanni concluded:

> I believe there must be a thorough reform of party rules and I do not believe that this should scandalize anyone. We have broken away from the traditional concept of the unity of the international workers' movement and this has certainly had a profound impact on many comrades' feelings, but it was important to do so for the sake of the development of the party . . . they understood that we had to become an adult party and could not relinquish our originality for the sake of aligning with the leading state and the leading party . . . I believe it is necessary to continue in the same direction. I am fully aware of the seriousness of the issue and of its significance to many, many comrades who experienced democratic centralism as a constituent element of their own identity as communists. But I am convinced that it is necessary to move forward for the party's sake. (Ibid.)

A similar demand came from the opposite quarter and was articulated by Armando Cossutta, a party veteran and member of the Directorate who had dissented in previous years from party policy and who was well known for his pro-Soviet stance. Speaking during the Central Committee meeting of 24 July, Cossutta said,

> The extraordinary importance of the decisions we are preparing to make demands that the entire party take part in the debate . . . We are not frightened by the different tendencies. Let them be expressed and compared clearly and with the involvement of the entire party. I am more worried about conformism which often exploits the comrades' enthusiasm for party unity. Dissenters are not opposed to unity and do not violate it. If anything, they ask for different majorities to be allowed to exist on different decisions. It is their right since no pre-determined majorities exist during a congress phase. Those who jeopardize unity are those who hinder and bureaucratize a genuine, frank and honest debate and attempt to confine it to the top . . . the debate must involve the entire party to extricate it from its malaise. (*L'Unità*, 24 July)

The debate within the party became increasingly open during the year. The Central Committee meeting held in mid-December to approve the theses for the spring 1986 congress represented a major change with respect to the past. During several days of debate, over 400 amendments were presented and voted on in an open manner (*La Repubblica*, 12 December). These changes in the rules and procedures were widely praised by independent observers who identified the presence of a number of groups within the party. These included a large majority of "reformists"—for example, Natta, Giorgio Napolitano, Alfredo Reichlin, and a number of former associates of Enrico Berlinguer, the PCI secretary general from 1972 to 1984. Two minor factions represented the right and left wings, respectively. The latter was divided into a pro-Soviet group headed by Cossutta and a more radical faction (*Corriere della Sera*, 12 December). These divisions appeared to be present in the debates held at the federation level, but only the debate and the ballotting in the forthcoming congress will determine the numerical strength of the various alignments.

Domestic Affairs. Elections for regional and local offices were held in Italy on 12–13 May. Some 70,000 candidates competed in 15 out of 20 regions, 86 out of 95 provinces, and approximately 6,500 municipalities. Although no parliamentary seats were at stake, the elections were widely regarded as a test of the popularity of the government led by Socialist prime minister Bettino Craxi. Moreover, in the elections for the European Parliament held in June 1984 the PCI had overtaken the Christian Democratic Party (DC) for the first time in postwar history; the May 1985 elections were therefore viewed with apprehension by the parties in the governmental coalition and with some positive expectations on the part of the PCI. Whether or not the Communist Party would confirm "overtaking" ("il sorpasso") the DC was the single-most important issue surrounding the contest. Natta emphasized this aspect of the elections in an interview with members of the editorial staff of the left-wing paper *Il Manifesto*; he stated that in the event of a cabinet crisis following the elections, the PCI would be justified in requesting the task of forming a government (*L'Unità*, 22 February). The political import of the elections was explained by Craxi: "If the Communist opposition should win or, worse, if both the left- and right-wing oppositions should win and if the government parties should be defeated, the current balance of forces would crumble and the result would be a situation with unforeseeable developments" (ANSA, 20 April). On the eve of the elections the PCI daily stated that "the advance of the PCI is the primary condition and guarantee for having democratic leftist administrations that are efficient, diligent, and free of corruption, thereby maturing and affirming a democratic alternative that is necessary for the nation" (*L'Unità*, 12 May). The possibility that the PCI might emerge as the single largest political group turned out to be a great asset for the DC and other parties of the coalition, and it served to reinforce the cohesion among the governmental parties.

The returns dashed the Communists' hope of confirming the success of 1984. In the races for regional offices—widely regarded as the most important ones—the PCI polled 30.2 percent and the DC 35.1 percent. Compared to the returns of the regional elections of 1980, the PCI performance represented only a modest loss (1.3 percent). Most observers and politicians, however, compared the returns with the results of 1984, and against this benchmark the decline of the PCI loomed larger (3.1 percent). The outcome of the races for provincial and municipal councils was similar; the PCI declined from 31.5 to 29.9 percent. More important than the overall results, however, were the returns in a number of major cities in which the PCI had traditionally done well. In Rome the PCI was overtaken by the DC; in Genoa and Turin it lost four percentage points; even in Bologna—a traditional stronghold—the party suffered a small decline.

PCI leaders admitted that the outcome represented a "heavy blow" and stressed the need to "begin without delay and with a completely open mind the task of understanding the results" (*L'Unità*, 15 May). The causes of the defeat were attributed, in part, to the "climate of alarm artificially created by the DC and its allies" and to the "overwhelming superiority of propagandist means" (ibid., 14 May). The returns were also blamed on the lackluster performance of local governments of which the PCI was part. As Natta put it, "There has been a loss of focus on the part of left-wing councils, a loss of impetus, and a lesser ability to adapt and even maintain contact with social change, to perceive the new needs of the citizens" (ibid., 19 May).

The impact of the elections was twofold. First, the outcome reinforced the ruling coalition and frustrated the PCI's hope of playing a governmental role at the national level. Second, the PCI lost control of a number of local governments, most noticeably in the cities of Milan, Rome, and Turin. This second development was due only in part to the electoral defeat. It also had to do with the changed attitudes of the PSI, which in the past had been the traditional partner of the PCI in many local governments. In 1985 the PSI adopted a policy of replacing left-wing coalitions with center-left coalitions composed of the same parties in power at the national level. The breakup of the traditional PCI-PSI alliance further strained the already embittered relations between the two.

Less than a month after the regional and local elections, Italian voters were called to the polls again. The issue this time was the abrogation of a law passed in 1984 that modified the system of wage indexing and reduced, to some extent, the impact of the automatic wage escalator. The provisions, aimed at curbing inflation, were first adopted by the government in early 1984 and later approved by parliament over the fierce opposition of the PCI. Defeated in the legislative branch, the PCI proposed a referendum and actively campaigned to collect the 500,000 signatures needed to place the proposition before the voters. In the view of PCI leaders, the proposed referendum was a weapon directed more to pressure the government to reconsider the matter than to provoke a major electoral confrontation. When the Craxi government refused to budge, the PCI faced the prospect of another battle—a difficult one given the fact that two major unions refused to endorse the referendum. Even the PCI-dominated Confederation of Labor (CGIL) gave a lukewarm reaction; its leader, Luciano Lama, feared that a loss would weaken the union movement (*NYT*, 9 June).

Like the May elections, the June referendum became a test of political strength. Craxi went so far as to announce a week before the vote that he would resign "in a minute" if the government lost the issue (ibid.). For its part, the PCI saw in the referendum a chance of recovering from the defeat suffered in May. The issue seemed a potentially popular one since a repeal of the law would have added some $15 a month to the paycheck of each worker. The campaign was short but intense, and it pitched the five parties of the governmental coalition against opposition groups on both the left and the right. The PCI thus found itself on the same side as the Movimento Sociale Italiano (the neofascist party) for the first time in the history of the country. On 9–10 June, almost 34 million voters (or over 78 percent of the electorate) went to the polls, and 54.3 percent of them rejected the Communists' proposal for the abrogation of the law. The outcome was seen as a victory for the five-party coalition, but the fact that almost 46 percent of the people had voted in favor of the position held by the PCI made this second electoral defeat of the year somewhat more palatable.

The election of the president of the republic scheduled for late June provided the PCI with another opportunity to play a major role in the political life of the country. The mandate of aging President Sandro Pertini (a Socialist) was due to expire at the beginning of July, and it was widely expected that the leading DC would insist on having one of its own leaders in the prestigious position. The DC candidate, Senate president Francesco Cossiga, could not be elected on the first ballot (in which a two-thirds majority is required) with the votes of only the five-party coalition. For a first ballot election the PCI would have to throw its support behind the candidate. This situation strengthened the hand of the PCI. When the special assembly—made up of members of parliament and regional representatives—met on 24 June for the presidential election, the PCI parliamentary group unanimously approved a document endorsing the choice of Cossiga "as the candidate of all the forces that established the Republic and forged the Constitution." The document continued: "The Communists' approval of Francesco Cossiga's candidacy . . . reflects a careful and balanced assessment and confidence in the candidate's ability to discharge the duties of impartial and supreme guarantor proper to the office of president of the republic" (*L'Unità*, 25 June). The document did not hide the PCI's satisfaction that it had "been called upon to make a decisive contribution" and stressed that "the Communists have always fought to ensure that the election stems from a broad understanding among the political parties . . . and the fact [that] on this occasion such an understanding was sought from the outset marks a major innovation" (ibid.). The position taken by the PCI meant that, barring unforeseen circumstances, the DC candidate could be elected on the first ballot. Indeed, on 24 June Cossiga succeeded Pertini as the eighth president of the republic.

In October the hijacking of the cruise boat *Achille Lauro* created serious tensions within the government coalition as well as between the government and the opposition. In the debate between Prime Minister Craxi and Defense Minister Spadolini over the handling of the incident, the PCI, in spite of tense relations with the PSI, clearly sided with Craxi. After the prime minister explained the government action in parliament, the PCI issued a "positive assessment of Craxi's remarks, both for the thoroughness of the information and facts provided and for the line of conduct that they reveal"

(*L'Unità*, 18 October). The party also indicated that it could not ignore the "serious nature of the blows dealt over the past few days to our dignity and national sovereignty by the intolerable initiatives and reactions by the U.S. administration as emerged from the Craxi report" (ibid.). Two days later, in the midst of the cabinet crisis caused by the resignation of Spadolini, Natta said: "We have fought this government unyieldingly when it seemed to us to err on matters of economic and social policy . . . We have also unambiguously censored the conduct of the individual members of the government on specific issues. But this has not prevented us in the past from expressing our support for some aspects of the country's foreign policy. In the same way now, with the *Achille Lauro* affair, we have openly supported a generally correct line aimed at saving so many lives and defending the national sovereignty and interests of our country in the Mediterranean sea" (ibid., 20 October). According to some observers, during the brief diplomatic confrontation between Rome and Washington Craxi had emerged as "the hero of the left for appearing to stand up to American pressure," and by praising him "[the] PCI has sought to use the American-Italian feud in search for a political opening" (*NYT*, 20 October).

The patching up of differences among the coalition parties and the rapid solution of the governmental crisis, however, quickly ended the PCI's hopes that the *Achille Lauro* affair would prove fatal for the center-left coalition and provide a political opening for the Communists. The PCI continued to press for the formation of a government open to different political groups and based on platforms and policy stands rather than coalition alignments, but at the end of 1985 the party was no closer to its goal than it had been at the beginning.

Foreign Affairs. Toward the end of 1984, the journal *Problemy Mira i Sotsialisma* proposed convening a conference of the communist parties of the world. The first response from the PCI was given in Serbo-Croatian on the Yugoslav radio by Luciano Gruppi, member of the PCI Central Control Commission. Gruppi thought that the proposal was not "an important one at this time," and he went on to explain: "We participated, despite a number of reservations, in the latest world conference of communist and workers parties in 1969 and we did so because we did not want to be absent. But we voted only one article of the final document. Now we are afraid that another such meeting would lead to general propagandistic assessments that create an illusory unity behind which all differences remain. We ask ourselves whether the Communist Party of China and other parties would agree to participate in such a meeting. If they did not then the conference would have mostly a negative influence" (Belgrade Domestic Service, 27 December 1984).

This was not, however, the only response. At the end of January, Armando Cossutta made the case for participating in such a world conference. There is, Cossutta said in a speech to the Central Committee, "a world movement which moves in the direction of emancipation mapped out by the October Revolution, expresses the most genuine anxiety for change, and does its utmost on its behalf, albeit with differences, shortcomings and errors . . . I do not see why we should issue a categorical rejection of a possible meeting . . . The meeting would provide an opportunity for frank discussion despite divergencies" (*L'Unità*, 1 February). Cossutta went on to suggest that the refusal by the leadership probably hid the intention of "giving priority in international contacts to the Social Democratic parties" (ibid.). In answering Cossutta, PCI secretary Natta—who had already made his views known in a 27 January article in the Yugoslav periodical *Nin*—restated his case: the conference was "inopportune" and "dangerous" because of the existence of "profound divergencies . . . conflicts and disagreements" to the point where the "very concept of an international movement must be reappraised" (*L'Unità*, 2 February). "One cannot really say," Natta concluded, "that we have to loosen our relations with the communist parties in order to further intensify relations with socialist and social democratic parties. Our option is to maintain relations with all forces which truly represent and organize the workers movement in Europe" (ibid.).

Contacts and dialogues with noncommunist parties were indeed taking place. Perhaps the most significant step was the friendly exchange between Horst Ehmke of the West German Social Democratic Party (SPD) and Giorgio Napolitano of the PCI Directorate. The dialogue between the two leaders took place through articles published in *Die Neue Gesellschaft*, the theoretical journal of the SPD. After stating that the changes undergone by the PCI under the leadership of Berlinguer "were one of the most fascinating chapters in the history of the European workers movement," Ehmke invited the PCI to contribute to the proposed revision of the SPD Bad Godesberg program. He wrote that "It is not our intention to involve the PCI in shaping our strategy. What we propose is to ask the Italian Communists a certain number of questions on this subject. Berlinguer laid the foundations on which significant and useful talks of this kind can take place and we pay a respectful tribute to his memory" (ibid., 5 February).

In response, Napolitano accepted the invitation on behalf of his party and pointed out that "in the past Italian Communists had considered social democracy to be the antithesis of the struggle for socialism" but that this was no longer the case. The new approach involved the abandonment of taboos and barriers erected in the past. The "third way" proposed by the PCI, as explained by Napolitano, meant to "go beyond the historically outdated and indisputably negative elements of both the social democratic tradition and the communist tradition." He added, "For us there is no third way between the efforts to achieve the ideals of socialism in democracy, through democratic reforms, and the denial of fundamental liberties and rights in the name of socialism" (ibid.). Napolitano ended by suggesting that it was time to develop bilateral meetings among the more important parties of the European left.

The changes in the leadership of the Soviet Communist Party (CPSU) were viewed as positive by PCI leaders. Commenting on the inaugural address by Mikhail Gorbachev, Natta said, "His speech is very important because it does not contain polemics with the United States over the star-wars [Strategic Defense Initiative] proposals" (ANSA, 13 March). Emanuele Macaluso, editor of *L'Unità*, gave the following assessment of the change in the CPSU leadership. "Gorbachev can do it. He is the right choice. But will he do it? This is the question. We have the impression that Soviet society and its major vital forces are at present held in check but are pressing for innovation and for new developments . . . [Gorbachev's] emphasis made clear to us that there are within Soviet society demands for equity and justice . . . The nub of the problem is political and institutional and affects relationships between the citizens and the state and therefore the nature of Soviet democracy . . . they are complex and difficult problems partly because they call into question the relation between the party and the state and . . . they involve a network of interests that have become established and rooted over the years" (*L'Unità*, 17 March). Asked whether the advent of new leaders in the USSR would change the relations between the two parties, Italian officials who attended Chernenko's funeral stressed the "independence" and "autonomy" of the parties. "We do not think we have to justify or criticize everything the Soviet party does," said Natta (ibid.).

It was clear nevertheless that changes in the CPSU leadership might facilitate a rapprochement between the two parties after the tensions of previous years. A sign of Soviet interest in normalizing relations with the PCI was the unscheduled meeting between Gorbachev and Gianni Cervetti of the PCI Directorate, who had traveled to Moscow in the end of May in his capacity of chairman of the Communist group in the European Parliament. Cervetti reported, "I think that on the Soviet side there was a desire to make a gesture of goodwill towards our party and at the same time to emphasize their particular interest in Italy and Western Europe." The fact that *Pravda* carried a front-page report on the meeting was taken as another sign of Soviet interest. As for relations between the two parties, Cervetti denied that the purpose of the talk was to "heal the breach" between them and stressed that the expression coined at the time of the PCI condemnation of the USSR intervention in Poland was "inappropriate." He went on to say that "the autonomy of each party is the foundation of a new relationship and precisely this is the import of the things said in the conversations with Gorbachev and with other leaders. The general secretary of the CPSU himself chose to emphasize the absolute freedom of movement with which the USSR conducts relations with numerous progressive forces in Europe. 'The days of the Comintern are gone,' said Gorbachev" (ibid., 22 March).

During the year there were numerous pronouncements by PCI leaders on the issue of arms control. The party continued to oppose vigorously the Strategic Defense Initiative proposed by the U.S. administration "mainly for propaganda purposes" (ibid., 20 March). According to party officials, a possible proliferation of strategic defense systems would provoke a new phase of nuclear rearmament and contribute to destabilization. The test carried out by the United States of antisatellite weapons in space was viewed with "extreme concern" by Natta (Tass, 16 September).

In April the party strongly supported the USSR initiative on the European theater missiles. In the past, said Romano Ledda, "relations between the superpowers in the nuclear sphere had followed a different direction [than] one measure in exchange for another . . . measures, countermeasures, and countercountermeasures have followed each other in a continuous and paranoiac race without any break and with a growing fear of the other side's defensive and offensive capabilities . . . deterrence has gradually lost its initial connotation of strategic stability (however dangerous) and has become the source of increasingly destabilizing nuclear weapons. One of the superpowers is now breaking the vicious circle for a few months with a unilateral moratorium" (*L'Unità*, 9 April). Natta praised the Soviet initiative and suggested that Italy should suspend the deployment of missiles in Comiso, Sicily. He said, "We consider it indispensable that in a matter so very crucial to the future of the world any signal of detente be met with a constructive response" (ibid., 11 April).

PCI officials also had many opportunities to express their views on Central America and especially on the situation in Nicaragua. In May, on returning from a trip to Managua, Gianni Cervetti gave his impressions of the visit and stated the position of the party on Nicaragua: "It is a crucial issue involving a very large number of principles: the respect for national sovereignty and independence, relations between the countries of the North and South, and European-U.S. relations . . . The embargo against Nicaragua decided by Reagan is a very serious act . . . because an attempt is being made to terminate the independent and original experiment of a sovereign country . . . There must be an immediate and clear response, and it must come first and foremost from the whole of Europe . . . It is absolutely indispensable that Nicaragua become the subject of constant political initiatives on the part of the European left and of the PCI in particular. A new season of struggles and mobilization must begin. We cannot regard the Nicaraguan question as just another of the many problems of the world" (ibid., 3 May).

The polemics between the PCI and communist parties of Eastern Europe were less evident in 1985 than in previous years. This does not mean, however, that the PCI has changed its views of the nature of some communist regimes referred to as the countries of "real socialism." In August, Adriano Guerra, head of the PCI research institute, published an article in the party weekly in which he analyzed the significance of the Soviet invasion of Czechoslovakia and the formation of the independent union in Poland in 1980. After comparing the situation in both countries and analyzing their differences, Guerra concluded that "in both cases it is not possible to discern anything that would allow us to say that the lacerations of the past are no longer of central importance, or even that they are in the process of becoming less important" (*Rinascita*, 24 August). He went on to describe Czechoslovakia as a country "still suffering from the consequences of a policy of 'normalization' that precisely because it came from the outside [was] cut off from what one might call the normal flow of blood to the living body of a society." In short, a country that appears to be "distant from everything, as if isolated from our time, from what is said and done elsewhere, in either the East or the West" (ibid.). As for Poland, Guerra stated that this nation had "stubbornly refused to accept normalization . . . [and] the 'Baltic Coast' wave has been halted but not eliminated. The banners most widely displayed in Poland are still those of Solidarity" (ibid.). Guerra concluded that changes were badly needed in these countries and could come only from a changing attitude in the Soviet Union. A positive signal was the fact that "something seems to have changed or to be in the process of changing in Moscow," although Gorbachev had not yet addressed the issue of reforms for East European regimes.

International Party Contacts. As in previous years, PCI leaders and delegations met with a large number of officials of other parties throughout the world. At the beginning of the year, Giancarlo Pajetta, a member of the Secretariat, traveled to Cuba. Meetings were held with Fidel Castro, Cuban Communist Party Politburo member Carlos Raphael Rodriguez, and others. The meetings were devoted to discussing the international situation with particular reference to Central America and the Caribbean (*L'Unità*, 9 January). Pajetta then went on to Managua, where he held talks with Nicaraguan leaders Daniel Ortega, Thomás Borge, and Carlos Núñez (ibid., 20 January). While Pajetta was in Central America, a CPSU delegation headed by Mikhail Nenashev, chief editor of the newspaper *Sovetskaya Rossiya*, held talks at PCI headquarters in Rome with Secretariat member Alfredo Reichlin and other officials. The Soviet delegation also met with leaders and activists from the federations of Bologna, Florence, and Milan (*Pravda*, 10 January).

In February a PCI delegation traveled to Hanoi at the invitation of the Central Committee of the Communist Party of Vietnam (CPV). According to Hanoi sources, "The PCI delegation expressed its admiration for the correct leadership of the CPV . . . and held that the successes and experiences of the Vietnamese revolution contributed not only to national liberation movements but also to the revolutionary cause of Italy" (VNA, 19 February). The impressions gathered by the Italian visitors were less positive, however. Directorate member Giglia Tedesco offered a balanced assessment of the problems of Vietnam and concluded that "they have taken steps forward in the social field . . . even if they only eat a bowl of rice a day at least everyone eats. But they could take the great leap forward to development on their own and this is why it has not taken place" (*L'Unità*, 1 May).

In March two PCI officials, Antonio Rubbi and Massimo Micucci, met with Palestine Liberation Organization (PLO) leader Yasir Arafat in Tunis. The two Italian representatives reconfirmed the commitment of Italian Communists to a negotiated solution, the self-determination of the Palestinian people, and the recognition of the PLO (ANSA, 1 April). In September a delegation of Chinese Communist Party (CPC) officials was invited to attend the closing ceremony of the Unità Festival. After talks between Italian and Chinese leaders, Natta told them that "Your presence is the symbol of friendship and good relations between our two parties" (*Xinhua*, 20 September). Shortly afterward, Natta traveled to Beijing for talks with CPC leader Deng Xiaoping. On that occasion, the Chinese leader stated that "We oppose whoever pursues hegemony; we cooperate with whoever befriends us"; he added that the independent policies pursued by both China and Europe are conducive to world peace (ibid., 16 October). In November, Alvaro Cunhal, leader of the Portuguese Communist Party, traveled to Rome at the invitation of the PCI. Cunhal and Natta held talks on the international situation and on domestic developments in their respective countries.

A number of other meetings took place during the year. They included conversations in Rome with members of a Lebanese Progressive Socialist Party delegation (*L'Unità*, 21 February); a visit by officials of the Rome PCI federation to Berlin at the invitation of the Socialist Unity Party (SED) (*Neues Deutschland*, 10 March); a meeting between a delegation of the French Communist Party and PCI officials in Rome (*L'Unità*, 11 April); a visit of PCI activists to Beijing where they were received by Hu Qili, a member of the Secretariat of the CPC (*Xinhua*, 30 July); an encounter in Varna between Adalberto Minucci of the PCI Secretariat and Milko Balev, Politburo member of the Bulgarian Communist Party (BTA, 12 August); a meeting between Sarath Huttegana of the Communist Party of Sri Lanka and PCI foreign section chief Antonio Rubbi (*L'Unità*, 7 August); a visit to the PCI headquarters by a delegation of officials of the Communist Party of Japan (*L'Unità*, 19 September); and a meeting between an Italian delegation headed by Giuseppe Chiarante, editor of *Rinascita*, and members of the staff of the Soviet weekly *Kommunist* (*Pravda*, 28 October).

Other Communist Groups. After the merger of the Party of Proletarian Unity for Communism (PDUP) with the PCI in 1984, there remains only one other left-wing group with parliamentary representation, Proletarian Democracy (DP). In the elections of June 1983, DP received 1.5 percent of the popular vote and obtained seven seats in the 630-member lower house. DP also presented lists for the June 1984 elections for the European Parliament. It received 1.4 percent of the vote and sent one representative to the European Assembly.

Terrorist Groups. Episodes of political violence carried out by self-styled "true communist" groups had become less frequent in the early 1980s. This led observers to believe that the government had won the fight against terrorism. The fact that the major figures had been apprehended and were serving long prison sentences lent weight to this thesis, even though magistrates prosecuting cases of terrorism had warned that underground organizations were regrouping and might strike again. In 1985 the government scored further successes largely because of the help of former terrorists who have turned state's evidence. At the same time, it became clear that terrorism was still very much of a threat.

In January a 28-year-old police agent involved in antiterrorist work was shot to death. The murder was claimed by an anonymous caller who stated that the slaying was an act of revenge for the shooting of a terrorist suspect on 14 December 1984 (ANSA, 10 January).

On 27 March, Ezio Tarantelli, a well-known professor of economics at the University of Rome and an adviser to the Catholic labor union CISL, was shot in a parking lot of the campus. Responsibility was claimed by both the Red Brigades and a group called Armed Proletarian Nuclei. A long document detailing the philosophy and strategy of the groups was found near Tarantelli's body. It was widely believed that the victim was chosen for his outspoken criticism of the system used in Italy for adjusting wages to inflation.

During the year many alleged terrorists were arrested and others were brought to trial. In June police arrested the last member of the Red Brigades still at large, Barbara Balzerani. She had been sought since late 1978 for a number of terrorist acts, including the 1978 kidnap and murder of former prime minister Aldo Moro and the kidnap of U.S. brigadier general James L. Dozier. Balzerani had been tried in absentia and sentenced to life imprisonment (*Los Angeles Times*, 20 June).

In July a Venice court handed life sentences to eight members of the Red Brigades for the kidnapping and murder of Giuseppe Taliercio, director of Italy's largest chemical firm. Another 65 defendants, charged with complicity, received sentences adding up to 264 years in prison (AFP, 20 July). In October a Genoa court convicted Red Brigades terrorist Adriana Faranda to seven years in prison for the kidnap of shipowner Pietro Costa. Faranda was already serving a 30-year sentence for the murder of Moro (ibid., 30 October).

Giacomo Sani
Ohio State University

Luxembourg

Population. 367,000
Party. Communist Party of Luxembourg (Parti communiste Luxembourgeois; CPL)
Founded. 1921
Membership. 600 (estimated)
Chairman. Réne Urbany
Honorary Chairman. Dominique Urbany
Executive Committee. 10 members: Aloyse Bisdorff, François Hoffmann, Fernand Hübsch, Marianne Passeri, Marcel Putz, René Urbany, Jean Wesquet, Serge Urbany, André Moes, Babette Ruckert
Secretariat. 2 members: René Urbany, Dominique Urbany
Central Committee. 31 full and 7 candidate members
Status. Legal
Last Congress. Twenty-fourth, 4–5 February 1984
Last Election. 1979, 5.0 percent, 2 of 64 seats
Auxiliary Organizations. Jeunesse communiste Luxembourgeoise; Union des femmes Luxembourgeoises
Publications. *Zeitung vum Lëtzeburger Vollek* (Newspaper of the Luxembourgian People), official CPL organ, daily, 1,000–1,500 copies (CPL's claim: 15,000–20,000)

The pro-Soviet CPL played an insignificant political role in Luxembourg prior to World War II. After 1945 the CPL's position improved: Communists were elected to serve in parliament and in several communities. From 1945 to 1947 Luxembourg's cabinet included one communist minister. The best election results were achieved in 1968, but the communist vote declined steadily in 1974 and 1979. On 10 June 1979, in the first elections to the European Parliament, the CPL obtained 5.1 percent; in the second elections on 17 June 1984, the communist vote share declined to 4.1 percent. In municipal elections in 1981 the CPL received 7.2 percent, as compared with 16 percent in 1975.

The CPL leadership is dominated by the Urbany family. René Urbany succeeded his father, Dominique, as chairman at the first meeting of the Central Committee after the Twenty-second Congress in

1977. Dominique Urbany remained in the CPL as honorary chairman. Members of the Urbany family hold many key positions in the party and its auxiliaries, and René Urbany is also the director of the party press.

Party membership cards were exchanged in 1985. The Central Committee of the CPL claims that the number of party members and supporters has increased. It is further asserted that this improvement in turn strengthened the party's influence in parliament and municipal councils and enterprises. The Central Committee reported that the campaign for subscriptions of the party's official organ, *Zeitung vum Lëtzeburger Vollek*, was successful, although it continued to ask for financial contributions to the communist press fund (*WMR*, June). It appears that a front organization, the Society for the Development of the Press and Printing Industry, which was founded a few years ago by the Socialist Unity Party of Germany (the East German Communist Party), continues its financial support of communist publishing houses in noncommunist-ruled countries in Europe (*Die Welt*, 11 February 1984).

COPE, the CPL's publishing company, prints the French edition of the *World Marxist Review*. COPE's new and modern technical equipment and production facilities, which exceed local requirements, serve communist parties and organizations in several other countries.

The CPL, like other communist parties in Western Europe, supported Soviet foreign policy objectives in its "mass publications" and its effort to promote "joint actions against the threat of war."

Contacts with fraternal parties were maintained during 1985. A delegation from the Communist Party of the Soviet Union (CPSU)—led by Boris Yeltsin, secretary of the CPSU Central Committee—visited Luxembourg on 10–14 July. Yeltsin met with René Urbany, members of the CPL Central Committee, and Luxembourgian officials and businessmen (Tass, 10 July, *FBIS*, 15 July). Urbany called for further strengthening of the fraternal ties with the CPSU and of their common struggle for peace and socialism (*Pravda*, 15 July; *FBIS*, 16 July). Urbany also continued his personal visits to leaders of ruling communist parties. Accompanied to East Berlin by John Castengnaro, president of the Confederation of Independent Trade Unions of Luxembourg, Urbany visited Harry Tisch, chairman of the Free German Trade Unions (FDGB). They agreed to intensify the activities of all trade unions, regardless of their views and international affiliations, in the peace movement (East Berlin, Voice of the GDR Domestic Service, 17 August; *FBIS*, 19 August). On 19 August, Urbany met Todor Zhivkov, secretary general of the Central Committee of the Bulgarian Communist Party and discussed his party's support of the "antiwar movement" in his country. (Sofia, BIA, 19 August; *FBIS*, 9 September). A meeting between Urbany and Nicolae Ceauşescu, secretary general of the Romanian Communist Party, took place on 24 August in Romania. Both leaders agreed to enhance the unity of action of communist and workers' parties, democratic and progressive forces, and peoples everywhere in the struggle to build a world of peace, detente, and cooperation (Bucharest Domestic Service, 24 August; *FBIS*, 28 August).

Luxembourg also witnessed violent activities committed by terrorists. It was reported that between May and October thirteen bombings were directed against public installations, such as airports and government buildings (*Frankfurter Allgemeine Zeitung*, 11 November).

Eric Waldman
University of Calgary

Malta

Population. 332,002 (Malta Central Office of Statistics)
Party. Communist Party of Malta (Partit Komunista Malti; CPM)
Founded. 1969
Membership. 200 (estimated)
Secretary-General. Anthony Vassallo (61)
Central Committee. 11 members: Anthony Baldacchino (president; 45), Lino Vella (vice president), Anthony Vassallo, Karmenu Gerada (international secretary; 44), Mario Mifsud (propaganda secretary; 32), Dominic Zammit (financial secretary; 25), Victor Degiovanni (assistant secretary general), Joseph Cachia (assistant international secretary), Michael Schembri (assistant propaganda secretary), Francis Z. Caruana (assistant financial secretary), Paul Agius
Status. Legal
Last Congress. Extraordinary Congress, 18–25 May 1984
Last Election. 1981 (CPM did not contest)
Auxiliary Organizations. Peace and Solidarity Council of Malta; Malta-USSR Friendship and Cultural Society; Malta-Czechoslovakia Friendship Society; Malta-Cuba Friendship and Cultural Society; Communist Youth League (CYL); Malta-Korea Friendship and Cultural Society
Publications. *Zminijietna* (Our Times), a monthly tabloid, part in English and part in Maltese, Anthony Vassallo, editor; *International Political Review*, monthly, English-language edition of *World Marxist Review*; *Problemi ta Paci u Socjalizmu*, quarterly, Maltese-language abstract of same; *Bandiera Hamra* (Red Flag), issued by CYL; *Bridge of Friendship and Culture Malta-USSR*, quarterly in English, issued by the Malta-USSR Friendship and Cultural Society

The love-hate relationship between the CPM and the Malta Labor Party (MLP) government, led by Prime Minister Carmelo Mifsud Bonnici, crystallized in 1985. The CPM has now declared its intention to contest the next elections, which are expected to be held in early 1987. The party kept a relatively low profile during the year but was strongly supported by its auxiliary organizations, notably by the Malta-USSR Friendship and Cultural Society. There was repeated evidence of mutual disenchantment arising from the Malta-USSR three-year trade agreement signed in March 1984. Nevertheless, the Soviet embassy and the governments of the Soviet satellite states maintained intensive activity in Malta out of proportion to the size of the island.

Malta Government Policies. Since Mifsud Bonnici assumed office in December 1984, he has tried to reopen a dialogue with the European Common Market and various Western powers. The links with communist countries have also intensified. As a member of the group of nonaligned countries, Malta has taken a stance against Soviet policy on specific issues, such as the occupation of Afghanistan and Kampuchea, which was denounced by foreign Minister Alex Sceberras Trigona when he addressed the U.N. General Assembly during the 40th session in October. Malta claims to maintain a policy of "equidistance" from the two superpowers and seeks to invite the interest of the world's democracies by urging them to demonstrate the same interest in Malta as that shown by the

Soviets and their satellites. This policy appears to be counterproductive, insofar as increasing Maltese commitments with the communist community discourages greater Western investment and business confidence. This view was emphasized in a *WSJ* editorial of 25 October. Any initiatives to dispel the impressions prevailing in Western quarters must come from Malta but, unfortunately, Mifsud Bonnici has been more enigmatic than clear on this vital issue. When he addressed the biennial General Workers' Union (GWU) national conference in October, he denied that Malta was "moving to the East." He explained that "in its efforts to be equidistant from the two military blocs, Malta had moved away from the West toward the center. In doing this, it had naturally moved Eastward. With Malta in the center, the Eastern countries were moving closer to Malta, answering Malta's call for help in order to generate more jobs for its unemployed. The West could do the same." Mifsud Bonnici insisted that Malta wanted to remain equidistant, neutral, and unaligned, but he added that "since the sun rises in the east, Malta would look toward the East" (Malta, *Sunday Times*, 6 October). Whether this oracular pronouncement will clear doubts and suspicions in business and diplomatic quarters is debatable.

Mifsud Bonnici has only been in the limelight of the Malta political scene for little more than a year. He has not had too many opportunities to expound his basic philosophy on the theme of communism and its practical significance in real life. He did express himself fleetingly on this subject when he spoke in parliament on the demise of Soviet president Konstantin Chernenko; in the context of his speech he declared that "the working class in the Soviet Union is an inspiration to the workers of the whole world to unite and fight for their rights" (Malta, *Orizzont*, 12 March). This statement drew strong criticism from the opposition Nationalist Party. Yet at that time the government was sending a delegation to Moscow to clinch a Soviet order for eight timber carriers to be built in Malta drydocks.

In the climate of intensifying communist activity in Malta on the one hand and evidence of Western suspicion on the other, the Mifsud Bonnici government has had to work hard to convince the chancelleries of the West of Malta's neutrality. Existing doubts have not been allayed by unexplained contacts with European communist functionaries who, while visiting Malta during the year, had talks with MLP and GWU officials (as distinct from Malta government representatives). There were also visits by Sujka Bogumil, head of the international relations department of the Polish United Workers Party (*Orizzont*, 22 May); by Dr. Bauer Roland from the Socialist Unity Party of Germany (SED) (Malta, *Times*, 6 June; and by a delegation from the International Department of the Central Committee of the Communist Party of the Soviet Union (CPSU). The latter delegation was headed by Anatoly Chernyayev, deputy head of the International Department (Malta, *Hajja*, 12 June). All these visitors were scheduled to meet MLP and GWU officials during a relatively short period of time. No information was released after any of these meetings as to the nature of the discussions. Their significance is a matter of conjecture.

Domestic Party Affairs. Toward the end of the year, *Zminijietna* announced the resignation of Mario Vella from the Central Committee and from the party. Vella, who holds a doctorate of philosophy and was considered to be the CPM's theoretical guru, had earlier been appointed head of research of the Malta Development Corporation, which is a government-controlled organization. His post was taken up by Mario Mifsud, who was upgraded from financial secretary. The vacancy in the Central Committee was filled by Francis Z. Caruana soon after returning to Malta from a twenty-day visit to the USSR as a guest of the CPSU.

In the January issue of the *World Marxist Review*, Anthony Vassallo had some blunt things to say against the ruling MLP. He accused the government of "acting in many cases against the interests of the working people and refusing to resolve some important social problems." He added that "under the Labor government, there has been a significant growth of corruption" and that "long years in power have made MLP leaders arrogant." He also claimed that the GWU, which is statutorily fused to the MLP, "is now entirely subservient to the government." He underlined the fact that "as noted at the last CPM congress, many Maltese now no longer see Labor policy as a genuine alternative to the course steered by the opposition Nationalist Party."

Vassallo claimed that this put the CPM "in a quandary—that of appearing to the workers in a role supporting the government on the one hand and criticizing it on the other." He stressed that this was the correct course, because "the Maltese government's policy of nonalignment and its efforts to improve the political situation in the Mediterranean and promote relations with countries of the socialist community are helping to strengthen peace and security in Europe."

This stance—of both support and criticism—was consistently maintained by the CPM during 1985. The party publications promoted Soviet foreign policy objectives; a number of public resolutions were issued to express solidarity with Nicaragua, condemn the Israeli raid on the PLO headquarters in Tunisia, and inveigh against the installation of cruise missiles in Comiso, Sicily. The party kept a low profile insofar as domestic policy was concerned.

On 4 May, while addressing student journalists at the University of Malta, Vassallo announced that his party intended to contest the 1987 elections (*Times*, 5 May). This was confirmed in the October issue of *Zminijietna*; in a front-page article Vassallo declared that the CPM electoral program was being drawn up, with an emphasis on social problems. He claimed that every vote cast for the CPM would strengthen the left and prevent the MLP from committing further mistakes; he added that the MLP has been captured by the rich and by a new class of businessmen. Writing in the same issue, Assistant Secretary General Victor Degiovanni complained that the MLP claims to be a workers' party but is, in fact, a bourgeoisie party. The main concern of the CPM as he saw it is to free the workers of "state exploitation." Simultaneously with this development, Malta-USSR trade relations showed signs of strain, and these events could conceivably be linked.

The text of the three-year trade agreement of 1984 was never published by either side. However, when the chairman of the Malta Development Corporation, Paul Xuereb, was opening a Soviet trade exhibition in November 1984, he disclosed that "it has been agreed that Malta will sell to the Soviet Union 265 million dollars worth of Maltese products and, in turn, purchase 140 million dollars worth of Soviet products" (Malta, *Commercial Courier*, 19 December 1984). These targets have proved to be beyond reach and the two sides are blaming each other.

The Maltese minister of industry, Karmenu Vella, led a high-level delegation to Moscow to give momentum to the trade protocol (*Orizzont*, 4 April). He returned without reporting any progress. A two-man friendship delegation led by the Soviet deputy minister for heavy industry, Victor Zabelin, then visited Malta in May, and Maltese concern was expressed in forthright terms on the subject of trade. The Maltese minister of foreign affairs, Sceberras Trigona, "emphasized the importance of strengthening trade relations and advanced his own ideas about possible future initiatives" (*Orizzont*, 10 May). At a press conference before leaving Malta, Zabelin disclosed that among the suggestions put to him was one for a more substantial trade protocol. He promised to convey the message (ibid., 11 May).

The official Soviet response was not long in coming. Mikhail Filippov of the Moscow Department of Trade with Western Countries visited Malta on the occasion of the Malta International Fair. He addressed a seminar held in the offices of the Soviet commerical counsellor and complained of "one-way traffic." He declared that "if one excludes the deliveries of oil and petroleum products to Maltese firms, one would find that Soviet exports were almost stagnant over the past few years, both in terms of costs and range of goods. Even if oil and petroleum are to be included, the total exports from the USSR to Malta dropped all the same." He stressed that "despite the list of Soviet export goods attached to the protocol, its clauses largely fail to be carried out." Filippov spelled out his grievance in concise terms. He said that "we are either [being] denied import licenses for a whole number of goods in general or licenses are issued for limited quotas, which make the deal economically disadvantageous. This concerns Soviet-made refrigerators, electrical appliances, and motors. The Maltese side has repeatedly taken an unconstructive attitude toward potential purchases of Soviet oil and petroleum products, which casts doubts on the conclusion of a deal in general. The talks on the purchases of Soviet timber are lingering. Quite unwittingly, the question arises: what about the Malta-USSR protocol?. . . Authorized Maltese organizations should evidently give some thought to a new approach to the tackling of business with partners under bilateral, intergovernmental trade protocols" (*Zminijietna*, August). In terms of economic diplomacy, this approximated the language of exasperation.

Since that time, the Malta government has maintained its pressure on the Soviet government to step up its purchases from Malta. When the president of Malta, Agatha Barbara, made an overnight stop in Moscow on her way to China and North Korea, she brought up the subject with the top Kremlin leaders. Sceberras Trigona, who was a member of Barbara's party and who returned home ahead of her, declared at an airport interview that, in Moscow "we found precisely the agreement we were seeking, namely the space for Maltese exports in an enormous market" (*Orizzont*, 29 August). Yet no developments materialized by year's end. To the contrary, Karmenu Vella made a subsequent trip to Moscow at the head of another delegation; one of his purposes was to have further talks on the trade protocol (*Orizzont*, 23 September), but he returned without claiming any progress.

It is pertinent to point out that Malta's economy is in distress with high and persistent unemployment, a sharp drop in investment, a slump in tourism (compared to the 1980 peak), and, for the first time, a decline in the Malta Central Bank total external reserves. At the same time, the island is beginning to look toward the next elections.

The questions that arise are whether the Soviet Union is holding back on the trade protocol in an attempt to twist the arm of the Malta government and whether the decision of the CPM to contest the elections is yet another twist of the screw that would, to a lesser or greater extent, threaten to weaken the MLP's performance. Yet it is just as conceivable that the CPM's decision is motivated by the necessity of having an autonomous left-wing voice in the Maltese political leadership, in case the MLP should stand up to the Soviets on the issue of the protocol and threaten to turn to the West for more dependable economic ties.

The CPM's chief public activity was a "permanent seminar" in the form of a weekly discussion, open to the public at its headquarters, to examine various social issues such as the electoral system, women's rights, and workers' grievances. One of its other initiatives was to organize Malta's national representation at the Moscow Youth Festival. MLP and GWU representatives formed part of the Malta contingent.

The three CPM publications—*Zminijietna*, *International Political Review*, and *Problemi ta Paci u Socjalizmu*—were issued regularly and available for free distribution.

Auxiliary and Front Organizations. The Malta-USSR Friendship and Cultural Society was by far the most active. For example, scholarships were offered for study in the Soviet Union; a competition was organized and a free trip to the USSR offered as a prize, in connection with the 40th anniversary of the victory over Nazism and fascism; the society continued to organize Russian-language lessons and distributed literature to all quarters; the secretary of the society, Remig Sacco, has broadcast a long radio series on "The Soviet Union After the Revolution"; and the president, Anton Cassar, and honorary president, Geraldu Azzopardi, represented the society at a Vienna conference of USSR friendship societies (Malta, *Torca*, 2 June). The vice president of the society, Paul Agius, was presented with a medal on the occasion of the anniversary of the Soviet victory over fascism (Malta, *Weekend Chronicle*, 31 August).

The Malta-USSR Friendship Society openly clashed with the Malta government over an article in the society's journal, *The Bridge*. The first quarterly issue of this publication was devoted to Dom Mintoff's visit to the Soviet Union toward the end of 1984. One of the feature articles was by William Mkrtchyan, former Tass resident correspondent in Malta and now vice president of the friendship society in Moscow. Mkrtchyan wrote on "USSR-Malta Mutual Understanding and Cooperation" and quoted the Maltese charge d'affaires in Moscow, Dr. Guzeppi Schembri, attributing to him statements derogatory to Western countries. A special May issue of *The Bridge* was published soon afterwards with a disclaimer by Schembri.

The Malta-Czechoslovakia, Malta-Cuba, and Malta-Korea friendship societies ran nominal programs but the Malta Peace and Solidarity Council showed greater initiative during the year. The council issued a number of statements and sent a delegation to a high-level World Peace Council meeting in Moscow in March. Its delegation consisted of Victor Degiovanni (CPM) and Ray Lanzon, member of the MLP Executive Committee (*Zminijietna*, April).

International Activities, Views and Positions. Communist interest and activities in Malta were maintained at a high pitch during 1985. The Soviet embassy was the spearhead of a sustained propaganda program intended to give visibility to the Soviet image. A long-term contract was signed in Moscow for the building of eight timber carriers in Malta drydocks. Although there was a blaze of publicity around this news item, work on the first ship has yet to start. Some belated orders were made to the government-controlled foundry (*Orizzont*, 18 October), and plans were announced for the use of Malta as a home base for Soviet Mediterranean cruise ships (*Torca*, 13 October). Five scholarships were offered through the Ministry of Culture, book presentations were made to schools, and more films than ever have been shown on Malta television and news stories placed in local newspapers. Soviet folk groups gave performances at the GWU headquarters and other places, and facilities were provided for Maltese participation at a Moscow film festival and for a Maltese photographer to hold an exhibition in the USSR. The Soviet Union had a large stand at the Malta International Fair and held a special exhibition to commemorate the 40th anniversary of the end of the "War against Fascism." The show was opened by the president of the republic and, curiously, was boycotted by government ministers and other officials.

The prime minister of Bulgaria, Grisha Filipov, paid a 24-hour visit to Malta at the head of a large delegation in February. The Bulgarian deputy minister of foreign trade, A. Ginov, preceded him and signed an agreement on trade and economic cooperation with the Maltese minister of trade and economic planning, Lino Spiteri.

A Czech commercial delegation held a round of little-publicized talks in Malta at the end of February. A brief news item in *Orizzont* of 1 May reported that these talks involved officials from the Malta government, the Malta Development Corporation, and the Central Bank of Malta. The Czech deputy foreign minister, Jarimir Joannes, visited the island to discuss possibilities of expanding bilateral trade (*Orizzont*, 19 September). The Slovak minister of health, Emil Matejicek, also visited Malta to sign a health agreement that was to provide opportunities for Maltese doctors and paramedical staff to train in Czechoslovakia, for Czech doctors and university lecturers to continue to work on the island, and for Maltese technicians to be trained in the maintenance of hospital equipment (*Times*, 3 October).

The most significant relations are those being established and expanded between the GWU, which is an affiliate of the International Confederation of Free Trade Unions (ICFTU), and the Revolutionary Trade Union Movement (ROH) of Czechoslovakia, which is a leading affiliate of the World Federation of Trade Unions (WFTU). The WFTU is universally recognized as an international communist-front organization. The GWU and ROH signed a protocol providing for relays of Maltese trade unionists to undergo "courses in trade unionism" in Prague. The Czechs sent a number of trade unionists of their own for an educational holiday in Malta (*International Report to the GWU National Conference 1985–87*, p. 145).

The Maltese minister of finance, Wistin Abela, held talks in Warsaw with the Polish deputy prime minister and his colleagues on the purchase of coal and shipbuilding equipment (*Sunday Times*, 10 March).

President Agatha Barbara paid a state visit to Romania in July. In the final communiqué, Romanian president Nicolae Ceauşescu and Barbara expressed their satisfaction "at the ascending evolution of Maltese-Romanian relations" and at "the similar stand of the two countries on main international problems" (*Times*, 11 July). Nicu Ceauşescu, Romanian minister of youth affairs, visited Malta and presided over a meeting of the fourth Mediterranean Youth Camp in the Valletta Conference Center. He also held talks with the Ministry of Foreign Affairs and visited the Malta Trade Fair as well as some educational establishments (*Times*, 13 July). The Maltese minister of tourism, Joe Grima, visited Bucharest for a meeting of the Maltese-Romanian Mixed Economic Commission (*Orizzont*, 5 May). As a result of that meeting, the two countries reportedly decided to launch a joint venture in the form of a health resort, with Romania contributing 20 percent of the equity. The Malta government is preparing to invite public participation in this investment project (*Orizzont*, 28 October).

Malta's close relationship with North Korea was symbolized by a ten-day state visit to that country by President Barbara. In the course of the visit, Barbara conferred Malta's highest honor, *Gieh ir-Repubblika*, on Kim il-Sung, and she was in turn decorated by the North Korean leader with the Order of the National Banner, First Class (*Torca*, 1 September). This trip was punctuated with frequent expressions of mutual friendship, all of which was given great publicity by media supporting the government.

Relations with China continued to be warm, but Chinese assistance to Malta might conceivably be scaled down in the future. Malta has started to pay back the $40 million interest-free loan of 1972. About $11 million had been paid back by October (*Times*, 24 October). The Chinese technical experts engaged in the Marsaxlokk transshipment harbor project will soon finish their assignment, since the breakwater project is almost complete (*Times*, 26 September). Malta's friendship with China was sealed by a ten-day state visit by President Barbara. Beijing University conferred an honorary doctorate on Barbara, who toured extensive parts of China and held official talks with top Chinese leaders (*Weekend Chronicle*, 31 August). It was announced after Barbara's visit that China ordered two more small ships to be built in Malta's drydocks.

J. G. E. Hugh
Valletta, Malta

Netherlands

Population. 14,529,000 (Centraal Bureau voor de Statistiek, in *Het Parool*, 31 December, No. 12531)
Party. Communist Party of the Netherlands (Communistische Partij van Nederland; CPN)
Founded. 1909
Membership. 12,000 (estimated)
Chairperson. Elli Izeboud
Executive Committee (Partijbestuur). 11 members: Elli Izeboud, John Geelen (secretary), Fenna Bolding (party organization), Siem van der Helm (propaganda and information), Frank Biesboer (social-economic developments), Jan Berghuis (social-economic developments), Boe Thio (treasurer), Ina Brouwer (peace and security commission; member of Parliament), Ton van Hoek (coalition politics), Leo Molenaar (representative of Cruise No Committee [KKN]), Pau Wouters
Central Committee. 46 members (John Geelen, secretary; Ton van Hoek, international secretary)
Status. Legal
Last Congress. Twenty-ninth, 1–3 March 1985, in Amsterdam
Last Election. 1982, 1.8 percent, 3 of 150 seats in lower house; European Parliament elections, 14 June 1984, Green Progressive Accord, 5.6 percent
Auxiliary Organizations. General Netherlands Youth Organization (ANJV), CPN Women, Stop the N-Bomb/Stop the Nuclear Arms Race, CPN Youth Platform, Scholing en Onderwijs, Women Against Nuclear Weapons
Publications. *De Waarheid* (Truth), official daily, circulation between 9,000 and 14,000, Paul Wouters, editor; *CPN-Leden krant*, published ten times annually for CPN members; *Politiek en Cultuur*, theoretical journal published ten times yearly; *Komma*, quarterly, issued by CPN's Institute for Political and Social Research. CPN owns Pegasus Publishers.

The CPN was founded in 1909 as the Social Democratic Party (Sociaal-Democratische Partij) by radical Marxists. It assumed the name Communist Party of Holland (Communistische Partij Holland) in 1919 when the party affiliated with the Comintern. The present name dates from 1935. Except during World War II, the party has always been legal.

According to CPN chairperson Elli Izeboud, the Twenty-ninth Congress on 1–3 March was to take place with most of the problems confronting the party behind them. She said in early January that "the renewal of the party has come to a new phase; we first discussed old ideas whereby we made clear what we did not want, and now it is time to formulate what we do want" (*NRC Handelsblad*, 5 January). These words reflected the task that the CPN placed before itself for the year.

The first event of 1985 was a CPN meeting in January in Amsterdam where more than 2,000 CPN members gathered to set the stage for the March congress. At this meeting, CPN veteran Marcus Bakker called on "all communists" who left the party in 1984 to rejoin (*De Volkskrant*, 4 February). Thus, a second event of great importance to the CPN took place: the founding by the "horizontalists" within the CPN of the Confederation of Communists in the Netherlands (VCN) because of renewed growth in CPN membership. In the eyes of many orthodox Communists of the Stalinist line, this renewal effectively destroyed the meaning of communism as a movement. By the end of 1985, some 1,500 former CPN members had joined the VCN. At the same time, many of the more radical "renewers"—that is, those who wished to see the CPN become the pacifist-feminist party of the Netherlands—left the party because change did not come quickly enough.

The March congress was attended by 457 authorized delegates. About 50 percent of the delegates were women and 73 percent were between the ages of 25 and 45. The most important issues of the congress were the election by democratic vote of the 46-member Central Committee and the adoption, without the tumult of the past two congresses, of a party program. A decision was also made to work for a coalition with the "small left-wing" parties. One independent observer described the congress as lacking the "élan" of the past (*CPN–Leden krant*, March, no. 3, p. 2).

The issues, in order of importance, that concerned the CPN during 1985 were the deployment of cruise missiles on Dutch territory, which was assented to by the Cabinet of Prime Minister Ruud Lubbers on 1 November; the adoption of an eventual 25-hour workweek; a defense of the Dutch social security system, which the CPN believed was under attack by the "rightist" coalition government under Lubbers; activities toward the prevention of any new nuclear power plants to be built in the country; solidarity with the peoples of Nicaragua and against apartheid in South Africa; the attempt to form a coalition with small left-wing parties; and, finally, the whole question as to whether the party newspaper, *De Waarheid*, was succeeding in its effort to be a newspaper for all of the left as laid down by the Twenty-eighth Congress in November 1982 (ibid.; *Neues Deutschland*, March, no. 52).

In contrast to the CPN of the past, these objectives were to be attained by methods that fit within the democratic system of the country and that reflected the pluralism of the society in which the party was active. In each case, the CPN strove to join with other progressive forces in society. This emphasis on cooperation with the larger movement was also the subject of discussions in Moscow during a visit by Izeboud in late December 1984. She told Boris Ponomarev, a member of the Soviet Communist Party (CPSU) Secretariat, and Vadim V. Zagladin, deputy head of the CPSU Central Committee International Department, that the CPN disapproved of the attempts by both the United States and the Soviet Union to guarantee peace by maintaining a balance of power. Rather, the emphasis should be placed on "mutual security." In this context, cooperation with the peace movement in the East and West was of paramount importance in achieving peace (*CPN–Leden krant*, February, no. 1, p. 2).

While the threat of a split within the communist ranks has become real, it has thus far not had the disastrous effect some had predicted. The CPN has turned away from democratic centralism, from the official line of Marxist-Leninism, and from Eastern bloc countries such as Poland and Czechoslovakia; it has accepted a degree of openness in decision-making, emphasized pluralism within the party, striven for the rights of women, and confirmed the democratic process in the Netherlands. The leader of the Labor Party (PvdA), Joop Den Uyl, has observed that most of the members in the CPN could now belong to his own organization.

The horizontalists who left the party to join the VCN managed to maintain their organization, but they have not attracted the following they expected. The CPN lost members during the year and *De Waarheid* ran into some financial and editorial problems. However, while the future of the party in Parliament may have been in doubt, there was no question that the CPN would continue to operate as a left-wing party influenced by Marxism-Leninism. The attempt to join with other left-wing parties was still in its initial phase and, for historical and doctrinaire reasons, it will take time, but the three main parties to the left of the PvdA—the CPN, Political Radical Party (PPR), and Pacific Socialist Party (PSP)—were all of the opinion that cooperation with one another will be necessary.

Party Internal Affairs. Whereas the Twenty-eighth Congress had been devoted to a change of doctrinal views, the Twenty-ninth Congress began the implementation of new tasks set down by the CPN. In her opening address to the congress, Izeboud stated that a "breakthrough in the habit of depending on authoritarian structures" should "move toward an association of progressive forces for the promotion of the concrete interests of the people" and the "development of an alternative that, in form and perspective, offers peace, crisis management, and renewal in society" (ibid., March, no. 2, p. 2).

The proposal to join with the PPR and PSP on a joint election list for the municipal elections on 19 March 1986 and the parliamentary elections on 21 May 1986 was accepted by the congress without opposition. The real problem facing the delegates was whether unity and organizational capacity could be restored after the serious conflicts at the Twenty-eighth Congress and at the Extraordinary Congress in February 1984.

The 1985 congress confirmed the course of renewal as laid out by the Extraordinary Congress in 1984. In choosing the new Central Committee at the Twenty-ninth Congress, the party leadership eliminated the extreme wings, the radical renewers, and the Groningen orthodox Communists; the congressional delegates decided that the Central Committee should be composed of not less than 40 nor more than 55 members. To be chosen, a member had to receive more than half of the votes during the first ballot.

The vote on a list of 110 candidates was surprising in that Izeboud received only 334 votes, as compared to 426 for Marius Ernsting. Of the members from the orthodox districts, only two were chosen from Groningen and one from North Holland. Hoogenberg—the man behind the Enkhuizer Consultations, which was an attempt to keep the orthodox members from leaving the party—was not returned to the Central Committee (ibid., no. 3, p. 11; *Het Parool*, 4 March; *De Waarheid*, 4 March).

The congress accepted all proposals put forward by the leadership. However, on the issue of the right of foreign workers in the Netherlands to vote in the municipal elections, Marcus Bakker and the leadership were opposed because, as Bakker stated, "Foreigners who do not choose for the Dutch nationality may not choose for the national administration" (*CPN–Leden krant*, March, no. 3, p. 11; *NRC Handelsblad*, 4 March; *De Volkskrant*, 4 March). Nevertheless, a majority of the delegates voted for the proposal.

The most lively part of the congress came when a mineworker from Kent in England received a loud ovation for talking about "the lies and propaganda of the capitalist press of Fleet Street" and "indecisive attitude of the trade union council."

Additional members elected to the Central Committee were Oedayray Sing Varma Tara, originally from the Netherlands Antilles with 417 votes; Messaoudy Malik, from Morocco, with 416 votes; and Member of Parliament Ina Brouwer with 410 votes. Messoudy said his election to the Central Committee was "the first time that a party in Europe chose a foreigner in its executive . . . that means a recognition of the problems foreign workers have here" (*CPN–Leden krant*, March, no. 3, p. 11; *NRC Handelsblad*, 4 March; *De Volkskrant*, 4 March).

The missing voices at the congress were those who sympathized with the horizontalists but had not joined the VCN and those who wanted the CPN to merge with other left-wing parties. In commenting on the congress, an editorial in *De Waarheid* on 4 March stated that "those for a breakthrough and horizontalists—people on the wings—say their influence has waned . . . which does not mean that a new colorless middle group has won out. Among the new leaders of the party are primarily youth, reform-minded trade unionists, feminists, and members of minority groups" (*CPN–Leden krant*, March, no. 3, p. 11; *De Groene Amsterdammer*, 6 March, pp. 6–7).

The relationship of the CPN to *De Waarheid* also reflected tensions within the party. The Extraordinary Congress of 1984 called for a communist party that would be of significance for the whole of the left. This meant that *De Waarheid* should have its own journalistic responsibility and be relatively independent of CPN influence. Yet this effort at reform came to a halt when the chief editor, Constant Vecht, left the paper in early December; the primary problem was that the new formula was not bringing in new subscribers to replace those who had left. In the 8 November issue of the paper, Izeboud said that "the existence of *De Waarheid* is not to be taken for granted." In order to keep the newspaper afloat, the format was cut back to tabloid form and a new editor—Paul Wouters, 34—was appointed with the approval of the executive head of the Bepenak Foundation, the publisher of *De Waarheid*. Wouters was a biochemist with little journalistic experience, but he was the head of the Amsterdam district of the CPN and a member of the CPN Executive Committee. Vecht had been the only editor of the paper not to be a member of the Executive Committee; thus, the appointment of Wouters restored this break in continuity.

The change has been seen by some as an attempt by the party to regain its influence over the paper in order to strengthen its position for the elections in 1986. Izeboud said that *De Waarheid* was "a paper which has distanced itself from being an organ for the party and now wants to be a newspaper for the whole of the left. Also, therefore, for us. And, indeed, just this step appears to have cost it its head" (*De Waarheid*, 8 November; *Trouw*, 10 November; *De Volkskrant*, 16 December).

A further threat to the CPN took more solid form when the VCN managed to gather 1,000 members at the traditional meeting place of Communists in Amsterdam, "de Hoeksteen." The VCN has claimed to be the re-establishment of the Communist Party in the Netherlands. It sees itself as the true inheritor of the spirit of communism, wherein "class struggle" are the key words. The natural support for the VCN comes from the workers and the civil service trade unions in Amsterdam. The VCN has a party newspaper, *Manifest*, with a reported 3,500 subscribers. Its chief editor, Laurens Mertens, is also the leader of the VCN (*De Volkskrant*, 4 November; *NRC Handelsblad*, 1 November).

In the sectarian politics of the Netherlands, the CPN has taken on the appearances of a normal political party. Its opponent, the VCN, retains its purity but is essentially a splinter group that reflects only the views of the traditional working class, a group that is quickly disappearing in the Netherlands. The first real test of whether the VCN does constitute a threat to the CPN will be the municipal elections on 19 March 1986.

Domestic Affairs. In each of the domestic areas designated by the Twenty-ninth Congress to be of crucial importance for the party, the CPN took positions that were held by a large segment of the Dutch population. For example, the most important objective of the CPN was to prevent the government from permitting the deployment of cruise missiles on Dutch territory. The first paragraph of Chapter One of the program adopted by the CPN at the congress read: "The CPN remains unconditionally in resistance to the deployment of cruise missiles in the Netherlands. It shall strive to do its utmost to bring the campaign to the people to which it is directed" (*CPN-Leden krant*, March, no. 3, p. 6).

The CPN directed its energy against the cruise missiles through the umbrella organization, KKN, which was composed of a variety of political parties, including the Netherlands Federation of Labor (FNV) and the Inter-Church Peace Council (IKV). CPN participation in the KKN was an integral part of their coalition policy. The major campaign of the KKN—or, globally speaking, the peace movement—was the People's Petition. The CPN was active in this campaign; party member Joop Wolf sat on the Credentials Committee.

The CPN saw its role within the peace movement as an opportunity to contribute to "détente and disarmament" (ibid., August, no. 6, p. 1). The People's Petition was waged as a test of democracy, or the will of the majority against the government. Ton van Hoek referred to the People's Petition as a "clear expression of the Dutch people to the government that the Cabinet of Lubbers was expected to carry out an indirect policy of peace and that the non-deployment of cruise missiles in the Netherlands is a demand of democracy" (ibid., April, no. 4, p. 8). The CPN argued that its objectives must be obtained through joint effort with others.

In response to the government assent to cruise missiles on 1 November in spite of the 3.8 million signatures collected in the People's Petition, the CPN Central Committee stated on 1 December that it would remain active in its attempt to persuade the government to change its mind. The party made an appeal to the democratic conscience of legislators, and it gave its "support to initiatives for a peaceful and effective boycott of all that has to do with the construction of the installations at Woensdrecht." The CPN continued to support all those groups that comprise the KKN. This again reflects the central theme of the CPN new style in the Netherlands. "The point of departure for the CPN is the political significance of the emergence of the broadly based peace movement as witnessed again in grandiose style with the People's Petition" (ibid.).

The first event on the social-economic calendar for the CPN was the Third National Women's Conference on 19–20 January. At this meeting, reference was made to a "new situation," "anxiety and rage," "feminism on the offensive," and "breakthrough." Some 1,000 women participated, representing all of the views within the party. A declaration formulated by the participants stated that the "CPN Conference of Women was formed to change the causes of the conflict between the sexes" and that the group exists because of the CPN (ibid., February, no. 1, p. 9).

The Twenty-ninth Congress laid out the priorities for the social-economic policies of the CPN in 1986. The highest priority was given to the shorter workweek in order to create an "expansion of employment, interest in the social security system, and a tax system that everyone could afford" (ibid., March, no. 3, p. 2). Some 200 amendments were entered on the chapter before its discussion at the congress.

Another key to new-style CPN politics in 1985 was the emphasis the party placed on forming a joint election list with the PSP and PPR. Originally, it had been the intention of the CPN to share its election program with the Evangelical Peoples Party (EVP) and the PvdA (*NRC Handelsblad*, 1 April).

Izeboud had stated at the beginning of the year that "the renewal of the CPN is in a new phase. Until now it has been characterized by a polemic toward the past; now we are to work out what we want and less of what we do not want." This meant, she said, that "under the influence of the actions against, among others, the threat of the deployment of the cruise missile and the reductions in social security, it has become necessary to become stronger through cooperation" (ibid., 5 January).

The first test of cooperation with the left came from the EVP, which had one seat in the lower house. At a party congress in late March, the EVP did not give priority for cooperation with the left, especially with the CPN; it was decided to first pursue another course of action (ibid., 1 April; *De Volkskrant*, 1 April).

The second test occurred at a meeting between the three "small left-wing" parties in Amsterdam on 1 June. The general conclusion was that further cooperation between the three would depend on a decision by the PSP. There were two issues at this conference that one could say defined the intention of the CPN. First, the CPN and PPR were considering participation in a left-wing majority government together with the PvdA. The PSP, however, preferred the opposition. Second, the CPN—in order to reach some kind of agreement with the other two left-wing parties in order to achieve its aim—was willing to be more pragmatic, such as easing its demands for a shorter workweek from 25 hours by 1990 to 32 hours (*Het Parool*, 3 June).

In an important *De Volkskrant* article on 29 June, Izeboud set out quite definitely the intention of the CPN. She maintained that the CPN did not wish to exclude itself from eventual participation in forming a government with the PvdA. Yet she also defended the CPN against accusations that it was not radical enough. "Up to now, there has been no known example wherein the left exercised effective, inspirational, and democratic governmental power. In this area, there is much more of a challenge for the creative development of new ways than the choice between unsatisfactory existing examples." She went on to argue for a strengthened parliamentary democracy and for intense cooperation between the left-wing parties.

Nevertheless, the EVP decided on 29 June against cooperation with the PPR and CPN. The PSP, however, after expressing its doubts about working with the CPN and PPR, elected a new leader of the party at a congress on 14 December. This new leader, Andrée van Es, was a member of Parliament and a proponent of left-wing cooperation. At the congress, van Es said, "I only want the PSP to open the window, look and listen to what is going on in other radical left-wing parties and movements, and see if differences can be bridged" (*De Volkskrant*, 16 December).

Because of objections from the PSP, the CPN had earlier decided to seek joint election lists where possible for the 1986 municipal elections and parliamentary elections but to enter the election campaign on its own. Yet closer relations may be possible between the three small left-wing parties in the future and, depending on the PvdA—which has thus far rejected all cooperation with the CPN—this could lead to a left-wing cabinet. This, of course, will depend on the elections. According to current opinion polls in December, CPN representation would be reduced to no more than one seat in the lower house.

Foreign Affairs and International Party Contacts. The CPN's standpoint under the new, more pragmatic course of the party toward Eastern Europe was succinctly put by the party's parliamentary chairman, Ina Brouwer: "We are against the violation of human rights wherever they are violated in the world. How should you give your support to the democratic movements in Eastern Europe? In the draft election program, there is something in the concluding framework agreements with East European countries that may be taken as an implementation of the Helsinki Accords. I would gladly meet with representatives of Solidarnosc and Charter 77 to see what other possibilities there may be" (*De Waarheid*, 28 November).

A delegation of the CPN led by Izeboud visited Moscow in late December 1984. According to the CPN, Izeboud explained to Boris Ponomarev and Vadim V. Zagladin about the cruise missile situation in the Netherlands and the importance to the CPN of participating in the broad-based peace movement. She emphasized that this way of mutual security offered more chance of success than either of the present courses currently followed by the United States and Soviet Union. She told the Soviets that the CPN did not think SS-20s in the western part of the Soviet Union were contributing to peace in Europe. Differences of opinion arose regarding the causes of the arms race, the role played by the two military blocs in Europe, and the reasoning behind the balance-of-power strategies.

On bilateral party relations, the view was expressed that despite wide-ranging differences in a variety of areas, there was agreement on the autonomy of both the CPSU and the CPN, and the CPN emphasized it wanted openness to prevail in discussions between the two parties. The CPN criticized the CPSU for its "diplomatic" style of discussion wherein the CPSU expressed only the view of the state. The Soviets responded to this by saying that the next party congress of the CPSU would address itself to these questions (*CPN-Leden krant*, February, no. 2, p. 2).

The second-most important visit of the year was to the People's Republic of China in mid-May, after which the delegation traveled to North Korea (ibid., August, no. 6, p. 2). It was the first official visit of a CPN delegation to China since 1982. Other contacts during the year included a visit to Moscow on the fortieth anniversary of the victory over fascism and another visit in October to Moscow by Ton van Hoek, participation at an international peace conference in Japan by Leo Molenaar, and visits by members of the Communist parties of Romania and Cuba to the Netherlands. A new characteristic of these talks was that "they are no longer limited to providing information about the activities and standpoints of the CPN." The visitors to Amsterdam received "a view of daily life, the social-economic situation, the political relationships, and the general conditions under which the CPN must execute its tasks" (ibid., November 9, p. 4).

Robert I. Weitzel
Amsterdam

Norway

Population. 4,160,000

Parties. Norwegian Communist Party (Norges Kommunistiske Parti; NKP); Socialist Left Party (Sosialistisk Venstreparti; SV); Workers' Communist Party (Arbeidernes Kommunistiske Parti; AKP), runs as Red Electoral Alliance (Rod Valgallians; RV) in elections

Founded. NKP: 1923; SV: 1976; AKP: 1973

Membership. NKP: 5,500; SV: 2,000; AKP: 10,000 (all estimated)

Chairman. NKP: Hans I. Kleven; SV: Theo Koritzinsky; AKP: Kjersti Ericsson

Central Committee. NKP. 14 full members: Hans I. Kleven, Ingrid Negard (deputy chairman), Bjorn Naustvik (organizational secretary), Arne Jorgensen, Trygve Horgen, Grete Trondsen, Asmund Langsether (trade-union affairs), Rolf Dahl, Gunnar Wahl, Kare Andre Nilsen, Arvid Borglund, Gunnar Sorbo, Kirsti Kristiansen, Ornulf Godager (*Friheten*, 20 September 1984); 6 alternate members: Martin Gunnar Knutsen (former party chairman), L. Hammerstad, H. P. Hansen, Sturla Indregard, Fredrik Kristensen, Knut Johansen

Status. Legal

Last Congress. NKP: Eighteenth, 30 March–2 April 1984, in Oslo; SV: March 1985, in Trondheim; AKP: December 1984, "somewhere in Norway" (*Arbeiderbladet*, 18 December 1984)

Last Election. 1985; NKP: 0.2 percent, no representation; SV: 5.4 percent, 6 of 157 representatives; AKP: 0 percent, no representation

Auxiliary Organizations. NKP: Norwegian Communist Youth League (NKU)

Publications. NKP: *Friheten* (Freedom), semiweekly, Arne Jorgensen, editor; *Vart Arbeid*, internal organ; AKP: *Klassekampen* (Class Struggle), daily

Until 1979 the Norwegian Labor Party (Det Norske Arbeiderparti; DNA)—a moderate social-democratic reform movement—dominated postwar Norwegian politics. During this era, the DNA was the main governing party and all but monopolized the left in the country's politics. Three Marxist parties have stood to the left of the DNA: the pro-Soviet NKP and SV and the Maoist AKP, which has campaigned in parliamentary elections as the RV. In the 1981 elections the DNA was ousted from power by a center-right coalition led by Conservative Party leader Kaare Willoch.

Willoch's coalition was re-elected in the general election of 9 September, and he became the first conservative prime minister ever to win a second term in Norway. His coalition held only a one-seat majority in the Storting (parliament), however, and was forced to depend for support on the two representatives of the right-wing Progressive Party (which advocated the dismantling of the Norwegian welfare state). The DNA made a significant but incomplete comeback in the elections.

The Norwegian Communist Party. The NKP began as a small splinter group of radical trade unionists and politicians who left the DNA in 1923. It experienced many lean years until after World War II, when its support for the war effort against Nazi Germany and the Soviet liberation of northern Norway boosted the NKP's popularity at the polls (eleven seats in the first postwar parliament). However, the party's fortunes fell with the onset of the Cold War.

The weakness of the NKP was due, in large part, to its decision in 1975 to remain a staunchly pro-Soviet, Stalinist party. Its membership and popularity dwindled when Reidar Larsen, then its chairman, and several other leaders abandoned the NKP and established the SV.

Although differences still exist between the NKP and the SV, NKP chairman Hans I. Kleven looks favorably upon SV chairman Theo Koritzinsky's call for a broad united front of left-wing parties in Norway. Kleven believes that it is especially important to establish unity of action in the labor movement, both in the unions themselves and in the political parties close to labor—the DNA, SV, and NKP.

In addition, Kleven supports Koritzinsky's proposals for electoral cooperation between the NKP and the SV. Kleven has suggested running SV and NKP candidates on joint election lists. The NKP chairman has also backed Koritzinsky's idea for the NKP and SV to cooperate on specific issues in order to reshape Norwegian society in a socialist direction.

The NKP continues to be one of the weakest communist parties in Western Europe. It received a mere 7,025 votes (0.3 percent) in the last parliamentary elections in 1981, far short of the number needed to win a seat in the Storting. In the local elections of 1983 the NKP captured only 0.4 percent of the vote, and in the general elections of September 1985 the party polled just 0.2 percent.

The Nuclear Issue. At its Seventeenth Congress in 1981, the NKP formally adopted a peace offensive. Its essence was the struggle against the deployment of new nuclear weapons in Europe and for a nuclear-free northern Europe. The party advocated a nuclear-free zone encompassing Norway, Sweden, Denmark, and Finland, formalized by a treaty guaranteed by the great powers (*WMR*, April 1983). The NKP was active in preparations for Peace March 1983, a twenty-day affair that began on 10 July in Eidsvoll, in southern Norway, and finished in the northern city of Trondheim. The slogans were "No to nuclear weapons in Norway" and "No to the deployment of new missiles in Europe." NKP-affiliated sponsors of the march included the Norwegian Peace Committee (a branch of the Soviet-controlled World Peace Council) and the Women's Committee for Peace.

The NKP supported the unsuccessful vote in October 1982 by the Labor Party against NATO infrastructure appropriations needed to prepare sites for new U.S. missiles in Europe. The Communists also praised the findings of the DNA commission, released in January 1983, that came out against the deployment of U.S. Pershing II and cruise missiles in Western Europe and in favor of a nuclear freeze and the creation of nuclear-free zones in northern Europe.

According to the NKP, the conservative-led coalition that came to power in 1981 has increased Norway's subordination to the United States and exacerbated relations between Norway and the USSR, which share a border. The NKP accuses the Norwegian government of involvement in "U.S. militarist plans" and demands that it pursue an "independent security and defense policy" (*WMR*, April 1983; *Aftenposten*, 9 March 1983; *JPRS*, 20 April 1983).

Differences have emerged between the NKP and

the DNA on the issue of Soviet responsibility for the growing nuclear threat in Europe. In particular, the NKP has criticized the DNA's call for reductions in Soviet medium-range missiles on the continent. The NKP has also backed the ongoing appeal by the Socialist bloc to the United States to follow the Soviet example and pledge no-first-use of atomic weapons.

At the beginning of 1984, a subtle shift in the NKP's position on nuclear issues became apparent. On 8 January, *Aftenposten* printed a lengthy statement by Kleven, who had just chaired an NKP Politburo session on missiles and the peace movement in Europe. The bulk of Kleven's statement was strongly anti-American, as typified by the following passage: "The new U.S. missiles in Europe have brought us one step closer to disaster . . . The Norwegian Communist Party wants to stigmatize those who carry the main responsibility for this: the U.S. government and the arms industry . . . Moreover, the U.S. NATO allies, among them the Willoch government, carry joint responsibility for the deterioration of the international situation." Kleven demanded the withdrawal of the missiles and a return to the status quo that existed in Europe before their deployment. Nevertheless, he stipulated that, parallel to the withdrawal of the U.S. missiles, "counterefforts by the Warsaw Pact [to deploy its own missiles] must cease" and there must be a "halt to all testing, production and deployment of new nuclear weapons," presumably by the Soviets as well as the Americans.

The NKP has continued to promote an October 1982 directive from the Central Board of Communists in the trade unions to link the struggle for better working and living conditions with demands for cuts in military spending. The NKP advocates switching funds earmarked for military purposes to civilian needs.

In July the NKP issued a statement calling on the Norwegian government to bar nuclear-armed U.S. naval vessels from the country's ports. The statement was inspired by the example of New Zealand, which effectively barred all U.S. warships, inasmuch as the United States refuses to divulge which of its ships carry nuclear weapons.

The Eighteenth NKP Congress and Its Aftermath. Peace and jobs were the major themes at the NKP's Eighteenth Congress, held 30 March–2 April 1984. Kleven raised the familiar issues of U.S. nuclear missiles in Europe and the need for a Nordic nuclear-free zone. He proposed a conference of European communist parties to discuss concrete measures to ease world tension. At the same time, he urged the Norwegian government to initiate negotiations with the other Scandinavian countries to bring about a treaty for a nuclear-free zone in northern Europe. Kleven declared that NATO "does not give us protection; it means increased danger instead." Nevertheless, he conceded that the majority of Norwegian citizens favor continued participation in the NATO alliance (Oslo, *Arbeiderbladet*, 31 March 1984).

Kleven's speech expressed optimism that war could be averted in Europe. He cited the alleged shift in the "correlation of forces" away from "imperialism," the peace initiatives of the Socialist bloc, and the upsurge of the antiwar movement in Europe. Terminating the deployment of U.S. missiles on the continent and forcing the withdrawal of those already deployed would remain the key task of the peace movement, Kleven asserted (Tass, 30 March 1984).

On the issue of jobs, former NKP deputy chairman Trygve Horgen reminded the congress of the party's ten-point program to fight unemployment and of its pressure on the government to uphold the right to work. He also reiterated the labor movement's responsibility to struggle against war and militarism. On 3 April, the day after the close of the congress, *Friheten* published an editorial headlined "To Work, Comrades!" In it, the NKP called for a short-term program of creating a national plan to deal with unemployment—a program to be financed by the government with 5 billion kroner annually. Over the longer term, the NKP cited the need "to abolish the capitalist system and bring in a Socialist planned economy in which such crises will not take place."

On international issues, the NKP supported the Soviet stance not only on European issues but also on areas of crisis around the world. For example, the congress adopted a unanimous resolution of solidarity with Central America in its struggle against the allegedly aggressive actions of the United States (*Pravda*, 3 April 1984). A plenum of the NKP's Central Committee in May 1984 passed resolutions opposing the Pol Pot insurgents in Cambodia and the persecution of Communists in Iran, to cite examples of the party's international concerns (ibid., 9 May 1984).

Kleven was re-elected party chairman at the congress, but elections for most of the NKP's other leading officials were postponed as a result of sharp personality conflicts. The post of deputy chairman, for example, was the object of a contest between Asmund Langsether, an academic backed by Kleven, and Trygve Horgen, a workingman supported by *Friheten* editor Arne Jorgensen, among others. Another contentious issue was Kleven's reported proposal to exclude Martin Gunnar Knutsen, the former party chairman, from the Central Committee (*Arbeiderbladet*, 1 June 1984).

Former Central Committee member John Atle Krogstad sent a remarkable letter to Norwegian newspapers in June 1984 that reflected disillusionment with the interparty struggles. "There is an atmosphere of distrust among leading party members," he wrote. "Personality conflicts in the [Central Committee] have convinced me to withdraw from the party . . . The party is permeated with personality conflicts, despite the unanimous agreements at the national congress . . . and despite the fact that the chairman was chosen unanimously." Krogstad added, "The NKP is digging its own grave . . . [because of] the party's lack of ability to discuss and solve its differences" (ibid., 16 June 1984).

On 19 June 1984, Kleven published a "Letter to Members of the Norwegian Communist Party" in *Friheten*. It acknowledged the damage done to the NKP by "internal conflicts and disputes, which in most instances have generally been personal rather than political and ideological differences . . . It is most regrettable that we are losing members and officeholders who support the party's policies and ideology. We cannot afford this. We can only solve our differences in a productive manner . . . by means of open, objective and thorough debate." Kleven appointed a temporary eight-man Central Committee, including Horgen, to serve until final selections could be made.

Magne Mortensen, the NKP's national director, sent a letter to *Friheten* (13 September) that summed up the leadership crisis as it evolved during 1984. The letter accused Kleven of divisive tactics and overweening personal ambition. Mortensen charged that the chairman had transformed normal differences and conflicts among party members on various issues into a debilitating contest of personalities (*Friheten*, 13 September 1984).

In October 1984 the Central Committee passed a resolution that the party's infighting could no longer be aired on the pages of *Friheten*. The resolution was justified in the name of "democratic centralism," that is, adherence to the NKP's decisions once they were debated and adopted. The decision to gag *Friheten* reportedly was taken in the face of four "nay" votes in the Central Committee. Jorgensen was among the dissenters, but he decided to remain as *Friheten*'s editor (*Aftenposten*, 16 October 1984). He declared that "the political debate will carry on in the paper's columns. But if it is decided that such a debate will not be permitted, well, then I will have to go" (ibid.).

The NKP's Central Committee held a plenum in December 1984 at which a "liveable" compromise was reached to end the internecine disputes in the party (*Aftenposten*, 18 December 1984). It was agreed that the quarrel over the composition of the Central Committee would cease but that interparty discussions in the future would be more free.

No sooner had the divisive debate over the composition of the NKP's Central Committee been relegated to history than a new crisis racked the party. This time the focal point was international issues, particularly relations with the Soviet Union. According to an article in *Klassekampen* (30 January):

> A new storm is brewing in the Norwegian Communist Party (NKP). Outwardly, there is an impression of calm, but internally the situation is extremely tense. The conflicts that led to an uncontrolled eruption last fall continue to tear the party apart. One group within the party wants it to reject the Soviet system. Another group is calling for closer relations with Eastern Europe and the Soviet Union . . . Many NKP members see support for "proletarian internationalism," i.e., Soviet foreign policy, as vital to the party's existence. On the other hand, strong forces within the party say that it will be destroyed unless it severs its ties with the Soviet Union.

The split within the NKP, which had previously seemed merely to pit the supporters of Kleven against those of former chairman Knutsen, has acquired an extra dimension. Kleven, widely regarded as a political opportunist, heads the majority faction; Knutsen and Jorgensen lead a strongly pro-Soviet faction; and the party's youth group, NKU, represents a Eurocommunist-style faction. The main supporter of the latter faction on the party's Central Committee is Kirsti Kristiansen.

The continuing factional struggle in the NKP has severely affected the party's efforts not only to attract new members but also to remain a viable organization:

> The Norwegian Communist Party . . . has never been weaker in Norway than it is today. The party has some influence in the peace movement and in the labor movement, but that is all. Many members have left the

> party during the past year. Many others are making up their minds. Some members have gone over to the Labor Party. Other have gone into passivity. (Ibid.)

Party members and supporters emphasize that the factionalism can no longer be papered over, since it involves not only personalities but also major policy questions. As one interested observer pointed out:

> If the party leadership tries to avoid a battle with the Soviet faction, it will be a tragic mistake. The party leadership must realize how serious the situation is. We must discuss our relationship to the Soviet Communist Party and the Soviet Union. It is the party's national credibility that is at stake. (Ibid.)

The worsening of the internecine struggle in the NKP came at a peculiarly bad time, for the party was preparing to participate in the national elections. The electoral campaign was the primary topic under discussion at the NKP's national conference, which took place in Oslo in March. Bolstering the unity of all "progressive" and democratic forces in the country was deemed the most important task facing the NKP (*Pravda*, 4 March). The party issued an election manifesto, which recommended the formation of election pacts among the NKP, the SV, and the Labor Party to contest the Storting elections scheduled for September. In addition, the party conference called for a cutback in the work week to 35 hours, flexible retirement ages for Norwegians over the age of 62, higher taxes on unearned income, the use of petrodollars to create up to 20,000 new jobs, and, in the international arena, the establishment of a Nordic nuclear-free zone ratified by the major world powers (*Aftenposten*, 4, 6 March).

Bjorn Naustvik, the NKP's organizational secretary, urged party members to seek contacts with Labor Party and SV representatives in each county of Norway, with the goal of forging electoral alliances; he also enlisted the help of the trade-union movement in this endeavor (*Aftenposten*, 11 June).

Kleven has conceded that the NKP must cooperate with other parties ("given the actual situation in the country, only the Norwegian Labor Party offers a real alternative to Conservative rule"), but must also carve out its own role, especially in the struggles for peace and improvement of conditions for the working class. He lamented that

> our party is small, it is not represented in the Storting and has virtually no access to the mass media. Still, advancing their election programs and delivering their speeches, Communists try to convince voters that there is a need for them to support the Communist Party.

A vote for the NKP, he declared,

> is not lost. It is a ballot cast for a policy of peace and detente, of fighting against unemployment, the crisis and inflation. Election of Communists to parliament will mean greater opportunities for . . . upholding working people's interests . . . The role of Communist parties in the trade union and antiwar movements . . . confirms that even a numerically small party can be a highly dynamic and elective social force. (*WMR*, March, pp. 34–35)

The NKP's international links revolve largely around meetings of the Nordic communist parties and consultations with the Soviet and East European parties. During 1985, however, delegations from the NKP visited China (in January) and North Korea (in October). The wide-ranging issues discussed at Nordic Communist gatherings were typified in a communiqué published after the parley of northern European communist parties in Finland in November 1982. The document covered, inter alia, the inability of capitalism to solve unemployment problems in Scandinavia, the campaign for peace, disarmament, and a Nordic nuclear-free zone, and the right of the Palestinians to establish a state of their own (*IB*, February 1983, p. 38).

In October 1984 Kleven led a party delegation to Sofia, where he held talks with Todor Zhivkov, general secretary of the Bulgarian Communist Party. They reportedly focused special attention on issues relating to peace and security in Europe (Sofia, BTA, 26 October 1984). In December of that year the NKP participated in a meeting in Czechoslovakia of world communist parties under the auspices of the journal *Problems of Peace and Socialism* (*World Marxist Review*). In February 1985 a delegation under Kleven's leadership visited Czechoslovakia for talks with General Secretary Gustáv Husák. They condemned "U.S. imperialism," demanded an end to the arms race, and called for celebrating the 40th anniversary of the defeat of Nazi Germany by renewing the struggle for international peace and detente (*FBIS—Eastern Europe*, 22 February, p. D1). In May the NKP organized a series of events commemorating the World War II victory. The Soviets sent a delegation headed by D. B. Golovko, secretary of the

Kiev section of the Ukrainian Communist Party (*Pravda*, 8 May).

The Socialist Left Party. The SV is the strongest Marxist party to the left of the DNA. In the 1981 parliamentary elections, it received 4.9 percent of the vote and four seats in the Storting. The SV campaigned as a parliamentary ally of the DNA in the local elections of September 1983 (in which it received 5.2 percent of the vote) and in the general election of September 1985 (in which it won 5.4 percent and 6 parliamentary seats).

Leadership and Organization. In January 1983 party leader Berge Furre was replaced by Theo Koritzinsky, who had been chairman of the Socialist Youth League. The SV congress in March of that year produced almost a completely new leadership. Koritzinsky was confirmed as chairman, Tora Houg and Einar Nyheim were selected as the new deputy chairmen, Erik Solheim continued to serve as party secretary, and a new Executive Committee was formed, including veteran Finn Gustavsen.

In the summer of 1984 a struggle broke out between Koritzinsky and Gustavsen (called by his detractors "a Social Democrat in a red coat") over who would be nominated to fill an upcoming vacancy in the Oslo delegation to the Storting (*Aftenposten*, 2 June 1984). The struggle revolved around personalities as well as policies. Women's groups within the SV, for example, announced their opposition to Gustavsen because he opposed SV participation in the campaign against pornography.

The main shift in leadership that occurred at the SV's congress in March 1985 was the replacement of Solheim—evidently at his own request—by Hilde Vogt. The congress also reaffirmed Einar Nyheim's role as the individual in charge of trade-union affairs and Kirsti Nost's position as head of women's issues (*Aftenposten*, 7 March).

Views and Activities. In January 1983, just before his replacement as party leader, Berge Furre presented the SV Executive Committee's draft for a working program for the 1980s. The program called for stronger state power, increased government subsidies, and a further expansion of the public sector. It demanded higher taxes and wages, more housing, and nationalizations, as well as "self-sufficiency" and increased "power for the workers" (*Aftenposten*, 29 January 1983; *JPRS*, 23 February 1983).

Shortly after he assumed the party chairmanship, Koritzinsky came out in favor of broad case-by-case cooperation with the left, especially between the SV and the NKP. Koritzinsky has advocated cooperation among peace, environmental, women's, and labor-union groups. He has emphasized, however, that such cooperation must be under the control of local party groups and must not be aimed at party unifications (*Friheten*, 26 January 1983; *JPRS*, 3 March 1983). Hanna Kvanmo, the SV's parliamentary leader, has declared that she will not permit the impression to evolve that the SV is a "support party" for the DNA, with which it has an electoral pact (*Aftenposten*, 7 March).

Unlike the NKP, the SV favors reforms rather than total rejection of current Norwegian institutions. Nevertheless, Koritzinsky stresses that reforms must be structural in nature, with a transfer of power to popularly elected delegates and organized labor. This program implies greater municipal and county authority and stronger company democracy. Koritzinsky says that the SV is considering the concept of wage-earner funds, which would give unions and elected delegates more control over capital. In general, however, the SV's "new" working program appears to be simply a repackaging of old ideas.

The SV congress of 1983 focused on the struggle against growing unemployment in Norway and the struggle for women's equality (*FBIS—Western Europe*, 14 March 1983). It also passed a resolution urging party members to participate in local peace marches against several airports in Norway that the SV claims are a part of U.S. nuclear strategy, "so that the civilian population in the districts concerned understands the dangers it is exposed to" (*Aftenposten*, 14 March 1983; *JPRS*, 20 April 1983). On the international front, the congress issued a strongly worded statement condemning the Soviet war in Afghanistan (ibid.).

At its 1985 congress, the SV declared that keeping Norway free of nuclear weapons, combatting unemployment, and bringing about a fairer distribution of the material goods of society constituted its top priorities, both in its day-to-day policy and in the national election campaign that was already underway. Probably the most controversial aspect of the party's proposals was the call for a six-hour workday, to be instituted before 1992. In addition, the party congress called for a lowering of the age for pension eligibility, the nationalizing of key industries and credit institutions, greater sympathy on the part of the government for women's rights, and a prohibition on visits to Norwegian ports by nuclear-armed ships (*Aftenposten*, 8, 11 March). Outgoing party secretary Erik Solheim told the congress that "SV's influence cannot be measured in our number of election votes alone." He recalled the "countless issues that SV has pushed forth, and others have harvested the benefits" (ibid., 11 March).

The Workers' Communist Party. The AKP was born in the late 1960s as an amalgam of various Maoist organizations that were disenchanted with the Soviet economic model and with Soviet foreign policy. The AKP was founded as a formal organization in 1973. Its electoral front, the RV, has not fared well, and the party has never garnered enough votes for even a single seat in the Storting.

A book by AKP member Dag Solstad provided a rare glimpse of life inside the party. Entitled *High School Teacher Pedersen's Account of the Big Political Revival in Our Country*, the book maintained that constant squabbling characterized the AKP during the early 1980s. A good deal of the squabbling may have involved the role of women in the organization, because at the party's congress in December 1984, women captured the leadership. Kjersti Ericsson, a university instructor, succeeded Pal Steigan as the AKP's chairman. Women also gained several other high-ranking posts, including that of political vice chairman, which went to a teacher named Jorun Gulbrandsen. Ericsson contends that "the women's struggle has been underestimated in the communist movement" and that Norwegian women will finally be able to exercise the role they deserve in the campaign for a communist revolution (Oslo, *Arbeiderbladet*, 18 December 1984). The 1984 congress, which was held in an undisclosed location to preclude intervention by security officials, passed a resolution stipulating that women must comprise half the membership of the AKP's Central Committee and half the delegates to party congresses (ibid.). With regard to the party's composition, it was also revealed that half the members come from the working classes—a term that was not further defined (*Klassekampen*, 5 January).

According to the 5 January issue of *Klassekampen*, "anti-Soviet AKP has taken the lead in making a six-hour workday the watchword from start to finish as a women's issue within the labor movement . . . AKP also has had great and decisive significance for important campaigns in the battle to save jobs." At a press conference held shortly after its congress, the AKP emphasized that it continues to advocate armed revolution and a dictatorship of the proletariat (*Aftenposten*, 18 December 1984). On other issues, the party opposes Norway's membership in NATO, calls for a strong, independent defense posture, and asserts that the AKP has been too servile toward China (ibid.; *Arbeiderbladet*, 18 December 1984).

The Red Electoral Alliance. The RV is no longer simply an offshoot of the AKP. It is a coalition of the AKP and independent Socialists. The RV has numerous representatives on municipal and county councils. The third annual RV congress was held in April 1983, at which time the independent Socialists in the RV and some AKP members pushed through a resolution guaranteeing "real, not just formal" democratic rights for working people after the revolution in Norway. The RV's electoral manifesto of that year stipulated that a postrevolutionary socialist government must allow "freedom of speech and organization, independent trade unions, the right to strike, legal protection, and control by the workers over state and production organs" (*Aftenposten*, 18 April 1983).

A debate developed at the congress over Norway's membership in NATO. A motion on the country's withdrawal from the alliance was defeated by a vote of 54 to 35 (ibid.). As part of its manifesto, the RV agreed on a plank calling for strengthening the conventional defenses of Western Europe and building a strong independent defense system outside NATO. The RV argued that "the prospect of being rescued from across the Atlantic is doubtful. For this reason, the RV proposes that Norway must get out of NATO's integrated military cooperation" (*Aftenposten*, 16 April 1983).

The RV discounts the Soviet "guarantee" not to use nuclear arms against the Nordic region. It also warns against relying on Soviet advocacy of arms reduction and argues for strong international pressure on the USSR to force it to destroy its SS-20 missiles under international supervision (ibid.). The RV's manifesto was critical of both superpowers, but, according to the RV, the Soviet Union is the most aggressive power. Soviet power is regarded as ascendant and U.S. power as in decline. Thus, with no counterforce to Soviet combativeness, the threats of Soviet occupation of Europe and of a new world war are becoming greater (ibid.).

The RV manifesto maintained that real socialism could be introduced into Norway only through a socialist revolution in which the working class assumes state power after a prolonged struggle. The RV, therefore, is ultimately a revolutionary rather than a reform-minded party. Although it participates in elections, it contends that Norway "will never get socialism through the ballot box" (*Aftenposten*, 13 April 1983).

Major points in the RV's platform for the general election of 1985 included demands for a six-hour workday, a campaign against pornography, a prohibition on shutting down state-owned enterprises, and the use of oil revenues to narrow the gap between the rich and poor in Norway (*Aftenposten*, 1 July). The RV placed great emphasis on winning votes among women and laborers but emphasized that a vote cast by any citizen for the RV would not be a lost vote. Stressing its own independent stance on a number of important issues, the RV has criticized the SV for entering into electoral pacts with the Labor Party without insisting on certain preconditions to ensure its separate identity (ibid.).

Marian Leighton
Defense Intelligence Agency

Portugal

Population. 10,045,000
Party. Portuguese Communist Party (Partido Comunista Português; PCP)
Founded. 1921
Membership. 200,753 (claimed, December 1983)
Secretary General. Álvaro Cunhal (since 1961)
Secretariat. 8 full members: Álvaro Cunhal, Carlos Costa, Domingos Abrantes, Fernando Blanqui Teixeira, Joaquim Gomes, Jorge Araújo, Octávio Pato, Sérgio Vilarigues; 2 alternate members: Jaime Félix, Luísa Araújo
Political Secretariat. 5 members: Álvaro Cunhal, Carlos Brito, Carlos Costa, Domingos Abrantes, Octávio Pato
Political Commission. 18 full members: Álvaro Cunhal, Ângelo Veloso, Dias Lourenço, António Gervásio, Carlos Brito, Carlos Costa, Diniz Miranda, Domingos Abrantes, Fernando Blanqui Teixeira, Jaime Serra, Joaquim Gomes, Jorge Araújo, José Soeiro, José Casanova, José Vitoriano, Octávio Pato, Raimundo Cabral, Sérgio Vilarigues; 7 alternate members: António Lopes, António Orcinha, Artur Vidal Pinto, Bernardina Sebastião, Carlos Ramildes, Edgar Correia, Zita Seabra
Central Committee. 91 full and 74 alternate members
Status. Legal
Last Congress. Tenth, 8–11 December 1983, in Oporto
Last Election. 1985, United People's Alliance (communist coalition), 15.49 percent, 38 of 250 seats (*FBIS*, 31 October)
Auxiliary Organizations. General Confederation of Portuguese Workers (Confederação Geral de Trabalhadores Portugueses–Intersindical Nacional; CGTP), Portugal's largest labor grouping; National Confederation of Farmers (Confederação Nacional de Agricultores), comprising 400 peasant organizations; Popular Democratic Movement/Democratic Electoral Commission (Movimento Democrático Popular/Comissão Eleitoral Democrático; MDP/CED), said to be a communist-front "satellite" party
Publications. *Avante!*, weekly newspaper; *O Militante*, theoretical journal; *O Diário*, semiofficial daily newspaper; all published in Lisbon

Western Europe's most Stalinist and pro-Soviet party dominates the communist movement in Portugal, controls about half of the unionized labor force, and has a significant, though declining, electoral following. It has been excluded from the government since an aborted 1976 coup attempt. Most radical-left groups, which thrived after 1974 and which opposed the "revisionist" PCP, have languished in recent years. A terrorist group active since 1980 and condemned by the PCP is the Popular Forces of the 25th of April (Fôrças Populares do 25 de abril; FP-25).

Domestic Affairs. The fall of the government headed by Mário Soares was welcomed by the Communists as the deserved and inevitable consequence of "ruinous" official policies. A "brutal offensive" against nationalized sectors and against agrarian reform had only exacerbated all the grave national problems, said Álvaro Cunhal, causing the "cronies" in the coalition cabinet to blame each other for their resulting unpopularity (*Avante!*, 13 June; *FBIS*, 21 June). The Social Democrats withdrew from the cabinet in May, charging that the Socialists were delaying liberal economic reforms (*WP*, 1 July).

One observer described the Communists as exasperated with Soares and his Socialist Party for having utterly ignored them. The only other possibility they purportedly saw for dialogue that might open political doors for them was through President António Ramalho Eanes (*Expresso*, 24 August; *JPRS*, 23 September). For months the PCP had been pressing him to call new elections, in which it expected to be strengthened, and to replace the cabinet with a "democratic government of national salvation" to include Communists—now the "only" active defenders of the nation's revolutionary achievements (Tass, 6 February; Warsaw, *Trybuna Ludu*, 1 March; *FBIS*, 8 February and 5 March). The president, in fact, was reluctant to call new elections for parliament even when the cabinet fell but was forced to do so when all the major parties, including the PCP, refused to support a "consensus government" (*WP*, 1 July).

The PCP was encouraged by the formation in March of the Democratic Renewal Party (Partido Renovador Democrático; PRD), which it was expected Eanes would head as soon as his presidential term ended in January 1986. Cunhal anticipated that the new party could play a key role in ending the "monopoly of right-wing coalitions" by drawing votes away from the Socialists and Social Democrats and collaborating with the Communists (*CSM*, 7 March; *Diário de Lisboa*, 28 March; *JPRS*, 23 April). The PRD's chairman was not sanguine about the possibility of a future coalition with Communists "in light of the PCP's political practices," but said such an alliance would depend on election results (*Expresso*, 24 August; *FBIS*, 5 September). The new party, called by Cunhal more pragmatic than ideological, was considered by most observers to be left of center—somewhere between the Socialists and the Communists (*CSM*, 7 March; *Diário de Notícias*, 8 July; *FBIS*, 16 July).

October elections confirmed Cunhal's expectation that the Socialist Party would be weakened since it lost almost half of its seats in the National Assembly, mostly to the PRD. Yet the Social Democratic Party (Partido Social Democrático; PSD) gained ten seats and the Communists lost eight (*FBIS*, 31 October). Cunhal was gratified that there was now "no basis" for setting up a right-wing coalition and that in spite of his own party's setback, the now pivotal role of the PRD opened up positive prospects for the PCP (Lisbon domestic service, 11 October; *FBIS*, 16 October). The new prime minister, PSD leader Aníbal Cavaco Silva, formed a cabinet entirely from his own party, which had won only a third of the seats in the new assembly. Cunhal concluded that the precariousness of the new government strengthened the foundations for setting up his proposed "democratic government of national salvation" (Lisbon domestic service, 11 October; Tass, 29 October; *FBIS*, 16 and 31 October).

Cunhal rejoiced that the decline in popular support for the Socialist Party had jeopardized Soares's presidential candidacy for elections scheduled for January 1986 (Lisbon domestic service, 11 October; *FBIS*, 16 October). To ensure the victory of a "democrat," Cunhal said that the voters who reelected Eanes in 1980 had to be rallied together. The Communists nominated as their candidate Ângelo Veloso, a member of the PCP Central Committee, but Cunhal said this was done only to facilitate a negotiated consensus around another candidate with a real chance to win the election (*Diário de Notícias*, 12 August; *JPRS*, 2 October; Lisbon domestic service, 15 November; *FBIS*, 18 November).

In a poll of Portuguese opinions about communism taken early in the year only 3.5 percent of the adult population considered communist countries the best models for Portugal even while 22 percent professed some support or sympathy for the PCP. Some 11 percent thought of communism as the wave of the future (*Diário de Notícias*, 24 February; *JPRS*, 26 March). In October elections, support for communist candidates declined from 18 percent in 1983 to 15.5 percent (*FBIS*, 31 October). Cunhal, meanwhile, claimed in February that in the previous few months more than 10,000 Portuguese, mostly young, had joined the PCP (ibid., 25 February). Of the total membership of over 200,000, more than 100,000 were workers and over 45,000 were women, he said (*Expresso*, 30 March; *JPRS*, 13 May).

Auxiliary and Front Organizations. Cunhal described as a significant cause of the Soares cabinet's fall a series of nation-wide strikes in June that called for the dismissal of the government. The communist-controlled CGTP staged these protests as well as earlier rallies and marches by tens of thousands of workers challenging the government's economic policies (*NYT*, 17 March and 5 June; *Avante!*, 6 June; *FBIS*, 21 June).

In May the MDP/CED again agreed to ally itself with the PCP in an electoral coalition as the United People's Alliance (*Diário de Notícias*, 27 May; *JPRS*, 9 July). There had been some speculation that the MDP/CDE was seeking ties with other parties in order to counter the widespread perception that it was merely a disguised cell of the PCP. An MDP/CDE spokesman considered that the PCP had made a "serious error" in criticizing his party's proposal in late 1984 for dialogue with the Soares government (see *YICA*, 1985, p. 521); all the same, it was claimed, there should be no surprise that the two parties sometimes disagreed since they were "two autonomous blocs" (*Expresso*, 10 and 24 November 1984; *Diário de Notícias*, 27 May; *Tempo*, 30 May; *JPRS*, 4 January and 9 July).

International Views and Activities. Communist deputies offered the only dissent to parliament's overwhelming approval in July of Portugal's entry into the European Economic Community. The PCP protested that since the assembly was being dissolved it was not qualified to ratify the integration treaty (*NYT*, 12 July). This decision, it said, was an act of national capitulation that would ruin the Portuguese economy and facilitate the restoration of monopolies and fascist estates (*Avante!*, 18 April; *FBIS*, 24 April). The PCP was said to hope for dissolution of parliament before ratification of the treaty, thereby making it unlikely that Portugal could meet the 1 January deadline for acceptance (*Diário de Notícias*, 11 May; *JPRS*, 28 June).

The PCP demanded in July that the government reject the appointment of Frank Shakespeare as the new U.S. ambassador to Lisbon because of the latter's "intended" interference in Portuguese life. The proposed envoy had reportedly stated that two of the problems he would confront were the electoral weight of the PCP and the present size of the state apparatus in Portugal's economy (Lisbon domestic service, 3 July; *FBIS*, 5 August). Communists also continued to oppose defense agreements permitting U.S. deployment of nuclear weapons and use of military facilities—especially of a radar station for tracking weapons in space—on Portuguese territory (Tass, 23 August; Lisbon domestic service, 4 November; *FBIS*, 26 August and 7 November).

PCP officials held consultations during 1985 with the communist parties of the Soviet Union (Cunhal conferred directly with Mikhail Gorbachev), East Germany, Poland, Hungary, Spain, Cuba, Syria, Yemen, China, Vietnam, Kampuchea, and Korea. While emphasizing that Korean Communists were building socialism successfully, Cunhal noted the contrast between the Koreans' "strong personality cult" and Portuguese emphasis on "collective work" (*Avante!*, 24 January; *FBIS*, 30 January). The PCP participated in a Paris conference of West European communist parties in May to discuss the "communist crisis" in each country (*Le Drapeau Rouge*, 15–16 June).

Other Far-Left Groups. Lt. Col. Otelo Saraiva de Carvalho, hero of the 1974 revolution, went on trial in July, along with 72 other suspects, for responsibility in terrorist activities carried out over the previous five years through the FP-25. These acts included bomb explosions in March that damaged several foreign businesses and homes in Lisbon and Evora; they took place soon after the government announced plans to permit private investment in nationalized companies. Carvalho denied charges of secretly directing the guerrillas. However, he conceded that members, with ideological convictions similar to his own, had infiltrated the Armed Civilian Structure, which he had organized as the embryo of a "revolutionary army." Said by police to be a front for the FP-25 were the Forces of Popular Unity(Fôrças de Unidade Popular; FUP), an extreme leftist political group formed by Carvalho in 1980, the same year the FP-25 emerged (*CSM*, 6 February; *NYT*, 12 March and 22 July; Lisbon domestic service, 24 October; *FBIS*, 30 October).

While extreme leftist elements in Portugal accused the government of persecuting Carvalho, the PCP condemned the acts of the FP-25 for providing the government with a pretext for taking repressive measures against workers and "popular movements" (Warsaw, *Trybuna Ludu*, 4 March; *FBIS*, 18 March; *NYT*, 22 July). In December the new government of Prime Minister Cavaco Silva dismissed the state television network's management board for "lack of objectivity" in having authorized the transmission of an FP-25 press briefing (*NYT*, 18 December).

Responsibility for a bomb explosion outside the South African Embassy in Lisbon in July was claimed by the left-wing, anti-apartheid Revolutionary Autonomous Groups, a previously unknown organization (*FBIS*, 29 July).

H. Leslie Robinson
University of the Pacific

Spain

Population. 38,629,000
Party. Spanish Communist Party (Partido Comunista de España; PCE)
Founded. 1920
Membership. 86,000 (*Mundo Obrero*, 24–30 October; *FBIS*, 13 November), down from 240,000 in 1977
Secretary General. Gerardo Iglesias
President. Dolores Ibárruri (legendary La Pasionaria of Civil War days)
Secretariat. 11 members: Andreu Claret Serra, José María Coronas, Enrique Curiel Alonso, Francisco Frutos, Gerardo Iglesias, Francisco Palero, Juan Francisco Pla, Pedro Antonio Ríos, Francisco Romero Marín, Simón Sánchez Montero, Nicolás Sartorius
Executive Committee. 28 members
Central Committee. 102 members
Status. Legal
Last Congress. Eleventh, 14–18 December 1983, in Madrid
Last Election. 1982, 3.8 percent, 4 of 350 seats
Auxiliary Organization. Workers' Commissions (Comisiones Obreras; CC OO), Marcelino Camacho, chairman
Publications. *Mundo Obrero* (Labor World), weekly; *Nuestra Bandera* (Our Flag), bimonthly ideological journal; *Ahora Hora*, magazine of minority faction, edited by Santiago Carrillo; all published in Madrid

The Spanish communist movement is the most deeply divided in Europe, now split into two main rival parties as well as numerous minor ones. The PCE is further rent by challenges from within posed by former Secretary General Santiago Carrillo and by Basque, Catalan, and Galician regionalists. Ideology in the various groups ranges from pro-Soviet, Marxist-Leninist orthodoxy to variations of

Eurocommunist commitment. Marxist Basques continue to press their separatist cause with terrorist acts.

Organization and Leadership. Santiago Carrillo intensified his public assault on the leadership of his successor as secretary general, Gerardo Iglesias, to the point of boycotting PCE conferences and organizing his own platform for a "party within the party." This insubordination provoked the Central Committee in April to purge Carrillo and 18 of his supporters from the Central and Executive committees and to strip the onetime leader of his role as party spokesman in parliament. Regional officials loyal to him were displaced through elections organized in Madrid, Valencia, and Galicia by the central leadership (*WP*, 19 April; *NYT*, 21 April; *RFE Research*, 28 October).

The principal bone of contention was Iglesias's proposed strategy of seeking an electoral convergence between the PCE and other leftist groups to oppose the governing Spanish Socialist Workers' Party (Partido Socialista Obrero Español; PSOE). In place of such a "disastrous" policy, Carrillo insisted on "revolutionary orthodoxy" and more vehement confrontation with the government. It took political courage, he said, to disregard the party's "formal majority" but the life of the PCE and the future of the workers' movement required a different tack from the official one. He felt compelled to alert his comrades to "those philistines in the temple" who wanted to isolate the "real communists." His followers were said to make up almost a fourth of the party membership (*Mundo Obrero*, 3–9 January; *JPRS*, 28 February; *El País*, 31 March; Madrid domestic service, 14 April; *FBIS*, 5 and 15 April; London, *Economist*, 20 April; *NYT*, 28 April).

The secretary general recalled that Carrillo himself had in previous years encouraged tactics similar to the convergence approach of which he was now so critical (Madrid domestic service, 7 March; *FBIS*, 8 March). "Shuddering" at antics that could only blunt the party's impact on society, Iglesias admonished his predecessor that the PCE was not a boxing ring nor anyone's personal property (*Mundo Obrero*, 14–20 March; *FBIS*, 3 April). Having repeatedly renounced the use of sanctions against dissidents, a practice "of the past," he sought to explain Carrillo's exclusion as self-inflicted by the latter's refusal to heed a party ultimatum to conform (Milan, *L'Unità*, 16 January; Madrid domestic service, 31 March and 14 April; *FBIS*, 18 January and 2, 15 April).

The expectation of party leaders that Carrillo might now form a splinter party seemed to be confirmed in October with the announcement by the Interior Ministry that a Marxist-Revolutionary Spanish Communist Party (Partido Comunista de España, Marxista-Revolucionario; PCE-MR) had been registered. The former party leader hedged that the disclosure was premature and misleading; he was not really preparing to resign from the PCE and to found still another communist party. This and similar titles had been registered merely as a "precautionary" measure in case agreement could not be reached with other Communists to join his "centrist" faction in an electoral alliance. He then convened a "national assembly" to elect a board, said to be tantamount to a Central Committee, and to mobilize support for "communist unity." Ignacio Gallego of the rival Communist Party (Partido Comunista; PC) responded that unity could not be achieved by an electoral alliance that put aside ideological considerations. He concluded that the communist crisis had reached "rock bottom" (*NYT*, 28 April; *El País*, 13 September; *FBIS*, 4 October; *RFE Research*, 28 October). Iglesias lamented that by permitting the registration of the new political group under the PCE name, the government was demonstrating to what extent it was aiming to weaken the PCE (*Mundo Obrero*, 17–23 October; *FBIS*, 21 October).

Domestic Affairs. Spain's fractious Communists were at least agreed in finding intolerable the government's "antisocial," "essentially right-wing" policies, which were imposed on a society that was "mostly left-wing." Prime Minister Felipe González abandoned his "progressive" program once elected, and this was attributed by Iglesias to the former's accommodation with the second strongest party in parliament, the conservative Popular Alliance (Alianza Popular; AP). A power vacuum on the left created by the Communist Party crisis, by government manipulation of labor, and by widespread public apathy, he said, had permitted González to veer to the right in a "sofa pact" with AP leader Manuel Fraga Iribarne. The latter was thereby neutralized as a credible opposition, since he could not criticize a program that he himself favored (*Mundo Obrero*, 27 June–3 July; *El País*, 22 October; *FBIS*, 12 July and 12 November).

The PCE's principal strategy for overcoming the

paralysis of the left was to try to negotiate an electoral alliance with other left-wing parties and disaffected Socialists as well as with pacifists, feminists, and ecologists. Iglesias stressed that the goal was not to absorb or represent the other forces but to converge with them in order to avoid being "marginalized" by the Socialists (*NYT*, 28 April). Communists were also urged to be sensitive, not just to the problems of the workplace, but also to those of youth, of women, and of the large and growing underprivileged classes as well as to the defense of the environment. Alternative policies must be suggested and society "mobilized" (*Mundo Obrero*, 13 June; *JPRS*, 22 August; *El País*, 22 October; *FBIS*, 12 November).

Auxiliary Organization. Communists were at least able to mobilize some labor protest through the CC OO, said by Iglesias to be the only effective tool for the defense of Spanish workers (*Mundo Obrero*, 13 June; *JPRS*, 22 August). Moderately successful was a one-day general strike called in June to protest proposed government austerity measures that would reduce pension eligibility and make dismissals easier. The CC OO claimed that 75 percent of industrial workers and 65 percent of service and transportation workers struck, "exceeding expectations." The government said only 10 percent of the workforce went out, and a Socialist-controlled General Workers' Union spokesman, who accused the CC OO of political opportunism, declared "unequivocally" that the strike had failed in its objective. Socialist and communist unions did agree to join in a massive protest march in Madrid and almost 50 other cities and towns. Socialists were sufficiently pressured by the march and strike to offer a revision of the bill being considered by parliament (*NYT*, 21 June and 7 July).

The communist and socialist labor confederations reportedly each control about a third of Spain's organized workers, with the CC OO claiming membership of 500,000 to 600,000. Of the 50 members on the CC OO Executive Committee, 27 are said to be supporters of Chairman Marcelino Camacho, 14 of Carrillo, 8 of Gallego, and one is a Trotskyist (*El País*, 21 April; *JPRS*, 25 May; *NYT*, 7 July). According to 1983 figures, all labor unions represent perhaps only a quarter of the labor force (*World Fact Book, 1985*, May).

International Views and Activities. The PCE stepped up its campaign against Spanish membership in NATO as well as against "repeated and scandalous" interference in Spanish political life by the United States. The report that Washington intended to deploy nuclear weapons in Spain in the event of an emergency was cited by the PCE as evidence that the United States subordinated the country to the dictates of its own foreign policy (*Mundo Obrero*, 21–27 February; *FBIS*, 28 February; *NYT*, 28 April). Communists also took part in massive demonstrations against President Reagan's visit to Madrid in May (*NYT*, 5 May; *FBIS*, 9 May). The replacement of an intellectual Marxist with a former top Francoist official as foreign minister was assailed by a PCE spokesman as "Reagan's revenge." He said this cabinet shakeup was a clear signal that the prime minister intended to keep Spain in the NATO alliance (*San Francisco Sunday Examiner and Chronicle*, 14 July).

Another visit to Spain in May—by President Daniel Ortega of Nicaragua—was greeted with enthusiastic support by approximately twenty left-wing parties and organizations that included the PCE, the CC OO, and communist youth groups. They held a rally in front of the U.S. Embassy in Madrid to protest American intervention in Central America (Madrid, Spanish News Agency [EFE], 8 May; *FBIS*, 10 May). Also in May, following consultations with members of the Communist Party of Cuba, Iglesias exulted over the "unusually high level of mutual understanding" between Cuban and Spanish Communists (*Mundo Obrero*, 16–22 May; *JPRS*, 19 June). Iglesias paid "visits of friendship" to Yugoslavia and Romania, and a *Mundo Obrero* delegation visited Chinese Communists in Beijing.

A PCE Executive Committee member returned from a visit to the Soviet Union in March with a very favorable impression of President Mikhail Gorbachev, citing his image as a "strong and reformist" leader. He speculated that economic reforms would be tackled along lines similar to those undertaken in Hungary in favor of greater decentralization (*Mundo Obrero*, 21–27 March; *FBIS*, 27 March). The secretary general did not himself visit Moscow, although he expressed his intention of doing so (*RFE Research*, 29 August).

In June a PCE group attended a Paris conference of West European communist parties to analyze the crisis of the communist parties of each country (*Le Drapeau Rouge*, 15–16 June).

Rival Communist Party. Soviet Communists continued to show a decisive preference for the PC over the PCE, while appearing to take pains to avoid officially "disowning" the latter. Gallego and other

PC members had numerous official interparty talks with the Soviets, Czechs, and East Germans when Gallego was a guest at a Crimean youth camp celebration attended by Gorbachev. There were also reports unofficially attributed to the Spanish government that the PC was being amply subsidized by Moscow (*Cambio 16*, 29 July; *JPRS*, 25 September; *RFE Research*, 29 August and 28 October).

Resisting overtures for any kind of alliance with either Iglesias or Carrillo, Gallego insisted that neither the party's unity nor its restoration were possible based on a platform of Eurocommunism, which he saw as the cause of the PCE's present crisis. He said the campaign for a convergence of the left was only a cover-up for the liquidationist policy of the PCE leadership (Tass, 4 April; *FBIS*, 5 April). While the PC secretary general claimed for his party only 35,000 militants, another member spoke of 50,000 activists, mostly young, with new ones joining every day. One day "we will run the country," he boasted (Prague, *Mlada Fronta*, 28 January; *FBIS*, 11 February; *Cambio 16*, 29 July; *JPRS*, 25 September).

The PC was at the forefront of the hostile demonstrations against President Reagan's visit to Spain, and it charged that the latter's aim was to blackmail the socialist government into not permitting the promised referendum on Spanish membership in NATO (Tass, 4 April; *FBIS*, 5 April; *National Review*, 20 September).

Left-Wing Terrorist Groups. Bombing attacks by the terrorist group Basque Homeland and Liberty (Euzkadi ta Askatasuna; ETA) resulted in new killings that brought the seventeen-year total to nearly 500 (*NYT*, 19 November). Special targets were tourist resorts on Spain's Mediterranean coast, and the victims included a number of civil guardsmen, a retired general, and the chief of the Basque region's police force (ibid., 8 March, 3, 7 May, and 24 December; EFE, 23 February; *FBIS*, 26 February). González called the terrorists assassins of hope and enemies of democracy (*NYT*, 13 June). In December there was a general strike and a rash of violent protests in the Basque area following the death of an ETA suspect while in police custody (ibid., 19 and 24 December).

Spanish authorities were adamant in resisting a demand of the Beirut hijackers of a TWA jetliner in June that two Lebanese terrorists jailed in Madrid be released. The terrorists were charged with having shot and wounded a Libyan diplomat in Spain in 1984, for which they were sentenced to more than 23 years in jail. The government feared that freeing them would set a precedent that could undermine its campaign against ETA (ibid., 24 and 26 June).

The government intelligence agency, the Interior Brigade, acknowledged that it had infiltrated various extremist groups; it was also accused of spying on opposition political parties represented in parliament. Government officials said this would be investigated (ibid., 15 May).

H. Leslie Robinson
University of the Pacific

Sweden

Population. 8,335,000
Party. Left Party Communists (Vänsterpartiet Komunisterna; VPK)
Founded. 1921 (VPK, 1967)
Membership. 17,500, principally in the far north, Stockholm, and Göteborg
Chairman. Lars Werner

Executive Committee. 9 members: Lars Werner, Viola Claesson, Bertil Mabrink (vice chairman), Kenneth Kvist (secretary), Gudrun Schyman, Brit Rundberg, Lars-Ove Hagberg, Bror Engstrom, Lennart Beijer
Party Board. 35 members
Status. Legal
Last Congress. Twenty-seventh, 2–6 January 1985
Last Election. September 1985, 5.4 percent, 19 out of 349 seats
Auxiliary Organization. Communist Youth (KU)
Publications. *Ny Day* (New Day), semiweekly; *Socialistisk Debatt* (Socialist Debate), monthly; both published in Stockholm

The ancestor of the VPK, Sweden's Communist Party (Sveriges Kommunistiska Partiet), was established in 1921, but a number of divisions adversely affected it in the 1920s. Its greatest moment came right after World War II when it obtained 11.2 percent of the vote in local elections. This result was largely due to the popularity of the Soviet Union at the end of the war. Since then, the Communist Party has usually garnered around 4–5 percent of the vote. The party has had a marginal influence in Swedish politics. It has never made a truly major contribution to communist history. Perhaps its most important role has been to allow the Social Democrats to govern during much of Sweden's recent history. During the past half-century, the Swedish Social Democrats have been Europe's most dominant social-democratic party, and during many of their years in power they have relied on a combined majority with the Communists in the Riksdag (parliament). The Communists have never, however, been a part of the government.

In Sweden a party has to clear a 4-percent threshold in order to be represented in parliament, and after the bitter reaction to the Soviet invasion of Czechoslovakia in 1968, the VPK went under the 4 percent mark and was not represented. In the 1970 and 1976 elections it received 4.8 percent, and in 1979 and 1982, 5.6 percent of the vote. The VPK dropped slightly to 5.4 percent in 1985.

The Communists changed both the name and direction of the party congress in 1967. Blue-collar workers constituted the majority of the communist electorate in previous years, but increasingly the VPK is attracting white-collar workers and younger people. Voting studies indicate no significant age differentials among the voters of various parties except for the VPK. In the 1979 election, approximately half of the VPK voters were under the age of 30. Most of the party's new white-collar supporters were in cultural, educational, and health-related occupations.

The VPK projects a Marxist image, even though it has disassociated itself from Moscow and is generally regarded as one of the more moderate West European communist parties. Its program states: "The party's foundation is scientific socialism, the revolutionary theory of Marx and Lenin. It seeks to apply this theory, develop it, infuse it with the struggle of the Swedish working class. The party's goal is to have the struggle of the working class and of the people, guided by the ideas of revolutionary socialism, lead to victory over capitalism and to a classless society."

Party Internal Affairs. The Twenty-seventh Congress of the VPK, held 2–6 January, turned out to be one of the more lively and fractious congresses. The party secretary, Bo Hammar, the object of considerable internal party criticism, did not stand for re-election. Kenneth Kvist replaced him as party secretary. Three other members of the nine-member Executive Committee, Jörn Svensson, Marie-Ann Johansson, and Margo Ingvardsson, also did not run for re-election and were replaced by Gudrun Schyman, Brit Rundberg, and Lars-Ove Hagberg. Two new vice chairmen, Viola Claesson and Bertil Mabrink, were elected. The latter leveled a heavy barrage at both Hammar and the party chairman, Lars Werner, several days before the party congress in the internal paper, *VPK Information* (reported in *Dagens Nyheter*, 22 December 1984). Mabrink said that "Hammar is politically capable but he cannot handle organization work." Mabrink also criticized Werner "for not arousing enthusiasm among party members for political demands." Some speculated that Mabrink's appointment to the post of vice chairman was a tactical move on the part of Werner to co-opt his leading critic (*Dagens Nyheter*, 2 February). Hagberg, new member of the Executive Committee, was also a critic of Werner.

The basic disagreements that surfaced before and during the party congress related to what role a

Communist Party should play in a multiparty democracy. Werner has leaned toward trying to influence policy in the short term by employing parliamentary methods. As *Svenska Dagbladet* (23 December 1984) commented in an editorial, Mabrink favored "the more orthodox line based on placing long-range ideological goals in the foreground of all party efforts."

In his lengthy speech at the opening of the party congress, Werner took note of the internal criticism and said that "general agitation for socialism is necessary, but it will never be credible if it cannot be combined with concrete results in the daily struggle" (*Dagens Nyheter*, 3 January). Werner also criticized the Social Democratic (SK) government for "leaning toward the right." The party chairman pointed out that his limited arrangements with the Social Democrats has helped to raise the child allowance and reduce the gasoline tax. He also alluded to the government having to withdraw three bills due to VPK pressure.

At the same time, Werner did admit shortcomings. He admitted deficiencies in recruiting new members and a decline in support by women and youth. He also included in his self-criticism the fact that he had been guilty of "presumptuousness" but said that he was "now humble" (*Dagens Nyheter*, 3 January). He urged the labor movement to go on the offensive against the reactionary policies of the conservatives. Werner's laundry list of priorities for the government was to use the high profits of the capitalists to create new work, build day-care centers and new dwellings, and invest more for care of sick and elderly persons. He also asked for more money for the environment and less for the military, as well as a reduction in the value-added tax. Another priority item was a reduction in the work hours.

Werner was re-elected unanimously to serve another three-year term, although three candidates were nominated to oppose him. The three withdrew their names but the nomination of opposition candidates was unprecedented in modern VPK history (*Dagens Nyheter*, 4 January).

Domestic Affairs. The major domestic event of 1985 was the election, which found the SK government under Olof Palme retaining power, but by a slightly reduced margin. The Social Democrats lost 7 of their 166 seats, and the VPK lost one of its 20 seats. The combined SK-VPK total of 178 was still enough to retain slender control of the 349-member Riksdag. In the previous parliament, the Social Democrats had a three-vote margin over the three so-called bourgeois parties, without the help of the Communists. Now, with the loss of seven seats, Palme's party is dependent on VPK support for a majority vote in the Riksdag, with the implication that the VPK has more leverage. The SK percentage slipped from 45.6 to 45.1 and the VPK dropped slightly from 5.6 to 5.4. Thus, the combined left had 50.5 percent of the vote. As parties have to win at least 4 percent of the vote to be represented in the Riksdag, there was speculation in every election that some Social Democrats voted VPK in order to ensure that the VPK would cross the 4 percent threshold. A study done by the Swedish Central Bureau of Statistics (reported by *Svenska Dagbladet*, 27 January) suggested that almost 2 percent of the 1982 VPK vote was contributed by Social Democrats who wanted to make sure that the party reached 4 percent.

The most startling gains were made by the Liberal Party (Volkpartiet), under the new leadership of Bengt Westerberg, which increased its number of seats from 21 to 51. This is one of the largest advances in modern Swedish history. The Liberal Party (considered slightly right of center in the Swedish political spectrum) campaigned on the theme of "social responsibility without socialism." Westerberg called for greater freedom of individual choice in public services, such as health care. The Liberal Party, like the other two right-of-center parties, the Moderate Party (Moderata) and the Center Party (Centerpartiet), campaigned vigorously against the so-called wage-earner funds, which was also a major issue in the 1982 election. The three "bourgeois parties" called the funds a form of socialization of private business.

The vote of Ulf Adelsohn's Moderate Party, the largest of the nonsocialist parties, fell from a postwar peak of 23.6 percent to 21.3 percent. The biggest loser was the former prime minister, Thorbjorn Falldin, the leader of the Center Party. His party's vote fell for the fifth consecutive election, to 12.5 percent.

Olof Palme has largely ignored the Communists during the time that he has been in office, but during the campaign he indicated that there might be a possibility of making deals on specific issues with the VPK, under a "revisionist" leader such as Werner. There was some speculation immediately after the election that Palme could always make arrangements with either the Liberals or the Center Party, rather than depend on the VPK (*Economist*, 21 September).

Foreign Affairs. The Soviet submarine issue, which had been a major one since the Soviet submarine went aground near a naval base at Karlskrona in October 1981, cooled down somewhat during 1985. The issue had been percolating since 1981 as news of sightings of Soviet submarines, real or imagined, was frequently before the public. A parliamentary inquiry after a 1982 incident revealed evidence that six Soviet submarines had been involved. This led to a strong protest from Palme to Moscow. During the past year, Palme and his new foreign minister, Sten Andersson, have been trying to improve relations with the Kremlin and thus have played down the submarine issue. This led thirteen senior Swedish naval officers to write letters to *Svenska Dagbladet* complaining about the continuing presence of Soviet submarines in Swedish waters and about the lack of funding for proper naval equipment to catch the alleged intruders (*Economist*, 16 November).

In his speech to the party congress on 2 January, Werner was somewhat oblique in his portrayal of the USSR's role in the world. Werner did criticize the Soviet intervention in Afghanistan, but he seemed to suggest that it was an exception in an otherwise peaceful policy. He defended the Soviet nuclear-arms buildup as a necessary response to the U.S. buildup. Werner passed over the Soviet role in Poland and other East European countries. He said that "the analysis of conditions of socialist countries must be a task for their own peoples—it is far too difficult for the VPK" (*Dagens Nyheter*, 3 January).

International Party Contacts. Although the Soviets were not harshly criticized at the Twenty-seventh Congress, there were also no official representatives from the Soviet Union (who are normally invited to attend). There were, however, many Soviet observers in the press gallery. Only the Nordic "fraternal" parties were invited to the congress. Even members of the embattled Stalinist party minority from Finland were not invited (*Dagens Nyheter*, 3 January). Tass (1 January) and *Neues Deutschland* (2 January) did report messages of formal greetings from the Soviet Union and the German Democratic Republic, respectively, to the congress.

VPK party secretary Kvist had a meeting with Ji Pengfei, member of the Standing Committee of the Chinese Communist Party, in Beijing on 24 June. The VPK also participated in a meeting of West European communist parties in Paris on 12–13 June. The meeting focused on analysis of the crisis of the communist parties in each country (*L'Humanité*, 22 January).

Rival Communist Groups. The pro-Soviet Communist Workers' Party (APK), which was founded in 1977, decided to withdraw from the elections less than one month before the date of the election. APK leader Rolf Hagel said that it was important not to split the socialist vote, which would result in a right-wing victory. In the 1982 election the APK received 5,877 votes, or less than 0.1 percent of all votes in the election. This was half the 1979 figure (*Dagens Nyheter*, 16 August). In June, Hagel met in Sofia, Bulgaria, with Milko Balev, secretary of the Central Committee of the Bulgarian Communist Party (*JPRS-EPS*, 23 July).

Peter Grothe
Monterey Institute of International Studies

Switzerland

Population. 6,512,000
Party. Swiss Labor Party (Partei der Arbeit der Schweiz/Parti suisse du travail/Partito Svizzero del Lavoro; PdAS)
Founded. 1921; outlawed 1940; re-established 1944
Membership. 4,500 (estimated)
General Secretary. Armand Magnin
Honorary President. Jean Vincent
Politburo. 14 members
Secretariat. 5 members
Central Committee. 50 members
Status. Legal
Last Congress. Twelfth, 21–22 May 1983
Last Election. 1983, 0.9 percent, 1 of 200 seats
Auxiliary Organizations. Communist Youth League of Switzerland (KVJS), Marxist Student League, Swiss Women's Organization for Peace and Progress, Swiss Peace Movement, Swiss–Soviet Union Society, Swiss-Cuban Society, Central Sanitaire Swiss
Publications. *Voix Ouvrière* (Geneva), weekly, circulation 8,000 copies; *Vorwärts* (Basel), weekly, circulation 6,000 copies; *Il Lavatore*, Italian-language edition; *Zunder*, KVJS organ

Switzerland has three communist parties of some significance: PdAS, with most of its followers in the western part of the country; the Progressive Organizations Switzerland (POCH), which replaced its former Marxist-Leninist ideological concepts with those of the Greens; and the Trotskyist Socialist Workers' Party (Sozialistische Arbeiterpartei/Parti Socialiste ouvrière; SAP), which is active only in some urban centers. During 1985 these parties lost influence, as demonstrated in the substantial loss of votes in cantonal and municipal elections. The Social Democratic Party of Switzerland (SPS) also suffered considerable election losses. Left-extremist SPS members gained greater influence within the party leadership, causing a decline in the following of the traditionalist trade unions (*Schweizerisches Ostinstitut, Links in der Schweiz—Informationen fur 1984/85*, letter to author, November).

The pro-Soviet PdAS is the oldest of the communist parties in Switzerland. It was founded on 5 March 1921 as the Swiss Communist Party. The party was outlawed in 1940 and re-established on 15 October 1944 under its present name. The PdAS is in a deep crisis as a result of further election defeats in 1985 after having lost two of its three seats in the lower house (*Nationalrat*) in the 1983 federal elections. In the 13 October elections in canton of Geneva, the party lost two seats of the ten it had previously held; it polled 8.2 percent of the vote in 1985 as compared to 10.4 percent in 1981 (*Neue Züricher Zeitung [NZZ]*, 14 October). A worse defeat were the municipal elections in Lausanne on 27 October. The PdAS, once the strongest party in the city parliament, lost all of its eight seats; it received 4.65 percent of the 1985 vote as compared to 7.3 percent in 1981 (*NZZ*, 30 October).

There are several reasons for the decline of the party. The PdAS never openly rejected the Soviet interventions in Berlin, Hungary, Czechoslovakia, Poland, and Afghanistan. The PdAS's close relations with the Italian Communist Party were gradually replaced by those with the French party. Another reason was the inability of the party to replace its aging leadership: the leader of the canton of Waadt is 75-year-old André Muret; the secretary general of the party, Armand Magnin, is 64. In 1969 about one hundred young intellectuals left the party and founded the revolutionary Marxist League, thus depriving the PdAS of its future intellectual leadership. Yet probably the main reason for the crisis is the party's failure to adjust to the sociological revolution of the recent decades. The Communists still address themselves with the old class-struggle vocabulary to the "working class" and the "proletariat," whereas the Swiss employees, with an increasing number employed in the service industries, have aspired to be part of the middle class (*NZZ*, 2 October 1984).

The PdAS maintained its relations with fraternal parties. The party participated in the Paris meeting of the communist parties of capitalist Europe on 12–13 June (*L'Humanité*, 22 June; *JPRS-WER*, 85-064, 7 August). Honorary president of the PdAS, Jean Vincent, conferred in Beijing on 21 June with Hu Yaobang, secretary general of the Chinese Communist Party (Beijing, *Xinhua*, 21 June; *FBIS*, 25 June).

The POCH was founded in 1972 by student dissidents from thc PdAS who rejected the party's adherence to the world communist movement and the sterile policies of the old party. In spite of POCH's emphasis on its independence, it supports Soviet policies. During the founding phase, the Basel branch held the leadership position. Since 1973 the party's Secretariat has been in Zürich. Total membership is about 10,000, of which 65 percent are women. It publishes the weekly *POCH-Zeitung* with a circulation of about 10,000 copies.

POCH's new policies along Green Party lines proved, at least in the short run, successful. Its aggressive campaign style attracted support from the academic professions and from youth. In the 1983 federal elections, POCH increased its representation from two to three seats (*Schweizerisches Ostinstitut*, November).

A POCH subsidiary, the Organization for Women's Affairs, is the most important women's group in Switzerland. It emerged from Progressive Women Switzerland. The organization's magazine is the weekly *Emanzipation*. Other organizations affiliated with POCH are the Solidarity Committee for Africa, Asia, and Latin America and the Swiss Society for Social Health.

The SAP adopted its new name at the Fifth Congress of the Revolutionary Marxist League in 1980. The league was founded in 1969 by a group of young Trotskyists who left the PdAS. The SAP is the Swiss section of the Fourth International (Trotskyist) with headquarters in Brussels, and it advocates the revolutionary class struggle in production centers. It aims at the eventual control of enterprises, a policy similar to former revolutionary syndicalism. Its leading theoretician is Fritz Osterwalder, and membership is about 6,000. The youth organization of the SAP, *Maulwurf* (Mole), was dissolved in the late 1970s but reactivated in 1983 as the Revolutionary Socialist Youth Organization (RSJ). The SAP obtained 0.4 percent of the votes in the 1983 federal elections and has an insignificant number of elected representatives at local levels (*Schweizerisches Ostinstitut*, November). SAP publications includes *Bresche* (German), *La Brèche* (French), *Rosso* (Italian), and *Roia* (Spanish).

The SAP is quite active in the anti–nuclear power plant movement. In 1982 the party was instrumental in organizing the Group for a Switzerland Without Military (*Gruppe Schweiz ohne Armee*; GSoA). On 21 March the GSoA started collecting signatures for a referendum calling for the abolishment of the military. The goal is to obtain 100,000 signatures of eligible voters by September 1986 in order to place the referendum before the people (ibid.). The text of the referendum had been published on 12 March. Although that action is supported by the SAP, Swiss Peace Council, Soldiers' Committee, POCH, RSJ, Greens, and Jusos (Young Socialists) (*Tagesanzeiger*, 22 March), it is doubtful that it will succeed.

The SAP organized an Eastern Europe symposium in Bern (2–3 November) with the topic "Peace Movement and Solidarnosc: Alternatives to the Dictatorship of the Blocs?" (*Infotch, Information zur Neuen Politik*, October). Members of the SAP, PdAS, Greens, trade unions, and social organizations agreed on a "resistance list" of candidates for the forthcoming municipal elections in Zürich in 1986. As of November, about 100 persons had signed the appeal. Among them are representatives of several left radical committees such as the Central America Committee, Association of Concerned Parents, and students' groups (*Infotch*, November).

The Autonomous Socialist Party (Autonome Sozialistische Partei/Parti socialiste autonome/Partito Socialista Autonomo; PSA) is the outcome of a split within the Socialist Party of the canton of Tessin in 1960. Although the dissidents obtained majority support at the party congress in 1966, they were unable to assert themselves against the entrenched leadership and so founded the PSA in April 1969. Its membership is about 1,000 and its secretary general is Werner Carrobbio. The party considers itself an autonomous component of the world communist movement and rejects social democracy, Trotskyism, and spontaneity. In the federal elections in 1983, the PSA received 10 percent of the vote in Tessin, giving it one seat in the Nationalrat. This brought the strength of the PdAS/POCH/PSA parliamentary faction to five seats. The PSA is concerned that in the next elections it might lose its only seat, and it therefore indicated its readiness to merge with the SPS. However, the positive reaction of some SPS members to the proposed merger led to intraparty dissension and to the termination of further negotiations (*Schweizerisches Ostinstitut*, November). The PSA publishes *Politika Nuova*.

Other communist organizations, such as the Communist Party of Switzerland Marxist-Leninist (KPS/ML) and the Communist Organization–Labor Party, have shown no sign of activity during 1985 (ibid.).

The *Schweizerische Friedensbewegung* (SFB), the Swiss section of the World Peace Council that is controlled by the PdAS, was unable to organize mass demonstrations except the "Easter March" in the border region of Basel. About 2,000 demonstrators came from five countries (in 1983, about 12,000 demonstrators had participated in the march). The previously active feminist organization Women for Peace was dormant (ibid.).

The peace demonstrations at the Geneva Summit Conference in November between President Ronald Reagan and Soviet leader Mikhail Gorbachev drew about 10,000 persons. A great number of the participants came from the German part of Switzerland and from abroad. "Anti-imperialist" Turkish and Latin American groups advocating the "revolution of liberation" were especially articulate. Most of the demonstrators belonged to one of the many guest workers' groups and left-wing organizations. The Socialists and Communists were represented with about 500 persons. Petra Kelly, a Green party member of the German Bundestag, was among the main speakers (*NZZ*, 18 November).

The initiators and organizers of the Geneva "peace manifesto"—the left-pacifist Peace Committee (Comité Paix), the SFB, and the Swiss branch of the International Women's League for Peace and Freedom (IFFF), which has close ties to the SFB—were divided on the text of the appeal. The original proclamation contained the demand for the dissolution of both NATO and the Warsaw Pact. The PdAS, SFB, and IFFF published their own pro-Soviet appeal, which blamed the "imperialist West" for the arms race. The Swiss Peace Council and the SPS supported both appeals (*NZZ*, 16–17 November).

Some of the numerous left-radical and pacifist groups cooperated on several occasions. For example, at an address by NATO secretary general Lord Carrington on 25 June at the University of Zürich, an anti-NATO demonstration was sponsored by the GSoA Zürich, the Committee Against Isolation Confinement (KGI; the legal organization in Switzerland of the German terrorist Red Army Faction), the Group Switzerland-Philippines, the anti-imperialist ZH/BS, Latin American groups, the SAP, the RSJ, and the Frente Izquierda Revolucionaria (FIR) (*Infotch*, August).

There was also occasional cooperation between members of autonomous and terrorist groups and activists of communist parties and their youth organizations. An example of this is the Nicaragua/El Salvador–Committee Zürich, a close associate of the other Latin American committees. The "liberation front" FMLN/FDR maintains an office in Brussels. One of its seven representatives, Louis Alonso Enriques, is the delegate for Switzerland. As representative of the Commission de Solidaridad International (CSI), he participates at the meetings of the Zürich Committee (*Infotch*, March).

Anti-apartheid activists in Switzerland are organized in several groups, among them Fighting Africa (PAC/Maoist) and the Anti-Apartheid Movement (AAB; ANC-Moscow loyal). The Secretariat of the AAB is in Zürich at the Students' Center ("Junge europäische Schüler- und Studenteninitiative der Schweiz," *Rundbrief*, October).

Additional left-extremist publications are the left-radical *Wochen-Zeitung* (circulation about 10,000 copies), the monthly or quarterly *plädoyer* (Democratic Jurists), *Infrarot* (Jusos), and *Zeit-Dienst* (cadre paper of the left faction of the SPS). *Tell*, the monthly publication of the 68-Movement was terminated in April, and no replacement has been noted (*Schweizerisches Ostinstitut*, November).

No new information was available about the reactivated anarchist activities.

Eric Waldman
University of Calgary

Turkey

Population. 51,259,000
Party. Communist Party of Turkey (TCP)
Founded. 1920
Membership. Negligible
Secretary General. Haydar Kutlu
Leading Bodies. No data
Status. Illegal
Last Congress. Fifth, October or November 1983
Last Election. N/a
Auxiliary Organizations. No data
Publications. *Atilim* (according to Voice of the Turkish Communist Party, this was a monthly publication slated to become weekly; no other information is available).

The year was politically a relatively quiet one in Turkey, although the trends of previous years continued. Political parties continued their attempts to gain advantageous positions in succession to the banned parties of the pre-1980 era. The dominant position of the ruling Motherland Party, led by Prime Minister Turgut Ozal, remained fundamentally unshaken despite charges of misconduct and minor cabinet reshuffling. The opposition parties made efforts to overcome the anomalous split between those represented in the parliament and those excluded.

An agreement was achieved to merge the relatively weak Populist Party with the stronger, extraparliamentary Social Democratic Party (SODEP). There were reports of a similar development involving the conservative Nationalist Democracy Party with the extraparliamentary True Path Party. The last-named party is informally backed by former prime minister Suleyman Demirel. His former rival, Bulent Ecevit, continued to stir the boiling pot on the political left through the activities of his wife in organizing a new party to be known as the Democratic Left Party. It was widely believed that the Ecevits' efforts would have a spoiler effect, since they threatened to split the democratic left rather than unify it.

New elections, which might test the relative strength of these political formations, are still as much as three years in the future. The most recent local elections, held in the spring of 1984, had confirmed the dominant position of the Motherland Party and the strength of SODEP as the second party.

Economic growth and stability continued to be the major testing ground for the Ozal regime. The record in 1985 was mixed. While exports had grown substantially during 1984 (by 24.5 percent), imports had also increased, leaving a large negative trade balance. Inflation continued to exceed targets, and foreign investment failed to come up to expectations. Yet the Gross Domestic Product did continue to grow, and the regime's efforts to privatize some prominent public enterprises (such as the Bosphorus Bridge and the Keban hydro-electric dam) through the sale of public shares were apparently successful. Nonetheless, critics continued to charge that the Friedmanite policies of the regime were increasing the gap between the rich and the poor.

Internal security remained a sensitive issue for the regime. Martial law was dismantled in stages until, late in the year, there were only nine southeastern provinces still affected (*NYT*, 20 November). The lifting of martial law did not mean a return to complete normality, however. A number of provinces in which martial law was lifted remained under an emergency regime. In addition, a new law was passed that granted the police enhanced powers to detain and interrogate suspects and that liberalized the regulations governing their use of armed force and general powers of surveillance. Moreover, the maintenance of a martial-law regime in the southeast reflected the continuation of guerrilla activities of Kurdish dissidents ("separatists" in official Turkish parlance) in that border region. According to the minister of the interior, between August 1984 and September 1985 there were 132 incidents in the southeast that resulted in 133 deaths, 59 of which were members of government security forces (*FBIS*, 21 October). He also stated that 108 "bandits" had been killed and 442 captured in the course of these incidents. He claimed that 650 "bandits" were receiving training in "certain neighboring countries" (presumably referring to Syria, Iraq, and Iran) but added that security forces operating under martial law were continuing their efforts to counter these groups; the forces were reinforced with new troops and "nighttime observation equipment." Contacts with the concerned neighboring governments were also under way (ibid.). Earlier in the year Foreign Minister Halefoglu had visited Baghdad, where he signed a cross-border agreement with Iraq allowing each of the two governments to penetrate the territory of the other in pursuit of guerrillas up to a depth of five kilometers for a maximum of three days without prior notification (*Keesing's*, March, p. 33497).

The TCP has been illegal for almost its entire 65-year history. It is therefore extremely difficult to accurately trace its political activities. The Turkish authorities almost invariably accuse those who are arrested and tried on charges of subversion or sedition as extreme leftists or Communists—save for those exceptional cases when militant right-wing extremists run afoul of the law. Conversely, the TCP accuses the authorities of anticommunism, as though it were indeed the main target of such prosecutions.

Turkish relations with the governments of the communist world were reasonably good during 1985. Soviet prime minister Nikolai Tikhonov paid an official state visit to Ankara in December 1984, the first since Kosygin's visit of 1975. Although agreements to enhance trade were signed on this occasion, the failure to agree on a final communiqué signified continuing political differences.

There was also considerable unhappiness in Turkey over the treatment of the Muslim Turkish minority in the neighboring Soviet satellite of Bulgaria. Ethnic Turks are estimated to account for 10 percent of the population of Bulgaria. In the recent past, large numbers of these Turks have been allowed to settle in Turkey by mutual agreement of the two governments. It seems the Bulgarian government has put renewed pressure on those who remained to give up their ethnic identity. One hundred people reportedly died as the result of ensuing clashes. These incidents aroused public anger in Turkey, leading to a mass meeting reportedly attended by 40,000 in Istanbul. The Turkish government recalled its ambassador from Sofia and pressed for a high-level meeting to begin discussions for a new accord regulating migration between the two countries. Bulgaria rejected this proposal and denied allegations concerning mistreatment of the Turkish minority.

TCP broadcasts (on the clandestine wavelengths of Our Radio and the Voice of the TCP) maintained a steady stream of comment on these and other developments. The failure of the Tikhonov visit to produce more notable results was blamed on imperialist opposition. Turkish complaints about alleged persecution by the Bulgarian regime was dismissed as a U.S.-inspired reactionary campaign. By contrast, a formal meeting between TCP secretary general Haydar Kutlu and Bulgarian chief Zhivkov occurred late in July without a hint regarding these incidents.

The Voice of the TCP reported the results of a trial of its own members by the Turkish government, under the "fascist" Articles 141 and 142 of the Penal Code that outlaw communism and associated ideologies. Two hundred sentences of up to seventeen years were allegedly meted out. It was also reported that members of the outlawed Nationalist Action Party, an extreme right-wing group led by Colonel Alpaslan Turkes, had been freed and allowed to assume important government positions (*FBIS*, 8 May).

In February, Our Radio called for early elections under conditions of full freedom in Turkey, claiming that there would be no other way to bring an end to the reactionary Evren-Ozal "dictatorship." In May, Our Radio reported a statement issued by the TCP Central Committee at its fourth plenum; the statement noted that "though its strength is declining, the fascist dictatorship continues to survive. The movement for democracy is expanding, and though the forces opposing the Evren-Ozal dictatorship have not retreated in the face of all the pressures and intrigues, they have not yet reached the strength that will allow the dictatorship to be overthrown or democracy to be achieved." The statement specifically called for a general political amnesty, restoration of "all democratic rights and liberties," "a national democratic constitution," and "an intensification of the peace movement's struggle against the extension of the joint defense cooperation agreement with the United States and the existence of U.S. bases in our country." The statement promised to continue "the struggle for an early election" as well (ibid., 9 May).

The new police law was denounced as "fascism without martial law." In a joint statement, the TCP and the Iraq Communist Party attacked the cross-border agreement between the two countries and strongly identified with the Kurdish groups whose activities were the target. The anti-Kurdish drive by the two governments was alleged to have the backing of the United States and NATO (*FBIS*, 27 June).

On the 65th anniversary of the party in September, the Voice of the TCP broadcast an interview with Kutlu, in the course of which he set forth the following opinions: a merger between SODEP and the Populist Party would be pointless unless it included all the forces of the left; organized labor also required unification, since Turk Is—the single remaining labor federation—engaged in collaboration with the government; former military officers in the Evren regime were corrupt; and secret agreements underlie construction of military bases in eastern Turkey. Moreover, Kutlu characterized these bases as planned outposts for attacks on the Soviet Union and Middle Eastern neighbors of Turkey. He alleged that there were plans to establish a laser base on Mt. Ararat, overlooking the Turkish border with Iran and the Soviet Union, as part of the U.S. Strategic Defense Initiative.

Frank Tachau
University of Illinois at Chicago

Select Bibliography, 1984–1985

GENERAL

Adamek, Josef. *Centrally Planned Economies: Economic Overview 1984*. New York: Conference Board, 1984. 72 pp.

Adamson, Walter L. *Marx and the Disillusionment of Marxism*. Berkeley: University of California Press, 1985. 258 pp.

Avineri, Shlomo. *Moses Hess, Prophet of Communism and Zionism*. New York: New York University Press, 1985. 266 pp.

Baier, Lothar, et al. *Die Linke neu denken: acht Lockerungen*. Berlin: Wagenbach, 1984. 157 pp.

Baranski, Zygmunt G., and John R. Short. *Developing Contemporary Marxism*. London: Macmillan, 1985. 308 pp.

Beetham, David, comp. *Marxists in Face of Fascism*. Totowa, N.J.: Barnes and Noble, 1984. 381 pp.

Benton, Ted. *The Rise and Fall of Structural Marxism: Althusser and His Influence*. New York: St. Martin's Press, 1984. 259 pp.

Berezovaia, L. G. *Partiia bolshevikov i demokraticheskaia intelligentsiia v gody novogo revoliutsionnogo podema*. Moscow: "Vysshaia shkola," 1985. 76 pp.

Bertsch, Gary K. *Power and Policy in Communist Systems*. 3rd ed. New York: Wiley, 1985. 181 pp.

Bethlen, Istvan, and Ivan Völgyes, eds. *Europe and the Superpowers: Political, Economic and Military Policies in the 1980s*. Boulder, Colo.: Westview Press, 1985. 164 pp.

Bideleux, Robert. *Communism and Development*. New York: Methuen, 1985. 313 pp.

Bien, Joseph. *History, Revolution and Human Nature: Marx's Philosophical Anthropology*. Amsterdam: B. R. Gruner, 1984. 228 pp.

Billingsley, Lloyd. *The Generation That Knew Not Joseph: A Critique of Marxism and the Religious Left*. Portland, Oreg.: Multnomah Press, 1985. 217 pp.

Bodrova, Valentina, and Richard Anker, eds. *Working Women in Socialist Countries*. Geneva: International Labour Office, 1985. 234 pp.

Brown, Archie, ed. *Political Culture and Communist Studies*. Basingstoke, Hampshire: Macmillan, 1984. 211 pp.

Cameron, Kenneth Neill. *Marxism: The Science of Society*. South Hadley, Mass.: Bergin and Garvey, 1985. 222 pp.

Chirkin, V. E. *Revoliutsionno-demokraticheskoe gosudarstvo sovremennosti*. Moscow: Nauka, 1984. 295 pp.

Chukanov, Olimp A., ed. *Khoziaistvennyi mekhanizm v stranakh-chlenakh SEV: spravochnik*. Moscow: Politizdat, 1984. 299 pp.

Coker, Christopher. *NATO, the Warsaw Pact and Africa*. New York: St. Martin's Press, 1985. 302 pp.

Colletti, Lucio. *Déclin du marxisme*. Paris: PUF, 1984. 176 pp.

Conte, Arthur. *Les Dictateurs du vingtième siècle*. Paris: Laffont, 1984. 524 pp.

Crewe, Ivar, and David Denver, eds. *Electoral Change in Western Democracies*. London: Croom-Helm, Ltd., 1985. 438 pp.

Crozier, Brian; Drew Middleton; and Jeremy Murray-Brown. *This War Called Peace*. New York: Universe Books, 1985. 378 pp.

Fedorov, Igor F. *Tverdost i chistota partii*. Moscow: Politizdat, 1985. 94 pp.

Fedoseev, P. N., et al. *Nauchnyi kommunizm: Uchebnik dlia vuzov*. 7th ed. Moscow: Politizdat, 1985. 400 pp.

Fernandez Buey, Francisco. *Contribución a la critica del Marxismo Cientificista*. Barcelona: Edición de la Universidad de Barcelona, 1984. 346 pp.

First Congress of the Communist International: Proceedings, Resolutions and Related Materials. New York: Monad Press, 1985. 450 pp.

Galkin, A. A., chief ed. *Rabochii klass v mirovom revoliutsionnom protsesse*. Moscow: Nauka, 1985. 372 pp.

Gastil, Raymond D. *Freedom in the World: Political Rights and Civil Liberties, 1984–1985*. Westport, Conn.: Greenwood Press, 1985. 438 pp.

Gumpel, Werner, ed. *Das Leben in kommunistischen Staaten: Symposium*. Cologne: Bachem, 1985. 215 pp.

Havriliuk, O. Iu. *Freedom of Conscience in a Socialist Society*. Kiev: Polividav Ukraini, 1984. 138 pp.

Hirszowicz, Maria. *Coercion and Control in Communist Society*. New York: St. Martin's Press, 1985. 256 pp.

Honecker, Erich. *Arbeitermacht zum Wohle des Volkes*. East Berlin: Dietz Verlag, 1984. 406 pp.

Huntington, Samuel P., and Joseph S. Nye, Jr., eds. *Global Dilemmas*. Lanham, Md.: University Press of America, 1985. 307 pp.

Ingersoll, David E., and Richard K. Matthews. *The Philosophic Roots of Modern Ideology*. Englewood Cliffs, N.J.: Prentice Hall, 1986. 286 pp.

Jay, Martin. *Marxism and Totality*. Berkeley: University of California Press, 1984. 576 pp.

Kapitonov, I. V. *Izbrannyie rechi i stat'i*. Moscow: Politizdat, 1985. 528 pp.

Keller, Theodore. *Marx's Truth and Its Consequences*. Daly City, Calif.: Prismatique Publications, 1985. 297 pp.

Kintner, William R. *The Front Is Everywhere: Militant Communism in Action*. Lanham, Md.: University Press of America, 1984. 276 pp.

Kosta, H. G. Jiri. *Wirtschaftssysteme des realen Sozialismus: Proben und Alternativen*. Cologne: Bund-Verlag, 1984. 268 pp.

Krasin, Iu. A., et al. *Revoliutsionnyi protsess: Natsional'noe i internatsional'noe*. Moscow: Mysl', 1985. 341 pp.

Labica, Georges. *Le Marxisme-leninisme: elements pour une critique*. Paris: B. Huisman, 1984. 142 pp.

Laurent, Eric. *La Corde pour les prendre . . .: relations entre milieux d'affaires occidentaux et regimes communistes de 1917 à nos jours*. Paris: Fayard, 1985. 305 pp.

Lavigne, Marie L. *Economie internationale des pays socialistes*. Paris: A. Colin, 1985. 254 pp.

Das Leben in den kommunistischen Staaten. Cologne: Hans Martin Schleyer, 1985. 215 pp.

Login, V. T., chief ed. *Opyt voin zashchity sotsialisticheskogo otechestva: Istoriko-teoreticheskoe issledovanie*. Moscow: Nauka, 1985. 256 pp.

Low, Konrad, ed. *Marxismus-Quellenlexikon*. Cologne: Kölner Universitätsverlag, 1985. 352 pp.

———. *Warum fasziniert Kommunismus? Eine systematische Untersuchung*. 4th enl. & rev. ed. Cologne: Deutscher Instituts-Verlag, 1985. 380 pp.

Lukes, Steven. *Marxism and Morality*. Oxford: Clarendon Press, 1985. 163 pp.

Marcellin, Raymond. *La guerre politique*. Paris: Plon, 1985. 250 pp.

Maresca, John J. *To Helsinki: The Conference on Security and Cooperation, 1973–1975*. Durham, N.C.: Duke University Press, 1985. 292 pp.

McCrea, Barbara P.; Jack C. Plano; and George Klein. *The Soviet and East European Political Dictionary*. Santa Barbara, Calif.: ABC-Clio, 1984. 367 pp.

Miniushev, F. I. *Fenomen sotsialisticheskoi lichnosti*. Moscow: Izd-vo Moskovskogo universiteta, 1985. 187 pp.

Muromtseva, L. P. *Deiatelnost' kommunisticheskoi partii po ukrepleniiu mestnykh sovetov (1946–1950 gg)*. Moscow: Izd-vo Moskovskogo universiteta, 1985. 133 pp.

Nauchnyi kommunizm: A Dictionary of Scientific Communism. Moscow: Progress Publishers, 1984. 288 pp.

Olekh, L. G. *Nauchnyi kommunizm: predmet i metod*. Edited by V. I. Boiko. Novosibirsk: Nauka sibirskoe otdelenie, 1985. 205 pp.

Parrott, Bruce, ed. *Trade, Technology and Soviet-American Relations*. Bloomington: Indiana University Press, 1985. 394 pp.

Ra'anan, Uri, et al. *Third World Marxist-Leninist Regimes*. Washington, D.C.: Pergamon-Brassey's, 1985. 130 pp.

Rockman, Bert A., and Ronald H. Linden, eds. *Elite Studies and Communist Politics: Essays in Memory of Carl Beck*. Pittsburgh, Pa.: University of Pittsburgh Press, Center for International Studies, 1984. 352 pp.

Rutkevich, Michael. *Towards Social Homogeneity*. Moscow: Progress, 1984. 247 pp.

Rydenfelt, Sven. *A Pattern for Failure: Socialist Economies in Crisis*. San Diego: Harcourt Brace Jovanovich, 1984. 175 pp.

Sazonov, V. V. *On the "Manifesto of the Communist Party" of Marx and Engels*. Moscow: Progress, 1984. 103 pp.

Schaff, Adam. *Wohin führt der Weg?* Munich: Europaverlag, 1985. 185 pp.

Schlacht, Richard. *Alienation*. Lanham, Md.: University Press of America, 1984. 356 pp.

Schroeder, Friedrich-Christian; Boris Meissner; and Klaus Westen, eds. *Kontinuität und Wandel in der kommunitschen Staatstheorie*. Berlin: Verlag Arno Spitz, 1985. 151 pp.

Seleznev, Leonid. *What Is Scientific Communism?* Moscow: Progress, 1985. 173 pp.

Shaw, Martin, ed. *Marxist Sociology Revisited: A Critical Assessment*. Basingstoke, Hampshire: Macmillan, 1985. 276 pp.

Solovev, A. I. *Avtoritet kommunista*. Moscow: Politizdat, 1984. 141 pp.

Sowell, Thomas. *Marxism: Philosophy and Economics*. New York: William Morrow and Co., 1984. 281 pp.

Staar, Richard F., ed. *1985 Yearbook on International Communist Affairs*. Stanford, Calif.: Hoover Institution Press, 1985. 578 pp.

Suvorova, M. I. *Kritika Kominternom revizionistskikh vzgliadov na ekonomiku sotsializma*. Moscow: Izd-vo Moskovskogo universiteta, 1985. 114 pp.

Terzuolo, Eric R. *Red Adriatic: The Communist Parties of Italy and Yugoslavia*. Boulder, Colo.: Westview Press, 1985. 255 pp.

Thobaben, Robert G., and Nicholas Piediscalzi. *Three Worlds of Christian-Marxist Encounters*. Philadelphia, Pa.: Fortress Press, 1985. 220 pp.

Tiersky, Ronald S. *Ordinary Stalinism: Democratic Centralism and the Question of Communist Political Development*. London: Allen and Unwin, 1985. 209 pp.

Volkov, F. M., and L. Novotnyi, eds. *Sistema kommunisticheskogo vospitaniia studentov v uchebnom protsesse*. Moscow: Izd-vo Moskovskogo universiteta, 1984. 190 pp.

Zagladin, Vadim V., ed. *Mirovoe kommunisticheskoe dvizhenie*. 2nd rev. ed. Moscow: Politizdat, 1984. 432 pp.

Zinoviev, Aleksandr. *The Reality of Communism*. 1st American edition. New York: Schocken Books, 1984. 259 pp.

AFRICA

Angolan Women Building the Future: From National Liberation to Women's Emancipation. London: Zed Books, 1984. 151 pp.

Asiwaju, A. I., ed. *Partitioned Africans: Ethnic Relations Across Africa's International Boundaries*. London: C. Hurst, 1984. 45 pp.

Bolton, Dianne. *Nationalization: A Road to Socialism? The Lessons of Tanzania*. London: Zed Books, 1985. 178 pp.

Burness, Don, ed. *Wanasema: Conversation with African Writers*. Athens: Ohio University, Center for International Studies, 1985. 95 pp.

Calvocoressi, Peter. *Independent Africa and the World*. London: Longman, 1985. 151 pp.

Carter, Gwendolen M., and Patrick O'Meara, eds. *African Independence: The First Twenty-five Years*. Bloomington: Indiana University Press, 1985. 364 pp.

Cilliers, J. K. *Counter-Insurgency in Rhodesia*. London: Croom Helm, 1985. 266 pp.

Davies, Robert H. *The Struggle for South Africa: A Reference Guide to Movements, Organizations and Institutions*. London: Zed Books, 1984. 2 vols.
Donham, Donald L. *Work and Power in Maale, Ethiopia*. Ann Arbor, Mich.: UMI Research Press, 1985. 196 pp.
Firebrace, James, and Stuart Holland. *Never Kneel Down: Drought, Development and Liberation in Eritrea*. Trenton, N.J.: Red Sea Press, 1985. 191 pp.
Fituni, Leonid L. *Narodnaia Respublika Angola: spravochnik*. Moscow: Nauka, 1985. 204 pp.
Freund, Bill. *The Making of Contemporary Africa: The Development of African Society since 1800*. Bloomington: University of Indiana Press, 1984. 357 pp.
Gabou, Alexis. *Les Constitutions congolaises*. Paris: Librarie générale du droit et de jurisprudence, 1984. 547 pp.
Gavrilov, N. I. *Strany severnoi Afriki: Problemy politicheskogo, ekonomicheskogo i sotsial'nogo razvitiia*. Moscow: Nauka, 1984. 224 pp.
Gromyko, A. A., chief ed. *Afrika: strany sotsialisticheskoi orientatsii v revoliutsionnom protsesse*. Moscow: Nauka, 1984. 272 pp.
Gutkind, Peter C. W., and Immanuel Wallerstein, eds. *Political Economy of Contemporary Africa*. Beverly Hills, Calif.: Sage Publications, 1985. 344 pp.
Harrison, David. *The White Tribe of Africa: South Africa in Perspective*. Berkeley: University of California Press, 1984. 310 pp.
The Implications of Ideological and Institutional Change in Angola and Mozambique, 1974–1984. Stellenbosch: University of Stellenbosch, Institute for the Study of Marxism, 1984. 1 vol. (photocopy of typed conference papers)
Jewsiewicki, B., ed. *Etat indépendant du Congo, Congo belge, République démocratique du Congo, République du Zaire*. Quebec: SAFI, 1984. 162 pp.
Jouve, Edmond. *L'Organisation de l'unité africaine*. Paris: Presses Universitaires de France, 1984. 284 pp.
Kasfir, Nelson, ed. *State and Class in Africa*. London: Cass, 1984. 125 pp.
Koshukin, Nikolai D. *Revolutionary Democracy in Africa: Its Ideology and Policy*. Moscow: Progress, 1985. 166 pp.
Machel, Samora. *Samora Machel, an African Revolutionary: Selected Speeches and Writings*. Edited by Barry Munslow. London: Zed Press, 1985. 201 pp.
Maksimov, S. L., and L. S. Stoklitskaia. *Naimenee razvitye strany Afriki: problemy i perspektivy*. Moscow: Nauka, 1984. 120 pp.
Malwal, Bona. *The Sudan: A Second Challenge to Nationhood*. New York: Thornton Books, 1985. 42 pp.
Mandela, Winnie. *Part of My Soul Went with Him*. Edited by Anne Benjamin. New York: Norton, 1985. 164 pp.
Meredith, Martin. *The First Dance of Freedom: Black Africa in the Post-War Era*. New York: Harper, 1985. 412 pp.
Moseiko, Aida N. *Ideologiia v stranakh Tropicheskoi Afriki: traditsii i sovremennost*. Moscow: Nauka, 1985. 21 pp.
Nelson, Harold D., ed. *Mozambique: A Country Study*. Washington, D.C.: American University Foreign Area Studies, 1984. 342 pp.
Ngara, Emmanuel. *Art and Ideology in the African Novel: A Study of the Influence of Marxism on African Writing*. London: Heinemann, 1985. 126 pp.
Nkomo, Mokubung O. *Student Culture and Activism in Black South African Universities: The Roots of Resistance*. Westport, Conn.: Greenwood Press, 1984. 209 pp.
Nzouankeu, Jacques Mariel. *Les partis politiques sénégalais*. Dakar: Editions Clairafrique, 1984. 146 pp.
Pike, Henry R. *A History of Communism in South Africa*. Germiston, South Africa: Christian Mission International of South Africa, 1985. 601 pp.
Ranger, Terence. *Peasant Consciousness and Guerrilla War in Zimbabwe*. London: James Currey, Ltd., 1985. 377 pp.
Saul, John S., ed. *A Difficult Road: The Transition to Socialism in Mozambique*. New York: Monthly Review Press, 1985. 420 pp.

Schatzberg, Michael G., ed. *The Political Economy of Zimbabwe*. New York: Praeger, 1984. 288 pp.
Schwab, Peter. *Ethiopia: Politics, Economics, and Society*. Boulder, Colo.: Lynn Rienner, 1985. 134 pp.
Thompson, Virginia, and Richard Adloff. *Historical Dictionary of the People's Republic of the Congo*. 2nd ed. Metuchen, N.J.: Scarecrow Press, 1984. 239 pp.
Tordoff, William. *Government and Politics in Africa*. Bloomington: Indiana University Press, 1985. 352 pp.
Voll, John Obert, and Sara Potts Voll. *The Sudan: Unity and Diversity in a Multicultural State*. Boulder, Colo.: Westview Press, 1985. 178 pp.
The Whole Truth about SWAPO: Idealistic Christians and Heroes of Freedom and Justice? Or Instruments of International Communist Aggression? Pleasantville, N.Y.: American Society for the Defense of Tradition, Family and Property, 1984. 66 pp.

THE AMERICAS

Alfonso, Pablo M. *Cuba, Castro y los católicos: del humanismo revolucionario al marxismo totalitario*. Miami, Fla.: Ediciones Hispanamerican Books, 1985. 228 pp.
Arevalo, Oscar. *El camino de los comunistas*. Buenos Aires: Anteo, 1984. 33 pp.
———. *Lucha de ideas y organizacion para la lucha*. Buenos Aires: Anteo, 1984. 123 pp.
Arismendi, Rodney. *Palabras a la Union de la Juventud Comunista del Uruguay en Argentina*. Buenos Aires: Centro Artigas de Residentes Uruguayos en Argentina, 1984. 47 pp.
Arnaudo, Florencio José. *Liberalismo, marxismo, socialcristianismo, tres visiones del mundo*. Buenos Aires: Editoreal Pleamar, 1984. 254 pp.
Barrenechea, Ramiro. *Dos proyectos en pugna: el poder las masas, o sin masas ni poder*. La Paz: Partido Comunista Boliviana, 1984. 80 pp.
Benjamin, Medea; Joseph Collins; and Michael Scott. *No Free Lunch: Food and Revolution in Cuba Today*. San Francisco: Institute for Food and Development Policy, 1984. 240 pp.
Berryman, Philip. *Inside Central America*. New York: Pantheon, 1985. 142 pp.
Bessarab, Maiia. *Strana moego serdtsa: povest o Dzhone Ride*. Moscow: Sov. pisatel, 1984. 286 pp.
Bolivia. Partido Comunista de Bolivia. *Estatuto organico del Partido Comunista de Bolivia*. La Paz: Unidad, 1985. 21 pp.
Botey, Aná Maria, and Rodolfo Cisneros. *La Crisis de las 1929 y la fundacion del Partido Comunista de Costa Rica*. San Jose: Editorial Costa Rica, 1984. 144 pp.
Burgas, Miguel. *Miguel Burgas, el primer diputado comunista*. Buenos Aires: Anteo, 1984. 92 pp.
Cabezas, Omar. *Fire from the Mountain: The Making of a Sandinista*. New York: Crown, 1985. 233 pp. (published by Cuba in Spanish, 1982, 255 pp.)
Calvert, Peter. *Guatemala: A Nation in Turmoil*. Boulder, Colo.: Westview Press, 1985. 239 pp.
Cheroni, Alcion. *Los partidos marxistas en el Uruguay desde sus origenes hasta 1973*. Montevideo: Centro Latinoamericano de Economia Humana, 1984. 23 pp.
Christian, Shirley. *Nicaragua: Revolution in the Family*. New York: Random House, 1985. 337 pp.
Coggiola Osvaldo. *Historia del trotskismo argentino (1929–1960)*. Buenos Aires: Centro Editor de Americana Latina, 1985. 159 pp.
Cuello H., Jose Israel. *El Partido Comunista Dominicano*. Santo Domingo: Ediciones de Taller, 1984. 296 pp.
D'Angelo, Edward, ed. *Cuban and North American Marxism*. Amsterdam: B. R. Gruner, 1984. 214 pp.
Davis, Nathaniel. *The Last Two Years of Salvador Allende*. Ithaca, N.Y.: Cornell University Press, 1985. 480 pp.
Dias, Giocondo. *Una alternativa democratica para crise brasileira: encontro nacional pela legalide do PCB*. São Paulo: Novos Romos, 1984. 109 pp.
Dolsen, James H. *Bucking the Ruling Class*. The author, 1984. 128 pp.
Fauriol, Georges, ed. *Latin American Insurgencies*. Washington, D.C.: Georgetown University, Center for Strategic and International Studies and The National Defense University, 1985. 214 pp.
Foster, Charles R., and Albert Valdman, eds. *Haiti—Today and Tomorrow*. New York: University Press of America, 1984. 389 pp.

Garthoff, Raymond L. *Détente and Confrontation: American-Soviet Relations from Nixon to Reagan*. Washington, D.C.: Brookings Institution, 1985. 1,147 pp.

Green, Gil. *Cold War Fugitive: A Personal Story of the McCarthy Years*. New York: International Publishers, 1984. 275 pp.

Grinevich, E. A., and B. I. Gvosdarev. *Kuba v mirovoi politike*. Moscow: Mezhdunarodnye otnosheniia, 1984. 576 pp.

Grossman, Karl. *Nicaragua: America's New Vietnam?* London: Permanent Press, 1984. 227 pp.

Hall, Gus. *Fighting Racism: Selected Writings*. New York: International Publishers, 1985. 304 pp.

Judson, C. Fred. *Cuba and the Revolutionary Myth*. Boulder, Colo.: Westview Press, 1984. 294 pp.

Keraly, Hugues. *S.O.S. Nicaragua: voyage au pays du communisme à langage chrétien*. Grez-en-Bouere: Dominique Martin Morin, 1985. 133 pp.

Key Sanchez, Fernando. *Fundacion del Partido Comunista de Venezuela*. 2nd enl. ed. Caracas: Fondo Editorial "Carlos Aponte," 1984. 94 pp.

Kivisto, Peter. *Immigrant Socialists in the United States: The Case of the Finns and the Left*. Rutherford, N.J.: Farleigh Dickinson University Press, 1984. 243 pp.

Konder, Leandro. *O marxismo na batalha das ideias*. Rio de Janeiro: Editore Nova Frontera, 1984. 103 pp.

Langley, Lester D. *Central America: The Real Stakes*. New York: Crown, 1985. 280 pp.

Leiken, Robert S., ed. *Central America: Anatomy of Conflict*. New York: Pergamon Press, 1984. 351 pp.

Levesque, Andrée. *Virage à gauche interdit: Les communistes, les socialistes et leur ennemies au Quebec 1929–1939*. Montreal: Boreal Express, 1984. 186 pp.

Lima, Haroldo. *Historia da Acao Popular: da JUC ao PC do B*. São Paulo: Editorials, 1984. 176 pp.

Lora, Guillermo. *Lecciones de la Asamblea Popular*. La Paz, Bolivia: n.p., 1984. 47 pp.

Manasov, M. A., chief ed. *Respublika Kuba*. Moscow: Nauka, 1984. 336 pp.

Marin, Juan Carlos. *Los hechos armados: un ejercicio posible*. Buenos Aires: CICSO, 1984. 233 pp.

Martinez Verdugo, Arnoldo, ed. *Historia del comunismo en Mexico*. Mexico City: Editorial Grijalbo, 1985. 501 pp.

McGinnis, James. *Solidarity with the People of Nicaragua*. Maryknoll, N.Y.: Orbis Books, 1985. 162 pp.

Medina, Javier. *Ni Marx, ni menos: dos notas a propositio de la tesis socialista de la COB*. La Paz: Ediciones el Tigre de Papel, 1984. 75 pp.

Merin, B. M., ed. *Proletariat i revoliutsionnyi protsess v Latinskoi Amerike*. Moscow: Nauka, 1985. 374 pp.

Montaner, Carlos Alberto. *Cuba, Castro and the Caribbean*. New Brunswick, N.J.: Transaction Press, 1985. 116 pp.

Nelson, Harold D., ed. *Costa Rica: A Country Study*. Washington, D.C.: American University Foreign Area Studies, 1984. 355 pp.

Newcombe, Pat. *The Peace Movement and the Communist Party of Canada*. Toronto: Citizens for Foreign Aid Reform, 1984. 87 pp.

Nicholls, David. *Haiti in Caribbean Context: Ethnicity, Economy and Revolt*. New York: St. Martin's Press, 1985. 282 pp.

O'Brien, Philip, and Paul Cammack, eds. *Generals in Retreat: The Crisis of Military Rule in Latin America*. Dover, N.H.: Manchester University Press, 1985. 208 pp.

Ochoa, T. and Juan M. *Sistema que sigue: el vertice de capitalismo y comunismo*. Mexico, D.F.: Edamex, 1984. 100 pp.

Partido Comunista Dominicano. Comite Central. *Informe del Comite Central saliente al tercer Congreso del Partido Comunista Dominicano*. Santo Domingo: PCD, 1984. 128 pp.

El Partido Comunista en el Uruguay. Montevideo: Centro Militar, 1984. 31 pp.

Partido Comunista Peruano. *La trayectoria del Partido Comunista Peruano y los heroes de nuestro tiempo*. Lima: PCP, 1985. 31 pp.

Payne, Anthony. *Grenada: Revolution and Invasion*. New York: St. Martin's Press, 1984. 233 pp.

Prado, Jorge del. *¿Quien gano y quien perdio el 14 de abril?: informe politico a la XIV Sesion Plenaria del Comite Central del PCP*. Lima: Ediciones Unidad, 1985. 42 pp.

El Presidio politico en Cuba comunista: testimonio. Miami: Ediciones Universal, 1984. 511 pp.

Riquelme, Alfredo. *Vision des Estados Unidos en el Partido Comunista Chileano*. Santiago de Chile: Facultad Latinoamericana de Ciencias Sociales, 1985. vol. 1.

Ropp, Steve C., and James A. Morris, eds. *Central America: Crisis and Adaptation*. Albuquerque: University of New Mexico Press, 1984. 311 pp.

Rosales, Juan. *Cristo y/o Marx? los comunistas y la religion*. Buenos Aires: Editorial Cartago, 1984. 211 pp.

Rosenberg, Mark B., and Philip L. Shepherd, eds. *Honduras Confronts Its Future: Contending Perspectives on Critical Issues*. Boulder, Colo.: Lynne Rienner, 1985. 275 pp.

Rudolph, James D. *Honduras: A Country Study*. 2nd ed. Washington, D.C.: American University Foreign Area Studies, 1984. 294 pp.

Sanford, Gregory W. *Grenada: The Untold Story*. Lanham, Md.: Madison Books, 1984. 180 pp.

Schoenhals, Kai P., and Richard A. Melanson. *Revolution and Intervention in Grenada*. Boulder, Colo.: Westview Press, 1985. 211 pp.

Seabury, Paul, and Walter A. McDougall, eds. *The Grenada Papers*. San Francisco: Institute for Contemporary Studies Press, 1984. 346 pp.

Steinberg, Peter L. *The Great "Red Menace": The United States Prosecution of American Communists, 1947–1952*. Westport, Conn.: Greenwood Press, 1984. 311 pp.

Thorndike, Tony. *Grenada: Politics, Economy and Society*. Boulder, Colo.: Lynne Rienner, 1985. 206 pp.

United States. Central Intelligence Agency. Directorate of Intelligence. *Directory of Officials of the Republic of Cuba*. Washington, D.C.: National Technical Information Service, November 1985. 243 pp.

Wiarda, Howard J., and Harvey F. Kline, eds. *Latin American Politics and Development*. 2nd ed. Boulder, Colo.: Westview Press, 1985. 671 pp.

Zwerling, Philip, and Connie Martin. *A New Kind of Revolution*. Westport, Conn.: Lawrence Hill, 1985. 231 pp.

ASIA AND THE PACIFIC

Allen, James S. *The Radical Left on the Eve of War: A Political Memoir*. Quezon City, Philippines: Foundation for Nationalist Studies, 1985. 121 pp.

Amnesty International. *China: Violations of Human Rights*. London: Amnesty International, 1984. 129 pp.

Babin, A. I., ed.-in-chief. *Vooruzhennaia bor'ba narodov Azii za svobodu i nezavisimost', 1945–1980*. Moscow: Nauka, 1984. 341 pp.

Barnett, A. Doak. *The Making of Foreign Policy in China: Structure and Processes*. Boulder, Colo.: Westview Press, 1985. 160 pp.

Bartke, Wolfgang, and Peter Schier. *China's New Party Leadership: Biographies of the Twelfth Central Committee of the Chinese Communist Party*. Armonk, N.Y.: M. E. Sharpe, 1985. 289 pp.

Brugger, Bill, ed. *Chinese Marxism in Flux, 1978–1984*. Armonk, N.Y.: M. E. Sharpe, 1985. 218 pp.

Bunge, Frederica M., ed. *Malaysia: A Country Study*. 4th ed. Washington, D.C.: American University Foreign Area Studies, 1985. 366 pp.

Clutterbuck, Richard. *Conflict and Violence in Singapore and Malaysia, 1945–1983*. Boulder, Colo.: Westview Press, 1984. 412 pp.

Copper, John F.; Franz Michael; and Yuan-li Wu. *Human Rights in Post-Mao China*. Boulder, Colo.: Westview Press, 1985. 117 pp.

Day, Alan J., ed. *China and the Soviet Union, 1949–84*. New York: Facts on File Publications, 1985. 202 pp.

Gankovskii, Iu. V., ed.-in-chief. *Afghanistan: Ekonomika, politika, istoriia*. Moscow: Nauka, 1984. 262 pp.

Garrett, Banning N., and Bonnie S. Glaser. *War and Peace: The Views from Moscow and Beijing*. Berkeley: Institute of International Studies, University of California, 1984. 151 pp.

Geisherik, Ia. B., ed. *Revoliutsionnaia demokratiia i kommunisty vostoka*. Moscow: Glavnaia redaktsiia vostochnoi literatury, 1984. 378 pp.

Glasunov, E. P., and M. P. Isaev. *Strany Indokitaia: put' bor'by i svershenii*. Moscow: Mysl', 1984. 271 pp.

Goldstein, Steve M., ed. *China Briefing, 1984*. Boulder, Colo.: Westview Press, 1985. 125 pp.

Gregor, A. James. *Crisis in the Philippines: A Threat to U.S. Interests*. Washington, D.C.: Ethics and Public Policy Center, 1984. 110 pp.

Harris, Lillian Craig. *China's Foreign Policy Toward the Third World*. New York: Praeger, 1985. 121 pp.

Hollingworth, Clare. *Mao and the Men Against Him*. London: Jonathan Cape, 1985. 372 pp.

India. Communist Party of India. National Council. *Report and Resolutions Adopted by the National Council of the Communist Party of India, New Delhi, October 10–13, 1984*. New Delhi: Communist Party Publications, 1984. 63 pp.

Japanese Communist Party. Central Committee. *Sixty Years of the Japanese Communist Party*. Tokyo: Japan Press Service, 1984. 714 pp.

Joseph, William. *The Critique of Ultra-leftism in China, 1981–1985*. Stanford, Calif.: Stanford University Press, 1984. 312 pp.

Kiernan, Ben. *How Pol Pot Came to Power*. Cambridge: Cambridge University Press, 1985. 430 pp.

Kim, Samuel S., ed. *China and the World: Chinese Foreign Policy in the Post-Mao Era*. Boulder, Colo.: Westview Press, 1984. 354 pp.

Knox, Donald. *The Korean War: Pusan to Chosin*. New York: Harcourt Brace Jovanovich, 1985. 697 pp.

Kobelev, E V., chief ed. *Kampuchiia: spravochnik*. Moscow: Nauka, 1985. 184 pp.

Kutsobin, P. V. *Adzhoi Gkhosh i kommunisticheskoe dvizhenie v Indii*. Moscow: Mysl', 1985. 248 pp.

Mackerras, Colin, and Nick Knight, eds. *Marxism in Asia*. New York: St. Martin's Press, 1985. 297 pp.

Marxist Perspectives. Trivandrum, Kerala, India: Social Scientist Press, 1984. 146 pp.

Mikheev, Iu. Ia. *Laosskaia Narodno-Demokraticheskaia Respublika (LNDR): spravochnik*. Moscow: Politizdat, 1985. 111 pp.

Mkhitarian, S. A., ed.-in-chief. *Noveishaia istoriia V'etnama*. Moscow: Nauka, 1984. 424 pp.

Mosher, Steven W. *Journey to the Forbidden China*. New York: Free Press (Macmillan), 1985. 180 pp.

Nathan, Andrew J. *Chinese Democracy*. New York: Alfred A. Knopf, 1985. 313 pp.

O'Donnell, Charles Peter. *Bangladesh: Biography of a Muslim Nation*. Boulder, Colo.: Westview Press, 1984. 332 pp.

Parish, William L., ed. *Chinese Rural Development: The Great Transformation*. Armonk, N.Y.: M. E. Sharpe, 1985. 278 pp.

Peck, Stacey. *Halls of Jade, Walls of Stone: Women in China Today*. London: Franklin Watts, 1985. 321 pp.

Prizzia, Ross. *Thailand in Transition: The Role of Oppositional Forces*. Honolulu: University of Hawaii Press, 1985. 124 pp.

Quested, R. K. I. *Sino-Russian Relations*. London: Allen and Unwin, 1984. 194 pp.

Richardson, Jim. *The Genesis of the Philippine Communist Party*. London: University of London Press, 1984. 376 pp.

Rozman, Gilbert. *A Mirror of Socialism: Soviet Criticisms of China*. Princeton, N.J.: Princeton University Press, 1985. 292 pp.

Salisbury, Harrison E. *The Long March: The Untold Story*. New York: Harper and Row, 1985. 419 pp.

Schell, Orville. *To Get Rich Is Glorious: China in the 80s*. New York: Pantheon, 1984. 210 pp.

Segal, Gerald. *Defending China*. New York: Oxford University Press, 1985. 264 pp.

Segal, Gerald, and William T. Tow, eds. *Chinese Defense Policy*. Champaign: University of Illinois Press, 1984. 286 pp.

Shalom, Stephen Risskamm. *Deaths in China Due to Communist Propaganda Versus Reality*. Tempe: Arizona State University Press, 1984. 234 pp.

Shambaugh, David L. *The Making of a Premier: Zhao Zyang's Provincial Career*. Boulder, Colo.: Westview Press, 1984. 157 pp.

Shaw, Yu-ming, ed. *Power and Policy of the PRC*. Boulder, Colo.: Westview Press, 1985. 370 pp.

Sladkovskii, M. I., chief ed. *Kitaiskaia Narodnaia Respublika v 1980 godu*. Moscow: Nauka, 1984. 256 pp.

Snow, Helen F. *My China Years: A Memoir*. New York: Morrow, 1984. 349 pp.

Song, Du-Yul. *Sowjetunion und China: Egalisierung und Differenzierung im Sozialismus*. Frankfurt and New York: Campus Verlag, 1984. 255 pp.

Tang Tsou. *The Cultural Revolution and Post-Mao Reform*. Chicago: University of Chicago Press, 1985. 440 pp.

Third World Studies. *Marxism in the Philippines: Marx Centennial Lectures*. Quezon City, Philippines: Third World Studies Center, 1984. 242 pp.

Truong Nhu Tang et al. *A Vietcong Memoir*. San Diego: Harcourt Brace Jovanovich, 1985. 350 pp.

United States. Central Intelligence Agency. Directorate of Intelligence. *Directory of Chinese Officials: National Level Organizations, June 1985*. Washington, D.C.: National Technical Information Service, 1985. 166 pp.

———. *Directory of Officials of the Democratic People's Republic of Korea, April 1985*. Washington, D.C.: National Technical Information Service, 1985. 108 pp.

———. *Directory of Officials of Vietnam*. Washington, D.C.: National Technical Information Service, July 1985. 139 pp.

———. *Who's Who in Cambodia: A Reference Aid* (Wallchart CR 85-10625). Washington, D.C.: National Technical Information Service, 1985.

Vasil'ev, V. F., chief ed. *Iugo-Vostochnaia Aziia: sovremennoe politicheskoe razvitie*. Moscow: Nauka, 1984. 294 pp.

Wolf, Margery. *Revolution Postponed: Women in Contemporary China*. Stanford, Calif.: Stanford University Press, 1985. 285 pp.

EASTERN EUROPE

Aczél, György. *Socialism and the Freedom of Culture*. Budapest: Corvina Kiado, 1984. 485 pp.

Adam, Jan. *Employment and Wage Policies in Poland, Czechoslovakia and Hungary since 1950*. New York: St. Martin's Press, 1985. 251 pp.

Aleksievets, N. M. *GDR: kursom razvitogo sotsializma*. L'vov: Vishcha shkola, 1984. 166 pp.

Andrews, Nicholas G. *Poland, 1980–81: Solidarity Versus the Party*. Washington, D.C.: National Defense University Press, 1985. 351 pp.

Aslund, Anders. *Private Enterprise in Eastern Europe: The Non-Agricultural Private Sector in Poland and the GDR*. New York: St. Martin's Press, 1985. 294 pp.

Badstübner, Rolf. *Geschichte der Deutschen Demokratischen Republik*. East Berlin: Deutscher Verlag der Wissenschaften, 1984. 402 pp.

Beliaev, Iu. N. *Strany SEV v mirovoi ekonomike*. Moscow: Mezhdunarodnye otnosheniia, 1984. 272 pp.

Bell, John D. *The Bulgarian Communist Party: From Blagoev to Zhivkov*. Histories of Ruling Communist Parties. Stanford, Calif.: Hoover Institution Press, 1985. 396 pp.

Beloff, Nora. *Tito's Flawed Legacy*. London: Gollancz, 1985. 287 pp.

Benser, Günter. *Die KPD im Jahre der Befreiung: Vorbereitung und Aufbau der legalen kommunistischen Massenpartei*. East Berlin: Dietz, 1985. 580 pp.

Berend, Ivan R., and György Ránki. *The Hungarian Economy in the Twentieth Century*. New York: St. Martin's Press, 1985. 336 pp.

Bethell, Nicholas William. *The Great Betrayal: The Untold Story of Kim Philby's Biggest Coup*. London: Hodder and Stoughton, 1984. 213 pp.

Bingen, Dietrich, ed. *Polen, 1980–1984: Dauerkrise oder Stabilisierung?* Baden-Baden: Nomos Verlag, 1985. 401 pp.

Biondi, Lawrence, and Frank Mocha, eds. *Poland's Solidarity Movement*. Chicago: Loyola University Press, 1984. 236 pp.

Blobaum, Robert. *Feliks Dzierzynski and the SDKPiL: A Study of the Origins of Polish Communism*. Boulder, Colo.: East European Monographs, 1984. 307 pp.

Brandt, Hans-Jürgen, and Martin Dinges. *Kaderpolitik und Kaderarbeit in den "bürgerlichen" Parteien und den Massenorganisationenen in der DDR*. Berlin: A. Spitz, 1984. 88 pp.

Bryson, Phillip J. *The Consumer Under Socialist Planning: The East German Case*. New York: Praeger, 1984. 207 pp.

Bulgarian Academy of Sciences. *Information Bulgaria: A Short Encyclopaedia of the People's Republic of Bulgaria*. New York: Pergamon Press, 1985. 976 pp.

Charlton, Michael. *The Eagle and the Small Birds: Crisis in the Soviet Empire from Yalta to Solidarity*. Chicago: University of Chicago Press, 1985. 192 pp.

Cioranescu, George. *Bessarabia: Disputed Land Between East and West*. Munich: Ion Dumitru Verlag, 1985. 372 pp.

Council for Mutual Economic Assistance. *Obzor deiatel'nosti SEV mezhdu XXXVII i XXXIX zasedaniiami sessii soveta*. Moscow: CMEA Secretariat, 1984. 61 pp.

Daubenton, Annie. *La Pologne: un pays dans la tête*. Paris: Encre, 1984. 214 pp.

Davies, Norman. *Heart of Europe: A Short History of Poland*. Oxford: Clarendon Press, 1984. 511 pp.

Djilas, Milovan. *Rise and Fall*. San Diego: Harcourt Brace Jovanovich, 1985. 424 pp.

Eckart, Gabriele. *So sehe ich die Sache: Protokolle aus der DDR*. Cologne: Kiepenhauer und Witsch, 1984. 118 pp.

Edwards, G. E. *GDR Society and Social Institutions*. London: Macmillan, 1985. 244 pp.

Gremion, Pierre. *Paris-Prague: la gauche face au renouveau et la regression tchecoslovaques* [sic], *1968–1978*. Paris: Julliard, 1985. 367 pp.

Handbuch der DDR: Jubiläumsausgabe 1984. Leipzig: VEB Bibliographisches Institut, 1984. 744 pp.

Hazan, Baruch A. *The East European Political System*. Boulder, Colo.: Westview Press, 1985. 396 pp.

Helwig, Gisela. *Jugend und Familie in der DDR: Leitbild und Alltag im Widerspruch*. Cologne: Wissenschaft und Politik, 1984. 126 pp.

Hirsch, Helga. *Bewegung für Demokratie und Unabhängigkeit in Polen, 1976–1980*. Mainz: Kaiser-Grünwald, 1985. 175 pp.

Holzer, Jerzy. *Solidarität*. Munich: Verlag C. B. Beck, 1984. 441 pp.

Horak, Stephan M., et al. *East European National Minorities, 1919–1980: A Handbook*. Littleton, Colo.: Libraries Unlimited, 1985. 274 pp.

Hoxha, Enver. *Laying the Foundation of the New Albania*. Tirana: 8 Nëntori Publishing House, 1984. 581 pp.

———. *Two Friendly People*. Tirana: 8 Nëntori Publishing House, 1985. 451 pp.

———. *Selected Works, November 1976–June 1981*. vol. 5. Tirana: 8 Nëntori Publishing House, 1985. 1,043 pp.

Kádár, János. *Selected Speeches and Interviews*. Budapest: Akadémiai Kiadó, 1985. 469 pp.

Kaie, V. A., ed.-in-chief. *Chechoslovatskaia Sotsialisticheskaia Respublika*. Moscow: Nauka, 1984. 317 pp.

Kaplan, Karel. *The Short March: The Communist Takeover of Power in Czechoslovakia, 1945–48*. London: C. Hurst, 1985. 240 pp.

Kertész, Stephen. *Between Russia and the West: Hungary and the Illusion of Peacemaking, 1945–47*. Notre Dame, Ind.: Notre Dame University Press, 1984. 299 pp.

Király, Béla; Barbara Lotze; and Nándor F. Dreisziger, eds. *The First War Between Socialist States: The Hungarian Revolution and Its Impact*. New York: Brooklyn College Press (distributed by Columbia University Press), 1984. 608 pp.

Klima, Ivan. *My Merry Mornings*. New York: Readers International, 1985. 154 pp.

Kolosov, V. A., ed.-in-chief. *Germanskaia Demokraticheskaia Respublika: Ekonomiko-geograficheskaia kharakteristika*. Moscow: Mysl', 1984. 240 pp.

Kommunistische Partei Deutschlands. *Protokoll des Gründungsparteitages der Kommunistischen Partei Deutschlands (30 Dez. 1918–1 Jan. 1919)*. Berlin: Dietz Verlag, 1985. 345 pp.

Köves, András. *The CMEA Countries in the World Economy*. Budapest: Akadémiai Kiadó, 1985. 247 pp.

Krisch, Henry. *The Democratic German Republic*. Boulder, Colo.: Westview Press, 1985. 105 pp.

Landau, Zbigniew, and Jerzy Tomaszewski. *The Polish Economy in the Twentieth Century*. New York: St. Martin's Press, 1985. 346 pp.

Lange, Ernst. *DDR—und Deutschlandforschung in der Bundesrepublik Deutschland einschliesslich Berlin*. Bonn: Gesamtdeutsches Institut, Bundesanstalt für gesamtdeutsche Aufgaben, 1984. 409 pp.

Lendvai, Paul. *Das einsame Albanien*. Zurich: Edition Interfrom, 1985. 118 pp.

Lewis, Paul G., ed. *Eastern Europe: Political Crisis and Legitimation*. New York: St. Martin's Press, 1984. 202 pp.

Manusevich, A. Ia., chief ed. *Narodnyie i natsional'nye fronty v antifashistskoi osvoboditel'noi bor'be i revoliutsiiakh 40-kh godov*. Moscow: Nauka, 1985. 638 pp.

Markovski, Venko. *Goli Otok: Island of Death*. Boulder, Colo.: East European Monographs, 1984. 229 pp.

Mason, David S. *Public Opinion and Political Change in Poland, 1980–1982*. New York: Cambridge University Press, 1985. 256 pp.

Max, Stanley M. *The United States, Great Britain, and the Sovietization of Hungary, 1945–1948*. Boulder, Colo.: East European Monographs, 1985. 195 pp.

McArdle, Arthur W., and Bruce Boenau. *East Germany: A New Nation under Socialism?* Washington, D.C.: University Press of America, 1984. 364 pp.

Micewski, Andrzej. *Cardinal Wyszynski: A Biography*. San Diego: Harcourt Brace Jovanovich, 1984. 496 pp.

Misztal, Bronislaw, ed. *Poland After Solidarity*. New Brunswick, N.J.: Transaction Books, 1985. 167 pp.

Mur, Jan. *A Prisoner of Martial Law: Poland, 1981–1982*. San Diego: Harcourt Brace Jovanovich, 1984. 311 pp.

Nagy, László. *The Socialist Collective Agreement*. Budapest: Akadémiai Kiadó, 1984. 258 pp.

Oldberg, Ingmar, ed. *Unity and Conflict in the Warsaw Pact*. Stockholm: Swedish National Defense Research Institute, 1984. 158 pp.

Omrcanin, Ivo. *Enigma Tito*. Washington, D.C.: Samizdat, 1984. 465 pp.

Piskol, Joachim, et al. *Anti-faschistisch-demokratische Umwälzung auf dem Lande (1945–1949)*. Berlin: VEB Deutscher Landwirtschaftsverlag, 1984. 207 pp.

Plaudis, Arturs, ed. *The Dead Accuse: Collection of Letters from Behind the Iron Curtain*. Park Orchards, Australia: JAJM Fund, 1984. 152 pp.

Pollman, Bernhard. *Daten zur Geschichte der Deutschen Demokratischen Republik*. Düsseldorf: Econ Verlag, 1984. 267 pp.

Potapov, Vladimir Il'ich. *Sotsialisticheskaia Respublika Rumyniia: spravochnik*. 3rd rev. ed. Moscow: Politizdat, 1984. 141 pp.

Raina, Peter. *Poland 1981: Towards Social Renewal*. London: Allen and Unwin, 1985. 472 pp.

Rakowska-Harmstone, Teresa, et al. *Warsaw Pact, the Question of Cohesion: Phase II*. Ottawa, Canada: Department of National Defence, Operational Research and Analysis Establishment, 1984. 2 vols.

Rakowski, Mieczyslaw F. *Ein schwieriger Dialog: Aufzeichnungen zu Ereignissen in Polen 1981–1984*. Düsseldorf: Econ Verlag, 1985. 269 pp.

Ramet, Pedro. *Nationalism and Federalism in Yugoslavia, 1963–1983*. Bloomington: Indiana University Press, 1984. 299 pp.

———, ed. *Yugoslavia in the 1980s*. Boulder, Colo.: Westview Press, 1985. 355 pp.

Rice, Condoleezza. *The Soviet Union and the Czechoslovak Army, 1948–1983: Uncertain Allegiance*. Princeton, N.J.: Princeton University Press, 1984. 303 pp.

Ronge, Volker. *Von drüben nach hüben: DDR Bürger im Westen*. Wuppertal: Hartman Verlag, 1986. 107 pp.

Sampson, Steven L. *National Integration Through Socialist Planning: An Anthropological Study of a Romanian New Town*. Boulder, Colo.: East European Monographs, 1984. 352 pp.

Scharf, Bradley. *Politics and Change in East Germany*. Boulder, Colo.: Westview Press, 1984. 219 pp.

Scharf, Wilfried. *Das Bild der Bundesrepublik Deutschland in den Massenmedien der DDR: eine empirische Untersuchung von Tageszeitungen, Hörfunk und Fernsehen*. Frankfurt am Main: Lang, 1985. 256 pp.

Schulze, G. *DDR—Bürgerinteresse als Staatspolitik*. Vienna: Verlag für Gesellschaftskritik, 1984. 161 pp.

Shafir, Michael. *Romania, Politics, Economics and Society: Political Stagnation and Simulated Change*. London: F. Pinter, 1985. 232 pp.

Shalamanov, S., ed. *Narodna Respublika Bolgariia v sotsialisticheskoi ekonomicheskoi integratsii: struktura i politika*. Moscow: Progress, 1984. 248 pp.

Simecka, Milan. *The Restoration of Order: The Normalization of Czechoslovakia, 1969–1976*. London: Verso, 1985. 167 pp.

Simon, Jeffrey. *Warsaw Pact Forces: Problems of Command and Control*. Boulder, Colo.: Westview Press, 1985. 246 pp.

Singleton, Fred. *A Short History of the Yugoslav Peoples*. Cambridge: Cambridge University Press, 1985. 309 pp.

Skorodenko, P. P. *Vo glave boevogo soiuza: kommunisticheskie partii—sozdateli i rukovoditeli Organizatsii Varshavskogo Dogovora*. Moscow: Voenizdat, 1985. 224 pp.

Smiley, David. *Albanian Assignment*. London: Hogarth Press, 1984. 170 pp.

Sozialistische Einheitspartei Deutschlands. *Dokumente der SED: Beschlüsse und Erklärungen des Zentralkomites und seines Sekretetäriats*, vol. XIX, 1982–83. East Berlin: Dietz Verlag, 1984. 424 pp.

Staritz, Dietrich. *Die Gründung der DDR*. Munich: Deutscher Taschenbuch Verlag, 1984. 245 pp.

Stent, Angela E., ed. *Economic Relations with the Soviet Union*. Boulder, Colo.: Westview Press, 1985. 181 pp.

Stevens, John N. *Czechoslovakia at the Crossroads: The Economic Dilemmas of Communism in Postwar Czechoslovakia*. Boulder, Colo.: East European Monographs, 1985. 349 pp.

Szymanski, Albert. *Class Struggle in Socialist Poland*. New York: Praeger, 1984. 265 pp.

Taras, Ray. *Ideology in a Socialist State: Poland 1956–1983*. New York: Cambridge University Press, 1984. 299 pp.

Terry, Sarah Meiklejohn. *Soviet Foreign Policy in Eastern Europe*. New Haven, Conn.: Yale University Press, 1984. 375 pp.

Tontsch, Günther H. *Das Verhältnis von Partei und Staat in Romänien: Kontinuität und Wandel, 1944–1982*. Cologne: Verlag Wissenschaft und Politik, 1985. 201 pp.

United States. Central Intelligence Agency. Directorate of Intelligence. *Bulgarian Communist Party* (Reference Aid; Chart). Washington, D.C.: National Technical Information Service, May 1985.

———. *Directory of Albanian Officials*. Washington, D.C.: National Technical Information Service, June 1985. 91 pp.

———. *Directory of Czechoslovak Officials*. Washington, D.C.: National Technical Information Service, September 1985. 166 pp.

———. *Directory of Hungarian Officials*. Washington, D.C.: National Technical Information Service, December 1985. 130 pp.

———. *Directory of Romanian Officials*. Washington, D.C.: National Technical Information Service, June 1985. 145 pp.

———. *Directory of Yugoslav Officials*. Washington, D.C.: National Technical Information Service, December 1985. 215 pp.

———. *Government of the People's Republic of Bulgaria* (Reference Aid; Chart). Washington, D.C.: National Technical Information Service, May 1985.

———. *Hungarian Socialist Workers' Party* (Reference Aid; Chart). Washington, D.C.: National Technical Information Service, August 1985.

Vienna Institute for Comparative Economic Studies, ed. *COMECON Data, 1983*. Westport, Conn.: Greenwood Press, 1984. 491 pp.

Völgyes, Iván. *Politics in Eastern Europe*. Chicago: Dorsey Press, 1986. 368 pp.

Volkogonov, D. A., ed. *Armii stran Varshavskogo Dogovora: spravochnik*. Moscow: Voenizdat, 1985. 223 pp.

Voss, Eugen, ed. *Die Religionsfreiheit in Osteuropa*. Zollikon: G-2-W Verlag, 1984. 272 pp.

Vree, Dale. *From Berkeley to East Berlin and Back*. Nashville, Tenn.: Nelson, 1985. 168 pp.

Vukcevic, Radoje. *General Mihailovic*. Chicago: Serbian Historical and Cultural Society, "Njegos," 1984. 158 pp.

Wallace, Ian, ed. *The GDR in the 1980s*. Loughborough: Loughborough University Press, 1984. 132 pp.

Wolchik, Sharon L., and Alfred G. Meyer, eds. *Women, State and Party in Eastern Europe*. Durham, N.C.: Duke University Press, 1985. 366 pp.
Zhivkov, Todor. *Marxist Concepts and Practices*. New York: Pergamon Press, 1984. 201 pp.
———. *Statesman and Builder of New Bulgaria*. 2nd rev. ed. New York: Oxford University Press, 1985. 519 pp.

USSR

Alexeyeva, Ludmilla. *Soviet Dissent*. Middletown, Conn.: Wesleyan University Press, 1985. 521 pp.
Alford, Jonathan, ed. *The Soviet Union: Security Policies and Constraints*. New York: St. Martin's Press, 1985. 180 pp.
Baller, Eleazar. *Communism and Cultural Heritage*. Moscow: Progress Publishers, 1984. 267 pp.
Berg, Gerard Pieter van den. *Organisation und Arbeitsweise der sowjetischen Regierung*. Baden-Baden: Nomos Verlag, 1984. 381 pp.
Bittman, Ladislav. *The KGB and Soviet Disinformation: An Insider's View*. Washington, D.C.: Pergamon-Brassey's, 1985. 226 pp.
Bloch, Sidney, and Peter Reddaway. *Soviet Psychiatric Abuse: The Shadow over World Psychiatry*. London: Gollancz, 1984. 288 pp.
Bogomolov, Oleg Timofeevich. *Strany sotsializma v mezhdunarodnom razdelenii truda*. Moscow: Nauka, 1985. 362 pp.
Bruchis, Michael. *Nations—Nationalities—People: A Study of the Nationalities Policy of the Communist Party in Soviet Moldavia*. Boulder, Colo.: East European Monographs, 1984. 230 pp.
Butko, V. V., et al.; N. I. Rodionova, comp. *Soratniki: Biografii aktivnykh uchastnikov revoliutsionnogo dvizheniia v Moskve i Moskovskoi oblasti*. Moscow: Moskovskii rabochii, 1985. 510 pp.
Butson, Thomas G. *Gorbachev: A Biography*. New York: Stein and Day, 1985. 168 pp.
———. *The Tsar's Lieutenant: The Soviet Marshal*. New York: Praeger, 1984. 281 pp.
Caldwell, Dan. *Soviet International Behavior and U.S. Policy Options*. Lexington, Mass.: Lexington Books/D.C. Heath, 1985. 291 pp.
Chernenko, Konstantin U. *Po puti sovershenstvovaniia razvitogo sotsialisma*. Moscow: Politizdat, 1985. 367 pp.
———. *Soviet-U.S. Relations: The Selected Writings and Speeches*. New York: Praeger, 1984. 203 pp.
Cohen, Stephen F. *Rethinking the Soviet Experience: Politics and History since 1917*. New York: Oxford University Press, 1985. 222 pp.
Conquest, Robert. *Inside Stalin's Secret Police: NKVD Politics, 1936–39*. Stanford, Calif.: Hoover Institution Press, 1985. 222 pp.
Conquest, Robert, and Jon Manchip White. *What to Do When the Russians Come*. New York: Stein and Day, 1984. 177 pp.
Corson, William R., and Robert T. Crowley. *The New KGB: Engine of Soviet Power*. New York: William Morrow, 1985. 560 pp.
Dekan', L. F. *Sredstva massovoi informatsii i propagandy*. Moscow: Politizdat, 1984. 352 pp.
Dolot, Miron. *Execution by Hunger: The Hidden Holocaust*. New York: W. W. Norton, 1985. 231 pp.
Donchenko, V. N., et al. *Edinstvo ideino-politicheskogo, trudovogo i nravstvennogo vospitaniia studentov*. Moscow: "Vysshaia shkola," 1984. 221 pp.
Dunmore, Timothy. *Soviet Politics, 1945–1953*. New York: St. Martin's Press, 1984. 176 pp.
Elleinstein, Jean. *Staline*. Paris: Fayard, 1984. 568 pp.
Getty, J. Arch. *Origins of the Great Purges: The Soviet Communist Party Reconsidered, 1933–1938*. New York: Cambridge University Press, 1985. 276 pp.
Girardet, Edward. *Afghanistan: The Soviet War*. New York: St. Martin's Press, 1985. 256 pp.
Godson, Roy. *Labor in Soviet Global Strategy*. Rev. ed. New York: Crane Russak, 1984. 102 pp.

Golitsyn, Anatoliy. *New Lies for Old: The Communist Strategy of Deception and Disinformation*. New York: Dodd, Mead, 1984. 412 pp.

Gong, Gerrit W.; Angela E. Stent; and Rebecca V. Strode. *Areas of Challenge for Soviet Foreign Policy in the 1980s*. Bloomington: Indiana University Press, 1984. 142 pp.

Gorbachev, Mikhail S. *A Time for Peace*. New York: Richardson and Steinman, 1985. 297 pp.

Grishin, V. V. *Voprosy partiino-organizatsionnoi i ideologicheskoi raboty*. Moscow: Politizdat, 1984. 397 pp.

Gromyko, A. A. *Leninskim kursom mira*. Moscow: Politizdat, 1984. 734 pp.

Gusev, K. V., ed. *Intelligentsiia i revoliutsiia, XX vek*. Moscow: Nauka, 1985. 334 pp.

Haynes, Michael. *Nikolai Bukharin and the Transition from Capitalism to Socialism*. New York: Holmes and Meier Publishers, 1985. 136 pp.

Hazard, John N. *Recollections of a Pioneering Sovietologist*. New York: Oceana Publications, 1984. 139 pp.

Hoffmann, Erik P., ed. *The Soviet Union in the 1980s*. New York: Academy of Political Science, 1984. 244 pp.

Hoffmann, Erik P., and Robbin F. Laird. *Technocratic Socialism: The Soviet Union in the Advanced Industrial Era*. Durham, N.C.: Duke University Press, 1985. 229 pp.

Hutchings, Raymond. *The Structural Origins of Soviet Industrial Expansion*. New York: St. Martin's Press, 1984. 242 pp.

Huyn, Hans Graf von. *Sieg ohne Krieg: Moskaus Griff nach der Weltherrschaft*. Munich: Universitas, 1984. 407 pp.

Ivanov, V. M. *Marshal M. N. Tukhachevskii*. Moscow: Voenizdat, 1985. 318 pp.

Keeble, Curtis, ed. *The Soviet State*. Boulder, Colo.: Westview Press, 1985. 244 pp.

Khaldev, M. I., and G. I. Krivoshein, comps. *Partiinaia rabota na sele*. Moscow: Politizdat, 1984. 334 pp.

Khromov, S. S., ed. *Istoriia sovetskogo rabochego klassa*. Moscow: Nauka, 1984. 3 vols. (495, 511, 588 pp.)

Klimov, Iu. *Stories About the Party of Communists*. Moscow: Progress, 1984. 295 pp.

Klimov, S. N. *Voenno-organizatorskaia deiatelnost' Komunisticheskoi partii v srednei Azii*. N.p.: Nauch. "Uzbekistan," 1985. 184 pp.

Kort, Michael. *The Soviet Colossus: The History of the USSR*. New York: Charles Scribner's Sons, 1985. 318 pp.

Krawchenko, Bohdan. *Social Change and National Consciousness in Twentieth-Century Ukraine*. New York: St. Martin's Press, 1985. 256 pp.

Kremlin-PCF: conversations secrètes. Paris: Orban, 1984. 227 pp.

Kuz'min, E. L. *Voprosy demokratii i bor'ba idei na mezhdunarodnoi arene*. Moscow: Mezhdunarodnye otnosheniia, 1984. 280 pp.

Laïdi, Zaki. *L'URSS vue du Tiers Monde*. Paris: Editions Karthala, 1984. 185 pp.

Lane, David. *Soviet Economy and Society*. New York: New York University Press, 1985. 342 pp.

———. *State and Politics in the USSR*. Oxford: Basil Blackwell, 1985. 398 pp.

Lewin, Moshe. *The Making of the Soviet System*. New York: Pantheon Books, 1985. 354 pp.

Lewytzkyi, Boris. *Politics and Society in Soviet Ukraine, 1953–1980*. Edmonton: Canadian Institute of Ukrainian Studies, University of Alberta Press, 1984. 219 pp.

———. *Who's Who in the Soviet Union*. Munich: Saur, 1984. 428 pp.

Littlejohn, Gary. *A Sociology of the Soviet Union*. New York: St. Martin's Press, 1984. 300 pp.

Liubitskii, V. N., comp. *Pravo vesti za soboi*. Moscow: Politizdat, 1985. 223 pp.

Lubin, Nancy. *Labor and Nationality in Soviet Central Asia*. Princeton, N.J.: Princeton University Press, 1984. 305 pp.

Lukes, Steven. *Marxism and Morality*. Oxford: Clarendon Press, 1985. 163 pp.

Lukyanov, A., et al. *The Soviet Constitution and the Myth of Sovietologists*. Moscow: Progress, 1984. 244 pp.

Mal'tsev, V. F., et al. *Sovetsko-vengerskie otnosheniia, 1977–1982*. Moscow: Politizdat, 1984. 421 pp.

Mehta, Dalpat Singh. *USSR Through Indian Eyes*. Moscow: Progress, 1984. 196 pp.

Meissner, Boris. *Partei, Staat und Nation in der Sowjetunion*. Berlin: Duncker and Humblot, 1985. 543 pp.

Melnikov, A. I., comp. *Propagandisty leninskoi shkoly*. 3rd ed. Moscow: Politizdat, 1985. 349 pp.

Moskoff, William. *Labor and Leisure in the Soviet Union: The Conflict between Public and Private Decision-Making in a Planned Economy*. New York: St. Martin's Press, 1984. 225 pp.

Nogee, Joseph L., ed. *Soviet Politics: Russia After Brezhnev*. New York: Praeger, 1985. 238 pp.

Page, Stephen. *The Soviet Union and the Yemens: Influence in Asymmetrical Relationships*. New York: Praeger, 1985. 225 pp.

Pinkus, Benjamin. *The Soviet Government and the Jews, 1948–1967*. Cambridge: Cambridge University Press, 1984. 612 pp.

Polan, A. J. *Lenin and the End of Politics*. Berkeley: University of California Press, 1984. 229 pp.

Popov, Sergei I. *Socialism and Optimism*. Moscow: Progress, 1984. 287 pp.

Porter, Roger B. *The U.S.-USSR Grain Agreement*. New York: Cambridge University Press, 1984. 160 pp.

Rahr, Alexander G., comp. *Biographic Directory of 100 Leading Soviet Officials*. 2nd ed. Munich: Central Research RFE/RL, 1984. 245 pp.

Ramet, Pedro, ed. *Religion and Nationalism in the Soviet Union*. Durham, N.C.: Duke University Press, 1984. 282 pp.

Rapoport, Vitaly, and Yuri Alexeev. *Essays on the History of the Red Army, 1918–1938*. Durham, N.C.: Duke University Press, 1985. 456 pp.

Rigby, T. H.; Archie Brown; and Peter Reddaway, eds. *Authority, Power and Policy in the USSR*. New York: St. Martin's Press, 1985. 207 pp.

Rosenberg, William G., ed. *Bolshevik Visions: First Phase of the Cultural Revolution in Soviet Russia*. Ann Arbor, Mich.: Ardis, 1984. 501 pp.

Rositzke, Harry August. *Managing Moscow: Guns or Goods?* New York: Morrow, 1984. 240 pp.

Rubinstein, Alvin Z. *Soviet Foreign Policy Since World War II: Imperial and Global*. 2nd ed. Boston: Little, Brown, 1985. 344 pp.

Rumer, Boris Z. *Investment and Reindustrialization in the Soviet Economy*. Boulder, Colo.: Westview Press, 1984. 145 pp.

Saivetz, Carol R., and Sylvia Woodby. *Soviet–Third World Relations*. Boulder, Colo.: Westview Press, 1985. 245 pp.

Schlögel, Karl. *Der renitente Held: der Arbeiterprotest in der Sowjetunion, 1953–1983*. Hamburg: Junius, 1984. 323 pp.

Schmid, Alex P. *Military Interventions Since 1945*. New Brunswick, N.J.: Transaction Books, 1985. 223 pp.

Semenova, V. E. *Sotsialno-psikhologicheskie problemy nravstvennogo vospitaniia lichnosti*. Leningrad: Izd-vo Leningradskogo universiteta, 1984. 159 pp.

Service, Robert. *Lenin: A Political Life*. vol. 1. Bloomington: Indiana University Press, 1985. 246 pp.

Shanor, Donald R. *Behind the Lines: The Private War Against Soviet Censorship*. New York: St. Martin's Press, 1985. 179 pp.

Shevchenko, Arkady N. *Breaking with Moscow*. New York: Knopf, 1985. 378 pp.

Smith, Thomas B. *The Other Establishment*. Chicago: Regnery Gateway, 1984. 205 pp.

Sorokin, G. M. *Ocherki politicheskoi ekonomii sotsializma*. Moscow: Nauka, 1984. 327 pp.

Staar, Richard F. *USSR Foreign Policies After Détente*. Stanford, Calif.: Hoover Institution Press, 1985. 300 pp.

Swietochowski, Tadeusz. *Russian Azerbaijan, 1905–1920*. Cambridge: Cambridge University Press, 1985. 253 pp.

Taagepera, Rein. *Softening Without Liberalization in the Soviet Union: The Case of Jüri Kukk*. Lanham, Md.: University Press of America, 1984. 244 pp.

United States. Central Intelligence Agency. Directorate of Intelligence. *Directory of Soviet Officials: Republic Organizations*. Washington, D.C.: National Technical Information Service, January 1985. 341 pp.

———. *Directory of Soviet Officials: Science and Education*. Washington, D.C.: National Technical Information Service, September 1985. 405 pp.

van den Berg, Ger P. *Organisation und Arbeitsweise der sowjetischen Regierung*. Baden-Baden: Nomos Verlagsgesellschaft, 1984. 381 pp.

Veen, Hans-Joachim, ed. *Wohin entwickelt sich die Sowjetunion?* Melle: Verlag Ernst Knoth, 1984. 336 pp.

Volkov, V. K., and V. Ia. Sipols, chief eds. *SSSR i strany narodnoi demokratii: Stanovlenie otnoshenii druzhby i sotrudnichestva 1944–1949 gg*. Moscow: Nauka, 1985. 480 pp.

Willis, David K. *Klass: How Russians Really Live*. New York: St. Martin's Press, 1985. 328 pp.

Wimbush, Enders. *Soviet Nationalities in Strategic Perspective*. New York: St. Martin's Press, 1985. 256 pp.

Wixman, Ronald. *The Peoples of the USSR: An Ethnographic Handbook*. Armonk, N.Y.: M. E. Sharpe, 1984. 264 pp.

Yaacov, Ro'i, ed. *The USSR and the Muslim World*. London: Allen and Unwin, 1984. 298 pp.

Zaleski, Eugène. *La Planification Stalinienne*. Paris: Economica, 1984. 1,118 pp.

Zemtsov, Ilya. *Lexicon of Soviet Political Terms*. Fairfax, Va.: Hero Books, 1984. 279 pp.

THE MIDDLE EAST

Arnold, Anthony. *Afghanistan: The Soviet Invasion in Perspective*. Stanford, Calif.: Hoover Institution Press, 1985. 179 pp.

Azar, Edward E., et al. *The Emergence of a New Lebanon: Fantasy or Reality?* New York: Praeger, 1985. 292 pp.

Berenshtein, L. E., chief ed. *Sionism: Vrag mira i sotsial'nogo progressa*. Kiev: Naukova Dumka, 1984. 131 pp.

Bradley, C. Paul. *Parliamentary Elections in Israel: Three Case Studies*. Grantham, N.H.: Tompson Rutter (Shoestring Press), 1985. 208 pp.

Freedman, Robert O. *The Middle East Since Camp David*. Boulder, Colo.: Westview Press, 1984. 263 pp.

Gavrilov, N. I. *Strany severnoi Afriki: Problemy politicheskogo, ekonomicheskogo i sotsial'nogo razvitiia*. Moscow: Nauka, 1984. 224 pp.

Hart, Alan. *Arafat: Terrorist or Peacemaker?* London: Sidgwick and Jackson, 1985. 501 pp.

Hoxha, Enver. *Reflections on the Middle East, 1958–1983*. Tirana: 8 Nëntori Publishing House, 1984. 540 pp.

Kapuscinski, Ryszard. *Shah of Shahs*. San Diego: A Helen and Kurt Wolff Book/Harcourt Brace Jovanovich, 1985. 152 pp.

Klinghoffer, Arthur Jay. *Israel and the Soviet Union: Alienation or Reconciliation?* Boulder, Colo.: Westview Press, 1985. 303 pp.

Koshelev, V. S. *Egipet, uroki istorii: bor'ba protiv kolonial'nogo gospodstva i kontrrevoliutsii (1879–1981)*. Minsk: Universitetskoe izdatelstvo, 1984. 206 pp.

Lawless, Richard, and Allan Findlay. *North Africa: Contemporary Politics and Economic Development*. New York: St. Martin's Press, 1984. 275 pp.

Magnus, Ralph H. *Afghan Alternatives: Issues, Options, and Policies*. New Brunswick, N.J.: Transaction Books, 1985. 221 pp.

Marr, Phoebe. *The Modern History of Iraq*. Boulder, Colo.: Westview Press, 1985. 382 pp.

Nimschowski, Helmut. *Der nationale Befreiungskrieg des algerischen Volkes (1954–1962)*. East Berlin: Militärverlag der DDR, 1984. 96 pp.

Nyrop, Richard F., ed. *Saudi Arabia: A Country Study*. 4th ed. Washington, D.C.: American University: American University Foreign Area Studies, 1985. 409 pp.

Pridham, B. R., ed. *Contemporary Yemen: Politics and Historical Background*. New York: St. Martin's Press, 1984. 276 pp.

The Promised Defeat of Marxism: Confessions of Leader of the Dissolved Tudeh Party of Iran. Iran: n.p., 1984. vol. 1.

Rubenstein, Sondra Miller. *The Communist Movement in Palestine and Israel, 1919–1984*. Boulder, Colo.: Westview Press, 1985. 419 pp.

Shahrani, M. Nazif, and Robert L. Canfield, eds. *Revolutions in Afghanistan: Anthropological Perspectives*. Berkeley, Calif.: Institute of International Studies, 1984. 394 pp.

Wright, Robin. *Sacred Rage: The Wrath of Militant Islam*. New York: Simon and Schuster, 1985. 315 pp.

WESTERN EUROPE

Adereth, M. *The French Communist Party: A Critical History (1920–1984)*. Dover, N.H.: Manchester University Press, 1984. 326 pp.

Allison, Roy. *Finland's Relations with the Soviet Union, 1944–84*. New York: St. Martin's Press, 1985. 211 pp.

Alvarez, Santiago. *Castelao y nosostros los comunistas*. Sada: Ediciós Castro, 1984. 206 pp.

Baudrillard, Jean. *La Gauche divine*. Paris: Grasset, 1985. 165 pp.

Bethell, Nicholas. *The Great Betrayal: The Untold Story of Kim Philby's Biggest Coup*. London: Hodder and Stoughton, 1984. 214 pp.

Blum, Mark E. *The Austro-Marxists, 1890–1918*. Lexington: University of Kentucky Press, 1985. 254 pp.

Boddy, Martin, and Colin Fudge. *Local Socialism? Labor Councils and New Left Alternatives*. London: Macmillan, 1984. 290 pp.

Boggs, Carl. *The Two Revolutions: Antonio Gramsci and the Dilemmas of Western Marxism*. Boston, Mass.: South End Press, 1984. 311 pp.

Branson, Noreen. *History of the Communist Party of Great Britain, 1927–1941*. Salem, N.H.: Salem House, 1985. 350 pp.

Chauvel, Jean-François. *La guerre éclatée*. Paris: Mercure de France, 1985. 298 pp.

Chiaromonte, Gerardo. *Quatro anni difficili: il PCI e i sindicati, 1979–1983*. Rome: Editori Riuniti, 1984. 270 pp.

Clark, Robert P. *The Basque Insurgents: ETA, 1952–1980*. Madison: University of Wisconsin Press, 1984. 328 pp.

Coccopalmierio, Domenico. *Dogmatismo e storicitá del marxismo; politica e diritto nell'esperienza comunista*. Milan: Giuffré Editore, 1984. 213 pp.

Cot, Jean-Pierre. *A l'épreuve du pouvoir: le tiers-mondisme pour quoi faire?* Paris: Seuil, 1984. 218 pp.

Curti, Aurelio. *La vera alternativa al capitalismo ed al Marxismo*. Turin: G. Giappichelli, 1984. 203 pp.

Dallidet, Léon-Raymond. *1934–1984: Voyage d'un communiste*. Paris: Pensée universelle, 1984. 319 pp.

Delperrie de Bayac, Jacques. *Histoire du Front Populaire*. Verviers, Marabout, 1984. 539 pp.

Donneur, André. *L'Alliance fragile: socialistes et communistes français 1922–1983*. Montreal: Nouvelle Optique, 1984. 319 pp.

Durand, Yves, et al. *Le Gestapo contre le Parti communiste: rapports sur l'activité du PCF (décembre 1940–juin 1941)*. Paris: Editions Messidor/Editions Sociales, 1984. 234 pp.

Ebermann, Thomas. *Die Zukunft der Grünen: Ein realistisches Konzept für eine radikale Partei*. Hamburg: Konkret, 1984. 288 pp.

Farneti, Paolo. *The Italian Party System, 1945–1980*. New York: St. Martin's Press, 1985. 199 pp.

Fonseca Ferreira, Antonio, et al. *Os Caminos de liberdade: de idade de razão à idade da revolta*. Lisbon: Spaço Tempo, 1984. 185 pp.

Fourvel, Eugene. *Mémoires d'Eugene Fourvel: depute communiste du Puy-de-Dome*. Nonette: Editions CREER, 1984. 142 pp.

Gallagher, Michael. *Political Parties in the Republic of Ireland*. Dover, N.H.: Manchester University Press, 1985. 174 pp.

Gotto, Klaus, and Hans-Joachim Veen. *Die Grünen—Partei wider Willen*. Mainz: Hase and Kohler Verlag, 1984. 159 pp.

Graham, Robert. *Spain: Change of a Nation*. London: Michael Joseph, 1984. 327 pp.

Hallensleben, Anna. *Von der Grünen Liste zur Grünen Partei?* Göttingen: Muster-Schmidt, 1984. 325 pp.

Hirsch, Arthur. *The French Left: A History and Overview*. Montréal: Black Rose Books, 1984. 253 pp.

Ibarruri, Dolores. *Memorias de Pasionara 1939–1977: Me faltaba España*. Barcelona: Planeta, 1984. 228 pp.

Jenson, Jane, and George Ross. *The View from Inside: A French Communist Cell in Crisis*. Berkeley: University of California Press, 1984. 346 pp.

Jessop, Bob. *Nicos Poulantzas: Marxist Theory and Political Strategy*. London: Macmillan, 1985. 391 pp.

Joffrin, Laurent. *La Gauche en voie de disparition. Comment changer sans trahir?* Paris: Seuil, 1984. 189 pp.

Kanapa, Jean. *Kremlin PCF, conversations secrètes*. Paris: Olivier Orban, 1984. 227 pp.

Kelly, Petra. *Fighting for Hope*. Boston, Mass.: South End Press, 1984. 121 pp.

Kesselman, Mark. *French Workers' Movement*. Winchester, Mass.: Allen and Unwin, 1984. 350 pp.

Kiros, Teodros. *Toward the Construction of a Theory of Political Action: Antonio Gramsci, Consciousness, Participation and Hegemony*. Lanham, Md.: University Press of America, 1985. 290 pp.

Kramer, Steven Philip. *Socialism in Western Europe: The Experience of a Generation*. Boulder, Colo.: Westview Press, 1984. 229 pp.

Kriegel, Annie. *Le Système communist mondial*. Paris: Presses Universitaires, 1984. 271 pp.

———. *Les Communistes français dans leur premier demi-siècle, 1920–1970*. Paris: Editions du Seuil, 1985. 400 pp.

Langels, Otto. *Die ultralinke Opposition der KPD in der Weimarer Republik*. Frankfurt am Main: P. Lang, 1984. 341 pp.

Langguth, Gerd. *Der Grüne Faktor. Von der Bewegung zur Partei?* Osnabrück: Fromm, 1984. 138 pp.

Lehmann, Hans Georg. *Öffnung nach Osten*. Bonn: Verlag Neue Gesellschaft, 1984. 256 pp.

Le Pen, Jean-Marie. *Les Français d'abord*. Paris: Carrère-Lafont, 1984. 245 pp.

Longo, Luigi. *La nostra parte: scritti, scelti, 1921–1980*. Rome: Editori Riuniti, 1984. 437 pp.

Luks, Leonid. *Entstehung der kommunistischen Faschismustheorie: die Auseinandersetzung der Komintern mit Faschismus und Nationalsozialismus, 1920–1935*. Stuttgart: DVA, 1985. 310 pp.

MacLeod, Alex. *La Révolution inopportune: les partis communistes français et italien face à la revolution portugaise, 1973–75*. Montréal: Edition Nouvelle Optique, 1984. 242 pp.

Maqua, Mireille. *Rome-Moscou: L'Ostpolitik du Vatican*. Louvain-la-Neuve, Belgium: Cabay, 1984. 243 pp.

Marchais, Georges. *Nous sommes à l'heure de choix cruciaux: rapport au comité central du PCF, 18 janvier 1984*. Paris: PCF, 1984. 210 pp.

Marcilly, Jean. *Le Pen sans bandeau*. Paris: Jacques Grancher, 1984. 241 pp.

Martelli, Roger. *Communisme Français: histoire sincère du PCF, 1920–1984*. Paris: Messidor/Ed. Sociales, 1984. 249 pp.

Mauroy, Pierre. *A Gauche*. Paris: Albin Michel, 1985. 445 pp.

Mende, Hans-Jürgen. *Karl Kautsky—vom Marxisten zum Opportunisten: Studie zur Geschichte des historischen Materialismus*. East Berlin: Dietz, 1985. 192 pp.

Meolgrani, Piero. *Fascismo, communismo e revoluzione industriale*. Bari: Laterza, 1984. 175 pp.

Mitchell, Alex. *Behind the Crisis in British Stalinism*. Clapham/London: Clapham Publications, 1984. 128 pp.

Mitterrand, Jacques. *A gauche toute, citoyens!* Paris: Ed. Guy Roblot, 1984. 248 pp.

Mujal-León, Eusebio. *Communism and Political Change in Spain*. Bloomington: Indiana University Press, 1985. 288 pp.

Müller, Emil-Peter. *Die Grünen und das Parteiensystem*. Cologne: Deutscher Instituts Verlag, 1984. 183 pp.

Napoli, Mario. *Occupazione e politica del lavoro in Italia: profili della legislazione, 1947–1983*. Milan: Franco Angeli, 1984. 346 pp.

Partito Comunista Sanmarinese. *Ripensaria politica per un progetto di gestione democratica e partecipata della societá*. San Marino: Partito Comunista Sanmarinese, 1985. 101 pp.

Partito Comunista Italiano. *La Proposta di alternativa per il cambiamento*. Rome: Editrice "l'Unitá," 1985. 124 pp.

———. Comito Regionale. *Il Caso Calabria: quale progetto di alternativa al degrado?* Rome: G. Gangemi Editore, 1984. 492 pp.

Plissonnier, Gaston. *Une vie pour lutter: entretiens avec Danielle Bleitrach*. Paris: Editions Sociales, 1984. 223 pp.

Reif, Karlheinz, ed. *Ten European Elections*. Aldershot, England: Gower, 1985. 223 pp.

Revolutionary Road to Communism: Manifesto of the Revolutionary Communist Group. London: Larkin Publications, 1984. 159 pp.

Rigoulout, Pierre. *Des Français au goulag (1917–1984)*. Paris: Fayard, 1984. 367 pp.

Robrieux, Philippe. *La Secte*. Paris: Stock, 1985. 360 pp.

Rouch, Jean-Louis. *Proletaire en veston: une approche de Maurice Domanget*. Treignac: "Les Monediers," 1984. 231 pp.

Ruscio, A. *Les Communistes français et la guerre d'Indochine*. N.p., 1985. 422 pp.

Salvadori, Massimo. *Storia del pensioro comunista: da Lenin alla crisi dell'internazionalismo*. Milan: A. Mondadori Editore, 1984. 751 pp.

Scargill, the Stalinist: The Communist Role in the 1984 Miners' Strike. London: Oak Tree Books, 1984. 128 pp.

Schain, Martin A. *French Communism and Local Power*. London: Frances Pinter Publishers, 1985. 147 pp.

Sevilla Segura, Jose V. *Economia, politica de las crisis Española*. Barcelona: Editorial Critica, 1985. 183 pp.

Spriano, Paolo. *Stalin and European Communists*. London: Verso, 1985. 315 pp.

Tachau, Frank. *Turkey: The Politics of Authority, Democracy and Development*. New York: Praeger, 1984. 224 pp.

Valentini, Chiara. *Il Compagno Berlinguer*. Milan: Mursia, 1985. 233 pp.

Volk, Richard. *Die französischen Kommunisten und die Befreiung Frankreichs, 1943–1945*. Frankfurt am Main: P. Lang, 1984. 295 pp.

Wickman, Stephen B., ed. *Belgium: A Country Study*. 2nd ed. Washington, D.C.: American University Foreign Area Studies, 1985. 364 pp.

Cumulative Index of Biographies

Karmal, Babrak	Afghanistan	1980, p. 450
Kaysone, Phomvihane	Laos	1985, pp. 209–10
Kim Chong-il	Korea	1981, p. 465
Kim Il-Song	Korea	1983, p. 191
Kiselev, Tikhon Y.	USSR	1981, p. 463
Langer, Felicia	Israel	1984, p. 34
Le Duc Tho	Vietnam	1985, p. 244
Ligachev, Yegor K.	USSR	1984, p. 401; 1986, p. 369
Machel, Samora Moisés	Mozambique	1982, p. 42
Marchais, Georges	France	1983, pp. 427–28
Morán, Rolando, *see* Ramirez de Leon		
Mengistu, Haile Mariam	Ethiopia	1982, pp. 17–18
Muhyi al-Din, Khalid	Egypt	1984, pp. 20–21
Murakhovsky, Vsevolod S.	USSR	1986, p. 369
Núñez Tellez, Carlos	Nicaragua	1985, p. 115
Ortega Saavedra, Daniel	Nicaragua	1982, p. 130
Ortega Saavedra, Humberto	Nicaragua	1982, p. 130
Payet, Bruny	Réunion	1986, p. 26
Petkoff, Teodoro	Venezuela	1982, pp. 151–52
Planinc, Milka	Yugoslavia	1986, p. 384
Pol Pot	Kampuchea	1979, p. 451
Poungi, Ange Edouard	Congo	1985, pp. 11–12
Ramirez de Leon, Ricardo	Guatemala	1986, pp. 103–4
Romanov, Grigori V.	USSR	1984, p. 401
Ryzhkov, Nikolai I.	USSR	1986, pp. 369–70
Santos, José Eduardo dos	Angola	1983, pp. 9–10
Shevardnadze, Eduard A.	USSR	1986, p. 370
Sinuraya, Thomas	Indonesia	1985, pp. 189–90
Sokolov, Serge Leonidovich	USSR	1985, p. 367
Solomentsev, Mikhail S.	USSR	1984, pp. 401–2
Souvanna Phouma	Laos	1985, p. 209
Sychev, Vyacheslav	USSR (CMEA)	1984, p. 416
Talyzin, Nikolai V.	USSR	1986, p. 370
Tikhonov, Nikolai A.	USSR	1980, p. 450
Truong, Chin	Vietnam	1984, pp. 285–86
Van Tien Dung	Vietnam	1986, pp. 246–47
Villalobos, Joaquín	El Salvador	1985, p. 84
Vlajković, Radovan	Yugoslavia	1986, p. 384
Vorotnikov, Vitali I.	USSR	1984, p. 402
Wheelock Román, Jaime	Nicaragua	1982, pp. 130–31
Zarkovic, Vidoje	Yugoslavia	1986, p. 384
Zhao Ziyang	China–PRC	1981, p. 464

Index of Names

Index of Subjects